MW01127736

TO THE STUDENT: A partially progr̶a̶m̶m̶e̶d̶ study guide to this
textbook is available through you̶r̶ c̶o̶l̶l̶e̶g̶e̶ b̶o̶o̶k̶s̶t̶o̶r̶e̶ under
the title *Study Guide for Principles of Accounting* by
Loren A. Nikolai, David Gotlob, Jerry G. Kreuze, and
James S. Worthington. The Study Guide can help you with course
material by acting as a tutorial, review, and study aid. If
the Study Guide is not in stock, ask the book store manager to
order a copy for you.

PRINCIPLES OF ACCOUNTING

PRINCIPLES OF ACCOUNTING

Loren A. Nikolai, Ph.D., CPA
Professor, School of Accountancy
University of Missouri–Columbia

John D. Bazley, Ph.D., CPA
Associate Professor, School of Accountancy
University of Denver

James C. Stallman, Ph.D.
Professor, School of Accountancy
University of Missouri–Columbia

KENT PUBLISHING COMPANY

A Division of Wadsworth, Inc.

Boston, Massachusetts

Senior Editor: *David S. McEttrick*
Production Editor: *Ian M. List*
Interior Designer: *Anna Post*
Cover Designer: *Steve Snider*
Production Coordinator: *Linda Card*

Kent Publishing Company
A Division of Wadsworth, Inc.

Printed in the United States of America
2 3 4 5 6 7 8 9   85 84 83

Library of Congress Cataloging in Publication Data
Nikolai, Loren A.
    Principles of accounting.

    Includes index.
    1. Accounting.   I. Bazley, John D.
II. Stallman, James C.   III. Title.
HF5635.N693   657   81-18619
ISBN 0-534-01049-0   AACR2

Preface

Purpose

Our goal in writing this elementary text has been to provide students with a solid foundation in the dynamic and growing field of accounting. Accounting majors using this text will obtain a thorough understanding of financial and managerial accounting fundamentals. This will help to reduce the gap frequently encountered by students moving from beginning to intermediate and advanced courses. Non-accounting majors will find the thorough grounding in accounting presented in this text to be valuable in their future careers as bankers, managers, investors, or perhaps as owners of their own businesses.

General Overview

This textbook has been developed for a two-semester (3 quarter) sequence in elementary financial and managerial accounting. It is written with the same care and thought as our INTERMEDIATE ACCOUNTING textbook (by Nikolai, Bazley, Schroeder, Reynolds, KENT 1980). Our goal is to include the most educationally effective blend of theory and practice. Whereas practice is the main focus, we discuss financial and managerial accounting theory as it applies to the topics in each chapter. The financial accounting portion of the book is organized in a fairly traditional manner. We do not feel that rearranging the order of coverage, just for the sake of being different, is sound pedagogy. On the other hand, we have chosen to expand the treatment of some topics (e.g., inflation accounting, present value, and leases) while reducing that of other topics (e.g., consolidations) to provide a more realistic and useful introduction to accounting. We are also concerned that the managerial accounting portions of many principles texts lack sufficient attention to organization, content, and detail. We have devoted considerable care to overcoming these deficiencies while still maintaining a traditional mix of financial and managerial coverage.

Pedagogy

Although accounting principles are sometimes difficult for elementary students, we believe they can be made more understandable and interesting by using a clear, direct, building-block discussion that anticipates a student's learning process and that is written at the student's reading level. Each chapter begins with a set of learning objectives—what the student should understand after reading the chapter—and an introduction that presents the topics to be covered. Each topic is then discussed in a logical order. Generally each topic is introduced by a brief practical or conceptual overview, followed by a discussion of the related accounting practices. This discussion often includes the use of visuals; i.e., flowcharts, diagrams, or sets of steps designed to facilitate the student's understanding of the material. After the discussion, an example is presented to reinforce the student's learning process. Each example is straightforward, fully explained, and avoids quantum leaps that might confuse the student. Illustrations of journal entries, supporting schedules, and financial statements are abundant and meaningful. A conceptual summary concludes the discussion of many topics.

Within each chapter, headings split the material into logically ordered, understandable portions for the student. Key definitions are **boldfaced;** *italics* are used for emphasis. Each chapter has a glossary of key terms, carefully developed to be a concise but complete reference for the student. Review problems (and solutions) are included at the ends of all chapters except Chapter 6. The accounting practices of real companies are referred to often to relate the discussion to actual practice. The 1980 annual report of Royal Crown Companies, Inc. is included in Appendix A at the end of the text.

Coverage

The text consists of 27 chapters divided into five parts including: I. The Accounting Process, II. Accounting for Assets and Liabilities, III. Business Entities, IV. Financial Statements: Additional Aspects of Financial Reporting, and V. Managerial Accounting for Business Entities. For colleges and universities on a semester system the chapters are arranged so that Parts I and II can be covered in the first semester and Parts IV and V in the second semester. Part III can be covered in either semester depending on the instructor's preference. For schools on a quarter system, Chapters 1–9 (through current assets) can be covered in the first quarter, Chapters 10–18 (through the statement of changes in financial position) in the second quarter, and Chapters 19–27 in the last quarter.

Specific Features

In our combined 40 years of teaching experience we have identified many aspects of sound pedagogy; these have been incorporated into this textbook. Some of the major features are summarized below.

1. *Source documents.* In Part I the role of source documents is emphasized to give students a better understanding of where the information comes from for recording transactions (and for internal control). The importance of source documents is reinforced throughout the text.
2. *Nontechnical GAAP.* Broad, generally accepted accounting principles (GAAP) are introduced and explained in Chapter 1; others are introduced and explained in later chapters as specific topics arise. GAAP is presented in an understandable nontechnical language without repeatedly quoting formal pronouncements.
3. *Revenue and expense transactions.* Discussion of revenues and expenses is

deferred until Chapter 3, after a clear discussion of simple balance sheet transactions (Chapter 1) and accounts, journal entries, and postings for balance sheet transactions (Chapter 2), causing less confusion for the students.

4. *Corporations.* Parts I and II focus primarily on sole proprietorships, although many of the basic principles also apply to partnerships and corporations. Chapter 5, however, includes a section that identifies the basic accounting differences between sole proprietorships and corporations, allowing the instructor the flexibility of taking a more corporate approach throughout Part II, including coverage of marketable securities and income taxes. Partnerships and corporations are then fully discussed in Chapters 13, 14, and 15.

5. *Internal control and EDP systems.* Chapter 6 provides a comprehensive discussion of internal control, highlighting the importance and use of an efficient and effective accounting system and including internal control as it relates to authorizing, executing, and recording transactions, and overall accountability for assets. The EDP discussion goes beyond that in most texts by converting a manual illustration from a previous chapter to an EDP system and comparing (in nontechnical language) the differences in steps and documents.

6. *Receivables and liabilities.* Accounts receivable and notes receivable are thoroughly discussed together in Chapter 8; Current liabilities (including payroll) are also covered in one chapter (Chapter 10). This arrangement lessens the confusion often found in many texts that try to discuss the accounting principles for both receivables and payables at the same time.

7. *Tax issues integrated.* Rather than devoting an entire chapter to the specifics of income taxes (which many instructors do not cover in a principles course, given the complex and changeable nature of tax), a brief discussion of income tax is integrated in each chapter where it applies to specific topics (e.g., inventories and depreciation). This enables students to understand the general relationship of accounting principles and income taxes while leaving the detailed discussion of specifics to a separate tax course, often taken by both accounting and nonaccounting majors.

8. *Bonds payable and present value.* Bonds payable and the straight line method for premiums or discounts are discussed *before* present value. After present value is fully discussed, the effective interest method is described. This arrangement allows flexibility for the instructor and a more logical organization for the student.

9. *Present value concepts and techniques.* Present value is carefully introduced at an elementary level in Chapter 16 and later applied to bonds, mortgages, investments, leases, and capital budgeting, allowing a more realistic and relevant understanding of these topics.

10. *Consolidated financial statements.* In accordance with the recommendations of reviewers and a survey of principles instructors, only the underlying concepts and basic practices of this very technical topic are presented (as part of Chapter 17), rather than devoting a full chapter to it as in many texts. The important items affecting financial statements (e.g., goodwill and minority interest) are discussed while the complexities of preparation are not. This

enables valuable class time to be devoted to other topics more appropriate for the beginning level.

11. *Inflation accounting.* Since the issuance of FASB Statement 33, accounting for changing prices is here to stay. Chapter 20 presents an elementary yet thorough discussion of this important topic, including simple examples of comprehensively restated financial statements (using both constant dollar and current cost approaches) and simple examples of the minimum disclosure requirements of FASB Statement 33.

12. *Managerial accounting.* Part V of the text provides a better and more appropriate elementary managerial accounting coverage than is found in other principles texts. The discussion begins (Chapter 21) with an introduction to accounting for manufacturing companies. By emphasizing the periodic inventory system here, we familiarize students with the similarities and differences of merchandising and manufacturing companies. Complete introductory discussions of job order and process cost accounting systems follow in Chapter 22. These discussions emphasize the structure of practical cost accounting systems and reinforce the use of source documents, subsidiary ledgers, and the perpetual inventory method introduced in the financial accounting portion of the book.

13. *The concept of cost behavior.* Cost behavior and its use in cost estimation is introduced early in Chapter 23 and is reinforced and extended in the discussion of cost-volume-profit (CVP) analysis, budgeting, variance analysis, and both short and long-term decision making.

14. *Budgeting.* Budgeting and master budget schedules are comprehensively treated in Chapter 24 without complications. Cash budgeting is made more understandable through the use of budget schedules that show costs or revenues and their resulting cash payments or receipts.

15. *Standard setting, variance computations, and variance recording.* These topics are discussed separately in Chapter 25 for each element of cost (direct materials, direct labor, and factory overhead), providing an improved introduction to standard cost accounting. The discussion of overhead variances is also more understandable since students have already been exposed to the idea of a flexible budget for overhead costs in the preceding chapter on budgeting.

16. *Short-term and long-term decision making.* Each type is carefully developed in a full chapter treatment (Chapters 26 and 27), providing a solid background in the use of accounting information in decision making. Placing these chapters at the end of this section, after students fully appreciate the nature, measurement, and estimation of costs, allows a more complete discussion and enables the use of richer, more realistic, and more interesting illustrations. The solid discussion of present value presented in Chapter 16 makes possible a more straightforward discussion of present value considerations in long-term investment decisions.

17. *Assignment materials.* An abundance of end-of-chapter assignment materials are included, divided into questions, exercises, problems (Part A and B), and discussion cases. A **boldfaced** note beside each assignment indicates the

subject at issue. The questions address key concepts and terms; each exercise reinforces a topic at an elementary level. The problems either combine a number of topics or focus on a more in-depth study of a single topic. Many problems also require short discussion-type answers. The discussion cases require the students to integrate the topical materials.

Supplementary Materials

In addition to the textbook, several supplementary aids are available. For the student, these include:

1. A *Study Guide* prepared by Loren A. Nikolai, David Gotlob, and Jerry Kreuze, University of Missouri, and James W. Worthington, Auburn University. The study guide includes an outline of each chapter along with self-evaluation exercises and supplementary short-answer homework assignments, with solutions and post tests.
2. Partially completed *Working Papers* for all problems. (Vol. I, Chs. 1–15; Vol. II, Chs. 16–27.)
3. A *Checklist* of key answers to the problems.
4. Two *Practice Sets,* developed by Loren A. Nikolai and David Gotlob. Practice set I, "Boone Office Supply," focusing on accounting for a sole proprietorship retailing company, is designed to be used after Chapter 6. Practice set II, "Crockett Automotive Parts," deals with accounting for a wholesaling corporation and is to be used anytime after Chapter 18.

For the instructor, the supplementary aids include:

1. A *Solutions Manual* for all homework materials. The manual includes general notes for an instructional overview of each chapter, a suggested solution time for each problem, all supporting calculations, and helpful notes to the instructor concerning difficult areas students might encounter in each problem. (Vol. I, Chs. 1–15; Vol. II, Chs. 16–27.)
2. A *Test Bank* of examination materials for each chapter, including true-false and multiple-choice questions, completion statements, and short-answer problems.
3. A set of approximately 550 *Transparencies* (set in large type) for the solutions to selected homework materials. Also included are numerous "teaching visuals" for lecture purposes.

Acknowledgements

We wish to thank Eileen Huhmann, Ben-Hsien Bao, and Ron Henley for their invaluable technical assistance in the preparation of the book and supporting materials. We also wish to thank our graduate and undergraduate students, including Benjamin Y. K. Tai, Bernard D. Williams, Robert J. Hoffman, Stephen M. Moyer, and Marcia K. Jones and those students who have participated in the classroom use of the various chapters. We are sincerely indebted to our typists, Mary Thomas, Anita Blanchar, Jonalee Slaughter, Lisa Heuermann, Grace Butler, Merita Nettles, Sylvia Noordewier, and Karen Miles, whose quality work and perseverance enabled us to complete the manuscript in a timely and orderly fashion.

Appreciation is also extended to our editorial and production staffs, including David S. McEttrick, Ian List, Tina Samaha, and Ann Sleeper.

We are grateful to our respective Schools of Accountancy and to The Peat, Marwick, Mitchell Foundation for their support, and to the American Institute of Certified Public Accountants, the Financial Accounting Standards Board, and the many companies for granting us permission to quote from their respective pronouncements and financial statements. We are also grateful to our wives, children, and friends who provided us with considerable moral support and understanding during the entire manuscript production process.

Loren A. Nikolai
John D. Bazley
James C. Stallman

The authors wish to express their appreciation to the individuals who served as reviewers and who provided insightful comments and valuable suggestions in the development of the manuscript and careful checking of homework material and solutions:

Wilton T. Anderson
Oklahoma State University

Terry L. Arndt
Ball State University

James J. Benjamin
Texas A & M University

John T. Burke
Western Michigan University

James T. Hood
Northeast Louisiana University

Robert W. Ingram
University of South Carolina

Edward J. Krohn
Miami-Dade Community College

Anthony T. Krzystofik
University of Massachusets—Amherst

Richard W. Lott
Bentley College

Paul H. Mihalek
University of Connecticut

Daniel J. O'Mara
Villanova University

Philip M. J. Reckers
Arizona State University

H. Lee Schlorff
Bentley College

Richard Vangermeersch
University of Rhode Island

James S. Worthington
Auburn University

Contents

.

Current Marketable Securities. **Current Marketable Securities — Stocks.** The acquisition of Current Marketable Securities — Stocks. Subsequent Valuation of Current Marketable Securities — Stocks: Lower of Cost or Market Method. Sale of an Investment in Stocks. Revenue on an Investment in Stocks. **Current Marketable Securities — Bonds.** The Acquisition of Current Marketable Securities — Bonds. Subsequent Valuation of Current Marketable Securities — Bonds. Revenue on Current Marketable Securities — Bonds. Sale of Current Marketable Securities — Bonds. **Additional Considerations.** Income Tax Rules for Marketable Securities. Valuation of Marketable Securities at Market Value. **Review Problem. Solution to Review Problem. Glossary.**

PRINCIPLES OF ACCOUNTING

PART 1 | THE ACCOUNTING PROCESS

1 Accounting: Its Uses, Principles, and Practices

After reading this chapter, you should understand:

- The meaning of the term accounting
- The various specialized fields of accountancy
- The general concepts affecting financial accounting information
- The definitions of assets, liabilities, and owner's equity
- The accounting equation and the double entry rule
- Recording transactions in a simple accounting system
- Preparing a simple balance sheet

The tired joke, "old accountants never die, they just lose their balance," is as outdated as the image of an accountant wearing a green eyeshade and working at a dimly lit desk. Although some accounting still involves the computation of balances, a large part of accounting is the communication of information for use in many important decisions. There are now more than 500,000 professional accountants and they are engaged in several interesting areas of accounting specialities, some of which take many of them on national and worldwide travels.

We begin our study of accounting in this chapter by defining what accounting is and showing how accounting information affects decision making. Next we identify the various areas of accounting in which a person may wish to work. Then we introduce several broad concepts that are important to understanding the accounting process, and finally, we explore several basic practices in the accounting process.

ACCOUNTING AND DECISIONS

Accounting Defined

Accounting has been defined in many different ways and by combining these definitions we arrive at the following: **Accounting is the process of providing quantitative information about economic entities to aid users in making decisions concerning the allocation of economic resources.** This definition is quite long and can be best understood by briefly studying each phrase of the definition.

The process of providing means that there is a series of activities leading up to and including the communication of accounting information. These activities are

(1) identifying the information, and then (2) measuring, (3) recording, (4) retaining, and (5) communicating it. *Quantitative* means that the information is communicated by using numbers; in accounting, numbers are usually numbers of *dollars. Economic entities* means that accounting not only applies to all types of businesses, but also to churches, hospitals, charitable organizations, municipalities, governments, and other organizations.

Decisions concerning the allocation of economic resources include, among others, whether to buy, sell, or hold investments, whether to extend credit to a company desiring a loan, whether to manufacture and sell a particular product, or whether to modify the income tax regulations to stimulate business activities. These and other examples are discussed throughout this textbook to show how accounting information can be used in decision making.

As suggested by the variety of decisions listed above, there are many *users* of accounting information. Users may be categorized into two groups, external users and internal users. **External users are individuals and groups outside the business or other economic entity who need accounting information to decide whether or not to engage in some activity with the entity.** They include investors, bankers, suppliers, labor unions, and the local, state, and federal governments. **Internal users are persons within a business or other economic entity who need the accounting information to make decisions concerning the operations and activities of the entity.** These users include all levels of management, including departmental supervisors, sales personnel, divisional and regional managers, and "top management."

Decision Making by Internal and External Users

Decision making, whether by external or internal users, can be viewed as a four-stage process as shown in Exhibit 1-1.

The first step for the decision maker is to recognize that a problem exists for which a decision must be made. For example, assume a company applies for a bank loan of a certain amount for a specified time. When this request is made the banker (an *external* user of accounting information) recognizes that a decision must be made about granting the loan. Or in the case of an *internal* user, a manager of the business may need to decide whether or not to manufacture and sell Product X.

The second step is to identify the alternatives. For the banker there are many alternatives, including refusing the bank loan, granting a loan of a smaller or greater amount for a shorter or longer time, or granting the loan as requested. For the internal manager the alternatives include not manufacturing and selling the product, manufacturing and selling a few units of the product, or manufacturing and selling many units.

EXHIBIT 1-1
Stages in Decision Making

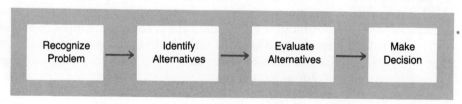

Recognize Problem → Identify Alternatives → Evaluate Alternatives → Make Decision

The third step is to evaluate the alternatives. Accounting information is used for this purpose. The banker must have information concerning the cash in the checking and savings accounts of the business, the cash the business must spend to pay its bills and the amount it expects to collect from its customers, the timing of these payments and collections, and the way in which the bank loan would be used. By gathering the related accounting information the banker can evaluate whether the business needs the bank loan, the amount and length of time of the loan, and the likelihood that the loan will be repaid. For the manager accounting information concerning the cost to manufacture and sell the product, the expected selling price and number of units sold, and the financial impact on the manufacture and sales of existing products must be known in order to evaluate the alternatives.

Once the alternatives have been evaluated a decision may be made. The banker makes the loan decision and the manager makes the product decision based, to a great extent, on the accounting information gathered in the *alternative evaluation* stage. Although these examples of decisions are overly simplified, we can see that accounting information is used by both internal and external users in the decision-making process.

Accounting Information and Decision Making The role of accounting information in the decision-making process is further illustrated by the diagram in Exhibit 1-2. This exhibit shows the continual nature of the accounting process; that is, accounting information about economic entities is accumulated and communicated to both internal and external users to assist them in decision making. Their decisions, in turn, have an impact on the economic entity, and the accounting information accumulation and communication process is repeated again. For the bank loan and product decisions, we can see that the decisions by both the internal and external users will affect the accounting information accumulated and communicated about the business. *Prior* to either decision,

EXHIBIT 1-2 Accounting Information and Decision Making

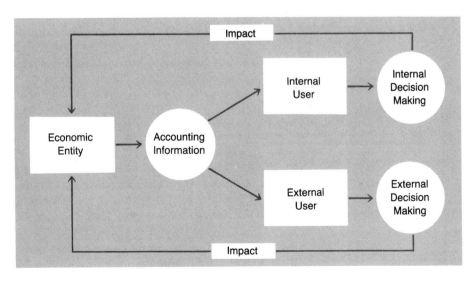

the information communicated would be the information needed to make the decisions as discussed earlier. *After* the decisions, whether or not the bank loan is granted and whether or not the product is manufactured and sold will change the future activities of the business and, in turn, result in different accounting information about the business.

Because there are many activities in the accounting process, many economic entities for which accounting information is prepared, and many users of accounting information, there are several *specialty* areas of accounting to satisfy the users' needs. They are discussed in the following section.

THE ACCOUNTANCY PROFESSION

Accountancy has emerged as a profession, alongside the professions of medicine and law. The study and practice of accountancy require a broad understanding of concepts in such areas as economics, sociology, psychology, and public administration as well as in-depth knowledge of specialized accounting areas. The three main fields of accountancy include (1) public accounting, (2) managerial accounting, and (3) governmental and quasi-governmental accounting, each of which has several accounting specialty areas. Standardized national examinations are given at regular intervals for people who desire to work in some of these areas. Each of these fields is discussed below and summarized in Exhibit 1-3.

Public Accounting

A public accountant is an independent professional person who provides accounting services to clients for a fee. Most of them are *certified public accountants* (CPAs), having met certain state requirements. In order to practice accountancy, each CPA must hold a license issued by the state in which the CPA works. Licensing is designed to help to ensure that high-quality, professional service is provided by accountants. Although the licensing requirements vary from state to state, all CPAs must pass the Uniform CPA Examination, a national examination given twice a year across the United States. The examination is administered by the American Institute of Certified Public Accountants and includes the topics of accounting theory, accounting practice, auditing, and business law. In addition, states often have minimum educational and practical experience requirements. Several specialty areas of public accounting are discussed below.

AUDITING.   Accounting information may be communicated in many different ways. One way is through the issuance of *financial statements* (which are discussed in greater detail throughout this text). Both the New York Stock Exchange and the American Stock Exchange, as well as the Securities and Exchange Commission, require certain businesses to issue an annual report. **An annual report is a report published by a business once a year that contains its audited financial statements.** In addition, banks may require a business to show its audited financial statements when applying for a loan. Other types of economic entities, such as universities and charitable organizations, also issue audited financial statements.

Auditing involves examining the accounting records of an economic entity and the resulting financial statements to attest to the fairness of the accounting

EXHIBIT 1-3
The Accounting
Profession

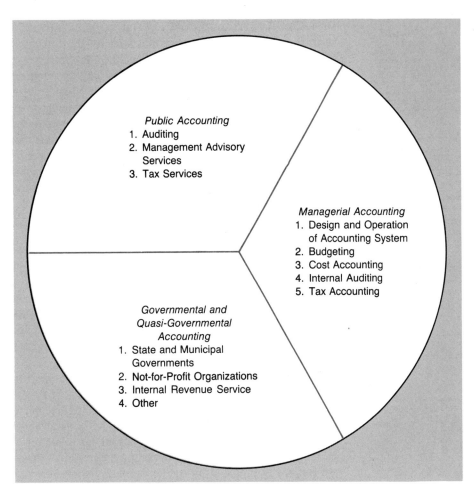

Public Accounting
1. Auditing
2. Management Advisory
   Services
3. Tax Services

Managerial Accounting
1. Design and Operation
   of Accounting System
2. Budgeting
3. Cost Accounting
4. Internal Auditing
5. Tax Accounting

Governmental and
Quasi-Governmental
Accounting
1. State and Municipal
   Governments
2. Not-for-Profit Organizations
3. Internal Revenue Service
4. Other

information in the statements. Auditing is necessary because financial statements are prepared by the management of the economic entity issuing the statements. Because of the potential bias of management, external users of the financial statements need assurance that the statements fairly present the accounting information about the entity. Consequently, these financial statements must be audited by a CPA because a CPA is the only person licensed to do so.

Auditing is the primary professional service offered by a CPA, who is an independent and unbiased observer. Based upon the evidence gathered in the auditing process, the CPA expresses a professional opinion as to the fairness of the financial statements. Because many users rely on the CPA's opinion, auditing plays an important role in society. Most CPAs work in CPA firms, and auditing is done by many local and regional CPA firms. In addition, the large size of many businesses, some of which span the United States as well as the world in their activities, has led to the growth of large CPA firms with offices in most major United States and international cities.

MANAGEMENT ADVISORY SERVICES.   During an audit by a CPA firm, a careful study is made of the accounting records kept by the business, which are part of its *management information system*. Thus the CPA firm has a good knowledge of the strengths and weaknesses of the operating activities and information system of the business. In addition to auditing departments, many CPA firms have established separate management advisory services departments to offer organizations constructive criticism about how to improve their internal operations.

Management advisory services in CPA firms include the design or improvement of the financial accounting system for identifying, measuring, recording, retaining, and reporting accounting information. These services also may include assistance in developing cost control systems, planning manufacturing facilities, and installing computer operations. These advisory services have required CPA firms to hire people with specialities other than accounting, for example, lawyers, industrial engineers, and electronic data processing experts.

TAX SERVICES.   The federal government as well as most state governments require the filing of income tax returns and the payment of taxes. The various federal and state tax regulations are designed to collect taxes in a fair manner and to stimulate (or discourage) certain activities and investments. The area of tax services is another natural offshoot of the auditing function. Many CPA firms have established tax services departments to provide both tax planning and tax return preparation services for their clients.

Because of the high tax rates, complex tax regulations, and special tax incentives today, most businesses (and individuals) can benefit from carefully planning their activities to minimize or postpone their tax payments. CPA firms employ tax professionals who are experts in the various federal and state tax regulations to assist these businesses and individuals in tax planning. Similarly, business or individual income tax returns, reflecting the results of these tax planning activities, are frequently prepared by the tax services department of the CPA firms.

Managerial Accounting

A managerial accountant is an accountant employed by an economic entity to perform its internal (managerial) accounting activities. A high-level manager usually coordinates these activities. This manager frequently reports directly to the top management of the organization, which is an indication of how important the accounting functions are to the organization's operations.

Another indication of the importance of managerial accounting is the Certificate in Management Accounting (CMA). The CMA is granted to persons who meet specific educational and professional standards and who pass a uniform CMA examination, administered twice yearly by the Institute of Management Accounting of the National Association of Accountants. The examination covers several topics, including business finance, organizations and behavior, public reporting standards, auditing and taxes, periodic reporting for internal and external purposes, and decision analysis. Although the CMA is not required as a license to practice, accountants holding the CMA are recognized as professional experts in the area of managerial accounting.

The accounting activities in managerial accounting encompass several areas: (1) design and operation of accounting systems, (2) budgeting, (3) cost accounting, (4) internal auditing, and (5) tax accounting. Each of these areas is briefly discussed below.

DESIGN AND OPERATION OF ACCOUNTING SYSTEM. An accounting system is a means by which accounting information about an organization's activities is identified, measured, recorded, and retained so that it can be reported in an accounting statement. As is shown in this textbook, certain general principles (rules) apply to the operation of an efficient accounting system for all organizations. Within these principles, however, each organization can design and operate its accounting system in the way that best meets its needs. One duty of the managerial accountant is to design and operate the organization's accounting system. This function is sometimes referred to as *general accounting* because of the wide variety of activities involved. These activities include, among others, determining the portion of the accounting system that will be manually or computer operated, integrating the accounting activities for different departments, designing accounting forms and reports, and establishing standard operating and recording procedures.

BUDGETING. The management of an organization includes two functions, planning and controlling. Planning means developing a plan of action for the short-, mid-, and long-term future of the organization. Planning enables the organization to develop strategies to meet its goals and to provide the resources required to implement these strategies. A business establishes strategies by identifying the quantities and types of products sold, determining how to produce these products, and setting the selling price. Providing the required resources means having the necessary personnel, facilities, supplies, and finances. **Budgeting is the process of quantifying the plans of management to show their impact on the organization's operating activities.** The quantification of a plan is known as a *budget* (or *forecast*).

Controlling is the process of making sure, to the extent that is reasonable, that the actual operations of the various parts of the organization achieve the established plans. As an aid in the control function, another aspect of budgeting is the frequent comparison of actual quantified results to the budget so that differences between actual and planned results may be seen and corrective action may be taken when necessary. Budgeting, as part of both the planning and control functions of management, is an important aspect of managerial accounting.

COST ACCOUNTING. **Cost accounting is the process of determining and accumulating the costs of certain activities within an organization.** For a business cost accounting is primarily concerned with product costs; that is, determining the cost of producing a unit of a product. Cost accounting may also involve calculating the cost of operating a particular department, a manufacturing process, or a marketing technique, however. Cost accounting cannot be separated from budgeting because the accounting information used to determine the unit cost of a product, for example, is the same information used in the controlling (comparing actual to planned costs) aspect of budgeting. The difference is that in cost accounting actual costs are computed for other purposes as well, such as establishing selling prices and determining operating profits. Cost accounting is an interesting area of managerial accounting because many costs apply to different products, processes, and departments. Even the definition of *costs* may vary depending on the circumstances. These applications and alternative definitions of costs are discussed later in the book.

INTERNAL AUDITING.   Earlier we discussed the design and operation of an accounting system. One part of the design is establishing good internal control. **Internal control involves the procedures to safeguard the organization's economic resources and to promote the efficient and effective operation of the accounting system.** Internal auditing establishes these internal control procedures and reviews operations to ensure that these procedures are being followed throughout the organization. Internal auditing is becoming increasingly important because the procedures for the external audit depend, to a great degree, on the quality of the internal control. As evidence of professionalism in internal auditing, an accountant may earn a Certificate of Internal Auditing (CIA). The CIA certificate is awarded by the Institute of Internal Auditors, Inc. Although it is not a license to practice, the certificate states that the holder has met strict educational and practical experience requirements and has passed a uniform CIA examination of four parts: principles of internal auditing, internal auditing techniques, principles of management, and disciplines related to internal auditing (e.g., economics, computer systems).

TAX ACCOUNTING.   Although businesses often assign their tax work to the tax services department of a CPA firm, many of them still maintain their own tax departments. This department is staffed by accountants with expertise in the tax laws relating to the business. These accountants handle income tax planning and the preparation of state and federal income tax returns. They also work on real estate taxes, personal property taxes, such as taxes on inventories, and other taxes.

Governmental and Quasi-Governmental Accounting

Certain governmental and quasi-governmental agencies employ accountants. These agencies include (1) state and municipal governments, (2) not-for-profit organizations, (3) the Internal Revenue Service, and (4) other quasi-governmental organizations.

STATE AND MUNICIPAL GOVERNMENTS.   Officials of state and municipal governments are responsible for the imposition, collection, and control of tax revenues and tax expenditures. Accountants are hired on the state and local levels to provide accounting information for use in the administration of these activities.

NOT-FOR-PROFIT ORGANIZATIONS.   Administrators of state and municipal organizations such as colleges and universities, hospitals, and mental health agencies are responsible for their efficient and effective operations. The accounting information needed by these organizations is the same in many respects as that needed by businesses. But because they are not-for-profit organizations financed in part by public funds, they are required to use slightly different accounting procedures. Accountants hired by these organizations design and operate the accounting systems of the organizations.

INTERNAL REVENUE SERVICE. The Internal Revenue Service (IRS) is responsible for administering the collection of federal income taxes. This role includes the processing of individual and corporation tax returns, payments, and refunds, as well as the investigation (auditing) of selected tax returns. The IRS also issues various regulations, based on research and other activities, designed to explain the Internal Revenue Code. State revenue agencies also perform similar functions. Many accountants are employed in these activities.

OTHER GOVERNMENTAL ORGANIZATIONS. Several other governmental organizations are involved in accounting activities. The Securities and Exchange Commission (SEC) has the responsibility of overseeing the financial statements of certain businesses and has the legal authority to establish accounting regulations for them. The SEC employs many accountants to identify appropriate accounting procedures and to verify that existing regulations are being followed. The General Accounting Office (GAO) has the responsibility of cooperating with various agencies of the federal government in the development and operation of their accounting systems to improve the management of these agencies. Other federal and state agencies also prepare and use accounting information, such as the Interstate Commerce Commission, the Environmental Protection Agency, and the Federal Communications Commission.

EMPHASIS OF THIS TEXTBOOK

At this point we have a general understanding of the accounting process and the accountancy profession, with its many specialty areas. Now we turn to the *fundamentals* to begin our study of the technical and conceptual aspects of accounting.

Accounting has been called the language of business. Throughout our early education we learned the vocabulary and other basic elements of the English language so that we would be able to communicate effectively. The same is true for accounting. Many students using this textbook will not become accountants, although they may be employed by or own businesses, become managers, bankers, or investors, and will use accounting information. In order to understand and to use accounting information most effectively, they must have a solid grounding in its fundamentals. For students who plan to pursue a career in accounting, a thorough understanding of accounting fundamentals is needed for more advanced study. Thus the emphasis of this textbook is on the basics, the "how to's" of accounting. An inquisitive mind, however, must also ask "why" and "why not," and these aspects of accounting information are discussed as well.

To orient our discussion we will narrow our study to business organizations, compare the meanings of the terms accounting and bookkeeping, and identify the differences between financial and managerial accounting and the placement of these topics in the text.

EXHIBIT 1-4   Types of Business Organizations (Companies)

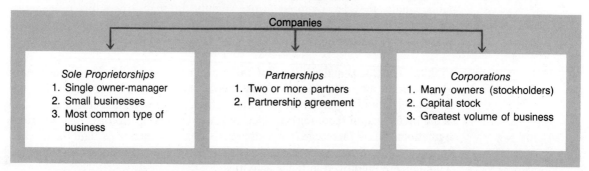

Business Organizations

Although we have discussed several types of organizations and the use of their accounting information, the emphasis in this textbook is on business organizations. These organizations are a significant aspect of the United States economy. A business may be organized in three ways: (1) a sole proprietorship, (2) a partnership, or (3) a corporation, as shown in Exhibit 1-4. **A sole proprietorship is a business owned by one individual who is the sole investor of money into the business.** The money invested is called *capital*. Usually the sole owner also acts as the manager of the business. This form of organization is frequently used by small retail stores and service firms. **A partnership is a business owned by two or more individuals who each invest capital.** The individuals are called partners, and their responsibilities, obligations, and benefits are usually described in a contract called a *partnership agreement*. CPA firms and law firms are examples of partnerships. **A corporation is a business incorporated as a separate legal entity according to the laws of the state in which it is based.** Shares of *capital stock* are issued to owners—called *stockholders*—as evidence of their investment of capital in the corporation; these shares are easily transferable. A corporation may be owned by a few or by many stockholders; certain large corporations have thousands of stockholders. Examples of corporations are General Motors and IBM Corporation.

The sole proprietorship is the most common type of business because it is easiest to organize and simplest to operate. The corporation, on the other hand, has the greatest volume of business in the United States. Its organization and legal structure are complex, requiring complex accounting procedures. Most basic accounting procedures apply to all types of businesses. Therefore in our discussion we use the general term *company* to apply to any business, unless the topic relates only to a specific type of business. In these cases we identify the type of business. *Company applies, therefore, to a sole proprietorship, partnership, or corporation.* Because the sole proprietorship is a simpler type of business, in the first half of the book we mainly study this type of business.

Accounting Versus Bookkeeping

The term *bookkeeping* has sometimes been confused with accounting. Recall that accounting includes external and internal auditing, management advisory services, income tax planning and preparation of returns, budgeting, and the design and operation of an accounting system. Recall also that the accounting process includes several phases, including identifying, measuring, recording, retaining, and communicating information. **Bookkeeping is the process of recording accounting information for a company according to a standard set of steps.** Thus bookkeeping is only one phase (i.e., the *recording* phase) in the accounting process. A person who understands bookkeeping may not necessarily be knowledgeable about accounting, but an accountant must always have a thorough knowledge of bookkeeping. In addition, a user of accounting information will find a basic knowledge of bookkeeping helpful in understanding the accounting information about a company.

The Differences Between Financial and Managerial Accounting

A common way of viewing accounting is to separate it into two types, financial accounting and managerial accounting. **Financial accounting is the aspect of accounting concerned with the recording, accumulation, and communication of a company's accounting information for external users in their various decisions.** In contrast, **managerial accounting involves the recording, accumulation, and communication of a company's accounting information for internal users in their managerial decision making.**

Much accounting information that is useful to an external user in making a decision (e.g., whether or not to extend a bank loan to a company) is not useful to a manager within the company in making a decision (e.g., should a certain product be produced and sold). Thus one set of accounting information is prepared for the external user and another set is prepared for the internal user, although at least some of the accounting information needed by the internal user is also helpful to the external user, and vice versa. (For example, the product may not be produced unless there is sufficient money to do so, and the likelihood of repayment of the bank loan may depend upon current and future sales of the product.) The different external and internal needs for accounting information and the overlap of this information are the concern of an accountant designing an accounting system.

In the first part of this textbook we study financial accounting and in the later parts of the text we shift our study to managerial acounting. Throughout the financial accounting part of the text, however, we continue to discuss the relationship between financial and managerial accounting information.

Because general principles that influence financial accounting have been established, a knowledge of these principles is helpful to learning financial accounting fundamentals. These principles are discussed in the next section.

GENERAL PRINCIPLES AND CONCEPTS OF FINANCIAL ACCOUNTING

Accounting is a dynamic and growing field, keeping pace with the rapidly changing business and economic environment. Over the years, owing to the activities of several professional accounting organizations, a set of guidelines for financial accounting has evolved. These guidelines are referred to as generally accepted accounting principles. **Generally accepted accounting principles, or GAAP, are the currently acceptable concepts, principles, procedures, and practices that should be used for financial accounting.**

Organizations Influential in Establishing GAAP

The organizations that have had a significant influence in establishing generally accepted accounting principles are the American Institute of Certified Public Accountants (AICPA), the Financial Accounting Standards Board (FASB), and the Securities and Exchange Commission (SEC).

The AICPA is the national professional association of CPAs. In 1938 the AICPA formed the Committee on Accounting Procedures, which issued fifty-one *Accounting Research Bulletins* identifying GAAP. This committee was replaced in 1959 by the Accounting Principles Board (APB) of the AICPA. The APB issued thirty-one *APB Opinions,* until it was phased out in 1973. At that time the FASB was created as an independent board of professional persons experienced in accounting. As of July 1, 1981 the FASB has issued 49 *Statements of Financial Accounting Standards,* 35 *Interpretations,* and 4 *Statements of Financial Accounting Concepts.* The SEC is an agency of the federal government created to administer legislation (including the filing of certain accounting reports) concerning the initial sale and later trading of corporate securities. The SEC sets up accounting principles in its *SEC Accounting Series Releases.*

Most of these pronouncements involving generally accepted accounting principles are still in effect, and many of them are complex and very technical in nature. As we discuss specific accounting issues in this textbook, the applicable generally accepted accounting principles are summarized in a manner that is easily understood by an accounting student. In addition, only the basic aspects of generally accepted accounting principles are introduced. It is important to recognize, however, that these principles are not set in concrete; they are modified as business practices and decisions change and as better accounting techniques are developed. Before we discuss the specific principles in the rest of the book, an explanation of several general underlying concepts of financial accounting is useful.

Relevance

The accounting information communicated to users must be relevant to their decision-making process. **Relevance is the capacity to influence a user's decision.** As we saw in the bank loan decision discussed earlier, the amount of cash in the company's checking and savings account and the cash it expected to collect and to pay were relevant information for the banker's decision. On the other hand, the cost of the typewriters owned by the company is probably not relevant to the banker and this accounting information would not be communicated. Relevance is a very important concept to be considered in accumulating and communicating accounting information.

Materiality

Materiality is like relevance in that both concepts are defined in terms of what influences or makes a difference to a user of accounting information. **Materiality is the concept that accounting information is useful when the monetary amount involved is large enough to make a difference in a user's decision.** Thus in the bank loan decision the amount of cash to be paid by the company for its employees' wages is material to the banker's decision. The cash to be paid by the company for typing paper is not material, however. Only material accounting information should be accumulated and communicated to users. (In this book we often use small numbers for convenience, but it is assumed in all cases that the amounts are material.)

Entity Concept

We noted earlier that individuals may own several types of businesses, including sole proprietorships, partnerships, or corporations. Furthermore, one individual may own all or part of several businesses. From an accounting standpoint each business is treated as a separate economic entity. **An entity is considered to be separate from its owners and from any other business.** Thus each business has its own accounting system and accounting records for identifying, measuring, recording, retaining, and communicating its accounting information. An owner's personal financial activities are *not* included within the accounting records of the business owned unless this activity has a *direct* impact upon the business. For instance, the purchase by an owner of an automobile for personal use would not affect the business's accounting records, but the purchase by the owner with personal funds of a delivery van to be used in the business would affect its records.

Transactions and Source Documents

Business transactions and source documents are very important to the overall financial accounting process. The identification, measurement, and recording phases of the accounting process usually begin as a result of a business transaction. **A transaction in accounting is an exchange of property or services by a business entity with an external party.** For example, the purchase of the delivery van in the previous paragraph involved an exchange of cash for property (the van). Events or activities other than a transaction may be recorded in the accounting process; they are discussed later in the text.

A **source document is a business record that serves as evidence that a transaction has occurred.** A source document may be a canceled check, a sales receipt, a bill from a supplier, a bill sent to a customer, a payroll timecard, or a record of the miles driven in the company's delivery truck. Although the accounting process begins when a transaction occurs, identifying, measuring, and recording the accounting information are based on an analysis of the source document. For instance, a review of a check written by a company would show the date of the transaction, the dollar amount, the payee, and possibly the reason for the check. Several source documents may be used as evidence of a single transaction.

Source documents also play an important part in auditing. In the auditing process, accountants use the term *objective* to refer to *recorded accounting information that is factual and capable of being verified*. To evaluate the fairness of a company's financial statements, an auditor verifies that the recorded transactions are supported by evidence in the form of source documents. In the early part of this textbook, as we discuss the accounting for various transactions, the source documents used in the analysis are identified.

Monetary Unit and Historical Cost

In the exchange of property or services, a unit of exchange value is used. Accounting information about these transactions must be recorded and communicated in a form that is understood by both external and internal users. This requirement has led to the concept of the monetary unit. **The monetary unit concept means that**

the results of transactions are recorded and communicated in monetary terms. In the United States the monetary unit is the dollar, and therefore financial statements are expressed in dollars. In other countries the monetary unit is the national currency of the particular country. The use of a monetary unit does not stop accountants from showing other important, but nonmonetary, information. This information may be expressed in numbers and descriptions as shown in later sections of this textbook.

Another important concept related to the monetary concept is the historical cost or, simply, the cost concept. **The historical cost concept means that transactions are recorded on the basis of the dollars exchanged (i.e., the cost) in the transaction.** Once a transaction is recorded, the *cost* involved in the transaction is retained in the accounting records regardless of whether the *value* of the property or services owned increases (or decreases). For instance, a company may acquire land for $10,000. Several years later the land may have increased in value to $13,000. Under the historical cost concept, the company would continue to show the land in its accounting records at $10,000, the acquisition cost.

The increase in the value of any item may be due to the effects of inflation. It may also be due to specific changes in the supply of and demand for that type of item. In the past the dollar has been a relatively stable measuring unit. With the recent high rates of inflation, however, everyone has experienced the reduction in the *purchasing power* of the dollar. There has also been rapid technological growth and change that have affected the supply of and demand for many items. Inflation and technological changes have been so great in recent years that accountants have modified both the monetary unit and the historical cost concept, although not in the financial statements. In the United States, *supplemental* information (in addition to the financial statements) concerning the effects of inflation and the effects of changes in supply and demand on the prices of certain items is currently presented. These supplemental disclosures are discussed later in the text, but until then, both the monetary unit and the historical cost concept will be followed.

Going Concern Concept

To meet its goals, a company enters into many transactions that require it to carry out future commitments. **The going concern concept is the general assumption made by accountants that the company will continue to operate long enough to meet these commitments.** It is also called the *continuity assumption*. The going concern concept is necessary for many of the accounting procedures that are discussed later. Obviously not all businesses are successful, but the going concern concept is valid in most cases. If the business appears on the verge of bankruptcy, this assumption should be discarded.

Diagram of General Concepts of Financial Accounting

We have discussed several general concepts of financial accounting that affect the information accumulated and communicated in the accounting process. These concepts are presented in Exhibit 1-5. These important general concepts should be kept in mind as we discuss the accounting process. Not all of the concepts affecting financial accounting have been introduced here; other concepts will be presented as they apply to topics discussed later in the book. We now turn to a discussion of the basics of the accounting process.

EXHIBIT 1-5
General Concepts
Affecting Financial
Accounting
Information

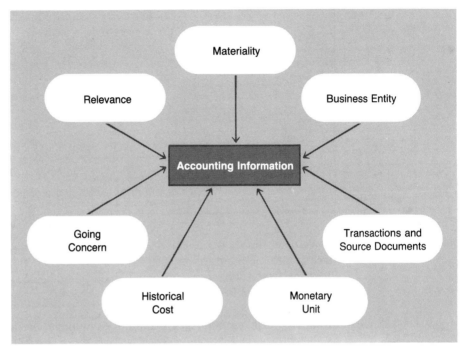

Materiality

Relevance

Business Entity

Accounting Information

Going
Concern

Transactions and
Source Documents

Historical
Cost

Monetary
Unit

FINANCIAL STATEMENTS

Businesses operate to achieve various goals. Companies may be interested in providing a healthy work environment for their employees, in achieving a high level of pollution control, or in making contributions to civic and social organizations and activities. To meet these goals, however, a company must achieve two *primary* objectives: (1) to earn a satisfactory profit and (2) to remain solvent. If a business fails to meet either of these primary objectives, it will not be able to survive in the long run.

Financial statements are accounting reports used to summarize and communicate financial information about a business. Two major financial statements, the income statement and the balance sheet, are used to report information about the company's primary objectives discussed in the previous paragraph. These financial statements are the end result of the accounting system. Each of these statements summarizes certain information that has been identified, measured, recorded, and retained during the accounting process.

Income Statement

An income statement is a financial statement summarizing the results of a company's income (profit) making activities for a specific time period. It shows the revenues, expenses, and net income of a company for this time period. Revenues are the prices charged to a company's customers for goods or services provided. Expenses are the costs of providing the goods or services. The net income is the difference between revenues and expenses. An example of an income statement for one type of company is shown in Exhibit 1-6.

EXHIBIT 1-6
Income Statement

JACKSON ADVERTISING AGENCY
Income Statement
For Month Ended July 31, 1983

Revenues:
  Advertising revenues $44,000

Expenses:
  Rent expense . . . . $ 9,600
  Salaries expense   11,700
  Office supplies expense   2,300
  Utilities expense   1,800
    Total expenses.   25,400
Net Income. $18,600

We defer further discussion of the income statement until Chapter 3. To introduce you to the basics of an accounting system we can look at a simple balance sheet for another type of company and then study the accounting process leading up to this type of financial statement.

Balance Sheet   **A balance sheet summarizes a company's financial position on a given date.** It is alternatively called a *statement of financial position*. A balance sheet lists the company's assets, liabilities, and owner's equity. A balance sheet for Turner's Laundry is shown in Exhibit 1-7.

Note that the balance sheet has a heading consisting of three lines, the name of the company, the title of the financial statement, and the date for which it was prepared. Note also that the balance sheet consists of three segments, the assets section, the liabilities section, and the owner's equity section. Finally, observe that the information is expressed in monetary terms and that the total (indicated by a double ruled line) of the assets ($36,000) is equal to the sum of the liabilities ($16,000) plus the owner's equity ($20,000). The balance sheet is so named, in fact, because both sides must be in balance (equal to each other).

EXHIBIT 1-7
Balance Sheet

TURNER'S LAUNDRY
Balance Sheet
December 31, 1983

Assets		*Liabilities*	
Cash	$ 1,000	Accounts payable	$ 4,000
Laundry supplies	800	Notes payable	12,000
Prepaid insurance.	700	Total Liabilities	$16,000
Building.	21,000		
Laundry equipment	3,500	*Owner's Equity*	
Land	9,000	P. Turner, capital	$20,000
		Total Liabilities and	
Total Assets	$36,000	Owner's Equity.	$36,000

ASSETS.   **Assets are the economic resources of a company that are expected to provide future benefits to the company.** A business may own many assets, some of which are physical in nature such as land, buildings, supplies to be used in the business, and goods (inventory) that the business expects to sell to its customers. Other assets do not possess physical characteristics, but are economic resources because of the legal rights they convey to the business. These assets include amounts owed by customers to the business (*accounts receivable*), the right to insurance protection (*prepaid insurance*), and investments made in other companies.

LIABILITIES.   **Liabilities are the economic obligations (debts) of the company.** The external parties to whom the economic obligations are owed are referred to as the *creditors* of the company. Usually, although not exclusively, legal documents serve as evidence of liabilities. These documents establish a claim (equity) by the creditors (the *creditors' equity*) against the assets of the company. Liabilities include such items as amounts owed to suppliers (*accounts payable*), amounts owed to employees for wages (wages payable), taxes payable, and mortgages owed on the company's property. A company may also borrow money from a bank on a short- or long-term basis by signing a legal document called a *note*, which specifies the terms of the loan. Amounts of loans would be listed as *notes payable*.

OWNER'S EQUITY.   **The owner's equity of a company is the owner's current investment in the assets of the company.** (For a partnership, the owners' equity might be referred to as the *partners' equity*; for a corporation, *stockholders' equity*.) As is shown later, the owner's equity is affected by the capital invested into the business by the owner, by the company's earnings from its operations, and by withdrawals of capital by the owner from the business. For a sole proprietorship, the owner's equity is shown by listing the owner's name, the word *capital*, and the amount of the current investment. The owners' equity of a partnership (partners' equity) and of a corporation (stockholders' equity) is shown slightly differently as discussed later. Owner's equity is sometimes referred to as *residual equity*, because creditors have first legal claim to a company's assets. Once the creditor's claims have been satisfied, the owner is entitled to the remainder (residual) of the assets. Sometimes the total of the liabilities (creditors' equity) is combined with the owner's equity and the result is referred to as the *total equity* of the company.

THE ACCOUNTING EQUATION AND DOUBLE ENTRY RULE

As noted on the Turner Laundry balance sheet, the total of the assets is equal to the total of the liabilities plus the owner's equity. This is true for any balance sheet because a company's economic resources are financed either by its creditors or by its owners.

This equality may be shown in equation form. The basic *accounting equation* (sometimes referred to as the *balance sheet equation*) is as follows:

Accounting Equation

ASSETS   =   LIABILITIES   +   OWNER'S EQUITY

In the case of the Turner Laundry, the equation in monetary terms is:

$$\$36,000 \quad = \quad \$16,000 \quad + \quad \$20,000$$

Like any equation, the components may be transposed. A common way of showing the equation is:

Assets   –   **Liabilities**   =   **Owner's Equity**

or

$$\$36,000 \quad - \quad \$16,000 \quad = \quad \$20,000$$

The accounting equation must always remain in balance—the two sides must always be equal. This rule is one of the basic rules in accounting. Since a transaction normally begins the accounting process, each transaction must be recorded so that this equality is maintained.

Double Entry Rule

A second rule, which complements the equality rule, is the double entry rule. **The double entry rule means that in recording a transaction at least two changes must be made in the assets, liabilities, or owner's equity.** These changes are made as *entries* in the accounting records; thus a double entry must always be made. For instance, if the owner invested $20,000 into the business, assets (cash) would be increased by $20,000 and owner's equity (owner's capital) would be increased by $20,000. The double entry rule is observed and the accounting equation is in balance.

The rule about a double entry does not mean that a transaction will always affect both sides of the equation—or even two components of the equation. A transaction may affect only one side by increasing one asset and decreasing another asset for the same amount, for example. A transaction could also affect only the right side. The rule does not specify in which direction a change is made. The left and right side totals may increase, decrease, or even remain the same. If assets and liabilities both go up, for example, the total of the equation increases, and if both go down, it decreases. But if one asset increases and another asset decreases, the total assets remain unchanged. It is essential, however, that the accounting equation as a whole remains in balance after the transaction.

The balance sheet shows the equality of the accounting equation. A balance sheet can be prepared at any point in the operations of a business, even following each transaction, and it should *always* show total assets equal to the total of the liabilities and owner's equity.

EXAMPLE OF RECORDING TRANSACTIONS

Let us assume that Anne Dixon opens a travel agency on January 1, 1983, by writing a $30,000 personal check and depositing the money in the checking account of the Dixon Travel Agency. This business checking account is separate, of course, from her personal account because of the entity concept. She decides to establish a simple accounting system by listing assets, liabilities, and owner's equity as headings of separate columns with subheadings for specific *kinds* of assets, liabilities, and owner's equity. Each transaction is recorded by entering the amounts in the appropriate columns. The source documents for the first transaction are Anne Dixon's check and the receipt issued by the Dixon Travel Agency to Dixon for her check. Anne Dixon's check does not serve as the only source document for the Dixon Travel Agency because the company's records are kept separate from the owner's, in accordance with the entity concept. This transaction is recorded as follows:

Trans.	Date	Assets		=	Liabilities	+	Owner's Equity
		Cash					A. Dixon, Capital
(1)	1/1/1983	+$30,000		=			+$30,000

As a result of this first transaction, the company now has an asset, Cash, worth $30,000 and owner's equity, A. Dixon, Capital, shows the $30,000 investment by the owner. Note that two entries were made to record this transaction—one to an asset and one to owner's equity—and that the accounting equation is in balance because both sides of the equation were increased by the same amount.

To conduct its operations, the Dixon Travel Agency purchased a small office building on January 2, 1983, paying $18,000 cash. Since such a major cash outlay is paid by check, the Dixon Travel Agency check and the legal documents relating to the purchase of the building serve as the source documents for this transaction. This second transaction is recorded as follows:

Trans.	Date	Assets		=	Liabilities	+	Owner's Equity
		Cash	Building				A. Dixon, Capital
(1)	1/1/1983	+$30,000					+$30,000
(2)	1/2/1983	− 18,000	+$18,000				
		$12,000	+$18,000	=	−0−	+	$30,000

The building is an economic resource expected to provide future benefit to the company by providing space for conducting its business. As a result the building is an asset and the $18,000 is recorded as an increase in the new asset, Building. Because cash was paid out, the asset Cash must be decreased by the same amount. This amount is subtracted from the previous amount of Cash to show the new amount, $12,000. After recording the transaction, the accounting equation must be checked to see that it remains in balance. This is done by adding the assets ($12,000 + $18,000) and comparing this figure to the total of the liabilities ($0) plus owner's equity ($30,000). Thus, the balance is maintained.

On January 5, 1983, Dixon Travel Agency purchased $700 of office supplies from City Supply Company, agreeing to pay for half the supplies on January 15 and the remainder on February 15. The invoice (a document listing the items purchased, the cost of each item, and the total cost) received with the supplies is the source document for the information recorded as follows:

Trans.	Date	Assets			=	Liabilities	+	Owner's Equity
		Cash	Building	Office Supplies		Accts. Payable		A. Dixon, Capital
(1)	1/1/1983	+$30,000						+$30,000
(2)	1/2/1983	− 18,000	+$18,000					
(3)	1/5/1983			+$700		+$700		
		$12,000	+ $18,000 +	$700	=	$700	+	$30,000

Because the office supplies will be used to conduct business, they are recorded as an asset, Office Supplies. This asset is increased by $700. Cash is not reduced, however, because none was paid out. Since Dixon Travel Agency has agreed to pay for half of the supplies on January 15 and the remainder on February 15, it has incurred a debt, or a liability. The liability is labeled Accounts Payable—because it is an amount to be paid by the company—and is increased for the total amount ($700). Note that the increase in the company's assets was financed by a creditor (the supply company), not the owner. As a result, no change was recorded in owner's equity. The accounting equation must remain in balance, however, and therefore the increase in assets on the left side is matched by an increase in liabilities on the right side. Also note that the total of the assets remains equal to the total of the liabilities and owner's equity.

On January 12, 1983, Dixon Travel Agency purchased office equipment from Ace Equipment Company at a cost of $3,000. It paid $1,000 down and signed a note, agreeing to pay the remaining $2,000 at the end of one year. The invoice, check, and note are used to record this fourth transaction as follows:

Trans.	Date	Assets				=	Liabilities		+	Owner's Equity
		Cash	Building	Office Supplies	Office Equipment		Accts. Payable	Notes Payable		A. Dixon, Capital
(1)	1/1/1983	+$30,000								+$30,000
(2)	1/2/1983	− 18,000	+$18,000							
(3)	1/5/1983			+$700			+$700			
(4)	1/12/1983	− 1,000			+$3,000			+$2,000		
		$11,000	+ $18,000 +	$700 +	$3,000	=	$700 +	$2,000	+	$30,000

Because the office equipment is an economic resource to be used in the business, the asset, Office Equipment, is increased by the total cost of $3,000. The asset Cash is decreased by the amount paid, $1,000. Since a $2,000 liability is incurred and a legal note has been issued, the liability, Notes Payable, is increased by this amount. Observe that this transaction affected two assets and a liability, but the accounting equation remains in balance.

On January 15, 1983, Dixon Travel Agency paid the City Supply Company half the amount owed for the supplies purchased on January 5, 1983, by issuing a check for $350. This fifth transaction is recorded as follows:

Trans.	Date	Assets				=	Liabilities		+	Owner's Equity
		Cash	Building	Office Supplies	Office Equipment		Accts. Payable	Notes Payable		A. Dixon, Capital
(1)	1/1/1983	+$30,000								+$30,000
(2)	1/2/1983	− 18,000	+$18,000							
(3)	1/5/1983			+$700			+$700			
(4)	1/12/1983	− 1,000			+$3,000			+$2,000		
(5)	1/15/1983	− 350					− 350			
		$10,650 +	$18,000 +	$700 +	$3,000	=	$350 +	$2,000 +		$30,000

Because the debt owed to City Supply Company was reduced, the liability Accounts Payable was decreased by $350. Because the company made a cash outlay, the asset Cash was decreased by $350. This transaction caused a decrease of the same amount in both sides of the accounting equation, and therefore the equation remained in balance.

Finally, on January 28, 1983, the Dixon Travel Agency decided that it did not need a desk that it had purchased on January 12. This desk had cost $400 and it was sold for this price to James Baker, an insurance agent, for use in his office. The insurance agent agreed to pay for the desk on February 7. This sixth transaction is recorded as follows:

Trans.	Date	Assets					=	Liabilities		+	Owner's Equity
		Cash	Building	Office Supplies	Office Equip.	Accts. Rec.		Accts. Payable	Notes Payable		A. Dixon, Capital
(1)	1/1/1983	+$30,000									+$30,000
(2)	1/2/1983	− 18,000	$18,000								
(3)	1/5/1983			+$700				+$700			
(4)	1/12/1983	− 1,000			+$3,000				+$2,000		
(5)	1/15/1983	− 350						− 350			
(6)	1/28/1983				− 400	+$400					
Balances	1/31/1983	$10,650 +	$18,000 +	$700 +	$2,600 +	$400	=	$350 +	$2,000 +		$30,000

Because the company sold one of its economic resources, the asset Office Equipment is decreased by $400, the cost of the desk. Since the amount to be received from the agent in February is a different economic resource for the Dixon Travel Agency, it also records an increase of $400 in the asset, Accounts Receivable. Again, note the equality of the accounting equation.

We have now recorded six typical transactions for the Dixon Travel Agency. In each case we identified, measured, recorded, and retained the monetary information from the transactions. Our accounting system now contains all the information relating to the company's financial position at the end of January. We can now summarize and communicate this information in a balance sheet. The January 31, 1983, balance sheet of the Dixon Travel Agency is shown in Exhibit 1-8.

The balance sheet lists the ending amounts for each item of assets, liabilities, and owner's equity recorded in the accounting system. Although Accounts Receivable

EXHIBIT 1-8
Balance Sheet

DIXON TRAVEL AGENCY
Balance Sheet
January 31, 1983

Assets			*Liabilities*	
Cash	$10,650		Accounts payable	$ 350
Accounts receivable	400		Notes payable	2,000
Office supplies	700		Total Liabilities	$ 2,350
Building	18,000			
Office equipment	2,600		*Owner's Equity*	
			A. Dixon, capital	$30,000
			Total Liabilities and	
Total Assets	$32,350		Owner's Equity	$32,350

was the last column in the assets section of our simple accounting system, the ending amount of Accounts Receivable is shown directly after Cash on the balance sheet. This procedure is typical because assets are listed in the order of their *liquidity*; that is, the ease of converting them into cash. Office supplies are listed next because they will be used in the business more quickly than the building or office equipment. As we noted throughout the example, in recording each transaction the double entry rule was followed to maintain the equality of the accounting equation. The end result is that total assets ($32,350) are equal to the total of the liabilities ($2,350) and the owner's equity ($30,000).

In the Dixon Travel Agency example, for simplicity we assumed that the company did not engage in any income (profit) making activities. In addition, we studied only basic balance sheet transactions. In the next chapter we introduce more complex transactions involving balance sheet items. Income statement transactions are introduced in Chapter 3. At this point you should be familiar with the basic concepts and principles underlying the accounting process, as well as the elementary procedures involved in completing this process.

REVIEW PROBLEM

On December 31, 1983, the following alphabetical list of items was contained in the records of the Midland Company:

Accounts payable	$ 4,000
Accounts receivable	3,700
Cash	2,600
Building	32,000
Equipment	10,400
G. Midland, capital	27,000
Notes payable	20,000
Prepaid insurance	1,000
Supplies	1,300

Required: Prepare a December 31, 1983, balance sheet for the Midland Company.

SOLUTION TO REVIEW PROBLEM

MIDLAND COMPANY
Balance Sheet
December 31, 1983

Assets		Liabilities	
Cash	$ 2,600	Accounts payable	$ 4,000
Accounts receivable	3,700	Notes payable	20,000
Supplies	1,300	Total Liabilities	$24,000
Prepaid insurance	1,000	*Owner's Equity*	
Building	32,000	G. Midland, capital	$27,000
Equipment	10,400	Total Liabilities and	
Total Assets	$51,000	Owner's Equity	$51,000

GLOSSARY

Accounting. The process of providing quantitative information about economic entities to aid users in making decisions. Financial accounting provides accounting information for external users. Managerial accounting provides accounting information for internal users.

Accounting Equation. Assets = Liabilities + Owner's Equity. This equation must always remain in balance (the two sides must always be equal).

Accounting Principles Board (APB). A committee of the AICPA that established generally accepted accounting principles from 1959 through 1973.

Accounting System. Means by which accounting information is identified, measured, recorded, and retained so that it can be reported in an accounting statement.

Accounts Payable. Liability showing amounts owed *by* a company to its suppliers.

Accounts Receivable. Asset showing amounts owed *to* a company by its customers.

American Institute of Certified Public Accountants (AICPA). A national professional organization of CPAs in the United States.

Annual Report. A yearly report published by a company that contains its audited financial statements.

Assets. Economic resources of a company that are expected to provide future benefits to the company.

Auditing. The primary professional service offered by a CPA. Involves examining the accounting records and resulting financial statements to attest to the fairness of the financial statements.

Balance Sheet. A financial statement used to summarize the financial position (assets, liabilities, and owner's equity) of a company on a given date. Also called a *statement of financial position*.

Certified Public Accountant (CPA). A licensed professional accountant who has met certain educational, experience, examination, and other requirements.

Corporation. A business incorporated as a separate legal entity according to the laws of the state in which it is based.

Double Entry Rule. Rule stating that for each transaction at least two entries must be recorded in the components of the accounting equation to maintain its equality.

Entity Concept. The concept that a company is considered as separate from its owners and from any other company.

Financial Accounting Standards Board (FASB).   An independent board of professional individuals experienced in accounting that establishes generally accepted accounting principles.

Financial Statements.   Accounting reports (income statement and balance sheet) used to summarize and communicate financial information about a company.

Generally Accepted Accounting Principles (GAAP).   The currently acceptable accounting concepts, principles, practices, and procedures that should be used in financial accounting.

Going Concern Concept (Continuity).   Assumption by accountants that a company will continue to operate long enough to meet its current commitments and obligations.

Historical Cost Concept.   Concept that all transactions are recorded at the cost involved in the transaction and that this cost is retained in the accounting records.

Liabilities.   Economic obligations of a company that have been incurred as a result of a transaction and which can be measured in monetary terms.

Materiality.   Concept that accounting information should be communicated only when the monetary amount is large enough to make a difference (be useful) in a user's decision.

Notes Payable.   Liability showing amounts owed by a company as a result of issuing legal documents called notes.

Objective.   Factual and capable of being verified. Important aspect of accounting information.

Owner's Equity.   The owner's current investment in the assets of a company.

Partnership.   A company owned by two or more individuals called partners.

Prepaid Insurance.   Asset showing amount paid for legal right to insurance protection in the future.

Relevance.   Concept that accounting information should be communicated only when it has the capacity to influence a user's decision.

Sole Proprietorship.   A company owned by one individual.

Securities and Exchange Commission (SEC).   An agency of the federal government that regulates the accounting by certain companies.

Source Document.   A business record that serves as evidence that a transaction has occurred.

Transaction.   An exchange of property or services by a company with an external party.

QUESTIONS

Q1-1   Define accounting. Briefly discuss each of the phrases included in your definition.

Q1-2   Who are external users? Give two examples of an economic decision made by an external user.

Q1-3   Who are internal users? Give two examples of an economic decision made by an internal user.

Q1-4 Draw a diagram of the decision-making process. Briefly discuss the steps in the process and indicate where in the process accounting information is used.

Q1-5 What is auditing? Why is an audit important to the external users of a company's financial statements?

Q1-6 List and briefly explain the subareas of public accounting.

Q1-7 What is internal control and how does it relate to internal auditing?

Q1-8 Differentiate accounting from bookkeeping.

Q1-9 Differentiate financial accounting from managerial accounting. How are they similar?

Q1-10 Identify and define the three types of companies. Which type is the most numerous? Which type conducts the greatest volume of business?

Q1-11 Identify the three organizations that have established generally accepted accounting principles. List the pronouncements used for this purpose by each organization.

Q1-12 Define relevance and materiality. How do these concepts relate to each other?

Q1-13 What is the entity concept and how does it affect the accounting for a specific business?

Q1-14 What is a transaction? A source document? Why are they important in accounting?

Q1-15 What is the historical cost concept? What is the going concern concept?

Q1-16 What is an income statement? Define the items included in an income statement.

Q1-17 What is a balance sheet? What is included in the heading of a balance sheet? What are the three segments of a balance sheet?

Q1-18 Define an asset. Give four examples.

Q1-19 Define a liability. Give two examples.

Q1-20 Define owner's equity. What items affect owner's equity?

Q1-21 What is the accounting equation? Why must it always be in balance?

Q1-22 What is the double entry rule? How does this rule relate to the accounting equation?

EXERCISES

E1-1 Accounting Equation. Each of the following cases is independent of the others:

Case	Assets	Liabilities	Owner's Equity
1	A	$16,000	$42,000
2	$65,000	B	28,000
3	28,000	9,000	C

Required: Determine the amounts of A, B, and C.

E1-2 Change in Accounting Equation. At the beginning of the year the Ellis Company had total assets of $52,000 and total liabilities of $20,000. During the year total assets increased by $18,000. At the end of the year owner's equity totaled $55,000.

Required: Determine (1) the owner's equity at the beginning of the year and (2) the total liabilities at the end of the year.

E1-3 Manipulate Accounting Equation. At the end of the year a company's total assets are $78,000 and its total owner's equity is $47,000. During the year the company's liabilities decreased by $11,000 while its assets increased by $8,000.

Required: Determine the company's (1) ending total liabilities, (2) beginning total assets, and (3) beginning owner's equity.

E1-4 Balance Sheet. On August 31, 1983, the Hernandez Company's records contained the following items (listed in alphabetical order):

Accounts payable	$ 9,300
Accounts receivable	14,000
Cash	5,200
L. Hernandez, capital	?
Notes payable	6,000
Office equipment	5,500
Office supplies	400
Prepaid insurance	600

Required: Prepare a balance sheet for the Hernandez Company at August 31, 1983. Insert the correct amount for L. Hernandez, capital.

E1-5 Balance Sheet. Listed below in random order are all the items included in the Ridge Company balance sheet on December 31, 1983:

Accounts receivable	$ 3,500
Cash	?
Supplies	900
Accounts payable	4,600
Building	19,000
A. Ridge, capital	?
Equipment	5,300
Notes payable	3,000

Total assets on December 31, 1983, are $29,900.

Required: Prepare a balance sheet for the Ridge Company on December 31, 1983. Insert the correct amounts for Cash and A. Ridge, capital.

E1-6 Impact on Accounting Equation. The following transactions are taken from the records of the Lee Company:

	Assets	Liabilities	Owner's Equity
(a) C. M. Lee, the owner, invested $10,000 cash in the business.			
(b) Paid $3,000 cash to acquire a small building for the business.			
(c) Received $600 cash from A. B. Jacobs, as payment for office equipment that Jacobs purchased from the company on credit last month.			
(d) Issued a $1,200 check in payment of a note issued last month.			

Required: Determine the overall effect of each transaction on the assets, liabilities and owner's equity of the Lee Company. Use the symbols *I* for increase, *D* for decrease, and *N* for no change. Also show the related dollar amounts.

E1-7 Recording Transactions. The Wilman Company entered into the following transactions during the month of June:

Date	Transaction
6/1	T. Wilman deposited $10,000 in the company's checking account.
6/10	Purchased $500 of office supplies from Timmer Supplies, agreeing to pay for half the supplies by June 30 and the remaining balance by July 15.
6/15	Purchased a 3-year fire insurance policy on a building owned by the company, paying $300 cash.
6/30	Paid Timmer Supplies half the amount owed for supplies purchased on June 10.

Required: Record the above transactions using the following accounting system (use subheadings for the specific kinds of assets, liabilities, and owner's equity):

Date	Assets	=	Liabilities	+	Owner's Equity

E1-8 Examples of Transactions. A transaction of a company may change the balances of the assets, liabilities, and owner's equity of the company.

Required: Give a transaction that will result in the following changes in the contents of a balance sheet:
(a) Increase in an asset and increase in a liability.
(b) Decrease in an asset and decrease in a liability.
(c) Increase in an asset and decrease in another asset.
(d) Increase in an asset and increase in owner's equity.

E1-9 Source Documents. Source documents are used by companies as a basis for recording business transactions.

Required: Name the source documents for each of the following transactions:
(a) Receipt of cash from the owner for additional investment in the business.
(b) Payment by check to purchase office equipment.
(c) Purchase of office supplies on credit.
(d) Sale of office equipment at its original purchase price to a local attorney.
(e) Purchase of fire and casualty insurance protection.

PROBLEMS

Part A

P1-1A Recording Transactions and Source Documents. The Parsons Company was established on June 1, 1983. The following transactions occurred during the month of June:

(a) E. Parsons, owner, started the business by investing $30,000 cash.
(b) Office equipment was purchased. The cash price of $2,600 was paid by writing a check to the supplier.
(c) An office building was acquired at a cost of $14,000. The company paid $4,000 down and signed a note for the remaining balance of $10,000. The note is due in 6 months.
(d) Office supplies totaling $250 were purchased on credit. The amount is due in 30 days.
(e) One piece of office equipment was sold for $600 cash to a real estate agent. The equipment had been purchased earlier this month at a cost of $600.
(f) Purchased a 1-year fire insurance policy for $300.

Required: 1. Record the transactions for the Parsons Company.
2. List the source documents that you would normally use in recording each of the transactions.

P1-2A Recording Transactions and Preparing Balance Sheet.

L. Snider, a young CPA, started an accounting practice on September 1, 1983. During the month of September, the following transactions took place:

(a) L. Snider invested $40,000 cash to start the new business.
(b) A building was purchased for the business at a cost of $25,000. The company made a down payment of $5,000 and signed a note for the remaining balance of $20,000. The note is due in 1 year.
(c) Office equipment totaling $3,500 was purchased for cash.
(d) One piece of office equipment was sold to D. Popper. The selling price, $550, was the same as the cost at which the office equipment was originally purchased. Popper agreed to pay the $550 at the end of October.
(e) Office supplies were purchased for a total price of $1,700. The amount was paid by writing a check to the supplier.

Required: 1. Record the transactions for the company, L. Snider, CPA.
2. Prepare a September 30, 1983 balance sheet for the company, L. Snider, CPA.

P1-3A Recording Transactions and Preparing Balance Sheets.

The Envoy Investment Company was recently established by the owner, G. Envoy. The following transactions took place during April:

(a) On April 1 G. Envoy set up the business by transferring $45,000 cash from his personal checking account to the newly opened checking account of the Envoy Investment Company.
(b) On April 3 a building was acquired to be used as the office. A note for the entire purchase price of $24,000 was signed and given to the seller. The note is due in 1 year.
(c) On April 6 several pieces of office equipment were purchased for a price of $4,200. A check for that amount was written and given to the seller.
(d) On April 15 office supplies totaling $640 were purchased on credit. The amount is due at the end of May.
(e) On April 23 one piece of office equipment was sold at a selling price equal to its original cost of $820. The amount was collected in cash.

Required: 1. Record the transactions for the Envoy Investment Company.
2. Prepare a balance sheet after each transaction has taken place (a total of five balance sheets is required).

P1-4A Analyzing Cash Transactions.

All the transactions that took place during the month of February for the Van Tassel Company are as follows:

(a) On February 1 L. Van Tassel started the business by investing $55,000 in the company. A checking account was opened in the name of the Van Tassel Company and the entire $55,000 was deposited in the newly opened account.
(b) An office building was purchased for $23,000. A down payment of $8,000 was paid by writing a check; a note was signed for the remaining $15,000. The note is due in 3 months.
(c) A $4,200 check was written to pay for the entire purchase price of office equipment.
(d) A check in the amount of $600 was written to acquire office supplies.
(e) One piece of office equipment was sold to D. Clark at its original purchase price, and the cash collected was deposited in the company's checking account.

Required: Assuming all the transactions of the Van Tassel Company in the month of February were properly recorded and the balance of the checking account at the end of February was found to be $42,930, compute the selling price of the piece of equipment sold in (e) above. Show your calculations.

P1-5A   Identifying Transactions from Successive Balance Sheets.   The bookkeeper of the Smith Company prepares a balance sheet immediately after each transaction is recorded. During March, the first month of operations, the following five balance sheets were prepared:

(a)

SMITH COMPANY
Balance Sheet
March 1, 1983

Assets		*Liabilities and Owner's Equity*	
Cash	$80,000	Jan Smith, capital	$80,000
		Total Liabilities and	
Total Assets	$80,000	Owner's Equity	$80,000

(b)

SMITH COMPANY
Balance Sheet
March 3, 1983

Assets		*Liabilities and Owner's Equity*	
Cash	$75,000	Notes payable	$15,000
Building	20,000	Jan Smith, capital	80,000
		Total Liabilities and	
Total Assets	$95,000	Owner's Equity	$95,000

(c)

SMITH COMPANY
Balance Sheet
March 7, 1983

Assets		*Liabilities and Owner's Equity*	
Cash	$75,000	Accounts payable	$ 1,300
Office supplies	1,300	Notes payable	15,000
Building	20,000	Total Liabilities	$16,300
		Jan Smith, capital	80,000
		Total Liabilities and	
Total Assets	$96,300	Owner's Equity	$96,300

(d)

SMITH COMPANY
Balance Sheet
March 8, 1983

Assets		*Liabilities and Owner's Equity*	
Cash	$71,500	Accounts payable	$ 1,300
Office supplies	1,300	Notes payable	15,000
Building	20,000	Total Liabilities	$16,300
Office equipment	3,500	Jan Smith, capital	80,000
		Total Liabilities and	
Total Assets	$96,300	Owner's Equity	$96,300

(e)

SMITH COMPANY
Balance Sheet
March 29, 1983

Assets		Liabilities and Owner's Equity	
Cash	$71,920	Accounts payable	$ 1,300
Office supplies	1,300	Notes payable	15,000
Building	20,000	Total Liabilities	$16,300
Office equipment	3,080	Jan Smith, capital	80,000
		Total Liabilities and	
Total Assets	$96,300	Owner's Equity	$96,300

Required: Describe the nature of the five transactions that took place during the month of March.

P1-6A Identifying Transactions. The five transactions that occurred during June, the first month of operations for the Brown Company, were recorded as follows:

		Assets				=	Liabilities		+	Owner's Equity
Trans.	Date	Cash +	Office Supplies +	Building +	Office Equipment =		Accts. Payable +	Notes Payable +		Tom Brown, Capital +
(a)	6/01/1983	+$75,000								+$75,000
(b)	6/05/1983	− 8,000		+$28,000				+$20,000		
(c)	6/08/1983	− 270	+$270							
(d)	6/17/1983	− 4,000			+$12,000			+ 8,000		
(e)	6/26/1983		+ 480				+$480			
Balances	6/30/1983	$62,730 +	$750 +	$28,000 +	$12,000 =		$480 +	$28,000 +		$75,000

Required:
1. Describe the nature of the five transactions that took place during the month of June.
2. Prepare a balance sheet at June 30, 1983.

PROBLEMS

Part B

P1-1B Recording Transactions and Source Documents. The Johnson Company was established on October 1, 1983. The following transactions occurred during the month of October:

(a) M. Johnson, the owner, started the business by investing $40,000 cash.
(b) An office building was acquired at a cost of $22,000. A down payment of $8,000 was made and a note for $14,000 was signed. The note is due in 1 year.
(c) Several pieces of office equipment were purchased for a cash price of $4,600. The amount was paid immediately.
(d) Office supplies totaling $850 were purchased on credit. The amount is due in early December.
(e) Two pieces of office equipment that had been acquired earlier in the month at a cost of $1,400 were sold to T. Jackson. The selling price of $1,400 was received in cash.
(f) Purchased a 1-year fire insurance policy for $200.

Required:
1. Record the transactions for the Johnson Company.
2. List the source documents that you would normally use in recording each of the transactions.

P1-2B Recording Transactions and Preparing a Balance Sheet. F. Ryan, a young attorney, decided to start a law firm on December 1, 1983. During the month of December the following transactions took place:

(a) F. Ryan invested $35,000 cash to start the new business.
(b) An office building was purchased. Out of the total purchase price of $18,000, $3,000 was paid in cash and a note for the remaining balance of $15,000 was signed and given to the seller. The note is due in three months.
(c) Office equipment was purchased for a cash price of $7,500.
(d) Office supplies were purchased on credit from a local supplier. The purchase price of $660 is due next month.
(e) One piece of office equipment that had been purchased earlier was sold at its original cost of $470. A check in the amount of $470 was received.

Required: 1. Record the transactions for the company, F. Ryan, Attorney.
   2. Prepare a December 31, 1983 balance sheet for the company, F. Ryan, Attorney.

P1-3B Recording Transactions and Preparing Balance Sheets. The Lawrence Travel Agency was established by the owner, K. Lawrence. The following transactions took place during July:

(a) On July 1 K. Lawrence set up the business by transferring $45,000 cash from his personal checking to the newly opened checking account of the Lawrence Travel Agency.
(b) On July 7 a building was acquired for a price of $27,000. A down payment of $7,000 was made and a note in the amount of $20,000 was signed. The note is due in 6 months.
(c) On July 13 office equipment was purchased for a total price of $5,500. A cash payment of $1,500 was made and the remaining balance of $4,000 is due in 30 days.
(d) On July 24 office supplies totaling $960 were purchased on credit. The amount is due at the end of August.
(e) On July 31 one piece of office equipment was sold at its original cost of $1,040. The amount was collected in cash.

Required: 1. Record the transactions for the Lawrence Travel Agency.
   2. Prepare a balance sheet after each transaction has taken place (a total of five balance sheets is required).

P1-4B Analyzing Cash Transactions. All the transactions that took place during the month of November for the Patrick Company are as follows:

(a) On November 1 T. Patrick set up the company by investing $35,000 in the business. A checking account in the name of the company was opened and the entire $35,000 was deposited in that account.
(b) An office building was purchased for the new business. A check in the amount of $4,500 was written to pay for the down payment and a 3-month note for the remaining $18,500 was signed.
(c) A check in the amount of $7,300 was written to pay for the entire purchase price of office equipment.
(d) One piece of equipment that had been purchased earlier was sold to J. Collins at its original cost of $1,200. The $1,200 was collected and deposited in the company's checking account.
(e) Office supplies were purchased and a check was written for the purchase price.

Required: Assuming all the transactions of the Patrick Company in the month of November were properly recorded and the balance of the checking account at the end of November was found to be $22,700, compute the purchase price of the office supplies in (e) above. Show your calculations.

P1-5B **Identifying Transactions from Successive Balance Sheets.** Lisa Wallace, owner of the Wallace Company, believes that current information is necessary for successful business operations. Accordingly, she requires that a balance sheet be prepared and submitted to her immediately after each transaction takes place. During the month of August, the following five balance sheets were prepared and submitted to her by the company's bookkeeper:

(a)

WALLACE COMPANY
Balance Sheet
August 1, 1983

Assets		Liabilities and Owner's Equity	
Cash	$65,000	Lisa Wallace, capital	$65,000
		Total Liabilities and	
Total Assets	$65,000	Owner's Equity	$65,000

(b)

WALLACE COMPANY
Balance Sheet
August 2, 1983

Assets		Liabilities and Owner's Equity	
Cash	$59,000	Notes payable	$15,000
Building	21,000	Lisa Wallace, capital	65,000
		Total Liabilities and	
Total Assets	$80,000	Owner's Equity	$80,000

(c)

WALLACE COMPANY
Balance Sheet
August 4, 1983

Assets		Liabilities and Owner's Equity	
Cash	$59,000	Accounts payable	$ 1,400
Office supplies	1,400	Notes payable	15,000
Building	21,000	Total Liabilities	$16,400
		Lisa Wallace, capital	65,000
		Total Liabilities and	
Total Assets	$81,400	Owner's Equity	$81,400

(d)

WALLACE COMPANY
Balance Sheet
August 9, 1983

Assets		Liabilities and Owner's Equity	
Cash	$56,000	Accounts payable	$ 1,400
Office supplies	1,400	Notes payable	25,000
Building	21,000	Total Liabilities	$26,400
Office equipment	13,000	Lisa Wallace, capital	65,000
		Total Liabilities and	
Total Assets	$91,400	Owner's Equity	$91,400

(e)

WALLACE COMPANY
Balance Sheet
August 24, 1983

Assets		*Liabilities and Owner's Equity*	
Cash	$52,800	Accounts payable	$ 1,400
Office supplies	4,600	Notes payable	25,000
Building	21,000	Total Liabilities	$26,400
Office equipment	13,000	Lisa Wallace, capital	65,000
		Total Liabilities and	
Total Assets	$91,400	Owner's Equity	$91,400

Required: Describe the nature of the five transactions that the bookkeeper recorded during the month of August.

P1-6B Identifying Transactions. The following transactions were recorded by the Sutton Company for the month of May, its first month of operations:

		Assets				=	Liabilities		+	Owner's Equity
Trans.	Date	Cash	+ Office Supplies +	Building +	Office Equipment =		Accts. Payable +	Notes Payable +		Steve Sutton, Capital
(a)	5/01/1983	+$55,000								+$55,000
(b)	5/02/1983	− 8,000		+$24,000				+$16,000		
(c)	5/07/1983	− 2,500			+$6,500			+ 4,000		
(d)	5/10/1983		+$1,100				+$1,100			
(e)	5/22/1983	+ 300			− 300					
Balances	5/31/1983	$44,800	+ $1,100 +	$24,000 +	$6,200 =		$1,100 +	$20,000 +		$55,000

Required: 1. Describe the nature of the five transactions that were recorded during the month of May.
2. Prepare a balance sheet at May 31, 1983.

2 | Recording and Reporting Accounting Information

After reading this chapter, you should understand:

- The terms account, chart of accounts, general ledger, general journal, and trial balance
- The debit and credit rules for assets, liabilities, and owner's equity
- The relationship between the double entry rule, the debit and credit rule, and the accounting equation
- Journalizing and posting transactions affecting the balance sheet
- Preparing a balance sheet from a trial balance
- The relationship between business documents and the steps in the accounting process of an accounting system

In Chapter 1 we used a simple columnar accounting system to record transactions and to prepare a balance sheet. Although this system was helpful for explaining the accounting process, it is not very practical in today's business world. Within the period of a month most companies have hundreds or thousands of transactions involving many assets, liabilities, and owner's equity items. These transactions not only affect the balance sheet but also the income statement. Setting up a column for recording transactions affecting all the assets, liabilities, and owner's equity items of most companies would result in a very large accounting record, which would not be very useful for an actual business.

A better system for processing accounting information is needed. This system would include a set of accounting procedures and documents for recording, retaining, and reporting all the information about each transaction. In this chapter we introduce a system for transactions affecting the balance sheet. After we have attained a good understanding of the accounting system described in this chapter, the system will be extended in Chapter 3 for income statement transactions. The accounting system shown here can be used for either manual or computer information processing. For ease of learning the discussion in this textbook mostly involves manual processing. Computer information processing is discussed in Chapter 6.

ACCOUNTS

We defined an accounting system as a means by which accounting information is identified, measured, recorded, and retained so that it can be reported in an accounting statement. In the example in the last chapter we used a separate column to record and retain the increases and decreases in each asset, liability, and owner's equity item. In an accounting system in the business world, an account is used for this purpose. **An account is a business document that is used to record and retain the monetary information from business transactions.** Separate accounts are used for each asset, liability, and owner's equity item. For example, a company may have accounts for Cash, Accounts Receivable, Notes Receivable, Office Supplies, Prepaid Insurance, Office Equipment, Delivery Equipment, Land, Buildings, Accounts Payable, Notes Payable, and A. Dixon, Capital, to name only a few. The number, types, and names of the accounts for each company depend upon the particular company's operations, whether it is a sole proprietorship, partnership, or corporation, and the types of assets it owns and liabilities it has incurred. **A general ledger is the entire set of accounts for a company.** For this reason, sometimes accounts are referred to as *ledger accounts*.

An account can take several physical forms. It might be a computer card, a location on a computer disk or tape, or a standardized business paper in the case of a manual system. The general ledger might be a deck of computer cards, a computer disk or tape, or a loose-leaf binder containing all the accounts of a manual system. Regardless of the physical form, all accounts are used for recording and retaining accounting information.

Components of an Account

No matter what physical form is used, the same logical format is used throughout for recording and retaining accounting information in the accounts. This format is easiest to understand for a manual system. A simple format for the accounts in a manual system is called a *T-account* because it looks like the capital letter T. As shown below, each T-account has three basic parts: (1) a place at the top for the *title* of the particular asset, liability, or owner's equity item, (2) a *left* side, called the *debit* side, and (3) a *right* side, called the *credit* side. The title of each account describes the nature of the account (e.g., Buildings, Notes Payable). The left (debit) and the right (credit) sides of each account are used for recording and retaining the monetary information from business transactions. **A debit entry is a monetary amount recorded (debited) in the left side of an account. A credit entry is a monetary amount recorded (credited) in the right side of an account.**

Title of Account	
Left (debit) side	Right (credit) side

Debit and Credit Rules

Each account accumulates information about both increases and decreases from various business transactions. There are two rules for recording these increases and decreases in the accounts. The first rule is that for each account all increases are recorded in one side of the account and all decreases are recorded in the other side of the account. This rule makes it easy to determine the total increases and decreases for a particular account. It does not indicate, however, whether the increases or decreases should be recorded in the debit or credit side of the account. A second rule is *the debit and credit rule*. This rule relates to the basic accounting equation; it states:

> **Asset accounts (accounts on the left side of the accounting equation) are increased by debit entries (i.e., recorded amounts on the left side) and decreased by credit entries.**
>
> **Liabilities and owners' equity accounts (accounts on the right side of the equation) are increased by credit entries (i.e., recorded amounts on the right side) and decreased by debit entries.**

This rule and its relationship to the accounting equation are illustrated as follows. (Since this rule applies to the accounts of a sole proprietorship, partnership, or corporation, the plural *owners'* equity is used here.)

Assets	=	Liabilities	+	Owners' Equity
Asset Accounts		*Liability Accounts*		*Owners' Equity Accounts*
(debit) / (credit)		(debit) / (credit)		(debit) / (credit)
Increase / Decrease		Decrease / Increase		Decrease / Increase
+ / −		− / +		− / +

This rule is essential for understanding how to record business transactions. It may be separated into parts as follows:

1. **Assets**
   (a) An increase in an asset is recorded in the left (debit) side of the asset account, by a debit entry.
   (b) A decrease in an asset is recorded in the right (credit) side of the asset account, by a credit entry.

2. **Liabilities**
   (a) An increase in a liability is recorded in the right (credit) side of the liability account, by a credit entry.
   (b) A decrease in a liability is recorded in the left (debit) side of the liability account, by a debit entry.

3. **Owners' Equity**
   (a) An increase in owners' equity is recorded in the right (credit) side of the owners' equity account, by a credit entry.
   (b) A decrease in owners' equity is recorded in the left (debit) side of the owners' equity account, by a debit entry.

Balance of an Account **The balance of an account is the difference between the total increases and decreases recorded in the account.** Usually the balance of each account is computed when the accounting information is to be communicated in an accounting report. Each asset account normally has a debit balance because the total increases (debits) exceed the total decreases (credits) in the account. Each liability and owners' equity account has a credit balance because the total credits (increases) exceed the total debits (decreases) in each account.

To illustrate, look at the Cash account (numbered 101, discussed later) shown below:

Cash			No. 101
6/1/83 Balance	2,000	6/2/83	900
6/4/83	5,000	6/10/83	3,000
		6/26/83	700
- - - - - - - - - - - - -		- - - - - - - - - - - - -	
6/30/83 Balance	2,400		

Note that on June 1, 1983, the account had a $2,000 debit balance (this was the ending balance for May, the difference between the total debits and credits in the account to that date). On June 4 a transaction occurred that increased (debited) the Cash account by $5,000, while on June 2, 10, and 26 the Cash account was decreased (credited) by $900, $3,000, and $700, respectively. The debit balance of the Cash account is $2,400 on June 30, 1983, because the total debits ($7,000) exceed the total credits ($4,600). The debit and credit entries in accounts are discussed in more detail later in the chapter.

Double Entry Rule

In Chapter 1 we introduced the double entry rule, which stated that to record a transaction, at least two entries must be made in the components of the accounting equation to keep both sides of the equation equal. At that time we had not learned the debit and credit rule. The double entry rule is now modified as follows: **The double entry rule states that when recording each transaction, the total amount of the debit entries must be equal to the total amount of the credit entries for that transaction.** Thus for each recorded transaction there must be at least one debit entry and one credit entry (although there could be more entries of each type), and the total amounts must be equal. For example, suppose a company purchased land for cash at a cost of $2,000. To record this transaction, an asset account Land would be increased by a debit entry for $2,000 and another asset account Cash would be decreased by a credit entry of $2,000. Thus the total debits equal the total credits in this transaction.

It is important to understand the consistent relationship between the accounting equation, the debit and credit rule, and the double entry rule. Recall that the accounting equation must always be in balance. Recall also that when recording a transaction, it is not necessary to affect both sides of the equation or even two components of the equation. It is possible to record a transaction as affecting only the left side, the right side, or both sides of the equation provided that the equation remains in balance. If the debit and credit rule and the double entry rule are followed, the accounting equation will *always* remain in balance. For instance, in the land example just given the debit entry *increased* the Land account while the credit entry *decreased* the Cash account. The total debits equaled the total credits, and thus the double entry rule was followed. Only the left side of the accounting equation (the asset component) was affected, but the equation remained in balance because there was no change in *total* assets. The left side of the equation therefore remained equal to the right side of the equation. Additional examples are presented later in the chapter.

Checklist of Important Rules

Up to this point we have stated several important rules that must be followed in an actual accounting system. These rules are summarized as follows to help you remember them and their relationship:

1. **The accounting equation (assets equal liabilities plus owners' equity) must always remain in balance.**
2. **All increases in an account are recorded on one side of the account; all decreases are recorded on the other side of the account.**
3. **The debit and credit rule states that:**
   (a) **Asset accounts are increased by debit entries and decreased by credit entries.**
   (b) **Liabilities and owners' equity accounts are increased by credit entries and decreased by debit entries.**
4. **The double entry rule states that for all recorded transactions, the total amount of the debit entries must be equal to the total amount of the credit entries.**

Illustration of Rules

To illustrate the rules that have been stated in this chapter, we use the Dixon Travel Agency example from Chapter 1. The agency entered into six transactions during January, 1983. Presented below are the date and description of each transaction, an analysis of the transaction, the applicable debit and credit rules, a summary of the entries to record the transaction, and the T-account debit and credit entries. The arrows show that the total amount of the debit and credit entries is equal for each transaction.

Transaction 1 (1/1/1983): Anne Dixon opened a travel agency by depositing a $30,000 personal check in the Dixon Travel Agency checking account.

Analysis: The asset account Cash is increased by $30,000 and the owner's equity account A. Dixon, Capital is increased by $30,000.

Debit and Credit Rules: Asset accounts are increased by debit entries; owner's equity accounts are increased by credit entries.

Summary of Entries: Cash is debited for $30,000 and A. Dixon, Capital is credited for $30,000.

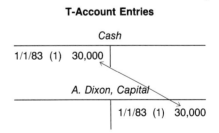

T-Account Entries

Cash

1/1/83 (1) 30,000

A. Dixon, Capital

1/1/83 (1) 30,000

Transaction 2 (1/2/1983):   Office building is purchased for $18,000.

Analysis: The asset account Building is increased by $18,000 and the asset account Cash is decreased by $18,000.

Debit and Credit Rules: Asset accounts are increased by debit entries; asset accounts are decreased by credit entries.

Summary of Entries: Building is debited for $18,000 and Cash is credited for $18,000.

T-Account Entries

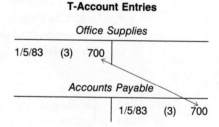

Building

| 1/2/83 | (2) 18,000 | |

Cash

| 1/1/83 | (1) 30,000 | 1/2/83 | (2) 18,000 |

Transaction 3 (1/5/1983):   Office supplies costing $700 are purchased on account from City Supply Company. Half the amount owed is to be paid for on January 15; the remainder is due on February 15.

Analysis: The asset account Office Supplies is increased by $700 and the liability account Accounts Payable is increased by $700.

Debit and Credit Rules: Asset accounts are increased by debit entries; liability accounts are increased by credit entries.

Summary of Entries: Office Supplies is debited for $700 and Accounts Payable is credited for $700.

T-Account Entries

Office Supplies

| 1/5/83 | (3) | 700 | |

Accounts Payable

| | | 1/5/83 | (3) | 700 |

Transaction 4 (1/12/1983):   Office equipment costing $3,000 is purchased from Ace Equipment Company by making a $1,000 down payment and signing a $2,000 note due at the end of one year.

Analysis: The asset account Office Equipment is increased by $3,000. The asset account Cash is decreased by $1,000 and the liability account Notes Payable is increased by $2,000.

Debit and Credit Rules: Asset accounts are increased by debit entries and decreased by credit entries. Liability accounts are increased by credit entries.

Summary of Entries: Office Equipment is debited for $3,000, Cash is credited for $1,000 and Notes Payable is credited for $2,000.

T-Account Entries

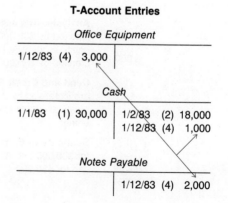

Office Equipment

| 1/12/83 | (4) | 3,000 | |

Cash

| 1/1/83 | (1) 30,000 | 1/2/83 | (2) 18,000 |
| | | 1/12/83 | (4) 1,000 |

Notes Payable

| | | 1/12/83 | (4) | 2,000 |

Transaction 5 (1/15/1983): $350 is paid to City Supply Company in partial payment of Accounts Payable.

Analysis: The liability account Accounts Payable is decreased by $350 and the asset account Cash is decreased by $350.

Debit and Credit Rules: Liability accounts are decreased by debit entries; asset accounts are decreased by credit entries.

Summary of Entries: Accounts Payable is debited for $350 and Cash is credited for $350.

T-Account Entries

Accounts Payable

1/15/83 (5)	350	1/5/83 (3) 700

Cash

1/1/83 (1) 30,000	1/2/83 (2) 18,000
	1/12/83 (4) 1,000
	1/15/83 (5) 350

Transaction 6 (1/28/1983): Office equipment (desk) that cost $400 is sold for $400 on account, the purchaser agreeing to pay the full amount on February 7.

Analysis: The asset account Accounts Receivable is increased by $400 and the asset account Office Equipment is decreased by $400.

Debit and Credit Rules: Asset accounts are increased by debit entries and decreased by credit entries.

Summary of Entries: Accounts Receivable is debited for $400 and Office Equipment is credited for $400.

T-Account Entries

Accounts Receivable

1/28/83 (6) 400	

Office Equipment

1/12/83 (4) 3,000	1/28/83 (6) 400

Note that the double entry rule was followed in recording each transaction. Now look at a summary of the impact of each transaction on the accounting equation (*dr* and *cr* in parentheses refer to debit and credit, respectively; they are common abbreviations and are used frequently throughout this textbook).

Transaction Number	Assets	=	Liabilities	+	Owner's Equity
1	+$30,000 (dr) Cash				+$30,000 (cr) A. Dixon, Capital
2	+ 18,000 (dr) Building				
	− 18,000 (cr) Cash				
3	+ 700 (dr) Office supplies		+$ 700 (cr) Accounts payable		
4	+ 3,000 (dr) Office equipment				
	− 1,000 (cr) Cash		+ 2,000 (cr) Notes payable		
5	− 350 (cr) Cash		− 350 (dr) Accounts payable		
6	+ 400 (dr) Accounts receivable				
	− 400 (cr) Office equipment				
Totals	$32,350	=	$2,350	+	$30,000

In this summary see that for each transaction the total debits always equaled the total credits. This was true even when there was more than one debit or credit entry (transaction 4 had two credit entries). See also that the accounting equation always remained in balance, even though (1) only one side of the equation may have been affected by a particular transaction and (2) a transaction may have caused an increase, a decrease, or no change in the equation. Furthermore, the total of each side of the equation is $32,350. Although we could compute the account balances and prepare a balance sheet at this point as we did in Chapter 1, first we will introduce several other accounting procedures.

THE GENERAL JOURNAL AND JOURNALIZING

Our example of the Dixon Travel Agency had only six transactions and each was summarized to keep the example simple. The agency had only eight T-accounts in which we directly recorded the transactions. In reality a company engages in hundreds or thousands of transactions and has many more than eight accounts. When the transactions occur they are not summarized as shown in the example. Recording the transactions directly in the accounts would lead to a high chance for error because of the numerous accounts in the general ledger. In addition, if the accountant reviews a debit entry in an account and wants to see the related credit entry of the transaction, it would not be possible. Finally, no written description of the transactions would exist if the transactions were recorded directly in the accounts. For these reasons, transactions are *not* initially recorded directly in a company's accounts.

General Journal

The business transactions of a company are first recorded in a journal, after which the information is transferred to the company's accounts. **A general journal is a business document in which are recorded the date of the transaction, the accounts to be debited and credited, the amounts of the debit and credit entries, and an explanation of each transaction.** In a manual accounting system the general journal is a book of columnar pages.

A general journal can be used to record all types of transactions. It is the main journal used throughout this textbook. Many companies have a number of *special journals,* each of which is designed for recording a particular type of business transaction. For instance, one special journal is the Cash Receipts Journal used to record all receipts of cash. Special journals are discussed in Chapter 6. The following discussion applies to all types of journals.

A journal entry is the recorded information for each transaction. Journalizing is the act of preparing the journal entry. A journal is often referred to as the *document of original entry* because each transaction is first, or originally, entered in the journal. (Before computers were widespread, a journal was called the *book* of original entry. But since a journal today may be a deck of computer cards or a magnetic tape or disk, the term *document* is more appropriate than the term book.)

There are many advantages to using a journal for initially recording a company's transactions. First, use of a journal helps to prevent errors. Since the accounts and the debit and credit amounts for each transaction are initially recorded on a single journal page rather than directly in the many accounts, this method makes it easier to prove that the debits and credits are equal. Second, all the information about the transactions (including the explanation) is recorded in one place, thereby providing a complete "picture" of the transaction. This is very useful during the auditing process or if an error is discovered later in the accounting process, because the accountant can look in the journal to see all of the accounts involved and find an explanation for the transaction. Finally, since the transactions are recorded chronologically (day by day), the journal also provides a chronological "history" of the company's financial transactions.

Key Procedures in Journalizing

Throughout this text you will study many journal entries. You will also prepare many journal entries in the general journal for your homework assignments. It is very important that you understand the form of the general journal and carefully learn the procedures for journalizing each transaction. Shown below is a partial page from a general journal. A completed general journal page is shown in Exhibit 2-2.

	GENERAL JOURNAL			Page 9
Date	Account Titles and Explanations	Acct. No.	Debit	Credit

Listed below are the journalizing procedures for each column of the general journal. Study them carefully, referring to the partial general journal page or to Exhibit 2-2. An illustration follows.

1. The month, day, and year of the first transaction are entered in the column entitled, "Date," with the year written above the month. It is not necessary to repeat the month and the year of subsequent transactions until a new journal page is begun or transactions for the next month are recorded.
2. The *exact* title of the account to be debited is entered at the far left of the column entitled, "Account Titles and Explanations." The amount of the debit to this account is entered in the debit column. Dollar signs are typically not used in the debit (or credit) column.
3. The *exact* title of the account to be credited is entered on the next line below the title of the debited account. The title of the credit account is indented slightly to the right so that when looking at the journal page, a reader can easily identify which account titles are to be credited and debited. The amount of the credit to this account is entered in the credit column.

4. As we have already seen, a transaction may be recorded that involves two or more debits, two or more credits, or both. (Remember that for each transaction the total amount of the debit entries must be equal to the total amount of the credit entries.) This type of entry is called a *compound entry*. When recording a compound entry, all the accounts (and amounts) to be debited are listed first (with each account listed on a separate line), followed by all the accounts to be credited (indented and also listed on a separate line). The January 12, 1983, transaction in Exhibit 2-2 is an example of a compound journal entry. In this entry Office Equipment was debited for $3,000 and both Cash and Notes Payable were credited for $1,000 and $2,000, respectively.

5. A brief explanation is entered on the line below the last credit entry of each transaction. The explanation is entered at the far left of the column entitled, "Account Titles and Explanations." A line is skipped before beginning another journal entry to set off each entry.

6. During the process of journalizing, *no* number is recorded in the column entitled, "Acct. No." (Account Number). A number will be entered in this column later.

Illustration of Journal Entries

To illustrate the general journal and journalizing, the six transactions of the Dixon Travel Agency for January 1983 are recorded in Exhibit 2-2, but first the transactions are briefly summarized in Exhibit 2-1. Also included are the source documents from which the accounting information was obtained for each transaction.

EXHIBIT 2-1 Source Documents and Summary of Transactions

Transaction Number	Date	Source Document	Transaction
1	1/1/1983	Receipt issued by Dixon Travel Agency	Anne Dixon invested $30,000 in the Dixon Travel Agency.
2	1/2/1983	Check and legal documents	Office building was purchased at a cost of $18,000.
3	1/5/1983	Invoice received with supplies	Office supplies costing $700 were purchased on account from City Supply Company. Half of this amount is to be paid on January 15, the remainder is due on February 15.
4	1/12/1983	Invoice received with office equipment, check, and note	Office equipment costing $3,000 is purchased from Ace Equipment Company by making a $1,000 down payment and signing a 1-year note for $2,000.
5	1/15/1983	Check	$350 is paid on account to City Supply Company.
6	1/28/1983	Written agreement summarizing sale and payment terms	Office equipment (desk) costing $400 is sold for $400 on account to James Baker. The full amount is due on February 7.

Exhibit 2-2 shows the journal entries in the Dixon Travel Agency general journal for each of the six transactions. In studying Exhibit 2-2 you should review each transaction listed in Exhibit 2-1, form a picture in your mind of the accounting information on the source documents, determine the debit and credit entries, think of the journalizing procedures, and compare these procedures to the journal entries made in Exhibit 2-2.

To illustrate the journalizing process, we look at the January 2, 1983, transaction (the purchase of the office building). To start the process, we examine the source

EXHIBIT 2-2
Dixon Travel Agency
General Journal

GENERAL JOURNAL				Page 1	
Date		Account Titles and Explanations	Acct. No.	Debit	Credit
1983 Jan.	1	Cash A. Dixon, Capital Owner invested cash into business.		30,000	30,000
	2	Building Cash Purchased office building in which to operate the travel agency.		18,000	18,000
	5	Office Supplies Accounts Payable Purchased office supplies on account from City Supply Company; agreed to pay half of the amount owed on January 15 and the remainder on February 15.		700	700

	12	Office Equipment
		    Cash
		    Notes Payable
		Purchased office equipment from Ace Equipment Company; made cash down payment and signed 1-year note.
				3,000	1,000
					2,000

	15	Accounts Payable Cash Paid City Supply Company half of the amount owed for office supplies purchased on January 5, 1983.		350	350
	28	Accounts Receivable Office Equipment Sold desk that cost $400 to James Baker on credit for $400; the full amount is to be collected on February 7.		400	400

documents, the Dixon Travel Agency check for $18,000 and the legal documents related to the event. The legal documents (deed, contract, etc.) verify that the check was written for the purchase of the building. Thus the asset account Building increased and should be debited for $18,000, while the asset account Cash decreased and should be credited for $18,000. Skipping a line after the previous transaction, we enter the date and the exact account title (Building) and amount ($18,000) to be debited. On the next line, we indent about an inch and enter the exact account title (Cash) and amount ($18,000) to be credited.[1] On the next line we write a brief explanation of the journal entry. In this explanation we could include the reference numbers (e.g., check number) to the source documents that are available. This is useful in the auditing process or in the case of an error, where a review of the original source documents would be useful. This process is followed for each transaction, and all the source documents are then filed in the company's records.

ACCOUNTS AND POSTING

In the journalizing process each transaction is initially entered in one record, the journal, to (1) minimize errors, (2) have all the debit and credit information for each transaction in one place, and (3) have a chronological list of all the company's financial transactions. However, the accounting information from each transaction is not yet recorded in the accounts, the so-called "storage units" for the company's accounting information. To do so, we must post the accounts from the journal to the ledger accounts. **Posting is the process of transferring the debit and credit information for each journal entry to the proper accounts in the general ledger.**

Account Formats

Earlier in the chapter we used T-accounts to show the process of recording and retaining information. Throughout the text we often use T-accounts as examples because they are simple and easy to understand. In a manual accounting system in the actual business world, however, an account usually has a format as shown in Exhibit 2-3.

**EXHIBIT 2-3
Illustration of a
Typical Account
Format**

Cash						Acct. No. 101
Date		Explanation	Jr. Ref.	Debit	Credit	Debit Balance

[1] We have not used a "cents" column in the debit and credit amount columns to avoid unnecessary detail. Both dollars and cents would be recorded in the general journal for actual transactions, however.

In this format the columns for the date, explanation, and journal reference (Jr. Ref.) are the first three columns in the account. The debit and credit columns are on the righthand side. A column entitled, "balance," which shows a running total of the debit or credit balance in the account, is at the far right side of the account. The column entitled "explanation," is used for only unusual and complicated entries, since an explanation of each entry in the account has already been made in the journal. The use of the journal reference column is explained later when posting is discussed.

Account Numbers and Chart of Accounts

To help in posting (and later accounting procedures), each account of a company is assigned a number. This number is listed to the right of the account title for both a T-account and the account format shown in Exhibit 2-3. The number is obtained from the company's chart of accounts. **The chart of accounts is a numbering system designed to organize the accounts efficiently and to reduce errors in the recording and retaining process.** The chart of accounts is generally set up so that the Cash account is given the lowest number, followed in order by all the other asset accounts, all the liability accounts, and then by the owner's equity account. Within the asset accounts, after Cash the remaining assets are given higher numbers in the order of their *liquidity* (i.e., their ease of conversion into cash) and according to their usual placement on the company's balance sheet. A similar scheme is used for the liability and owner's equity accounts. The accounts are then included in the general ledger in the order in which they are listed in the chart of accounts. The chart of accounts must be flexible enough so that as new asset, liability, or owner's equity accounts are needed, they can be properly placed in the general ledger.

Listed in Exhibit 2-4 is the chart of accounts of the Dixon Travel Agency. Notice that the asset account numbers begin at 101, the liabilities at 201, and owner's equity at 301. This numbering system is used to help identify and classify accounts. (Some large corporations use numbers as high as six digits for classifying their accounts.) Note also that the accounts are not consecutively numbered. This is because any new asset, liability, and owner's equity accounts can be inserted in the chart of accounts (and general ledger) later and given account numbers in their proper balance sheet order.

EXHIBIT 2-4
Dixon Travel Agency
Chart of Accounts

Account Title	Account Number
Cash	101
Accounts receivable	103
Office supplies	107
Building	122
Office equipment	124
Accounts payable	201
Notes payable	204
A. Dixon, capital	301

Summary of Posting Process and Illustration

Recall that the posting process involves transferring the information recorded in the general journal to the accounts in the general ledger. In a manual system posting is usually done at the end of each work day. As in the journalizing process, a set of key procedures should be learned for posting to the individual accounts. These procedures are summarized as follows:

1. In the general ledger, locate the first account of the transaction in the general journal to be posted. This is done by looking at the account title in the general ledger.
2. Enter the month, date, and year of the transaction (as listed in the general journal) in the *Date* column of the account. It is not necessary to repeat the year and month until a new account page is begun or a transaction for the next month is posted.
3. Enter the debit amount (as listed in the general journal) in the *Debit* column of the account and compute the new account balance. (Caution: Remember that assets have debit balances and liabilities and owner's equity accounts have credit balances.)
4. In the *Journal Reference* (Jr. Ref.) column, enter the *page number* of the general journal on which the journal entry was recorded. This is done to provide a *cross reference* between the general journal page and the posting to the account. This cross reference is useful in the auditing process or when an error has been discovered. (Caution: Remember that this procedure is completed *after* the amount is posted in the account.)
5. Go back to the general journal and enter in the *Account Number* (Acct. No.) column the number of the account in which the debit amount was posted. A number listed in the Account Number column indicates that the posting process has been completed for that *line* of the general journal; it is the last step before continuing with the posting of the next line. (Caution: Remember that this procedure is completed *after* the amount is posted in the account.)
6. For the next line of the transaction in the general journal (usually the credit entry, unless a compound entry is involved) repeat steps 1 through 5, except that the amount to be credited is recorded in the *Credit* column of the appropriate account.

Once the debit and credit entries for each transaction have been posted to the related accounts, the next journal entry for the day is posted and the process continued until the daily postings are completed. By strictly following these posting procedures, the chance of error is minimized.

The posting process is illustrated in Exhibit 2-5 for the January 1, 1983, transaction of the Dixon Travel Agency. The arrows numbered 2, 3, 4, and 5 refer to steps 2 through 5 (for both the debit and credit entries) in the list of posting procedures.

EXHIBIT 2-5
Illustration
of Posting

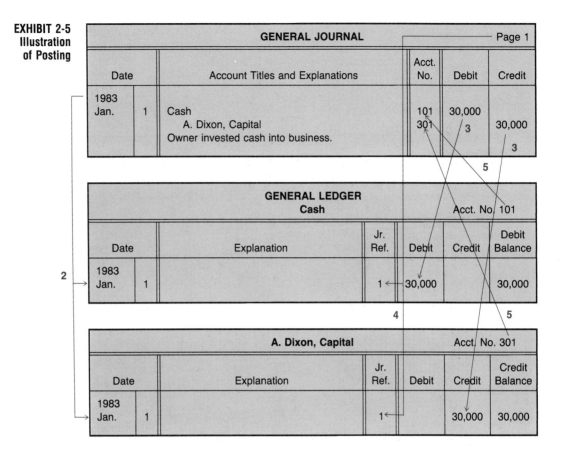

Note that the date of the transaction is transferred from the general journal to each ledger account. The amount of the debit ($30,000) is posted in the debit column[2] of the Cash account and the new balance is computed. (Since this is the first posting to the account, the balance is the same as the debit entry.) The credit entry ($30,000) and the new balance are posted in the A. Dixon, Capital account. The page number (1) of the general journal on which the transaction is journalized is listed in the journal reference column of each account, and the account numbers (101 and 301) are listed in the account number column of the general journal.

The posting process is completed at the end of each day of January. The accounts at the end of January are shown in Exhibit 2-6. They are listed as they would appear in the general ledger, which is according to the chart of accounts shown in Exhibit 2-4. You should study the postings to the accounts, referring to the journal entries listed in Exhibit 2-2. Note that in Exhibit 2-2 the account number column had not

---

[2] To avoid unnecessary detail, we again omitted the "cents" column in the debit and credit columns of the accounts. Both dollars and cents would be recorded in an actual account, however.

been completed at that time but would have been completed during the posting process. You should think of the numbers that would be listed in this column based on the account numbers in Exhibit 2-6.

EXHIBIT 2-6
Dixon Travel Agency
Postings and Account
Balances

Cash — Acct. No. 101

Date		Explanation	Jr. Ref.	Debit	Credit	Debit Balance
1983 Jan.	1		1	30,000		30,000
	2		1		18,000	12,000
	12		1		1,000	11,000
	15		1		350	10,650

Accounts Receivable — Acct. No. 103

Date		Explanation	Jr. Ref.	Debit	Credit	Debit Balance
1983 Jan.	28		1	400		400

Office Supplies — Acct. No. 107

Date		Explanation	Jr. Ref.	Debit	Credit	Debit Balance
1983 Jan.	5		1	700		700

Building — Acct. No. 122

Date		Explanation	Jr. Ref.	Debit	Credit	Debit Balance
1983 Jan.	2		1	18,000		18,000

Office Equipment — Acct. No. 124

Date		Explanation	Jr. Ref.	Debit	Credit	Debit Balance
1983 Jan.	12		1	3,000		3,000
	28		1		400	2,600

EXHIBIT 2-6
(Continued)

				Accounts Payable									Acct. No. 201	
Date				Explanation			Jr. Ref.		Debit		Credit		Credit Balance	
1983 Jan.	5						1				700		700	
	15						1		350				350	

				Notes Payable									Acct. No. 204	
Date				Explanation			Jr. Ref.		Debit		Credit		Credit Balance	
1983 Jan.	12						1				2,000		2,000	

				A. Dixon, Capital									Acct. No. 301	
Date				Explanation			Jr. Ref.		Debit		Credit		Credit Balance	
1983 Jan.	1						1				30,000		30,000	

THE TRIAL BALANCE

In discussing the journalizing and posting process we have set up procedures so that the double entry rule is followed; that is, the total amount of the debit entries is equal to the total amount of the credit entries. By following these procedures the accounting equation remains in balance and errors are minimized.

People can make mistakes, however, and therefore it is desirable to reduce the chance that a journalizing or posting error may be included in the financial statements used to communicate the accounting information. If we follow the double entry rule in journalizing and posting each transaction, the total of the debit balances in all the accounts should be equal to the total of the credit balances in all the accounts. Before preparing the financial statements, it is useful to perform an additional procedure to check for errors. This procedure involves proving the equality of the debit and credit account balances by preparing a trial balance.

A trial balance is a schedule that lists the titles of all the accounts in the general ledger, the debit or credit balance of each account, and the totals of the debit and credit balances. To prepare a trial balance the balance of each account in the general ledger is computed if this has not already been done. Next the accounts and debit or credit balances are listed on the trial balance according to the order in which the accounts are listed in the general ledger. Finally, the debit and credit columns are totaled to determine their equality. The trial balance of the Dixon Travel Agency is shown in Exhibit 2-7.

EXHIBIT 2-7
Trial Balance

DIXON TRAVEL AGENCY
Trial Balance
January 31, 1983

Account Titles	Debits	Credits
Cash	$10,650	
Accounts receivable	400	
Office supplies	700	
Building	18,000	
Office equipment	2,600	
Accounts payable		$ 350
Notes payable		2,000
A. Dixon, capital		30,000
Totals	$32,350	$32,350

The trial balance is an accounting working paper used to prove the equality of the debit and credit account balances in the accounts. It is *not* a formal accounting statement, but rather a type of source document. After it is prepared it is kept in the accounting records for future reference if necessary.

Error Detection

If a trial balance does not balance (i.e., the total debits are not equal to the total credits), an error has been made. To find the error, the debit and credit columns of the trial balance should be readded. If the column totals do not agree, the amounts in the debit and credit columns should be checked to be sure that a debit or credit account balance was not mistakenly listed in the wrong column.

If the error is still not found, the difference in the column totals should be computed and divided by 9. When the difference is evenly divisible by 9, there is a good chance that a *transposition* or a *slide* has occurred. A transposition occurs when two digits in a number are mistakenly reversed. For instance, if the $2,600 Office Equipment balance had been listed as $6,200 in Exhibit 2-7, the debit column would have totaled $35,950 instead of $32,350. The difference, $3,600, is evenly divisible by 9. A slide occurs when the digits are listed in the correct order but are mistakenly moved one decimal place to the left or right. For instance, if the $350 Accounts Payable balance had been listed as $35 in Exhibit 2-7, the credit column would have totaled $32,035 instead of $32,350. The $315 difference is evenly divisible by 9.

If a transposition or slide has occurred, the error may have been made when transferring the account balances from the accounts to the trial balance or when the account balances were initially computed. Thus the account balances listed on the trial balance should be compared with the account balances listed in the ledger. Then the ledger account balances should be recomputed, and if no error is found, the postings should be double checked. Finally, the journal entries should be reviewed for accuracy.

If the trial balance is in balance (i.e., the total debits are equal to the total credits), it is likely that: (1) equal debit entries and credit entries were recorded for each transaction; (2) the debit and credit entries were posted to the accounts; and (3) the account balances were correctly computed. The equality of the debit and credit totals, however, does not necessarily mean that the information in the accounting system is error free. Several types of errors are not found by a trial balance. First, an entire transaction may not have been journalized. Second, an entire transaction may not have been posted to the accounts. Third, equal debits and credits, but of the wrong amount, may have been recorded for a transaction. Fourth, a transaction may have been journalized to a wrong account. For instance, the purchase of land may have been debited to the Buildings account instead of the Land account. Finally, a journal entry may be posted to the wrong account. For instance, the debit in a journal entry to the Office Supplies account may be posted as a debit to the Office Equipment account. This is why it is very important that you carefully study each transaction and always follow the set procedures in the journalizing and posting process.

BALANCE SHEET

Once the trial balance has been completed, the financial statements may be prepared. Since we have discussed only balance sheet transactions up to this point, the focus here is on this financial statement. Recall that the accounts and account balances are listed on the trial balance in the order that they appear in the general ledger according to the chart of accounts. Recall also that the chart of accounts is set up so that assets are listed first in the order of their liquidity, followed by the liability and owner's equity accounts. Thus the listing of the accounts on the trial balance follows the order in which the accounts will appear on the balance sheet.

Another advantage of the trial balance is that it aids in the preparation of the balance sheet. The accounts and account balances as shown on the trial balance are simply recopied in a balance sheet format. The balance sheet of the Dixon Travel Agency shown in Exhibit 2-8 was prepared directly from the trial balance listed in Exhibit 2-7.

EXHIBIT 2-8
Balance Sheet

DIXON TRAVEL AGENCY
Balance Sheet
January 31, 1983

Assets		Liabilities	
Cash	$10,650	Accounts payable	$ 350
Accounts receivable	400	Notes payable	2,000
Office supplies	700	Total Liabilities	$ 2,350
Building	18,000		
Office equipment	2,600	*Owner's Equity*	
		A. Dixon, capital	$30,000
		Total Liabilities and	
Total Assets	$32,350	Owner's Equity	$32,350

COMPONENTS OF AN ACCOUNTING SYSTEM

We have now completed a simple accounting process for an accounting system. The steps in the process included examining source documents, journalizing, posting, preparing a trial balance, and completing a balance sheet. The business documents in the system include source documents, a general journal, ledger accounts, a trial balance, and the balance sheet. They are important steps and documents in any manual accounting system; their relationship is shown in Exhibit 2-9.

EXHIBIT 2-9   Accounting System: Documents and Process

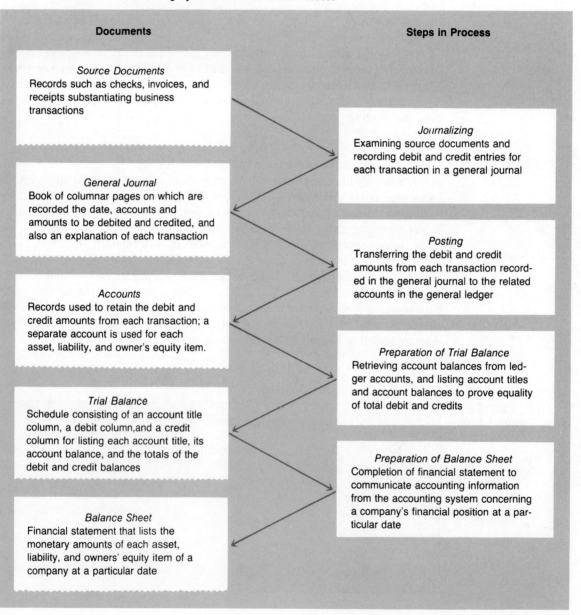

Documents

Source Documents
Records such as checks, invoices, and receipts substantiating business transactions

General Journal
Book of columnar pages on which are recorded the date, accounts and amounts to be debited and credited, and also an explanation of each transaction

Accounts
Records used to retain the debit and credit amounts from each transaction; a separate account is used for each asset, liability, and owner's equity item.

Trial Balance
Schedule consisting of an account title column, a debit column, and a credit column for listing each account title, its account balance, and the totals of the debit and credit balances

Balance Sheet
Financial statement that lists the monetary amounts of each asset, liability, and owners' equity item of a company at a particular date

Steps in Process

Journalizing
Examining source documents and recording debit and credit entries for each transaction in a general journal

Posting
Transferring the debit and credit amounts from each transaction recorded in the general journal to the related accounts in the general ledger

Preparation of Trial Balance
Retrieving account balances from ledger accounts, and listing account titles and account balances to prove equality of total debit and credits

Preparation of Balance Sheet
Completion of financial statement to communicate accounting information from the accounting system concerning a company's financial position at a particular date

The documents and steps in Exhibit 2-9 should be studied carefully. They are the main parts of each manual accounting system[3] and are important to understanding the remaining topics in this textbook. A review problem including these steps is presented next.

REVIEW PROBLEM

During the month of March 1983, Paul Campbell started the Campbell Insurance Agency, a sole proprietorship, and the company entered into the following transactions.

Date	Transaction
3/2/1983	Paul Campbell formed the Campbell Insurance Agency and invested $20,000 into the company.
3/6/1983	The company purchased land and a building for $35,000. The land was valued at $8,000 and the building at $27,000. The company made a $5,000 down payment and signed a 20-year mortgage for the remaining balance.
3/10/1983	The company purchased office equipment for $2,000 from the Tiger Office Supply Company, paying $500 down and agreeing to pay the remaining balance in 30 days.
3/14/1983	The company purchased a 2-year comprehensive insurance policy on the building and its contents, paying $300.
3/17/1983	The company sold half of the land purchased on March 6, 1983 for $4,000. The purchaser (Ace Realty Company) made a $1,000 down payment and signed a note requiring payment of the balance at the end of 1 year.
3/22/1983	The company purchased $600 of office supplies from the Tiger Office Supply Company on account; it agreed to pay the amount owed at the end of the month.
3/31/1983	The company paid Tiger Office Supply Company $600 for the supplies purchased on March 22.

The company established the following chart of accounts.

Account Titles	Account Number
Cash	101
Notes Receivable	104
Office Supplies	105
Prepaid Insurance	106
Land	120
Building	121
Office Equipment	123
Accounts Payable	201
Mortgage Payable	205
P. Campbell, Capital	301

Required: (1) prepare journal entries to record the March transactions, (2) post the journal entries to the proper accounts, (3) prepare a trial balance at the end of March, and (4) prepare a March 31, 1983, balance sheet.

[3] As we shall see, there are more documents (e.g., the income statement) and processes in an accounting system; they are discussed in Chapter 3.

SOLUTION TO REVIEW PROBLEM

Requirement 1: General Journal Entries.

GENERAL JOURNAL					Page 1
Date		Account Titles and Explanations	Acct. No.	Debit	Credit
1983 Mar.	2	Cash P. Campbell, Capital Owner invested cash into business.	101 301	20,000	 20,000

	6	Land
		Building
		    Cash
		    Mortgage Payable
		Invested in land and building. Made cash down payment and signed a 20-year mortgage for the balance owed.
			120
			121
			101
			205
				8,000
				27,000
					
					5,000
					30,000

	10	Office Equipment
		    Cash
		    Accounts Payable
		Purchased office equipment from Tiger Office Supply Company, making cash down payment and agreeing to pay balance owed at end of month.
			123
			101
			201
				2,000	
					500
					1,500

	14	Prepaid Insurance Cash Purchased a 2-year comprehensive insurance policy on building and contents.	106 101	300	 300
	17	Cash Notes Receivable Land Sold half of the land purchased on March 6, 1983, to Ace Realty Company, receiving a cash down payment and accepting a 1-year note for the balance owed.	101 104 120	1,000 3,000	 4,000
	22	Office Supplies Accounts Payable Purchased office supplies from the Tiger Office Supply Company, agreeing to pay the balance owed at the end of the month.	105 201	600	 600
	31	Accounts Payable Cash Paid Tiger Office Supply Company amount owed on account for office supplies purchased on March 22.	201 101	600	 600

Requirement 2: Postings to the Accounts. (Note: The Acct. No. column in the general journal is completed *after* the posting to the accounts.)

			Cash				Acct. No. 101

Date		Explanation	Jr. Ref.	Debit	Credit	Debit Balance
1983 Mar.	2		1	20,000		20,000
	6		1		5,000	15,000
	10		1		500	14,500
	14		1		300	14,200
	17		1	1,000		15,200
	31		1		600	14,600

			Notes Receivable				Acct. No. 104

Date		Explanation	Jr. Ref.	Debit	Credit	Debit Balance
1983 Mar.	17		1	3,000		3,000

			Office Supplies				Acct. No. 105

Date		Explanation	Jr. Ref.	Debit	Credit	Debit Balance
1983 Mar.	22		1	600		600

			Prepaid Insurance				Acct. No. 106

Date		Explanation	Jr. Ref.	Debit	Credit	Debit Balance
1983 Mar.	14		1	300		300

			Land				Acct. No. 120

Date		Explanation	Jr. Ref.	Debit	Credit	Debit Balance
1983 Mar.	6		1	8,000		8,000
	17		1		4,000	4,000

Requirement 2 (Continued):

Building   Acct. No. 121

Date		Explanation	Jr. Ref.	Debit	Credit	Debit Balance
1983 Mar.	6		1	27,000		27,000

Office Equipment   Acct. No. 123

Date		Explanation	Jr. Ref.	Debit	Credit	Debit Balance
1983 Mar.	10		1	2,000		2,000

Accounts Payable   Acct. No. 201

Date		Explanation	Jr. Ref.	Debit	Credit	Credit Balance
1983 Mar.	10		1		1,500	1,500
	22		1		600	2,100
	31		1	600		1,500

Mortgage Payable   Acct. No. 205

Date		Explanation	Jr. Ref.	Debit	Credit	Credit Balance
1983 Mar.	6		1		30,000	30,000

P. Campbell, Capital   Acct. No. 301

Date		Explanation	Jr. Ref.	Debit	Credit	Credit Balance
1983 Mar.	2		1		20,000	20,000

Requirement 3: Preparation of Trial Balance.

CAMPBELL INSURANCE AGENCY
Trial Balance
March 31, 1983

Account Titles	Debits	Credits
Cash	$14,600	
Notes receivable	3,000	
Office supplies	600	
Prepaid insurance	300	
Land	4,000	
Building	27,000	
Office equipment	2,000	
Accounts payable		$ 1,500
Mortgage payable		30,000
P. Campbell, capital		20,000
Totals	$51,500	$51,500

Requirement 4: Preparation of Balance Sheet.

CAMPBELL INSURANCE AGENCY
Balance Sheet
March 31, 1983

Assets		Liabilities	
Cash	$14,600	Accounts payable	$ 1,500
Notes receivable	3,000	Mortgage payable	30,000
Office supplies	600	Total Liabilities	$31,500
Prepaid insurance	300	*Owner's Equity*	
Land	4,000	P. Campbell, capital	20,000
Building	27,000		
Office equipment	2,000	Total Liabilities and	
Total Assets	$51,500	Owner's Equity	$51,500

GLOSSARY

Account.   Document used to record and retain the monetary information from a company's transactions. A separate account is used for each asset, liability, and owner's equity item.

Account Balance.   The difference between the total increases and total decreases in an account. Asset accounts have debit balances; liability and owner's equity accounts have credit balances.

Account Number.   The number assigned to each account from the company's chart of accounts.

Chart of Accounts.   A numbering system for a company's accounts in its general ledger. Helps reduce errors in the recording and retaining of the company's accounting information.

Compound Entry.   A journal entry in which two or more debit entries, two or more credit entries, or both, are made.

Credit Entry. Monetary amount recorded (credited) in the right side (or credit column) of an account or the credit column of a journal.

Cross Reference. Page number of general journal listed in the *journal reference* column of an account. Used to link the account entry to the general journal for auditing purposes and error detection.

Debit and Credit Rule. Rule that states that all asset accounts are increased by debits and decreased by credits and all liability and owner's equity accounts are increased by credits and decreased by debits.

Debit Entry. Monetary amount recorded (debited) in the left side (or debit column) of an account or the debit column of a journal.

Double Entry Rule. Rule that states that for all recorded transactions, the total amount of the debit entries must be equal to the total amount of the credit entries.

General Ledger. The set of accounts of a company listed in order according to the chart of accounts.

General Journal. A business document in which each transaction is initially recorded.

Journal Entry. An entry made in a journal listing the date, the account titles and amounts to be debited and credited, and an explanation of a transaction.

Journalizing. The process of recording a journal entry.

Posting. The process of transferring the debit and credit entries recorded in each journal entry to the related accounts in the general ledger.

T-Account. An account that looks like the capital letter T. The left side is used for recording debit entries and the right side for recording credit entries. T-accounts are used for illustrative purposes.

Trial Balance. Schedule used to prove the equality of the debit and credit account balances. It lists the titles of all the accounts, the debit or credit balance of each account, and the totals of the debit and credit columns.

QUESTIONS

Q2-1 What is an accounting system?

Q2-2 Define an account. What are the parts of a T-account? What is a set of accounts called?

Q2-3 What is the debit and credit rule? How does this rule relate to the accounting equation?

Q2-4 What is a debit entry? A credit entry?

Q2-5 How is an account balance computed? What accounts usually have debit balances and what accounts usually have credit balances?

Q2-6 What is a general ledger? What is a chart of accounts?

Q2-7 Explain the double entry rule. How (if at all) is this rule changed in the case of a compound entry?

Q2-8 What is a general journal (in a manual accounting system)? Why is a journal often referred to as a document of original entry?

Q2-9 List the advantages of initially recording all transactions in a journal.

Q2-10 What is journalizing? Briefly describe the journalizing process.

Q2-11 What is posting? Briefly describe the posting process.

Q2-12 What is a trial balance? What are the advantages of preparing a trial balance? In what order are the accounts listed on a trial balance? Why?

Q2-13 Describe the process that should be completed if a trial balance does not balance.

Q2-14 List the types of errors that would *not* be detected by a trial balance.

Q2-15 List the steps involved in completing the accounting process in their proper order. Relate these steps to the documents involved in the accounting system.

Q2-16 Indicate which accounts would be debited and credited in the following events:
  (a) Increase in asset and increase in owner's equity
  (b) Increase in asset and increase in liability
  (c) Increase in asset and decrease in another asset
  (d) Decrease in liability and decrease in asset
  (e) Decrease in liability and increase in owner's equity

EXERCISES

E2-1 Ending Cash Balance. On March 1 the Kaw Company showed a balance of $12,000 in its cash account. During the month it entered into the following transactions affecting cash:

Date	Transaction
Mar. 2	Purchased building for $8,000.
15	Owner deposited a $20,000 personal check in the Kaw Company checking account.
21	Office equipment costing $2,500 was purchased by making a $1,250 down payment and signing a $1,250 note due at the end of 1 year.
28	Paid March telephone bill in the amount of $212.

Required: Set up a T-account for Cash and, based on the above information, enter the beginning balance, record the changes in the account, and calculate the ending balance.

E2-2 Reconstruct Journal Entries. The general ledger of the Keller Company showed the following T-accounts on September 30 after all the transactions for the month of September had been recorded and posted.

	Cash				Accounts Receivable	
9/1	15,000	9/7	8,000	9/28	770	
		9/11	1,500			
		9/16	450			

	Office Supplies				Building	
9/16	450			9/7	8,000	

Office Equipment				Notes Payable	
9/11	6,500	9/28	770		
				9/11	5,000

W. A. Keller, Capital	
	9/1 15,000

Required: Prepare the journal entries that the company recorded during September.

E2-3 Accounting Equation and Debits and Credits. In each of the following situations, the total debits or credits for one component of the accounting equation are missing:

(a) Assets debited for $8,000; liabilities credited for $3,200.
(b) Liabilities debited for $2,000; owner's equity credited for $10,000.
(c) Assets credited for $5,500; owner's equity debited for $12,750.
(d) Owner's equity credited for $27,500; liabilities debited for $5,715.
(e) Assets debited for $11,525; owner's equity debited for $23,750.

Required: Using Assets: $60,000 = Liabilities: $20,000 + Owner's Equity: $40,000 as the beginning accounting equation, for each of the above situations determine (1) the total debits or credits for the missing component of the equation and (2) the amount of each component in the *ending* accounting equation. Treat each situation independently.

E2-4 Accounting Equation and Debits and Credits. The total debits or credits for one component of the accounting equation are missing in each situation that follows:

(a) Assets credited for $12,000; liabilities debited for $6,200.
(b) Owner's equity debited for $15,750; assets credited for $7,500.
(c) Liabilities credited for $1,000; owner's equity debited for $5,000.
(d) Owner's equity credited for $20,000; assets debited for $6,250.

Required: Using Assets: $45,000 = Liabilities: $15,000 + Owner's Equity: $30,000 as the beginning accounting equation, for each of the situations shown above determine (1) the total debits or credits for the missing component of the equation and (2) the amount of each component in the *ending* accounting equation. Treat each situation independently.

E2-5 Journal Entries. During the month of July the Sands Realty Company entered into the following transactions:

Date	Transaction
July 1	Nancy Sands deposited a $30,000 personal check in the company's checking account.
10	Purchased an office building at a cost of $21,000, paying $7,000 down and signing a $14,000 note due at the end of the year.
25	Purchased office supplies costing $400 on account.

Required: 1. Prepare the journal entries necessary to record the above transactions.
2. Name the source documents that you would normally use in recording each of the above transactions.

E2-6 Journal Entries. Albert Mitchell started Worldwide Travel Service on April 1 of the current year, and the company engaged in the following transactions during the month of April:

Date		Transaction
Apr.	1	Albert Mitchell opened the business by depositing a $45,000 personal check in the new company's checking account.
	3	Purchased a small office building for $30,000, paying $10,000 down and signing a 1-year note for $20,000.
	20	Purchased office equipment at a cost of $6,000. Half of the cost was paid in cash and the remainder is due at the end of May.

Required: 1. Prepare the necessary journal entries to record the above transactions.
2. Name the source documents that you would normally use in recording the above transactions.

E2-7 Journal Entries. Wiley Cato started Cato's Tax Service on January 1 of the current year, and the company engaged in the following transactions during the month of January:

Date		Transaction
Jan.	2	Wiley Cato deposited a $10,000 personal check in the company's checking account to start the business.
	2	Purchased building at a cost of $20,000, paying 15% down and signing a 10-year mortgage for the balance.
	3	Purchased office equipment costing $2,000 by paying $500 cash and signing a 90-day note for $1,500.
	4	Purchased $300 of office supplies on account.
	6	Purchased a 3-year insurance policy for $450 cash.
	10	Purchased office furniture at a cost of $900, paying 25% down with the balance due at the end of the month.
	15	Paid the amount due for office supplies purchased on January 4.
	30	Paid balance due on office furniture purchased on January 10.

Required: Prepare the necessary journal entries to record the above transactions.

E2-8 Posting and Trial Balance. The general journal and chart of accounts of the Miffler Company on May 31, 1983, are shown below:

GENERAL JOURNAL						Page 1
Date		Account Titles and Explanations	Acct. No.	Debit	Credit
1983 May	1	Cash		20,000	
		J. R. Miffler, Capital			20,000
		Owner invested cash into business.			
	5	Land		5,000	
		Cash			5,000
		Purchased land for future use.			

GENERAL JOURNAL (Continued)				Page 1
Date	Account Titles and Explanations	Acct. No.	Debit	Credit
10	Office Equipment		2,500	
	Cash			500
	Accounts Payable			2,000
	Purchased office equipment from Hav-all Supply Company, making cash down payment and agreeing to pay balance at end of month.			
15	Building		30,000	
	Cash			3,000
	Mortgage Payable			27,000
	Purchased building, making 10% down payment and signing a 10-year mortgage.			
31	Accounts Payable		2,000	
	Cash			2,000
	Paid Hav-all Supply Company amount owed on account for office equipment.			

MIFFLER COMPANY CHART OF ACCOUNTS

Account Title	Account Number
Cash	101
Land	110
Building	112
Office equipment	115
Accounts payable	201
Mortgage payable	205
J. R. Miffler, capital	301

Required: 1. Prepare general ledger accounts for each of the accounts in the chart of accounts.
2. Post the above journal entries to the proper accounts and prepare a trial balance.

E2-9 Recording in T-Accounts. The Waterloo Company began operations on January 2, 1983. During the month of January it entered into the following transactions:

Date	Transaction
Jan. 2	Ken Waterloo deposited $20,000 cash in the company's checking account.
7	Purchased a building for $8,000; $4,000 was paid in cash and a 10-year mortgage was signed for the remaining balance.
23	Office supplies were purchased at a cost of $2,100.
30	Equipment was purchased at a cost of $4,500, paying $1,125 down and signing a note for $3,375.

Required: 1. Set up T-accounts for each of these accounts: Cash, Office Supplies, Building, Equipment, Mortgage Payable, Notes Payable, and Ken Waterloo, Capital.
2. Record each of the above transactions directly in the T-accounts set up in requirement 1.

E2-10   Prepare Trial Balance from Accounts.   On May 31, 1983, the Broden Company showed the following account balances (listed in random order).

L. A. Broden, capital	$46,500
Accounts receivable	950
Office equipment	18,550
Cash	16,700
Mortgage payable	22,000
Buildings	25,000
Accounts payable	6,500
Prepaid insurance	1,000
Office supplies	7,300
Land	5,500

Required: Prepare in good form a trial balance for the Broden Company on May 31, 1983.

E2-11   Correction of Errors.   The trial balance of the Jordan Company that follows does not balance:

JORDAN COMPANY
Trial Balance
March 31, 1983

Account Titles	*Debits*	*Credits*
Cash	$ 8,000	
Notes receivable	3,000	
Office supplies	750	
Land	9,500	
Building	21,000	
Office equipment	3,750	
Accounts payable		$ 1,150
Jim Jordan, capital		45,000
Totals	$46,000	$46,150

Upon investigation, the following errors were discovered:

(a) On March 24 the company purchased office equipment at a cost of $1,500. The purchase was recorded by a debit of $1,500 to office equipment and a credit to accounts payable of $150.
(b) On March 31 the bookkeeper mistakenly posted a debit of $750 in cash to the credit side of the cash account.

Required: Assuming there are no other errors, prepare a corrected trial balance for the Jordan Company at March 31, 1983.

E2-12   Balance Sheet.   The following trial balance was prepared by the Cooper Company on June 30, 1983:

COOPER COMPANY
Trial Balance
June 30, 1983

Account Titles	Debits	Credits
Cash	$ 8,400	
Accounts receivable	4,700	
Office supplies	840	
Prepaid insurance	560	
Building	32,000	
Office equipment	6,500	
Accounts payable		$10,000
Susan Cooper, capital		43,000
Totals	$53,000	$53,000

Required: Prepare a balance sheet for the Cooper Company at June 30, 1983.

PROBLEMS

Part A

P2-1A   Recording in T-Accounts.   On August 1, 1983, Judy Kimberly started the Nu-Way Advertising Agency and the company engaged in the following transactions during August:

Date	Transaction
Aug. 1	Judy Kimberly deposited a $25,000 personal check into the agency's checking account.
2	Acquired an office building at a cost of $22,000. A down payment of $4,000 was made and a 1-year note was signed for the balance.
14	Purchased several pieces of office equipment at a cost of $2,500. The entire amount is due September 15.
26	Purchased office supplies at a cost of $900 cash.

Required: 1. Prepare T-accounts for the following accounts: Cash, Office Supplies, Building, Office Equipment, Accounts Payable, Notes Payable, and J. Kimberly, Capital.
2. Enter the above transactions directly in the T-accounts from requirement 1.
3. Prepare a trial balance for the Nu-way Advertising Agency at August 31, 1983.

P2-2A   Journal Entries and Posting.   The Cameron Company was recently set up by Joseph Cameron. The company's transactions during October, the first month of operations, were as follows:

Date	Transaction
Oct. 3	Joseph Cameron deposited $30,000 in the company's checking account.
4	Acquired an office building for $45,000, paying $5,000 cash and signing a 5-year mortgage.
15	Office equipment costing $8,000 was purchased on account from Office Equipment Company.
26	Office supplies costing $1,200 were purchased for cash.
27	Purchased office furniture costing $1,500 from Freddy's Furniture, paying $300 cash. The balance of $1,200 is due in 30 days.
28	Purchased a 3-year insurance policy for $600 cash.
31	Paid balance due to Office Equipment Company for equipment purchased on October 15.

Required: 1. Set up the following general ledger accounts (and account numbers): Cash (101), Office Supplies (105), Prepaid Insurance (106), Building (112), Office Equipment (114), Office Furniture (118), Accounts Payable (201), Mortgage Payable (220), and J. Cameron, Capital (301).
2. Record the above transactions in a general journal.
3. Post the journal entries to the general ledger accounts.

P2-3A   Journal Entries, Posting, and Trial Balance. On July 1, 1983, B. Bonzor started Bonzor's Barbeque Pit. During the month of July the company entered into the following transactions:

Date	Transaction
July 1	B. Bonzor deposited $40,000 cash into the business checking account.
2	Purchased building and land for $25,000, making a $5,000 down payment and signing a 15-year mortgage for the remaining balance. The land was valued at $6,000.
3	Purchased all necessary kitchen equipment for $10,000 cash.
5	Purchased tables and booths for the dining area at a cost of $6,500 by signing a 1-year note for the entire amount.
10	Purchased $500 of supplies on account from Gelone's Restaurant Supplies.
20	Purchased dining room equipment for $600 cash.

Required: 1. Set up the following general ledger accounts (and account numbers): Cash (101), Supplies (106), Land (110), Building (112), Kitchen Equipment (114), Tables and Booths (115), Dining Room Equipment (116), Accounts Payable (201), Notes Payable (210), Mortgage Payable (220), and B. Bonzor, Capital (301).
2. Record the above transactions in a general journal.
3. Post the journal entries to the general ledger accounts.
4. Prepare a trial balance for Bonzor's Barbeque Pit at July 31, 1983.

P2-4A   Journal Entries and Trial Balance. The general ledger of the Humphreys Company shows the following T-accounts on April 30, 1983 (all the transactions during April have been properly recorded and posted):

Cash				Accounts Receivable		
4/1	50,000	4/2	5,000	4/28	400	
		4/8	2,000			

Office Supplies			Land		
4/6	900		4/2	10,000	

Building			Office Equipment		
4/2	15,000		4/8	7,000	4/28	400

Accounts Payable			Notes Payable		
	4/6	900		4/8	5,000

Mortgage Payable			R. Humphreys, Capital		
	4/2	20,000		4/1	50,000

Required: 1. Prepare the journal entries that the company recorded during April.
2. Prepare a trial balance for the Humphreys Company at April 30, 1983.

P2-5A   Trial Balance and Balance Sheet. Shown below are the account balances of the Sheetel Company on May 31, 1983 (listed in random order):

Mortgage payable	$14,300
Notes receivable	925
P. Sheetel, capital	26,000
Office supplies	1,450
Land	8,500
Cash	10,750
Prepaid insurance	1,350
Accounts payable	1,115
Building	21,500
Notes payable	?

Required: 1. Prepare a trial balance in the proper order for the Sheetel Company at May 31, 1983 (insert the correct amount for Notes Payable).
2. Prepare a balance sheet for the Sheetel Company at May 31, 1983.

P2-6A   Correction of Errors. On July 31, one month after the Salisbury Company was established, the company's accounting records showed the following trial balance:

SALISBURY COMPANY
Trial Balance
July 31, 1983

Account Titles	Debits	Credits
Cash	$11,300	
Accounts receivable	600	
Office supplies		$ 1,100
Building	8,400	
Office equipment	6,700	
Notes payable		4,100
James Salisbury, capital		25,000
Totals	$27,000	$30,200

The following errors were found upon examination of the records:

(a) One piece of office equipment was sold at its original cost of $600 on July 16. In posting, the building account was credited erroneously instead of office equipment. The debit was posted correctly.
(b) When posting, $1,100 of supplies purchased on July 9 were entered erroneously in the credit side of the office supplies account. The cash payment was posted correctly.
(c) An addition error was made when determining the ending cash account balance on July 31. The error overstated the credits to cash by $1,000.

Required: 1. Prepare a corrected trial balance for the Salisbury Company at July 31, 1983.
2. Prepare a balance sheet for the company at July 31, 1983.

P2-7A   The Accounting Process. During the month of June 1983, E. Fliey established the Fliey Company, and the company entered into the following transactions:

Date	Transaction
June 1	E. Fliey deposited $40,000 cash in the company's checking account.
8	The company purchased land and a building for $27,500. The land was valued at $5,000 and the building at $22,500. A down payment of $6,875 was made and a 10-year mortgage signed for the balance.
9	The company purchased office equipment for $5,000, paying $500 down and agreeing to pay the balance due in 30 days.
15	The company purchased $1,200 of office supplies for cash.
30	The company purchased a 2-year comprehensive insurance policy on the building, paying $500.

Required:
1. Set up the following general ledger accounts (and account numbers): Cash (101), Office Supplies (105), Prepaid Insurance (106), Land (110), Building (112), Office Equipment (114), Accounts Payable (201), Mortgage Payable (220), and E. Fliey, Capital (301).
2. Prepare the necessary general journal entries to record the above transactions.
3. Post the journal entries to the proper accounts.
4. Prepare a trial balance at June 30, 1983.
5. Prepare a balance sheet at June 30, 1983.

PROBLEMS

Part B

P2-1B Recording in T-Accounts. On June 1, 1983, Jody Weis started the Weis Company. The company engaged in the following transactions during June:

Date	Transaction
June 1	Jody Weis deposited $37,000 cash in the company's checking account.
3	Purchased an office building for $33,500, paying $3,500 down and signing a 10-year mortgage for the balance.
16	Purchased $2,000 of office equipment, paying $1,000 and agreeing to pay the remaining $1,000 in 30 days.
24	Purchased office supplies for $1,200 cash.

Required:
1. Prepare T-accounts for the following accounts: Cash, Office Supplies, Building, Office Equipment, Accounts Payable, Mortgage Payable, and Jody Weis, Capital.
2. Enter the above transactions directly in the T-accounts set up in requirement 1.
3. Prepare a trial balance for the Weis Company at June 30, 1983.

P2-2B Journal Entries and Posting. The Polar Company was recently set up by P. T. Polar. During November 1983, the first month of operations, the company entered into the following transactions:

Date	Transaction
Nov. 1	P. T. Polar deposited $20,000 in the company's checking account.
4	Acquired land and building for $18,500. The land was valued at $3,500 and the building at $15,000. A $3,700 down payment was made and a 5-year mortgage was signed for the balance.
18	Office equipment costing $4,700 was purchased on account from Weller's Company.
23	Office supplies costing $900 were purchased for cash.
24	Purchased a 2-year insurance policy for $600 cash.
28	Purchased $2,000 of office furniture by signing a 90-day note for $1,500 and paying $500 cash.
30	Paid Weller's Company $2,350 on account for office equipment purchased on June 18.

Required: 1. Set up the following general ledger accounts (and account numbers): Cash (101), Office Supplies (105), Prepaid Insurance (106), Land (110), Building (112), Office Equipment (114), Office Furniture (116), Accounts Payable (201), Notes Payable (210), Mortgage Payable (220), and P. T. Polar, Capital (301).
2. Record the above transactions in a general journal.
3. Post the journal entries to the general ledger accounts.

P2-3B   Journal Entries, Posting, and Trial Balance.   P. Talleby started the Talleby Company on August 1, 1983, and the company entered into the following transactions during the month of August:

Date	Transaction
Aug. 1	P. Talleby deposited $15,000 into the company's checking account.
5	Purchased an office building for $28,000. The company made a $4,200 down payment and signed a mortgage for the balance.
8	Purchased a 3-year insurance policy on the building and its contents, paying $450 cash.
12	Purchased office equipment for $1,350 from Belle's Office Equipment Company, paying $350 cash and agreeing to pay the balance at the end of the month.
18	Purchased $500 of office supplies on account from Joe's Office Supplies.
30	Paid balance due Belle's Office Equipment Company for office equipment purchased on August 12.

Required: 1. Set up the following general ledger accounts (and account numbers): Cash (101), Office Supplies (106), Prepaid Insurance (108), Building (112), Office Equipment (114), Accounts Payable (201), Mortgage Payable (220), and P. Talleby, Capital (301).
2. Record the above transactions in a general journal.
3. Post the journal entries to the general ledger accounts.
4. Prepare a trial balance for the Talleby Company at August 31, 1983.

P2-4B   Journal Entries and Trial Balance.   The general ledger of the Lanards Company shows the following T-Accounts on October 31, 1983 (all the transactions during October have been properly recorded and posted):

	Cash				Accounts Receivable	
10/1	25,000	10/2	2,500	10/28	200	
		10/8	1,000			

	Office Supplies			Land	
10/6	450		10/2	5,000	

	Building			Office Equipment	
10/2	37,500		10/8	3,500	10/28	200

Accounts Payable			Notes Payable	
	10/6	450		10/8	2,500

Mortgage Payable			R. S. Lanards, Capital	
	10/2	40,000		10/1	25,000

Required: 1. Prepare the journal entries that the company recorded during October.

              2. Prepare a trial balance for the Lanards Company at October 31, 1983.

P2-5B   Trial Balance and Balance Sheet.   Shown below are the account balances of the Letel Company on March 31, 1983 (listed in random order):

Notes payable	$ 6,120
Building	53,000
Accounts payable	?
Prepaid insurance	2,700
Cash	11,500
Land	17,000
Office supplies	2,900
R. Letel, capital	50,000
Notes receivable	1,850
Mortgage payable	30,600

Required: 1. Prepare a trial balance in the proper order for the Letel Company at March 31, 1983 (insert the correct amount for Accounts Payable).

              2. Prepare a balance sheet for the Letel Company at March 31, 1983.

P2-6B   Correction of Errors.   After the February 28, 1983, trial balance was prepared, the owner of Chatam Laundry Service suspected the cash account was in error. The balance shown for the cash account was $18,750, whereas the February 28 bank statement for the company showed a balance of $15,780. Upon investigation the following errors were discovered in the company's records:

(a) When calculating the ending cash balance the bookkeeper made a mathematical error that overstated the balance by $100.

(b) On February 6 the company purchased office supplies for $650 cash. However, the bookkeeper erroneously credited Accounts Payable instead of Cash for $650.

(c) On February 17 the company sold laundry equipment at its original cost of $970 for cash. The bookkeeper erroneously debited Cash and credited Laundry Equipment for $790.

(d) When posting to the general ledger the bookkeeper carelessly entered a credit entry for cash of $1,200 to the debit side of the cash account.

Required: Starting with the cash account balance in a T-account make corrections in the account necessary to reconcile the difference between the cash balance and the balance shown on the bank statement. Assume the bank statement is accurate and current to date.

P2-7B   The Accounting Process.   During the month of August 1983, Z. Peeley established the Peeley Company, and the company entered into the following transactions:

Date		Transaction
Aug.	1	Z. Peeley deposited $22,000 cash in the company's checking account.
	6	Purchased land and a bulding for $13,750. The land was valued at $2,500 and the building at $11,250. A down payment of $1,375 was made and a 5-year mortgage signed for the balance.
	9	Purchased office equipment for $3,000, paying $400 down and agreeing to pay the balance due in 30 days.
	19	Purchased $600 of office supplies for cash.
	30	Purchased a 2-year comprehensive insurance policy on the building, paying $200.

Required: 1. Set up the following general ledger accounts (and account numbers): Cash (101), Office Supplies (105), Prepaid Insurance (106), Land (110), Building (112), Office

Equipment (114), Accounts Payable (201), Mortgage Payable (220), and Z. Peeley, Capital (301).

2. Prepare the necessary general journal entries to record the above transactions.
3. Post the journal entries to the proper accounts.
4. Prepare a trial balance at August 31, 1983.
5. Prepare an August 31, 1983, balance sheet.

DISCUSSION CASES

C2-1   Stolen Checkbook. On March 9, 1983, Peter Bailey started his own company by depositing $10,000 in the Bailey Company checking account at the local bank. On March 13, 1983, the Bailey Company checkbook was stolen. During that period of time the Bailey Company had entered into several transactions, but unfortunately it had not established an accounting system for recording the transactions. Bailey did save numerous source documents, however, which had been put into an old shoebox.

In the shoebox is a fire insurance policy dated March 11, 1983, on a building owned by the Bailey Company. Listed on the policy was an amount of $300 for 1 year of insurance. "Paid in Full" had been stamped on the policy by the insurance agent. Also included in the box was a deed for land and a building at 800 East Main. The deed was dated March 10, 1983, and showed an amount of $40,000 (of which $8,000 was for the land). The deed indicated that a down payment had been made by the Bailey Company and that a mortgage was signed by the company for the balance owed.

The shoebox also contained an invoice dated March 11, 1983, from the Ace Office Equipment Company for $600 of office equipment sold to the Bailey Company. The invoice indicates that the amount is to be paid at the end of the month. A $35,000 mortgage, dated March 10, 1983, and signed by the Bailey Company, for the purchase of land and a building is also included in the shoebox. Finally, a 30-day, $4,000 note receivable is included in the shoebox. It is dated March 13, 1983, and is issued to the Bailey Company by the Ret Company for "one-half of the land located at 800 East Main."

The Bailey Company has asked for your help in preparing a balance sheet as of March 13, 1983. Peter Bailey indicates that company checks have been issued for all cash payments. Bailey has called its bank. The bank's records indicate that the Bailey Company's checking account balance is $9,500, consisting of a $10,000 deposit, a $200 canceled check made out to the Finley Office Supply Company, and a $300 canceled check made out to the Patz Insurance Agency.

You notice that the Bailey Company has numerous office supplies on hand. Peter Bailey indicates that a company check was issued on March 9, 1983, to purchase the supplies, but none of the supplies had been used.

Required: Based on the above information prepare a balance sheet for the Bailey Company on March 13, 1983. Be prepared to support each amount shown.

C2-2   Components of an Accounting System. The new owner of a small company has come to you for advice in setting up an accounting system for his business. Having had book-keeping in high school, he vaguely remembers T-accounts but has no idea about the other components of an accounting system.

Required: Explain the components of an accounting system (e.g., the steps in the accounting process and the business documents related to each step).

C2-3   Erroneous Trial Balance. P. Softly recently opened Softly's Watch Repair. Since opening the business, he has recorded all the transactions relating to the business directly in T-accounts without dating or referencing the transactions in any way. Upon preparation of a trial balance Mr. Softly discovered that the trial balance is "out of balance" by $2,700 and he has no idea where the problem lies.

Required: What suggestions would you make to Mr. Softly in order to find the error? What suggestions would you make in order to prevent this type of problem from occurring in the future? Even if the trial balance had been in balance could Mr. Softly be certain that his accounting system is error free? Why or why not?

3 | Revenues, Expenses, and the Income Statement

After reading this chapter, you should understand:

- The definitions of revenues, expenses, and withdrawals
- The debit and credit rules for revenues, expenses, and withdrawals
- Recording revenue, expense, and withdrawals transactions
- The meanings of the matching principle, accrual accounting, and accounting period
- The preparation of an income statement, statement of changes in owner's equity, and a balance sheet
- The relationships between the items on an income statement, statement of changes in owner's equity, and balance sheet
- Preparing closing entries
- The steps in the accounting process and the business documents related to these steps

In Chapter 2 we introduced an accounting system, the accounting process, and accounting documents. The intent of any accounting system is to identify, measure, record, retain, and communicate the accounting information from business transactions. Until now we have focused on only a few types of transactions affecting the balance sheet accounts.

Companies also enter into other types of transactions to earn income, which is a major goal of every business enterprise. In this chapter we focus on these income-producing transactions. We do not change the basic accounting rules established in the previous chapter; instead, we extend these rules as they apply to additional types of transactions.

NET INCOME AND THE INCOME STATEMENT

A major goal of a company is to sell goods or services to customers at prices that are higher than the costs consumed to provide the goods or services and, as a result, provide satisfactory income to the owners. Users of financial statements need income information to evaluate a company's operating results. By recording the transactions of a company's day-to-day operations, accountants are able to develop this income information.

The income of a company is commonly referred to as net income. **Net income is the excess of revenues over expenses for a particular time period.** Net income is sometimes called *net profit, net earnings,* or simply *earnings.* **Revenues are the prices charged to a company's customers for goods or services provided during a particular time period. Expenses are the costs of providing the goods or services during the time period.** Net income may be shown in an equation as follows:

$$\text{Net Income} = \text{Revenues} - \text{Expenses}$$

If expenses are more than revenues, the resulting negative amount is called *net loss,* instead of net income. Because net income (net loss) is the difference between revenues and expenses, it is important to understand these items and their relationship.

Revenues

Because revenues are prices charged to customers, revenues result in increases in assets (or, as is shown later, decreases in liabilities). When goods or services are provided, the company either receives cash from the customer or the customer agrees to pay at a later date, and the company thus acquires an account receivable. In either case, (1) revenue has resulted and (2) assets (either cash or accounts receivable) have increased. It is very important to understand that the definition of revenue is *not* directly related to the inflow of cash. Cash *may* increase as a result of a revenue, but it is not necessary for cash to increase in order to record revenue. In addition, there are many times when cash increases but no revenue is recorded. For instance, cash would increase as a result of borrowing money from a bank and signing a note payable to be repaid at a future date; or if after a sale of goods to a customer on accounts receivable the receivable is collected. In either case, even though there is an increase in cash, no revenue would be recorded. In the first case the cash increased as a result of an increase in a liability. In the second case the cash increased as a result of a decrease in another asset, accounts receivable. (The revenue was recorded at the time of the sale; a common mistake among beginning accounting students is to record the revenue again at the time of the cash collection.) The requirement for recording revenue is that assets must have increased (or liabilities decreased) as a result of goods or services being provided to customers.

Expenses

Examples of expenses include the wages of employees, the cost of products sold, advertising, heat, light, and power expenditures, property taxes, and delivery costs. Because expenses are the costs of providing goods or services, expenses result in decreases in assets or increases in liabilities. When wages are paid to employees, for instance, an expense has resulted and an asset (Cash) has decreased.

It is important to remember two issues in regard to expenses. First, the outflow of cash is *not* a requirement to record an expense; that is, an expense may be incurred whether or not there is an outflow of cash. (This issue is discussed more fully later in the chapter.) Furthermore, there may be an outflow of cash (e.g., the purchase of office equipment for cash) without incurring an expense. The important point is that assets must have decreased (or liabilities increased) because of providing goods or services in a time period.

**EXHIBIT 3-1
Cost: Asset
or Expense**

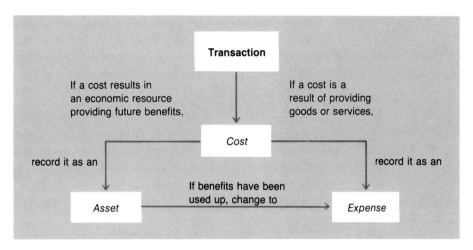

Second, it is important to distinguish between the terms *cost* and *expense*. Sometimes these terms have the same meaning, and at other times they do not. Recall from Chapter 1 that accounting is based upon the historical cost principle; that is, business transactions are recorded on the basis of the monetary value exchanged (i.e., the cost) in the transaction. Thus the term *cost* refers to the amount at which a transaction is recorded. The nature of the transaction determines *how* a cost is recorded in an accounting system. The cost involved in a transaction can be recorded as either (1) an asset or (2) an expense. A cost is recorded as an asset when, in a transaction, the company acquires an economic resource that is expected to provide future benefits to the company. A cost is recorded as an expense if it results from providing goods or services to customers in a time period. This difference in recording costs is illustrated in Exhibit 3-1.

When a cost is recorded as an asset, it may be referred to as an *unexpired* cost, and when it is recorded as an expense, it may be referred to as an *expired* cost. What is important to remember at this point is·that assets do not provide future benefits forever. Most assets eventually lose their potential for providing future benefits, and their status must be changed from an unexpired cost (asset) to an expired cost (expense). This concept is illustrated on the bottom line in Exhibit 3-1 and is also discussed later in the chapter.

**Accounting
Principles
Related to
Net Income**

Three principles are important for understanding the measurement of net income. They include the concept of an accounting period, the matching principle, and accrual accounting.

ACCOUNTING PERIOD.   Companies typically operate for many years. Financial statement users therefore need net income information on a regular basis in order to make economic decisions. Earlier, when defining net income, we referred to a *particular time period*. **An accounting period is the period of time for which the revenues and expenses of a company are computed.**

For financial accounting, a company usually uses a calendar year as its accounting period. Companies whose operations are seasonal also use a year, but a year that corresponds more closely to its seasonal operating activities. For instance, a company may use July 1, 1982, through June 30, 1983, as its accounting period. This period is often called a *fiscal* year or fiscal period. Certain companies are now required to compute and report their net income on a quarterly basis. These accounting periods (and others shorter than a year) are referred to as *interim* periods.

For managerial accounting most companies use a month as the accounting period, which enables the management of the company to have current income information available for operating decisions. In this text we often use a month as our accounting period. Although it is not realistic in terms of actual financial reporting, it saves time and space for illustrations and assignment material.

MATCHING PRINCIPLE.   In the computation of net income, expenses are subtracted from revenues. Another way of expressing this principle is to say that the costs are *matched* against the prices charged to customers to determine net income. **The matching principle states that to determine the net income of a company for an accounting period, the total expenses involved in obtaining the revenues of the period must be computed and matched against the revenues recorded in that period.**

ACCRUAL ACCOUNTING.   Accrual accounting is related to the matching principle and to our earlier discussion of the relationship between revenues and cash inflows, and expenses and cash outflows. **In accrual accounting, revenue and expense transactions are recorded in the accounting period when the goods or services are provided, regardless of whether cash is received or paid by the company.** To accrue means to accumulate. In accrual accounting a company must be certain that all revenues have been recorded at the end of each accounting period. Thus, it must record all revenues even if no cash inflow has been received. Similarly, the company must be certain that all expenses that should be matched against the revenue have been recorded even if no cash outflow has been made.

To illustrate this point, suppose a company purchased a two-year insurance policy at the beginning of 1982. At that time it properly recorded the cost as an asset, Prepaid Insurance. At the end of 1982 only one year of insurance coverage from the policy remains. Part of the insurance cost was for insurance coverage in 1982, an expense of doing business in that year. Thus, as we discussed earlier, a portion of the cost originally recorded as an asset (unexpired cost) must be recorded as an expense (expired cost) at the end of 1982.

Accrual accounting is important because it links the revenues of a company to the accounting period in which they were earned, and it matches the expenses against the revenues in the same period. This procedure makes the resulting accounting information especially useful to users in evaluating the performance of a particular company. The accounting procedures related to accrual accounting are discussed later in the chapter.

Some companies, particularly smaller companies, do not use accrual accounting. Instead they use cash basis accounting. **In cash basis accounting, the net income for the accounting period is computed by subtracting the cash payments from the cash receipts for operations.** This method may lead to incorrect evaluations of a company's operating results. The receipt and payment of cash may occur much earlier or later than the sale of goods or the providing of services to customers and the related costs. Accrual accounting eliminates distortions of operating results and is appropriate for companies of all sizes. For convenience, however, cash basis accounting may be used for small companies with a few employees in which the owner-manager finances all the operations.

Income Statement **An income statement is a financial statement summarizing the revenues, expenses, and net income (or net loss) of a company for its accounting period.** This statement is alternatively referred to as a *statement of income*, *statement of earnings*, *profit and loss statement*, or *statement of operations*. The income statement is an expansion of the income equation presented earlier:

Net Income = Revenues − Expenses

An illustration of a typical income statement for a service company (a company such as a travel agency or laundry selling a service instead of a product) is shown in Exhibit 3-2. An income statement always has a heading. The heading consists of three lines, the company's name, the title of the statement (i.e., *income statement*), and the accounting period for which the income statement is prepared. Within the income statement are two sections; one is for revenues and the other for

EXHIBIT 3-2
Income Statement

NORSTED LAUNDRY AND DRY CLEANING
Income Statement
For Year Ended December 31, 1983

Revenues:		
Laundry revenues		$28,200
Dry cleaning revenues		49,700
Total Revenues		$77,900
Expenses:		
Employees wages	$22,400	
Heat, light, and power	8,100	
Property taxes	1,200	
Depreciation expense: Washers and dryers	2,600	
Depreciation expense: Dry cleaning equipment	3,900	
Rent expense on building	9,600	
Insurance expense	500	
Supplies	4,300	
Total Expenses		52,600
Net Income		$25,300

expenses. In the revenues section the types and amounts of revenues for the period are listed. These amounts are summed to determine the total revenues. A service company often has only a single revenue (e.g., Travel Commissions Revenue or Laundry Revenue). In the expenses section the various types and amounts of expenses for the period are listed. These amounts are summed to determine the total expenses. Total expenses are then subtracted from total revenues to determine net income. (When total expenses exceed total revenues the format of the income statement is the same, although the resulting negative difference is entitled *net loss*.)

Since a major goal of each company is to earn a satisfactory income, it is not surprising that the income statement has become the most important financial statement. Owners, potential owners, creditors, and other users of accounting information rely on the information in the income statement to make important economic decisions concerning the current and likely future operating performance of a company.

Each income statement is an end result of a company's accounting system. To understand the accounting information contained in the income statement better, we return to the identifying, measuring, recording, and retaining processes that must be completed before the preparation of the income statement. First, however, we briefly discuss withdrawals and the relationship of net income to owner's equity.

WITHDRAWALS

When an owner invests in a company the owner contributes cash or other assets, and an increase is recorded in the company's assets and in owner's equity. This investment in assets is used in the company's operations in order to earn a satisfactory net income for the owner. In many businesses the owner is also the full-time manager. While operating the business the owner may require cash for personal expenditures or other investment opportunities. Cash may be periodically withdrawn from the company for this purpose.

Care must be taken to account properly for the owner's withdrawals of assets from a business. A withdrawal should be recorded in a manner opposite to that of recording an investment by the owner; that is, a withdrawal is recorded as a decrease in a company's assets and as a decrease in the company's owner's equity. Withdrawals should not be confused with expenses. *Withdrawals are not expenses just like investments are not revenues*.

This treatment of withdrawals is consistent with the business entity concept introduced in Chapter 1, in which we noted that a company is considered to be an economic entity separate from its owner. We observed that an owner's personal financial activities are not included within the accounting system of the company unless the activity has a direct impact on the business. The direct impact of a withdrawal is a *disinvestment* of assets by the owner. It is not considered an expense, but is instead treated as a direct reduction of assets and owner's equity. Withdrawals are therefore *not* included in an income statement. We discuss the recording and reporting of withdrawals later in this chapter.

RELATIONSHIP OF NET INCOME AND WITHDRAWALS TO OWNER'S EQUITY

In Chapter 1 we introduced the accounting equation: assets equal liabilities plus owner's equity. We noted that the equation must always remain in balance because assets are financed either by a company's creditors or by its owner. We have observed that owner's equity may increase as a result of the initial and subsequent investments by the owner. It may decrease as a result of withdrawals by the owner.

In this chapter we relate revenues to increases in assets (or decreases in liabilities) as a result of providing goods or services to customers during an accounting period. We relate expenses to decreases in assets (or increases in liabilities) from providing the goods or services. When revenues exceed expenses, resulting in net income, an increase in net assets (net assets are assets minus liabilities) also occurs. Since the net income of a company belongs to its owner, it is recorded as an increase in owner's equity (thereby keeping the accounting equation in balance).

We may now summarize the components of owner's equity. Owner's equity is increased by the initial and subsequent investments of the owner and by net income (revenues greater than expenses). Owner's equity is decreased by the withdrawals of the owner and by a net loss (expenses greater than revenues). This relationship is shown in Exhibit 3-3.

It is important to understand the relationship of the components (revenues and expenses) of net income to owner's equity. Exhibit 3-3 shows that net income increases owner's equity. Since revenues increase net income, it follows that *revenues increase owner's equity*. Since expenses decrease net income, it follows that *expenses decrease owner's equity*. In the case of a net loss, a decrease in owner's equity occurs because expenses (which decrease owner's equity) exceed revenues (which increase owner's equity). The relationship of revenues and expenses to owner's equity plays an important part in the recording process for these items.

**EXHIBIT 3-3
Components of
Owner's Equity**

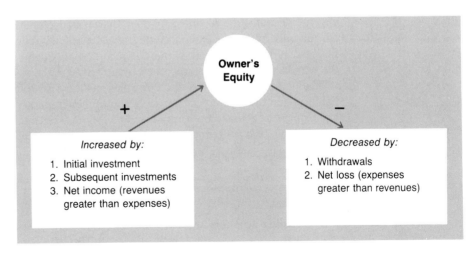

RECORDING, RETAINING, AND REPORTING NET INCOME AND WITHDRAWALS INFORMATION

Since net income affects owner's equity, it would be possible to record all the transactions of a company affecting revenues and expenses directly in the owner's capital account. Remember, however, that only the balance of an account is reported on a financial statement. Reporting the ending balance of the owner's capital account may be useful for certain purposes, but it would not be useful in reporting the company's net income. What is needed are additional accounts in the company's accounting system in which to record and retain the monetary amounts of the revenue and expense transactions so that an income statement for the accounting period can be prepared. These accounts are called *temporary* (or *nominal*) accounts because they are used only to compute the net income for the accounting period. These accounts are different from the *permanent* (or *real*) accounts that are listed on the balance sheet.

Withdrawals could also be deducted directly from the owner's capital account. It is important, however, to report the total withdrawals for the accounting period so that the owner will know exactly how much has been taken out of the business during the period. A *temporary* withdrawals account is used for this purpose.

Debit and Credit Rules

We already have several rules for a typical accounting system. They include maintaining the equality of the accounting equation, the debit and credit rules for assets, liabilities, and owner's equity accounts, and the double entry system. In creating new revenue and expense accounts and a withdrawals account, these accounts must *fit* into the accounting system so that none of these rules will be broken. Thus debit and credit rules have been made for revenues, expenses, and withdrawals based on their relationship to owner's equity.

Recall that the owner's capital account is on the right side of the accounting equation. It is therefore increased by credit entries and decreased by debit entries. Since revenues increase owner's equity, all revenue accounts are increased by credit entries and decreased by debit entries. Expenses, however, decrease owner's equity. As expenses increase, owner's equity decreases. Thus the debit and credit rule for expenses is the opposite of that for owner's equity; that is, increases in expense accounts are recorded by debit entries and decreases in expense accounts are recorded by credit entries. Withdrawals similarly reduce owner's equity. An increase in the withdrawals account is recorded by a debit entry and a decrease in the withdrawals account is recorded by a credit entry.

The entire set of debit and credit rules, as they relate to the permanent asset, liability, and owners' equity accounts and to the temporary withdrawals, revenue, and expense accounts, are summarized as follows (since the set of rules applies to the accounts of a sole proprietorship, partnership, or corporation, the plural *owners'* equity is used here):

1. **Asset accounts are increased by debit entries and decreased by credit entries.**

2. **Liability accounts are increased by credit entries and decreased by debit entries.**

Errata Sheet
Principles of Accounting
Second Printing
Nikolai, Bazley, and Stallman

Page   Correction

471   P12-6B. All dates on this page only should be reduced by
              one year (i.e., 1983 should be 1982, and 1984 should be
              1983).

733   Exhibit 19-9. All dates should be reduced by one year
              (i.e., 1983 should be 1982, 1984 should be 1983). In
              addition, on line 10 below Exhibit 19-9 the year 1984
              should be 1983.

802   P20-4A and P20-5A. All dates on this page only should be
              reduced by one year (i.e., 1980 should be 1979, 1984 should
              be 1983, etc.)

805-806   P20-3B, P20-4B and P20-5B. All dates on these pages only
              should be reduced by one year (i.e., 1980 should be 1979,
              1984 should be 1983, etc.)

Kent Publishing Company, Inc.

3. **Permanent owners' equity (capital) accounts are increased by credit entries and decreased by debit entries. Temporary owners' equity accounts have the following rules:**
   (a) **Withdrawal accounts are increased by debit entries and decreased by credit entries.**
   (b) **Revenue accounts are increased by credit entries and decreased by debit entries.**
   (c) **Expense accounts are increased by debit entries and decreased by credit entries.**

The remaining rules that have already been made are still used in the accounting system; that is, the accounting equation must always remain in balance and the double entry rule must be followed in recording all transactions.

The debit and credit rules, as they relate to the accounting equation, are illustrated in Exhibit 3-4.

EXHIBIT 3-4   Accounting Equation and Debit and Credit Rules

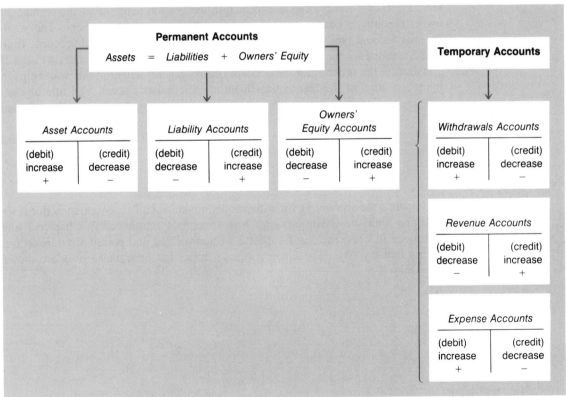

Recording and Posting Transactions

The rules for recording and posting also apply to revenue and expense transactions; that is, for each transaction the source documents are examined to determine the types of accounts affected and the monetary amount of the transaction. The transaction is initially recorded in the general journal by listing the date, the account to be debited and the amount, the account to be credited (remember this item is indented slightly) and the amount, and an explanation of the journal entry. Compound entries are recorded as discussed earlier.

The postings to the general ledger follow the same procedures as before. The journal entry is posted, line by line, to the related accounts. In the account is listed the date, the amount of the debit or credit entry, and the page number of the journal on which the transaction was initially recorded. The account number is listed in the account reference column of the general journal to complete the posting for that line. The posting is continued until each line for all the journal entries has been posted.

Chart of Accounts and Account Titles

As explained in Chapter 2, the chart of accounts is established so that the asset, liability, and owner's equity accounts are listed in order in the general ledger. Because withdrawals, revenue, and expense accounts are temporary accounts affecting owner's equity, they are located in the general ledger *after* the permanent owner's equity accounts and are assigned higher account numbers. The withdrawals account typically follows directly after the owner's capital account. Then all the revenue accounts are included, followed by the expense accounts. As we will see shortly, the ordering of the accounts in the general ledger in this way helps in the preparation of the income statement and the balance sheet. The title of each revenue and expense account is usually very descriptive. Thus Legal Fees Earned or Accounting Services Revenues might be titles used for the revenue accounts of a lawyer and CPA, respectively. Salaries Expense and Rent Expense are examples of the titles of expense accounts.

Illustration of Accounting for Withdrawals, Revenues, and Expenses

To illustrate the accounting for withdrawals, revenue, and expense transactions, we continue with the Dixon Travel Agency example introduced in Chapter 1 and continued in Chapter 2. In Chapter 2 we journalized and posted six transactions during January 1983. The January journal entries for these transactions are shown in Exhibit 3-5.

**EXHIBIT 3-5
General Journal
Entries for
January 1983**

GENERAL JOURNAL				Page 1
Date	Account Titles and Explanations	Acct. No.	Debit	Credit
1983 Jan. 1	Cash	101	30,000	
	A. Dixon, Capital	301		30,000
	Owner invested cash into business.			
2	Building	122	18,000	
	Cash	101		18,000
	Purchased office building in which to operate the travel agency.			
5	Office Supplies	107	700	
	Accounts Payable	201		700
	Purchased office supplies on account from City Supply Company; agreed to pay half of the amount owed on January 15 and the remainder on February 15.			
12	Office Equipment	124	3,000	
	Cash	101		1,000
	Notes Payable	204		2,000
	Purchased office equipment from Ace Equipment Company; made cash down payment and signed 1-year note.			
15	Accounts Payable	201	350	
	Cash	101		350
	Paid City Supply Company half of the amount owed for office supplies purchased January 5, 1983.			
28	Accounts Receivable	103	400	
	Office Equipment	124		400
	Sold desk that cost $400 to James Baker on credit for $400, the full amount is to be collected on February 7.			

At the beginning of February 1983 the Dixon Travel Agency hired one employee at a monthly salary of $600, payable at the end of each month, and began its operations. It added the following accounts and account numbers to its chart of accounts:

Account Titles		Account Numbers
Accumulated Depreciation:	Building	123
Accumulated Depreciation:	Office Equipment	125
A. Dixon, Withdrawals		304
Income Summary		306
Travel Commissions Revenues		401
Salary Expense		501
Telephone Expense		502
Utilities Expense		503
Office Supplies Expense		504
Depreciation Expense:	Building	505
Depreciation Expense:	Office Equipment	506

During February it entered into eight transactions. These transactions are summarized and analyzed in Exhibit 3-6.

EXHIBIT 3-6   Analysis of Transactions

Date	Source Document	Transaction	Analysis
2/3/1983	Receipts issued to customers and related paperwork	Made travel arrangements for several customers and collected $620 in commissions for services performed.	The asset Cash is increased as a result of services performed. Debit (increase) Cash and credit (increase) the revenue account, Travel Commissions Revenues.
2/7/1983	Check from James Baker	Collected $400, the amount owed by Baker for desk purchased on January 28.	The asset Cash is exchanged for the asset Accounts Receivable. No revenue is involved. Debit (increase) Cash and credit (decrease) Accounts Receivable.
2/10/1983	Bills sent to customers and related paperwork	Made travel arrangements for several customers. Customers agreed to pay the $680 commissions by March 10, 1983.	The asset Accounts Receivable is increased as a result of services performed. Debit (increase) Accounts Receivable and credit (increase) Travel Commissions Revenues.
2/15/1983	Check issued to supplier	Paid City Supply Company $350 on account for supplies purchased on January 5, 1983.	The liability Accounts Payable is paid. No expense is involved. Debit (decrease) Accounts Payable and credit (decrease) Cash.

EXHIBIT 3-6   (Continued)

Date	Source Document	Transaction	Analysis
2/20/1983	Check issued to Anne Dixon	Anne Dixon withdrew $450 cash from the business for her personal use.	The asset Cash is decreased as a result of withdrawal (disinvestment) by owner. Debit (increase) A. Dixon, Withdrawals and credit (decrease) Cash.
2/27/1983	Check issued to employee	Employee was paid $600 monthly salary.	The asset Cash is decreased as a result of an expense. Debit (increase) Salary Expense and credit (decrease) Cash.
2/28/1983	Bill from phone company	Paid phone company $100 for phone charges for month of February.	The asset Cash is decreased as a result of an expense. Debit (increase) the expense account, Telephone Expense and credit (decrease) Cash.
2/28/1983	Utility bill	Received the $170 utility bill (heat, light, and water) for February, to be paid by March 5, 1983.	The liability Accounts Payable is increased as a result of an expense. Debit (increase) Utilities Expense and credit (increase) Accounts Payable.

JOURNAL ENTRIES.   The journal entries to record the February transactions are listed in Exhibit 3-7. Notice that the January 1983 journal entries completely filled page 1 of the Dixon Travel Agency general journal and therefore the February transactions are recorded on page 2. Also remember that the Acct. No. (account number) column has been filled in because the journal entries have been posted to the respective accounts (shown in Exhibit 3-8).

The February 3 and 10 journal entries involve revenue transactions. In both cases assets were increased as a result of services performed. The February 3 entry involved Cash while the February 10 entry involved Accounts Receivable. On February 27 and 28 three expense transactions were recorded as a result of providing services. The first two transactions involved a decrease in the asset, Cash, while the third transaction resulted in an increase in a liability, Accounts Payable.

Note that the February 20 withdrawal was not recorded as an expense, but rather in the Withdrawals account. Although the February 7 and 15 journal entries involved

EXHIBIT 3-7
Journal Entries

		GENERAL JOURNAL			Page 2
Date		Account Titles and Explanations	Acct. No.	Debit	Credit
1983 Feb.	3	Cash Travel Commissions Revenues Made travel arrangements for customers and collected cash for services performed.	101 401	620	620
	7	Cash Accounts Receivable Collected cash from James Baker as amount owed for desk purchased in January.	101 103	400	400
	10	Accounts Receivable Travel Commissions Revenues Made travel arrangements for customers on account. Customers agreed to pay amounts owed by March 10, 1983.	103 401	680	680
	15	Accounts Payable Cash Paid City Supply Company for balance owed on account from purchase of office supplies on January 5.	201 101	350	350
	20	A. Dixon, Withdrawals Cash Owner withdrew cash for her personal use.	304 101	450	450
	27	Salary Expense Cash Paid employee's salary for February.	501 101	600	600
	28	Telephone Expense Cash Paid phone bill for the month of February.	502 101	100	100
	28	Utilities Expense Accounts Payable Incurred utilities for February to be paid by March 5, 1983.	503 201	170	170

a receipt and payment of cash, respectively, neither was a revenue nor an expense. The February 7 entry related to the collection of an account receivable while the February 15 entry involved a payment of an account payable.

POSTING. The postings of journal entries to the appropriate accounts for the February transactions are shown in Exhibit 3-8. Notice that the beginning February balance for each permanent (balance sheet) account is the ending balance for January (as computed in Chapter 2). Also notice that the Jr. Ref. (journal reference) in each account is to page 2 of the general journal and that the account numbers are listed in the general journal (Exhibit 3-7) as evidence that the postings are completed.

EXHIBIT 3-8 Postings and Account Balances

Cash						Acct. No. 101
Date		Explanation	Jr. Ref.	Debit	Credit	Debit Balance
1983 Jan.	1		1	30,000		30,000
	2		1		18,000	12,000
	12		1		1,000	11,000
	15		1		350	10,650
Feb.	3		2	620		11,270
	7		2	400		11,670
	15		2		350	11,320
	20		2		450	10,870
	27		2		600	10,270
	28		2		100	10,170

Accounts Receivable						Acct. No. 103
Date		Explanation	Jr. Ref.	·Debit	Credit	Debit Balance
1983 Jan.	28		1	400		400
Feb.	7		2		400	0
	10		2	680		680

Office Supplies						Acct. No. 107
Date		Explanation	Jr. Ref.	Debit	Credit	Debit Balance
1983 Jan.	5		1	700		700

**EXHIBIT 3-8
(Continued)**

Building   Acct. No. 122

Date		Explanation	Jr. Ref.	Debit	Credit	Debit Balance
1983 Jan.	2		1	18,000		18,000

Office Equipment   Acct. No. 124

Date		Explanation	Jr. Ref.	Debit	Credit	Debit Balance
1983 Jan.	12		1	3,000		3,000
	28		1		400	2,600

Accounts Payable   Acct. No. 201

Date		Explanation	Jr. Ref.	Debit	Credit	Credit Balance
1983 Jan.	5		1		700	700
	15		1	350		350
Feb.	15		2	350		0
	28		2		170	170

Notes Payable   Acct. No. 204

Date		Explanation	Jr. Ref.	Debit	Credit	Credit Balance
1983 Jan.	12		1		2,000	2,000

A. Dixon, Capital   Acct. No. 301

Date		Explanation	Jr. Ref.	Debit	Credit	Credit Balance
1983 Jan.	1		1		30,000	30,000

**EXHIBIT 3-8
(Continued)**

A. Dixon, Withdrawals — Acct. No. 304

Date		Explanation	Jr. Ref.	Debit	Credit	Debit Balance
1983 Feb.	20		2	450		450

Travel Commissions Revenues — Acct. No. 401

Date		Explanation	Jr. Ref.	Debit	Credit	Credit Balance
1983 Feb.	3		2		620	620
	10		2		680	1,300

Salary Expense — Acct. No. 501

Date		Explanation	Jr. Ref.	Debit	Credit	Debit Balance
1983 Feb.	27		2	600		600

Telephone Expense — Acct. No. 502

Date		Explanation	Jr. Ref.	Debit	Credit	Debit Balance
1983 Feb.	28		2	100		100

Utilities Expense — Acct. No. 503

Date		Explanation	Jr. Ref.	Debit	Credit	Debit Balance
1983 Feb.	28		2	170		170

EXHIBIT 3-9
Trial Balance

DIXON TRAVEL AGENCY
Trial Balance
February 28, 1983

Account Titles	Debits	Credits
Cash	$10,170	
Accounts receivable	680	
Office supplies	700	
Building	18,000	
Office equipment	2,600	
Accounts payable		$ 170
Notes payable		2,000
A. Dixon, capital		30,000
A. Dixon, withdrawals	450	
Travel commissions revenues		1,300
Salary expense	600	
Telephone expense	100	
Utilities expense	170	
Totals	$33,470	$33,470

TRIAL BALANCE. At the end of February a trial balance may be prepared to prove the equality of the debit and credit balances in the ledger accounts. This is shown in Exhibit 3-9.

Adjusting Entries

Earlier in the chapter when discussing accrual accounting, we pointed out that at the end of a company's accounting period the company must be certain that all revenues and expenses have been recorded. We stated that in journalizing a transaction, a *cost* may be recorded as an expense (expired cost) or as an asset (unexpired cost). We also observed that most assets eventually lose their potential for providing future benefits and must be changed to an expense. An adjusting entry is used for this purpose.

Adjusting entries are journal entries made at the end of an accounting period in order to bring the revenue and expense account balances up to date and to show the correct ending balances in the asset and liability accounts. There are many different types of adjusting entries, and they are discussed in detail in Chapter 4.

In the Dixon Travel Agency example we will assume that the month of February is the accounting period. Three adjusting entries must be made at the end of the month. These adjusting entries are shown in Exhibit 3-10 along with the postings and account balances. A further illustration is provided in the review problem at the end of the chapter. The adjusting entries are explained in the following paragraphs.

EXHIBIT 3-10
Adjusting Entries
and Postings

GENERAL JOURNAL					Page 2
Date		Account Titles and Explanations	Acct. No.	Debit	Credit
1983 Feb.	28	Office Supplies Expense	504	30	
		Office Supplies	107		30
		To record office supplies used during February.			
	28	Depreciation Expense: Building	505	50	
		Accumulated Depreciation: Building	123		50
		To record depreciation of office building.			
	28	Depreciation Expense: Office Equipment	506	27	
		Accumulated Depreciation: Office Equipment	125		27
		To record depreciation of office equipment.			

GENERAL LEDGER						
Office Supplies					Acct. No. 107	
Date		Explanation	Jr. Ref.	Debit	Credit	Debit Balance
1983 Jan.	5		1	700		700
Feb.	28		2		30	670

Accumulated Depreciation: Building					Acct. No. 123	
Date		Explanation	Jr. Ref.	Debit	Credit	Credit Balance
1983 Feb.	28		2		50	50

Accumulated Depreciation: Office Equipment					Acct. No. 125	
Date		Explanation	Jr. Ref.	Debit	Credit	Credit Balance
1983 Feb.	28		2		27	27

EXHIBIT 3-10
(Continued)

| Office Supplies Expense | | | | | Acct. No. 504 |

Date		Explanation	Jr. Ref.	Debit	Credit	Debit Balance
1983 Feb.	28		2	30		30

| Depreciation Expense: Building | | | | | Acct. No. 505 |

Date		Explanation	Jr. Ref.	Debit	Credit	Debit Balance
1983 Feb.	28		2	50		50

| Depreciation Expense: Office Equipment | | | | | Acct. No. 506 |

Date		Explanation	Jr. Ref.	Debit	Credit	Debit Balance
1983 Feb.	28		2	27		27

OFFICE SUPPLIES EXPENSE. Office supplies expense is the cost of the office supplies used during the accounting period. When the office supplies costing $700 were purchased on January 5, they were recorded as an asset, Office Supplies. By the end of February some of these supplies had been used in the operations of the travel agency. The office supplies used are an expense of doing business while the remaining supplies are still an asset. The expense amount and the reduction in the asset is recorded in an adjusting entry.

If the office supplies used during February amount to $30, the adjusting entry involves a debit (increase) to the expense account, Office Supplies Expense, for $30 and a credit (decrease) to the asset account, Office Supplies, for $30. It is important to understand that when the $30 credit to the Office Supplies account is subtracted from the $700 debit balance, a $670 ending debit balance results, which is the amount of office supplies still on hand at the end of February.

DEPRECIATION EXPENSE: BUILDING. When the office building was purchased, the asset account, Building, was increased for the $18,000 cost. The building was acquired for use in the operations of the travel agency. One expense of operating the agency involves the cost of using the building during the accounting period. **Depreciation expense is the part of the cost of a physical asset assigned as an expense to each accounting period in which the asset is used.**

Assume the depreciation expense for the office building is $50 per month.[1] The adjusting entry involves a $50 debit (increase) to Depreciation Expense: Building and a $50 credit (increase) to Accumulated Depreciation: Building. The Accumulated Depreciation: Building account is used to record the portion of the cost of the office building that has expired to date and has been assigned as depreciation expense. This account has a *credit* balance (and therefore is increased by a credit entry) because it is deducted from the Building account on the balance sheet to show the book value of the building. **The book value of an asset is the remaining unexpired cost of the physical asset (i.e., cost less accumulated depreciation).** The book value is also called the *carrying value*.

The remaining unexpired cost (book value) of the building on February 28, 1983, is $17,950. This amount would be reported on the Dixon Travel Agency balance sheet for that date as follows:

Building	$18,000	
Less: Accumulated depreciation	(50)	17,950

The complete balance sheet is shown in Exhibit 3-14. Each month, after the depreciation adjusting entry is recorded and posted, the Accumulated Depreciation account balance will increase and cause the book value of the building to decrease.

It is important to understand the usefulness of the Accumulated Depreciation account. The $50 credit in the adjusting entry *could* have been made directly to the Building account. In that case the Building account would have been listed on the balance sheet at its ending balance of $17,950. The reader of the balance sheet, however, would have no way of determining that the building had originally cost $18,000, with the $50 being assigned to date as depreciation. By using an Accumulated Depreciation account much more useful information can be presented on the balance sheet. This procedure is explained more fully in Chapter 4.

DEPRECIATION EXPENSE: OFFICE EQUIPMENT. When the office equipment was purchased the $2,600 cost was recorded as an asset. The office equipment was purchased to be used in the operations of the travel agency. As in the case of the building, a part of the cost of the office equipment must be assigned as depreciation expense in order to show all the operating expenses for the February accounting period.

Assume that the monthly depreciation for the office equipment is $27. The adjusting entry to record the depreciation involves a $27 debit (increase) to Depreciation Expense: Office Equipment and a $27 credit (increase) to Accumulated Depreciation: Office Equipment. The Accumulated Depreciation account balance

---

[1]The method of computing this amount is discussed in Chapter 4.

is subtracted from the Office Equipment account balance on the February 28, 1983, balance sheet (see Exhibit 3-14) to report the $2,573 book value of the office equipment on that date.

After the adjusting entries have been journalized and posted, all the account balances are up to date for the accounting period. Before preparing the financial statements, it is useful to prepare an adjusted trial balance. **An adjusted trial balance is a schedule prepared after the adjusting entries have been made to prove the equality of the debit and credit balances in the ledger accounts.** Like the trial balance, an adjusted trial balance is the accountant's working paper and not a financial statement.

An adjusted trial balance helps to prevent debit and credit errors from being included in the financial statements. (If the debit and credit columns do *not* balance, the procedures recommended in Chapter 2 should be followed.) An adjusted trial balance also makes it easier to prepare the financial statements. As we will see shortly, since the adjusted trial balance lists the accounts according to their place in the chart of accounts, different parts of the adjusted trial balance are used to prepare each financial statement. The adjusted trial balance of the Dixon Travel Agency is shown in Exhibit 3-11.

EXHIBIT 3-11
Adjusted
Trial Balance

DIXON TRAVEL AGENCY
Adjusted Trial Balance
February 28, 1983

Account Titles	Debits	Credits
Cash	$10,170	
Accounts receivable	680	
Office supplies	670	
Building	18,000	
Accumulated depreciation: building		$ 50
Office equipment	2,600	
Accumulated depreciation: office equipment		27
Accounts payable		170
Notes payable		2,000
A. Dixon, capital		30,000
A. Dixon, withdrawals	450	
Travel commissions revenues		1,300
Salary expense	600	
Telephone expense	100	
Utilities expense	170	
Office supplies expense	30	
Depreciation expense: building	50	
Depreciation expense: office equipment	27	
Totals	$33,547	$33,547

EXHIBIT 3-12
Income Statement

DIXON TRAVEL AGENCY Income Statement For Month Ended February 28, 1983		
Revenues:		
Travel commissions revenues		$1,300
Expenses:		
Salary expense	$600	
Telephone expense	100	
Utilities expense	170	
Office supplies expense	30	
Depreciation expense: building	50	
Depreciation expense: office equipment	27	
Total Expenses		977
Net Income		$ 323

Financial Statements

After completing the adjusted trial balance, the financial statements for the accounting period are prepared. The income statement is prepared first because the amount of net income (or net loss) affects the owner's capital account on the balance sheet. For a sole proprietorship the statement of changes in owner's equity, a supporting schedule to the balance sheet, is often prepared next. Finally, the balance sheet is prepared. A discussion of each statement follows.

INCOME STATEMENT. An income statement is the financial statement that summarizes the revenues, expenses, and net income of a company for its accounting period. The income statement of the Dixon Travel Agency for the month of February is shown in Exhibit 3-12.

The Dixon Travel Agency income statement was prepared from the accounts listed on the lower part of the adjusted trial balance shown in Exhibit 3-11. Because the revenue and expense accounts are listed at the end of each company's chart of accounts (and, therefore, its general ledger), these accounts are always listed in the lower portion of every company's adjusted trial balance. This procedure simplifies preparation of the income statement. The Dixon Travel Agency net income for February is $323, computed by deducting (matching) the $977 total expenses from the $1,300 total revenues.

STATEMENT OF CHANGES IN OWNER'S EQUITY. In order to disclose the impact on the owner's equity of any additional investments, the net income, and the withdrawals during the accounting period, a statement of changes in owner's equity is often prepared. This statement is presented as a supporting schedule to the owner's capital account balance listed on the balance sheet. The schedule starts with the beginning balance in the owner's capital account. To this balance are added the

EXHIBIT 3-13
Statement of Changes
in Owner's Equity

DIXON TRAVEL AGENCY
Statement of Changes in Owner's Equity
For Month Ended February 28, 1983

A. Dixon, capital, February 1, 1983	$30,000
Add: Net income for February	323
	$30,323
Less: Withdrawals for February	(450)
A. Dixon, capital, February 28, 1983	$29,873

additional investments (if any) by the owner and the net income[2] for the accounting period. From the resulting subtotal the amount of the owner's withdrawals for the period is subtracted to determine the ending balance in the owner's capital account. A similar schedule would be prepared for a partnership or a corporation. The Dixon Travel Agency statement of changes in owner's equity is shown in Exhibit 3-13.

Because withdrawals were more than net income for February, owner's equity decreased from $30,000 to $29,873. Although this decrease is undesirable, it is not unusual in the first month or even the first several months of the operation of a business. A good sign for future success is that the travel agency earned a net income in its first month of operations. Many small businesses fail and go bankrupt early in their operations because they cannot earn a net income or cannot keep a positive cash balance.

BALANCE SHEET.   A balance sheet reports the financial position of a company on a particular date. The balance sheet of the Dixon Travel Agency as of February 28, 1983, is shown in Exhibit 3-14.

Use of the adjusted trial balance makes the preparation of the balance sheet very easy. The assets, liabilities, and owner's capital accounts are the first accounts in a company's chart of accounts and in its general ledger. Therefore these accounts are always listed in the upper portion of the company's adjusted trial balance. It should be noted, however, that the amount listed as the owner's capital on the adjusted trial balance is *not* the amount to be listed on the ending balance sheet because it has not been updated for the company's net income or withdrawals. The ending amount of owner's capital is obtained instead from the statement of changes in owner's equity. In Exhibit 3-14 the $29,873 amount listed for A. Dixon, Capital was obtained from the statement of changes in owner's equity shown in Exhibit 3-13.

The balance sheet shown in Exhibit 3-14 is presented in report form. **In the report form the assets on the balance sheet are presented first, directly followed by the liabilities and owner's equity.** An alternative format is the account form of the balance sheet, as used in Exhibit 2-8 of Chapter 2. **In the account form the assets are presented on the left side and the liabilities and owner's equity are presented on the right side of the balance sheet.** Both forms of balance sheets are commonly used in practice today.

---

[2]A net loss for the accounting period would be subtracted in the computation.

EXHIBIT 3-14
Balance Sheet

DIXON TRAVEL AGENCY
Balance Sheet
February 28, 1983

Assets

Cash		$10,170
Accounts receivable		680
Office supplies		670
Building	$18,000	
Less: Accumulated depreciation	(50)	17,950
Office equipment	$ 2,600	
Less: Accumulated depreciation	(27)	2,573
Total Assets		$32,043

Liabilities

Accounts payable		$ 170
Notes payable		2,000
Total Liabilities		$ 2,170

Owner's Equity

A. Dixon, capital		29,873
Total Liabilities and Owner's Equity		$32,043

The relationships of the items on the adjusted trial balance, income statement, statement of changes in owner's equity, and balance sheet are shown in Exhibit 3-15.

EXHIBIT 3-15   Relationship of Financial Statements

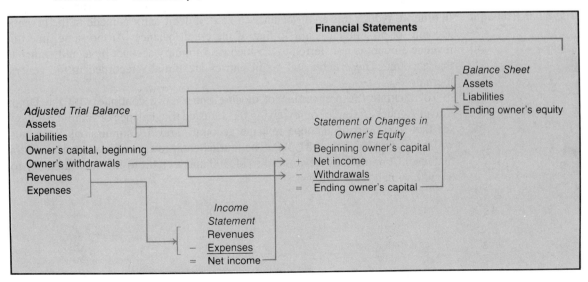

CLOSING ENTRIES

Earlier we noted two points. First, the revenue, expense, and withdrawals accounts are *temporary* accounts. These accounts are used to determine the changes in the owner's equity in the current accounting period as a result of net income (or net loss) and withdrawals. Second, the owner's capital account balance listed on the adjusted trial balance was *not* used in preparing the balance sheet because this account balance was not up to date for the net income and withdrawals of the accounting period.

To begin the next accounting period, it is important to (1) show the current balance in the owner's capital account and (2) show zero balances in the revenue, expense, and withdrawals accounts. The owner's capital account should be up to date to show the owner's current investment in the assets of the company. The revenue, expense, and withdrawals accounts will be used in the next accounting period to accumulate the net income and withdrawals information *for that period*. It is useful, therefore, to start with a zero balance in each of these accounts at the beginning of the period so that at the end of the period, the balances in the accounts will show the revenues, expenses, and withdrawals for only one period.

Closing entries are journal entries made at the end of an accounting period to create zero balances in each revenue, expense, and withdrawals account and to transfer these account balances to the owner's permanent capital account. Closing entries are made like any journal entry. They are recorded first in the general journal and then posted to the respective accounts. The revenue and expense account balances are not closed directly to the owner's capital account. These account balances are first transferred to an account entitled Income Summary. **The Income Summary account is a temporary account used in the closing process to accumulate the amount of net income (or net loss) before transferring this amount to the owner's capital account.** We discuss the closing of each type of account (revenues, expenses, and withdrawals) separately.

Closing the Revenue Accounts

Recall that each revenue account normally has a credit balance (prior to closing). In order to reduce this credit balance to zero, a debit entry is made in the revenue account for an amount *equal* to that of the credit balance. At the same time this revenue amount is transferred to the Income Summary account by a credit entry to that account. These debit and credit entries are initially recorded in the general journal.

To illustrate the preparation of closing entries, we continue with the Dixon Travel Agency example. In reviewing the adjusted trial balance of Exhibit 3-11, we see that the company has one revenue account, Travel Commissions Revenues, with an ending balance of $1,300. The journal entry to close this account is a debit to Travel Commissions Revenues for $1,300 and a credit to Income Summary for $1,300, which is as follows:

GENERAL JOURNAL					Page 3
Date		Account Titles and Explanations	Acct. No.	Debit	Credit
1983 Feb.	28	Travel Commissions Revenues		1,300	
		Income Summary			1,300
		To close the revenue account.			

The journal entry and the postings (identified by the arrows labeled A and B) are also shown in Exhibit 3-16. After the revenue closing entry has been journalized and posted, the Travel Commissions Revenues account has a zero balance and is ready to accumulate the revenues for the next accounting period. The total revenues of $1,300 have been transferred as a credit to the Income Summary account. If a company has more than one revenue account, it is typical to close all of the revenue accounts in a single compound journal entry.

Closing the Expense Accounts

Each expense account has a debit balance (prior to closing). To reduce each debit balance to zero, a credit entry is made in each expense account for an amount *equal* to that of the debit balance. This expense amount is transferred to the Income Summary account by a debit entry. Companies typically have many expense accounts, and therefore it is usual to close all the expense accounts by making a compound journal entry crediting each expense account for its balance and debiting the Income Summary account for the total expenses. (Remember, however, that the debit entry is always listed first in the general journal.)

The adjusted trial balance in Exhibit 3-11 shows six expense accounts with debit balances at the end of February. The journal entry to close these accounts involves a debit to Income Summary for $977 and a credit to each of the six expense accounts for the respective balance. This journal entry is as follows:

GENERAL JOURNAL					Page 3
Date		Account Titles and Explanations	Acct. No.	Debit	Credit
1983 Feb.	28	Income Summary		977	
		Salary Expense			600
		Telephone Expense			100
		Utilities Expense			170
		Office Supplies Expense			30
		Depreciation Expense: Building			50
		Depreciation Expense: Office Equipment			27
		To close the expense accounts.			

The journal entry and postings (identified by the arrows labeled C through I) are also shown in Exhibit 3-16. After the expenses closing entry has been journalized and posted, each of the expense accounts has a zero balance and is ready to accumulate the respective expenses for the next accounting period. The $977 total expenses has been transferred as a debit to Income Summary. The $323 *credit* balance in the Income Summary account represents the *net income* for February because the revenue credit entry of $1,300 exceeds the expenses debit entry of $977.

Closing the Income Summary Account

After the revenue and expense accounts have been closed to the Income Summary account, the balance in this account is the net income (or net loss). A credit balance indicates that the company has earned a net income for the accounting period because revenues exceeded expenses. A debit balance indicates a net loss because expenses exceed revenues.

The net income (or net loss) amount is now transferred to the owner's permanent capital account. For net income the journal entry is a debit to the Income Summary account for its balance and a credit to the owner's capital account for a like amount. The debit to Income Summary reduces the account balance to zero, and therefore it is ready for the closing entries of the next accounting period. The credit to the owner's capital account increases the account for the net income. A net loss would be handled in an opposite manner; that is, a debit to the owner's capital account for the amount of the net loss and a credit to the Income Summary account to reduce it to zero.

The journal entry to close the $323 credit balance in Income Summary account of the Dixon Travel Agency is as follows:

GENERAL JOURNAL					Page 3
Date		Account Titles and Explanations	Acct. No.	Debit	Credit
1983 Feb.	28	Income Summary A. Dixon, Capital To close the Income Summary account and transfer the net income to the owner's capital account.		323	323

The journal entry and postings (identified by the arrows labeled J and K) are shown in Exhibit 3-16. After posting this closing entry, the Income Summary account has a zero balance and the A. Dixon, Capital account is up to date for the net income of the accounting period, but *not* for the withdrawals.

Closing the Withdrawals Account

The debit balance of the withdrawals account is closed *directly* to the owner's permanent capital account. The closing entry is a debit to the owner's permanent capital account and a credit to the withdrawals account for the total withdrawals of the period. The debit entry brings the owner's capital account balance up to date at the end of the period. The credit to the withdrawals account reduces the account balance to zero so that it can accumulate the withdrawals of the next period.

The withdrawals by Anne Dixon totaled $450 during February, as shown in the adjusted trial balance of Exhibit 3-11. The journal entry to close the A. Dixon, Withdrawals account is as follows:

GENERAL JOURNAL					Page 3
Date		Account Titles and Explanations	Acct. No.	Debit	Credit
1983 Feb.	28	A. Dixon, Capital		450	
		A. Dixon, Withdrawals			450
		To close the withdrawals account.			

The journal entry and postings (identified by the arrows labeled L and M) are shown in Exhibit 3-16. After posting the withdrawals closing entry, the ending balance in the A. Dixon, Capital account is $29,873, the amount listed on the February 28, 1983, balance sheet shown in Exhibit 3-14. The $450 credit entry in the A. Dixon, Withdrawals account reduces the account balance to zero and completes the closing entries.

Illustration of Complete Closing and Posting Process

All of the closing entries, postings, and account balances for the Dixon Travel Agency are shown in Exhibit 3-16. The closing entries are the same as those discussed earlier in the separate sections on closing the revenue accounts, expense accounts, Income Summary account, and Withdrawals account.

GENERAL JOURNAL   Page 3

Date		Account Titles and Explanations	Acct. No.	Debit	Credit
1983 Feb.	28	Travel Commissions Revenues	401	1,300	
		Income Summary	306		1,300
		To close the revenue account.			
	28	Income Summary	306	977	
		Salary Expense	501		600
		Telephone Expense	502		100
		Utilities Expense	503		170
		Office Supplies Expense	504		30
		Depreciation Expense: Building	505		50
		Depreciation Expense: Office Equipment	506		27
		To close the expense accounts.			
	28	Income Summary	306	323	
		A. Dixon, Capital	301		323
		To close the Income Summary account and transfer the net income to the owner's capital account.			
	28	A. Dixon, Capital	301	450	
		A. Dixon, Withdrawals	304		450
		To close the withdrawals account.			

GENERAL LEDGER
A. Dixon, Capital   Acct. No. 301

Date		Explanation	Jr. Ref.	Debit	Credit	Credit Balance
1983 Jan.	1		1		30,000	30,000
1983 Feb.	28		3		323	30,323
	28		3	450		29,873

A. Dixon, Withdrawals   Acct. No. 304

Date		Explanation	Jr. Ref.	Debit	Credit	Debit Balance
1983 Feb.	20		2	450		450
	28		3		450	0

Income Summary   Acct. No. 306

Date		Explanation	Jr. Ref.	Debit	Credit	Credit Balance
1983 Feb.	28		3		1,300	1,300
	28		3	977		323
	28		3	323		0

Travel Commissions Revenues — Acct. No. 401

Date		Explanation	Jr. Ref.	Debit	Credit	Credit Balance
1983 Feb.	3	A	2		620	620
	10		2		680	1,300
	28		3	1,300		0

Salary Expense — Acct. No. 501

Date		Explanation	Jr. Ref.	Debit	Credit	Debit Balance
1983 Feb.	27		2	600		600
	28	D	3		600	0

Telephone Expense — Acct. No. 502

Date		Explanation	Jr. Ref.	Debit	Credit	Debit Balance
1983 Feb.	28		2	100		100
	28	E	3		100	0

Utilities Expense — Acct. No. 503

Date		Explanation	Jr. Ref.	Debit	Credit	Debit Balance
1983 Feb.	28	F	2	170		170
	28		3		170	0

Office Supplies Expense — Acct. No. 504

Date		Explanation	Jr. Ref.	Debit	Credit	Debit Balance
1983 Feb.	28		2	30		30
	28		3		30	0

Depreciation Expense: Building — Acct. No. 505

Date		Explanation	Jr. Ref.	Debit	Credit	Debit Balance
1983 Feb.	28		2	50		50
	28		3		50	0

Depreciation Expense: Office Equipment — Acct. No. 506

Date		Explanation	Jr. Ref.	Debit	Credit	Debit Balance
1983 Feb.	28		2	27		27
	28		3		27	0

G

H

EXHIBIT 3-17
Post-Closing
Trial Balance

DIXON TRAVEL AGENCY
Post-Closing Trial Balance
February 28, 1983

Account Titles	Debits	Credits
Cash	$10,170	
Accounts receivable	680	
Office supplies	670	
Building	18,000	
Accumulated depreciation: building		$ 50
Office equipment	2,600	
Accumulated depreciation: office equipment		27
Accounts payable		170
Notes payable		2,000
A. Dixon, capital		29,873
Totals	$32,120	$32,120

Post-Closing Trial Balance

After the closing entries have been journalized and posted, the only accounts with nonzero balances should be the permanent accounts; that is, the assets, liabilities, and owner's capital accounts. As a check to make sure that no debit or credit errors were made during the closing entries, a post-closing trial balance is prepared. **A post-closing trial balance is a schedule prepared after the closing entries have been made to prove the equality of the debit and credit balances in the asset, liability, and owner's capital accounts**.

The post-closing trial balance of the Dixon Travel Agency is shown in Exhibit 3-17.

Summary of Closing Process

The steps in the closing process at the end of each accounting period are as follows:

1. Close all the revenue accounts to a zero balance by debiting each revenue account for its balance and crediting the Income Summary account for the total revenues.
2. Close all the expense accounts to a zero balance by crediting each expense account for its balance and debiting the Income Summary account for the total expenses.
3. Compute the balance in the Income Summary account after completing steps 1 and 2. Close a credit balance (net income) in the account by debiting Income Summary and crediting the owner's capital account for the amount of the net income. Close a debit balance (net loss) in the account by crediting Income Summary and debiting the owner's capital account.
4. Close the owner's withdrawals account by crediting the account and debiting the owner's capital account for the balance of the withdrawals account.
5. Prepare a post-closing trial balance to prove the equality of the debit and credit balances in the asset, liability, and owner's capital account balances.

The closing entries for a partnership and a corporation are similar to the entries discussed for a sole proprietorship except that they are modified to apply to the particular type of business entity. They are discussed in later chapters.

THE ACCOUNTING PROCESS

In Exhibit 2-9 of Chapter 2 we listed a set of steps and business documents in the accounting process. In this chapter we added several new steps and documents. The complete set shown in Exhibit 3-18 makes up a typical manual accounting system designed to identify, measure, record, retain, and report accounting information. A good understanding of the sequence of steps, the business documents, and their relationship is very important for further study in this text.

EXHIBIT 3-18   Accounting System: Documents and Process

Documents	Steps in Process
Source Documents Records such as checks, invoices, and receipts substantiating business transactions	**Journalizing** Examine source documents and record debit and credit entries for each transaction in a general journal
General Journal Book of columnar pages on which are recorded the date, accounts and amounts to be debited and credited, and also an explanation of each transaction	**Posting** Transfer the debit and credit amounts from each transaction recorded in the general journal to the related accounts in the general ledger
Accounts Records used to retain the debit and credit amounts from each transaction; separate accounts used for each asset, liability, and owner's capital, withdrawals, revenue, and expense item	**Preparation of Trial Balance** Retrieve account balances from ledger accounts and list account titles and account balances to prove the equality of the total debits and credits
Trial Balance Schedule consisting of an account title column, a debit column, and a credit column for listing each account title, its account balance, and the totals of debit and credit balances; used to prove equality of debit and credit balances of accounts	**Preparation of Adjusting Entries and Adjusted Trial Balance** Journalize and post adjusting entries at the end of the accounting period to bring revenue and expense accounts up-to-date; prepare adjusted trial balance
Adjusted Trial Balance Schedule, like a trial balance, used to prove the equality of the debit and credit balances of ledger accounts; includes results of adjusting entries	**Preparation of Financial Statements** Income statement prepared first, followed by the statement of changes in owner's equity; balance sheet prepared last, including ending owner's capital account from statement of changes in owner's equity
Financial Statements 1. Income statement reporting results of operations for accounting period and 2. Balance sheet reporting financial position at end of accounting period; statement of changes in owner's equity, reporting changes in owner's capital account for accounting period, used as supporting schedule for balance sheet	**Preparation of Closing Entries and Post-Closing Trial Balance** Journalize and post closing entries at end of accounting period to close the revenue, expense, and withdrawals accounts and bring the owner's capital account up-to-date; prepare post-closing trial balance
Post-Closing Trial Balance Schedule, like a trial balance, used to verify the equality of the debit and credit balances in the asset, liability, and owner's capital accounts	

REVIEW PROBLEM

John Thompson operates Ace Insulating Company from a small rented office; he installs insulation for customers in their houses and buildings. The company has been in business for several years. On March 31, 1983, it prepared the following post-closing trial balance:

ACE INSULATING COMPANY
Post-Closing Trial Balance
March 31, 1983

Account Titles	Acct. No.	Debits	Credits
Cash	101	$ 1,000	
Accounts receivable	103	3,000	
Insulating supplies	105	2,400	
Prepaid rent	107	300	
Trucks	125	12,000	
Accumulated depreciation: trucks	126		$ 3,800
Accounts payable	201		1,200
J. Thompson, capital	301		13,700
Totals		$18,700	$18,700

In addition to the above accounts and account numbers, the following accounts are listed in the company's chart of accounts:

Account Titles	Account Numbers
J. Thompson, Withdrawals	302
Income Summary	303
Insulating Revenues	401
Salaries Expense	501
Utilities Expense	502
Insulating Supplies Expense	503
Gas, Oil, and Maintenance Expense	504
Rent Expense	505
Depreciation Expense: Trucks	506

During April the company engaged in the following transactions:

Date	Transaction
4/2/1983	Collected $700 on account from a customer for insulating work completed in March.
4/8/1983	Installed insulation for customer and collected $1,200 for services performed.
4/10/1983	Paid $600 on account for insulating supplies purchased in March.
4/15/1983	Thompson withdrew $500 cash for his personal use.
4/18/1983	Paid $80 to service station for gas, oil, and routine maintenance on trucks during April.
4/20/1983	Installed insulation for customer; customer agreed to pay the contract price of $1,500 in 30 days.
4/28/1983	Paid $40 for April utilities bill.
4/29/1983	Paid $450 to employees for April salaries.

At the end of April, the following information is available:

1. The company pays rent on its office for several months in advance. At the time of payment, the cost is recorded (debited) as an asset Prepaid Rent because it represents the legal right to use the office in the future. For April $50 of prepaid rent is now an expired cost and must be recorded as rent expense.
2. Insulating supplies used during April cost $580.
3. Depreciation expense on the trucks totals $200 for April.

Required: For April, (1) journalize and post entries to record the transactions, (2) journalize and post adjusting entries (a trial balance is not prepared here to save space), (3) prepare an adjusted trial balance, (4) prepare financial statements, and (5) journalize and post closing entries.

SOLUTION TO REVIEW PROBLEM

Requirements 1, 2, and 5: Journalize transactions, adjusting entries, and closing entries. (Note: The Acct. No. column is completed *after* posting to the accounts.)

GENERAL JOURNAL					Page 9
Date		Account Titles and Explanations	Acct. No.	Debit	Credit
1983 Apr.	2	Cash	101	700	
		Accounts Receivable	103		700
		Collected cash on account.			
	8	Cash	101	1,200	
		Insulating Revenues	401		1,200
		Installed insulation and collected contract price.			
	10	Accounts Payable	201	600	
		Cash	101		600
		Paid cash on account.			
	15	J. Thompson, Withdrawals	302	500	
		Cash	101		500
		Owner withdrew cash for personal use.			
	18	Gas, Oil, and Maintenance Expense	504	80	
		Cash	101		80
		Paid April bill owed to service station.			
	20	Accounts Receivable	103	1,500	
		Insulating Revenues	401		1,500
		Installed insulation; customer agreed to pay contract price in 30 days.			

GENERAL JOURNAL				Page 10

Date		Account Titles and Explanations	Acct. No.	Debit	Credit
1983 April	28	Utilities Expense	502	40	
		Cash	101		40
		Paid April utilities.			
	29	Salaries Expense	501	450	
		Cash	101		450
		Paid employees April salaries.			
		Adjusting Entries			
	30	Rent Expense	505	50	
		Prepaid Rent	107		50
		To record rent expense for April.			
	30	Insulating Supplies Expense	503	580	
		Insulating Supplies	105		580
		To record insulating supplies used during April.			
	30	Depreciation Expense: Trucks	506	200	
		Accumulated Depreciation: Trucks	126		200
		To record depreciation expense for April.			
		Closing Entries			
	30	Insulating Revenues	401	2,700	
		Income Summary	303		2,700
		To close revenue account.			
	30	Income Summary	303	1,400	
		Salaries Expense	501		450
		Utilities Expense	502		40
		Insulating Supplies Expense	503		580
		Gas, Oil, and Maintenance Expense	504		80
		Rent Expense	505		50
		Depreciation Expense: Trucks	506		200
		To close expense accounts.			
	30	Income Summary	303	1,300	
		J. Thompson, Capital	301		1,300
		To close net income to the owner's capital account.			
	30	J. Thompson, Capital	301	500	
		J. Thompson, Withdrawals	302		500
		To close withdrawals account.			

Requirement 3:

ACE INSULATING COMPANY
Adjusted Trial Balance
April 30, 1983

Account Titles	Debits	Credits
Cash	$ 1,230	
Accounts receivable	3,800	
Insulating supplies	1,820	
Prepaid rent	250	
Trucks	12,000	
Accumulated depreciation: trucks		$ 4,000
Accounts payable		600
J. Thompson, capital		13,700
J. Thompson, withdrawals	500	
Insulating revenues		2,700
Salaries expense	450	
Utilities expense	40	
Insulating supplies expense	580	
Gas, oil, and maintenance expense	80	
Rent expense	50	
Depreciation expense: trucks	200	
Totals	$21,000	$21,000

Requirement 4:

ACE INSULATING COMPANY
Income Statement
For Month Ended April 30, 1983

Revenues:		
Insulating revenues		$ 2,700
Expenses:		
Salaries expense	$ 450	
Utilities expense	40	
Insulating supplies expense	580	
Gas, oil, and maintenance expense	80	
Rent expense	50	
Depreciation expense: trucks	200	
Total Expenses		1,400
Net Income		$ 1,300

ACE INSULATING COMPANY
Statement of Changes in Owner's Equity
For Month Ended April 30, 1983

J. Thompson, capital, March 31, 1983	$13,700
Add: Net income for April	1,300
	$15,000
Less: Withdrawals for April	(500)
J. Thompson, capital, April 30, 1983	$14,500

ACE INSULATING COMPANY
Balance Sheet
April 30, 1983

Assets			*Liabilities*	
Cash	$ 1,230		Accounts payable	$ 600
Accounts receivable	3,800			
Insulating supplies	1,820			
Prepaid rent	250			
Trucks $12,000			*Owner's Equity*	
Less: Accumulated			J. Thompson, capital	14,500
depreciation (4,000)	8,000		Total Liabilities and	
Total Assets	$15,100		Owner's Equity	$15,100

Accounts after posting April transactions, adjusting, and closing entries:

Cash   Acct. No. 101

Date		Explanation	Jr. Ref.	Debit	Credit	Debit Balance
1983 Mar.	31					1,000
Apr.	2		9	700		1,700
	8		9	1,200		2,900
	10		9		600	2,300
	15		9		500	1,800
	18		9		80	1,720
	28		10		40	1,680
	29		10		450	1,230

Accounts Receivable   Acct. No. 103

Date		Explanation	Jr. Ref.	Debit	Credit	Debit Balance
1983 Mar.	31					3,000
Apr.	2		9		700	2,300
	20		9	1,500		3,800

Insulating Supplies   Acct. No. 105

Date		Explanation	Jr. Ref.	Debit	Credit	Debit Balance
1983 Mar.	31					2,400
Apr.	30		10		580	1,820

Prepaid Rent — Acct. No. 107

Date		Explanation	Jr. Ref.	Debit	Credit	Debit Balance
1983 Mar.	31					300
Apr.	30		10		50	250

Trucks — Acct. No. 125

Date		Explanation	Jr. Ref.	Debit	Credit	Debit Balance
1983 Mar.	31					12,000

Accumulated Depreciation: Trucks — Acct. No. 126

Date		Explanation	Jr. Ref.	Debit	Credit	Credit Balance
1983 Mar.	31					3,800
Apr.	30		10		200	4,000

Accounts Payable — Acct. No. 201

Date		Explanation	Jr. Ref.	Debit	Credit	Credit Balance
1983 Mar.	31					1,200
Apr.	10		9	600		600

J. Thompson, Capital — Acct. No. 301

Date		Explanation	Jr. Ref.	Debit	Credit	Credit Balance
1983 Mar.	31					13,700
Apr.	30		10		1,300	15,000
	30		10	500		14,500

J. Thompson, Withdrawals — Acct. No. 302

Date		Explanation	Jr. Ref.	Debit	Credit	Debit Balance
1983 Apr.	15		9	500		500
	30		10		500	0

Income Summary — Acct. No. 303

Date		Explanation	Jr. Ref.	Debit	Credit	Credit Balance
1983 Apr.	30		10		2,700	2,700
	30		10	1,400		1,300
	30		10	1,300		0

Insulating Revenues — Acct. No. 401

Date		Explanation	Jr. Ref.	Debit	Credit	Credit Balance
1983 Apr.	8		9		1,200	1,200
	20		9		1,500	2,700
	30		10	2,700		0

Salaries Expense — Acct. No. 501

Date		Explanation	Jr. Ref.	Debit	Credit	Debit Balance
1983 Apr.	29		10	450		450
	30		10		450	0

Utilities Expense — Acct. No. 502

Date		Explanation	Jr. Ref.	Debit	Credit	Debit Balance
1983 Apr.	28		10	40		40
	30		10		40	0

Insulating Supplies Expense				Acct. No. 503

Date	Explanation	Jr. Ref.	Debit	Credit	Debit Balance
1983 Apr. 30		10	580		580
30		10		580	0

Gas, Oil, and Maintenance Expense				Acct. No. 504

Date	Explanation	Jr. Ref.	Debit	Credit	Debit Balance
1983 Apr. 18		9	80		80
30		10		80	0

Rent Expense				Acct. No. 505

Date	Explanation	Jr. Ref.	Debit	Credit	Debit Balance
1983 Apr. 30		10	50		50
30		10		50	0

Depreciation Expense: Trucks				Acct. No. 506

Date	Explanation	Jr. Ref.	Debit	Credit	Debit Balance
1983 Apr. 30		10	200		200
30		10		200	0

GLOSSARY

Account Form. Form of balance sheet on which assets are reported on the left side and liabilities and owner's equity are reported on the right side.

Accounting Period. Period of time for which the revenues and expenses of a company are computed and reported on an income statement. Stated in the heading of the income statement.

Accrual Accounting. The principle that revenue and expense transactions are recorded in the accounting period when goods or services are provided, regardless of whether cash is received or paid.

Adjusted Trial Balance. A schedule prepared to prove the equality of the debit and credit balances in the ledger accounts after the adjusting entries have been made.

Adjusting Entries. Journal entries made at the end of an accounting period to bring the revenue and expense account balances up to date and to show the correct ending balances in the asset and liability accounts.

Cash Basis Accounting. Accounting practice in which net income of a company is computed by subtracting the cash payments from the cash receipts for operations during the accounting period.

Closing Entries. Journal entries made at the end of an accounting period to create zero balances in each revenue, expense, and withdrawals account and to transfer these account balances to the owner's capital account.

Cost. The amount at which a transaction is recorded. A cost may be recorded as an expense (expired cost) or as an asset (unexpired cost).

Expenses. Costs of a company to provide goods or services during an accounting period.

Income Statement. Financial statement summarizing the revenues, expenses, and net income of a company for its accounting period.

Income Summary Account. A temporary account used during the closing process to accumulate the revenue and expense balances before transferring the net income (or net loss) to the owner's capital account.

Matching Principle. States that expenses of an accounting period are subtracted from (matched against) the revenues earned during that period to determine net income.

Net Income. The amount by which the revenues of a company exceed the expenses during an accounting period.

Net Loss. The amount by which the expenses of a company exceed the revenues during an accounting period.

Permanent Accounts. Asset, liability, and owner's capital accounts that are not closed at the end of each accounting period. Permanent accounts are also called *real* accounts.

Post-Closing Trial Balance. Schedule prepared to prove the equality of the debit and credit balances in the asset, liability, and owner's capital accounts after the closing entries have been made.

Report Form. Form of balance sheet in which assets are listed first, after which liabilities and owner's equity are reported directly below the assets.

Revenues. Prices charged to a company's customers for goods or services provided during an accounting period.

Temporary Accounts. Revenue, expense, and withdrawals accounts used to determine the net income and withdrawals during an accounting period. These accounts are closed at the end of each accounting period. Also called *nominal* accounts.

Withdrawals Account. Account used to accumulate the amounts of assets withdrawn from a sole proprietorship by its owner during an accounting period.

QUESTIONS

Q3-1 How is net income computed? Where (if at all) do withdrawals fit into the net income calculation?

Q3-2 Define revenues. Define expenses. What is meant by *matching* expenses against revenues?

Q3-3 What is cost? When is a cost an asset and when is it an expense?

Q3-4 What is an accounting period? How long is a usual accounting period in actual financial reporting?

Q3-5 What is accrual accounting? What is cash basis accounting? Which is more useful?

Q3-6 Explain the matching principle and how it relates to the computation of net income.

Q3-7 Define an income statement. What are the two sections of an income statement?

Q3-8 What are withdrawals? How are they recorded?

Q3-9 Give the debit and credit rules for revenue, expense, and withdrawals accounts.

Q3-10 Why are revenue, expense, and withdrawals accounts called *temporary* accounts? What are permanent accounts?

Q3-11 Where are revenue, expense, and withdrawals accounts included in a company's chart of accounts? Why is the chart of accounts useful in preparing financial statements?

Q3-12 What are adjusting entries? Why are they necessary?

Q3-13 What is the book value of a physical asset? Show how the book value of a building would be reported on a balance sheet.

Q3-14 What is an adjusted trial balance? How is it used in preparing financial statements?

Q3-15 What is a statement of changes in owner's equity? Show the format of this schedule.

Q3-16 How does a report form of a balance sheet differ from an account form of a balance sheet?

Q3-17 What are closing entries? Describe how (a) revenue accounts, (b) expense accounts, and (c) the withdrawals account are closed.

Q3-18 What is a post-closing trial balance?

Q3-19 List the steps and related business documents in a manual accounting system.

EXERCISES

E3-1 **Income Statement.** On June 30, 1983, the Robinskon Consulting Company showed the following revenue and expense account balances for June:

Consulting service revenues	$1,800
Salaries expense	1,000
Telephone expense	125
Office supplies expense	25
Utilities expense	90
Rent expense	350
Depreciation expense: office equipment	15

Required: Prepare the June 1983, income statement for the Robinskon Consulting Company.

E3-2 Income Statement. The adjusted trial balance for the Benzer Diaper Service on February 28, 1983 (the end of its monthly accounting period), is as follows:

BENZER DIAPER SERVICE
Adjusted Trial Balance
February 28, 1983

Account Titles	Debits	Credits
Cash	$13,744	
Supplies	6,000	
Building	11,500	
Accumulated depreciation: building		$ 530
Equipment	10,000	
Accumulated depreciation: equipment		320
Accounts payable		1,560
B. D. Benzer, capital		39,000
B. D. Benzer, withdrawals	1,000	
Diaper service revenues		6,000
Salaries expense	3,000	
Supplies expense	1,250	
Telephone expense	45	
Utilities expense	785	
Depreciation expense: building	54	
Depreciation expense: equipment	32	
Totals	$47,410	$47,410

Required: Prepare the February 1983, income statement for the Benzer Diaper Service from the adjusted trial balance given above.

E3-3 Owner's Equity Account. Four independent cases related to the owner's equity account of the Cox Company are as follows:

Case	Laura Cox, Capital May 1, 1983	Net Income May 1983	Withdrawals in May	Laura Cox, Capital May 31, 1983
1	$ A	$2,700	$1,000	$26,700
2	37,000	B	1,720	38,750
3	26,000	900	C	24,800
4	34,000	1,820	1,500	D

Required: Determine the amounts of A, B, C, and D.

E3-4 Assets and Expenses. During the month of October the Wilson Company incurred the following costs:

(a) Paid $360 to an insurance company for a 2-year comprehensive insurance policy on the company's building.
(b) Purchased office supplies costing $770 on account from Bailey's Office Supplies.
(c) Paid the telephone company $90 for telephone service during the month of October.
(d) Paid the $770 owed to Bailey's Office Supplies.
(e) The owner withdrew $1,000 for personal use.
(f) Found that of the $770 of office supplies purchased in (b) above, only $700 remained at October 31.

Required: Which of the above transactions would be recorded as expenses by the Wilson Company for the month of October? Explain.

E3-5 Revenues. Gertz Rent-A-Car is in the business of providing customers with quality rental automobiles at low rates. The following transactions were engaged in by the company during the month of March:

(a) J. Gertz deposited an additional $1,500 of his personal cash into the agency's checking account.
(b) Collected $1,050 in car rental fees for the month of March.
(c) Borrowed $5,000 from the 1st National Bank to be repaid in 1 year.
(d) Completed arrangements to provide fleet service to a local company at a cost of $18,000 per year, payable in advance.

Required: Which of the above transactions would be recorded as revenues by Gertz Rent-A-Car for the month of March? Explain.

E3-6 Journal Entries. The Both Plumbing Company entered into the following transactions during the month of May:

Date	Transaction
May 4	Installed plumbing in new house under construction; contractor agreed to pay contract price of $1,500 in 30 days.
15	Made plumbing repairs for customer and collected $45 for services performed.
28	Paid $58 for May telephone bill.
31	Paid $800 to employees for May salaries.
31	Received $100 utility bill, to be paid in early June.

Required: Prepare the necessary journal entries to record the above transactions.

E3-7 Journal Entries. The Aline Taxi Service entered into the following transactions during the month of September:

Date	Transaction
Sept. 1	Paid $350 rent on garage for the month of September.
15	Cash receipts for taxi fares for the first half of the month totaled $1,230.
23	Paid $980 for September fuel bill from Wildcat Oil Company.
29	P. L. Aline withdrew $200 for personal use.
30	Paid salaries amounting to $1,500 to employees.
30	Cash receipts for taxi fares for the second half of the month totaled $1,340.

Required: Prepare journal entries to record the above transactions.

E3-8 Adjusting Entries and Adjusted Trial Balance. On June 30, 1983, the Washington Company showed the following trial balance:

Account Titles	Debits	Credits
Cash	$16,150	
Office supplies	345	
Office equipment	1,500	
Accounts payable		$ 295
D. L. Washington, capital		17,000
Service revenues		2,175
Salary expense	1,000	
Rent expense	300	
General expenses	175	
Totals	$19,470	$19,470

The following adjustments are needed:

(a) Office supplies used during the month of June totaled $45.

(b) Depreciation expense for the month of June on office equipment totaled $25.

June was the first month of operations for the Washington Company.

Required: 1. Prepare the necessary adjusting entries to record the above adjustments.
2. Prepare the June 30, 1983, adjusted trial balance for the Washington Company.

E3-9 Statement of Changes in Owner's Equity.
The beginning balance in the R. L. Barnun, Capital account on October 1, 1983 was $20,000. The Barnun Company reported total revenues for October of $3,000 and total expenses of $1,584. In addition, R. L. Barnun withdrew $1,200 for his personal use on October 25.

Required: Prepare a statement of changes in owner's equity for the month of October for the Barnun Company.

E3-10 Closing Entries and Post-Closing Trial Balance.
The adjusted trial balance of the Larkin Service Company on May 31, 1983 (the end of its monthly accounting period), is as follows:

Account Titles	Debits	Credits
Cash	$ 9,840	
Accounts receivable	1,500	
Equipment	4,200	
Accumulated depreciation: equipment		$ 140
Accounts payable		1,555
Joseph Larkin, capital		13,000
Joseph Larkin, withdrawals	500	
Service revenues		2,450
Salaries expense	600	
Rent expense	300	
Depreciation expense: equipment	70	
Utilities expense	78	
Telephone expense	57	
Totals	$17,145	$17,145

Required: 1. Prepare the closing entries for the Larkin Service Company on May 31, 1983.
2. Prepare the post-closing trial balance for the Larkin Service Company on May 31, 1983.

E3-11 Closing Entries.
The Cobbler Company shows the following revenue, expense, and withdrawals account balances on December 31, 1983, before closing:

	Debit	Credit
A. B. Cobbler, withdrawals	$ 750	
Shoe service revenues		$3,790
Salaries expense	2,300	
Utilities expense	199	
Supplies expense	125	
Rent expense	550	
Depreciation expense: equipment	28	

Required: Prepare closing entries.

E3-12 Balance Sheet.
Use the information in E3-10.

Required: Prepare a balance sheet (account form) for the Larkin Service Company on May 31, 1983.

PROBLEMS

Part A

P3-1A Journal Entries. The Riles Landscaping Service entered into the following transactions during the month of March:

Date	Transaction
Mar. 1	Paid 3 months' rent in advance at $150 per month.
2	Provided landscaping service for customer, collecting $275 cash.
5	Purchased $50 of repair parts on account from LT's, a small engine service company, to be used immediately in repairing one of the company's mowers.
6–10	Provided landscaping service for customer; customer agreed to pay the contract price of $1,350 in 15 days.
15	Paid $50 due to LT's for repair parts purchased on March 5.
25	Collected $1,350 from customer for service provided on March 6–10.
31	Paid $40 for March utilities bill.
31	Paid $1,000 to employees for March salaries.
31	Received $28 March telephone bill, to be paid in early April.

Required: Prepare the necessary journal entries to record the above transactions.

P3-2A Journal Entries, Postings, and Trial Balance. The Jardine Consulting Company was established on January 2, 1983. The following transactions took place during January.

Date	Transaction
Jan. 2	D. Jardine set up the company by investing $50,000 cash in the company's checking account.
3	Acquired a building at a cost of $24,000. A $4,000 down payment was made and a mortgage signed for the remaining balance.
5	Purchased office equipment costing $8,000 by signing a note due in 1 year.
10	Office supplies costing $735 were purchased for cash.
21	Performed consulting services for customer and collected $1,020.
31	Paid $450 for employee's salary.
31	Paid utilities bill for January of $88.
31	D. Jardine withdrew $350 cash for personal use.

Required:

1. Set up the following accounts (and account numbers): Cash (101), Office Supplies (105), Building (112), Office Equipment (115), Notes Payable (220), Mortgage Payable (221), D. Jardine, Capital (301), D. Jardine, Withdrawals (302), Consulting Service Revenues (401), Salary Expense (501), Utilities Expense (502).
2. Prepare the necessary journal entries to record the above transactions.
3. Post the journal entries to the accounts.
4. Prepare a trial balance at January 31, 1983.

P3-3A Financial Statements and Closing Entries. The adjusted trial balance for the Swire Advertising Services Company on November 30, 1983 (the end of its monthly accounting period) is as follows:

Account Titles	Debits	Credits
Cash	$11,167	
Accounts receivable	3,783	
Office supplies	1,074	
Prepaid insurance	1,540	
Building	33,400	
Accumulated depreciation: building		$ 130

Office equipment	2,880	
Accumulated depreciation: office equipment		40
Accounts payable		1,783
Mortgage payable		12,000
A. Swire, capital		40,000
A. Swire, withdrawals	600	
Advertising services revenues		1,834
Salaries expense	650	
Insurance expense	140	
Telephone expense	177	
Utilities expense	94	
Office supplies expense	112	
Depreciation expense: building	130	
Depreciation expense: office equipment	40	
Totals	$55,787	$55,787

Required: 1. Prepare a November income statement, statement of changes in owner's equity, and a November 30, 1983, balance sheet (account form) for the Swire Advertising Services Company.
2. Prepare the closing entries on November 30, 1983.
3. Prepare a post-closing trial balance.

P3-4A Closing Entries and Post-Closing Trial Balance.

On February 28, 1983 (the end of the first month of operations), the following adjusted trial balance for the Gammon Employment Agency was prepared:

Account Titles	Debits	Credits
Cash	$17,140	
Accounts receivable	575	
Office supplies	1,526	
Prepaid insurance	792	
Building	21,600	
Accumulated depreciation: building		$ 60
Office equipment	5,280	
Accumulated depreciation: office equipment		55
Accounts payable		1,640
Notes payable		15,000
M. Gammon, capital		30,000
M. Gammon, withdrawals	800	
Employment commissions revenues		1,997
Salaries expense	650	
Insurance expense	72	
Telephone expense	70	
Utilities expense	68	
Office supplies expense	64	
Depreciation expense: building	60	
Depreciation expense: office equipment	55	
Totals	$48,752	$48,752

Required: 1. Set up the following T-accounts: M. Gammon, capital, M. Gammon, withdrawals, Employment commissions revenues, Salaries expense, Insurance expense, Telephone expense, Utilities expense, Office supplies expense, Depreciation expense: building, Depreciation expense: office equipment, Income summary. Enter the account balances as listed on the adjusted trial balance.

2. Prepare closing entries for the Gammon Employment Agency on February 28, 1983.
3. Post the closing entries to the T-accounts.
4. Prepare a February 28, 1983, post-closing trial balance.

P3-5A Financial Statements. On May 31, 1983, the bookkeeper of Marina Boat Storage prepared the following closing entries for the month of May:

(a) Storage Revenues	2,635	
Income Summary		2,635
(b) Income Summary	1,824	
Depreciation Expense: Building		140
Depreciation Expense: Equipment		110
Supplies Expense		233
Salaries Expense		950
Telephone Expense		92
Utilities Expense		64
Insurance Expense		235
(c) Income Summary	811	
L. Marina, Capital		811
(d) L. Marina, Capital	615	
L. Marina, Withdrawals		615

In addition, the following post-closing trial balance was prepared:

Account Titles	Debits	Credits
Cash	$15,184	
Accounts receivable	735	
Supplies	1,117	
Land	16,000	
Building	25,200	
Accumulated depreciation: building		$ 140
Equipment	10,560	
Accumulated depreciation: equipment		110
Accounts payable		1,350
Notes payable		7,000
Mortgage payable		25,000
L. Marina, capital		35,196
Totals	$68,796	$68,796

Required:
1. Prepare an income statement for the month ended May 31, 1983.
2. Prepare a statement of changes in owner's equity for the month ended May 31, 1983.
3. Prepare a May 31, 1983, balance sheet (report form).

P3-6A Accounting Process. The June 30, 1983, trial balance of the Ruff Furniture Refurbishment Center is as follows:

Account Titles	Debits	Credits
Cash	$ 3,425	
Accounts receivable	152	
Supplies	500	
Equipment	5,160	
Accumulated depreciation: equipment		$ 989

Accounts payable		212
J. Ruff, capital		8,600
J. Ruff, withdrawals	850	
Refurbishment revenues		928
Rent expense	300	
Telephone expense	55	
Utilities expense	287	
Totals	$10,729	$10,729

Additional information:
(a) The temporary accounts reflect only June transactions.
(b) The supplies used during the month totaled $253.
(c) Depreciation expense on the equipment totals $43 for June.

Required:
1. Prepare adjusting entries on June 30, 1983.
2. Prepare a June 30, 1983, adjusted trial balance.
3. Prepare closing entries on June 30, 1983.
4. Prepare a statement of changes in owner's equity for the month ended June 30, 1983.
5. Prepare a June 30, 1983, post-closing trial balance.

PROBLEMS
Part B

P3-1B Journal Entries. Stevel Stor-All entered into the following transactions during the month of April:

Date	Transaction
Apr. 1	Purchased a 3-year insurance policy on the company's building for $280 cash.
6	Purchased office supplies on account at a cost of $87.
14	Paid $30 on account for supplies purchased on April 6.
15	Collected storage fees for the first half of the month totaling $630.
30	Paid April telephone bill of $55.
30	Collected storage fees for the last half of the month totaling $630.
30	Paid $600 to employee for April salary.
30	Received $98 April utility bill, to be paid in early May.

Required: Prepare the necessary journal entries to record the above transactions.

P3-2B Journal Entries and Trial Balance. The Salanar Service Company was established on March 1, 1983. The following transactions took place during March:

Date	Transaction
Mar. 1	P. Salanar set up the company by investing $25,000 cash in the company's checking account.
4	Acquired a building at a cost of $12,000. A $3,000 down payment was made and a mortgage was signed for the remaining balance.
7	Purchased office equipment costing $4,000 by signing a note due in 1 year.
8	Office supplies costing $330 were purchased for cash.
20	Collected $1,882 from customers for services performed.
31	Paid $523 for employee's salary.
31	Paid $82 for March utilities bill.
31	P. Salanar withdrew $200 cash for personal use.

Required: 1. Set up the following accounts (and account numbers): Cash (101), Office Supplies (106), Building (113), Office Equipment (116), Notes Payable (221), Mortgage Payable (222), P. Salanar, Capital (301), P. Salanar, Withdrawals (302), Service Revenues (401), Salary Expense (501), and Utilities Expense (502).
2. Prepare the necessary journal entries to record the above transactions.
3. Post the journal entries to the accounts.
4. Prepare a trial balance at March 31, 1983.

P3-3B Financial Statements and Closing Entries. The adjusted trial balance on June 30, 1983 (the end of the first month of operations), for Tellet Musicians Booking Agency is as follows:

Account Titles	Debits	Credits
Cash	$ 6,924	
Accounts receivable	1,892	
Office supplies	537	
Prepaid rent	215	
Building	15,700	
Accumulated depreciation: building		$ 65
Equipment	1,440	
Accumulated depreciation: equipment		20
Accounts payable		953
Mortgage payable		6,000
C. Tellet, capital		20,000
C. Tellet, withdrawals	300	
Musicians' booking revenues		857
Salaries expense	375	
Telephone expense	109	
Utilities expense	47	
Rent expense	215	
Office supplies expense	56	
Depreciation expense: building	65	
Depreciation expense: equipment	20	
Totals	$27,895	$27,895

Required: 1. Prepare a June income statement, statement of changes in owner's equity, and a June 30, 1983, balance sheet (report form) for Tellet Musicians' Booking Agency.
2. Prepare the closing entries on June 30, 1983.
3. Prepare a June 30, 1983, post-closing trial balance.

P3-4B Closing Entries and Post-Closing Trial Balance. The October 31, 1983, adjusted trial balance for Casey's Cleaners is as follows:

Account Titles	Debits	Credits
Cash	$25,710	
Accounts receivable	810	
Cleaning supplies	2,289	
Prepaid rent	1,240	
Building	32,400	
Accumulated depreciation: building		$ 90
Equipment	7,920	
Accumulated depreciation: equipment		82
Accounts payable		2,460

Notes payable		22,500
R. Casey, capital		45,000
R. Casey, withdrawals	1,200	
Cleaning service revenues		2,995
Salaries expense	775	
Telephone expense	58	
Utilities expense	132	
Rent expense	110	
Cleaning supplies expense	311	
Depreciation expense: building	90	
Depreciation expense: equipment	82	
Totals	$73,127	$73,127

Required: 1. Set up the following T-accounts: R. Casey, capital, R. Casey, withdrawals, Cleaning service revenues, Salaries expense, Telephone expense, Utilities expense, Rent expense, Cleaning supplies expense, Depreciation expense: building, Depreciation expense: equipment, Income summary. Enter the account balances as listed on the adjusted trial balance.
2. Prepare closing entries on October 31, 1983.
3. Post the closing entries to the T-accounts.
4. Prepare an October 31, 1983, post-closing trial balance.

P3-5B   Financial Statements.   On September 30, 1983, the bookkeeper of Kerrel Lawn Service prepared the following adjusted trial balance (the temporary accounts reflect only September transactions):

Account Titles	Debits	Credits
Cash	$ 1,387	
Supplies	838	
Prepaid rent	550	
Land	12,000	
Trucks	28,900	
Accumulated depreciation: trucks		$ 105
Lawn equipment	7,920	
Accumulated depreciation: lawn equipment		82
Accounts payable		1,028
Notes payable		5,250
T. Kerrel, capital		44,400
T. Kerrel, withdrawals	650	
Lawn service revenues		2,794
Salaries expense	515	
Gas and oil expense	200	
Supplies expense	100	
Telephone expense	67	
Utilities expense	70	
Rent expense	275	
Depreciation expense: trucks	105	
Depreciation expense: lawn equipment	82	
Totals	$53,659	$53,659

Required: 1. Prepare an income statement for the month ended September 30, 1983.
2. Prepare a statement of changes in owner's equity for the month ended September 30, 1983.
3. Prepare a September 30, 1983, balance sheet (report form).

P3-6B Accounting Process. The July 31, 1983, trial balance for the Cane Consulting Agency is as follows:

Account Titles	Debits	Credits
Cash	$ 3,890	
Accounts receivable	304	
Office supplies	1,000	
Office equipment	14,820	
Accumulated depreciation: office equipment		$ 1,956
Accounts payable		446
D. Cane, capital		16,000
D. Cane, withdrawals	500	
Consulting revenues		2,856
Telephone expense	70	
Rent expense	500	
Utilities expense	174	
Totals	$21,258	$21,258

Additional Information:
(a) The temporary accounts reflect only July transactions.
(b) The office supplies used during the month totaled $200.
(c) The depreciation expense on the office equipment amounted to $163 for the month.

Required: 1. Prepare adjusting entries on July 31, 1983.
2. Prepare an adjusted trial balance on July 31, 1983.
3. Prepare closing entries on July 31, 1983.
4. Prepare a statement of changes in owner's equity for the month ended July 31, 1983.
5. Prepare a July 31, 1983, post-closing trial balance.

DISCUSSION CASES

C3-1 Erroneous Financial Statements. The bookkeeper for the Powell Service Agency was confused when he prepared the following financial statements.

POWELL SERVICE AGENCY
Profit and Expense Statement
December 31, 1983

Expenses:		
Salaries expense	$19,000	
Utilities expense	2,300	
Accounts receivable	500	
C. Powell, withdrawals	16,000	
Office supplies	1,500	
Total Expenses		$39,300
Revenues:		
Service revenues	$43,000	
Accounts payable	800	
Accumulated depreciation: office equipment	1,800	
Total Revenues		45,600
Net Revenues		$6,300

POWELL SERVICE AGENCY
Balancing Statement
For Year Ended December 31, 1983

Liabilities		Assets	
Mortgage payable	$19,000	Building	$32,000
Accumulated depreciation:		Depreciation expense:	
building	6,400	building	1,600
Total Liabilities	$25,400	Office equipment	9,000
		Depreciation expense:	
C. Powell, capital[a]	21,000	office equipment	900
Total Liabilities and		Cash	2,900
Owner's Equity	$46,400	Total Assets	$46,400

[a] $14,700 beginning capital + $6,300 net revenues

C. Powell has asked you to examine the financial statements and related accounting records. You find that, with the exception of office supplies, the debit or credit *amount* of each account is correct even though the account might be incorrectly listed in the financial statements. You determine that the office supplies used during the year amount to $800 and the office supplies on hand at the end of the year amount to $700.

Required: 1. Review each financial statement and indicate any errors you find.
            2. Prepare a corrected 1983 income statement, statement of changes in owner's equity, and ending balance sheet.

C3-2 Confusion About Debit and Credit Rules. A friend of yours in this accounting class is confused and says, "I just don't understand revenues and expenses. I learned in the previous chapter that assets are increased by debits and liabilities are increased by credits. Now I read in this chapter that expenses are increased by debits and revenues are increased by credits. So the way I look at it, expenses must be assets and revenues must be liabilities. But then this book says that revenues increase assets and expenses decrease assets. And, if that isn't confusing enough, the book goes on to say that not all increases in assets are revenues and not all decreases in assets are expenses. Wow! Does this make sense to you?"

Your friend continues, "And these closing entries boggle my mind. Why are they necessary? The company isn't going to close down its business. How do I know which accounts to close? At first I thought all accounts are closed at the end of each accounting period but now I'm not so sure. And after learning that expenses are increased by debits (like assets) and revenues are increased by credits (like liabilities), I look at the closing entry example. There the revenues were debited and the expenses were credited! Furthermore, I thought withdrawals were expenses but then why isn't the withdrawals account listed with the expenses in the closing entries? Please help me! I know I need a good understanding of these issues before I read any further in the book."

Required: Prepare a written explanation for each issue raised by your friend. Use examples where needed.

4

Adjusting Entries and the Worksheet

After reading this chapter, you should understand:

- The need for adjusting entries
- Adjusting entries for the apportionment of depreciation and prepaid and unearned items
- Adjusting entries to record accrued expenses and accrued revenues
- The preparation of a worksheet
- The completion of the accounting process from a worksheet
- The use of reversing entries

In the first three chapters we developed an accounting system for recording, retaining, and reporting information about transactions. The discussion involved a company operating as a service business and entering into simple transactions. In this chapter we look at transactions that lead to more complex adjusting entries at the end of the period. We also introduce the worksheet, an accounting working paper designed to aid in several steps of the accounting process.

ADJUSTING ENTRIES

Most companies use the accrual basis of accounting, in which revenues are recorded in the accounting period when products are sold or services are performed for customers and not necessarily when cash is collected. All the related expenses are then matched against these revenues, regardless of the inflow or outflow of cash. In many cases not all revenue and expense account balances are up to date at the end of the accounting period. As introduced in Chapter 3, certain amounts must be *adjusted* to properly state the net income on the income statement and the ending financial position on the balance sheet. These adjustments are made by adjusting entries. **Adjusting entries are journal entries made at the end of the accounting period to bring the revenue and expense account balances up to date and to show the correct ending balances in the asset and liability accounts.**

An adjusting entry ordinarily affects both a permanent (balance sheet) and a temporary (income statement) account. Adjusting entries may be grouped into two types. The types of entries and the affected balance sheet accounts are listed as follows:

1. Apportionment of depreciable, prepaid, and unearned items:
   (a) Depreciable assets
   (b) Prepaid expenses
   (c) Unearned revenues
2. Recording of accrued items:
   (a) Accrued expenses
   (b) Accrued revenues

A discussion of the adjusting entries and illustrations for each category are presented in the following sections.

Apportionment of Depreciable Assets

In Chapter 3 we discussed the differences between the terms *cost, asset,* and *expense*. The cost refers to the amount at which a transaction is recorded. This cost may be recorded as an asset (unexpired cost) when a company acquires an economic resource that is expected to provide future benefits to the company. The cost may be recorded as an expense (expired cost) if it relates to selling goods or providing services to customers in an accounting period. If a cost is recorded as an asset, part or all of the related cost must be changed from an asset (unexpired cost) to an expense (expired cost). This procedure is necessary because most assets eventually lose their potential for providing future benefits. Another way of stating this concept is to say that the cost must be *apportioned* (allocated) between the assets (portion remaining) at the end of an accounting period and the expenses incurred (portion used up) during that period.

Companies frequently acquire physical economic resources that they expect to use for many years in their operating activities. These resources are recorded as assets at the acquisition cost. Examples of these assets are land, buildings, office equipment, trucks, machinery, and automobiles. These long-term physical assets are commonly called *property and equipment*. Alternative terms for these assets are *fixed assets* and *operational assets*. Most of these assets are also depreciable. **Depreciable assets are long-term physical assets whose expected economic benefits expire over the useful life of the asset.** The costs of these depreciable assets must be apportioned as expenses in the accounting period during which they are used. This expense is called depreciation expense. **Depreciation expense is the part of the cost of a long-term physical asset allocated as an expense to each accounting period in the asset's useful life.**[1] An adjusting entry is made at the end of the accounting period to record depreciation expense. The amount is calculated as discussed below.

CALCULATION OF DEPRECIATION EXPENSE.   There are several methods for computing depreciation expense, and these methods are fully discussed in Chapter 11. One

---

[1] Land, although a physical asset, is not depreciable because it is not considered to have a limited useful life.

method of depreciation is referred to as the straight line depreciation method. **The straight-line method records an equal portion of the cost of the asset as depreciation expense in each accounting period in which the asset is used.** The equation for computing annual straight-line depreciation is shown below.

$$\text{Annual Depreciation Expense} = \frac{\text{Cost} - \text{Estimated Residual Value}}{\text{Estimated Useful Life in Years}}$$

The cost is the amount recorded in the account for the physical asset. Thus the depreciable asset account balance serves as the source document for the depreciation calculation. The estimated residual value is the amount for which the asset is expected to be disposed of at the end of its useful life. Because of difficulties in making this estimate accurately, companies often assign a nominal or zero value to the residual value. In this chapter we assume the residual value is zero for all the depreciation calculations in the discussions and homework materials.

The estimated useful life is the number of years the asset is expected to be used before its disposal. When an asset is acquired in the middle of a year, the depreciation expense in the first year is determined by multiplying the annual depreciation expense times the fraction of the year (expressed in months) the asset was used.

To illustrate the calculation of depreciation, the adjusting entries for depreciation, and the resulting book values, we discuss the 1983 depreciation for two physical assets of the Stalley Company, which are described below.

1. **Building.**   On January 1, 1975, the company purchased a building at a cost of $60,000. The estimated useful life was 25 years at that date. Accumulated depreciation of $19,200 on January 1, 1983, resulted in a book value of $40,800 ($60,000 − $19,200) on that date.
2. **Store Equipment.**   On March 2, 1983, the company purchased store equipment at a cost of $12,000. The estimated life was 10 years on that date.

The company computes its 1983 depreciation expense (assuming a zero residual value) as shown below.

Building:

$$\text{Annual Depreciation Expense} = \frac{\$60,000 - \$0}{25 \text{ years}}$$

$$\text{1983 Depreciation Expense} = \$2,400$$

Store Equipment:

$$\text{Annual Depreciation Expense} = \frac{\$12,000 - \$0}{10 \text{ years}}$$

$$= \$1,200$$

$$\text{1983 Depreciation Expense} = \$1,200 \times 10/12$$

$$= \$1,000$$

For the store equipment, it would be incorrect to record $1,200 annual depreciation expense for 1983 because the store equipment was used only 10 months[2] during that period. Instead the 1983 depreciation of the store equipment is $1,000, computed by multiplying the $1,200 times 10/12 (the fraction of time, in months, the asset was used during the year).

Many companies prepare financial statements for accounting periods shorter than a year (e.g., for interim reports or for monthly budgeting purposes). These companies would compute the depreciation expense for the shorter period based on a fraction of the year, as discussed earlier.

DEPRECIATION ADJUSTING ENTRY.   The adjusting entry to record the depreciation expense for Buildings, for example, involves a debit (increase) to the expense account Depreciation Expense: Buildings and a credit (increase) to the account Accumulated Depreciation: Buildings. The last word of the account titles would be changed for other depreciable assets (e.g., Depreciation Expense: Store Equipment).

To illustrate this concept, the adjusting entries of the Stalley Company for the depreciation expense on the building and store equipment are shown next based on the amounts calculated earlier.[3]

```
1983
Dec. 31   Depreciation Expense: Building  . . . . . . . . . . .  2,400
              Accumulated Depreciation: Building  . . . . . . .         2,400
          To record depreciation on building.

      31  Depreciation Expense: Store Equipment. . . . . . .  1,000
              Accumulated Depreciation: Store Equipment. . .         1,000
          To record 10 months of depreciation on store
          equipment.
```

Each Depreciation Expense account is listed on the income statement to compute the net income for the accounting period. Each Depreciation Expense account is then closed at the end of the period.

BOOK VALUES.   Each Accumulated Depreciation account is a permanent account and is a contra (negative) account to its related physical asset. **A contra account is an account whose balance is subtracted from another related account in order to determine a resulting amount.** A contra account always has a balance

[2] Because depreciation is based upon an estimated useful life, it is typical not to count the exact days an asset is used. Depreciation is computed instead to the nearest whole month. Thus a common rule is that assets purchased from the 1st through the 15th of a month are considered as being acquired at the beginning of that month. Assets purchased from the 16th through the end of the month are considered as being acquired at the beginning of the *next* month. You should use this rule unless told otherwise.

[3] Throughout the remainder of the book, we will use a simpler format for general journal entries, which omits the column headings, account number column, and transaction date (unless the date is critical to the discussion).

opposite of the account to which it is related. The debit and credit rule that applies to a contra account is also the opposite of the rule that applies to the related account. Thus each Accumulated Depreciation account is increased by credit entries (and decreased by debit entries) and has a credit balance. The credit balance of each Accumulated Depreciation account is subtracted from the debit balance of its related long-term physical asset account on the ending balance sheet for the accounting period to determine the remaining *unexpired* cost. This unexpired cost is referred to as the book value of the asset. **The book value (or carrying value) is the cost of a depreciable asset less its related accumulated depreciation.** Each year, after the depreciation expense has been recorded for a physical asset, the related Accumulated Depreciation account balance increases and the book value decreases. Eventually, at the end of the asset's life, the Accumulated Depreciation account credit balance will be equal to the related asset account debit balance (assuming no residual value), and therefore the asset will have a zero book value.

To illustrate this procedure consider the depreciation adjusting entries recorded earlier for the Stalley Company. After the adjusting entry for the depreciation on the building has been posted, the Accumulated Depreciation: Buildings account has an ending balance of $21,600. This amount results from having depreciated the building for 8 years (1975 through 1982) at $2,400 per year totaling $19,200 and adding $2,400 depreciation for 1983. The resulting book value of the building on December 31, 1983, is $38,400 ($60,000 − $21,600). This book value would be reported on the company's December 31, 1983, balance sheet as follows:

Building	$60,000	
Less: Accumulated depreciation	(21,600)	$38,400

Note that the book value of the building has decreased from $40,800 ($60,000 − $19,200) on December 31, 1982, to $38,400 ($60,000 − $21,600) on December 31, 1983, because the Accumulated Depreciation account balance was increased by $2,400 in 1983. Note also that the $38,400 book value will be reduced to a book value of zero after $2,400 annual depreciation has been recorded in each of the remaining 16 years of the building's estimated useful life.

After the depreciation adjusting entry for the store equipment has been posted, the Accumulated Depreciation: Store Equipment account has an ending balance of $1,000 (since this is the first year that the store equipment was used). The resulting book value of the store equipment on December 31, 1983, is $11,000 and would be reported on the company's balance sheet for that date as follows:

Store equipment	$12,000	
Less: Accumulated depreciation	(1,000)	$11,000

As has been illustrated, by using an Accumulated Depreciation account instead of reducing (crediting) the asset account directly for the depreciation, the original cost of each long-term physical asset is retained in the accounts and reported on the balance sheet. In addition, the total unexpired cost (the book value) and the total expired cost (the Accumulated Depreciation) that have been recorded over the current and all previous accounting periods are also reported on the balance sheet.

In this way the reader of the balance sheet can see the original cost of the physical assets. By observing the book value, the Accumulated Depreciation, and the changes in these amounts each accounting period, the reader also can gain insights into the age of the physical assets. This information is useful to users of the balance sheet in evaluating the need for the company to replace its physical assets and the likely timing of this replacement.

Apportionment of Prepaid Expenses

Prepaid expenses are economic resources that are expected to be used in the near future. Prepaid expenses are similar in several ways to depreciable assets; that is, they are economic resources that a company has acquired and expects to use in its current and future operating activities. Prepaid expenses differ from depreciable assets because they may or may not be physical in nature and are expected to provide economic benefits for only a short period of time. Examples of prepaid expenses include prepaid insurance, prepaid rent, office supplies, and store supplies.

When goods or services involving a prepaid expense are acquired, the cost is usually recorded as an asset. At the end of the accounting period a part of the goods or services has been used in order to earn revenues. The expired cost must be matched, as an expense, against the revenues of the period, while the unexpired cost remains as an asset on the ending balance sheet. The apportionment (allocation) of the cost of each prepaid expense between an expense and an asset is recorded in an adjusting entry at the end of the accounting period.

PREPAID EXPENSE ADJUSTING ENTRY.   When a prepaid expense has been initially recorded as an asset, the related end-of-period adjusting entry involves a debit (increase) to an appropriately titled expense account (e.g., Rent Expense, obtained from the company's chart of accounts) and a credit (decrease) directly to the asset account (e.g., Prepaid Rent). A contra account, like Accumulated Depreciation, is *not* used with each prepaid expense because of the relatively short expected life of the asset.

The calculation of the amount of the adjusting entry depends upon the type of prepaid expense. In the case of prepaid insurance, for example, the total cost of insurance coverage (as determined by a review of the insurance policy source document) is apportioned on a *straight-line* basis similar to depreciation. The cost, however, is usually divided by the number of *months* of insurance coverage acquired instead of years. The resulting monthly insurance expense is then multiplied times the number of months in the accounting period that the insurance coverage was in force to determine the insurance expense for the period. In the case of prepaid rent, the total rent expense for the period is computed by multiplying the monthly rent (determined by a review of the rental agreement source document) times the months in the accounting period. For office supplies and store supplies, a physical count is made of the supplies and related costs on hand at the end of the accounting period. The difference between the cost of the supplies on hand at the end of the accounting period and the cost of the supplies available for use during the period is the supplies expense for the period.

To illustrate the accounting for prepaid expenses, assume that the Stalley Company acquires two prepaid expenses during 1983, summarized as follows:

1. **Office Supplies.**   On January 1, 1983, the company had $240 of office supplies on hand. On May 8, 1983, the company acquired an additional $80 of office supplies. A physical count on December 31, 1983, determines that $170 of office supplies are on hand on that date.
2. **Prepaid Insurance.**   On November 1, 1983, the company paid $540 for a 1-year comprehensive insurance policy.

The year-end adjusting entries based on this information for office supplies and prepaid insurance are explained below.

OFFICE SUPPLIES.   The office supplies purchased on May 8, 1983, were an economic resource to the company and were recorded as an asset by debiting (increasing) Office Supplies for $80 and crediting (decreasing) Cash for $80. After posting this entry, the Office Supplies account had a balance of $320 ($240 + $80), the office supplies available for use. On December 31, 1983, $170 of office supplies were still on hand. Since $320 of office supplies were available for use and $170 of office supplies were left, $150 ($320 − $170) of office supplies were used during the year. The December 31, 1983, adjusting entry to record the office supplies expense is as follows:

```
1983
Dec. 31   Office Supplies Expense  . . . . . . . . . . . . . . .      150
              Office Supplies  . . . . . . . . . . . . . . . . . . . .            150
          To record office supplies expense.
```

After the journal entry is posted, the $150 amount in the Office Supplies Expense account will be listed as an expense on the 1983 income statement. Note that the $150 credit (decrease) to the Office Supplies account, after it is deducted from the previous $320 debit balance, will result in a $170 ending debit balance that will be listed as an asset on the December 31, 1983, balance sheet.

PREPAID INSURANCE.   On November 1, 1983, when the company paid $540 for the 1-year insurance policy, the right to the insurance protection was an economic resource to the company. At that time the transaction was recorded by debiting (increasing) the asset account Prepaid Insurance for $540 and crediting (decreasing) Cash for the same amount. No further entries were made in the Prepaid Insurance account during the rest of the accounting period. At the end of the year, a review of the insurance policy related to this account reveals that 2 months of insurance protection (for November and December) or $90 [($540 ÷ 12) × 2 months] has expired and 10 months of insurance protection or $450 [($540 ÷ 12) × 10] remains in force (unexpired). The December 31, 1983, adjusting entry to record the insurance expense is as follows:

```
1983
Dec. 31   Insurance Expense  . . . . . . . . . . . . . . . . . . .    90
              Prepaid Insurance  . . . . . . . . . . . . . . . . . .          90
          To record insurance expense.
```

After the journal entry is posted, the $90 debit will be included as insurance expense on the 1983 income statement. The $90 credit (decrease) to Prepaid Insurance, when it is deducted from the $540 debit balance, will result in a $450 ending debit balance. This balance will be listed as an asset on the December 31, 1983, balance sheet.

ALTERNATIVE ACCOUNTING PROCEDURES.   A company may choose to establish a policy of *initially* recording the entire prepayment of a cost as an *expense* (expired cost) *instead* of as an *asset* (unexpired cost). In this case an adjusting entry is still necessary at the end of the accounting period, but it is different from the entries discussed earlier. The proper adjusting entry procedure is to calculate the correct ending balance that *should be* in the asset account and adjust the accounts accordingly. The adjusting entry must *reduce* the expense account and *increase* the asset account by this amount.

In the previous example, for instance, the Stalley Company *could* have recorded the November 1, 1983, payment for insurance as a debit (increase) to Insurance Expense for $540 and a credit (decrease) to Cash for a like amount. Since $450 of insurance remains prepaid at the end of the period, the adjusting entry would be a debit (increase) to Prepaid Insurance for $450 and a credit (decrease) to Insurance Expense for $450. This adjusting entry is as follows:

```
1983
Dec. 31   Prepaid Insurance  . . . . . . . . . . . . . . . . . . .    450
              Insurance Expense . . . . . . . . . . . . . . . . . .          450
          To record prepaid insurance.
```

After this journal entry is posted, Insurance Expense will have a balance of $90 ($540 − $450) and Prepaid Insurance will have a balance of $450. Note that the end result of this initial entry and adjusting entry is the same as that shown earlier. Care must be taken to determine the way in which a company initially records its prepayments before the proper adjusting entry is determined.

Apportionment of Unearned Revenues

In Chapter 3 we defined revenues as the prices charged to customers for goods or services provided during an accounting period. We also noted that the inflow of cash and the recording of revenue are not always directly related.

In some cases customers may make an advance payment to a company for goods or services to be provided in the future. At the time of the transaction, even though an asset, Cash, has increased, the company has not earned revenue because the goods or services have not yet been provided. Instead the company has incurred a liability because it has an obligation to provide the future goods or services. **An unearned revenue is an advance receipt for goods or services to be provided**

in the future and it is recorded as a liability. The liability is frequently entitled, *Unearned,* and is followed by an explanatory term (e.g., *Unearned Legal Fees*). At the end of each accounting period, all such liabilities and related source documents must be examined to determine whether the goods or services have been provided. If so, an adjusting entry must be made to reduce the liability and increase the revenues of the period. The journal entry involves a debit (decrease) to the unearned liability account (e.g., Unearned Legal Fees) and a credit (increase) to a related revenue account (e.g., Legal Fees Earned). As a result, the income statement shows all the revenues in the period in which they are earned and the ending balance sheet reports the remaining liabilities of the company.

EXAMPLE OF ADJUSTMENT OF UNEARNED REVENUE.   To illustrate, assume the building that the Stalley Company owns is too large for its current operations and therefore the company rents a portion of the building to another firm. On December 1, 1983, the other firm pays $720 in advance for 6 months rent ($120 per month). Upon receipt of the money, the Stalley Company incurred an economic obligation (liability) to provide the use of the rented space to the other firm for 6 months. No revenue should be recorded at this point because no service has been provided. Thus the company recorded this transaction as a debit (increase) to Cash for $720 and a credit (increase) to a liability account, Unearned Rent, for $720. No further entries were made in the Unearned Rent account during the accounting period. At the end of the period, a review of this account and the rental agreement reveals that 1 month of rent revenue or $120 has been earned and 5 months or $600 ($120 × 5) is still unearned. The December 31, 1983, adjusting entry to record the rent revenue is as follows:

```
1983
Dec. 31   Unearned Rent . . . . . . . . . . . . . . . . . . . . . . .   120
              Rent Revenue  . . . . . . . . . . . . . . . . . . . . .          120
          To record rent earned.
```

After the journal entry is posted, the $120 rent revenue will be included on the 1983 income statement. The $120 debit (decrease) to Unearned Rent, when it is deducted from the $720 credit balance, will result in a $600 ending credit balance. This balance will be listed as a liability on the December 31, 1983, balance sheet.

ALTERNATIVE ACCOUNTING PROCEDURES.   Instead of following the above procedures, a company may choose to establish a policy of *initially* recording the receipt of an advance payment for future goods or services as a revenue (instead of as a liability). In this case, an adjusting entry must be made at the end of the accounting period to *reduce* the revenue and *increase* a liability for the amount of goods or services that have not yet been provided.

In the previous example, for instance, the receipt of the $720 advance payment *could* have been recorded as a debit (increase) to Cash and a credit (increase) to Rent Revenue. Since $600 of rent remains unearned at the end of the accounting period, the adjusting entry would be a debit (decrease) to Rent Revenue for $600 and a credit (increase) to Unearned Rent for $600. This adjusting entry is as follows:

```
1983
Dec. 31   Rent Revenue  . . . . . . . . . . . . . . . . . . . . . .   600
              Unearned Rent  . . . . . . . . . . . . . . . . . . . .         600
          To record unearned rent.
```

After posting this journal entry, Rent Revenue will have a balance of $120 ($720 − $600) and Unearned Rent will have a balance of $600. The end result of this initial entry and adjusting entry is the same as that shown earlier. Care must be taken to determine the way in which a company initially records the receipt of advances from customers before the proper adjusting entry may be determined.

Recording of Accrued Expenses

Most of a company's expenses are recorded when payment is made. At the end of an accounting period a few expenses of the company have usually not yet been recorded, however. These expenses are called accrued expenses. **An accrued expense is an expense that has been incurred during the accounting period but has neither been paid nor recorded.** The most common type of accrued expense is unpaid employees' wages and salaries. Other common accrued expenses include unpaid interest, taxes, and utility bills. In order to match all expenses against revenues and to report all the liabilities at the end of the period, an adjusting entry must be made for each accrued expense. Two accrued expenses, salaries and interest, are discussed further. The accounting principles that apply to these accrued items also apply to the others.

ACCRUED SALARY EXPENSE.   Companies have different policies for payment of their employees' salaries. Employees are seldom paid in advance, and they are usually paid after completion of their duties in the pay period. Some employees of a company may be paid weekly, some twice a month, and others monthly. Seldom does an accounting period end on the same day as the salary payment date for all of the employees. Nevertheless, the salaries earned by the employees from the date of the last salary payment through the end of the accounting period are an expense of the period even though they will be paid in the next accounting period. An adjusting entry must be made at the end of the period to record the salary expense and liability. The journal entry is a debit (increase) to Salaries (or Wages) Expense and a credit (increase) to Salaries (Wages) Payable. The amount is determined by a review of the payroll records.

To illustrate, assume that the Stalley Company has six employees, each of whom earns $300 per week for a 5-day work week (Monday through Friday). The employees are paid every Wednesday at the end of the day. December 31, 1983, is on Saturday. The employees' salaries totaling $720 ($300 × 6 × 2/5) for the Thursday and Friday of the last week in December are an expense of 1983 even though they will not be paid until 1984. The December 31, 1983, adjusting entry to record the expense and the liability[4] is as follows:

```
1983
Dec. 31   Salaries Expense  . . . . . . . . . . . . . . . . . . .    720
              Salaries Payable  . . . . . . . . . . . . . . . . . .          720
              To record accrued salaries.
```

After the journal entry is posted, the Salaries Expense account will include the total employees' salaries for all of the 1983 accounting period and will be listed on the 1983 income statement. The $720 of Salaries Payable will be listed as a liability on the December 31, 1983, balance sheet.

When a company has recorded accrued salaries at the end of an accounting period, it must be careful to record the correct journal entry when the salaries are paid in the *next* accounting period. The journal entry must record the part of the total salaries for the new period as Salaries Expense and the part for the salaries of the previous period as a reduction of Salaries Payable. To illustrate, the Stalley Company will pay $1,800 ($300 × 6) of salaries on Wednesday, January 4, 1984. Of this amount, $1,080 ($300 × 6 × 3/5) is for the 3 days of January and is an expense of 1984. The remaining $720 is for the 2 days of December that was accrued in the adjusting entry on December 31, 1983. The January 4, 1984, journal entry for the payment of the weekly salary would be recorded as follows:

```
1984
Jan. 4   Salaries Expense  . . . . . . . . . . . . . . . . . . .   1,080
             Salaries Payable . . . . . . . . . . . . . . . . . . .     720
             Cash . . . . . . . . . . . . . . . . . . . . . . . . .          1,800
             To record salaries expense and eliminate accrued
             salaries.
```

After posting, the Salaries Expense account will have a debit balance of $1,080 for the 3 days of salaries for the new 1984 accounting period. (Remember that the Salaries Expense account was closed at the end of 1983.) The Salaries Payable account will have a zero balance because the $720 liability set up at the end of 1983 has now been eliminated.

ACCRUED INTEREST EXPENSE.   Many companies enter into transactions involving the issuance or receipt of a note. A note is a written legal document in which one party (the *issuer*) agrees to pay another party a certain amount of money (the *principal*) on an agreed future date (the *maturity date*). Notes may be exchanged for cash or for goods or services. Most notes are interest bearing. An *interest-bearing note* is a note for which the issuer is charged interest on the principal. The *annual* interest rate is printed on the note. In the case of an interest-bearing note, the issuer may pay both the principal and the interest on the maturity date. Between the date that

---

[4] In reality, a company would also record certain payroll taxes related to such items as unemployment benefits and social security. These items are ignored in this chapter, but they are discussed in Chapter 10.

the note is issued and the maturity date, interest accumulates (accrues) daily on an interest-bearing note.

If a company issues an interest-bearing note, the interest is an expense of doing business. Even though the interest accrues daily, however, interest expense is normally recorded when the note is paid on the maturity date. When a company has issued a note in the current accounting period but the maturity date is not until the next accounting period, part of the interest applies to the current period and part to the next period. An adjusting entry must be made at the end of the current period to record the accrued interest as an expense of the period and as a liability at the end of the period. The journal entry is a debit (increase) to Interest Expense and a credit (increase) to Interest Payable.

The amount of interest that has accrued on a note at any time is computed by multiplying the principal times the annual interest rate for the length of time the note has been issued. The information necessary to make this computation is determined by a review of the note. The computation of interest is discussed more fully in Chapter 8. For our purposes here you need only a basic understanding of interest calculation.

To illustrate, assume that on November 1, 1983, the Stalley Company borrowed $12,000 from a local bank. The company signed (issued) a $12,000, 3-month, 10% note requiring it to repay the principal plus $300 interest ($12,000 × 10% for 3/12 year) on February 1, 1984. At the date of issuance the company recorded the transaction by debiting (increasing) Cash for $12,000 and crediting (increasing) Notes Payable for $12,000. No further entries were made for the note during the accounting period. At the end of the period a review of the note reveals that an adjusting entry must be made to record the interest that has accrued but has not been recorded. Since two of the three months life of the note have passed, the amount of accrued interest is $200 ($300 total interest × 2/3). The journal entry to record the accrued interest is as follows:

```
1983
Dec. 31   Interest Expense . . . . . . . . . . . . . . . . . . . . . .   200
              Interest Payable  . . . . . . . . . . . . . . . . . . . .        200
          To record accrued interest on note payable.
```

The Interest Expense will be listed on the 1983 income statement and the Interest Payable will be listed as a liability on the December 31, 1983, balance sheet.

Recording of Accrued Revenues

Most revenues of a company are recorded at the time goods or services are provided to a customer. At the end of an accounting period, a few revenues of a company may have not yet been recorded. These revenues are called accrued revenues. **An accrued revenue is a revenue that has been earned during the accounting period but has been neither collected nor recorded.** An adjusting entry must be made for each accrued revenue at the end of the period in order to record all the revenues for the period and the ending assets of the period. The entry involves a debit (increase) to an appropriately titled asset account and a credit (increase) to an appropriately titled revenue account. The amount is determined by a review of the accounting records and related source documents. There are not many types of accrued revenues. One common accrued revenue is the interest that has accumulated on a note *received* by a company.

EXAMPLE OF ACCRUED REVENUE.   Assume that on May 1, 1983, the Stalley Company sold some land to the Trage Company for $9,000. The land had originally cost $9,000 and was recorded by the Stalley Company as an asset at the time it was purchased. The Trage Company paid $1,000 down and signed a 1-year, 12% note for the $8,000 balance. At that time the Stalley Company recorded the transaction by debiting (increasing) Cash for $1,000, debiting (increasing) Notes Receivable for $8,000 and crediting (decreasing) Land for $9,000. No further entries were made for the note during 1983. At the end of the accounting period an adjusting entry must be made to record the interest that has accrued on the note but which will not be collected until the maturity date. The note has been issued for 8 months (May through December), and therefore the accrued interest amounts to $640 ($8,000 × 12% for 8/12 year). The journal entry to record the accrued interest is as follows:

```
1983
Dec. 31   Interest Receivable  . . . . . . . . . . . . . . . . . . . .   640
              Interest Revenue . . . . . . . . . . . . . . . . . . . .          640
          To record accrued interest on note receivable.
```

The $640 of Interest Revenue will be included in the 1983 income statement and the $640 of Interest Receivable will be reported as an asset on the December 31, 1983, balance sheet. The journal entries to record the collection of the note and interest are discussed in Chapter 8.

When all the adjusting entries have been journalized and posted, an adjusted trial balance is prepared to prove the equality of the debit and credit account balances. After the adjusted trial balance is completed the financial statements and closing entries are prepared. To aid in these steps of the accounting process a worksheet may be prepared.

THE WORKSHEET

At the end of an accounting period a company must prepare adjusting entries, closing entries, and its financial statements. A worksheet is often prepared to aid in these accounting activities. **A worksheet is an accounting working paper used for initially preparing the trial balance, adjustments, adjusted trial balance, income statement, and balance sheet at the end of an accounting period.** A worksheet, which is a large columnar paper, is used to minimize errors, to simplify the journal recording of the adjusting and closing entries, and to make it easier to prepare the financial statements. Note that a worksheet is *not* a substitute for any formal accounting records or financial statements; it is an accounting working paper used only for the purposes just mentioned.

There are four steps in the completion of a worksheet. They include preparation of the: (1) trial balance, (2) worksheet adjustments, (3) adjusted trial balance, and

EXHIBIT 4-1
Worksheet

D. JONES, ATTORNEY
Worksheet
For Year Ended December 31, 1983

Account Titles	Trial Balance		Adjustments	
	Debit	Credit	Debit	Credit
Cash	4,200			
Accounts receivable	5,600			
Prepaid rent	600			(b) 400
Office supplies	470			(d) 300
Notes receivable	3,200			
Office equipment	7,500			
Accumulated depreciation		3,000		(a) 750
Accounts payable		1,900		
Unearned legal fees		800	(e) 500	
D. Jones, capital		13,940		
D. Jones, withdrawals	9,000			
Legal fees earned		21,170		(e) 500
Salaries expense	8,000		(c) 200	
Utilities expense	840			
Rent expense	800		(b) 400	
Telephone expense	600			
Totals	40,810	40,810		
Depreciation expense			(a) 750	
Salaries payable				(c) 200
Office supplies expense			(d) 300	
Interest receivable			(f) 320	
Interest revenue				(f) 320
			2,470	2,470
Net Income				

Explanations:
(a) Depreciation expense on office equipment for the year.
(b) Prepaid rent expired during the year.
(c) Accrued salaries at end of year.
(d) Office supplies used during the year.
(e) Legal fees earned during the year.
(f) Accrued interest earned during the year.

(4) worksheet financial statements. A completed worksheet of the law practice of D. Jones, Attorney for the year ended December 31, 1983, is shown in Exhibit 4-1. Each step in the completion of the worksheet is discussed next.

Adjusted Trial Balance		Income Statement		Balance Sheet	
Debit	Credit	Debit	Credit	Debit	Credit
4,200				4,200	
5,600				5,600	
200				200	
170				170	
3,200				3,200	
7,500				7,500	
	3,750				3,750
	1,900				1,900
	300				300
	13,940				13,940
9,000				9,000	
	21,670		21,670		
8,200		8,200			
840		840			
1,200		1,200			
600		600			
750		750			
	200				200
300		300			
320				320	
	320		320		
42,080	42,080	11,890	21,990	30,190	20,090
		10,100			10,100
		21,990	21,990	30,190	30,190

Preparation of Trial Balance (Step 1)   The first step in completing a worksheet is the preparation of a trial balance. All the account titles and account balances (prior to adjustments) are obtained from the general ledger. The account titles are listed in the Account Titles column of the worksheet. The debit or credit balance of each account is listed in the debit or credit column of the Trial Balance on the worksheet; the columns are then *footed* to prove the equality of the debit and credit totals. **To foot means to total a vertical column on the worksheet.** Double lines are drawn under the totals to indicate their equality. For D. Jones, Attorney, the account titles and balances were taken from the company's general ledger. The debit and credit columns of the trial balance total $40,810, as shown on Exhibit 4-1.

Preparation of Worksheet Adjustments (Step 2)

The second step involves analyzing the accounts to determine the adjustments needed at the end of the accounting period. These adjustments are made directly on the worksheet in the Adjustments columns. For each adjusting entry a letter of the alphabet is listed in front of the debit and credit amount to provide a cross reference and so to reduce the chance of error. If an adjusting entry involves an account that is not included in the trial balance, the account title is written on the first available line below the other account titles. An explanation for each entry (identified by the same letter of the alphabet) is also included at the bottom of the worksheet. The explanation may include the calculations for the adjusting entry. After all the adjusting entries are made on the worksheet, the Adjustments debit and credit columns are footed (totaled) to prove the equality of the debit and credit totals. It is important to understand that the entering of the adjusting entries on the worksheet is *not* the same as the preparation of adjusting entries in the general journal. As discussed later, the worksheet adjusting entries must be copied into the general journal and posted to bring the actual account balances up to date.

The worksheet adjusting entries of D. Jones, Attorney are shown in Exhibit 4-1. A summary of each adjusting entry is as follows:

(a) Jones owns office equipment costing $7,500. The office equipment has a 10-year life; therefore annual depreciation is $750. Since the account Depreciation Expense is not yet listed on the worksheet, this account title is written on the first available line and $750 is entered on that line in the debit column of the Adjustments. $750 is entered in the credit column of the Adjustments on the line entitled Accumulated Depreciation.

(b) On September 1, 1983, Jones had paid $600 for 6 months rent in advance for office space. (The previous 8 months rent had been paid monthly and recorded as Rent Expense.) At year end, 4 months rent ($400) has expired. Rent Expense is debited for $400 and Prepaid Rent is credited for $400 in the Adjustments columns of the worksheet.

(c) On December 31, 1983, salaries had accrued in the amount of $200. Salaries Expense is debited for $200 on the worksheet. Since the Salaries Payable account is not listed on the worksheet, it is listed on the first available line and $200 is entered on the line in the credit column of the Adjustments.

(d) Office supplies used during 1983 totaled $300. The account title Office Supplies Expense is entered on the worksheet and $300 is recorded in the debit column of the Adjustments. Office Supplies is credited for $300.

(e) During 1983 Jones had collected $800 of legal fees in advance and recorded them as Unearned Legal Fees. A review of the accounting and legal records shows that $500 of these fees are earned at the end of 1983 and the rest will be earned in 1984. In the Adjustments columns of the worksheet, Unearned Legal Fees is debited for $500 and Legal Fees Earned is credited for $500.

(f) On January 1, 1983, a client had issued Jones a $3,200, 2-year, 10% note for legal services recently provided. The interest is to be collected on the maturity date. To date, $320 ($3,200 × 10%) has been earned. Both the Interest Receivable and Interest Revenue account titles must be listed on the worksheet and debited and credited in the Adjustments columns for the $320, respectively.

The Adjustments debit and credit columns both total $2,470, proving the equality of the debit and credit entries of the adjustments.

Preparation of Adjusted Trial Balance (Step 3)

After completing the adjustments on the worksheet an adjusted trial balance is prepared. The trial balance debit or credit amount of each account is combined with the amount of any debit or credit adjustment to that account to determine the new account balance. **Crossfooting is the combining of these amounts for each account.** Care must be taken when crossfooting. For instance, when the debit balance of an account is combined with a credit entry in the adjustments, the credit entry must be *subtracted* to determine the new debit balance of the account. Each new account balance is listed in the correct debit or credit column of the Adjusted Trial Balance on the worksheet. The Adjusted Trial Balance columns are footed to prove the equality of the debit and credit totals.

In Exhibit 4-1 each line is crossfooted and the resulting account balance listed in one of the Adjusted Trial Balance columns. For instance, no adjustments were made to the Cash or Accounts Receivable accounts and therefore their balances of $4,200 and $5,600 are listed as debits in the Adjusted Trial Balance. The $600 debit balance of the Prepaid Rent account is combined with the $400 credit from adjusting entry (b) and the resulting $200 debit balance is listed in the debit column of the Adjusted Trial Balance. This process is continued until the last account balance (Interest Revenue of $320) has been listed in the Adjusted Trial Balance. Each column of the Adjusted Trial Balance is then footed. The columns total $42,080, proving the equality of the debit and credit totals.

Preparation of Worksheet Financial Statements (Step 4)

After the Adjusted Trial Balance has been completed, the income statement and balance sheet are prepared on the worksheet. The preparation of these statements involves transferring each account balance listed in the Adjusted Trial Balance columns to its respective Income Statement or Balance Sheet column.

The asset, liability, and owner's capital, as well as the owner's withdrawals, account balances are transferred to the Balance Sheet columns. For instance, in Exhibit 4-1 the $4,200 Cash account balance is listed in the Balance Sheet debit column while the $1,900 Accounts Payable balance is listed in the credit column. The transfer of the $9,000 D. Jones, Withdrawals account to the Balance Sheet *debit* column needs further explanation. Recall that a statement of changes in owner's equity is prepared as a supporting schedule to the *ending* owner's capital account balance listed on a company's balance sheet. This ending owner's capital account balance is computed by adding net income to and subtracting withdrawals from the beginning balance. The owner's capital account balance on the worksheet is the *beginning* balance. Since no columns of the worksheet are included for preparing the statement of changes in owner's equity (this would make the worksheet too wide), the net income and withdrawals must be included in the Balance Sheet columns of the worksheet. The withdrawals account is listed in the Balance Sheet debit column because it is a subtraction from the beginning credit balance of the capital account. The inclusion of net income is discussed next.

The revenue and expense account balances are transferred to the Income Statement columns. For instance, in Exhibit 4-1 the $21,670 Legal Fees Earned account balance is listed in the Income Statement credit column. The $8,200 Salaries Expense balance is listed in the debit column. Although the revenue and expense accounts are listed in the lower part of the Adjusted Trial Balance, some of the items in this lower part may *not* belong on the income statement. Recall that in preparing the adjusting entries on the worksheet, if an account title was not listed in the trial balance, it was written on the first available line of the worksheet. Worksheet adjusting entries often require listing an asset (e.g., the Interest Receivable of $320) or a liability (e.g., the Salaries Payable of $200) in the lower part of the worksheet. Care must be taken to transfer these asset and liability items to the Balance Sheet instead of the Income Statement on the worksheet, as shown in Exhibit 4-1.

After the account balances have been transferred to the Income Statement and Balance Sheet columns, each column is subtotaled. In Exhibit 4-1 the Income Statement debit and credit column subtotals are $11,890 and $21,990, respectively. The Balance Sheet debit and credit column subtotals are $30,190 and $20,090, respectively. Note that the subtotal of the Income Statement debit column does *not* equal the subtotal of the Income Statement credit column. In addition, the subtotal of the Balance Sheet debit column does *not* equal the subtotal of the Balance Sheet credit column. **The net income (or net loss) for the accounting period is the difference between the column subtotals of each financial statement.**

The $21,990 subtotal of the Income Statement credit column is the total revenues for the period. The $11,890 subtotal of the Income Statement debit column is the total expenses for the period. The difference is a $10,100 net income. To make these columns balance, the term *Net Income* (or when expenses are more than revenues, *Net Loss*) is written on the next line below the subtotals. The amount of net income ($10,100) is listed directly under the Income Statement debit column subtotal (a net loss would be listed under the credit column subtotal) and added to the subtotal to determine the $21,990 total of the Income Statement debit column. The Income Statement credit column subtotal is extended down to the same line as the debit total and it is listed as the $21,990 total of the Income Statement credit column. These two totals are now equal and a double line is drawn below the totals.

The Balance Sheet subtotals are not equal because the net income has not yet been transferred to the owner's capital account. All the amounts listed in the Balance Sheet columns are ending account balances except for the owner's capital account, which shows a beginning credit balance. Net income must be added and withdrawals subtracted to determine the ending balance. Since withdrawals are already included in the debit column of the Balance Sheet, net income must be added to the credit column to bring the owner's capital account balance up to date (i.e., to make the balance sheet "balance"). The amount of net income ($10,100) is listed directly under the Balance Sheet credit column subtotal (a net loss, which decreases owner's equity, would be listed under the debit column subtotal) and added to the subtotal to determine the $30,190 total of the Balance Sheet credit column. The Balance Sheet debit column subtotal is extended down to the same line as the credit column total and listed as the $30,190 total of the Balance Sheet debit column. These two totals are now equal and a double line is inserted below the totals. The worksheet is now complete.

Checking for Errors

There are several ways of reducing the chance of errors in the worksheet. The Trial Balance columns, Adjustments columns, and Adjusted Trial Balance columns are footed at the end of each step to prove the equality of the debit and credit column totals. If any of these sets of column totals are not equal, the error causing the inequality must be corrected before going on to the next step. This usually involves double checking, in reverse order, the work done in the previous step. For instance, if the Trial Balance and Adjustments columns are in balance (e.g., the column totals are equal) but the Adjusted Trial Balance column totals are not equal, the debit and credit columns should be re-added to prove their accuracy. If no error is found, each debit and credit account balance should be checked to be sure it has been listed in the correct debit or credit column. If the error still is not found, the mistake must be in the crossfooting of the accounts.

Sometimes the worksheet will not balance because an error has been made in completing the financial statement columns. This so-called imbalance occurs when the computed net income amount is added to the balance sheet credit column subtotal and the resulting credit column total does not equal the total of the debit column. This inequality does not always mean that an error was made in transferring the accounts from the adjusted trial balance to the Balance Sheet columns. An error could have been made in transferring accounts to the Income Statement columns, in which case an incorrect net income would have been computed. To correct for an error in the Income Statement or Balance Sheet columns the mathematical accuracy of each of the four columns should be checked. Each debit and credit account balance should be reviewed next to be sure it has been listed in the correct debit or credit column. Finally, each account title should be checked to be sure it has been listed in the correct financial statement.

Completing the Accounting Process from the Worksheet

Earlier we mentioned that the worksheet is used to aid in journalizing the adjusting and closing entries and in preparing the financial statements. We now discuss completing the accounting process from the information in the worksheet.

ADJUSTING ENTRIES.   Adjusting entries must be journalized in the general journal and posted to the general ledger to bring the account balances up to date at the end of the accounting period. The journalizing of the adjusting entries is very simple once a worksheet has been prepared. Each adjusting entry included in the worksheet is simply copied from the worksheet into the general journal. The explanation of each adjusting entry in the worksheet is used to prepare the explanation of the adjusting entry in the general journal. The posting of the adjusting entries is completed in the usual manner. The adjusting entries for D. Jones, Attorney are shown in Exhibit 4-2.

EXHIBIT 4-2
D. Jones, Attorney
Adjusting and
Closing Entries
for 1983

GENERAL JOURNAL				Page 87
Date		Account Titles and Explanations	Debit	Credit

Adjusting Entries

Date		Account Titles and Explanations	Debit	Credit
1983 Dec.	31	Depreciation Expense	750	
		Accumulated Depreciation		750
		To record depreciation of office equipment.		
	31	Rent Expense	400	
		Prepaid Rent		400
		To record prepaid rent expired during the year.		
	31	Salaries Expense	200	
		Salaries Payable		200
		To record accrued salaries at end of year.		
	31	Office Supplies Expense	300	
		Office Supplies		300
		To record office supplies used during the year.		
	31	Unearned Legal Fees	500	
		Legal Fees Earned		500
		To record legal fees earned during the year.		
	31	Interest Receivable	320	
		Interest Revenue		320
		To record accrued interest earned during the year.		

Closing Entries

Date		Account Titles and Explanations	Debit	Credit
	31	Legal Fees Earned	21,670	
		Interest Revenue	320	
		Income Summary		21,990
		To close the revenue accounts.		
	31	Income Summary	11,890	
		Salaries Expense		8,200
		Utilities Expense		840
		Rent Expense		1,200
		Telephone Expense		600
		Depreciation Expense		750
		Office Supplies Expense		300
		To close the expense accounts.		
	31	Income Summary	10,100	
		D. Jones, Capital		10,100
		To close the Income Summary account and transfer net income to the owner's capital account.		
	31	D. Jones, Capital	9,000	
		D. Jones, Withdrawals		9,000
		To close the withdrawals account.		

CLOSING ENTRIES. Closing entries must also be journalized and posted to bring the revenue, expense, and withdrawals accounts to zero and update the ending balance in the owner's capital account. The worksheet also aids in preparing the closing entries. The amounts of all the accounts listed in the Income Statement credit column of the worksheet (i.e., the revenue accounts) are debited in the first closing entry and the subtotal of the credit column is credited to Income Summary. Next the amounts of all the accounts listed in the Income Statement debit column (i.e., the expense accounts) are credited in the second closing entry and the subtotal of the debit column is debited to Income Summary. The amount of the net income listed on the worksheet is used to close the Income Summary account to the owner's capital account in the third closing entry. Finally, the amount of the withdrawals account listed in the Balance Sheet debit column is closed as a reduction (debit) to the owner's capital account. The posting of the closing entries is completed in the usual manner. The closing entries for D. Jones, Attorney are shown in Exhibit 4-2.

FINANCIAL STATEMENTS. The information on the worksheet also aids in preparing the financial statements. The income statement is prepared from the information contained in the Income Statement columns of the worksheet. The income statement of D. Jones, Attorney for 1983 is shown in Exhibit 4-3. Note that the income statement includes two parts, an Operating Income section and an Other Revenues and Expenses section. The Operating Income section of an income statement includes all the revenues earned and expenses incurred in the normal day-to-day operations of a company. The Other Revenues and Expenses section of an income statement includes any revenues and expenses that are not related to the primary operations of the company. A more detailed discussion of the sections of the income statement is presented in Chapter 5.

EXHIBIT 4-3
Income Statement

D. JONES, ATTORNEY
Income Statement
For Year Ended December 31, 1983

Revenues:		
Legal fees earned		$21,670
Expenses:		
Salaries expense	$8,200	
Utilities expense	840	
Rent expense	1,200	
Telephone expense	600	
Depreciation expense	750	
Office supplies expense	300	
Total Expenses		11,890
Operating Income		$ 9,780
Other Revenues and Expenses:		
Interest revenue		320
Net Income		$10,100

EXHIBIT 4-4
Balance Sheet and
Statement of Changes
in Owner's Equity

D. JONES, ATTORNEY
Balance Sheet
December 31, 1983

Assets			*Liabilities*		
Cash		$ 4,200	Accounts payable		1,900
Accounts receivable		5,600	Unearned legal fees		300
Office supplies		170	Salaries payable		200
Prepaid rent		200	Total Liabilities		$ 2,400
Notes receivable					
(due 1/1/1985)		3,200			
Interest receivable					
(due 1/1/1985)		320	*Owner's Equity*		
Office equipment .	$7,500		D. Jones, capital (see		
Less: Accumulated			Schedule A)		15,040
depreciation .	(3,750)	3,750	Total Liabilities and		
Total Assets		$17,440	Owner's Equity		$17,440

D. JONES, ATTORNEY
Schedule A
Statement of Changes in Owner's Equity
For Year Ended December 31, 1983

D. Jones, capital, January 1, 1983	$13,940
Add: Net income	10,100
	$24,040
Less: Withdrawals	(9,000)
D. Jones, capital, December 31, 1983	$15,040

The balance sheet is prepared from the information contained in the Balance Sheet columns of the worksheet, with one exception. Recall that the owner's capital account balance listed on the worksheet is the beginning balance. A separate supporting schedule, the statement of changes in owner's equity, must be completed to determine the ending balance of the owner's capital account. The net income and withdrawals information for this schedule is included on the worksheet. This schedule is shown in the lower part of Exhibit 4-4. In completing the balance sheet, the items in the lower part of the Balance Sheet columns of the worksheet must be put in the correct section of the balance sheet. The 1983 ending balance sheet of D. Jones, Attorney is shown in the upper part of Exhibit 4-4.

INTERIM STATEMENTS.   Companies normally use a year as their accounting period and journalize and post adjusting entries at the end of the year. Many companies also prepare interim financial statements. **Interim financial statements are financial statements prepared for a period of less than one year.** Interim financial statements for each quarter of the year are common. When a company prepares interim financial statements, the accounting information that is being gathered for the yearly accounting period should not be affected by actually journalizing and posting the adjusting entries for the interim period. Use of a worksheet is ideal for the preparation of interim financial statements. The interim period adjusting entries can be made only on the worksheet, without actually journalizing the entries. The interim financial statements can then be prepared from the worksheet information. It is not necessary to prepare closing entries since the accounts will be used to accumulate the accounting information for the rest of the year. By using a worksheet, interim financial statements can be prepared without affecting the yearly accounting process.

REVERSING ENTRIES

After the accounts have been adjusted and closed for the current accounting period, the accounting process is begun for the next period. Before journalizing the daily transactions of the new accounting period in the general journal, many companies prepare reversing entries. **A reversing entry is a journal entry that is the exact reverse (both account titles and amounts) of an adjusting entry.** Reversing entries are usually made at the same time as closing entries but are dated the first day of the *next* accounting period. Not all adjusting entries are reversed. Reversing entries are *optional* and have one purpose, to simplify the recording of a later transaction related to a particular adjusting entry. Reversing entries allow the later transaction to be recorded in a routine way, without the need for considering the impact of the related adjusting entry from the previous year.

To illustrate the preparation and use of reversing entries consider the December 31, 1983, adjusting entry presented earlier in regard to the $720 accrued salaries of the Stalley Company and the subsequent $1,800 payment of the salaries on January 4, 1984. These entries are reproduced in Exhibit 4-5. At the time of payment we noted that (if a reversing entry is not made) a careful analysis must be made to determine the portion of the $1,800 salaries relating to salaries expense ($1,080) for 1984 and the salaries payable ($720) for 1983. The use of a reversing entry eliminates this analysis. The payment of the salaries on January 4, 1984, is recorded in the usual manner as a debit for the entire amount ($1,800) to Salaries Expense and a credit to Cash, as shown in Exhibit 4-5.

Whether or not to make a reversing entry is a matter of judgment. The important consideration is whether or not the reversing entry will simplify the recording of a later transaction related to the adjusting entry. If it will do so, the reversing entry should be made. As a general rule a reversing entry should be made for any adjusting entry that creates a new balance sheet account.

Therefore, reversing entries *should be* made for:

1. Adjusting entries that establish accrued expenses or revenues to be paid or collected in the next accounting period (e.g., salaries payable, interest receivable)
2. Adjusting entries related to prepayments of costs initially recorded as *expenses* or receipts in advance initially recorded as *revenues*

Reversing entries *should not* be made for:

1. Adjusting entries related to prepayments of costs initially recorded as assets or receipts in advance initially recorded as liabilities (e.g., prepaid rent, unearned legal fees)
2. Adjusting entries for depreciation

Except where indicated in the homework materials at the end of this chapter, reversing entries are not used in this textbook.

EXHIBIT 4-5
Illustration of
Reversing Entry

Adjusting Entry

12/31/83	Salaries Expense	720	
	Salaries Payable		720
12/31/83	Revenues and expenses are CLOSED		

If reversing entry is not made:	*If reversing entry is made:*
Reversing Entry	**Reversing Entry**

1/1/84	None			1/1/84	Salaries Payable	720
					Salaries Expense	720

Subsequent Entry	**Subsequent Entry**

1/4/84	Salaries Expense	1,080		1/4/84	Salaries Expense	1,800
	Salaries Payable	720			Cash	1,800
	Cash	1,800				

Analysis of Subsequent Entry	**Analysis of Subsequent Entry**
Salaries of $1,800 are paid, but $720 was recorded in Salaries Payable at end of last period. Consequently, Salaries Payable must be debited for $720 and Salaries Expense debited for $1,080.	Salaries of $1,800 are paid and debited to Salaries Expense. Because a reversing entry was made for $720, the net result in Salaries Expense is a $1,080 debit balance.

REVIEW PROBLEM

The December 31, 1983, trial balance of the Sparkle Company included the following accounts and account balances:

Account Titles	Debits	Credits
Notes receivable	$ 2,000	
Store supplies	600	
Prepaid insurance	216	
Building	30,000	
Accumulated depreciation: building		$12,000
Unearned rent		2,400

A review of the accounting records and related source documents reveals the following information:

1. Interest of $100 has accrued on the notes receivable.
2. Store supplies on hand at year end total $80.
3. The prepaid insurance is for a 2-year insurance policy purchased on May 1, 1983.
4. The building was acquired in 1975 and is being depreciated over a 15-year life (no residual value).
5. The unearned rent is for 1 year of rent ($200 per month) collected in advance from the renter on October 1, 1983.
6. Accrued salaries total $500 at the end of 1983.

Required: Prepare year-end adjusting entries to record the above information.

SOLUTION TO REVIEW PROBLEM

GENERAL JOURNAL				Page 38	
Date			Account Titles and Explanations	Debit	Credit
1983 Dec.	31		Interest Receivable	100	
			Interest Revenue		100
			To record accrued interest earned during the year.		
	31		Store Supplies Expense	520	
			Store Supplies		520
			To record store supplies used ($600 − $80) during the year.		
	31		Insurance Expense	72	
			Prepaid Insurance		72
			To record insurance expense [($216 ÷ 24) × 8].		
	31		Depreciation Expense: Building	2,000	
			Accumulated Depreciation: Building		2,000
			To record depreciation of building ($30,000 ÷ 15).		
	31		Unearned Rent	600	
			Rent Revenue		600
			To record rent earned [($2,400 ÷ 12) × 3].		
	31		Salaries Expense	500	
			Salaries Payable		500
			To record accrued salaries at year end.		

GLOSSARY

Accrued Expense. Expense that has been incurred during the accounting period but has neither been paid nor recorded. An example is unpaid employees' salaries.

Accrued Revenue. Revenue that has been earned during the accounting period but has neither been collected nor recorded. An example is uncollected interest.

Adjusting Entries. Journal entries made at the end of an accounting period to bring the revenue and expense account balances up to date and to show the correct ending balances in the asset and liability accounts.

Book Value. The cost of a depreciable asset less its related accumulated depreciation. Also called *carrying value*.

Contra Account. Account whose balance is subtracted from another related account to determine a resulting amount. An example is accumulated depreciation.

Crossfooting. Combining the amount of an account with a debit or credit adjustment to the account on a worksheet. Horizontal addition or subtraction.

Depreciable Assets. Long-term physical assets whose expected economic benefits expire over the useful life of the assets. The related costs must be apportioned as depreciation expense in the accounting periods during which the assets are used.

Depreciation Expense. The part of the cost of a long-term physical asset allocated as an expense to each accounting period in the asset's useful life.

Foot. To total a vertical column of a worksheet.

Interest. Amount charged for the use of money. For an interest-bearing note the interest is computed by multiplying the principal times the annual interest rate for the length of time the note has been issued.

Interest Rate. Rate of interest charged on the principal of a note. Expressed as an annual percentage.

Interim Financial Statements. Financial statements prepared for a period of less than one year.

Prepaid Expense. Economic resource that is expected to be used in the near future. Examples are prepaid rent and office supplies.

Principal. Amount of a note.

Reversing Entry. Journal entry that is the exact reverse (both account titles and amounts) of an adjusting entry. Dated the first day of the new accounting period. It is optional and used to simplify the recording of a later transaction related to the adjusting entry.

Straight-Line. Method of depreciation that records an equal portion of the cost of an asset as depreciation expense in each accounting period in which the asset is used.

Unearned Revenue. Advance receipt for goods or services to be provided in the future. Recorded as a liability at the time of receipt. An example is unearned rent.

Worksheet. A large columnar accounting paper for initially preparing the trial balance, adjustments, adjusted trial balance, income statement, and balance sheet at the end of an accounting period.

QUESTIONS

Q4-1 What are adjusting entries? Why are they necessary?

Q4-2 What is a depreciable asset? How is annual straight-line depreciation expense computed?

Q4-3 What is a contra account? What is a book value? Show how the book value of a building costing $14,000 and having accumulated depreciation of $5,000 would be listed in a balance sheet.

Q4-4 What is a prepaid expense? Give an example of the journal entries to record the initial transaction and adjusting entry for a prepaid expense (dollar amounts are not necessary).

Q4-5 What is an unearned revenue? Give an example of the journal entries to record the initial transaction and adjusting entry for an unearned revenue (dollar amounts are not necessary).

Q4-6 What is an accrued expense? Give an example of an adjusting entry for an accrued expense (dollar amounts are not necessary).

Q4-7 Discuss the journal entry that would be made to record the salaries paid to employees at the beginning of a new accounting period if part of the salaries were accrued at the end of the last period. Assume reversing entries are not used.

Q4-8 What is an accrued revenue? Give an example of an adjusting entry for an accrued revenue (dollar amounts are not necessary).

Q4-9 When preparing adjusting entries why is it important to know if a company initially recorded the receipt of an advance payment from a customer as a liability or a revenue?

Q4-10 For an interest-bearing note define the following: (a) interest, (b) principal, (c) rate. How is interest computed?

Q4-11 What is a worksheet? Why is it used?

Q4-12 List and very briefly discuss the steps that must be completed in the preparation of a worksheet.

Q4-13 Briefly discuss what to do if a worksheet does not "balance."

Q4-14 What are interim financial statements? Why is a worksheet helpful in their preparation?

Q4-15 What steps in the accounting process are completed *after* a worksheet is prepared?

Q4-16 What are reversing entries? Why are they used? For what kinds of adjusting entries should they be made?

Q4-17 A company accrues salaries at the end of 1983 in the amount of $500. Salaries paid to its employees in the first pay period of 1984 total $1,800. Show the journal entry to record the 1984 payment assuming that: (a) reversing entries are not used and (b) reversing entries are used (also show the reversing entry).

EXERCISES   **E4-1** **Depreciation.**   On January 1, 1983, the McCartney Company purchased store equipment for $5,400 cash. The equipment has an estimated useful life of 9 years and a residual value of zero. The company uses the straight-line depreciation method.

Required: 1. Prepare journal entries to record:
  (a) The purchase of the store equipment on January 1, 1983.
  (b) The necessary adjusting entry at the end of 1983.
  2. If the adjusting entry had *not* been made in requirement 1(b) discuss what effect this error would have on the accounts and totals listed in the income statement and balance sheet.

E4-2 **Prepaid Expenses.**   On October 1, 1983, the Bourdon Company paid $800 for a 2-year comprehensive insurance policy on the company's building.

Required: Prepare the journal entry to record the purchase of this insurance policy and the adjusting entry at the end of 1983, assuming the cost of the policy was initially recorded as:
  1. An asset
  2. An expense

E4-3 **Unearned Revenues.**   On October 1, 1983, the Sagir Company received $1,560 in advance for 6 months rent of office space to the Land-Ho Real Estate Agency.

Required: 1. Prepare the Sagir Company journal entries to record:
  (a) The receipt of the payment (assume the company records any receipt in advance as a liability).
  (b) The adjustment for rent revenue at the end of 1983.
  2. If the adjusting entry had *not* been made in requirement 1(b) discuss what effect this error would have on the accounts and totals listed in the income statement and balance sheet.

E4-4 **Accrued Expense and Reversing Entry.**   The Clinkscales Company employs five employees, each of whom earns $250 per week for a 5-day work week (Monday through Friday). The employees are paid every Friday; November 30, 1983, the end of the company's fiscal year, falls on Wednesday.

Required: 1. Prepare the necessary adjusting entry for salaries on November 30, 1983.
  2. Prepare the journal entry for the payment of salaries on December 2, 1983 (assume a reversing entry is not made).
  3. Disregard requirement 2. Prepare the reversing entry related to requirement 1 and prepare the journal entry for the payment of salaries on December 2, 1983.

E4-5 **Accrued Interest Expense and Revenue.**   On October 1, 1983, the Scotch Company purchased 2 acres of land from the Irist Company at a cost of $10,000. The Scotch Company signed (issued) a 1-year, 10% note requiring it to repay the $10,000 principal plus $1,000 interest on October 1, 1984, to the Irist Company. The Irist Company had originally purchased the land for $10,000.

Required: Based on the foregoing information, prepare the October 1, 1983, entry and the adjusting entry for interest at the end of 1983 for:
  1. The Scotch Company
  2. The Irist Company

E4-6 Adjusting Entries. The following partial list of accounts and account balances has been taken from the trial balance and the adjusted trial balance of the Mane Company:

	Trial Balance		Adjusted Trial Balance	
Account Titles	Debit	Credit	Debit	Credit
Accumulated depreciation		$5,000		$6,200
Interest payable		0		218
Prepaid insurance	$350		$150	
Salaries payable		0		550

Required: Prepare the adjusting entry that caused the change in each account balance.

E4-7 Adjusting Entries. At the end of the current year the Rulem Company provides you with the following information:

(a) Depreciation expense on equipment totals $1,050 for the current year.
(b) Accrued interest on a note payable issued on October 1 amounts to $850 at year end.
(c) Unearned revenue in the amount of $1,200 has become earned (all receipts in advance are recorded in an unearned revenue account).
(d) Supplies used during the year total $250 (all purchases of office supplies are recorded in an asset account).

Required: Prepare adjusting entries at the end of the current year based on the above information.

E4-8 Worksheet. The June 30, 1983, trial balance for the Shelen Company is shown on the partially completed worksheet below.

SHELEN COMPANY
Worksheet
For Month Ended June 30, 1983

Account Titles	Trial Balance		Adjustments		Adjusted Trial Balance		Income Statement		Balance Sheet	
	Debit	Credit	Debit	Credit	Debit	Credit	Debit	Credit	Debit	Credit
Cash	30,000									
Accounts receivable	3,740									
Prepaid rent	2,100									
Office supplies	450									
Office equipment	6,000									
Accumulated depreciation		600								
Accounts payable		1,200								
F. Shelen, capital		40,000								
F. Shelen, withdrawals	1,000									
Service revenues		5,435								
Salaries expense	3,575									
Utilities expense	230									
Telephone expense	140									
Totals	47,235	47,235								

Additional Information:

(a) Prepaid rent in the amount of $300 has expired during June.
(b) Salaries at month end that have accumulated but have not been paid total $525.
(c) Monthly straight-line depreciation on office equipment is based on a cost of $6,000, an estimated useful life of 5 years, and no residual value.
(d) Office supplies used during the month of June totaled $75.

Required: Complete the worksheet for the month of June.

E4-9 Worksheet. The September 30, 1983 trial balance for the Conrad Company is shown on the partially completed worksheet below.

CONRAD COMPANY
Worksheet
For Month Ended September 30, 1983

Account Titles	Trial Balance		Adjustments		Adjusted Trial Balance		Income Statement		Balance Sheet	
	Debit	Credit	Debit	Credit	Debit	Credit	Debit	Credit	Debit	Credit
Cash	40,000									
Accounts receivable	1,000									
Supplies	6,500									
Building	90,000									
Accumulated depreciation: building		10,000								
Accounts payable		3,280								
Unearned rent revenues		4,500								
D. Conrad, capital		95,500								
Rent revenues		26,900								
Salaries expense	2,200									
Utilities expense	400									
Telephone expense	80									
Totals	140,180	140,180								

Additional Information:

(a) Monthly depreciation on the building is computed on a straight-line basis with an estimated life of 15 years and no residual value.
(b) Supplies on hand on September 30, 1983, total $6,150.
(c) Unearned rent revenue that was earned during September totaled $700.

Required: Complete the worksheet for the month of September.

E4-10 Adjusting and Closing Entries from Worksheet. At the end of 1983 the Crandle Company prepared the worksheet below.

CRANDLE COMPANY
Worksheet
For Year Ended December 31, 1983

Account Titles	Trial Balance Debit	Trial Balance Credit	Adjustments Debit	Adjustments Credit	Adjusted Trial Balance Debit	Adjusted Trial Balance Credit	Income Statement Debit	Income Statement Credit	Balance Sheet Debit	Balance Sheet Credit
Cash	8,145				8,145				8,145	
Accounts receivable	1,400				1,400				1,400	
Prepaid rent	750			(b) 750						
Supplies	1,310			(d) 1,270	40				40	
Equipment	5,000				5,000				5,000	
Accumulated depreciation		1,000		(a) 1,000		2,000				2,000
Accounts payable		475				475				475
Unearned cleaning revenue		1,000	(e) 850			150				150
G. Crandle, capital		10,000				10,000				10,000
G. Crandle, withdrawals	7,000				7,000				7,000	
Cleaning revenue		22,180		(e) 850		23,030		23,030		
Salaries expense	9,000		(c) 500		9,500		9,500			
Utilities expense	800				800		800			
Rent expense	750		(b) 750		1,500		1,500			
Telephone expense	500				500		500			
Totals	34,655	34,655								
Depreciation expense			(a) 1,000		1,000		1,000			
Salaries payable				(c) 500		500				500
Supplies expense			(d) 1,270		1,270		1,270			
			4,370	4,370	36,155	36,155	14,570	23,030	21,585	13,125
Net Income							8,460			8,460
							23,030	23,030	21,585	21,585

Explanations:
(a) Depreciation expense on equipment for the year.
(b) Prepaid rent expired during the year.
(c) Accrued salaries at end of year.
(d) Supplies used during the year.
(e) Unearned cleaning fees earned during the year.

Required: 1. Prepare adjusting entries from the worksheet.
2. Prepare closing entries from the worksheet.

E4-11 Financial Statements. Refer to the data in E4-10.

Required: From the information on the worksheet:
1. Prepare a 1983 income statement.
2. Prepare a 1983 statement of changes in owner's equity.
3. Prepare a December 31, 1983, balance sheet (account form).

E4-12   Reversing Entries. On December 31, 1983, the Bluen Company made the following adjusting entries for its annual accounting period:

Depreciation Expense	1,500	
Accumulated Depreciation		1,500

To record depreciation on equipment.

Interest Receivable	80	
Interest Revenue		80

To record interest on note receivable due on February 1, 1984.

Salaries Expense	280	
Salaries Payable		280

To record salaries accumulated but not paid.

Rent Expense	400	
Prepaid Rent		400

To record expired prepaid rent.

Required: Prepare whatever reversing entries are appropriate.

PROBLEMS

Part A

P4-1A   Adjusting Entries. The trial balance of the Halsey Company on December 31, 1983 (the end of its annual accounting period), included the following account balances *before* adjustments:

Note receivable	$12,000	debit
Prepaid insurance	7,200	debit
Equipment	18,000	debit
Building	90,000	debit
Unearned rent	6,480	credit
Note payable	10,000	credit
Supplies	1,500	debit

In reviewing the company's recorded transactions and accounting records for 1983, you find the following data pertaining to the December 31, 1983, adjustments:

(a) On July 1, 1983, the company had accepted a $12,000, 1-year, 10% note receivable from a customer. The interest is to be collected when the note is collected.
(b) On October 1, 1983, the company had paid $7,200 for a 3-year insurance policy.
(c) The building was acquired on January 1, 1975, and is being depreciated using the straight-line method over a 20-year life with no residual value.
(d) The equipment was purchased on April 1, 1983. It is to be depreciated using the straight-line method over a 15-year life with no residual value.
(e) On July 1, 1983, the company had received 2 years rent in advance for a portion of its building rented to the Shields Company.
(f) On November 1, 1983, the company had issued a $10,000, 3-month, 9% note payable to a supplier. The $225 total interest is to be paid when the note is paid.
(g) On January 1, 1983, the company had $200 of supplies on hand. During 1983 the company purchased $1,300 of supplies. A physical count on December 31, 1983, revealed that there are $90 of supplies still on hand.

Required: Prepare the adjusting entries that are necessary to bring the Halsey Company accounts up to date on December 31, 1983. Each journal entry explanation should summarize your calculations.

P4-2A Adjusting Entries. Several transactions of the Paribus Company that occurred during 1983 and which were recorded in balance sheet accounts are as follows:

Date	Transaction
Mar. 1	Purchased equipment for $12,000, paying $3,000 down, and issuing a 1-year, 10% note payable for the $9,000 balance. The equipment has an estimated life of 8 years and a zero residual value. The interest on the note will be paid on the maturity date.
May 24	Purchased $340 of office supplies. The office supplies on hand at the beginning of the year totaled $160.
June 2	Purchased a 2-year comprehensive insurance policy for $960.
Sept. 1	Received 6 months rent in advance at $350 per month and recorded the $2,100 receipt as unearned rent revenue.
Oct. 1	Accepted a $3,000, 6-month, 10% note receivable from a customer. The $150 total interest is to be collected when the note is collected.

Additional Information:
(a) On December 31, 1983, the office supplies on hand totaled $47.
(b) All employees work Monday through Friday. The weekly payroll of the Paribus Company amounts to $5,000. All employees are paid at the close of business each Thursday for the previous 5 working days (including Thursday). December 31, 1983, falls on a Saturday.

Required: On the basis of the above information prepare journal entries to record whatever adjustments are necessary on December 31, 1983. Each journal entry explanation should show any related computations.

P4-3A Adjusting Entries. A partial list of accounts and account balances taken from the December 31, 1983, trial balance and adjusted trial balance of the Rowland Company is as follows:

Account Titles	Trial Balance Debit	Trial Balance Credit	Adjusted Trial Balance Debit	Adjusted Trial Balance Credit
Supplies	$1,200		$ 82	
Prepaid insurance	500		50	
Accumulated depreciation: building		$5,000		$7,500
Accumulated depreciation: equipment		800		1,000
Interest payable		0		78
Salaries payable		0		573
Unearned rent		2,250		750

Required: Prepare the adjusting entry that caused the change in each account balance.

P4-4A Worksheet and Closing Entries. Shown on the following page is the December 31, 1983, worksheet (partially complete) for Gundy's Repair Service.

Required: 1. Complete the worksheet.
2. Prepare an income statement for the year ended December 31, 1983.
3. Prepare closing entries on December 31, 1983.

GUNDY'S REPAIR SERVICE
Worksheet
For Year Ended December 31, 1983

Account Titles	Trial Balance Debit	Trial Balance Credit	Adjustments Debit	Adjustments Credit	Adjusted Trial Balance Debit	Adjusted Trial Balance Credit	Income Statement Debit	Income Statement Credit	Balance Sheet Debit	Balance Sheet Credit
Cash	44,650				44,650					
Prepaid rent	2,100			(a) 1,050	1,050					
Prepaid insurance	500			(d) 250	250					
Supplies	3,100			(c) 2,400	700					
Notes receivable	8,000				8,000					
Equipment	40,000				40,000					
Accumulated depreciation		4,000		(b) 2,000		6,000				
Accounts payable		1,080				1,080				
H. Gundy, capital		50,000				50,000				
H. Gundy, withdrawals	8,000				8,000					
Repair service revenues		204,390				204,390				
Salaries expense	150,000				150,000					
Utilities expense	2,160				2,160					
Telephone expense	960				960					
Totals	259,470	259,470								
Rent expense			(a) 1,050		1,050					
Depreciation expense			(b) 2,000		2,000					
Supplies expense			(c) 2,400		2,400					
Insurance expense			(d) 250		250					
Interest receivable			(e) 400		400					
Interest revenue				(e) 400		400				
			6,100	6,100	261,870	261,870				

Explanations:
(a) Prepaid rent expired during the year.
(b) Depreciation expense on equipment for the year.
(c) Supplies used during the year.
(d) Prepaid insurance expired during the year.
(e) Accrued interest earned during the year.

P4-5A   Worksheet. The McKinnon Company prepared a trial balance on the partially completed worksheet shown on the following page for the year ended December 31, 1983.

Additional Information:
(a) The equipment is being depreciated on a straight-line basis over a 12-year life, no residual value.
(b) The building is being depreciated on a straight-line basis over a 20-year life, no residual value.
(c) Salaries accrued but not recorded total $300.
(d) Supplies on hand at December 31, 1983, total $973.
(e) On October 1, 1983, the company had paid $1,000 for a 1-year comprehensive insurance policy.
(f) On July 1, 1983, the company borrowed $10,000 from a local bank. The company signed

(issued) a $10,000, 1-year, 10% note. The $500 year-end accrued interest is to be paid when the note is paid.

(g) Unearned service revenues that were earned by the end of the year totaled $975.

Required: Complete the worksheet.

McKINNON COMPANY **Worksheet** **For Year Ended December 31, 1983**											
	Trial Balance		Adjustments		Adjusted Trial Balance		Income Statement		Balance Sheet		
Account Titles	Debit	Credit	Debit	Credit	Debit	Credit	Debit	Credit	Debit	Credit	
Cash	19,050										
Accounts receivable	5,500										
Prepaid insurance	1,000										
Supplies	3,000										
Building	35,000										
Accumulated depreciation: building		8,750									
Equipment	15,000										
Accumulated depreciation: equipment		6,250									
Accounts payable		850									
Note payable		10,000									
Unearned service revenues		1,200									
Z. McKinnon, capital		40,000									
Z. McKinnon, withdrawals	17,000										
Service revenues		75,000									
Salaries expense	45,000										
Utilities expense	960										
Telephone expense	540										
Totals	142,050	142,050									

P4-6A **Comprehensive.** The Dickinson Employment Agency has prepared a trial balance on the partially completed worksheet shown on the following page for the year ended December 31, 1983.

Additional Information:
(a) Prepaid rent expired during the year totaled $2,250.
(b) Supplies on hand on December 31, 1983, totaled $800.
(c) Depreciation expense on equipment for the year amounted to $600.
(d) Salaries accrued but not recorded total $375.

Required: 1. Complete the worksheet.
2. Make any adjusting entries needed on December 31, 1983.
3. Prepare an income statement for the year ended December 31, 1983.
4. Prepare a statement of changes in owner's equity for the year ended December 31, 1983.
5. Prepare a balance sheet (account form) at December 31, 1983.
6. Prepare closing entries on December 31, 1983.
7. Prepare whatever reversing entries are appropriate.

| | DICKINSON EMPLOYMENT AGENCY
Worksheet
For Year Ended December 31, 1983 | | | | | | | | | |
| | Trial Balance | | Adjustments | | Adjusted
Trial Balance | | Income
Statement | | Balance
Sheet | |
Account Titles	Debit	Credit	Debit	Credit	Debit	Credit	Debit	Credit	Debit	Credit
Cash	7,105									
Prepaid rent	3,000									
Supplies	2,800									
Equipment	15,400									
Accumulated depreciation		1,200								
Accounts payable		1,085								
P. Dickinson, capital		15,000								
P. Dickinson, withdrawals	2,500									
Employment service fees		25,480								
Salaries expense	10,400									
Utilities expense	960									
Telephone expense	600									
Totals	42,765	42,765								

PROBLEMS

Part B

P4-1B   Adjusting Entries.   The trial balance of the Cronell Company on December 31, 1983 (the end of its annual accounting period), included the following account balances before adjustments:

Note receivable	$6,000	debit
Prepaid rent	4,200	debit
Supplies	2,000	debit
Equipment	9,000	debit
Unearned service revenues	1,025	credit
Note payable	5,000	credit

Upon reviewing the company's accounting records, you find the following data pertaining to the December 31, 1983, adjustments:

(a) On October 1, 1983, the company had accepted a $6,000, 6-month, 10% note receivable from a customer. The $300 total interest is to be collected when the note is collected.

(b) On January 2, 1983, the company paid for 1 year of rent in advance at $350 per month.

(c) On January 1, 1983, $400 of supplies were on hand. During 1983 the company purchased $1,600 of supplies. A physical count on December 31, 1983, revealed that there are $210 of supplies on hand.

(d) The equipment was purchased on July 1, 1983. It is to be depreciated using the straight-line method over a 5-year life with no residual value.

(e) On October 1, 1983, the company received $1,025 in advance for services to be rendered. On December 31, 1983, $225 remained unearned.

(f) On April 1, 1983, the company had issued a $5,000, 1-year, 10% note payable to a supplier. Interest is to be paid when the note is paid.

Required: Prepare the adjusting entries necessary to bring the Cronell Company accounts up to date on December 31, 1983. Each journal entry explanation should summarize your calculations.

P4-2B **Adjusting Entries.** Several transactions of the Marlin Company that occurred during 1983 and which were recorded in balance sheet accounts are as follows:

Date	Transaction
Apr. 2	Purchased equipment for $15,000 paying $3,000 down and issuing a 1-year, 10% note payable for the $12,000 balance. The equipment has an estimated life of 15 years and a zero residual value. The interest on the note will be paid on the maturity date.
June 14	Purchased $750 of office supplies. The office supplies on hand at the beginning of 1983 totaled $150.
July 1	Received 6 months rent in advance at $300 per month and recorded the $1,800 receipt as unearned rent revenue.
Nov. 1	Accepted a $3,750, 6-month, 8% note receivable from a customer. The $150 total interest is to be collected when the note is collected.

Additional Information:
(a) On December 31, 1983, the office supplies on hand totaled $200.
(b) All employees work Monday through Friday. The weekly payroll of the company amounts to $4,000. All employees are paid at the close of business each Wednesday for the previous 5 working days (including Wednesday). December 31, 1983, falls on a Saturday.

Required: On the basis of the above information, prepare journal entries to record whatever adjustments are necessary on December 31, 1983.

P4-3B **Worksheet.** The Conon Advertising Service Company prepared a trial balance on the partially completed worksheet shown below for the year ended December 31, 1983.

CONON ADVERTISING SERVICE COMPANY
Worksheet
For Year Ended December 31, 1983

Account Titles	Trial Balance Debit	Trial Balance Credit	Adjustments Debit	Adjustments Credit	Adjusted Trial Balance Debit	Adjusted Trial Balance Credit	Income Statement Debit	Income Statement Credit	Balance Sheet Debit	Balance Sheet Credit
Cash	9,020									
Accounts receivable	6,240									
Prepaid rent	3,000									
Office supplies	2,500									
Note receivable	5,000									
Office equipment	7,500									
Accumulated depreciation		3,125								
Accounts payable		1,250								
Unearned revenues		2,000								
Q. Conon, capital		30,000								
Q. Conon, withdrawals	3,000									
Advertising service revenues		20,625								
Rent expense	4,000									
Salaries expense	15,600									
Utilities expense	660									
Telephone expense	480									
Totals	57,000	57,000								

Additional Information:

(a) The office equipment is being depreciated on a straight-line basis over a 12-year life, no residual value.

(b) On October 1, 1983, the company accepted a $5,000, 6-month, 10% note from a customer. The $250 total interest is to be collected when the note is collected.

(c) Salaries accrued but not recorded total $150.

(d) Office supplies on hand on December 31, 1983, total $300.

(e) On September 1, 1983, the company paid 6 months rent in advance at $500 per month.

(f) Unearned revenues that were earned by completing advertising services during the year total $975.

Required: Complete the worksheet.

P4-4B   Worksheet and Closing Entries.   Shown below is the December 31, 1983, worksheet (partially complete) for the Sundal Travel Agency.

SUNDAL TRAVEL AGENCY
Worksheet
For Year Ended December 31, 1983

Account Titles	Trial Balance Debit	Trial Balance Credit	Adjustments Debit	Adjustments Credit	Adjusted Trial Balance Debit	Adjusted Trial Balance Credit	Income Statement Debit	Income Statement Credit	Balance Sheet Debit	Balance Sheet Credit
Cash	8,270				8,270					
Prepaid rent	5,400			(a) 5,400						
Supplies	1,300			(c) 1,200	100					
Equipment	4,000				4,000					
Accumulated depreciation		1,000		(b) 500		1,500				
Accounts payable		270				270				
T. Sundal, capital		12,000				12,000				
T. Sundal, withdrawals	1,000				1,000					
Travel arrangement fees		19,130				19,130				
Salaries expense	10,000				10,000					
Utilities expense	950				950					
Telephone expense	1,480				1,480					
Totals	32,400	32,400								
Rent expense			(a) 5,400		5,400					
Depreciation expense			(b) 500		500					
Supplies expense			(c) 1,200		1,200					
			7,100	7,100	32,900	32,900				

Explanations:
(a) Prepaid rent expired during the year.
(b) Depreciation expense on equipment for the year.
(c) Supplies used during the year.

Required: 1. Complete the worksheet.
2. Prepare an income statement for the year ended December 31, 1983.
3. Prepare closing entries on December 31, 1983.

P4-5B Adjusting Entries. A partial list of accounts and account balances taken from the December 31, 1983, trial balance and adjusted trial balance of the Triton Company is as follows:

	Trial Balance		Adjusted Trial Balance	
Account Titles	Debit	Credit	Debit	Credit
Office supplies	$ 675		$23	
Prepaid rent	3,300		0	
Accumulated depreciation		$1,000		$1,500
Interest receivable	0		98	
Salaries payable		0		325
Unearned revenue		1,275		275

Required: Prepare the adjusting entry that caused the change in each account balance.

P4-6B Comprehensive. Shown below is the December 31, 1983, trial balance prepared on a partially completed worksheet for the Raffensager Consulting Agency.

RAFFENSAGER CONSULTING AGENCY **Worksheet** **For Year Ended December 31, 1983**												
	Trial Balance		Adjustments		Adjusted Trial Balance		Income Statement		Balance Sheet			
Account Titles	Debit	Credit	Debit	Credit	Debit	Credit	Debit	Credit	Debit	Credit		
Cash	3,295											
Accounts receivable	1,570											
Office supplies	3,000											
Building	17,000											
Accumulated depreciation: building		2,500										
Office equipment	6,000											
Accumulated depreciation: office equipment		1,500										
Accounts payable		1,915										
F. Raffensager, capital		18,000										
F. Raffensager, withdrawals	4,000											
Consulting revenues		27,830										
Salaries expense	14,600											
Utilities expense	1,080											
Telephone expense	1,200											
Totals	51,745	51,745										

Additional Information:
(a) Depreciation expense on the building for the year amounts to $500.
(b) Depreciation expense on the office equipment for the year amounts to $300.
(c) Salaries accrued but not recorded total $125.
(d) Supplies on hand on December 31, 1983, total $500.

Required: 1. Complete the worksheet.

2. Prepare the necessary adjusting entries on December 31, 1983.
3. Prepare an income statement for the year ended December 31, 1983.
4. Prepare a statement of changes in owner's equity for the year ended December 31, 1983.
5. Prepare a balance sheet (account form) at December 31, 1983.
6. Prepare closing entries on December 31, 1983.
7. Prepare whatever reversing entries are appropriate.

DISCUSSION CASES

C4-1 Faulty Financial Statements. Ray Young owns and operates a repair service called Ray's Rapid Repairs. It is the end of the year and his bookkeeper has recently resigned to move to a warmer climate. Knowing only a little about accounting, Ray prepared the following financial statements, based upon the ending balances in the company's accounts on December 31, 1983:

RAY'S RAPID REPAIRS
Income Statement
For Year Ended December 31, 1983

Repair service revenues		$28,000
Operating expenses:		
Rent expense	$ 3,600	
Salaries expense	9,900	
Utilities expense	1,200	
R. Young, withdrawals	15,000	
Total operating expenses		29,700
Net Loss		$ (1,700)

RAY'S RAPID REPAIRS
Balance Sheet
December 31, 1983

Assets		Liabilities and Owner's Equity	
Cash	$ 1,900	Accounts payable	$ 1,600
Repair supplies	2,000	Note payable (due 1/1/1985)	10,000
Repair equipment	14,000	Total Liabilities	$11,600
		R. Young, capital[a]	6,300
		Total Liabilities and	
Total Assets	$17,900	Owner's Equity	$17,900

[a] Beginning capital − net loss.

Ray is upset and says to you, "I don't know how I could have a net loss in 1983. Maybe I did something wrong when I made out these financial statements. Could you help me? My business has been good in 1983. In these times of rising prices, people have been getting their appliances and other items repaired by me instead of buying new ones. I used to have to rent my repair equipment, but business was so good that I purchased $14,000 of repair equipment at the beginning of the year. I know this equipment will last 10 years even though it won't be worth anything at the end of that time. I did have to sign a note for $10,000 of the purchase price, but the amount (plus 10% annual interest) will not be due until the beginning of 1985. I still have to rent my repair shop, but I paid $3,600 for 2 years of rent in advance at the beginning of 1983, so I am OK there. And besides, I just counted my repair supplies and I have $700 of supplies left from 1983 which I can use in 1984."

He continues, "I'm not too worried about my cash balance. I know that customers owe me $600 for repair work I just completed in 1983. These are good customers and always pay, but I never tell my bookkeeper about this until I collect the cash. I am sure I will collect in 1984, and that will also make 1984 revenues look good. In fact, it will just about offset the $800 I collected in advance (and recorded as a revenue) from a customer for repair work I said I would do in 1984. I still have to write a check to pay my bookkeeper for his last month's salary, but he was my only employee in 1983. In 1984 I am only going to hire someone on a part-time basis to keep my accounting records. You can have the job, if you can determine whether the net loss is correct, and if not, what it should be and what I am doing wrong."

Required: 1. Prepare any adjusting entries you think are appropriate for 1983. Show any calculations in your explanations.
2. Prepare closing entries for 1983.
3. Prepare a corrected 1983 income statement, statement of changes in owner's equity, and ending balance sheet (report form).
4. Write a brief report to Ray Young summarizing your suggestions for improving his accounting practices.

C4-2   Effects of Adjusting Entry Errors.   During the current accounting period the book-keeper for the Nallen Company made the following errors in the year-end adjusting entries:

			Effect of Error on:			
Error	Revenues	Expenses	Net Income	Assets	Liabilities	Owner's Equity
Example: Failed to record $200 of accrued salaries	N	U $200	O $200	N	U $200	O $200
1. Failed to adjust prepaid insurance for $300 of expired insurance.						
2. Failed to record $500 of interest expense that had accrued during the period.						
3. Inadvertently recorded $400 of annual depreciation twice for the same equipment.						
4. Failed to record $100 of interest revenue that had accrued during the period.						
5. Failed to reduce unearned revenues for $600 of revenues that were earned during the period.						

Required: Assuming that the errors are not discovered, indicate the effect of each error on revenues, expenses, net income, assets, liabilities, and owner's equity at the end of the accounting period. Use the following code: O = Overstated, U = Understated, and N = No effect. Include dollar amounts. Be prepared to explain your answers.

5 | Accounting for a Merchandising Company

After reading this chapter, you should understand:

- How to record sales, sales discounts, and sales returns and allowances
- How to record purchases, purchases discounts, and purchases returns and allowances
- How to compute cost of goods sold for a merchandising company
- The sections (and items in each section) of a classified income statement and classified balance sheet
- How to prepare closing entries for a merchandising company
- How to prepare a worksheet for a merchandising company

In the first four chapters we developed an accounting system and accounting process for service companies. A service company provides a service to its customers and records the related revenues and expenses to determine its net income. Another type of business entity, the merchandising company, is very important in business today. **A merchandising company is a business entity that purchases goods (*merchandise*) for resale to its customers in order to earn a net income.** Merchandising companies can be *retailers*, such as shoestores, department stores, or automobile dealerships, which sell their goods directly to the final consumer. Or they can be *wholesalers*, such as plumbing supply stores, electrical suppliers, or beverage distributors, which primarily sell their goods to retailers or other commercial users. Whether these merchandising companies are retailers or wholesalers, the accounting systems used are similar to, but more extensive than, systems used for service companies. An accounting system for a merchandising company must record, retain, and report information about the purchase and sale of its merchandise. These accounting issues are the main focus of this chapter.

SALES

A merchandising company sells goods to customers either for cash or on account. Occasionally these goods are returned by customers or are found to be damaged. When goods are sold on credit some merchandising companies offer incentives for prompt payment. These aspects of sales are discussed next.

Sales Revenues Whether the customer buys goods for cash or on credit most merchandising companies use a revenue account entitled *Sales Revenues,* or simply, *Sales,* to record the transaction. For instance, a cash sale of merchandise for $300 is recorded as:

```
1983
May 9   Cash . . . . . . . . . . . . . . . . . . . . . . . . . . . . .   300
             Sales . . . . . . . . . . . . . . . . . . . . . . . . . . .          300
        To record the cash sale of merchandise.
```

Alternatively, if the same sale had been made on account it would be recorded as:

```
1983
May 9   Accounts Receivable  . . . . . . . . . . . . . . . . . .   300
             Sales . . . . . . . . . . . . . . . . . . . . . . . . . . .          300
        To record the sale of merchandise on account.
```

For a sale on account the source document for the transaction is called a sales invoice, or simply, an invoice. **An invoice is a business document that lists the terms of a sale, including the customer's name and address, date of sale, items sold and selling price, total amount, payment terms, and other information.** (The source document for a purchase, which is discussed later, is the same invoice made out by the supplier.) An example of an invoice is shown in Exhibit 5-1.

EXHIBIT 5-1   Example of Sales Invoice

GIBBS HOME FURNISHINGS, INC., Providence Plaza, 203 E. Leslie Lane, Columbia, Mo. 65201, (314) 449-1716

SOLD TO
Mr. Roger Younger
2802 Middlebush Drive
Columbia, Missouri 65201

SHIPPED TO
Same

Date	Date Shipped	Shipped Via	Your Order No.	F.O.B.	Terms	Invoice No.
3/2/83	Same	Local	—	Destination	n/30	**002676**

Quantity	Description		Price	Amount
1	43411-120 Triple Dresser / 43411-220 Mirror / 43411-311 Chest / 43411-120 H Board	Reg. $1,198.00 Sale	$ 799.00	
1	5/0 Mattress		278.00	
1	5/0 Box Spring			
1	R.O. Bed Frame W/Center Support		36.00	
	Subtotal		$1,113.00	
	Sales Tax		51.48	
	Total			$1,164.48

Reprinted with permission.

Sales Returns and Allowances

When merchandise is sold to a customer, it is assumed by both the merchandising company and the customer that the merchandise is not damaged and is acceptable to the customer. Occasionally, upon checking the merchandise after purchase, the customer may find that it is damaged, of inferior quality, or simply the wrong size or color. Most merchandising companies have a *satisfaction guaranteed* policy and allow the customer to return the merchandise or make an adjustment in the sales price. **A sales return is the return of previously purchased merchandise by a customer.** The effect of a sales return is to cancel the sale. **A sales allowance occurs when the customer agrees to keep the merchandise, and an adjustment (reduction) is made in the original sales price.** In either case a source document called a credit memo is prepared. **A credit memo is a business document that lists the information for a sales return or allowance.** A credit memo includes the customer's name and address, how the original sale was made (cash or on account), the reason for the sales return or allowance, the items returned or upon which the allowance is given, and the amount of the return or allowance.

When the merchandise was originally sold the revenue account Sales was increased (credited) for the amount of the sale. For a sales return, the Sales account could be decreased (debited) for the amount of the return. For a sales allowance, the Sales account also could be decreased for the amount of the allowance. Both transactions are reductions of sales recorded earlier. Most merchandising companies do *not* reduce the Sales account directly, however. **A Sales Returns and Allowances account is used to record the total sales returns and allowances.** This account is a contra account to the Sales account and thus has a debit balance and is increased by debit entries and decreased by credit entries. The Sales Returns and Allowances account provides useful information to the managers of a merchandising company and to other users about customer satisfaction with the company's merchandise.

The credit memo is used as the source document to record the return or allowance. The amount is listed on the credit memo. If the original sale had been made for cash, a cash refund is typically given to the customer. If the original sale had been made on account and the account has not been collected, the customer's account is reduced (credited) by the amount of the return or allowance. (The source document is called a *credit* memo because it lists the *credit* to the Cash or Accounts Receivable account.)

To illustrate this procedure assume that a customer returns merchandise that had been sold to the customer on account for $100. The following entry would be made to record the return:

```
1983
June 8   Sales Returns and Allowances . . . . . . . . . . . .   100
              Accounts Receivable . . . . . . . . . . . . . . .          100
         To record return of merchandise originally sold on
         account.
```

Assume that another customer purchased goods for $80 cash and, upon unpacking the goods, found that they had been slightly damaged. The customer agrees to keep the goods but is allowed a $20 reduction (i.e., allowance) in the original sales price. A cash refund is given and the following entry would be made:

```
1983
July 19   Sales Returns and Allowances . . . . . . . . . . . . .   20
            Cash . . . . . . . . . . . . . . . . . . . . . . . . . . . . .          20
          To record allowance given to customer for damaged
          merchandise.
```

The recording of sales returns and allowances, as discussed, is consistent with the definition of revenues. Revenues include the prices charged to a company's customers for goods sold during an accounting period. When sales returns or allowances are recorded in the Sales Returns and Allowances account, since this account is a contra account to Sales, revenues are reduced because part (or all) of the prices charged to customers is returned to them.

Sales Discounts

When merchandise is sold on account the terms of payment are normally listed on the sales invoice. These terms vary from company to company, although most competing companies tend to have similar credit terms. Many companies offer a cash discount as an incentive for early payment of accounts by customers. **A cash discount is a percentage reduction of the invoice price for payment of the invoice within a specified time period.**

The payment terms for an invoice are usually expressed in a standard format. For instance, a common payment term is n/10/EOM. This term means that the total amount (n) of the invoice is due 10 days after the end of the month (EOM) in which the sale occurred. Thus if a credit sale is made on July 7, 1983, payment of the invoice is due by the 10th of August.

In the previous example no cash discount was allowed for early payment. Cash discount terms might read 2/10, n/30. The first number is the percentage discount (2%) and the second number (10) is the number of days in the discount period. **The discount period is the period of time from the date of the invoice within which the customer must pay the invoice to receive the cash discount.** The term n/30 means that full payment of the invoice is due within 30 days of the invoice date. Thus 2/10, n/30 is read as "a 2% discount is allowed if the invoice is paid within 10 days and the total amount of the invoice is due within 30 days." If a $500 sale on account is made with terms of 2/10, n/30 and the customer pays the invoice within 10 days, $490 would be collected [$500 − (.02 × $500)].

When a sale is made on account and the terms of payment include cash discount terms, Accounts Receivable is increased (debited) and Sales is increased (credited) for the full invoice price because the merchandising company does not know whether the customer will pay within the discount period. If the customer pays the invoice (less the discount) within the discount period, the cash collected from the sale is less than the accounts receivable initially recorded. The sales revenue initially recorded at the time of the sale was essentially overstated. **Sales Discounts, which is a contra account to Sales, is used to record the amount of cash**

discounts taken by customers in the accounting period. This account is used instead of reducing the Sales account directly. Because Sales Discounts is a contra account to Sales, this account has a debit balance.

To illustrate this procedure assume that on March 16, 1983, a customer purchased $1,000 of merchandise on account, with terms of 3/10, n/30. The customer remitted a check for $970 [$1,000 − (.03 × $1,000)] on March 25, 1983. The entries to record the sale and collection are as follows:

```
1983
Mar. 16   Accounts Receivable  . . . . . . . . . . . . . . .   1,000
              Sales . . . . . . . . . . . . . . . . . . . . .           1,000
          To record sales on account.

      25  Cash . . . . . . . . . . . . . . . . . . . . . . .     970
          Sales Discounts  . . . . . . . . . . . . . . . .        30
              Accounts Receivable . . . . . . . . . . . . .           1,000
          To record collection of March 16 invoice, less 3% cash
          discount.
```

Two additional points are important for sales discounts. First, if a sales return or allowance is allowed on an invoice, the cash discount terms apply to the amount owed on the invoice *after* deducting the return or allowance. This is because the cash discount is allowed only on the amount of the goods actually purchased by the customer. Second, if a customer pays for an invoice after the discount period has expired, the collection of the total invoice price is recorded in the usual manner as a debit (increase) to Cash and a credit (decrease) to Accounts Receivable.

Net Sales Because contra accounts for sales returns and allowances and sales discounts are used to reduce the total amount of sales revenues, the revenues section of a merchandising company's income statement must be expanded to include these items. On the income statement both the Sales Returns and Allowances account and the Sales Discounts account are deducted from the Sales account to determine Net Sales. The Sales account is frequently entitled *Gross Sales* on the income statement to show that it is not the same as the Net Sales. Exhibit 5-2 illustrates the revenues section of a typical merchandising company.

EXHIBIT 5-2
Partial Income
Statement

HINES DEPARTMENT STORE		
Partial Income Statement		
For Year Ended December 31, 1983		
Revenues:		
Gross sales		$89,200
Less: Sales returns and allowances	$2,900	
Sales discounts	3,600	6,500
Net sales		$82,700

Since the Sales Returns and Allowances and Sales Discounts accounts are used to accumulate the returns and allowances and discounts *during* the accounting period, they are temporary accounts. These accounts are closed along with the Sales account at the end of the period. Closing entries for a merchandising company are discussed later in the chapter.

COST OF GOODS SOLD

In the previous section we discussed the additional issues involved in recording the revenues of a merchandising company. In this section we focus on the issues involving the expenses of a merchandising company. Expenses are the costs of providing goods or services during an accounting period. These expenses are matched against the revenues of the period to determine the net income. One of the major expenses of a merchandising company is the cost of goods sold. **Cost of goods sold is the cost of the merchandise (goods) that a merchandising company has sold to its customers during an accounting period.** The way a company determines the amount of cost of goods sold that it reports on its income statement depends upon whether the company uses a perpetual inventory system or a periodic inventory system. **Inventory is the merchandise being held for resale by a merchandising company.** Some companies use the term *merchandise inventory* to refer to these goods.

Perpetual Inventory System

Some merchandising companies use a perpetual inventory system. **A perpetual inventory system is a system in which a continuous record is kept of the cost of inventory on hand and the cost of inventory sold.** When an item of inventory is purchased for resale a journal entry is recorded to increase (debit) the asset account, Inventory (or Merchandise Inventory), for the invoice cost of the merchandise. When merchandise is sold, not only is a journal entry made to record the sale, but a journal entry is also made to reduce (credit) the Inventory account and to increase (debit) an expense account entitled Cost of Goods Sold. Hence the Inventory and Cost of Goods Sold accounts are perpetually up to date. In addition, a written record is also kept of the physical quantities of inventory purchased and sold, and therefore the physical quantity of inventory on hand is always known.

To illustrate this procedure assume on April 4, 1983, a company makes a $2,000 cash purchase of goods for resale. On April 8, 1983, it sells $500 of these goods to customers at a cash selling price of $900. If the company used a perpetual inventory system, the following journal entries would be made to record the purchase and subsequent sale of the goods:

```
1983
Apr. 4  Inventory . . . . . . . . . . . . . . . . . . . . . . . . . .   2,000
            Cash . . . . . . . . . . . . . . . . . . . . . . . . . . .          2,000
        To record the purchase of merchandise.
```

Apr. 8	Cash	900	
	Sales		900
	To record the cash sale of merchandise.		
8	Cost of Goods Sold	500	
	Inventory		500
	To record the cost of merchandise sold.		

Note that on April 8 the company made two journal entries. The first was made to record the inflow of assets and revenue based on the *selling price* of the merchandise. The second was made to record the outflow of assets and the expense based on the *cost* of the merchandise that was sold.

The ending balance of the Cost of Goods Sold account would be listed on the income statement in a separate section as a deduction from Net Sales. Since the Cost of Goods Sold account is a temporary account used to accumulate the expense of the merchandise sold during the period, the account is closed at the end of each accounting period. Both the income statement and closing entries are discussed later in this chapter.

The perpetual inventory system is usually used when a merchandising company sells relatively few items at a high selling price and the cost of each item sold is easily determined. Examples of merchandising companies using this system are automobile dealers, jewelers, and appliance retailers. A perpetual system is less common when a merchandising company sells a high volume of low-priced items because the cost of each item may not be easily determined. Perpetual inventory systems are discussed in more detail in Chapter 9. The remainder of this section deals with the accounting for a merchandising company that uses a periodic inventory system.

Periodic Inventory System   **A periodic inventory system is a system in which a continuous record of the inventory on hand is not kept and a physical count of the inventory is taken periodically at the end of each accounting period.**[1] The only time that the cost of the inventory on hand is known is when the periodic inventory is taken. Each time a sale is made, a record of the cost of goods sold is *not* made. The cost of goods sold for the accounting period is calculated by deducting the ending inventory from the cost of goods available for sale during the period. The items that are included in this calculation are as follows:

Cost of Goods Available for Sale = **Beginning Inventory + Purchases**
                     − Purchases Returns and Allowances
                     − Purchase Discounts Taken
                     + Transportation-In

Cost of Goods Sold = **Cost of Goods Available for Sale**
                     − Ending Inventory

---

[1] The process of taking the inventory is discussed in Chapter 9.

**EXHIBIT 5-3
Partial Income
Statement**

HINES DEPARTMENT STORE Partial Income Statement For Year Ended December 31, 1983		
Cost of Goods Sold:		
Inventory, January 1, 1983		$10,300
Purchases	$47,200	
Less: Purchases returns and allowances	(1,800)	
Purchases discounts taken	(3,100)	
Plus: Transportation-in	4,300	
Net purchases		46,600
Cost of goods available for sale		$56,900
Less: Inventory, December 31, 1983		11,600
Cost of Goods Sold		$45,300

These calculations are shown directly on the income statement, as illustrated in Exhibit 5-3. Each component of cost of goods sold is discussed next.

INVENTORY. In the periodic inventory system a physical count of the inventory is taken at the end of each accounting period. At that time the goods on hand are counted and their costs determined. This amount is then recorded in the Inventory account. (This procedure is discussed later.) Thus, as opposed to the perpetual inventory system, the Inventory account in a periodic system is up to date only at the time of the periodic count at the end of the accounting period. This ending inventory of the current period is also the beginning inventory of the next period. Thus in Exhibit 5-3 the January 1, 1983, beginning inventory of $10,300 was the December 31, 1982, ending inventory on the 1982 income statement. The December 31, 1983, ending inventory of $11,600 will also be the January 1, 1984, beginning inventory on the 1984 income statement. Inventories, as well as the other components of cost of goods sold, are discussed in more detail in Chapter 9.

PURCHASES. The cost of merchandise purchased during an accounting period is not recorded directly in the Inventory account. A temporary account is used instead. **The Purchases account is used to record the invoice cost of the merchandise acquired for resale during an accounting period.** Since the Purchases account is used to increase cost of goods sold (an expense of operations), the Purchases account has a debit balance and is increased by debit entries. All purchases of merchandise for resale, whether for cash or on account, are included in the Purchases account. The source document used to record the purchase is an invoice from the supplier.

To illustrate this procedure assume that on June 7 and 9, 1983, a company purchased merchandise costing $400 and $700, respectively. The first purchase was for cash, and the second was on account. The journal entries made to record these purchases are as follows:

1983

June 7   Purchases   400
              Cash   400
          To record cash purchases.

      9   Purchases   700
              Accounts Payable   700
          To record purchases on account.

It is important to remember that the Purchases account shows only the invoice cost of the goods purchased for resale during the accounting period. The balance or change in the account at any time or for any period does *not* disclose any information about whether the goods purchased during the period are still on hand or have been sold. The Purchases account is closed at the end of each accounting period.

PURCHASES RETURNS AND ALLOWANCES.   When merchandise for resale is purchased from a supplier both the supplier and the merchandising company assume that the goods will be of acceptable quality. For various reasons, after a purchase has been recorded, it may be discovered that certain merchandise is unacceptable to the merchandising company. (Often this discovery is made when a customer of the merchandising company is granted a sales return or allowance.) **A purchases return is a return of the merchandise to the supplier and a cancellation of the purchase. A purchases allowance is an adjustment (reduction) in the purchase price that is made when the merchandising company agrees to keep the goods**. In either case a debit memo is prepared. **A debit memo is a business document that lists the information for a purchases return or allowance.** A debit memo includes the supplier's name and address, the terms of the original purchase, the reason for the purchases return or allowance, and the items and amount involved.

Control of purchases returns and allowances is very important to the efficient management of a merchandising company. Customer satisfaction with the quality of goods offered for sale by a merchandising company is directly affected by the quality of merchandise purchased from suppliers. In addition, the return (or allowance) of purchased merchandise is a time-consuming and costly process. An initial step in this control process is to keep an accurate record of the cost of any purchases returns and allowances. **A Purchases Returns and Allowances account is used to record the total purchases returns and allowances.** This account is used instead of reducing Purchases directly for these costs. The Purchases Returns and Allowances account is a contra account to Purchases, and therefore it has a credit balance.

The debit memo (so called because it lists the *debit* to Cash or Accounts Payable) is used as the source document to record the return or allowance. If the original purchase was for cash, a cash refund is received from the supplier. If the purchase was on account, accounts payable is reduced (debited). To illustrate this procedure suppose that merchandise which had been previously purchased on account is found to be of inferior quality and the supplier grants an allowance of $80. The merchandising company would record the allowance as follows:

```
1983
Feb.  4   Accounts Payable  . . . . . . . . . . . . . . . . . . . . . . . .    80
               Purchases Returns and Allowances  . . . . . . . . . .         80
          To record allowance given by supplier for inferior
          merchandise.
```

If $60 of goods previously purchased for cash are returned to a supplier, a cash refund would be received and the following entry recorded:

```
1983
Nov.  8   Cash . . . . . . . . . . . . . . . . . . . . . . . . . . . . . .    60
               Purchases Returns and Allowances  . . . . . . . . . .         60
          To record goods returned to supplier for cash refund.
```

Since the Purchases Returns and Allowances account is used to accumulate the total returns and allowances for the accounting period, it is deducted from Purchases on the income statement and is closed at the end of the period.

PURCHASES DISCOUNTS TAKEN.   When merchandise is purchased on account, the payment terms are listed on the invoice. Many suppliers offer a cash discount[2] if payment is made within the specified discount period. These terms are expressed as discussed earlier, for example, 2/10, n/30. All cash discounts on purchases should be taken because of the high annual interest rate involved, and many companies establish procedures designed to make sure that this is done. The interest rate and payment procedures are discussed in Chapters 9 and 10.

When a purchase is made on account and cash discount terms are involved, Purchases is increased (debited) and Accounts Payable is increased (credited) for the full invoice amount.[3] If payment is made within the discount period the Purchases account is not directly reduced. **A Purchases Discounts Taken account is used instead to record all cash discounts taken.** This account is a contra account to Purchases, and therefore it has a credit balance.

To illustrate this procedure assume that on October 11, 1983, a merchandising company purchased $2,000 of goods from a supplier on account, with terms 2/10, n/30. The company remitted (issued) a check for $1,960 [$2,000 − (.02 × $2,000)] on October 21, 1983. The entries to record the purchase and payment are as follows:

---

[2] Another type of discount is the trade discount. **Trade discounts are reductions in the list or catalog price of a merchandise item, and are usually shown as a percentage of the list price.** For example, if goods with a list price of $1,000 subject to a 20% discount are purchased, the invoice price is $800 [$1,000 − (.20 × $1,000)]. Trade discounts are *not* recorded by the merchandising company; thus the above purchase would be recorded at $800. Trade discounts are discussed more fully in Chapter 9.

[3] Some companies initially record their purchases and accounts payable at the net amount after deducting the cash discount. This method of handling cash discounts is discussed in Chapter 9.

```
1983
Oct. 11   Purchases  . . . . . . . . . . . . . . . . . . . . . . .   2,000
              Accounts Payable  . . . . . . . . . . . . . . .              2,000
          To record purchases on account; terms 2/10, n/30.

     21   Accounts Payable  . . . . . . . . . . . . . . . . .   2,000
              Purchases Discounts Taken . . . . . . . . . . .                40
              Cash . . . . . . . . . . . . . . . . . . . . . .             1,960
          To record payment of October 11 invoice, less 2%
          cash discount.
```

Two additional points are important for purchases discounts. First, if a purchases return or allowance is granted on an invoice the cash discount terms apply to the amount owed on the invoice *after* deducting the return or allowance. Second, if payment is made after the discount period has expired the payment of the total invoice price is recorded in the usual manner as a debit (decrease) to Accounts Payable and a credit (decrease) to Cash. The balance of the Purchases Discounts Taken account is deducted from Purchases on the income statement and is closed at the end of the accounting period.

TRANSPORTATION COSTS.   When merchandise is purchased for resale it must be shipped from the supplier to the merchandising company. With the increase in energy costs, shipping costs have become more significant. Whether the supplier or the purchaser is responsible for payment of the freight charges associated with purchased merchandise depends upon the terms agreed to at the time of purchase. These terms are typically included on the purchase invoice.[4] When the merchandising company agrees to pay the freight charges, these costs are, in effect, a cost of purchasing the merchandise. **Transportation-In (or Freight-In) is an account used to record the freight charges incurred for shipments of merchandise purchased from suppliers.** This account is used instead of including the freight charges directly in the Purchases account. The Transportation-In account has a debit balance since it increases the total cost of purchases for the period. The freight bill presented by the freight company is the source document used to record the transportation charges.

To illustrate this procedure suppose that a merchandising company agrees to pay freight charges on goods purchased from a supplier. The merchandising company is billed $70 by the freight company for the delivered merchandise. The journal entry to record the payment of the freight charges on August 9, 1983, is as follows:

---

[4] As can be seen in Exhibit 5-1, freight terms are expressed as *FOB destination*, which means the supplier is responsible for paying the freight, or *FOB shipping point*, which means the purchaser is responsible for payment of the freight charges. These terms are discussed more fully in Chapter 9.

```
1983
Aug.  9   Transportation-In . . . . . . . . . . . . . . . . . . . . . . . .  70
            Cash . . . . . . . . . . . . . . . . . . . . . . . . . . . . . . . .       70
          To record payment of freight charges on purchases.
```

The balance of Transportation-In is added to Purchases on the income statement and is closed at the end of the accounting period.

It is important to distinguish clearly between the payment of freight charges on purchased goods from the payment of freight charges on goods shipped to customers. When the merchandising company agrees to pay the freight charges on shipments of merchandise to customers, these freight charges are a delivery expense of the accounting period. **Transportation-Out (or Freight-Out) is the account used to record the freight charges incurred for shipments of merchandise sold to customers.**

To illustrate this procedure suppose that a merchandising company ships merchandise to customers and is billed $40 by the freight company for the delivery. The journal entry to record the payment of the freight charges on May 4, 1983, is as follows:

```
1983
May  4   Transportation-Out . . . . . . . . . . . . . . . . . . . . . .  40
            Cash . . . . . . . . . . . . . . . . . . . . . . . . . . . . . . . .       40
          To record payment of freight charges on merchandise
          shipped to customers.
```

Transportation-Out is a selling expense (discussed later) on the income statement and is closed at the end of the accounting period.

COST OF GOODS AVAILABLE AND SOLD.   As we noted in the previous discussion, in a periodic inventory system Transportation-In is added to Purchases and Purchases Returns and Allowances and Purchases Discounts Taken are subtracted. These calculations are shown on the income statement, and the end result is entitled *Net Purchases*. The net purchases are added to the beginning inventory (remember that this inventory is the ending inventory of the previous accounting period) to determine the Cost of Goods Available for Sale during the current accounting period. The ending inventory (determined by a physical count at the end of the period) is subtracted from the cost of goods available for sale to derive Cost of Goods Sold. These calculations were shown in Exhibit 5-3.

CLASSIFIED FINANCIAL STATEMENTS

In the early chapters we used only a limited number of accounts in our discussion. Regardless of whether a business entity is a service or merchandising company, as a general rule the larger the company the more accounts it needs in its chart of accounts. These accounts are necessary to record and retain the financial information from the many types of transactions of the company. When a company prepares its financial statements, it is useful to group the accounts on each financial statement in a way that will help the readers of the financial statement in decision making. **A classified financial statement is a statement in which the accounts are grouped into selected categories to provide more useful information for the users of the statement.** The groupings in a classified financial statement will depend upon the way the company is organized and its type of operations. Basic classifications have been developed, however, and the way in which they apply to a merchandising company is the focus of this section.

Classified Income Statement

A classified income statement of a company has two parts: an *operating income* component and an *other revenues and expenses* component. **Operating income includes all the revenues earned and expenses incurred in the normal day-to-day operating activities of the company.** This is true regardless of whether a business is a merchandising or service company. **Other revenues and expenses include any items of revenue and expense that are not related to the primary operations of the company.** The operating income component of a merchandising company is usually much more complex than that of a service company and has three sections: (1) revenues, (2) cost of goods sold, and (3) operating expenses. The complete 1983 income statement of the Hines Department Store is presented in Exhibit 5-4. The items on the income statement are discussed next.

REVENUES. The revenues section includes the revenues earned from the sale of merchandise to customers. This section begins with gross sales from which sales returns and allowances given to customers and sales discounts taken by credit customers are subtracted. The end result is entitled net sales and amounts to $82,700 for the Hines Department Store.

COST OF GOODS SOLD AND GROSS PROFIT. Cost of goods sold is the total cost of the merchandise that has been sold to customers during the accounting period. Because the cost of goods sold is such an important expense of a merchandising company, it is listed in a separate section of the income statement, directly below the revenues section and above the operating expenses section. For a company using a perpetual inventory system, the amount of cost of goods sold is the ending balance in the cost of goods sold account. For companies using a periodic inventory system, the amount of cost of goods sold is calculated directly on the income statement, as shown in Exhibit 5-4. The amount of cost of goods sold is subtracted from net sales to determine the *gross profit* (or *gross margin*). For the Hines Department Store, the $45,300 cost of goods sold is deducted from the $82,700 net sales to derive a gross profit of $37,400.

The gross profit is sometimes referred to as the portion of profits remaining to cover the operating expenses. Although cost of goods sold is shown separately from the other expenses to determine gross profit, nonetheless it is still an expense. Although some expenses are more "avoidable" than cost of goods sold, *all* expenses must be covered in order to earn a net income and there is no priority in the coverage of expenses.

OPERATING EXPENSES. The operating expenses are the expenses (other than cost of goods sold) incurred in the normal day-to-day operations of the merchandising

EXHIBIT 5-4
Income Statement

HINES DEPARTMENT STORE
Income Statement
For Year Ended December 31, 1983

Revenues:			
Gross sales			$89,200
Less: Sales returns and allowances		$ 2,900	
Sales discounts		3,600	6,500
Net sales			$82,700
Cost of Goods Sold:			
Inventory, January 1, 1983		$10,300	
Purchases	$47,200		
Less: Purchases returns and allowances	(1,800)		
Purchases discounts taken	(3,100)		
Plus: Transportation-in	4,300		
Net purchases		46,600	
Cost of goods available for sale		$56,900	
Less: Inventory, December 31, 1983		11,600	
Cost of goods sold			45,300
Gross profit			$37,400
Operating Expenses:			
Selling expenses:			
Depreciation expense: store equipment	$ 1,400		
Depreciation expense: building (sales space)	2,500		
Advertising expense	3,900		
Sales salaries expense	4,200		
Transportation-out	1,100		
Store supplies used	600		
Total selling expenses		$13,700	
General and administrative expenses:			
Depreciation expense: office equipment	$ 1,200		
Depreciation expense: building (office space)	900		
Office salaries expense	2,700		
Administrative salaries expense	3,600		
Office supplies expense	800		
Insurance expense	200		
Total general and administrative expenses		9,400	
Total operating expenses			23,100
Operating income			$14,300
Other Revenues and Expenses:			
Interest revenue		$ 1,300	
Rent revenue (from specialty shop in store)		900	
Interest expense		(700)	
Nonoperating income			1,500
Net Income			$15,800

company. The operating expenses section of the income statement is frequently separated into two parts, selling expenses and general and administrative expenses. **Selling expenses are the operating expenses directly related or allocated to the sales activities of a company.** Sales activities are activities involved in the actual sale and delivery of merchandise to customers. Selling expenses include such items as sales salaries expense, advertising expense, and transportation-out. **General and administrative expenses are the operating expenses directly related or allocated to the general management of a company.** They include such items as office salaries expense, insurance expense, and office supplies expense.

Sometimes an operating expense is not directly related to either the sales activities or the general management of the company. The total expense, however, may be allocated to selling expenses and general and administrative expenses on a reasonable basis. For instance, many merchandising companies that have their sales floor and offices in the same building will allocate the depreciation expense for the building between selling expenses and general and administrative expenses based upon the proportion of the floor space used for sales activities and office activities. This method is followed by the Hines Department Store in Exhibit 5-4.

The total selling expenses are added to the total general and administrative expenses to determine the total operating expenses. The total operating expenses are deducted from gross profit to determine operating income. The selling expenses of the Hines Department Store total $13,700 while the general and administrative expenses amount to $9,400. The total operating expenses of $23,100 are deducted from the $37,400 gross profit to get the operating income of $14,300.

OTHER REVENUES AND EXPENSES.   The other revenues and expenses (sometimes called the *nonoperating income*) section of the income statement includes the revenues and expenses that are not related to the primary operations of the company. Included in this section are revenues and expenses related to financing the company's operations (e.g., interest revenue and interest expense), revenues and expenses (called gains and losses) from selling depreciable assets for more or less than their book value, and other incidental items (e.g., miscellaneous rent revenue, losses due to theft or fire). These items are discussed more fully later in the book.

NET INCOME.   For a sole proprietorship or partnership, the total amount of the other revenues and expenses (nonoperating income) is added to the operating income to determine the net income. The net income of the Hines Department Store (a sole proprietorship) is $15,800, which was determined by adding the $1,500 nonoperating income to the $14,300 operating income.

Sole proprietorships and partnerships are not subject to income taxes (although, of course, the owners are taxed on the income from the business included in their personal income). Corporations, however, must pay income taxes because they are separate legal entities. These income taxes are an expense of doing business and are computed as a percentage of income before income taxes (the total of operating and nonoperating income). Income tax expense is deducted as the last item in the computation of a corporation's net income. Since a corporation *pays* its income taxes in the next period,[5] income taxes are also shown as a liability on the balance sheet (discussed later).

Since the owners of a corporation hold shares of capital stock, a corporation also reports earnings per share on its income statement, which is shown directly below net income. **Earnings per share is the net income divided by the number of capital shares held by stockholders.** To illustrate earnings per share and income taxes assume that the Hines Department Store is a corporation that has issued 4,000 shares of capital stock to its owners and the company is subject to a 40% income tax rate. The lower portion of the income statement shown in Exhibit 5-4 would be modified as follows:

Income before income taxes	$15,800
Income tax expense	6,320
Net Income	$ 9,480
Earnings per share (4,000 shares)	$ 2.37

The $6,320 would also be shown as income taxes payable on the balance sheet of the corporation. These and other items in a corporation's income statement and balance sheet are discussed more fully in Chapter 15. Because corporations are taxed at such a high rate (nearly 50% in some cases), in later chapters we frequently discuss the impact of accounting practices upon the income taxes of corporations.

Classified Balance Sheet

A classified balance sheet of a sole proprietorship has three major sections: the assets, liabilities, and owner's equity. Within each section the items are classified in an informative manner. Regardless of whether a business entity is a service or merchandising company, a common classification scheme on its balance sheet is as follows:

1. *Assets*
   (a) Current assets
   (b) Long-term investments
   (c) Property and equipment

2. *Liabilities*
   (a) Current liabilities
   (b) Noncurrent liabilities

3. *Owner's Equity*
   (a) Owner's capital account

Even though not every company uses all of these classifications, a discussion of the classification scheme helps in understanding the contents of a classified balance sheet. Each classification is briefly discussed next, and the items within each section are more fully discussed in later chapters. An example of a classified balance sheet (report form) for the Hines Department Store is presented in Exhibit 5-5.

---

[5] Many corporations actually have to pay their income taxes on a quarterly basis, but these payments are beyond the scope of this text. We will assume that all the income taxes for a current period are paid in the next period.

EXHIBIT 5-5
Balance Sheet

HINES DEPARTMENT STORE
Balance Sheet
December 31, 1983

Assets

Current Assets
Cash		$ 5,200
Marketable securities		4,400
Receivables		
Accounts receivable		22,900
Notes receivable (due 7/1/1984)		5,000
Interest receivable (due 7/1/1984)		200
Inventory		11,600
Prepaid items		
Insurance	$ 500	
Store supplies	400	
Office supplies	900	1,800
Total current assets		$ 51,100

Long-term Investments
Government bonds (due 12/31/1990)	$ 6,000	
Notes receivable (due 12/31/1985)	4,000	
Total long-term investments		10,000

Property and Equipment

	Cost	Accumulated Depreciation	Book Value		
Land	$ 8,200	–	$ 8,200		
Building	49,000	$10,900	38,100		
Store equipment	15,500	3,600	11,900		
Office equipment	11,700	2,400	9,300		
Totals	$84,400	$16,900	$67,500		
Total property and equipment					67,500
Total Assets					$128,600

Liabilities

Current Liabilities
Accounts payable	$19,100	
Salaries payable	300	
Notes payable (due 3/1/1984)	3,000	
Interest payable (due 3/1/1984)	100	
Unearned rent	800	
Total current liabilities		$ 23,300

Noncurrent Liabilities
Note payable (due 12/31/1988)	$ 7,000	
Mortgage payable	19,800	
Total noncurrent liabilities		26,800
Total Liabilities		$ 50,100

Owner's Equity

T. Hines, capital (see Schedule A)	78,500
Total Liabilities and Owner's Equity	$128,600

CURRENT ASSETS.   **Current assets are cash and other assets that are reasonably expected to be converted into cash, sold, or consumed within the normal operating cycle or 1 year, whichever is longer.**[6] **An operating cycle is the average time taken by a company to spend cash for inventory, sell the inventory, and collect the receivables, converting them back into cash.** Most companies have operating cycles of a year or less. A few companies such as lumber, distillery, and tobacco companies have operating cycles that are longer than 1 year. In this case the longer time period should be used to determine the current assets. The following items are classified as current assets: (1) cash, (2) marketable securities, (3) receivables, (4) inventory, and (5) prepaid items. These items are presented in the current assets section in the order of their liquidity; that is, according to how quickly they can be converted into cash.

Cash includes cash on hand and in checking and savings accounts. *Marketable securities* are items such as government bonds and capital stock and bonds (these securities are a type of legal note that pays interest) of corporations in which the company has temporarily invested. Alternative captions are *temporary investments* and *short-term investments*. *Receivables* include accounts receivable, notes receivable, and interest receivable with maturity dates of less than 1 year. *Inventory* is goods held for resale. *Prepaid items* such as insurance, rent, office supplies, and store supplies will not be converted into cash but will be consumed. In theory prepaid items should not be classified as current assets in the sense that they are not convertible into cash and do not directly enter into the operating cycle. They are included as current assets, however, because if they had not been paid in advance, cash would have been paid out within the cycle. Furthermore, even though a 2-year prepayment of insurance would extend over more than an annual operating cycle, the payment is usually classified as a current asset for convenience. The current assets of the Hines Department Store total $51,100 as shown in Exhibit 5-5.

Assets that are not classified as current assets are called noncurrent assets. Noncurrent assets include long-term investments and property and equipment.

LONG-TERM INVESTMENTS.   Long-term investments include items such as notes receivable, government bonds, and bonds of corporations with maturity dates more than a year in advance, capital stock of corporations, and other securities. To be classified in the long-term investments section, the company must intend to hold the investment for more than 1 year or the operating cycle, whichever is longer. The long-term investments of Hines Department Store total $10,000 as shown in Exhibit 5-5.

PROPERTY AND EQUIPMENT.   The property and equipment section of the balance sheet includes all the physical, long-term assets used in the operations of the

---

[6]"Restatement and Revision of Accounting Research Bulletins," *Accounting Research and Terminology Bulletins*, Final Edition, No. 43 (New York: AICPA, 1961), ch. 3, sec. A, par. 4.

company. Often these assets are referred to as the *fixed assets* or *operating assets* because of their relative permanency in the company's operations. Assets that have a physical existence such as land, buildings, equipment, and furniture are listed in this category. Except for land, all the fixed assets are depreciable. Land is listed at its original cost while the remaining fixed assets are listed at their book values. A contra account, accumulated depreciation, is used to reduce the fixed assets to their book values while still reporting the historical cost.

Certain long-term lease contracts relating to leased property and equipment are also included in this section. Long-term leases of assets have become a popular way by which a lessee company may acquire the rights to the use of the assets without the initial cash outlay to finance the acquisitions. Since certain leases give the lessee company relatively unrestricted rights to the use of an asset for an extended period of time, the rights are economic resources to the company and an asset is recorded even though the asset is not legally owned. The property and equipment section of the Hines Department Store totals $67,500 as shown on Exhibit 5-5.

CURRENT LIABILITIES.   **Current liabilities are obligations that are expected to be paid within the next year (or operating cycle, if longer) and whose payment is reasonably expected to require the use of existing current assets.**

The following types of liabilities should be included as current liabilities:

1. Obligations for items (goods or services) that have entered the operating cycle. These obligations would include accounts payable, salaries payable, and the like.
2. Advance collections for the future delivery of goods or performance of services, for instance, unearned rent and unearned legal fees. These items are referred to as unearned revenues.
3. Other obligations that will be paid within 1 year or the operating cycle, such as short-term notes payable and interest payable, and income taxes payable (for corporations).[7]

The current liabilities of the Hines Department Store total $23,300 as shown in Exhibit 5-5.

NONCURRENT LIABILITIES.   Noncurrent liabilities are obligations that are not expected to require the use of current assets within the next year or operating cycle (if longer than a year). Noncurrent liabilities are also called *long-term* liabilities because usually these obligations are outstanding for several years. Included in this category are such items as long-term notes payable, obligations for long-term lease contracts, mortgages payable, and bonds payable (in the case of corporations). The noncurrent liabilities of the Hines Department Store are $26,800 as shown in Exhibit 5-5.

---

[7] Ibid., par. 7.

EXHIBIT 5-6
Statement of Changes
in Owner's Equity

HINES DEPARTMENT STORE
Schedule A
Statement of Changes in Owner's Equity
For Year Ended December 31, 1983

T. Hines, capital, January 1, 1983	$70,700
Add: Net income	15,800
	$86,500
Less: Withdrawals	(8,000)
T. Hines, capital, December 31, 1983	$78,500

OWNER'S EQUITY. Owner's equity is the current investment of the owner in the assets of the company; that is, the equity of the owner is the company's assets less the liabilities. For a sole proprietorship, whether the business entity is a service or merchandising company, the total ending owner's equity is listed in a single *capital* account. For a partnership the total ending owners' equity is divided into separate partner's capital accounts. The ending balance in the capital account(s) may be affected by additional investments, net income, or withdrawals. To report these items, a separate schedule, the statement of changes in owner's equity (for a sole proprietorship) or the statement of changes in partners' equity (for a partnership) is prepared. This schedule is a supporting schedule to the balance sheet. An example is presented in Exhibit 5-6. The Hines Department Store owner's equity totals $78,500 as shown in Exhibit 5-5.

MODIFICATIONS OF OWNERS' EQUITY FOR CORPORATIONS. A corporation is a separate legal entity that must adhere to the laws of the state in which it is based. Many state laws affect the accounting for stockholders' equity (the term used for owners' equity) on the balance sheet of a corporation. To adhere to these laws stockholders' equity is separated into two sections, contributed capital and retained earnings.

Contributed capital is the total dollar amount of investments made by stockholders into the corporation. Various types of stock are issued to the owners (called stockholders); collectively they are called capital stock. **Capital stock is the term used for shares issued to the owners of a corporation as legal evidence of their ownership.** Accounting for capital stock transactions is fully discussed in Chapter 14. Here it is sufficient to know that for certain capital stock, the total amount invested by stockholders in the corporation is reported in a separate account called Capital Stock. Thus, in the contributed capital section of stockholders' equity, the item Capital Stock, $26,000, means that stockholders have invested this amount in the corporation.

Retained earnings is the total lifetime earnings (net income) of a corporation that has not been distributed to stockholders as dividends. Dividends are the amounts distributed to stockholders as a reward (incentive) for investing in the corporation. Each corporation has a Retained Earnings account and may have a

Dividends account. The Retained Earnings account has a credit balance that is reported on a corporate balance sheet in the stockholders' equity section. A Dividends account for a corporation has a debit balance and is similar to the Withdrawals accounts of a sole proprietorship or partnership.

The ending balance in the Capital Stock account is affected by additional stockholders' investments. The ending balance in the Retained Earnings account is affected by the net income and dividends of the current period. To report these items a separate schedule, the statement of changes in stockholders' equity, is prepared as a supporting schedule to the balance sheet of a corporation. This schedule is not illustrated in this chapter but is discussed in Chapter 14.

If the Hines Department Store had been a corporation instead of a sole proprietorship, the stockholders' equity section of the balance sheet in Exhibit 5-5 might appear as follows:

Stockholders' Equity

Contributed capital	
Capital stock	$26,000
Retained earnings	46,180
Total Stockholders' Equity	$72,180

It is important to note that the total stockholders' equity of $72,180 is *not* the same as the $78,500 owners' equity shown in Exhibit 5-5. This is because the net income of the corporation is only $9,480 (as computed earlier) compared to the $15,800 net income shown in Exhibit 5-4, due to the income taxes of $6,320. The balance sheet still "balances," however, because the $6,320 would be listed as a current liability, income taxes payable. Thus as a corporation the Hines Department Store would list current liabilities of $29,620 ($6,320 + $23,300) and total liabilities of $56,420 ($29,620 + $26,800). The total liabilities and stockholders' equity would be $128,600 ($56,420 + $72,180), the same amount as shown in Exhibit 5-5.

WORKING CAPITAL. The working capital of a company relates primarily to the financial resources utilized in its operating cycle. **Working capital is the excess of a company's current assets over its current liabilities.** Although working capital is seldom disclosed on the balance sheet, it is an indicator of the short-run solvency of the company and is often computed by creditors and other users. Often a slightly different computation, the current ratio, is used for the same purpose. **The current ratio is the current assets divided by the current liabilities.** A common "rule of thumb" is that a company's current ratio should be around 2 to 1. A satisfactory current ratio depends upon the type of company, however. Some companies have current assets that are more "liquid" (more easily converted into cash) than other companies. For instance, a company with a high percentage of prepaid items is not as liquid as a company without any prepaid items. The working capital of the Hines Department Store is $27,800 ($51,100 − $23,300) while its current ratio is 2.2 to 1 ($51,100 ÷ $23,300).

A complete set of financial statements of the Royal Crown Companies, Inc. is shown in Appendix A. Some of the items included in the financial statements and related notes are discussed in the later chapters of the book. In reviewing these financial statements, however, you should recognize that we have introduced many of the items in these first five chapters.

CLOSING ENTRIES

Because of the many contra accounts and the importance of cost of goods sold, the closing entries for a merchandising company are more complex than for a service company. The objective is still the same, however, to close the temporary income statement and withdrawals accounts and to update the permanent balance sheet accounts. The 1983 closing entries of the Hines Department Store, a sole proprietorship, are shown in Exhibit 5-7 (based on the account balances shown in Exhibit 5-4) and are discussed next. The closing entries of partnerships and corporations are discussed in later chapters.

Cost of Goods Sold Closing Entries

Because cost of goods sold is such an important operating expense, a merchandising company that uses a periodic inventory system usually uses a Cost of Goods Sold *closing* account in addition to the Income Summary account. (Remember that a company has a Cost of Goods Sold account during the accounting period only if it uses a perpetual inventory system.) For a periodic inventory system all of the accounts used to compute cost of goods sold are first closed to the Cost of Goods Sold account. The balance of the Cost of Goods Sold account is then closed with the remaining expenses to the Income Summary account.

The first two closing entries in Exhibit 5-7 are used to compute the 1983 cost of goods sold. The first closing entry closes the temporary accounts with debit balances (Purchases, Transportation-In, and beginning Inventory) to the Cost of Goods Sold account. It is important to understand the handling of the Inventory account in the closing entries of a company using a periodic inventory system. Under this system the beginning Inventory account balance (remember that this amount is the ending inventory of the previous period) has not changed throughout the entire accounting period. The actual cost of inventory on hand is not known until the end of the accounting period when the periodic inventory is taken. At this point the beginning Inventory account balance is outdated and must be replaced by the cost of the ending inventory. To do this the first step is to close out the beginning inventory by crediting the Inventory account for its beginning balance ($10,300 in this case).

The second closing entry closes the temporary accounts with credit balances (Purchases Returns and Allowances and Purchases Discounts Taken) and records the cost of the ending inventory (as determined by the physical count in the periodic inventory) in the Inventory account. After the two journal entries have been posted, the Purchases, Transportation-In, Purchases Returns and Allowances, and Purchases Discounts Taken accounts all have zero balances. The Cost of Goods Sold account has a $45,300 debit balance ($61,800 − $16,500), which is the 1983 cost of goods sold as shown in the income statement in Exhibit 5-4. The Inventory account has a debit balance of $11,600, the cost of the ending inventory. This is

EXHIBIT 5-7
Hines Department
Store
Closing Entries

		GENERAL JOURNAL		Page 92
Date		Account Titles and Explanations	Debit	Credit
		Closing Entries		
1983 Dec.	31	Cost of Goods Sold	61,800	
		Purchases		47,200
		Transportation-In		4,300
		Inventory (January 1, 1983)		10,300
		To close merchandise costs to cost of goods sold.		
	31	Purchases Returns and Allowances	1,800	
		Purchases Discounts Taken	3,100	
		Inventory (December 31, 1983)	11,600	
		Cost of Goods Sold		16,500
		To close the accounts that reduced the merchandise costs and to establish the ending inventory.		
	31	Sales	89,200	
		Interest Revenue	1,300	
		Rent Revenue	900	
		Income Summary		91,400
		To close the revenue accounts.		
	31	Income Summary	75,600	
		Cost of Goods Sold		45,300
		Sales Returns and Allowances		2,900
		Sales Discounts		3,600
		Depreciation Expense: Store Equipment		1,400
		Depreciation Expense: Building (sales and office space)		3,400
		Advertising Expense		3,900
		Sales Salaries Expense		4,200
		Transportation-Out		1,100
		Store Supplies Used		600
		Depreciation Expense: Office Equipment		1,200
		Office Salaries Expense		2,700
		Administrative Salaries Expense		3,600
		Office Supplies Expense		800
		Insurance Expense		200
		Interest Expense		700
		To close the temporary accounts with debit balances.		
	31	Income Summary	15,800	
		T. Hines, Capital		15,800
		To close Income Summary account and transfer net income to owner's capital account.		
	31	T. Hines, Capital	8,000	
		T. Hines, Withdrawals		8,000
		To close the withdrawals account.		

the result of closing out the beginning balance and establishing the ending balance in the closing entries. The postings to the Inventory account are as follows:

		Inventory		
Balance, 1/1/83	10,300	12/31/83		10,300
12/31/83	11,600			
Balance, 12/31/83	11,600			

Remaining Closing Entries

Once the Cost of Goods Sold account balance has been determined, it is closed to the Income Summary account along with the rest of the revenue and expense accounts. These closing entries for a merchandising company are the same as the entries for a service company, except that they also include the additional contra accounts, Sales Returns and Allowances and Sales Discounts, and the Cost of Goods Sold account. The remaining closing entries for the Hines Department Store are shown in Exhibit 5-7 below the cost of goods sold closing entries (the $8,000 withdrawals information was obtained from Exhibit 5-6).

WORKSHEET FOR MERCHANDISING COMPANY

A merchandising company may use a worksheet to aid in preparing its adjusting entries, closing entries, and financial statements. The steps in completing a worksheet for a merchandising company that uses a periodic inventory system are almost identical to the steps shown in Chapter 4 for a service company. An extra step must be included for a merchandising company, however. The steps to be completed for this worksheet are discussed below as they relate to Exhibit 5-8:

Step 1:   Prepare the trial balance in the trial balance columns. List the account titles and ending account balances from the general ledger. Remember that the Inventory account in the trial balance is the *beginning* balance because no entries have been made in this account during the year. The trial balance for the Cohen Company in Exhibit 5-8 totals $128,300.

Step 2:   Prepare the worksheet adjusting entries. Analyze the accounts and make whatever adjusting entries are necessary to bring the accounts up to date at the end of the period. Use letters of the alphabet to identify each entry and list an explanation for each entry at the bottom of the worksheet. Total the adjustments columns to prove the equality of the total debits and credits. In Exhibit 5-8 two adjusting entries for $1,500 depreciation and $200 accrued salaries were made. The adjustments columns total $1,700.

Step 3:   Prepare an adjusted trial balance. Crossfoot (combine) the trial balance amount of each account with any adjustments to the account. The adjusted trial balance columns total $130,000 in Exhibit 5-8.

Step 4:   Transfer each account balance listed in the adjusted trial balance columns to its respective income statement or balance sheet columns. The beginning inventory account balance is transferred to the *income statement* debit column instead of to the balance sheet. This may be seen for the $18,000 beginning inventory in Exhibit 5-8. It is important to understand why this is the case. Recall that the inventory listed on the adjusted trial balance is the *beginning* inventory. The beginning inventory is added to purchases on the income statement in the calculation of cost of goods available for sale. Therefore it is listed in the income statement debit column. The *ending* inventory will be included on the balance sheet as shown in Step 5.

In transferring the accounts to the respective financial statement columns, special attention should be paid to the new accounts introduced in this chapter (Sales Returns and Allowances, Sales Discounts, Purchases, Transportation-In and -Out, Purchases Returns and Allowances, and Purchases Discounts Taken). All of them are income statement accounts; many of them are contra accounts. A common error is to list one of these account balances in the wrong income statement column (e.g., debit instead of credit column) or to include it in the balance sheet. Be careful when transferring these accounts!

Step 5: Enter the ending inventory on the worksheet. This is the additional step for a merchandising company using a periodic inventory system. The term *Inventory* (and the ending date) is written in the account titles column on the first line below the totals of the adjustments columns and the adjusted trial balance columns. The ending inventory amount (as determined by a physical count) is entered in two columns. First, it is entered in the *credit* column of the income statement. Second, it is entered in the *debit* column of the balance sheet. This may be seen in Exhibit 5-8 for the $21,000 ending inventory (12/31/1983) of the Cohen Company.

It is important to understand why the ending inventory is included in both the income statement and balance sheet. The ending inventory is included in the income statement credit column because it is deducted from cost of goods available for sale in computing cost of goods sold. Since the beginning inventory and purchases (which are used to determine cost of goods available for sale) are listed in the income statement debit column, it is necessary to list the ending inventory in the credit column in order to determine accurately the cost of goods sold and net income. The amount of the ending inventory is listed in the debit column of the balance sheet because this amount will replace the beginning inventory when the closing entries are prepared and will be included in the ending balance sheet.

Step 6: Complete the financial statement columns on the worksheet. Subtotal the income statement columns and the balance sheet columns. The difference between the subtotals of each set of columns is the net income (or net loss). Enter the term *Net Income* in the account titles column. List the amount of the net income directly below the income statement debit column subtotal and the balance sheet credit column subtotal and total each set of columns.[8] The net income of the Cohen Company is $12,000 as shown in Exhibit 5-8. The worksheet is now complete.

---

[8] A net loss would be listed below the income statement *credit* column subtotal and the balance sheet *debit* column subtotal.

EXHIBIT 5-8
Worksheet for a
Merchandising
Company

	COHEN COMPANY Worksheet For Year Ended December 31, 1983				
Account Titles	Trial Balance		Adjustments		
	Debit	Credit	Debit	Credit	
Cash	5,400				
Accounts receivable	9,600				
Inventory (1/1/1983)	18,000				
Property and equipment	30,000				
Accumulated depreciation		12,000		(a) 1,500	
Accounts payable		13,700			
S. Cohen, capital		36,500			
S. Cohen, withdrawals	9,900				
Sales		62,000			
Sales returns and allowances	3,000				
Sales discounts	1,200				
Purchases	40,300				
Purchases returns and allowances		2,800			
Purchases discounts taken		1,300			
Transportation-in	2,400				
Advertising expense	2,300				
Salaries expense	4,400		(b) 200		
Transportation-out	800				
Utilities expense	1,000				
Totals	128,300	128,300			
Depreciation expense			(a) 1,500		
Salaries payable				(b) 200	
			1,700	1,700	
Inventory (12/31/1983)					
Net Income					

Explanations:
(a) To record the annual depreciation expense.
(b) To record accrued salaries at the end of the year.

Once the worksheet is completed, the adjusting entries, closing entries, and financial statements are prepared. The adjusting entries are copied from the worksheet to the general journal (the explanations from the worksheet are used to prepare the explanations in the general journal). The closing entries (as discussed earlier)

Adjusted Trial Balance		Income Statement		Balance Sheet	
Debit	Credit	Debit	Credit	Debit	Credit
5,400				5,400	
9,600				9,600	
18,000		18,000			
30,000				30,000	
	13,500				13,500
	13,700				13,700
	36,500				36,500
9,900				9,900	
	62,000		62,000		
3,000		3,000			
1,200		1,200			
40,300		40,300			
	2,800		2,800		
	1,300		1,300		
2,400		2,400			
2,300		2,300			
4,600		4,600			
800		800			
1,000		1,000			
1,500		1,500			
	200				200
130,000	130,000				
			21,000	21,000	
		75,100	87,100	75,900	63,900
		12,000			12,000
		87,100	87,100	75,900	75,900

are prepared in the general journal based on the amounts in the income statement columns (and the withdrawals amount). The financial statements (including the statement of changes in owner's equity) are prepared from the information in the income statement and balance sheet columns of the worksheet.

REVIEW PROBLEM

The Houston Company has the following adjusted trial balance on December 31, 1983:

Account Titles	Debits	Credits
Cash	$ 1.000	
Accounts receivable	2,700	
Inventory (January 1, 1983)	5,100	
Prepaid insurance	800	
Land	3,200	
Buildings and equipment	31,000	
Accumulated depreciation		$15,000
Accounts payable		3,300
Salaries payable		420
Notes payable (due July 1, 1985)		5,000
Interest payable (due July 1, 1985)		400
Unearned rent		360
A. Roe, capital		16,020
A. Roe, withdrawals	1,200	
Sales		30,000
Sales returns and allowances	2,100	
Rent revenue		1,440
Purchases	15,900	
Purchases returns and allowances		1,240
Freight-in	1,780	
Selling expenses	4,800	
General and administrative expenses	3,200	
Interest expense	400	
Totals	$73,180	$73,180

In addition, the company took its annual physical inventory on December 31, 1983. It determined that its ending inventory is $5,600.

Required: Prepare the following items for 1983:
1. A classified income statement
2. A statement of changes in owner's equity
3. A classified ending balance sheet (report form)
4. Closing entries

**SOLUTION TO
REVIEW
PROBLEM**

Requirement 1:

HOUSTON COMPANY
Income Statement
For Year Ended December 31, 1983

Revenues:			
Sales			$30,000
Less: Sales returns and allowances			2,100
Net sales			$27,900
Cost of Goods Sold:			
Beginning inventory, 1/1/1983		$ 5,100	
Purchases	$15,900		
Less: Purchases returns and allowances	(1,240)		
Plus: Freight-in	1,780		
Net purchases		16,440	
Cost of goods available for sale		$21,540	
Less: Ending inventory, 12/31/1983		5,600	
Cost of goods sold . . . . :			15,940
Gross profit			$11,960
Operating Expenses:			
Selling expenses		$ 4,800	
General and administrative expenses		3,200	
Total operating expenses			8,000
Operating income			$ 3,960
Other Revenues and Expenses:			
Rent revenue		$ 1,440	
Interest expense		(400)	
Nonoperating income			1,040
Net Income			$ 5,000

Requirement 2:

HOUSTON COMPANY
Schedule A
Statement of Changes in Owner's Equity
For Year Ended December 31, 1983

A. Roe, capital, January 1, 1983	$16,020
Add: 1983 net income	5,000
	$21,020
Less: 1983 withdrawals	(1,200)
A. Roe, capital, December 31, 1983	$19,820

Requirement 3:

HOUSTON COMPANY
Balance Sheet
December 31, 1983

Assets

Current Assets
Cash . . . . $ 1,000
Accounts receivable 2,700
Inventory 5,600
Prepaid insurance 800
    Total current assets $10,100

Property and Equipment
Land . . . . $ 3,200
Buildings and equipment $31,000
Less: Accumulated depreciation . . . . (15,000)   16,000
    Total property and equipment $19,200
    Total Assets $29,300

Liabilities

Current Liabilities
Accounts payable . . . . $ 3,300
Salaries payable 420
Unearned rent 360
    Total current liabilities . . . . $ 4,080

Noncurrent Liabilities
Notes payable (due 7/1/1985) . . . . $ 5,000
Interest payable (due 7/1/1985) 400
    Total noncurrent liabilities . . . . $ 5,400
    Total Liabilities . . . . $ 9,480

Owner's Equity

A. Roe, capital (see Schedule A) $19,820
    Total Liabilities and Owner's Equity $29,300

Requirement 4:

GENERAL JOURNAL				Page 79	
Date		Account Titles and Explanations		Debit	Credit
		Closing Entries			
1983 Dec.	31	Cost of Goods Sold		22,780	
		Purchases			15,900
		Freight-In			1,780
		Inventory (January 1, 1983)			5,100
		To close merchandise costs to cost of goods sold.			

31	Purchases Returns and Allowances Inventory (December 31, 1983) Cost of Goods Sold	1,240 5,600	 6,840
	To close account that reduced merchandise costs and to establish the ending inventory.		
31	Sales Rent Revenue Income Summary	30,000 1,440	 31,440
	To close the revenue accounts.		

31	Income Summary
	   Cost of Goods Sold
	   Sales Returns and Allowances
	   Selling Expenses[a]
	   General and Administrative Expenses[a]
	   Interest Expense
		26,440	
			15,940
			2,100
			4,800
			3,200
			400

	To close temporary accounts with debit balances.		
31	Income Summary A. Roe, Capital	5,000	 5,000
	To close net income to the owner's capital account.		
31	A. Roe, Capital A. Roe, Withdrawals	1,200	 1,200
	To close the withdrawals account.		

[a] Each selling expense and general and administrative expense would normally be listed separately on the income statement and closed separately in the closing entries. To save space in this review problem only the totals are listed and closed.

GLOSSARY
Cash Discount. Percentage reduction of the invoice price for payment within the discount period.

Capital Stock. Term used for shares issued to the owners of a corporation as legal evidence of their ownership.

Cost of Goods Available for Sale. Beginning inventory plus purchases and transportation-in, less purchases returns and allowances and purchases discounts taken.

Cost of Goods Sold. Cost of the merchandise (goods) that have been sold to customers during an accounting period. For a periodic inventory system, cost of goods sold equals cost of goods available for sale less ending inventory.

Credit Memo.   Business document used to list the information for a sales return or allowance. Called a credit memo because it shows the amount of the credit (decrease) to cash or accounts receivable.

Current Assets.   Cash and other assets that are reasonably expected to be converted into cash, sold, or consumed during the normal operating cycle or 1 year, whichever is longer. Current assets include cash, marketable securities, receivables, inventory, and prepaid items.

Current Liabilities.   The obligations that are expected to be paid in the next year (or operating cycle, if longer) and whose payment is reasonably expected to require the use of existing current assets. Examples are accounts payable and salaries payable.

Current Ratio.   Current assets divided by current liabilities. Indicator of short-run solvency of a company.

Debit Memo.   Business document used to list the information for a purchases return or allowance. Called a debit memo because it shows the amount of the debit to cash or accounts payable.

General and Administrative Expenses.   Section on a classified income statement. Includes operating expenses directly related or allocated to the general management of a company.

Gross Profit.   Net sales less cost of goods sold.

Income Tax Expense.   Account used to record the income tax expense of a corporation for the accounting period. Deducted from income before income taxes to determine net income.

Inventory.   Merchandise (goods) being held for resale by a merchandising company. Sometimes referred to as *merchandise inventory*.

Invoice.   Business document used to list the information for a sale of merchandise.

Long-Term Investments.   Section on a classified balance sheet for investments in items that a company intends to hold for more than 1 year or the operating cycle, whichever is longer. Examples are investments in government bonds, noncurrent notes receivable, and capital stock and bonds of corporations.

Merchandising Company.   Business entity that purchases goods (merchandise) for resale to its customers. May be a retailer or wholesaler.

Net Sales.   Sales less sales returns and allowances and sales discounts.

Noncurrent Assets.   Assets not classified as current assets. Included are long-term investments and property and equipment.

Noncurrent Liabilities.   Obligations that are not classified as current liabilities. Examples are long-term notes payable and mortgages payable.

Operating Cycle.   Average time taken by a company to spend cash for inventory, sell the inventory, and collect the receivables, converting them back into cash.

Operating Income.   Section of classified income statement that includes all the revenues earned and expenses incurred in the normal day-to-day operating activities of the company.

Other Revenues and Expenses.   Section of classified income statement that includes any items of revenue and expense that are not related to the primary operations of the company.

Periodic Inventory System.   System in which a continuous record is not kept of the cost of inventory on hand and sold during the accounting period. Ending inventory is determined by a physical count.

Perpetual Inventory System.   System in which a continuous record is kept of the cost of inventory on hand and the cost of inventory sold during the accounting period.

Purchases.   Account used in a periodic inventory system to record the cost of goods purchased for resale to customers.

Purchases Discounts Taken.   Contra account to the Purchases account. Used to record the reduction in the amount paid for purchases on account as a result of payment within the discount period.

Purchases Returns and Allowances.   Contra account to the Purchases account. Used to record the cost of goods returned to suppliers or the adjustments (reductions) given by suppliers in the cost of goods purchased because of inferior quality.

Sales.   Revenue account used to record the selling price of goods sold for cash or on account to customers during an accounting period.

Sales Discounts.   Contra account to the Sales account. Used to record the cash discounts taken by credit customers for payment of an invoice within the discount period.

Sales Returns and Allowances.   Contra account to the Sales account. Used to record the selling price of goods returned by customers or allowances (reductions in the sales price) made to customers because of dissatisfaction with the goods.

Selling Expenses.   Section on a classified income statement. Includes operating expenses directly related or allocated to the sales activities of a company.

Transportation-In.   Account used to record the freight charges incurred for shipment of goods purchased from suppliers. Also referred to as *Freight-In*.

Transportation-Out.   Selling expense. Account used to record the freight charges incurred for shipments of merchandise sold to customers. Also referred to as *Freight-Out*.

Working Capital.   Current assets minus current liabilities. Indicator of short-run solvency of a company.

QUESTIONS

Q5-1   What is a merchandising company? Distinguish between a retailer and a wholesaler.

Q5-2   List and define the components of net sales.

Q5-3   Give and explain the debit and credit rules for recording sales returns and allowances and sales discounts.

Q5-4   What is the difference between a sales return and a sales allowance?

Q5-5   What is a cash discount? A discount period? Explain the meaning of the terms 2/10, n/30, and n/15/EOM.

Q5-6   Distinguish between a perpetual and a periodic inventory system. Which is more useful?

Q5-7   For a periodic inventory system give the equations for (1) cost of goods available for sale and (2) cost of goods sold.

Q5-8   List and define the components of net purchases.

Q5-9   Give and explain the debit and credit rules for recording purchases returns and allowances and purchases discounts taken.

Q5-10 What is the difference between transportation-in and transportation-out? Where is each reported on the income statement?

Q5-11 What are classified financial statements?

Q5-12 List the sections of a classified income statement for a merchandising company (sole proprietorship). What items are included in each section? Assume the use of a periodic inventory system.

Q5-13 How does the lower portion of the income statement for a corporation differ from that of a sole proprietorship? Where are income taxes payable reported in the classified financial statements of a corporation?

Q5-14 List the major sections of assets and liabilities in a classified balance sheet. What items are included in each section?

Q5-15 What are the major items included in current assets? Current liabilities? What is working capital? How is the current ratio computed?

Q5-16 What are the differences (if any) in the owners' equity of a (a) sole proprietorship, (b) partnership, and (c) corporation?

Q5-17 For a corporation define the following terms: (a) earnings per share, (b) contributed capital, (c) capital stock, (d) retained earnings, and (e) dividends.

Q5-18 Discuss how the amounts of the beginning and ending inventory are entered on a work-sheet.

EXERCISES

E5-1   Sales and Sales Returns. On April 6 the Piper Company sold $1,025 of merchandise to a customer. On April 8 the customer returned $95 of the merchandise purchased on April 6 because it was defective.

Required: 1. Prepare the journal entries to record this information assuming:
   (a) The merchandise was sold for cash.
   (b) The merchandise was sold on account.
2. What source documents would be used to record each transaction?

E5-2   Sales Discounts. On June 4 the Shearson Company sold $1,500 of merchandise on account to a customer, with terms of 3/10, n/30.

Required: Prepare journal entries to record the sale and later payment assuming:
1. The customer remits payment on June 13.
2. The customer remits payment on June 30.

E5-3 Sales Returns and Discounts. On May 8 Hernandez Company sold $1,000 of merchandise on account to a customer, with terms of 2/10, n/30. On May 12 the customer returned $200 of the merchandise.

Required:
1. Prepare journal entries to record the sale, return, and collection assuming:
    (a) The customer remits payment on May 17.
    (b) The customer remits payment on May 29.
2. What source documents would be used to record each transaction?

E5-4 Purchases and Purchases Allowances. On July 1, 1983, the Nikko Company purchased merchandise costing $12,000. Upon inspection of the merchandise some of it was found to be of inferior quality. Instead of returning the merchandise to the supplier the Nikko Company was granted an allowance of $1,500, and it planned to sell the merchandise at its annual "sidewalk sale." The Nikko Company uses a periodic inventory system.

Required:
1. Prepare journal entries to record this information assuming:
    (a) The merchandise was purchased for cash.
    (b) The merchandise was purchased on account.
2. What source documents would be used to record each transaction?

E5-5 Purchases Discounts. On September 2, 1983, the Morgan Company purchased $8,000 of merchandise from a supplier on account, with terms 4/10, n/30. The Morgan Company uses a periodic inventory system.

Required: Prepare journal entries to record this information assuming:
1. The Morgan Company remits payment on September 12, 1983.
2. The Morgan Company remits payment on September 30, 1983.

E5-6 Purchases Returns and Discounts. On June 4, 1983, the Klein Company purchased $2,000 of merchandise on account, with terms of 2/10, n/30. On June 6 Klein returned $300 of the merchandise to the supplier. The Klein Company uses a periodic inventory system.

Required:
1. Prepare journal entries to record the purchase, return, and payment assuming:
    (a) The Klein Company remits payment on June 12, 1983.
    (b) The Klein Company remits payment on June 25, 1983.
2. What source documents would be used to record each transaction?

E5-7 Cost of Goods Sold. You are given the following information:

Ending inventory	$15,000
Purchases	62,000
Transportation-in	3,000
Beginning inventory	12,000
Sales returns and allowances	5,000

Required: Compute the cost of goods sold.

E5-8 Cost of Goods Sold. The following data are available for the Arnhold Company for the year:

Beginning inventory	$ 40,000
Ending inventory	50,000
Purchases	101,000
Purchases returns and allowances	4,000
Purchases discounts taken	500
Transportation-in	5,000

Required: Prepare a schedule that computes the cost of goods sold for the year.

E5-9   Perpetual Inventory System. On July 1 Drexel's Appliance purchased $5,000 of goods for resale. On July 15 it sold $2,600 of these goods to customers at a selling price of $4,000. The company uses the perpetual inventory system.

Required: Prepare journal entries to record this information.

E5-10   Income Statement. Shown below are items that appeared in the income statement of the Harburg Company for the month ended October 31, 1983. The company is a sole proprietorship and uses the periodic inventory system.

Beginning inventory	?
Sales	$85,000
Purchases	41,000
Purchases returns and allowances	1,500
Ending inventory	10,000
Cost of goods sold	50,000
Sales returns	5,000
Selling expenses	7,000
General and administrative expenses	?
Transportation-in	500
Net Income	12,000

Required: From the information given determine the amounts of the beginning inventory and general and administrative expenses. (Hint: Preparation of an income statement will help you determine the answers.)

E5-11   Classified Income Statement. Shown below are selected accounts and account balances of Foile's Music Store for the year ended December 31, 1983. The company is a sole proprietorship, uses the periodic inventory system, and has made all necessary adjusting entries.

Beginning inventory	$ 5,300
Depreciation expense: office equipment	1,500
Ending inventory	6,500
Interest revenue	675
Interest expense	250
Purchases	56,000
Purchases returns and allowances	1,000
Sales	97,000
Sales returns and allowances	2,900
Transportation-in	1,300
Office supplies expense	600
Depreciation expense: store equipment	2,200
Office salaries expense	4,000
Sales salaries expense	7,200
Advertising expense	360
Rent expense	1,800

Of the rent expense, $\frac{5}{6}$ is applicable to the store and $\frac{1}{6}$ is applicable to the office.

Required: Prepare, in good form, a classified income statement for Foile's Music Store for the year ended December 31, 1983.

E5-12 Classifying Accounts. At the end of 1983 the Jaffray Company showed the following accounts on its post-closing trial balance:

> Accounts payable
> Accounts receivable
> Buildings and equipment
> Accumulated depreciation: buildings and equipment
> Cash
> Marketable securities
> Inventory
> Prepaid insurance
> Notes payable (due 12/31/1985)
> Government bonds (due 12/31/1986)
> Salaries payable
> Unearned rent
> P. Jaffray, capital

Required: Using the common classifications presented in the chapter prepare a classified balance sheet (report form) for the Jaffray Company on December 31, 1983. Use XXX's for dollar amounts.

E5-13 Worksheet. The trial balance of the Becker Company for the year ended December 31, 1983, is shown on a partially completed worksheet below.

	BECKER COMPANY Worksheet For Year Ended December 31, 1983										
	Trial Balance		Adjustments		Adjusted Trial Balance		Income Statement		Balance Sheet	
Account Titles	Debit	Credit	Debit	Credit	Debit	Credit	Debit	Credit	Debit	Credit
Cash	2,100									
Accounts receivable	4,000									
Inventory, 1/1/1983	6,800									
Prepaid rent	3,600									
Equipment	30,000									
Accumulated depreciation		12,000								
Accounts payable		3,100								
E. Becker, capital		24,400								
E. Becker, withdrawals	1,000									
Sales		45,000								
Purchases	22,400									
Salaries expense	7,100									
Utilities expense	2,900									
Advertising expense	4,600									
Totals	84,500	84,500								

Additional Information:

(a) The equipment is being depreciated on a straight-line basis over a 10-year life, with no residual value.

(b) On January 1, 1983, the company had paid 3 years rent in advance at $100 per month.

(c) The December 31, 1983, inventory is $8,200.

Required: Complete the worksheet.

E5-14 Corporation's Net Income. For the year ended December 31, 1983, the Newhard Corporation had operating income of $21,000 and other revenues of $3,500. The company is subject to a 40% income tax rate and currently has 10,000 shares of capital stock held by stockholders.

Required: Calculate the Newhard Corporation's net income and earnings per share for the year ended December 31, 1983. Prepare your solution in the form of a partial income statement, starting with operating income.

E5-15 Stockholders' Equity. On January 1, 1983, the ACE Corporation showed the following account balances:

Capital stock $100,000
Retained earnings   57,850

During 1983, the following events occurred:

(a) The company issued $10,000 of additional capital stock.

(b) Net income for the year was $32,000.

(c) Dividends in the amount of $12,000 were paid to stockholders.

Required: Prepare the stockholders' equity section of the ACE Corporation's balance sheet on December 31, 1983. (Hint: The beginning balance of capital stock and retained earnings must be changed for the events occurring during the year.)

PROBLEMS

Part A

P5-1A   Journal Entries. The Morg Retail Company entered into the following transactions (the company uses the periodic inventory system):

Date	Transaction
Sept. 1	Purchased $1,000 of merchandise on account from the Doe Company, with terms 4/10, n/30.
2	Returned $50 of defective merchandise purchased on September 1 from the Doe Company for credit.
5	Sold $300 of merchandise to customer for cash.
6	Purchased $350 of merchandise for cash.
6	Granted $70 allowance to customer for minor defects found in merchandise sold on September 5.
10	Paid balance due to Doe Company for purchase of September 1 and related transaction.
21	Sold $1,200 of merchandise on account to R. Bailey, with terms 3/10, n/30.
30	Received balance due from R. Bailey for merchandise purchased on September 21.

Required: 1. Prepare the necessary journal entries to record these transactions.
2. What were the net sales for the month?
3. What were the net purchases for the month?

P5-2A   Journal Entries. The Steed Company entered into the following transactions during the month of August (the company uses the periodic inventory system):

Date	Transaction
Aug. 1	Purchased $1,000 of merchandise for cash.
4	Sold $1,800 of merchandise on account to P. Tarlet, with terms n/15. The Steed Company agreed to pay all shipping charges.
4	Paid freight charges incurred in the shipping of merchandise sold to P. Tarlet, $80.
6	Purchased $4,000 of merchandise on account from the Rony Company, with terms n/20. The Steed Company agreed to pay all freight charges.
6	Paid freight charges related to merchandise purchased from the Rony Company, $150.
10	Returned, for credit, $200 of defective merchandise purchased on August 6 from the Rony Company.
12	Sold $450 of merchandise to customer for cash.
13	Granted $50 allowance to customer for damaged merchandise sold on August 12.
15	Received balance due from P. Tarlet for merchandise sold on account on August 4.
25	Paid balance due to the Rony Company for purchase on August 6.

Required: Prepare the necessary journal entries to record these transactions.

P5-3A   Income Statement Calculations. The income statement information, for 1982 and 1983, of the Weeden Company is as follows:

	1982	1983
Beginning inventory	$ 1	$ 4
Sales	200,000	5
Purchases	110,000	130,000
Purchases returns and allowances	5,000	4,000
Ending inventory	50,000	6
Sales returns and allowances	3,000	15,000
Gross profit	2	95,000
Cost of goods sold	107,000	100,000
Operating expenses	50,000	7
Transportation-in	1,000	6,000
Net income	3	65,000

Required: Fill in the blanks numbered 1 through 7. All the necessary information is listed. (Hint: It is not necessary to do your answers in numerical order.)

P5-4A   Corporation. The Finestein Corporation showed the following balances on January 1, 1983:

Capital stock (4,000 shares)	$40,000
Retained earnings	$64,000

On January 2, 1983, the company issued 1,000 shares of capital stock for $10,000. For the year ended December 31, 1983, the company had operating income of $23,000 and other revenues of $3,000. In addition, the company paid dividends of $5,000 on December 31. The Finestein Corporation is subject to a 40% income tax rate.

Required: 1. Prepare a partial income statement, starting with operating income, for the year ended December 31, 1983. Include earnings per share information based on the total capital stock for 1983.
2. Prepare the stockholders' equity section of the December 31, 1983, balance sheet. (Hint: The beginning balances of capital stock and retained earnings must be changed for the events occurring during the year.)

P5-5A Worksheet and Financial Statements. The Bulse Clothing Company, a retail clothing store, prepared the following partially completed worksheet for the year ended December 31, 1983:

	BULSE CLOTHING COMPANY Worksheet For Year Ended December 31, 1983										
	Trial Balance		Adjustments		Adjusted Trial Balance		Income Statement		Balance Sheet	
Account Titles	Debit	Credit	Debit	Credit	Debit	Credit	Debit	Credit	Debit	Credit
Cash	4,500									
Accounts receivable	3,500									
Inventory (1/1/1983)	8,000									
Store supplies	550									
Prepaid insurance	1,000									
Property and equipment	30,000									
Accumulated depreciation		3,000								
Accounts payable		1,160								
H. Bulse, capital		40,000								
H. Bulse, withdrawals	8,500									
Sales		81,000								
Sales returns and allowances	3,650									
Purchases	50,000									
Purchases returns and allowances		1,000								
Transportation-in	2,600									
Salaries expense	11,700									
Advertising expense	960									
Utilities expense	840									
Telephone expense	360									
Totals	126,160	126,160								

Additional Information:
(a) The property and equipment is being depreciated using the straight-line method with an estimated life of 20 years and no residual value.
(b) Store supplies on hand at December 31, 1983, totaled $150.
(c) Prepaid insurance expired during the year in the amount of $500.
(d) Inventory on December 31, 1983, totaled $13,000.

Required: 1. Complete the worksheet.
2. Prepare an income statement for the year ended December 31, 1983 (do *not* separate the operating expenses section into two parts).
3. Prepare a statement of changes in owner's equity for the year ended December 31, 1983.
4. Prepare a December 31, 1983 balance sheet (report form).

P5-6A Income Statement and Closing Entries. The adjusted trial balance of the Werthiem Company on December 31, 1983, is as follows (the company uses the periodic inventory system):

Account Titles	Debit	Credit
Cash	$ 6,400	
Accounts receivable	9,700	
Inventory (1/1/1983)	18,500	
Property and equipment	40,000	
Accumulated depreciation		$ 16,000
Accounts payable		13,900
T. Werthiem, capital		45,000
T. Werthiem, withdrawals	8,800	
Sales		71,000
Sales returns and allowances	3,000	
Purchases	42,500	
Purchases returns and allowances		2,500
Transportation-in	2,600	
Advertising expense	3,000	
Salaries expense	8,000	
Telephone expense	940	
Utilities expense	960	
Depreciation expense	4,000	
Totals	$148,400	$148,400

The inventory on December 31, 1983, amounted to $23,000.

Required: 1. Prepare an income statement for the year ended December 31, 1983 (do *not* separate the operating expenses section into two parts).
2. Prepare closing entries on December 31, 1983.

P5-7A Classified Income Statement. The December 31, 1983, adjusted trial balance and other accounting records of Lyon's Hardware showed the following items (the company is a sole proprietorship and uses the periodic inventory system):

Advertising expense	$ 4,300
Beginning inventory	?
Depreciation expense: store equipment	1,800
Depreciation expense: building (store)	2,700
Depreciation expense: office equipment	1,500
Depreciation expense: building (office)	1,000
Ending inventory	10,000
Interest revenue	1,600
Interest expense	1,100
Insurance expense	350
Sales returns and allowances	1,020
Freight-out	1,400
Sales	93,000
Cost of goods sold	55,700
Office supplies expense	480
Sales discounts	2,040
Purchases	50,000
Store supplies expense	800
Sales salaries expense	7,800
Freight-in	5,300
Office salaries expense	2,600
Purchases returns and allowances	600

Required: Prepare, in good form, a classified income statement for Lyon's Hardware for the year ended December 31, 1983 (insert the correct amount for the beginning inventory).

P5-8A Classified Balance Sheet. The following accounts and account balances appeared in the accounting records of the Merkin Company on December 31, 1983:

Accounts receivable	$ 2,900
Accounts payable	3,200
Building	12,000
Cash	2,400
Delivery equipment	30,000
Inventory (12/31/1983)	8,500
Accumulated depreciation: delivery equipment	6,000
L. Merkin, capital	36,300
Mortgage payable	26,000
Marketable securities	1,000
Accumulated depreciation: office equipment	1,600
Notes payable (due 10/1/1984)	10,000
Office supplies	1,800
Land	8,000
Notes receivable (due 12/31/1985)	6,000
Accumulated depreciation: building	2,000
Office equipment	8,000
Prepaid insurance	2,100
Notes payable (due 12/31/1985)	12,000
Interest payable (due 10/1/1984)	1,000
Unearned revenue	3,000
Government bonds (due 12/31/1990)	19,000
Salaries payable	600

All necessary adjustments have been made.

Required: 1. Prepare, in good form, a classified balance sheet (report form) on December 31, 1983.
2. The Merkin Company is applying for a short-term loan at a local bank. If you were the banker would you grant a loan to the company? Explain your decision. (Hint: Look at such items as the current ratio and working capital of the company.)

PROBLEMS

Part B

P5-1B Journal Entries. Nomura Sales, a medical supplies wholesaler, entered into the following transactions (the company uses the periodic inventory system):

Date	Transaction
Aug. 1	Purchased $5,500 of medical supplies on account from the Nead Company, with terms 3/10, n/30.
3	Returned $100 of defective medical supplies purchased on August 1 from the Nead Company for credit.
5	Sold $2,000 of medical supplies on account to P & H Drugs, with terms 2/10, n/30.
8	Granted $200 credit to P & H Drugs for return of medical supplies purchased on August 5.

Aug.	9	Purchased $1,000 of medical supplies for cash.
	10	Paid balance due to the Nead Company for purchase of August 1 and related transaction.
	15	Received balance due from P & H Drugs for medical supplies purchased on August 5.
	30	Sold $500 of merchandise to customer for cash.

Required: 1. Prepare the necessary journal entries to record these transactions.
2. What were the net sales for the month?
3. What were the net purchases for the month?

P5-2B   Journal Entries.   The Kerem Company entered into the following transactions during the month of July (the company uses the periodic inventory system):

Date	Transaction
July 1	Sold $280 of merchandise for cash.
3	Purchased $1,600 of merchandise for cash from the Jokem Supply Company.
4	Received $250 cash allowance from the Jokem Supply Company for defective merchandise purchased on July 3.
6	Sold $800 of merchandise on account to Q. Reemy with terms n/10. The Kerem Company agreed to pay all transportation charges.
6	Paid $60 in transportation charges to ship merchandise sold to Q. Reemy.
8	Q. Reemy returned $40 of defective merchandise sold on July 6 for credit.
12	Purchased $1,200 of merchandise on account from Duwell Supplies, with terms n/15. The Kerem Company agreed to pay all transportation charges.
12	Paid transportation charges related to merchandise purchased from Duwell Supplies, $85.
16	Received balance due from Q. Reemy for merchandise sold on July 6.
25	Paid balance due to Duwell Supplies for merchandise purchased on July 12.

Required: Prepare the necessary journal entries to record these transactions.

P5-3B   Income Statement Calculations.   The income statement information of the Lernette Company for 1982 and 1983, is as follows:

	1982	1983
Ending inventory	$ 75,000	$ 4
Sales	300,000	315,000
Freight-in	1,500	9,000
Sales returns and allowances	4,500	5
Purchases returns and allowances	7,500	6,000
Beginning inventory	74,000	6
Operating expenses	1	45,000
Purchases	2	195,000
Gross profit	135,000	142,500
Net income	60,000	7
Cost of goods sold	3	150,000

Required: Fill in the blanks numbered 1 through 7. All the necessary information is listed. (Hint: It is not necessary to do your answers in numerical order.)

P5-4B Income Statement and Closing Entries. The adjusted trial balance of the Hyphon Company on December 31, 1983, is as follows (the company uses the periodic inventory system):

Account Titles	Debit	Credit
Cash	$ 8,000	
Accounts receivable	12,125	
Inventory (1/1/1983)	23,150	
Property and equipment	50,000	
Accumulated depreciation		$ 20,000
Accounts payable		17,375
T. Hyphon, capital		56,250
T. Hyphon, withdrawals	11,000	
Sales		88,750
Sales returns and allowances	3,750	
Purchases	53,100	
Purchases returns and allowances		3,125
Freight-in	3,250	
Advertising expense	3,750	
Salaries expense	10,000	
Telephone expense	1,175	
Utilities expense	1,200	
Depreciation expense	5,000	
Totals	$185,500	$185,500

The inventory on December 31, 1983, amounted to $28,750.

Required: 1. Prepare an income statement for the year ended December 31, 1983. (Do *not* separate the operating expenses section into two parts.)
2. Prepare closing entries on December 31, 1983.

P5-5B Classified Income Statement. The December 31, 1983, adjusted trial balance and other accounting records of the Oppenel Company showed the following items (the company is a sole proprietorship and uses the periodic inventory system):

Purchases returns and allowances	$ 4,400
Office salaries expense	6,900
Transportation-in	5,600
Sales salaries expense	9,700
Store supplies expense	900
Purchases	45,000
Sales discounts	1,000
Office supplies expense	500
Cost of goods sold	50,900
Sales	89,300
Transportation-out	1,500
Advertising expense	4,800
Beginning inventory	15,700
Depreciation expense: store equipment	2,300
Depreciation expense: building (store)	2,900
Depreciation expense: office equipment	800
Depreciation expense: building (office)	1,100
Ending inventory	?
Interest revenue	1,760
Interest expense	1,060
Insurance expense	700
Sales returns and allowances	6,200

Required: Prepare, in good form, a classified income statement for the year ended December 31, 1983. Insert the correct amount for the ending inventory.

P5-6B **Worksheet and Financial Statements.** The Amary Company prepared the following partially completed worksheet for the year ended December 31, 1983:

		AMARY COMPANY									
		Worksheet									
		For Year Ended December 31, 1983									

Account Titles	Trial Balance		Adjustments		Adjusted Trial Balance		Income Statement		Balance Sheet	
	Debit	Credit	Debit	Credit	Debit	Credit	Debit	Credit	Debit	Credit
Cash	6,200									
Accounts receivable	4,900									
Inventory (1/1/1983)	11,200									
Supplies	870									
Prepaid insurance	1,400									
Property and equipment	42,000									
Accumulated depreciation		4,200								
Accounts payable		8,624								
B. Amary, capital		56,000								
B. Amary, withdrawals	7,700									
Sales		102,200								
Sales returns and allowances	5,110									
Purchases	70,000									
Purchases returns and allowances		1,400								
Transportation-in	3,640									
Salaries expense	16,380									
Advertising expense	1,344									
Utilities expense	1,176									
Telephone expense	504									
Totals	172,424	172,424								

Additional Information:

(a) The property and equipment is being depreciated using the straight-line method with an estimated life of 20 years and no residual value.

(b) Supplies on hand at December 31, 1983, totaled $175.

(c) Prepaid insurance expired during the year in the amount of $750.

(d) Inventory on December 31, 1983, totaled $19,500.

Required: 1. Complete the worksheet.

2. Prepare an income statement for the year ended December 31, 1983. (Do *not* separate the operating expenses section into two parts.)

3. Prepare a statement of changes in owner's equity for the year ended December 31, 1983.

4. Prepare a December 31, 1983, balance sheet (report form).

P5-7B **Classified Balance Sheet.** The following accounts and account balances appeared in the accounting records of the Rigons Company on December 31, 1983:

Salaries payable	$ 900
Accounts receivable	10,500
Government bonds (due 12/31/1987)	30,000
Accounts payable	6,800
Unearned revenue	1,000
Building	45,000
Interest payable (due 9/1/1984)	200
Cash	6,600
Notes payable (due 12/31/1985)	15,000
Store equipment	18,000
Prepaid insurance	1,000
Office equipment	12,000
Inventory (12/31/1983)	12,750
Accumulated depreciation: store equipment	3,000
Accumulated depreciation: building	9,000
Notes receivable (due 12/31/1986)	7,500
P. Rigons, capital	91,250
Land	12,000
Mortgage payable	22,500
Office and store supplies	2,700
Marketable securities	2,000
Notes payable (due 9/1/1984)	8,000
Accumulated depreciation: office equipment	2,400

All necessary adjustments have been made.

Required: 1. Prepare a classified balance sheet (report form) on December 31, 1983.
2. The Rigons Company is applying for a $2,000 short-term loan at a local bank. If you were the banker would you grant a loan to the company? Explain. (Hint: Look at such items as the company's current ratio and working capital.)

DISCUSSION CASES

C5-1   Financial Statements from Incomplete Records. On January 1, 1983, Paula Randolph opened a boutique called P.R.'s Boutique. At that time she invested $30,000 cash in the business. With this cash the business immediately purchased $8,000 of inventory and $12,000 of store equipment, and paid two years rent in advance for store space. Paula estimated the store equipment would last for 8 years and after that it would be worthless.

During the year the boutique appeared to operate successfully. Paula did not know anything about accounting, although she did keep an accurate checkbook. Her checkbook showed the following summarized items on December 31, 1983:

Payment of 2 years rent for store space	$ 2,400
Receipts from cash sales	31,000
Payments for purchases of merchandise	15,000
Payments for operating expenses	12,000
Withdrawals of cash for personal use	10,000

Paula has asked for your assistance. She says, "The ending cash balance in the company checkbook is $1,600. Since the beginning cash balance was $30,000, the company seems to have had a net loss of $28,400. Something must be wrong. I am sure the company did better than that. Please find out what the company's earnings were for 1983 and its financial position at the end of 1983."

You agree to help Paula. She has just finished "taking inventory" and indicates the cost of the ending inventory is $9,000. She has kept copies of invoices made out to customers who purchased merchandise on account. These uncollected invoices total $13,000. Paula also has a file of unpaid invoices of suppliers. These unpaid invoices add up to $6,000. Just as you begin your calculations, Paula says, "Oh yes, I also owe my employees $400 of salaries that they have earned this week."

Required: Prepare a 1983 income statement and a December 31, 1983, balance sheet for P.R.'s Boutique. Include explanations for all amounts shown.

C5-2 Corrections to Balance Sheet.

The bookkeeper of the Washet Company prepared the following balance sheet as of December 31, 1983:

WASHET COMPANY
Balance Sheet
For Year Ended December 31, 1983

Working capital	$ 23,100	Noncurrent liabilities	$ 25,400
Other assets	121,400	Owner's equity	119,100
Total	$144,500	Total	$144,500

Your analysis of these accounts reveals the following information for each item (the amounts in parentheses indicate deductions from each item):

(a) Working capital consists of:

Equipment	$ 30,000
Land	10,000
Accounts due to suppliers	(32,000)
Inventory, including office supplies of $3,700	34,700
Salaries owed to employees	(2,600)
Note owed to bank (due December 31, 1985)	(17,000)
	$ 23,100

(b) Other assets include:

Cash	$ 9,000
Prepaid insurance	2,400
Buildings	70,000
Long-term investment in government bonds	29,000
A. Washet, withdrawals	11,000
	$121,400

(c) Noncurrent liabilities consist of:

Mortgage payable	$ 33,000
Accumulated depreciation: equipment	16,000
Accounts due from customers	(16,600)
Notes receivable (due December 31, 1986)	(7,000)
	$ 25,400

(d) Owner's equity includes:

A. Washet, capital	$103,400
Accumulated depreciation: buildings	24,000
Securities held as a temporary investment	(10,000)
Interest payable (due July 1, 1984)	1,700
	$119,100

Required: Based on your analysis prepare a properly classified December 31, 1983, balance sheet (report form) for the Washet Company.

6 | Internal Control, Special Journals, and EDP Systems

After reading this chapter, you should understand:

- The definition of internal control
- Internal control for authorizing, executing, and recording transactions, and for accountability for assets
- General internal control principles
- Subsidiary ledgers
- The advantages of using special journals
- Recording transactions in the sales journal, purchases journal, cash receipts journal, and cash payments journal
- The accounting system using electronic data processing

In Chapter 1 we defined an accounting system as a means by which accounting information is identified, measured, recorded, and retained so that it can be reported in an accounting statement. We also said that internal control involved procedures to safeguard a company's economic resources and to promote the efficient and effective operation of the accounting system. In Chapters 2 through 5 we introduced a manual accounting system using a general journal, first as it applied to a service company and then as it applied to a merchandising company. We limited our discussion of internal control to the use of source documents as evidence of a company's transactions.

In this chapter we extend our discussion to the assignment of responsibilities, documentation, and routines and procedures needed for sound internal control. We discuss how a company might use special journals in addition to its general journal to make its accounting system more efficient. Finally, we look at how the steps and documents of a company's accounting system would be different if it used electronic data processing (i.e., a computer) in its operations.

INTERNAL CONTROL

The definition of internal control can be expanded slightly from the definition given in Chapter 1. **Internal control consists of the policies and procedures used to safeguard a company's assets and to ensure that reliable financial statements are the end result of an efficient accounting system.** Safeguarding assets means that a company's assets are protected against loss from unintentional or intentional errors (involving fraud and theft) in processing transactions and handling the assets.

Establishing and maintaining a good system of internal control is the responsibility of the management of a company, and accountants can assist in fulfilling this responsibility. The purpose of this section is to discuss several general principles of good internal control. In later chapters we discuss the aspects of internal control that apply to specific assets or parts of the accounting system.

To meet the goal of safeguarding assets and having an efficient accounting system, there are four subgoals of internal control:

1. To ensure that transactions are carried out according to management's general and specific policies.
2. To ensure that transactions are recorded as needed (a) so that financial statements are prepared according to generally accepted accounting principles (GAAP) and (b) so that specified employees are held accountable for the various assets of the company.
3. To ensure that only authorized individuals have access to assets.
4. To ensure that the accounting records of the company's assets agree with the actual existing assets under the company's control.[1]

The term *to ensure* does not mean that management always uses internal control procedures to protect each and every asset, for example. Promoting an efficient accounting system and protecting assets costs time and money. The advantages of doing so must be greater than the costs incurred. Management must make sure, *within reason,* that efficiency is promoted and assets are protected. For instance, it is more important to safeguard a desk calculator than a box of paperclips even though both are assets.

Because transactions are the basis of a company's operations, they are the main concern of internal control. Transactions not only include exchanges with external parties but also include the use of assets (or services) within a company. Revenue and expense transactions are also included because they involve assets (e.g., sale of items from inventory for cash or accounts receivable, incurrence of an expense by payment of cash). In establishing good internal control, consideration must be given to: (1) authorizing transactions, (2) executing transactions, (3) recording transactions, and (4) the accountability for the resulting assets.[2] Each of these factors is discussed below.

Authorization for Transactions

The final authority for business transactions is the owner or owners of a company. The owner frequently delegates authority to different managers in the company, however. **Authorization means permission to exchange or use assets for specific purposes under given conditions.** Good internal control must include policies that indicate who can enter into different kinds of transactions and provide guidelines about the price, quantity, timing, and other aspects of each transaction.

---

[1] *Statement on Auditing Standards No. 1* (New York: AICPA, 1979), par. 320.28.
[2] Ibid., par. 320.20.

For instance, general policies may indicate who is authorized to make sales to customers, who may make purchases of inventory, who may enter into transactions to acquire equipment, buildings, and marketable securities, and who may purchase office supplies. Such policies assign responsibilities for certain transactions to specific employees and help to prevent other employees from making unauthorized purchases or sales. Authorization policies may also be specific and include guidelines for the selling price to each customer, whether some customers are entitled to a cash discount, which customers can make purchases on account, when to reorder inventory, which suppliers to purchase from, and how many alternatives must be considered when a major product is purchased. These policies ensure that similar procedures are followed for similar transactions and minimize the chance of an unintentional error (such as giving a trade discount to a customer not entitled to a lower selling price).

Execution of Transactions

The execution of transactions means the set of steps needed to complete the exchange of assets or use of assets in the company. A well-established set of steps to be followed for each major type of transaction is important to good internal control. Two common transactions, the sale of merchandise and the purchase of merchandise, can be used to illustrate these steps.

SALE OF MERCHANDISE. The routine procedures for the sale of merchandise to a customer vary from company to company, depending upon the size and type of company, size of customer, size of order, and so on. A general description of the steps for good internal control can be presented, however. Assume that a wholesaler accepts orders from retailers through the mail. The steps would include acceptance of the order, assembling, packing and shipment of the inventory, and billing and collection of the sales price.

Acceptance of the order would begin with the receipt of a retailer's order form, a source document, in the mail. Since retailers normally purchase on account, approval would first be obtained from the company's credit department (a department in the company responsible for checking potential and current customer's *credit ratings* and collecting past due accounts) before proceeding. This credit check helps to avoid the unintentional error of making a credit sale to a customer that is late in paying its account. Upon credit approval, a sales invoice (illustrated in Chapter 5) indicating the items ordered is prepared by the accounting department. An original invoice and three copies of the invoice are typically prepared and used for internal control, as illustrated in Exhibit 6-1.

Copies 1 and 2 are sent to the inventory department where the ordered items are assembled and packed for shipment. Copy 1 is included in the shipment. Copy 2 is initialed by the employees who assembled and packed the items and is returned to the accounting department. Copy 3 is retained by the accounting department. The accounting department enters the items shipped (based on Copy 2), price, discount terms, and other information on Copy 3 and the original invoice. The original invoice is then mailed as a bill to the retailer and Copy 3 is used to record the sales transaction.

EXHIBIT 6-1
Flow of
Sales Invoice
Copies for
Internal Control

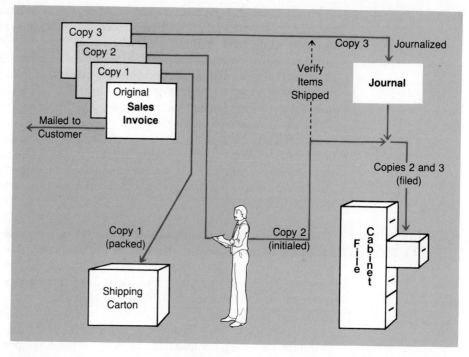

Copies 2 and 3 are then kept in the company's records. They indicate that the asset (inventory) has been shipped and identify which employees were responsible for the asset as it went through the company's assembling, packing, and shipping operations. Copy 3 is also used later as a source document for preparing and mailing a monthly statement to the retailer and recording the collection of the retail customer's account. These steps help to ensure that operations are run efficiently, that only authorized individuals have access to the company's assets (inventory and accounts receivable), and that these assets are protected from theft or misplacement throughout the execution of the sale, assembly, shipment, billing, and collection activities.

PURCHASE OF MERCHANDISE.   The procedures for purchases of merchandise also vary from company to company. A general description is presented for a retailer purchasing inventory on credit from a wholesaler. The steps include a requisition of the inventory, issuing the purchase order, receiving the inventory, and paying the purchase price.

Processing of the order begins with a purchase requisition. **A purchase requisition is an internal business document requesting that certain items of inventory be purchased.** This document is usually prepared by the manager in charge of the department selling the inventory items. This purchase requisition is sent to the purchasing department, which then prepares a purchase order. **A purchase order is a business document authorizing a supplier to ship the items listed at a specified price.** Exhibit 6-2 shows an example of a purchase order.

EXHIBIT 6-2
Purchase Order

Purchase Order

Order No. 129

Jay Sports Company
1200 East Main Street
Columbia, Missouri

Date ___5/18/1983___
Shipping Instructions ___UPS___
Authorization ___Al Knox___

To: Smith Supply Company
3000 South James Street
Kansas City, Missouri

Please ship the following items:

	Description	Quantity	Price	Total
#472	Tennis racket	10	$20.00	$200.00
# 68	Tennis balls (24 cans per box)	20 boxes	24.00	480.00
#124	Nylon racket covers (12 per box)	2 boxes	18.00	36.00
				$716.00

An original and three copies of the purchase order are usually prepared by the purchasing department. The original purchase order is mailed to the wholesaler, Copy 1 is sent to the receiving department (the department responsible for receiving and unpacking inventory shipped from suppliers), Copy 3 is sent to the accounting department, and Copy 2 is kept by the purchasing department.

The multiple copies of the purchase order are used for internal control as shown in Exhibit 6-3. When the inventory is received by the receiving department from the wholesaler, the quantity and condition are checked. Copy 1 of the purchase order (sometimes called the *receiving report*) is initialed and sent with the inventory to the sales department. An employee in the sales department checks the inventory for quality and style, initials Copy 1 of the purchase order, and sends it to the accounting department. The accounting department notifies the purchasing department that the order is received and collects Copy 2 of the purchase order. Copies 1 and 2 are compared with Copy 3 to verify that the items ordered have been received in the proper condition. By this time the original invoice from the supplier has been received in the mail. The accounting department checks the invoice against Copy 3 of the purchase order for accuracy and approves (1) the recording of the purchase transaction and (2) the payment of the invoice (less any applicable cash discounts) on the due date.

These steps help to ensure that purchasing activities are efficient, that no unauthorized individual has access to the assets (inventory and cash), and that the company's assets are protected from theft or misplacement throughout all the purchase activities. They also help to ensure that the company's accounting records show the actual existing assets under the company's control. Similar internal control steps for the acquisition and disposal of operating assets such as office equipment and sales equipment are also important for safeguarding assets and proper operation of the accounting system.

**EXHIBIT 6-3
Flow of Purchase
Order Copies for
Internal Control**

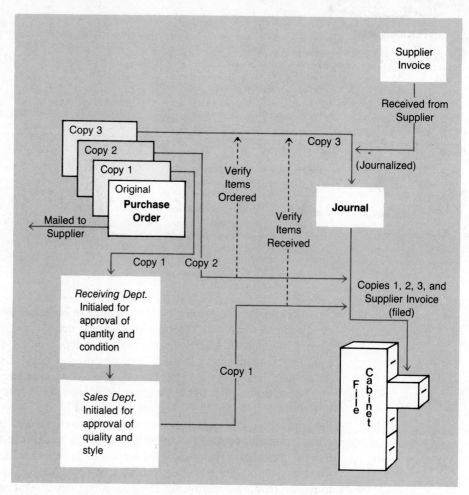

Recording of Transactions

Recording includes journalizing and posting transactions, and keeping up-to-date records of a company's assets. There are several concerns important to internal control: (1) that all executed transactions are recorded in the correct amounts and the correct accounting period, (2) that no unauthorized transactions are recorded, and (3) that the transactions are recorded in the proper accounts. Good internal control procedures for recording transactions are independent of the method of data processing used. Thus these procedures apply equally to manual or electronic data processing. Besides protecting a company's assets, good internal control for recording transactions helps to ensure that the resulting financial statements are prepared according to generally accepted accounting principles.

Three factors, the use of source documents, subsidiary ledgers, and special journals, help in the internal control for recording transactions. The first two factors are discussed next. Special journals are discussed later in the chapter.

SOURCE DOCUMENTS. Source documents play an important part in recording transactions. As we have often mentioned in the first five chapters, all recorded transactions must be supported by source documents. Source documents help to ensure that all executed transactions are recorded in the correct amounts, accounts, and accounting period. They also provide evidence that no unauthorized transactions have been recorded.

We have discussed many source documents in previous chapters. These source documents include sales invoices, canceled checks, freight bills, sales returns and allowances credit memos, purchases returns and allowances debit memos, legal notes, and purchase requisitions, to name a few. As a general rule source documents prepared by *independent* external parties are more useful in internal control than documents prepared internally. Thus an invoice received from another company for inventory delivered is better evidence of an executed transaction than simply a purchase order prepared within the company. Assembling several source documents for a transaction is the best evidence, however. For instance, in our earlier example the wholesaler's invoice combined with the retailer's purchase order provide strong evidence for recording the purchase transaction and the resulting payment for the purchase.

SUBSIDIARY LEDGERS AND CONTROL ACCOUNTS. Recall from Chapter 2 that a company's general ledger includes all the accounts listed in its chart of accounts. As a company increases in size so does its general ledger increase because of the additional accounts needed to record the accounting information. A larger company, for example, is likely to own more and different types of physical assets. In addition, it will have more customer accounts for sales on credit and supplier accounts for purchases on credit.

In order to (1) reduce the size of the general ledger, (2) minimize errors, (3) improve efficiency in recording transactions, and (4) keep up-to-date records of dealings with charge customers and suppliers, a company sets up subsidiary ledgers. **A subsidiary ledger is a group of similar accounts that show the detail of one specific company activity.** Most companies have separate subsidiary ledgers for accounts receivable and accounts payable. These ledgers enable a company to have better information about the amounts due from customers and the amounts owed to suppliers.

The *accounts receivable* subsidiary ledger contains the individual accounts of all the company's charge (credit) customers; that is, all of the individual customer accounts are taken out of the general ledger and are included in the accounts receivable subsidiary ledger. The customer accounts can be listed either alphabetically or numerically in the subsidiary ledger. Whenever a credit sale is made to a customer, the increase (debit) in the customer's account is recorded in this subsidiary ledger. When a customer pays its account, the decrease (credit) in the customer's account is recorded in this ledger. Thus at all times the company knows the balance in each customer's account. This information is very helpful in deciding whether or not to extend additional credit to a customer and in determining which customers need to be reminded to pay their bills.

Since the individual customer accounts normally have debit balances (because sales on account are made before collections on the accounts), it follows that the accounts receivable subsidiary ledger has a *total* debit balance. When an accounts receivable subsidiary ledger is used, a single Accounts Receivable account is still kept in the general ledger (to keep the general ledger in balance in accordance with the accounting equation). **The Accounts Receivable account is referred to as a control account because it takes the place of (controls) the individual customer accounts, which have been removed and placed in the subsidiary ledger.** *The debit balance of the Accounts Receivable control account must always be equal to the debit total of the accounts receivable subsidiary ledger on each balance sheet date.* Thus after a company records a sale on account (or collection of an account or a credit sales return or allowance) in its general journal, *two* postings must be made for the receivable. One posting is made to the control account in the general ledger and another is made to the subsidiary ledger. To illustrate this procedure suppose a $1,000 credit sale was made to James Franklin. The journal entry and postings are shown below. The check mark ($\sqrt{}$) in the general journal indicates the posting has been made in the subsidiary ledger. (In this and following examples and the exercises and problems the accounts in the subsidiary ledgers are listed alphabetically so that no account number is necessary. In more complex accounting systems subsidiary account numbers would be used.) The accounting equation remains in balance because the $1,000 debit to Accounts Receivable is equal to the $1,000 credit to Sales (since the James Franklin customer account is *not* in the general ledger, the $1,000 debit in the subsidiary ledger does not affect the accounting equation). The balance of the control account remains in agreement with the balance of the subsidiary ledger because a $1,000 debit entry was recorded in each.

GENERAL JOURNAL					Page 4
Date		Account Titles and Explanations	Acct. No.	Debit	Credit
1983 Jan.	3	Accounts Receivable: James Franklin	103/√	1,000	
		Sales	401		1,000
		To record sale on account.			

GENERAL LEDGER

Accounts Receivable   No. 103

1/3/83	1,000		

Sales   No. 401

		1/3/83	1,000

ACCOUNTS RECEIVABLE SUBSIDIARY LEDGER

James Franklin

1/3/83	1,000		

Before preparing a trial balance, at the end of each accounting period a schedule is prepared that lists the balance of each customer account in the accounts receivable subsidiary ledger. These balances are totaled and the total is compared with the balance of Accounts Receivable to prove the equality of the control account and subsidiary ledger. Exhibit 6-4 shows a schedule and comparison for a company's accounts receivable.

The *accounts payable* subsidiary ledger contains the individual accounts of all the company's charge (credit) suppliers and works in the same manner as an accounts receivable subsidiary ledger. Whenever a purchase on account or a payment of a supplier account is made, it is recorded in the individual supplier account in the subsidiary ledger. An Accounts Payable *control account* is kept in the general ledger to control the individual supplier accounts in the subsidiary ledger. *The credit balance of the Accounts Payable control account must always be equal to the credit total of the accounts payable subsidiary ledger on each balance sheet date.* Thus after recording credit purchases, credit purchases returns and allowances, or payments on account in the general journal, *two* postings must be made for the payable, one to the control account and the other to the subsidiary ledger shown as follows. (Note that since the Trale Supply Company account is *not* in the general ledger, the $800 credit in the subsidiary ledger does not affect the accounting equation.)

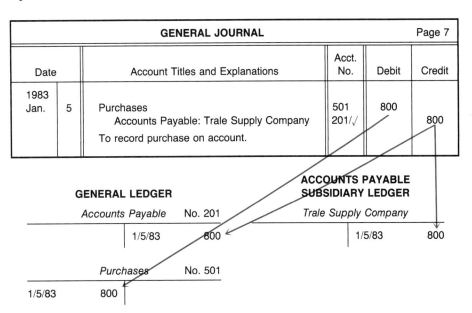

At the end of the period, before preparing the trial balance a schedule is prepared listing the balance of each supplier account in the subsidiary ledger. The total is compared to the Accounts Payable balance to prove the equality of the control account and subsidiary ledger.

Many companies also use subsidiary ledgers for such major items as property

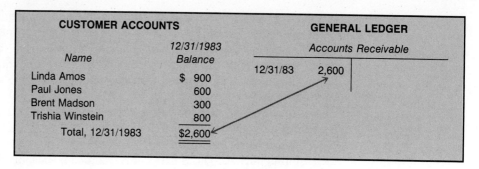

and equipment, selling expenses, and general and administrative expenses. Control accounts again replace the individual asset and expense accounts in the general ledger and the accounting procedures are similar to the procedures discussed earlier. For a subsidiary ledger for property and equipment, each piece of physical equipment is listed, along with its cost, acquisition date, book value, residual value, life, and depreciation method. In addition, the individual employee responsible for the control of each piece of physical equipment is usually listed. This is an added feature of internal control because the accounting records report who is accountable for each physical asset of the company.

Subsidiary ledgers are helpful in internal control for recording transactions because they help to ensure that similar transactions are recorded in a similar way in the proper accounts.[3] They also help to minimize errors and improve the efficiency of the accounting system because one person can be trained to, say, record all accounts receivable transactions. Subsidiary ledgers are also helpful in internal control, because up-to-date records are kept of a company's assets and the individuals accountable for the assets. Subsidiary ledgers may be used with or without special journals, as discussed later.

Accountability for Assets

In internal control, accountability involves keeping track of assets from the time of their acquisition in one transaction until their disposal or use in another transaction.[4] This is to ensure that the assets are used for their intended purpose, that they are not misplaced, that they are maintained in proper operating condition, and that they are not stolen. This means that adequate records must be kept of who is responsible for each asset and periodic checks must be made to ensure that the records agree with the actual assets. Policies must be established concerning which individuals are authorized to have access to assets; periodic checks must be made to ensure compliance with these policies.

---

[3] For simplicity, in the remainder of the text (except Chapters 8 and 10 dealing with accounts receivable and accounts payable, respectively) when general journal entries are used to illustrate transactions, subsidiary ledger accounts will not be shown.

[4] Op. cit., par. 320.25.

We have already mentioned several internal control procedures in this regard. When inventory is sold, for instance, employees in the inventory department must initial a copy of the sales invoice to verify that the correct amount and type of inventory was assembled and shipped. For a purchase, employees in the receiving department and sales department must initial a copy of the purchase invoice to verify the receipt of the inventory. The property and equipment subsidiary ledger lists the individual responsible for each physical asset.

Policies concerning which individuals are authorized to have access to assets depend on the nature and importance of the assets and how likely the assets are to be lost through unintentional errors or fraud or theft. Because cash is very easy and tempting to steal, for instance, very strict policies should be established for its control (these policies are briefly discussed later in the chapter and more fully in Chapter 7). Some items of inventory such as thin gold necklaces or other jewelry are also easy to misplace or steal; careful internal control policies for these items (such as always keeping them in locked display cases or drawers) are also important. On the other hand, an inventory of items like wastebaskets or cement blocks needs less restrictive policies of internal control.

The frequency of periodic checks of the agreement of the accounting records with the actual assets also depends on the nature and importance of the assets and the likelihood of loss. A comparison of a company's cash records and its bank account records, for example, is usually made on a monthly basis. Companies on a perpetual inventory system normally take a physical count of their inventory at least once a year. For certain kinds of inventory, such as gold jewelry, this physical count may be made much more often. Checks of operating assets are made at regular intervals, the time depending in part on whether the assets are likely to break down or malfunction if not properly maintained. Comparisons of the accounting records with the actual office desks of a company may be made every several years, whereas checks of the office typewriters and calculators may be made over shorter time periods.

Internal Control Principles

Internal control is concerned with protecting assets from unintentional errors as well as from fraud or theft, which may arise in authorizing, executing, or recording transactions or in controlling the use of the assets. Several principles have been developed that help in promoting good internal control. They are general principles not necessarily relating to a single aspect of internal control and are briefly discussed next.

COMPETENT AND RESPONSIBLE EMPLOYEES. The key to a good system of internal control lies in the employees of the company. Responsibilities must be clearly defined and employees must be technically competent for their assigned tasks and willing to accept responsibility for their performance. It is helpful if they understand the importance of strong internal control procedures and the need to follow these procedures in all cases. Employees must have high integrity because dishonest employees can undermine even the best internal control system. Technical competence, willingness to accept responsibility, and high integrity can be identified through sound personnel hiring programs and can be improved by on-going employee training programs.

SEPARATION OF DUTIES.   An important principle of internal control is that no one person should be responsible for recording transactions involving an asset and also be responsible for control of that asset. Anyone who has both responsibilities is in a position to make an unintentional error (e.g., misplacing the asset) or an intentional error (e.g., stealing the asset) that are difficult to detect. For instance, an employee who is responsible for both depositing customer checks and recording the receipt of the checks might inadvertently lose a customer's check and fail to record it. Or an employee responsible for authorizing payments for purchases as well as writing checks may prepare a fictitious invoice, write a company check to a fictitious supplier, and cash the check. Assets are better protected by separating the recording duties from the asset control duties, whether for cash, marketable securities, inventory (as discussed earlier), or other assets. The employee responsible for the recording duties serves as a monitor or double check over the employee controlling the asset, thus reducing unintentional errors and also minimizing intentional errors. This procedure helps to prevent theft or fraud unless collusion exists between two or more employees. It is a commonly held belief that two (or more) people acting together are less likely to commit theft or fraud than one person acting alone.

ROTATION OF DUTIES.   When practical, duties should be rotated among employees because rotation can uncover unintentional or intentional errors. The knowledge that an employee's duties soon will be performed by another employee is likely, in fact, to encourage the employee to follow established policies and procedures. Employees should also be required to take annual vacations so that their duties will be taken over by another employee for the vacation period. This procedure also helps to uncover errors. Any rotation, of course, must always involve competent employees with technical knowledge of the duties.

RULES FOR CONTROL OF ASSETS.   In addition to the separation of duties, rules are useful in keeping good internal control over assets. For instance, rules may be established that identify who may use specific physical assets and who has access to an inventory warehouse. Many companies restrict employees from bringing purses, coats, and bags into working areas to discourage theft of company property.

Other rules are helpful in controlling cash. For cash receipts the rule is to deposit all cash receipts daily in the company's bank. This reduces the amount of cash on hand and results in a double record of cash inflows, one in the company's cash records and the other in the bank's records. Another policy involves establishing a maximum cash balance that a company should keep in its checking account.

When this balance is exceeded many companies require that the excess cash be invested in short-term marketable securities. This makes efficient use of the excess cash and discourages misuse. Cash payments should be made only by check, using a check-writing machine and accompanied by independent source documents. This discourages unauthorized cash payments. Accounts payable should also be arranged and filed according to due date so that all cash discounts can be taken. Additional procedures for cash receipts and payments are discussed in Chapters 7 and 10.

WELL-DESIGNED SOURCE DOCUMENTS.   Each type of source document used in the company should be properly designed. This includes preprinting the source documents, having spaces for authorization signatures, and using serial numbers. Invoices, checks, purchase orders, purchases return and allowance debit memos and sales return and allowance credit memos, as well as other frequently used forms, should each be serially numbered when they are printed. In this way all source documents must be accounted for. If a check or invoice is misplaced or stolen, the missing number in the sequence will highlight the discrepancy.

INTERNAL AUDITING.   Many companies have an internal auditing staff, which consists of accountants who establish the internal control procedures and who review operations to ensure that these procedures are being followed throughout the organization. This is an important element of internal control because improvements can be made on a regular basis to the internal control system. In addition, employees who know that their activities are being monitored are more likely to follow prescribed procedures.

This form of control is also important to the CPA firm that audits the company in order to be able to express an opinion concerning the fairness of the company's financial statements. If the CPA firm knows that the company has a good internal auditing staff, it can feel more confident that the financial statements fairly present the accounting information about the company.

Diagram of Internal Control   Shown in Exhibit 6-5 is a diagram of the goals and subgoals of internal control, the concerns of internal control in regard to transactions, and the general principles of good internal control. We will discuss more internal control principles as they apply to different topics throughout the book.

Limitations of Internal Control   The design of an internal control system should be based on the current operations of the company. Regardless of how careful management is in establishing internal control, however, there are always limitations. Unintentional errors may still arise from a misunderstanding of instructions, mistakes of judgment, personal care-

**EXHIBIT 6-5
Internal Control**

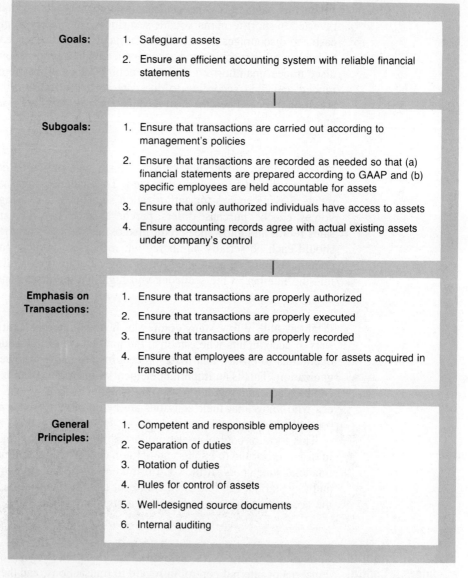

Goals:
1. Safeguard assets
2. Ensure an efficient accounting system with reliable financial statements

Subgoals:
1. Ensure that transactions are carried out according to management's policies
2. Ensure that transactions are recorded as needed so that (a) financial statements are prepared according to GAAP and (b) specific employees are held accountable for assets
3. Ensure that only authorized individuals have access to assets
4. Ensure accounting records agree with actual existing assets under company's control

Emphasis on Transactions:
1. Ensure that transactions are properly authorized
2. Ensure that transactions are properly executed
3. Ensure that transactions are properly recorded
4. Ensure that employees are accountable for assets acquired in transactions

General Principles:
1. Competent and responsible employees
2. Separation of duties
3. Rotation of duties
4. Rules for control of assets
5. Well-designed source documents
6. Internal auditing

lessness, distractions, or fatigue.[5] Theft and fraud, even with the separation of duties, can still occur if collusion takes place. Finally, a good internal control system for efficient current operations may become weak because of changes in future operating conditions. These conditions may arise from increasing sales that require additional purchases of inventory and different operating assets. Management must always be alert for improvements in its internal control and accountants should make every effort to assist in this activity.

[5] Ibid., par. 320.34.

SPECIAL JOURNALS

Just as a company's increasing size causes the need for subsidiary ledgers, it also creates the need for internal control procedures to record and summarize many daily transactions efficiently. Special journals are used for this purpose. **A special journal is a journal used to record major recurring transactions.** Use of these journals (1) allows the accounting task to be divided (in accordance with good internal control principles), (2) reduces the time needed to complete the various accounting activities, and (3) provides for a chronological list of similar transactions. Since operating procedures and business transactions are different from company to company, each company organizes its special journals in the way that is best for its operations. Most recurring transactions for a merchandising company, however, can be classified into one of four types: (1) sales of merchandise on account, (2) purchases of merchandise on account, (3) cash receipts, and (4) cash payments. Special journals are usually established to record these transactions. A general journal is still necessary to record various other transactions.

The major journals and their uses are as follows:

1. **Sales Journal.**   Used to record all (and only) sales of merchandise on account.
2. **Purchases Journal.**   Used to record all (and only) purchases of merchandise on account.
3. **Cash Receipts Journal.**   Used to record all cash receipts.
4. **Cash Payments Journal.**   Used to record all cash payments.
5. **General Journal.**   Used to record adjusting, closing, and reversing entries and other transactions not recorded in the special journals (such as the purchase of equipment on account).

The use of special journals does not affect the information in the general or subsidiary ledgers, although the postings to the ledgers are made at different times. Each of these journals is discussed in the following sections.

Sales Journal

Companies make sales of merchandise on credit or for cash. The sales journal is used to record all sales of merchandise on account (cash sales are recorded in the cash receipts journal, which is discussed later). Recall that recording a sale on credit increases (debits) an individual customer's account (account receivable) and increases (credits) the Sales account. A sales journal has columns for the date, customer account debited, invoice number, posting reference, and the amount of the sale. A sales journal[6] is shown in Exhibit 6-6. A sale on credit is recorded by simply listing the date, the customer's name, the invoice number, and the amount. For example, on June 1 a $400 credit sale was made to Ann Alcott on sales invoice number 229.

The amounts from the sales journal are posted at two different times. Since each credit sale increases (debits) a customer's account, each line in the sales journal is posted daily as a debit to the customer's account in the accounts receivable subsidiary ledger, as shown in Exhibit 6-6. By using this posting procedure each

---

[6] It should be noted that in this and later journals, for simplicity, only a few transactions are shown. In reality, however, each journal could have hundreds of recorded transactions.

**EXHIBIT 6-6
Sales Journal
and Postings**

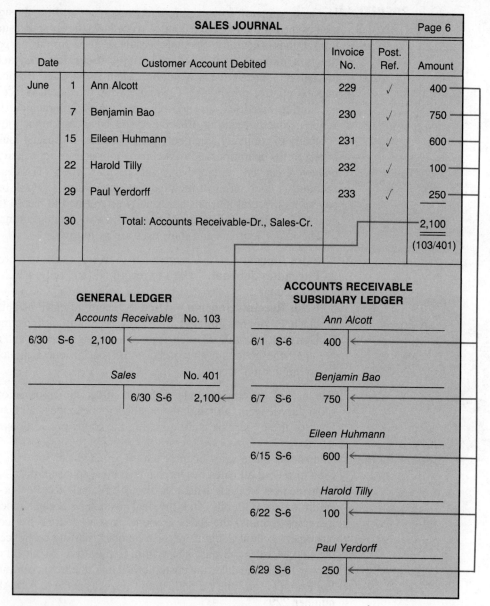

SALES JOURNAL				Page 6
Date	Customer Account Debited	Invoice No.	Post. Ref.	Amount
June 1	Ann Alcott	229	√	400
7	Benjamin Bao	230	√	750
15	Eileen Huhmann	231	√	600
22	Harold Tilly	232	√	100
29	Paul Yerdorff	233	√	250
30	Total: Accounts Receivable-Dr., Sales-Cr.			2,100
				(103/401)

GENERAL LEDGER

Accounts Receivable   No. 103

6/30 S-6   2,100

Sales   No. 401

6/30 S-6   2,100

ACCOUNTS RECEIVABLE SUBSIDIARY LEDGER

Ann Alcott

6/1 S-6   400

Benjamin Bao

6/7 S-6   750

Eileen Huhmann

6/15 S-6   600

Harold Tilly

6/22 S-6   100

Paul Yerdorff

6/29 S-6   250

customer account balance is always current. A check mark (√) is placed in the posting reference column to indicate that the daily posting has been made to the customer account.

Except for decisions involving the extension of credit and efforts to collect cash from credit customers, the balances in a company's accounts need be up to date only when the company prepares its financial statements. Most companies prepare interim financial statements on a monthly basis for managerial accounting purposes. Therefore the accounts need to have current balances only at the end of the month. At the end of the month the amount column of the sales journal is totaled. The total is the credit sales for the entire month and is posted to two accounts in the general ledger. First, the total is posted as a debit to the Accounts Receivable control account. This posting updates the control account for the monthly customer charges and brings it into agreement with the totals of the daily postings to the customer accounts in the subsidiary ledger. Second, the total is posted as a credit to the Sales account to update it for the credit sales of the month. These postings are shown in Exhibit 6-6. Note that the account numbers are listed in parentheses below the total to indicate that the postings have been made. Note also that the journal reference in each account is S-6, indicating that the postings were made from the Sales (S) journal, page 6.

Purchases Journal

Companies make purchases of merchandise for cash or on credit. The purchases journal is used to record all purchases of merchandise on account (cash purchases are recorded in the cash payments journal, which is discussed later). Recall that a purchase on credit increases (debits) the Purchases account and increases (credits) an individual supplier's account (account payable). A purchases journal is very similar to a sales journal. It includes columns for the date, supplier account credited, invoice date, posting reference, and the amount of the purchase. A purchases journal is shown in Exhibit 6-7. Each purchase on credit is recorded by listing the date, the supplier's name, the supplier's invoice date, and the amount.

The amounts from the purchases journal are posted at two different times. Each line is posted daily as a credit to the supplier's account in the accounts payable subsidiary ledger, thus keeping these accounts up to date on a daily basis. At the end of the month the amount column is totaled. The total credit purchases for the month are posted to two accounts in the general ledger. First, the total is posted as a debit to the Purchases account to update it for the current credit purchases. Second, the total is posted as a credit to the Accounts Payable control account to bring it into agreement with the totals of the daily postings to the supplier accounts in the subsidiary ledger. Note that the journal reference in each account is P-8, indicating that the postings were made from the Purchases (P) journal, page 8.

Cash Receipts Journal

All transactions involving the receipt of cash are recorded in the cash receipts journal. A Cash debit column is used for this purpose. Since many transactions involve cash receipts, each company determines exactly which accounts are frequently credited and accordingly establishes column headings for these accounts. A Miscellaneous credit column is then used for recording the credit amounts of infrequent transactions. Because many cash receipts are from cash sales and collections of accounts receivable (less the sales discounts) column headings are frequently provided for these accounts. Columns for the date, explanation, and posting references complete the cash receipts journal. A cash receipts journal is shown in Exhibit 6-8.

EXHIBIT 6-7
Purchases Journal
and Postings

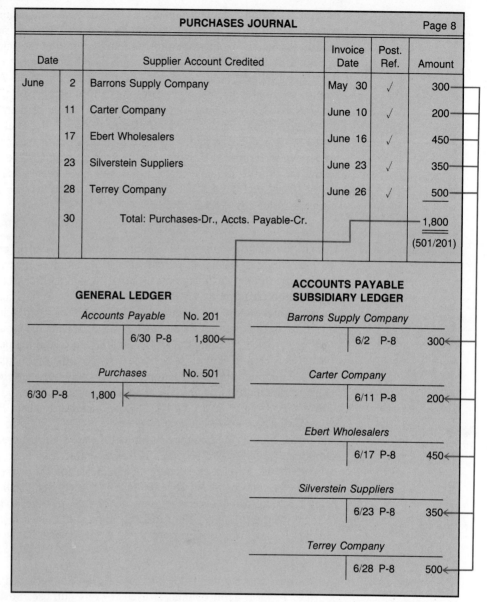

To record a cash receipt transaction, it is necessary to list the title of the account to be credited only if the amount of the credited account must be listed in the Miscellaneous credit column or if an individual customer account is credited in the subsidiary ledger. For instance, on June 2 D. Perry invested $3,000 into the company. Since no credit column is used for the D. Perry, Capital account, the account title is listed and the $3,000 credit is listed in the Miscellaneous credit

EXHIBIT 6-8   Cash Receipts Journal and Postings

		CASH RECEIPTS JOURNAL								Page 9
Date	Explanation (or Account Title)	Cash Debit	Sales Disc. Debit	Post. Ref.	Acct. Rec. Credit	Sales Credit	Post. Ref.	Misc. Credit
June 2	D. Perry, Capital, investment	3,000					301	3,000
4	Cash sales	1,500				1,500		
10	Ann Alcott, Invoice 229 less 2%	392	8	√	400			
16	Cash sales	1,600				1,600		
24	Land; sale at cost	2,000					111	2,000
27	Benjamin Bao, Invoice 230	750		√	750			
30	Totals	9,242	8		1,150	3,100		5,000
		(101)	(403)		(103)	(401)		(√)

GENERAL LEDGER

Cash   No. 101

6/30 CR-9   9,242

Accounts Receivable   No. 103

6/30 S-6   2,100 | 6/30 CR-9   1,150

Land   No. 111

Bal.   2,000 | 6/24 CR-9   2,000

D. Perry, Capital   No. 301

6/2   CR-9   3,000

Sales   No. 401

6/30   S-6   2,100
6/30   CR-9   3,100

Sales Discounts   No. 403

6/30 CR-9   8

ACCOUNTS RECEIVABLE SUBSIDIARY LEDGER

Ann Alcott

6/1   S-6   400 | 6/10 CR-9   400

Benjamin Bao

6/7   S-6   750 | 6/27 CR-9   750

Eileen Huhmann

6/15 S-6   600

Harold Tilly

6/22 S-6   100

Paul Yerdorff

6/29 S-6   250

column. A similar recording is made for the sale of land on June 24. On June 10 and 27 two customers paid their accounts and the customer account titles in the accounts receivable subsidiary ledger are listed. Account titles are *not* needed for amounts listed in the columns set up for specific accounts in the general ledger; explanations are usually provided, however. For the June 4 and 16 entries, explanations indicate these amounts are for cash sales.

Certain items in the cash receipts journal are posted on a daily basis and the remaining items are typically posted monthly. The entries to the individual customer accounts are posted daily. This daily posting keeps the customer account balances in the subsidiary ledger up to date. A check mark is placed in the accounts receivable posting reference column to indicate that the postings have been completed. In Exhibit 6-8 the June 10 and 27 credit entries are posted on those dates, respectively, as reductions to the Ann Alcott and Benjamin Bao customer accounts as shown (note the debit entries in the accounts from the sales journal). The individual amounts in the Miscellaneous credit column are typically posted daily (or at convenient intervals during the month) to the account titles listed. Thus the $3,000 credit to D. Perry, Capital on June 2 and the $2,000 credit to Land on June 24 are posted on the respective dates. The account numbers are listed in the posting reference column to indicate that the postings have been completed.

At the end of the month all the columns are totaled, and the total of the debit columns is compared with the total of the credit columns to prove their equality. The totals of the Cash and Sales Discounts columns are posted as debits to each of these accounts, respectively. The total of the Accounts Receivable column is posted as a credit to the control account to bring it into agreement with the subsidiary ledger. [Note the debit posting in the control account from the sales journal; also note that the debit and credit postings in the control account total $950 ($2,100 − $1,150), the same amount as the total of the postings to the subsidiary ledger accounts.] Finally, the total of the Sales column is posted as a credit to the Sales account to record the total cash sales. (The $3,100 cash sales, when combined with the $2,100 credit sales posted from the sales journal, amount to $5,200 total sales for June.) The total of the Miscellaneous column is *not* posted since the individual miscellaneous accounts were previously posted. The account numbers are listed below the column totals to indicate that the totals have been posted. A check mark is shown under the Miscellaneous column to indicate that it was not posted. The CR-9 listed beside each posting in the accounts indicates that the amount came from the cash receipts (CR) journal, page 9.

Cash Payments Journal

All transactions involving the payment of cash are recorded in the cash payments journal. The form of this journal as well as the entry and posting procedures are similar to the cash receipts journal. A Cash credit column is used to record the amount of each cash payment. Column headings are established for accounts that are frequently debited, and Miscellaneous debit and credit columns are used to record amounts of infrequent transactions. Since cash payments often involve cash purchases and payments of accounts payable (less the purchases discounts taken) column headings are usually provided for these accounts. Columns for the date, explanation, and posting references complete the cash payments journal. A cash payments journal is shown in Exhibit 6-9. Note that the *credit* columns are listed *before* the debit columns because so many credit entries are recorded in the Cash credit column. By placing this column and the other credit columns on the left side, time is saved in recording cash payment transactions.

To record a cash payment transaction the account title is listed only if the amount must be recorded in the Miscellaneous debit or credit column or if an individual supplier account is debited in the subsidiary ledger. For instance, on June 18 the purchase of the equipment requires a debit to Equipment for $4,500 and credits to Notes Payable and Cash for $3,500 and $1,000, respectively. Both the Equipment and the Notes Payable account titles must be listed since the respective amounts are recorded in the Miscellaneous columns (two lines are needed for this transaction). Similar entries are made for the Salaries Expense on June 20 and the Sales Returns and Allowances on June 22. On June 8 and June 21 payments are made to suppliers, and each supplier's account title in the subsidiary ledger is listed. Explanations are provided for amounts listed in the columns established for specific accounts in the general ledger (see the June 3 and 28 entries).

Certain items in the cash payments journal are posted daily, whereas other items are posted monthly. The entries to the individual supplier accounts are posted daily to keep the accounts payable subsidiary ledger up to date. In Exhibit 6-9 the June 8 and 21 debit entries are posted on those dates to the Barrons Supply Company and Carter Company supplier accounts as shown (note the credit entries in the accounts from the purchases journal). The individual amounts in the Miscellaneous debit and credit columns are typically posted daily (or at convenient intervals during the month) to the account titles as shown.

At the end of the month all the columns are totaled, and the total debits are compared with the total credits to prove their equality. The totals of the Cash and Purchases Discounts Taken columns are posted as credits to these accounts. The Accounts Payable column total is posted as a debit to the control account to bring it into agreement with the subsidiary ledger. [Note the credit posting in the control account from the purchases journal; also note that the $1,300 ($1,800 − $500) difference in the postings to the control account is the same as the total of the postings to the subsidiary ledger accounts.] Finally, the debit total of the Purchases column is posted to the Purchases account. (The $1,800 credit purchases from the purchases journal combined with the $600 cash purchases amounts to $2,400 total purchases for June.) The totals of the Miscellaneous columns are not posted since the individual amounts in these columns were previously posted. The CP-7 listings indicate that each posting came from the cash payments (CP) journal, page 7.

General Journal The general journal is required even when special journals are used. The general journal is used for recording adjusting, closing, and reversing entries, as well as for certain other transactions that do not occur very often. These transactions include purchases returns and allowances on account, sales returns and allowances on account, and also the purchase or sale of assets (other than merchandise) on account. The journalizing and posting process is the same as that described in earlier chapters, but with one exception. If subsidiary ledgers are used, any debit

EXHIBIT 6-9 Cash Payments Journal and Postings

CASH PAYMENTS JOURNAL
Page 7

Date		Explanation (or Account Title)	Cash Credit	Purch. Disc. Taken Credit	Post. Ref.	Misc. Credit	Post. Ref.	Accts. Pay. Debit	Purch. Debit	Post. Ref.	Misc. Debit
June	3	Cash purchases	200						200		
	8	Barrons Supply Co., no discount	300				√	300			
	18	Equipment Notes Payable Purchased with note and cash down payment.	1,000		203	3,500				114	4,500
	20	Salaries expense	900							511	900
	21	Carter Company, less 2% discount	196	4			√	200			
	22	Sales Returns and Allowances for cash	34							402	34
	28	Cash purchases	400						400		
	30	Totals	3,030	4		3,500		500	600		5,434
			(101)	(503)		(√)		(201)	(501)		(√)

GENERAL LEDGER

Cash   No. 101
6/30 CR-9 9,242	6/30 CP-7 3,030

Equipment   No. 114
6/18 CP-7 4,500

Accounts Payable   No. 201
6/30 CP-7 500	6/30 P-8 1,800

Notes Payable   No. 203
	6/18 CP-7 3,500

Sales Returns & Allowances   No. 402
6/22 CP-7 34

Purchases   No. 501
6/30 P-8 1,800
6/30 CP-7 600

Purchases Discounts Taken   No. 503
6/30 CP-7 4

Salaries Expense   No. 511
6/20 CP-7 900

ACCOUNTS PAYABLE SUBSIDIARY LEDGER

Barrons Supply Company
6/8 CP-7 300	6/2 P-8 300

Carter Company
6/21 CP-7 200	6/11 P-8 200

Ebert Wholesalers
	6/17 P-8 450

Silverstein Suppliers
	6/23 P-8 350

Terrey Company
	6/28 P-8 500

or credit to accounts receivable or accounts payable must be posted *twice*, once to the appropriate control account and once to the individual subsidiary account that is not part of the double-entry system.

For example, suppose that a $50 purchase allowance is granted on June 30 by Ebert Wholesalers for goods purchased on account on June 17. This entry would be recorded in the general journal. (If a *cash* purchase allowance had been given, the entry would have been recorded in the cash receipts journal.) The journal entry and postings are as follows (the other amounts in the control account and supplier account are from the cash payments and purchases journals; the G-5 refers to general (G) journal, page 5):

	GENERAL JOURNAL			Page 5
Date	Account Titles and Explanations	Acct. No.	Debit	Credit
June 30	Accounts Payable: Ebert Wholesalers	201/✓	50	
	Purchases Returns and Allowances	502		50
	To record purchase allowance on June 17 invoice.			

GENERAL LEDGER

Accounts Payable   No. 201

6/30 CP-7	500	6/30 P-8	1,800
6/30 G-5	50		

Purchases Returns
and Allowances   No. 502

	6/30 G-5 50

ACCOUNTS PAYABLE SUBSIDIARY LEDGER (PARTIAL)

Ebert Wholesalers

6/30 G-5	50	6/17 P-8	450

Modifications in Special Journals

As indicated earlier special journals are designed to fit the needs of each company. They are based on each company's common transactions; that is, the more often a company records transactions in a specific account, the more useful it is to establish a column for that account in the appropriate special journal. For instance, a company might include a Sales Tax column in its sales journal. It might also include a Sales Returns and Allowances column in its sales journal, or it might create a separate special journal for these items. Similar adjustments could be made to the purchases journal for purchases returns and allowances or transportation-in.

The cash payments journal might include additional columns for the Selling Expenses control account and the General and Administrative Expenses control account if these accounts are used. Or the Purchases column might be omitted from the cash payments journal if a company makes almost all its purchases on account.

In fact, if a company uses a voucher system as discussed in Chapter 7, the purchases journal is greatly expanded into a special journal called a voucher register. In addition, the columns in the cash payments journal are reduced in number, and this journal is then called a check register. The important point to remember is that although the special journals illustrated in this chapter are commonly used, each company designs its own special journals to fit its needs.

Advantages of Special Journals (with Subsidiary Ledgers)

There are several advantages to using special journals in conjunction with subsidiary ledgers. Some of the advantages are as follows:

1. **Time Is Saved in Recording.**   Usually only one line is used in recording each journal entry. Since the column headings list the main accounts to be debited or credited, this procedure reduces the amount of recording required. In addition, no explanations are needed in the sales and purchases journals.

2. **Time Is Saved in Posting.**   In the sales and purchases journals only two postings for the monthly totals are made in the general ledger. In the cash receipts and cash payments journals, postings are also reduced because only monthly postings are needed for most columns.

3. **Customer and Supplier Accounts Are Always Up to Date.**   Since postings are made daily to the subsidiary ledgers from the special journals, the current balance is always known for each customer or supplier account. Current customer account balances are useful to the credit department in (a) determining whether or not to extend additional credit to a customer; (b) watching for slow-paying customers so that they can be contacted about paying their accounts; and (c) answering customer questions about their account balances. Current supplier account balances are useful in ensuring that all cash discounts are taken and that payments are made when invoices are due.

4. **Similar Transactions Are Listed in Chronological Order.**   All sales on credit and purchases on credit are listed in chronological order in the sales and purchases journals. This procedure is useful in tracing inconsistencies between the records of a company and the records of its customers or suppliers when disagreements have arisen. It is also useful in the auditing process of verifying the total amounts of the sales and purchases transactions.

5. **Division of Accounting Tasks.**   Since several special journals are usually used, this procedure allows several employees to journalize and post at the same time in the separate journals. It also allows employees to "specialize" in recording certain transactions, thereby making the accounting process more efficient and minimizing errors.

ELECTRONIC DATA PROCESSING

Throughout this text we have used and will continue to use a manual accounting system. In the business world, however, companies look for ways to speed up and make the processing of accounting information more efficient. Some companies use mechanical bookkeeping machines that can prepare journals, invoices, and other records. With the reduction in (1) the cost of acquiring a computer and (2) the physical size of a computer (some minicomputers fit on the top of a desk), many companies are using electronic data processing for their accounting information. **In electronic data processing (EDP) a computer is used to record, retain, and report a company's financial and managerial accounting information.** EDP systems as they apply to financial accounting are briefly discussed in this section.[7]

Components of an EDP System

A computer is a high-speed electronic machine that can record, retain, process, and report information on the basis of a set of stored instructions. A computer is only one part of an EDP system. An EDP system consists of three main components: (1) input devices to transfer information and instructions into the central processing unit, (2) a central processing unit (the computer), and (3) output devices to transfer information out of the central processing unit. A diagram of the main components of an EDP system is shown in Exhibit 6-10.

INPUT DEVICES.   Input devices are necessary in an EDP system to transfer information and instructions to the computer. An input device can be a terminal or a reader of punched cards, punched paper tapes, magnetic tapes, or magnetic disks. Terminals are keyboard devices that are similar to a typewriter by which information is sent directly to the central processing unit. Examples of terminals are cash registers, which are used by retail companies such as Sears and J. C. Penney, that are an integral part of the EDP system. Readers "read" information from physical input items such as punched cards, magnetic tapes, or magnetic disks and send this information to the central processing unit.

A punched card is an 80-column data card in which small rectangular holes are punched in specified positions. The placement of the holes indicates specific information (punched cards are used in a later illustration). Magnetic tape is like tape used in a tape recorder, except that it is wider and more expensive; information is recorded and stored on this tape. A magnetic disk is similar to a musical record album; information is recorded and stored in spots on the disk. Pictures of a magnetic tape and magnetic disk are shown in Exhibit 6-11.

The information contained in the physical input items (punched cards, tapes, or disks) may be data from transactions, data from accounts, or computer programs. **A computer program is a detailed set of instructions (commands) to the computer about how to record, retain, process, and report information.** Even though computers are highly sophisticated and complex, nevertheless they are machines that must be operated by a person. The type, quality, and quantity of work done by a computer depends on the quality of the programs (instructions) and other input that the operator communicates to the computer.

Instructions must be communicated by means of language, and in computer programming several special languages are used. Some of these computer lan-

---

[7] There are numerous EDP systems that can be purchased from many companies, such as the Apple Computer Company and IBM Corporation. These systems, which are sold as a package, are designed to perform all or various aspects of the accounting process. The more common tasks include maintaining a company's accounts receivable, accounts payable, and payroll records.

**EXHIBIT 6-10
Main Components of
a Computer (EDP)
System**

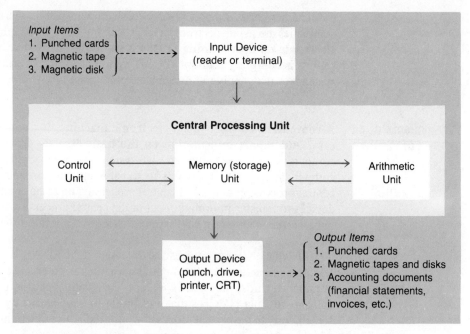

Input Items
1. Punched cards
2. Magnetic tape
3. Magnetic disk

Input Device
(reader or terminal)

Central Processing Unit

Control
Unit

Memory (storage)
Unit

Arithmetic
Unit

Output Device
(punch, drive,
printer, CRT)

Output Items
1. Punched cards
2. Magnetic tapes and disks
3. Accounting documents
   (financial statements,
   invoices, etc.)

EXHIBIT 6-11   Magnetic Tape and Magnetic Disk

Magnetic Tape

Magnetic Disk

Courtesy of International Business Machines Corporation.

guages are called RPGII, FORTRAN, BASIC, PL/1, and COBOL. In this text we do not discuss computer languages, although parts of several programs used to instruct the computer to perform various accounting steps are shown. In these programs COBOL is used (i.e., Common Business-Oriented Language) because it is widely used in business applications and consists of English phrases. Thus the sets of steps in the instructions can be more easily understood than if the instructions were given in some of the other computer languages.

CENTRAL PROCESSING UNIT. The central processing unit (CPU) of an EDP system consists of three parts: (1) the control unit, (2) the memory (storage) unit, and (3) the arithmetic unit. The control unit reads, interprets, and carries out the instructions given in the computer program. The arithmetic unit does the actual computing; that is, it adds, subtracts, multiplies, divides, and performs other computations (at extremely fast speeds). The memory unit stores program instructions and accounting information (e.g., results of recorded transactions, account balances). It is the largest and most expensive part of the central processing unit. When computers were first made vacuum tubes (like the tubes in old radios) were used in memory units. These units took up considerable space (rooms in some cases) and were very expensive. With the advent of transistors, printed circuitry, and chips, the memory units of computers and therefore the computers themselves have been significantly reduced in size. *Minicomputers* that fit on a desk top are now being used. (*Microcomputers,* which are run by hand calculators, are also available.) A picture of a conventional computer system and of a minicomputer are shown in Exhibits 6-12 and 6-13, respectively.

EXHIBIT 6-12   Conventional Computer System

Courtesy of International Business Machines Corporation.

EXHIBIT 6-13
Minicomputer

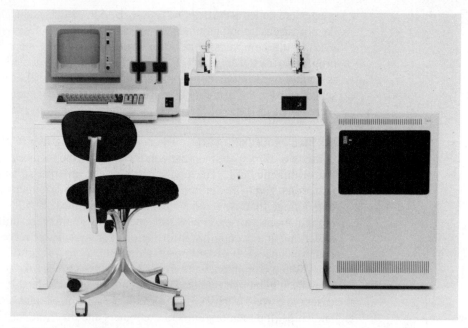

Courtesy of International Business Machines Corporation.

OUTPUT DEVICES. Output devices are necessary in an EDP system to transfer information out of the computer. Output devices include card and paper tape punches, magnetic tape and disk drives, printers, and CRT (cathode ray tube) screens. Card punches punch holes in data cards similar to the process discussed earlier for input documents. Tape or disk drives record output information on magnetic tapes or disks. Although cards, tapes, and disks are commonly used, before the output information can be understood by a person it must be converted into a human language. Printers are used for this purpose. Printers print output information in readable form on standard computer printout paper. CRT screens are similar to television sets and show the output on a televisionlike screen.

Printers can print out accounting information in whatever form is programmed into the computer. For financial accounting this information would include trial balances, financial statements, adjusting and closing entries, and so on. Printers can also print source documents such as sales invoices, purchase orders, and payroll checks.

Illustration of Electronic Data Processing

Whether a company uses a manual or EDP system, the steps that must be completed to record, retain, and report accounting information are the same. The difference lies in the *way* in which the steps are completed. In a manual system the steps are done by hand and are usually based on a set of written procedures. In an EDP system the steps are performed electronically by a machine and are based on programs written in computer language. Another difference between manual and electronic data processing is the *form* of the accounting documents used in the process. In a manual system, between the time a source document is used to first record a transaction until the time the accounting information is reported in a financial statement, accounting documents are listed on pieces of paper. These documents are easily readable by individuals and include the general journal, accounts, trial balances, and worksheets. In an EDP system the documents are cards, tapes, or disks, which are easily readable by a computer but not readable by a person.

To illustrate the differences in the instructions used to complete the steps and the accounting documents in the accounting process, we refer to a diagram and review problem in Chapter 3. In Chapter 3, Exhibit 3-18 showed a diagram of the steps and documents for a manual accounting system and the review problem and solution showed the manual journalizing and posting of several transactions and the preparation of an adjusted trial balance and financial statements. Because of space limitations these items are not reproduced here in entirety, and therefore at this time (and periodically during the later discussion) you should refer to the review problem and solution in Chapter 3. In Exhibit 6-14 the diagram from Exhibit 3-18 is reproduced (in abbreviated form), showing the differences between a manual and an EDP system. In the related discussion it is assumed that information is input into the computer with punched cards, the information is stored on a magnetic tape, and a printer is used for output.[8] The differences between the manual and EDP systems are discussed next.

JOURNALIZING AND THE GENERAL JOURNAL.   In a manual system journal entries are recorded (which is the first step) in a general journal (which is the resulting document). The journalizing procedures discussed in Chapter 2 (e.g., recording the debit entry on the first line and indenting the credit entry) are usually given as instructions (i.e., a so-called manual program) in a written procedures manual. In the EDP system a manual program is still necessary to instruct employees how to punch the transactions information on the data cards. This program would include instructions about the columns in which to punch the date, account number, amounts, and so on. The first two April journal entries from the review problem at the end of Chapter 3 are shown on page 249, in both general journal and punched card form. The arrows indicate where the same information (date, account number, account title, amount, and debit entry or credit entry) that is recorded in the general journal for a manual system would be recorded on punched cards for an EDP system.

---

[8] Many EDP systems (especially minicomputers) use CRT terminals and magnetic disks instead of punched cards and tapes. But because it is easier to "see" punched cards and tapes they are used in our example.

EXHIBIT 6-14   Differences Between Manual and Electronic Data Processing (Using Punched Cards and Tapes)

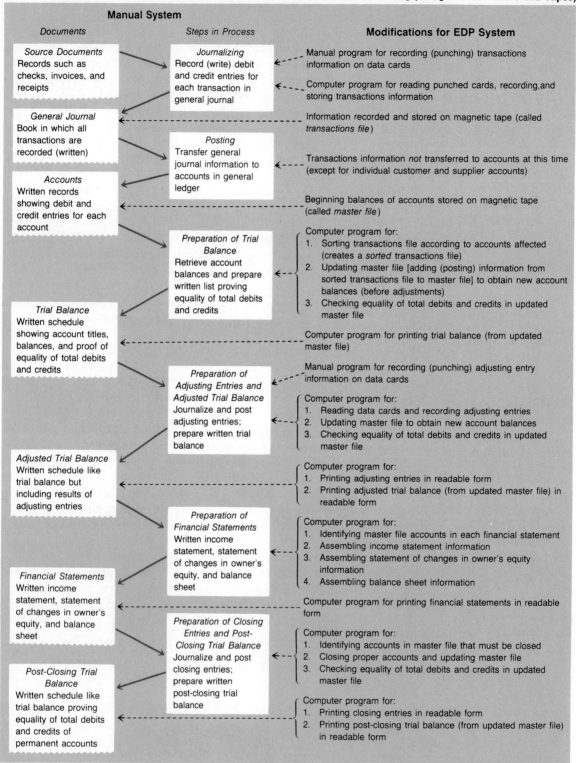

Manual System

Documents

Steps in Process

Modifications for EDP System

Source Documents
Records such as checks, invoices, and receipts

Journalizing
Record (write) debit and credit entries for each transaction in general journal

Manual program for recording (punching) transactions information on data cards

Computer program for reading punched cards, recording, and storing transactions information

Information recorded and stored on magnetic tape (called *transactions file*)

General Journal
Book in which all transactions are recorded (written)

Posting
Transfer general journal information to accounts in general ledger

Transactions information *not* transferred to accounts at this time (except for individual customer and supplier accounts)

Accounts
Written records showing debit and credit entries for each account

Beginning balances of accounts stored on magnetic tape (called *master file*)

Preparation of Trial Balance
Retrieve account balances and prepare written list proving equality of total debits and credits

Computer program for:
1. Sorting transactions file according to accounts affected (creates a *sorted* transactions file)
2. Updating master file [adding (posting) information from sorted transactions file to master file] to obtain new account balances (before adjustments)
3. Checking equality of total debits and credits in updated master file

Trial Balance
Written schedule showing account titles, balances, and proof of equality of total debits and credits

Computer program for printing trial balance (from updated master file)

Manual program for recording (punching) adjusting entry information on data cards

Preparation of Adjusting Entries and Adjusted Trial Balance
Journalize and post adjusting entries; prepare written trial balance

Computer program for:
1. Reading data cards and recording adjusting entries
2. Updating master file to obtain new account balances
3. Checking equality of total debits and credits in updated master file

Adjusted Trial Balance
Written schedule like trial balance but including results of adjusting entries

Computer program for:
1. Printing adjusting entries in readable form
2. Printing adjusted trial balance (from updated master file) in readable form

Preparation of Financial Statements
Written income statement, statement of changes in owner's equity, and balance sheet

Computer program for:
1. Identifying master file accounts in each financial statement
2. Assembling income statement information
3. Assembling statement of changes in owner's equity information
4. Assembling balance sheet information

Financial Statements
Written income statement, statement of changes in owner's equity, and balance sheet

Computer program for printing financial statements in readable form

Preparation of Closing Entries and Post-Closing Trial Balance
Journalize and post closing entries; prepare written post-closing trial balance

Computer program for:
1. Identifying accounts in master file that must be closed
2. Closing proper accounts and updating master file
3. Checking equality of total debits and credits in updated master file

Post-Closing Trial Balance
Written schedule like trial balance proving equality of total debits and credits of permanent accounts

Computer program for:
1. Printing closing entries in readable form
2. Printing post-closing trial balance (from updated master file) in readable form

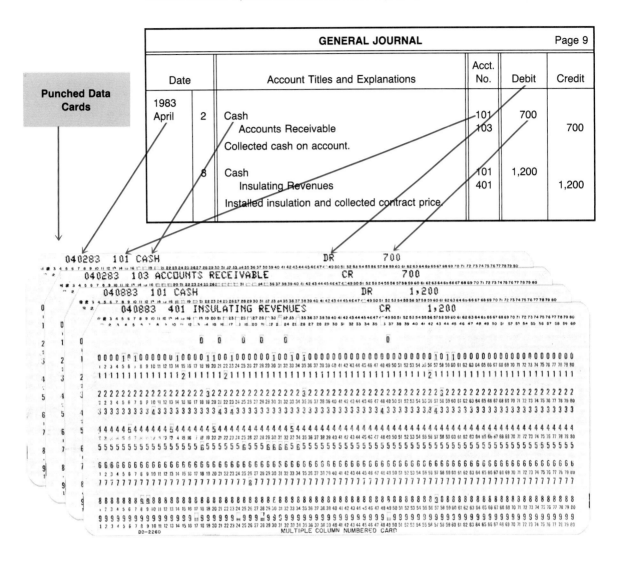

For purposes of illustration the punched card information is overly simplified. It may not be necessary to list the account titles because the computer may be programmed to read the account numbers. In addition, in an EDP system the account numbers would probably have more digits for identification purposes in later computer programs. Additional information could also be recorded on the cards. For instance, if the company purchased a depreciable asset, the estimated life and residual value of this asset could be included on the cards so that the computer could be programmed to calculate depreciation expense.

A computer program is necessary to tell the computer how to read, record, and store the transactions information from the punched data cards. The data division and procedure division of a partial program are as follows:

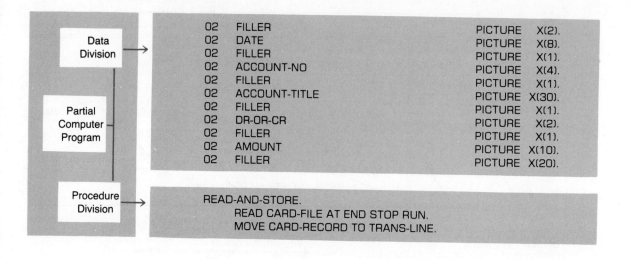

02	FILLER		PICTURE	X(2).
02	DATE		PICTURE	X(8).
02	FILLER		PICTURE	X(1).
02	ACCOUNT-NO		PICTURE	X(4).
02	FILLER		PICTURE	X(1).
02	ACCOUNT-TITLE		PICTURE	X(30).
02	FILLER		PICTURE	X(1).
02	DR-OR-CR		PICTURE	X(2).
02	FILLER		PICTURE	X(1).
02	AMOUNT		PICTURE	X(10).
02	FILLER		PICTURE	X(20).

```
READ-AND-STORE.
     READ CARD-FILE AT END STOP RUN.
     MOVE CARD-RECORD TO TRANS-LINE.
```

This partial program is written in COBOL so that you can understand the instructions given to the computer. At times programs have to be very long (sometimes hundreds of instructions) because a computer cannot think. The computer must be instructed, step by step, in a logical and painstaking fashion. In this illustration the partial program is short. The data division of the program indicates to the computer the format and meanings of the information punched in the columns of the data card. For example, FILLER means columns are left blank for spaces between items while DATE means the date is recorded in the following columns. Then more columns are left blank (FILLER), followed by the account number (ACCOUNT-NO). The second portion of the program is the procedure division (entitled READ-AND-STORE in this program), which contains the processing instructions for the computer. The first line instructs the computer to read a deck of punched cards (CARD-FILE) and to stop running after it reads the last card. The second line instructs the computer to move the information from each punched card (CARD-RECORD) to a transactions file for storage.

A transactions file is a magnetic tape (or other storage medium) in an EDP system on which all transactions information is stored. It takes the place of a general journal in a manual system. Although the information on a magnetic tape cannot actually be seen, part of the tape can be depicted as shown on the following pages.

The arrows from the punch card to the tape indicate that the information on the tape is in the order in which the transactions were recorded. Although space was left between the items in the example, on an actual magnetic tape each item of information would usually be stored immediately after the preceding item with a gap between the records (the information from each punched card).

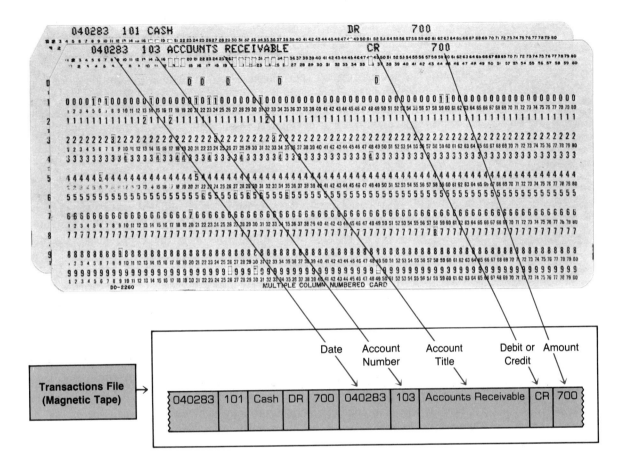

Transactions File (Magnetic Tape)

POSTING AND ACCOUNTS. In a manual system, after journalizing, the information is posted to the accounts and the account balances are brought up to date. This procedure is *not* followed in an EDP system. The *beginning* account balances are stored on a master file. **A master file is a magnetic tape (or other storage medium) on which permanent records are stored and which is periodically updated.** This method of information storage is a key difference between a manual and EDP system. In a manual system at any given time an account contains the beginning balance, changes in the account, and its current balance. In an EDP system the *master* file (until it is updated) contains the beginning balance of each account whereas the *transactions* file contains the changes in the accounts.[9] This

---

[9] It should be noted that the accounts receivable and accounts payable subsidiary ledger files *would* be updated on a daily (or more frequent) basis to ensure that current information is maintained on customer and supplier account balances. The computer program for this procedure is not shown.

difference is not important, however, because the computer can almost instantly update the accounts when needed.

PREPARATION AND LISTING OF TRIAL BALANCE.   In a manual system a written trial balance is prepared from the current account balances based on instructions in a procedures manual (these steps were discussed in Chapter 2). In an EDP system the account balances in the master file are not current. Therefore the computer must complete several steps based on instructions in a computer program. A *sorted* transactions file must first be made from the initial transactions file. A sorted transactions file contains the same information as the initial transactions file, but the transactions are sorted so that those affecting *each* account are listed together in chronological order. The account balances must be updated next by *merging* the sorted transactions file with the initial master file. (Merging in an EDP system is similar in essence to posting in a manual system.) After merging, the updated master file contains the current account balances (before adjustments). These steps are depicted in Exhibit 6-15.

The upper portion of Exhibit 6-15 shows part of the unsorted transactions file (continued on two lines). The portion of the sorted transactions file illustrated (continued on four lines) contains the seven chronological entries to the Cash account from the April transactions of the review problem. These debit and credit entries are merged with the $1,000 beginning Cash balance in the master file and result in the $1,230 Cash balance in the updated master file.

Finally, the program instructs the computer to check the equality of the total debits and credits in the updated master file. Because this equality check cannot be "seen" by a person, another computer program (which would usually be part of the previous program) instructs the computer to print a trial balance in readable form. To save space the programs and the trial balance are not shown here.

PREPARATION OF ADJUSTING ENTRIES AND ADJUSTED TRIAL BALANCE.   In a manual system the accountant scans the accounts and identifies the accounts that need adjusting, journalizes the adjusting entries, and prepares the adjusted trial balance. In a sophisticated EDP system the computer can be programmed to scan the accounts and prepare adjusting entries. For instance, we said earlier that data cards could include information for depreciable assets so that a computer program could be included to prepare the depreciation adjusting entry. Other more simple EDP systems require inputs (punched cards) to provide the computer with the necessary adjusting information; this requirement is assumed in the illustration.

A computer program must instruct the computer to read the data cards, record the adjusting entries, update the master file, and check the debit and credit equality in the updated master file. Another program instructs the computer to print the adjusting entries and the adjusted trial balance in readable form. These programs are not shown here. The adjusting entries are shown on the computer printout on the top of page 254.

EXHIBIT 6-15 Depiction of Sorting and Merging Process

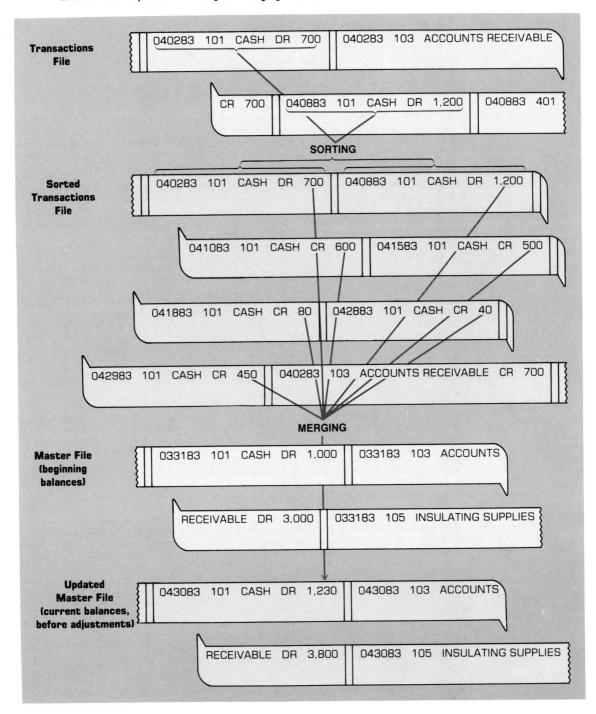

		ADJUSTING ENTRIES			
043083	505	RENT EXPENSE	DR	50	A
043083	107	PREPAID RENT	CR	50	A
043083	503	INSULATING SUPPLIES EXPENSE	DR	580	A
043083	105	INSULATING SUPPLIES	CR	580	A
043083	506	DEPRECIATION EXPENSE: TRUCKS	DR	200	A
043083	126	ACCUMULATED DEPREC.: TRUCKS	CR	200	A

Computer Printout of Adjusting Entries →

Note that the adjusting entries are not in a typical general journal form, but include the date, account numbers, account titles, debits and credits, and amounts. The printout of the adjusted trial balance is as follows:

ACE INSULATING COMPANY
ADJUSTED TRIAL BALANCE
APRIL 30, 1983

ACCOUNT TITLES	DEBIT	CREDIT
CASH	$ 1,230	
ACCOUNTS RECEIVABLE	3,800	
INSULATING SUPPLIES	1,820	
PREPAID RENT	250	
TRUCKS	12,000	
ACCUMULATED DEPRECIATION: TRUCKS		$ 4,000
ACCOUNTS PAYABLE		600
J. THOMPSON, CAPITAL		13,700
J. THOMPSON, WITHDRAWALS	500	
INSULATING REVENUES		2,700
SALARIES EXPENSE	450	
UTILITIES EXPENSE	40	
INSULATING SUPPLIES EXPENSE	580	
GAS, OIL, AND MAINTENANCE EXPENSE	80	
RENT EXPENSE	50	
DEPRECIATION EXPENSE: TRUCKS	200	
TOTALS	$21,000	$21,000

Note that this trial balance is the same as the trial balance shown in the review problem in Chapter 3.

PREPARATION AND LISTING OF FINANCIAL STATEMENTS. In an EDP system a computer program must instruct the computer to identify the accounts in the master file that belong on each financial statement (which is usually done by account number) and assemble (prepare) each financial statement. Part of the computer program is as follows:

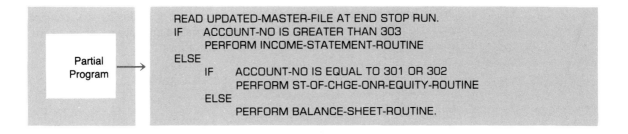

```
READ UPDATED-MASTER-FILE AT END STOP RUN.
IF    ACCOUNT-NO IS GREATER THAN 303
      PERFORM INCOME-STATEMENT-ROUTINE
ELSE
      IF    ACCOUNT-NO IS EQUAL TO 301 OR 302
            PERFORM ST-OF-CHGE-ONR-EQUITY-ROUTINE
      ELSE
            PERFORM BALANCE-SHEET-ROUTINE.
```

Recall from Chapter 3 that accounts are assigned account numbers from the chart of accounts in a specific order to facilitate preparation of the financial statements. Recall also that the income statement is prepared first, followed next by the statement of changes in owner's equity, and then by the balance sheet. This partial program instructs the computer to read each account number and, depending on its number, include it in the preparation of the income statement, statement of changes in owner's equity, or balance sheet. For instance, accounts with numbers greater than 303 (i.e., revenue and expense accounts) would be included in the income statement. To save space the programs (routines) for preparing the financial statements are not included here. The computer must then be told to print the financial statements in a readable form. To save space only a computer printout of the income statement is shown as follows (it is the same as the income statement in Chapter 3):

ACE INSULATING COMPANY
INCOME STATEMENT
FOR MONTH ENDED APRIL 30, 1983

REVENUES:		
INSULATING REVENUES		$2,700
EXPENSES:		
SALARIES EXPENSE	$450	
UTILITIES EXPENSE	40	
INSULATING SUPPLIES EXPENSE	580	
GAS, OIL, AND MAINTENANCE EXPENSE	80	
RENT EXPENSE	50	
DEPRECIATION EXPENSE: TRUCKS	200	
TOTAL EXPENSES		1,400
NET INCOME		$1,300

PREPARATION OF CLOSING ENTRIES AND POST-CLOSING TRIAL BALANCE. A computer program must instruct the computer to identify the accounts (by account numbers) in the master file that must be closed. The computer must then be told to close these accounts and update the master file, to check the debit and credit equality in the updated master file, and to print the closing entries and post-closing trial balance in a readable form. This program and post-closing trial balance are not shown here; the computer printout of the closing entries is as follows:

			CLOSING ENTRIES		
043083	401	INSULATING REVENUES		DR	2,700
043083	501	SALARIES EXPENSE		CR	450
043083	502	UTILITIES EXPENSE		CR	40
043083	503	INSULATING SUPPLIES EXPENSE		CR	580
043083	504	GAS, OIL, AND MAINTENANCE EXP.		CR	80
043083	505	RENT EXPENSE		CR	50
043083	506	DEPRECIATION EXPENSE: TRUCKS		CR	200
043083	301	J. THOMPSON, CAPITAL		CR	800
043083	302	J. THOMPSON, WITHDRAWALS		CR	500

Note that an Income Summary account is not used and that the J. Thompson, Capital account is increased (credited) directly for $800 (the difference between the $1,300 net income and the $500 withdrawals).

SUMMARY. Although computers are very efficient machines, they are machines nevertheless. The sizes of computers and numbers and sophistication of computer programs may vary from company to company. The quality of the accounting information (the output), however, depends on the quality of the computer programs and the quality of the employees operating the system. There is an old saying, "garbage-in, garbage-out," which is very true for EDP systems. It is one of the reasons why special attention is placed on evaluating the strength of internal control for these systems in the auditing process.

GLOSSARY

Authorization. Permission to exchange or use assets for specific purposes under given conditions in a company. Used for internal control purposes.

Cash Payments Journal. Special journal used to record all cash payments.

Cash Receipts Journal. Special journal used to record all cash receipts.

Computer. High-speed electronic machine that can record, retain, process, and report information on the basis of a set of stored instructions.

Computer Program. Detailed set of instructions to the computer about how to record, retain, process, and report information.

Control Account. Account in the general ledger that takes the place of certain accounts that have been removed and placed in a subsidiary ledger. Examples are Accounts Receivable and Accounts Payable.

Electronic Data Processing (EDP). Use of a computer to record, retain, and report a company's accounting information.

Execution. The set of steps needed to complete the exchange of assets or use of assets in a company. Used for internal control purposes.

Internal Control. Policies and procedures used by a company to safeguard its assets and to ensure that reliable financial statements are the end result of an efficient accounting system.

Master File. A storage medium (e.g., magnetic tape or disk) in an EDP system on which permanent records are stored and which is periodically updated.

Purchase Order. Business document authorizing a supplier to ship the items listed at a specified price.

Purchase Requisition. Internal business document requesting that certain items of inventory be purchased.

Purchases Journal. Special journal used to record all purchases on account.

Recording. Includes journalizing and posting transactions, and keeping up-to-date records of a company's assets. Used for internal control purposes.

Sales Journal. Special journal used to record all sales on account.

Special Journal. Journal used to record major recurring transactions. Examples are sales journal, purchases journal, cash receipts journal, and cash payments journal.

Subsidiary Ledger. Group of similar accounts that show the detail of one specific company activity. Examples are accounts receivable and accounts payable subsidiary ledgers.

Transactions File. A storage medium (e.g., magnetic tape or disk) in an EDP system, on which all transactions information is stored.

QUESTIONS

Q6-1 What is the definition of internal control? What is meant by "safeguarding assets"?

Q6-2 List the four subgoals of internal control.

Q6-3 For internal control, what is meant by (1) authorizing, (2) executing, and (3) recording transactions? What internal control policies would be established for each of them?

Q6-4 List the major concerns of internal control in regard to recording transactions.

Q6-5 What is a subsidiary ledger? What is a control account? Why are subsidiary ledgers used for accounts receivable and accounts payable?

Q6-6 Reply to this statement: "When all the customer accounts are taken from the general journal and placed in a subsidiary ledger, the general journal will no longer balance."

Q6-7 What is meant by "accountability for assets"? Why is it important for internal control?

Q6-8 What is a special journal? When special journals are used, list the major journals and the transactions recorded in each journal.

Q6-9 How are transactions journalized in the sales journal? When is the sales journal posted?

Q6-10 How are transactions journalized in the purchases journal? When is the purchases journal posted?

Q6-11 Discuss the recording and posting process for the cash receipts journal.

Q6-12   Discuss the recording and posting process for the cash payments journal.

Q6-13   Which types of journal entries are recorded in a general journal when a company uses special journals?

Q6-14   List and briefly discuss the advantages of using special journals.

Q6-15   Distinguish between manual and electronic data processing.

Q6-16   What is electronic data processing? Define: computer, computer program, transactions file, and master file.

Q6-17   List and briefly discuss the three main components of an EDP system.

Q6-18   Name the three parts of a central processing unit (CPU) of a computer. For what is each part used?

EXERCISES

E6-1   Internal Control Principles. Internal control is concerned with promoting an efficient accounting system and safeguarding a company's assets. Several general principles have been developed to help in establishing and maintaining good internal control.

Required: List and discuss the general principles of internal control presented in this chapter.

E6-2   Separation of Duties. The Leonibus Company is concerned about maintaining internal control over selected accounting duties. The company has three competent employees (Employees A, B, and C) who must perform the following tasks:

(a) Write checks to suppliers.
(b) Record transactions in the sales journal and the accounts receivable subsidiary ledger.
(c) Deposit customers' checks received in payment of their accounts.
(d) Issue credit memos to customers for sales returns and allowances on account.
(e) Record transactions in the purchases journal and the accounts payable subsidiary ledger.
(f) Issue debit memos to suppliers for purchases returns and allowances on account.

Required: 1. Explain what is meant by separation of duties. Why is it important for internal control?
2. Show how you would divide the above tasks among Employees A, B, and C for *good* internal control. Explain your reasoning.
3. Show how you would divide the above tasks among Employees A, B, and C for *poor* internal control. Explain your reasoning.

E6-3   Internal Control Weaknesses. Listed below are several internal control weaknesses of a retail store:

(a) One employee is responsible for depositing customer checks and for recording their receipt in both the cash receipts journal and the accounts receivable subsidiary ledger.
(b) Credit sales of a large dollar amount can be approved by any sales employee.
(c) Sales invoices are not prenumbered.
(d) Some purchases are made by phone and no purchase order is written up.
(e) Employees are allowed to bring coats, bags, and purses into working areas.
(f) One employee is responsible for recording purchases in the purchases journal and for writing checks.
(g) The inventory of gold jewelry for sale is kept in unlocked display cases.
(h) Whenever inventory is low, any sales employee can prepare a purchase order to reorder the items and send the purchase order to the purchasing department.

Required: 1. For each internal control weakness explain how the weakness might result in a loss of the company's assets or an inefficient accounting system.
2. For each internal control weakness explain what action could be taken to correct the weakness.

E6-4 Matching Transactions with Special Journals. The following journals are used by a company:

A. Cash Receipts
B. Cash Payments
C. Sales
D. Purchases
E. General

During a month the company entered into the following transactions:

1. Sold merchandise on account.
2. Paid utilities expense.
3. Owner invested an additional $5,000 in the company.
4. Purchased merchandise on account.
5. Returned defective merchandise for cash refund.
6. Sold merchandise for cash.
7. Paid cash to customer for return of faulty merchandise previously sold to the customer.
8. Purchased land by issuing note payable.
9. Purchased merchandise for cash.
10. Prepared closing entries.
11. Returned defective merchandise to supplier for adjustment to account.
12. Purchased equipment with note payable and cash down payment.

Required: Match each of these transactions with the appropriate journal (A through E) in which it would be recorded.

E6-5 Special Journals and Accounts. Below are ten transactions of a company that uses special journals:

Transaction	Journal	Accounts
(a) Purchase of equipment for cash	————	————
(b) Sale of merchandise on account	————	————
(c) Preparation of adjusting entries	————	————
(d) Sales allowance for cash	————	————
(e) Purchase of merchandise on account	————	————
(f) Sale of merchandise for cash	————	————
(g) Payment of advertising expense	————	————
(h) Purchase of merchandise for cash	————	————
(i) Payment on accounts payable	————	————
(j) Return of defective merchandise to supplier for adjustment to account	————	————

Required: In the space provided:
1. Indicate in which of the following journals the transaction would be recorded: sales, purchases, cash receipts, cash payments, and general journal.

2. Indicate the accounts that would be debited or credited in the journal for each transaction.

E6-6 Special Journals and Accounts. Shown below are ten transactions of a company that uses special journals:

Transaction	Journal	Accounts
(a) Purchase of merchandise for cash	_____	_____
(b) Payment of telephone expense	_____	_____
(c) Additional investment by owner	_____	_____
(d) Sale of merchandise on account	_____	_____
(e) Preparation of closing entries	_____	_____
(f) Purchase of merchandise on account	_____	_____
(g) Payment of salary expense	_____	_____
(h) Purchase of equipment by issuing note payable	_____	_____
(i) Sale of merchandise for cash	_____	_____
(j) Payment on account payable, less discount	_____	_____

Required: 1. Indicate in which of the following journals the transaction would be recorded: sales, purchases, cash payments, cash receipts, and general journal.
2. Indicate the accounts that would be debited or credited in the journal for each transaction.

E6-7 Cash Receipts Journal. The Boggler Company entered into the following transactions during the month of May:

Date	Transaction
May 1	Sold $1,000 of merchandise to W. Moehler for cash.
5	Received payment from P. Ott on account receivable of $450 less 2% discount.
13	Sold land at its original cost of $1,500.
24	T. Boggler invested an additional $1,000 cash in the company.
30	Received payment from V. Sidnel on account receivable in the amount of $300.

Required: Using the format shown in the text prepare a cash receipts journal and record the Boggler Company transactions in it.

E6-8 Cash Payments Journal. The Foily Company entered into the following transactions during the month of April:

Date	Transaction
Apr. 2	Refunded $50 cash to a customer, Tolley Company, for faulty merchandise returned.
5	Purchased $1,200 of merchandise for cash.
15	Paid advertising expense of $100 for the first two weeks of the month.
20	Purchased $1,300 of equipment making a $300 cash down payment and signing a $1,000 note.
26	Paid $1,000 account payable to Caner Company, less 2% discount.

Required: Using the format shown in the text prepare a cash payments journal and enter the Foily Company transactions in it.

E6-9 Posting from Journals. The sales journal and purchases journal of the Atheon Company for July are as follows:

SALES JOURNAL					Page 8
Date		Customer Account Debited	Invoice No.	Post. Ref.	Amount
July	1	Van Haley	640		60
	6	Faye Dunday	641		103
	14	Howard Carren	642		47
	29	Gayle Francis	643		206
	31	Total			416

PURCHASES JOURNAL					Page 4
Date		Supplier Account Credited	Invoice Date	Post. Ref.	Amount
July	3	Lalel Company	June 30		400
	12	Deiter's Supply Company	July 12		300
	24	Foiler Suppliers	July 22		200
	30	Longaker Company	July 29		500
	31	Total			1,400

The company shows the following accounts in its general ledger:

| *Accounts Receivable* No. 103 | *Accounts Payable* No. 201 | *Sales* No. 401 | *Purchases* No. 501 |

Required: Assuming that the Atheon Company uses subsidiary ledgers for accounts receivable and accounts payable, make the necessary daily and monthly postings to the appropriate accounts.

E6-10 Posting from Cash Receipts Journal. The cash receipts journal of the TR Company for May is as follows:

CASH RECEIPTS JOURNAL									Page 2
Date	Explanation (or Account Title)	Cash Debit	Sales Disc. Debit	Post. Ref.	Acct. Rec. Credit	Sales Credit	Post. Ref.	Misc. Credit
May 3	Cash sales	350				350		
10	P. Tari, Invoice 302 less 2%	490	10		500			
20	Randall Quepy, Invoice 306	300			300			
28	Land; sale at cost	5,000						5,000
31	Totals	6,140	10		800	350		5,000

The company uses a subsidiary ledger for accounts receivable, and it shows the following accounts in its general ledger:

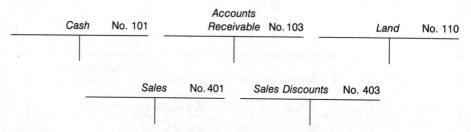

Cash   No. 101   *Accounts Receivable* No. 103   *Land*   No. 110

Sales   No. 401   *Sales Discounts*   No. 403

Required: Make all the necessary postings from the cash receipts journal.

E6-11   Posting from Cash Payments Journal.   The cash payments journal used by the Polex Company is shown below. The company uses a subsidiary ledger for accounts payable and shows the accounts on the following page in its general ledger.

CASH PAYMENTS JOURNAL										Page 6
Date	Explanation (or Account Title)	Cash Credit	Purch. Disc. Taken Credit	Post. Ref.	Misc. Credit	Post. Ref.	Accts. Pay. Debit	Purch. Debit	Post. Ref.	Misc. Debit
May 1	Land { Purchase with note and Notes Payable { cash down payment	1,000			4,000					5,000
10	Utilities Expense	180								180
20	Porter Company, less 2% discount	490	10				500			
30	Cash purchases	475						475		
31	Barrows Company	600					600			
31	Totals	2,745	10		4,000		1,100	475		5,180

Account Title	Account Number
Cash	101
Land	110
Accounts Payable	201
Notes Payable	210
Purchases	501
Purchases Discounts Taken	503
Utilities Expense	521

Required: Set up T-accounts for the Polex Company account titles and the accounts payable subsidiary ledger and make all the necessary postings from the cash payments journal.

PROBLEMS

Part A

P6-1A Internal Control and Purchases. The Anibonita Company is a retail store with several sales departments. It also has an accounting department, a purchasing department, and a receiving department. All inventory is kept in the sales departments. When the inventory of a specific item is low, the manager of the sales department that sells the item notifies the purchasing department, which then orders the merchandise. All purchases are made on credit. Anibonita Company pays the freight charges on all its purchases after being notified of the cost by the freight company. When the inventory is delivered, it is checked in by the receiving department and then sent to the sales department where it is placed on the sales shelves. The company uses special journals and subsidiary ledgers.

Required:
1. Briefly explain what is meant by authorization, execution, recording, and accountability in relation to internal control over the Anibonita Company's purchasing process.
2. Describe what source documents are needed, as well as how they should be used, to maintain internal control over the purchasing process.

P6-2A Evaluation of Internal Control. Listed below are several independent situations, each of which may or may not have one or more internal control weaknesses.

(a) All sales made by Company A, whether they are for cash or on account, are "rung up" on a single cash register. Employee X is responsible for collecting the cash receipts from sales and customer charge slips at the end of each day. The employee carefully counts the cash, preparing a "cash receipts" slip for the total. The employee compares the total of the cash receipts slip and the customer charge slips to the total sales on the cash register tape to verify the total sales for the day. The cash register tape is then discarded and the cash is deposited in the bank. The cash receipts slip and the customer charge slips are turned over to a different employee who records the cash and credit sales in the general journal.

(b) To reduce the paperwork in Company B, orders for purchases of inventory from suppliers are made by phone. No purchase order is prepared. When the goods arrive at the company they are immediately brought to the sales floor. An employee then authorizes payment based on the supplier's invoice, writes and signs a check, and mails payment to the supplier. Another employee uses the paid invoice to record the purchase and payment in the general journal.

(c) Employee Y is in charge of employee records for Company C. Whenever a new employee is hired, the new employee's name, address, salary, and other relevant information are properly recorded. Every payday all employees are paid by check. At this time Employee Y makes out each employee's check, signs it, and gives it to each employee. After distributing the paychecks, Employee Y makes an entry in the general journal debiting Salaries Expense and crediting Cash for the total amount of the salary checks.

(d) Company D owns a delivery van for deliveries of sales to customers. No mileage is kept of the deliveries, although all gas and oil receipts are carefully checked before being paid. To advertise the store, two signs with the store's name have been printed and hung on each side of the van. These signs are easily removable so that the van can be periodically cleaned without damaging the signs. The company allows employees to borrow the van at night or on the weekends if they need the van for personal hauling. No mileage is kept of the personal hauling, but the employee who borrowed the van must fill the gas tank before returning the van.

(e) In Company E one employee is responsible for counting and recording all the receipts received in the mail from customers paying their accounts. Usually customers pay by check but occasionally they mail cash. Every day after the mail is delivered this employee opens the envelopes containing payments by customers. She carefully counts all remittances and places the checks and cash in a bag. She then lists the amount of each check or cash received and the customer's name on a sheet of paper. After totaling the cash and checks received she records the receipts in the cash receipts journal, endorses the checks in the company's name, and deposits the checks and cash in the bank.

(f) Company F has purchased several small calculators for use by the office and sales employees. So that these hand calculators will be available to any employee who needs one they are kept in an unlocked storage cabinet in the office. Anyone who takes and uses a calculator "signs out" the calculator by writing his or her name on a sheet of paper posted near the cabinet. When the calculator is returned the employee crosses out his or her name on the sheet.

Required: 1. List the internal control weakness or weaknesses you find in each of the above independent situations. If no weakness can be found explain why the internal control is good.
2. Describe how you would remedy each situation in which there is an internal control weakness to improve the internal control.

P6-3A   Special Journals, Journalizing and Posting.   The transactions that the Boco Company completed during the month of May are as follows:

Date	Transaction
May 1	Paid May rent of $500 and recorded as rent expense.
2	Sold merchandise on credit to T. Crone, Invoice No. 80, $400. Terms 2/10, n/30.
4	Purchased merchandise for cash, $300.
5	Sold merchandise for cash, $150.
7	Purchased merchandise on credit from Barnum Supply Company, $850, invoice dated May 6. Terms 2/10, n/30.
9	Received $392 from T. Crone in payment of Invoice No. 80, less cash discount.
11	Sold land at cost, $2,000.
12	Paid Barnum Supply Company for merchandise received on May 7, less cash discount.
14	Sold merchandise on credit to R. Holen, Invoice No. 81, $350. Terms 2/10, n/30.
15	Purchased merchandise on credit from Walthem's Company $1,600, invoice dated today. Terms n/30.
18	Received $100 credit on account with Walthem's Company for defective merchandise purchased on May 15.
20	Received payment from R. Holen for Invoice No. 81, less cash discount.
24	Purchased store equipment by paying $600 cash and signing a note payable for $1,000.
28	Sold merchandise for cash, $280.
30	Paid May utilities bill, $120.

The company shows the following accounts in its general ledger:

Account Title	Account Number
Cash	101
Accounts Receivable	103
Land	110
Store Equipment	114
Accounts Payable	201
Notes Payable	210
Sales	401
Sales Discounts	403
Purchases	501
Purchases Discounts Taken	503
Purchases Returns and Allowances	506
Utilities Expense	521
Rent Expense	523

Required:
1. Prepare a sales journal, purchases journal, cash receipts journal, cash payments journal, and general journal as shown in the text.
2. Record the Boco Company transactions in the appropriate journals.
3. Set up the general ledger accounts and subsidiary ledgers for accounts receivable and accounts payable.
4. Make all the necessary postings during and at the end of the month.

P6-4A   Cash Receipts Journal.   During the month of February the Mobac Company entered into the following transactions related to cash receipts:

Date	Transaction
Feb. 1	The owner, T. Mobac, invested an additional $5,000 cash in the business.
3	Sold $600 of merchandise for cash.
3	Returned $50 of defective merchandise to supplier for cash refund.
5	Collected $500 from B. Teer for payment on account.
8	Sold $450 of merchandise for cash.
11	Received $600 less 2% discount from T. Beem for payment on account.
13	Sold land at cost, $6,000.
14	Received $1,015 in payment of a $1,000 note receivable, plus current interest revenue of $15.
16	Collected $375 from R. Cooke in payment of account.
20	Sold $250 of merchandise for cash.
23	Received $700 less 2% discount from Q. Tempe for payment on account.
28	Borrowed $1,500 from local bank by signing a 3-month note.

The company uses a subsidiary ledger for its accounts receivable and on January 31 showed the following accounts (and selected account balances) in its books:

GENERAL LEDGER

Cash No. 101	Accounts Receivable No. 103	Notes Receivable No. 106
	Bal. 2,445	Bal. 1,000

Land No. 110	Notes Payable No. 210	T. Mobac, Capital No. 301
Bal. 6,000		

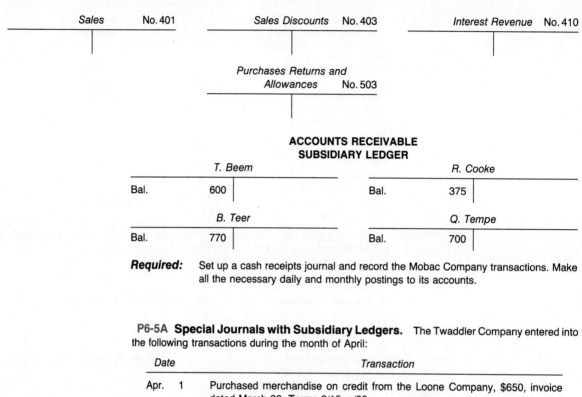

Sales	No. 401		Sales Discounts	No. 403		Interest Revenue	No. 410

Purchases Returns and
Allowances   No. 503

**ACCOUNTS RECEIVABLE
SUBSIDIARY LEDGER**

	T. Beem			R. Cooke	
Bal.	600		Bal.	375	

	B. Teer			Q. Tempe	
Bal.	770		Bal.	700	

Required: Set up a cash receipts journal and record the Mobac Company transactions. Make all the necessary daily and monthly postings to its accounts.

P6-5A Special Journals with Subsidiary Ledgers.   The Twaddler Company entered into the following transactions during the month of April:

Date		Transaction
Apr.	1	Purchased merchandise on credit from the Loone Company, $650, invoice dated March 30. Terms 2/15, n/30.
	1	Paid April rent of $500 and recorded as rent expense.
	2	Sold merchandise on credit to Norm Waters, Invoice No. 302, $350. Terms 2/10, n/30.
	3	Received $50 credit on account from Loone Company for defective merchandise purchased on April 1.
	5	Sold merchandise for cash, $1,400.
	6	Purchased store equipment on credit from XYZ Supply Company, $500.
	8	Purchased $800 of merchandise for cash.
	9	Received payment from Norm Waters for Invoice No. 302, less cash discount.
	10	Sold merchandise on credit to Lee Dillard, Invoice No. 303, $600. Terms 2/15, n/30.
	10	Paid balance due on merchandise purchased from Loone Company on April 1, less cash discount.
	12	Sold store equipment at cost, $50.
	12	Purchased merchandise on credit from Scroggs Company, invoice dated today, $1,200. Terms 2/10, n/30.
	14	Purchased land by paying $2,000 cash and signing an $8,000 note payable.
	16	Sold merchandise for cash, $500.
	18	Borrowed $6,000 from local bank, issuing a 90-day note payable.
	19	Paid balance due on merchandise purchased from Scroggs Company on April 12, less cash discount.
	20	The owner, T. Twaddler, invested an additional $2,500 cash in the business.
	24	Received balance due from Lee Dillard for Invoice No. 303, less cash discount.
	28	Paid monthly salaries, $3,000.
	30	Paid April utility bill, $100.

Required:
    1. Prepare a sales journal, a purchases journal, a cash receipts journal, a cash payments journal, and a general journal as shown in the text.
    2. Record the Twaddler Company transactions in the appropriate journals.
    3. Prepare subsidiary ledgers for accounts receivable and accounts payable.
    4. Make the daily postings to the subsidiary ledgers.

PROBLEMS
Part B

P6-1B Internal Control and Sales. The JeBean Company is a wholesale company that makes only sales on account to retail customers who order through the mail. The company has an accounting department, credit department, inventory department, and shipping department. After approval of the order by the credit department, the merchandise is assembled in the inventory department and then sent to the shipping department. The shipping department packs the merchandise in cardboard boxes after which it is picked up by the freight company and shipped to the customer. JeBean Company pays for freight charges on all items shipped to customers after being notified of the cost by the freight company. The company uses special journals and subsidiary ledgers.

Required:
    1. Briefly explain what is meant by authorization, execution, recording, and accountability in relation to internal control of the JeBean Company's sales process.
    2. Describe what source documents are needed, as well as how they should be used, to maintain internal control over the sales process.

P6-2B Internal Control over Purchases. Oliver Bauer, owner of Bauer's Retail Store, has been very careful to establish good internal control over purchases for his store. The store has several employees and since Ollie cannot devote as much time as he would like to running the store, he has entrusted a long-time employee with the task of purchasing inventory. This employee has worked for Ollie for 15 years and knows all of the store's suppliers. Whenever inventory must be purchased the employee prepares a purchase order and mails it to the supplier. When a rush order is needed the employee occasionally calls in the order and does not prepare a purchase order. This procedure is acceptable to the suppliers because they know the employee. When the goods are received from the supplier this employee carefully checks in each item to verify the correct quantity and quality. This job is usually done at night after the store is closed, thus allowing the employee to help with sales to customers during regular working hours. After checking in the items the employee initials the copy of the supplier invoice received with the goods, staples the copy to the purchase order (if there is one), journalizes the purchase, and prepares a check for payment. Oliver Bauer examines the source documents (purchase order and initialed invoice) at this point, signs the checks, and the employee journalizes the payment. Ollie has become concerned about the store's gross profit, which has been steadily decreasing even though he has heard customers complaining that the store's selling prices are too high. In a discussion with the employee, the employee says, "I'm doing my best to hold down costs. I will continue to do my purchasing job as efficiently as possible (even though I am overworked). However, I think you should hire another sales person and spend more on advertising. This will increase your sales and, in turn, your gross profit."

Required:
    Why do you think the gross profit of the store has gone down? Prepare a report for Oliver Bauer that summarizes any internal control weaknesses existing in the purchasing procedure and explain what the end result might be. Make suggestions for improving any weaknesses you uncover.

P6-3B Special Journals with Subsidiary Ledgers. The Noval Company entered into the following transactions during the month of June:

Date	Transaction
June 1	Paid June rent of $350 and recorded as rent expense.
3	Sold merchandise for cash, $400.
5	Purchased equipment on credit from Ziemar Company for $800.
7	Purchased merchandise on credit from the Kaas Company, $1,300, invoice dated June 5. Terms 2/10, n/30.
8	Sold merchandise on credit to B. Coton, Invoice No. 501, $800. Terms 2/10, n/30.
10	Received $100 credit on account from Kaas Company for faulty merchandise purchased on June 7.
12	Sold equipment at cost, $250.
15	Received payment from B. Coton for Invoice No. 501, less cash discount.
18	Purchased $1,200 of merchandise for cash.
19	Paid balance due on merchandise purchased from Kaas Company on June 7, less cash discount.
20	Sold merchandise on credit to R. Hagin, Invoice No. 502, $1,500. Terms 2/10, n/30.
21	Sold merchandise for cash, $750.
23	Purchased land by paying $3,000 cash and signing a $9,000 note payable.
25	Purchased merchandise on credit from Peol Company, invoice dated today, $1,800. Terms 2/10, n/30.
26	The owner T. Noval invested an additional $5,000 cash in the business.
28	Received balance due from R. Hagin for Invoice No. 502, less cash discount.
28	Borrowed $10,000 from local bank, issuing a 6-month note payable.
29	Paid balance due for merchandise purchased from Peol Company on June 25, less cash discount.
30	Paid monthly salaries, $8,000.
30	Paid June telephone bill, $85.

Required:
1. Prepare a sales journal, a purchases journal, a cash receipts journal, a cash payments journal, and a general journal as shown in the text.
2. Record the transactions of the Noval Company in the appropriate journals.
3. Prepare subsidiary ledgers for accounts receivable and accounts payable.
4. Make the daily postings to the subsidiary ledgers.

P6-4B Cash Payments Journal. The Shoer Company entered into the following transactions during the month of January:

Date	Transaction
Jan. 2	Purchased new equipment by signing a $1,000 note payable and paying $500 cash.
2	Purchased $1,200 of merchandise for cash.
4	Paid January rent of $500 and recorded as rent expense.
6	Paid balance due to Willis Company, $800, less 2% discount.
12	Refunded $80 cash to customer upon return of defective merchandise sold earlier in the month.
12	Paid $600 to Value Suppliers on account.
15	Paid $50 for advertisement in local newspaper.
19	Paid Quine Supply Company $750, less 2% discount.
20	Purchased $200 of merchandise for cash.
25	Paid Tailer Company $800 on account.
30	Paid January utility bill in the amount of $110.
31	Paid monthly salaries of $2,500.

The company uses a subsidiary ledger for accounts payable and shows the following accounts (and selected account balances) on its books:

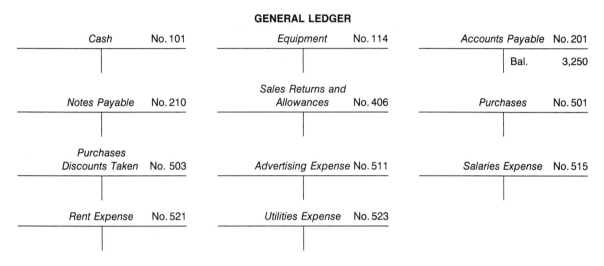

GENERAL LEDGER

Cash	No. 101		Equipment	No. 114		Accounts Payable	No. 201
						Bal.	3,250

Notes Payable	No. 210		Sales Returns and Allowances	No. 406		Purchases	No. 501

Purchases Discounts Taken	No. 503		Advertising Expense	No. 511		Salaries Expense	No. 515

Rent Expense	No. 521		Utilities Expense	No. 523

**ACCOUNTS PAYABLE
SUBSIDIARY LEDGER**

Quine Supply Company			Tailer Company	
Bal.	750		Bal.	1,000

Value Suppliers			Willis Company	
Bal.	700		Bal.	800

Required: Set up a cash payments journal and record the transactions of the Shoer Company. Make all the necessary daily and monthly postings to its accounts.

6-5B Special Journals, Journalizing and Posting. The transactions completed by the Photope Company during the month of June are as follows:

Date	Transaction
June 1	Sold merchandise on account to R. Crush, Invoice No. 180, $800. Terms 2/15, n/30.
3	Paid June rent of $600 and recorded as rent expense.
6	Sold merchandise for cash, $225.
8	Refunded $50 cash for defective merchandise sold on June 6.
10	Purchased merchandise on account from LT Supply Company, $1,200; invoice dated today. Terms 2/15, n/30.
12	Received payment of Invoice No. 180 from R. Crush, less cash discount.
16	Sold delivery equipment at cost, $200.
19	Purchased merchandise on account from Prones Company $1,100, invoice dated June 17. Terms n/30.
21	Paid LT Supply Company for merchandise purchased on June 10, less cash discount.

June	22	Purchased delivery equipment on account from Peats', $300. Terms n/30.
	25	Sold merchandise on account to L. Lind, Invoice No. 181, $300. Terms 2/10, n/30.
	27	Sold merchandise for cash, $420.
	29	Purchased land by paying $1,000 cash and issuing a $2,000 note payable.
	29	Paid June telephone bill, $85.
	30	Received payment from L. Lind for Invoice No. 181, less cash discount.
	30	Purchased merchandise for cash, $500.

The company shows the following accounts in its general ledger:

Account Title	Account Number
Cash	101
Accounts Receivable	103
Land	110
Delivery Equipment	114
Accounts Payable	201
Notes Payable	210
Sales	401
Sales Discounts	403
Sales Returns and Allowances	406
Purchases	501
Purchases Discounts Taken	503
Telephone Expense	521
Rent Expense	525

Required:
1. Prepare a sales journal, purchases journal, cash receipts journal, cash payments journal, and general journal as shown in the text.
2. Record the transactions of the Photope Company in the appropriate journals.
3. Set up the general ledger accounts and subsidiary ledgers for accounts receivable and accounts payable.
4. Make all the necessary postings during and at the end of the month.

DISCUSSION CASES

C6-1   EDP System.   Brian Baker, owner of Baker Company, has come to you for advice. He says, "I have been using a manual accounting system with a general journal and general ledger for years. Recently a computer salesperson suggested that I should switch to an electronic data processing system. I might consider doing so, but I don't know anything about computers. He said I could use punched cards as input to the CPU, which could be 'programmed' to do my accounting process. He talked about magnetic tape, transactions files, master files, updated master files, and output. At this point I was lost. I didn't really understand the meanings of these words. It sounded to me like I would not have a general journal or a general ledger. This is confusing to me. How can I have an accounting system when there is no general journal or general ledger? And how can I prepare any financial statements without them? If you can explain to me in simple terms how an EDP system works and what these words mean, then I will be more informed when the salesperson comes back next week."

Required: Based upon the discussion in this chapter, prepare a report for Brian Baker that explains how an EDP system works. Be sure to define all the terms you use in the report.

PART 2 | ACCOUNTING FOR ASSETS AND LIABILITIES

7 | Cash and Marketable Securities

After reading this chapter, you should understand:

- The definition of cash
- The basic concepts underlying internal control of cash
- A voucher system
- The accounting for a petty cash fund
- How to perform a bank reconciliation
- The accounting for current marketable securities

Cash and marketable securities are the assets that are usually listed first on a balance sheet because they are the most liquid current assets. Current assets are cash and other assets that are reasonably expected to be converted into cash, sold, or consumed within 1 year or the normal operating cycle, whichever is longer. Current assets are usually listed on the balance sheet in the order of their liquidity. **Liquidity is the measure of the time in which the asset will be converted into cash.** The most liquid asset is the asset that can most easily be converted into cash. Since marketable securities can be sold very quickly, they are normally listed immediately after cash. Cash is a very important resource for a company in the same way that it is for an individual. When a company has a temporary excess of cash it often invests in marketable securities to earn a higher income than could be obtained from leaving the cash in a checking or savings account. In this chapter we discuss the nature of cash, procedures used to control cash, petty cash, the bank reconciliation, and the accounting procedures used for marketable securities.

CASH

Cash includes coins and currency on hand, deposits in checking and savings accounts, and checks that have been received but not yet deposited. When in doubt include in cash anything that a bank will accept as a deposit. Thus postage stamps and postdated checks (checks that are dated in the future and cannot be deposited) are not cash, but they should be classified as supplies and accounts receivable, respectively. Cash is received from customers who have purchased goods or services, bank loans, and investments by owners. Cash must be available to pay suppliers, employees, and taxes, to purchase new assets, to repay loans, and for withdrawals. In addition to being such an integral part of a business, cash is also the most likely asset for employees and others to steal. For example, cash received from customers in a retail store has no identification marks that have been recorded by the store, and therefore once the money has been removed from the store it is very difficult to prove that it was stolen. Cash that is illegally transferred from a company bank account involves no physical possession of the cash by the thief, and if the records can be concealed or destroyed the money may not be traceable. Although internal control procedures are necessary for all phases of a company's business, they are usually most important for cash.

INTERNAL CONTROL OF CASH

Internal control of cash consists of the policies and procedures developed by management to ensure that transactions are handled and recorded correctly to prevent theft or other loss of cash and to ensure the correct processing of transactions that involve cash. In addition to the general principles of internal control discussed in Chapter 6, special procedures are used to control the receipt and payment of cash.

The purpose of internal control procedures for cash is to prevent both the unintentional loss and the theft of cash. The basic rule for good internal control of cash is to have all payments made by check. A very small business that is operated by the owner may have little need for additional internal control procedures. The owner is involved in purchasing goods, signing checks in payment, and paying employees by check. Perhaps the only other control procedure that may be needed is in regard to the cash register to ensure that each sale is rung up, a receipt is given to each customer, and that the amount of cash collected is matched against the cash register tape at the end of each employee's work shift.

As a business grows, the owner delegates authority and loses direct knowledge of all aspects of operations. The internal control procedures must grow along with the increased delegation of authority. As already discussed, the internal control procedures should prevent fraud and theft, but they should also ensure compliance with prescribed management policies in an efficient manner and the preparation of accurate and useful accounting information in a timely fashion. There is no universal set of internal control procedures for cash because it is necessary to adopt policies that are suitable for the particular operating environment and the management style of the company. There are several principles that should be embodied in all systems for the control of cash, however. We discuss the establishment of responsibilities, the need to maintain good records, the separation of duties, the use of mechanical devices and established routines, and the necessity for physical safety and insurance. In addition, the special problems of cash receipts and payments are discussed.

Establishing Responsibilities

The responsibilities of every person involved with cash in the operation of an accounting system must be clearly established and the procedures to be followed should be defined. An example is discussed in the section on cash receipts. Unfortunately there is an inherent conflict between establishing an accounting system in which every procedure is clearly and completely defined and a system in which individuals are allowed discretion in solving problems caused by unusual situations. The first type of accounting system may establish better internal control, whereas the second type may provide greater motivation to employees and perhaps lead to a less expensive overall system because of greater efficiency. For a cash system, however, it is usually necessary to define responsibilities very clearly and to establish controls that continuously monitor the activities of the employees.

Maintaining Good Records

A sound internal control system for cash requires that accurate and complete records be maintained so that management can determine whether the system is actually operating in compliance with the established procedures, and so that employees know that documents are available for reviewing their activities. For example, copies of invoices can be reviewed to ensure that unauthorized payments have not been made. Such reviews should be performed periodically on a routine basis, and also whenever a special investigation is warranted, so that the correct operation of the system can be verified. Of course, the records must be maintained outside the control of the employees who are performing the functions. For example, the employee responsible for preparing checks should not have routine access to paid invoices to prevent possible changes being made to the invoices.

The maintenance of good records for cash receipts and payments is desirable for reasons other than internal control. For example, good records assist in the preparation of financial statements and income tax returns. If an audit is performed by the Internal Revenue Service the availability of good records may prevent the assessment of additional taxes.

Separation of Duties

A fundamental characteristic of a good internal control system for cash is that the duties to be performed in the company involving cash should be separated so that more than one employee is involved in each transaction. When cash record keeping is the responsibility of a different employee from the employee performing the activity, there is a separation of duties. For example, a person who authorizes an expenditure should not be the same person who prepares the check, and preferably still another person should sign the check. In this way each employee monitors another employee, which is similar to the double-entry system in which one entry acts as a check on another entry.

Separation of duties enhances internal control of cash because it is more likely that errors will be discovered as a result of employees monitoring the activities of other employees than by any other method. In addition, fraud or theft of cash would require collusion among employees, and it is therefore less likely than when one employee performs all the duties.

Mechanical Devices and Established Routines

The use of mechanical devices, such as cash registers and check-writing machines, enhances internal control over cash because these devices reduce the likelihood of error from the unintentional loss of cash as well as the opportunities for employees to alter records to conceal the theft of cash. A cash register records the amount of each sale, which can then be totaled and compared to the cash received. A check-writing machine is a device used to print the amounts and signatures on the checks. Its use under the control of a single employee should prevent the unauthorized writing of checks.

The establishment of certain routines is also a useful aspect of internal control over cash. For example, sequential numbering of checks assists in the tracing of all checks written. Employees who operate cash registers should keep the money given to them by the customer out of the cash register until change has been given to minimize errors in determining the correct change. In this way the customer cannot dispute either the original amount given or the amount of change received.

Physical Safety and Insurance

Assets such as cash, which are subject to theft or destruction by an accident such as a fire, should be kept in a physically secure place like a safe to reduce the likelihood of loss. A checkbook should be similarly kept in a physically secure place like a locked drawer to prevent unauthorized use.

Insurance should be maintained on all assets including cash in case of loss. In addition, employees should be bonded because bonding provides insurance against employee theft. When an employee is bonded the company pays an insurance premium to the bonding company, which then pays for any losses caused by the bonded employees. Bonding is particularly important for employees who have access to cash.

Cash Received from Cash Sales

At the beginning of each sales employee's daily work period, a set amount of cash (for giving change) should be placed in each cash register. Cash sales should be rung up on a cash register as each sale is made. Note that cash refers to both currency and checks. The amount of the sale should be clearly visible to the customer and a receipt should be given to the customer. Each cash register should have a locked-in tape on which each sale is recorded and which is checked against the cash in the register every time there is a change in the employee operating the register. If large amounts of cash are collected during the day, it may be desirable for a supervisor to remove the cash from the cash register periodically during the day. This procedure should not be performed by the person who operates the register, although it may be useful for the clerk to count the cash before turning it over to the supervisor to be counted again. In this way two people count the cash, and the clerk also has some protection against theft by the supervisor. If possible, a third employee should be the only person to have access to the tape, thus creating further separation of duties.

At the end of each day cash should be removed from the cash registers and deposited in the bank. Banks have night deposit boxes so that deposits can be made at any time. The cash received from customers should never be used to make payments of any kind. All payments should be made by check except for some minor items that can be paid out of a petty cash fund, which is discussed later in the chapter.

Cash Received by Mail

Many customers make purchases on account and then pay the invoice by mail. The system for handling the receipt of checks in the mail for payment of these accounts receivable should involve three people. A mail clerk should open the mail and prepare a list of the checks (customer payments by cash should be discouraged) received along with the name of the sender (customer) and the reason for the payment. This information should be available because the person or the company sending the check should include a copy of the invoice with the payment. A copy of this list should be kept by the mail clerk so that a review of the receipts can be made later. The list of the checks received is also sent to the cashier and the bookkeeper. The cashier is responsible for depositing the cash and the bookkeeper for updating the cash receipts journal, which was discussed in Chapter 6. In this way the bookkeeper never has control of the cash and the cashier never has control of the accounting records. A bank reconciliation, which is discussed later in the chapter, provides a further check on the accuracy of the process.

Cash Payments

Control over cash payments is perhaps more important than control over receipts because many cases of theft have involved payment of fictitious invoices after which the checks are deposited in bank accounts controlled by employees. All payments should be made by check except for payments from the petty cash fund. Each payment should be based upon adequate source documents that provide verification of the obligation. Separation of the authorization, check preparation, and check-signing functions is desirable, and it is often accomplished by using a voucher system.

Voucher System

A voucher system is a method of providing internal control over the function of purchasing goods or services, paying for them, and ensuring that the correct accounts are debited and credited. The elements of a voucher system are the voucher, the voucher register, the check register, the unpaid voucher file, and the paid voucher file. **A voucher is a document used to summarize a transaction and approve payment and recording.** A typical voucher is illustrated in Exhibit 7-1 and consists of two parts. One part includes the voucher number, the payee's name and address, and the details of the invoice including the net amount payable (discussed in Chapter 5). The other part includes the accounts debited when the payment is made, a payment summary, the check number used in payment, the date of payment, and the signature of the person approving payment. These aspects are discussed more fully later in the chapter.

Correct use of the voucher system ensures that a procedure for incurring and paying obligations is established. The operation of a typical voucher system involves the following sequence of events:

1. **Approval for Incurring an Obligation (An Acquisition).** Only specified departments and individuals are allowed to incur obligations that result in cash

EXHIBIT 7-1 Voucher

FRONT	**BACK**

MOUNTAIN RETAIL COMPANY

Voucher No. ___312___

Date: ___June 1, 1983___

Payee: ___Adams Co.___

Street: ___1500 Elm St.___

City: ___Denver___

State: ___CO 80222___

Date of Invoice	Terms	Invoice Number	Amount
June 1	n/30	60752	320.00

Accounting Distribution

Account Debited	Acct. No.	Amount
Purchases	501	300.00
Transportation-In	504	20.00

Payment Summary

Total cost   320.00

Discount   –0–

Net payment $320.00

Check No. ___573___
Date of Check ___6/10/83___

Payment Approved

David Jackson

disbursements. For example, in a retail store only the purchasing department may be allowed to incur obligations for the purchase of merchandise. Although requests for purchases may come from employees in many different areas of the company, all of them must be routed through the purchasing department. A purchase order is prepared by the purchasing department and sent to the supplier.

2. **Receipt of the Goods Ordered.** When goods that have been ordered are received, they must be checked against the purchase order to ensure that the correct items have been sent by the supplier. In addition, the supplier sends an invoice, as illustrated in Chapter 5 (Exhibit 5-1), which includes a description

of the goods, the amount that must be paid, freight terms, discount terms, and payment dates. A copy of the invoice is typically included with the goods that are shipped and should also be compared with the purchase order when the goods are received to verify the quantities, prices, and terms of the purchase.

3. **Preparation of the Voucher.** When the ordered goods are received, a voucher is prepared. As shown in Exhibit 7-1 the front of the voucher includes the following information:

   (a) The voucher number. The vouchers should be sequentially numbered so that reference to, and checking of, vouchers can be accomplished easily.

   (b) The date the voucher is prepared.

   (c) The name of the company (or individual) to which payment is to be made.

   (d) The terms such as the date of the invoice, the invoice number, the cash discount available, the last date for payment if the cash discount is to be received (the date of the invoice plus the discount period), and the amount to be paid. In this example there are no discounts for prompt payment. Such discounts were introduced in Chapter 5 and are discussed more fully in Chapter 9.

The voucher is often in the form of a jacket in which supporting documents, such as the invoice, can be placed. The back of the voucher illustrated in Exhibit 7-1 includes the following information:

   (a) The account distribution, which describes the account(s) and account numbers in which the transaction is recorded. An asset, expense, or purchases account is debited, depending on whether the goods are considered the acquisition of an asset, the incurrence of an expense, or the purchase of goods for resale. If the company pays for the transportation, a Transportation-In account is also debited. The accompanying credit is to Vouchers Payable. **Vouchers Payable is the liability account that substitutes for Accounts Payable when a voucher system is used.** The title Accounts Payable is still used in the balance sheet.

   (b) The payment summary that lists the amount to be paid, which is the amount of the invoice, corrected for any adjustments, such as rejection of goods incorrectly sent or damaged in transit, and reduced by any discount for prompt payment. Accounting for a purchases return and allowance is discussed in the section on the voucher register and accounting for a discount is discussed in the section on the check register. The payment summary also lists the number of the check used for payment, the date the check was written, and includes space for an employee to approve the payment. The employee is an officer of the company who has specific responsibilities for vouchers and who checks the supporting documents to ensure that the correct amount is being paid.

The Voucher Register   **A voucher register is a multicolumn journal used to record all the vouchers that are prepared.** A voucher register is illustrated in Exhibit 7-2. The vouchers are listed in numerical order. One voucher is listed on each line. The date each

EXHIBIT 7-2
Voucher Register

		Voucher No.	Payee	Date Paid	Check No.	Vouchers Payable Credit	Purchases Debit
Date							
June	1	312	Adams Company	June 10	573	320.00	300.00
	8	313	David Finney	June 8	570	600.00	
	8	314	Karen Miles	June 8	571	800.00	
	8	315	Steven Smith	June 8	572	400.00	
	10	316	Mountain Telephone	June 20	574	120.00	
	15	317	Falstaff Company	June 25	575	140.00	
	22	318	Sherman Company	July 1	577	850.00	800.00
	26	319	First Bank	June 26	576	75.00	
	30	320	Castle Company	July 15	578	410.00	400.00
	30		Totals			3,715.00	1,500.00

voucher is prepared is listed first, followed by the voucher number, the name of the payee, the date paid, and the check number. The vouchers payable column lists the amounts of all vouchers approved for payment. The remainder of the register includes columns for the accounts that are regularly debited; the totals of these columns are posted monthly. Each amount in the Other Accounts Debit column is posted daily. The voucher register is very similar to the cash payments journal (discussed in Chapter 6) and replaces this journal when a voucher system is used.

PURCHASES RETURNS AND ALLOWANCES. When purchases returns and allowances are made *before* the voucher is entered in the register, the amount of the return or allowance is entered on the voucher and the net amount owed is entered in the register. When an item is returned *after* the voucher is recorded, a general journal entry would be made as follows:

Vouchers Payable 20
    Purchases Returns and Allowances 20
    Return of defective unit.

The amount of the return is shown on the voucher so that the correct amount will be paid. A reference is made to the general journal entry and the Purchases Returns and Allowances debit memo is placed in the voucher jacket.

Check Register   **A check register is a special journal in which all the checks issued are recorded.** A check register for June is illustrated in Exhibit 7-3. The date of payment, the check number used for payment, and the payee are recorded first along with the voucher number. The amount of the debit to the Vouchers Payable

Transpor- tation-In Debit	Wages Expense Debit	Adminis- trative Expense Debit	Other Accounts Debit		
			Account Name	Acct. No.	Amount Debit
20.00					
	600.00				
	800.00				
	400.00				
		120.00			
		140.00			
50.00			Interest Expense	550	75.00
10.00					
80.00	1,800.00	260.00			75.00

account is listed and should be equal to the vouchers payable credit amount listed in the voucher register. When a purchases discount is taken, it is recorded in a separate column. The amount of the check is recorded in the final column. The totals of the columns would be posted monthly.

Vouchers Unpaid and Vouchers Paid Files In a voucher system some vouchers are paid as soon as they are recorded, as for example the wages in the voucher register in Exhibit 7-2. Vouchers that are not paid immediately are placed in an unpaid vouchers file. This file takes the place of the Accounts Payable subsidiary ledger discussed in Chapter 6. The vouchers in the file

EXHIBIT 7-3
Check Register

			CHECK REGISTER				
Date		Check No.	Payee	Voucher No.	Vouchers Payable Debit	Purchases Discounts Taken Credit	Cash Credit
June	8	570	David Finney	313	600.00		600.00
	8	571	Karen Miles	314	800.00		800.00
	8	572	Steven Smith	315	400.00		400.00
	10	573	Adams Company	312	320.00		320.00
	20	574	Mountain Telephone	316	120.00		120.00
	25	575	Falstaff Company	317	140.00	2.80	137.20
	26	576	First Bank	319	75.00		75.00
	30		Totals		2,455.00	2.80	2,452.20

should be organized by the date they are due to be paid to ensure that all discounts are taken and no accounts become past due.

A vouchers paid file is maintained for all the vouchers that have been paid. This file is useful in the case of an audit or a question about a payment. The specific procedures followed by companies depend on their particular organizational structure and policies. The illustration just discussed is a simple example of a typical system and indicates how internal control over the acquisition and payment for goods is established.

THE PETTY CASH FUND

Although a voucher system, or a similar set of procedures, is necessary for establishing good internal control, it is a costly and time-consuming system. Therefore it is inefficient to use a voucher system for various small expenditures that can be better paid in cash. **A petty cash fund is a cash fund established under the control of an employee and is used for making small cash expenditures not included in the voucher system.** A petty cash fund is also used because some payments, such as taxi fares, collect telegrams, and small amounts of supplies, can be made only in cash, or because writing a check would be cumbersome. There is obviously less control over such expenditures, but the allowable amount for spending should be sufficiently small so that an employee will not be tempted to steal. In addition, we will see that the procedures used in a petty cash fund discourage both intentional and unintentional loss of cash.

A typical petty cash system includes the following elements:

1. **The Petty Cash Fund Is Established.** An employee is appointed to control the cash fund and make disbursements. A check is approved for payment to the employee. The amount of the check is based on an estimate of the cash that will be needed for approved payments over a short period of time, for example, a month. If this amount is $200, the journal entry to record this transaction is as follows:

Petty Cash Fund	200	
Cash		200

    To establish the petty cash fund.

2. **Petty Cash Vouchers. Petty cash vouchers are the control documents to record payments made from the petty cash fund.** A petty cash voucher is illustrated in Exhibit 7-4. It requires the recording of the date, the recipient of the money, an explanation of the reason for the payment, the account to be debited, the amount of the payment, and the person approving the payment.

    Internal control can readily be exercised because the cash remaining in the fund after some payments have been made, plus the amount of the petty cash vouchers, should always be equal to the amount of the petty cash fund ($200 in this example). Therefore the fund can be checked at any time to ensure that it is not being misused.

    It should be noted that no entries are made in the accounting system when

EXHIBIT 7-4
Petty Cash
Voucher

NO. 101   DATE ____January 9____ , 19<u>83</u>

PETTY CASH VOUCHER

EXPLANATION ___Taxi Fare_____

_____

DEBIT TO _____Transportation Expense_____ ACCOUNT

AMOUNT _____$25.42_____

APPROVED BY: PAYMENT RECEIVED BY:

Karen S. Miles   *Carmen J. Mangis*

a payment is made from the petty cash fund. In addition, the petty cash vouchers are prenumbered and should always be filed in numerical order to lessen the possibility of the loss or misuse of a voucher.

3. **Replenishment of the Petty Cash Fund.** When the cash in the petty cash fund becomes low the fund must be replenished, and it is necessary to determine the categories of expenses that have been incurred so that the accounting system may be properly updated. The petty cash fund must also be replenished and the expenses recorded at the end of each accounting period so that the financial statements will be correct. To illustrate the replenishment of the fund and recording the appropriate amounts in the various accounts, suppose that an examination of the petty cash vouchers indicates that the following payments had been made:

Postage	$55.27
Office Supplies	82.68
Taxi Fares	25.42

The journal entry to record these expenses is as follows:

Postage Expense	55.27	
Office Supplies	82.68	
Transportation Expense	25.42	
Cash		163.37

Replenishment of the petty cash fund.

A check for $163.37 is written to the employee controlling the petty cash fund, who then cashes it and deposits the cash in the fund. Note that the expense accounts are debited and *not* the Petty Cash Fund account. Therefore the accounting system indicates that there is always $200 in the petty cash fund, and every time the fund is replenished the cash payment and the appropriate amounts in the various accounts are recorded.

4. **Errors in the Petty Cash Fund.** Because the petty cash fund operates on a day-to-day basis it is inevitable that some mistakes will be made. An error will become known when the sum of the vouchers plus the remaining cash does not equal the amount of the petty cash fund. If the error cannot be traced and collected, the amount of the error is charged to a Cash Over and Short account. **The Cash Over and Short account is used to record the unresolved errors that are the result of a difference between the cash held and the cash recorded in the accounting records.** For example, suppose that after the above replenishment the balance in the fund is only $198.45 and no reason for the error can be determined. The shortage of $1.55 is recorded as follows:

Cash Over and Short	1.55	
Cash		1.55

To record shortage of petty cash fund and to replenish fund.

This entry would normally be combined with the earlier entry to record the expenses, and therefore a check for a total of $164.92 ($163.37 + $1.55) would be issued to the employee who controls the fund. Although a shortage in the fund may be caused by errors, it may also result from theft. Thus the size of the shortage should be reviewed periodically to see if there is a pattern to the shortages that might indicate theft.

The Cash Over and Short account may *also* be used to record any unexplained difference between the cash collected in the cash register and the amount recorded in the register tape. For example, if cash sales of $826.55 are "rung up" and $830.55 is in the cash register, the entry to record the sales is as follows:

Cash	830.55	
Cash Over and Short		4.00
Sales		826.55

To record sales.

Although this overage is possible, it is more likely that shortages occur because customers are less likely to report being given too much change than they are to report being given too little change. Therefore the Cash Over and Short account usually has a debit balance. It is closed at the end of each accounting period and, if it has a debit balance, this amount is included as a miscellaneous expense on the income statement. If it has a credit balance, this amount would be included as a miscellaneous revenue on the income statement.

Despite all the procedures used to control the receipt and payment of cash, errors in a company's records can still occur. In addition, there are differences between the timing of receipts and payments recorded by the bank and the company. Therefore a bank reconciliation is necessary to determine the accuracy of a company's cash balance.

BANK RECONCILIATION

A bank reconciliation is a schedule prepared to analyze the difference between the ending cash balance in the company's accounting records and the ending cash balance reported by the bank in a bank statement to discover errors and to adjust for timing differences in the recorded cash receipts and cash payments. The bank reconciliation enables the company's correct cash balance to be determined for inclusion in the balance sheet.

Every month banks send a statement to each depositor summarizing the activities that have taken place in the depositor's checking account. These activities include deposits, checks written, miscellaneous items, and the ending balance in the checking account. Each company has a checking account and maintains its own accounting records for its deposits and checks. Because of the various causes of differences discussed next, it can be expected that the bank statement and the company's accounting records will not be in complete agreement. When the bank statement is received each month, the company prepares a bank reconciliation to compare the bank statement balance and the company's cash balance so that they may be reconciled.

Causes of the Difference

The causes of the difference between the cash balance listed on the bank statement and the balance shown in the company's cash account include the following factors:

1. **Outstanding Checks.   An outstanding check is a check that has been deducted from the company's cash balance but has not yet been deducted from the balance reported in the bank statement.** On the date a company issues a check, it records a reduction in the balance of the Cash account in its general ledger. A period of time is necessary for the check to be received by the payee (the recipient of the check), to be deposited in the payee's bank, and to be forwarded by the payee's bank to the company's bank to be subtracted from the company's bank balance. Therefore a company has a certain number of outstanding checks at the end of each month that cause the company's cash account balance to be less than the balance on the bank statement.

2. **Deposits in Transit.   A deposit in transit is a cash receipt that has been added to the company's cash balance but has not yet been added to the balance reported on the bank statement.** When a company receives a check it records an addition to its Cash account. A period of time passes before the check is deposited by the company and is recorded by the bank. At the end of each month there may be deposits in transit (either cash or checks) that cause the company's cash balance to be greater than the balance reported on the bank statement.

3. **Charges Made Directly by the Bank.**   A bank frequently imposes a service charge for a depositor's checking account and deducts this charge directly from the account. Banks also charge for the cost of printing checks according to an agreed price. The company is informed of the amount of the charge when it receives the bank statement, which includes a document stating the amount of the deduction.

When a customer's check is received by the company it is deposited in the company's bank account for collection. The company (as well as the bank) records this check as a cash receipt even though the cash has not been transferred from the customer's bank account to the company's bank account. The company's bank is occasionally unable to collect the amount of the customer's check. **NSF (not sufficient funds) is the term used for a customer's check that has been deposited in a company's bank account but has not been paid by the customer's bank because there are insufficient funds in the customer's account.** Because the bank has not received payment from the customer it deducts this amount from the company's bank account. Although the bank should inform the company immediately of each NSF check and the company should correct its accounting records, there may be some NSF checks included in the bank statement that have not been recorded by the company.

At the end of the month each of the above charges made directly by the bank are listed as deductions from the company's cash balance on the bank statement even though they may not have been deducted from the company's cash balance in its accounting records. Therefore the bank statement balance is less than the balance in the company's cash account in this case.

4. **Collections Made Directly by the Bank.**   A bank often acts as a collecting agency for its customers on items such as notes receivable. When these amounts are collected the bank records the principal and interest as an increase in the company's bank account. Although the bank should immediately inform the company of the deposit and the company should update its records, the bank statement may include deposits recorded by the bank that have not yet been recorded in the company's accounting records. The bank statement balance is greater than the balance in the company's cash account in this case.

5. **Errors.**   Despite the internal control procedures established by the bank and the company, errors may arise in either the bank's records or the company's records and they may not be discovered until the bank reconciliation is performed. For example, a bank may include a deposit or a check in the wrong customer's account or make an error in recording an amount. A company may similarly make an error in recording an amount. For example, a common error is to transpose two numbers so that the correct amount of $426 is recorded as $462.

To bring the bank statement balance and the balance in the company's Cash account into agreement, the following additions and subtractions must be made:

Ending Balance in the Company's Cash Account

$+$ Unrecorded Collections Made Directly by the Bank

$-$ Unrecorded Charges Made Directly by the Bank

$\pm$ Errors Made by the Company

$=$ Ending Reconciled Cash Balance

	Ending Cash Balance from the Bank Statement
+	Deposits in Transit
−	Outstanding Checks
±	Errors Made by the Bank
=	Ending Reconciled Cash Balance

The ending reconciled cash balance calculated in these two ways must be equal; otherwise the reconciliation is not complete. The ending reconciled cash balance is the correct cash balance that should be reported in the company's balance sheet.

Procedures for Preparing a Bank Reconciliation

Now that we have identified the items that might cause a difference between the company's ending cash balance and the bank statement ending balance, we can develop a list of procedures to be followed in preparing a bank reconciliation:

1. *Compare the deposits listed on the company's records with the deposits shown on the bank statement.* Determine whether the deposits in transit included in the *last* month's bank reconciliation are included in this month's bank statement. These deposits do not need any adjustment in the bank reconciliation. Identify any deposits not listed on the bank statement and include them in the bank reconciliation. In the reconciliation the amounts of the deposits in transit are added to the ending cash balance of the bank statement.
2. *Compare the checks listed on the company's records with the checks shown on the bank statement.* Determine that the outstanding checks included in last month's bank reconciliation are included in this month's bank statement. These checks do not need any adjustment in the bank reconciliation. Identify any checks not deducted in the current bank statement. The amounts of these outstanding checks are subtracted from the ending cash balance of the bank statement in the reconciliation.
3. *Note any collections or charges made directly by the bank that are not included on the company's records.* These items include service charges, NSF checks, collections of notes receivable, and so on, which are listed on the bank statement. The collections or charges must be added to or subtracted from the company's ending cash balance in the bank reconciliation.
4. *Determine the effect of any errors.* If an error is found the nature of the error determines whether the error is added to or subtracted from the company's ending cash balance or from the ending cash balance of the bank statement.
5. *Complete the bank reconciliation and accompanying journal entries* (which are illustrated next).

Illustration of a Bank Reconciliation

The Perrin Company is performing a bank reconciliation on June 30, 1983. The following facts are determined:

Balance in the cash account, June 30 . . . . $1,575
Cash balance from the bank statement, June 30 1,542
Outstanding checks: No. 165 130
                 No. 168 80
Deposit in transit, June 30 272
Bank service charge unrecorded by the company 10
NSF check from David Johnson unrecorded by the company 112
Note of $180 collected by the bank, plus interest of $10 and less collection
   fee of $12 (unrecorded by the company) 178

The bank recorded a deposit of $242 as $224.
The company recorded check No. 160, written for $132, as $123. The check
   was for the purchase of supplies.

The bank reconciliation would be prepared as follows:

PERRIN COMPANY
Bank Reconciliation
June 30, 1983

Cash balance from the company's records, June 30 . . . . $1,575
Add:
  Unrecorded collection of $180 note, plus interest of $10,
  less collection fee of $12   178
                                           $1,753
Deduct:
  Bank service charge unrecorded by the company . . . . $ 10
  NSF check unrecorded by the company   112
  Error: Check No. 160 written for $132 recorded as $123   9   131
Reconciled Cash Balance, June 30 . . . . $1,622

Cash balance from the bank statement, June 30 . . . . $1,542
Add:
  Deposit in transit   272
  Error: Deposit of $242 recorded as $224   18
                                       $1,832
Deduct:
  Outstanding checks: No. 165 . . . . $ 130
               No. 168   80   210
Reconciled Cash Balance, June 30 . . . . $1,622

Since the Perrin Company has a recorded cash balance of $1,575 but the correct cash balance is $1,622, it must make several adjustments to its accounting records. The note collected by the bank must be recorded as follows:

Cash   178
Collection Expense   12
  Interest Revenue   10
  Note Receivable   180
To record collection of note by bank.

The previously unrecorded bank service charge is recorded as follows:

Miscellaneous Expense   10
  Cash   10
To record the bank service charge.

The check from David Johnson that subsequently became an NSF check would have been recorded as a collection of an account receivable when it was originally deposited. The fact that the check was not collected is recorded by reversing the entry used to record the apparent collection as follows:

Accounts Receivable: David Johnson	112	
Cash		112
To record an NSF check of David Johnson.		

The company will continue to attempt to collect the $112 from David Johnson, of course.

The error in recording check No. 160 means that a payment of $132 was recorded as only $123. Since this check was for payment of supplies the supplies are understated by $9. The entry to correct this error is as follows:

Supplies	9	
Cash		9
To correct the recording of check No. 160.		

These four entries will bring the company's cash balance to its correct ending amount of $1,622. This amount would be listed on the June 30, 1983, balance sheet. It is not necessary for the company to make any additional entries since the deposits in transit and the outstanding checks will eventually appear correctly in the bank statement. The company will, of course, want to inform the bank of the error the bank made in recording the deposit.

MARKETABLE SECURITIES

Often a company has excess cash for a short period that it does not need for its current operations. It may not wish to invest in long-term assets or reduce liabilities, however, because the company realizes that it will need the money in the near future for operations. Instead of depositing the excess cash in a savings account that earns relatively low interest, many companies invest in marketable securities that provide a higher rate of return. **Marketable securities are investments in capital stocks, bonds, or commercial paper that are readily saleable.** These securities are classified as current if it is intended that they be sold within a year or the normal operating cycle, whichever is longer. Many companies are becoming increasingly sophisticated in their approach to cash management, and since some of the securities are so easy to acquire or sell, a company may invest its excess cash for as short a period of time as one day. Examples of marketable securities are:

1. **Stocks of Other Companies.** For example, the capital stock of a corporation (discussed in Chapter 5) may be purchased on the stock market by another company. Capital stock is the term used for the shares of stock issued by a corporation as evidence of an ownership interest in the corporation. Corporations usually pay dividends each period on the capital stock they have issued, and the company (or individual) holding the capital stock collects the dividends.

2. **Bonds of Other Companies.**   A bond is a written promise by a company to repay a specific amount at some date (usually many years in the future) and to pay interest (usually semiannually) each year. The company (or individual) that purchases these bonds collects the interest each period.

3. **Commercial Paper.**   Commercial paper is short-term notes issued by corporations that is not included as notes receivable because it is not received in the normal course of the operations of the company. Commercial paper also pays interest and companies holding the commercial paper collect the interest.

Market Prices of Stocks and Bonds

An investment in stocks or bonds of publicly traded companies can be made very easily by dealing through a stockbroker. A stockbroker is a person or company that buys and sells (*trades*) stocks, bonds, and similar types of investments for other people or companies. The stocks and bonds of large companies are traded on organized securities exchanges, such as the New York Stock Exchange or the American Stock Exchange. The stocks and bonds of smaller companies are traded in the over-the-counter market in which brokers deal directly with each other rather than through a stock exchange.

The market prices of such stocks and bonds are quoted daily and reported in many newspapers. For example, the stock of IBM was recently listed as follows:

52 Weeks		Dividend	Yield, %	Sales, 100s	High	Low	Close	Net Change
High	Low							
$78\frac{1}{2}$	$50\frac{3}{8}$	3.44	6.4	5708	$54\frac{1}{8}$	$52\frac{3}{4}$	$53\frac{3}{4}$	$+\frac{7}{8}$

This information indicates that the stock has sold at a high of $78\frac{1}{2}$ per share and a low of $50\frac{3}{8}$ per share in the last 52 weeks. The annual dividend is $3.44 per share, which is a yield of 6.4% (the dividend as a percentage of the market price) on the closing market price. On the date of this quotation, 570,800 shares were traded, the high price for the day was $54\frac{1}{8}$ per share, the low price $52\frac{3}{4}$ per share, and the closing price $53\frac{3}{4}$ per share, which was an increase in price of $\frac{7}{8}$ over the closing price of the previous day.

Bonds of IBM were also listed as follows:

Bonds	Current Yield	Volume	High	Low	Close	Net Change
$9\frac{3}{8}$ 04	10	94	$90\frac{1}{2}$	$89\frac{1}{2}$	$90\frac{1}{8}$	$-\frac{1}{8}$

This information indicates that the bonds have an interest rate of $9\frac{3}{8}\%$ and mature in the year 2004. The bonds currently yield 10% (the annual interest as a percentage of the market price) and on the date of this quotation 94 bonds were traded. The high price for the day was $90\frac{1}{2}$, the low price $89\frac{1}{2}$, the closing price $90\frac{1}{8}$, which represents a decrease of $\frac{1}{8}$ from the closing price of the previous day. These bond prices are quoted as percentages of the face value of the bond and not as dollar amounts. Since bonds have a face value of $1,000 these quotes represent prices of $905 ($90\frac{1}{2}\% \times \$1,000$), $895 ($89\frac{1}{2}\% \times \$1,000$), and $901.25 ($90\frac{1}{8}\% \times \$1,000$).

These quoted market prices indicate the price a company would have to pay to purchase the securities or the price at which they can be sold. In addition, the company would have to pay a fee to the stockbroker to make a purchase or a sale, and for bonds the company will also have to pay accrued interest since the last interest payment date.

Accounting for Current Marketable Securities

When a company acquires stocks or bonds of other companies it may intend to sell them soon or hold them as a longer-term investment. The acquisition is therefore called a *current* marketable security if the intent is to sell the security within a year or the normal operating cycle, whichever is longer, if excess cash is needed. The acquisition is classified as a *noncurrent* marketable security if the intent is to hold the security for more than a year or the normal operating cycle, whichever is longer. (Since the classification is only important when financial statements are issued, the criterion of a year extends from the balance sheet date). In this chapter we are concerned with current marketable securities. Noncurrent marketable securities are discussed in Chapter 17.

Two general questions arise in accounting for current marketable securities. First, how should the asset be recorded in the balance sheet? Second, when is the revenue from the investment recognized?[1] The answers to both questions unfortunately vary between stocks and bonds. Current investments in stocks are reported in the balance sheet at the lower of cost or market, whereas current investments in bonds are usually reported at cost, although they may be recorded at the lower of cost or market. In this book we assume that current investments in bonds are reported at cost. Dividends paid by the corporation issuing the stock are recorded as revenue by the owner of the stock only when the dividends are declared periodically (as discussed later). Interest paid by the corporation issuing bonds is recorded as revenue by the owner of the bonds for the period they are owned. To put it simply, interest accrues continuously over time, whereas dividends are periodic payments.

CURRENT MARKETABLE SECURITIES — STOCKS

Accounting for the acquisition, valuation, sale, and income from current investments in marketable securities — stocks is discussed in the following sections. Investments in bonds are discussed later in the chapter.

The Acquisition of Current Marketable Securities — Stocks

All marketable securities are recorded at the cost of acquisition, which is the purchase price, including commissions to the stockbroker, and any transfer taxes that are imposed. Although total current marketable securities are usually reported as a single figure in the balance sheet, it is desirable to record acquisitions of stock in a separate account from acquisitions of bonds because of the different valuation procedures used for balance sheet reporting. Furthermore, if a company owns several different stocks or bonds, it is necessary to maintain a subsidiary ledger in which the cost, the number of securities, and the cost per security is recorded for each type of security.

Suppose that on October 1, 1983, the Lennon Company purchases 100 shares of the capital stock of General Motors when the market price is $40 per share and

---

[1] In accounting, the terms *recognized* and *recorded* are often used interchangeably. We will do so in this text.

50 shares of the capital stock of United Airlines when the market price is $20 per share. Stockbroker's fees and transfer taxes are ignored in this example. The total acquisition cost of $5,000 [(100 × $40) + (50 × $20)] is recorded as follows:

Current Marketable Securities —Stocks	5,000	
Cash		5,000
Acquired 100 shares of General Motors and 50 shares of United Airlines.		

Thus the Lennon Company has exchanged one current asset, cash, for another current asset, marketable securities.

Subsequent Valuation of Current Marketable Securities — Stocks: Lower of Cost or Market Method

The subsequent valuation of current marketable securities — stocks utilizes the lower of cost or market method based on the current portfolio of stocks owned.[2] **The portfolio is all the investments in capital stock of other companies. The current portfolio includes the investments in capital stock that are classified as current. The lower of cost or market is a valuation method in which an asset is valued at the lower of its original cost or its current market value.** That is, if the total cost of the current portfolio of investments in capital stock is less than the total market value of the portfolio, the Current Marketable Securities — Stocks are carried at cost. Alternatively, if the market value of the portfolio is less than the cost of the portfolio, the Current Marketable Securities — Stocks are carried at market value. This procedure is consistent with the conservatism principle.

The conservatism principle holds that accounting principles should be developed so that there is little likelihood that assets or income are overstated. This principle does *not* state that assets or income should be understated, but when there is a doubt about the likely effect of an accounting method the bias should be toward the conservative method. The rationale for the conservatism principle is that the users of financial statements are least likely to be misled if the least favorable alternative valuation is used; conservatism also tends to offset the optimistic view of management. Many accountants disagree with the conservatism principle, however, because they believe that accounting should strive to obtain the best valuation with a bias neither toward nor against conservatism. It is also possible that conservatism may be unfair to present stockholders and biased in favor of prospective stockholders because of the lower valuation. Furthermore, since the long-term income of the company is the same whether conservatism is applied or not, reducing income or asset values in the current period will inevitably result in higher income in the future than would otherwise have been reported. Nevertheless, this principle has affected several accounting practices, including the lower of cost or market method.

To illustrate the application of the lower of cost or market method, suppose that the Lennon Company's current investments in capital stock had the following

---

[2] "Accounting for Certain Marketable Securities," *FASB Statement No. 12* (Stamford, Conn.: FASB, 1975).

values at December 31, 1983, determined from current stock market prices as discussed earlier:

	Number of Shares	Cost per Share	Market Value per Share	Total Cost	Total Market Value
General Motors	100	$40	$30	$4,000	$3,000
United Airlines	50	20	25	1,000	1,250
				$5,000	$4,250

Since the total value of the current portfolio is $4,250 and the cost was $5,000, the portfolio must be valued at $4,250 in the balance sheet and a loss of $750 ($5,000 − $4,250) included in the income statement. A loss is reported because there is a decline in the value of the assets of the company, and this decline in value accrues to the owners of the company. The loss is included in the income statement in the Other Revenues and Expenses category. The entry to record the decline in value is as follows:

Unrealized Loss on Decline in Value of Current		
Marketable Securities — Stocks	750	
Allowance for Decline in Value of Current Marketable		
Securities — Stocks		750

To record current marketable securities — stocks at lower of cost or market.

The Unrealized Loss on Decline in Value of Current Marketable Securities — Stocks is the loss from holding current marketable securities (stocks) that has not been realized through a sale. Therefore the loss is called an *unrealized loss*. The Allowance for Decline in Value of Current Marketable Securities — Stocks is a contra-asset account used to record the amount by which the market value of Current Marketable Securities — Stocks is less than the cost. The account has the effect of reducing the asset value in the balance sheet. The cost of the portfolio of Current Marketable Securities — Stocks, however, is also reported (usually on the face of the balance sheet) so that the users of the financial statements know both the cost and the market value. For example, the Lennon Company might disclose its current marketable securities as follows:

Current Assets		
Marketable securities — stocks, at cost	$5,000	
Less: Allowance for decline in value	750	
Marketable securities — stocks, at lower of cost		
or market	$4,250	

If the market price of the portfolio continues to fall, a loss must again be recognized. The loss would be equal to the additional decline in value and would be the amount necessary to obtain the correct balance in the Allowance account. The general rule is that the loss in any period is equal to the decline in the recorded value of the portfolio during the period under the lower of cost or market method. For example, suppose that the Lennon Company is preparing its quarterly financial statements on March 31, 1984, and the portfolio has the following market values:

	Number of Shares	Market Value per Share	Total Market Value
General Motors	100	$27	$2,700
United Airlines	50	26	1,300
			$4,000

Note that although the market price of the United Airlines stock went up from $25 to $26 per share, it is the *total* market value of the current portfolio that is compared to the previously recorded value of the portfolio. Since the previously recorded market value was $4,250, the entry to record the additional decline in value to $4,000 is as follows:

Unrealized Loss on Decline in Value of Current Marketable Securities — Stocks	250	
Allowance for Decline in Value of Current Marketable Securities — Stocks		250

To record current marketable securities — stocks at lower of cost or market.

The balance in the Allowance account is now $1,000 ($750 + $250) and therefore the net value of the Current Marketable Securities — Stocks is $4,000 ($5,000 − $1,000).

If the market price of the portfolio subsequently rises the gain in value is recognized, but the gain cannot exceed previously recognized losses. That is, the portfolio cannot be valued above cost. The general rule is that the gain in any period is equal to the increase in the recorded value of the portfolio during the period under the lower of cost or market method provided that the recorded value does not exceed cost. For example, suppose that the Lennon Company is preparing its quarterly financial statements on June 30, 1984. At this time the portfolio has the following market values:

	Number of Shares	Market Value per Share	Total Market Value
General Motors	100	$33	$3,300
United Airlines	50	26	1,300
			$4,600

Since the market value of the portfolio is still below the cost of $5,000, the value of $4,600 is used in the balance sheet and the increase in value of $600 ($4,600 − $4,000) since the last balance sheet date is recognized. The required journal entry is as follows:

```
Allowance for Decline in Value of Current
        Marketable Securities — Stocks . . . . . . . . . . . . . . .   600
Unrealized Gain on Increase in Value of Current
        Marketable Securities — Stocks . . . . . . . . . . . . . .          600
```
To record current marketable securities — stocks at lower of cost or market.

The gain of $600 appears in the income statement for the quarterly period in the Other Revenues and Expenses category and the balance sheet includes the value of the portfolio as follows:

```
Current Assets
    Marketable securities — stocks, at cost . . . . . . . .   $5,000
    Less: Allowance for decline in value  . . . . . . . . .      400
    Marketable securities — stocks, at lower of cost
        or market . . . . . . . . . . . . . . . . . . . . .   $4,600
```

If the total market value of the current marketable securities is $5,500 on September 30, 1984, when the next quarterly financial statements are prepared, a gain of only $400 is recorded and therefore the Allowance account is eliminated. That is, when the market value of the portfolio goes *above* the cost, the gain is computed by the company as the difference between the previous market value ($4,600) and the cost ($5,000) of the portfolio. Therefore the marketable securities are now recorded at their cost of $5,000 and *not* at the market value of $5,500 because the market value is *higher* than the cost. The Lennon Company would disclose the following information in its balance sheet:

```
Current Assets
    Marketable securities — stocks, at cost
        (market value is $5,500)  . . . . . . . . . . . . .   $5,000
```

Sale of an Investment in Stocks

When additional cash is needed for a company's operations, a current investment in capital stock may be sold. The gain or loss on the sale is the difference between the selling price and the *cost* of the capital stock. That is, the balance in the Allowance account is *ignored*. The gain or loss is *not* measured as the difference between the selling price of the securities and their most recent market value because *individual* stocks are not carried at their market value. It is the *total* portfolio that is being carried at the lower of cost or market. At the end of the period the portfolio of stocks is valued again, and the balance in the Allowance account is adjusted accordingly. Suppose the Lennon Company sells the 100 shares of General Motors capital stock for $35 per share (ignoring the stockbroker's commission and transfer taxes). The Lennon Company will receive $3,500 (100 × $35) and will recognize a loss of $500 (the $4,000 original cost − $3,500) as follows:

```
Cash . . . . . . . . . . . . . . . . . . . . . . . . . . .   3,500
Loss on Sale of Current Marketable Securities — Stocks . . .    500
    Current Marketable Securities — Stocks . . . . . . . . .          4,000
```
Sold 100 shares of General Motors stock.

Revenue on an Investment in Stocks

A corporation has no obligation to pay dividends on its issued capital stock. Dividends are a discretionary payment that must be voted by the board of directors as discussed in Chapter 15. Thus the purchaser of stock has no right to receive dividends, and therefore receives no revenue, until the dividends are *declared* by the corporation. When a corporation decides to pay dividends it first declares that it will pay dividends. This act creates a legal obligation to pay the dividends. The dividends are actually paid about a month later. The reasons for different declaration and payment dates are discussed in Chapter 15. Since the declaration creates a legal obligation at that time, the owner of the capital shares should recognize revenue. Suppose United Airlines declares a dividend of $1 per share. The Lennon Company now has revenue of $50 (50 shares × $1), which is recorded as follows:

Dividends Receivable	50	
Dividend Revenue		50

To record dividend declared on the current investment in United Airlines stock.

The Dividend Revenue is included in the Other Revenues and Expenses category in the income statement. When the dividends are paid the receipt of cash is recorded as follows:

Cash	50	
Dividends Receivable		50

Receipt of dividends previously declared.

Since the revenue was recognized at the time of declaration, note that no revenue is recognized when the dividends are received. Some companies do not record Dividends Receivable at the time of the dividend declaration, but instead record Dividend Revenue when the cash is received.

CURRENT MARKETABLE SECURITIES — BONDS

The Acquisition of Current Marketable Securities — Bonds

As with stocks an investment in Current Marketable Securities — Bonds is recorded at the acquisition cost. For example, suppose that on September 1, 1983, the Lennon Company purchased 12 Exxon Company bonds when they were selling at 98. Remember that bonds have a face value of $1,000 and the selling price is quoted as a percentage of the face value. Thus the company is purchasing bonds with a face value of $12,000 for 98% of the face value, or $11,760. If stockbrokers' fees of $150 are also paid the cost of the bonds is $11,910. An additional complication arises with the acquisition of bonds, however, because interest on the bonds accrues continuously but is paid periodically. Therefore when purchasing the bonds the Lennon Company will be charged by the previous owner for the interest that has accrued to the owner since the last interest payment. Suppose that the Exxon Company bonds have an *annual* interest rate of 10% and pay interest *semiannually* on June 30 and December 31. On September 1 (the purchase date) 2 months of interest has accrued since June 30, which amounts to $200 ($12,000 × 10% × $\frac{2}{12}$). The previous owner of the bonds has earned the interest for 2 months, but the

Lennon Company will receive the interest payment for the entire 6 months at December 31, 1983. Therefore the Lennon Company pays the previous owner of the bonds for the 2 months interest and would pay a total of $12,110 ($11,910 + $200). The acquisition would be recorded as follows:

Current Marketable Securities — Bonds	11,910	
Interest Receivable	200	
Cash		12,110

Acquired 12 Exxon 10% bonds and paid 2 months accrued interest.

The interest is recorded as a receivable because the interest accrues over time and the Lennon Company will receive the interest when Exxon makes the next interest payment. Note that in accordance with the accrual basis of accounting the Lennon Company is recognizing interest *revenue* on a separate basis from interest *received*. This procedure is discussed in greater detail later.

Subsequent Valuation of Current Marketable Securities — Bonds

The accounting principles used for the subsequent valuation and reporting of Current Marketable Securities — Bonds are not as clearly defined as the principles for stocks. Most companies use the *cost method*, which simply means that the investment is reported in the balance sheet at the acquisition cost no matter whether the market value is higher or lower. Therefore no adjusting entries are required. The lower of cost or market method, however, is allowed for current investments in bonds in which case the adjustment procedure described for stocks would be used. In this textbook we use the cost method. Thus on the December 31, 1983, balance sheet the investment in the Exxon bonds would be shown as follows:

Current Assets
Marketable securities — bonds, at cost $11,910

Revenue on Current Marketable Securities — Bonds

As discussed earlier interest on bonds accrues continuously over time, and therefore the investor in Current Marketable Securities — Bonds earns revenue continuously. Whenever financial statements are prepared the investor must recognize the correct amount of interest revenue for the period. Continuing with the example in the previous section, Exxon will pay 6 months interest of $600 ($12,000 × 10% × $\frac{6}{12}$) on December 31, 1983, to the Lennon Company. Since the Lennon Company has owned the bonds for only 4 months, however, interest for only 4 months should be recognized as revenue. The receipt of the other 2 months interest would be payment of the Interest Receivable recorded at the time of acquisition. The receipt of the interest is recorded as follows:

Cash	600	
Interest Receivable		200
Interest Revenue		400

Received interest payment on Exxon bonds.

Thus of the $600 cash received only $400 is included in revenue of the period, and the remaining $200 is receipt of an asset recognized at the time of the acquisition of the bonds. The Interest Revenue would be included in Other Revenues and Expenses on the income statement.

Sale of Current Marketable Securities — Bonds

When additional cash is needed for the operations of a company a current investment in bonds may be sold. Because interest accrues over time it is necessary to recognize the interest earned between the last interest payment date and the date of sale. Suppose that the Lennon Company sells its investment in the Exxon bonds on January 31, 1984, at 102 plus accrued interest. The company will receive $12,240 ($12,000 × 1.02) for the bonds plus the interest that has been earned since the last payment date. The company has earned interest of $100 ($12,000 × 10% × $\frac{1}{12}$) since the last interest payment on December 31, 1983. Since the company sells the bonds for $12,240 plus accrued interest, and interest revenue of $100 had been earned during January, total cash of $12,340 is received. Because the bonds were being carried at their cost of $11,910, the Lennon Company has a gain of $330 on the sale ($12,240 − $11,910). The entry to record the sale is as follows:

Cash	12,340	
Gain on Sale of Current Marketable Securities —		
Bonds		330
Interest Revenue		100
Current Marketable Securities — Bonds		11,910
Sale of Exxon bonds.		

Both the Gain on Sale and the Interest Revenue would be included in the Other Revenues and Expenses category on the income statement. It is important to differentiate between the two amounts because they result from different causes. The gain on the sale is the result of advantageous buying and selling decisions whereas the interest revenue is the amount earned on the investment over time.

ADDITIONAL CONSIDERATIONS

Income Tax Rules for Marketable Securities

Federal income tax rules do not allow the use of the lower of cost or market method for income tax reporting purposes. Thus an unrealized loss on a decline in the value of current marketable securities is not a tax-deductible expense, and subsequent gains up to the original cost are not taxable income. The gain or loss on the sale of current marketable securities for tax purposes is the difference between the selling price and the cost and therefore is the same amount as we discussed in this chapter. Such a gain is taxable income and a loss is deducted from taxable income.

Valuation of Marketable Securities at Market Value

Although the valuation and reporting of current marketable securities at market values is not allowed under generally accepted accounting principles (except when market is less than cost), many accountants argue that marketable securities should always be reported in a company's balance sheet at their market value and cost should be ignored. The major arguments in favor of using market values are:

1. It is intended that the securities will be sold in the relatively near future (because

they are classified as current) and the current market value is a better indicator than cost of the eventual amount of cash to be received from the sale.
2. The market value of the securities may be received easily through a sale without interfering with the productive operations of the company.
3. Changes in market value are an indicator of the success of the investment strategy of the management of the company and the resulting gains and losses should be reported in the income statement.
4. The market price can be easily and objectively determined.

Although companies are not allowed to use market value in the financial statements,[3] the market value of the total current marketable securities should be disclosed in the financial statements as shown earlier. The market value is normally disclosed in parentheses on the face of the balance sheet, but it may also be disclosed in the footnotes to the financial statements.

**REVIEW
PROBLEM**

The Drake Company invests its temporary excess cash in marketable securities. At the end of 1982 Drake's portfolio of current marketable securities is as follows:

Security	Number of Shares or Bonds	Cost per Share or Bond	Market Value per Share or Bond
Texaco	200 shares	$ 45	$ 44
Coca Cola	100 shares	35	36
DuPont	300 shares	40	38
U.S. Steel	Twelve 10% bonds	950	940

All securities were purchased during the last quarter of 1982, and no securities had previously been owned during the year. During the first quarter of 1983 the company engaged in the following transactions:

Date	Transaction
Feb. 5	Sold the Coca Cola shares for $33 each.
Mar. 2	Purchased 100 shares of Anheuser-Busch for $30 each.
Mar. 31	Dividends of $200 were received, interest was recorded, and the market prices on this date were:

Security	Market Value per Share or Bond
Texaco	$ 42
Anheuser-Busch	25
DuPont	41
U.S. Steel	930

During the second quarter of 1983 the company engaged in the following transactions:

---

[3] Some companies in special industries, such as mutual funds and brokerage companies, report investments in securities at their current market value.

Date	Transaction
Apr. 6	Sold the Texaco shares for $47 each.
May 31	Sold the U.S. Steel bonds at 98 plus accrued interest.
June 30	Dividends of $250 were received, and the market prices on this date were:

Security	Market Value per Share
DuPont	$39
Anheuser-Busch	31

The company records dividend revenue when the cash is received and uses the cost method to account for its investments in bonds. The bonds pay interest on June 30 and December 31.

Required:
1. What is the balance in the Allowance for Decline in Value of Current Marketable Securities — Stocks on December 31, 1982?
2. Prepare journal entries to record the above events for 1983.
3. Show how the income recognized for each period and the value of the marketable securities reported in the balance sheet at the end of each period would be disclosed on the interim financial statements for 1983.

SOLUTION TO REVIEW PROBLEM

Requirement 1: The balance in the Allowance for Decline in Value of Current Marketable Securities — Stocks on December 31, 1982, may be calculated as follows (because all the securities were purchased in the last quarter of 1982 and no securities had previously been owned during the year):

Security	Number of Shares	Cost per Share	Market Value per Share	Total Cost	Total Market Value
Texaco	200	$45	$44	$ 9,000	$ 8,800
Coca Cola	100	35	36	3,500	3,600
DuPont	300	40	38	12,000	11,400
				$24,500	$23,800

The balance in the Allowance account is $700 ($24,500 − $23,800) at December 31, 1982. (Note: Only the shares are included because the bonds are accounted for by the cost method.)

Requirement 2:

Feb. 5	Cash	3,300
	Loss on Sale of Current Marketable Securities — Stocks	200
	Current Marketable Securities — Stocks	3,500
	Sold 100 Coca Cola shares.	

| Mar. | 2 | Current Marketable Securities — Stocks . . . . | 3,000 | |
| | | Cash . . . . | | 3,000 |

Purchased 100 shares of Anheuser-Busch.

| Mar. | 31 | Cash . . . . | 200 | |
| | | Dividend Revenue . . . . | | 200 |

Received dividends on current marketable securities.

| | | Interest Receivable . . . . | 300 | |
| | | Interest Revenue . . . . | | 300 |

To record interest revenue of $12,000 \times 10\% \times \frac{3}{12}$.

| | | Unrealized Loss on Decline in Value of Current Marketable Securities — Stocks . . . . | 100 | |
| | | Allowance for Decline in Value of Current Marketable Securities — Stocks . . . . | | 100 |

To record current marketable securities—stocks at the lower of cost or market.

Security	Number of Shares	Cost per Share	Market Value per Share	Total Cost	Total Market Value
Texaco	200	$45	$42	$ 9,000	$ 8,400
DuPont	300	40	41	12,000	12,300
Anheuser-Busch	100	30	25	3,000	2,500
				$24,000	$23,200

The balance in the Allowance account needs to be $800. The balance before the adjusting entry is $700, and therefore an unrealized loss of $100 is recognized.

Apr.	6	Cash	9,400	
		Current Marketable Securities — Stocks		9,000
		Gain on Sale of Current Marketable Securities — Stocks		400

Sold 200 Texaco shares.

May	31	Cash	12,260[c]	
		Gain on Sale of Current Marketable Securities — Bonds		360[d]
		Interest Receivable		300
		Interest Revenue		200[a]
		Current Marketable Securities — Bonds		11,400[b]

Sold U.S. Steel bonds.

[a] $12,000 \times 10\% \times \frac{2}{12}$.
[b] $12 \times \$950$.
[c] $12,000 \times \frac{98}{100} + \$500$.
[d] $12 \times (\$980 - \$950)$.

```
June 30   Cash  . . . . . . . . . . . . . . . . . . . . . . . . .      250
              Dividend Revenue  . . . . . . . . . . . . . . . .              250
          Received dividends.

          Allowance for Decline in Value of Current
                  Marketable Securities — Stocks  . . . . . . . .    600
              Unrealized Gain on Increase in Value of Current
                  Marketable Securities — Stocks  . . . . . . . .            600
          To record current marketable securities at the
          lower of cost or market.
```

Security	Number of Shares	Cost per Share	Market Value per Share	Total Cost	Total Market Value
DuPont	300	$40	$39	$12,000	$11,700
Anheuser-Busch	100	30	31	3,000	3,100
				$15,000	$14,800

The balance in the Allowance account needs to be $200. The balance before the adjusting entry is $800, and therefore an unrealized gain of $600 is recognized.

Requirement 3:

Income Statement	First Quarter	Second Quarter
Other revenues and expenses		
Gain (loss) on sale of current marketable securities	$ (200)	$ 760
Revenue on current marketable securities	500[a]	450[b]
Unrealized gain (loss) on increase (decline) in value		
of current marketable securities.	(100)	600
	$ 200	$ 1,810

Balance Sheet		
Marketable securities — stocks, at cost	$24,000	$15,000
Less: Allowance for decline in value	800	200
Marketable securities — stocks, at the lower		
of cost or market	$23,200	$14,800
Marketable securities — bonds at cost	11,400	–
Total marketable securities	$34,600	$14,800

[a] Dividends, $200 plus interest, $300.
[b] Dividends, $250 plus interest, $200.

GLOSSARY

Allowance for Decline in Value of Current Marketable Securities. A contra asset account used to record the amount by which the market value of Current Marketable Securities—Stocks is less than the cost (see lower of cost or market).

Bank Reconciliation. A schedule prepared to analyze the difference between the ending cash balance in the accounting records and the ending cash balance reported by the bank in a bank statement to determine the correct ending cash balance.

Cash. An asset that includes coins and currency on hand, deposits in checking and savings accounts, and checks received but not yet deposited.

Cash Over and Short. An account used to record the unresolved errors that are the result of a difference between the cash held and the cash recorded in the accounting records.

Check Register. A special journal in which the checks issued are recorded.

Conservatism Principle. Holds that accounting principles should be developed so that there is little likelihood that assets or income are currently overstated.

Deposit in Transit. A deposit added to a company's cash account that has not yet been recorded by the bank.

Lower of Cost or Market. A valuation method in which an asset is valued at the lower of its original cost or its current market value.

Marketable Securities. Investments in securities such as capital stock, bonds, or commercial paper that are readily saleable. They are classified as current if it is intended that they be sold within a year or the normal operating cycle, whichever is longer.

NSF (Not Sufficient Funds). The term used for a customer's check that has been deposited in a company's bank account but has not been paid by the customer's bank because there are insufficient funds in the customer's account.

Outstanding Check. A check that has been written by a company and deducted from its cash account but has not yet been recorded as a deduction by the bank.

Petty Cash Fund. A cash fund used for the payment of small expenditures.

Petty Cash Voucher. The control document used to record payments from the petty cash fund.

Portfolio. All the investments in capital stock of other companies.

Unrealized Gain or Loss on Decline in Value of Current Marketable Securities. A gain or loss from holding current marketable securities (stocks) that has not been realized through a sale. It is measured by the difference between the cost and market value of the portfolio of the current marketable securities (stocks).

Voucher. A document used to summarize a transaction and approve payment and recording.

Vouchers Payable. The liability account that substitutes for the Accounts Payable account in a voucher system.

Voucher Register. A journal that is used to record all the vouchers that are prepared.

Voucher System. An accounting system used to provide internal control over the function of purchasing goods or services, paying for them, and ensuring that the correct accounts are debited and credited.

QUESTIONS

Q7-1   What items are included in the Cash account balance on a balance sheet? Give examples of two items that are similar to cash but would be excluded from cash.

Q7-2   What is the purpose of internal control for cash? List the main principles used in a good internal control system for cash.

Q7-3　　Why is the separation of duties a common element of internal control?

Q7-4　　What is the purpose of bonding employees?

Q7-5　　What is the purpose of a voucher system? List the basic elements of a voucher system?

Q7-6　　Why does a company have a petty cash fund?

Q7-7　　When are the payments made out of a petty cash fund recorded as an expense? How often is a debit made to the petty cash fund?

Q7-8　　What is the purpose of a Cash Over and Short account? Will it normally have a debit or credit balance? What happens to the balance in the account at the end of the period?

Q7-9　　Why does a company perform a bank reconciliation? Name five items that might appear in a bank reconciliation.

Q7-10　　What are the procedures that should be followed in a bank reconciliation?

Q7-11　　Why might a company make journal entries after performing a bank reconciliation?

Q7-12　　Why does a company invest in current marketable securities? Give examples of the securities in which a company might invest.

Q7-13　　How is a current investment in marketable securities (stocks) accounted for subsequent to acquisition? A current investment in marketable securities—bonds?

Q7-14　　What is an Unrealized Loss on Decline in Value of Current Marketable Securities—Stocks account and where is it disclosed on the financial statements?

Q7-15　　What is an Allowance for Decline in Value of Current Marketable Securities—Stocks account and where is it disclosed on the financial statements?

Q7-16　　How is revenue on an investment in stocks accounted for? Revenue on an investment in bonds?

Q7-17　　How is the gain or loss on the sale of an investment in stocks determined? An investment in bonds?

Q7-18　　Why does a purchaser of bonds pay for "accrued interest" whereas a purchaser of stocks does not pay for "accrued dividends?"

Q7-19　　Are unrealized losses on the valuation of current marketable securities included in the determination of taxable income? Explain.

EXERCISES

E7-1　**Items Included in Cash.**　The accountant of the Sherman Company is considering whether or not the following items should be included in the company's cash balance at December 31, 1983:

(a) The Sherman Company bid on a contract on December 14, 1983. It included a "good faith" check of $5,000 dated January 14, 1984, with the bid. The bid was rejected on January 10, 1984, and the check was returned.

(b) A petty cash fund has been established in the amount of $150. At December 31 a count of the cash in the fund showed a balance of $48, and a count of the petty cash vouchers totaled $100. The correct year-end adjusting entry has been made.

(c) Two checks of $125 were received in December from a customer for payment of its $125 account balance. One of the checks was returned in January.

(d) A check was received and deposited for $130 in December. The check was returned by the bank in January marked NSF.

(e) A check from a customer for $87 was received and deposited in December. In January it was discovered that it was in payment of an invoice in the amount of $78. A check for $9 was issued and mailed by the Sherman Company to the customer.

Required: For each of the items indicate how much, if any, should have been included in the cash balance on the balance sheet at December 31, 1983, assuming that all the information was obtained from the bank reconciliation for the month ending December 31, 1983.

E7-2   Internal Control.   The following independent situations exist:

(a) The mail is delivered to the bookkeeper who distributes it unopened to various employees around the company, including the cash receipts clerk.

(b) Cash is often received in the mail without an accompanying invoice for purchases made by customers. The bookkeeper opens this mail.

(c) A manager prepares the invoices and signs the checks for items purchased.

(d) In a retail store the cash in the cash register is not counted before each employee's work period.

(e) The company does not perform a bank reconciliation because it trusts that the bank will not make a mistake.

Required: For each of the situations explain the weakness in the internal control and suggest how it could be overcome.

E7-3   Voucher System.   The Palas Company uses a voucher system. During March 1983 the following vouchers were prepared:

Date	Voucher No.	Payee	Amount	Check No.	Date Paid	Explanation
5	574	Thomas Co.	$300	414	March 12	Purchase
7	575	INP Co.	200	413	March 11	Rent for month
10	576	Peter Jay	280	412	March 10	Travel
15	577	Catch Co.	420	417	April 5	Typewriter
30	578	David Finch	900	415	March 30	Salary
30	579	Rose Hill	950	416	March 30	Salary

The purchase from the Thomas Company was on terms of 2/10, n/30. The discount was taken.

Required: 1. Prepare a voucher register for March.
2. Prepare a check register for March.

E7-4   Petty Cash Fund.   The Huron Company maintains a petty cash fund of $500. On June 30 the fund contained cash of $372.55 and the following petty cash vouchers:

Taxi fares	$51.06
Payment to employee for entertainment expenses . . .	50.00
Office supplies	26.52

Required: 1. If the company's fiscal year ends on June 30 should the petty cash fund be replenished on June 30?
2. Prepare the journal entry to record the reimbursement of the petty cash fund on June 30.

E7-5 Petty Cash Fund. The Crestone Company established a $100 petty cash fund on January 9. On September 28 there was $20.53 in the fund, along with the following vouchers:

Freight charge on purchases	$31.28
Office supplies	15.39
Postage	16.12
Miscellaneous	16.68

Required:
1. How much cash is needed to replenish the fund?
2. How much are the expenses for the period?
3. Prepare the journal entry needed to record the reimbursement of the petty cash fund on September 28.

E7-6 Bank Reconciliation. A company is performing a bank reconciliation and discovers the following items:

(a) Outstanding checks.
(b) Deposits in transit.
(c) Unrecorded charges made directly by the bank.
(d) Unrecorded collections made directly by the bank.
(e) The erroneous underrecording by the bank of a deposit.
(f) The erroneous underrecording by the company of a check written.

Required: Indicate how each of these items would be used to adjust:
1. The company's cash balance.
2. The bank balance to calculate the reconciled cash balance.

E7-7 Bank Reconciliation. At the end of March 1983 the Elbert Company's books showed a cash balance of $5,472. When comparing the March 31, 1983, bank statement with the company's cash account, it was discovered that outstanding checks totaled $827, deposits in transit were $725, unrecorded bank service charges were $28, and unrecorded NSF checks totaled $182.

Required:
1. Compute the March 31, 1983, reconciled cash balance of the Elbert Company.
2. Compute the unadjusted cash balance listed on the March 31, 1983, bank statement.
3. Prepare appropriate journal entries for the Elbert Company on March 31, 1983.

E7-8 Bank Reconciliation. At the end of September 1983 the Bross Company's books showed a cash balance of $2,135. When comparing the September 30, 1983, bank statement, which showed a cash balance of $1,860, with the company's cash account, it was discovered that outstanding checks were $462, unrecorded bank service charges were $23, and unrecorded NSF checks totaled $93.

Required:
1. Compute the September 30, 1983, reconciled cash balance of the Bross Company.
2. Compute the September deposits in transit.
3. Prepare the appropriate journal entries for the Bross Company on September 30, 1983.

E7-9 Current Marketable Securities—Stocks. The Castle Company purchased a portfolio of current marketable securities that were all capital stocks on January 14, 1983. The company bought and sold shares during the next year, and the portfolio had the following costs and market values at the end of each quarter during the year:

	Cost	Market Value
March 31, 1983	$87,500	$88,200
June 30, 1983	82,000	80,000
September 30, 1983	95,000	87,000
December 31, 1983	64,000	66,000

Required: 1. How much unrealized loss or gain will be reported in each of the quarterly income statements prepared on the above dates?

2. Prepare the journal entries required on each of the above dates.

E7-10   Current Marketable Securities—Stocks.   On January 5, 1983, the Belford Company purchased a portfolio of current marketable securities that were all capital stocks for $38,000. At the end of the company's fiscal year on June 30, 1983, the market value of the portfolio was $35,000. On August 25, 1983, the company sold one of the stocks in its portfolio, which had cost $10,000, for $12,000. On June 30, 1983, this security had a market value of $9,500.

Required: 1. How much income will the Belford Company recognize from January 5, 1983, through August 25, 1983, as a result of these events?

2. Prepare journal entries required to record these events.

E7-11   Current Marketable Securities—Bonds.   On February 1, 1983, the Grays Company purchased 10 Torres Company 8% $1,000 bonds at 105 plus accrued interest, and paid stockbroker's fees of $200. The bonds pay interest on June 30 and December 31 each year. On August 31, 1983, the company sold the bonds at 106 plus accrued interest.

Required: 1. Compute the total amount paid for the bonds.

2. Compute the interest earned on the bonds by the Grays Company during 1983.

3. For the sale of the bonds, compute the amount received and the gain or loss.

4. Prepare the journal entries required to account for the bonds during 1983.

E7-12   Current Marketable Securities—Bonds.   On March 1, 1983, the Harsh Company purchased Elm Company bonds with a face value of $5,000. The bonds pay interest at a 10% annual interest rate on June 30 and December 31 each year. The Harsh Company paid 97 plus accrued interest, plus a stockbroker's commission of $150. The Harsh Company sold the bonds on November 1, 1983, at 101 plus accrued interest.

Required: 1. Compute the amount paid for the bonds.

2. Compute the interest earned on the bonds by the Harsh Company during 1983.

3. For the sale of the bonds, compute the amount received and the gain or loss.

4. Prepare the journal entries required to account for the bonds during 1983.

PROBLEMS

Part A

P7-1A   Petty Cash Fund.   On October 10 the Dixon Company established a petty cash fund of $300 under the control of an employee. During the year the following transactions occurred:

Date	Transaction
Oct. 15	Purchased office supplies, $20.
27	Paid floral maintenance service for the office plants, $14.
Nov. 5	Purchased postage stamps, $8.
15	Paid UPS delivery charges, $10.
29	Purchased office supplies, $15.

Date	Transaction
Dec. 1	Reimbursed employee for taxi fare, $8.
5	Paid COD delivery charges, $5.
12	Paid for office cleaning, $26.
24	Paid for employee taxi fares, $50.
31	Replenished petty cash fund.

Required: 1. How much is required to replenish the petty cash fund assuming no cash is over or short?

2. If $130 was in the petty cash fund before it was replenished, prepare the journal entry on December 31 to record the expenses and replenish the petty cash fund.

P7-2A Bank Reconciliation. An examination of the accounting records and the bank statement of the Evans Company at March 31, 1983, provides the following information:

(a) The cash account has a balance of $5,682.38.

(b) The bank statement shows a bank balance of $3,446.81.

(c) The company's petty cash account has a balance of $300 and was replenished on March 31.

(d) The March 31 cash receipts of $3,268.95 were deposited at the bank but were not recorded by the bank until April 1.

(e) Checks issued and mailed in March but not included among the checks listed on the bank statement were:

Check No. 706	$872.38
Check No. 717	212.00

(f) A bank service charge of $28 had not been recorded by the company.

(g) A check received from a customer for $182 and deposited by the Evans Company was returned marked NSF. The nonpayment had not been previously recorded by the Evans Company.

(h) The bank collected a note of $200 and charged a collection fee of $5. The cash receipt had not previously been recorded by the Evans Company.

(i) The Evans Company discovered that Check No. 701, which was written for the March rent, was recorded as $526 when it had been correctly written as $562.

Required: 1. Prepare a bank reconciliation at March 31, 1983.

2. Prepare the journal entries required to correct the Evans Company's cash account.

P7-3A Bank Reconciliation. The Carson Company received the following bank statement for February 1983:

Carson Company
1313 Williams St.
Denver, Co. 80218

Mid-Town Bank
Denver, Co. 80222

Date	Checks	Deposits	Balance
Feb. 1			3,264.01
5	2,700.33	8,642.61	
10	3,484.81		
12	6.00SC	350.00CM	
17	274.09		
19	4,133.60	3,385.49	
23	69.69NSF		
28			5,684.38

SC = Service Charge   NSF = Check Returned
CM = Credit Memo   DM = Debit Memo

The receipt of $350 on February 12 was for a note of $345 collected by the bank, plus $10 current interest, less a $5 service charge. The company's accounting records contained the following information:

Cash Balance on February 28 from the books: $2,060.42

Cash Disbursements		Cash Receipts	
Check No. 155	$2,700.33	Feb. 4	$8,624.61
156	3,484.81	18	3,385.49
157	274.09		
158	589.02	All receipts are verified and correct.	
159	4,133.60		
160	2,742.63		

Required: 1. Prepare a bank reconciliation on February 28 for the Carson Company.
2. Prepare the journal entries that the Carson Company should record as a result of the reconciliation.

P7-4A   Marketable Securities.   The Wilson Company invests its temporary excess funds in marketable securities. At the end of 1982 Wilson's portfolio of current marketable securities (capital stock) is as follows:

Security	Number of Shares	Cost per Share	Market Value per Share
Bierstadt Company	500	$25	$28
Lindsey Company	400	35	37
Pyramid Company	800	20	20

During the first quarter of 1983 the company engaged in the following transactions:

Date	Transaction
Feb. 10	Sold one-half of the Pyramid shares for $26 per share.
Mar. 18	Purchased 700 shares of Maroon Company stock for $18 per share.
Mar. 31	Received dividends of $1,400 on the marketable securities during the period for which the market prices on this date are:

Security	Market Value per Share
Bierstadt Company	$24
Lindsey Company	33
Pyramid Company	22
Maroon Company	17

During the second quarter of 1983 the company engaged in the following transactions:

Date	Transaction
Apr. 18	Purchased 300 shares of the Huron Company stock for $30 per share.
May 15	Sold the Lindsey Company shares for $37 per share.
June 30	Received dividends of $1,800 on the marketable securities during the period for which the market prices on this date are:

Security	Market Value per Share
Bierstadt Company	$26
Pyramid Company	19
Maroon Company	21
Huron Company	32

Required: 1. Prepare journal entries to record these events. The company records dividend revenue when the cash is received.
2. Show how the income recognized each quarter and the value of the marketable securities reported in the balance sheet at the end of each quarter would be disclosed on the interim financial statements.

P7-5A Investments in Current Marketable Securities.
The Windom Company purchased and sold several marketable securities that were classified as current. The acquisitions, sales, and market values were as follows:

Security	Acquisition Date	Cost	Market Value 12/31/1982	Market Value 12/31/1983	Sale Date	Selling Price
1,000 shares	1/10/1982	$10,000	$ 9,000	–	1/10/1983	$11,000
2,000 shares	3/25/1982	15,000	14,000	–	2/11/1983	13,000
Twenty 10% bonds	4/1/1982	22,000	21,000	$23,000	3/1/1984	24,000
500 shares	3/10/1983	11,000	–	12,000	4/20/1984	8,000
Ten 8% bonds	6/1/1983	9,000	–	6,000	5/1/1984	6,000
100 shares	10/4/1984	5,000	–	–	6/5/1985	8,000

Assume that the bonds are accounted for by the cost method and pay interest on June 30 and December 31 of each year. The cost of the bonds excludes the accrued interest that was also paid at the time of purchase. The selling price listed above for the bonds excludes the accrued interest collected at the time of the sale. The last purchase of 100 shares has a market value on December 31, 1984, of $6,000. No dividends have been paid or declared on the shares.

Required: 1. Prepare journal entries to record these events for the period 1982 through 1985.
2. Show how the income reported each year by the Windom Company as a result of these transactions would be disclosed on its income statement.
3. Show how the value of the Current Marketable Securities would appear in the balance sheet at the end of each year.
4. Some of the securities were held for more than a year. Does this mean that they should not have been included in the current portfolio?

PROBLEMS
Part B

P7-1B Petty Cash Fund.
On November 6 the Checker Company established a petty cash fund of $500 under the control of an employee. During the year the following transactions occurred:

Date	Transaction
Nov. 10	Purchased postage stamps, $15.
21	Paid COD charges, $5.
24	Paid for office cleaning, $17.
30	Paid janitorial service, $16.
Dec. 5	Purchased office supplies, $8.
9	Paid UPS delivery charges, $10.
12	Paid employee's taxi fare, $12.
18	Paid floral maintenance service for the office plants, $25.
20	Purchased office supplies, $28.
31	Replenished petty cash fund.

Required: 1. How much is required to replenish the petty cash fund assuming that there is no cash over or short?
2. If $350 was in the petty cash fund before it was replenished, prepare the journal entry on December 31 to record the expenses and replenish the petty cash fund.

P7-2B **Bank Reconciliation.** An examination of the accounting records and the bank statement of the Rancher Company at May 31, 1983, provides the following information:

(a) The cash account has a balance of $7,149.27.
(b) The bank statement shows a bank balance of $3,443.89.
(c) The company's petty cash account has a balance of $450 and was replenished on May 31.
(d) The May 31 cash receipts of $4,599.13 were deposited but were not recorded by the bank until June 1.
(e) Checks issued and mailed in May but not included among the checks listed on the bank statement were:

Check No. 949	$518.65
Check No. 957	$372.90

(f) A bank service charge of $27 had not been recorded by the company.
(g) A check received from a customer for $241 and deposited by the Rancher Company was returned marked NSF. The nonpayment had not been previously recorded by Rancher Company.
(h) The bank collected a note of $300 and charged a collection fee of $10. The cash receipt had not been previously recorded by the Rancher Company.
(i) The Rancher Company discovered that Check No. 941, which was correctly written for the May utilities bill, was recorded as $627.41 although it had been correctly written as $647.21.

Required: 1. Prepare a bank reconciliation at May 31, 1983.
2. Prepare the journal entries required to correct the Rancher Company's cash account.

P7-3B **Bank Reconciliation.** The Oomph Company received the following bank statement for the month of August 1983:

	Oomph Company **Denver, Co. 80223**		**Downtown Bank** **Denver, Co. 80001**	
Date	Checks		Deposits	Balance
Aug. 1				4,075.25
4	1,314.88		4,769.32	
11	773.56			
14	10.00SC		1,000.00CM	
20	3,200.00			
24	6,198.43		9,703.22	
26	275.00NSF			
29				7,775.92

SC = Service Charge   CM = Credit Memo   NSF = Check Returned   DM = Debit Memo

The receipt of $1,000 on August 14 was for a note of $940 collected by the bank, plus current interest of $75, less a $15 service charge. The company's accounting records contained the following information:

Cash Balance on August 31 from the books: $4,806.08

Cash Disbursements		*Cash Receipts*	
Check No. 311	$1,314.88	Aug. 3	$4,679.32
312	773.56	20	9,703.22
313	3,200.00	All receipts are verified and correct.	
314	1,736.98		
315	6,198.43		
316	427.86		

Required: 1. Prepare an August 31 bank reconciliation for the Oomph Company.
2. Prepare any journal entries necessary after the reconciliation.

P7-4B Marketable Securities. The Streeter Company invests its temporary excess funds in marketable securities. At the end of 1982 Streeter's portfolio of current marketable securities (capital stock) is as follows:

Security	Number of Shares	Cost per Share	Market Value per Share
Parham Company	500	$20	$23
Beckman Company	400	30	32
Traub Company	800	15	15

During the first quarter of 1983 the company engaged in the following transactions:

Date	Transactions
Mar. 11	Sold one-half of the Parham shares for $21 per share.
Mar. 17	Purchased 700 shares of the Gilman Company for $10 per share.
Mar. 31	Received dividends of $1,500 on the marketable securities during the period, and the market prices on this date are:

Security	Market Value per Share
Parham Company	$19
Beckman Company	28
Traub Company	17
Gilman Company	9

During the second quarter of 1983 the company engaged in the following transactions:

Date	Transactions
May 16	Purchased 300 shares of the Hagge Company stock for $25 per share.
June 9	Sold the Beckman Company stock for $32 per share.
June 30	Received dividends of $2,000 on the marketable securities during the period, and the market prices on this date are:

Security	Market Value per Share
Parham Company	$21
Traub Company	14
Gilman Company	13
Hagge Company	27

Required: 1. Prepare journal entries to record these events. The company records dividend revenue when the cash is received.
2. Show how the income recognized each quarter and the value of the marketable securities reported in the balance sheet at the end of each quarter would be disclosed on the interim financial statements.

P7-5B Investments in Current Marketable Securities. The Martell Company purchased and sold several marketable securities that were classified as current. The acquisitions, sales, and market values were as follows:

Security	Acquisition Date	Cost	Market Value 12/31/1982	Market Value 12/31/1983	Sale Date	Selling Price
1,000 shares	2/17/1982	$14,000	$12,000	–	2/17/1983	$16,000
2,500 shares	4/6/1982	20,000	19,000	–	3/11/1983	17,000
Fifteen 10% bonds	5/1/1982	16,000	15,000	$17,000	4/1/1984	18,000
600 shares	3/19/1983	12,000	–	13,000	5/1/1984	7,000
Twenty 8% bonds	6/1/1983	18,000	–	15,000	6/1/1984	17,000
120 shares	10/19/1984	6,000	–	–	7/9/1985	8,000

Assume that the bonds are accounted for by the cost method and pay interest on June 30 and December 31 each year. The cost of the bonds excludes the accrued interest, which was also paid at the time of purchase. The selling price listed above for the bonds excludes the accrued interest collected at the time of the sale. The last purchase of 120 shares has a market value on December 31, 1984, of $7,000. No dividends have been declared or paid on the shares.

Required: 1. Prepare journal entries to record these events for the period 1982 through 1985.
2. Show how the income reported each year by the Martell Company as a result of these transactions would be disclosed on its income statement.
3. Show how the value of the Current Marketable Securities would appear in the balance sheet at the end of each year.
4. Some of the securities were held for more than one year. Does this mean that they should not have been included in the current portfolio?

DISCUSSION CASES

C7-1 Internal Control. Sam Lewis has been operating a service station for several years. Although he has occasionally employed students part-time, he has collected the cash for gas and service work himself. He has now decided to open a second service station and put himself more in the role of a manager, and therefore he will hire employees to run the service stations and to pump gas and do repair work.

Required: How could Sam Lewis implement the principles of internal control for cash? If any of the principles are not applicable in this situation, does it mean that Sam Lewis has to accept that he cannot have control over the financial aspects of the business?

C7-2 Marketable Securities. The Board of Directors of the Oxford Company is discussing the method that should be used for the valuation of the company's current marketable securities. Some of the comments are as follows:

"We should use cost, because until we sell the securities, we don't know if we have made any money."

"If we use cost we are effectively lying to the shareholders, and as a member of the Board of Directors I don't feel I'm fulfilling my responsibilities."

"Market value is too pessimistic. If the price is up in one period and down in the next, we will report a loss in the second period although we may have a profit overall. That's misleading."

Required: Describe what the speaker of each of these comments means and prepare a counterargument for each of them. (Ignore the requirements of generally accepted accounting principles.)

8 Accounts Receivable and Notes Receivable

After reading this chapter, you should understand:

- Credit sales, sales discounts, and sales returns and allowances
- The allowance method and the direct write-off method of accounting for bad debts
- How to compute the amount of bad debt expense under the percent of sales method and the aging method
- How to account for credit card sales
- A promissory note (receivable) and how to calculate interest on a note
- How to determine the maturity date of a note
- Notes receivable, including discounting a note
- How accounts receivable and notes receivable are disclosed in financial statements

As we have seen in earlier chapters companies do not always engage in cash transactions; instead they make purchases and sales on credit. In this chapter we discuss some of the accounting issues associated with the receivables that result from making sales on credit. These issues include the valuation of accounts receivable and the bad debt expense resulting from the noncollection of accounts receivable. Also included is accounting for notes receivable, which involves discussions of calculating and recognizing interest, discounting a note at a bank, and dishonored notes.

CREDIT SALES AND COLLECTIONS

Companies make sales on credit for two primary reasons. The first is that it may be more convenient to sell on credit than for cash (as discussed in the last chapter checks received at the time of a sale are considered to be cash). For example, when a company is selling a product that has to be shipped it is a common business practice for the purchaser to pay for the goods after receiving them. Between the time that the purchaser acquires title to the goods and the time payment is received by the seller, credit has been extended by the seller to the purchaser.

The second reason why credit sales are made is that management may believe that offering credit will encourage a purchaser to acquire an item that would not otherwise be purchased. This is particularly common in retail sales when the purchaser may not have sufficient cash available to make the purchase. The seller, or retail store, offers credit terms so that the purchaser will agree to the sale. The disadvantage of credit sales is that they may require a significant management effort because the company must make credit investigations, prepare and mail bills, and ensure collection from the customers. All of these activities involve a cost to the company in money and employee time.

Accounting for credit sales, which was first discussed in Chapter 3, would lead to the following journal entries to record a sale of $1,000 to Diane Matt and later collection of the accounts receivable resulting from the sale (assuming no sales discount):

```
Accounts Receivable: Diane Matt . . . . . . . . . . . . . . . .    1,000
    Sales . . . . . . . . . . . . . . . . . . . . . . . . . . . . . . .           1,000
To record the sale of merchandise on account.

Cash . . . . . . . . . . . . . . . . . . . . . . . . . . . . . . . .    1,000
    Accounts Receivable: Diane Matt . . . . . . . . . . . . .              1,000
Collection of accounts receivable.
```

These entries are the entries that would be recorded in the general journal or in the sales journal and cash receipts journal if special journals are used. In addition, entries would be recorded in the accounts receivable subsidiary ledger for the individual customers who have increased and decreased their particular account balances.

Sales discounts and sales returns and allowances were discussed in Chapter 5. To briefly review these topics, recall that neither affects the initial recording of the sales revenue and the accounts receivable. If a sales discount is taken by a customer, the company receives less cash than the amount of the account receivable and the difference is the sales discount taken. For example, if a company makes the sale for $1,000 to Diane Matt on terms of 1/10, n/30 and she takes the discount, the journal entry to record the cash collection is as follows:

```
Cash . . . . . . . . . . . . . . . . . . . . . . . . . . . . . . . .    990
Sales Discounts  . . . . . . . . . . . . . . . . . . . . . . . . .    10
    Accounts Receivable: Diane Matt . . . . . . . . . . . . . .             1,000
Collected sale of $1,000, made on terms of 1/10, n/30.
```

Sales returns and allowances extended to customers result in a reduction in accounts receivable without cash being collected. For example, if a company gives an allowance of $50 on the sale because of damage caused during delivery the journal entry to record the allowance is as follows:

```
Sales Returns and Allowances . . . . . . . . . . . . . . . . . .    50
    Accounts Receivable: Diane Matt . . . . . . . . . . . . . . .            50
To record sales returns and allowances.
```

Both the sales discounts taken and the sales returns and allowances are deducted from sales revenue in the income statement.

When credit sales are made to facilitate or encourage sales, there is always a chance that the seller will not collect the full amount of its accounts receivable because the purchaser does not pay. It should be recognized that the existence of uncollectible accounts does not indicate that the company should not have made credit sales. As long as the gross profit generated from the additional credit sales less the cost of operating the credit activities exceeds the loss from not collecting certain accounts, the policy of offering credit sales may be considered to be advantageous. Suppose that because a company offers credit terms its sales increase by $80,000 and the gross profit on sales is $15,000. If the operations of the credit department cost $10,000, the increase in profit is $5,000 ($15,000 − $10,000). If the company does not collect 2% of these additional credit sales, it loses $1,600 (2% × $80,000). The company is still better off by $3,400 ($5,000 − $1,600), however. Accounting for such uncollectible accounts receivables is discussed in the next section.

UNCOLLECTIBLE ACCOUNTS RECEIVABLE

Uncollectible accounts receivable are the accounts receivable that a company does not collect. At the time of the credit sales, the company does not know which customers will not pay because, of course, if it knew then that the customers would not pay it would never have made the sale in the first place. Although a company agrees to sell on credit based on a customer's credit references, the references indicate only the past record of the customer's payments and do not guarantee that the customer will pay in the future. Thus a period of time, perhaps several months or even years, may pass before the company knows for sure that it will not collect a particular account. When it is known the account is *written off*, which means that attempts to collect the account are minimal even though hope for eventual collection may continue. Since the original sale was recorded as revenue for the company, it is clear that the uncollectibility of an account receivable must be recorded as a reduction in income.

Accounting for uncollectible accounts receivable raises three basic questions. The first is whether the uncollectibility should be recorded as a contra revenue or as an expense. The second relates to the period in which the uncollectibility should be recognized. The third is the value that should be shown for accounts receivable on the balance sheet at the end of the accounting period. Each of these questions is discussed in the next three sections.

How Should the Uncollectibility Be Recognized in the Income Statement?

Sound arguments can be made for the recognition of an uncollectible account receivable as either a contra revenue or an expense. Since the sale was recorded as a revenue it may be argued that the noncollection of the sale price means that the sale should never have been recognized. Rather than reducing the sales revenue account directly, a contra-revenue account would be used and the amount in the account deducted from sales revenue in the income statement.

Alternatively, it can be argued that the uncollectibility of certain sales is part of the cost of doing business and therefore should be considered an expense. This is probably a sounder argument because it is consistent with the two major reasons for making credit sales, which were discussed earlier. Whether credit sales are made for convenience or to attract customers the costs associated with making these sales should be an expense. **Bad debt expense is the expense for the accounting period due to the eventual noncollection of accounts receivable.** Recording these costs as bad debt expense is consistent with the treatment of other costs associated with the sale that are also treated as expenses. Although there is no rule that specifies how a company must classify the uncollectibility of a receivable in the income statement, it is more common to include the amount as an operating expense in the category of general and administrative expenses. Since the decision to grant credit is normally made by the credit department rather than by the selling department, it is appropriate to classify bad debt expense as an administrative expense rather than a selling expense.

When Should the Uncollectibility Be Recognized?

As mentioned, a period of time elapses between recording the sale and knowing that the particular receivable will not be collected. Sometimes these two events occur in the same accounting period, in which case there is no problem. More often, however, the sale is recorded in one accounting period and the knowledge of the uncollectibility of the related account occurs in a later period. This suggests two alternatives for the time period in which the bad debt expense could be recognized. The expense could be recognized in the time period in which the sale is made or the time period in which the uncollectibility is known, that is, the period of the write-off. For example, suppose that the Marlin Company sells a product in August 1982 to John Jones for $150. John Jones later encounters financial difficulty and declares bankruptcy in July 1983 before he has paid Marlin. Should Marlin recognize this expense in 1982 or 1983?

A review of the matching principle, which was first discussed in Chapter 3, should make it very clear which answer is correct. The matching principle requires that the cost of generating sales revenue be matched against the revenue in the period in which the revenue is recognized. We have clearly seen this principle being applied when the cost of the product sold (the cost of goods sold) is matched against the sales revenue in the period of the sale even though the purchase may have been made in an earlier period and the cash payment made in an earlier or later period. The cost of goods sold is *not* recognized in, for example, the period of the purchase or the cash payment, but rather the period in which the product is sold. Similarly, the bad debt expense that is associated with the sales of a period should be matched against the sales of that period.

In order to adhere to the matching concept the allowance method of accounting for uncollectible accounts receivable is used. **The allowance method requires the recognition of the bad debt expense in the period of the sale and *not* in the period of uncollectibility.** Referring to the example in the previous paragraph, the Marlin Company has a bad debt expense in 1982 and *not* in 1983. Since the uncollectibility will not be known until 1983, however, the bad debt expense for 1982 must be *estimated* (this estimate is discussed in the next section). Once again the recognition of accounting expenses is being separated from the related cash flow, or in this case the lack of a cash flow.

Recognition of Bad Debt Expense

Before explaining in the next section the problem of estimating the amount of the bad debt expense (before the write-off occurs) under the allowance method, let us review how the financial statements are affected by the recognition of a bad debt expense in the period of sale.

When the bad debt expense is recognized the company is accepting the fact that a portion of the accounts receivable will not be collected. Therefore the value of the accounts receivable should also be reduced because otherwise the value of the asset would be overstated. An allowance for uncollectible accounts is used for this purpose. **Allowance for Uncollectible Accounts is a contra-asset account in which the amount of accounts receivable that a company estimates will not be collected is recorded.** The Allowance account is subtracted from Accounts Receivable to give net accounts receivable, which is reported in the balance sheet. In the Marlin Company example we discussed the uncollectibility in terms of a single account; in actual practice, however, companies evaluate the uncollectibility of their entire accounts receivable at once. Thus a single journal entry is used to recognize the expense and the reduction of the asset value for all the company's estimated uncollectible accounts. This is accomplished by an adjusting entry made at the end of the year (for the entire year) as follows (using assumed amounts):

Bad Debt Expense	2,500	
Allowance for Uncollectible Accounts		2,500

To record the estimated bad debt expense for the period.

Note that the credit to the Allowance account has the same effect as a credit to the Accounts Receivable account would have; that is, because the Allowance account is increased net accounts receivable is decreased. The advantage of using the contra-asset account is that the Accounts Receivable account will still include the total amount that the company is legally entitled to receive. In addition, if the Accounts Receivable account were credited directly it would not have the same balance as the accounts receivable subsidiary ledger. This is so because it is not possible to write down individual accounts in the subsidiary ledger since the individual customers who will not pay are not known. If the individual customers who failed to pay could have been known the company would never have made the sales to them. The net accounts receivable, the balance of the Accounts Receivable less the balance of the Allowance for Uncollectible Accounts, indicates the company's *estimate* of the amount of cash it will actually receive. It is also the amount that would be disclosed on the ending balance sheet as follows (using assumed numbers):

Accounts receivable	$95,000
Less: Allowance for uncollectible accounts	3,200
Net accounts receivable	$91,800

Write-Off of an Uncollectible Account

Eventually certain individual customer accounts will be judged to be uncollectible. When a company writes off an account receivable it is recognizing the non-collection of an amount that was included in its previous estimation of uncollectible accounts. Therefore this recognition does *not* affect the total assets or expenses of the company. The expense and the reduction in the asset were both recorded at the time of the estimate by means of the adjusting entry. Therefore the write-off of a specific uncollectible account receivable of Ann Blake of $220 is recorded in the following journal entry:

Allowance for Uncollectible Accounts   220
    Accounts Receivable: Ann Blake   220
To record the write-off of uncollectible account receivable.

Note that the effect of this entry is to reduce (debit) a contra asset, Allowance for Uncollectible Accounts, and reduce (credit) an asset, Accounts Receivable. Therefore the net effect on the assets of the company is zero. At the same time as this journal entry is made, the individual customer's account in the accounts receivable subsidiary ledger will be credited for the nonpayment of the account. Since a company usually refers to its customer accounts in the subsidiary ledger when deciding whether or not to extend additional credit, this write-off should have the effect of causing the company to refuse credit to this customer in the future.

The Direct Write-Off Method

Although the allowance method is required by generally accepted accounting principles, some companies use the direct write-off method. **The direct write-off method recognizes the bad debt expense in the period when the account is written off because it is uncollectible.** Therefore no estimate of bad debt expense is made in the period of sale. The direct write-off method is *not* a generally accepted accounting principle because it violates the matching concept. The method may be used, however, in three circumstances. First, it may be used if the effect on the financial statements is not materially different from using the allowance method (materiality was discussed in Chapter 1). Thus if the effect of using the direct write-off method instead of the allowance method does not result in a materially different measure of income or assets, its use is acceptable. Second, many companies are not required to follow generally accepted accounting principles in the preparation of their financial statements and therefore may use the direct write-off method. For example, sole proprietorships, partnerships, and corporations whose stock is not publicly traded are not *required* to follow generally accepted accounting principles. It may be a very shortsighted policy, however, not to follow generally accepted accounting principles. Whenever the company comes into contact with third parties such as banks and various regulatory authorities, the absence of generally accepted accounting principles may cause considerable difficulties. In addition, the eventual conversion to generally accepted accounting principles may be expensive and time-consuming. Third, the direct write-off method is often used for federal income tax reporting.

Accounting for the direct write-off method is simpler than for the allowance method. No estimate of bad debt expense is made, and no allowance account is used. When an account receivable is judged to be uncollectible, the bad debt expense is recognized and the account receivable written off. For example, if a company writes off a $300 account receivable from Carl Norbeck, the following journal entry would be made:

Bad Debt Expense   300
    Accounts Receivable: Carl Norbeck   300
To record the bad debt expense.

Although the direct write-off method may be simpler for a smaller company that is not required to follow generally accepted accounting principles, management should be careful to keep track of accounts receivable to avoid incurring unnecessary losses. In the rest of the chapter we will assume that the allowance method is being used.

MEASUREMENT OF THE BAD DEBT EXPENSE

An obvious problem arises when the bad debt expense is recognized in the period of the sale and not in the period that the account is written off. How is the amount that is eventually to be written off known in the period the sale is made? The amount is not known for certain, but the company can *estimate* how much it will not collect in the future. Two methods of estimation are used. The percent of sales method uses an estimate that is based on the sales of the current period. The aging method uses an estimate that is based on the balance in accounts receivable.

The Percent of Sales Method of Estimating Bad Debt Expense

A company can estimate its bad debt expense by using the percent of sales method. **The percent of sales method requires the company to estimate the bad debt expense by multiplying the net credit sales of the period by the percent estimated to be uncollectible.** Net credit sales are credit sales less sales discounts and sales returns and allowances. The estimate can be based on the past experience of the company or on the experiences of other companies published in a trade journal. For example, suppose that a company has net credit sales of $200,000 in 1983 and its past experience indicates that $1\frac{1}{2}\%$ of its net credit sales are never collected. Therefore in order to match expenses against revenues the company must recognize a bad debt expense of $3,000 ($1\frac{1}{2}\% \times \$200,000$) in 1983. The adjusting entry at the end of the year to record this expense is as follows:

Bad Debt Expense   3,000
    Allowance for Uncollectible Accounts   3,000
To record the estimated bad debt expense for 1983.

The effect of this entry is to reduce income for 1983 and reduce the value of accounts receivable. If a specific account should be considered uncollectible the write-off is recorded as discussed earlier by reducing (debiting) the Allowance for Uncollectible Accounts and reducing (crediting) Accounts Receivable. The write-off would also be recorded in the accounts receivable subsidiary ledger.

While the percent of sales method matches the bad debt expense against the sales revenue in the current period, a major disadvantage is that there is no verification of the reasonableness of the balance of the Allowance for Uncollectible Accounts. Recall that the account is increased (credited) when the estimate is made and reduced (debited) when the write-off occurs. Therefore if the company over-estimates the bad debts (the estimated amount exceeds the write-offs) the allowance account will have a credit balance remaining in it that exceeds the value of the accounts that will be written off in the future. If this overestimation is not offset by an equal underestimation in subsequent periods the balance will never be removed. Such a *permanent* balance leads to an incorrect valuation of the accounts receivable and indicates that the bad debt expense of previous periods has been estimated incorrectly. While it is possible for the company to periodically eliminate any balance that has accumulated in the allowance account, the aging method of estimating the bad debt expense prevents such an incorrect balance from being created in the account.

The Aging Method of Estimating Bad Debt Expense

Instead of basing the estimate of bad debt expense on net credit sales, the aging method bases the estimate of the balance in the allowance for uncollectibles account on the age of the individual accounts included in the ending balance of the accounts receivable account. The rationale for this method is that the bad debts result from the accounts receivable that are outstanding rather than from the sales themselves. Therefore an excessive balance cannot build up in the Allowance for Uncollectible Accounts because each period's estimate of the amounts uncollectible is based on the particular accounts receivable balance at the end of that period. The aging method is also generally considered to be more accurate for valuing the net accounts receivable collectible at the end of the period because the estimate is based on the age of the specific customer's accounts receivable outstanding. As the length of time a customer's account has been outstanding increases, the likelihood of the account not being collected is increased. For example, a company is much more likely to collect an account that is 30 days old than an account that is 360 days old. Therefore as the proportion of old accounts increases, the balance in the Allowance for Uncollectible Accounts should also increase in proportion to the larger expected write-offs.

The aging method requires that a company categorize individual accounts into age groups based on the length of time they have been outstanding and then multiply the amount in each age group by a historically developed bad debts percentage to give the estimate of the uncollectible accounts in each age group and finally sum those amounts to determine the required ending balance in the Allowance for Uncollectible Accounts. As with the percent of sales method these estimates would be based on the past experience of the company, or on the experiences of other companies that have been published in a trade journal. To illustrate the application of the aging method suppose that the Joyce Company makes credit sales during 1983 and has a balance in accounts receivable of $100,000 at the end of 1983. This total balance is made up of amounts within each age group and percents expected to be uncollectible as follows:

Age Group	Amount	Estimated Percent Uncollectible	Estimated Amount Uncollectible
Not yet due	$ 40,000	$\frac{1}{2}$%	$ 200
1–30 days past due	25,000	1	250
31–60 days past due	20,000	2	400
61–120 days past due	10,000	5	500
More than 120 days past due	5,000	20	1,000
Total	$100,000		$2,350

Since the Joyce Company has accounts receivable of $40,000 that are not yet due, and the company's experience shows that $\frac{1}{2}$% of these accounts will become uncollectible, the expected amount uncollectible is $200 ($\frac{1}{2}$% × $40,000). Applying this analysis to each age group provides a total estimated amount uncollectible of $2,350. Therefore the expected collectible amount is $97,650 ($100,000 − $2,350) and would be shown in the balance sheet as follows:

```
Accounts receivable  . . . . . . . . . . . . . . . . . . .   $100,000
Less: Allowance for uncollectible accounts . . . . . . .       2,350
Net accounts receivable  . . . . . . . . . . . . . . . .   $ 97,650
```

It is important to realize that the amount of $2,350 is the required *balance* of the Allowance for Uncollectible Accounts and *not* the amount of the Bad Debt Expense. The Bad Debt Expense is instead the amount that is needed to increase the existing balance of the Allowance for Uncollectible Accounts up to the required ending balance of $2,350. Therefore if it is assumed that the Joyce Company had a credit balance in the account of $400 before it performed the aging analysis, the bad debt expense for the year is $1,950 ($2,350 − $400) and would be recorded by an adjusting entry at year end as follows:

```
Bad Debt Expense . . . . . . . . . . . . . . . . . . . . . . .   1,950
    Allowance for Uncollectible Accounts . . . . . . . . . . .           1,950
To record the estimated bad debt expense for 1983.
```

It is important to understand why there is a $400 credit balance in the Allowance for Uncollectible Accounts before the year-end adjusting entry. The $400 in the Allowance for Uncollectible Accounts results from the estimates of uncollectible accounts from previous years less the amounts written off to date. The addition of $1,950 to the credit balance in the Allowance account of $400 results in the correct ending balance of $2,350. Thus the ending accounts receivable is properly valued at the expected amount collectible of $97,650. Note that use of the aging method does *not* consider the sales for the period. Consequently, the use of the aging method avoids the possibility of creating an incorrect ending balance in the Allowance for Uncollectible Accounts as is possible with the percent of sales method.

While the aging method is a more accurate method for valuing accounts receivable than the percent of sales method, it requires more information for its application. This added knowledge of the estimated percent of uncollectibles by age groups, however, is useful information that management should know for effective control of its credit operations. As individual accounts move to older age groups the credit department should make increasing efforts to collect the accounts.

Recovery of Accounts Written Off

Now that we have seen how to estimate and account for bad debt expense and the write-off of accounts receivable, an additional item needs to be considered. After a company has written off an account receivable, the receivable may subsequently be collected. This recovery of a previously written off account receivable requires a two-step process. First, the journal entry used to write off the account must be reversed. Second, the collection of cash on the reinstated account receivable must be recognized. Suppose that the Joyce Company recovers the $150 account of Thomas Martin that it had previously written off. The following journal entries are required:

Accounts Receivable: Thomas Martin	150	
Allowance for Uncollectible Accounts		150
To reverse the write-off of the account of Thomas Martin.		

Cash	150	
Accounts Receivable: Thomas Martin		150
Collection of past due account of Thomas Martin.		

Note that these two entries have no effect on total assets although one asset, cash, has been increased and another asset, accounts receivable, has been decreased. The first entry increases (debits) an asset, accounts receivable, and increases (credits) a contra asset, allowance for uncollectible accounts, and the second entry increases (debits) an asset, cash, and decreases (credits) another asset, accounts receivable.

Since the net effect of the two entries is to increase cash and decrease accounts receivable, it is important to recognize why two entries are made instead of a single combined entry (debiting cash and crediting accounts receivable). When a debit or credit entry is made in the accounts receivable control account, an entry is also made in the accounts receivable subsidiary ledger. The first entry is necessary to reinstate the balance in the customer's subsidiary account and the second entry is necessary to record the account as paid. This two-entry process provides a complete record of the customer's account that may be useful in determining whether or not to offer credit to this customer in the future.

In the previous example if the company had used the direct write-off method to write off the Thomas Martin account initially, the subsequent recovery of this account would be recorded as follows:

Accounts Receivable: Thomas Martin	150	
Bad Debt Expense		150
To reverse the write-off of the account of Thomas Martin.		

Cash	150	
Accounts Receivable: Thomas Martin		150
Collection of past due account of Thomas Martin.		

Summary of Percent of Sales and Aging Methods

In summary, it can be said that the percent of sales method is an income statement approach that properly matches expenses against revenues, although it tends to ignore the valuation of the accounts receivable in the ending balance sheet. In contrast, the aging method focuses on the valuation of the account receivable in the balance sheet, although it puts less emphasis on the expense in the income statement. Whichever method is used the entries that are made in the two accounts, Accounts Receivable and the Allowance for Uncollectible Accounts, can be summarized in general ledger form as follows:

Accounts Receivable		Allowance for Uncollectible Accounts	
Beginning balance	Cash received	Accounts written off	Beginning balance
Credit sales	Accounts written off		Amount recorded as bad debt expense
Amounts recovered from write-offs			
			Amounts recovered from write-offs
- - - - - - - - - - - - - - - - - - - -		- - - - - - - - - - - - - - - - - - -	
Ending Balance			Ending balance

CREDIT CARD SALES

Many retail companies sell products or services to customers who use credit cards such as VISA and Mastercard to pay for their purchases. To be able to make such sales the company must have made an agreement with the credit card company. Credit card sales and collections follow several steps. First, the retail company records the credit card sale and bills the credit card company. The retail company then receives payment from the credit card company less a service charge, which is generally between 2% and 8%. The credit card company bills the customer who makes the payment directly to the credit card company. This arrangement is advantageous from the retail company's perspective because it (1) enables the company to attract customers who might not otherwise make purchases, (2) enables the company to collect cash from the credit card company sooner than it could collect from the customer, and (3) frees the company from being concerned with the problems of credit investigation, billing, and collection.

There is a time period, which is perhaps very short, between the sale to the customer and the collection of cash from the credit card company. If the customer pays with a bank credit card, such as VISA or Mastercard, the retailer may be able to deposit the credit card receipt along with checks and cash in its bank and therefore the sale can be immediately recorded as a cash sale rather than as an account receivable. The receipt for other types of credit cards, such as American Express or Diner's Club, which are typically accepted by companies operating airlines, hotels, and restaurants, cannot be deposited directly in the bank and therefore results in an account receivable. In both situations a credit card expense is also recognized at the same time as the transaction is recorded.

Suppose that the Carson Travel Agency sells an airline ticket for $100 to a customer who pays with a credit card. If the service charge is 8% the company will receive only $92 and the $8 is considered to be a credit card expense. This transaction would be recorded at the time of sale as follows:

Credit Card Accounts Receivable (or Cash)	92	
Credit Card Expense	8	
Sales		100

To record a credit card sale less the service charge.

When sales discounts were discussed in Chapter 5 the accounts receivable amount was recorded at the full amount. When the customer took the discount (and less cash was received) the difference between the cash and the accounts receivable balance was recorded as a Sales Discount Taken. This procedure was followed because it was not known at the time of the sale whether or not the discount would be taken. In contrast, with credit card sales it is known at the time of the sale that a lesser amount will be received by the retail company, and therefore it is appropriate to record the lesser amount when the sale is made. A company may also find it more convenient to record the account receivable at the full amount and recognize the expense when payment is received. Although this procedure is not as accurate and also is not consistent with the matching concept, it may be more desirable if it lessens record keeping because an expense does not have to be computed for every sale.

NOTES RECEIVABLE

When a company sells on credit in the routine course of business, it expects to receive payment in a relatively short time. Many companies, however, also sell to customers under an agreement in which payment will not be received for a much longer period. In this situation the selling company usually requires the purchaser to sign a promissory note. This note can be referred to if there is a legal dispute over the collection of the note. In addition, a major reason for requiring a note is that it can be converted into cash by selling it to a bank.

Promissory Note

A promissory note is a written legal document in which one party (the issuer) makes an unconditional promise to pay another party a certain amount of money on demand or on an agreed future date. Exhibit 8-1 includes an example of a note in which John Burgen agrees to pay the Morgan Company $10,000, plus interest of 12% on the maturity date. **The principal (also known as the face value) is the amount that is stated on the face of the note.** In this example the principal is $10,000. **The maturity date is the date on which the note and any interest are due and payable.** In our example the maturity date is February 1, 1984, which is 6 months after the date the note was signed on August 1, 1983. **The maker of the note is the person or company that signs the note and agrees to pay it on the maturity date. The payee is the person or company to whom the note is payable.** In this example John Burgen is the maker (or issuer) of the note and the Morgan Company is the payee.

Notes Receivable is the account used to record promissory notes held by the company. Thus when the Morgan Company makes the sale and receives the note it records sales revenue and a note receivable as follows:

Notes Receivable	10,000	
Sales		10,000

Note received in a sale to John Burgen.

This entry is identical to the entry made to record a credit sale except for the change in the title of the asset account from Accounts Receivable to Notes Receivable. In addition, a company generally does not use a subsidiary ledger for notes receivable because it can use the physical existence of the note for the necessary supporting documentation.

It is stated on the note that interest of 12% will be paid. It should always be assumed that the quoted interest rate is an *annual* rate, unless otherwise stated. The interest is paid on the principal of the note. Consequently, John Burgen has agreed to pay annual interest of 12% for a 6-month period. Since the annual interest would be $1,200 (12% × $10,000), on the maturity date John Burgen will pay $600 ($1,200 × $\frac{6}{12}$) interest for the 6 months. **The maturity value of a note is the principal plus the interest due on the maturity date.** In this example the maturity value is $10,600 ($10,000 principal plus $600 interest).

The payment of interest represents an expense to John Burgen and interest revenue to the Morgan Company. A complication arises, however, because at the end of the Morgan Company's fiscal year (December 31, 1983) the company has earned interest revenue for the period it has held the note even though it has not received any cash. This interest is for 5 months, from August through December, and therefore is equal to $\frac{5}{12}$ of the annual interest, or $500 ($1,200 × $\frac{5}{12}$). The interest is recorded as follows by an adjusting entry at the end of the year:

Interest Receivable	500	
Interest Revenue		500

To record accrual of interest on John Burgen's note.

EXHIBIT 8-1 Promissory Note

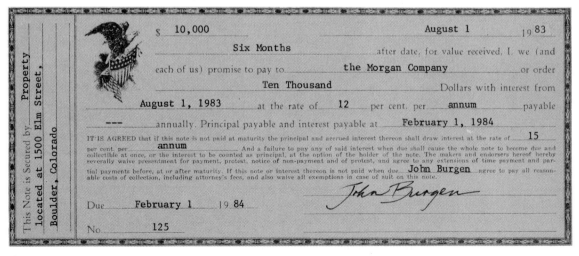

Reprinted with permission.

In the journal entry the company has recognized revenue because the interest was earned over a 5-month period; it also has recognized a receivable because John Burgen has a legal obligation to pay that amount on the maturity date. The Interest Revenue would be included in the Other Revenues and Expenses category of the income statement, and the Interest Receivable would be listed as a Current Asset in the balance sheet.

The note is due on February 1, 1984, and at that time the Morgan Company will receive $10,600 cash from John Burgen, consisting of the $10,000 principal and interest for 6 months of $600. In 1984, however, interest for only 1 month is earned, which is equal to $\frac{1}{12}$ of the annual interest, or $100 ($1,200 $\times \frac{1}{12}$). The remaining $500 is the collection of the interest earned in 1983 and recorded as Interest Receivable at the end of 1983. Therefore the following journal entry is used to recognize the receipt of the $10,600 cash:

Cash	10,600	
Interest Receivable		500
Interest Revenue		100
Notes Receivable		10,000

Received principal and interest on John Burgen's note.

In summary, the Morgan Company is increasing its assets by $100 ($10,600 − $10,500), recognizing revenue of $100, and exchanging two assets, notes receivable and interest receivable, for cash.

General Rule for Computing Interest and the Maturity Date

The previous example used a simple situation in which the note was outstanding for exactly 6 months. In many situations, however, notes are outstanding for periods that include partial months. When the note is issued with the life of the note stated but the maturity date not specified, two computations are necessary. First, the maturity date of the note must be determined, and second, the interest must be computed for the correct period of time.

MATURITY DATE. The maturity date of a note is computed by counting the exact number of days between the date the note was signed and the date it is due. In this calculation the day the note is signed is omitted, but the day the note is paid is included. To illustrate this rule suppose that a $2,000, 10%, 90-day note is signed on October 9 and is due 90 days after the signing. The maturity date is calculated as follows:

Life of the note		90
Number of days in October	31	
Minus the day of the note	9	
The number of days for the note in October		22
Number of days in November		30
Number of days in December		31
		83
Maturity date in January		7

The maturity date of the note is determined to be January 7.

COMPUTING INTEREST. The general rule for computing interest is:

$$\text{Interest} = \begin{array}{c}\textbf{Principal of}\\ \textbf{the Note}\end{array} \times \begin{array}{c}\textbf{Annual Rate}\\ \textbf{of Interest}\end{array} \times \begin{array}{c}\textbf{Period of Time the Note}\\ \textbf{Is Outstanding in Years}\\ \textbf{or Fraction of a Year}\end{array}$$

When a note is outstanding for several whole months the fraction of the year may be expressed by the number of months divided by 12, or in the earlier example of a $10,000, 12%, 6-month note:

$$\text{Interest} = \$10{,}000 \times 12\% \times \frac{6}{12}$$
$$= \$600$$

The usual rule for the computation of interest for a period other than a whole number of months is to assume that the year consists of 360 days (12 months of 30 days each). Using this 360-day rule the interest on the $2,000, 90-day, 10% note would be computed as follows:

$$\text{Interest} = \$2{,}000 \times 10\% \times \frac{90}{360}$$
$$= \$50$$

There may appear to be some inconsistency in computing *interest* on the basis of a 360-day year and the *maturity date* on the basis of the exact number of days. Nevertheless, these procedures are typical business practices and do not result in material errors in the interest calculation.

ACCRUAL OF INTEREST. At the end of each accounting period the interest that has accrued on any note must be recognized. The number of days the note has been outstanding must be determined and the interest computed according to the rule just explained. To continue the above example, on December 31 interest on the note must be accrued. At that time the $2,000 note will have been outstanding for 83 days (22 days in October + 30 days in November + 31 days in December) and 10% interest is computed as follows:

$$\text{Interest} = \$2{,}000 \times 10\% \times \frac{83}{360}$$
$$= \$46.11$$

The year-end adjusting entry to record the interest would be as follows:

Interest Receivable	46.11	
Interest Revenue		46.11

To accrue interest on a $2,000, 10% note.

Interest on Accounts Receivable

If a retail company chooses to operate its own credit department rather than accepting national credit cards, interest may be charged on the outstanding accounts receivable balance. The recognition of interest revenue would then follow the same principles as discussed for notes receivable.

Dishonored Notes Receivable

Just as accounts receivable are not always paid, notes receivable are sometimes not paid. **A dishonored note is a note that the maker fails to pay at the maturity date.** The maker is still responsible for payment, of course, but it is desirable for the payee to classify dishonored notes receivable separately from notes receivable that have not yet become due. For example, if John Burgen had failed to pay his note on February 1, 1984, he would have owed the Morgan Company $10,600 (the $10,000 principal plus the $600 interest). Since the interest for 1984 of $100 would not yet have been recorded in the accounts, the entry to record the dishonored note is as follows:

Notes Receivable Dishonored	10,600	
Notes Receivable		10,000
Interest Receivable		500
Interest Revenue		100

To record John Burgen's note as dishonored.

Apart from the recognition of interest revenue this entry has no effect on total assets. Nevertheless, it is a useful reclassification of the accounts. As an alternative to using the Notes Receivable Dishonored account, it may be desirable to debit the Accounts Receivable account and establish John Burgen's subsidiary ledger account so that this account may be charged with the dishonored amount. This entry should prevent the Morgan Company from extending additional credit to John Burgen.

It is questionable whether interest revenue should be recognized when collection is in doubt. Since the maker of the note owes interest as well as the principal, however, and the note is a legal document, which should increase the probability of collection, it is normal to record the interest revenue so that the Notes Receivable Dishonored asset amount reflects the full amount owed.

DISCOUNTING A NOTE RECEIVABLE

One of the advantages of a note that was mentioned earlier is that it can be converted into cash before maturity. Thus management has the opportunity of obtaining additional cash without having to apply for a loan. This is accomplished by discounting the note with a bank. **Discounting a note is a process in which the payee of a note assigns it over to a bank in exchange for cash.** The bank will then collect the note and interest from the maker on the maturity date. The payee usually remains responsible to the bank for the ultimate payment of the note should the maker default, however. That is, if the maker fails to pay the bank, the payee must pay the bank. This liability of the payee is known as a contingent liability. **A contingent liability is a liability that may or may not be paid depending on whether or not a future event occurs.** Discounting a note creates a contingent liability because the legal obligation the payee has to the bank is a liability, and the liability is contingent because it will have to be paid only if the maker fails to pay.

When a note is discounted at a bank it is first necessary to compute the maturity value at the maturity date. The maturity value is the sum of the principal and the interest. Since the maturity value is the amount the bank will receive from the maker on the maturity date, the bank then computes interest on this amount for the period between the date the note is discounted to the bank and the maturity date. This interest is deducted from the maturity value to determine the amount to pay the payee. It should be noted that the interest rate charged by the bank bears no relation to the rate listed on the note.

To illustrate the discounting of a note suppose that Susan Davis signs a $1,000, 10%, 6-month note on March 31 payable to the Williams Company as payment for a purchase of furniture. At that time the Williams Company recorded the transaction by increasing (debiting) Notes Receivable and increasing (crediting) Sales for $1,000. The Williams Company holds the note until April 30 when it is discounted at the bank. The bank charges the Williams Company 12% interest on the maturity value of the note. The bank will collect the maturity value of the note from Susan Davis on September 30. The maturity value is calculated as follows:

Principal	$1,000
Interest ($1,000 × 10% × $\frac{6}{12}$)	50
Maturity value	$1,050

Since the bank will collect the $1,050, 5 months after receipt of the note, it charges interest to Williams for 5 months at 12%. This interest is computed as follows:

$$\text{Interest} = \$1,050 \times 12\% \times \frac{5}{12}$$
$$= \$52.50$$

Therefore the bank will pay to the Williams Company the maturity value less the interest it charges, or $997.50 ($1,050 − $52.50). The effects of discounting this note can be illustrated as follows:

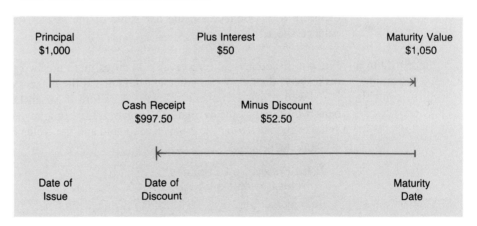

Since the $997.50 total payment on the note is less than the $1,000 principal, there is an interest expense to the Williams Company of $2.50. The Williams Company will record the discounting of the note as follows:

Cash	997.50	
Interest Expense	2.50	
Notes Receivable Discounted		1,000
To record the discounting of the Susan Davis note.		

Two points should be noted. First, the Williams Company has a *net* interest expense because the interest cost ($52.50) to the company from discounting the note is higher than the interest earned ($50) on the note. The interest expense of $2.50 consists of the following components:

Interest charged on the note, April 30–September 30	
($1,050 × 12% × $\frac{5}{12}$)	$52.50
Less: Interest given up, April 30–September 30	
($1,000 × 10% × $\frac{5}{12}$)	41.67
Interest cost	$10.83
Less: Interest earned, March 31–April 30	
($1,000 × 10% × $\frac{1}{12}$)	8.33
Net interest expense	$ 2.50

It is entirely possible that the proceeds from discounting the note will exceed the principal of the note, in which case Interest Revenue would be recognized (credited) for the net difference.

The second point is that the credit in the above journal entry is made to a Notes Receivable Discounted account rather than to the Notes Receivable account. The Notes Receivable Discounted account is a contra account to Notes Receivable and is deducted from Notes Receivable on the balance sheet. (An example of this is shown later.) The purpose of this separate classification is to recognize the existence of the contingent liability discussed earlier. If the Notes Receivable account had been credited instead the note would no longer be recorded anywhere in the accounting system. Using the Notes Receivable Discounted account retains two references to the note in the accounting system. The net value of the Notes Receivable less the Notes Receivable Discounted for a *particular* note is zero and therefore does not increase the net value of the asset, Notes Receivable, in the balance sheet.

Maturity of a Discounted Note Receivable

When a discounted note receivable matures there are two possibilities: either the maker pays the note as scheduled or defaults. If the maker pays the bank the payee is relieved of its contingent liability. Therefore if Susan Davis pays the note the bank would notify the Williams Company. The company would then remove the value of the note from the Notes Receivable and the Notes Receivable Discounted accounts as follows:

Notes Receivable Discounted	1,000	
Notes Receivable		1,000
To remove contingent liability for the Susan Davis note.		

There is no interest to recognize at the maturity date because the interest was accounted for when the note was discounted.

If the note is dishonored the bank will claim payment from the payee, which will include the principal and interest, plus a service charge for processing the dishonored note. Therefore if Susan Davis defaults on her note the bank will claim the $1,000 principal of the note, the $50 interest accrued, plus a service charge from the Williams Company. If the service charge is $10 the total amount will be $1,060

($1,000 + $50 + $10), and the Williams Company will record the payment of the dishonored note as follows:

Notes Receivable Dishonored	1,060	
Cash		1,060
Payment on the Susan Davis dishonored note.		

As discussed earlier it may be desirable to record the asset as Accounts Receivable rather than Notes Receivable Dishonored. In addition, since the note and the contingent liability are no longer outstanding, the Williams Company will eliminate the related accounts as follows:

Notes Receivable Discounted	1,000	
Notes Receivable		1,000
To remove contingent liability for the Susan Davis note.		

On receipt of the cash the bank will deliver the dishonored note to the Williams Company. Susan Davis, of course, is still legally obligated to pay the company, which will make every attempt to collect the full amount owed to it. If the note is collected, the following entry would be made:

Cash	1,060	
Notes Receivable Dishonored		1,060
Collection of the Susan Davis note.		

If a company has doubts about its ability to collect notes receivable, a Bad Debt Expense and an Allowance for Uncollectible Notes Receivable should be established in exactly the same way as accounts receivable. If the note is not collected, it would then be written off in the same way as an uncollectible account receivable. If an Allowance account has not been established, the Note Receivable would be written off (credited) and a Bad Debt Expense would be recorded (debited).

Disclosure of Accounts and Notes Receivable in the Financial Statements

As we have seen, both accounts receivable and notes receivable have an impact on the financial statements. Both the bad debt expense and interest revenue are included in the income statement. The balance sheet includes the net value for each type of receivable. For example, if the Aspen Company has accounts receivable of $30,000, an allowance for uncollectible accounts of $2,000, and notes receivable of $20,000, of which $15,000 have been discounted, the balance sheet would typically include the following items in current assets (assuming all items are expected to be collected within one year or the operating cycle, whichever is longer):

Current Assets		
Accounts receivable	$30,000	
Less: Allowance for uncollectible accounts	2,000	
Net accounts receivable		$28,000
Notes receivable	$20,000	
Less: Notes receivable discounted	15,000	
Net notes receivable		5,000

Alternatively, instead of showing both the Notes Receivable and the Notes Receivable Discounted accounts in the balance sheet, the notes receivable can be included in the balance sheet at their net value of $5,000 ($20,000 − $15,000). The contingent liability associated with the discounted notes receivable then would be disclosed in the footnotes as follows:

Footnotes to the Financial Statements
    The Aspen Company is contingently liable for $15,000 of notes receivable that have been discounted.

REVIEW PROBLEM

On December 31, 1982, the Holstrum Company had the following balances in selected accounts:

Accounts Receivable	$50,000
Allowance for Uncollectible Accounts	3,000
Interest Receivable	1,400
Notes Receivable	20,000

The note was a 12%, 1-year note due on May 31, 1983. During 1983, the company made credit sales of $120,000 and collected $124,000. In addition, the following transactions occurred in 1983:

Date	Transaction
Jan. 15	Wrote off an uncollectible account of $4,000 due from Donald Eastwood.
Mar. 1	Sold goods worth $10,000 and received a 6-month, 10% note as payment (not included in the credit sales of $120,000).
July 1	Discounted the note received on March 1 to a bank that charged 14% interest.
Aug. 20	Half of the account written off on January 15 was collected.
Sept. 1	The March 1 note was dishonored. The bank made a service charge of $20.
Sept. 30	The dishonored note was collected, along with all the accrued interest and the service charge.
Dec. 31	The age of the accounts receivable and the percentage estimated to be uncollectible was as follows:

Age Group	Amount	Estimated Percentage Uncollectible
Not yet due	$20,000	1%
1–30 days past due	8,000	3
31–90 days past due	4,000	6
More than 90 days past due	10,000	10

Required: 1. Prepare journal entries to record these events.
              2. Show how the net amount of the accounts receivable would be reported on the December 31, 1983, balance sheet.

SOLUTION TO
REVIEW
PROBLEM

Requirement 1:

Summary journal entries for sales and cash collections:

Accounts Receivable[a]	120,000	
Sales		120,000
To record the sale of merchandise on account.		

[a] For the summary journal entries individual account names are omitted.

Cash	124,000	
Accounts Receivable		124,000
Collection of accounts receivable during the year.		

Jan. 15	Allowance for Uncollectible Accounts	4,000	
	Accounts Receivable: Donald Eastwood .		4,000
	To record the write-off of uncollectible account receivable.		

Mar. 1	Notes Receivable	10,000	
	Sales		10,000
	Sold goods and received 6-month, 10% note.		

May 31	Cash	22,400	
	Notes Receivable		20,000
	Interest Receivable		1,400
	Interest Revenue		1,000[a]
	Collected 12% note and accrued interest.		

[a] $20,000 \times 12\% \times \frac{5}{12}$

July 1	Cash	10,255[a]	
	Interest Revenue		255
	Notes Receivable Discounted		10,000
	To record the discounted note.		

[a] Maturity value = $10,000 + ($10,000 \times 10\% \times \frac{6}{12})$ = $10,500
Proceeds = $10,500 - ($10,500 \times 14\% \times \frac{2}{12})$ = $10,255

Aug. 20	Accounts Receivable: Donald Eastwood . . .	2,000	
	Allowance for Uncollectible Accounts . . .		2,000
	To reverse the write-off of half the account of Donald Eastwood.		

	Cash	2,000	
	Accounts Receivable: Donald Eastwood		2,000
	Collection of half the account of Donald Eastwood previously written off.		

Sept. 1	Notes Receivable Dishonored	10,520	
	Cash		10,520
	Payment on the dishonored note.		
	Notes Receivable Discounted	10,000	
	Notes Receivable		10,000
	To remove contingent liability for the discounted note.		
Sept. 30	Cash	10,520	
	Notes Receivable Dishonored		10,520
	Collection of the dishonored note receivable.		
Dec. 31	Bad Debt Expense	680	
	Allowance for Uncollectible Accounts . . .		680
	To record the bad debt expense for the year.		

Age Group	Amount	Estimated Percent Uncollectible	Estimated Amount Uncollectible
Not yet due	$20,000	1%	$ 200
1–30 days past due	8,000	3	240
31–90 days past due	4,000	6	240
More than 90 days past due	10,000	10	1,000
Total	$42,000		$1,680

$$\text{Bad debt expense} = \text{Required balance} - \text{Existing balance}$$
$$= \$1,680 - \$1,000$$
$$= \$680$$

Requirement 2:

Accounts receivable	$42,000
Less: Allowance for uncollectible accounts	1,680
Net accounts receivable	$40,320

GLOSSARY

Aging Accounts Receivable. A method of estimating the allowance for uncollectible accounts, and therefore the bad debt expense. Accounts receivable are classified into age groups, and the balance in each age group is multiplied by the estimated percentage of the accounts that are uncollectible. The resulting amounts are summed to determine the ending balance in Allowance for Uncollectible Accounts.

Allowance for Uncollectible Accounts. An account used to show the amount of accounts receivable that a company estimates will not be collected.

Allowance Method. A method of accounting for uncollectible accounts in which bad debt expense is recognized in the period of the sale.

Bad Debt Expense. The expense for the accounting period due to the eventual noncollection of accounts receivable. It is recorded by means of an adjusting entry at the end of the period.

Contingent Liability. A liability that may or may not be paid depending on whether or not a future event occurs.

Direct Write-Off Method. A method of accounting for uncollectible accounts in which bad debt expense is recognized at the time an account is written off. This method is inconsistent with the accrual concept of accounting.

Discounting a Note. A process in which the payee of a note assigns it to a bank in exchange for cash. The bank then collects the maturity value of the note from the maker on the maturity date.

Dishonored Note. A note that the maker has failed to pay at the maturity date.

Maker of a Note. The person or company that signs a note and agrees to pay the maturity value on the maturity date.

Maturity Date of a Note. The date on which a note and any interest are due and payable.

Maturity Value of a Note. The principal of the note plus the interest due on the maturity date.

Notes Receivable. The asset account used to record promissory notes held by a company.

Payee. The person or company to whom a note is payable.

Percent of Sales Method. A method of estimating bad debt expense. The amount is computed by multiplying the net credit sales for the accounting period by the percent estimated to be uncollectible.

Principal of a Note. The amount stated on the face of a note. Also called the *face value*.

Promissory Note. A written legal document in which one party makes an unconditional promise to pay another party a certain sum of money on demand or on an agreed future date.

QUESTIONS

Q8-1 For what two reasons might a company choose to make credit sales? If a company does not collect some of its accounts receivable does it mean that the company's policy of making credit sales is wrong?

Q8-2 What are the arguments for recognizing the estimate of bad debts as a contra revenue? As an expense? Which alternative is most commonly used?

Q8-3 How can the use of the direct write-off method be justified?

Q8-4 What accounting principle supports the use of an estimate of bad debt expense? Explain.

Q8-5 Why is it desirable to keep the amount of a company's uncollectible accounts in the Allowance for Uncollectible Accounts?

Q8-6 Explain how the financial statements are affected by recording the estimated accounts receivable that will not be collected. How are the financial statements affected by recording the eventual write-off of an account receivable? By the recovery of a receivable previously written off?

Q8-7 How is bad debt expense estimated when the percent of sales method is used? When the aging method is used?

Q8-8 Which method of estimating bad debt expense is considered to be an income statement approach? Which is considered to be a balance sheet approach? Why?

Q8-9 How do credit card sales differ from other types of sales on credit?

Q8-10 What is a promissory note? Who is the maker? Who is the payee? What are the principal and the maturity date?

Q8-11 Why might a company prefer to hold a note receivable rather than an account receivable?

Q8-12 Describe how interest on a note receivable is computed.

Q8-13 What is meant by the term dishonored note receivable?

Q8-14 Why might a company discount a note receivable?

Q8-15 How does a bank determine the cash it will pay on a discounted note?

Q8-16 What is a contingent liability? Why should it be reported differently from a liability such as an account payable?

Q8-17 How is a discounted note receivable disclosed on a company's balance sheet?

EXERCISES

E8-1 **Percent of Sales Method.** The Redford Company uses the percent of sales method for estimating its bad debt expense. In 1983 the company made credit sales of $200,000 and had sales returns and allowances for credit of $20,000. In past years approximately 2% of net credit sales have been uncollectible. At the end of the year, before the bad debt expense is recorded, the accounts receivable balance was $40,000 and the credit balance in the allowance for uncollectible accounts was $300.

Required: 1. Compute the bad debt expense for 1983 using the percent of sales method.
2. Prepare journal entries to record all these events in 1983, including the bad debt expense.
3. Show how the net accounts receivable would be reported in the balance sheet at the end of 1983.

E8-2 **Aging Method.** Use the facts for the Redford Company in E8-1. In addition, the company has found that 2% of accounts receivable that are not overdue at the end of any particular year are never collected and 6% of accounts receivable that are overdue at year end are never collected. Of the accounts receivable balance at the end of 1983, 40% are not overdue.

Required: 1. Compute the bad debt expense for 1983 using the aging method.
2. Prepare the journal entry to record the bad debt expense.
3. Show how the net accounts receivable would be reported in the balance sheet at the end of 1983.

E8-3 **Aging Method.** At the end of the year the accounts receivable of the Andrews Company were categorized as follows:

Age Group	Amount	Estimated Percentage Uncollectible
Not yet due	$ 60,000	$\frac{1}{2}$%
1–30 days past due	30,000	1
31–60 days past due	20,000	2
61–90 days past due	10,000	4
More than 90 days past due	8,000	7
	$128,000	

Before recording the bad debt expense the credit balance in the Allowance for Uncollectible Accounts was $800.

Required: 1. Prepare the journal entry to record the bad debt expense.
2. Show how the net accounts receivable would be reported in the balance sheet at the end of the year.

E8-4 Direct Write-Off Method. The Newman Company made credit sales of $100,000 during the year. In addition, the company wrote off $3,000 of uncollectible accounts receivable in 1983 and uncollectible accounts receivable have averaged 4% of the ending balance of accounts receivable in recent years. The ending balance of accounts receivable is $30,000.

Required: 1. Compute the bad debt expense for 1983 using the direct write-off method.
2. Show how the net accounts receivable would be reported in the balance sheet at the end of 1983.

E8-5 Sales Transactions. During 1983 the Hopkins Company made credit sales of $60,000 and gave sales returns and allowances on credit of $5,000. In addition, sales discounts taken by credit customers were $200, which was 2% of the accounts collected. At the end of the year the company estimated that 3% of net credit sales would be uncollectible. The Hopkins Company uses the percent of sales method for estimating bad debts.

Required: Prepare journal entries to record these events.

E8-6 Write-Off and Recovery of Uncollectible Accounts. During 1983 the Ross Company wrote off uncollectible accounts of $700 and recovered accounts of $300 that had been written off in 1982. In addition, the following information is available:

	December 31, 1982	December 31, 1983
Accounts receivable	$30,000	$40,000
Allowance for uncollectible accounts	1,000	1,500

Required: 1. Prepare the journal entries to record the write-off and recovery of the uncollectible accounts in 1983.
2. How much bad debt expense was recorded in 1983?

E8-7 Credit Card Sales. On June 10 the Sweep Company made a sale of $300 to a customer who used a bank credit card. The credit card company makes a service charge of 3%, and the company deposited the credit card receipts in the bank along with its deposit of cash from cash sales. The Sweep Company also made a sale of $600 to a customer who used an American Express card. The credit card company makes a service charge of 4%, and the credit card receipt had to be sent to the credit card company to obtain reimbursement.

Required: Prepare journal entries to record the two sales.

E8-8 Interest Revenue. The Nicholson Company has the following current notes receivable during 1983:

Amount	Date Issued	Date Due	Interest Rate
$5,000	January 5	March 15	10%
7,000	May 13	August 3	12%
9,000	September 17	November 12	9%

Required: Compute the interest revenue earned by the Nicholson Company during 1983.

E8-9 Maturity Date and Interest Revenue. The Cunningham Company has the following notes receivable during 1983:

Amount	Date Issued	Life	Interest Rate
$2,000	October 18	90 days	12%
4,000	November 5	45 days	8%
1,000	December 12	80 days	10%

Required: 1. What is the maturity date of each note?
2. Compute the interest revenue earned by the Cunningham Company during 1983.

E8-10 Notes Receivable. On April 1, 1983, the O'Neill Farm Equipment Company sold a tractor to Klemme Farms for $50,000 and agreed to delay collection of the selling price for 6 months until after the harvest. Klemme Farms issued a note dated April 1, 1983, that had a stated interest rate of 10%. The note was paid on schedule.

Required: Prepare the journal entries for the O'Neill Farm Equipment Company during 1983.

E8-11 Dishonored Notes Receivable. Use the facts in E8-10.

Required: Prepare the journal entries that the O'Neill Farm Equipment Company would make if Klemme Farms did not pay the note as scheduled.

E8-12 Discounting Notes Receivable. The Gome Company received a 6-month, 10% note of $50,000 dated May 1, 1983, as a result of a current sale. The company discounted the note at a bank on July 1, 1983. The bank charges 12% interest. The issuer of the note pays it on the maturity date and the bank notifies the Gome Company.

Required: Prepare the journal entries for the Gome Company for 1983.

PROBLEMS

Part A

P8-1A Accounts Receivable and the Aging Method. The Newman Company operates a retail store in which most of its sales are made on credit. In 1983 the company had credit sales of $500,000, sales returns and allowances on credit sales of $12,000, and gave sales discounts of $560 on collections of accounts receivable of $28,000. Additional collections of accounts receivable were made with no sales discounts. During 1983 the company has written off accounts amounting to $1,200 and recovered accounts of $300 that had been written off in 1982. In addition, the following information is available:

	December 31, 1982	December 31, 1983
Accounts receivable	$80,000	$92,000
Allowance for uncollectible accounts	500(credit)	?

The accounts receivable at the end of 1983 were classified as follows:

Age Group	Balance	Estimated Percentage Uncollectible
Not yet due	$45,000	$\frac{1}{2}$%
1–30 days past due	22,000	1
31–60 days past due	8,000	2
61–120 days past due	5,000	5
More than 120 days past due	12,000	20

Required: 1. Prepare the journal entries to record these events, including the bad debt expense.
2. Show how the net accounts receivable would be reported on the December 31, 1983, balance sheet.
3. Is the aging method or the percent of sales method more desirable to use in the financial statements?

P8-2A **Accounts Receivable and Percent of Sales Method.** During January 1983 the following events occurred for the Radner Company:

Jan. 1   Accounts Receivable balance $30,000; Allowance for Uncollectible Accounts balance, $300 (credit).

Jan. 2   Wrote off the $500 account of Kevin Habit when he declared bankruptcy.

Jan. 12   Recovered the $200 account of Patricia Brake that had previously been written off.

Jan. 18   Accepted a 10% note for the $700 account of Brent Gray that was overdue.

Jan. 31   Sales for the month were as follows:

Cash	$ 5,000
Credit	50,000
Credit cards	12,000 (The credit card company charges an 8% fee.)

The credit card receipts had to be sent to the credit card company for reimbursement. The Radner Company estimates that 2% of its net credit sales (excluding credit card sales) will be uncollectible.

Required: 1. Prepare journal entries for January for the Radner Company including the accrual of interest.
2. Explain how each of the events affects the financial statements for January.

P8-3A **Credit Card Sales.** The Beatty Company had the following selected transactions involving the Christie Credit Card Company for 1983:

Date	Transaction
Feb. 21	Sold merchandise for $300 to a customer using a Christiecard. Christie Credit Card Company charges a fee of 5%.
Mar. 10	Received reimbursement from Christie.
Aug. 7	Sold merchandise for $700 to a customer using a Christiecard.
Aug. 15	Received notification from the Christie Credit Card Company that the card used for the $700 purchase was a stolen card. Because the Beatty Company had not called Christie to check the card at the time of the sale, no reimbursement will be made by Christie until it collects payment.
Nov. 20	Received payment of the $700 account from Christie. Owing to the difficulty and expense of collecting this payment, Christie charged an extra 15% fee.
Dec. 3	Sold merchandise for $500 to a customer using a Christiecard. Under a new arrangement with the Christie Credit Card Company, the receipt was deposited directly in Beatty Company's bank account.

Required: 1. Prepare the journal entries to record these transactions.
2. Considering that a seller does not receive the full price of merchandise sold to customers using a credit card, why do sellers accept credit cards?

P8-4A   Notes Receivable. The Reynolds Company had the following transactions affecting its notes receivable during 1983:

Date	Transaction
Jan. 5	Sold merchandise for $10,000 to the Fields Company and received a 6-month, 10% note.
Mar. 5	Discounted the note from the Fields Company at a bank that charged interest of 12%.
Mar. 17	Sold merchandise on credit for $5,000 to the Shore Company.
Apr. 15	Sold merchandise for $20,000 to the Clayburgh Company and received an 8-month, 12% note.
June 1	Sold merchandise for $3,000 to the Carne Company and received a 12-month, 9% note.
July 1	Received a $5,000, 12-month, 10% note from the Shore Company when it was unable to pay its overdue account.
Aug. 1	Discounted the note from the Carne Company at a bank that charged interest of 8%.

The interest on each note is due on the maturity date.

Required: 1. Prepare the journal entries to record the above transactions for the Reynolds Company. The Fields and Clayburgh notes were paid on their due dates.
2. Show how the above events would be reported on the financial statements for 1983.

P8-5A   Notes Receivable Discounted and Dishonored. Use the facts in P8-4A, except that the Fields and Clayburgh notes were dishonored. The bank charged a $10 fee on the Fields note. The Clayburgh note was paid in full on December 29. The Fields Company declared bankruptcy on December 10, and the Reynolds Company did not expect to collect any amount on the note.

Required: Prepare the journal entries to record the events related to the dishonored notes.

PROBLEMS

Part B

P8-1B   Accounts Receivable and the Percent of Sales Method. During August 1983 the following events occurred for the Olivier Company:

Aug. 1	Accounts Receivable balance $46,000; Allowance for Uncollectible Accounts balance, $750 (credit).
Aug. 5	Accepted a 13% note for the $1,000 account of Erin Dudley that was overdue.
Aug. 10	Wrote off the $6,000 account of Darcy Mitchell when she declared bankruptcy.
Aug. 21	Recovered the $3,000 account of John Gatti that had previously been written off.
Aug. 31	Sales for the month were:

Credit $ 90,000
Credit cards $110,000   (The credit card company charges a 6% fee.)

The credit card receipts had to be sent to the credit card company for reimbursement. The Olivier Company estimates that 4% of its net credit sales (excluding credit card sales) will be uncollectible.

Required: 1. Prepare journal entries for August including the accrual of interest.
2. Explain how each of the events affects the financial statements for August.

P8-2B   Accounts Receivable and the Aging Method. The Gere Company operates a wholesale outlet that makes most of its sales on credit. In 1983 the company had credit sales of $950,000, sales returns and allowances on credit sales of $21,000, and gave sales discounts of $400 on collections of accounts receivable of $40,000. Additional collections of accounts receivable were made with no sales discounts. During 1983 the company has written off accounts totaling $35,000 and recovered accounts of $12,000 that had been written off in 1982. In addition, the following information is available:

	December 31, 1982	December 31, 1983
Accounts receivable	$190,000	$300,000
Allowance for uncollectible accounts	5,000(credit)	?

The accounts receivable at the end of 1983 were classified as follows:

Age Group	Balance	Estimated Percentage Uncollectible
Not yet due	$120,000	3%
1–30 days past due	70,000	5
31–60 days past due	50,000	8
61–120 days past due	20,000	15
More than 120 days past due	40,000	30

Required: 1. Prepare the journal entries to record these events, including the 1983 bad debt expense.
2. Show how the net accounts receivable would be reported on the December 31, 1983, balance sheet.
3. Do you think that the Gere Company's credit policy is adequate? What, if any, changes would you suggest? Explain.

P8-3B   Credit Card Sales. The Campbell Company had the following transactions involving the Tucker Credit Card Company during 1983:

Date	Transaction
Mar. 7	Sold merchandise for $500. The customer charged the goods on his Tucker card. Tucker charges a fee of 4%.
Mar. 20	Received reimbursement from Tucker.
July 15	Sold merchandise for $400 to a customer using a Tucker card.
July 22	Received notification from Tucker that the card used for the $400 purchase had been a stolen card. Because the Campbell Company had not called to verify the card at the time of the sale, no reimbursement will be made by Tucker until it collects payment.
Dec. 7	Received payment of the $400 account from Tucker. Owing to the trouble and expense of collecting this payment, Tucker charged an extra 20% fee.
Dec. 9	Sold merchandise for $200 to a customer using a Tucker card. Under a new arrangement with the Tucker Credit Card Company, the receipt was deposited directly in the Campbell Company's bank account.

Required: 1. Prepare the journal entries to record these transactions.
2. Why would a seller accept credit cards when it does not collect the full amount of a sale?

P8-4B **Notes Receivable.** The Charles Company had the following transactions affecting its notes receivable during 1983:

Date	Transaction
Feb. 2	Received a $150,000, 12-month, 10% note from the Duncan Company in payment for merchandise sold on this date.
Apr. 2	Sold merchandise to the Wells Company and received an $80,000, 6-month, 8% note.
June 2	Discounted the Duncan and Wells notes at a bank that charged interest of 12%.
July 19	Received a $30,000, 2-month, 13% note from the Munroe Company when it was unable to pay its overdue account.

The interest on each note is due on the maturity date.

Required: 1. Prepare the journal entries to record these transactions for the Charles Company. The notes were paid when due.
2. Show how the above events would be reported on the financial statements for 1983.

P8-5B **Notes Receivable Discounted and Dishonored.** Use the facts in P8-4B, except that the Wells and Munroe notes were dishonored. The bank charges a $20 fee on all dishonored notes. The Munroe Company declared bankruptcy on November 5, and the Charles Company did not expect to collect any amount on the note. The Wells note was paid in full on November 27, including the bank fee.

Required: Prepare the journal entries to record the events related to the dishonored notes.

DISCUSSION CASES

C8-1 **Accounts Receivable.** The Midler Boutique has expanded its sales significantly in recent years by offering a liberal credit policy. As a result bad debt losses have also increased. The following summarized income statements have been prepared:

	1980	1981	1982	1983
Sales on credit	$30,000	$50,000	$70,000	$90,000
Cost of goods sold	12,000	19,000	26,000	33,000
Bad debt expense	1,200	2,100	3,080	4,140
Other expenses	10,000	12,000	14,000	16,000
Net Income	$ 6,800	$16,900	$26,920	$36,860
Accounts written off	$ 200	$ 1,000	$ 1,600	$ 2,000

The company uses the percent of sales method to calculate its bad debt expense. The accounts written off each year relate to credit sales made in the previous period.

Required: Prepare a report for Ms. Midler that explains the trend in bad debts as compared to other items in the income statement. Does it appear that the liberal credit policy is successful? What do you think the bad debt expense for 1984 should be if credit sales were $120,000 that year?

C8-2 **Accounting for Bad Debts.** Your friend has been operating a business for two years and has been making many sales on credit. His accountant has told your friend that an estimate of amounts that will be uncollectible in the future must be included in this year's financial statements. Your friend is upset because he does not want "guesses" appearing in the financial statements and he knows that accounting information should be objective and verifiable. Since he knows that you are currently studying accounting, he buys you dinner and before picking up the check asks you for your opinion.

Required: How would you answer your friend? Explain in detail why the accountant is suggesting that an estimate of uncollectible accounts be included in this year's financial statements and why your friend's concerns are not critical.

9 | Inventories and Cost of Goods Sold

After reading this chapter, you should understand:

- How to determine inventory quantities
- The differences between the periodic and perpetual inventory systems
- How to determine the cost of inventory
- The differences between the gross and net methods of accounting for purchases discounts
- The alternative cost flow assumptions, including specific identification, FIFO, average, and LIFO
- The lower of cost or market method
- How to estimate the cost of inventory by the gross profit method and the retail inventory method
- The effects of errors in the recording of inventory

Inventory is the assets of a company that are being held for sale in the ordinary course of business. For a manufacturing company, inventory also includes materials being held for use in the production process or goods that are in the process of production. In this chapter we discuss inventory by using the example of a merchandising company. A merchandising company is a company engaged in a retail or wholesale business; it does not change the physical characteristics of the goods it sells. The principles discussed also apply to a manufacturing company (that does change the physical characteristics of the goods); the additional problems specifically associated with accounting for manufactured inventories are discussed in Chapter 21.

In this chapter we consider the factors that affect the calculation of the cost of the ending inventory. We discuss the computation of the quantity of units in the ending inventory and the cost assigned to each unit acquired during the period. We will see that accounting in this area is well defined, and that all companies should follow the same principles. Finally, we discuss the method by which the costs of the units are included in the cost of goods sold and the ending inventory. Here we

347

will see that several alternative principles are allowed, and therefore the management of a company can select one method from several methods that give significantly different amounts of net income and assets on its financial statements.

THE IMPORTANCE OF INVENTORY

Inventory, sometimes called *merchandise inventory*, is a very important asset for a company and is of particular interest to users of the company's financial statements. Inventory is typically the largest current asset and represents a source of revenue in the near future through sales of the merchandise. The challenge facing the accountant is to determine correctly (a) the quantities of items that should be included in the inventory, (b) the cost to attach to each unit included in the inventory, and (c) the method of including these costs in the income statement or the balance sheet; that is, the way that the costs are matched against the revenue of the current and subsequent periods. Before we discuss each of these tasks in detail, however, it is important to realize the significant impact that the inventory figure has on the financial statements.

As discussed in Chapter 5, the cost of goods available for sale is the sum of the beginning inventory for the period and the costs of the net purchases made during the period. In a periodic inventory system when the cost of the ending inventory is determined, it is subtracted from the cost of goods available for sale to compute the cost of the goods sold. The cost of goods sold is then subtracted from net sales to determine the gross profit. This relationship may be stated in the following three equations:

COST OF GOODS AVAILABLE FOR SALE = BEGINNING INVENTORY
+ PURCHASES (NET)

COST OF GOODS SOLD = COST OF GOODS AVAILABLE FOR SALE − ENDING INVENTORY

GROSS PROFIT = SALES (NET) − COST OF GOODS SOLD

Once the cost of goods available for sale has been found, any change in the costs assigned to the ending inventory will change the cost of goods sold, and vice versa (how the cost of the inventory is determined is discussed later in the chapter). Any change in the cost of goods sold, in turn, will have a corresponding effect on gross profit. In addition, since the ending inventory of one accounting period is the beginning inventory of the next period, the cost assigned to the ending inventory will also affect the cost of goods available for sale, the cost of goods sold, and the gross profit of the next period. Thus we can see that the determination of the cost of the ending inventory has a major impact on current and future balance sheets and income statements of the company and therefore may affect the perceptions that the users of the financial statements have of the company. In summary, if ending inventory is overstated (understated) income for the period is overstated (understated).

For example, suppose that a company has the partial income statement shown

EXHIBIT 9-1
Effect of Ending
Inventory
Valuation on the
Gross Profit

	Alternative 1		Alternative 2	
Sales (net)		$10,000		$10,000
Beginning inventory	$ 800		$ 800	
Purchases (net)	9,700		9,700	
Cost of goods available for sale	$10,500		$10,500	
Less: Ending inventory	1,000		1,200	
Cost of goods sold		9,500		9,300
Gross Profit		$ 500		$ 700

in Alternative 1 of Exhibit 9-1. Now suppose that ending inventory was computed instead as $1,200, which is an increase of $200 or 20%. As can be seen from Alternative 2, gross profit is increased by $200, which is an increase of 40% ($700 ÷ $500 = 1.40). In this case a percentage change in the value of ending inventory has had a *proportionately* much larger percentage impact on the gross profit.

Now that we have examined the importance of inventory valuation, we discuss the components of this valuation.

ALTERNATIVE INVENTORY SYSTEMS

The first step in the computation of the cost of the inventory of a company is the determination of the quantity of inventory that is on hand during and at the end of the period. The two methods that are used to account for inventory are the periodic system and the perpetual system.

Periodic Inventory System

The periodic inventory system is a system of accounting for inventory in which a continuous record is not kept of the physical quantities (or costs) of inventory on hand during the period. A record of the cost of goods sold is *not* made each time a sale is made (revenue from the sale is recorded in the normal manner). The only time that the physical quantity of inventory on hand (and therefore the quantity sold) is known is when a physical inventory is taken. **A physical inventory is the counting by employees of the physical quantity of each item held in inventory.** A physical inventory enables the quantity sold to be computed as follows:

QUANTITY SOLD	=	QUANTITY IN BEGINNING INVENTORY	+	QUANTITY PURCHASED	−	QUANTITY IN ENDING INVENTORY

As a minimum, a physical inventory must be taken at the end of the annual accounting period so that the financial statements can be prepared. The cost of the ending inventory, and therefore the cost of goods sold, is then found by attaching costs to these physical quantities based on the cost flow assumptions used (as discussed later in the chapter).

For example, if a company has an inventory on January 1, 1983, of 20,000 units and then purchases 70,000 units, the number of units available for sale is 90,000. Although the company has made sales, and therefore has incurred a cost of goods sold, the number of units sold is not known until the physical inventory is taken at the end of the year. If the physical inventory at the end of the year is found to be 30,000 units, the cost of goods sold would include 60,000 units (90,000 − 30,000). The costs attached to these units are discussed later in the chapter. If interim financial statements are prepared during the period (e.g., quarterly financial statements), a physical inventory is usually *not* taken. The cost of the quarterly ending inventory can be found by using one of the estimation methods discussed later in the chapter.

THE PURCHASES ACCOUNT.   The beginning inventory of a period that is recorded in the Inventory account is the ending inventory from the previous period. The cost of inventory purchased during the current period usually is not debited directly to the Inventory account in the periodic system. Such a procedure would lead to the account indicating more inventory than the company actually had on hand because the account is not reduced (credited) during the period in which sales of the inventory items are made. Therefore the Purchases account is used to record purchases of inventory in a periodic system. The account is a temporary account to which acquisitions of inventory are added (debited) while the beginning inventory remains in the Inventory account. For example, the purchase of merchandise inventory on account is recorded[1] as follows (using assumed amounts):

```
Purchases . . . . . . . . . . . . . . . . . . . . . . . . . . . . . .    3,200
    Accounts Payable . . . . . . . . . . . . . . . . . . . . . . . . .          3,200
To record purchase of merchandise.
```

If a company returns some of the items it has purchased during the period or is granted a reduction in the purchase price due to damaged or inferior goods, it would record these returns or allowances by a credit to a separate account, Purchases Returns and Allowances. The advantage of recording purchases returns and allowances in a separate account is that management can keep track of the returns and allowances as a proportion of purchases. This relationship gives an indication of the quality of the goods provided by its various suppliers, thereby enabling the effectiveness of the company's purchasing activities to be monitored. Purchases on account that are returned would be recorded as follows:

```
Accounts Payable  . . . . . . . . . . . . . . . . . . . . . . . . .    600
    Purchases Returns and Allowances  . . . . . . . . . . . . .          600
To record return of purchases.
```

The net purchases for the period are the debit balance in the Purchases account less the credit balance in the Purchases Returns and Allowances account. In addition,

---

[1] Recall from Chapter 6 that we are not using subsidiary ledger accounts in these subsequent chapters (except for Chapters 8 and 10). If a subsidiary ledger was being used, an entry would be made in the accounts payable subsidiary ledger at the same time.

as discussed in Chapter 5 net purchases include Transportation-In, whereas Purchases Discounts Taken are subtracted.

At the end of the period the Inventory account will have a balance that is still equal to the beginning inventory for the period, and the Purchases and Purchases Returns and Allowances accounts will have balances that reflect the activities for the period. All these accounts are closed at the end of the period as first discussed in Chapter 5. This closing process is illustrated in summary form in the journal entries later in the chapter.

Perpetual Inventory System

A perpetual inventory system is a system of accounting for inventory in which a continuous record is kept of the physical quantities in inventory and the number of units sold. In addition, a continuous record of the cost of the units in inventory and sold is frequently maintained. A system that operates only in terms of quantities is simpler, and less expensive, and may provide sufficient information for management. The inclusion of costs facilitates the preparation of financial statements and is assumed in the remaining discussion. The inclusion of costs is becoming more common with the increased sophistication and lower cost of computer-based accounting systems. Many retail stores (e.g., J. C. Penney and Sears) use "point-of-sale" systems in which each item of inventory has a unique code that is entered into the system through the cash register as every unit is sold. Although the perpetual inventory system provides a continual update of the inventory, it is still necessary to verify the physical count and the cost of the ending inventory by taking a physical inventory periodically.

When a perpetual inventory system is used to maintain a record of the cost of the inventory, purchases and the cost of inventory sold are recorded directly in the Inventory account. Each purchase and related transportation charge is added (debited) directly to the Inventory account. Each time a sale is made the reduction (credit) in the Inventory account and the addition (debit) to the Cost of Goods Sold account are recorded. If a company has purchases returns and allowances during the period, the Inventory account is usually reduced (credited) directly; these returns and allowances can be maintained in a separate Purchases Returns and Allowances account that has a credit balance, however.

Differences Between the Periodic and Perpetual Inventory Systems

The differences between the periodic and perpetual inventory systems can be illustrated by equations and journal entries (using assumed amounts) as shown on the following pages.

Note that in this case the cost of goods sold and ending inventory are the same in the two methods. The sequence of their computation is different, however. In the perpetual inventory system the cost of goods sold of $9,450 is obtained directly. The ending inventory of $4,000 is determined by adding the $10,000 purchases and $150 transportation charges to the $3,500 beginning inventory, and then subtracting the $200 purchases returns and allowances and the $9,450 cost of goods sold. In the periodic system the $4,000 ending inventory is determined by a physical count, and the $9,450 cost of goods sold is the net amount of the two closing entries ($13,450 − $4,000 = $9,450).

PERIODIC INVENTORY SYSTEM

Cost of Goods Sold = Beginning Inventory +   Purchases (net)   − Ending Inventory
$$\$9,450 \quad = \quad \$3,500 \quad + (\$10,000 + \$150 - \$200) - \quad \$4,000$$

Journal Entries

Purchase of Merchandise

Purchases	10,000	
Cash or Accounts Payable		10,000

To record purchase of merchandise.

Payment of Transportation Charges

Transportation–In	150	
Cash		150

To record payment for transportation of units purchased.

Return or Allowance on Purchases

Cash or Accounts Payable	200	
Purchases Returns and Allowances		200

To record return of, or allowance on, purchase.

Sale of Merchandise

Cash or Accounts Receivable	20,000	
Sales		20,000

To record the sale of merchandise.

Computing the Cost of Goods Available for Sale

Purchases Returns and Allowances	200	
Cost of Goods Sold	13,450	
Purchases		10,000
Transportation-In		150
Inventory (beginning)		3,500

To determine the cost of goods available for sale by transferring the net Purchases to the Cost of Goods Sold closing
account and to close the beginning inventory *at the end of
the period* (normally included in the closing entries).

Recording the Ending Inventory

Inventory (ending)	4,000	
Cost of Goods Sold		4,000

To determine the cost of goods sold ($9,450 = $13,450 −
$4,000) by recording the ending inventory *at the end of the
period* (normally included in the closing entries).

PERPETUAL INVENTORY SYSTEM

Ending Inventory = Beginning Inventory +   Purchases (net)   − Cost of Goods Sold
      $4,000   = $3,500   + ($10,000 + $150 − $200) − $9,450

Journal Entries

Purchase of Merchandise

Inventory	10,000	
Cash or Accounts Payable		10,000

To record the purchase of merchandise.

Payment of Transportation Charges

Inventory	150	
Cash		150

To record payment for transportation of units purchased.

Return or Allowance on Purchases

Cash or Accounts Payable	200	
Inventory		200

To record return of, or allowances on, purchases.

Sale of Merchandise

Cash or Accounts Receivable	20,000	
Sales		20,000

To record the sale of merchandise.

Cost of Goods Sold

Cost of Goods Sold	9,450	
Inventory		9,450

To record the cost of goods sold as each sale is made during the period.

Evaluation of the Two Methods

Both the periodic and perpetual inventory systems result in approximately the same ending inventory and cost of goods sold for the year, and therefore the financial statements are not significantly affected by the choice of either method.[2] The selection by management of the periodic or perpetual system depends on other factors. The advantage of the periodic system is that it is less expensive and simpler to operate. Its disadvantage is that the inventory and cost of goods sold can be found only by taking a physical count of the inventory, or by an estimation technique.

The periodic system is most appropriate for relatively low-cost inventory items, because in these cases it is not as important for management to know continually the physical inventory for control and reordering purposes. Although the perpetual

---

[2] In the above example the ending inventory and cost of goods sold were the same for both systems because the first-in, first-out cost flow method (discussed later) was used. When other inventory cost flow methods are used, the periodic and perpetual inventory systems will result in a slightly different ending inventory and cost of goods sold.

system is more expensive to operate, it allows management to exercise better control over the operations of the company, because the cost of goods sold and inventory are continually known and can be used for inventory control and in evaluating the performance of the company whenever management chooses to do so. It should also be noted that a perpetual *physical* inventory system can be maintained without integration with the accounting system that maintains the *cost* of *each* item. In this case the quantities are known, although the cost associated with these quantities is not known.

When the perpetual inventory system is used, a difference may arise between the ending inventory according to the balance of the inventory account and the ending inventory determined when the physical inventory is taken. This difference provides a measure of the amount of theft, breakage, and spoilage that has occurred during the period. Management may consider this information to be useful in that it will help in the control of the company's activities. Information about the amount of theft, breakage, and spoilage cannot be obtained when the periodic system is used because the only value of the ending inventory is the value obtained from the physical inventory.

Taking a Physical Inventory

As we have seen, taking a physical inventory is essential under either the perpetual or periodic inventory system. The purpose of taking the inventory varies according to the system used. When the periodic system is used, the physical inventory is necessary to determine the ending inventory and the cost of goods sold. When the perpetual system is used, the taking of a physical inventory acts as a check on the accuracy of the ending inventory included in the perpetual records and indicates the extent of losses from theft, breakage, or spoilage. At a minimum, the taking of a physical inventory occurs at the end of each fiscal year. In many businesses a physical inventory is taken more frequently, perhaps as often as each month, although this count may be for only part of the inventory. Management must evaluate the tradeoff between the cost of taking the inventory and the information that results. It is usual to take the inventory outside of regular business hours so that the counting is not affected by goods being sold or received while the count is in progress.

The taking of a physical inventory should be carefully planned and supervised to prevent some items being omitted from the count, or other items being counted twice. The physical location of the items must be identified (e.g., on the sales floor, in the warehouse, or in the department responsible for receiving the goods), and movement of the items must be prevented during the count. It is usual to plan the inventory count so that one person checks the accuracy of the work of another person. Accuracy can be achieved by counting all the merchandise twice, but a less expensive way is to double check the counts of selected samples of merchandise, perhaps placing special emphasis on high-cost items.

Inventory counts are often performed by two-person teams. One person counts the merchandise and tells the other person the quantity and description. The second person records this information on an inventory sheet, or perhaps on a tape recorder. **Inventory tags are tags attached to each item of merchandise counted**

during a physical inventory to ensure that each item is counted and only counted once. The person making the count of each item initials the inventory tag. Similarly, if a second count is made the tag is initialed a second time. After completion of the individual counts all the tags are collected. The items on each tag are listed and summed on a master sheet to determine the total physical count of the inventory.

Items in Transit and on Consignment

The taking of a physical inventory determines the quantity of inventory actually in the possession of the company in its stores and warehouses. The company may also own additional units of inventory that are in transit or have been sent out on consignment (as discussed next). If the company is the legal owner of such items, they should be included in inventory.

Goods may be purchased or sold under terms of FOB (free on board) shipping point or FOB destination. **FOB shipping point means that transfer of ownership from the seller to the buyer occurs at the place of sale (shipping point).** The selling company should exclude such items from its inventory because they have been sold, whereas the purchasing company should include such items in its inventory. For goods shipped FOB shipping point, the purchasing company is responsible for any transportation charges incurred to deliver the goods. The cost of the transportation would be recorded in the Transportation-In account of the purchaser. **FOB destination means that transfer of ownership occurs when the items are delivered to the purchaser.** The selling company should include such items in its inventory until delivery takes place, whereas the purchasing company should exclude them. For goods shipped FOB destination, the selling company is responsible for any transportation charges incurred to deliver the goods. The cost of the transportation would be recorded in the Transportation-Out account of the seller. The terms are normally agreed to by the purchaser and the seller at the time the sale is negotiated and are listed on the sales invoice of the seller.

Some companies choose to sell on consignment. In this situation the company (the consignor) ships the goods to a retailer (the consignee) who acts as a selling agent. The retailer does not purchase the goods, and therefore the consignor must include such items in its inventory until they are sold by the retailer, or returned. The retailer does not include these goods in its inventory because it is not the legal owner.

THE DETER-MINATION OF THE COST OF INVENTORY

The cost of inventory includes all the costs incurred in bringing the items to their existing condition and location. Thus the cost of inventory includes the purchase price (giving consideration to purchases discounts), sales tax, transportation costs, insurance, customs duties, and similar costs. When a cost is difficult to associate with a particular inventory item, such as the cost of ordering the inventory, it may be allocated to each purchase, or as is more common the cost may be expensed directly as a general and administrative expense.

When a purchases discount is offered by the seller of the merchandise, the purchaser can use either the gross method or the net method to account for the discount.

Purchases Discounts: The Gross Method

Purchases discounts, which are offered by sellers to encourage prompt payment of amounts owed, should be deducted from the cost of purchases. One method of accounting for discounts is the gross method. **The gross method requires the purchases and accounts payable accounts to be recorded at their gross amounts and the purchase discount to be recorded when the discount is taken at the time of cash payment.** For example, suppose that the Wembley Company purchases merchandise for $1,000 and the seller offers a 2% discount if payment is made within 10 days. If the discount is not taken, full payment is required within 30 days. These terms are usually abbreviated as 2/10, n/30. The purchase and payment within 10 days would be recorded in a periodic system as follows (the account titles in parentheses indicate the accounts used in the perpetual system):

Purchases (or Inventory)	1,000	
Accounts Payable		1,000

To record purchase of merchandise using the gross method.

Accounts Payable	1,000	
Purchases Discounts Taken (or Inventory)		20
Cash		980

To record payment within 10 days.

The Purchases Discounts Taken account is a contra account to Purchases and therefore has a credit balance. It represents a reduction in the cost of purchases and is included in the calculation of net purchases. The discounts taken are normally recorded in a separate account so that management will know the total amount of the discounts taken. For example, if the discounts taken decrease over time as a proportion of purchases, it may indicate that the company is being less efficient in its payments and is losing discounts that it should have taken. If payment was not made within 10 days, it would be recorded as follows:

Accounts Payable	1,000	
Cash		1,000

To record payment after the discount period has expired.

The Purchases Discounts Taken account is closed at the same time as the Purchases, Purchases Returns and Allowances, and Transportation-In accounts are closed.

Purchases Discounts: The Net Method

An alternative method of accounting for purchase discounts is the net method. **The net method requires the purchase discount available to be deducted at the time of the purchase and the purchases and accounts payable to be recorded at their net amounts.** The net amount is the gross amount less the purchase discounts available. For example, the Wembley Company would record the purchase of merchandise for $1,000 on terms of 2/10, n/30 at the net amount of $980 [$1,000 − (2% × $1,000)] as follows:

Purchases (or Inventory)	980	
Accounts Payable		980

To record purchase of merchandise using the net method.

If payment is made within the discount period of 10 days, the payment is recorded as follows:

Accounts Payable   980
   Cash   980
To record payment within 10 days.

If payment is not made within the discount period, the cash paid is greater than the balance in the Accounts Payable account and the difference is recorded in the Purchases Discounts Lost account as follows:

Accounts Payable   980
Purchases Discounts Lost   20
   Cash   1,000
To record payment after the discount period has expired.

The balance in the Purchases Discounts Lost account would be included in the income statement as a financing expense (similar to interest expense).

Implications for Management

Although the gross method is used more frequently, the net method has definite advantages for the management of a company. The decision not to take advantage of a purchase discount is very costly. Consider the Wembley Company example. If the company does not take advantage of the discount, it delays payment by 20 days (the 30 days allowed as a maximum minus the 10-day discount period). For this privilege it pays 2% extra. Therefore the company is incurring a cost of 2% to delay payment by 20 days. This is an approximate annual cost of 36% (2% $\times$ 360 $\div$ 20). It would be less expensive for the company to borrow money from a bank to pay for the purchases within the discount period.

Given the high cost of not taking a discount, management should be very interested in knowing if any discounts have not been taken. The net method indicates this fact directly because any discounts not taken are included in the Purchases Discounts Lost account. In contrast, the gross method includes in the Purchases Discounts Taken account only the discounts that were available and were taken. It does not indicate the discounts that were available but *not* taken.

Trade Discounts

It is important to distinguish between cash discounts for prompt payment and trade discounts. **A trade discount is a reduction in the invoice price from a catalog or list price.** Trade discounts are given to preferred customers, to customers who purchase large quantities, to assist in the rapid sale of merchandise, or to reduce the retail price to a wholesaler. Trade discounts are quoted as percentages of the list price. For example, the price might be quoted as $50 less 20%, 10%. This quoted price indicates that the list price of $50 is subject to discounts of 20% and 10% under certain circumstances. Each discount applies to the net price *after* deducting any previous discounts. For example, if a purchaser is allowed both discounts, the invoice price would be:

List price		$50
Less 20% discount ($50 × 0.2)		10
		$40
Less 10% discount ($40 × 0.1)		4
Net Invoice Price		$36

Trade discounts are *not* recognized for financial accounting purposes because they are used to establish a pricing policy. The purchase of goods subject to trade discounts is recorded at the net invoice price, or $36 in our example. A cash discount for prompt payment would be applied to the net invoice price.

INVENTORY COST FLOW ASSUMPTIONS

The cost of each unit of inventory is determined by a review of the source documents (e.g., invoices) used to record the initial acquisition of the inventory. Once a company has determined the number of units in the ending inventory and the cost of the units purchased during the period, it is necessary to decide how the total cost of the units for the period (the cost of goods available for sale) will be divided among the ending inventory (balance sheet) and the cost of goods sold (income statement). This relationship is shown by the following diagram:

```
Cost of Beginning  ⎫                              ⎧  Cost of Ending  ───────→  Balance
Inventory          ⎪                              ⎪  Inventory                 Sheet
                   ⎬ =  Cost of Goods             ⎪
   +               ⎪    Available for  =  ⎨            +
                   ⎪    Sale                       ⎪
Cost of Purchases  ⎭                              ⎪  Cost of Goods   ───────→  Income
                                                  ⎩  Sold                      Statement
```

The difficulty of determining the costs to be included in the ending inventory and the cost of goods sold arises when costs incurred to acquire the units in inventory have changed during the period. Such changes (usually increases) occur frequently in the current economic environment. The four alternative cost flow assumptions that are commonly used are specific identification (although it may be more accurate to state that specific identification is an actual cost flow rather than a cost flow assumption), first-in, first-out (FIFO), average cost, and last-in, first-out (LIFO). Each of these methods is discussed for the Davis Company using the information in Exhibit 9-2.

The company has a beginning inventory of $500 and made two purchases during January that had a total cost of $815 ($275 + $540). Therefore the cost of goods available for sale is $1,315 ($500 + $815), which must be divided between the 130 units sold (the cost of goods sold) and the ending inventory of 110 units. It is assumed that the Davis Company uses the periodic inventory system, but the principles of the alternative cost flow assumptions are not changed if the perpetual system is used.

Although each of the four inventory cost flow methods produces different amounts for the cost of goods sold and ending inventory, each of the methods is based on actual costs incurred and is an acceptable interpretation of the historical

EXHIBIT 9-2
Inventory Information

DAVIS COMPANY
Inventory Information

Beginning inventory, January 1	100 units @ $5.00 per unit	$ 500
January 10, purchase	50 units @ $5.50 per unit	275
January 22, purchase	90 units @ $6.00 per unit	540
	240 units	$1,315
Sales during January	130 units	
Ending inventory, January 31	110 units	

Notes: 1. The units are sold for $13 per unit.
       2. The Davis Company uses the periodic inventory system. For computational simplicity, it is assumed that the physical inventory is taken monthly.

cost principle. The computations to determine the cost of goods sold and ending inventory under each method are discussed in the following sections.

Specific Identification

Specific identification is a method of assigning costs to cost of goods sold and ending inventory by identifying a specific cost incurred with each unit sold and each unit in ending inventory. If a unit has been sold, the cost is included in cost of goods sold; if a unit remains in inventory, the related cost is included in the cost of the ending inventory. For example, when the Davis Company sells a unit during January, the following three alternatives are possible:

	Sell a Unit from the Beginning inventory	Sell a Unit from the January 10 Purchase	Sell a Unit from the January 22 Purchase
Sales	$13.00	$13.00	$13.00
Cost of goods sold	5.00	5.50	6.00
Gross Profit	$ 8.00	$ 7.50	$ 7.00

Depending on the unit selected, the gross profit can vary from a low of $7 to a high of $8, which is a difference of 14.3% ($8 ÷ $7 = 1.143). The specific identification method is particularly appropriate for a company with a small volume of separately identifiable units in inventory, such as an automobile dealership. When a company has an inventory consisting of large quantities of similar items, however, the method may be inefficient, time-consuming, and perhaps impossible to use. For example, the specific identification method would not be suitable for the inventory of canned peas of a large grocery store. When identical units are carried in inventory, the specific identification method is very arbitrary and perhaps may be manipulated by management to change gross profits as particular units with different costs are selected for sale. Although the specific identification method could be used with the periodic inventory system, it is more compatible with the perpetual system, in which the cost of each unit is identified as it is sold.

EXHIBIT 9-3
Davis Company: FIFO

DAVIS COMPANY
First-In, First-Out Cost Flow Assumption

Ending Inventory (110 units)

90 units @ $6.00 per unit (from January 22 purchase)	$540
20 units @ $5.50 per unit (from January 10 purchase)	110
110	$650

Cost of Goods Sold	=	Beginning Inventory	+	Purchases	−	Ending Inventory
$665	=	$500	+	$815	−	$650

First-In,
First-Out

The first-in, first-out (FIFO) cost flow assumption includes the earliest costs incurred in the cost of goods sold and the latest costs are included in the ending inventory. Under this method the Davis Company computes the ending inventory to be $650 and the cost of goods sold to be $665, as shown in Exhibit 9-3. (Note that since the company is using the periodic inventory system the ending inventory is computed first.)

The Davis Company has an ending inventory of 110 units and the costs of these units are assumed in the FIFO method to be the latest costs incurred, which include the cost of the 90 units from the purchase on January 22 and the cost of the 20 units remaining from the purchase on January 10. Consequently, the cost of goods sold includes the earliest costs, that is, the cost of the 100 units from the beginning inventory and the cost of the 30 units from the purchase made on January 10.

Average Cost

The average cost flow assumption allocates the average cost for the period to both the ending inventory and the cost of goods sold. As shown in Exhibit 9-4,

EXHIBIT 9-4
Davis Company:
Average Cost

DAVIS COMPANY
Average Cost Flow Assumption

Average Cost per Unit	=	Cost of Goods Available for Sale	÷	Number of Units Available for Sale
	=	$1,315 ÷ 240		
	=	$5.48 per Unit (rounded)		

Ending Inventory	=	Number of Units	×	Average Cost per Unit
	=	110 × $5.48		
	=	$603 (rounded to the nearest dollar)		

Cost of Goods Sold	=	Beginning Inventory	+	Purchases	−	Ending Inventory
$712	=	$500	+	$815	−	$603

EXHIBIT 9-5
Davis Company: LIFO

DAVIS COMPANY
Last-In, First-Out Cost Flow Assumption

Ending Inventory (110 units)

100 units @ $5.00 per unit (from beginning inventory)	$500
10 units @ $5.50 per unit (from January 10 purchase)	55
110	$555

Cost of Goods Sold	=	Beginning Inventory	+	Purchases	−	Ending Inventory
$760	=	$500	+	$815	−	$555

the average cost per unit of $5.48 for the Davis Company is calculated by dividing the total cost of goods available for sale ($1,315) by the number of units available for sale (240, which includes the 100 units in the beginning inventory plus the 140 units purchased).

The ending inventory is computed as $603 for the 110 units on hand at the average cost of $5.48 per unit and the cost of goods sold as $712, which includes the 130 units sold at the average cost of $5.48 per unit.

Last-In, **The last-in, first-out (LIFO) cost flow assumption includes the latest costs**
First-Out **incurred in the cost of goods sold and the earliest costs (part or all of which**
are costs incurred in previous periods) are included in the ending inventory.
The Davis Company computes the ending inventory to be $555 and the cost of goods sold to be $760, as shown in Exhibit 9-5. The company has an ending inventory of 110 units and the costs of these units are assumed in the LIFO method to be the earliest costs incurred, which include the cost of the entire beginning inventory and the cost of the 10 units remaining from the January 10 purchase. Consequently, the cost of goods sold includes the latest costs, that is, the cost of the goods from the January 22 purchase ($540) and the cost of 40 units from the January 10 purchase ($220).

Additional   To further illustrate the differences among FIFO, average cost, and LIFO, we
Illustration continue the Davis Company example through February. The inventory information for the Davis Company for February is shown in Exhibit 9-6. The cost of the ending inventory on February 28 and the cost of goods sold for February are shown for the FIFO, average, and LIFO cost flow assumptions. It is important to note that the beginning inventory for February is the ending inventory for January, and therefore the amount is different for each cost flow assumption. The calculations otherwise follow the same procedures as for January.

EXHIBIT 9-6
Davis Company:
February

DAVIS COMPANY
Ending Inventory and Cost of Goods Sold for February

Additional Information

Beginning inventory, February 1	110 units	
February 5, purchase	40 units @ $6.20 per unit	$248
February 20, purchase	80 units @ $6.40 per unit	$512
	230 units	
Sales during February	100 units	
Ending inventory, February 28	130 units	

First-In, First-Out

Beginning Inventory = 20 units @ $5.50 per unit + 90 units @ $6.00 per unit
(from Exhibit 9-3)
= $650

Ending Inventory = 80 units @ $6.40 per unit
+ 40 units @ $6.20 per unit
+ 10 units @ $6.00 per unit
= $820

Cost of Goods Sold = Beginning Inventory + Purchases − Ending Inventory
= $650 + $760 (i.e., $248 + $512) − $820
= $590

Average Cost

Average Cost per Unit = Cost of Goods Available ÷ Number of Units Available
for Sale for Sale
= [$603 (from Exhibit 9-4) + $760] ÷ [110 + 120]
= $5.93 per unit (rounded)

Ending Inventory = Number of Units × Average Cost per Unit
= 130 × $5.93
= $771 (rounded to the nearest dollar)

Cost of Goods Sold = Beginning Inventory + Purchases − Ending Inventory
= $603 + $760 − $771
= $592 (or 100 units × $5.93 allowing for a $1 rounding error)

Last-In, First-Out

Beginning Inventory = 100 units @ $5 per unit + 10 units @ $5.50 per unit
= $555 (from Exhibit 9-5)

Ending Inventory = 100 units @ $5 per unit
+ 10 units @ $5.50 per unit
+ 20 units @ $6.20 per unit
= $679

Cost of Goods Sold = Beginning Inventory + Purchases − Ending Inventory
= $555 + $760 − $679
= $636

EVALUATION OF THE THREE ALTERNATIVES

The advantages and disadvantages of the FIFO, average, and LIFO cost flow assumptions are discussed in this section (the advantages and disadvantages of the specific identification method were discussed earlier).

The choice made by management to adopt any one of the three cost flow assumptions has an impact on both the income statement and the balance sheet. If prices are rising income will be highest under FIFO and lowest under LIFO, whereas inventory will be highest under FIFO and lowest under LIFO. The average cost figures will be between those of FIFO and LIFO. If prices are falling the relationships are reversed. Using the Davis Company example, the following comparative gross profit figures result from selling 130 units for $1,690 in *January* (assuming a selling price of $13 per unit):

	FIFO		Average Cost		LIFO	
Sales		$1,690		$1,690		$1,690
Cost of goods available for sale	$1,315		$1,315		$1,315	
Ending inventory	(650)		(603)		(555)	
Cost of goods sold		665		712		760
Gross profit		$1,025		$ 978		$ 930

It should be noted that there is a simplifying assumption included in the Davis Company example for January that has made the differences less than they might otherwise be. It was assumed that the beginning inventory consisted of 100 units at $5 under all three alternatives. Recall, however, that the beginning inventory of the period is the ending inventory of the previous period. Therefore if each method had been used in the previous period and prices had changed during that period, the beginning inventory would be different under each of the alternatives, just as the ending inventory for January is different under each method. This relationship can be clearly seen in the calculations for February in which the beginning inventory is different in all three situations. This factor can become very significant when the LIFO cost flow assumption is used. If the number of units in the inventory increases during each period, the costs included in the beginning inventory are carried over for each period. As years pass, however, these costs may become very outdated. For example, many companies adopted LIFO in the late 1930s and others during the period of high inflation in the middle of the 1970s. Therefore the inventories disclosed in the balance sheets of the 1980s may include elements of costs from many years ago.

Earlier it was stated that during periods of rising prices, use of LIFO will result in a lower income figure than FIFO or average cost. There is one exception to this general rule. **A liquidation of LIFO layers occurs when a company using LIFO decreases the number of units in inventory over a period.** This occurs when unit sales exceed unit purchases during the period. As a result, costs assigned to the beginning inventory are included in cost of goods sold for the period. Following LIFO principles, the first costs included in cost of goods sold will be the last costs added to the inventory. Therefore the greater the decline in inventory, the older the costs that will be included in the cost of goods sold. In times of rising prices, these older costs will be lower and therefore income will be higher. **Liquidation profit**

is the additional profit that arises when a liquidation of LIFO layers occurs. It is measured by the difference between the current period's latest cost and the historical LIFO cost of the units of inventory from previous periods that are sold in the current period. For example, if the Davis Company had sold 160 units during February, the ending inventory would be 70 units (230 − 160). The cost of the ending inventory would have been $350 (70 units @ $5 per unit) and the cost of goods sold would have been $965 ($555 + $760 − $350). Note that the cost of goods sold includes 120 units purchased in February and 40 units from the beginning February inventory (consisting of 30 units from the beginning January inventory at $5 and 10 units purchased in January for $5.50 per unit). There has been a LIFO liquidation profit of $42 on the 30 units from January's beginning inventory, which is the difference between the LIFO cost of $5 per unit and the most recent purchase price of $6.40 per unit. There is also a LIFO liquidation profit of $9 [($6.40 − $5.50) × 10] on the 10 units purchased in January. As LIFO is used over a long period of time, the effect of a LIFO liquidation may become very significant. For example, in 1980 Interlake, Inc., reported that its income was increased by $5.6 million as a result of a LIFO liquidation. The company's profit was $19.4 million compared with $13.7 million in the previous year, and thus the LIFO liquidation provided almost all the profit increase.

Why would the management of a company select LIFO when it results in lower reported income (except when a liquidation profit results from a liquidation of LIFO layers)? There are two reasons. First, if the company is a corporation, LIFO is allowable for income tax purposes only if it is also used for financial statements. Assuming rising prices, the use of LIFO results in lower taxable income and consequently in the payment of less income taxes. (Any of the other methods discussed may be used for calculating corporate taxable income regardless of which method is used for financial reporting.) For example, a recent article in the *Wall Street Journal* reported that:

> According to their latest annual reports, three long time LIFO users—Amoco, General Electric, and U.S. Steel—have together saved more than $3 billion in taxes compared to what they would have paid using FIFO.[3]

Second, many accountants argue that LIFO results in a better measure of income. To illustrate this point, consider the Davis Company in *January*. If the company uses the FIFO method, it would be selling units and recording a cost of $5 per unit and a gross profit of $8 per unit during January (the $13 selling price less the $5 cost). The company has to replace the inventory during the month by paying $5.50 or $6 per unit, however. Therefore, $.50 or $1 of the profit must be used to buy the replacement units of inventory, and only $7.50 or $7 represents the real profit of the Davis Company. **A holding gain, or inventory profit, is the illusory profit that results from recording cost of goods sold at lower historical costs than the**

---

[3] "Paying FIFO Taxes: Your Favorite Charity?" by Gary C. Biddle, *Wall Street Journal*, January 22, 1981

replacement cost of the unit sold. In this example, the holding gain is $.50 or $1 per unit sold. Since the holding gain cannot be distributed to the owners as withdrawals (dividends) without reducing the ability of the company to replace the units of inventory sold, many accountants argue that the holding gain should be excluded from income. A more complete discussion of the problems of accounting under conditions of changing prices is included in Chapter 20.

Although a company is able to select one of the four cost flow assumptions to account for its inventory, it is expected that once the selection is made the method will be consistently applied from period to period. If a change is made the effects of the change must be fully disclosed in the financial statements.

THE LOWER OF COST OR MARKET RULE

The requirement that inventory be recorded at its historical cost is modified in one situation. When the market value of the inventory falls below the cost, the inventory should be written down to its market value and the corresponding loss should be included in the income statement.[4] The use of the term *market* may lead to confusion. It should be clearly understood that it refers to the cost of replacing the item and *not* the selling price.

The cost of replacing the item is known as the replacement cost. **The replacement cost is the cost that would have to be paid at the present time to purchase an item of inventory in normal quantities from the usual suppliers, including any transportation costs ordinarily incurred.** A decline in the replacement cost of the inventory may result from physical deterioration, obsolescence, or perhaps a declining price level.

For example, suppose that the Barnhill Company has 100 units of inventory for which it paid $50 per unit. If the replacement cost declines to $40 per unit, the inventory should be included in the balance sheet at $40 per unit because the $50 cost is an overstatement of the value of the inventory. Similarly, the company has lost $10 per unit by owning the inventory while its cost declined. If it had delayed the purchase, it could have acquired the inventory for only $40 per unit. The lower of cost or market method is an example of the application of the conservatism principle discussed in Chapter 7.

Another argument in favor of the lower of cost or market method is based on the assumption that the relationship between cost and selling price remains fairly constant. That is, a common practice is to set the selling price at a certain percentage (called the *markup*) above the cost of the inventory. For example, if the Barnhill Company normally sells for $100 the units that cost $50 it is receiving a markup of 100% of cost. If the replacement cost drops to $40, it might be expected that the selling price will drop to $80, thus maintaining the 100% markup on cost. Continuing to value the inventory at $50 per unit would reduce the markup to 60% ($80 ÷ $50 = 1.60). Use of the lower of cost or market method thus separates

---

[4] There are upper and lower limits to the market value that can be used. See Nikolai, Bazley, Schroeder, and Reynolds, *Intermediate Accounting,* 2nd ed. (Boston: Kent Publishing Co., 1983), chapter 9.

the loss on holding the inventory from the gross profit that results from selling the inventory.

The lower of cost or market method is normally applied separately to each item in inventory as indicated in the following example:

	Quantity	Unit Cost	Unit Market	Total Cost	Total Market	Lower of Cost or Market
Item A	100	$20	$18	$ 2,000	$ 1,800	$ 1,800
Item B	200	30	31	6,000	6,200	6,000
Item C	200	25	20	5,000	4,000	4,000
Item D	100	40	43	4,000	4,300	4,000
				$17,000	$16,300	$15,800

The value of the inventory under the lower of cost or market method applied to individual items is $15,800. In this case a loss of $1,200 ($17,000 − $15,800) is recorded as follows:

Loss on Reduction of Inventory to Market   1,200
    Allowance for Reduction of Inventory to Market   1,200
To record valuation of inventory at lower of cost or market.

The inventory would be included in the balance sheet at its cost less the allowance as follows:

Inventory, at cost $17,000
Less: Allowance for reduction to market value   1,200
                                                    $15,800

A less conservative method of application is to record the lower of cost or market of the inventory as a whole. The inventory would be valued at $16,300 and a loss of $700 recorded under this alternative. In either case the loss would be included in the Other Revenues and Expenses section of the income statement.

When the conservatism principle was discussed in Chapter 7, it was pointed out that the reduction in income in the current period is offset by higher income in later periods than would otherwise have been reported. In the first example, income in the second year will be $1,200 higher than it would otherwise have been because the beginning inventory is $1,200 lower, resulting in a lower cost of goods sold.

METHODS OF ESTIMATING INVENTORY COSTS

It is sometimes necessary to estimate the cost of inventory. If a company is using the periodic inventory system, the management may need to estimate the cost of the inventory during the year for the preparation of interim financial statements without going to the expense of taking a physical inventory. If a company experiences a loss of inventory in a fire or theft, or if the accounting records are destroyed, it may also need to estimate the remaining inventory (and corresponding loss) without taking a physical inventory. There are two commonly used methods of estimating the cost of inventory. The gross profit method is often used in the special situations just described, whereas the retail inventory method is routinely used by retailing companies, such as supermarkets and department stores.

The Gross Profit Method

The gross profit method is used to estimate the cost of inventory by applying a gross profit rate (gross profit ÷ net sales) based on the income statements of previous periods to the net sales of the current period. The resulting estimated gross profit is deducted from the net sales to determine the estimated cost of goods sold. The estimate of the cost of goods sold is then subtracted from the cost of goods available for sale to provide the estimate of the ending inventory.

For example, suppose that the beginning inventory of a company is $12,000, net purchases are $28,000, and net sales are $50,000. If the gross profit rate based on the company's income statements of previous periods is 40%, the ending inventory is computed by four steps as follows:

Step 1:   Gross Profit = Gross Profit Rate × Net Sales
$$= 40\% \times \$50,000$$
$$= \$20,000$$

Step 2:   Cost of Goods Sold = Net Sales − Gross Profit
$$= \$50,000 - \$20,000$$
$$= \$30,000$$

Step 3:   Cost of Goods Available for Sale = Beginning Inventory
$$+ \text{ Net Purchases}$$
$$= \$12,000 + \$28,000$$
$$= \$40,000$$

Step 4:   Ending Inventory = Cost of Goods Available for Sale
$$- \text{ Cost of Goods Sold}$$
$$= \$40,000 - \$30,000$$
$$= \$10,000$$

These relationships can be illustrated in income statement format as follows (Steps 1–4 are listed in parentheses):

Net sales		$50,000 (100%)
Beginning inventory	$12,000	
Net purchases	28,000	
Cost of goods available for sale (actual)	(3) $40,000	
Less: Ending inventory (estimated)	(4) 10,000	
Cost of goods sold (estimated)		(2) 30,000 (60%)
Gross Profit (estimated)		(1) $20,000 (40%)

The validity of the gross profit method depends on the reasonableness of the estimate of the gross profit rate. Since the rate is based on the gross profit and net sales relationships of past periods, it is a valid indicator of the gross profit rate of the current period only if the gross profit relationships are largely unchanged. If it is known that conditions have changed, the gross profit rate should be adjusted so that the estimate of the cost of the ending inventory will be more accurate.

The Retail Inventory Method

Retail companies generally find it easier and less expensive to base their inventory accounting systems on the retail value of the inventory being sold. The merchandise is marked and put on display at the retail price; it is then easier to count the inventory at retail prices than to attempt to identify the cost of each item. The *cost* of the inventory must be included in the financial statements, however.

The retail inventory method is used to estimate the cost of inventory by multiplying the retail value of the ending inventory by the cost-to-retail ratio of the current period. To apply this method, the cost-to-retail ratio for the current period is found by comparing the cost and retail value of the goods available for sale. Detailed records of the beginning inventory and the net purchases at both cost and retail prices are necessary to establish this rate. Net purchases at cost are purchases at cost minus purchases returns and allowances at cost, while net purchases at retail are purchases at retail minus purchases returns and allowances at retail. The ending inventory at retail is computed by subtracting net sales (sales minus sales returns and allowances) from the retail value of the goods available for sale. The ending inventory at retail is then multiplied by the cost-to-retail ratio to determine the ending inventory at cost. This procedure is illustrated for a company by the following example:

	Cost	Retail
Beginning inventory	$ 20,000	$ 55,000
Purchases (net)	60,000	145,000
Goods available for sale	$ 80,000	$200,000

Cost-to-retail ratio $\dfrac{\$ \ 80,000}{\$200,000} = 0.40$

Less: Sales (net)		150,000
Ending Inventory at Retail		$ 50,000
Ending Inventory at Cost (0.40 × $50,000)	$ 20,000	

Goods with a retail value of $200,000 were available for sale during the period, and net sales of $150,000 were made. Therefore the ending inventory has a retail value of $50,000. Since costs are 40% of the retail value, the cost of the ending inventory is $20,000.

The use of a single ratio of 0.40 implies that the retail value of every item consists of 40% cost and 60% gross profit. Obviously, that is unlikely to be true, but the method develops an acceptable cost of the inventory if it can be assumed that the weighted average of the items included in the goods available for sale and the ending inventory is the same. If this is an unreasonable assumption, separate cost-to-retail ratios should be developed and applied to the items in each category of inventory.

It should be noted that the retail inventory method is an estimating procedure and is useful for interim financial statements. It does not eliminate the need for taking a periodic physical inventory, however, especially at the end of the fiscal year. For example, if the company in the preceding example took a physical inventory and found that the retail value of the inventory was $48,000, the cost of the inventory included in the balance sheet would be $19,200 (0.40 × $48,000), because this figure is more accurate than the amount of $20,000 computed earlier. The difference of $800 would be included in cost of goods sold for the period.

ERRORS IN RECORDING INVENTORY

As an additional way of understanding the interrelationships between inventory valuation, income, and assets, we can consider the effects of errors in the valuation of inventory on the income and assets. For example, suppose that at the end of 1983 a company overstates its inventory; that is, it erroneously records the ending inventory at $60,000 instead of $50,000. If the company is using the periodic inventory system the following effects result:

1. Cost of goods available for sale for 1983 is correct.
2. Ending inventory for 1983 is overstated by $10,000.
3. Cost of goods sold for 1983 is understated by $10,000.
4. Gross profit for 1983 is overstated by $10,000.
5. Net income for 1983 is overstated by $10,000.
6. Cost of goods available for sale for 1984 is overstated by $10,000 because the beginning inventory (the ending inventory for 1983) is overstated.
7. Ending inventory for 1984 is correct (because the company took a physical inventory).
8. Cost of goods sold is overstated for 1984 by $10,000.
9. Gross profit for 1984 is understated by $10,000.
10. Net income for 1984 is understated by $10,000.

These relationships can also be stated in equation form as follows:

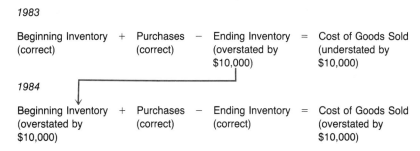

1983

| Beginning Inventory | + | Purchases | − | Ending Inventory | = | Cost of Goods Sold |
| (correct) | | (correct) | | (overstated by $10,000) | | (understated by $10,000) |

1984

| Beginning Inventory | + | Purchases | − | Ending Inventory | = | Cost of Goods Sold |
| (overstated by $10,000) | | (correct) | | (correct) | | (overstated by $10,000) |

Note that by the end of 1984 the error has counterbalanced. The overstatement of the gross profit and net income in 1983 has been counterbalanced by the understatement of the gross profit and net income in 1984. The inventory in the balance sheet at the end of 1984 is correct, and therefore the future financial statements are unaffected by the error. It should be remembered that if the financial statements for 1983 and 1984 are presented in the future for comparative purposes, however, they should be corrected for the effects of the error. Users of the financial statements who make an analysis of trends over time would be misled if such corrections were not made.

The effects of errors in the valuation of inventory on net income of the current period may be summarized as follows:

1. If the ending inventory is overstated, net income for the current period is overstated.
2. If the ending inventory is understated, net income for the current period is understated.
3. If the beginning inventory is overstated, net income for the current period is understated.
4. If the beginning inventory is understated, net income for the current period is overstated.

For a corporation, the dollar amount of the effect on net income will not be the same as the dollar amount of the effect on inventory. The difference arises because of the income tax effect on the change in the gross profit. For example, if ending inventory is overstated by $10,000, the gross profit is overstated by $10,000. If the corporate income tax rate is 40%, income tax expense (and liability) is overstated by $4,000, and therefore net income will be overstated by only $6,000.

DISCLOSURE IN THE FINANCIAL STATEMENTS

Inventory is included in the current assets section of the balance sheet, usually immediately after receivables. The inventory cost flow assumption (FIFO, average, or LIFO) and the method of valuing the inventory (cost or lower of cost or market) should be disclosed either by a parenthetical note in the balance sheet or in a footnote to the financial statements. Similarly, cost of goods sold is reported in the income statement. Exhibit 9-7 includes examples of alternative forms of disclosure of the inventory cost flow assumption.

EXHIBIT 9-7 Alternative Forms of Disclosure

Bird & Son, Inc.

Footnotes (in part):
    Inventories—Inventories are stated at the lower of cost (generally determined on a first-in, first-out basis) or market.

GAF Corporation

    Inventories—Inventories are valued at the lower of cost (principally average) or market.

United Technologies Corporation

Footnotes (in part):
    A substantial portion of the Corporation's inventories in its industrial products business is valued under the LIFO method. If such inventories had been valued at the lower of replacement value or cost under the first-in, first-out method, they would have been higher by $212,720,000 at December 31, 1980 ($159,120,000 at December 31, 1979).

The Peters Company made the following purchases and sales in 1983 and 1984:

Purchases, 1983		
	100 units @ $40 per unit =	$ 4,000
	120 units @ $41 per unit =	4,920
	220	$ 8,920

Sales, 1983	200 units

Purchases, 1984		
	150 units @ $42 per unit =	$ 6,300
	90 units @ $43 per unit =	3,870
	240	$10,170

Sales, 1984	220 units

The FIFO, average, and LIFO cost per unit of the 1983 beginning inventory of 60 units is $39, $38, and $30, respectively. The company uses the periodic inventory system.

Required:
1. Compute the units in inventory at the end of 1983 and 1984.
2. Compute the ending inventory and cost of goods sold for 1983 and 1984 if the company uses:
   (a) The FIFO cost flow assumption.
   (b) The average cost flow assumption.
   (c) The LIFO cost flow assumption.

SOLUTION TO
REVIEW
PROBLEM

Requirement 1:

1983:
Quantity in Ending Inventory = Quantity in Beginning Inventory + Quantity Purchased − Quantity Sold
= 60 + 220 − 200
= 80 units

1984:
Quantity in Ending Inventory = 80 + 240 − 220
= 100 units

Requirement 2:

(a) *First-in, First-out*

1983: Beginning Inventory = 60 units @ $39 per unit
= $2,340

Purchases = 100 units @ $40 per unit + 120 units @ $41 per unit
= $8,920

Ending Inventory = 80 units @ $41 per unit
= $3,280

Cost of Goods Sold = Beginning Inventory + Purchases − Ending Inventory
= $2,340 + $8,920 − $3,280
= $7,980

1984: Beginning Inventory   =   80 units @ $41 per unit
                                = $3,280

        Purchases   =   150 units @ $42 per unit   +   90 units @ $43 per unit
                                  = $10,170

        Ending Inventory   =   90 units @ $43 per unit   +   10 units @ $42 per unit
                                  = $4,290

        Cost of Goods Sold   =   Beginning Inventory   +   Purchases   −   Ending Inventory
                                  = $3,280   + $10,170   − $4,290
                                  = $9,160

(b) *Average cost*

1983: Average Cost per Unit   =   Cost of Goods Available for Sale   ÷   Number of Units Available for Sale

$$= \frac{[(60 \times \$38) + (100 \times \$40) + (120 \times \$41)]}{(60 + 100 + 120)}$$

                                  = $11,200   ÷   280
                                  = $40

        Ending Inventory   =   Number of Units   ×   Average Cost per Unit
                                  =   80   × $40
                                  = $3,200

        Cost of Goods Sold   =   Beginning Inventory   +   Purchases   −   Ending Inventory
                                  = $2,280   + $8,920   − $3,200
                                  = $8,000 (or 200 units   × $40)

1984: Average Cost per Unit   = $\frac{[(80 \times \$40) + (150 \times \$42) + (90 \times \$43)]}{(80 + 150 + 90)}$
                                  = $13,370   ÷   320
                                  = $41.78 (rounded)

        Ending Inventory   =   Number of Units   ×   Average Cost per Unit
                                  =   100   × $41.78
                                  = $4,178

        Cost of Goods Sold   =   Beginning Inventory   +   Purchases   −   Ending Inventory
                                  = $3,200   + $10,170   − $4,178
                                  = $9,192 (or 220 units   × $41.78)

(c) *Last-in, First-out*

1983: Beginning Inventory = 60 units @ \$30 per unit
                                 = \$1,800

      Purchases = 100 units @ \$40 per unit + 120 units @ \$41 per unit
                     = \$8,920

      Ending Inventory = 60 units @ \$30 per unit + 20 units @ \$40 per unit
                     = \$2,600

      Cost of Goods Sold = Beginning Inventory + Purchases − Ending Inventory
                     = \$1,800 + \$8,920 − \$2,600
                     = \$8,120

1984: Beginning Inventory = 60 units @ \$30 per unit + 20 units @ \$40 per unit
                                 = \$2,600

      Purchases = 150 units @ \$42 per unit + 90 units @ \$43 per unit
                     = \$10,170

      Ending Inventory = 60 units @ \$30 per unit + 20 units @ \$40 per unit +
                     20 units @ \$42 per unit
                     = \$3,440

      Cost of Goods Sold = Beginning Inventory + Purchases − Ending Inventory
                     = \$2,600 + \$10,170 − \$3,440
                     = \$9,330

GLOSSARY

Average Cost. An inventory cost flow assumption in which an average cost for the period is calculated and assigned to the number of units in cost of goods sold and ending inventory.

Consignee. The company that receives goods to sell on consignment without taking ownership.

Consignor. The company that ships goods to a retailer to sell on consignment without relinquishing ownership.

FIFO. An inventory cost flow assumption in which the first costs incurred (including the beginning inventory) during a period are assigned to cost of goods sold, and the latest costs are assigned to ending inventory.

FOB Destination. Terms for shipping goods in which transfer of ownership occurs at the point of destination.

FOB Shipping Point. Terms for shipping goods in which transfer of ownership occurs at the original shipping point.

Gross Profit Method. A method of estimating the cost of ending inventory by applying the historical gross profit rate to net sales of the current period to compute the estimated gross profit. The estimated gross profit is deducted from the net sales to determine the estimated cost of goods sold. The estimated cost of goods sold is deducted from cost of goods available for sale to give the estimated ending inventory.

Holding Gain.   The illusory profit that results from recording cost of goods sold at lower historical costs than the replacement cost of the items sold. Also called *inventory profit*.

Inventory.   Items being held for sale in the ordinary course of business. Sometimes called *merchandise inventory*. In the case of a manufacturing company, inventory also includes items being held for use in the production process or items that are in the process of production.

Inventory Tags.   Attached to items of inventory during the taking of a physical inventory to ensure that each item is counted only once.

LIFO.   An inventory cost flow assumption in which the latest costs incurred during a period are assigned to cost of goods sold, and the earliest costs are assigned to ending inventory.

Liquidation of LIFO Layers.   A reduction in the number of units in inventory, because the number of units sold exceeds the number of units purchased by a company using LIFO.

Liquidation Profit.   The additional profit that arises when a liquidation of LIFO layers occurs; it is measured by the difference between the current period's latest cost and the historical LIFO cost for the units of inventory from previous periods sold in the current period.

Periodic Inventory System.   A system of accounting for inventory in which a continuous record of the physical quantities (and costs) is not maintained.

Perpetual Inventory System.   A system of accounting for inventory in which a continuous record of the physical quantities (and costs) on hand and sold is maintained.

Physical Inventory.   The counting of the physical quantity of each item held in inventory.

Retail Inventory Method.   A method of accounting for inventory commonly used by retail companies in which the ending inventory is calculated on the basis of retail prices, and is then converted to cost by use of a cost-to-retail ratio.

Replacement Cost.   The cost of replacing (purchasing) an item of inventory.

Specific Identification.   A method of assigning costs to cost of goods sold and ending inventory by identifying a specific cost incurred with each unit sold and on hand.

Trade Discount.   A reduction in invoice price below the catalog or list price.

QUESTIONS   **Q9-1**   If the ending inventory for 1983 is understated, what effect does the understatement have on the financial statements for 1983? 1984?

Q9-2   Describe the periodic inventory system. How does it differ from the perpetual inventory system? What are the advantages of each system?

Q9-3 In which of the following types of businesses would a perpetual inventory system be practical: (a) an automobile dealer, (b) an auto parts store, (c) a bookstore, and (d) a restaurant?

Q9-4 What is the Purchases account used for? Is it used with the periodic or perpetual inventory system?

Q9-5 What is the Purchases Returns and Allowances account used for? How does the amount in the account affect the income statement?

Q9-6 What is the purpose of taking a physical inventory? How often should a physical inventory be taken?

Q9-7 Company X purchases units of inventory under terms FOB destination from Company Y, and the goods are still in transit. Which company should include the units in inventory? How would your answer change if the purchase had been made under terms of FOB shipping point?

Q9-8 A company purchases inventory for $10,000 under terms of 1/10, n/30. How much is the discount that is available? When must payment be made to receive the discount?

Q9-9 Describe the difference between the gross method and the net method of accounting for purchases discounts. Which method provides more useful information to management? Explain.

Q9-10 How is the cost of the ending inventory determined under the FIFO cost flow assumption? Average cost? LIFO? Does the use of any method affect the quantities included in the ending inventory?

Q9-11 If costs are rising, which cost flow assumption will give the lowest net income in the current accounting period? The highest net income? The lowest inventory cost? The highest inventory cost? An inventory cost closest to the current replacement cost?

Q9-12 What are the advantages and disadvantages of the specific identification method?

Q9-13 Why might the management of a company choose the LIFO cost flow assumption even though its use causes the company's net income to be lower?

Q9-14 What is the liquidation of a LIFO layer? What is a liquidation profit? How does a liquidation profit affect net income?

Q9-15 What is a holding gain? Why do some accountants believe holding gains should be excluded from net income?

Q9-16 If the ending inventory for 1983 is valued at market under the lower of cost or market rule, what is the effect on the financial statements for 1983? 1984? What is the meaning of the term market?

Q9-17 Describe how ending inventory is estimated using the gross profit method. When might the method be used?

Q9-18 Describe how ending inventory is computed under the retail inventory method. What are the advantages of the method?

Q9-19 What is meant by the phrase "inventory errors correct themselves?" If the errors correct themselves, why are accountants concerned with them?

EXERCISES

E9-1 Cost of Goods Sold. The following information for the Clark Company is available:

Beginning inventory	$10,000
Sales	52,000
Purchases	27,000
Purchases returns and allowances	1,100
Purchases discounts taken	700
Transportation-in	500
Ending inventory	12,000

Required: Compute the cost of goods available for sale, the cost of goods sold, and the gross profit.

E9-2 Beginning Inventory. The following information of the Mears Company is available:

Sales	$70,000
Purchases	30,000
Purchases discounts taken	600
Sales returns and allowances	1,000
Ending inventory	20,000
Cost of goods sold	32,000

Required: Compute the beginning inventory and the gross profit.

E9-3 Perpetual and Periodic Inventory. The financial statements of the Steward Company include the following information:

Beginning inventory	$15,000
Sales	60,000
Purchases	40,000
Ending inventory	12,000

Required: Assuming that all purchases and sales are for cash, prepare journal entries to record the purchases, sales, and closing entries for the period if the company uses (1) the perpetual inventory system and (2) the periodic inventory system.

E9-4 Items Included in Inventory. While taking a physical inventory for the Hawthorn Company you discover the following items:

1. Purchases ordered FOB destination are in transit.
2. Purchases ordered FOB shipping point are in transit.
3. Items for sale are being held on consignment by the company.
4. An item of inventory is ready for shipment on the last day of the fiscal year. A completed order for the product from the customer had been received.

Required: Indicate whether each item should be included in the ending inventory. Explain your reasoning.

E9-5 Discounts. The Collins Company made purchases of $50,000 during the year on terms of 2/10, n/30. The company took advantage of the discount on 60% of the purchases. It paid for the remainder after the discount period had expired. The company uses the periodic inventory system.

Required: 1. Prepare journal entries to record the purchase and both payments under (a) the gross method and (b) the net method.
2. If half the purchases are still in the inventory at the end of the year, what is the cost of the ending inventory under both methods?

E9-6 Alternative Cost Flow Assumptions. The Moss Company uses the perpetual inventory system and makes the following purchases and sales during March:

Mar.	1	Inventory	100 units	@	$10	=	$1,000
Mar.	5	Purchases	50 units	@	$11	=	550
Mar.	12	Sales	40 units				
Mar.	23	Purchases	80 units	@	$12	=	960
Mar.	26	Sales	70 units				

Required: Compute the cost of goods sold and ending inventory if the company uses:

  1. The FIFO cost flow assumption.
  2. The LIFO cost flow assumption.

E9-7 Alternative Cost Flow Assumptions. The Foyt Company uses the periodic inventory system and makes the following purchases and sales during September:

Sept.	1	Inventory	200 units	@	$25	=	$5,000
Sept.	10	Purchases	100 units	@	$27	=	2,700
Sept.	15	Sales	150 units				
Sept.	22	Purchases	80 units	@	$30	=	2,400
Sept.	28	Sales	50 units				

Required: Compute the ending inventory and the cost of goods sold if the company uses:

  1. The FIFO cost flow assumption.
  2. The average cost flow assumption.
  3. The LIFO cost flow assumption.

E9-8 Periodic and Perpetual Inventory Systems and FIFO and LIFO. The Schukter Company makes the following purchases and sales during May:

May	1	Inventory	300 units	@	$ 6	=	$1,800
May	5	Purchases	120 units	@	$ 7	=	840
May	12	Sales	160 units				
May	22	Purchases	150 units	@	$ 8	=	1,200
May	25	Sales	80 units				

Required: Compute the ending inventory and the cost of goods sold if the company uses:

  1. The periodic inventory system and the FIFO cost flow assumption.
  2. The periodic inventory system and the LIFO cost flow assumption.
  3. The perpetual inventory system and the FIFO cost flow assumption.
  4. The perpetual inventory system and the LIFO cost flow assumption.

E9-9 Lower of Cost or Market. The Brabham Company had the following costs and replacement costs of units in inventory:

Item	Number of Units	Unit Cost	Unit Replacement Cost
804	100	$10	$ 9
603	150	12	13
331	320	6	5
928	70	20	18

Required:
  1. Compute the value of the ending inventory under the lower of cost or market method, applied to the individual items.
  2. How will the financial statements be affected by the application of the lower of cost or market method?
  3. Show how the ending inventory would be reported on the balance sheet.

E9-10   Gross Profit Method.   On March 31, 1983, the Ireland Company needed to estimate its ending inventory for preparation of its first quarter's financial statements. The following information is available:

Inventory, January 1, 1983	$25,000
Purchases (net)	35,000
Sales (net)	80,000

An examination of past income statements indicates that a gross profit rate of 30% of net sales is appropriate.

Required: Compute the cost of goods sold and the ending inventory.

E9-11   Retail Inventory Method.   The Hunt Boutique uses the retail inventory method. At the end of the year, the following information is available:

	Cost	Retail
Beginning inventory	$ 6,000	$15,000
Purchases (net)	14,000	35,000
Sales (net)		40,000

Required: Compute the cost of the ending inventory and the gross profit using the retail inventory method.

E9-12   Errors.   The Jones Company had a beginning inventory of $25,000, net purchases of $47,000, an ending inventory of $28,000, and sales of $80,000.

Required:
1. Compute the cost of goods sold.
2. If an error was made in the physical inventory and the ending inventory should have been $32,000, what is the correct cost of goods sold? What is the percentage change in the gross profit?
3. What is the effect of the error in Requirement 2 on the financial statements of the next year?

PROBLEMS

Part A

P9-1A   Cost of Goods Sold.   The Redman Company uses the FIFO cost flow assumption, and the following summary information was available at the end of the year:

Beginning inventory	$20,000
Purchases	50,000
Sales	86,000
Transportation-in	1,500
Sales discounts	3,000
Purchases returns and allowances	4,500
Sales returns and allowances	2,000
Ordering costs	500
Ending inventory	22,000

The company followed a policy of expensing the ordering costs rather than allocating them to the units of inventory. Discounts of 2/10, n/30 were available on all the purchases, but the company took advantage of only half of them. The purchases returns and allowances were for items on which discounts were not taken. The company uses the gross method of accounting for discounts.

Required:
1. Prepare an income statement through to the calculation of gross profit.
2. The management of the company is considering changing from the FIFO method. They estimate that the ending inventory under average cost and LIFO would have been $20,000 and $15,000, respectively. What would the percentage increase or decrease in the gross profit be from changing to each alternative?

P9-2A Discounts. The Gurney Company purchased inventory for $18,000 on terms of 2/10, n/30. The company paid for half the purchase within 10 days and paid for the remainder after the discount period had expired. The company uses the periodic inventory system.

Required: 1. Prepare journal entries to record the above events using (a) the gross method and (b) the net method of accounting for purchases discounts.
2. If the company sold half the inventory for $20,000, how much would its gross profit be under each method?
3. How much would the gross profit be if the company deducted all the discounts available from the cost of the inventory under each method?

P9-3A Alternative Cost Flow Assumptions: Periodic. The Ginther Company made the following purchases and sales during January and February and uses the periodic inventory system:

Jan. 1	Inventory	100 units
Jan. 10	Purchases	50 units for $100 each
Jan. 20	Purchases	40 units for $102 each
Feb. 5	Purchases	20 units for $104 each
Feb. 18	Purchases	60 units for $108 each

Sales during January and February were 70 units and 90 units, respectively. The FIFO, average, and LIFO cost of each unit in the beginning inventory was $95, $93, and $60, respectively.

Required: 1. Compute the ending inventory and the cost of goods sold for each month if the company uses:
(a) The FIFO cost flow assumption.
(b) The average cost flow assumption.
(c) The LIFO cost flow assumption.
2. Which cost flow assumption provides the more realistic balance sheet valuation? Which provides the more realistic measure of income? Why?

P9-4A Alternative Cost Flow Assumptions: Perpetual. The Russell Company made the following purchases and sales during April and May, and uses the perpetual inventory system.

Apr. 1	Inventory	160 units
Apr. 9	Purchases	20 units for $12 each
Apr. 17	Sales	30 units
Apr. 24	Purchases	50 units for $13 each
Apr. 26	Sales	20 units
May 8	Sales	30 units
May 15	Purchases	60 units for $14 each
May 22	Sales	40 units

The FIFO and LIFO cost of each unit in the beginning inventory was $10 and $6, respectively.

Required: 1. Compute the cost of goods sold and the ending inventory for each month if the company uses:
(a) The FIFO cost flow assumption.
(b) The LIFO cost flow assumption.
2. Which cost flow assumption provides the more realistic balance sheet valuation? Which provides the more realistic measure of income? Why?

P9-5A Lower of Cost or Market. The Seaman Company's ending inventory included the following items:

Item	Number of Units	Unit Cost	Unit Replacement Cost
A12B	50	$100	$90
L15C	100	80	82
P27X	200	50	48
W08S	400	10	9

Required:
1. Compute the value of the ending inventory under the lower of cost or market rule applied to individual items.
2. Prepare the journal entry to record the reduction of the inventory to its market value.
3. Show how the ending inventory would be reported on the balance sheet.
4. If the lower of cost or market method is applied to the inventory as a whole, how would your answer to Requirement 1 change?
5. If at the end of the next year none of the items in inventory has a market value below cost, how will the financial statements for the second year be affected by application of the lower of cost or market method in the first year?

P9-6A   Retail Inventory Method.   The Scheckter Department Store uses the retail inventory method. At the end of the first quarter, the following information was available:

	Cost	Retail
Inventory, Jan. 1	$10,000	$18,000
Purchases	40,000	82,000
Purchases returns	2,000	4,000
Sales		80,000
Sales returns		4,000

Required:
1. Compute the cost of the ending inventory and the gross profit for the first quarter.
2. If the company took a physical inventory at the end of the first quarter and the retail value was $18,000, what is the cost of the ending inventory?
3. What may have caused the difference in the answers for Requirements 1 and 2?

P9-7A   Gross Profit Method.   The Lotus Company estimates its ending inventory for its quarterly financial statements by using the gross profit method. The following information is available:

	First Quarter	Second Quarter
Inventory, Jan. 1	$25,000	
Purchases	38,000	$45,000
Purchases returns	3,000	5,000
Sales	68,000	76,000
Sales returns	2,000	1,000

The company uses a gross profit rate of 30% of net sales.

Required: Compute the cost of goods sold and the ending inventory for each quarter.

P9-8A   Errors.   The accounting records of the Hill Company, which uses the periodic inventory system, showed the following information at the end of the year:

Beginning inventory	$19,500
Purchases	42,000
Purchases returns	1,500
Sales	98,000
Sales returns	2,700
Ending inventory	22,000

Required: 1. Using an income statement format compute the cost of goods sold and the gross profit.
2. Suppose a mistake was made in taking the physical inventory and the ending inventory should be $18,000. Using an income statement format compute the resulting cost of goods sold and the gross profit.
3. A purchase of $2,500 was erroneously recorded at $5,200. What is the effect of the error on the financial statements of the current year. (The answer to Requirement 3 is independent of the answer to Requirement 2.)

PROBLEMS

Part B

P9-1B   Cost of Goods Sold.   The Perth Company uses the LIFO cost flow assumption and the periodic inventory system. The following summary information was available at the end of the year:

Beginning inventory	$15,000
Purchases	64,000
Sales	97,000
Transportation–in	1,500
Sales discounts	1,000
Purchases returns and allowances	3,000
Sales returns and allowances	5,000
Ordering costs	500
Ending inventory	28,000

The company followed a policy of expensing its ordering costs rather than allocating them to the units of inventory. Discounts of 1/10, n/30 were available on all purchases, but the company took advantage of only 60% of them. The purchases returns and allowances were for items on which discounts were not taken. The company uses the gross method of accounting for discounts.

Required: 1. Prepare an income statement through to the calculation of gross profit.
2. The management at Perth is considering changing from the LIFO method. They estimate that the ending inventory would have been $34,000 under FIFO and $30,000 under average cost. What would be the percentage increase or decrease in the gross profit from changing to each alternative?

P9-2B   Discounts.   The Bellemere Company purchased inventory for $60,000 on terms of 2/10, n/30. The company paid for two-thirds of the purchases within 10 days and paid for the remainder after the discount period had expired. The company uses the periodic inventory system.

Required: 1. Prepare journal entries to record the above events using (a) the gross method and (b) the net method of accounting for purchases discounts.
2. If the company sold half of the inventory for $50,000, how much would its gross profit be under each method?
3. How much would the gross profit be if the company deducted all of the discounts available from the cost of the inventory under each method?

P9-3B   Alternative Cost Flow Assumptions: Periodic.   The Johnson Company made the following purchases and sales during July and August, and uses the periodic inventory system:

July	1	Inventory	250 units
July	8	Purchases	40 units for $20 each
July	27	Purchases	90 units for $21 each
Aug.	18	Purchases	50 units for $22 each
Aug.	24	Purchases	60 units for $23 each

Sales during July and August were 150 units and 100 units, respectively. The FIFO, average, and LIFO inventory cost of each unit in the beginning inventory was $19, $18, and $13, respectively.

Required: 1. Compute the ending inventory and the cost of goods sold for each month if the company uses:
(a) The FIFO cost flow assumption.
(b) The average cost flow assumption.
(c) The LIFO cost flow assumption.
2. Which cost flow assumption provides the more realistic balance sheet valuation? Which provides the more realistic measure of income? Why?

P9-4B   Alternative Cost Flow Assumptions: Perpetual.   The Caldwell Company made the following purchases and sales during November and December and uses the perpetual inventory system:

Nov. 1	Inventory	50 units
Nov. 12	Sales	40 units
Nov. 20	Purchases	100 units for $60 each
Nov. 29	Sales	80 units
Dec. 4	Purchases	100 units for $70 each
Dec. 10	Purchases	50 units for $75 each
Dec. 16	Sales	140 units

The FIFO and LIFO cost of each unit in the beginning inventory was $58 and $44, respectively.

Required: 1. Compute the cost of goods sold and ending inventory for each month if the company uses:
(a) The FIFO cost flow assumption.
(b) The LIFO cost flow assumption.
2. Which cost flow assumption provides the more realistic balance sheet valuation? Which provides the more realistic measure of income? Why?

P9-5B   Lower of Cost or Market.   The Thodes Company's ending inventory included the following items:

Item	Number of Units	Unit Cost	Unit Replacement Cost
SP5	20	$500	$400
CX3	300	60	50
TL9	95	200	180
FN6	250	80	90

Required: 1. Compute the value of the ending inventory under the lower of cost or market rule applied to the inventory as a whole.
2. Prepare the journal entry to record the reduction of the inventory to its market value.
3. Show how the ending inventory would be reported on the balance sheet.
4. If the lower of cost or market rule is applied to the inventory on an individual item basis, how would your answer to Requirement 1 change?
5. If at the end of the next year none of the items in the inventory has a market value below cost, how will the financial statements for the second year be affected by the application of the lower of cost or market method in the first year?

P9-6B   Retail Inventory Method.   The Burris Department Store uses the retail inventory method. At the end of the first quarter, the following information was available:

	Cost	Retail
Inventory, January 1	$ 5,000	$ 9,000
Purchases	30,000	63,000
Purchases returns	1,000	2,000
Sales		60,000
Sales returns		2,000

Required: 1. Compute the cost of the ending inventory and the gross profit for the first quarter.
2. If the company took a physical inventory at the end of the first quarter and the retail value was $10,000, what is the cost of the ending inventory?
3. What may have caused the difference in the answers for Requirements 1 and 2?

P9-7B Gross Profit Method. The Williams Company estimates its ending inventory for its quarterly financial statements by using the gross profit method. The following information is available:

	First Quarter	Second Quarter	Third Quarter
Inventory, January 1	$20,000		
Purchases	50,000	$55,000	$60,000
Purchases returns	1,000	2,000	1,000
Sales	95,000	90,000	98,000
Sales returns	2,000	1,000	3,000

The company used a gross profit rate of 40% of net sales in the first two quarters, but in the third quarter the cost of the company's purchases increased by 10%. The company did not increase its prices, however.

Required: Compute the cost of goods sold and the ending inventory for each quarter.

P9-8B Errors. The accounting records of the Kirkpatrick Company, which uses the periodic inventory system, showed the following information at the end of the year:

Beginning inventory	$ 35,000
Purchases	85,000
Purchases returns	3,000
Sales	160,000
Sales returns	2,000
Ending inventory	46,000

Required: 1. Using an income statement format compute the cost of goods sold and the gross profit.
2. Suppose a mistake was made in taking the physical inventory and the ending inventory has a cost of $40,000. Using an income statement format compute the resulting cost of goods sold and the gross profit.
3. A purchase of $6,200 was erroneously recorded at $2,600. What is the effect of the error on the cost of goods sold, gross profit, and ending inventory? (The answer to Requirement 3 is independent of the answer to Requirement 2.)

DISCUSSION CASES

C9-1 Estimate of Inventory Lost in Theft. When Janet Guthrie arrived at her dress shop on the morning of June 15, 1983, she found that thieves had broken in overnight and stolen much of her merchandise. The agent of the Alright Insurance Company agreed to visit in the afternoon and promised he would write out a check for the amount of the loss if she could verify it. Since it would be very time-consuming to take a physical inventory, Ms. Guthrie needed to make an estimate of the loss so that she could collect the insurance money and buy new merchandise. She asked for your help and you agreed to look at her accounting records. She told you that the store had been in business since January 1, 1982, and she does not use the retail method of accounting. You obtain the following information:

Inventory, January 1, 1982	$ 5,000
Purchases (net), 1982	30,000
Purchases (net), 1983	20,000
Sales (net), 1982	80,000
Sales (net), 1983	45,000
Delivery charges on purchases, 1982	2,000
Delivery charges on purchases, 1983	1,500
Inventory, January 1, 1983	15,000

Required: How much would you recommend that Ms. Guthrie settle for with the insurance company? What is the major assumption underlying your answer?

C9-2 Inventory and Holding Gains. The Birkin Company uses the FIFO inventory cost flow assumption. The following amounts are included in the company's financial statements:

Inventory, January 1	$100,000
Purchases	300,000
Cost of goods sold	250,000
Inventory, December 31	150,000

The company sells only one product, and purchases and sales are made evenly throughout the year. The replacement cost of the inventory at January 1 and December 31 is $120,000 and $180,000, respectively. The cost of the company's purchases was 20% higher at the end of the year than at the beginning.

Required: The owner of the Birkin Company asks you to analyze the above information and tell her the following:

1. How much would the cost of goods sold be if it were computed on the basis of the average replacement cost for the period?
2. What is the holding gain (inventory profit) included in the income computed on a FIFO basis?
3. Did the number of units in inventory increase or decrease during the year?

10 Current Liabilities and Payrolls

After reading this chapter, you should understand:

- Accounts payable
- Unearned revenue
- Accrued liabilities including premium or coupon liability, warranty liability, sales tax payable, property taxes payable, income taxes payable, and dividends payable
- The nature of a note payable and how to compute interest on the note
- How to account for money borrowed from a bank
- Payroll accounting, including federal income taxes, social security taxes, and unemployment taxes
- How to record the payroll, including use of the payroll register

In the previous three chapters the current assets of cash, marketable securities, accounts receivable, and inventory were discussed. The concept of working capital (current assets minus current liabilities) was introduced earlier in the book. In this chapter current liabilities are discussed. **Current liabilities are liabilities that will be paid, or eliminated, within one year or the normal operating cycle, whichever is longer.**

In the normal course of their operating activities companies incur many current liabilities. Some of these liabilities have been discussed previously as they arose through acquisitions, such as accounts payable, or through accruing expenses at the end of the year. Others include unearned revenue, warranty liabilities, and sales tax payable. To finance operations companies often borrow money for short periods of time. Accounting for these notes payable is also discussed in this chapter. Finally, accounting for payroll and the accompanying liabilities is discussed.

PURCHASING ON CREDIT

As explained in Chapter 8 companies often sell on credit to customers. These credit sales result in accounts receivable. Similarly, companies often make purchases on credit, which give rise to either accounts payable or notes payable. (Accounting for purchases was discussed in Chapter 9.) The reasons for purchasing on credit are similar to the reasons for selling on credit. The first reason is that it is often more convenient to purchase on credit than for cash. For example, if a company places an order with a supplier and the supplier ships the goods, the purchaser records the inventory when it acquires legal ownership. At this point a liability is also created and remains outstanding until the purchaser pays the supplier, usually by mailing a check.

The second reason for purchasing on credit is to delay paying for purchases and, by so doing, obtaining a short-term "loan" from the supplier. Many companies, particularly small companies, often suffer from a cash shortage and find it difficult to pay for their purchases immediately. The management of the company therefore tries to delay payment until the cash is received from the eventual sale of the product; it then uses this cash to pay the liability created by the purchase. This is why many suppliers offer cash discounts to encourage prompt payment.

Since accounts payable and notes payable for one company are accounts receivable and notes receivable for another company, the accounting for the liabilities is very similar to the accounting for the assets. It is virtually a "mirror image." Accounting for accounts and notes receivable was discussed in Chapter 8, and it may be useful to refer to this chapter to reinforce the similarities. In addition, accounts payable and accrued liabilities have been included in parts of previous chapters, and therefore only a brief review of these items is included in this chapter. It is useful for the reader, however, to understand clearly the nature of these current liabilities which appear on the balance sheet.

Accounts Payable

Accounts payable is the title of the liability created by the normal activities of a company in purchasing items such as inventory and supplies. The liability is recorded at the same time as the inventory is recorded; that is, when the inventory (or invoice) is received if the terms are FOB destination, or when it is shipped if the terms are FOB shipping point. When the liability is recorded, the Purchases (or Inventory) account is increased (debited) and Accounts Payable is increased (credited). If the gross method of accounting for purchases discounts is used, the purchases and the accounts payable are recorded at the gross amount. If the purchases discounts lost method (the net method) is used, they are recorded at the net amount.

As discussed in Chapter 5, companies occasionally return purchases or receive an allowance on the amount to be paid because of damage or defects or because an incorrect item was sent. When a purchases return or allowance is made on credit, the journal entry involves a decrease (debit) to Accounts Payable (and to the supplier's account in the accounts payable subsidiary ledger) and an increase (credit) to the contra-purchases account, Purchases Returns and Allowances. If the gross method is being used, the return is recorded at the gross amount; it is recorded at the net amount if the net method is being used. Care must be taken to record the proper amount so that the correct accounts payable balance is reflected in the supplier's account in the accounts payable subsidiary ledger.

The balance of the Accounts Payable is eliminated (debited) when payment is made. If the gross method is being used and a discount for prompt payment is taken, the payment is less than the amount at which the account payable was recorded, with the difference being the purchases discount taken. Note that the discount would be taken on the amount of the purchases *after* deducting purchase returns and allowances. For example, if the Homestake Company purchases goods from Smith Supply Company for $12,000 on terms of 1/10, n/30, returns $2,000 of the goods, uses the gross method, and pays within 10 days, the following entry would be made to record the payment:

Accounts Payable: Smith Supply Company	10,000	
Purchases Discounts Taken		
[($12,000 − $2,000) × .01]		100
Cash		9,900

To record payment within the discount period of $12,000 purchase less $2,000 purchase return.

If payment was not made until after the discount period had expired, a payment of $10,000 would be necessary to eliminate the accounts payable liability.

If the Homestake Company had been using the net method, the purchase would have been recorded at $11,880 [$12,000 − (.01 × $12,000)], the purchases return would have been recorded at $1,980 [$2,000 − (.01 × $2,000)], and the accounts payable balance would have been $9,900. If payment is made within 10 days, it would be recorded as follows:

Accounts Payable: Smith Supply Company	9,900	
Cash		9,900

To record payment within the discount period of $11,880 purchase less $1,980 purchase return.

If payment is made after the discount period has expired, the payment of $10,000 must be made and is recorded as follows:

Accounts Payable: Smith Supply Company	9,900	
Purchases Discounts Lost	100	
Cash		10,000

To record payment made after the discount period has expired.

Accounting for discounts was discussed in greater detail in Chapter 9, and the reader should review that material if necessary.

UNEARNED REVENUE AND ACCRUED LIABILITIES

Many of the operating activities of a company lead to current liabilities being incurred. Interest payable and wages payable are discussed later in the chapter in the section on notes payable and payroll accounting. **Unearned revenue is the liability representing an obligation to provide goods and services in the future as a result of receiving cash in advance. An accrued liability represents an obligation at the end of the period that has arisen during the accounting period but has not yet been paid or recorded.** Several accrued liabilities have arisen in transactions discussed earlier in the book. These liabilities were called accrued expenses in Chapter 4 because then we were focusing on matching expenses and revenues. In this chapter we use the term *accrued liabilities* because we are focusing on the liability portion of the journal entry. Unearned revenue and commonly occurring accrued liabilities are discussed in the following sections.

Unearned Revenue

A company usually receives payment from a customer at the time of the sale or after the sale. A company, however, may require payment in advance for an item it will sell in the future. In this situation it is inappropriate to record revenue at the time of the cash receipt, because the service or product has not yet been provided. A liability, unearned revenue, is created instead because the company has an obligation to provide goods or services in the future. When the goods are sold or the services are provided in the future, the revenue is recognized.

A common example involves magazine publishing companies, which require the subscriber to pay the subscription in advance. When the cash is received by the company, it has performed no service because it has not sent any magazines to the subscriber; therefore it should not recognize any revenue. Instead, when the cash is received by the company a liability (unearned revenue) is created that represents the obligation to deliver magazines in the future.

The liability is reduced each time the publishing company delivers a magazine. As the liability is reduced, revenue could be recognized. As discussed in Chapter 4, however, it is more efficient for the company to wait until the end of the accounting period and record all of the revenue earned by that date by means of an adjusting entry. For example, suppose that the Outdoors Publishing Company receives a check for $36 from Susan Chamberlain for a subscription for 12 issues of Outdoor magazine. The journal entry to record the cash receipt is:

```
Cash . . . . . . . . . . . . . . . . . . . . . . . . . . . . . . 36
     Subscriptions Collected in Advance  . . . . . . . . . . . . . . .     36
Subscription received for 1 year from Susan Chamberlain.
```

The Subscriptions Collected in Advance account is a current liability representing the unearned revenue related to the subscription. At the end of the period, the liability is reduced based on the number of magazines delivered. If five issues have been delivered to Susan Chamberlain, the liability is reduced by $15 ($36 × 5/12) and is recorded as follows:

```
Subscriptions Collected in Advance  . . . . . . . . . . . . . . . . . . 15
     Subscriptions Revenue  . . . . . . . . . . . . . . . . . . . . . .     15
To record revenue at year end.
```

Subscriptions Revenue would be included in the revenues section of the income statement and the remaining $21 ($36 − $15) balance in Subscriptions Collected in Advance is a current liability in the ending balance sheet. This illustration is for a single subscriber, but in practice the company would make a single adjusting entry to recognize revenue for the period from delivering magazines to all its customers.

Premiums and Coupons

Many companies that produce consumer goods, especially grocery products, offer premiums ("send in five labels and receive an electric carving knife") and coupons ("50 cents off on your next purchase"). These premiums and coupons are usually attached to a product container or are printed in newspapers and magazines. They are provided as an inducement to the consumer so that the company's sales will increase and the additional profit from the sales in the long run will exceed the cost of the premiums or coupons.

When a company offers such premiums and coupons in the current period, the cost of fulfilling the terms of the offer is an expense of the period. As the premiums or coupons are redeemed in the current period, an expense is recorded. In many cases the expiration date does not occur until the next period, and not all the premiums and coupons are redeemed in the current period. Nevertheless, the company has still incurred an expense for these items during the current period because the offer was made with the intention of increasing current sales. The matching principle requires that the expense be subtracted from the revenues in the period of the sale, even though fulfillment of the terms will not be made until a later period. The company also has a liability at the end of the period that represents the cost of fulfilling the terms of the premium or coupon offer in the future. Thus an adjusting entry to record an expense and a liability is necessary.

For example, suppose that in 1983 a company attaches a coupon to a product it sells offering a $1 cash refund if the coupon is mailed to the company by June 30, 1984. The company estimates that 60% of the total coupons issued will be redeemed by customers. During 1983 the company sold 100,000 units of the product. If customers redeemed 40,000 coupons in 1983, the journal entry to record the cash paid would be:

Coupon Expense	40,000	
Cash		40,000
Paid customers under terms of coupon offer.		

At the end of 1983, since the company expects 60% of the *total* coupons to be redeemed and 40,000 coupons have already been returned by customers, another 20,000 coupons are expected to be returned next year that were attached to products sold in 1983 [(100,000 × 0.60) − 40,000]. Therefore an expense and liability of $20,000 (20,000 × $1) must be recognized at the end of 1983 as follows:

Coupon Expense	20,000	
Coupon Liability		20,000
To record liability for future coupon redemptions.		

In situations in which a premium is to be sent to customers, the company must first acquire the premiums. At that time a premium inventory is increased (debited). When the premium is sent to the customer during the period, the inventory is reduced (credited) and an expense is recorded (debited). In addition, if the customer is required to send cash, the cash receipt will also be recorded. For example, suppose that a company agrees to send an electric carving knife to any customer who purchases a product during the period if the customer sends $10. The knife is purchased by the company at a cost of $18. Therefore the expense to the company of each knife sent to a customer is $8 ($18 − $10). The company expects to distribute 2,000 knives. The journal entry to record the acquisition of the 2,000 knives is as follows:

```
Premium Inventory . . . . . . . . . . . . . . . . . . . . . . .    36,000
    Cash (2,000 × $18)  . . . . . . . . . . . . . . . . . . .               36,000
Purchased 2,000 knives for premium offer.
```

If the company distributes 1,500 knives during the period, the following journal entry is made:

```
Cash (1,500 × $10)  . . . . . . . . . . . . . . . . . . . . .    15,000
Premium Expense (1,500 × $8)  . . . . . . . . . . . . . .    12,000
    Premium Inventory (1,500 × $18)  . . . . . . . . . . . .              27,000
Sent 1,500 knives to customers.
```

At the end of the period the company has a liability related to the remaining 500 knives that the company expects to distribute. This liability is recorded by means of an adjusting entry. An expense is also recognized because the company has incurred a cost associated with the sales of the current period. The amount of the adjusting entry is $4,000 based on the $8 net cost ($18 − $10) of the knives, and it is recorded as follows:

```
Premium Expense (500 × $8)  . . . . . . . . . . . . . . . .    4,000
    Premium Liability . . . . . . . . . . . . . . . . . . . . . .             4,000
To record liability for future premium redemptions.
```

The Premium or Coupon Expense would be included in the income statement as a selling expense. The balance in the Premium or Coupon Liability account would be included as a current liability in the ending balance sheet.

Warranties

A very similar situation to that of premiums and coupons arises with warranties. When a company offers a warranty on a product it sells, it agrees to repair or replace the product for a specified period of time. The cost of providing the warranty should be matched against the revenues in the period of the sale. When the warranty is fulfilled during the same period in which the sale was made, the following journal entry is made (amounts assumed):

```
Warranty Expense . . . . . . . . . . . . . . . . . . . . . . .    8,000
    Cash . . . . . . . . . . . . . . . . . . . . . . . . . . . . .             8,000
Fulfilled terms of warranty.
```

If all the warranties have not expired at the end of the period, an expense and a liability must be recognized. The cost of providing the unexpired warranty is not known in the period of the sale and therefore must be estimated. The estimated cost of fulfilling the terms of the warranty in the future is recorded at the end of the period as follows (using assumed amounts):

| Warranty Expense . . . . | 5,400 | |
| Warranty Liability . . . . | | 5,400 |

To record liability for future warranty costs.

The warranty expense would be included in the income statement as a selling expense, and the balance in the warranty liability account is included as a current liability on the ending balance sheet.

Sales Tax

Most states impose a sales tax on many types of products sold in the state. The tax is typically collected by the seller from the customer at the time of the sale and is paid to the state at a later date. Since the company is acting as a collection agency for the state, at the time of the sale there is no revenue or expense to the company with respect to the sales tax. The collection of the tax from the customer creates a liability for the company because it has received cash that it owes to the state. The liability is eliminated when payment is made to the state. The summary journal entries to record the collection of the sales tax from customers at the time of the sale and the later payment of the tax to the state are as follows (using assumed amounts):

Cash (or Accounts Receivable)	21,000	
Sales		20,000
Sales Tax Payable		1,000

To record sales and related sales tax.

| Sales Tax Payable . . . . | 1,000 | |
| Cash . . . . | | 1,000 |

Sales tax remitted to the state.

Any unremitted Sales Tax Payable at the end of the period is reported as a current liability in the ending balance sheet.

Property Taxes

Property taxes are assessed by municipal, county, and some state governments on the value of property owned, such as land and buildings. On the date that the taxes are legally assessed, the company owning the property has incurred a liability. The property taxes are assessed for the governmental agency's fiscal year, although this fiscal year may not coincide with a company's accounting period. Furthermore, the taxes may not be assessed until the middle of the fiscal year. Whatever the taxing situation, the expense associated with the taxes should be recognized over the accounting period of the company. For example, the city of Denver has a fiscal year of July 1 to June 30. The city assesses taxes on January 1, which is in the middle of its fiscal year. For a company with an accounting period ending December 31, this company must include a property tax expense in its calendar year income statement and also report a liability at the end of its accounting period. To do so, it may have to accrue the expense before the assessed taxes are known. Fortunately, because tax rates are well publicized and not subject to sudden changes, a company can usually make an accurate estimate of its future property taxes. In the previous example, at December 31 it is necessary to recognize an expense for the July 1 to December 31 portion of the property taxes. (The January 1 to June 30 property taxes would be known and would already have been expensed on the basis of the tax assessment from the previous year.) If the company estimates its annual property taxes to be $5,000, one-half, or $2,500, would be recorded as follows:

Property Tax Expense	2,500	
Property Tax Payable		2,500
To accrue property taxes.		

The property tax expense should be included on the income statement in the same section of the statement as the depreciation expense of the asset on which the taxes are being paid. Thus it might be included as a selling or as a general and administrative expense. Property Tax Payable is a current liability on the ending balance sheet. When the property taxes are paid in the next accounting period, the liability is eliminated and the remaining part of the payment is an expense for that accounting period. The payment is recorded as follows:

Property Tax Payable	2,500	
Property Tax Expense	2,500	
Cash		5,000
Payment of assessed property taxes.		

Income Taxes A corporation is required to compute the income tax expense related to its *income before income taxes* for the accounting period. Since the payment usually takes place after the end of the accounting period, the company will accrue an expense and a liability through an adjusting entry at the end of the period as follows (using assumed amounts):

Income Tax Expense	9,200	
Income Taxes Payable		9,200
To accrue income taxes.		

Unlike individuals who typically pay income taxes once a year, corporations usually are required to pay income taxes every quarter. Since corporations often prepare quarterly financial statements, the expense and amount payable are recognized each quarter. The income tax expense is deducted from income before income taxes to determine the quarterly net income. The income tax liability would be included as a current liability on the balance sheet at the end of the quarter. When the income taxes are paid the liability is eliminated. Income taxes are discussed more fully in Chapter 15.

Cash Dividends Cash dividends are paid by a corporation to its owners (stockholders) as a reward or incentive for investing in the capital stock of the corporation. Cash dividends become a liability when they are legally declared by a corporation, which is discussed briefly in Chapter 7 and more fully in Chapter 15. When dividends are declared, stockholders' equity is also reduced. The journal entry to record the declaration of a dividend is to increase (debit) Dividends Declared and to increase (credit) Dividends Payable. The Dividends Declared account is similar to the Withdrawals account and is closed at the end of the accounting period. Dividends are usually paid about a month after they are declared. When the accounting period ends between the date the dividends are declared and the date they are paid, the balance in the Dividends Payable account is listed as a current liability on the ending balance sheet. The liability is eliminated when the payment is made to the shareholders. The journal entries to record the declaration of the dividends and the subsequent payment are as follows (using assumed amounts):

```
Dividends Declared  . . . . . . . . . . . . . . . . . . . . . . . .   10,000
    Dividends Payable  . . . . . . . . . . . . . . . . . . . . .               10,000
Dividends declared on the capital stock.

Dividends Payable  . . . . . . . . . . . . . . . . . . . . . . . .   10,000
    Cash . . . . . . . . . . . . . . . . . . . . . . . . . . . . . .             10,000
To record dividends paid to stockholders.
```

In typical situations, all the unearned revenue and the accrued liabilities that have been discussed are classified as current liabilities on the balance sheet. It should be recognized that the current liability classification will also include the portion of any long-term liability that is to be paid in the current year.

NOTES PAYABLE

Just as companies sometimes require a note to be signed by a customer, thus creating a note receivable, so are companies also at times the customers at the other end of the transaction. That is, the officers of the company sign and deliver a note to make a purchase or to extend the time for payment of an account payable, thus creating a liability for the company. As discussed in Chapter 8, a promissory note is a written legal document in which one party makes an unconditional promise to pay another party a certain amount of money on demand or an agreed future date. Notes Payable is the account used to record promissory notes issued by a company. Another common way in which a note payable is created is when a company borrows money from a bank for a short period. Again in this situation, a note is signed and delivered to the bank when the cash is received. Each of these situations is discussed in the following sections.

Note Given to Make a Purchase or Extend Payment Time on an Account Payable

When a note is given to a supplier either to make a purchase or to extend the time allowed for payment, a note payable is recorded as a liability accompanied by recording purchases or inventory, or the removal of a liability (accounts payable). For example, suppose that on July 15, 1983, the Simba Company has a $700 account payable with the Avanti Company that is overdue and the Avanti Company agrees to accept a 12%, 90-day note. The Simba Company will record the issuance of the note as follows:

```
1983
July 15   Accounts Payable: Avanti Company  . . . . . . . .    700
            Notes Payable  . . . . . . . . . . . . . . . . .            700
          Issued a 12%, 90-day note to extend payment on an
          account with Avanti Company.
```

Simba has not paid the debt but has simply transformed it into a more formal liability and has agreed to pay interest on the liability. When the note is paid in 90 days, interest of $21 ($700 × 12% × 90/360) will be paid. At that time the following entry will be made to record the payment of the note:

```
1983
Oct. 13   Notes Payable  . . . . . . . . . . . . . . . . . .    700
          Interest Expense  . . . . . . . . . . . . . . . .     21
            Cash . . . . . . . . . . . . . . . . . . . . . .          721
          To record payment of note and interest due to the
          Avanti Company on maturity date.
```

Note Given to Borrow Money from a Bank

When a bank loans money to a company, it will require that the interest either be paid at the maturity date of the note or be deducted from the amount of money that is paid to the company. To illustrate the accounting for the two types of loans, suppose that the Simba Company borrows $20,000 at 10% for 6 months on August 1, 1983.

INTEREST PAID WHEN THE NOTE MATURES.   If interest is to be paid at the maturity date of the note, the journal entry to record the borrowing by Simba is as follows:

```
1983
Aug. 1   Cash . . . . . . . . . . . . . . . . . . . . . . . .  20,000
            Notes Payable  . . . . . . . . . . . . . . . .          20,000
         Borrowed $20,000 on a 10% 6 month note.
```

No interest is recorded at the date of issuance because the Simba Company is not legally liable for interest at this time. The liability for interest accrues each day for the life of the loan. Therefore interest must be accrued at the end of the Simba Company's fiscal year on December 31, 1983, even though it will not be paid until 1984. The interest expense for 5 months and the accompanying liability are recognized as follows:

```
1983
Dec. 31  Interest Expense  . . . . . . . . . . . . . . . .    833
           Interest Payable . . . . . . . . . . . . . . . .            833
         To record interest expense ($20,000 × 10% × 5/12).
```

The interest expense is included in Other Revenues and Expenses on the income statement. Interest payable is included as a current liability on the ending balance sheet. When the note becomes due on February 1, 1984, a payment of $21,000 must be made, consisting of the principal of $20,000 and interest of $1,000

($20,000 $\times$ 10% $\times$ 6/12). Since an interest expense of $833 has been recognized in 1983 only $167 ($20,000 $\times$ 10% $\times$ 1/12) is interest expense for 1984. The entry to record the payment is as follows:

```
1984
Feb. 1   Interest Payable  . . . . . . . . . . . . . . . . . . . .      833
         Interest Expense  . . . . . . . . . . . . . . . . . . .      167
         Notes Payable  . . . . . . . . . . . . . . . . . . . .    20,000
             Cash . . . . . . . . . . . . . . . . . . . . . . .              21,000
         To record payment of note and interest due on
         maturity date.
```

INTEREST DEDUCTED AT TIME OF ISSUANCE.   As shown in the above example, Simba paid $21,000 to the bank when the note matured, consisting of the $20,000 principal and interest of $1,000. Alternatively, the bank can deduct the interest from the amount loaned to the borrower. In this case the note has a face value of the total principal and interest to be paid at maturity ($21,000), and the bank issues a check for the net amount ($20,000) of the maturity value ($21,000) less interest ($1,000) to Simba. The difference of $1,000 represents the interest to be incurred in the future over the life of the note. Since this interest is *not* an expense at the time the note is signed (remember that interest accrues over time), it is recorded in a Discount on Notes Payable account as follows:

```
1983
Aug. 1   Cash . . . . . . . . . . . . . . . . . . . . . . . . . .    20,000
         Discount on Notes Payable  . . . . . . . . . . . .     1,000
             Notes Payable . . . . . . . . . . . . . . . . . .              21,000
         Borrowed $20,000 at 10% for 6 months
         with interest deducted in advance.
```

The Discount on Notes Payable account (in which future interest costs on a note are recorded) is a contra-liability account because the amount borrowed is only $20,000. It is *not* a prepaid expense because the $1,000 has not yet been paid. The net amount of the liability is $20,000 and would be reported in the balance sheet on the date of issuance as follows:

Notes payable	$21,000
Less: Discount on notes payable	1,000
	$20,000

Because the Discount on Notes Payable represents the future interest charges on the note, the Discount account is reduced whenever interest expense is recorded and therefore the balance in the account represents the future interest that still remains. On December 31, 1983, Simba would recognize interest of $833 (calculated in the same way as before) by reducing the Discount account as follows:

```
1983
Dec. 31   Interest Expense  . . . . . . . . . . . . . . . . . . .      833
              Discount on Notes Payable  . . . . . . . . . .              833
          To record interest expense.
```

At this point the net amount of the notes payable is $20,833, which consists of the Notes Payable account of $21,000 less the remaining balance in the Discount on Notes Payable account of $167 ($1,000 − $833). Although the $20,833 is listed as the net amount of the notes payable, it effectively represents the amount borrowed ($20,000) plus the interest payable to date ($833).

When the note is paid at maturity, the remaining interest expense is recognized and the remaining Discount is removed because no future interest remains. The face value of the note is also eliminated by the payment of $21,000, which is recorded as follows:

```
1984
Feb. 1   Interest Expense  . . . . . . . . . . . . . . . . . . . .        167
         Notes Payable  . . . . . . . . . . . . . . . . . . . .      21,000
              Discount on Notes Payable  . . . . . . . . . .                    167
              Cash . . . . . . . . . . . . . . . . . . . . . . .               21,000
         To record payment of note on maturity date.
```

Comparison of the Two Types of Loans

The two types of loans have the same effect on the financial statements because the same amount ($20,000) is borrowed for the same time period at the same rate. The interest expense shown on the income statement is the same under both situations since it amounts to $167 per month, or $833 for the 5 months from August 1 through December 31, 1983 and $167 in January 1984.

The net amount of the liability included in the balance sheet is the same under both situations, but there is a slightly different classification for each type of loan as illustrated by the following partial disclosures:

Interest Paid When the Note Matures		Interest Deducted at Time of Issuance	
August 1, 1983			
Current liabilities:		Current liabilities:	
Notes payable	$20,000	Notes payable	$21,000
		Less: Discount on notes payable	1,000
			$20,000
December 31, 1983			
Current liabilities:		Current liabilities:	
Notes payable	$20,000	Notes payable	$21,000
		Less: Discount on notes payable	167
Interest payable	833		
	$20,833		$20,833

PAYROLL ACCOUNTING

Payroll accounting is a very important, and often complex, aspect of a company's operations. Initially an employee's gross pay must be determined, which is either based on the length of the pay period for a salaried employee, or on the hours worked and the hourly rate of pay for an employee paid on an hourly basis. Numerous deductions are made from gross pay for such items as the employee's federal and state income taxes, federal social security taxes, and contributions to pension plans, union dues, medical insurance, and charitable contributions. These deductions are withheld from the employee, who is then paid the *net pay*. The deductions are later paid by the company to the appropriate agencies on behalf of the employees. In addition, the employer must pay federal social security taxes, federal and state unemployment taxes, and also may make contributions to pension plans, hospital insurance and match charitable contributions on behalf of employees. Each of these deductions is discussed below.

Federal and State Income Taxes

The computation of the federal and state income taxes that must be paid by individuals is very complex. The determination of the amount of the taxes owed, as well as the payment of the taxes, is the responsibility of the employee, not the employer. The employer, however, is required to withhold federal and state income taxes from the employee's pay and to send the money withheld at periodic intervals to the appropriate tax authorities. The purpose of this pay-as-you-go withholding of taxes is to increase the likelihood that the taxing authorities will collect the taxes from the individual taxpayer, because if there were no withholding of taxes many individuals would not save enough to pay their taxes. Since state income tax laws vary from state to state, the discussion will focus on the federal income tax.

The amount of federal income tax to be withheld from an employee's pay is a function of two factors. First, the number of exemptions (or withholding allowances) claimed by the employee affects the amount withheld. **An exemption is an exclusion of earned income from taxable income.** An individual is allowed an exemption for him- or herself, an additional exemption for each dependent, and additional exemptions for being over 65 or blind (and for the spouse being over 65 or blind if a joint return is filed). At the time of writing, each exemption results in $1,000 being exempted from taxable income. Thus an employee who earns $15,000 and claims four exemptions has a taxable income of $11,000. Each employee is required to file an Employee's Withholding Allowance Certificate, called a Form W-4, with the employer. **The Employee's Withholding Allowance Certificate (Form W-4) reports the number of the exemptions claimed by the employee.** It is illustrated in Exhibit 10-1.

The second factor that affects the amount of federal income tax to be withheld is the pay level of the employee. Since tax rates are higher for higher incomes, progressively larger amounts are withheld at higher pay levels. An excerpt from the federal income tax withholding table is shown in Exhibit 10-2. For example, if a married employee with two exemptions (withholding allowances) earns $800 biweekly, income taxes of $124.60 are withheld from each biweekly paycheck.

Once the appropriate federal income taxes are withheld, employers must periodically remit the taxes to the Internal Revenue Service. Each quarter they must also file a report showing the taxes withheld. After the end of the year a Wage and Tax Statement, Form W-2, is prepared by the company.

The Wage and Tax Statement (Form W-2) is a form provided by the employer to the employee and the Internal Revenue Service that reports the employee's total wages and salary, wages subject to FICA taxes, state and

federal income taxes withheld, and FICA taxes withheld. (FICA taxes are discussed below.) The W-2 form is illustrated in Exhibit 10-3.

EXHIBIT 10-1
Employee's Withholding Allowance Certificate (W-4)

Form **W-4** (Rev. October 1979)	Department of the Treasury—Internal Revenue Service **Employee's Withholding Allowance Certificate**

Print your full name ▶   Your social security number ▶

Address (including ZIP code) ▶

Marital status: ☐ Single   ☐ Married   ☐ Married, but withhold at higher Single rate

Note: *If married, but legally separated, or spouse is a nonresident alien, check the single block.*

1 Total number of allowances you are claiming (from line F of the worksheet on page 2) . . . .

2 Additional amount, if any, you want deducted from each pay (if your employer agrees) . . . . $

3 I claim exemption from withholding because (see instructions and check boxes below that apply):
   a ☐ Last year I did not owe any Federal income tax and had a right to a full refund of ALL income tax withheld, AND
   b ☐ This year I do not expect to owe any Federal income tax and expect to have a right to a full refund of ALL income tax withheld. If both
     a and b apply, enter "EXEMPT" here . . . . ▶
   c If you entered "EXEMPT" on line 3b, are you a full-time student? . . . . ☐ Yes ☐ No

Under the penalties of perjury, I certify that I am entitled to the number of withholding allowances claimed on this certificate, or if claiming exemption from withholding, that I am entitled to claim the exempt status.

Employee's signature ▶   Date ▶   , 19

Employer's name and address (including ZIP code) **(FOR EMPLOYER'S USE ONLY)**   Employer identification number

EXHIBIT 10-2
Excerpt From Federal Income Tax Withholding Table

MARRIED Persons — BIWEEKLY Payroll Period

And the wages are—		And the number of withholding allowances claimed is—										
At least	But less than	0	1	2	3	4	5	6	7	8	9	10 or more
		The amount of income tax to be withheld shall be—										
$600	$620	$95.10	$86.00	$77.90	$69.80	$61.80	$53.70	$46.80	$39.90	$33.00	$26.00	$20.00
620	640	99.90	90.60	82.10	74.00	66.00	57.90	50.40	43.50	36.60	29.60	23.00
640	660	104.70	95.40	86.30	78.20	70.20	62.10	54.00	47.10	40.20	33.20	26.30
660	680	109.50	100.20	91.00	82.40	74.40	66.30	58.20	50.70	43.80	36.80	29.90
680	700	114.30	105.00	95.80	86.60	78.60	70.50	62.40	54.30	47.40	40.40	33.50
700	720	119.10	109.80	100.60	91.40	82.80	74.70	66.60	58.50	51.00	44.00	37.10
720	740	123.90	114.60	105.40	96.20	87.00	78.90	70.80	62.70	54.60	47.60	40.70
740	760	129.10	119.40	110.20	101.00	91.70	83.10	75.00	66.90	58.80	51.20	44.30
760	780	134.70	124.20	115.00	105.80	96.50	87.30	79.20	71.10	63.00	55.00	47.90
780	800	140.30	129.50	119.80	110.60	101.30	92.10	83.40	75.30	67.20	59.20	51.50
800	820	145.90	135.10	124.60	115.40	106.10	96.90	87.70	79.50	71.40	63.40	55.30
820	840	151.50	140.70	130.00	120.20	110.90	101.70	92.50	83.70	75.60	67.60	59.50
840	860	157.10	146.30	135.60	125.00	115.70	106.50	97.30	88.00	79.80	71.80	63.70
860	880	162.70	151.90	141.20	130.40	120.50	111.30	102.10	92.80	84.00	76.00	67.90
880	900	168.30	157.50	146.80	136.00	125.30	116.10	106.90	97.60	88.40	80.20	72.10
900	920	174.00	163.10	152.40	141.60	130.80	120.90	111.70	102.40	93.20	84.40	76.30
920	940	180.40	168.70	158.00	147.20	136.40	125.70	116.50	107.20	98.00	88.80	80.50
940	960	186.80	174.50	163.60	152.80	142.00	131.30	121.30	112.00	102.80	93.60	84.70
960	980	193.20	180.90	169.20	158.40	147.60	136.90	126.10	116.80	107.60	98.40	89.10
980	1,000	199.60	187.30	175.00	164.00	153.20	142.50	131.70	121.60	112.40	103.20	93.90
1,000	1,020	206.00	193.70	181.40	169.60	158.80	148.10	137.30	126.50	117.20	108.00	98.70
1,020	1,040	212.40	200.10	187.80	175.50	164.40	153.70	142.90	132.10	122.00	112.80	103.50
1,040	1,060	218.80	206.50	194.20	181.90	170.00	159.30	148.50	137.70	127.00	117.60	108.30
1,060	1,080	225.20	212.90	200.60	188.30	176.00	164.90	154.10	143.30	132.60	122.40	113.10
1,080	1,100	231.60	219.30	207.00	194.70	182.40	170.50	159.70	148.90	138.20	127.40	117.90
1,100	1,120	238.00	225.70	213.40	201.10	188.80	176.50	165.30	154.50	143.80	133.00	122.70
1,120	1,140	245.30	232.10	219.80	207.50	195.20	182.90	170.90	160.10	149.40	138.60	127.80
1,140	1,160	252.70	238.50	226.20	213.90	201.60	189.30	177.00	165.70	155.00	144.20	133.40
1,160	1,180	260.10	245.90	232.60	220.30	208.00	195.70	183.40	171.30	160.60	149.80	139.00
1,180	1,200	267.50	253.30	239.10	226.70	214.40	202.10	189.80	177.50	166.20	155.40	144.60

EXHIBIT 10-3
Wage and
Tax Statement

1 Control number			
22222			

2 Employer's name, address, and ZIP code	3 Employer's identification number	4 Employer's State number

	5 Stat. employee ☐　Deceased ☐　Pension plan ☐　Legal rep. ☐　942 emp. ☐　Subtotal ☐　Correction ☐　Void ☐
	6	7 Advance EIC payment

8 Employee's social security number	9 Federal income tax withheld	10 Wages, tips, other compensation	11 FICA tax withheld

12 Employee's name, address, and ZIP code	13 FICA wages	14 FICA tips
	16 Employer's use	
	17 State income tax	18 State wages, tips, etc.	19 Name of State
	20 Local income tax	21 Local wages, tips, etc.	22 Name of locality

Wage and Tax Statement 1980　　Copy 1 For State, City, or Local Tax Department ☐
Employee's and employer's copy compared.

Federal Social Security Taxes

At the time of writing the Social Security Act provides that qualified participants will receive monthly retirement benefits after reaching the age of 62, certain medical benefits after reaching the age of 65, and benefits to the family of the participant in the case of death. The benefits are based on the average earnings during the employee's (participant's) years of employment. The Social Security System is basically a pay-as-you-go system, which means that the money collected during the current period from employed people is used to pay benefits to retired people in the same period. **Social security taxes are assessed against employees and employers under the Federal Insurance Contributions Act (FICA) to pay for benefits of retired employees.** They are often referred to as *FICA taxes.* They are levied at a set rate on annual wages and salaries up to a maximum amount (*limit*). These taxes are projected at rates and on maximum amounts (limits) of earnings as follows:

Year	Tax on Employee	Tax on Employer	Annual Maximum Compensation per Employee Subject to Tax
1982	6.70%	6.70%	$31,800
1983	6.70	6.70	33,900
1984	6.70	6.70	36,000
1985	7.05	7.05	38,100
1986	7.15	7.15	40,200
1987	7.15	7.15	42,600

The employer is required to withhold the employee's social security tax at the appropriate rate from each employee's pay until the annual salary limit is reached. The employer must also pay its equal share of the tax. It must periodically remit both amounts to the Internal Revenue Service. Periodic reports have to be filed, and the taxes withheld are reported on Form W-2.

Federal and State Unemployment Taxes

The federal and state governments participate in a joint unemployment insurance program. The state government operates the program to provide benefits to the unemployed in the form of cash payments made for a specified period of time. **The Federal Unemployment Tax Act (FUTA) taxes are assessed at a maximum rate of 3.4% levied on the employer on the basis of the first $6,000 paid to each employee in each year.** These taxes are often referred to as *FUTA taxes*. Of the 3.4%, 2.7% is paid to the state if the state levies an approved unemployment insurance tax; thus 0.7% is left for the federal government. Most states allow for a reduction of the 2.7% tax through merit-rating plans for employers who do not lay off employees, because steady employment reduces the unemployment funds paid by the state.

Other Employee Deductions

Often employees pay for programs such as medical insurance, union dues, and charitable contributions (e.g., United Fund) through payroll deductions. The employer must keep track of the appropriate deductions from each employee's pay and remit the correct amounts to the various agencies. In addition, the company itself may contribute to the cost of the program and therefore must calculate and pay its share.

EXHIBIT 10-4   Payroll Register

<table>
<tr><td colspan="7" align="center">KASPER COMPANY
Payroll Register
For Week Ended March 5, 1983</td></tr>
<tr><td></td><td></td><td></td><td></td><td colspan="3" align="center">Earnings</td></tr>
<tr><td>Employee Name
and Social
Security Number</td><td>Hours
Worked</td><td>Overtime
Hours</td><td>Pay
Rate</td><td>Regular
Pay</td><td>Overtime
Pay</td><td>Gross
Pay</td></tr>
<tr><td>Linda Jones
453-61-5261</td><td>40</td><td></td><td>5.00</td><td>200.00</td><td></td><td>200.00</td></tr>
<tr><td>David Kennedy
523-06-9143</td><td>40</td><td></td><td>8.00</td><td>320.00</td><td></td><td>320.00</td></tr>
<tr><td>Peter Morgan
468-21-6842</td><td>45</td><td>5</td><td>6.00</td><td>240.00</td><td>45.00</td><td>285.00</td></tr>
<tr><td>Kathleen Thomas
521-26-0374</td><td>40</td><td></td><td>7.50</td><td>300.00</td><td></td><td>300.00</td></tr>
<tr><td>Michael Williams
621-55-3164</td><td>40</td><td></td><td>6.00</td><td>240.00</td><td></td><td>240.00</td></tr>
<tr><td>Total</td><td></td><td></td><td></td><td>1,300.00</td><td>45.00</td><td>1,345.00</td></tr>
</table>

RECORDING THE PAYROLL

The procedures followed in accounting for payroll vary from company to company, although they have some common elements. These elements are discussed in the following sections. Although most companies have automated payroll accounting systems, the elements are described in the form of a nonautomated record-keeping system. The information contained in either type of system is essentially the same.

Payroll Register

The payroll register is a record in which details of each employee's pay and deductions for the period are entered. A typical payroll register is illustrated for the Kasper Company in Exhibit 10-4. The register includes each employee's name, social security number, pay rate, total hours worked, and hours of overtime, which in this case are paid at 150% of the regular rate. The gross pay is determined from the hours worked and the pay rate. Federal and state income tax deductions, FICA tax deductions (at an assumed 6.7% rate), and medical insurance deductions are all listed. The total deductions subtracted from the gross pay indicate the net amount to be paid to the employee. Upon payment, the number of the check used for payment is recorded. The last column indicates the distribution of the cost; that is, the expense account in which the pay will be recorded.

Recording the Journal Entry for the Payroll

When the Kasper Company has completed the payroll register for all its employees, it prepares a journal entry (on the following page) at the time of the cash payment for the employee's salaries:

	Deductions				Payment		
Federal Income Tax	State Income Tax	FICA Taxes	Medical Insurance	Total Deductions	Net Pay	Check No.	Distribution
21.30	3.20	13.40	15.00	52.90	147.10	609	Office Salaries Expense
50.60	5.15	21.44	15.00	92.19	227.81	610	Sales Salaries Expense
44.20	4.85	19.10	18.00	86.15	198.85	611	Maintenance Salaries Expense
36.20	3.82	20.10	15.00	75.12	224.88	612	Accounting Salaries Expense
20.60	2.90	16.08	20.00	59.58	180.42	613	Office Salaries Expense
172.90	19.92	90.12	83.00	365.94	979.06		

Office Salaries Expense ($200 + $240)	440.00	
Sales Salaries Expense	320.00	
Maintenance Salaries Expense	285.00	
Accounting Salaries Expense	300.00	
Federal Income Tax Payable		172.90
State Income Tax Payable		19.92
FICA Taxes Payable		90.12
Medical Insurance Payable		83.00
Cash		979.06

Payroll for week ending March 5, 1983.

Note that the amount of each salary expense is based on the *gross* pay because that is the cost to the company of each employee. When the company remits the appropriate amounts withheld to the various agencies, the related liability is reduced (debited) as the cash is paid (credited).

Frequently the date of payment of the wages and salaries does not coincide with the end of the accounting period. In this case it is necessary to calculate the wages and salaries earned between the last payment date and the end of the period in order to record the related expense and liability. For example, if salaries were last paid on December 27, any salaries earned between that date and December 31 should be recognized by an adjusting entry. The adjusting entry would have the same format as the entry above, except that Salaries Payable would be credited instead of Cash because payment will not be made until January of the next year. When payment is made the Salaries Payable account is debited and Cash is credited.

Payroll Taxes Paid by the Employer

As discussed earlier, some payroll taxes are levied directly on the employer. These taxes include the employer's share of social security taxes and unemployment taxes. In addition, although they are not really taxes, the employer may pay a share (or all) of such items as medical insurance and pension plan payments.

Continuing the above example, the Kasper Company would have to pay FICA taxes of $90.12 (6.7% × $1,345.00), assuming the salary levels of the employees have not reached the FICA limit; federal unemployment taxes of $9.42 (0.7% × $1,345.00), assuming that the salary levels of the employee have not reached the $6,000 FUTA limit; state unemployment taxes of $36.31 (2.7% × $1,345.00), assuming that the company has no merit-rating reduction; and medical insurance of $83.00, assuming that the Kasper Company matches the employee's insurance payment. The journal entry to record the $218.85 ($90.12 + $9.42 + $36.31 + $83.00) payroll tax expenses would be:

Office Salaries Expense	79.44	
Sales Salaries Expense	47.32	
Maintenance Salaries Expense	46.79	
Accounting Salaries Expense	45.30	
FICA Taxes Payable		90.12
Federal Unemployment Taxes Payable		9.42
State Unemployment Taxes Payable		36.31
Medical Insurance Payable		83.00

Payroll tax expenses for week ended March 5, 1983.

The amounts should be divided among each salary expense category in the same way as the payments made to the employees. For example, the sales salaries expense of $47.32 is calculated as follows:

FICA Taxes	$21.44 (6.7% × $320)
Federal Unemployment Taxes	2.24 (0.7% × $320)
State Unemployment Taxes	8.64 (2.7% × $320)
Medical Insurance	15.00
	$47.32

The total expense for the employee's salaries for the Kasper Company is the sum of the expenses recorded in the two journal entries. Thus the total sales salaries expense is $367.32 ($320.00 + $47.32). The total salaries expense included in the income statement for this pay period is $1,563.85 ($1,345.00 + $218.85). The sales salaries expense would be included as part of sales expenses and the other three expense items would be included in general and administrative expenses.

As an alternative to the treatment discussed above, the company could isolate all the payroll costs in a single account such as Payroll Tax Expense. The effect of this practice would be to reduce the expense in each categorized expense account, but the total expenses for the period would be the same since the Payroll Tax Expense is reported separately.

REVIEW PROBLEM

During 1983 The Cameron Company engaged in the following summarized transactions:

1. The company received $12,000 during the year for subscriptions to a trade magazine it publishes monthly. This amount represented payment for 200 one-year subscriptions. By December 31, 1983, the company had delivered 800 copies of the magazine to the various subscribers.
2. The company attached coupons to an electronic game it sells. The coupon, which offered a $1 rebate, had to be redeemed by July 1, 1984. The company expected 60% of the coupons to be redeemed. During 1983 the company sold 20,000 electronic games (included in the sales listed in item 4 below). By December 31, 1983, customers had redeemed 3,000 coupons.
3. The company offers a warranty on its products. It expects to receive 200 claims at an average amount of $20 on the items it sold in 1983. During 1983, 30 of these claims were satisfied at a total cost of $600.
4. The company collected a sales tax of 6% from customers on its cash sales of $210,000. Of the amount collected for the sales tax 80% has been remitted to the state.
5. The company paid property taxes on April 5 of $20,000. These property taxes covered the period July 1, 1982, to June 30, 1983. The company estimates that property taxes for July 1, 1983, to June 30, 1984, will be $22,000.
6. On September 1 the company borrowed $10,000 for 6 months from a bank that charged 12% interest. The company issued a $10,600 note. The bank deducted

interest at the time the note was issued and issued a check to the company for $10,000.

7. During 1983, the company paid salaries as follows:

Sales clerks	$80,000
Office employees	60,000

FICA taxes were assessed at a rate of 6.70%, and none of the employees exceeded the annual maximum amount on which taxes are assessed. The company's FUTA taxes are 1.9% of which 1.2% is paid to the state. Salaries subject to FUTA taxes were $54,000, of which $30,000 was for sales clerks. The federal income tax withholding rate is 15% of gross pay. Union dues paid by the employees and withheld from their paychecks totaled $6,000, of which $4,000 was for sales clerks. All the deductions and payroll costs have been paid.

8. The company estimated that its income tax expense for 1983 is $12,000. The taxes will be paid in April 1984.

9. The company declared a dividend of $15,000 on December 28, 1983, to be paid on January 10, 1984.

Required: Prepare journal entries to record the above events.

SOLUTION TO REVIEW PROBLEM

1.

During Year

Cash	12,000	
Subscriptions Collected in Advance		12,000
Subscriptions received.		

At End of Year

Subscriptions Collected in Advance	4,000[a]	
Subscriptions Revenue		4,000
To record revenue at year end.		

[a] $800/(12 \times 200) \times \$12,000$.

2.

During Year

Coupon Expense	3,000	
Cash		3,000
Paid customers under terms of coupon offer.		

At End of Year

Coupon Expense $[(20,000 \times 0.60) - 3,000] \times \$1$	9,000	
Coupon Liability		9,000
To record liability for future coupon redemptions.		

3.

During Year

Warranty Expense	600	
Cash		600

Fulfilled terms of warranty.

At End of Year

Warranty Expense [$20 × (200 − 30)]	3,400	
Warranty Liability		3,400

To record liability for future warranty costs.

4.

During Year

Cash	222,600	
Sales		210,000
Sales Tax Payable ($210,000 × 0.06)		12,600

To record sales and related sales taxes.

Sales Tax Payable ($12,600 × 0.80)	10,080	
Cash		10,080

Sales tax remitted to the state.

5.

1983

Apr. 5	Property Tax Payable[a]	10,000	
	Property Tax Expense	10,000	
	Cash		20,000

    Paid property taxes.

      [a] Accrued at the end of 1982.

1983

Dec. 31	Property Tax Expense ($22,000 × 6/12)	11,000	
	Property Tax Payable		11,000

    To accrue property taxes.

6.

1983

Sept. 1	Cash	10,000	
	Discount on Notes Payable		
	($10,000 × 12% × 6/12)	600	
	Notes Payable		10,600

    Borrowed $10,000 from the bank by issuing 6-month
    note with interest deducted in advance.

1983

Dec. 31	Interest Expense ($10,000 × 12% × 4/12)	400	
	Discount on Notes Payable		400

    To record interest expense.

7.
Payroll entry

Sales Salaries Expense	80,000	
Office Salaries Expense	60,000	
Federal Income Taxes Payable		21,000[a]
FICA Taxes Payable		9,380[b]
Union Dues Payable		6,000
Cash		103,620

Payroll for the year.

[a] $140,000 \times 15\%$
[b] $140,000 \times 6.7\%$

Payroll tax entry

Sales Salaries Expense	5,930[a]	
Office Salaries Expense	4,476[b]	
FICA Taxes Payable		9,380[c]
Federal Unemployment Taxes Payable		378[d]
State Unemployment Taxes Payable		648[e]

Payroll tax expenses for the year.

[a] $(\$80,000 \times 6.7\%) + (\$30,000 \times 0.7\%) + (\$30,000 \times 1.2\%)$
[b] $(\$60,000 \times 6.7\%) + (\$24,000 \times 0.7\%) + (\$24,000 \times 1.2\%)$
[c] $\$140,000 \times 6.7\%$
[d] $\$54,000 \times 0.7\%$
[e] $\$54,000 \times 1.2\%$

Payroll tax payment entry

Federal Income Taxes Payable	21,000	
Union Dues Payable	6,000	
FICA Taxes Payable ($9,380 + $9,380)	18,760	
Federal Unemployment Taxes Payable	378	
State Unemployment Taxes Payable	648	
Cash		46,786

Remitted the payroll tax withholdings.

8.
Income tax entry

Income Tax Expense	12,000	
Income Taxes Payable		12,000

To accrue income taxes.

9.
Dividends entry

Dividends Declared	15,000	
Dividends Payable		15,000

Dividend declared on the capital stock.

GLOSSARY

Accrued Liability. A liability outstanding at the end of the period that has arisen during the accounting period but has not yet been paid. Also called an *accrued expense*.

Discount on Notes Payable. A contra liability account in which the future interest costs on a note are recorded. It arises only when the Notes Payable account is recorded at the maturity value (principal plus interest) of the note.

Employee's Withholding Allowance Certificate (Form W-4). A form filed by the employee with the employer that reports the number of exemptions claimed by the employee.

Exemption. An exclusion of earned income from taxable income.

Federal Unemployment Tax Act (FUTA). Federal unemployment taxes assessed at 3.4% of the first $6,000 of each employee's income in a given year; 2.7% is paid to the state, leaving 0.7% for the federal government.

Notes Payable. The liability account used to record promissory notes issued by a company.

Payroll Register. A record in which details of each employee's pay and deductions for the period are entered.

Social Security Taxes (FICA Taxes). Taxes assessed against employees and employers to pay for benefits of retired employees. The amount of the tax is determined by multiplying a set rate times the annual wages and salaries earned by an employee, up to a maximum amount.

Unearned Revenue. A liability representing an obligation to provide goods and services in the future as a result of receiving cash in advance.

Wage and Tax Statement (Form W-2). A form provided by the employer to the employee and to the Internal Revenue Service that reports the employee's total wages and salary, wages subject to FICA taxes, state and federal income taxes withheld, and FICA taxes withheld.

QUESTIONS

Q10-1 Why do companies often purchase merchandise on credit?

Q10-2 When a company makes a purchase return or receives a purchase allowance on goods purchased on credit and subject to a cash discount, how is the amount of the return or allowance accounted for under (a) the gross method and (b) the net method of accounting for cash discounts assuming the discount period has not expired?

Q10-3 Why is a liability created when cash is received in advance for rent charged on a building that is being leased to others?

Q10-4 "When we offer coupons to customers, there is no liability because we don't know which customers will use them." Do you agree with this statement? Explain.

Q10-5 If a company offers a warranty on a product it sells, why may a liability exist at the end of the accounting period?

Q10-6 "Since sales taxes are paid by the customer and not by us, there cannot be a liability on our balance sheet for sales taxes payable." Do you agree with this statement? Explain.

Q10-7 What problem may a company face in determining the correct amount of property tax expense for the current accounting period?

Q10-8 If a company borrows money from a bank and issues a note, describe the difference between a note on which the interest is paid at maturity and a note on which the interest is deducted when the money is borrowed. Is there any difference in how these notes and the related interest are reported in the company's financial statements?

Q10-9 Why does the employer deduct federal and state income taxes from the employee's paycheck if it is the employee's responsibility to pay these taxes?

Q10-10 What is an exemption for federal income tax purposes? For what is an exemption given?

Q10-11 What is the purpose of an Employee's Withholding Allowance Certificate? What information does it include?

Q10-12 What is the purpose of a Wage and Tax Statement? What information does it include?

Q10-13 What is the purpose of social security taxes (FICA)? Who pays these taxes?

Q10-14 Who pays federal unemployment taxes (FUTA)? At what rate are FUTA taxes paid? How may the portion paid to the state be reduced by a company?

Q10-15 A company paid its employees on December 26. What must the company do in regard to the payroll if its accounting period ends on December 31?

EXERCISES

E10-1 Purchase with Discount Available. The Sherman Company uses a periodic inventory system and purchased inventory costing $5,500 on terms of 2/15, n/30. Purchases of $500 were returned during the discount period. Payment was made within 15 days.

Required: 1. Prepare journal entries to record the above events using each of the following methods to account for cash discounts:
   (a) The gross method.
   (b) The net method.
   2. Prepare the journal entry to record the payment under each method if payment was made in 30 days.

E10-2 Subscriptions Received in Advance. On June 20 the Madison Company received $60 for a 2-year subscription to a monthly magazine. The first copy is delivered on July 10.

Required: 1. Prepare the journal entry to record the receipt of the cash.
   2. Prepare any adjusting entries necessary at the end of the year. Where would any resulting liability be disclosed?

E10-3 Premiums. On January 10 the Grant Company offered a premium to purchasers of its frozen pizzas. It offered a free beach blanket to any customer who sent in 10 labels before March 31 of the next year and expects 100,000 labels to be returned. The company purchased 5,000 blankets on February 25 for $2 each. It plans to buy the remaining blankets later. By the end of the year, 20,000 labels were returned by customers and the appropriate number of blankets sent to the customers.

Required: 1. Prepare journal entries to record the above events.
            2. What is the amount of the liability at the end of the year? Where would it be disclosed?

E10-4   Coupons.   On April 12 the Monroe Company decided to attach a coupon to a product it sells. The coupon offered a $1 cash refund and had to be returned by June 30 of the next year. The company expects 120,000 coupons to be returned by customers. By December 31, 80,000 coupons had been returned by customers and the company had mailed checks to these customers.

Required: 1. Prepare journal entries to record the above events.
            2. What is the amount of the liability at the end of the year? Where would it be disclosed?

E10-5   Warranties.   During 1983 the Ryan Company sold electric toasters with 1-year warranties. It was expected that 500 of the toasters would be returned for repair and that each repair would cost $8. By the end of the year, 200 toasters had been repaired at an average cost of $8 each.

Required: 1. Prepare journal entries to record the above events for 1983.
            2. What is the amount of the liability at the end of the year? Where would it be disclosed?

E10-6   Sales Tax.   During 1983 the Caran Company made sales of $80,000 on which a 6% sales tax was imposed. The sales tax was collected from the customer at the time of each sale. By the end of the year, 80% of the sales taxes collected had been remitted to the state.

Required: 1. Prepare journal entries to record the above events for 1983.
            2. What is the amount of the liability at the end of the year? Where would it be disclosed?

E10-7   Property Taxes.   On December 31, 1982, the Adams Company was preparing its financial statements and estimated that its property taxes for the period from July 1, 1982, to June 30, 1983, would be $30,000. On February 10, 1983, it receives its property tax bill for $30,000 and the bill is paid.

Required: Prepare journal entries to record the above events.

E10-8   Note Given to Make a Purchase.   On August 1, 1983, the Taft Company purchased inventory for $40,000 and gave a 12%, 6-month note to the seller. The company uses the periodic inventory system.

Required: 1. Prepare the journal entries to record the purchase, the accrual of interest at year end, and the repayment of the note.
            2. What are the amounts of the liabilities at the end of the year? Where would they be disclosed?

E10-9   Interest Deducted at Borrowing.   On September 1, 1983, the Wilson Company borrowed $10,000 cash from a bank that charges 10% interest. The company issued a 6-month note in the amount of $10,500 and the bank remitted $10,000 to the company when the note was issued.

Required: 1. What is the face value of the note?
            2. Prepare journal entries to record the borrowing, the interest expense at year end, and the repayment of the money.
            3. What is the amount of the liability at the end of 1983? Where would it be disclosed?

E10-10   Calculation of Net Pay.   For employees of the McKinley Company, the gross pay and the federal income tax withheld in the first week of February 1983 were as follows:

Employee	Gross Pay	Federal Income Tax Withheld
Carver, James	$200	$42
Webb, Steve	250	54
Bailey, Doreen	300	77

FICA taxes were withheld at a 6.70% rate. FUTA taxes are 3.4%, and the company has no reduction in the portion paid to the state. Each employee has a $5 union fee deducted from every paycheck.

Required: Assuming that no maximum amounts (limits) have been reached, compute the net amount paid to each employee.

E10-11   Calculation of Payroll Expense.   Use the information in E10-10.

Required: 1. Compute the total salaries expense incurred by the McKinley Company for the first week of February.
2. Prepare a journal entry to record the salaries, assuming that Carver is a salesman and the other two employees are office employees.

E10-12   Net Pay and Payroll Expense.   Anthony Hopkins is an employee of the Seasons Company. His annual salary is $60,000, which is earned evenly over the year. During November the federal income tax withheld was $700. FUTA taxes are 3.4%, and the company has no reduction in the portion paid to the state. The FICA tax rate is 6.7% up to a maximum salary of $36,000. Hopkins pays $50 per month for medical insurance; the company withholds this amount and also contributes an equal amount.

Required: 1. Compute the net amount paid to Hopkins in November.
2. Compute the salary expense of Hopkins for the Seasons Company in November.

PROBLEMS

Part A

P10-1A   Purchases.   During 1983 the Keel Company purchased inventory at a cost of $50,000 on terms of 2/10, n/30; $5,000 of the purchases were returned during the discount period. The company paid for 60% of the net purchases within the discount period and the remainder was paid after the discount period had expired. The company also purchased inventory that cost $20,000 on terms of n/30; $3,000 of these purchases were returned. Payment of the remainder was made within 30 days. The Keel Company uses the gross method of accounting for cash discounts. The company uses the periodic inventory system.

Required: Prepare journal entries to record the above events.

P10-2A   Accrued Liabilities.   The following events occurred for the Brake Company during 1983:

(a) Recorded cash sales of Product X in the amount of $100,000. A sales tax of 6% was collected on these sales. Three-quarters of these taxes have been remitted to the state.
(b) Offered a 1-year warranty on Product X sales. It is expected that the cost of fulfilling the warranty on Product X sold in (a) will amount to 5% of the sales price. During 1983, $3,000 costs (all cash) were incurred to fulfill the terms of the warranty.
(c) A property tax bill of $12,000 was received and paid early in 1983 for the period July 1, 1982, to June 30, 1983. Of this amount $6,000 had been accrued at the end of 1982. It is expected that the bill to be received in 1984 will be for $15,000.

(d) An offer was made to sell a cooler chest for $1 to any customer who purchased a $20 electronic game before April 1, 1984. It was expected that half of the customers would respond to the offer, and 5,000 chests were purchased in 1983 for $3 each. During 1983, 3,000 chests have been sent to customers. During 1983 the company had total sales of the game of $200,000.

(e) On September 30 a building owned by the company was rented to another company for $300 per month. A year's rent was received in advance.

Required: Prepare journal entries to record all the above events. Where possible record the initial event separately from any adjusting entry required at year end.

P10-3A Notes Payable. During 1983 the Birch Company engaged in the following transactions:

Date	Transaction
Aug. 12	Purchased a warehouse for $40,000. Paid 20% down and gave a 10% note due February 8 for the balance.
Sept. 1	Gave a 12%, 90-day note to the Maple Company to extend an overdue account of $2,000.
Oct. 15	Borrowed $10,000 at 10% from the First State Bank. The interest will be paid when the note is repaid on April 13, 1984.
Nov. 1	Borrowed $5,000 for 120 days at 12% from the MetroBank. Issued a $5,200 note and the bank remitted $5,000 since interest was deducted by the bank when the note was signed.

Required:
1. Prepare journal entries to record the above events for 1983 and 1984, including the accrual of interest at December 31, 1983. Assume that all notes are paid on schedule. All interest rates are annual rates, and the company computes interest based on a 360-day year for the exact number of days.
2. Show how the notes would be disclosed on the December 31, 1983, balance sheet.

P10-4A Payroll Register. The Linden Company has three employees. The payroll information about them is as follows:

Name	Pay Rate per Hour	Medical Insurance per Week	Charitable Contributions per Week	Gross Pay Year to Date	Department
A. Snap	$10	$5	$2	$11,000	Sales
D. Crackle	12	3	3	12,000	Office
Z. Pop	8	5	1	4,000	Maintenance

During the first week of July 1983, each employee worked 40 hours except for Pop, who worked 42 hours. Overtime is paid at 150% of the regular rate. FICA taxes are assessed at 6.70%, FUTA taxes are 2.4%; 0.7% is paid to the federal government and 1.7% is paid to the state. For simplicity, assume that the federal income tax withholding is 15% of gross pay and the state income tax withholding is 2% of gross pay. The company contributes an equal amount for both the medical insurance costs and the charitable contributions paid by the employees as listed above.

Required:
1. Prepare a payroll register for the Linden Company for the first week of July.
2. Compute the total payroll expense for the Linden Company in the first week of July.
3. Prepare journal entries to record the salaries expense for the first week of July.

P10-5A Accrued Liabilities. The following events occurred for the Ryan Company during 1983 (the company uses a periodic inventory system):

(a) Purchased $600,000 of inventory on account on terms of n/30, of which two-thirds has been paid for.

(b) Cash sales of $1 million were made. Sales tax collected was 5%, of which half has been remitted to the state by the end of 1983.

(c) Included in the sales in item (b) were sales of 10,000 cameras. Coupons were attached to each camera offering a $10 rebate from the purchase price. The offer expires on March 31, 1984. The company expected that 90% of the purchasers would return the coupons for rebates. By the end of the year 3,000 rebates had been mailed to customers.

(d) Income taxes for the year were estimated to be $100,000. None of this amount has been paid yet.

(e) Dividends of $50,000 were declared. They will be paid in 1984.

Required: 1. Prepare journal entries to record the above events. Where possible record the initial entry separately from any adjusting entry required at year end.
2. What is the total amount of current liabilities at year end?

PROBLEMS

Part B

P10-1B   Purchases.   During 1983 the Mast Company purchased inventory at a cost of $40,000 on terms of 1/10, n/30; $2,000 of the purchases were returned within the discount period. The company paid for 80% of the net purchases within the discount period and the remainder was paid after the discount period had expired. The company also purchased inventory that cost $16,000 on terms of n/30; $1,000 of these purchases were returned. Payment of the remainder was made within 30 days. The Mast Company uses the net method of accounting for cash discounts. The company uses the periodic inventory system.

Required: Prepare journal entries to record the above events.

P10-2B   Accrued Liabilities.   The following events were recorded by the Poundloss Weight Control Company in 1983:

(a) Sold 5,000 take-home Poundloss kits to customers. The kits sold for $20 each and were subject to a 6% sales tax. All the sales tax collected has been remitted to the state.

(b) Offered a money-back guarantee that weight loss will be maintained for 6 months after a week's stay at a Poundloss residential program. It is expected that the cost of fulfilling the guarantee will amount to 10% of service revenues. During 1983, 5,000 people paid $1,000 each for a week at Poundloss, and $200,000 was paid to customers who did not maintain their weight loss.

(c) A property tax bill of $54,000 was received and paid in January for the period September 1, 1982, to August 31, 1983. One-third of the property taxes had been accrued at the end of 1982. It is expected that the bill to be received in 1984 will be for $60,000.

(d) An offer was made to sell a calorie calculator for $5 to any Poundloss residential program customer who lost at least 30 pounds during his or her stay and maintained the weight loss for 6 months. It was expected that 4,000 customers who attended the program during 1983 would respond to the offer. Therefore 4,000 calculators were purchased for $8 each; 2,500 calorie calculators have been sold to customers by the end of 1983.

(e) By December 31, 1983, 3,000 people had made reservations for the 1984 Poundloss season. A total of $200,000 had been received as deposits.

Required: Prepare journal entries to record all the above events. The company's accounting period ends on December 31. Where possible record the initial event separately from any adjusting entry required at year end.

P10-3B   Notes Payable.   During 1983 the Sycamore Company engaged in the following transactions:

Date	Transaction
Jan. 17	Purchased a tract of land for $70,000. Paid 10% down and gave an 8% note due October 14 for the balance.
July 6	Borrowed $50,000 at 10% from Second State Bank. Issued a $52,500 note and the bank remitted $50,000 since the interest was deducted when the note was signed. The note is due on January 2, 1984.
July 19	Borrowed $20,000 at 9% for 90 days from Outer Metro Bank. The interest will be paid at maturity.
Nov. 4	Gave a 6% note, due January 3, 1984, to the Waze Company to extend an overdue account of $7,000.

Required: 1. Prepare journal entries to record all the above events for 1983 and 1984, including the accrual of interest at year end. Assume that all the notes were paid on schedule. All interest rates are annual rates, and the company computes interest based on a 360-day year for the exact number of days.

2. Show how the notes would be disclosed on the December 31, 1983, balance sheet.

P10-4B   Payroll Register.   The Ash Company has three employees. The payroll information about them is as follows:

Name	Pay Rate per Hour	Medical Insurance per Week	Charitable Contributions per Week	Gross Pay Year to Date	Department
Jones	$13	$5.33	$2	$12,000	Sales
Smith	10	3.33	2	3,000	Maintenance
Zinski	15	4.00	1	5,000	Office

From June 2 through June 6 each employee worked 40 hours except for Jones, who worked 42. Overtime is paid at 200% of the regular rate. FICA taxes are assessed at 6.70%. FUTA taxes are 2.9%; 0.7% is paid to the federal government and 2.2% is paid to the state. For simplicity, assume that the federal income tax withholding rate is 15% of gross pay and that the state income tax withholding rate is 2% of gross pay. The company contributes half the amount of medical insurance costs listed and an amount equal to the charitable contributions paid by the employees as shown above.

Required: 1. Prepare a payroll register for the week of June 2 through June 6.
2. Compute the total payroll expense for the Ash Company during the week of June 2 through June 6.
3. Prepare journal entries to record the salaries expense for the week of June 2 through June 6.

P10-5B   Accrued Liabilities.   The following events occurred for the Eastman Company during 1983 (the company uses the periodic inventory system):

(a) Purchased $500,000 of inventory on account, of which one-fourth has been paid for.
(b) Cash sales of $900,000 were made. Sales tax collected was 9%; by the end of 1983, one-third had been remitted to the state.
(c) Included in the sales in item (b) were sales of 60,000 toasters. Coupons were attached to each toaster offering a $5 refund off the purchase price. The offer expires on June 30, 1984. The company expects that 25% of the purchasers will return the coupons for refunds. By the end of 1983 refunds have been paid to 12,000 customers.
(d) Income taxes for the year were estimated to be $40,000. None of this amount has been paid yet.
(e) Dividends of $50,000 were declared. They will be paid in 1984.

Required: 1. Prepare journal entries to record the above events. Where possible record the initial entry separately from any adjusting entry required at year end.

2. What is the total amount of the current liabilities at year end?

DISCUSSION CASE

C10-1 Payroll Costs. The Zanzibar Company has a significant increase in business around Christmas. In past years it has hired 10 extra employees for December, with each employee working 200 hours. As a result of using seasonal employees, the company pays the full 2.7% of the 3.4% FUTA tax to the state on these salaries as well as on the salaries of its 20 year-round employees. The company is confident that if it did not have this seasonal employment problem, it could achieve a merit rating and pay only 1.9% to the state for the FUTA tax. The company estimates that it costs $20 in interviewing and processing costs to hire each employee.

As an alternative for 1983 the Zanzibar Company is considering using employees provided by Temphelp, a company that specializes in providing temporary employees. Zanzibar would have to pay Temphelp $6 per hour per employee, but Temphelp would pay all social security and federal and state unemployment taxes.

Required: Using the rates provided in this chapter for 1983, what is the company wage rate at which it would make no difference to the Zanzibar Company if it hired its own employees or used Temphelp? Provide supporting calculations for your answer.

11 Property, Plant, and Equipment: Acquisition and Depreciation

After reading this chapter, you should understand:

- The characteristics of property, plant, and equipment
- How to compute the acquisition cost of property, plant, and equipment
- The concept of depreciation
- How to compute the amount of depreciation under the straight-line, sum-of-the-years'-digits, double-declining balance, and activity methods
- How to compute depreciation for fractional periods
- The accounting for expenditures incurred after the acquisition of property, plant, and equipment

The title Property and Equipment was used in a classified balance sheet to disclose the operational assets for a service or merchandising company in Chapter 5. The title of Property, Plant, and Equipment is more general because it also applies to manufacturing companies that own plant facilities for manufacturing.

Property, plant, and equipment is a very important component of a company's operating activities. In physical terms, they include assets that are necessary for a merchandising company to conduct its business, such as land, stores, warehouses, and delivery vehicles. A manufacturing company has similar assets, including factories, machinery, and equipment, that are generally accounted for in a way similar to a merchandising company. The special accounting aspects of these manufacturing companies are discussed in Chapter 21. In financial terms, property, plant, and equipment are usually a major portion of the total assets of a company, and therefore an understanding of the accounting principles used is essential to an understanding of financial statements.

**CHARACTER-
ISTICS OF
PROPERTY,
PLANT, AND
EQUIPMENT**

Property, plant, and equipment are the long-term physical assets acquired for use in the operations of a company. These assets include such items as land, buildings, machinery, furniture, office equipment, and automobiles. An asset classified as property, plant, and equipment must have the following three characteristics:

1. *The asset must be used in the operating activities of the company.* To be included in property, plant, and equipment an asset does not have to be used continuously, and therefore machinery owned for standby purposes in case of breakdowns would be included. It is also possible that a particular asset may be categorized as property, plant, and equipment by one company and as inventory by another. For example, an automobile owned by a car dealer that is intended for resale is included in inventory. The same type of automobile used by an employee of a company would be a part of property, plant, and equipment. Land owned by a real estate company that is intended for resale is included in inventory, whereas similar land on which a company builds a warehouse is categorized as property, plant, and equipment.

2. *The asset must have a life of more than 1 year.* The asset represents a bundle of future services that will be received by the company over the life of the asset. To be included in property, plant, and equipment, the benefits must extend for more than 1 year, and therefore the asset is distinguished from other assets, such as supplies, that are expected to be consumed in the current year. For example, a truck may have an expected life of 100,000 miles and the company will receive the benefits from operating the truck over more than a year. In addition, a company owning a building can expect to receive benefits from that building for more than a year.

3. *The asset must be tangible in nature.* The asset must have a physical substance that can be seen and touched. Intangible assets, in contrast, which are discussed in Chapter 12, do not have a physical substance.

There are several accounting issues associated with property, plant, and equipment. In this chapter we are concerned with the initial cost of such assets, the treatment of subsequent expenditures on these assets, and the depreciation of the assets.

**ACQUISITION
COST OF
PROPERTY,
PLANT, AND
EQUIPMENT**

The acquisition cost of an asset includes all the expenditures that are necessary and reasonable to acquire the asset and prepare the asset for its intended use. For an asset included in property, plant, and equipment these costs include the invoice price, less any discounts available, plus freight, sales tax, installation, and testing costs. Installation and testing costs include the cost of salaries and materials directly associated with these activities. Thus these costs are included in the cost of the asset and not in salaries expense or cost of goods sold. The invoice price is used rather than the list price because it represents the actual cost paid for the asset. The list price may be only an advertised price that is used as a basis for negotiating the invoice price. Transportation costs are included in the cost of the asset if it is shipped FOB shipping point. If the asset is shipped FOB destination, the supplier pays the transportation costs and they are not included in the cost of the asset. Costs that are unnecessary and unreasonable such as damage during transportation are excluded from the cost of the asset and are recorded as an expense in the current period (unless reimbursed by the transportation company or the supplier). Sales discounts *should* be deducted from the acquisition cost, whether or not they are taken. If they are not taken, they are treated as an interest (or financing) expense because management decided to forego early payment. The added cost should not be included in the cost of the asset because it was not a necessary cost of the acquisition. To avoid unnecessary detail some companies, however, do not deduct from the acquisition cost discounts that are not taken. This inconsistency is similar to the inconsistency that arises when some companies use the gross method of recording cash discounts on purchases and other companies use the net method.

Types of Property, Plant, and Equipment

There are several types of property, plant, and equipment, including land, buildings, machinery and equipment, leased assets, and leasehold improvements. Each type is discussed below.

LAND.   The acquisition cost of land includes: (1) the purchase price, (2) the cost of closing the transaction and obtaining title, including real estate commissions, legal fees for examining the correct ownership of the property, and past-due taxes, (3) the costs of surveys, and (4) the costs of preparing the land for its particular use, such as clearing, grading, and razing old buildings (net of the proceeds for any salvaged items), when such improvements have an indefinite life. The costs of improvements with a limited economic life, such as landscaping, streets, sidewalks, and sewers, should be recorded (debited) to a Land Improvements account and depreciated over their economic lives (as discussed later in the chapter).

BUILDINGS.   The acquisition cost of buildings includes: (1) the contract price, (2) the costs of excavation for the specific building (if not included in the contract price), (3) architectural costs and the cost of building permits, and (4) legal fees associated with the acquisition. If a used building is purchased, the costs of remodeling and reconditioning necessary to prepare the building for its intended use are included in the acquisition cost.

MACHINERY AND EQUIPMENT.   The acquisition cost of machinery and equipment includes: (1) the purchase price, and (2) installation and testing costs that are necessary to prepare the machinery and equipment for its intended use.

LEASED ASSETS.   Many companies lease property, plant, and equipment rather than purchasing these assets. Although these leases do not transfer legal ownership of the asset, they do enable the company to obtain the use of the asset for an extended period of time. Consequently, many leases result in the recording of an asset that is included in property, plant, and equipment on the balance sheet. Leases are discussed in Chapter 17.

LEASEHOLD IMPROVEMENTS.   When leased assets are improved by the lessee, the expenditures should be recorded as an asset in a separate Leasehold Improvements account and expensed over the life of the lease or the life of the improvements, if it is shorter. This is necessary because the company no longer has the use of the leasehold improvements after the end of the life of the lease, and therefore it does not receive any more benefits.

Illustration of Accounting for Acquisition Cost

To illustrate the journal entries necessary to record the acquisition of an asset, suppose that the Gentry Company purchases a machine with an invoice price of $10,000 on terms of 2/10, n/30. It incurs transportation costs of $1,500 and installation and testing costs of $1,000. The discount of $200 (2% × $10,000) is deducted and the net invoice price is $9,800 ($10,000 − $200). Remember that the discount should be deducted whether or not it is taken. In this example it is assumed that the discount is taken, and therefore the cash payment is $9,800. Sales tax is 5% of the invoice price, or $500 (5% × $10,000). During the transportation of the machine uninsured damages of $100 were incurred in an accident, and they were paid by the company. The following summary journal entry would be made to record these items:

Machine	12,800	
Repair Expense	100	
Cash		12,900

To record acquisition of machine and damages incurred.

The cost of the machine is calculated as follows:

Invoice price	$10,000
Sales tax	500
Transportation	1,500
Installation and testing	1,000
Less: Cash discount	(200)
	$12,800

The transportation, sales tax, installation, and testing costs are included in the cost of the asset because they are necessary for the asset to be able to produce the benefits for which it was purchased. The cost of repairing the damages is excluded from the cost of the asset because it was not necessary to incur these costs to receive the benefits associated with the machine. If the discount of $200 had not been taken, the cash payment would have increased by $200 and interest expense of $200 would have been recorded (debited). As mentioned earlier, for convenience some companies would include the extra $200 in the cost of the asset.

Acquisition Cost in a Lump-Sum Purchase

Frequently, land and buildings are purchased in a single package. In this case it is necessary to separate the cost of the land from the cost of the buildings because the buildings have a limited economic life and are depreciated, whereas land is considered to have an indefinite life and is not depreciated. The cost of each component is determined by its relative fair market value, which may be implicit in the purchase contract or may have to be determined by an appraisal. For example, suppose that land and a building are purchased for $200,000 and an independent appraisal shows that the land would be worth $100,000 and the building $140,000 if they were acquired separately. The cost at which to record each asset is determined as follows:

	Appraisal Value	Relative Fair Market Value	×	Total Cost	=	Allocated Cost
Land	$100,000	$100,000 ÷ $240,000	×	$200,000	=	$ 83,333
Building	140,000	140,000 ÷ 240,000	×	200,000	=	116,667
	$240,000					$200,000

The journal entry to record the acquisition is:

Land	83,333	
Building	116,667	
Cash		200,000

To record the acquisition of land and building.

Note that the sum of the amounts recorded for the land and the building is $200,000, which is the total acquisition cost and *not* the total appraisal value of $240,000.

Acquisition by Self-Construction

Many companies construct assets for their own use. For example, utilities often construct their own generating plants over a period of several years or a manufacturing company may make a special purpose machine for its own use. Two special accounting issues arise in these situations.

INTEREST DURING CONSTRUCTION. During construction a company often borrows money to finance the costs incurred. The question arises whether these interest costs should be expensed as they are incurred or included in the cost of the asset. Accounting principles require that any interest costs actually incurred during the construction period should be included in the cost of the asset. Thus if a loan is negotiated specifically to finance the construction, the interest would be included in the cost of the asset. If a company does not acquire a special loan, but has debt outstanding, such as long-term notes payable, the average interest cost on the debt would be included in the cost of the asset. The reason for using outstanding debt if a special loan was not obtained is that companies often do not borrow for specific projects. Instead they plan their overall level of operations, and then they decide what amount of money needs to be borrowed to support that level of operations.

The average interest cost to be included in the asset cost for the construction period is calculated by multiplying the average interest rate by the average cost incurred for construction during the period. For example, suppose that a company borrows money at 10% to finance a construction project that is started at the beginning of the year. By the end of the year construction costs of $80,000 have been incurred. The interest included in the cost of the asset would be $4,000 [10% × ($0 construction costs at the beginning of the year + $80,000 construction costs at year end) ÷ 2]. This amount is included in the cost of the asset rather than being recorded as interest expense.

If the company has not borrowed any money it cannot impute an interest cost and include that amount in the cost of an asset. Therefore, other things being equal, if two companies build identical assets and one borrows money to finance the construction and the other has no liabilities on which it is paying interest, the cost of the assets will be different.

PROFIT ON SELF-CONSTRUCTION.   If a company builds an asset for less than it would have cost to purchase the same asset should it recognize a profit of the difference between the two costs? Accounting principles allow the recognition of profit only when sales are made and not for the acquisition of an asset. In addition, accounting is based on actions taken, not on what might have occurred. The savings obtained by building rather than purchasing the asset are *not* recognized as profit, but they will be reflected by a lower depreciation expense each year over the life of the asset, since depreciation is based on the lower recorded cost of the asset.

DEPRECIATION

As we have already discussed, assets included in property, plant, and equipment provide benefits to the company owning (or leasing) the items for more than one year. The *matching* principle, which was discussed in Chapter 3, requires that the costs of generating revenue be matched against the revenue in the accounting period when the revenue is earned. As we saw in Chapter 9, the cost of inventory (cost of goods sold) is matched against the sales revenue in each accounting period, and therefore the amount of the income provides a fair measurement of the success of the company. Similarly, the cost of using the property, plant, and equipment (except land) acquired by a company must be matched in each accounting period against the revenue that these assets help to produce. This cost is the depreciation expense. **The depreciation expense is the part of the cost of a long-term physical asset allocated as an expense to each accounting period in the asset's useful life.** For a merchandising company, the store, the warehouse, the checkout equipment, and delivery vehicles are all examples of items of property, plant, and equipment that are necessary for making sales, and therefore their acquisition cost should be matched against the sales revenue they help to produce over their productive lives. First we review a simple and commonly used method for computing depreciation expense, the straight-line method, which was introduced in Chapter 3, and then we discuss several principles that affect our understanding of depreciation. Finally, we explain the other methods of computing depreciation that are used in practice.

Straight-Line Depreciation

The straight-line depreciation method is a method of depreciating an asset in which the cost of an asset less its estimated residual value is allocated equally to each period of the asset's life. It is the simplest and most commonly used way of calculating the amount of depreciation expense. There are three factors involved in the calculation of the amount of depreciation: **(1) the cost of the asset; (2) the estimated service life of the asset, which is the life over which the asset is expected to be useful; and (3) the estimated residual value of the asset, which**

is the estimated proceeds from the sale or disposal of an asset at the end of its estimated service life. The cost of the asset is determined according to the principles discussed earlier. The service life and the residual value must be estimated when the asset is acquired. The factors affecting these estimates are discussed later, but it should be recognized that these estimates may be difficult to make in practice and they may involve some fairly arbitrary assumptions. The amount of the depreciation was first discussed in Chapter 5 and is computed as follows:

$$\text{Depreciation per Year} = \frac{\text{Cost} - \text{Estimated Residual Value}}{\text{Estimated Service Life}}$$

The numerator of this depreciation equation is known as the depreciable cost. **The depreciable cost is the cost less the estimated residual value.** It is the estimated total portion of the acquisition cost that will be allocated to depreciation expense over the service life.

For example, suppose that the Marbal Company buys a copying machine for $12,000 on January 1, 1983, and estimates that it will be sold for $1,000 (the residual value) after being used for 5 years (the service life). The depreciable cost of the copying machine to the company is the acquisition cost of $12,000 less the $1,000 it expects to obtain when the asset is sold after 5 years. This $11,000 is allocated equally to each year of the asset's life, or at the rate of $2,200 per year. The depreciation expense is computed as follows:

$$\text{Depreciation per year} = \frac{\$12,000 - \$1,000}{5 \text{ years}} = \$2,200$$

Each year the recording of the depreciation expense reduces the book value of the asset. **Accumulated depreciation is the total depreciation recorded on an asset to date. The book value of an asset is the cost of the asset less the accumulated depreciation.** A summary of the straight-line depreciation over the life of the asset is as follows:

STRAIGHT-LINE DEPRECIATION SCHEDULE

Year	Depreciation Expense	Accumulated Depreciation	Book Value at the End of the Year
1983	$2,200	$ 2,200	$9,800
1984	2,200	4,400	7,600
1985	2,200	6,600	5,400
1986	2,200	8,800	3,200
1987	2,200	11,000	1,000

Effects of Depreciation on the Financial Statements

The journal entry required to record the annual depreciation calculated above is as follows:

Depreciation Expense: Machine	2,200	
Accumulated Depreciation: Machine		2,200

To record depreciation for the year on the copying machine.

Recording depreciation has two effects on the financial statements. The cost that is matched against the revenues in a particular accounting period is included as an expense in the income statement. Therefore it is debited to the Depreciation Expense account. This expired cost also represents a reduction in the book value of the asset (acquisition cost − accumulated depreciation). Rather than reduce (credit) the asset account directly, the normal procedure is to increase (credit) a contra-asset account, Accumulated Depreciation (contra-asset accounts were first discussed in Chapter 4). Either procedure has the same effect of reducing the book value of the asset, but the use of the contra-asset account is preferable because it aids in preparing the financial statements, in which both the acquisition cost and the sum of the accumulated depreciation to date have to be disclosed in the balance sheet. For example, the Marbal Company would disclose the following information in its balance sheet for December 31, 1983:

Machinery, cost	$12,000
Less: Accumulated depreciation	2,200
	$ 9,800

Recording the cost and the accumulated depreciation in separate accounts makes the information more readily available.

Each year the Depreciation Expense account balance is closed to Income Summary, and the balance in the Accumulated Depreciation account grows until the asset is fully depreciated. Therefore at the end of the estimated service life, the book value of the asset is equal to its expected residual value. For example, in the straight-line depreciation situation the book value at the end of 1987 is $1,000, the same as the estimated residual value.

As a reminder, the debit to Depreciation Expense is included as an expense that is matched against sales revenue in the income statement, and the credit to Accumulated Depreciation reduces the book value of the asset in the balance sheet. Separate depreciation expense and accumulated depreciation accounts should be maintained for each class of asset. The differences that arise when assets used in manufacturing are depreciated are discussed in Chapter 21.

Causes of Depreciation

The service life of an asset, which is the period over which the asset is expected to provide benefits, may be limited by several factors, which can be divided into the categories of physical causes and functional causes.

PHYSICAL CAUSES. Physical causes include wear and tear due to operational *use*, deterioration and decay caused by the passage of *time*, and damage and destruction.

FUNCTIONAL CAUSES. Functional causes limit the life of the asset, even though the physical life is not exhausted. *Obsolescence* is a common occurrence in a technologically advanced economy when an asset is made obsolete by the introduction of new technology. *Inadequacy* occurs when an asset is no longer suitable for the company's operations even though it may still be physically sound.

The lives of most assets are not limited by a single factor operating alone. In most cases a primary cause can be identified, however. For example, the life of a delivery truck is primarily limited by physical causes, in which wear and tear, deterioration and decay, and damage and destruction may all be expected to contribute. In contrast, the useful life of a computer is likely to be limited by a functional cause, whether it be obsolescence resulting from the availability of newer more efficient computers, or inadequacy resulting from the needs of the company outgrowing the capacity of the computer.

The straight-line method of depreciation discussed earlier is appropriate when the usefulness of the asset is expected to be equal each period. If the benefits are equal each period, the total *remaining* benefits decline equally each period. This kind of depreciation occurs when physical deterioration and decay occur at a steady rate over the life of the asset, or when the usefulness is reduced by a functional cause. Then it is reasonable to record an equal amount of depreciation expense each period by using the straight-line method.

Service Life and Residual Value

The estimated service life of an asset is affected by the perceptions of the company's management of the various causes discussed above. This estimated service life also directly affects the estimate of the residual value. In some cases it may be management's intention to keep the asset until its physical life is exhausted. In this case the estimated residual value will be close to zero (or it may even be negative if disposal costs are significant and exceed the value of any salvaged material, such as for a nuclear power plant). Alternatively, management may dispose of the asset well before its physical life is exhausted, in which case the estimated residual value may be very large. For example, airlines usually sell their planes long before the end of their physical lives. The Internal Revenue Service publishes the estimated service lives of many assets for use in computing depreciation for income tax purposes, and these estimates are often used for convenience in the computation of depreciation expense for financial reporting.

Allocation of Cost Not Valuation

As we discussed earlier, the process of depreciation involves the matching of the acquisition cost of the asset as an expense against the revenue. It is *not* an attempt to provide an estimate of the value of the asset at any given time. As we saw with the straight-line method, the purpose of depreciation is to allocate the cost of an asset as an expense over its service life and in so doing reduce the book value of the asset to its estimated residual value (which is an estimate of the market value of the asset at the *end* of its life). Depreciating an asset, however, is *not* an attempt to estimate the market value of an asset *during* its life. Therefore it is only at the time of acquisition and at the end of the life of an asset (if the original estimate of the residual value is accurate) that the book value can be expected to equal the asset's market value. Certain supplemental disclosures of the current values of property, plant, and equipment are now required in annual reports. We will discuss these disclosures in Chapter 20.

Systematic and Rational Allocation of Costs

Since depreciation is not an attempt to measure the value of an asset, it is reasonable to ask, "What is the purpose?" Remember the discussion of matching expenses with revenues with which we introduced the subject of depreciation. The cost of the asset should be matched as an expense against the revenues (benefits) it helps to produce. Since it is usually impossible to measure precisely the benefits that a particular asset provides, the underlying principle is that costs should be matched in a "systematic and rational"[1] manner against revenues. The term *systematic* is used to indicate that the calculation should follow a formula and not be determined in an arbitrary manner. The straight-line method and the alternative methods discussed below are all considered systematic. The term *rational* is used to indicate that the amount of the depreciation should relate to the benefits that the asset produces in any period. Thus the straight-line method should be used when it may be reasonably assumed that the asset produces equal benefits each period. Then an equal cost each period is matched as an expense against an equal benefit (revenues) each period. A declining-charge method should be used when it is considered that the benefits generated by an asset decline in each succeeding period. **A declining-charge depreciation method is a method of depreciation in which the amount of depreciation declines in each succeeding period.**

It is sometimes suggested that the management of a company has a free hand in the selection of a depreciation method. The above discussion should have made it clear that the selection of a particular method is based on specific criteria that management should follow.

Declining-Charge Depreciation Methods

Two declining-charge depreciation methods, the double-declining balance and the sum-of-the-years'-digits methods, are often used. These methods are also known as *accelerated* methods because they accelerate the recognition of depreciation, or in other words recognize more depreciation expense early in the life of the asset than the straight-line method. This early recognition of a higher depreciation expense, however, is offset by recognizing less depreciation expense later in the life of the asset, and therefore the *total* depreciation expense recognized over the life of the asset is always the same (the total expense equals the depreciable cost, which is the cost less the estimated residual value). Each of these accelerated methods is discussed below.

DOUBLE-DECLINING BALANCE METHOD.   **The double-declining balance method is a declining-charge depreciation method in which the depreciation expense is computed by multiplying the book value of the asset at the beginning of the period by twice the straight-line rate.** Note that the method uses twice the *rate* that is used for the straight-line method (*not* twice the amount) and that the residual value is *not* considered in the calculation of the depreciation. The asset, however, should never be depreciated below the estimated residual value, which is discussed later. The depreciation expense on an asset in any year is computed as follows:

---

[1] *Accounting Terminology Bulletin No. 1* (New York: AICPA, 1953), par. 56.

Depreciation per Year $= 2 \times$ Straight-Line Rate $\times$ Book Value at the Beginning of the Year

$$= 2 \times \frac{1}{\text{Life}} \times \text{Book Value at the Beginning of the Year}$$

For example, consider the Marbal Company example introduced when straight-line depreciation was discussed. The copying machine was purchased at the beginning of 1983 and had the following characteristics:

Cost	$12,000
Estimated residual value	1,000
Estimated service life	5 years

Since the asset has a life of 5 years, the straight-line depreciation rate is 20% per year (one-fifth of the cost is depreciated each year). Therefore the double-declining balance depreciation rate is 40% per year, and the depreciation expense each year is calculated as follows:

DOUBLE-DECLINING BALANCE DEPRECIATION SCHEDULE

Year	Book Value at the Beginning of the Year	Depreciation Calculation	Depreciation Expense	Accumulated Depreciation	Book Value at the End of the Year
1983	$12,000	40% × $12,000	$4,800	$ 4,800	$7,200
1984	7,200	40% × 7,200	2,880	7,680	4,320
1985	4,320	40% × 4,320	1,728	9,408	2,592
1986	2,592	40% × 2,592	1,037	10,445	1,555
1987	1,555		555[a]	11,000	1,000

[a] 40% × $1,555 = $622, but depreciation expense is limited to $555. See discussion below.

Note that the calculation of the depreciation in the first year was based on the total acquisition cost of $12,000 and *not* on the acquisition cost less the estimated residual value. In 1987 a modification has to be made to the usual calculations because the asset should not be depreciated below its estimated residual value. Therefore in 1987 the depreciation expense should be only $555 (instead of 40% × $1,555, or $622), which reduces the book value to $1,000 at the end of the year so that it is equal to the estimated residual value.

The double-declining balance method is the most accelerated method of depreciation that is allowed under generally accepted accounting principles. Another declining balance method that is sometimes used is the 150% declining balance method. This method is applied in exactly the same way as the double-declining method, except that, as the name implies, the rate that is used is $1\frac{1}{2}$ times the straight-line method. If the Marbal Company used this method it would depreciate the book value of the copying machine at the rate of 30% per year ($1\frac{1}{2} \times 20\%$), and the depreciation expense in 1983 would be $3,600 (30% × $12,000).

SUM-OF-THE-YEARS'-DIGITS METHOD. **The sum-of-the-years'-digits depreciation method is a declining-charge depreciation method in which the depreciation is**

computed by multiplying the depreciable cost by a fraction that declines each year. The fraction each year is calculated as follows:

$$\text{Fraction} = \frac{\text{Number of Years Remaining in the Asset's Life at the Beginning of the Year}}{\text{Sum of the Years' Digits}}$$

The sum of the years' digits for an asset with a 5-year life is $5 + 4 + 3 + 2 + 1 = 15.$[2] The annual depreciation expense for the Marbal Company's copying machine with a depreciable cost of \$11,000 (\$12,000 − \$1,000) would be computed as follows:

SUM-OF-THE-YEARS'-DIGITS DEPRECIATION SCHEDULE

Year	Depreciation Calculation	Depreciation Expense	Book Value at the End of the Year
1983	$11,000 × 5/15	$3,667	$8,333
1984	11,000 × 4/15	2,933	5,400
1985	11,000 × 3/15	2,200	3,200
1986	11,000 × 2/15	1,467	1,733
1987	11,000 × 1/15	733	1,000

Note that the book value at the end of the last year of the asset's life equals \$1,000, which is the estimated residual value of the asset. This value results because the sum of the fractions used in the calculation of the depreciation total 15/15, and the amount being depreciated is the cost less the estimated residual value.

The effect of the straight-line and the two declining-charge depreciation methods on depreciation expense and book value for the Marbal Company's machine is illustrated by the diagrams on the following page.

The depreciation methods discussed so far — the straight-line, double-declining balance, and the sum-of-the-years'-digits methods — are all based on the life of the asset measured in years. It may be more reasonable, however, to measure the life of the asset in terms of its expected physical activity, and therefore to base the depreciation expense on that activity.

Activity Depreciation Methods

An activity depreciation method is a depreciation method in which the depreciation expense is based on the level of physical activity of the asset. The activity (or use) of an asset may be measured in terms of the number of units the asset is expected to produce, or perhaps the number of hours it is expected to operate. For example, the Marbal Company might estimate that its copying machine would be expected to produce 500,000 copies or operate for 10,000 hours during its useful

[2] The general formula to compute the sum of the years' digits is $n(n + 1) \div 2$. Thus for an asset with a 20-year life, the sum is $(20 \times 21) \div 2 = 210$.

life. The depreciation *rate* could be computed on the basis of the number of copies or the hours as follows:

$$\text{Depreciation Rate} = \frac{\text{Cost} - \text{Estimated Residual Value}}{\text{Total Lifetime Activity Level}}$$

$$= \frac{\$12,000 - \$1,000}{500,000 \text{ copies}} = \$0.022 \text{ per copy}$$

or

$$\text{Depreciation Rate} = \frac{\$12,000 - \$1,000}{10,000 \text{ hours}} = \$1.10 \text{ per hour}$$

When the depreciation is based on the activity level of the asset, it is sometimes referred to as the *units-of-production* method. The depreciation expense for the year is computed by multiplying the rate times the activity level for the year. For example, if the Marbal Company makes 110,000 copies and operates the machine

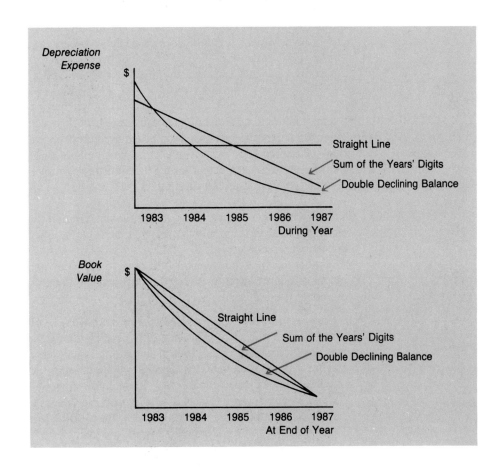

for 1,900 hours in 1983, the depreciation expense would be computed under the two alternatives, as follows:

$$
\begin{aligned}
\text{Depreciation Expense} \ &= \ \text{Rate per Copy} \ \times \ \text{Number of Copies} \\
&= \ \$0.022 \ \times \ 110{,}000 \text{ copies} \\
&= \ \$2{,}420
\end{aligned}
$$

or

$$
\begin{aligned}
\text{Depreciation Expense} \ &= \ \text{Rate per Hour} \ \times \ \text{Number of Hours} \\
&= \ \$1.10 \ \times \ 1{,}900 \text{ hours} \\
&= \ \$2{,}090
\end{aligned}
$$

Although in this example we illustrate depreciation based on both activity levels, it should be noted that the company has to select one measure of the activity level and use that measure consistently for its computation of depreciation. The effect of these activity methods on the financial statements should be compared to the straight-line method. The activity methods produce a constant depreciation rate per *unit* (hour or copy in this example), but the total depreciation expense will vary per *year* as the activity level varies. In contrast, the straight-line method produces a constant depreciation expense per *year,* but the amount will vary per *unit* as the activity level varies. It can be seen from this comparison that an activity method is more appropriate when the service life of the asset is limited by physical reasons (especially wear and tear) and the level of activity varies from period to period.

ADDITIONAL DEPRECIATION CONSIDERATIONS

Several additional considerations are discussed in this section. The calculation of depreciation expense when an asset is acquired or disposed of during a period, the effect of depreciation on income taxes, the relationship between depreciation, inflation, and replacement of an asset, and a revision of the estimate of residual value or service life are all discussed.

Depreciation and Fractional Periods

In the discussion of depreciation so far, we have implicitly assumed that the asset was acquired at the beginning of the year and therefore a full year's depreciation expense was recorded in the year of acquisition. Assets are usually purchased throughout the year, however, and rules have to be developed for determining the amount of depreciation to record for each period in such situations. Three of the commonly used alternatives are as follows:

1. *Compute depreciation expense to the nearest whole month.* An asset purchased on or before the 15th of the month is depreciated for the whole month, and an asset purchased after the 15th of the month is not depreciated in the month of acquisition. For example, if an asset is purchased on May 20, depreciation is recorded in the first year for June through December, or 7 months.
2. *Compute depreciation expense to the nearest whole year.* Record a full year's depreciation in the year of acquisition if the asset is acquired in the first half of the fiscal year and no depreciation in that year if the asset is acquired in the second half of the fiscal year. Record a full year's depreciation in the year of disposal if the asset is disposed of in the second half of the fiscal year and no

depreciation in that year if the asset is disposed of in the first half of the fiscal year.

3. *Record one-half year's depreciation expense on all assets purchased or sold during the year.* No matter when the asset is acquired or disposed of during the fiscal year, one-half year's depreciation is recorded in both the year of acquisition and the year of disposal.

To illustrate these three alternatives, suppose that a company with an accounting period ending on December 31 purchases a machine on September 28, 1983, for $6,000. The machine has an estimated life of 3 years and no estimated residual value. The asset is disposed of on September 20, 1986. Straight-line depreciation expense would be computed as follows:

Year	Compute Depreciation to the Nearest Whole Month	Compute Depreciation to the Nearest Whole Year	Record One-Half Year's Depreciation on All Assets Purchased or Sold During the Year
1983	$ 500[a]	$ 0[d]	$1,000[f]
1984	2,000[b]	2,000	2,000
1985	2,000	2,000	2,000
1986	1,500[c]	2,000[e]	1,000[f]

[a] $3/12 \times [(Cost - Residual) \div Life] = 3/12[(\$6,000 - \$0) \div 3]$.
[b] $(\$6,000 - \$0) \div 3$.
[c] $9/12 \times [(\$6,000 - \$0) \div 3]$.
[d] Asset acquired in the second half of the year; depreciation expense is zero.
[e] Asset sold in second half of the year; depreciation expense is for full year, or $2,000.
[f] Asset acquired or sold during the year; depreciation expense is $2,000 \times \frac{1}{2}$.

Depreciation and Income Taxes

Depreciation is an expense that is deducted in the income statement shown in a corporation's annual report, and it is also deducted by a corporation in reporting its taxable income under the provisions of the Internal Revenue Code. In many situations, however, the amounts of depreciation expense in any year for accounting and for income tax reporting are different (as discussed below). It should not be surprising that the amounts can be different because the objectives of financial accounting and the Internal Revenue Code are quite different. The objective of the generally accepted accounting principles used in the preparation of the income statement is to prepare statements that fairly present the income-producing activities of the company and are useful to decision makers. In contrast, the objectives of the Internal Revenue Code, among others, are to obtain revenue for the operation of the federal government and to provide certain kinds of investment incentives to business.

Management has a responsibility to minimize the taxes paid by the corporation without violating the law. Therefore it is desirable for a corporation to record, for income tax purposes, as much depreciation as possible early in the life of an asset. This method reduces the corporation's taxable income, and therefore the taxes that must be paid are also reduced. There are two ways in which the depreciation deducted for tax purposes may be greater than the depreciation deducted in the financial statements. First, as mentioned earlier, the Internal Revenue Code defines the life over which the asset may be depreciated for tax purposes, which is often shorter than the estimated service life that is appropriate for financial reporting. Second, the Internal Revenue Code allows the use of declining-charge methods, whereas the straight-line method is most commonly used in financial reporting. Thus management should require that the fastest possible method of depreciation be used by the corporation for computing taxable income. For example, many companies use the double-declining balance method for computing corporate income taxes and the straight-line method for computing the net income that is presented in the income statement.[3] If a company uses a different depreciation method for income tax purposes from the method it uses for financial reporting purposes, it is required to disclose the effects of the difference in the footnotes to the financial statements. For example, consider the Marbal Company machine discussed earlier in the chapter. Suppose that the company uses the straight-line method for computing depreciation for its income statement but uses the double-declining balance method for computing its taxable income. In 1983 the depreciation expense included on its income statement would be $2,200, whereas the depreciation expense included in the computation of its taxable income would be $4,800. Therefore the company's taxable income would be $2,600 ($4,800 − $2,200) less than its income reported in the income statement.

You should remember that the total depreciation expense over the life of the asset is the same for all depreciation methods. Therefore the income included in the income statement and the income for tax purposes will be the same over the life of the asset. The use of the accelerated method for tax calculations delays the payment of income taxes until later in the life of the asset.

Depreciation, Inflation, and the Replacement of an Asset

As we have seen, depreciation expense is based on the acquisition cost, estimated residual value, and estimated service life of the asset. The effect of depreciation upon the various elements of the financial statements of a corporation over the *total life* of the asset and the equations to determine the amount of each effect are as follows:

Effect on Elements of Financial Statements	Calculation of the Total Amount of the Effect over Life of Asset
Depreciation expense is increased.	Cost − Residual value
Income before income taxes is reduced.	Cost − Residual value
Income tax expense is reduced.	(Cost − Residual value) × Tax rate
Net income is reduced.	(Cost − Residual value) × (1 − Tax rate)
Owners' equity is reduced.	(Cost − Residual value) × (1 − Tax rate)
Noncurrent assets are reduced.	Cost − Residual value
Income taxes paid are reduced.	(Cost − Residual value) × Tax rate
Cash is greater (due to tax savings).	(Cost − Residual value) × Tax rate

[3] According to *Accounting Trends and Techniques* (New York: AICPA, 1981), 560 of the 600 surveyed companies used the straight-line method in 1980.

To illustrate the above relationships, consider the following example:

Asset cost: $60,000
Estimated service life: 5 years
Estimated residual value: $10,000
Income tax rate: 40%

Over the life of the asset the following would occur:

Depreciation expense is increased by $50,000 ($60,000 − $10,000).
Income before income taxes is reduced by $50,000.
Income tax expense is reduced by $20,000 ($50,000 × 40%).
Net income is reduced by $30,000 [$50,000 × (1 − 40%)].
Owners' equity is reduced by $30,000 [$50,000 × (1 − 40%)].
Noncurrent assets are reduced by $50,000 ($60,000 − $10,000).
Income taxes paid are reduced by $20,000 ($50,000 × 40%).
Cash is greater by $20,000 ($50,000 × 40%) due to tax savings.

It is sometimes suggested that recording depreciation ensures that sufficient cash will be available to replace the asset. The above example should make it clear that this is incorrect. The cash is greater than it *would have been* if no depreciation expense was recorded, because income taxes paid are reduced and therefore the cash held by the company is increased. It should be clearly recognized, however, that this does *not* mean that sufficient cash is available at the end of the life of the asset to replace it. First, the cash would have to be on hand for the replacement of the asset. The cash saved by the company in income taxes may have been used for other purposes. Second, the cash is much less than the cost of the asset. Third, the effects of inflation are likely to cause the cost of replacing the asset to be considerably higher than the cash saved in income taxes. It should be clear that planning for the replacement of an asset and also for financing the acquisition require explicit decisions by management.

The Revision of Estimates

As we have seen, the calculation of depreciation depends on making estimates of the service life and the residual value of an asset. Sometimes these estimates have to be revised because new knowledge is acquired or operating conditions change. When estimates are changed depreciation is computed on the basis of the revised amounts, and therefore the remaining undepreciated cost is depreciated over the remaining service life. For example, suppose that a building has the following characteristics at the time of acquisition:

Acquisition cost	$90,000
Date of purchase	January 1, 1981
Estimated residual value	$10,000
Estimated service life	40 years
Annual depreciation expense (straight line).	$2,000 [($90,000 − $10,000) ÷ 40]

At December 31, 1985, the accumulated depreciation and book value are:

Accumulated depreciation	$10,000 (5 × $2,000)
Book value	$80,000 ($90,000 − $10,000)

At the beginning of 1986 (after 5 years), the following revised estimates are made:

Estimated residual value $20,000
Estimated remaining service life . . . .   20 years (for a total life of 25 years)

The depreciation per year is computed, using the remaining book value and the revised estimates, as follows:

$$\text{Annual Depreciation Expense} = \frac{\text{Book Value} - \text{Estimated Residual Value}}{\text{Estimated Remaining Service Life}}$$

$$= \frac{\$80,000 - \$20,000}{20}$$

$$= \$3,000 \text{ per year}$$

This revised amount of depreciation expense would be recorded each year for the remainder of the asset's life.

SUBSEQUENT EXPENDITURES

After an asset has been acquired, further expenditures on the asset are often made during the life of the asset. These expenditures and their appropriate accounting treatment can be categorized as follows:

1. **Capital expenditures. Capital expenditures are expenditures that increase the benefits to be obtained from an asset and should be capitalized. Capitalization is the recording of the cost as an increase in the asset account.** An increase in assets may be accomplished by an increase (debit) in an asset account or a decrease (debit) in an accumulated depreciation account, as discussed below. If the expenditure increases the usefulness of the asset, it should be added (debited) to the asset account; and if it extends the life of the asset, it should be subtracted from (debited to) the accumulated depreciation account.
2. **Revenue expenditures. Revenue expenditures are expenditures that only maintain the benefits that were originally expected to be obtained from the asset and should be expensed.**

Capital Expenditures

Examples of capital expenditures are additions, improvements, replacements, and extraordinary repairs such as adding a new wing to a building, installing additional insulation, replacing the roof of a building so that the life of the building is longer than originally expected, or repairing a boiler in such an extensive way that its life is extended. All costs associated with these items, which are often called "renewals and betterments," should be capitalized.

Ideally, capital expenditures should be accounted for by removing from the accounts (in the manner discussed in the next chapter) the cost and accumulated depreciation that relate to the part of the old asset being replaced or improved. Then the expenditure would be added (debited) to the appropriate asset account. Since the cost and accumulated depreciation on the part of the asset being replaced or improved are often impossible to determine, however, the common practice is to add the cost to the asset account if the expenditure is being made to increase the usefulness of the asset. Alternatively, the cost is subtracted from the accumulated depreciation account if the expenditure is being made to extend the life of the asset. The effect of this latter entry is to *decrease* the Accumulated Depreciation account, thereby *increasing* the book value of the asset by the amount of the expenditure. For example, a capital expenditure of $20,000 to replace a roof on a warehouse, thereby extending the life of the warehouse, would be recorded as follows:

Accumulated Depreciation: Warehouse	20,000	
Cash		20,000

Replaced roof on the warehouse.

Alternatively, if an expenditure of $20,000 to enlarge a warehouse increases the usefulness of the warehouse, the cost would be added to the asset account as follows:

Warehouse	20,000	
Cash		20,000

Enlarged warehouse.

It should be noted that the net effect of both entries is to increase the book value of the asset by $20,000. One entry decreases the accumulated depreciation, and the other entry increases the balance in the asset account.

Revenue Expenditures

Expenditures that maintain the benefits that were originally expected from the asset should be expensed when incurred. These expenditures are known as revenue expenditures. The major item in this category is routine repair and maintenance costs. For example, if a company buys an automobile that it expects to use for 60,000 miles, it knows that it will have to perform repairs and maintenance during that time. Consequently, each routine repair merely maintains the ability of the car to last for 60,000 miles and does not extend its life beyond the 60,000 miles. To illustrate, if a company had a tuneup on one of its cars at a cost of $60, it would be recorded as follows:

Repair Expense	60	
Cash		60

Tuneup on car.

Some items that should be considered capital expenditures are often accounted for as revenue expenditures because the dollar amounts are so small as to be considered immaterial. For example, the company owning the car mentioned above might decide to buy a new engine for the car at 50,000 miles so that the car can be used for another 30,000 miles. This is a capital expenditure because it extends the life of the car beyond the original 60,000 miles, although it would typically be accounted for as a revenue expenditure (i.e., it is recorded as an expense).

DISCLOSURE IN THE FINANCIAL STATEMENTS

We have used the title Property, Plant, and Equipment in this chapter because it is the most frequently used caption in the balance sheet. Variations of this title are sometimes used, however, such as Plant and Machinery, Land and Buildings, or for a merchandising company, Property and Equipment. Companies are required to disclose the following items in the financial statements or in the footnotes accompanying these statements:

1. Depreciation expense for the period.
2. Balances of major classes of depreciable assets by nature (such as land, buildings, equipment) or function (such as petroleum exploration, chemical, construction) at the balance sheet date.
3. Accumulated depreciation, either by major classes of assets or in total, at the balance sheet date.
4. A general description of the method or methods used in computing depreciation with respect to major classes of depreciable assets.

For example, the Dr Pepper Company satisfies these disclosure requirements as shown in Exhibit 11-1.

EXHIBIT 11-1
Example of Disclosure

DR PEPPER COMPANY AND SUBSIDIARIES
Balance Sheets (Partial)
December 31, 1980 and 1979

Assets	1980	1979
Land held for investment, at cost	1,787,000	1,787,000
Property, plant and equipment — at cost:		
Land	5,747,000	4,594,000
Buildings and improvements	35,398,000	24,386,000
Machinery, equipment and furniture	65,927,000	55,820,000
	107,072,000	84,800,000
Less accumulated depreciation	34,122,000	27,620,000
Net property, plant and equipment	72,950,000	57,180,000

Consolidated Statements of Changes in Financial Position (Partial)
Years ended December 31, 1980 and 1979

	1980	1979
Depreciation of property, plant and equipment	8,987,000	8,141,000

Notes to Consolidated Financial Statements

Property, Plant, and Equipment. The Company and its subsidiaries provide for depreciation of property, plant and equipment on a straight-line basis over the estimated useful life of the asset.

Maintenance and repairs are charged to operations as incurred; renewals and betterments are capitalized and depreciated. The cost and accumulated depreciation of properties sold or disposed of are removed from the accounts. The resultant profit or loss on such transactions is credited or charged to earnings.

REVIEW PROBLEM

On January 1, 1983, the Matt Company purchased a machine for $70,000. The machine had an estimated service life of 6 years and an estimated salvage value of $7,000.

Required: Prepare a schedule to show the depreciation expense, the accumulated depreciation, and the book value at the end of the year for each of the following methods:

1. Straight line.
2. Sum of the years' digits.
3. Double declining balance.

SOLUTION TO REVIEW PROBLEM

1. *Straight line*

Year	Depreciation Expense	Accumulated Depreciation	Book Value at the End of the Year
1983	$10,500[a]	$10,500	$59,500
1984	10,500	21,000	49,000
1985	10,500	31,500	38,500
1986	10,500	42,000	28,000
1987	10,500	52,500	17,500
1988	10,500	63,000	7,000

[a] $$\frac{\$70,000 - \$7,000}{6}$$

2. *Sum of the years' digits*

The total of the sum of the years' digits for a life of 6 years

$$= 6 + 5 + 4 + 3 + 2 + 1$$
$$= 21$$

or $n(n + 1) \div 2 = 21$

Year	Depreciation Calculation	Depreciation Expense	Accumulated Depreciation	Book Value at the End of the Year
1983	$63,000 × 6/21	$18,000	$18,000	$52,000
1984	63,000 × 5/21	15,000	33,000	37,000
1985	63,000 × 4/21	12,000	45,000	25,000
1986	63,000 × 3/21	9,000	54,000	16,000
1987	63,000 × 2/21	6,000	60,000	10,000
1988	63,000 × 1/21	3,000	63,000	7,000

3. *Double declining balance (rounded to the nearest dollar)*

Straight line rate = $1/6 = 16\frac{2}{3}\%$

Double declining rate = $2 \times 16\frac{2}{3}\%$
$$= 33\frac{1}{3}\%$$

Year	Book Value at the Beginning of the Year	Depreciation Calculation	Depreciation Expense	Accumulated Depreciation	Book Value at the End of the Year
1983	$70,000	$33\frac{1}{3}\%$ × $70,000	$23,333	$23,333	$46,667
1984	46,667	$33\frac{1}{3}\%$ × $46,667	15,556	38,889	31,111
1985	31,111	$33\frac{1}{3}\%$ × $31,111	10,370	49,259	20,741
1986	20,741	$33\frac{1}{3}\%$ × $20,741	6,914	56,173	13,827
1987	13,827	$33\frac{1}{3}\%$ × $13,827	4,609	60,782	9,218
1988	9,218		2,218[a]	63,000	7,000

[a] The depreciation expense is $2,218 rather than $3,073 ($33\frac{1}{3}\%$ × $9,218) to reduce the book value to the expected residual value of $7,000.

GLOSSARY

Accumulated Depreciation. The total depreciation recorded on an asset to date.

Acquisition Cost. The total expenditures that are necessary and reasonable to acquire an asset and prepare it for its intended use.

Activity Depreciation Methods. Methods of depreciation that are based on the level of physical activity of the asset. The depreciation rate is determined by dividing the depreciable cost by the total lifetime activity level. The depreciation expense is computed by multiplying the depreciation rate times the activity level for the period. Examples are the units-of-production method based on the number of units the asset is expected to produce or the number of hours the asset is expected to operate.

Book Value. The cost of an asset less the accumulated depreciation to date.

Capital Expenditure. An expenditure that increases the benefits to be obtained from a productive asset and which is capitalized.

Capitalization. Recording a cost as an asset.

Declining-Charge Depreciation Methods. Methods of depreciation in which the amount of depreciation declines in each succeeding period. Examples are double-declining depreciation and sum-of-the-years'-digits depreciation. Also known as accelerated depreciation methods.

Depreciable Cost. The acquisition cost less the estimated residual value.

Depreciation Expense. The allocation of a portion of the depreciable cost of an asset as an expense to each accounting period in the asset's useful life.

Double-Declining Balance Depreciation. A declining-charge depreciation method in which the depreciation expense is computed by multiplying the book value of the asset at the beginning of the period by twice the straight-line rate.

Property, Plant, and Equipment. Long-term physical assets that are held for use in the operations of a company.

Residual Value. The estimated proceeds from the sale (disposal) of an asset at the end of its estimated service life.

Revenue Expenditure. An expenditure that maintains the benefits that were originally expected to be derived from a productive asset and which is expensed.

Service Life. The estimated life over which an asset will be useful.

Straight-Line Depreciation. A method of depreciating an asset in which the cost of an asset less its estimated residual value (the depreciable cost) is allocated equally to each period of the asset's life.

Sum-of-the-Years'-Digits Depreciation.   A declining-charge depreciation method in which the depreciation is computed by multiplying the depreciable cost by a fraction that declines each year. The numerator of the fraction is the number of years remaining in the life of the asset at the beginning of the year. The denominator of the fraction is the sum of the years' digits.

QUESTIONS   Q11-1   What are the characteristics that an asset must have to be included in property, plant, and equipment?

Q11-2   What items are normally included in the acquisition cost of land? Of a building?

Q11-3   If a company purchases an asset for $20,000 on terms of 2/10, n/30 and does not take advantage of the discount, what is the acquisition cost of the asset? How should the purchases discount lost be treated?

Q11-4   What criteria should a company use to choose a depreciation method?

Q11-5   Describe how the acquisition cost of each asset is calculated when a lump-sum purchase occurs. Why is it necessary to determine the cost of each asset?

Q11-6   Does the straight-line method produce a constant or variable depreciation amount per unit? Is your answer different for the units-of-production method?

Q11-7   May a company include interest in the cost of constructing an asset for its own use? How much may it include?

Q11-8   "Depreciation is an attempt to measure the value of an asset." Do you agree with this statement? Why or why not? Should depreciation on a building be recorded in a year when the market value of the building rises? Discuss.

Q11-9   Is the life of a truck more likely to be affected by physical or functional causes? The life of a computer? Explain.

Q11-10   If a company uses a declining-charge method of depreciation for a building rather than the straight-line method, what effect does that choice have on the financial statements in the year of acquisition?

Q11-11   What factors affect the amount of depreciation recorded on an asset?

Q11-12   If a company purchases an asset in the middle of the year and uses the straight-line method, what alternative approaches may be used to record the first year's depreciation?

Q11-13   What is the equation used for computing depreciation under (1) the straight-line method, (2) the sum-of-the-years'-digits method, and (3) the double-declining balance method?

Q11-14   Is the estimated residual value included in the calculation of sum-of-the-years'-digits depreciation? Double declining balance? Straight line?

Q11-15   What is a revenue expenditure? How does it differ from a capital expenditure? Give an example of each type of expenditure. Why might a capital expenditure not be capitalized?

Q11-16   For a corporation does the same depreciation method have to be used for financial
statements in its annual report and the calculation of federal income taxes? Why or why
not? If different methods are used, what must the corporation disclose in a footnote to the
financial statements?

Q11-17   "We will be able to buy the new machine that costs $80,000 because we have over
$100,000 of accumulated depreciation." Do you agree?

Q11-18   If a company changes its estimate of the residual value or service life of an asset, how
is the change accounted for?

Q11-19   What is the nature of the Accumulated Depreciation account? What is meant by the term
book value? How is the book value disclosed in the balance sheet?

EXERCISES

E11-1   Assets Included in Property, Plant, and Equipment.   The Young Company
owned the following assets at the end of its accounting period:

(a) Land on which a warehouse had been built.
(b) Land on which it is planning to build a new store two years from now.
(c) A retail store.
(d) Shelving in the store used for the display of products.
(e) Old cash registers that had been replaced by point-of-sale systems and will be sold next year.
(f) Goods held in a warehouse for later sale.

Required: Which of the assets should be considered as property, plant, or equipment? Explain
your reasoning.

E11-2   Acquisition Cost of an Asset.   The Hawkins Company acquired a new copying
machine. The machine had an invoice price of $5,000 and was purchased on terms of 2/10, n/30.
The bill was paid within 10 days. The sales tax rate is 6% on the invoice price. Delivery costs paid
by the Hawkins Company were $200. Modifications to the room in which the copier was installed
were $150, of which $30 was the result of damage caused by an accident. After a month of use, a
service representative repaired damage caused by an employee unfamiliar with the machine at a
cost of $50.

Required: What is the acquisition cost of the copying machine? Explain.

E11-3   Lump Sum Purchase.   The Gibson Company purchased a building and some
machinery on January 1, 1983, by paying $120,000 cash. The building was appraised for $90,000
and the machinery for $45,000. The estimated lives of the building and machinery were 20 years and
8 years, respectively, and the estimated residual values were zero. The straight-line depreciation
method is used.

Required: 1. Prepare the journal entry to record the acquisition of the building and machinery
on January 1, 1983.
2. Prepare the journal entry to record the depreciation expense for 1983.

E11-4   Lump Sum Purchase.   An acre of land and a building were acquired by the Evans
Company for $80,000 cash. The land and building were appraised for $30,000 and $70,000,
respectively.

Required: Prepare the journal entry to record the acquisition.

E11-5   Acquisition Cost of Assets.   The Jarrett Company purchased three machines. The
machines had list prices totaling $50,000, but the company was able to acquire them for $48,000
because it purchased all three of them at once. Machines A, B, and C had list prices of $25,000,

$20,000, and $5,000, respectively. Delivery costs of $1,000 were paid in cash. A discount of 1/10, n/30 was offered, but the company did not pay until 30 days after the receipt of the invoice.

Required: Prepare the journal entry to record the acquisition of the machines.

E11-6 Self-Construction of Assets. The Pepper Company decided to build its own warehouse over a 6-month period. The lowest bid by a construction company was $70,000. During construction the Pepper Company incurred related wage costs of $30,000 and material costs of $20,000. The company borrowed all construction funds from a bank at an annual rate of 10% and withdrew the money at an even rate over the construction period.

Required: At what cost should the warehouse be recorded?

E11-7 Capital and Revenue Expenditures. The following events occurred in a company during the year:

(a) Installed a solar energy collector in a warehouse.
(b) Installed a hydraulic lift door in a delivery truck.
(c) Put a new roof on a warehouse.
(d) Painted a new advertising logo on the fleet of the company trucks.
(e) Redecorated offices.
(f) Repaired a company automobile involved in an accident; the car was not covered by insurance.

Required: Classify the above items as capital or revenue expenditures. Explain your reasoning.

E11-8 Depreciation Methods. The Mingus Company purchased a delivery truck on January 1, 1983, for $15,000. The truck was expected to be used for 8,000 hours, be driven 100,000 miles, and be sold for $3,000 at the end of 1986. The truck was used for 1,800 hours and driven 20,000 miles in 1983.

Required: Compute the depreciation for 1983 under each of the following methods:
    1. Straight line.
    2. Units of production based on (a) hours and (b) miles driven.

E11-9 Depreciation Methods. The Jackson Company purchased a milling machine on January 1, 1983, for $30,000. The machine had an expected life of 10 years or 40,000 hours and a residual value of $2,000. During 1983 and 1984 the machine was used for 3,500 and 4,200 hours, respectively.

Required: Compute the depreciation for 1983 and 1984 under each of the following methods:
    1. Units of production: hours used.
    2. Straight line.
    3. Double declining balance.

E11-10 Depreciation Methods. The Tatum Company purchases a minicomputer on January 1, 1983, for $50,000. The computer was expected to be used for 4 years and have a residual value of $6,000.

Required: Prepare a depreciation schedule for the life of the asset under each of the following methods:
    1. Straight line.
    2. Double declining balance.
    3. Sum of the years' digits.

E11-11 Depreciation and Partial Periods. The Monk Company purchased a typewriter for $1,200 on March 31, 1983. The estimated life and residual value of the typewriter were 4 years and $200, respectively. The straight-line depreciation method is used. The company sells the typewriter on March 31, 1987.

Required: Compute the depreciation for each fiscal year over the life of the typewriter under each of the following conditions:
1. Depreciation is computed to the nearest month.
2. One-half year's depreciation is recorded in the year of acquisition and the year of disposal.
3. Depreciation is computed to the nearest whole year.

E11-12 Revision of Estimates.
The Peterson Company purchased a computer on January 1, 1982, for $30,000. The economic life and the residual value are estimated to be 10 years and $5,000, respectively. The straight-line depreciation method is used. In January 1983, because of advances in technology, the company adjusts its estimates to a 6-year total life and a residual value of $500.

Required: Compute the depreciation expense for 1983.

PROBLEMS

Part A

P11-1A Acquisition Cost of Assets.
The Goodman Company purchased land to build a new retail store. The following costs were incurred in regard to the land and building:

Land	$20,000
Legal fees to purchase land	1,000
Cost incurred to cut down trees cleared from land . .	700
Proceeds from sale of trees	100
Architect's fee for building	5,000
Payment to building contractor for construction.	60,000
Payment for landscaping	4,000
Paving parking lot	2,000

Required:
1. Indicate whether each of the above costs should be recorded in the land or building account.
2. Calculate the total cost to be recorded in the land and building accounts.
3. Prepare the journal entries to record each of the above costs if all the transactions were paid in cash.

P11-2A Lump Sum Purchase.
On January 1, 1983, the Morton Company purchased land, a warehouse, and a retail store for $150,000 cash. An appraisal shows that the land, warehouse, and retail store were valued at $40,000, $60,000 and $100,000, respectively. The estimated lives of the warehouse and retail store were 20 years and 15 years, respectively, and each had an estimated residual value of $5,000. The land was expected to be sold in 5 years for $50,000. The company uses straight-line depreciation.

Required:
1. Prepare the journal entry to record the acquisition.
2. Why is it necessary to record the separate components of the acquisition?
3. The president of the corporation wants to record the assets at $200,000. Why do you think the president wants to do this? Is this procedure acceptable?
4. Prepare the journal entries to record the depreciation expense for 1983.
5. Prepare the Property and Equipment section of the balance sheet on December 31, 1983.

P11-3A Capital and Revenue Expenditures.
The Jackson Company paid for the following items in cash during 1983:

(a) Rearrangement of the office layout, $1,000.
(b) Uninsured repairs to company truck after accident, $500.
(c) Routine service on company car, $100.

(d) Overhaul of machine to extend its life by 2 years, $5,000.
(e) Repainting the showroom, $800.
(f) Installation of facilities for handicapped employees, $1,200.

Required: Prepare journal entries to record the above events. Explain your reason for the method of recording each item.

P11-4A Depreciation Methods. The Desmond Company purchased a machine on January 1, 1983, for $50,000. The estimated life and residual value are 10 years and $10,000, respectively. It is expected that the machine will operate for 20,000 hours and produce 100,000 units.

During 1983 the machine was operated for 2,200 hours and produced 10,500 units. During 1984 there was a strike and the machine operated for only 1,600 hours and produced only 7,500 units.

Required: 1. Compute the depreciation expense for 1983 and 1984 under each of the following methods:
     (a) Activity level: units produced.
     (b) Activity level: hours used.
     (c) Straight line.
     (d) Sum of the years' digits.
     (e) Double declining balance.
  2. Show how the asset would be disclosed in the balance sheet at December 31, 1983, under each method.
  3. Should the strike affect the application of any of the above depreciation methods? Explain.

P11-5A Depreciation and Changes in Estimates. The Davis Company purchased a building at the beginning of 1978 for $60,000. It was estimated that the building would be used for 20 years, after which it would be sold for $20,000. Straight-line depreciation is used.

Required: 1. Compute the depreciation expense for 1982 and prepare the related journal entry.
  2. At the beginning of 1983 it was decided that the building would be used for another 25 years. Compute the depreciation expense for 1983 and prepare the related journal entry.
  3. Ignore the change in Requirement 2. At the beginning of 1983, because of the increase in real estate prices, it was expected that the building would be sold for $30,000 at the end of its life. Compute the depreciation expense for 1983. Show how the asset would be disclosed in the balance sheet at December 31, 1983.

P11-6A Comprehensive Problem. The Terry Company purchased a building for $160,000 on January 1, 1982. The building had an estimated service life and residual value of 20 years and $20,000, respectively. The company uses straight-line depreciation. On January 1, 1984, the company spent $10,000 to replace the roof and therefore estimated that the building would have a total economic life of 25 years.

Required: Prepare all the necessary journal entries for the Terry Company in 1982, 1983, and 1984.

P11-7A Comprehensive Problem. On August 1, 1982, the Ellington Company purchased two used machines, A and B, at an auction for $60,000. Machine A was newer and worth twice as much as Machine B. It also had an expected remaining life of 10 years compared to four years for B. The company decided to use the sum-of-the-years'-digits depreciation for Machine B and the straight-line method for Machine A with no residual value on either machine.

On October 10, 1982, maintenance was done on both machines. The costs were $800 and $300 for A and B, respectively. On February 1, 1985, the company spent $4,000 on a major overhaul of A and thereby extended its life by an extra 2 years. The company's accounting period ends on December 31, and it computes depreciation to the nearest whole year.

Required: Prepare journal entries for 1982 through the end of 1985.

PROBLEMS

Part B

P11-1B   Acquisition Cost of Assets. The Hughes Company purchased land to build a warehouse. The following costs were incurred in regard to the land and the building:

Land	$50,000
Legal fees to purchase land	1,000
Real estate commission on land	300
Cost to demolish old building	500
Salvage proceeds from old building	200
Architect's fee for building	10,000
Payment to building contractor for construction	80,000
Payment for landscaping	9,000
Paving parking lot	4,000

Required: 1. Indicate whether each of the above costs should be recorded in the land or building account.
2. Calculate the total cost to be recorded in the land and building accounts.
3. Prepare the journal entries to record each of the above costs if all the transactions were paid in cash.

P11-2B   Lump Sum Purchase. On January 1, 1983, the Stewart Company purchased three machines, A, B, and C, for $300,000 on terms of 2/10, n/30. An appraisal shows that they were worth $200,000, $160,000, and $40,000, respectively. Sales tax of $3,000 was added to the invoice. The company paid shipping charges of $20,000, and it paid for the machines 2 weeks after delivery. The estimated lives of machines A, B, and C were 10 years, 6 years, and 8 years, respectively. Each machine had a residual value of $1,000. The company uses straight-line depreciation.

Required: 1. Prepare the journal entries to record the acquisition.
2. Why is it necessary to record the separate components of the acquisition?
3. The president of the corporation wants to record the assets at $400,000. Why do you think the president wants to do this? Is this procedure acceptable?
4. Prepare the journal entries to record the depreciation expense for 1983.
5. Prepare the Property and Equipment section of the balance sheet on December 31, 1983.

P11-3B   Capital and Revenue Expenditures. The Brooks Company paid for the following items in cash during 1983:

(a) Installation of energy-efficient windows in office, $4,500.
(b) Overhaul of machine to extend its original life by 3 years, $1,000.
(c) Replacement of dead trees on landscaping around office building, $500.
(d) Repair of all office typewriters, $2,000.
(e) Installation of facilities for handicapped employees, $800.
(f) Replacement of tires on all company trucks, $5,600.

Required: Prepare journal entries to record the above events. Explain your reason for the method of recording each item.

P11-4B   Depreciation Methods. The Prentiss Company purchased a machine on January 1, 1983, for $14,000. The estimated life and residual value are 4 years and $2,000, respectively. The machine is expected to operate for 30,000 hours and produce 200,000 units. During 1983 the machine was operated for 6,500 hours and produced 50,000 units. During 1984 there was a strike and the machine operated for only 3,300 hours and produced only 24,000 units.

Required: 1. Compute the depreciation expense for 1983 and 1984 under each of the following methods:
    (a) Activity level: units produced.
    (b) Activity level: hours used.

(c) Straight line.

(d) Sum of the years' digits.

(e) Double declining balance.

2. Prepare the journal entries to record depreciation in 1983 and 1984 under each method.

3. Should the strike affect the application of any of the above depreciation methods? Explain.

P11-5B   Depreciation and Changes in Estimates.   The Bauer Company purchased an airplane at the beginning of 1980 for $200,000. It was estimated that the airplane would be used for 10 years, after which it would be sold for $50,000. The company uses straight-line depreciation.

Required: 1. Compute the depreciation expense for 1982 and prepare the related journal entry.

2. At the beginning of 1983 it was decided that the airplane would be used for only 2 more years. Compute the depreciation expense for 1983 and prepare the related journal entry.

3. Ignore the change in Requirement 2. Because of an increase in the demand for this type of airplane, it was decided at the beginning of 1983 that the plane's residual value would be $80,000 at the end of its life. Compute the depreciation expense for 1983. Show how the asset would be disclosed in the balance sheet at December 31, 1983.

P11-6B   Comprehensive Problem.   The Roland Company purchased a machine for $30,000 on January 1, 1980. The estimated service life and residual value were 10 years and $5,000, respectively. The company uses the sum-of-the-years'-digits depreciation method. On January 1, 1983, the company modifies the machine at a cost of $6,000 so that it can be used in a new production process.

Required: 1. What is the book value of the machine on January 1, 1983?

2. Prepare all the necessary journal entries for the Roland Company in 1983.

P11-7B   Depreciation, Income Taxes, and Cash Flow.   On January 1, 1983, the Peterson Corporation purchased a typewriter for $5,500. It had an expected life of 5 years, a $500 residual value, and straight-line depreciation was used. The income tax rate is 40%.

Required: 1. For each of the following, compute the amounts for 1983 and for the entire 5-year life of the asset:

(a) Depreciation expense.

(b) The effect of the depreciation expense on income before income taxes.

(c) The effect of the depreciation expense on income tax expense and income taxes paid.

(d) The effect of the depreciation expense on net income.

(e) The effect of the depreciation expense on property, plant, and equipment, owners' equity, and cash.

2. The president of the corporation said at a meeting: "We have to plan only to finance our expansion because depreciation takes care of paying for the replacement of the assets we currently own." Evaluate the president's statement.

**DISCUSSION
CASES**

C11-1   Choice of Depreciation Method.   Coltrane Corporation is a newly formed company and has purchased a building, office equipment, a machine to be used in production, and three company cars. The company is considering which depreciation method to select for each asset for financial reporting.

The president wants to report the highest possible net income and pay the lowest possible income taxes. He also argues that the building is unlikely to go down in value in the next five years, so there is no need to depreciate for that time. He wants to "save the depreciation" until later in the life of the building when the value will go down. The chief accountant agrees that it is possible to minimize the payment of income taxes, but argues that it is incorrect to select a depreciation method in order to maximize net income or to relate to the value of an asset.

Required: 1. Evaluate the correctness of each argument.
2. Which depreciation method is it likely that the chief accountant would suggest for each asset? Explain.

C11-2   Depreciation and Replacement of Assets.   Ten years ago, the Davis Corporation purchased some equipment for $100,000. The equipment has been depreciated on a straight-line basis and is now about to be replaced. The income tax rate has been 40%. The president is shocked to find out that the company does not have enough cash available to replace the equipment because the selling price has doubled. The president lends the company enough money to buy the new equipment, but says that "now we will record twice as much depreciation as before so that we don't have this problem again."

Required: 1. Considering only the above facts, by how much will the cash balance of the company have changed over the life of the equipment?
2. Can the company implement the president's proposed depreciation policy? Do you agree that it would be desirable?

C11-3   Effect of Depreciation on Financial Statements.   Charles Parker is considering purchasing either the Gordon Company or the Rollins Company. Both companies started business 5 years ago, and at that time each company purchased property, plant, and equipment for $110,000 that are being depreciated over 10 years with no residual value. The Gordon Company is using straight-line depreciation and the Rollins Company is using sum-of-the-years'-digits depreciation. The two companies have very similar products and reputations, and their total assets (other than property, plant, and equipment) and total liabilities on the balance sheet are also very similar.

Required: 1. Compute the book value of the property, plant, and equipment for each company at the end of 5 years.
2. Which company represents the more desirable purchase? Explain your reasoning. Ignore income taxes.

12 | Property, Plant, and Equipment: Disposals, Intangibles, and Natural Resources

After reading this chapter, you should understand:

- How to account for the disposal by sale or exchange of property, plant, and equipment
- The characteristics of intangible assets
- The nature of research and development costs
- Patents, trademarks and tradenames, franchises, organization costs, and goodwill
- The difference between cost depletion and percentage depletion

Continuing the discussion of the previous chapter, we are initially concerned here with accounting for the disposal of tangible assets included in property, plant, and equipment. Disposal may be in the form of a sale of an asset, or an exchange of one asset for another. The discussion then moves to intangible assets, which are another type of economic resource essential to the operation of many companies. Finally, the special accounting problems that arise with regard to natural resource assets are discussed.

DISPOSALS OF PROPERTY, PLANT, AND EQUIPMENT

The recording of the acquisition cost of an asset included in property, plant, and equipment and the depreciation of that asset over its useful life were discussed in the previous chapter. When the asset is disposed of at the end of its useful life to the company, the disposal must be properly recorded. Three alternative situations may arise: the asset may be sold for an amount equal to the book value; an amount greater or less than the book value, in which case a gain or loss is recognized; or exchanged for a similar asset, in which case a loss but no gain may be recognized.

All disposals have some characteristics in common. Depreciation for the fraction of the year up to the date of disposal should be recorded. In the following discussion it is assumed that the necessary depreciation entries, which were discussed in the previous chapter, have been made. At the time of the disposal, the balances in the asset account and its related accumulated depreciation account must be removed. This is accomplished by reducing (crediting) the Asset account by an amount equal to its recorded acquisition cost and reducing (debiting) the Accumulated Depreciation account by an amount equal to the current credit balance in the account. Both the Asset and the Accumulated Depreciation accounts will then have a zero balance because the entry at disposal exactly offsets the balance being carried in each account before disposal. These debit and credit entries may comprise all or part of the disposal journal entry. Disposals range from the very simple, where there is no cash involved and the book value is zero, to more complex transactions in which gains or losses on the disposal must be recognized.

Disposal of a Fully Depreciated Asset with No Cash Proceeds

In the simplest situation an asset that is fully depreciated to a zero residual value is discarded. That is, it is disposed of and no cash is received. For example, suppose that a machine that originally cost $10,000 and is fully depreciated to a zero residual value is discarded and no cash is received. The asset and the related accumulated depreciation are removed from the books by the following entry:

Accumulated Depreciation: Machine	10,000	
Machine		10,000
To record disposal of machine.		

Note that this entry has no effect on the total assets in the balance sheet. The entry simply reduces (credits) an asset account and reduces (debits) a contra-asset account for the same amount.

Sale at an Amount Equal to the Residual Value

Suppose that the machine in the previous example has an estimated residual value of $1,000, is fully depreciated to that amount, and is sold for $1,000 cash. Then the following entry is made to record the sale:

Cash	1,000	
Accumulated Depreciation: Machine	9,000	
Machine		10,000
To record sale of machine for $1,000.		

In this situation, an asset with a book value of $1,000 ($10,000 − $9,000) that is included in property, plant, and equipment is removed and another asset, cash, is debited for $1,000. Thus a noncurrent asset has been replaced by a current asset.

Sale Above Book Value (Gain)

In most practical situations, assets are not sold for an amount equal to the book value. Therefore suppose that the same machine as discussed above is sold for $1,500 instead of $1,000. The following entry is required to record the sale:

Cash	1,500	
Accumulated Depreciation: Machine	9,000	
Machine		10,000
Gain on Sale of Machine		500
To record sale of machine with a book value of $1,000 for $1,500.		

In this situation, a machine with a book value of $1,000 is sold for $1,500 and therefore a gain of $500 is recognized on the sale. The gain arises because the original estimate of the residual value, made at the time the asset was acquired, was incorrect. This is not surprising given the difficulty of making such estimates, but it does mean that the amount of depreciation recorded in previous years is technically incorrect. Changing the amount of depreciation recorded in the financial statements of previous years, however, might be very confusing to the users of the statements. Therefore the gain is considered to be an increase in income for the period of the sale. The total amount included in the income statements over the life of the asset by recording depreciation each period and the gain on the sale in the period of the sale is the difference between the acquisition cost and the actual disposal value. The gain is recorded by a credit to an account, Gain on Sale of Machine. When the financial statements are prepared, the gain is included in the income statement in the Other Revenues and Expenses section. It should *not* be included as sales revenue because it is not part of the sale of goods or services in the normal course of business.

Sale Below Book Value (Loss)

If the same machine were sold for $700, the company would incur a loss of $300 ($1,000 book value − $700 proceeds) on the sale, which would be recorded as follows:

Cash	700	
Accumulated Depreciation: Machine	9,000	
Loss on Sale of Machine	300	
Machine		10,000

To record the sale of machine with a book value of $1,000 for $700.

The loss would be included in the income statement as a negative component of Other Revenues and Expenses.

Sale Before the End of the Estimated Service Life

It was assumed in the above examples that the asset had been depreciated to its estimated residual value before disposal. A company may decide to sell an asset earlier than originally anticipated, however, and therefore before the asset has been fully depreciated. The principles underlying the recording of the disposal are not changed. The depreciation must be brought up to date using one of the fractional period methods discussed in the previous chapter. The reduction of both the Asset account (credit) and the Accumulated Depreciation account (debit) removes the balances in these accounts. The gain or loss on the sale is still the difference between the book value of the asset and the cash received. For example, suppose that a company sells a machine with the following characteristics:

Original cost	$20,000
Date of purchase	Jan. 1, 1978
Estimated life	10 years
Estimated residual value	Zero
Depreciation method	Straight line
Cash proceeds from sale	$10,000
Date of disposal	July 10, 1983

If the company computes depreciation to the nearest month it is necessary to record depreciation for 6 months in 1983. The amount of depreciation is $1,000 [($20,000 ÷ 10) × 6/12] and is recorded as follows:

```
1983
July 10    Depreciation Expense: Machine . . . . . . . . . . .    1,000
                Accumulated Depreciation: Machine  . . . . . .            1,000
           To record depreciation on the machine for 6 months
           in 1983 prior to sale.
```

Since the machine now has had 5½ years' depreciation (1978 through half of 1983) recorded on it, the Accumulated Depreciation account has a balance of $11,000 ($2,000 per year for the 5½ years) and the asset has a book value of $9,000 ($20,000 − $11,000). When the machine is sold for $10,000 a gain of $1,000 ($10,000 proceeds − $9,000 book value) is recorded as follows:

```
1983
July 10    Cash . . . . . . . . . . . . . . . . . . . . . . . . .   10,000
           Accumulated Depreciation: Machine  . . . . . . . .   11,000
                Machine  . . . . . . . . . . . . . . . . . . . . .            20,000
                Gain on Sale of Machine . . . . . . . . . . . .             1,000
           To record the sale of a machine with a book
           value of $9,000 for $10,000.
```

In addition, it should be noted that an entry to record the disposal is recorded only when an asset is sold, *not* when it is fully depreciated to its estimated residual value. An asset that is fully depreciated but is still being used is kept in the accounting records at a book value equal to the estimated residual value (the asset minus the accumulated depreciation equals the estimated residual value). This provides evidence of the continued existence of the asset and is necessary for the operation of the internal control function, which ensures that assets listed in the accounting records are in the physical control of the company, and for the reporting of property taxes.

If the disposal occurs because the asset has been stolen or destroyed by an accident or fire, the procedures are the same as those described above except that the gain or loss account would have an appropriate title, such as Loss Due to Fire, or Gain Due to Accident. Note that this latter title does not indicate that the company has "gained" from the accident, but only that the recovery value of the asset, the cash received from the insurance company, is greater than the book value. Although the insurance company pays the fair value of the used asset, the company may not have gained anything. The company will almost certainly have suffered an economic loss because of other incidental costs related to the accident, such as a disruption in normal activities. In addition, the company may have to replace the used asset with a new asset that is likely to require a greater cash outlay than the amount received from the insurance company.

Exchange of Property, Plant, and Equipment
When a company decides to dispose of an asset, it may choose to trade in the asset for a new asset. For example, a used delivery van is often exchanged for a new van. The trade-in allowance (assumed to be equal to the fair market value of the asset) is deducted from the cost of the new delivery van, and the balance owed is paid according to the terms of the agreement. **Boot is the cash paid in the exchange of assets.** Thus the company acquires a new asset by giving up an old asset and paying boot.

Productive assets are assets used in the production of goods and services.[1] **Dissimilar productive assets are assets that are not of the same general type, that do not perform the same function, or that are not employed in the same line of business.** When dissimilar productive assets are exchanged (e.g., trading in a delivery van toward the acquisition of a building), the exchange is considered as two separate transactions. The disposal of the old asset is recorded as discussed earlier in this chapter (with the proceeds being the fair market value of the old asset rather than the cash paid), and the acquisition of the new asset is recorded as discussed in the previous chapter (i.e., at the acquisition cost), although both the disposal and acquisition are recorded in one journal entry. For example, suppose that a delivery van is traded in for a building and the transaction has the following characteristics:

Original cost of van	$10,000
Accumulated depreciation to date	6,000
Cost of building	40,000
Cash paid	37,000

Since the van and cash of $37,000 are exchanged for the building, which costs $40,000, the van must be worth $3,000. The van has a book value of $4,000 (the cost of $10,000 less the accumulated depreciation of $6,000), and therefore there is a loss of $1,000 on the disposal of the van ($4,000 book value − $3,000 fair market value). The journal entry to record the exchange is:

Building	40,000	
Accumulated Depreciation: Delivery Van	6,000	
Loss on Disposal of Delivery Van	1,000	
Delivery Van		10,000
Cash		37,000
To record acquisition of building in exchange for delivery van and cash.		

Similar productive assets are assets of the same general type, that perform the same function, or that are employed in the same line of business. When similar productive assets are exchanged, special accounting practices are used. For example, the trade of player contracts by professional sports organizations or the trade of a used delivery truck for a new delivery truck would be considered exchanges of similar productive assets.

---

[1] "Accounting for Nonmonetary Transactions," *APB Opinion No. 29* (New York: AICPA, 1973), par. 3.

The special accounting procedure for an exchange of similar productive assets is that a gain on the trade-in of the old asset is *not* recognized. This is justified because the earning process on the old asset has not been completed. For example, suppose that a company buys a warehouse that has an expected life of 20 years. The expectation is that the company will get 20 years of benefits. Suppose that the company exchanges the warehouse for another warehouse after 5 years. Since the 20-year productive life of the original warehouse will be completed by the new warehouse, any "gain" on the trade is ignored.

To illustrate accounting for similar asset exchanges, suppose that the following facts relate to the exchange of two delivery trucks by a company:

Original cost of old truck	$20,000
Accumulated depreciation on old truck	4,500
Book value of old truck	15,500
Invoice price for new truck	22,000
Cash paid (boot)	4,000

Since the new delivery truck has an invoice price of $22,000 but only $4,000 is paid, the trade-in allowance on the old truck must be $18,000. Therefore the seller has an implied gain of $2,500 (trade-in of $18,000 − book value of $15,500) on the old truck, but this is ignored, and the new truck is recorded as follows:

$$\text{Book Value of New Asset} = \text{Book Value of Old Asset} + \text{Cash Paid}$$
$$= \$15,500 + \$4,000$$
$$= \$19,500$$

The journal entry to record the exchange is:

Truck (New)	19,500	
Accumulated Depreciation: Truck	4,500	
Truck (Old)		20,000
Cash		4,000

To record the exchange of an old truck for a new truck.

The effect of ignoring the gain at the time of the exchange is to reduce the cost of the new asset and therefore the amount of depreciation to be recorded over the life of the newly acquired asset. Thus the "gain" is spread out over the life of the new asset because the lower recorded cost results in lower depreciation expense and higher net income over that life.

Many accountants disagree with this procedure because they argue that the substance of the transaction (the gain) is ignored. If similar productive assets are exchanged in the future and no loss is ever incurred, a virtually permanent non-recognition of subsequent gains may be possible.

It must be emphasized that this special procedure applies only when there is an implicit gain on the exchange. A *loss* is recognized by the normal procedure discussed earlier. The recognition of a loss is justified by the conservatism principle, which was discussed in Chapter 7.

Federal Income Tax and the Exchange of Similar Productive Assets

For corporate income tax purposes, the Internal Revenue Code requires both a loss and a gain to be *ignored* when similar productive assets are exchanged and cash is *paid* by the company acquiring the new asset. (Special procedures, which are beyond the scope of this text, apply when cash is *received* by the company that has a gain. These special procedures also apply to financial reporting.) Thus there is a difference between financial and income tax reporting, because a loss is not recognized for income tax purposes, whereas, as we have seen, it is recognized for financial reporting purposes. This difference would be reported in the footnotes to the financial statements.

INTANGIBLE ASSETS

In addition to property, plant, and equipment, many companies have another category of noncurrent assets called intangible assets. **Intangible assets are noncurrent assets that do not have a physical substance.** Their value to the company results from the use of the legal rights associated with the intangible asset rather than from physical use. Examples of intangibles are patents, copyrights, trademarks and tradenames, franchises, organization costs, and goodwill. It should be noted that the recording of intangibles does not change the accounting principles discussed earlier in this book. For example, advertising costs are expensed in the period incurred and are not considered to be an intangible asset, because they convey no legal rights to the company even though long-lasting benefits may result from the expenditures on advertising.

Intangible assets are similar in many ways to the tangible assets, property, plant, and equipment; because (1) they are used in activities related to the production process and they are not held for investment; (2) they have an expected life of more than one year; (3) they derive their value from their ability to generate revenue for their owners; and (4) they should be expensed in the periods in which their benefits are received.

Intangible assets generally have five characteristics that distinguish them from tangible assets:

1. Intangible assets do not have a physical substance but more often, though not exclusively, result from legal rights.
2. There is generally a higher degree of uncertainty regarding the future benefits that can be expected to be derived from them.
3. Their value is subject to wider fluctuations because it may depend to a considerable extent on competitive conditions.
4. They may have value only to a particular company.
5. They may have expected lives that are very difficult to determine.

Before each kind of intangible asset is discussed, accounting for research and development is presented because it may affect the dollar amounts included as intangible assets.

Research and Development Costs

Many companies engage in research and development to improve their products. Expenditures on research and development by technologically oriented companies may represent a significant part of their total expenditures each period.

Research is a planned search or critical investigation aimed at discovery of new knowledge; development is the translation of research findings into a plan or design for a new product or process.[2] Costs incurred for research and development (R&D) are required to be *expensed as incurred,* and the amount must be disclosed directly in the financial statements or in the footnotes to these financial statements. The costs included in R&D are those for such items as materials, equipment, and facilities used in R&D projects, the salaries of R&D employees, and a reasonable allocation of general and administrative costs.

Each year companies spend large amounts of money on R&D because they expect to receive total future benefits that exceed the costs incurred. While total future benefits are expected to exceed the total costs incurred, not all R&D projects are successful. Some projects will be unsuccessful (costs exceed benefits), and others will be successful (benefits exceed costs) so that, overall, the benefits are expected to exceed the costs. If benefits are expected to exist for many periods in the future, it might be expected that the cost of acquiring these benefits would be recorded as an asset. The decision to require the expensing of all R&D costs was made to avoid the complexity of capitalizing (recording as an asset) any such costs expected to provide future benefits. For example, if accounting principles required the capitalization of R&D projects that were expected to be successful and the expensing of unsuccessful projects, many difficult problems would arise. How reliable would be such decisions on the expected success of projects? Who would make the decisions? How would the accountant verify the decisions? What is the expected life of the benefits? What is the pattern of the expected benefits? It was because of the difficulty of answering these kinds of questions that the FASB required the expensing of all R&D costs. This requirement has the advantage of generating uniformity among all companies even though it may not be the most conceptually sound alternative when future benefits are expected. The creation of uniformity may enhance comparability between companies and therefore help users of financial statements.

To illustrate the accounting for R&D suppose that a company incurs the following costs for R&D activities:

Materials used from inventory	$ 50,000
Wages and salaries	120,000
Allocation of general and administrative costs	20,000
Depreciation on building housing R&D activities	25,000

All these costs are included in R&D expenses, and therefore the journal entry is as follows:

---

[2] "Accounting for Research and Development Costs," *FASB Statement No. 2* (Stamford, Conn.: FASB, 1974), par. 8.

Research and Development Expenses	215,000	
Cash, Payables, etc.		140,000
Inventory		50,000
Accumulated Depreciation: Building		25,000

To record research and development costs.

Patents

A patent is an exclusive right granted by the federal government giving its owner the control of the manufacture, sale, or other use of an invention for 17 years. Patents cannot be renewed, but their effective life is often extended by obtaining new patents on modifications and improvements to the original invention. As a general rule the costs of obtaining a patent are capitalized; that is, they are recorded in an intangible asset account, entitled Patents. Since all the research and development costs associated with the internal development of an invention are expensed, however, the costs that are capitalized primarily consist of the costs of acquiring the patent, such as the costs of processing the patent application and any legal costs incurred. Alternatively, if a patent is purchased from another company, the entire acquisition cost is capitalized. If a company incurs a cost for the successful defense of a patent against infringement by another company, the cost is added (debited) to the Patent account. Of course, if the patent defense is unsuccessful, the costs would have to be expensed and the remaining balance in the Patent account would have to be removed (credited) and a loss recognized (debited) because the patent would no longer have value.

Copyrights

A copyright is an exclusive right granted by the federal government covering the right to publish, sell, or otherwise control literary or artistic products for the life of the author plus an additional 50 years. Copyrights cover such items as books, music, and films. As with patents, the costs of obtaining the copyright are capitalized in a Copyrights account. The cost of producing the item under copyright would be accounted for separately. For example, the costs of producing a film are accounted for separately from the copyright on the film and therefore are recorded as an asset entitled, say, Film Production. This asset would be depreciated over its revenue-producing life.

Trademarks and Tradenames

A trademark or tradename is registered with the U.S. Patent Office and establishes a right to exclusive use of a name, symbol, or other device used for product identification. Pepsi and Kleenex, for example, are tradenames. The right lasts for 20 years and is renewable indefinitely as long as the trademark or tradename is used continuously. Again, only the costs directly associated with obtaining the trademark or tradename are capitalized. The costs of promoting the name and producing the product are accounted for separately as advertising expense and inventory, respectively.

Franchises

Franchises are agreements entered into by two parties in which, for a fee, one party (the franchisor) gives the other party (the franchisee) rights to perform certain functions or sell certain products or services. In addition, the franchisor may agree to provide certain services to the franchisee. For example, many Mc-Donald's restaurants are locally owned and operated under a franchise agreement with the McDonald's Company. As with other intangibles, the cost incurred by the franchisee to acquire the franchise is capitalized as an intangible asset.

Organization Costs

Organization costs are the costs associated with the formation of a corporation. When a corporation is formed (incorporated) certain costs are incurred, such as legal fees, stock certificate costs, accounting fees, and fees associated with promoting the sale of the stock. These organization costs are also capitalized as an intangible asset entitled Organization Costs. While it may be argued that this asset has an expected life equal to the life of the company, Organization Costs must be amortized over a period not to exceed 40 years, as discussed below. In practice, however, most corporations amortize organization costs over 5 years, because this is the shortest time period allowed by the Internal Revenue Service for federal income tax purposes.

Amortization of Intangibles

Since the costs of the intangible assets discussed above are capitalized, they must be expensed over the expected useful life of the benefits they produce. **Amortization expense is the allocation of a portion of the acquisition cost of an intangible asset as an expense.** Therefore it is exactly the same concept as depreciation expense, with only a change in the title. Since it is unlikely that an intangible asset will have a residual value, none will be used in this chapter. Note that the cost of an intangible is amortized over its expected *useful* life and not necessarily over its legal life. For example, although a patent has a maximum legal life of 17 years, its expected economic life may be less than 17 years. The patent would be expensed over the lesser of the two periods, its actual economic life or its legal life of 17 years. As we have seen, some intangibles have very long lives, and in the case of trademarks and tradenames a potentially indefinite life. Because of the difficulty of determining the likelihood of benefits so far into the future, however, an arbitrary maximum economic life of 40 years has been imposed. *The general rule for amortization of intangibles, therefore, is that the expected life of the intangible is the lesser of the economic life or the legal life, up to a maximum of 40 years.* In addition, the *straight-line* amortization method should be used unless there is convincing evidence that an alternative method provides a better matching of revenues and expenses.

To illustrate, suppose that a company acquires a patent on a new type of production process at the beginning of the year for $10,000. The production process is expected to be useful for 10 years, after which newer technology will replace it. For this reason, the patent is amortized over the 10-year expected economic life rather than the 17-year legal life. The acquisition of the patent is recorded as follows:

Patent	10,000	
Cash		10,000

To record the acquisition of a patent.

At the end of the year, the amortization is recorded as follows:

Amortization Expense	1,000	
Patent (or Accumulated Amortization)		1,000

To record the first year's amortization on the patent.

Intangible assets are usually listed on the balance sheet in a separate section called Intangibles. This section is presented below Property, Plant, and Equipment. Intangible assets are valued at cost less the accumulated amortization. This book value is usually shown as a single net amount because disclosure of both the cost and the accumulated amortization is not required. That is why the credit entry can be made directly to the asset account as shown in the example above. An example of the disclosure of intangible assets is shown in Exhibit 12-1. It should be recognized that the market value of intangibles is often much greater than their book value disclosed on the balance sheet.

Although an intangible asset is amortized on the basis of its expected economic life at the time of acquisition, this life should be reviewed periodically to ensure that it is reasonable. For example, before the trucking industry was deregulated in 1980, many trucking companies included in their balance sheets an intangible asset relating to the franchises they owned allowing them to engage in interstate trucking. When the industry was deregulated these franchises became worthless, and therefore the asset had to be removed from the accounts and a loss recognized.

EXHIBIT 12-1
Example of
Intangible Asset
Disclosure

ESMARK, INC.
Balance Sheets (Partial)

	December 31, 1980	December 31, 1979
Patents and trademarks	64,660,000	68,968,000

Footnotes (in part):
    Intangible assets — patents and trademarks, primarily acquired in the purchase of Playtex and STP, are being amortized on the straight-line method over their expected useful lives but not in excess of forty years.

HUGHES TOOL COMPANY
Balance Sheets (Partial)

	December 31, 1980	December 31, 1979
Patents (less accumulated amortization		
1980, $3,542,000;		
1979 $2,536,000)	8,229,000	8,117,000

Footnotes (in part):
    Research and development expenditures are charged to operations as incurred. The cost of purchased patents is being amortized over the statutory lives of the patents on the straight-line method.
    Research and development expense was $18,729,000 in 1980 and $11,898,000 in 1979.

Goodwill   Goodwill is another intangible asset that might appear on the balance sheet. Goodwill is recorded when a company purchases another company or a significant portion of another company. Goodwill is often called "excess of cost over net assets of acquired companies." **Goodwill is the difference between the price paid to buy a company and the fair market value of the identifiable net assets (assets less liabilities) acquired.** The reason why a purchaser may be willing to pay more than the market value of the identifiable net assets is that there are some "assets" that are not recorded under generally accepted accounting principles, and therefore the purchaser can expect to obtain higher than normal earnings. For example, a company may have established a reputation for high-quality products and service on those products, or it may have recruited and trained employees who are above average. These characteristics make the company more valuable than the sum of the recorded net assets, and so the purchaser of the company should be willing to pay more than the fair market value of the net assets that are included on the balance sheet. The following accounting steps should be completed to determine the goodwill involved in the acquisition of another company:

1. Identify any assets and liabilities that are not included on the financial statements of the company being acquired, but which should be recorded (under generally accepted accounting principles).
2. Determine the fair market value of the assets and liabilities recorded on the financial statements of the company being acquired, as well as the fair market value of the assets and liabilities identified in Step 1.
3. Compute the value of goodwill as the difference between the purchase price of the company and the amount determined from Step 2.

For example, suppose that the balance sheet of the Windsor Company includes assets of $200,000 and liabilities of $75,000. Thus the book value of the recorded net assets (assets minus liabilities) is $125,000. Furthermore, assume that the fair market value of these net assets is $185,000 and that the company has unrecorded intangible assets with a fair market value of $25,000. If the Castle Company decides to purchase the Windsor Company for $240,000, the goodwill would be computed as follows:

Purchase price		$240,000
Book value of the recorded net assets	$125,000	
Excess of fair market value over book value of recorded net assets ($185,000 − $125,000)	60,000	
Fair market value of unrecorded identifiable intangible assets	25,000	
Value of identifiable net assets		210,000
Value of Goodwill Purchased		$ 30,000

The identifiable tangible and intangible net assets would be individually recorded at their respective fair market values totaling $210,000, and the purchased goodwill would be separately recorded as an intangible asset at its purchase price of $30,000.

It would then be amortized over its expected economic life (not to exceed 40 years). Amortization of goodwill is not an expense that can be deducted when computing corporate federal income taxes. The acquisition of one company by another is discussed further in Chapter 17.

NATURAL RESOURCE ASSETS

In addition to property, plant, and equipment and intangible assets, many companies have natural resource assets. **A natural resource asset is a productive asset that is physically consumed as it is converted into inventory.** Examples of natural resource assets are oil, coal, gravel, and timber. Natural resource assets are usually disclosed in a separate section of the balance sheet. They may appear above or below property, plant, and equipment, depending on the relative importance of the two categories of assets to the particular company. These assets are accounted for in the same manner as the other categories of productive assets. That is, their acquisition costs are capitalized and expensed over their expected economic lives. **Depletion expense is the allocation of a portion of the acquisition cost (less the estimated residual value) of a natural resource asset as an expense.** Thus we see that one concept has three different titles — depreciation for property, plant, and equipment, amortization for intangible assets, and depletion for natural resource assets. There are three special aspects of natural resource assets that require further consideration.

Method of Computing Depletion Expense

Depletion expense is computed using the units-of-production method discussed in Chapter 11. That is, the depletable cost (cost minus residual value) is expensed according to the estimate of the production to be obtained from the asset. This method is usually considered appropriate because it results in an equal depletion expense for every unit produced. For example, suppose that a coal mine is purchased for $100,000. The following journal entry is used to record the acquisition:

```
Coal Mine . . . . . . . . . . . . . . . . . . . . . . . . . . . . .    100,000
     Cash . . . . . . . . . . . . . . . . . . . . . . . . . . . . .               100,000
To record the purchase of a coal mine.
```

If the mine is expected to produce 10,000 tons of coal and the residual value is zero, the depletion per ton of coal mined would be computed as follows:

$$\text{Depletion per Unit} = \frac{\text{Cost} - \text{Residual Value}}{\text{Units of Production}}$$

$$= \frac{\$100,000 - \$0}{10,000 \text{ tons}}$$

$$= \$10 \text{ per ton}$$

If the company produces and sells 1,200 tons in the first year, the following journal entry would be made:

Depletion Expense ($10 × 1,200)   12,000
    Coal Mine (or Accumulated Depletion)   12,000
To record depletion of the first year's production.

Note that the credit is usually made directly to the asset account, Coal Mine, because separate disclosure in the financial statements of the accumulated depletion is not required. When a company produces more than it sells during a period, part of the depletion cost would be included in the ending inventory, thereby reducing the amount of depletion expense in the income statement for the period. To illustrate, suppose that in the example above only 1,000 tons of coal were sold, with 200 tons remaining in inventory. The expense would be $10,000 ($10 × 1,000), and the inventory would include depletion cost of $2,000 ($10 × 200).

Often a company purchases or builds tangible assets that have a life that is dependent on the life of the natural resource asset. Such assets should be depreciated over the life of the natural resource. For example, if a company builds housing that has a life of 20 years at a mine that has a life of 10 years, the housing should be depreciated over the expected life of the mine, or 10 years, because the housing will have no use after the mine is exhausted. The depreciation expense on the housing may also be calculated by using the units-of-production method since the usefulness of the housing expires as the coal is mined rather than through the passage of time. As with depletion, if a company produces more than it sells, part of the depreciation cost would be included in inventory.

Revised Estimates of Productive Capacity

Because it is often difficult to measure the expected lifetime productive capacity of a natural resource asset, revisions in the estimates are frequently required. Continuing the above example, suppose that at the beginning of the second year the company discovers that by spending an additional $14,600 it can increase the capacity of the mine by 2,000 tons. Assuming this additional cost is incurred, the new depletion rate is computed as follows:

$$\text{Depletion per Unit} = \frac{\text{Book Value} + \text{Additional Costs} - \text{Residual Value}}{\text{Remaining Units of Production (including additional units)}}$$

$$= \frac{(\$100,000 - \$12,000) + \$14,600 - \$0}{(10,000 - 1,200) + 2,000 \text{ tons}}$$

$$= \frac{\$102,600}{10,800 \text{ tons}}$$

$$= \$9.50 \text{ per ton}$$

If the company produces and sells 1,300 tons in the second year, the depletion expense will be $12,350 ($9.50 × 1,300). Again, if the company does not sell all the coal it produces, part of the annual depletion will be included in the cost of the ending inventory.

Cost Depletion and Percentage Depletion

For financial statement purposes, depletion expense is based on the initial cost of the asset, and over the life of the asset the total depletion expense is limited to the acquisition cost less the expected residual value. It is known as *cost* depletion and is related to the expected pattern of benefits produced by the asset. This is the method discussed above.

For corporate federal income tax purposes, depletion expense involves a different concept. **Percentage (or statutory) depletion is computed by multiplying a corporation's "gross income" from a natural resources asset by a statutory percentage.** Gross income is essentially the selling price of the natural resource; the statutory percentage varies, depending on the type of natural resource, from a minimum of 5% to a maximum of 15% (complexities in the computation of the percentage depletion expense are beyond the scope of this book). Since the percentage depletion expense is based only on the stated percentage and gross income, the total percentage depletion expense over the life of the asset for federal income tax purposes is *not* limited by the depreciable cost of the asset.

The special income tax laws for depletion are intended to encourage exploration and development of natural resources, whereas depletion expense for financial statement purposes is intended to match the costs against the benefits derived from the asset. There has been much discussion about whether or not percentage depletion encourages exploration and development, with the natural resource companies supporting the method and many consumer groups objecting to it. Although there does not appear to be any definitive evidence of its success, the percentage depletion method is still allowed for income tax purposes. Therefore most corporations compute a different amount of depletion expense for income tax purposes than for financial statements. The difference between cost depletion and percentage depletion is required to be disclosed in the footnotes to the financial statements.

REVIEW PROBLEM

Note: This review problem includes material from Chapters 11 and 12.

On December 31, 1982, the Vail Company owned the following assets:

Asset	Date of Purchase	Cost	Accumulated Depreciation	Life in Years	Residual Value	Depreciation Method
Building	1/1/1980	$50,000	$ 3,750	40	$ 0	Straight line
Office machinery	1/1/1980	20,000	9,760	10	2,000	Double declining balance
Office fixtures	1/1/1980	30,000	20,000	5	5,000	Sum of the years' digits

The company computes depreciation and amortization expense to the *nearest whole year* (explained in Chapter 11). During 1983, the following events occurred:

Date	Transaction
Jan. 2	Extended the building at a cost of $10,000. As a result, the total useful life of the building is extended to 50 years. (Debit the Building account.)

Mar. 6   Sold a piece of office machinery that had originally cost $4,000 and that had accumulated depreciation of $1,952 on December 31, 1982. The machine was sold for $3,000.

Apr. 28   The company obtained a patent on an invention by paying $2,000. It was expected that the patent would provide protection against competition for 10 years.

May 15   Purchased office fixtures and office machinery for $9,200. The supplier reduced the price because of the joint purchase. If purchased separately, the office fixtures would have cost $6,000 and the office machinery $4,000. Delivery charges paid by Vail were $200. The machinery was accidentally damaged during installation and cost $120 to repair. The office fixtures have an estimated life of 5 years and a residual value of $250. The office machinery has an estimated life of 10 years and a residual value of $500.

Aug. 10   The president's desk (classified as office fixtures) was exchanged for another desk. The desk had cost $600 and had accumulated depreciation on December 31, 1982, of $400 and an estimated residual value of $100. The new desk had a list price of $900 and $700 cash was paid.

Oct. 20   A manufacturer's representative serviced and adjusted the office machinery at a cost of $75.

Required:
1. Check the accuracy of the accumulated depreciation balances at December 31, 1982.
2. Prepare journal entries to record the above events in 1983 as well as the year-end recording of depreciation expense.
3. Prepare an accumulated depreciation account for each category of assets, enter the beginning balance, post the journal entries from Requirement 2, and compute the ending balance.

SOLUTION TO REVIEW PROBLEM

Requirement 1:

Each category of assets has been depreciated from January 1, 1980, to December 31, 1982, a total of 3 years.

Building:

$$\text{Annual Depreciation Expense} = \frac{\text{Cost} - \text{Estimated Residual Value}}{\text{Estimated Service Life}}$$

$$= \frac{\$50,000 - \$0}{40}$$

$$= \$1,250 \text{ per year}$$

$$\text{Accumulated Depreciation at December 31, 1982} = 3 \times \$1,250$$

$$= \underline{\underline{\$3,750}}$$

Office Machinery:

$$\text{Double-Declining Rate} = 2 \times \text{Straight-Line Rate}$$
$$= 2 \times 1/10$$
$$= 20\%$$

$$\text{Depreciation Expense, 1980} = \text{Double-Declining Rate} \times \text{Book Value at the Beginning of the Year}$$
$$= 20\% \times \$20{,}000^a$$
$$= \$4{,}000$$

$$\text{Depreciation Expense, 1981} = 20\% \times (\$20{,}000 - \$4{,}000)$$
$$= \$3{,}200$$

$$\text{Depreciation Expense, 1982} = 20\% \times (\$20{,}000 - \$7{,}200)$$
$$= \$2{,}560$$

$$\text{Accumulated Depreciation at December 31, 1982} = \$4{,}000 + \$3{,}200 + \$2{,}560$$
$$= \$9{,}760$$

[a] Estimated residual value is disregarded in computing double-declining balance depreciation.

Office Fixtures:

$$\text{Sum of the Years' Digits} = n(n + 1)/2$$
$$= (5 \times 6)/2$$
$$= 15$$

$$\text{Depreciation Expense, 1980} = 5/15 \times (\$30{,}000 - \$5{,}000) = \$\ 8{,}333$$
$$\text{Depreciation Expense, 1981} = 4/15 \times (\$30{,}000 - \$5{,}000) = \$\ 6{,}667$$
$$\text{Depreciation Expense, 1982} = 3/15 \times (\$30{,}000 - \$5{,}000) = \$\ 5{,}000$$

$$\text{Accumulated Depreciation at December 31, 1982} = \$20{,}000$$

Requirement 2:

1983

Jan.	2	Building	10,000	
		Cash (or other accounts)		10,000
		Extended the building. The new estimated total life is 50 years.		

Mar.	6	Cash	3,000	
		Accumulated Depreciation: Office Machinery[a] .	1,952	
		Office Machinery		4,000
		Gain on Disposal of Office Machinery		952
		Sold office machinery.		

[a] No depreciation expense is recorded because the asset is sold in the first half of the year. Accumulated depreciation is 20% ($4,000 cost ÷ $20,000 total office machinery) × $9,760 total accumulated depreciation (from requirement 1).

Apr. 28	Patent	2,000	
	Cash		2,000
	Purchased patent.		

May 15	Office Fixtures	5,640[a]	
	Office Machinery	3,760[a]	
	Repair Expense	120	
	Cash		9,520
	Purchased office fixtures and office machinery and incurred repair expense on damage during installation.		

[a] Total acquisition cost = Purchase price + delivery charges
= \$9,200 + \$200 = \$9,400
Cost of office fixtures = (\$6,000/\$10,000) × \$9,400 = \$5,640
Cost of office machinery = (\$4,000/\$10,000) × \$9,400 = \$3,760

Aug. 10	Depreciation Expense: Office Fixtures	67[a]	
	Accumulated Depreciation: Office Fixtures . .		67
	To record depreciation on the asset being exchanged.		

[a] The exchange of office fixtures occurred in the second half of the year, therefore, a full year's depreciation is recorded on the original asset. Depreciation expense on office fixtures purchased on 1/1/1980 = 2/15 (\$600 − \$100) = \$67 (rounded).

Aug. 10	Office Fixtures	833[a]	
	Accumulated Depreciation: Office Fixtures . . .	467[b]	
	Cash		700
	Office Fixtures		600
	Exchanged office fixtures and paid \$250.		

[a] Since boot is given, the new asset is recorded at the \$133 book value of the old asset (\$600 − \$467) plus the cash paid (\$700).
[b] \$400 accumulated depreciation (12/31/1982) + \$67.

Oct. 20	Repair Expense	75	
	Cash		75
	Service of office machinery.		

Dec. 31	Depreciation Expense: Building	1,197[a]	
	Depreciation Expense: Office Machinery	2,390[b]	
	Depreciation Expense: Office Fixtures	5,064[c]	
	Accumulated Depreciation: Building		1,197
	Accumulated Depreciation: Office Machinery .		2,390
	Accumulated Depreciation: Office Fixtures . .		5,064
	To record depreciation expense for the year.		

[a] $\dfrac{(\$50,000 - \$3,750) + \$10,000 - \$0}{47*} = \underline{\underline{\$1,197}}$ (rounded)

* Total life is extended to 50 years. Since the asset has been depreciated for 3 years, 47 years remain.

[b] The sale of office machinery on March 6 occurred in the first half of the year, and therefore no depreciation is recorded on that item.

Cost of remaining office machinery purchased on 1/1/1980 = \$20,000 − \$4,000 = \$16,000.

Accumulated depreciation on remaining office machinery = $9,760 − $1,952 = $7,808.

Depreciation expense on remaining office machinery purchased on 1/1/1980 = 20% ($16,000 − $7,808) = $1,638 (rounded).

The purchase of office machinery on May 15 occurred in the first half of the year, and therefore a full year's depreciation is recorded.

Depreciation expense on office machinery purchased on 5/15/1983 = 20% × $3,760 = $752.

Total depreciation expense = $1,638 + $752 = $2,390.

The purchase of office fixtures on May 15 occurred in the first half of the year, and therefore a full year's depreciation is recorded.

Depreciation expense = 5/15 × ($5,640 − $250) = $1,797 (rounded).

Depreciation on the office fixtures acquired by exchange is not recorded because the asset was acquired in the second half of the year, and depreciation on the asset disposed of was recorded on August 10.

Depreciation on the office fixtures acquired at 1/1/1980 is
2/15[($30,000 − $600) − ($5,000 − $100)] = $3,267 (rounded).

Total depreciation expense = $1,797 + $3,267 = $5,064.

Dec. 31	Amortization Expense	200
	Patent	200
	Amortization of patent (acquired in the first half of the year) over the estimated economic life of 10 years.	

Requirement 3:

Accumulated Depreciation: Building

		Bal. 12/31/82	3,750
		12/31/83	1,197
		Bal. 12/31/83	4,947

Accumulated Depreciation: Office Machinery

3/6/83	1,952	Bal. 12/31/82	9,760
		12/31/83	2,390
		Bal. 12/31/83	10,198

Accumulated Depreciation: Office Fixtures

8/10/83	467	Bal. 12/31/82	20,000
		8/10/83	67
		12/31/83	5,064
		Bal. 12/31/83	24,664

GLOSSARY

Amortization Expense. The allocation of a portion of the acquisition cost of an intangible asset as an expense.

Boot. Cash paid as part of an exchange of assets.

Copyright. An exclusive right granted by the federal government for publishing, selling, and controlling literary or artistic products for the life of the author plus an additional 50 years. The cost of acquiring the copyright is recorded as an asset.

Development. The translation of research findings into a plan or design for a new product or process. Development costs are expensed in the period incurred.

Depletion Expense. The allocation of a portion of the acquisition cost (less the estimated residual value) of a natural resource asset as an expense. Also called *cost* depletion.

Dissimilar Productive Assets. Productive assets that are not of the same general type, that do not perform the same function, or that are not employed in the same line of business.

Franchise. Agreement in which the franchisor assigns to the franchisee rights to perform certain functions or sell certain products or services. The cost of acquiring a franchise is recorded as an asset.

Gain (Loss) on Sale (Disposal) of an Asset. The amount by which the proceeds from the sale exceed (are less than) the depreciated cost (book value) of an asset.

Goodwill. An intangible asset representing the excess of the cost of acquiring a company over the fair market value of the identifiable net assets.

Intangible Assets. Noncurrent assets that do not have a physical substance. Their value results from the use of the legal rights associated with the intangible asset rather than from physical use.

Natural Resource Asset. A productive asset that is physically consumed as it is converted into inventory.

Organization Costs. Costs associated with the formation of a corporation. Capitalized as an asset.

Patent. An exclusive right granted by the federal government giving its owner the control of the manufacture, sale, or other use of an invention for 17 years. The cost of acquiring a patent is recorded as an asset.

Productive Assets. Assets used in the production of goods and services.

Percentage Depletion Expense. A method of computing depletion expense as a percentage of the gross income produced by a natural resource asset; it is used for corporate federal income tax purposes.

R&D Costs. An abbreviation for research and development costs.

Research. Planned search or critical investigation aimed at discovery of new knowledge. Research costs are expensed in the period incurred.

Similar Productive Assets. Productive assets that are of the same general type, that perform the same function, or that are employed in the same line of business.

Trademark and Tradename. A right to the exclusive use of a name, symbol, or other device that is used for product identification. The cost is recorded as an asset.

QUESTIONS

Q12-1 How is the gain or loss from the disposal of an asset determined when the asset is sold in the middle of the year?

Q12-2 Are gains and losses from disposals of assets reported in the income statement in the same way as depreciation expense? If not, how are they reported?

Q12-3 If a corporation traded in a machine on a new model and the trade-in value of the old machine is greater than its book value would the corporation recognize a gain? If the trade-in value is less than the book value would the corporation recognize a loss? Would your answer change for the corporation's federal income tax reports?

Q12-4 How is an exchange of dissimilar assets recorded?

Q12-5 When a gain is not recognized on the exchange of similar productive assets will the company's financial statements be affected in the long run because the company did not include a gain in the income statement?

Q12-6 An asset cost $50,000 and had an estimated residual value of $5,000. The accumulated depreciation account has a balance of $45,000. If the asset is still being used should depreciation be recorded on the asset? Should the asset and accumulated depreciation accounts be removed from the books?

Q12-7 What is meant by the terms research and development?

Q12-8 What characteristics distinguish intangible assets from tangible assets? What characteristics are similar?

Q12-9 Define the terms: (a) patent; (b) copyright; (c) franchise; (d) trademark; and (e) organization costs.

Q12-10 What is the correct life to use for the amortization of intangible assets?

Q12-11 Which amortization method should be used for intangible assets?

Q12-12 What is the maximum life over which the following intangible assets should be amortized: (a) patent; (b) copyright; (c) franchise; and (d) goodwill.

Q12-13 What is meant by the term goodwill? Describe two factors that might cause a purchaser to pay more than the fair market value of the net assets of a company.

Q12-14 Under what conditions is goodwill recorded?

Q12-15 What is a natural resource asset? How is it accounted for?

Q12-16 What are the similarities and differences between the terms depreciation, amortization, and depletion?

Q12-17 Describe how depletion expense is calculated under the cost depletion method. How does the calculation differ under percentage depletion?

EXERCISES

E12-1 **Disposal of an Asset.** The Brown Company owns a machine that had originally cost $20,000. The accumulated depreciation account now has a balance of $18,000.

Required: Prepare journal entries to record the disposal of the machine if it is sold for:
1. $2,000.
2. $1,000.
3. $3,000.

E12-2   Disposal of an Asset.
The Snowdon Company purchased a machine for $60,000 on January 1, 1980. It is being depreciated on a straight-line basis over 5 years to a zero residual value. On December 31, 1983, the machine is sold.

Required: Prepare journal entries to record the depreciation expense for 1983 and the disposal of the machine if it is sold for:
1. $12,000.
2. $9,000.
3. $14,000.

E12-3   Exchange of Similar Productive Assets.
The Whillans Company owns a machine that had an original cost of $40,000 and accumulated depreciation of $30,000. The company trades in the machine on a new model, which has an invoice price of $25,000 and pays cash of $12,000.

Required: 1. What is the acquisition cost of the new machine? Prepare the journal entry to record the acquisition.
2. If instead the company traded in the old machine and paid $17,000 in the exchange, what is the acquisition cost of the new machine? Prepare the journal entry to record the acquisition.

E12-4   Exchange of Dissimilar Assets.
The Scafell Company owns a machine that had an original cost of $60,000 and accumulated depreciation of $12,000. The company trades in the machine on a piece of land and pays $6,000. The machine has a fair market value of $46,000.

Required: 1. What is the acquisition cost of the land? Prepare the journal entry to record the exchange.
2. If the company paid $11,000 on the exchange what is the acquisition cost of the land? Prepare the journal entry to record the exchange.

E12-5   Exchange of Dissimilar Assets.
The Everst Company owns a delivery truck that had an original cost of $20,000 and accumulated depreciation of $12,000. The company trades in the truck on a machine that has a cost of $30,000.

Required: 1. Prepare the journal entry to record the transaction if the company pays $18,000 cash.
2. Prepare the journal entry to record the transaction if the company pays $25,000 cash.

E12-6   Intangible Assets.
The Noyce Company was involved in the following transactions:

(a) Purchased a patent from another company.
(b) Developed a design for a new type of machine for use in its production process.
(c) Purchased a franchise for exclusive regional sale of a product.
(d) Developed an advertising campaign for a new product.
(e) Purchased another company for more than the fair market value of its identifiable net assets.

Required: Explain whether each of the above items requires the company to record an intangible asset. If not, how would each item be recorded?

E12-7   Accounting for Intangible Assets.
The Langdale Company incurred the following costs:

(a) Purchased a patent from the Pike Company for $25,000.
(b) Developed a design for a new product at a cost of $80,000.
(c) Paid $90,000 to an actor to promote the company's new products.

Required: 1. Prepare the journal entries to record the above events assuming all payments are in cash.
2. For each item recorded as an asset, indicate the maximum life over which it may be amortized.

E12-8   Accounting for Intangible Assets. The Patey Company incurred the following costs:

(a) Legal costs associated with the formation of the company, $16,000.
(b) Purchased a Giantburger franchise for $50,000.
(c) Advertised the opening of their new restaurant at a cost of $10,000.

Required: 1. Prepare the journal entries to record the above events.
2. For each item recorded as an asset indicate the maximum life over which it may be amortized.

E12-9   Amortization of Intangible Assets. The Nevis Company held the following intangible assets:

(a) Organization costs, $6,000.
(b) A patent purchased for $34,000.
(c) A copyright purchased for $16,000.
(d) A trademark purchased for $30,000.
(e) A franchise purchased for $50,000.

The company amortizes the assets by using the straight-line method over the maximum allowable life.

Required: Prepare journal entries to record the amortization in the first year of each asset's life.

E12-10   Natural Resources. The Skiddaw Company purchased land for $10 million. The company expected to be able to mine 1 million tons of molybdenum from this land over the next 20 years, at which time the residual value would be zero. During the first 2 years of the mine's operation 30,000 tons were mined each year and sold for $80 per ton. The estimate of the total lifetime capacity of the mine was raised to 1.2 million tons at the beginning of the third year and the residual value was estimated to be $1 million. During the third year, 50,000 tons were mined and sold for $85 per ton.

Required: Compute the depletion expense for each of the 3 years and prepare the journal entry to record the depletion expense in each year.

E12-11   Natural Resources. The Bonnington Company purchased land for $1.2 million. The company expected to be able to mine 500,000 tons of coal from this land over the next 10 years, after which the land would be sold for $200,000. During the first year of the mine's operations 20,000 tons of coal were mined and sold for $50 per ton. The estimate of the total lifetime capacity of the mine was raised to 600,000 tons at the beginning of the second year, and 40,000 tons were mined and sold for $60 per ton during the year.

Required: Compute the depletion expense for the first and second years and prepare the journal entry to record the depletion expense in each year.

E12-12   Cost and Percentage Depletion. In a given year a mine owned by the Eskdale Corporation that had a cost of $800,000 and had an expected residual value of $160,000 produced 40,000 tons of ore out of its lifetime expected capacity of 320,000 tons. The ore was sold for $26 per ton. The percentage depletion rate is 15%.

Required: 1. Compute the cost depletion expense and the percentage depletion expense for the year.
2. If the selling price and costs remain constant is it advantageous for the corporation to use percentage depletion for federal income tax purposes over the life of the mine?

PROBLEMS

Part A

P12-1A   Disposal of Assets.   On January 1, 1983, The Hillary Company owns the following two assets:

(a) The president's car, which was purchased in 1980 for $14,000; the car was being depreciated on the basis of the miles driven. The original estimate was that the car would be driven for 50,000 miles and then sold for $4,000. On January 1, 1983, the car had been driven 40,000 miles. By May 20 it had been driven another 5,000 miles and was sold for $4,000.
(b) A machine purchased on January 1, 1978, for $40,000; it was being depreciated to a residual value of $4,000 over a period of 6 years by using the straight-line method. On August 31, 1983, it was sold for $8,000 and depreciation for 8 months was recorded.

Required: 1. Prepare journal entries to record the above events in 1983.
2. Show how the relevant items would affect the financial statements for 1983.

P12-2A   Exchange of Similar Productive Assets.   On January 1, 1983, the Haston Corporation owns two cars. Both cars were purchased on January 1, 1980. The president's car cost $15,000 and the salesman's car cost $8,000. The expected residual values at the end of their expected lives of 4 years are $5,000 and $2,000, respectively. The straight-line depreciation method is used for both cars. On December 31, 1983, both cars are traded for new cars. The president's car is exchanged for a new car with a cost of $18,000, and $12,000 cash is paid. The salesman's car is exchanged for a new car with a cost of $10,000, and $8,500 cash is paid.

Required: 1. Prepare journal entries to record the above events for 1983.
2. Show how the relevant items would be reported in the financial statements for 1983.
3. Prepare the journal entries to record depreciation in 1984 if an expected life of 5 years and a zero residual value is assumed for each new car.
4. State how your computation for Requirement 1 would change for federal income tax reporting (do not prepare journal entries).

P12-3A   Accidental Destruction of Assets.   On December 30, 1983, a building and machinery owned by the Messner Company were destroyed in a fire. The building had cost $100,000 at the beginning of 1975 and was being depreciated over 40 years to a zero residual value by the straight-line method. The machinery had been purchased at the beginning of 1980 for $40,000 and was being depreciated to a zero residual value over a 10-year life by the sum-of-the-years'-digits method. The salvageable materials from the fire were sold for $10,000 and the company collected $100,000 from its insurance company.

Required: 1. Prepare journal entries for 1983.
2. What is the meaning of the gain or loss that is recognized?

P12-4A   Intangible Assets.   The Shipton Company was involved in the following transactions during the current year:

(a) Developed a design for a new production process at a cost of $80,000. Legal costs to apply for a patent were $5,000.
(b) Paid $20,000 to employees who worked on the development of the design for the new production process.

(c) Paid $18,000 legal costs to successfully defend a copyright against infringement by another company. The original copyright was purchased 4 years ago at a cost of $30,000 and was being amortized over a 10-year life.
(d) Agreed to pay $80,000 to a racing driver to have the company name prominently displayed on his car for the year.
(e) Acquired the copyright to a novel for $30,000.

Required: 1. Prepare journal entries to record the above transactions.
2. Prepare journal entries to record the first year's amortization of intangible assets. Use the maximum life allowable unless a shorter life is indicated.

P12-5A Goodwill. The Caraway Company acquired the Forester Company for $100,000. The balance sheet of the Forester Company showed assets of $90,000 and liabilities of $30,000. The fair market value of the assets was $10,000 higher than the book value. In addition, an intangible asset that was not included on the balance sheet had a fair market value of $5,000.

Required: 1. How much goodwill would the Caraway Company record in regard to the purchase of the Forester Company?
2. Where would the goodwill appear in the financial statements of the Caraway Company?
3. Over what life should the goodwill be amortized?

P12-6A Natural Resource Assets. On January 1, 1982, the Eiger Company purchased a developed mine for $10 million. The expected capacity of the mine was 1 million tons. The cost of restoring the land at the end of the life of the mine was estimated to be $2 million. In addition, the company built housing for the miners for $100,000 that had a life of 20 years but which would have no value after the capacity of the mine has been exhausted. In 1982 the company incurred labor costs of $500,000 to mine and sell 100,000 tons at $25 per ton.

In January 1983 additional costs of $250,000 were incurred, which resulted in the capacity of the mine being increased to 100,000 tons greater than originally expected. In 1983 the company mined 150,000 tons, sold 120,000 tons at $30 per ton, and incurred related labor costs of $700,000.

The labor costs are expensed each period. Ignore income taxes.

Required: 1. Prepare income statements for 1982 and 1983.
2. How much depletion and depreciation is included in the inventory on the balance sheet of December 31, 1983?

PROBLEMS

Part B

P12-1B Disposal of Assets. On January 1, 1983, the Double Entries rock band owns the following two assets:

(a) A guitar, purchased in 1980 for $7,000, which was being depreciated on the basis of hours played. The original estimate was that the guitar would be played for 2,500 hours and then be sold for $2,000. By January 1, 1983, the guitar had been played for 2,000 hours. By June 3 it had been played for another 200 hours and was sold for $3,000.
(b) A sound system purchased on January 1, 1980, for $600,000, which was being depreciated to a residual value of $100,000 over a period of 5 years by using the straight-line method. On June 30, 1983, it was sold for $200,000 and depreciation for 6 months was recorded.

Required: 1. Prepare journal entries to record the above events in 1983.
2. Show how the above events would affect the financial statements for 1983.

P12-2B Exchange of Similar Productive Assets. On January 1, 1983, the Townsend Corporation owns two airplanes, both of which were purchased on January 1, 1980. The president's jet cost $1 million and the regional manager's biplane cost $130,000. The expected residual values at the end of their expected lives of 4 years are $200,000 and $30,000, respectively. The straight-line depreciation method is used for both planes. On December 31, 1983, both planes are traded for new planes. The president's new plane has a cost of $1.5 million, and $1.4 million cash is paid. The regional manager's biplane is exchanged for another plane with a cost of $60,000, and $20,000 cash is paid.

Required: 1. Prepare journal entries to record the above events in 1983.
2. Show how the relevant items would be reported on the financial statements for 1983.
3. Prepare the journal entries to record depreciation in 1984 if an expected life of 5 years and a zero residual value is assumed for both new planes.
4. State how your computation for Requirement 1 would change for federal income tax reporting (do not prepare journal entries).

P12-3B Accidental Destruction of Assets. On December 30, 1983, a movie theatre and projection machinery owned by the Emerson Company were destroyed by a tornado. The building had cost $250,000 at the beginning of 1975 and was being depreciated over 40 years to a zero residual value by means of the straight-line method. The projection machinery had been purchased at the beginning of 1980 for $55,000 and was being depreciated to a zero residual value over a 10-year life by means of the sum-of-the-years'-digits method. After the tornado the salvageable materials were sold for $20,000, and the company collected $200,000 from its insurance company.

Required: 1. Prepare journal entries for 1983.
2. What is the meaning of the gain or loss that is recognized?

P12-4B Intangible Assets. The Richards Company was involved in the following transactions during the current year:

(a) Developed a process for producing a new type of breakfast cereal at a cost of $200,000. Legal costs to apply for a patent were $40,000.
(b) Paid $50,000 to employees who worked on the development of the process for producing the breakfast cereal.
(c) Paid $20,000 legal costs to successfully defend a copyright, which was purchased 3 years ago, against infringement by another company. The original copyright cost $20,000 and was being amortized over a 20-year life.
(d) Agreed to pay $100,000 to have the company name flashed on the scoreboard at football games during this season.
(e) Acquired the copyright to a comic strip for $40,000.

Required: 1. Prepare journal entries to record the above transactions.
2. Prepare journal entries to record the first year's amortization of the intangible assets. Use the maximum allowable life unless a shorter life is indicated.

P12-5B Goodwill. The Floyd Company acquired the Palmer Company for $300,000. The balance sheet of the Palmer Company showed assets of $400,000 and liabilities of $200,000. The fair market value of the assets was $40,000 higher than the book value. In addition, an intangible asset that was not included on the balance sheet had a fair market value of $10,000.

Required: 1. How much goodwill would the Floyd Company record in regard to the purchase of the Palmer Company?
2. Where would the goodwill appear in the financial statements of the Floyd Company?
3. Over what life should the goodwill be amortized?

P12-6B Natural Resource Assets. On January 1, 1982, the Newton Company purchased a developed mine for $5 million. The expected capacity of the mine was 500,000 tons. The cost of restoring the land after the mine would be exhausted was estimated to be $100,000. In addition, the company built housing for the miners for $50,000 that had a life of 20 years but which would have no value after the capacity of the mine has been exhausted. In 1983 the company incurred labor costs of $100,000 to mine and sell 60,000 tons at $15 per ton.

In January 1984 additional costs of $70,000 were incurred, which resulted in the capacity of the mine being increased to 100,000 tons greater than originally expected. In 1984 the company mined 100,000 tons, sold 90,000 tons at $20 per ton, and incurred related labor costs of $200,000.

The labor costs are expensed each period. Ignore income taxes.

Required: 1. Prepare income statements for 1983 and 1984.
       2. How much depletion and depreciation would be included in the inventory on the balance sheet at December 31, 1984?

DISCUSSION CASES

C12-1 Intangible Assets. The Internal Revenue Service has the following rules regarding the amortization of intangibles for federal income tax purposes:

Patents:	17 years maximum
Copyrights:	40 years maximum
Franchises:	Length of franchise
Research and development:	Write off in period incurred

Intangible assets that have indefinite lives may not be amortized (including goodwill).

Required: 1. Explain clearly how the above rules differ from the rules for the preparation of financial statements.
       2. In each case in which there is a difference, explain how net income and income computed for federal income tax purposes by a corporation would differ.
       3. In each case in which there is a difference which alternative do you think is best for financial reporting?

C12-2 Goodwill. The Fastgro Company has increased its profits to five times the level of 6 years ago. The board of directors is meeting to discuss the sale of the company to a larger competitor. The following comments are made during the meeting:

"We should add some goodwill on the balance sheet, and then we can sell the company at a price equal to the net assets" (assets minus liabilities).

"We can't add goodwill to the balance sheet because that would violate generally accepted accounting principles. However, the company that buys us will record goodwill. I don't see why they can and we can't."

"It doesn't matter whether we add goodwill or not, because the price paid to buy this company will not be affected by the goodwill being on the balance sheet or not."

"You mentioned that the buyer will record goodwill on its balance sheet. I was wondering how they will decide how much the goodwill is, how they will decide whether or not to amortize it, and over what life?"

Required: Explain how you would respond to each of the comments.

PART 3 | BUSINESS ENTITIES

13 | Partnership Accounting

After reading this chapter, you should understand:

- The characteristics of a partnership
- Reasons for the formation of a partnership
- The alternative ways partnership earnings may be distributed among the partners
- The financial statements of a partnership
- How to account for the admission of a new partner
- How to account for the withdrawal of a partner
- How to account for the liquidation of a partnership

There are three principal forms of business organization: the sole proprietorship, the partnership, and the corporation. The discussion in the first five chapters of this book was based on a sole proprietorship, although the differences between a sole proprietorship and a corporation were briefly explained in Chapter 5. Chapter 6 through 12 and 16 through 27 discuss areas of accounting that are independent of the form of business organization. In Chapters 14 and 15 accounting for the corporation is explained. In this chapter the accounting principles that relate to partnerships are discussed. In order to help in understanding these principles it is useful to consider some of the characteristics of partnerships and the reasons for their existence.

CHARACTER-ISTICS OF A PARTNERSHIP

The Uniform Partnership Act is an act adopted by most states that governs the formation, operation, and liquidation of partnerships. A partnership is an association of two or more persons to carry on as co-owners a business for profit. Two or more people engaging in business transactions with other parties, therefore, could be operating as a partnership without realizing it and without having made any formal agreement about how to operate their business. In such cases any disputes would be resolved by reference to the Uniform Partnership Act. Most individuals who form a partnership prefer to specify in writing the terms of their business relationship in order to limit the potential for disagreements.

Partnership Agreement

A partnership agreement is an agreement among the parties that specifies the terms of the formation, operation, and liquidation of a partnership. The terms of the agreement supersede the Uniform Partnership Act, which is used only in areas not covered by the agreement. The agreement should define the nature of the business, the types and number of partners, the capital contributions required, the duties of each partner, the conditions for admission or withdrawal of a partner, the method of distributing earnings to each partner, and the allocation of assets in the liquidation of the partnership. Many of these topics are discussed in this chapter. Whatever the specific terms included in the partnership agreement, there are several characteristics common to all partnerships.

General and Limited Partners

Unless otherwise specified, all partners of the partnership are designated as general partners. **A general partner is a partner who has unlimited liability with respect to the debts of the partnership.** In some states partnerships are allowed to have limited partners. **A limited partner is a partner whose liability is limited to the assets contributed to the partnership by the specific partner.** The status of a limited partner is especially attractive to wealthy individuals who can contribute assets to the partnership without risking all of their personal assets.

Unlimited Liability

Unlimited liability is a characteristic of a partnership meaning that *each* general partner is liable for *all* the debts of the partnership. A creditor's claim on the partnership would first be satisfied by the assets of the partnership, but if these assets are insufficient to pay the claim, each partner's personal assets may be used to satisfy the claim. The only personal assets of a partner that are excluded are assets protected by bankruptcy laws. If one of the partners uses personal assets to pay the debts of the partnership, that partner has a right to claim a share of the payment from the other partners. This unlimited liability is a distinct contrast to the limited liability feature of a corporation discussed in the next chapter.

Income Tax

One of the primary reasons that an individual might prefer to invest in a partnership rather than a corporation is to avoid the double taxation imposed on a corporation. Double taxation refers to the taxing of the income earned by the corporation and the additional taxing of the dividends *paid* to the owners of the corporation. This is discussed more fully in Chapter 15. In contrast, income taxes are not assessed against the income of a partnership. Instead, the total earnings (including losses) of the partnership (*not* the withdrawals of the partners) are allocated to each partner, who then includes the allocated amount in his or her personal income for the computation of individual income tax for the year.

Voluntary Association

A partnership is a voluntary association that a person cannot be forced into against his or her will. Since a partner is responsible for the acts of fellow partners and has unlimited liability, it is reasonable that such responsibilities should be accepted only voluntarily. Thus a partner can leave a partnership at any time, unless the partnership agreement specifies otherwise.

Mutual Agency Each partner is an agent of the partnership. **An agent is a person who has the authority to act for another.** Thus a partner has the power to enter into and bind the partnership, and therefore all the partners, to any contract within the apparent scope of the business. Thus a partner in a grocery store can bind the partnership to contracts to purchase merchandise, hire employees, lease a building, purchase fixtures, and borrow money, because these activities are all within the normal scope of a grocery business. The partner, however, could not bind the partnership to contracts to buy an airplane or manage a musical group because these activities are outside the normal activities of a grocery business.

To provide protection for all the partners, they may agree to limit the type or size of contracts that an individual partner can enter into without prior consultation with the other partners. While such an agreement is binding on the partners and outsiders who know of its existence, outsiders who are unaware of it are not bound by its terms and can therefore assume that each partner acts as an unrestricted agent of the partnership.

Limited Life The life of every partnership is limited. The admission of a new partner, or the death, bankruptcy, incapacity, or withdrawal of an existing partner, automatically terminates the partnership. In addition, if the purpose for which the partnership was formed is completed, the partnership is terminated. If the partnership agreement is for a specified period of time, the partnership ends at the specified date. Finally, if there is no specified time limit and the purpose for which the business was formed continues indefinitely, the partnership may be terminated at any time by the withdrawal of a partner. This characteristic of a limited life is the opposite of the unlimited life of a corporation discussed in Chapter 14.

REASONS FOR THE FORMATION OF A PARTNERSHIP Partnerships are formed in two common situations. First, partnerships exist in many professional fields, such as accountancy, medicine, and law. In these professions the accountant, doctor, or lawyer has a personal responsibility to the client, and this responsibility is strengthened because the partnership has unlimited liability. Many states prohibit, or limit, the ability of professionals in many fields to form corporations, and therefore they must either be sole practitioners or form partnerships. Partnerships of this type may become very large. For example, some of the international accounting firms have over 500 partners as well as thousands of employees. The second common situation is when a sole proprietor is expanding his or her business and requires additional capital, or desires to attract another individual who has useful skills to participate in the business. A partnership rather than a corporation will be formed in these situations if the advantages of a partnership exceed the disadvantages.

The advantages of a partnership are that it is a very flexible form of organization, is easier and less expensive to form than a corporation, is less likely to be required to report to state and federal regulatory agencies, and avoids double taxation. The disadvantages of a partnership are the unlimited liability and the limited life which enables a partner at any time to terminate the partnership and withdraw his or her assets.

478 CHAPTER 13

ACCOUNTING FOR PARTNERSHIP EQUITY

Accounting for a partnership differs primarily from that of a sole proprietorship or a corporation in the way in which owners' equity is treated. Because ownership is divided among the partners and each partner engages in separate transactions with the partnership, it is necessary to have both a Capital account and a Withdrawals account for each partner.

The Capital and Withdrawals Accounts for Each Partner

A separate capital account is maintained for each partner. The capital account is used to record the capital balance of each partner. Each capital account is affected by the investments the partner makes, the partner's share of the net income of the partnership, and the partner's withdrawals.

A separate Withdrawals account is maintained for each partner. The Withdrawals account is used to record the assets withdrawn by each partner during the accounting period. All withdrawals of assets from the partnership made by each partner during the accounting period are recorded in that partner's withdrawals account. The balance of each partner's withdrawals account is closed to the partner's capital account at the end of each accounting period.

The effect of investments, net income, and withdrawals on the partner's capital and withdrawals accounts is shown below.

1. *Investments by the Partner Increase the Capital Account.* The initial investment or subsequent investments by the partner are recorded as follows (using assumed amounts):

```
Cash (or other asset accounts) . . . . . . . . . . . . . . . .   40,000
    J. Jones, Capital . . . . . . . . . . . . . . . . . . . . . . .         40,000
Investment by J. Jones into partnership.
```

2. *The Partner's Share of the Net Income (or Loss) of the Partnership Increases (or Decreases) the Capital Account.* Each partner's share of the net income is recorded in the process of closing the Income Summary account as follows (using assumed amounts):

```
Income Summary . . . . . . . . . . . . . . . . . . . . . . .   22,000
    J. Jones, Capital . . . . . . . . . . . . . . . . . . . . . .         11,000
    F. Smith, Capital . . . . . . . . . . . . . . . . . . . . . .         11,000
To close the Income Summary account and distribute the
earnings.
```

If there is a loss the entry will be the reverse of the entry shown. The share of the net income (or loss) is determined by the partnership agreement, and the computation may be complex as discussed later in this chapter.

3. *The Partner's Withdrawals During the Period Are Recorded in the Withdrawals Account.* The withdrawal of assets from the partnership by a partner is recorded as follows (using assumed amounts):

```
J. Jones, Withdrawals . . . . . . . . . . . . . . . . . . . . .   18,000
    Cash (or other assets) . . . . . . . . . . . . . . . . . . .         18,000
Withdrawal of cash by J. Jones for personal use.
```

The balance of the Withdrawals account is closed to the Capital account at the end of the period as illustrated below. Of course, the partnership agreement should specify the conditions under which withdrawals can be made and the allowable amounts that may be withdrawn. If merchandise (or other assets) may be withdrawn, the agreement should specify whether the cost (in which case an asset account such as inventory is credited) or the market value (in which case the sales account is credited) should be used.

4. *Withdrawals by the Partner Decrease the Capital Account.* One of the closing entries of the partnership is used to close each partner's Withdrawals account and reduce the partner's Capital account as follows (using assumed amounts):

J. Jones, Capital	18,000	
J. Jones, Withdrawals		18,000
To close the Withdrawals account.		

The balance in the Capital account at the end of the period is the sum of the investments made by the partner and the partner's share of net income (or loss) of the partnership, less the amount withdrawn by the partner.

PARTNERSHIP EARNINGS

Partnership earnings may be distributed in any proportions agreed to by the partners. In the absence of an agreement the Uniform Partnership Act requires that net income be distributed equally. Most partnerships have an earnings agreement that involves one or all of three basic factors: (1) allocation by a set ratio, (2) provision for interest on each partner's capital balance, and (3) recognition of salaries for each partner.

A set ratio may be appropriate when the total contribution of each partner is approximately equal. Partners do not invest in a partnership to earn interest, but the distribution of earnings may include a component that represents interest on the capital invested by the partner in the partnership. Similarly, as a member of a partnership, a partner cannot enter into an employer–employee relationship with him- or herself. Therefore no salary can be paid in the legal sense of the term. The distribution of partnership earnings, however, may recognize a payment for services provided to the partnership during the period and be effectively the same as a salary. These allowances for salary and interest on capital may be necessary for a fair distribution of net income. For example, one partner may contribute much more capital than another, whereas another partner may contribute more valuable services to the operations of the partnership. Losses may be divided in a different ratio than profits, but in the absence of a specific agreement it is assumed that losses are divided in the same way as profits. Each of the three basic methods of dividing earnings is discussed in the following sections.

Earnings Divided According to a Set Ratio

The simplest method of dividing earnings is according to a set ratio. Examples of the ratios that might be agreed to by the partners are:

1. Equally among all partners
2. A ratio other than equal

3. The ratio of partners' beginning (or ending) capital balances
4. The ratio of partners' weighted average capital balances.

To illustrate these alternatives, we will use the facts given in Exhibit 13-1 for the Lyme and Dorset partnership.

EARNINGS DIVIDED EQUALLY.   In this situation each partner would receive an equal share of the net income of the partnership. Since there are two partners, each would receive half the total 1983 net income of $40,000, or $20,000 each. The journal entry to record the distribution of net income is as follows:

Income Summary	40,000	
H. Lyme, Capital		20,000
R. Dorset, Capital		20,000

To close the Income Summary account and distribute the earnings.

In each of the subsequent earnings distributions, the accounts that are debited and credited are the same and only the amounts distributed to each partner are different. Therefore the journal entry will not be repeated.

A RATIO OTHER THAN EQUAL.   Suppose instead that the partners agree to distribute net income on the basis of three-fifths to Lyme and two-fifths to Dorset. In this situation, Lyme will be allocated $24,000 ($40,000 × $\frac{3}{5}$) and Dorset will be allocated $16,000 ($40,000 × $\frac{2}{5}$) of the $40,000 net income.

THE RATIO OF PARTNERS' BEGINNING CAPITAL BALANCES.   Suppose instead that the partners agree to distribute net income on the basis of each partner's capital balance at the beginning of the period. Lyme and Dorset have capital balances on January 1, 1983, of $30,000 and $50,000, respectively, or a total of $80,000. Therefore Lyme will be allocated $15,000 [$40,000 × ($30,000 ÷ $80,000)] and Dorset will be allocated $25,000 [$40,000 × ($50,000 ÷ $80,000)].

EXHIBIT 13-1   Information for Lyme and Dorset Partnership

LYME AND DORSET PARTNERSHIP						
		Investments		Withdrawals		Capital December 31, 1983 (before earnings distribution)
Partners	Capital January 1, 1983	Date	Amount	Date	Amount	
H. Lyme	$30,000	Apr. 13	$10,000	June 30	$15,000	$25,000
R. Dorset	50,000	June 1	20,000	Apr. 20	10,000	
				Aug. 30	12,000	48,000
Partnership net income for 1983: $40,000						

THE RATIO OF PARTNERS' WEIGHTED AVERAGE CAPITAL BALANCES. Suppose instead that the partners agree to distribute net income on the basis of each partner's weighted average capital balance during the period. In this example we will assume that the weighted average capital balance will be computed to the nearest whole month. Thus the withdrawal by Lyme on April 13 will be treated as if it occurred on April 1. To apply this alternative it is first necessary to compute the weighted average capital balance of each partner. Withdrawals are deducted in determining capital balances at the time of the withdrawal even though they would not be closed to the capital account until the end of the period. Thus the April 20 withdrawal of Dorset (treated as if it occurred on May 1) reduces his capital balance for the computation by $10,000 (from $50,000 to $40,000) even though this amount would be recorded in the Withdrawals account. The weighted average capital balances are computed as follows:

Lyme

Capital Balance		Months		
$30,000	×	3	=	$ 90,000
40,000	×	3	=	120,000
25,000	×	6	=	150,000
		12		$360,000

Weighted average capital balance = $30,000 (i.e., $360,000 ÷ 12)

Dorset

Capital Balance		Months		
$50,000	×	4	=	$200,000
40,000	×	1	=	40,000
60,000	×	3	=	180,000
48,000	×	4	=	192,000
		12		$612,000

Weighted average capital balance = $51,000 (i.e., $612,000 ÷ 12)

Based on these weighted average calculations, the average total capital is $81,000 ($30,000 + $51,000). The partnership net income of $40,000 will be allocated in the amounts of $14,815 [$40,000 × ($30,000 ÷ $81,000)] to Lyme and $25,185 [$40,000 × ($51,000 ÷ $81,000)] to Dorset.

Interest Provided on Capital When partners have provided unequal amounts of capital to the partnership, they may agree that it is desirable to include a provision for interest on the capital balances of each partner in the earnings distribution calculation. It is important to note that the interest is a distribution of earnings and is *not* an expense of the partnership. If the partnership agreement does not specify an interest provision on the partner's capital balances, no interest is computed. The remaining net income after the provision for interest on capital is divided among the partners in an agreed ratio. The distribution of the income is recorded by a single journal entry, as illustrated earlier.

The interest may be computed on the basis of the capital balances at the beginning of the period or on the average capital balance. To illustrate these two alternatives, assume that the Lyme and Dorset partnership earnings agreement stipulates an initial allocation of earnings at an interest rate of 10% and that the remaining net income is to be distributed equally after the interest provision has been deducted.

INTEREST PROVIDED ON BEGINNING CAPITAL BALANCES. When the interest is provided on the beginning capital balances, the distribution of the net income of $40,000 is computed as follows:

	Lyme	Dorset	Total
Interest			
Lyme (10% × $30,000)	$ 3,000		
Dorset (10% × $50,000)		$ 5,000	
Total			$ 8,000
Balance allocated equally			
Lyme ($32,000ª × ½)	16,000		
Dorset ($32,000 × ½)		16,000	
Total			32,000
Income Distribution	$19,000	$21,000	$40,000

ª $40,000 net income − $8,000 interest provision.

INTEREST PROVIDED ON AVERAGE CAPITAL BALANCES. It is usually more equitable to compute interest on the basis of the average capital balances during the period because this is a better measure of the investment of each partner. In this case the average capital balances of $30,000 and $51,000 for Lyme and Dorset, respectively, would be computed by the weighted average calculation illustrated earlier. The distribution of net income of $40,000 would be computed as follows:

	Lyme	Dorset	Total
Interest			
Lyme (10% × $30,000)	$ 3,000		
Dorset (10% × $51,000)		$ 5,100	
Total			$ 8,100
Balance allocated equally			
Lyme ($31,900ª × ½)	15,950		
Dorset ($31,900 × ½)		15,950	
Total			31,900
Income Distribution	$18,950	$21,050	$40,000

ª $40,000 net income − $8,100 interest provision.

Recognition of Salaries for Partners

Partners may agree to allocate a portion of earnings as salaries to provide rewards for different levels of effort or ability. Such allocations are *not* expenses of the partnership but are distributions of earnings. If the partnership agreement does not specify that salaries may be allocated to partners, no salary distribution is then made.

To illustrate, suppose that Lyme and Dorset are allocated salaries of $18,000 and $15,000, respectively. Assuming that the remaining balance of the $40,000 net income is distributed equally, the total distribution would be computed as follows:

	Lyme	Dorset	Total
Salaries	$18,000	$15,000	$33,000
Balance allocated equally			
Lyme ($7,000[a] × ½)	3,500		
Dorset ($7,000 × ½)		3,500	
Total			7,000
Income Distribution	$21,500	$18,500	$40,000

[a] $40,000 net income − $33,000 salary provision.

Salaries and Interest

The partners may agree to make provisions for the allocation of both salaries and interest in the earnings distribution, with the balance of the net income to be distributed in a set ratio. To illustrate, suppose that Lyme and Dorset agreed to distribute earnings based upon 8% interest on the average capital balances during the period, salaries of $12,000 and $10,000, respectively, with the remainder being distributed 40% to Lyme and 60% to Dorset. The distribution of the $40,000 net income would be as follows:

	Lyme	Dorset	Total
Salaries	$12,000	$10,000	$22,000
Interest			
Lyme (8% × $30,000)	2,400		
Dorset (8% × $51,000)		4,080	
Total			6,480
Balance allocated			
Lyme ($11,520[a] × 0.40)	4,608		
Dorset ($11,520 × 0.60)		6,912	
Total			11,520
Income Distribution	$19,008	$20,992	$40,000

[a] $40,000 net income − $22,000 salaries distribution − $6,480 interest provision.

It is important to recognize that when salaries and interest are included in the distribution of earnings, they are typically allocated even if they exceed the net income of the partnership. The resulting "loss" is then distributed in the agreed ratio. For example, assume the same facts as in the example above, except that the partnership net income is only $20,000. After allocation of the salaries and interest, which total $28,480 ($22,000 + $6,480), there is a "loss" of $8,480 ($20,000 − $28,480), which is divided in the agreed ratio as follows:

Lyme ($8,480 × 0.40)	$3,392 loss allocation
Dorset ($8,480 × 0.60)	$5,088 loss allocation

Therefore the total distributions to each partner are:

	Lyme	Dorset	Total
Salaries	$12,000	$10,000	$22,000
Interest	2,400	4,080	6,480
Balance	(3,392)	(5,088)	(8,480)
Income Distribution	$11,008	$ 8,992	$20,000

It should be noted that even though the "loss" of $8,480 was distributed to the partners in accordance with the earnings agreement, the total net income of $20,000 would be closed to the partners' capital accounts in the usual fashion and no "loss" would be shown in the partnership income statement. The journal entry to record the distribution would be:

```
Income Summary . . . . . . . . . . . . . . . . . . . . . . . .   20,000
      H. Lyme, Capital  . . . . . . . . . . . . . . . . . . . . .            11,008
      R. Dorset, Capital . . . . . . . . . . . . . . . . . . . . .             8,992
To close the income summary account and distribute the
earnings.
```

It should be emphasized that the alternative distributions of net income discussed above are distributions that are commonly used in practice, but partners may agree to a distribution in any way they wish.

FINANCIAL STATEMENTS OF A PARTNERSHIP

The financial statements of a partnership are very similar to the financial statements of a sole proprietorship engaged in the same type of business. The differences between these statements that do occur are discussed for each financial statement in the following sections.

Income Statement

Remember that salaries allocated to partners and interest distributed on capital balances in accordance with the partnership earnings agreement are *not* considered to be expenses, and therefore they are not included in the computation of net income in the income statement. It is common to add a section to the bottom of the income statement that shows the allocation of the income to the partners. To illustrate, refer to the last example of the Lyme and Dorset partnership in which it earned $20,000. This additional section of the income statement is illustrated in Exhibit 13-2.

EXHIBIT 13-2 Partial Income Statement

LYME AND DORSET
Partial Income Statement
For the Year Ended December 31, 1983

	Lyme	Dorset	Total
Net Income			$20,000
Allocation of net income to the partners			
Salary allowances	$12,000	$10,000	$22,000
Interest at 8% on average capital balances	2,400	4,080	6,480
Distribution of remainder (40%; 60%)	(3,392)	(5,088)	(8,480)
Income Distribution	$11,008	$ 8,992	$20,000

EXHIBIT 13-3
Statement of Changes
in Partners' Equity

LYME AND DORSET
Statement of Changes in Partners' Equity
For the Year Ended December 31, 1983

	Lyme	Dorset	Total
Balances, January 1, 1983	$30,000	$50,000	$80,000
Add: Additional investments	10,000	20,000	30,000
Less: Withdrawals	(15,000)	(22,000)	(37,000)
Capital balances before earnings distribution	$25,000	$48,000	$73,000
Earnings distribution:			
Salary allowances	12,000	10,000	22,000
Interest allocation	2,400	4,080	6,480
Distribution of remainder	(3,392)	(5,088)	(8,480)
Balances, December 31, 1983	$36,008	$56,992	$93,000

Balance Sheet The only difference between the balance sheet of a partnership and the balance sheet of a sole proprietorship is that the owners' equity section of a partnership balance sheet includes a separate capital account for each partner. If the number of partners is so large that including each partner's capital account in the balance sheet becomes unwieldy, a single partnership capital balance could be presented. In this case the amount of each partner's capital account would be listed on a separate schedule.

Statement of Changes in Partners' Equity At the end of each accounting period a statement of the changes in partners' equity should be prepared. **The statement of changes in partners' equity is a supplementary statement that lists the investments, withdrawals, and earnings distribution for each partner during the accounting period.** It is similar to the statement of change in owner's equity for a sole proprietorship illustrated in Chapter 5. The statement for Lyme and Dorset is shown in Exhibit 13-3, using the information listed in Exhibits 13-1 and 13-2. The statement shows greater detail than could be included conveniently in the balance sheet. Only the partners' ending capital balances are shown in the balance sheet.

The distribution of earnings and withdrawals by partners are typical changes in the partners' equity. Other changes may be caused by the admission of a new partner, the withdrawal of an existing partner, or the liquidation of the partnership. Each of these factors is discussed in the following sections.

ADMISSION OF A NEW PARTNER As discussed earlier an existing partnership is ended whenever there is a change in the partners, either by the admission of a new partner or the withdrawal of an existing partner. From an accounting perspective, however, the business entity is assumed to continue, with the only change being reflected in the capital balances of the partners affected by the change of ownership. In this section we discuss the admission of a new partner; the withdrawal of a partner is discussed in the next section. Liquidation of a partnership is discussed in the final section of the chapter.

Four alternatives may arise when a new partner is admitted to a partnership:

1. The new partner purchases an interest from an existing partner.
2. The new partner invests assets in the partnership and is assigned a capital balance equal to the assets contributed.
3. The new partner invests assets in the partnership and is assigned a capital balance less than the assets contributed. Therefore a "bonus" is assigned to the continuing partners.
4. The new partner invests assets in the partnership and is assigned a capital balance greater than the assets contributed. Therefore a "bonus" is assigned to the new partner.

Each of these alternatives is discussed in the following sections.

New Partner Purchases Interest from Existing Partner

When a new partner purchases an interest from an existing partner, the transaction is directly between the two partners, usually with the agreement of all the other partners. The new partner contributes no assets to the partnership, and therefore the assets and the liabilities of the partnership remain unchanged. The only payment by the new partner is to the existing partner. In accordance with the business entity concept, the only effect on the accounts of the partnership is the assignment of a part or all of the balance in the capital account from the name of the selling partner to the name of the new partner.

For example, suppose that Hardy and Laurel are partners with capital balances of $50,000 and $60,000, respectively. If Chaplin purchases a $20,000 interest in the partnership from Laurel, the journal entry on the partnership's books is as follows:

Laurel, Capital	20,000	
Chaplin, Capital		20,000

To record the transfer of a $20,000 interest in the partnership from Laurel to Chaplin.

Note that no mention has been made of the price paid by Chaplin to Laurel. It could be less than, equal to, or more than $20,000. In any case, the price paid has no effect on the partnership because it is simply a transfer of personal assets between two individuals. In addition to the above journal entry, some of the partnership agreement (e.g., the earnings distribution agreement) must be changed to reflect the admission of the new partner.

Existing partners cannot prevent the sale of a partnership interest by one partner to another individual. If the existing partners do not accept the new partner one of two alternatives may apply. Under common law the partnership must be liquidated, and the new partner receives only the liquidation rights of the selling partner. In many states the Uniform Partnership Act has replaced common law, and the Act requires that the new partner share in the earnings and losses of the partnership and in the liquidation of the partnership, but cannot participate in management.

EXHIBIT 13-4
Balance Sheet

HARDY AND LAUREL
Balance Sheet
January 1, 1983

Assets		Liabilities and Owners' Equity	
Cash	$ 25,000	Liabilities	$ 25,000
Other assets	110,000	Hardy, capital	50,000
		Laurel, capital	60,000
		Total Liabilities and	
Total Assets	$135,000	Owners' Equity . . .	$135,000

New Partner Assigned Capital Balance Equal to Assets Contributed

A partner may be admitted to a partnership by contributing assets to the partnership. In this situation the assets and the total partnership equity increase by the same amount. In the simplest case the new partner is assigned a capital balance equal to the assets contributed to the partnership. In the following examples it will be assumed that the new partner contributes cash to the partnership, but any asset could be contributed, such as inventory or a building.

To illustrate, assume that the Hardy and Laurel partnership has the condensed balance sheet shown in Exhibit 13-4. If Hardy and Laurel agree to admit Chaplin to a 20% interest in the partnership upon payment of a certain amount of cash, and Chaplin is to be assigned a capital balance equal to the cash amount, how much must Chaplin invest? The existing capital of the partnership is $110,000 ($50,000 + $60,000), but Chaplin is purchasing a 20% interest in the new partnership, *after* the contribution of Chaplin's assets to the partnership. Since Chaplin's share is to be 20%, the existing partners will own 80% of the new partnership. Their total capital balances of $110,000 therefore represent an 80% share of the new partnership, and the total capital of the new partnership is $137,500 ($110,000 ÷ 0.80). Thus Chaplin must contribute $27,500, which increases the partnership assets by that amount and increases the partnership capital by $27,500 to $137,500 ($110,000 + $27,500). This calculation may be summarized as follows:

Capital of continuing partners	$110,000
Investment of new partner	27,500
Total Capital of New Partnership	$137,500
New Partner's Capital (20% × $137,500)	$ 27,500

The journal entry that is used by the partnership to record the admission of Chaplin is:

Cash	27,500	
Chaplin, Capital		27,500
Chaplin admitted to the partnership.		

After the admission, the condensed balance sheet of the partnership would be as follows:

HARDY, LAUREL, AND CHAPLIN
Balance Sheet
January 1, 1983

Assets		Liabilities and Owners' Equity	
Cash	$ 52,500	Liabilities	$ 25,000
Other assets	110,000	Hardy, capital	50,000
		Laurel, capital	60,000
		Chaplin, capital	27,500
		Total Liabilities and	
Total Assets	$162,500	Owners' Equity	$162,500

While Chaplin has a 20% ownership in the partnership, he does not have a right to 20% of the earnings. The division of net income is subject to a separate earnings agreement among the partners and may be completely unrelated to the capital balances. If the partnership agreement does not specify the distribution of earnings, it is assumed that the partners intend to share profits and losses equally.

Bonus to Existing Partners

If the capital balance assigned to the new partner is not equal to the assets contributed by that partner, a bonus exists. **A bonus is the difference between the assets contributed by a new partner and the capital balance assigned to the new partner.** The bonus is assigned either to the existing partners or the new partner as follows:

— Bonus is assigned to the continuing partners if the capital balance assigned to the new partner is less than the assets contributed by the new partner.
— Bonus is assigned to new partner if the capital balance assigned to the new partner is greater than the assets contributed by the new partner.

To illustrate a bonus assigned to the existing partners, assume that Chaplin invests $30,000 for a 20% share of the partnership and that Hardy and Laurel share net income on the basis of 60% and 40%, respectively. Chaplin's investment raises the capital of the partnership to $140,000 ($110,000 + $30,000) but Chaplin's capital is only $28,000 ($140,000 × 0.20). The difference between the investment and the capital balance is $2,000 ($30,000 investment − $28,000 Chaplin's capital) and is the bonus assigned to the existing partners. The bonus is divided according to the earnings distribution ratio, and therefore Hardy receives $1,200 ($2,000 × 0.60) and Laurel receives $800 ($2,000 × 0.40). The journal entry used by the partnership to record the admission of Chaplin is:

Cash	30,000	
Chaplin, Capital		28,000
Hardy, Capital		1,200
Laurel, Capital		800

Chaplin admitted to the partnership.

It is fairly common for a bonus to be assigned to the continuing partners because the new partner has the advantage of entering an ongoing partnership with an established business.

Bonus to New Partner

Sometimes a new partner brings unusual benefits to the partnership, perhaps in the form of special skills or business contacts. In such situations a bonus may be assigned to the new partner. For example, assume that Chaplin invests $30,000 for a 30% share of the partnership. The capital assignment to Chaplin is calculated as follows:

Capital of continuing partners	$110,000
Investment of new partner	30,000
Total Capital of New Partnership	$140,000
New Partner's Capital ($140,000 × 0.30)	$ 42,000

Under these terms Chaplin receives a bonus of $12,000 ($42,000 Chaplin's capital − $30,000 investment). This bonus is subtracted from (debited to) the capital balances of the continuing partners in their earnings distribution ratios. Hardy's share is $7,200 ($12,000 × 0.60) and Laurel's share is $4,800 ($12,000 × 0.40). The journal entry used by the partnership to record the admission of Chaplin is:

Cash	30,000	
Hardy, Capital	7,200	
Laurel, Capital	4,800	
Chaplin, Capital		42,000
Chaplin admitted to the partnership.		

Again, the distribution of net income in the earnings agreement is a separate decision of the partners.

WITHDRAWAL OF A PARTNER

The partnership agreement should specify the procedures to be followed in the event of the withdrawal of a partner from the partnership. Usually the agreement calls for an audit and a revaluation of the partnership's assets to their market value. Instead of this revaluation process, the withdrawing partner may be allowed to withdraw assets less than, or greater than, the book value of his or her capital. Each of these three alternatives is discussed in the following sections.

Assets Revalued and Partner Receives Book Value of Equity

When the assets of the partnership are revalued, the difference between the market value and the book value is allocated to the partners' capital accounts in their earnings distribution ratios. The partners' capital accounts then reflect the current value of their equity, and the withdrawing partner receives assets equal to the value in his or her capital account.

To illustrate this procedure, assume that Palmer is retiring from the partnership of Lake, Palmer, and Emerson on January 9, 1983. The partners have shared

EXHIBIT 13-5
Balance Sheet

LAKE, PALMER, AND EMERSON
Balance Sheet
January 9, 1983

Assets		Liabilities and Owners' Equity	
Cash	$ 60,000	Liabilities	$ 10,000
Accounts receivable	20,000		
Inventory	35,000		
Property and equipment	90,000	Lake, capital	80,000
Less: Accumulated		Palmer, capital	50,000
depreciation	(25,000)	Emerson, capital	40,000
		Total Liabilities and	
Total Assets	$180,000	Owners' Equity	$180,000

earnings in the ratio of 50%, 25%, and 25%, respectively. The balance sheet of the partnership before the audit and revaluation is shown in Exhibit 13-5.

The audit and revaluation indicate that an allowance for uncollectible accounts of $2,000 should be established and that the property and equipment are undervalued by $10,000. The net increase in the value of the assets of $8,000 is divided among the partners in their earnings sharing ratio. It is fair to allocate the net gain in the earnings sharing ratio because the impact of the revaluation will eventually appear in the income statement through changes in the expenses recorded in future periods. The journal entry to record these revaluations is as follows:

Property and Equipment	10,000	
Allowance for Uncollectible Accounts		2,000
Lake, Capital		4,000
Palmer, Capital		2,000
Emerson, Capital		2,000

To revalue the assets.

After the revaluation the balance sheet would be as follows:

LAKE, PALMER, AND EMERSON
Balance Sheet
January 9, 1983

Assets		Liabilities and Owners' Equity	
Cash	$ 60,000	Liabilities	$ 10,000
Accounts receivable	20,000		
Less: Allowance for			
uncollectible accounts	(2,000)		
Inventory	35,000		
Property and equipment	100,000	Lake, capital	84,000
Less: Accumulated		Palmer, capital	52,000
depreciation	(25,000)	Emerson, capital	42,000
		Total Liabilities and	
Total Assets	$188,000	Owners' Equity	$188,000

Palmer withdraws from the partnership and receives cash equal to his equity of $52,000, which is recorded as follows:

Palmer, Capital	52,000	
Cash		52,000

Palmer withdraws from partnership.

The withdrawing partner does not have to take cash as settlement but may take any combination of assets or receive a promissory note from the partnership.

Partner Receives Assets Less Than the Book Value of Equity

The partnership agreement may specify that a withdrawing partner receive less than the book value of his or her equity. The assets may, or may not, be revalued first in the same way as above. Receipt of less than the book value may have been agreed on, for example, to discourage withdrawals. Alternatively, the partners may believe the assets to be overvalued or the partner may be very anxious to withdraw from the partnership. When withdrawing assets that are less than his or her equity, the partner is leaving part of his or her equity in the partnership. The amount left is distributed among the remaining partners in their earnings distribution ratio.

For example, suppose instead that Palmer withdraws from the partnership *without* a revaluation of the assets and receives assets of $41,000. This leaves $9,000 ($50,000 capital balance $-$ $41,000) to be allocated to the remaining partners. Since the original earnings distribution ratio was 50%, 25%, 25% or 2 : 1 : 1, the remaining partners will distribute net income on a 2 : 1 ratio or 66 $\frac{2}{3}$% to 33 $\frac{1}{3}$%. Thus Lake would be allocated $6,000 ($9,000 $\times$ 66 $\frac{2}{3}$%) and Emerson $3,000 ($9,000 $\times$ 33 $\frac{1}{3}$%). The journal entry to record the withdrawal of Palmer is:

Palmer, Capital	50,000	
Cash		41,000
Lake, Capital		6,000
Emerson, Capital		3,000

Palmer withdraws from the partnership.

After the withdrawal of Palmer, Lake and Emerson could change the earnings distribution agreement or any other aspect of the partnership agreement.

Partner Receives Assets Greater Than the Book Value of Equity

The partnership agreement may specify that a withdrawing partner receive more than the book value of his or her equity. This may be done to avoid the expense of revaluing the assets while attempting to approximate the market value of the partner's equity. Alternatively, the remaining partners may be so anxious for the partner to withdraw that they are willing to pay more than the book value of his or her equity. The effect of withdrawing assets greater than the book value of the equity is that the withdrawing partner is also withdrawing a portion of the equity of the other partners.

For example, suppose that Palmer withdraws from the partnership *without* a revaluation of the assets and receives assets of $62,000. The excess of $12,000 ($62,000 $-$ $50,000 capital balance) is removed from the capital accounts of the remaining partners in their earnings distribution ratios. Therefore $8,000

($12,000 $\times$ 66 $\frac{2}{3}$%) will be deducted from Lake's capital account and $4,000 ($12,000 $\times$ 33 $\frac{1}{3}$%) from Emerson's capital account. The journal entry to record the withdrawal of Palmer is:

Palmer, Capital	50,000	
Lake, Capital	8,000	
Emerson, Capital	4,000	
Cash		62,000

Palmer withdraws from the partnership.

LIQUIDATION OF A PARTNERSHIP

Liquidation is the dissolution of a partnership by selling the assets, paying the liabilities, and closing each partner's capital account. The liquidation of a partnership may occur for one of the following five reasons:

1. The purpose for which the partnership was formed is accomplished.
2. The time for which the partnership was formed has expired.
3. An agreement among the partners has been made to terminate the partnership.
4. A partner has declared bankruptcy.
5. A partner has died or withdrawn from the partnership.

Regardless of the reason for liquidation, the following sequence of events always occurs:

1. The noncash assets are sold or converted into cash and the gain or loss is distributed among the partners.
2. The liabilities of the partnership are paid.
3. The remaining cash (or assets not sold) are distributed to the partners and the partnership accounts are closed.

A liquidation may take place over a long period of time, in which case several partial distributions of cash may be made. Because the procedures to be followed are beyond the scope of this book, it will be assumed in the following examples that a single distribution of cash is made after all the assets have been converted into cash.

When a liquidation occurs the assets may be sold at a gain or a loss, there may or may not be sufficient cash to pay the liabilities, or a partner may have a negative capital balance. Each of these three situations is discussed in the following sections, using the balance sheet of the Lowe and Lerner partnership in Exhibit 13-6. Lowe and Lerner are allocated 60% and 40% of the partnership's earnings, respectively.

Assets Sold at a Gain

If the assets are sold at a gain, the gain is allocated to the partners in their earnings distribution ratio. The liabilities are paid off and the remaining cash is distributed to the partners in accordance with their capital balances and *not* in the earnings distribution ratio.

EXHIBIT 13-6
Balance Sheet

LOWE AND LERNER
Balance Sheet
July 15, 1983

Assets		*Liabilities and Owners' Equity*	
Cash	$10,000	Accounts payable	$20,000
Accounts receivable	8,000		
Inventory	25,000		
Property and equipment . . .	70,000		
Less: Accumulated		Lowe, capital	38,000
depreciation	(35,000)	Lerner, capital	20,000
		Total Liabilities and	
Total Assets	$78,000	Owners' Equity	$78,000

To illustrate, assume that the Lowe and Lerner partnership sold the assets *other than cash* for $80,000, resulting in a gain of $12,000 ($80,000 − $68,000). The gain allocated to Lowe is $7,200 ($12,000 × 0.60) and to Lerner is $4,800 ($12,000 × 0.40). Note that it is the gain, and *not* the proceeds, from the sale of the assets that is allocated to the partners. The journal entry to record the sale of the assets and the distribution of the gain is as follows:

Cash	80,000	
Accumulated Depreciation	35,000	
Accounts Receivable		8,000
Inventory		25,000
Property and Equipment		70,000
Lowe, Capital		7,200
Lerner, Capital		4,800
Sale of assets.		

Normally assets would be sold individually and would result in many gains and losses. For simplicity the above journal entry assumes a single sale and therefore a single gain or loss. The journal entry to record the payment of the liabilities is:

Accounts Payable	20,000	
Cash		20,000
Payment of liabilities.		

At this point the partnership has cash of $70,000 ($10,000 + $80,000 − $20,000) and the capital balances of Lowe and Lerner are $45,200 ($38,000 + $7,200) and $24,800 ($20,000 + $4,800), respectively. The cash is distributed to the partners according to their capital balances as follows:

Lowe, Capital	45,200	
Lerner, Capital	24,800	
Cash		70,000
Distribution of cash to partners.		

EXHIBIT 13-7   Liquidation Schedule

	Cash	Accounts Receivable	Inventory	Property and Equipment	Accumulated Depreciation	Accounts Payable	Lowe, Capital	Lerner, Capital
LOWE AND LERNER PARTNERSHIP **Liquidation Schedule**								
Balances, July 15, 1983	$ 10,000	$ 8,000	$ 25,000	$ 70,000	$(35,000)	$(20,000)	$(38,000)	$(20,000)
Sale of assets	80,000	(8,000)	(25,000)	(70,000)	35,000	0	(7,200)	(4,800)
	$ 90,000	$ 0	$ 0	$ 0	$ 0	$(20,000)	$(45,200)	$(24,800)
Payment of liabilities	(20,000)					20,000		
	$ 70,000					$ 0		
Distribution to partners	(70,000)						45,200	24,800
	$ 0						$ 0	$ 0

A schedule of the steps contained in the liquidation is illustrated in Exhibit 13-7. The schedule is based on the journal entries but with the changes in the account balances listed in the respective columns. Credit amounts are shown in parentheses. It should be noted that the amounts in each line have a net total of zero because at all times the debit balances equal the credit balances.

Assets Sold at a Loss   When assets are sold at a loss the same procedures are followed except that the loss on the sale (as opposed to the gain) is allocated among the partners in their earnings distribution ratio. For example, suppose that the assets *other than cash* are sold for $50,000, resulting in a loss of $18,000 ($68,000 − $50,000). The loss allocated to Lowe is $10,800 ($18,000 × 0.60) and $7,200 ($18,000 × 0.40) to Lerner. The journal entries to record the liquidation are as follows:

Cash	50,000	
Accumulated Depreciation	35,000	
Lowe, Capital	10,800	
Lerner, Capital	7,200	
Accounts Receivable		8,000
Inventory		25,000
Property and Equipment		70,000
Sale of assets.		

| Accounts Payable | 20,000 | |
| Cash | | 20,000 |

Payment of liabilities.

Lowe, Capital ($38,000 − $10,800)	27,200	
Lerner, Capital ($20,000 − $7,200)	12,800	
Cash		40,000

Distribution of cash to the partners.

Partner Has Negative Capital Balance

In some situations the loss on the sale of the assets is so large that a partner's capital balance is negative after the share of the loss has been allocated to it. After payment of the liabilities the cash available for distribution to the partners with positive (credit) balances will be insufficient until the partner with the negative (debit) capital balance has contributed cash to the partnership equal to the balance. If the partner with the negative balance is unable to pay the amount owed because of personal bankruptcy, the remaining partners must allocate this loss among themselves.

For example, suppose that the Lowe and Lerner partnership could sell their assets other than cash for only $8,000, resulting in a loss of $60,000 ($68,000 − $8,000). The loss allocated to Lowe is $36,000 ($60,000 × 0.60) and to Lerner is $24,000 ($60,000 × 0.40). The journal entry to record the sale of the assets is as follows:

Cash	8,000	
Accumulated Depreciation	35,000	
Lowe, Capital	36,000	
Lerner, Capital	24,000	
Accounts Receivable		8,000
Inventory		25,000
Property and Equipment		70,000

Sale of assets.

At this point Lerner's capital balance has a negative (debit) balance of $4,000 ($20,000 − $24,000). Lerner must therefore contribute cash to the partnership to remove the negative balance. If this occurs the journal entry to record the additional contribution is as follows:

| Cash | 4,000 | |
| Lerner, Capital | | 4,000 |

Contribution by Lerner.

After the additional contribution the partnership would have the following account balances:

Cash $22,000 ($10,000 + $8,000 + $4,000)
Accounts payable $20,000
Lowe, capital $2,000 ($38,000 − $36,000)
Lerner, capital $0 ($20,000 − $24,000 + $4,000)

The cash is used to pay the liabilities and Lowe. The journal entry to record the payment is as follows:

Accounts Payable	20,000	
Lowe, Capital	2,000	
Cash		22,000

Payment of liabilities and cash distribution to Lowe.

If Lerner is unable to pay the $4,000 to the partnership to cover the negative capital balance, the debit balance in the account is allocated to the remaining partners, Lowe in this case. The journal entry to record the allocation is:

Lowe, Capital	4,000	
Lerner, Capital		4,000

To assign Lerner's deficit to Lowe.

Lowe's capital account now has a negative balance of $2,000 ($38,000 − $40,000), which Lowe must remove by paying $2,000 to the partnership:

Cash	2,000	
Lowe, Capital		2,000

Contribution by Lowe.

Lowe's capital account now has a zero balance and the remaining cash is used to pay off the liabilities:

Accounts Payable	20,000	
Cash		20,000

Payment of liabilities.

Now all the accounts of the partnership have zero balances.

Insufficient Cash to Pay the Liabilities

The previous two examples have illustrated the concept of unlimited liability. The partners had to contribute assets to the partnership to cover negative balances in their capital accounts and to cover the negative balances in the accounts of partners who were personally insolvent. The effect is that the partner is paying cash from his or her personal resources to cover his or her "debts" to the partnership, either for payment to other partners or to pay the liabilities.

A more extreme situation might arise in which none of the partners is able to contribute sufficient assets to the partnership so that the liabilities can be paid. In a situation such as this any payments by the partnership to the liability holders would be decided under the provision of the bankruptcy laws applied to the partners.

REVIEW PROBLEM

On December 31, 1982, the balance sheet of the partnership of Spice and Sugar, who share earnings in a 2 to 1 ratio, was as follows:

SPICE AND SUGAR
Balance Sheet
December 31, 1982

Assets		Liabilities and Owners' Equity	
Cash	$ 50,000	Accounts payable	$ 25,000
Accounts receivable	30,000		
Property and equipment	60,000		
Less: Accumulated		Spice, capital	60,000
depreciation	(25,000)	Sugar, capital	30,000
		Total Liabilities and	
Total Assets	$115,000	Owners' Equity	$115,000

On January 1, 1983, Salt was admitted to the partnership. She paid $15,000 for a 10% share of the partnership. On June 30 the three partners each withdrew $10,000. During 1983 the partnership had sales of $90,000 on account, paid wages to employees of $22,000, and collected accounts receivable of $80,000. Depreciation expense for 1983 was $8,000. Assume accounts payable remained unchanged. The partners distribute earnings as follows:

Salaries: Spice, $10,000; Sugar, $8,000; Salt, $5,000
Interest: 10% of capital balances on January 1 (after admission of Salt)
Balance: In the new earnings distribution ratio of 6 : 3 : 1

On January 1, 1984, the partnership was liquidated. The assets other than cash were sold for $47,000, the accounts payable were paid, and the remaining cash was distributed to the partners.

Required: 1. Prepare journal entries to record the above events in 1983.
2. Prepare a balance sheet for the partnership at December 31, 1983.
3. Prepare the journal entries to record the liquidation.

SOLUTION TO REVIEW PROBLEM

Requirement 1:

1983
Jan. 1 Cash 15,000
    Salt, Capital .... 10,500[a]
    Spice, Capital ($\frac{2}{3}$ × $4,500) 3,000
    Sugar, Capital ($\frac{1}{3}$ × $4,500) 1,500
    Salt admitted to partnership.

[a] Capital of continuing partners .... $ 90,000
Investment of new partner 15,000
Total Capital of New Partnership $105,000
New Partner's Capital (10% × $105,000) .... $ 10,500

June 30 Spice, Withdrawals 10,000
    Sugar, Withdrawals 10,000
    Salt, Withdrawals 10,000
    Cash 30,000
    Withdrawals by partners.

During 1983	Accounts Receivable		90,000	
	Sales			90,000
	To record sales for the year.			

During 1983	Wages Expense		22,000	
	Cash			22,000
	To record wages paid for the year.			

During 1983	Cash		80,000	
	Accounts Receivable			80,000
	To record cash collections for the year.			

Dec. 31	Depreciation Expense		8,000	
	Accumulated Depreciation			8,000
	To record depreciation for the year.			

Dec. 31	Sales		90,000	
	Income Summary			90,000
	To close the sales account.			

Dec. 31	Income Summary		30,000	
	Wages Expense			22,000
	Depreciation Expense			8,000
	To close the expense accounts.			

Dec. 31	Income Summary[a]		60,000	
	Spice, Capital			32,200
	Sugar, Capital			19,100
	Salt, Capital			8,700
	To close the Income Summary account and distribute the earnings.			

[a] Schedule for Distribution of Income

	Spice	Sugar	Salt	Total
Salaries	$10,000	$ 8,000	$5,000	$23,000
Interest:				
Spice ($60,000 + $3,000) × 10%	6,300			
Sugar ($30,000 + $1,500) × 10%		3,150		
Salt ($10,500 × 10%)			1,050	
Total				10,500
Balance Allocated:				
Spice ($26,500* × 60%)	15,900			
Sugar ($26,500 × 30%)		7,950		
Salt ($26,500 × 10%)			2,650	
Total				26,500
Income Distribution	$32,200	$19,100	$8,700	$60,000

* $60,000 − $23,000 − $10,500 = $26,500

Dec. 31	Spice, Capital	10,000	
	Sugar, Capital	10,000	
	Salt, Capital	10,000	
	Spice, Withdrawals		10,000
	Sugar, Withdrawals		10,000
	Salt, Withdrawals		10,000
	To close the withdrawals accounts.		

Requirement 2:

SPICE, SUGAR, AND SALT
Balance Sheet
December 31, 1983

Assets		Liabilities and Owners' Equity	
Cash	$ 93,000[a]	Accounts payable	$ 25,000
Accounts receivable	40,000[b]		
Property and equipment . . .	60,000	Spice, capital	85,200[d]
Less: Accumulated		Sugar, capital	40,600[e]
depreciation	(33,000)[c]	Salt, capital	9,200[f]
		Total Liabilities and	
Total Assets	$160,000	Owner's Equity . . .	$160,000

[a] $50,000 + $15,000 − $30,000 − $22,000 + $80,000
[b] $30,000 + $90,000 − $80,000
[c] $25,000 + $8,000
[d] $60,000 + $3,000 − $10,000 + $32,200
[e] $30,000 + $1,500 − $10,000 + $19,100
[f] $10,500 − $10,000 + $8,700

Requirement 3:

1984			
Jan. 1	Cash	47,000	
	Accumulated Depreciation	33,000	
	Spice, Capital [($67,000 − $47,000) × 60%] . .	12,000[a]	
	Sugar, Capital [($67,000 − $47,000) × 30%] . .	6,000	
	Salt, Capital [($67,000 − $47,000) × 10%] . . .	2,000	
	Accounts Receivable		40,000
	Property and Equipment		60,000
	To record the sale of the assets and loss of $20,000.		

[a] Since the liquidation occurs on January 1, no recognition of salaries or interest is necessary.

Jan. 1	Accounts Payable	25,000	
	Cash		25,000
	To record the payment of liabilities.		

Jan.	1	Spice, Capital ($85,200 − $12,000)	73,200	
		Sugar, Capital ($40,600 − $6,000)	34,600	
		Salt, Capital ($9,200 − $2,000)	7,200	
		Cash		115,000

To record the distribution of remaining cash
to the partners.

GLOSSARY

Agent. A person who has the authority to act for another person.

Bonus. The difference between the assets contributed by a new partner and the capital balance assigned to the new partner.

Earnings Distribution Ratio. The ratio agreed by the partners that is used to distribute the earnings of the partnership to each partner (after the provisions for salaries and interest, if any).

General Partner. A partner who has unlimited liability.

Interest Allocated to Partners. A method of distributing a portion of the earnings of a partnership that compensates each partner for the capital contributed. Not an expense of the partnership.

Limited Partner. A partner who has limited liability.

Liquidation. The dissolution of a partnership by selling the assets, paying the liabilities, and closing the partners' capital accounts.

Partner's Capital Account. An account used by a partnership to record the capital balance of each partner.

Partner's Withdrawal Account. An account used by a partnership to record the assets withdrawn by each partner during the accounting period.

Partnership. An association of two or more persons to carry on as co-owners a business for profit.

Partnership Agreement. An agreement among the partners specifying the formation, operation, and liquidation of a partnership.

Salaries Distributed to Partners. A method of distributing a portion of the earnings of a partnership that compensates each partner for his or her contribution to the operations of the partnership. Not an expense of the partnership.

Statement of Changes in Partners' Equity. A supplementary statement that lists the investments, withdrawals, and earnings distribution for each partner during the accounting period.

Uniform Partnership Act. An act adopted by most states that governs the formation, operation, and liquidation of a partnership. It is superseded by the partnership agreement.

Unlimited Liability. A characteristic of a partnership meaning that each partner is liable for all the debts of the partnership.

QUESTIONS

Q13-1 What is a partnership? Can a partnership exist without a written agreement?

Q13-2 What is a partnership agreement? What is typically included in the agreement?

Q13-3 What are the characteristics that are common to all partnerships?

Q13-4 What is meant by *unlimited liability*? How does this affect a partner as compared to a person with an ownership interest in a corporation?

Q13-5 What is the difference between a general and a limited partner?

Q13-6 Does a partnership have to pay income taxes on its profits? Explain.

Q13-7 What is an *agent*? Can an agent bind other partners to all contracts?

Q13-8 A partner in a legal firm orders a tractor. Can the seller force the partnership to pay? Would your answer change if the partnership was involved in farming?

Q13-9 When does the life of a partnership end? Does a corporation have a limited life?

Q13-10 Why might two people form a partnership? What are the disadvantages?

Q13-11 What transactions directly affect the Capital account of each partner?

Q13-12 What is the purpose of the Withdrawals account of each partner?

Q13-13 What factors might be used to determine the distribution of the earnings of a partnership?

Q13-14 What are the alternatives by which a new partner may be admitted to a partnership?

Q13-15 Upon admission of a new partner when is a bonus assigned to the continuing partners? To the new partner?

Q13-16 When a partner withdraws from a partnership does it affect the capital balances of the other partners? If so, how?

Q13-17 A partner is withdrawing from a partnership. He claims that in addition to receiving assets equal to his capital balance, he should also receive an amount equal to a reasonable salary and interest on the capital he invested while a partner. Is this a valid claim? Explain.

Q13-18 Why might a partnership be liquidated? After the assets have been sold and the liabilities paid, will the remaining cash balance equal the sum of the partners' capital accounts?

Q13-19 If a partner has a negative capital balance when a partnership is liquidated, what is the correct procedure to follow?

EXERCISES

E13-1 Capital Account. During 1983 Susan Chambers was admitted to a partnership on payment of $40,000. She received a capital balance equal to her investment. During the year her share of the net income of the partnership was $18,000 and she withdrew $15,000.

Required: Prepare journal entries to record the above events. The partnership uses a Withdrawals account for each partner.

E13-2 Earnings Distribution. During 1983 the Clark, Hill, and Chapman partnership had a net income of $30,000.

Required: Prepare the journal entry to close the income summary account and distribute the net income if:
1. Earnings are divided equally.
2. Earnings are divided in the ratio 5 : 3 : 2 to Clark, Hill, and Chapman, respectively.

E13-3   Earnings Distribution Based on Capital Balances.   The following information is for the Simon and Art partnership:

	Capital	Investments		Withdrawals	
Partner	1/1/1983	Amount	Date	Amount	Date
Simon	$60,000	$10,000	June 30	$24,000	Nov. 1
Art	35,000	2,000	Apr. 1	18,000	Oct. 1

Required: 1. Prepare the journal entry to close the income summary account and distribute the net income of $40,000 if:
 (a) The partnership earnings are divided on the basis of beginning capital balances.
 (b) The partnership earnings are divided on the basis of average capital balances.
2. Prepare a statement of the changes in the partners' equity when the earnings distribution is based on the average capital balances.

E13-4   Interest on Capital Balances.   Use the same information as in E13-3. The partnership's net income in 1983 was $40,000. Interest of 10% was allowed on capital balances, with the remaining earnings being divided equally.

Required: 1. Prepare the journal entry to close the income summary account and distribute the net income if:
 (a) Interest is allowed on the beginning capital balances.
 (b) Interest is allowed on the average capital balances.
2. Is the interest recorded as interest expense on the partnership's income statement? Why or why not?

E13-5   Recognition of Salaries.   During 1983 the Carter and Hawkins partnership had a net income of $80,000. Salaries of $30,000 and $20,000 are allowed to Carter and Hawkins, with the remaining profits being distributed equally.

Required: 1. Prepare the journal entry to close the income summary account and distribute the net income.
2. Instead, prepare the closing entry assuming the partnership had a net income of $40,000.
3. Are the salaries recorded as salaries expense on the partnership's income statement? Why or why not?

E13-6   Admission of a New Partner.   The Chamberlain and Cambridge partnership decides to admit a new partner, Hart. Hart will pay $30,000 and will be assigned a capital balance of the same amount. Chamberlain and Cambridge have capital balances of $60,000 and $50,000, respectively, and share earnings equally.

Required: Prepare the journal entry to record the admission of Hart if:
1. Hart contributes assets of $30,000 to the partnership.
2. Hart purchases one-half of Chamberlain's share directly from him.

E13-7   Admission of a New Partner.   Use the information in E13-6, except that Hart does not receive a capital balance equal to $30,000.

Required: 1. Prepare the journal entry to record the admission of Hart if:
    (a) Hart purchases a 20% share of the partnership.
    (b) Hart purchases a 40% share of the partnership.
  2. What is the justification for Hart not receiving a capital balance equal to the assets contributed?

E13-8 Withdrawal of a Partner. Cameron decides to withdraw from the Taylor, Durrant, and Cameron partnership. He will receive cash equal to his capital balance after revaluation. The partners have an audit and revaluation that indicates that the inventory should be reduced by $2,000 and property and equipment increased by $15,000. Taylor, Durrant, and Cameron share in earnings 60%, 30%, and 10% and have capital balances of $70,000, $30,000 and $15,000, respectively.

Required: Prepare journal entries to record the revaluation and withdrawal.

E13-9 Withdrawal of a Partner. Use the information in E13-8, except that Cameron does not receive cash equal to his capital balance.

Required: Prepare journal entries to record the revaluation and withdrawal if:
  1. Cameron receives cash of $8,000.
  2. Cameron receives cash of $20,000.

E13-10 Liquidation of a Partnership. The Upps and Downs partnership has the following balance sheet on November 10, 1983:

UPPS AND DOWNS
Balance Sheet
November 10, 1983

Assets		*Liabilities and Owners' Equity*	
Cash	$10,000	Accounts payable	$15,000
Inventory	30,000		
Property and equipment . . .	40,000		
Less: Accumulated		Upps, capital	25,000
depreciation	(20,000)	Downs, capital	20,000
		Total Liabilities and	
Total Assets	$60,000	Owners' Equity	$60,000

The partners, who share earnings equally, decide to liquidate the partnership. The inventory is sold for $35,000 and the property and equipment for $12,000.

Required: Prepare journal entries to record the liquidation.

E13-11 Statement of Changes in Partners' Equity. Snowdon and Peak had capital balances on January 1, 1983, of $20,000 and $40,000, respectively. During 1983 Snowdon and Peak made additional investments of $15,000 and $12,000 and withdrawals of $8,000 and $9,000, respectively. In the distribution of earnings at the end of the year, Snowdon received a salary allowance of $12,000 and an interest allocation of $2,000. Peak received a salary allowance of $11,000 and an interest allocation of $4,000. The remaining $6,000 of partnership earnings were divided equally.

Required: Prepare a statement of the changes in partners' equity for 1983.

PROBLEMS

Part A

P13-1A Distribution of Earnings. Carson and Rickles had capital balances on January 1, 1983, of $48,000 and $25,000, respectively. On June 1 Carson contributed $10,000 cash to the partnership. On August 1, 1983, Rickles contributed a car worth $8,000 to the partnership. On March 31, 1983, Carson and Rickles withdrew $10,000 and $8,000, respectively. On September 30, 1983, they withdrew $12,000 and $9,000, respectively. The net income for 1983 was $30,000.

Required: 1. Prepare journal entries to record the closing of the income summary account and distribution of the partnership net income under each of the following independent alternatives:

(a) Earnings are divided equally.

(b) Earnings are divided 60% to Carson and 40% to Rickles.

(c) Earnings are divided in the ratio of the partners' average capital balances.

(d) Interest of 10% is provided on the average capital balances with the remainder divided equally.

(e) Salaries of $18,000 and $15,000 are allocated to Carson and Rickles, with the remainder divided equally.

(f) Salaries of $15,000 and 10,000 are allocated to Carson and Rickles, interest of 10% is provided on beginning capital balances, and the remainder is divided equally.

2. For your answer to Requirement 1, part f, prepare a partial income statement showing the allocation of net income to the partners.

P13-2A   Admission of a New Partner.   Howard and Castle are partners with capital balances of $70,000 and $50,000, respectively. The partnership has assets consisting of cash of $30,000, inventory of $40,000, and property and equipment of $77,000. Liabilities total $27,000. Howard receives 70% of the partnership's earnings, with the remainder going to Castle. A new partner, Duke, is admitted to the partnership by paying $30,000.

Required: 1. Prepare journal entries to record the admission of Duke to the partnership under each of the following independent alternatives:

(a) Duke pays $30,000 to Howard and Castle directly for 20% of each of their interests.

(b) Duke pays $30,000 to the partnership and is assigned a capital balance of $30,000.

(c) Duke pays $30,000 to the partnership and is assigned a capital balance of $24,000.

(d) Duke pays $30,000 to the partnership and is assigned a capital balance of $33,000.

2. Prepare a condensed balance sheet for the partnership immediately after the admission of Duke for each of the alternatives.

P13-3A   Withdrawal of a Partner.   The balance sheet of the Mays, Young, and Hodges partnership on June 30, 1983, is as follows:

MAYS, YOUNG, AND HODGES
Balance Sheet
June 30, 1983

Assets		*Liabilities and Owners' Equity*	
Cash	$15,000	Accounts payable	$10,000
Accounts receivable	20,000	Note payable	5,000
Inventory	10,000	Mays, capital	20,000
Property and equipment . . .	40,000		
Less: Accumulated		Young, capital	10,000
depreciation	(10,000)	Hodges, capital	30,000
		Total Liabilities and	
Total Assets	$75,000	Owners' Equity	$75,000

Earnings are distributed among Mays, Young, and Hodges in a 2 : 1 : 3 ratio. Young decides to withdraw from the partnership. An audit reveals that an allowance for uncollectible accounts of 10% of accounts receivable should be established and that the property and equipment is worth $38,000.

Required: 1. Prepare the journal entry to record the revaluation.
2. Prepare the journal entry to record the withdrawal of Young under each of the following independent alternatives:
   (a) Young receives partnership cash equal to her capital balance.
   (b) Young receives partnership cash equal to 80% of her capital balance.
   (c) Young receives partnership cash equal to 120% of her capital balance.
   (d) Young receives partnership cash equal to her capital balance and also receives inventory with a cost of $4,000.
   (e) Young sells her interest to Mays who pays her $45,000.

P13-4A Liquidation of a Partnership. The balance sheet of the Evans and Monk partnership on April 15, 1983, is as follows:

EVANS AND MONK
Balance Sheet
April 15, 1983

Assets		*Liabilities and Owners' Equity*	
Cash	$ 5,000	Accounts payable	$ 5,000
Accounts receivable	10,000	Notes payable	7,000
Prepaid rent	2,000		
Equipment	30,000		
Less: Accumulated		Evans, capital	8,000
depreciation	(25,000)	Monk, capital	2,000
		Total Liabilities and	
Total Assets	$22,000	Owners' Equity	$22,000

The amount shown in accounts receivable is for services performed for a client who is now in jail and is unlikely to be paid. The prepaid rent is for the next 2 months, and the partners do not expect to be able to rent the building to others. The equipment is sold for $10,000. Interest on the notes payable is accrued to date and is included in the notes payable balance. The partners share earnings equally.

Required: 1. Prepare journal entries to record the liquidation of the partnership if both partners can contribute cash to the partnership.
2. Prepare journal entries to record the liquidation of the partnership if Monk cannot contribute cash to the partnership.

P13-5A Comprehensive Problem. The balance sheet of the Haston, Brown, and Ward partnership on January 1, 1983, is as follows:

HASTON, BROWN, AND WARD
Balance Sheet
January 1, 1983

Assets		*Liabilities and Owners' Equity*	
Cash	$30,000	Accounts payable	$35,000
Accounts receivable	15,000		
Inventory	40,000		
Property and equipment . . .	30,000	Haston, capital	18,000
Less: Accumulated		Brown, capital	10,000
depreciation	(20,000)	Ward, capital	32,000
		Total Liabilities and	
Total Assets	$95,000	Owners' Equity	$95,000

Haston, Brown, and Ward share earnings in the ratio 50%, 30%, and 20%, respectively, after a salary allocation of $12,000, $10,000, and $8,000, respectively, and an interest provision of 10% on beginning capital balances. The following summarized events occurred during 1983:

(a) Sales of $92,000 on account.

(b) Collected accounts receivable of $87,000.

(c) Purchased inventory on account for $32,000.

(d) Paid accounts payable of $33,000.

(e) Wages paid to employees were $15,000.

(f) The property and equipment is being depreciated on a straight-line basis over 15 years to a zero residual value.

(g) Ending inventory was $46,000.

On January 1, 1984, Haston withdrew from the partnership. At that time the value of the accounts receivable was reduced by $2,000 and the value of the property and equipment increased by $6,000. Haston received cash equal to 90% of the value of her equity after revaluation.

On January 2, 1984, Gold was admitted to the partnership by paying $20,000 to the partnership for a capital balance of $16,000. His share of the earnings is to be 30% after a salary allocation of $6,000 and an interest provision of 10% on his beginning capital balance. Brown and Ward's salary allocations and interest provisions remain the same as in 1983. Their share of the earnings after the salary allocations and interest provisions are 42% and 28%, respectively. Between January 1, 1984, and March 31, 1984, the following summarized events occurred:

(a) Sales of $35,000 on account.

(b) Wages paid to employees were $4,000.

(c) Ending inventory was $5,000.

On March 31, 1984, the partnership was liquidated. All noncash assets were sold at an auction for $64,000. All three partners were able to contribute cash to the partnership to cover any negative capital balances. Salary distributions and interest allocations were made on a proportional basis for the partial year. Gold receives an interest allocation on the basis of his $16,000 initial capital balance. The partnership uses the periodic inventory system.

Required: 1. Prepare journal entries (including closing entries) to record the above events for each year.

2. Prepare the 1983 partnership income statement, the 1983 statement of changes in partners' equity, and the balance sheet at December 31, 1983.

PROBLEMS
Part B

P13-1B   Distribution of Earnings.   Peters and Ladd had capital balances of $120,000 and $180,000, respectively, on January 1, 1983. On July 1 Peters contributed $12,000 cash to the partnership. On September 1 Ladd contributed a machine worth $50,000 to the partnership. On April 1 Peters and Ladd withdrew $30,000 and $60,000, respectively. On October 1 Ladd contributed $25,000 to the partnership. The net income for 1983 was $200,000.

Required: 1. Prepare the journal entries to close the income summary account and distribute the partnership net income under each of the following independent alternatives:

(a) Earnings are distributed equally.

(b) Earnings are distributed 30% to Peters and 70% to Ladd.

(c) Earnings are distributed in the ratio of the partners' average capital balances.

(d) Interest of 15% is provided on the average capital balances, with the remainder distributed equally.

(e) Salaries of $50,000 and $75,000 are allocated to Peters and Ladd, with the remainder divided 30% to Peters and 70% to Ladd.

(f) Salaries of $50,000 and $75,000 are allocated to Peters and Ladd, interest of 15% is provided on average capital balances, and the remainder is divided equally.

2. For your answer to Requirement 1, part f, prepare a partial income statement showing the allocation of net income to the partners.

P13-2B   Admission of a New Partner. Dreves and Guthrie are partners with capital balances of $45,000 and $32,000, respectively. The partnership has assets consisting of cash of $10,000, inventory of $30,000, and property and equipment of $49,000. Liabilities total $12,000. Dreves receives 60% of the partnership's earnings, with the remainder going to Guthrie. A new partner, Dolph, is admitted to the partnership by paying $15,000.

Required: 1. Prepare the journal entries to record the admission of Dolph to the partnership under each of the following independent alternatives:
(a) Dolph pays $15,000 to Dreves and Guthrie directly for 30% of each of their interests.
(b) Dolph pays $15,000 to the partnership and is assigned a capital balance of $15,000.
(c) Dolph pays $15,000 to the partnership and is assigned a capital balance of $10,000.
(d) Dolph pays $15,000 to the partnership and is assigned a capital balance of $22,000.
2. Prepare a condensed balance sheet for the partnership immediately after the admission of Dolph for each of the alternatives.

P13-3B   Withdrawal of a Partner. The unaudited balance sheet of the Webster, Reeves, and Koontz partnership on April 30, 1983, is as follows;

WEBSTER, REEVES, AND KOONTZ
Balance Sheet
April 30, 1983

Assets		Liabilities and Owners' Equity	
Cash	$ 70,000	Accounts payable	$ 44,000
Accounts receivable	30,000	Rent payable	13,000
Inventory	26,000		
Property and equipment . .	95,000	Webster, capital	62,000
Less: Accumulated		Reeves, capital	30,000
depreciation	(31,000)	Koontz, capital	41,000
		Total Liabilities and	
Total Assets	$190,000	Owners' Equity	$190,000

Earnings are distributed among Webster, Reeves, and Koontz in a 2 : 1 : 2 ratio. Koontz decides to withdraw from the partnership. An audit reveals that an allowance for uncollectible accounts of 8% of accounts receivable should be established, that the inventory is worth $21,000, and that property and equipment is worth $70,000.

Required: 1. Prepare the journal entry to record the revaluation.
2. Prepare the journal entry to record the withdrawal of Koontz under each of the following independent alternatives:
(a) Koontz receives partnership cash equal to her capital balance.
(b) Koontz receives partnership cash equal to 75% of her capital balance.
(c) Koontz receives partnership cash equal to 130% of her capital balance.
(d) Koontz receives $25,000 cash and inventory with a cost of $20,000.
(e) Koontz sells 30% of her interest to Reeves and 70% to Webster and receives $20,000 from Reeves and $30,000 from Webster.

P13-4B   Liquidation of a Partnership. The balance sheet for the Price and Iverson partnership on September 15, 1983, is as follows:

PRICE AND IVERSON
Balance Sheet
September 15, 1983

Assets		Liabilities and Owners' Equity	
Cash	$ 50,000	Accounts payable	$ 23,000
Accounts receivable	15,000	Notes payable	27,000
Prepaid rent	8,000		
Equipment	110,000		
Less: Accumulated		Price, capital	43,000
depreciation	(83,000)	Iverson, capital	7,000
		Total Liabilities and	
Total Assets	$100,000	Owner's Equity	$100,000

The amount in accounts receivable is for services performed for a company that has since declared bankruptcy and is unlikely to be paid. The prepaid rent is for next month, and the partners do not expect to be able to rent their office space to others. The equipment is sold for $5,000. Interest on the notes payable is accrued to date and is included in the notes payable balance. Price and Iverson share earnings in a 2 : 1 ratio.

Required: 1. Prepare journal entries to record the liquidation of the partnership if both partners can contribute cash to the partnership.
2. Prepare journal entries to record the liquidation of the partnership if Iverson cannot contribute cash to the partnership.

P13-5B   Comprehensive Problem. The balance sheet for the Larson, Hayes, and Little partnership on January 1, 1983, is as follows:

LARSON, HAYES, AND LITTLE
Balance Sheet
January 1, 1983

Assets		Liabilities and Owners' Equity	
Cash	$100,000	Accounts payable	$130,000
Accounts receivable	120,000		
Inventory	60,000		
Property and equipment . .	80,000	Larson, capital	80,000
Less: Accumulated		Hayes, capital	65,000
depreciation	(40,000)	Little, capital	45,000
		Total Liabilities and	
Total Assets	$320,000	Owners' Equity	$320,000

Larson, Hayes, and Little share earnings in a 3 : 1 : 1 ratio, respectively, after a salary distribution of $30,000, $20,000, and $10,000, respectively, and an interest allocation of 10% on beginning capital balances. The following summarized events occurred during 1983:

(a) Sales of $404,000 on account.
(b) Collected accounts receivable of $450,000.
(c) Purchased inventory on account for $210,000.
(d) Paid accounts payable of $235,000.
(e) Wages paid to employees were $130,000.
(f) The property and equipment is being depreciated on a straight-line basis over 20 years to a zero residual value.
(g) Ending inventory was $90,000.

On January 1, 1984, Hayes withdrew from the partnership. At that time the value of the inventory was increased by $10,000 and the value of the property and equipment was reduced by $20,000. Hayes received cash equal to 110% of the value of her equity after revaluation. On January 2, 1984, Grant was admitted to the partnership by paying $50,000 to the partnership for a capital balance of $40,000. His share of the earnings is to be one-fifth after a salary distribution of $15,000 and an interest provision of 10% on his beginning capital balance. Larson and Little's salary allocations and interest provisions remain the same as in 1983. Their share of the earnings after the salary allocations and interest provisions are 60% and 20%, respectively. Between January 1, 1984, and April 30, 1984, the following summarized events occurred:

(a) Sales of $80,000 on account.
(b) Wages paid to employees were $40,000.
(c) Ending inventory was $10,000.

On April 30, 1984, the partnership was liquidated. All noncash assets were sold at an auction for $55,000. All three partners were able to contribute cash to the partnership to cover any negative capital balances. Salary distributions and interest allocations were made on a proportional basis for the partial year. Grant receives an interest allocation on the basis of his $40,000 initial capital balance. The partnership uses the periodic inventory method.

Required: 1. Prepare journal entries (including closing entries) to record the above events for each year.
2. Prepare the 1983 partnership income statement, the 1983 statement of changes in partners' equity, and the balance sheet at December 31, 1983.

DISCUSSION CASES

C13-1   Admission to a Partnership.   Anton and Derek have operated a partnership for many years. Anton's capital balance is $65,000, and she receives a salary allocation of $16,000. Derek's capital balance is $40,000, and he receives a salary allocation of $12,000. Interest of 10% is provided each year on each partner's beginning capital balance. Remaining earnings and losses are distributed 60% to Anton and 40% to Derek. The net income of the partnership has averaged $80,000 per year in recent years.

Tiegs has worked for the partnership for 10 years and has built an excellent relationship with the customers. She is currently being paid a salary of $16,000, but she has received an offer from a competitor for $20,000.

Since they are anxious to retain Tiegs in the business, Anton and Derek offer her a share of the partnership under the following terms:

1. She will be admitted to the partnership by paying $15,000 cash and signing a 2-year 8% note payable for $8,000. She will be assigned a capital balance of $20,000.
2. Interest of 10% on her capital balance will be provided, and she will receive a salary allocation of $12,000. Anton and Derek will continue to receive the same interest and salary allocations as before.
3. Remaining earnings will be distributed to Anton, Derek, and Tiegs in the ratio of 50%, 30%, and 20%, respectively.

Required: Tiegs has come to you for advice on whether she should become a partner or take the offer from the competitor. Prepare a report for Tiegs that analyzes the advantages and disadvantages of becoming a partner.

C13-2   Withdrawal from a Partnership.   Andrews and Moore have operated a partnership for a few years. Andrews and Moore receive salary allocations of $12,000 and $9,000, respectively, and interest of 10% is provided on their capital balances of $8,000 and $6,000, respectively. The remaining earnings are shared in the ratio of 70% and 30%, respectively.

The partnership has never been very successful, and this year there has been a loss of $1,000. The partnership agreement does not specify how losses are to be distributed. Moore decides to withdraw from the partnership and suggests the following:

1. The loss will be distributed equally with no interest or salary allocations being made.
2. The $13,000 assets of the partnership remaining after payment of the liabilities will be distributed equally.

Required: Prepare a report for Andrews advising him whether he should accept the terms offered by Moore.

14 | Corporations: Capital Stock and Contributed Capital

After reading this chapter, you should understand:

- The characteristics, advantages, and disadvantages of a corporation
- The differences between par value, stated value, and no-par stock
- Accounting for the issuance of stock for cash, for subscriptions, and in noncash exchanges
- Accounting for donated capital, the conversion of preferred stock to common stock, and stock splits
- The characteristics of treasury stock
- Accounting for treasury stock
- Preparing the statement of changes in stockholders' equity

In the earlier chapters we focused primarily on accounting for sole proprietorships. In Chapter 13 we discussed the specific accounting issues of partnerships. Although sole proprietorships and partnerships outnumber corporations in the number of existing entities, corporations produce and sell far more goods and services. To accumulate sufficient capital to finance its activities, a corporation may enter into many different transactions involving the issuance of its capital stock. In this chapter the main focus is on understanding corporations, their capital stock transactions, and the impact of these transactions upon the owners' equity of a corporation.

CORPORATE FORM OF ORGANIZATION

In 1819 Chief Justice John Marshall defined a corporation as "an artificial being, invisible, intangible, and existing only in contemplation of the law." Today, although a corporation is a collection of individual owners, it is treated as a separate entity according to the law. **A corporation is treated as an artificial entity, with a continuous life, and separate from and independent of the individual owners.** Thus ownership in a corporation may be transferred from one individual to another. An owner ordinarily has no personal liability for the corporation's debts and frequently plays no active part in the management of the corporation. As a result, the success of the corporation depends on its ability to attract large amounts of capital (from a diverse set of owners), which is controlled by its professional management group for an indefinite period of time.

Procedures for Incorporation

To operate as a corporation in the United States, a business entity must incorporate in one of the states. **To incorporate means to file the necessary documents and obtain permission to operate as a corporation.** Each state has its own laws of incorporation; many of these laws are uniform throughout the country, whereas others are not. Normally one or more individuals may apply to the appropriate state officials for approval to form a corporation. The application includes the names of the individual incorporators; the corporate name, address, and nature of business; the types, legal value (if any), and number of capital shares to be authorized for issuance; and any other information required by the state's laws. The application may also include the names and addresses of the initial subscribers (subscriptions are discussed later) to the capital stock, the number of subscribed shares, the subscription price, and the down payment (if any). **An approved application to form a corporation is referred to as the articles of incorporation (or corporate charter).** A meeting may then be held at which the initial issuance of capital stock is made to the incorporators, a board of directors is elected, a set of rules (bylaws) regulating the corporate operations is established, and the board appoints the executive officers (i.e., the *top management*) of the corporation. These terms are more fully discussed later in the chapter.

In order for a corporation to conduct its operations, the state gives it various rights and powers, including the right to enter into contracts, to hold, buy, and sell property, to sue and be sued, and to have a continuous life. These rights and powers are accompanied by a number of responsibilities. A corporation may engage only in the activities for which it was established; it must safeguard the corporate capital; it must adhere to all state and federal laws; it must adhere to state regulations concerning the distribution of net income; it must pay its debts; and it must pay local, state, and federal taxes.

Ownership and Management of a Corporation

Capital stock is the ownership unit in a corporation. A stock certificate is evidence of ownership in a corporation. **A stock certificate is a serially numbered legal document that indicates the number of shares of capital stock owned by a stockholder and the par (legal) value, if any.** It may also include additional information concerning the method of transferring the capital stock to any other owner. An illustration of a stock certificate is presented in Exhibit 14-1. **The owners of a corporation are referred to as the stockholders (or shareholders).**

Since shares of stock are transferable between individuals, the owners of a corporation may be a diverse set of stockholders who are not involved in the management of the corporation. Because of this separation of ownership and management, each stockholder has been given five rights. These rights are:

1. The right to attend stockholders' meetings and to vote in setting and approving major policies and actions of the corporation. Included are policies and actions

EXHIBIT 14-1   Illustration of Stock Certificate

Reprinted with permission.

concerning such items as mergers with other companies, acquisitions of other companies, sales of major portions of the corporation, and the issuance of additional stock and bonds (discussed in Chapter 16).

2. The right to vote in the election of the board of directors. **A board of directors is a group of individuals that has the responsibility and authority to supervise the corporation's ordinary business activities, make future plans, and take whatever action is necessary in the current management of the corporation.** Voting to elect the board of directors (and the *chairman of the board*) also takes place at the stockholders' meetings.

3. The right to share in net income by receiving dividends from the corporation. The payment of dividends, however, is determined by the board of directors.

4. The right to purchase additional capital stock if it is issued. This is called the preemptive right. **The preemptive right is the right to maintain a proportionate percentage of ownership of the corporation by purchasing a proportionate (pro rata) share of additional capital stock if it is issued.**

5. The right to share in the distribution of the assets of the corporation if it is liquidated (terminated). If a corporation is terminated creditors are given first priority in the collection of their claims; any remaining assets are then distributed to stockholders.

The separation of ownership and management has resulted in the need for a *chain of command* for operating and managing the corporation. A typical chain of command is illustrated in the organization chart presented in Exhibit 14-2.

Stockholders vote on major corporate policies and actions. They also vote in the election of the board of directors, thus indirectly influencing the supervision of the corporation's business activities. The board of directors appoints the president, who is the top (chief) executive officer in the organization. The president is responsible for the planning and control of all the corporate activities. Several vice presidents usually assist the president in the planning and control of operations, however. For instance, the vice president of marketing deals with sales, advertising, and marketing research. The vice president of production is responsible for purchasing, manufacturing, and quality control. The vice president of finance may oversee both the treasurer and controller. The treasurer is responsible for short- and long-term financing, credit and collections, and short- and long-term investments. The controller is responsible for internal control, the general supervision of accounting, and the preparation and issuance of accounting reports. The secretary is responsible for the corporate records, including keeping the minutes of the stockholders' meetings and the board of directors' meetings, and maintaining the stockholders' records.

EXHIBIT 14-2
Typical Corporate
Organization Chart

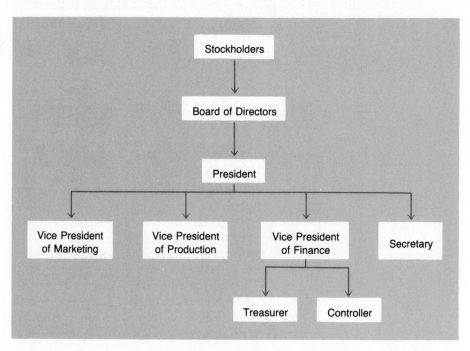

Because stock certificates may be transferred from one individual to another, state laws require that each corporation maintain records of its stockholders. **The stockholders' ledger contains a record for each stockholder that shows the stockholder's name, address, and number of shares held.** This information enables the corporation to notify stockholders of all stockholders' meetings and to pay the correct amount of dividends to the proper stockholders. Whenever new shares are issued or shares are exchanged between stockholders, the stockholders' ledger must be updated. Exchanges of stock are initially recorded in a stock transfer journal. **A stock transfer journal contains the names and addresses of the new and former stockholders involved in each stock transfer, the date of exchange, the stock certificate numbers, and the number of shares exchanged.** Many corporations used to employ an independent *transfer agent* to issue the stock certificates as well as a *registrar* to maintain the stockholder records. With the advent of high-speed computer-based systems, however, more and more corporations are doing these tasks themselves.

Advantages of a Corporation

The corporation has become so prominent because it offers five primary advantages:

1. **Limited Liability.**   Under the law a corporation is a separate legal entity, independent of its owners, and responsible for paying its obligations. Stockholders cannot be held personally responsible for the corporation's debts. This difference is the most important advantage over sole proprietorships and partnerships, in which creditors may be able to satisfy their claims by use of the owners' personal assets.
2. **Ease of Transferability of Ownership.**   The capital stock of many corporations sells on organized stock markets like the New York and American Stock Exchanges. Because shares of stock are transferable, it is relatively easy for an owner to dispose of his or her ownership should the need arise. This is not the case in a sole proprietorship or partnership.
3. **Ability to Attract Large Amounts of Ownership Capital.**   The operation of a major corporation requires a large amount of capital invested by owners. Because ownership in a corporation is transferable and stockholders have limited liability, corporations usually are able to attract the large amounts of capital necessary for their operations.
4. **Ability to Attract Top Quality Management.**   Most owners of corporations have neither the talent nor desire to manage its operations. These owners willingly give these management duties to the corporation's board of directors. The directors, in turn, can hire the highest-quality *management team* necessary to ensure successful operations.
5. **Continuity of Life.**   As a separate legal entity a corporation has a continuous life. In contrast to a sole proprietorship or partnership, the activities of a corporation are normally not affected or disrupted by the death or withdrawal of an owner.

**Disadvantages of
a Corporation**

Although the advantages of a corporation generally are very important, there are three primary disadvantages:

1. **Significant Taxation.**   Sole proprietorships and partnerships, as business entities, are not subject to income taxes. The owners of a sole proprietorship or partnership are taxed on their personal income from the business. Corporations, however, are treated as separate legal entities subject to federal and state income taxes. Since the maximum federal income tax rate for corporations is currently 46%, and many of them pay state income taxes, it is not unusual for income taxes to approach or exceed 50% of a corporation's income before income taxes. When the earnings of the corporation are distributed to stockholders as dividends, the stockholders may again be taxed on this personal income. This is referred to as *double taxation* and is the most significant disadvantage of a corporation.

2. **Government Control and Regulation.**   In order to protect creditors and stockholders, laws have been enacted to control and regulate corporations. For instance, the payment of dividends by a corporation is usually limited to a specified amount established by the laws of the state in which it is incorporated. In addition, corporations are restricted in the purchase of their own stock. If a corporation's capital stock is sold on a stock market certain reports must be filed by the corporation. Additional reports are required to be filed for such items as employee's safety and health and the corporation's environmental activities.

3. **Restricted Ability to Attract Creditor Capital.**   For a sole proprietorship or partnership, the creditors may use the personal assets of the owners to satisfy their claims. The owners of a corporation have limited liability, however. As a result, a corporation (particularly a smaller one) may have a more difficult time borrowing money on a short- or long-term basis because creditors may perceive their investment to be less safe.

The advantages of a corporation usually exceed the disadvantages when a business grows to a reasonable size. Because a corporation's management has the responsibility to abide by state and federal laws and to safeguard and ensure the proper use of capital invested by a diverse set of owners, accounting for the invested capital has become an important activity in itself. The remainder of this chapter deals with this accounting process.

**CORPORATE
CAPITAL
STRUCTURE**

In a sole proprietorship or partnership there are usually only a few owners. An owner's capital account is used for each owner, to report the owner's equity on the balance sheet. The ending balance of each owner's capital account includes the investments by the owner, plus the owner's share of the net income earned to date less the owner's withdrawals. There are usually many owners of a corporation, making it almost impossible to establish separate capital accounts for each owner like those of a sole proprietorship or partnership. Furthermore, state laws require special accounting procedures for the owners' equity of a corporation; these laws have been established to protect the absentee owners of a corporation as well as its creditors.

Stockholders' equity is the term used for the owners' equity of a corporation. The stockholders' equity on a corporation's balance sheet is usually separated into two components: contributed capital and retained earnings. This division of stockholders' equity is established in adherence to state laws. The basic format (with assumed numbers of shares and dollar amounts) of the stockholders' equity section on a corporation's balance sheet is shown below:

Stockholders' Equity

Contributed capital		
Capital stock, $5 par, 20,000 shares		
authorized, 10,000 shares issued and outstanding	$50,000	
Additional paid-in capital	70,000	
Total contributed capital		$120,000
Retained earnings		90,000
Total Stockholders' Equity		$210,000

The total amount of investments made by stockholders into the corporation is reported in the contributed capital section. Each of the accounts (capital stock and additional paid-in capital) and the information about the number of shares (authorized, issued, and outstanding) included in this section are discussed below. The balance in retained earnings reports the total lifetime corporate earnings that have been reinvested in the corporation and not distributed to stockholders as dividends. The accounting issues relating to retained earnings were briefly introduced in Chapter 5 and are discussed in Chapter 15.

Capital Stock and Legal Capital

Capital stock refers to the ownership units in the corporation. Capital stock may be issued by the corporation for cash, in installmentlike sales, in noncash exchanges, and in other transactions. The dollar amount recorded in the Capital Stock account by a corporation for each capital stock transaction depends on the laws of the state in which it is incorporated. Because capital stockholders have a *limited liability*, to protect creditors state laws usually set a legal capital for all corporations. **Legal capital is the amount of stockholders' equity that cannot be distributed to stockholders.** A corporation may not pay dividends or reacquire capital stock if these activities will reduce the legal capital. The definition of legal capital varies from state to state. In most states, however, the total par value or stated value of the issued capital stock is the legal capital.

PAR VALUE STOCK. Historically, the usual way legal capital has been established is by requiring that all capital stock have a par value. **The par value of capital stock is a monetary amount that is designated as the legal capital per share in the articles of incorporation and is printed on each stock certificate.** The total legal capital of a corporation is determined by multiplying the par value per share times the number of shares issued. Generally, states require that a separate accounting be made of the legal capital. Consequently, as we will see shortly, for each issuance of capital stock the total dollar amount of the par value is recorded in a capital stock account.

NO-PAR STOCK. Most states also allow the issuance of no-par capital stock. **No-par capital stock does not have a par value.** When no-par stock is issued, some states require that the entire proceeds received by the corporation for the issued shares be designated as legal capital, and accounting practices have been established for this situation. Many states, however, allow the corporation's board of directors to establish a stated value per share of no-par stock. **The stated value of no-par stock is the legal capital per share of stock.** The stated value per share, when multiplied times the number of shares issued, is the total amount of legal capital. Accounting for stated value, no-par stock is very similar to accounting for par value stock, and the total dollar amount of the stated value is recorded in a capital stock account.

The concept of legal capital has had a significant impact upon corporate accounting practices, particularly as they apply to stockholders' equity. Capital stock accounts are established to record the legal capital, and additional paid-in capital accounts are used for the remainder of the total amount of capital contributed by stockholders.

Additional Paid-in Capital

The par value of a share of capital stock often is set very low — perhaps $10, $2, or even less per share. Since capital stock normally will be issued at a price far in excess of par value, the legal capital is usually only a small part of the total proceeds received. The total proceeds received is the *market* value, the price at which the stock is issued. It is very important to understand that the par value of capital stock has *no* direct relationship to its market value at any time.

A corporation may issue capital stock in a variety of transactions. In addition to following state laws for recording the par or stated value in a capital stock account, it is also sound accounting practice (as well as state law in certain states) to record the excess value received. The excess value received is called additional paid-in capital. **Additional paid-in capital is the difference between the market value and the par value in each stock transaction and is recorded in an Additional Paid-in Capital account.** (How this is recorded is discussed later.) This account is alternatively entitled *Additional Paid-in Capital on Capital Stock, Additional Paid-in Capital in Excess of Par (or Stated) Value, Premium on Capital Stock*, or *Contributed Capital in Excess of Par (or Stated) Value*. Additional paid-in capital sometimes arises from transactions not involving the original issuance of capital stock. These transactions are discussed later in the chapter.

Classes of Capital Stock

Corporations may issue two classes of capital stock, common stock and preferred stock. If a corporation issues only one class of capital stock, it is frequently referred to as common stock. **Common stock is capital stock that shares in all the stockholders' rights.** If a corporation issues more than one class of stock, the other class of stock (in addition to common stock) is called preferred stock. **Preferred stock is capital stock for which certain additional rights are given to the stockholders in exchange for giving up some of the usual stockholders' rights.** The additional rights may involve the right to a set dividend rate on the preferred stock and the right to convert the preferred stock to common stock at a later date. The right to vote may be given up in exchange for these additional rights. Dividends on preferred stock are discussed more fully in Chapter 15. The conversion of preferred stock to common stock is briefly discussed later in this chapter.

Preferred stock is typically issued with a par value. When a corporation issues both common stock and preferred stock, it will use a Common Stock account and a Preferred Stock account to record the legal capital of each kind of stock. It will also use an Additional Paid-in Capital on Common Stock account and an Additional Paid-in Capital on Preferred Stock account for the difference between the market values received and the par values, respectively. We also use these account titles in this book. When a corporation issues both classes of stock, the contributed capital component of stockholders' equity would be expanded to include the additional accounts as shown below (using assumed numbers of shares and dollar amounts):

Stockholders' Equity

Contributed capital
Preferred stock, $100 par, 2,000 shares authorized,
    600 shares issued and outstanding $60,000
Common stock, $10 par, 30,000 shares authorized,
    9,000 shares issued and outstanding 90,000
Additional paid-in capital on preferred stock 72,000
Additional paid-in capital on common stock 43,000
    Total contributed capital $265,000
Retained earnings 173,000
    Total Stockholders' Equity $438,000

With this background in mind, we now turn to recording the various types of capital stock transactions. Since most capital stock is common stock, our examples are in terms of common stock. The journal entries shown would be the same for preferred stock, however, except for the necessary changes in the account titles. The review problem at the end of the chapter includes transactions involving preferred stock.

CAPITAL STOCK TRANSACTIONS

Common stock is authorized for issuance in the articles of incorporation after which it may be issued for cash, in installmentlike sales, in noncash exchanges, and in other transactions. Each of these alternatives is discussed below.

Authorization

The corporate charter contains the authorization to issue capital stock. This authorization lists the classes of stock that may be issued, the par or stated value, the number of authorized shares, and in the case of preferred stock, any preference provisions. Once a corporation has issued all of its authorized stock, it must reapply to the state for approval to issue more shares. Consequently, a corporation usually obtains authorization to issue more stock than it initially plans to sell.

It is important to understand the difference between authorized capital stock and issued capital stock. **Authorized capital stock is the number of shares of capital stock (both common and preferred) that the corporation *may* legally issue.**

Issued capital stock is the number of shares of capital stock that a corporation *has* legally issued to its stockholders on a specific date. As shown earlier, the numbers of shares authorized and issued for each class of stock are reported in the stockholders' equity section of a corporation's balance sheet.

Issuance for Cash

Capital stock may be issued with a par value, as no-par stock with a stated value, or as true no-par stock. In the case of par value stock issued for cash, when the cash received is equal to the par value, the journal entry is simply a debit (increase) to cash and a credit (increase) to the capital stock account for the amount of cash received. In the more usual case, when the cash received is more than the total par value, the difference is recorded in an additional paid-in capital account. To illustrate, assume that a corporation issues 300 shares of its $10 par common stock for $16 per share. The following journal entry would be made to record the transaction:

```
Cash ($16 × 300) . . . . . . . . . . . . . . . . . . . . . . . .      4,800
    Common Stock, $10 par ($10 × 300)  . . . . . . . . . . . .              3,000
    Additional Paid-in Capital on Common Stock  . . . . . . . .              1,800
To record issuance of common stock.
```

If, instead, the stock were no-par stock with a stated value of $10 per share, the above transaction would be recorded as follows:

```
Cash . . . . . . . . . . . . . . . . . . . . . . . . . . . . . .      4,800
    Common Stock, $10 stated value . . . . . . . . . . . . . .              3,000
    Additional Paid-in Capital on Common Stock  . . . . . . . .              1,800
To record issuance of common stock.
```

Note that, except for the title of the capital stock account, accounting for the issuance of no-par stock with a stated value is identical to that of par value stock.

Alternatively, the company may be authorized to issue no-par stock without a stated value. In this case the entire amount of the cash received is the legal capital and is recorded in the capital stock account. If the above transaction had involved no-par common stock, with no stated value, the following journal entry would have been made:

```
Cash . . . . . . . . . . . . . . . . . . . . . . . . . . . . . .      4,800
    Common Stock, no-par . . . . . . . . . . . . . . . . . . . .              4,800
To record issuance of 300 shares of common stock.
```

Note that in the explanation of this journal entry the number of *shares* issued was included. This was necessary because the number of shares issued in this transaction could not be determined by dividing the total increase in the Common Stock account by the par value per share. The remaining examples of stock issuances assume a par value.

Although most states prohibit such transactions, capital stock could be issued at a price *below* its par or stated value. In this case the stock sells at a *discount*, and the original stockholder may be required to pay into the corporation the amount of the discount should the corporation be unable to meet its financial obligations. When the stock is issued the difference between the cash received and the par value would be *debited* to an account entitled Discount on Common Stock. The Discount on Common Stock account would be listed as a contra (negative) account in the Contributed Capital section of stockholders' equity.

Miscellaneous costs may be incurred for the issuance of common stock. They include legal fees, accounting fees, stock certificate costs, and other costs. As discussed in Chapter 12, these costs associated with the *initial* issuance of stock at incorporation should be recorded (debited) as an intangible asset entitled Organization Costs. When these costs are associated with *subsequent* issuances of common stock, they reduce the proceeds received and should be debited to the Additional Paid-in Capital account.

Stock Subscriptions Investors sometimes agree to purchase capital stock on an "installment" basis. In this case the corporation and the future stockholder enter into a legally binding subscription contract. **In a subscription contract the subscriber (investor) agrees to buy a certain number of shares at a set price, with the payment spread over a specified time period.** The contract often requires a down payment and may contain provisions for any defaults (nonpayments) by the subscriber. The shares of capital stock are not issued to a subscriber until the subscriber has completed full payment of the subscription price.

To illustrate, assume that a corporation enters into a subscription contract with several subscribers that involves the purchase of 400 shares of $5 par common stock at a price of $9 per share. The contract requires a down payment of $2 per share, with the remaining $7 per share collectible at the end of 1 month. The stock will be issued to each subscriber upon full payment. The journal entry to record the subscription is as follows:

Cash ($2 × 400)	800	
Subscriptions Receivable: Common Stock ($7 × 400)	2,800	
Common Stock Subscribed ($5 × 400)		2,000
Additional Paid-in Capital on Common Stock		
[($9 − $5) × 400]		1,600

To record subscription to common stock.

Note that the balance to be received ($2,800) is recorded in a Subscriptions Receivable account. This account is usually listed as a current asset because the subscription contract ordinarily requires full payment within a year.

The Common Stock Subscribed account is increased (credited) for the $2,000 par value of the shares subscribed. This account is used because the shares have not yet been legally issued, although the corporation has contracted to issue additional stock. If a balance sheet is issued after a subscription contract but before the subscribed shares have been issued, the Common Stock Subscribed account is listed in the Contributed Capital section of stockholders' equity. Additional Paid-in Capital is increased (credited) for the entire difference ($1,600) between the subscription price (the proceeds) and the par value of the subscribed stock under the assumption that the legal contract will be completed and the stock fully paid for.

To illustrate the reporting of common stock subscribed in stockholders' equity, assume that the above corporation had issued 1,000 shares of the $5 par common stock for $6 per share prior to entering into the subscription. If a balance sheet were prepared immediately after entering into the subscription contract, stockholders' equity would appear as follows:

Stockholders' Equity

Contributed capital
Common stock, $5 par, 10,000 shares authorized
    1,000 shares issued and outstanding $5,000
Common stock subscribed (400 shares)   2,000
Additional paid-in capital on common stock
    ($1,000 + $1,600)   2,600
      Total contributed capital . . . . $ 9,600
Retained earnings (assumed)   6,000
      Total Stockholders' Equity $15,600

If no-par common stock with no stated value is used in a stock subscription, the entire subscription price is credited to the Common Stock Subscribed account. No-par stock with a stated value and preferred stock are accounted for as in the example, with suitable changes in account titles.

When the remaining payments on the stock subscription are received, Cash is increased (debited) and Subscriptions Receivable is decreased (credited). At the final payment by each subscriber, stock certificates are issued for the number of fully paid subscribed shares. At that time a journal entry is made decreasing (debiting) Common Stock Subscribed and increasing (crediting) Common Stock for the par value of the issued shares. To illustrate, assume that the $7 per share final payment on the 400 shares was received at the end of the month. The journal entries to record the receipt and the issuance of the shares are as follows:

Cash ($7 × 400)   2,800
    Subscriptions Receivable: Common Stock   2,800
To record receipt of final payment on subscription contract.

Common Stock Subscribed   2,000
    Common Stock, $5 par   2,000
To record issuance of fully paid subscribed shares.

Occasionally a subscriber will not make the entire payments required by the subscription contract. When a default occurs the accounting is determined by the subscription contract provisions, such as: (1) return to the subscriber the entire amount paid in; (2) return to the subscriber the amount paid in, less any costs incurred by the corporation to reissue the stock; (3) issue to the subscriber a lesser number of shares based upon the total amount of payment received; or (4) require the forfeiture of all amounts paid in. If the subscription contract does not include a provision for subscription defaults, the laws of the state in which the corporation is incorporated usually provide for one of these alternatives. The journal entries are beyond the scope of this textbook.

Noncash Issuance of Stock

Sometimes capital stock is issued for assets other than cash, or for services performed. When this occurs a correct value must be used to record the transaction. This is a thorny issue when it involves intangible assets such as patents, copyrights, or organization costs because of the difficulty in valuing these assets. A general rule useful in these cases is to record the transaction at the fair market value of the stock issued or the assets received, whichever can be more objectively determined. For instance, at the time of the transaction the stock may be selling on the stock market at a specified price. In this case the stock has a known value (the stock market price), and therefore this value would be used to record the transaction.

To illustrate, suppose that a corporation issues 100 shares of $10 par common stock in exchange for a patent. The stock is currently selling for $18 per share on the stock market. A value of $1,800 would be used to record the transaction as follows:

Patent	1,800	
Common Stock, $10 par ($10 × 100)		1,000
Additional Paid-in Capital on Common Stock		
[($18 − $10) × 100]		800

To record issuance of common stock for patent.

Alternatively, the corporation's stock may not be actively traded on a stock market. In this case the fair market value of the assets received may be used to record the transaction. This value may be based on a review of recent transactions involving similar assets or on an appraisal by a competent, independent appraiser. To illustrate, assume that a corporation issues 1,000 shares of $4 par common stock that is not widely traded in exchange for an acre of land. An independent appraiser indicates the land has a value of $16,000. The journal entry to record the transaction is shown below:

Land	16,000	
Common Stock, $4 par ($4 × 1,000)		4,000
Additional Paid-in Capital on Common Stock		
($16,000 − $4,000)		12,000

To record issuance of common stock for land.

Sometimes shares of capital stock are issued by a corporation as payment for legal or accounting services performed in its incorporation process. As we indicated earlier, the costs of these services are recorded as an intangible asset Organization Costs because these services will benefit the corporation in the future. The transaction should be recorded at the agreed-upon contract price for the services by increasing (debiting) Organization Costs for the contract price, increasing (crediting) Common Stock for the par value, and recording the difference between the contract price and the par value as an increase (credit) to Additional Paid-in Capital.

It is important to understand the impact on the financial statements of an error in recording the noncash issuance of capital stock. Suppose, for instance, that stock was issued for equipment and the transaction was recorded at too high a value. In this case both the assets and stockholders' equity of the corporation would be overstated. In addition, since equipment is a depreciable asset the initial error would cause an overstatement each year in the depreciation expense, resulting in an understatement of net income. The financial statements would be correct only at the end of the asset's useful life. If the equipment was initially recorded at too low a value, opposite errors would result. Good judgment must be used in recording noncash issuances of capital stock to avoid errors in the financial statements of current and later periods.

OTHER CHANGES IN CONTRIBUTED CAPITAL

Several other items may affect contributed capital. Each of these items is discussed below.

Donated Capital

In a few instances a corporation may increase contributed capital for events not related to the issuance of capital stock. These increases are rare because, generally, they do not conform to the historical cost principle. For example, it is possible for a corporation to receive donated assets, such as a plant site, to induce it to locate in an "industrial park" of a community. Some communities do this to increase the employment opportunities for their citizens and to increase the collection of property taxes. In this case the corporation should record the donation as an increase (debit) in its assets at the fair market value (as determined by, say, an independent appraisal). The credit portion of the journal entry would involve an increase (credit) to an account entitled Additional Paid-in Capital from Donations. This is appropriate because the assets of the corporation have increased without an increase in liabilities; the entire value belongs to the stockholders. To illustrate, suppose that a community donated land worth $8,000 to a corporation. The corporation would record the event as follows:

Land	8,000	
Additional Paid-in Capital from Donations		8,000
To record donated land at its fair market value.		

Whether cash or noncash assets are received as a result of donations, the balance of the Additional Paid-in Capital from Donations account is listed as an item in the contributed capital section of the balance sheet. It is added to the balances of the capital stock and other additional paid-in capital accounts to determine the total contributed capital.

Conversion of Preferred Stock to Common Stock

Earlier we mentioned that a corporation may issue two classes of stock, common and preferred. One of the preferences that might be extended to preferred stockholders is the right to exchange (convert) the preferred stock for common stock at a later date. **Preferred stock that is exchangeable into common stock is called convertible preferred stock.** Usually the number of common shares into which each preferred share is convertible is established at the time the preferred stock is issued. For instance, General Telephone & Electronics Corporation (GTE) has issued 763,760 shares of $50 par convertible preferred stock that is convertible into 660,247 shares of common stock.

Another preference involves the right to a set dividend. Both the conversion preference and the dividend preference are an advantage to the preferred stockholder. Since the preferred stock is convertible into a specified amount of common stock, the market price of the convertible preferred stock tends to rise in proportion to any rise in the market price of the common stock. When the market price of the common stock is falling, however, the right to a set dividend on the preferred stock tends to stabilize the market value of the preferred stock.

The issuance of preferred stock (whether or not it is convertible) is accounted for in the same manner (except for changes in account titles) as the issuance of common stock. Accounting for the conversion of preferred to common stock is very straightforward. The par value of the converted preferred stock and the additional paid-in capital on the preferred stock are eliminated (debited) and replaced with the par value of the common stock and the additional paid-in capital on the common stock.

To illustrate, assume that a corporation had previously issued 40 shares of $100 par convertible preferred stock for $110 per share. At the time of issuance the corporation recorded the following journal entry:

Cash (40 × $110)	4,400	
Preferred Stock, $100 par (40 × $100)		4,000
Additional Paid-in Capital on Preferred Stock (40 × $10) . .		400
To record issuance of preferred stock.		

Assume that each share of preferred stock is convertible into 6 shares of $10 par common stock and that 30 shares are converted. The journal entry to record the conversion is as follows:

Preferred Stock, $100 par (30 × $100)	3,000	
Additional Paid-in Capital on Preferred Stock (30 × $10) . . .	300	
Common Stock, $10 par (30 × 6 × $10)		1,800
Additional Paid-in Capital on Common Stock		
($3,300 − $1,800)		1,500
To record conversion of 30 shares of preferred stock to 180 shares of common stock.		

Note that the conversion of preferred stock to common stock affects the components of contributed capital but it does not affect the total contributed capital. The $3,300 contributed capital of the preferred stock was simply replaced by an equal amount of contributed capital for the common stock.

Stock Splits   Sometimes the market price of a corporation's common stock increases to the point where some investors are unwilling to buy the stock. Many corporations believe a wide distribution of ownership improves their public image and increases their product sales to their stockholders. To reduce the market price so that it falls within the *trading range* (the price per share investors are willing to pay for common stock) of most investors, the board of directors may authorize a stock split. **A stock**

split is a decrease in the par value per share of stock and a proportional increase in the number of shares authorized and issued. For example, in May 1981, Exxon Corporation issued a 2 for 1 stock split of its common stock.

Since a stock split affects the number of authorized shares and the legal capital, each stock split must be approved by the state in which the corporation is incorporated. To illustrate a stock split, suppose a corporation that has issued 50,000 shares of $10 par common stock declares a 2 for 1 stock split with a reduction to a $5 par value. After the split a total of 100,000 shares of $5 common stock have been issued. A stockholder who previously owned 40 shares of $10 par common stock will own 80 shares of $5 par common stock after the stock split. The additional number of shares participating in the same amount of corporate earnings will cause a proportional decrease in the market price per share.

A stock split has no impact upon the dollar amount of any element of stockholders' equity and consequently it has no effect on total stockholders' equity. In the previous example the total par value of the common stock is $500,000 before and after the stock split. Even though a stock split does not affect the balance of any account, a memorandum entry[1] is necessary to maintain a chronological history of the corporation's financial activities in the general journal. For the above stock split, the memorandum entry in the general journal might appear as follows (assuming the corporation was authorized to issue 80,000 shares before the stock split):

> On January 1, 1983, with approval by the state, the board of directors authorized a 2 for 1 stock split, reducing the par value of the common stock from $10 per share to $5 per share. The number of authorized shares increased from 80,000 to 160,000 shares, and the issued common stock increased from 50,000 to 100,000 shares.

This concludes our discussion of the main transactions involving the *issuance* of capital stock and their impact on contributed capital. We now turn to the accounting for the *reacquisition* of a corporation's capital stock.

TREASURY STOCK

In most states a corporation may reacquire its own previously issued capital stock, after which the stock is held by the corporation in its treasury. **Treasury stock is a corporation's own capital stock that (1) has been fully paid for by stockholders, (2) has been legally issued, (3) is reacquired by the corporation, and (4) is being held by the corporation.** For instance, at the end of 1980, Emerson Electric Company held 225,977 shares of its common stock as treasury stock.

Overview

A corporation may acquire treasury stock for various reasons: (1) to have shares available for employee purchase plans; (2) to issue stock in the conversion of convertible preferred stock; (3) to invest excess cash and help to maintain the

---

[1] **A memorandum entry is a written description of an event involving the corporation's financial activities.** It is recorded in the general journal but does not involve a debit or credit amount.

market price of its stock; (4) to issue stock in the acquisition of other companies; (5) to reduce the number of shares outstanding and increase the earnings per share (discussed in Chapter 15); or (6) to use in the issuance of a stock dividend (discussed in Chapter 15). Each of these transactions is subject to legal, governmental, and stock exchange regulations.

Treasury stock is clearly *not* an asset; a corporation cannot own itself. A corporation cannot recognize a gain or loss when reacquiring its own stock, which restricts a corporation from influencing its net income by buying and selling its own stock. Consequently, treasury stock is accounted for as a reduction of stockholders' equity as discussed below. Treasury stock does not generally have the stockholders' rights discussed earlier; it has no voting or preemptive rights, cannot participate in dividends, and has no rights at liquidation. It does participate in stock splits, however, since the par value must be reduced. When treasury stock is acquired, the amount of retained earnings available for dividends must ordinarily be restricted by the cost of the treasury stock held so that the payment of dividends will not reduce contributed capital.

Just as the original issuance of capital stock represents an increase in stockholders' equity and the number of shares outstanding, its reacquisition has an opposite effect. Stockholders' equity (and the number of shares outstanding) is reduced. It is important to understand the difference between issued capital stock and outstanding capital stock. Recall that issued capital stock is the number of shares that a corporation has issued to stockholders. **Outstanding capital stock is the number of shares that have been issued to stockholders and that are still being held by them as of a specific date.** Thus the difference between *issued* capital stock and *outstanding* capital stock is the number of shares being held by a corporation as treasury stock. Treasury stock may be reissued by a corporation for the purposes cited earlier. Upon reissuance stockholders' equity and the number of shares outstanding are again increased.

Accounting for Reacquisition

When capital stock is reacquired, the *cost* of the reacquisition[2] is recorded as an increase (debit) to an account entitled Treasury Stock and a decrease (credit) to Cash. Since treasury stock is capital stock that has already been legally issued, the par value of the stock is disregarded in recording the reacquisition. During the period between reacquisition and reissuance, the Treasury Stock account is treated as a contra-stockholders' equity account. If a balance sheet is issued during this period, the cost of the treasury stock would be deducted from the total of contributed capital and retained earnings.

To illustrate, suppose that a corporation has previously issued 5,000 shares of $10 par common stock for $12 per share. The corporation decides to reacquire 400 shares of this common stock, and it purchases these shares on the stock market at a cost of $14 per share. The journal entry to record the reacquisition of the stock is shown on the following page.

---

[2] This cost method is the most common way of accounting for treasury stock. Other accounting methods are sometimes used, but they are much less common and are not discussed in this text.

Treasury Stock ($14 × 400)   5,600
  Cash   5,600

To record reacquisition of 400 shares of common stock as
treasury stock.

Note that the treasury stock was recorded at its *cost* per share and that its par value
was disregarded. Note also that the explanation indicates the number of shares
reacquired. If the corporation prepared a balance sheet before reissuing these
shares, the stockholders' equity would appear as follows:

Stockholders' Equity

Contributed capital
  Common stock, $10 par, 40,000 shares authorized,
    5,000 shares issued, 4,600 shares outstanding $50,000
  Additional paid-in capital on common stock (5,000 × $2) . . .   10,000
      Total contributed capital $60,000
Retained earnings[a] (assumed)   35,000
      Total contributed capital and retained earnings $95,000
Less: Treasury stock (400 shares at $14 per share) . . . .   (5,600)
      Total Stockholders' Equity $89,400

[a] Note: Retained earnings are restricted regarding dividends in the amount of $5,600, the cost of
the treasury stock.

In the example the $5,600 cost of the treasury stock is subtracted from the
$95,000 total of contributed capital and retained earnings to determine the $89,400
total stockholders' equity. The numbers of shares authorized, issued, and outstanding are shown after the common stock account. The amount of retained
earnings available for dividends must be restricted in the amount of the cost of the
treasury stock so that the payment of dividends will not reduce contributed capital.
This is typically disclosed by means of a footnote as shown. Restrictions of retained
earnings are discussed more fully in Chapter 15.

Accounting for   When treasury stock is reissued it may be reissued at a price above, below, or equal
Reissuance   to the cost of reacquisition. Upon reissuance the Treasury Stock account is reduced
(credited) for the *cost* of the shares reissued, and the difference between the
proceeds received and this cost is treated as an adjustment of stockholders' equity.
When the proceeds exceed the cost of the reissued treasury stock, the excess is
treated as an increase (credit) in an account entitled Additional Paid-in Capital from
Treasury Stock. The balance of this account is included in the contributed capital
section in the balance sheet. If the proceeds are less than the cost, this Additional
Paid-in Capital from Treasury Stock account is reduced by the amount of the
difference. If this account should have too small a balance to absorb the difference,
the remainder should be recorded as a reduction in retained earnings. Since treasury
stock may be reacquired at different dates and at different costs, companies keep
records so that the cost information is available when the stock is reissued.

  To illustrate the reissuance, assume that 300 shares of the treasury stock from
our earlier example are reissued at $15 per share. The journal entry to record this
reissuance is as follows:

Cash ($15 × 300)	4,500	
Treasury Stock ($14 × 300)		4,200
Additional Paid-in Capital from Treasury Stock		300

To record reissuance of 300 shares of treasury stock.

In this journal entry the Treasury Stock account was reduced by the $4,200 cost of the reissued shares, and the difference between the $4,500 proceeds and this cost was credited to Additional Paid-in Capital from Treasury Stock. The number of shares reissued was identified in the explanation for the journal entry. After this transaction the stockholders' equity would appear as follows:

Stockholders' Equity

Contributed capital		
Common stock, $10 par, 40,000 shares authorized,		
5,000 shares issued, 4,900 shares outstanding	$50,000	
Additional paid-in capital on common stock (5,000 × $2) . . .	10,000	
Additional paid-in capital from treasury stock	300	
Total contributed capital		$60,300
Retained earnings[a] (assumed)		35,000
Total contributed capital and retained earnings		$95,300
Less: Treasury stock (100 shares at $14 per share)		(1,400)
Total Stockholders' Equity		$93,900

[a] Note: Retained earnings are restricted regarding dividends in the amount of $1,400, the cost of the treasury stock.

In this stockholders' equity section observe that the Additional Paid-in Capital from Treasury Stock is included in contributed capital. As long as this account has an ending balance, it is included in contributed capital even if a company has reissued all of its treasury stock. This is because stockholders have contributed more than the company paid for its treasury stock and this excess is a part of contributed capital. Also observe that the number of shares outstanding has increased (to 4,900) from the previous example.

To continue, suppose that the remaining 100 shares of treasury stock were reissued at $13 per share. The journal entry to record this reissuance is as follows:

Cash ($13 × 100)	1,300	
Additional Paid-in Capital from Treasury Stock	100	
Treasury Stock ($14 × 100)		1,400

To record reissuance of treasury stock.

In this case the $1,300 proceeds were less than the $1,400 cost of the treasury stock and therefore Additional Paid-in Capital from Treasury Stock was reduced for the $100 difference.

No-Par or Preferred Treasury Stock

In the previous examples we used common stock with a par value to illustrate the accounting for the reacquisition and reissuance of treasury stock. The reacquisition and reissuance of no-par common stock with or without a stated value is accounted for in the same manner. Companies also may occasionally reacquire preferred stock as treasury stock. The same accounting principles also apply to the reacquisition and reissuance of preferred shares as treasury stock.

Summary of Treasury Stock Characteristics

For treasury stock the following items are important:

1. Treasury stock is not an asset; it is accounted for as a reduction in stockholders' equity.
2. Treasury stock has no vote, has no preemptive right, does not share in dividends, and does not participate in assets at liquidation.
3. Treasury stock transactions do not result in gains or losses on the income statement so that a corporation cannot influence its net income by buying and selling its own stock.
4. Treasury stock reissuances increase additional paid-in capital when the proceeds exceed the cost of the reissued shares.
5. Treasury stock reissuances decrease additional paid-in capital (and occasionally retained earnings) when the proceeds are less than the cost of the reissued shares.
6. The cost of treasury stock is deducted from the sum of contributed capital and retained earnings to determine total stockholders' equity on the balance sheet.
7. Retained earnings usually must be restricted as to dividends by the cost of treasury stock held.

EXHIBIT 14-3   Statement of Changes in Stockholders' Equity

BARTH CORPORATION
Statement of Changes in Stockholders' Equity
Schedule A
For Year Ended December 31, 1983

Explanation	Common Stock — Shares Issued	Common Stock — $10 Par Value	Common Stock Subscribed	Additional Paid-in Capital — On Common Stock	Additional Paid-in Capital — From Treasury Stock	Additional Paid-in Capital — From Donations	Retained Earnings	Treasury Stock
Balances, 1/1/1983	6,000	$60,000	–0–	$24,000	$2,000	–0–	$67,000	$(4,500)
Issued for cash	1,000	10,000		8,000				
Reissued treasury stock (100 shares at $17, cost $15)					200			1,500
Subscription to 500 shares at $18 per share			$5,000	4,000				
Accepted donated land for plant site						$6,000		
Net income							49,000	
Dividends							(20,000)	
Balances, 12/31/1983	7,000	$70,000	$5,000	$36,000	$2,200	$6,000	$96,000	$(3,000)

STATEMENT OF CHANGES IN STOCKHOLDERS' EQUITY

As can be seen from the discussion in this chapter, in a single accounting period a corporation may have many transactions affecting some component of contributed capital. In addition, as we briefly introduced in Chapter 5, the retained earnings of a corporation are increased by the net income and decreased by the dividends of the accounting period. To disclose its corporate capital activities, each corporation reports the changes in the different classes of capital stock (including the number of shares issued), in each additional paid-in capital account, in capital stock subscribed, in treasury stock, and in retained earnings. Most corporations disclose this information on a statement of changes in stockholders' equity. **A statement of changes in stockholders' equity is a supporting schedule to the stockholders' equity section of the balance sheet.**

The statement of changes in stockholders' equity of the Barth Corporation is shown in Exhibit 14-3, using assumed figures.

In Exhibit 14-3 each of the transactions that affected the components of stockholders' equity is briefly explained in the explanation column. The shares issued and dollar amounts are included under the appropriate column. For instance, the second line indicates that the $18,000 proceeds received from issuing 1,000 shares of common stock were allocated in the amounts of $10,000 to the common stock account and $8,000 to additional paid-in capital. Note that the amounts in the treasury stock column are listed in parentheses because treasury stock is a negative component of stockholders' equity. The columns are then totaled, and the column headings and totals are included in the stockholders' equity section of the balance sheet, as shown in Exhibit 14-4. Observe that the items and amounts listed in stockholders' equity in Exhibit 14-4 correspond to the columns and totals presented in Exhibit 14-3.

EXHIBIT 14-4
Stockholders' Equity

BARTH CORPORATION
Stockholders' Equity
December 31, 1983

Contributed capital (see Schedule A)		
Common stock, $10 par, 30,000 shares authorized,		
7,000 shares issued, 6,800 shares outstanding	$70,000	
Common stock subscribed (500 shares)	5,000	
Additional paid-in capital on common stock	36,000	
Additional paid-in capital from treasury stock	2,200	
Additional paid-in capital from donations (land)	6,000	
Total contributed capital		$119,200
Retained earnings[a] (see Schedule A)		96,000
Total contributed capital and retained earnings		$215,200
Less: Treasury stock (200 shares at a cost of $15 per share) . . .		(3,000)
Total Stockholders' Equity		$212,200

[a] Note: Retained earnings are restricted regarding dividends in the amount of $3,000, the cost of the treasury stock.

REVIEW PROBLEM

Coral Corporation is authorized to issue 5,000 shares of $100 par preferred stock and 20,000 shares of $5 par common stock. Its December 31, 1982, stockholders' equity accounts showed the following balances.

Common stock, $5 par	$50,000
Additional paid-in capital on common stock	30,000
Retained earnings	60,000

During 1983 it entered into the following capital stock transactions:

Date	Transaction
Jan. 3	Issued 400 shares of preferred stock for $120 per share.
Mar. 11	Issued 600 shares of common stock in exchange for land valued at $5,400.
June 23	Reacquired 500 common shares as treasury stock for $10 per share.
Sept. 6	Reissued 300 shares of treasury stock for $11 per share.
Nov. 15	Agreed to a subscription contract for 800 shares of common stock for $12 per share. The subscription contract requires a down payment of $2 per share and a $4 per share payment on December 15. The balance is due on January 15, 1984, after which the stock will be issued.
Dec. 15	Collected the $4 per share payment on the subscription contract.

Required:
1. Prepare journal entries to record the above transactions.
2. Prepare a statement of changes in stockholders' equity (assume 1983 net income of $40,000 and dividends of $18,000).
3. Prepare the stockholders' equity section of the December 31, 1983, balance sheet.

SOLUTION TO REVIEW PROBLEM

Requirement 1:

1983
Jan. 3   Cash ($120 × 400) 48,000
              Preferred Stock, $100 par ($100 × 400) . . .   40,000
              Additional Paid-in Capital on Preferred
                 Stock   8,000
         To record issuance of preferred stock.

Mar. 11 Land 5,400
              Common Stock, $5 par ($5 × 600)   3,000
              Additional Paid-in Capital on Common
                 Stock ($5,400 − $3,000)   2,400
         To record issuance of common stock for land.

June 23 Treasury Stock 5,000
              Cash ($10 × 500)   5,000
         To record reacquisition of 500 shares of common
         stock as treasury stock.

Sept. 6	Cash ($11 × 300)	3,300	
	Treasury Stock ($10 × 300)		3,000
	Additional Paid-in Capital from Treasury		
	Stock		300
	To record reissuance of 300 shares of treasury stock.		
Nov. 15	Cash ($2 × 800)	1,600	
	Subscriptions Receivable: Common Stock		
	($10 × 800)	8,000	
	Common Stock Subscribed ($5 × 800)		4,000
	Additional Paid-in Capital on Common		
	Stock		5,600
	To record subscription to common stock.		
Dec. 15	Cash ($4 × 800)	3,200	
	Subscriptions Receivable: Common Stock . .		3,200
	To record receipt of payment on stock subscription.		

Requirement 2:

CORAL CORPORATION
Statement of Changes in Stockholders' Equity
Schedule A
For Year Ended December 31, 1983

	Preferred Stock		Common Stock		Common Stock Subscribed	Additional Paid-in Capital			Retained Earnings	Treasury Stock
Explanation	Shares Issued	$100 Par Value	Shares Issued	$5 Par Value		On Preferred Stock	On Common Stock	From Treasury Stock		
Balances, 12/31/1982	–0–	–0–	10,000	$50,000	–0–	–0–	$30,000	–0–	$60,000	–0–
Issued for cash	400	$40,000				$8,000				
Issued for land			600	3,000			2,400			
Reacquired 500 common shares as treasury stock										$(5,000)
Reissued 300 shares of treasury stock								$300		3,000
Subscription to 800 common shares at $12 per share					$4,000		5,600			
Net income									40,000	
Dividends									(18,000)	
Balances, 12/31/1983	400	$40,000	10,600	$53,000	$4,000	$8,000	$38,000	$300	$82,000	$(2,000)

Requirement 3:

Stockholders' Equity

Contributed capital (see Schedule A):

Preferred stock, $100 par, 5,000 shares authorized, 400 shares issued and outstanding	$40,000	
Common stock, $5 par, 20,000 shares authorized, 10,600 shares issued, 10,400 shares outstanding	53,000	
Common stock subscribed (800 shares)	4,000	
Additional paid-in capital on preferred stock	8,000	
Additional paid-in capital on common stock	38,000	
Additional paid-in capital from treasury stock	300	
Total contributed capital		$143,300
Retained earnings[a] (see Schedule A)		82,000
Total contributed capital and retained earnings		$225,300
Less: Treasury stock (200 shares at $10 per share)		(2,000)
Total Stockholders' Equity		$223,300

[a] Note: Retained earnings are restricted regarding dividends in the amount of $2,000, the cost of the treasury stock.

GLOSSARY

Additional Paid-in Capital on Common (or Preferred) Stock. Difference between the legal capital and the proceeds received from the issuance of common (preferred) stock.

Articles of Incorporation. Legal document containing information about a corporation, including the names of the incorporators, the corporate name, address, and nature of business, the types, legal value, and number of capital shares authorized for issuance. Also called a *corporate charter*.

Capital Stock. Unit of ownership in a corporation. There are two classes of capital stock, preferred stock and common stock.

Common Stock. Class of capital stock that shares in all the stockholders' rights including the preemptive right, right to vote, right to share in net income, and right to share in assets upon liquidation.

Common Stock Subscribed. A contributed capital account used to record the par value of common stock that has been subscribed to but not yet fully paid for. A Preferred Stock Subscribed account is used in the same manner.

Contributed Capital. Component of stockholders' equity listing the balances of the capital stock accounts and the additional paid-in capital accounts. Represents the total capital invested by stockholders.

Convertible Preferred Stock. Preferred stock that is exchangeable into common stock.

Corporation. Business entity with a continuous life that is treated legally as independent and separate from its owners, called stockholders.

Legal Capital. The amount of stockholders' equity that cannot be distributed to stockholders. Intended to protect the corporation's creditors.

Memorandum Entry. Written description of a financial event of a company, not involving a debit or credit amount. Recorded in the general journal.

No-Par Stock. Capital stock that does not have a par value. May have a *stated value* that is treated like par value.

Par Value. Monetary amount that is designated as the legal capital per share. Total legal capital of a corporation is determined by multiplying the par value per share times the number of shares issued.

Preemptive Right. Stockholder's right to maintain a proportionate percentage of ownership of a corporation by purchasing a pro rata share of additional capital stock, should it be issued.

Preferred Stock. Class of capital stock for which certain additional rights are given to its stockholders in exchange for giving up some of the usual stockholders' rights. Additional rights may include the right to a set dividend or to convert the preferred stock to common stock.

Stated Value. Legal capital assigned to a share of no-par stock.

Statement of Changes in Stockholders' Equity. Schedule in which a corporation reports the changes in all of its stockholders' equity accounts and the changes in the number of capital shares issued during each accounting period.

Stock Certificate. Serially numbered legal document that indicates the number of capital shares owned by a stockholder, the legal value per share, and other relevant information.

Stockholders. Holders of capital stock. Owners of a corporation.

Stockholders' Equity. Owners' equity section in a corporate balance sheet. Consists of two parts, contributed capital and retained earnings.

Stockholders' Ledger. Corporate record in which is kept the name, address, and number of shares owned by each stockholder.

Stock Split. Decrease in the par value of a corporation's capital stock and a proportionate increase in the number of shares authorized and issued.

Stock Transfer Journal. Corporate record containing the names, addresses, stock certificate numbers, and other pertinent information for the exchange of capital stock between old and new stockholders.

Subscription Contract. Contract in which an investor (subscriber) agrees to purchase a certain number of shares of capital stock at an agreed-upon price, with the payment spread over a specified time period.

Subscriptions Receivable. Asset account used to record the amount owed by subscribers in a subscription contract for capital stock.

Treasury Stock. A corporation's own capital stock that (1) has been fully paid for by stockholders, (2) has been legally issued, (3) is reacquired by the corporation, and (4) is being held by the corporation.

QUESTIONS

Q14-1 What information is included in a corporation's articles of incorporation?

Q14-2 Define the following terms: (a) stock certificate, (b) stockholders' ledger, (c) stock transfer journal.

Q14-3 What is capital stock? How does preferred stock differ from common stock?

Q14-4   List the basic rights of a stockholder. Which right do you consider to be the most important?

Q14-5   What is stockholders' equity? Identify the two major components of stockholders' equity.

Q14-6   Identify the accounts included in contributed capital.

Q14-7   What is legal capital and why is it important?

Q14-8   How is the total legal capital of a corporation determined, assuming capital stock has (a) a par value, (b) a stated value, or (c) no par or stated value?

Q14-9   What is the meaning of the following terms: authorized capital stock, issued capital stock, outstanding capital stock, and treasury stock? What is the difference between issued and outstanding capital stock?

Q14-10   What is a stock subscription? How are the accounts Common Stock Subscribed and Subscriptions Receivable classified in a balance sheet? Why are they so classified?

Q14-11   If capital stock is issued for an asset other than cash, what amount would you use to record the transaction?

Q14-12   How would you record the donation of an asset to a corporation on the corporation's books? Why?

Q14-13   What is convertible preferred stock? How is the conversion of preferred stock to common stock recorded on the corporation's books?

Q14-14   What is a stock split? How does a corporation record a stock split? What impact does a stock split have on the dollar amounts of the elements and the total of stockholders' equity?

Q14-15   What is treasury stock? Why might a corporation wish to acquire treasury stock?

Q14-16   Briefly explain the accounting for the reacquisition and reissuance of treasury stock.

Q14-17   How is treasury stock reported in a balance sheet? What footnote is included for retained earnings in regard to treasury stock?

Q14-18   What is a statement of changes in stockholders' equity? What changes in specific accounts are reported in this statement?

EXERCISES

E14-1   Par Value and No-Par Stock Issuance.   Ryland Corporation is authorized to issue 100,000 shares of common stock. It sells 40,000 shares at $12 per share.

Required: Prepare the journal entries to record the sale of the common stock, given the following independent assumptions:
1. The stock has a par value of $5 per share.
2. The stock is no-par stock, but has been assigned a stated value of $4 per share.
3. The stock has no par and no stated value.

E14-2   Stock Subscription.   On July 1, 1983, the Mark Corporation enters into a subscription contract with subscribers for 8,000 shares of $5 par common stock at a price of $6 per share. The contract requires a down payment of $2 per share, with the remaining balance to be paid in full on December 1, 1983. The stock will be issued to each subscriber upon full payment.

Required: Prepare journal entries to record the following:
1. The July 1 receipt of the down payment upon the signing of the contract.
2. The December 1 receipt of the remaining balance of $4 per share.
3. The issuance of the stock upon full payment.

E14-3 Noncash Issuance of Stock. The Antley Company issued 200 shares of $100 par preferred stock in exchange for 5 acres of land.

Required: Prepare the journal entry to record the acquisition of the land for each independent situation given below.
1. The preferred stock is currently selling on the market for $130 per share. No appraisal is available on the land.
2. The land is appraised at $25,000. The preferred stock is not actively traded on the stock market.

E14-4 Various Journal Entries. Webster Corporation is authorized to issue 50,000 shares of $3 par common stock. During the current period it engaged in the following transactions:

(a) Entered into a subscription contract for 5,000 shares of common stock at $10 per share and received a 20% down payment.
(b) Collected the remaining balance of the subscription contract and issued the common stock.
(c) Acquired 30 acres of land by issuing 10,000 shares of common stock. The common stock was selling on the market for $15 per share. No appraisal value was available for the land.
(d) Sold 1,000 shares of common stock at $14 per share.

Required: Prepare the journal entries to record the above transactions.

E14-5 Various Journal Entries. Thompson Corporation is authorized to issue 60,000 shares of no-par, $5 stated value common stock and 3,000 shares of $100 par preferred stock. It enters into the following transactions:

(a) Sells 10,000 shares of common stock at $11 per share.
(b) Sells 1,000 shares of preferred stock at $120 per share.
(c) Acquires a building by paying $10,000 cash and issuing 5,000 shares of common stock and 500 shares of preferred stock. Common stock is currently selling for $15 per share; preferred stock is selling for $125 per share. No appraisal value is available for the building.
(d) Enters into a subscription contract for 15,000 shares of common stock at $14 per share and receives a $6 per share down payment.
(e) Collects the remaining balance of the subscription contract and issues the common stock.

Required: Prepare the journal entries to record the above transactions.

E14-6 Donated Capital. The community of Happy Rock donated land to the Jipem Corporation for the site of a new factory. The land was valued at $10,000.

Required: Prepare the journal entry to record the donation of the land on the Jipem Corporation's books.

E14-7 Convertible Preferred Stock. On January 1, 1983, the Gasser Corporation issued 75 shares of $50 par convertible preferred stock at $104 per share. Each share of preferred stock is convertible into three shares of $5 par common stock. On January 12, 1984, all of the preferred stock was converted to common stock.

Required: 1. Prepare the journal entry to record the issuance of the preferred stock on January 1, 1983.
2. Prepare the journal entry to record the conversion of the preferred stock to common stock on January 12, 1984.

E14-8　Stock Split.　Bloom Company is authorized to issue 30,000 shares of $4 par common stock. To date it has issued 10,000 shares for $10 per share. On May 8, 1983, the board of directors authorized a 2 for 1 stock split with a reduction in par value to $2 per share.

Required:　1. Prepare the entry to record the stock split.
　　　　　　　2. What is the effect on the stockholders' equity accounts as a result of the stock split?

E14-9　Treasury Stock.　On January 1, 1983, the Amitroy Company had 10,000 shares of $5 par common stock outstanding. These shares were originally issued at a price of $12 per share. During 1983 the following stock transactions occurred:

(a) March 3, 1983: The company reacquired 2,000 shares of its common stock at a cost of $10 per share.
(b) April 23, 1983: The company sold 1,000 shares of the treasury stock for $11 per share.
(c) July 25, 1983: The company sold the remaining 1,000 shares of the treasury stock for $9.50 per share.

Required:　Prepare the journal entries to record the above transactions.

E14-10　Treasury Stock and Stockholders' Equity.　On January 1, 1983, the Rollo Corporation had 5,000 shares of $10 par common stock outstanding. These shares were originally issued at $25 per share. During 1983 the Rollo Corporation entered into the following transactions:

(a) Reacquired 2,500 shares of its common stock for $23 per share.
(b) Sold 1,250 shares of the treasury stock for $26 per share.
(c) Sold 750 shares of the treasury stock for $20 per share.

Required:　1. Prepare journal entries to record the above stock transactions.
　　　　　　　2. Prepare, in good form, the stockholders' equity section of the Rollo Corporation's balance sheet at December 31, 1983 (assume 40,000 shares are authorized and retained earnings is $40,000).

E14-11　Contributed Capital.　Below is a list of selected accounts and ending account balances taken from the accounting records of the Dean Company on December 31, 1983:

Account Title	Amount
Additional paid-in capital on preferred stock	$ 7,500
Common stock	80,000
Subscriptions receivable: preferred stock	6,750
Additional paid-in capital from treasury stock	1,000
Preferred stock	25,000
Treasury stock	6,000
Preferred stock subscribed	5,000
Retained earnings	90,000
Additional paid-in capital on common stock	40,000

Additional Information:

(a) Common stock has a $10 par value, 10,000 shares are authorized, 8,000 shares have been issued and are outstanding.
(b) Preferred stock has a $50 par value, 1,000 shares are authorized, 500 shares have been issued and are outstanding. One hundred shares have been subscribed at $75 per share.
(c) During 1983, 1,500 shares of common stock were reacquired at $12 per share; 1,000 shares were reissued at $13 per share.

Required:　Prepare the contributed capital section of the December 31, 1983, balance sheet for the Dean Company. Include an appropriate footnote in regard to the treasury stock.

E14-12 Changes in Stockholders' Equity. Fliter Company is authorized to issue 10,000 shares of $10 par common stock. On January 1, 1983, 5,800 shares of common stock were outstanding. These shares had been issued at $21 per share. The retained earnings account has a beginning balance of $93,000. During 1983 the following transactions took place:

Date	Transaction
Jan. 15	Issued 300 shares of common stock at $23 per share.
Mar. 30	Purchased land by issuing 2,100 shares of common stock. The stock had a current market price of $22 per share, which was used to record the transaction.
June 10	Reacquired 250 shares of common stock at $21 per share.

Required: Prepare a statement of changes in stockholders' equity for the year ended December 31, 1983 (assume net income for 1983 was $13,000 and dividends were $1,500).

E14-13 Changes in Stockholders' Equity. Clook Corporation is authorized to issue 25,000 shares of $5 stated value common stock. At the beginning of 1984, 11,000 shares were outstanding. These shares had been issued at $35 per share. The retained earnings account has a beginning balance of $420,000. During 1984 the following transactions took place:

Date	Transaction
Jan. 14	Issued 1,000 shares of common stock for $38 per share.
Apr. 17	Reacquired 850 shares of its common stock for $39 per share.
July 25	Issued 1,200 shares of common stock in exchange for a patent. The stock was selling at $40 per share on the market, and this price was used to record the transaction.
Sept. 12	Sold 850 shares of the treasury stock for $42 per share.

Required: 1. Prepare a statement of changes in stockholders' equity for the year ended December 31, 1984 (assume net income was $93,000 and dividends were $43,000).
2. Prepare the stockholders' equity section of the December 31, 1984, balance sheet for the Clook Corporation.

PROBLEMS

Part A

P14-1A Stock Transactions. The Cary Company is authorized to issue 100,000 shares of $7 par common stock. At the beginning of 1983, 18,000 shares of common stock were issued and outstanding. These shares had been issued at $14 per share. During 1983 the company entered into the following transactions:

Date	Transaction
Jan. 16	Issued 1,250 shares of common stock at $15 per share.
Mar. 21	Exchanged 14,000 shares of common stock for a building. The common stock was selling at $16 per share.
May 7	Reacquired 500 shares of its common stock at $16 per share.
July 1	Accepted subscriptions to 1,000 shares of common stock at $17 per share. The contract called for a 10% down payment, with the balance due December 1.
Sept. 20	Sold 500 shares of treasury stock at $18 per share.
Dec. 1	Collected the balance due on the July 1 subscriptions and issued the stock.

Required: 1. Prepare the journal entries to record the above transactions.
2. Prepare the stockholders' equity section of the December 31, 1983, balance sheet (assume ending retained earnings for 1983 is $122,000).

P14-2A Stock Transactions. The Crane Corporation was organized and started business on January 1, 1983. It is authorized to issue 100,000 shares of $2 par common stock and 50,000 shares of $100 par preferred stock. During 1983 the Crane Corporation entered into the following stock transactions:

Date	Transaction
Jan. 1	Issued 20,000 shares of common stock at $15 per share and 10,000 shares of preferred stock at $125 per share.
Jan. 5	Issued 10,000 shares of common stock in payment of various organization costs totaling $140,000. Since the stock had not been on the market long enough to establish a price, the total amount of $140,000 was used to record the transaction.
Mar. 6	Issued 30,000 shares of common stock at $16 per share and 15,000 shares of preferred stock at $127 per share.
June 24	Purchased land by issuing 1,000 shares of common stock and 500 shares of preferred stock. Common and preferred stock were selling on the market at $16 and $128 per share, respectively, and these prices were used to record the purchase.
Sept. 11	Issued 5,000 shares of common stock at $17 per share.
Oct. 18	Issued 600 shares of preferred stock at $126 per share.

Required: 1. Prepare the journal entries to record the above transactions.
2. Prepare the contributed capital section of the December 31, 1983, balance sheet.

P14-3A Treasury Stock. Mulky Company reported the following data on its December 31, 1982 balance sheet:

Preferred stock, $50 par	
(4,000 shares authorized)	$100,000
Additional paid-in capital on preferred stock	8,000
Common stock, $10 par	
(30,000 shares authorized)	50,000
Additional paid-in capital on common stock	25,000
Retained earnings	85,000

During 1983 the company entered into the following transactions:

(a) Reacquired 200 shares of its own preferred stock at $55 per share.
(b) Reacquired 500 shares of its own common stock at $16 per share.
(c) Sold 100 shares of preferred treasury stock at $56 per share.
(d) Sold 300 shares of common treasury stock at $19 per share.
(e) Sold 200 shares of common treasury stock at $14 per share.

The company maintains separate treasury stock accounts and related additional paid-in capital accounts for each class of stock.

Required: 1. Prepare the journal entries required to record the above treasury stock transactions.
2. Assuming the company earned a net income in 1983 of $30,000 and declared and paid dividends of $10,000, prepare the stockholders' equity section of the balance sheet at December 31, 1983.

P14-4A Contributed Capital. A partial list of the accounts and ending account balances taken from the post-closing trial balance of the Harley Company on December 31, 1983, is shown as follows:

Account Title	*Amount*
Retained earnings	$ 30,000
Accounts payable	9,000
Common stock subscribed	25,000
Accounts receivable	125,000
Additional paid-in capital on common stock	430,000
Additional paid-in capital from treasury stock	2,500
Common stock	150,000
Subscriptions receivable: common stock	95,000
Additional paid-in capital on preferred stock	94,500
Preferred stock	175,000

Additional Information:

(a) Common stock is no-par, with a stated value of $5 per share. 80,000 shares are authorized, 30,000 shares have been issued and are outstanding, and 5,000 shares have been subscribed at a price of $19 per share.

(b) 500 shares of common stock were reacquired in 1983 at $18 per share, and reissued later at $23 per share.

(c) Preferred stock has a $50 par value; 7,000 shares are authorized, and 3,500 shares have been issued and are outstanding.

Required: Prepare the contributed capital section of the December 31, 1983, balance sheet for the Harley Company.

P14-5A Changes in Stockholders' Equity. The Fife Corporation is authorized to issue 10,000 shares of $10 par common stock and 1,000 shares of $50 par preferred stock. The December 31, 1982, stockholders' equity accounts showed the following balances.

Common stock, $10 par	$60,000
Additional paid-in capital on common stock	48,000
Retained earnings	40,000

During 1983 the corporation engaged in the following capital stock transactions:

Date	*Transaction*
Jan. 15	Issued 250 shares of preferred stock at $82 per share.
Apr. 1	Issued 2,000 shares of common stock at $20 per share.
July 5	Accepted donated land valued at $10,000 for a plant site.
Sept. 30	Reacquired 650 shares of common stock at $15 per share.
Nov. 17	Accepted subscription contract for 1,000 shares of common stock at $22 per share. The contract calls for a 25% down payment and the balance to be paid on December 15.
Dec. 15	Received balance due on November 17 subscription contract.

Required: Prepare a statement of changes in stockholders' equity for the year ended December 31, 1983 (assume net income was $25,000 and dividends were $5,000).

P14-6A Various Journal Entries. The Walt-Ben Corporation is authorized to issue 8,000 shares of $50 par convertible preferred stock and 30,000 shares of $10 stated value common stock. As of December 31, 1982, there were 3,300 shares of preferred stock and 18,000 shares of common stock outstanding. These shares had been issued at $66 and $22 per share for the preferred and common stock, respectively. During 1983 the following transactions took place:

Date	Transaction
Jan. 4	Issued 1,000 shares of common stock at $23 per share.
Jan. 21	Issued 500 shares of preferred stock at $68 per share.
Mar. 6	Holders of 600 shares of preferred stock converted their shares to common stock in a ratio of 3 to 1 (i.e., three common shares for every one preferred share held). The 600 shares had originally been issued at $66 per share.
June 13	Accepted donation of four acres of land for future building site. The land had a fair market value of $8,000.
Sept. 3	Issued 550 shares of common stock at $24 per share.
Dec. 31	Declared a 2 for 1 stock split on the common stock, reducing the stated value to $5 per share and increasing the authorized shares to 60,000.

Required: 1. Prepare the journal entries to record the above transactions.
2. Prepare the contributed capital section of the December 31, 1983, balance sheet for the Walt-Ben Corporation.

P14-7A   Stock Subscriptions.   On September 1, 1983, the Tonley Company accepts separate subscriptions for 500 shares of $100 par preferred stock at $103 per share and 2,000 shares of $10 par common stock at $22 per share. The subscription contracts call for a 25% down payment, with the balance due by December 1, 1983. Shares are to be issued to each subscriber upon full payment.

On December 1 the company received the remaining balances due on all the preferred stock and common stock. The shares were issued on this date.

Required: Prepare journal entries to record all the transactions related to:
1. Preferred stock.
2. Common stock.

PROBLEMS

Part B

P14-1B   Stock Transactions.   The Rane Corporation is authorized to issue 100,000 shares of $10 par common stock. At the beginning of 1983, 30,000 shares of common stock were issued and outstanding. These shares had been issued at $26 per share. Listed below are the stock transactions entered into by the corporation during 1983:

Date	Transaction
Jan. 1	Issued 1,000 shares of common stock at $27 per share.
Mar. 4	Purchased a patent by issuing 2,000 shares of common stock. Common stock was selling at $27 per share, and no value was available for the patent.
Apr. 15	Reacquired 750 shares of common stock at $26 per share.
June 1	Accepted subscription contract for 1,500 shares of common stock at $26 per share. The contract calls for a $12 per share down payment and the balance to be paid in two equal payments on September 1, 1983, and January 1, 1984, respectively.
Aug. 18	Sold 500 shares of treasury stock at $28 per share.
Sept. 1	Collected payment due on June 1 subscription.

Required: 1. Prepare the journal entries to record the above transactions.
2. Prepare the stockholders' equity section of the December 31, 1983, balance sheet (assume retained earnings is $95,500).

P14-2B   Stock Transactions.   The Bain Company was organized and started business on January 1, 1983. It is authorized to issue 45,000 shares of $50 par preferred stock and 100,000 shares of $5 stated value common stock. During 1983, the Bain Company entered into the following stock transactions:

Date	Transaction
Jan. 1	Issued 5,000 shares of common stock in payment of miscellaneous organization costs. The stated value was used in recording the transaction.
Jan. 2	Issued 12,000 shares of common stock at $6 per share and 8,000 shares of preferred stock at $76 per share.
Jan. 9	Purchased equipment by issuing 15,000 shares of common stock. The equipment was valued at $105,000, and this amount was used to record the purchase.
May 25	Issued 30,000 shares of common stock at $12 per share.
July 25	Issued 21,000 shares of preferred stock at $78 per share.
Oct. 30	Acquired a building by issuing 2,000 shares of common stock and 575 shares of preferred stock. Common and preferred stock were selling on the market for $13 and $80 per share, respectively, and these prices were used to record the purchase.
Dec. 4	Issued 2,500 shares of common stock at $13 per share.

Required: 1. Prepare the journal entries to record the above transactions.
2. Prepare the contributed capital section of the December 31, 1983, balance sheet.

P14-3B Treasury Stock. Langy Electronics Corporation is authorized to issue 40,000 shares of $5 par common stock and 5,000 shares of $100 par preferred stock. At the beginning of 1983 there were 10,000 shares of common stock and 2,500 shares of preferred stock issued and outstanding. These shares had been issued at $14 and $104 per share for the common and preferred stock, respectively. During 1983 the corporation entered into the following transactions:

Date	Transaction
Jan. 14	Reacquired 750 shares of its common stock at $17 per share.
Jan. 24	Reacquired 400 shares of its preferred stock at $110 per share.
May 6	Sold 250 shares of common treasury stock at $19 per share.
June 17	Sold 250 shares of preferred treasury stock at $112 per share.
Aug. 20	Sold 150 shares of preferred treasury stock at $109 per share.

The company maintains separate treasury stock accounts and related additional paid-in capital accounts for each class of stock.

Required: 1. Prepare the journal entries to record the above treasury stock transactions.
2. Prepare the stockholders' equity section of the balance sheet at December 31, 1983 (assume retained earnings is $260,000).

P14-4B Contributed Capital. A partial list of the accounts and ending account balances taken from the post-closing trial balance of the Suitcom Corporation on December 31, 1983, is shown below.

Account Title	Amount
Common stock	$ 540,000
Subscriptions receivable: common stock	22,500
Additional paid-in capital on preferred stock	29,600
Common stock subscribed	10,000
Equipment	1,000,000
Additional paid-in capital from treasury stock	1,500
Preferred stock	672,500
Additional paid-in capital on common stock	717,000
Wages payable	145,000
Retained earnings	40,000

Additional Information:

(a) 750 shares of common stock were reacquired in 1983 at $24 per share. The treasury stock was later resold at $26 per share.

(b) Preferred stock has a $100 par value, 10,000 shares are authorized, and 6,725 shares have been issued and are outstanding.

(c) Common stock has a $10 par value, 100,000 shares are authorized, and 54,000 shares have been issued and are outstanding. 1,000 shares have been subscribed at $25 per share.

Required: Prepare the contributed capital section of the December 31, 1983, balance sheet for the Suitcom Corporation.

P14-5B   Changes in Stockholders' Equity. The Dought Corporation is authorized to issue 2,000 shares of $100 par preferred stock and 50,000 shares of $5 stated value common stock. As of December 31, 1982, Dought's stockholders' equity accounts showed the following balances:

Preferred stock, $100 par	$125,000
Common stock, $5 stated value	125,000
Additional paid-in capital on preferred stock	18,750
Additional paid-in capital on common stock	400,000
Retained earnings	75,000

During 1983 Dought entered into the following transactions affecting stockholders' equity:

(a) Issued 200 shares of preferred stock at $115 per share.

(b) Reacquired 500 shares of common stock for $20 per share.

(c) Sold 250 shares of the treasury stock for $20 per share.

(d) Issued 1,000 shares of common stock in exchange for 10 acres of land. At this time the common stock was selling for $23 per share, and no appraisal value was available for the land.

Required: 1. Prepare a statement of changes in stockholders' equity for the year ended December 31, 1983 (assume 1983 net income was $113,000 and dividends were $23,000).

2. Prepare the stockholders' equity section of the December 31, 1983, balance sheet for the Dought Corporation.

P14-6B   Various Journal Entries. The GoGro Company is authorized to issue 50,000 shares of $10 par common stock and 10,000 shares of $100 par convertible preferred stock. Each share of preferred stock is convertible into four shares of common stock. At the beginning of 1983, 30,000 shares of common stock (issued at $17 per share) and 3,000 shares of preferred stock (issued at $109 per share) were outstanding. During 1983 the following transactions took place:

Date	Transaction
Jan. 1	Accepted donation of a building and land to open a new warehouse. The building was valued at $18,000 and the land at $2,000.
Apr. 2	Issued 400 shares of preferred stock at $112 per share.
May 12	Holders of 2,000 shares of preferred stock converted their shares to common stock. The preferred stock had been originally issued at $109 per share.
Sept. 6	Issued 1,000 shares of preferred stock at $104 per share.
Dec. 31	Declared a 2 for 1 stock split on the common stock, reducing the par value to $5 per share and increasing the authorized shares to 100,000.

Required: 1. Prepare the journal entries to record the above transactions.

2. Prepare the contributed capital section of the December 31, 1983, balance sheet for the GoGro Company.

P14-7B   Various Journal Entries. The stockholders' equity section of the January 1, 1983, balance sheet for the M-T Corporation is shown as follows:

Stockholders' Equity

Contributed capital
　Preferred stock, $50 par, 5,000 shares authorized, 2,000
　　shares issued and outstanding $100,000
　Common stock, no-par, 50,000 shares authorized, 12,000
　　shares issued and outstanding   252,000
　Additional paid-in capital on preferred stock   20,000
　　　Total contributed capital $372,000
Retained earnings   123,000
　　　Total Stockholders' Equity $495,000

During 1983 the corporation entered into the following transactions:

Date	Transaction
Mar. 2	Issued 300 shares of preferred stock at $61 per share.
June 16	Issued 200 shares of preferred stock and 1,000 shares of common stock in exchange for a patent. At the time of the exchange the preferred and common stock were selling at $62 and $20 per share, respectively. The total value of the stock was used to record the exchange.
July 23	Reacquired 500 shares of common stock at $22 per share.
Sept. 5	Issued 750 shares of common stock at $23 per share.
Oct. 13	Sold 450 shares of treasury stock at $23 per share.
Dec. 21	Issued 250 shares of preferred stock at $63 per share.

Required: 　1. Prepare the journal entries to record the above transactions.
　　　　　　　2. Prepare the stockholders' equity section of the December 31, 1983, balance sheet for the M-T Corporation (assume 1983 net income was $65,000 and dividends were $22,000).

DISCUSSION CASES

C14-1　Exchange of Stock for Asset.　At the beginning of the current year the Blong Company issued common stock in exchange for equipment. The president of the company has asked your advice. He states, "I don't know how the company should record this transaction. However, even if the company recorded the transaction at too high or too low a price, it should not make any difference. This transaction does not affect net income for the current accounting period because it does not involve a revenue or expense account. Furthermore, since it occurs during the current accounting period, the future financial statements of the company will not be affected."

Required: 　Prepare a written evaluation of the president's comments. Include a suggestion for recording the transaction.

C14-2　Stock Subscriptions.　The Downs Company is considering whether or not to issue more common stock. One of the executives of the company has been advised that the company should sell its stock on the "installment basis," in which the investor agrees to buy a certain number of shares, makes a down payment, and then agrees to pay the remainder in the future. The executive has not heard of this procedure and makes the following statement, "I don't see how this installment sale would work. It seems to me that it would result in an understatement of assets at the time of the agreement because the company would show only the cash down payment. Furthermore, since the stock is issued at the time of the agreement, we would have too many shares outstanding for the amount of money paid in. And, on top of all this, what if an investor decides not to pay in full? How would we handle this and how would we get our stock back?"

Required: 　Prepare a written explanation of installment sales of stock, responding to each of the issues raised by the executive.

C14-3   Treasury Stock.   At the beginning of 1983 the Zing Corporation reacquired 500 shares of its own common stock for $20 per share. During 1983 it reissued 200 of these treasury shares for $25 per share. As of December 31, 1983, the company had not yet reissued the remaining treasury stock.

The president of Zing Corporation has suggested that the 300 shares of treasury stock be shown as an asset on the corporation's December 31, 1983, balance sheet and that the $1,000 "gain" be shown in the income statement. He also feels the treasury stock should be considered as outstanding shares and should not be distinguished from common stock issued.

Required:
1. Define treasury stock.
2. Why would a corporation acquire treasury stock?
3. What is common stock outstanding? What is the difference between common stock issued and common stock outstanding?
4. Identify how the president of Zing Corporation arrived at the $1,000 gain. Explain why he is wrong in suggesting that treasury stock be shown as an asset and that the gain be shown in the income statement.
5. In response to the suggestions by Zing Corporation's president, how would you recommend that the treasury stock and the gain be disclosed on the corporation's 1983 financial statements?

15

Corporations: Earnings, Retained Earnings, and Dividends

After reading this chapter, you should understand:

- The components and items in each component of a corporation's income statement
- The differences between income from continuing operations, results of discontinued operations, and extraordinary gains and losses
- How to compute earnings per share
- The closing entries of a corporation
- How to record cash dividends and stock dividends
- How to compute dividends on cumulative preferred stock and participating preferred stock
- Prior period adjustments for correcting entries
- Appropriations of retained earnings
- The statement of retained earnings

The stockholders' equity section of a corporate balance sheet includes a contributed capital component and a retained earnings component. Contributed capital reports the total amount of investments made by stockholders into the corporation. The transactions involving the issuance of capital stock and the resulting impact on contributed capital and stockholders' equity were discussed in Chapter 14. In this chapter the focus is on retained earnings. Retained earnings includes the lifetime earnings of the corporation not distributed as dividends to stockholders. Corporate earnings are reported differently from the earnings of a sole proprietorship or partnership because of the effect of income taxes, discontinued operations, extraordinary items, and the disclosure of earnings per share. Dividends may be distributed to both preferred and common stockholders, after having been "declared" at an earlier date. Dividends may be paid out in cash or distributed as stock dividends. Retained earnings may also be affected by corrections of errors made in previous earnings and by appropriations. Each of these topics is discussed in this chapter.

CORPORATE EARNINGS

Net income (loss) is the amount of earnings transferred to the Retained Earnings account as a result of a corporation's income-producing activities during its accounting period. This net income is reported in the corporation's income statement for the period. In contrast to the income statements of a sole proprietorship or partnership, the income statement of a corporation has several major components. Shown below is an outline of these components and the items within each component.

1. Income from continuing operations
   (a) Operating income
   (b) Nonoperating income (other revenues and expenses)
   (c) Income tax expense related to continuing operations
2. Results of discontinued operations
   (a) Income (loss) from operations of a discontinued segment (net of income taxes)
   (b) Gain (loss) on disposal of discontinued segment (net of income taxes)
3. Extraordinary gains or losses (net of income taxes)
4. Net income (the sum of items 1, 2, and 3)
5. Earnings per share

Not every corporate income statement contains each of these components. An example of a corporate income statement that includes each component is shown in Exhibit 15-1; these components are discussed below. In addition, since corporate net income may include several additional items and retained earnings is used to report the lifetime corporate earnings (less dividends), the closing entries of a corporation differ slightly from those of a sole proprietorship or partnership. These differences are also discussed below.

Income from Continuing Operations

This component of a corporate income statement is similar to that of any business entity. Included here is operating income, determined by subtracting cost of goods sold from net sales to obtain gross profit, and then deducting the selling expenses and general and administrative expenses. Also included is the nonoperating income (or expense), which is the sum of the other revenues and expenses. These other revenues and expenses include significant recurring items such as interest expense and revenue which are not part of the corporation's primary operations. They also include ordinary (as opposed to extraordinary) gains and losses (discussed later) such as those related to the sale of equipment or to the writedown of inventory to its lower of cost or market value.

The total of the operating income and the nonoperating income is entitled "income before income taxes" *if* the corporation does not report results of discontinued operations or extraordinary items (discussed later). If either of these items is reported, the total of the operating income and nonoperating income is entitled "pretax income from continuing operations." For instance, Colgate-Palmolive Company reported pretax income from continuing operations of $366,827,000 for 1980. In Exhibit 15-1 the Glanton Corporation's operating income is $11,000, its

EXHIBIT 15-1
Income Statement

GLANTON CORPORATION
Income Statement
For Year Ended December 31, 1983

Sales (net)		$100,000
Cost of goods sold		60,000
Gross profit		$ 40,000
Operating expenses		
Selling expenses	$16,000	
General and administrative expenses	13,000	
Total operating expenses		29,000
Operating income		$ 11,000
Other revenues and expenses		
Gain on sale of equipment	$ 500	
Interest revenue	700	
Interest expense	(200)	
Nonoperating income		1,000
Pretax income from continuing operations		$ 12,000
Income tax expense of continuing operations		4,800
Income from continuing operations		$ 7,200
Results of discontinued operations		
Loss from operations of discontinued		
Segment X (net of $200 income tax credit)	$ (300)	
Gain on sale of discontinued Segment X		
(net of $600 income tax expense)	900	600
Income before extraordinary loss		$ 7,800
Extraordinary loss from tornado (net of $800 income		
tax credit)		(1,200)
Net Income		$ 6,600
Earnings per common share (see Note A)		
Income from continuing operations		$ 2.61
Results of discontinued operations		.26
Extraordinary loss from tornado		(.52)
Earnings per common share		$ 2.35

Note A: Preferred dividends of $1,200 were deducted from net income and income from continuing operations in computing earnings per share. The weighted average number of common shares outstanding is 2,300 shares.

nonoperating income is $1,000, and its pretax income from continuing operations totals $12,000.

Income Taxes The earnings (net income) of sole proprietorships and partnerships are not subject to income taxes because, for tax purposes, these business entities are not considered to be independent of their owners. The owners of sole proprietorships and partnerships are, of course, taxed as individuals on their personal earnings from the business. A corporation, on the other hand, is considered to be a legal entity that is separate and distinct from its owners. Consequently, the earnings of a corporation are subject to federal and, in many cases, state and foreign income taxes. Since the maximum federal corporate income tax rate is 46% at the time of writing, it is not unusual for a corporation's income tax rate to approach or exceed 50% of its income before income taxes. Because actual income tax computations are very complex, for simplicity we will assume an income tax rate of 40% for all discussion and homework materials.

Income taxes are imposed on a corporation's "taxable income," which consists of the sum of its pretax income from continuing operations, results from discontinued operations, and extraordinary items.[1] To determine a corporation's *total* income taxes, its taxable income is multiplied times the income tax rate. Because it is necessary to report on the income statement the income tax expense (or income tax credit in the case of a loss) related to each of these components, a separate income tax computation for each component is required.

To illustrate, assume that in 1983 the Glanton Corporation reports pretax income from continuing operations of $12,000, a pretax loss from operations of discontinued Segment X of $500, a pretax gain on the sale of discontinued Segment X of $1,500, and a pretax extraordinary loss of $2,000. It computes its total income taxes and the income taxes related to each item as shown in Exhibit 15-2 (assuming a 40% income tax rate). Note that the two items of loss reduced the income taxes in the amounts of $200 and $800, respectively. These amounts are called *income tax credits*.

Income taxes are an expense for a corporation. Because this expense is usually so large in total and the amount is determined on the basis of several items, the components are separately reported on the income statement by intraperiod income

EXHIBIT 15-2
Income Tax
Computation

GLANTON CORPORATION Computation of Income Taxes for 1983					
	Pretax Amount	×	Income Tax Rate	=	Income Taxes
Pretax income from continuing operations	$12,000	×	.40	=	$4,800
Pretax loss from operations of discontinued segment	(500)	×	.40	=	(200)
Gain (pretax) on sale of discontinued segment	1,500	×	.40	=	600
Extraordinary loss (pretax)	(2,000)	×	.40	=	(800)
Taxable Income and Income Taxes	$11,000	×	.40	=	$4,400

[1] It is not necessary to understand the meaning of both *results from discontinued operations* and *extraordinary items* for computing income taxes. It may be helpful, however, to read the later sections of this chapter dealing with these items in conjunction with the remainder of this section.

tax allocation. **Intraperiod income tax allocation is the process of matching a portion of the total income tax expense against the pretax: (1) income from continuing operations, (2) income (loss) from the operations of a discontinued segment, (3) gain (loss) from the disposal of a discontinued segment, and (4) gain (loss) from an extraordinary item.** The reason for intraperiod income tax allocation is quite simple; the allocation is necessary to give a fair presentation of the after-tax impact of the major components of net income.

The portion of the income tax expense for continuing operations is listed as a separate item on the income statement and is deducted from pretax income from continuing operations (or income before income taxes if there are no additional components of net income) to determine income from continuing operations. (If there are no additional components the resulting amount is the net income.) As shown on Exhibit 15-1 for the Glanton Corporation, the $4,800 income tax expense of continuing operations, as computed in Exhibit 15-2, is deducted from the $12,000 pretax income from continuing operations to determine the $7,200 income from continuing operations.

Any items included in the results from discontinued operations or as extraordinary items are shown *net* of income taxes. That is, for each of these items the income tax expense (or income tax credit, in the case of a loss) is deducted directly from each item, and only the after-tax amount is included in the computation of net income. The income tax expense or credit is shown parenthetically on the income statement, however. In Exhibit 15-1 the loss from operations of discontinued Segment X is shown at its after-tax amount of $300 ($500 less the income tax credit of $200 from Exhibit 15-2), the gain on sale of discontinued Segment X is listed at $900 ($1,500 − $600), and the extraordinary loss at $1,200 ($2,000 − $800). The income tax expense or credit related to each item, as computed in Exhibit 15-2, is shown parenthetically in Exhibit 15-1.

A corporation, like an individual, is required to *pay* income taxes several months after the end of the accounting period.[2] In recording the amount of the income taxes in the general journal, an Income Tax Expense account is increased (debited) for the *total* income taxes and Income Taxes Payable is increased (credited) for a like amount. The Income Taxes Payable account is classified on a corporate balance sheet as a current liability because it will be paid within 1 year. The journal entry to record the Glanton Corporation income taxes based on the computations in Exhibit 15-2 is shown below:

```
1983
Dec. 31  Income Tax Expense  . . . . . . . . . . . . . . . . .   4,400
             Income Taxes Payable . . . . . . . . . . . . . .              4,400
         To record income taxes for the year.
```

[2] Some corporations are required to pay income taxes on a quarterly basis but this situation is beyond the scope of the financial accounting section of this textbook. For convenience, in this section we will assume that the entire amount of corporate income taxes is paid at one time, as indicated. We will modify this assumption in our discussion of budgeting for managerial accounting.

When the corporate income taxes are paid in the next year, the Income Taxes Payable account is decreased (debited) and Cash is decreased (credited) for the amount of the payment.

Results of Discontinued Operations

Many corporations, sometimes called *conglomerates,* have several major divisions (segments) that sell different products or services. A corporation occasionally disposes of one of these segments; this is referred to as a *disposal of a discontinued segment.* The disposal is usually made because the segment is not making a sufficient profit (or is operating at a loss). **A segment is a component of a corporation whose activities involve a separate major line of business and whose assets, results of operations, and activities can be clearly separated from the rest of the corporation.**[3] Examples of transactions involving the disposal of a segment include the sale by a communications company of all its radio stations or the disposal by a food distributor of its wholesale supermarket division.

The disposal of a discontinued segment is an important event for a corporation because the disposal potentially affects its future earnings potential. For this reason certain information about the discontinued segment is reported separately on the corporation's income statement. This information is reported in a section entitled "Results of discontinued operations." Two items are included in this section: (1) the income (or loss) from the operations of the discontinued segment for the accounting period and (2) the gain (or loss) from the disposal of the discontinued segment. For instance, Colgate-Palmolive Company disposed of several of its lines of business, including Helena Rubinstein, Inc., in 1980. The company reported an operating loss of $3,149,000 from the 1980 operations of these segments and a $19,878,000 loss from the disposal of these segments in the results of discontinued operations section of its income statement for 1980.

When the corporation operates the segment for part of the accounting period before its disposal, the pretax income (loss) from these operations must be calculated. The related income taxes are deducted from this pretax income (loss), and the after-tax income (loss) from the operations of the discontinued segment is shown on the income statement. As we discussed earlier, in Exhibit 15-1 the Glanton Corporation reported a $300 loss (after an income tax credit of $200) from the operations of discontinued Segment X.

When the assets of the discontinued segment are sold, a gain or loss (the difference between the selling price and the book value of the assets) is recorded. This gain or loss is computed in the same way as for an individual asset as discussed in Chapter 12. The related income taxes are deducted from this pretax gain (loss) and the after-tax gain (loss) is shown on the income statement. The after-tax gain (loss) on the disposal and the operating income (loss) of the discontinued segment are added together in the results of discontinued operations section of the income statement. For the Glanton Corporation, in Exhibit 15-1 the $900 gain (after income taxes of $600) is added to the $300 operating loss (net of an income tax credit of $200) to determine the $600 results of discontinued operations. The $600 is added

---

[3] "Reporting the Results of Operations," *APB Opinion No. 30* (New York: AICPA, 1973), par. 13.

to the $7,200 income from continuing operations to determine the income before extraordinary loss of $7,800.

Extraordinary Gains and Losses

Sometimes an event or transaction occurs that causes a gain or loss for a corporation and that is defined as an extraordinary item. **An extraordinary item is an event or transaction that is both unusual in nature *and* infrequent in occurrence, taking into consideration the political, legal, and physical environment within which the corporation operates.** Both criteria (*unusual* and *infrequent*) must be met in order to classify an event or transaction as extraordinary in nature.[4]

Examples of events that are likely to be extraordinary items are an earthquake, tornado, flood, expropriation of assets by a foreign country, and a prohibition under a newly enacted law. These extraordinary items are so abnormal in regard to a corporation's current and potential earnings that the related gains or losses are reported separately on its income statement. **Extraordinary gains or losses result from extraordinary items and are shown, net of income taxes, in a separate section of the income statement.** This section is located directly below the results of discontinued operations section (or, if there is no such section, after income from continuing operations). For instance, in its income statement for 1980 the Boise Cascade Corporation reported a $12,500,000 extraordinary gain, net of income taxes, due to the settlement of a claim against the People's Republic of China for the takeover (expropriation) of a power plant of the company in that country. In Exhibit 15-1, The Glanton Corporation shows a $1,200 extraordinary loss from a tornado (after deducting an $800 income tax credit).

Most gains and losses are not considered to be extraordinary. For example, the writedown of receivables or inventories and the sale of property, plant, and equipment results in ordinary gains and losses.[5] These are listed in the nonoperating income section as other revenues and expenses and are included in pretax income from continuing operations.

Earnings per Share

The owners (stockholders) of a corporation hold shares of stock as evidence of ownership. Because these shares are readily transferable, the stock of many corporations sells on organized stock markets like the New York and American Stock Exchanges. As discussed in Chapter 7, daily prices are listed for these shares of stock to help current and potential stockholders determine whether to buy, sell, or hold capital stock. Stockholders invest (or sell their investments) in a corporation for many reasons, including the likelihood of receiving future dividends or participating in any future increase in the stock market price. Both these factors are influenced by the corporation's current and future earnings.

To predict a corporation's future earnings, dividends, and stock market price, investors prepare many kinds of analyses (discussed in Chapter 19). One of the items of financial information that is used in these analyses is the corporation's *earnings per share*. Each corporation discloses its earnings per share on its income

[4] Ibid., par. 20.
[5] Ibid., par. 23.

statement, directly below the net income. For instance, Polaroid Corporation reported earnings per share of $2.60 on its income statement for 1980, based on net income of $85,406,000 and common shares of 32,855,000.

The figure for earnings per share is probably the most frequently cited information in a financial analysis of a corporation. In its simplest form, earnings per share is computed by dividing the corporation's net income by the number of common shares outstanding throughout the entire year. Many corporations, however, report several components of net income and have preferred stock outstanding that has first priority to dividends (discussed later in the chapter). They also may have shares of common stock outstanding for only a portion of a year as a result of stock issuances during the year.

Earnings per share computations can be very complicated; only the basic earnings per share computations are discussed here. The earnings per share computation may be expressed in an equation as shown below. A discussion of each element of the equation follows.

$$\text{Earnings per Common Share Outstanding} = \frac{\text{Net Income} - \text{Preferred Dividends}}{\text{Weighted Average Number of Common Shares Outstanding}}$$

NET INCOME AND PREFERRED DIVIDENDS.   Common stockholders are considered to be the *residual* owners of the corporation. Therefore earnings per share applies only to common shares, and only the earnings available to common stockholders are used in the numerator of the earnings per share computation. If a corporation has no preferred shares outstanding, the net income is used as the numerator in computing earnings per share. If there is outstanding preferred stock, however, the preferred dividends for the current period are deducted from the net income to determine the earnings available to common stockholders. To illustrate the computation of the numerator, suppose that the Glanton Corporation (from Exhibit 15-1) had preferred stock outstanding during all of 1983 and the dividends on this preferred stock amounted to $1,200. The numerator of the Glanton Corporation's 1983 earnings per share is $5,400, computed by subtracting the $1,200 preferred dividends from the $6,600 net income.

WEIGHTED AVERAGE COMMON SHARES.   Since a corporation earns its net income over the entire year, the earnings should be related to the weighted average number of common shares outstanding during the year. If a corporation has not issued any common shares during the year, the common shares outstanding for the year are used as the denominator. When common shares have been issued during the year, these shares are multiplied times the fraction of the year (in months) they are outstanding. The result is added to the beginning number of shares to determine the weighted average number of common shares outstanding during the year. This number is used as the denominator in the earnings per share calculation.

To illustrate, assume that the Glanton Corporation had 1,800 common shares that were outstanding during all of 1983. On August 1, 1983, it issued an additional

EXHIBIT 15-3
Weighted Average
Common Shares

Months Shares Are Outstanding	Shares Outstanding	×	Fraction of Year Outstanding	=	Weighted Average
January–December	1,800		$\frac{12}{12}$		1,800
August–December	1,200		$\frac{5}{12}$		500
			Total Weighted Average Common Shares		2,300

1,200 common shares so that it had 3,000 common shares outstanding at the end of the year. Its weighted average number of common shares outstanding during 1983 is 2,300, determined by adding 1,800 + 500 (1,200 × 5/12). These computations are shown in Exhibit 15-3.

COMPUTATION AND DISCLOSURE. The earnings per share figure is computed by dividing the earnings available to common stockholders (i.e., net income less preferred dividends) by the weighted average number of common shares outstanding. This earnings per share figure is disclosed on the income statement directly below net income. In addition, the earnings per share related to the major components of net income are also disclosed. The earnings per share for the income from continuing operations is calculated by subtracting the preferred dividends from the income from continuing operations and dividing the result by the weighted average common shares. The earnings per share figures for the results of discontinued operations and extraordinary items are computed by dividing the respective amounts (disregarding the preferred dividends) by the weighted average common shares. The amount of the preferred dividends deducted from the numerator and the weighted average number of common shares used in the denominator should be disclosed in a note to the income statement.

The earnings per share of the Glanton Corporation for 1983 are $2.35, as calculated below. Also shown below are the earnings per share for each component of the income statement. The earnings per share figures, of course, total $2.35 and are shown in Exhibit 15-1.

Earnings per share	$2.35	=	$\frac{\$6,600 - \$1,200}{2,300}$
Components:			
Income from continuing operations	$2.61	=	$\frac{\$7,200 - \$1,200}{2,300}$
Results of discontinued operations	.26	=	$\frac{\$600}{2,300}$
Extraordinary loss from tornado	(.52)	=	$\frac{\$(1,200)}{2,300}$
	$2.35		

The note to the Glanton Corporation income statement discloses the preferred dividends and weighted average shares.

Closing Entries   The revenue and expense accounts of a company are closed at the end of each accounting period. These accounts are first closed to the Income Summary account; then the balance of the Income Summary account (the net income or net loss) is closed to a permanent owners' equity account. There are two differences between the closing entries for the net income of a corporation as compared to a sole proprietorship or partnership. First, for a sole proprietorship or partnership the balance is closed to the owners' capital accounts; whereas for a corporation the balance is closed to the Retained Earnings account. Second, because corporations are subject to income taxes and report the results of discontinued operations and extraordinary items, the related accounts must also be closed in the closing entries. These accounts are closed in the usual manner with the other revenues and expenses.

As an example the December 31, 1983, closing entries of the Glanton Corporation (which uses a perpetual inventory system and control accounts for its net sales, selling, and general and administrative expenses) are shown below. The information for the closing entries was taken from Exhibits 15-1 and 15-2.

1983			
Dec. 31	Sales (net)	100,000	
	Interest Revenue	700	
	Gain on Sale of Discontinued Segment X		
	(*pretax*)	1,500	
	Gain on Sale of Equipment (*pretax*)	500	
	Income Summary		102,700
	To close the revenue accounts.		
31	Income Summary	96,100	
	Cost of Goods Sold		60,000
	Selling Expenses		16,000
	General and Administrative Expenses . . .		13,000
	Interest Expense		200
	Income Tax Expense (*total*)		4,400
	Loss From Operations of Discontinued		
	Segment X (*pretax*)		500
	Extraordinary Loss From Tornado (*pretax*)		2,000
	To close the expense accounts.		
31	Income Summary	6,600	
	Retained Earnings		6,600
	To close the Income Summary account and		
	transfer the net income to retained earnings.		

Note that the *pretax* amounts of the various gains and losses are used in the closing entries because the Income Tax Expense account contains the *total* of the related income taxes. The closing entry for dividends is discussed in a later section of the chapter.

DIVIDENDS

Cash dividends are the most common type of dividends distributed by a corporation. (Stock dividends are another "type" of dividend, discussed later in the chapter.) Whereas net income increases the assets of the corporation and this increase is recorded in retained earnings, the distribution of cash dividends has the opposite effect. The distribution reduces the assets of the corporation and is also recorded as a reduction in retained earnings. Thus the phrase, "retained earnings paid out in dividends," which is often used in discussing dividends, is somewhat misleading. Cash dividends are paid out of *cash* and retained earnings are reduced because the payment is a return of capital to the stockholders.

In order to pay dividends a company must meet legal requirements and have enough cash available. The setting of a corporation's dividend policy is the responsibility of the board of directors. The board determines the amount and timing of the dividends, considering legal requirements, compliance with contractual agreements, and the financial well-being of the corporation.

Legal requirements vary from state to state, with most states requiring a positive (credit) balance in retained earnings before dividends may be declared. (**A deficit is the term used to describe a *negative* retained earnings balance.** This occurs when the account has a *debit* balance, the result of accumulated prior net losses or dividends in excess of earnings.) Usually the amount of retained earnings available for dividends is also restricted by the cost of the treasury shares held.

In considering the financial well-being of the corporation, the board of directors should consult the corporate financial personnel, including the accountants. Consideration should be given to the impact of the payment of a dividend upon cash, current assets, and working capital, the ability to finance corporate expansion projects with the remaining assets, and the effect of the dividend on the stock market price per share. Payment of dividends should be in the financial long- and short-term best interests of the corporate stockholders.

In this section we discuss the important dates and journal entries for cash dividends, contrast these dividends with stock dividends, and examine the impact of preferred stock characteristics upon dividends.

Cash Dividends

Withdrawals in a sole proprietorship or partnership can be made very quickly. When the owner wants to withdraw cash, a check is written to the owner from the company's checking account, a journal entry is made to record (debit) the withdrawal and reduction (credit) in cash, and the owner cashes the check for personal use. In contrast, the distribution of dividends by a corporation cannot be made so quickly. There may be many stockholders of a corporation, and therefore extensive record keeping may be required by the corporation for its dividends. As a result the dividend process is usually spread out over a period of several weeks.

Three dates are significant for a cash dividend (or any type of dividend): (1) the date of declaration, (2) the date of record, and (3) the date of payment. For instance, on January 13, 1981, Procter & Gamble Company declared a 95¢ per share quarterly dividend, payable on February 14, 1981, to stockholders of record on January 23, 1981.

On the date of declaration, the board of directors formally declares that a

dividend will be paid to stockholders of record on a specified future date, typically 4 to 6 weeks later. On the declaration date the corporation becomes legally liable to pay the future dividend, and a journal entry is made to reduce retained earnings and establish the current liability. It normally takes a corporation some time to process the dividend checks and for investors to determine whether they desire to buy or sell the stock based on the dividends. Thus a *cut-off* date is needed — the date of record. **On the date of record, only investors listed as stockholders of the corporation (the stockholders of record) can participate in the dividend.** The date of record usually occurs several weeks after the declaration date and several weeks before the payment date, as specified in the dividend provisions. On the date of record no journal entry is necessary, although the corporation may make a memorandum entry in the general journal indicating that the date of record has been reached; it also begins processing the dividend checks. **On the date of payment, the corporation mails the dividend checks.** A journal entry is also made on this date to eliminate the liability and reduce the cash.

On the date of declaration the total amount of the dividend liability to common stockholders, as well as any dividend liability to preferred stockholders (discussed later), is determined. Dividends are normally declared on a *per share basis*. That is, a set dollar amount per common share outstanding is established at the time of declaration. The total amount of the dividend liability is determined by multiplying the dividends per share times the number of common shares outstanding on the date of declaration. The Retained Earnings account is usually reduced (debited) directly. (Some companies prefer to increase (debit) a contra-retained earnings account entitled Dividends Declared; however, this procedure will not be used in this chapter.) A liability, Dividends Payable, is also established (credited).

To illustrate, assume that on November 15, 1983, a corporation declared a 60¢ per share dividend on its 4,000 outstanding common shares. These dividends are payable on December 30, 1983, to stockholders of record as of December 15, 1983. The journal entry to record the declaration of the $2,400 dividends (4,000 × $.60) is shown below:

```
1983
Nov. 15   Retained Earnings . . . . . . . . . . . . . . . . . .   2,400
              Dividends Payable . . . . . . . . . . . . . . . .          2,400
          To record the declaration of cash dividends.
```

The journal entry to record the payment of the dividends is as follows:

```
1983
Dec. 30   Dividends Payable . . . . . . . . . . . . . . . . . .   2,400
              Cash . . . . . . . . . . . . . . . . . . . . . . .          2,400
          To record the payment of dividends.
```

If a Dividends Declared account had been used to record the declaration of the dividends, this account would be closed at the end of the year in the closing entries. The balance of the account would be closed by a debit to Retained Earnings and a credit to the Dividends Declared account. If the accounting period had ended between the date of declaration and the date of payment, the Dividends Payable account would be classified as a current liability on the corporate balance sheet.

Stock Dividends   Occasionally a corporation may declare and distribute a stock dividend. **A stock dividend is a pro rata (proportional) distribution of additional shares of a corporation's own stock to its stockholders.** For instance, early in 1981 Tootsie Roll Industries, Inc., issued a 3% stock dividend to its common stockholders.

A stock dividend usually consists of the same class of shares; that is, a common stock dividend is declared on common stock outstanding. Stock dividends most frequently are issued out of authorized but unissued shares, although treasury stock shares may be used. Unlike cash dividends, the declaration of a stock dividend usually can be legally rescinded.

A stock dividend differs from a cash dividend in that no corporate assets are distributed. Each stockholder holds the same percentage of ownership in the corporation as was held prior to the distribution. For instance, assume that a corporation has 10,000 common shares outstanding, one stockholder owns 2,000 shares, and the corporation issues a 10% stock dividend. After the stock dividend 11,000 shares will be outstanding (10,000 × 1.10), and the stockholder will now own 2,200 (2,000 × 1.10) shares. The stockholder owned 20% of the outstanding common stock *both prior to and after* the stock dividend. What occurs, from an accounting standpoint, is a rearrangement of stockholders' equity. Total stockholders' equity does not change, but retained earnings is decreased by the amount of the dividend and contributed capital is increased by the same amount because of the additional number of shares issued. A stock dividend also differs from a stock split (discussed in Chapter 14). Although both transactions increase the number of shares outstanding and neither causes any change in total stockholders' equity, a stock split does not affect total retained earnings or total contributed capital.

Stock dividends are often viewed favorably by stockholders even though: (1) they receive no corporate assets; (2) theoretically, the total market value of their investment will not increase because the increased number of shares will be offset by a decrease in the stock market price per share due to a larger number of shares participating in the same corporate earnings; and (3) future cash dividends may be limited because retained earnings is decreased by the amount of the stock dividend, and most states set legal dividend restrictions based on positive retained earnings. Some stockholders, however, welcome stock dividends because: (1) they see them as evidence of corporate growth and sound financial policy; (2) other investors may also look favorably on the stock dividends and purchase the stock, causing the stock market price *not* to decrease proportionally; (3) the corporation may continue to pay the same cash dividend per share, in which case stockholders will receive higher total dividends; and (4) the market price may decrease to a lower trading range, making the stock more attractive to additional investors.

In accounting for a stock dividend by a corporation, a distinction is made between a *small* and a *large* stock dividend and generally accepted accounting principles have been established for each of them. **A small stock dividend is less**

than or equal to 20% of the previously outstanding common shares.[6] It is argued that for a small stock dividend the size of the dividend does not significantly affect the stock market price of the outstanding shares. Thus the "value" of the stock issued in the stock dividend is considered to be the current stock market price, and therefore the stock dividend is recorded at this price. For a small stock dividend, retained earnings is reduced and contributed capital is increased by an amount equal to the current market value for the additional shares of the stock dividend.

A large stock dividend is greater than 20% of the previously outstanding common shares. The size of a large stock dividend is likely to cause a substantial decrease in the stock market price of the outstanding shares. Therefore the current market price is *not* appropriate for recording such a stock dividend. The *par* (or *stated*) value of the stock is used instead. For a large stock dividend, retained earnings is reduced and contributed capital is increased by the total par value for the additional shares of the stock dividend.

To illustrate the accounting for the two sizes of stock dividends, assume that a corporation has the following stockholders' equity prior to a stock dividend:

Stockholders' Equity

Contributed capital	
Common stock, $10 par, 40,000 shares authorized,	
10,000 shares issued and outstanding	$100,000
Additional paid-in capital on common stock	70,000
Total contributed capital	$170,000
Retained earnings	80,000
Total Stockholders' Equity	$250,000

SMALL STOCK DIVIDEND. Assume that the corporation declares and issues a 10% stock dividend. On the date of declaration the stock is selling for $19 per share. The 1,000 share (10,000 shares × 10%) stock dividend is recorded at the current market value of $19,000 as follows:

Date of Declaration

Retained Earnings (1,000 × $19)	19,000	
Common Stock To Be Distributed (1,000 × $10)		10,000
Additional Paid-in Capital from Stock Dividend		9,000
To record declaration of small stock dividend.		

Date of Issuance

Common Stock To Be Distributed	10,000	
Common Stock, $10 par		10,000
To record issuance of stock for stock dividend.		

---

[6] Generally accepted accounting principles state that a small stock dividend is less than 20% or 25%. Because this is confusing we will use 20%.

The resulting stockholders' equity would appear as follows:

Stockholders' Equity

Contributed capital	
Common stock, $10 par, 40,000 shares authorized,	
11,000 shares issued and outstanding	$110,000
Additional paid-in capital on common stock	70,000
Additional paid-in capital from stock dividend	9,000
Total contributed capital	$189,000
Retained earnings	61,000
Total Stockholders' Equity	$250,000

On the date of declaration, since the common stock will not be issued until later, a temporary contributed capital account, Common Stock To Be Distributed, is used to record the par value of the stock. If a balance sheet is prepared after the declaration but prior to the issuance of the stock dividend, the Common Stock To Be Distributed account would be listed as a component of contributed capital. The account is *not* a liability like the dividend payable account for cash dividends. It is is a temporary stockholders' equity item showing the legal capital of the stock to be issued. As illustrated, it is eliminated when the stock is issued. The Additional Paid-in Capital from Stock Dividend is also added to the other additional paid-in capital accounts in the contributed capital section. Note that there is no difference in the $250,000 total stockholders' equity prior to and after the stock dividend. Only the components are changed, with retained earnings decreasing by $19,000 and contributed capital increasing by the same amount (and the issued shares increasing to 11,000).

LARGE STOCK DIVIDEND. Assume, *instead*, that the corporation declares and issues a 30% stock dividend when the stock is selling for $19 per share. In this case the market value is disregarded, and the par value of $30,000 for the 3,000 shares (10,000 shares × 30% × $10) is used to record the stock dividend. The declaration and issuance of the large stock dividend are recorded as follows:

Date of Declaration

Retained Earnings (3,000 × $10)	30,000	
Common Stock To Be Distributed		30,000
To record declaration of large stock dividend.		

Date of Issuance

Common Stock To Be Distributed	30,000	
Common Stock, $10 par		30,000
To record issuance of stock for stock dividend.		

The resulting stockholders' equity is shown on the following page:

Stockholders' Equity

Contributed capital
  Common stock, $10 par, 40,000 shares authorized,
    13,000 shares issued and outstanding $130,000
  Additional paid-in capital on common stock 70,000
    Total contributed capital $200,000
  Retained earnings 50,000
    Total Stockholders' Equity $250,000

Again there is no difference between the $250,000 total stockholders' equity prior to and after the stock dividend. Only the components are changed, with retained earnings decreasing by $30,000 and contributed capital increasing by the same amount (and the number of issued shares increasing to 13,000).

Dividends on Preferred Stock

As we indicated in the previous chapter, some investors consider certain stockholder rights to be more important than others. To appeal to these investors, preferred stock may be issued. The rights of preferred stockholders are included in the stock certificate. Three of these rights are important for dividends. They include: (1) a preference to dividends, (2) accumulation of dividends, and (3) participation in excess dividends. Preferred stock may be issued with one or a combination of these rights. Each of these rights is discussed below.

PREFERENCE AS TO DIVIDENDS.   Holders of preferred stock have a preference as to dividends. **A dividend preference is a right of preferred stockholders to receive a dividend before a dividend can be paid to common stockholders.** Preferred stock is usually issued with a par or stated value and the dividends are expressed as a percentage of this value. For instance, assume that a corporation has outstanding 1,000 shares of 10%, $50 par preferred stock. The corporation must pay $5 per share ($50 par × 10%), which totals $5,000 ($5 × 1,000 shares), as dividends to preferred stockholders before it can pay *any* dividends to common stockholders.

Such a preference to dividends does *not* guarantee that a preferred dividend will be paid in any given year since the board of directors can decide not to pay any dividends. To protect preferred stockholders further, a provision may be included in the preferred stock certificate that requires the accumulation of dividends.

CUMULATIVE PREFERRED STOCK.   Stockholders are not legally entitled to share in dividends unless these dividends have been declared by the corporate board of directors. If dividends are not declared in a given year, a holder of noncumulative preferred stock will never be paid that dividend. For this reason noncumulative preferred stock is seldom issued, because investors consider this feature to be a distinct disadvantage.

Most preferred stock is cumulative. **Cumulative preferred stock is preferred stock that must be paid all dividends of the current and past periods before any dividends can be paid to common stockholders. Any dividends not declared on**

cumulative preferred stock in a given period become dividends in arrears. Dividends in arrears accumulate from period to period. The dividends in arrears are *not* a liability to the corporation because no liability exists until the dividend declaration. Any dividends in arrears, however, are very important to investors and other interested parties and should be disclosed in a note to the balance sheet.

To illustrate dividends in arrears, assume that a corporation has 2,000 shares of 8%, $100 par cumulative preferred stock outstanding. Each share of stock is entitled to an $8 annual dividend (computed by multiplying the 8% by the $100 par value). If dividends are not declared in 1981 and 1982, preferred stockholders would be entitled to dividends in arrears of $16,000 (2,000 × $8) at the end of 1981 and $32,000 (2,000 × $8 × 2 years) at the end of 1982. At the end of 1983 dividends of $48,000 (for 3 years) would have to be paid to preferred stockholders before any dividend payments could be made to common stockholders.

PARTICIPATING PREFERRED STOCK.   **Participating preferred stock is preferred stock that shares with the common stock in any *extra* dividends.** Extra dividends are paid only after preferred stockholders have been paid their stated dividend rate (on the *preferred* par value) and common stockholders have been paid at a rate (on the *common* par value) equal to that paid on the preferred stock. For example, if a corporation has 9%, $50 par participating preferred stock and $10 par common stock outstanding, it must first pay preferred stockholders $4.50 per share (9% times the $50 par) and common stockholders 90¢ per share (9% times the $10 par). If the total dividend to be paid then exceeds the amount needed to meet these dividend requirements, an extra dividend arises.

To illustrate further, assume that a corporation has issued 8% participating cumulative preferred stock with a par value of $20,000 and common stock with a par value of $30,000. Of the $50,000 total par value, therefore, 40% is for preferred stock and 60% is for common stock. The company wants to distribute cash dividends of $5,000, and there are no dividends in arrears. The dividend distribution is shown in Exhibit 15-4. In the calculations, common stock initially receives a rate equal to preferred stock *for the current year.* Had any preferred stock dividends been in arrears, these dividends would have been distributed before any participation calculations. Common stock does not share in any dividends in arrears.

EXHIBIT 15-4
Dividend Distribution

		Preferred	Common
8% dividend to preferred (on $20,000 par)		$1,600	
Common dividend (equal to 8% of $30,000 par) . .			$2,400
Extra dividend proportionate to par values:			
Total to allocate	$5,000		
Allocated ($1,600 + $2,400)	4,000		
Remainder (40% to preferred, 60% to common)	$1,000	400	600
Dividends to Each Class of Stock		$2,000	$3,000

Participating preferred stock is rare. Corporations generally agree that preferred stockholders receive too many rights if they are given first preferences to dividends and are also allowed to participate in all dividends.

ACCOUNTING FOR PREFERRED DIVIDENDS. Cash dividends on preferred stock are usually declared and paid at the same time as the cash dividends on common stock. When both classes of stock are outstanding, separate dividends payable accounts should be used for each class of stock. For instance, if a corporation declared and paid preferred and common dividends as calculated in Exhibit 15-4, the following journal entries would be made:

Date of Declaration

Retained Earnings	5,000	
Dividends Payable: Preferred		2,000
Dividends Payable: Common		3,000

To record the declaration of cash dividends.

Date of Payment

Dividends Payable: Preferred	2,000	
Dividends Payable: Common	3,000	
Cash		5,000

To record the payment of dividends.

PRIOR PERIOD ADJUSTMENTS: CORRECTIONS OF ERRORS

Corporations sometimes make changes in their accounting practices that require an adjustment of their accounting records of prior years. Some of these adjustments are called prior period adjustments. They include certain changes in accounting principles (e.g., a change from LIFO to FIFO for inventory) or a correction of an error made in a prior period. We discuss only error corrections here.

A corporation may make an error in the revenue or expense accounts (with a related error in the asset or liability accounts) of one accounting period that is not discovered until a later period. These errors may result from an oversight, the incorrect use of existing facts, or a mistake in mathematics. Such errors are corrected with correcting entries.

Correcting Entries

The correction of an error made in a previous period is recorded as a prior period adjustment to the beginning retained earnings balance in the period of correction. That is, the asset or liability account balance in error at the beginning of the period is corrected (debited or credited) and the offsetting debit or credit is recorded directly in the Retained Earnings account. This is because the error in the prior year's revenue or expense accounts was closed to retained earnings and the error does not affect the revenues or expenses of the current period. Any related impact on the prior year's income taxes should also be recorded in a similar way.

To illustrate, suppose that in 1983 the Slusher Corporation discovered that it inadvertently recorded too much depreciation expense in the amount of $5,000 in 1982. This error understated 1982 income before income taxes by $5,000. Thus retained earnings must be increased by $5,000 in the correcting entry. Assuming a 40% income tax rate, the 1982 income tax expense (previously closed to retained earnings) was understated, and therefore the corporation also owes an additional $2,000 of income taxes for 1982. The journal entries that would be made to record the corrections to the accounts are as follows:

Accumulated Depreciation	5,000	
Retained Earnings		5,000

To record the correction of the overstatement of the 1982 depreciation.

Retained Earnings	2,000	
Income Taxes Payable		2,000

To record the additional income taxes resulting from the correction of the 1982 depreciation overstatement.

The debit to Accumulated Depreciation in the first entry reduces the account balance for the overstatement recorded in 1982. The credit to Retained Earnings increases the account to correct it for the understatement of 1982 income before income taxes (remember that 1982 net income has been closed to retained earnings). The second entry records the effect of the error correction on prior income taxes. The debit to Retained Earnings reduces the account for the additional income tax expense related to 1982 income. The credit to Income Taxes Payable shows the additional taxes owed for 1982 but not yet paid. Alternatively, if the depreciation had been understated in 1982, the correcting entry would reduce (debit) Retained Earnings and increase (credit) Accumulated Depreciation. The correction for taxes would involve an increase (credit) in Retained Earnings (to correct for the prior overstatement of income tax expense) and an increase (debit) in a current asset account entitled Income Tax Refund Receivable for the overpayment of 1982 income taxes.

Financial Statement Disclosure

Prior period adjustments (e.g., error corrections) are reported, in the year of the correction, as an adjustment to the corporation's beginning retained earnings in its statement of retained earnings (discussed at the end of this chapter). The prior period adjustment, net of income taxes (the income taxes are shown in parentheses), is added to (or subtracted from) the beginning retained earnings balance to determine the *adjusted* beginning retained earnings. The correction of the overstatement of depreciation in our example is shown as a prior period adjustment in Exhibit 15-6 at the end of the chapter.

APPRO-PRIATIONS OF RETAINED EARNINGS

When setting dividend policy the board of directors of a corporation should consider both legal requirements and sound financial practice. Stockholders sometimes look at only the legal requirements, and as the Retained Earnings account balance increases, they may expect to receive more dividends. The *assets* of the corporation, however, must be used for a variety of corporate activities, including financing ongoing operations and long-term expansion projects, meeting principal and interest payments on bonds (discussed in Chapter 16), and making dividend payments.

To indicate that a part of retained earnings is unavailable for dividends, a corporation may appropriate (restrict) retained earnings. **An appropriation of retained earnings is the restriction of an amount of retained earnings by the board of directors so that this amount is not available for the declaration of dividends.** It is important to note that such a policy does *not* directly restrict the use of any assets; it merely requires that the corporation not distribute any assets that would reduce the restricted retained earnings. A corporation may still declare and pay dividends, reducing unappropriated retained earnings.

Reasons for Appropriations

A board of directors may appropriate retained earnings (1) to meet *legal* requirements, (2) to meet *contractual* restrictions, or (3) because of *discretionary* actions. Corporations must follow the laws of the state in which they are incorporated. States usually require restrictions of retained earnings when a corporation reacquires its own stock as treasury stock, the appropriation of retained earnings being an amount equal to the cost of the treasury shares. The argument for this appropriation is that the corporation, by acquiring treasury stock, reduces the amount of invested (permanent) capital. By restricting retained earnings for an equal amount, permanent capital is protected.

Retained earnings may also be restricted as a result of a contractual agreement. Such an agreement is often made when a corporation issues long-term bonds. To provide some assurance that excessive dividends will not be distributed which would endanger bondholders' claims, the bond provisions may require the periodic appropriation of a certain amount of retained earnings.

Finally, retained earnings may be appropriated as a result of management discretion. This type of restriction may be related to planning for future expansion. That is, a company may be planning to build a new plant or to add to existing facilities. It may be desirable to finance this activity through internally generated funds (i.e., funds that the corporation already holds or will receive from operations in the near future) rather than seek external funding from creditors or through the issuance of more capital stock. To indicate that these internal funds are being held as assets within the corporation for this purpose and are unavailable for dividends, the board of directors may appropriate a portion of retained earnings.

Alternative Accounting for Appropriations

Appropriations of retained earnings may be accounted for by (1) making journal entries or (2) reporting the restrictions in a footnote to stockholders' equity. If an appropriation of retained earnings is to be accounted for by a journal entry, an *Appropriated Retained Earnings* account is established (credited) and the Retained Earnings account is reduced (debited). When the appropriation is no longer needed the initial entry is reversed, thereby eliminating the appropriated retained earnings balance and increasing unappropriated retained earnings. To illustrate suppose that a corporation has a $200,000 retained earnings balance when it acquires treasury stock at a cost of $40,000. The journal entry to record a restriction of retained earnings would be as follows:

Retained Earnings	40,000	
Retained Earnings Appropriated for Treasury Stock . . .		40,000

To restrict retained earnings for the cost of treasury stock.

Note that the journal entry involves *no* assets; only retained earnings accounts are affected. Furthermore, when journal entries are used for appropriations the *total* retained earnings does not change. It is merely separated into two elements. On the balance sheet, retained earnings would be shown as follows:

Retained earnings, unappropriated	$160,000
Retained earnings appropriated for treasury stock . .	40,000
Total retained earnings	$200,000

When the treasury stock is reissued and the board of directors cancels the appropriation, the following journal entry would be made:

Retained Earnings Appropriated for Treasury Stock	40,000	
Retained Earnings		40,000

To cancel appropriation of retained earnings.

Again no change occurs in the assets or in total retained earnings. The Appropriated Retained Earnings account balance is canceled and the amount transferred back to unappropriated Retained Earnings. The same accounting entries (with slightly different account titles) would be made for appropriations resulting from contractual agreements or management discretion.

A major disadvantage of using journal entries to disclose appropriations of retained earnings is that stockholders still may be confused about the availability of dividends. In the last example, for instance, when stockholders see "Retained Earnings, Unappropriated" in the amount of $160,000 on the balance sheet, they may expect dividends to be paid in that amount. In order to improve the reporting of retained earnings appropriations, most companies now report this information by means of a footnote to the retained earnings in the stockholders' equity section of the balance sheet.

Footnote disclosure of appropriations (restrictions) of retained earnings is the practice recommended by the authors. When a footnote is used, a clear description of the legal, contractual, or discretionary provisions and the amount of the appropriation is necessary. When the appropriation is canceled, the note is removed from the financial statements. To illustrate, the $200,000 retained earnings balance from above and the footnote for the treasury stock would appear as follows:

Retained earnings (see Note A)	$200,000

Note A: Retained earnings are restricted regarding dividends in the amount of $40,000, the cost of the treasury stock.

STATEMENT OF RETAINED EARNINGS

The statement of retained earnings is an important part of the financial statements. This schedule reports the impact of the net income, dividends, and prior period adjustments for the accounting period on retained earnings. To show the impact of these items, the format in Exhibit 15-5 is used.

EXHIBIT 15-5
Format for
Statement of Retained
Earnings

Statement of Retained Earnings
For Year Ended December 31, 1983
Retained earnings, January 1, 1983
Plus (minus): Prior period adjustments (net of income tax effect)
Adjusted retained earnings, January 1, 1983
Plus (minus): Net income (net loss)
Minus: Cash dividends (identified for each class of stock, including per share amounts)
Stock dividends
Retained earnings, December 31, 1983

The retained earnings statement may be prepared as a separate schedule to the balance sheet, as a schedule directly beneath the income statement, or as is common, included in the statement of changes in stockholders' equity discussed in Chapter 14. Any restrictions (appropriations) of retained earnings would be disclosed by means of a footnote to the Retained Earnings account in stockholders' equity.

Exhibit 15-6 provides an illustration of a retained earnings statement (all amounts are assumed).

EXHIBIT 15-6
Statement of Retained
Earnings

SLUSHER CORPORATION
Statement of Retained Earnings
For Year Ended December 31, 1983

Retained earnings, January 1, 1983		$78,000
Add: Correction of understatement in 1982 net income due to overstatement of depreciation (net of $2,000 income tax expense)		3,000
Adjusted retained earnings, January 1, 1983		$ 81,000
Add: Net income		39,000
		$120,000
Less: Cash dividend on common stock ($4 per share)	$9,300	
Cash dividend on preferred stock ($6 per share)	7,200	
Stock dividend on common stock	2,500	(19,000)
Retained earnings, December 31, 1983		$101,000

On January 1, 1983, the Fairview Corporation had 1,200 shares of common stock outstanding and a retained earnings balance of $50,800. On that date the company issued 300 shares of 8%, $100 par preferred stock. On March 1, 1983, the company issued an additional 960 shares of common stock. During 1983 the company discovered it had not recorded bad debt expense of $3,000 in 1982. The company properly recorded the correction (including the effect on prior income taxes). At the end of 1983 the company records showed the following alphabetical list of items. The company is subject to a 40% income tax rate.

Cost of goods sold	$52,000
Dividends declared and paid: Common stock	2,160
Dividends declared and paid: Preferred stock	2,400
General and administrative expenses	8,000
Interest expense	1,400
Interest revenue	400
Sales	90,000
Selling expenses	14,000

Required: Prepare (1) an income statement, (2) closing entries, and (3) a statement of retained earnings.

SOLUTION TO
REVIEW
PROBLEM

Requirement 1:

FAIRVIEW CORPORATION
Income Statement
For Year Ended December 31, 1983

Sales		$90,000
Cost of goods sold		52,000
Gross profit		$38,000
Operating expenses		
Selling expenses	$14,000	
General and administrative expenses	8,000	
Total operating expenses		22,000
Operating income		$16,000
Other revenues and expenses		
Interest revenue	$ 400	
Interest expense	(1,400)	
Nonoperating loss		1,000
Income before income taxes		$15,000
Income tax expense (40%)		6,000
Net Income		$ 9,000
Earnings per common share (see Note A)		$ 3.30

Note A: Preferred dividends of $2,400 were deducted from net income in computing earnings per share. The weighted average number of common shares outstanding is 2,000 shares [(1,200 × 12/12) + (960 × 10/12)]

Requirement 2:

```
1983
Dec. 31   Sales  . . . . . . . . . . . . . . . . . . . . . . . . . .       90,000
          Interest Revenue . . . . . . . . . . . . . . . . . .         400
              Income Summary . . . . . . . . . . . . . . . .                   90,400
          To close the revenue accounts.


     31   Income Summary  . . . . . . . . . . . . . . . . .        81,400
              Cost of Goods Sold  . . . . . . . . . . . . . .                   52,000
              Selling Expenses . . . . . . . . . . . . . . . .                  14,000
              General and Administrative Expenses  . . . . .                     8,000
              Interest Expense  . . . . . . . . . . . . . . . .                  1,400
              Income Tax Expense . . . . . . . . . . . . . . .                   6,000
          To close the expense accounts.


     31   Income Summary  . . . . . . . . . . . . . . . . .         9,000
              Retained Earnings  . . . . . . . . . . . . . . .                   9,000
          To close the Income Summary account and
          transfer the net income to retained earnings.
```

Note: It is assumed that when the dividends were declared, Retained Earnings was reduced directly. Therefore no closing entry is necessary for dividends.

Requirement 3:

FAIRVIEW CORPORATION
Statement of Retained Earnings
For Year Ended December 31, 1983

Retained earnings, January 1, 1983		$50,800
Less: Correction of overstatement of 1982 net income due to understatement of bad debt expense (net of $1,200 income tax credit)		(1,800)
Adjusted retained earnings, January 1, 1983		$49,000
Add: Net income		9,000
		$58,000
Less: Cash dividends on common stock ($1 per share)	$2,160	
Cash dividends on preferred stock ($8 per share)	2,400	(4,560)
Retained earnings, December 31, 1983		$53,440

GLOSSARY

Appropriation of Retained Earnings. Restriction of amount of retained earnings by board of directors so that this amount is not available for the declaration of dividends. Retained earnings is appropriated for legal requirements, contractual restrictions, or discretionary actions. Recorded by using an Appropriated Retained Earnings account or by reporting in a footnote to the financial statements.

Common Stock To Be Distributed. Account used on the date of declaration to record the total par value of common stock to be issued in a stock dividend. Temporary contributed capital account.

Cumulative Preferred Stock. Preferred stock that must be paid all preferred dividends from current and past periods (dividends in arrears) before dividends can be paid to common stockholders.

Date of Declaration. Date on which a dividend is declared by the corporate board of directors. Dividend becomes legal liability of corporation at this time.

Date of Payment. Date on which dividends are paid to stockholders.

Date of Record. Date on which an investor must be listed as a stockholder of the corporation in order to participate in the payment of the corporation's dividends.

Deficit. Term used for a negative (debit) balance in the Retained Earnings account.

Dividend. Cash or capital stock distributed to stockholders as a return on their investment in a corporation.

Dividends in Arrears. Dividends on cumulative preferred stock that have not been declared.

Dividends Payable. Current liability account used to record the amount of cash dividends owed on the date of declaration of the dividends.

Dividend Preference. Right of preferred stockholders to receive a dividend before a dividend is paid to common stockholders.

Earnings per Share. Net income (less preferred dividends) divided by weighted average number of common shares outstanding. Disclosed on the income statement below net income.

Extraordinary Gain or Loss. Gain or loss resulting from extraordinary event or transaction that is both unusual in nature and infrequent in occurrence. Shown on the income statement as a separate item (net of income taxes) below results of discontinued operations.

Income from Continuing Operations. Component of income statement showing the net amount of the operating income, nonoperating income, and the income tax expense of operations.

Income Tax Expense. Account showing total amount of corporate income tax expense for the year. Allocated to components of net income by intraperiod income tax allocation. Closed at end of accounting period.

Income Tax Expense of Continuing Operations. The portion of total income tax expense that is matched against pretax income from continuing operations.

Income Taxes Payable. Current liability showing the total amount of income taxes owed to federal, state, and foreign governments.

Intraperiod Income Tax Allocation. Process of matching the total corporate income tax expense against pretax income from continuing operations, the results of discontinued operations, and extraordinary gains or losses.

Large Stock Dividend. Stock dividend greater than 20% of the previously outstanding common shares. Recorded at par (or stated) value of the stock.

Participating Preferred Stock. Preferred stock that participates with common stock in any extra dividends (dividends paid in excess of the preferred rate on preferred and common stock).

Prior Period Adjustment.   Adjustment of the beginning retained earnings balance for the correction of an error of a prior period. Shown, net of income taxes, on statement of retained earnings.

Retained Earnings.   Account used to accumulate the total lifetime earnings of a corporation that have not been distributed to stockholders as dividends. Component of stockholders' equity on the balance sheet of a corporation.

Results of Discontinued Operations.   Component of income statement showing the after-tax income (loss) from the operations of a discontinued segment and the after-tax gain (loss) from the disposal of the discontinued segment.

Small Stock Dividend.   Stock dividend of less than or equal to 20% of the previously outstanding common shares. Recorded at current market value of the stock.

Statement of Retained Earnings.   Schedule that reports the impact on retained earnings of the net income, dividends, and prior period adjustments for the accounting period.

Stock Dividend.   Dividend in which a pro rata (proportional) distribution of additional shares of a corporation's own common stock is made to its stockholders.

QUESTIONS

Q15-1   What are the major components and items in each component on a corporate income statement?

Q15-2   What is a segment of a corporation? What information for a discontinued segment is disclosed on an income statement and where is it disclosed?

Q15-3   What is an extraordinary item? Where and how are gains or losses from extraordinary items disclosed on an income statement?

Q15-4   What is intraperiod income tax allocation? Why is it necessary?

Q15-5   How is earnings per common share outstanding computed? How is it disclosed on a corporate income statement?

Q15-6   What is the weighted average number of common shares outstanding for computing earnings per share and how is it determined?

Q15-7   How do the closing entries of a corporation differ from those of a sole proprietorship or partnership?

Q15-8   What are the three dates of importance in regard to dividends? What journal entry is made on each date?

Q15-9   What is a stock dividend? Distinguish between a large and a small stock dividend and explain what amounts are used to record the declaration of each dividend.

Q15-10   How are a stock dividend and a stock split alike? How are they different?

Q15-11 Define the following terms regarding preferred stock: (a) dividend preference, (b) cumulative, (c) participating.

Q15-12 What does it mean when preferred dividends are "in arrears"? What journal entry is made to record dividends in arrears?

Q15-13 How does the declaration and payment of cash dividends on preferred stock differ from that for cash dividends on common stock?

Q15-14 What two journal entries must be made to record a correction of an error made in a prior period?

Q15-15 How is a correction of an error made in a prior period reported in the current period's financial statements?

Q15-16 What is an appropriation of retained earnings? For what reasons would retained earnings be appropriated?

Q15-17 What alternative accounting methods might be used for an appropriation of retained earnings? Briefly explain each method.

Q15-18 What is the format used for the statement of retained earnings?

EXERCISES

E15-1 Income Statement. The records of the Gliten Corporation for the year ended December 31, 1983, show the following items:

Operating income	$13,000
Nonoperating income	2,000

Additional Information:
(a) The weighted average number of common shares outstanding for the year is 6,000 shares.
(b) The company is subject to a 40% income tax rate.
(c) There is no preferred stock outstanding and the company has no discontinued segments or extraordinary items.

Required: Prepare the lower portion of the income statement of the Gliten Corporation for 1983, starting with operating income. Be sure to include earnings per share.

E15-2 Income Statement. The records of the Crowney Corporation for the year ended December 31, 1983, show the following items:

Pretax income from continuing operations	$90,000
Loss from operations of discontinued	
Segment Z (pretax)	(1,500)
Gain on sale of discontinued Segment Z (pretax) . . .	2,200
Extraordinary loss from flood (pretax)	(30,000)

Additional Information:
(a) The corporation had 10,000 shares of common stock outstanding during all of 1983.
(b) There is no preferred stock outstanding.
(c) The corporation is subject to a 40% income tax rate.

Required: Prepare the lower portion of the income statement of the Crowney Corporation for 1983, starting with pretax income from continuing operations. Be sure to include earnings per share.

E15-3 Weighted Average Shares. At the beginning of the current year the Stepher Corporation had 1,000 shares of $10 par common stock outstanding. During the year it engaged in the following transactions related to its common stock:

Date	Transaction
Apr. 1	Issued 600 shares of stock
July 1	Issued 460 shares of stock

Required: Determine the weighted average number of common shares outstanding for computing the earnings per share.

E15-4 Computation of Earnings per Share. The Neese Corporation reported net income in 1983 of $42,000. The company paid dividends for the current year on 200 shares of 6%, $100 par preferred stock and had 12,000 shares of common stock outstanding for the entire year.

Required: Compute the earnings per share of the Neese Corporation for 1983.

E15-5 Disclosure of Earnings per Share. The Rondale Corporation reported net income in 1983 of $28,000, consisting of income from continuing operations of $26,000, results of discontinued operations (net of tax) of $4,000, and an extraordinary *loss* (net of tax) of $2,000. The corporation paid dividends for the current year on 100 shares of 8%, $100 par preferred stock and had 10,000 shares of common stock outstanding for the entire year.

Required: Compute the earnings per share of the Rondale Corporation for 1983 and show how it would be reported on the income statement.

E15-6 Earnings per Share. At the beginning of 1983 the Davels Corporation had 1,000 shares of 8%, $50 par preferred stock and 16,500 shares of common stock outstanding. On June 1 Davels issued 3,000 additional shares of common stock. On December 31, 1983, Davels reported net income of $37,000 and paid the dividends for the current year on preferred stock.

Required: Compute the earnings per share of the Davels Corporation for 1983.

E15-7 Closing Entries. The Collier Corporation has the following revenue and expense accounts before its closing entries are made:

	Debit	Credit
Cost of goods sold	$ 9,000	
General and administrative expenses	6,000	
Interest expense	2,000	
Interest revenue		$ 5,000
Income tax expense	13,400	
Loss from operations of discontinued Segment X	3,000	
Gain from sale of discontinued Segment X		3,500
Sales		57,000
Selling expenses	10,000	
Extraordinary loss	2,000	

Required: Prepare closing entries for the revenues and expenses of the Collier Corporation.

E15-8 Cash Dividends. On October 1, 1983, the Sewel Corporation declared a cash dividend on its 1,500 outstanding shares of 7%, $100 par preferred stock. These dividends are payable on December 1, 1983, to stockholders of record as of November 15, 1983. On November 1, 1983, the company declared a 75¢ per share cash dividend on its 9,000 outstanding shares of common stock. These dividends are payable on December 15, 1983, to stockholders of record as of November 30, 1983.

Required: Prepare the journal entries for the Sewel Corporation to record the declaration and the payment of each of the above dividends.

E15-9   Stock Dividend. The stockholders' equity section of the January 1, 1983, balance sheet for the Turner Corporation is shown below:

Contributed capital
   Common stock, $10 par, 50,000 shares authorized,

20,000 shares issued and outstanding	$200,000
Additional paid-in capital on common stock	100,000
Total contributed capital	$300,000
Retained earnings	75,000
Total Stockholders' Equity	$375,000

On June 1, 1983, the corporation declared a 15% stock dividend to be distributed on July 15, 1983. The market value of the stock on June 1 is $17 per share. No additional shares of common stock were issued between January 1 and June 1, 1983.

Required: 1. Prepare the journal entry at the date of declaration.
              2. Prepare the journal entry at the date of issuance.
              3. Prepare the stockholders' equity section of the July 15, 1983 balance sheet for the Turner Corporation after the issuance of the stock dividend.

E15-10   Stock Dividend. The stockholders' equity section of the January 1, 1983, balance sheet for the Rutler Corporation is shown below:

Contributed capital
   Common stock, $5 par, 60,000 shares authorized,

30,000 shares issued and outstanding	$150,000
Additional paid-in capital on common stock	480,000
Total contributed capital	$630,000
Retained earnings	225,000
Total Stockholders' Equity	$855,000

On June 1, 1983, the corporation declared a 32% stock dividend to be distributed on July 1, 1983. On the date of declaration the stock had a current market value of $22 per share. No additional shares of common stock were issued between January 1 and June 1, 1983.

Required: 1. Prepare the journal entries to record the declaration and issuance of the stock dividend.
              2. Prepare the stockholders' equity section of the July 1, 1983 balance sheet for the Rutler Corporation after the issuance of the stock dividend.

E15-11   Dividends in Arrears. The Ithaca Corporation has 3,000 shares of 8%, $100 par cumulative preferred stock outstanding. Dividends on this stock have *not* been declared for the past 4 years. This year the corporation wishes to pay dividends to its common stockholders.

Required: What amount of preferred dividends must be paid before the Ithaca Corporation can pay dividends on common stock? Show your calculations.

E15-12   Participating Preferred Stock. The Asher Corporation has outstanding 9% participating cumulative preferred stock with a total par value of $25,000 and common stock with a total par value of $50,000. The company wishes to distribute cash dividends of $8,250; there are no dividends in arrears.

Required: Determine how the $8,250 in cash dividends will be distributed between preferred and common stock. Show all calculations.

E15-13 Prior Period Adjustment. In 1983 the Closel Corporation discovered that it had not recorded $3,000 of depreciation expense in 1982. The corporation is subject to a 40% income tax rate.

Required: 1. Prepare the journal entries for the Closel Corporation in 1983 to correct its accounting records.
2. Where would the correction be disclosed in the corporation's financial statements for 1983?

E15-14 Retained Earnings Statement. The Donner Corporation began 1983 with a retained earnings balance of $84,000. During the year the following events occurred:

(a) The corporation earned net income of $62,000.
(b) Current dividends totaling $8,000 on common and $4,000 on preferred stock were declared and paid.
(c) The corporation discovered that the depreciation expense had been overstated by $2,000 in 1982. The correcting entry increased retained earnings by $1,200 after related income taxes of $800.

Required: Prepare a statement of retained earnings for the Donner Corporation for the year ended December 31, 1983.

E15-15 Appropriations. On January 1, 1983, the Bloner Corporation had a retained earnings balance of $125,000. On June 1, 1983, the corporation acquired treasury stock at a cost of $27,000. The treasury stock is still being held at the end of 1983.

Required: 1. If the corporation makes journal entries to recognize appropriations of retained earnings, prepare the journal entry in regard to the treasury stock.
2. If the corporation, instead, recognizes appropriations of retained earnings by means of footnotes, prepare the footnote to accompany the December 31, 1983, balance sheet.
3. During 1984 all of the treasury stock was reissued and the appropriation of retained earnings was canceled. How would the cancellation be recorded if: (a) the company had used a journal entry to recognize the appropriation or (b) the company had recognized the appropriation by means of a footnote?

PROBLEMS

Part A

P15-1A Income Statement. The records of the Stringer Corporation show the following items on December 31, 1983:

Cost of goods sold	$40,000
Extraordinary loss from tornado (pretax)	1,500
General and administrative expenses	8,000
Interest revenue	400
Interest expense	200
Gain on sale of discontinued Segment R (pretax)	633
Loss from operations of discontinued Segment R (pretax)	1,000
Selling expenses	12,000
Sales	75,000

Additional Information:
(a) There were 2,000 shares of common stock outstanding on January 1, 1983. On July 1, 1983, the corporation issued 4,000 common shares.
(b) The corporation paid dividends for the current year on 200 shares of 8%, $100 par preferred stock outstanding. No dividends were paid to common stockholders.
(c) The corporation is subject to a 40% income tax rate.

Required: 1. Prepare the income statement of the Stringer Corporation for 1983.
2. Prepare the closing entries on December 31, 1983.

P15-2A Income Statement, Lower Portion. On January 1, 1983, the Eshroe Corporation had 2,200 shares of common stock outstanding and a retained earnings balance of $35,400. On June 1, 1983, another 2,400 shares of common stock were issued. On December 31, 1983, the company's records showed the following items:

Operating income	$18,000
Nonoperating income	4,500¢
Loss from operations of discontinued Segment Y (pretax)	2,200
Gain on sale of discontinued Segment Y (pretax)	2,500
Extraordinary loss from flood (pretax)	3,300
Dividends declared and paid: Preferred stock	3,000
Dividends declared and paid: Common stock	2,880

During 1983 it was discovered that the depreciation expense for 1982 had been overstated by $2,000 (pretax). Correcting entries were made for the error and related income taxes.

Required: Assuming the Eshroe Corporation is subject to a 40% income tax rate, prepare:
1. The lower portion of the income statement for 1983 starting with operating income.
2. A statement of retained earnings for 1983.

P15-3A Dividends. The stockholders' equity accounts of the Quiser Corporation on January 1, 1983, are shown below:

Preferred stock, 7%, $100 par (5,000 shares authorized)	$100,000
Common stock, $10 par (80,000 shares authorized)	200,000
Additional paid-in capital on preferred stock	7,000
Additional paid-in capital on common stock	10,000
Retained earnings	172,000
	$489,000

The company entered into the following transactions during 1983:

Date	Transaction
Jan. 1	Declared the annual cash dividend on the outstanding preferred stock and a 75¢ per share dividend on the outstanding common stock. These dividends are to be paid on February 15, 1983.
Feb. 15	Paid the cash dividend declared on January 1.
May 15	Declared a 15% stock dividend on the common stock outstanding on this date. The stock is to be distributed on June 30. The common stock is currently selling for $17 per share.
June 30	Issued the stock dividend declared on May 15.
July 1	Split the common stock 2 for 1, reducing the par value to $5 per share and increasing the authorized shares to 160,000.
Aug. 5	Declared a 35% stock dividend on the common stock outstanding on this date. The stock is to be distributed on September 25, 1983.
Sept. 25	Issued the stock dividend declared on August 5.
Dec. 31	Discovered that the 1982 depreciation expense had been understated by $2,500.

Required: 1. Prepare the journal entries of the Quiser Corporation to record the above transactions (the corporation is subject to a 40% income tax rate).
2. Prepare the stockholders' equity section of the December 31, 1983, balance sheet for the Quiser Corporation (assume that 1983 net income was $83,000).

P15-4A Retained Earnings. The records of the Warner Corporation show the following items as of December 31, 1983.

Income from continuing operations	$33,000
Loss from operations of discontinued Segment P (net of tax)	3,000
Gain on sale of discontinued Segment P (net of tax)	6,000
Extraordinary loss from expropriation of assets (net of tax)	2,500
Dividends declared and paid: Preferred stock	1,200
Dividends declared and paid: Common stock	1,850
Prior period adjustment: Overstatement of 1982 depreciation (net of $1,600 income tax)	2,400
Additional paid-in capital: Treasury stock	10,000
Stock dividend declared and issued	20,000
Treasury stock	12,000

Required: Prepare a statement of retained earnings for the Warner Corporation for the year ended December 31, 1983 (assume that the beginning retained earnings balance for 1983 was $69,750).

P15-5A Dividends. The Gunther Corporation has outstanding 1,000 shares of 8%, $100 par preferred stock and 40,000 shares of $10 par common stock. The company has $50,000 to distribute in dividends.

Required:
1. Assuming that the preferred stock is cumulative and that dividends are 2 years in arrears, (a) compute the amount of the preferred and common dividends and (b) prepare the journal entries to record the declaration and payment of the dividends.
2. Assuming, instead, that the preferred stock is participating but noncumulative, (a) compute the dividend distribution between preferred stock and common stock and (b) prepare the journal entries to record the declaration and payment of the dividends.

P15-6A Income and Retained Earnings Statements. The Grotwohl Corporation lists the following items on December 31, 1983:

Cost of goods sold	$138,000
Extraordinary loss from earthquake (net of tax)	4,000
General and administrative expenses	11,000
Interest revenue	1,850
Interest expense	650
Gain on sale of discontinued Segment L (net of tax)	1,200
Loss from operations of discontinued Segment L (net of tax)	400
Selling expenses	12,900
Sales (net)	230,000

Additional Information:
(a) There were 18,000 shares of common stock outstanding on January 1, 1983. On September 1, 1983, the company issued 6,000 more common shares.
(b) The company paid current cash dividends on 850 shares of 6%, $100 par preferred stock outstanding and an 80¢ per share dividend on the common stock outstanding on December 31, 1983.
(c) During 1983 a mathematical error was discovered in the computation of a gain on the sale of machinery recorded in 1982. The 1982 gain was understated by $900 (net of tax). The correcting entry was made for the error and related income taxes.

Required: 1. Prepare the income statement of the Grotwohl Corporation for the year ended December 31, 1983. Include earnings per share information (assume a 40% income tax rate).
2. Prepare a statement of retained earnings for the year ended December 31, 1983 (assume the beginning retained earnings for 1983 was $68,000).

PROBLEMS

Part B

P15-1B   Income Statement. The records of the Lundgren Corporation show the following items on December 31, 1983:

Cost of goods sold	$ 60,000
Extraordinary loss from flood (pretax)	2,250
General and administrative expenses	12,000
Interest revenue	600
Interest expense	300
Loss on sale of discontinued Segment Q (pretax)	250
Income from operations of discontinued Segment Q (pretax)	800
Selling expenses	18,000
Sales	112,500

Additional Information:

(a) There were 3,000 shares of common stock outstanding on January 1, 1983. On July 1, 1983, the company issued 6,000 common shares.

(b) The company paid dividends for the current year on 500 shares of 7%, $100 par preferred stock outstanding. No dividends were paid on common stock.

Required: 1. Prepare the income statement of the Lundgren Corporation for 1983. Assume a 40% income tax rate.
2. Prepare the closing entries on December 31, 1983.

P15-2B   Income Statement, Lower Portion. On January 1, 1983, the Conler Corporation had 3,600 shares of common stock outstanding and a retained earnings balance of $52,500. On April 1, 1983, another 1,600 shares of common stock were issued. During 1983 it was discovered that the depreciation expense for 1982 had been understated by $1,500 (pretax). Correcting entries were made for the error and related income taxes. On December 31, 1983, the company's records showed the following items:

Operating income	$33,000
Nonoperating income	3,500
Income from operations of discontinued Segment C (pretax)	1,850
Loss on sale of discontinued Segment C (pretax)	2,750
Extraordinary loss from earthquake (pretax)	4,500
Dividends declared and paid: Preferred stock	3,400
Dividends declared and paid: Common stock	3,600

Required: Assuming the Conler Corporation is subject to a 40% income tax rate, prepare:
1. The lower portion of the income statement for 1983 starting with operating income.
2. A statement of retained earnings for 1983.

P15-3B   Dividends. The stockholders' equity accounts of the Kahler Corporation on January 1, 1983, are shown below:

Preferred stock, 8%, $100 par (8,000 shares authorized)	$ 200,000
Common stock, $10 par (200,000 shares authorized)	450,000
Additional paid-in capital on preferred stock	28,000
Additional paid-in capital on common stock	255,000
Retained earnings	400,000
	$1,303,000

The company entered into the following transactions during 1983:

Date	Transaction
Jan. 1	Declared the annual cash dividend on the outstanding preferred stock and an 80¢ per share dividend on the outstanding common stock, to be paid on January 30, 1983.
Jan. 30	Paid the cash dividend declared on January 1.
Mar. 1	Declared a 30% stock dividend on the common stock outstanding on this date. The stock is to be distributed on April 15, 1983.
Apr. 15	Issued the stock dividend declared on March 1.
May 15	Split the common stock 2 for 1, reducing the par value to $5 per share and increasing the authorized shares to 400,000.
June 1	Declared a 10% stock dividend on the common stock outstanding on this date. The stock is to be distributed on July 1, 1983. The common stock is currently selling for $15 per share.
July 1	Issued the stock dividend declared on June 1.
Dec. 31	Discovered that an error was made in calculating the 1982 depreciation expense. This error understated 1982 net income by $3,000 (pretax).

Required:
1. Prepare the journal entries of the Kahler Corporation to record the above transactions (the corporation is subject to a 40% income tax rate).
2. Prepare the stockholders' equity section of the December 31, 1983, balance sheet for the Kahler Corporation (assume that the 1983 net income was $320,000).

P15-4B   Retained Earnings. The records of the Borg Corporation show the following items as of December 31, 1983:

Income from continuing operations	$62,000
Loss from operations of discontinued Segment B (net of tax)	5,500
Gain on sale of discontinued Segment B (net of tax)	11,000
Extraordinary loss from explosion (net of tax)	5,000
Dividends declared and paid: Preferred stock	2,200
Dividends declared and paid: Common stock	4,200
Accounts receivable	26,000
Additional paid-in capital from treasury stock	41,000
Stock dividend declared and issued	20,000
Prior period adjustment: Understatement of 1982 depreciation (net of $600 income tax credit)	900

Required: Prepare a statement of retained earnings for the Borg Corporation for the year ended December 31, 1983 (assume that the beginning retained earnings balance for 1983 was $84,000).

P15-5B **Dividends.** The stockholders' equity of the Landers Corporation is shown below:

Contributed capital
Preferred stock, 7%, $100 par	$ 300,000
Common stock, $10 par	900,000
Additional paid-in capital on preferred stock	24,000
Additional paid-in capital on common stock	360,000
Total contributed capital	$1,584,000
Retained earnings	716,000
Total Stockholders' Equity	$2,300,000

The company wishes to distribute $100,000 in dividends this year.

Required: 1. Assuming that the preferred stock is participating, (a) compute the amount of dividends to be distributed to preferred and common stock and (b) prepare the journal entries to record the declaration and payment of the dividends.
2. Assuming, instead, that the preferred stock is cumulative but nonparticipating and that dividends are 2 years in arrears, (a) compute the amount of dividends to be distributed to preferred and common stock and (b) prepare the journal entries to record the declaration and payment of the dividends.

P15-6B **Appropriations.** The December 31, 1983, stockholders' equity for the Benzer Corporation is shown below:

Contributed capital
Common stock, $10 par, 90,000 shares authorized,	
40,000 shares issued and outstanding	$ 400,000
Additional paid-in capital on common stock	800,000
Total contributed capital	$1,200,000
Retained earnings	1,300,000
Total Stockholders' Equity	$2,500,000

On this date the board of directors voted to appropriate $500,000 of retained earnings for future expansion.

Required: 1. Assuming that the Benzer Corporation makes journal entries to recognize appropriations, (a) prepare the journal entry to record the above appropriation and, (b) prepare the stockholders' equity section of the December 31, 1983, balance sheet for the Benzer Corporation after the appropriation.
2. If, instead, the corporation discloses appropriations by means of a footnote, prepare the footnote and the stockholders' equity section of the December 31, 1983, balance sheet after the above appropriation.

DISCUSSION CASES

C15-1 **Dividends.** The Small Corporation shows the following items of stockholders' equity:

Common stock, $10 par (40,000 shares authorized,	
10,000 shares issued and outstanding)	$100,000
Additional paid-in capital on common stock	80,000
Retained earnings	160,000

The company's common stock is currently selling for $20 per share on the stock market. The board of directors is considering the following *alternative* actions in regard to "dividends":

(a) Payment of a $1 per share cash dividend.
(b) Distribution of a 10% stock dividend.
(c) Distribution of a 40% stock dividend.
(d) Distribution of a 2 for 1 stock split, reducing the par value to $5 per share.

The board has always paid a cash dividend and is not very familiar with stock dividends and stock splits. It is also unsure of the effect of each of these alternatives upon stockholders' equity and has asked for your advice.

Required: 1. Explain what is meant by a stock dividend and a stock split, including which, if any, is really a "dividend."
　　　　2. Explain what is likely to happen to the market price per share of common stock as a result of a stock dividend or stock split.
　　　　3. For each *alternative,* determine the amount of each item of stockholders' equity for the Small Corporation immediately *after* the cash payment or the issuance of the common stock. Show your calculations for each amount that changed.

C15-2   Misclassifications. The bookkeeper for the Cortez Company prepared the following income statement and retained earnings statement for the year ended December 31, 1983:

CORTEZ COMPANY
December 31, 1983
Expense and Profits Statement

Sales (net)		$200,000
Less: Selling expenses		(19,200)
Net sales		$180,800
Add: Interest revenue		1,300
Add: Gain on sale of equipment		3,200
Gross sales revenues		$185,300
Less: Costs of operations		
Cost of goods sold	$121,100	
Correction of overstatement in last year's income due		
to error (net of $2,200 income tax credit)	3,300	
Dividend costs ($0.50 per share for 8,300 common		
shares outstanding the entire year)	4,150	
Extraordinary loss due to earthquake (net of $2,400		
income tax credit)	3,600	(132,150)
Taxable revenues		$ 53,150
Less: Income tax on continuing income		(14,800)
Net income		$ 38,350
Miscellaneous deductions:		
Loss from operations of discontinued Segment L		
(net of $1,200 income tax credit)	$ 1,800	
Administrative expenses	25,800	(27,600)
Net Revenues		$ 10,750

CORTEZ COMPANY
Retained Revenues Statement
For Year Ended December 31, 1983

Beginning retained earnings	$63,000
Add: Gain on sale of Segment L (net of $1,800 income tax expense)	2,700
Recalculated retained earnings	$65,700
Add: Net revenues	10,750
	$76,450
Less: Interest expense	(1,400)
Ending retained earnings	$75,050

You determine that the above account *balances* are correct but, in certain instances, have been incorrectly titled or classified.

Required: 1. Review both statements and indicate where each incorrectly classified item should be classified. Also indicate any other errors you find.

                 2. Prepare a corrected 1983 income statement and retained earnings statement for the Cortez Company.

PART 4 | FINANCIAL STATEMENTS: ADDITIONAL ASPECTS OF FINANCIAL REPORTING

16

Bonds Payable and Present Value

After reading this chapter, you should understand:

- The nature of bonds
- Why bonds might be issued rather than stock being sold
- The accounting for bonds sold at par
- The accounting for bonds sold at a discount or a premium
- The straight-line method of amortizing a premium or discount
- The concepts of present value and future value
- How to compute present values and future values
- The effective interest method of amortizing a premium or discount
- Retirement of bonds at maturity, or prior to maturity
- The conversion of bonds into common stock
- Mortgages payable

The nature of bonds, why bonds are issued, and accounting for bonds issued at par are discussed in the first section of the chapter. Because bonds are not always sold at par but instead at a premium or discount, the straight-line method of amortizing the premium or discount is explained next. The concepts of present and future value are then discussed. An understanding of these concepts is essential when evaluating decisions involving amounts of money received or paid at different time periods. In addition, the concept of present value is used in several areas of financial accounting, two of which, bonds payable (the selling price and the effective interest method of amortizing a premium or a discount) and mortgages payable, are discussed in this chapter.

BONDS PAYABLE

Companies frequently borrow money. When such a borrowing is for a large amount of money for a long period of time, it usually involves the issuance of bonds by the company. **A bond is a type of note in which a company agrees to pay the holder the face value at the maturity date and to pay interest periodically at a specified rate on the face value.** Thus the company that issues the bonds is borrowing money from the holder of the bonds, who is the lender. **The face value** (also called the par value) is the amount of money that the issuer will pay at maturity. It is the same concept as the principal of a note. The maturity date is the date on which the issuer of the bond agrees to pay the face value to the holder. The issuer also agrees to pay interest each period. The contract rate is the rate at which the issuer of the bond pays interest each period until maturity. The contract rate is also called the *stated or nominal* rate. Corporate bonds are nearly always issued so that each bond has a face value of $1,000. The entire bond issue may be sold to one purchaser or to numerous individual purchasers. Thus a $1 million dollar bond issue will consist of 1,000 bonds, each with a $1,000 face value. In addition, interest is usually paid twice each year (semiannually), although the interest rate is expressed in annual terms. Therefore the annual rate must be halved to obtain the interest rate per semiannual period. For example, a 10%, $1,000 bond will pay interest of $100 (10% × $1,000) per year or $50 (10% × $\frac{1}{2}$ × $1,000) every 6 months. A face value of $1,000 per bond and semi-annual interest payments will be assumed throughout this chapter.

Why Bonds Are Issued

There are two primary ways in which a company can obtain large amounts of money (capital) for long periods of time. One is by selling common stock (or preferred stock), which was discussed in Chapter 14. Selling common stock provides the company with permanent capital since there is no obligation to repay the stockholders. In addition, there is no legal obligation to make periodic dividend payments although many companies choose to do so. Because the stockholders are owners, selling additional stock spreads ownership, voting rights, and the earnings over more shares. The second way of obtaining long-term capital is to issue bonds, which obligates the company to repay the amount borrowed and also to pay interest each period. The payment of interest is a legal obligation, and if the company issuing the bonds (the borrower) fails to pay the interest on the principal, the holder of the bonds (the lender) can take legal action to enforce payment, which may cause the borrower to declare bankruptcy. The bondholders do not become owners of the company and have no voting rights.

The primary reason why the management of a company may decide to issue bonds instead of common stock is that the earnings available to the common stockholders can be increased through leverage. Leverage is the use of borrowing by a company to increase the return to common stockholders. It is also called *trading on equity*. If a corporation can borrow money by issuing bonds and using the money to invest in a project that provides greater income than the interest that must be paid on the bonds, the company and its stockholders will be better off (they will earn a higher income). One measure of the return to common stockholders is earnings per share, which was discussed in Chapter 15. When a company successfully uses leverage, earnings per share will increase.

To illustrate this concept, assume that a company currently has 10,000 shares of common stock outstanding, income before income taxes of $100,000, and an income tax rate of 40%. The management has decided to expand its operations by building a factory for $200,000. The factory will provide additional pretax income

EXHIBIT 16-1
Use of Leverage

	Before Expansion	Bond Financing	Stock Financing
Earnings before interest and income taxes	$100,000	$140,000	$140,000
Interest expense	–	20,000	–
Income before income taxes	$100,000	$120,000	$140,000
Income tax expense	40,000	48,000	56,000
Net Income	$ 60,000	$ 72,000	$ 84,000
Earnings per share	$6.00	$7.20	$5.60

of $40,000 per year. The company is considering selling 5,000 additional shares for $40 each or issuing bonds at par with a face value of $200,000 and a 10% interest rate. The effects of the two alternatives are illustrated in Exhibit 16-1.

The interest expense on the bonds is an expense on the income statement, and therefore income before income taxes is reduced when bonds are used for financing. Income tax expense is also reduced so that the net effect of the bond financing alternative is that net income is increased by $12,000 ($72,000 − $60,000) when bond financing is used. When stock financing is used, although net income increases by $24,000, the number of common shares is increased to 15,000 so that earnings per share declines from $6.00 to $5.60 ($84,000 ÷ 15,000 = $5.60). The company may choose to pay dividends to the stockholders, but the payments do not affect the computation of net income. When bond financing is used, earnings per share increases to $7.20 ($72,000 ÷ 10,000 = $7.20). Therefore, although financing by issuing bonds does not increase net income by as much as by selling stock, in this case it has a more favorable impact on earnings per share of present stockholders and is of greater benefit to the stockholders.

The reason for this advantageous result is that the new factory is expected to earn a pretax return (earnings ÷ investment) of 20% ($40,000 ÷ $200,000), whereas the pretax interest cost on the bonds is only 10%. Borrowing money at 10% to earn a return of 20% provides the leverage that is advantageous to the owners of the company. While it may be advantageous to borrow money, there is a limit to the amount of money a company can borrow. As the amount of money borrowed increases, the risk of default increases and therefore the interest rate the company will have to pay increases. At some point the interest rate will exceed the rate that can be earned from an investment, lenders will refuse to lend more money, or management will decide the risk of borrowing has become too high. Thus, all companies have a limit on the amount of borrowing that they can undertake.

It should be recognized that the selling of bonds can result in lower earnings per share if the project is not successful. For example, suppose that the expansion turns out to be disastrous and the earnings before interest expense and income taxes are

**EXHIBIT 16-2
Lower Earnings per
Share Through Bond
Financing**

	Bond Financing	Stock Financing
Earnings before interest and income taxes	$50,000	$50,000
Interest expense	20,000	–
Income before income taxes	$30,000	$50,000
Income tax expense	12,000	20,000
Net Income	$18,000	$30,000
Earnings per share	$1.80	$2.00

reduced to $50,000. The earnings per share if stock financing is used is reduced to $2.00 ($30,000 ÷ 15,000), whereas if bond financing is used earnings per share is only $1.80 ($18,000 ÷ 10,000) as shown in Exhibit 16-2.

Characteristics of Bonds

Companies issue bonds that may have different characteristics. Some of the more common types of bonds and their characteristics are:

Debenture bonds are bonds that are not secured by specific property. That is, the holder of the bonds (the lender of the money) is considered as a general creditor with the same rights as other creditors if the issuer fails to pay the interest or principal and declares bankruptcy.

Mortgage bonds are bonds that are secured with specific property. That is, the lender has a priority right to the specific property if the company fails to pay the interest or principal.

Registered bonds are bonds whose ownership is registered with the company. That is, the company maintains a record of the holder of each bond, and therefore payment of the interest and principal can be made without such payment being requested by the holder.

Coupon bonds are unregistered bonds on which interest is claimed by the holder presenting a coupon to the company.

Serial bonds are bonds issued at one time, but portions of the total face value mature at different future dates. For example, a bond issued in 1983 may have a face value of $50,000 and bonds with a face value of $10,000 mature each year from 1990 through 1994.

Sinking fund bonds are bonds for which the company must pay into a sinking fund over the life of the bonds. The amount paid in should be sufficient to retire the bonds at maturity. Sinking fund is the term used to describe the account into which the cash is paid.

Callable bonds are bonds that are callable by the company at a predetermined price. That is, the company may require the holder to return the bonds before the maturity date, with the company paying the predetermined price and interest to date.

Convertible bonds are bonds that are convertible into a predetermined number of common shares.

Although companies may issue bonds with these various characteristics, we focus on the accounting for debenture bonds in this chapter.

Bonds Issued at Par

In certain situations bonds are sold at par (i.e., at face value). Accounting for bonds sold at par is relatively simple because the cash received from the sale equals the face value. The semiannual interest expense also equals the interest paid.

Suppose that the Homestake Company sells 10% bonds with a face value of $100,000 for $100,000. The journal entry to record the sale of the bonds is as follows:

Cash	100,000	
Bonds Payable		100,000
Issued 10% bonds at par.		

The bonds payable are reported as a noncurrent liability in the balance sheet.

The interest must be computed on each interest payment date. Since bonds pay interest semiannually, the semiannual interest payment is computed as follows:

$$\begin{matrix} \text{Semiannual interest} \\ \text{payment} \end{matrix} = \begin{matrix} \text{Face value} \\ \text{of bonds} \end{matrix} \times \left(\begin{matrix} \text{Annual} \\ \text{contract rate} \end{matrix} \div \begin{matrix} \text{Number of interest} \\ \text{payments per year} \end{matrix} \right)$$

For the Homestake Company, the calculation is as follows:

$$\begin{aligned} \text{Semiannual interest payment} &= \$100,000 \times (10\% \div 2) \\ &= \$5,000 \end{aligned}$$

The journal entry to record the interest expense and cash payment is as follows:

Interest Expense	5,000	
Cash		5,000
To record interest paid on bonds.		

The interest expense is included in Other Revenues and Expenses in the income statement.

Interest Rates

In the above example of a bond issued at par, it was assumed that a 10% interest rate is appropriate. The determination of an appropriate interest rate depends on several factors and may vary significantly from the 10% rate assumed for our example.

An interest rate paid on bonds is affected by many factors such as the policies of the Federal Reserve Board, which affect the supply and demand for money in the national economy, federal regulations, and the budget surplus or deficit of the federal government. Interest rates, however, are generally considered to include three primary factors:

— The risk-free rate

— The risk premium

— The expected inflation rate

The risk-free rate is the rate that would be paid by a borrower, and received by a lender, in a situation in which there is no risk of default by the borrower and no inflation is expected. The risk premium is the additional interest that must be paid when there is a possibility of default by the borrower. The higher the risk of default, of course, the higher the risk premium. The third component is the expected inflation rate, which is included so that additional interest must be paid by the borrower to compensate for the expected inflation over the life of the borrowing. Inflation causes the value of the dollar that is eventually repaid to be worth less than the dollar that was originally lent, and the added interest compensates for this decline.

To illustrate the nature of these three components, at the time of writing this book the following rates were being paid on selected borrowings:

Maturity Date	Borrower	Interest Rate
1986	Federal government	9 %
1986	IBM	$9\frac{1}{2}$%
2004	IBM	10 %
1995	Ford	11 %

Since the United States is not inflation free, there are no situations in which only risk-free borrowings occur. Thus we can see only the effect of the risk-free rate plus the expected inflation rate. This is illustrated by borrowings of the federal government, which are considered to be risk free but occur in an inflationary environment. Thus the risk-free rate plus the inflation expectation is 9%. Since IBM does have some risk of default, the risk premium associated with the borrowing that will mature in 1986 is $\frac{1}{2}$%. The risk premium for the 2004 borrowing of IBM is 1% because there is a longer time period in which IBM can have financial problems. The risk premium for Ford is 2%, which indicates the greater likelihood that Ford rather than IBM will default. While it is not expected that the reader will be able to compute an interest rate for a particular situation, an understanding of the components should increase the understanding of bonds and the present and future value calculations later in the chapter.

Bonds Issued at a Discount or Premium

When a company decides to issue bonds, it may offer them to the public or offer them privately to an institution such as an insurance company or a pension fund. When the bonds are offered to the public, the company usually deals with a stockbrokerage firm (or an investment banker). The stockbroker, or a group of brokers, agrees on a price for the bonds and pays the company for them. The stockbroker then sells the bonds to its clients. The stockbroker, of course, collects a fee for this service, but the company issuing the bonds avoids the problem of having to find the purchasers and be involved in cash transactions with each purchaser.

There are certain steps a company must follow when it issues bonds. The company must receive approval from the regulatory authorities such as the Securities and Exchange Commission. It must also set the terms of the bond issue such as the contract rate and the maturity date. It must also make a public announcement of its intent to sell the bonds on a particular date and print the bond certificates. At the time of the sale the stockbrokerage firm negotiates with the company to determine an appropriate selling price. The selling price is based on the terms of the bond issue and the components of the interest rate as discussed earlier. The stockbrokerage firm determines the rate that it believes best reflects current market conditions. This market rate of interest is called a yield. **The yield is the market rate at which the bonds are issued.** Although the yield is stated as a percentage, it is usually referred to as a yield instead of a yield rate. The yield is also sometimes called the *effective rate*. The yield on the bonds may be different from the contract rate set by the company and printed on the bond certificates. Such a difference may result from a difference of opinion between the stockbroker and the company about the correct yield, or a change of economic conditions between the date the company announced the bond issue, set the contract rate and had the rate printed on the bond certificates, and the date it was issued.

Once the terms of the bond issue have been set and the yield determined, the selling price of the bonds may be calculated. The calculation is illustrated later in the chapter. If the yield is *more* than the contract rate, the purchasers of the bonds will pay *less* than the face value of the bonds; that is, the bonds are sold at a *discount*. Alternatively, if the yield is *less* than the contract rate, the purchasers of the bonds will pay *more* than the face value of the bonds; that is, the bonds are sold at a *premium*.

It is important to understand why bonds sell at a price different from the face value when the yield is different from the contract rate. This is because the difference between the price paid and the face value will enable the purchaser to earn a return on the bonds equal to the yield at the time the bonds were purchased. For instance, bonds are sold at a discount because the yield is higher than the contract rate. The "savings" (i.e., the discount) between the lower selling price and the face value, coupled with the contract interest received by the purchaser each interest period, results in a return equal to the higher yield. Alternatively, bonds are sold at a premium because the yield is lower than the contract rate. The "excess" (i.e., the premium) between the higher selling price and the face value, coupled with the contract interest received by the purchaser each interest period, results in a return equal to the lower yield.

Because purchasers of bonds are effectively earning a yield either higher (for bonds sold at a discount) or lower (for bonds sold at a premium) than the contract rate, the interest *expense* recorded by the issuing company each period is different from the interest *paid*. When bonds are sold at a *discount* the interest expense is *more* than the interest paid. When bonds are sold at a *premium* the interest expense is *less* than the interest paid. The difference between the interest expense and the interest payment is the amount of the discount or premium amortized in the period (discussed later).

BONDS ISSUED AT A DISCOUNT. To illustrate the sale of bonds at a discount and the computation of the interest expense, suppose that the Homestake Company sells a bond issue with the following characteristics:

Date of sale	April 1, 1983
Maturity date	March 31, 1988
Face value	$100,000
Contract rate	10%
Interest payment dates	September 30 and March 31

If the yield on the bonds is 12%, the selling price of the 10% bonds is $92,639.93 (the calculation is explained later in the chapter). Thus the bonds sell at a discount because the yield required by investors is higher than the contract rate.

When a company issues bonds at a discount, it receives cash and incurs a liability for the same amount. It is customary, however, to record the liability in two accounts. The face value is recorded in the Bonds Payable account. The excess of the face value over the selling price is recorded in the Discount on Bonds Payable account. Therefore the journal entry to record the issue of the Homestake Company bonds on April 1, 1983 is:

```
1983
Apr.  1   Cash . . . . . . . . . . . . . . . . . . . .   92,639.93
          Discount on Bonds Payable . . . . . . .    7,360.07
             Bonds Payable . . . . . . . . . . . .               100,000.00
          Issued 10% bonds at a discount.
```

The Discount on Bonds Payable is a contra account to Bonds Payable and is subtracted from the Bonds Payable account in the balance sheet to determine the book value of the bonds. **The book value of the bonds is the balance in the Bonds Payable account less the balance in the Discount on Bonds Payable account.**

As mentioned earlier, when bonds are sold at a discount the interest expense each period is higher than the interest paid, the difference being the amount of the discount amortized in the period. **Amortization is the process of writing off the discount (or premium) as an adjustment of interest expense over the life of the bonds. The straight-line method is a method of amortizing a discount or premium by an equal amount each period.** The amount of the semiannual discount amortization is *added* to the semiannual interest payment to determine the semiannual interest expense. The remaining balance in the Discount account is often referred to as the *unamortized* Discount on Bonds Payable. The Homestake Company bonds were sold at a $7,360.07 discount, and this discount must be amortized over the life of the bonds. Because the Homestake Company bonds have a 5-year life and pay interest semiannually, there are 10 semiannual interest periods. Therefore $736.01 ($7,360.07 ÷ 10, rounded) of the discount is amortized each semiannual period. The interest paid is $5,000 ($100,000 × 10% × ½) each semiannual period. Thus the interest expense is $5,736.01 ($5,000 + $736.01) each semiannual period. The journal entry to record the interest expense on September 30, 1983, is as follows:

```
1983
Sept. 30    Interest Expense. . . . . . . . . . . . . . .    5,736.01
                Discount on Bonds Payable. . . . . . .                  736.01
                Cash. . . . . . . . . . . . . . . . . . . .            5,000.00
            To record interest paid on bonds and dis-
            count amortized by the straight-line method.
```

At this point, the Discount on Bonds Payable account has a balance of $6,624.06 ($7,360.07 − $736.01) and the book value has increased from $92,639.93 to $93,375.94 ($100,000 − $6,624.06).

The interest expense on bonds payable is typically recorded by a company on each interest payment date. In many cases, however, an interest payment date will not coincide with the end of the company's accounting period. In such a case, the company must make an adjusting entry at the end of the accounting period to record the interest that has accrued from the last interest payment date. This is the case for the Homestake Company, whose accounting period ends on December 31, 1983. At that time it must record the interest that has accrued on its bonds from September 30, 1983, through the end of December. The interest expense for these 3 months is determined by computing the interest for 6 months, as discussed above, and then allocating this amount proportionately over the 6 months as follows:

```
Interest expense for    =   Semiannual interest expense   ×   Fraction of period since
fraction of period                                             previous recognition of
                                                               interest expense
                        =   $5,736.01   ×   3/6
                        =   $2,868 (rounded)
```

The amortization of the discount is calculated as follows:

```
Amortization of discount   =   Semiannual amortization   ×   Fraction of period since
on bonds payable                                              previous recognition of
for fraction of period                                        interest expense
                           =   $736.01   ×   3/6
                           =   $368 (rounded)
```

The amount of interest owed at this date is calculated as follows:

```
Interest payable for    =   Semiannual interest payment   ×   Fraction of period
fraction of period                                             since previous payment
                        =   $5,000   ×   3/6
                        =   $2,500
```

The journal entry to record the interest at December 31, 1983, is:

```
1983
Dec.  31    Interest Expense. . . . . . . . . . . . . . .    2,868.00
                Discount on Bonds Payable. . . . . . .                  368.00
                Interest Payable . . . . . . . . . . . . .            2,500.00
            To accrue interest at the end of the year.
```

The balance in the Discount on Bonds Payable account is now $6,256.06 ($7,360.07 − $736.01 − $368.00) and the book value of the bonds is now $93,743.94. These amounts would be reported on the December 31, 1983, balance sheet in the noncurrent liability section as follows:

10% Bonds payable, due 3/31/1988.	$100,000.00
Less: Discount on bonds payable	6,256.06
	$ 93,743.94

The total interest expense of $8,604.01 ($5,736.01 from the first payment on September 30 and $2,868.00 from the December 31 accrual) would be shown on the income statement for 1983 in the Other Revenues and Expenses section.

On March 31, 1984, the second semiannual interest payment of $5,000 occurs. The interest expense to be recognized at this time is the remaining portion of the semiannual interest expense not recognized at December 31, 1983, which amounts to $2,868.01 ($5,736.01 − $2,868.00). Therefore the journal entry to record the interest payment is:

1984			
Mar. 31	Interest Expense.	2,868.01	
	Interest Payable	2,500.00	
	Discount on Bonds Payable.		368.01
	Cash.		5,000.00
	To record interest paid on bonds and discount amortized by the straight-line method.		

To summarize the interest expense for each 6-month period, a discount amortization schedule can be prepared as shown in Exhibit 16-3. For simplicity, the accrual of interest at December 31 of each year has been omitted. At the end of the life of the bonds on March 31, 1988, the discount has been completely amortized so that the book value of the bonds is equal to the face value of $100,000.

BONDS ISSUED AT A PREMIUM.   As we saw in the above example, a bond may be sold at a price below its face value. A bond may also be sold at a price above its face value, that is, at a premium. A premium is the excess of the selling price over the face value. As discussed earlier, bonds sell at a premium when the yield required by investors is lower than the contract rate.

To illustrate a bond sold at a premium consider the same bond issue by the Homestake Company, except that instead the yield is 8%. The selling price of the 10% bonds is assumed to be $108,110.88 (the calculation is explained later in the chapter). When bonds are sold at a premium it is customary to record the liability in two accounts. The face value is recorded in the Bonds Payable account and the excess of the selling price over the face value is recorded in the Premium

EXHIBIT 16-3
Bond Discount
Amortization Schedule

		HOMESTAKE COMPANY Bond Discount Amortization Schedule Straight-Line Method		
Date	Cash Paid[a] (credit)	Amortization of Discount on Bonds Payable[b] (credit)	Interest Expense[c] (debit)	Book Value of Bonds[d]
4/1/1983				$ 92,639.93
9/30/1983	$5,000	$736.01	$5,736.01	93,375.94
3/31/1984	5,000	736.01	5,736.01	94,111.95
9/30/1984	5,000	736.01	5,736.01	94,847.96
3/31/1985	5,000	736.01	5,736.01	95,583.97
9/30/1985	5,000	736.01	5,736.01	96,319.98
3/31/1986	5,000	736.01	5,736.01	97,055.99
9/30/1986	5,000	736.01	5,736.01	97,792.00
3/31/1987	5,000	736.01	5,736.01	98,528.01
9/30/1987	5,000	736.01	5,736.01	99,264.02
3/31/1988	5,000	735.98[e]	5,735.98	100,000.00

[a] Face value × (Annual contract rate ÷ Number of interest payments per year), or $100,000 × (10% ÷ 2).

[b] (Face value − Selling price) ÷ (Number of interest payments per year × Life of the bond in years), or ($100,000 − $92,639.93) ÷ (2 × 5).

[c] Cash paid + Amortization of discount on bonds payable, or $5,000 + $736.01.

[d] Previous book value + Amortization of discount on bonds payable.

[e] Adjusted for rounding error of $.03.

on Bonds Payable account. The journal entry to record the issue of the Homestake Company bonds on April 1, 1983, is shown below:

```
1983
Apr.   1   Cash . . . . . . . . . . . . . . . . . .      108,110.88
               Bonds Payable . . . . . . . . . . . .                    100,000.00
               Premium on Bonds Payable. . . . . .                        8,110.88
           Issued 10% bonds at a premium.
```

The Premium on Bonds Payable is an adjunct account to the Bonds Payable account. **An adjunct account is an account added to another account to determine the book value.** This account is in contrast to a contra account, which is subtracted from another account to determine the book value. Thus the book value of the bonds is the balance in the Bonds Payable account plus the balance in the Premium on Bonds Payable account. If the Homestake Company prepared a balance sheet immediately after selling the bonds, the following information would be disclosed in the noncurrent liability section:

```
10% Bonds payable, due 3/31/1988 . . . . . . . .     $100,000.00
Plus: Premium on bonds payable . . . . . . . . .         8,110.88
                                                     $108,110.88
```

As mentioned earlier, when bonds are sold at a premium the interest expense each period is lower than the interest paid, the difference being the amount of the premium amortized in the period. Under the straight-line method, the amount of the semiannual premium amortization is *subtracted* from the semiannual interest payment to determine the semiannual interest expense. For the Homestake Company the premium of $8,110.88 must be amortized over 10 semiannual interest periods. Therefore $811.09 (rounded) is amortized each semiannual period. Since the interest paid each semiannual period is $5,000, the interest expense each semiannual period is $4,188.91 ($5,000 − $811.09). The journal entry to record the interest expense on September 30, 1983, would be:

```
1983
Sept. 30   Interest Expense. . . . . . . . . . . . . . . .   4,188.91
           Premium on Bonds Payable . . . . . . . . .    811.09
             Cash. . . . . . . . . . . . . . . . . . . . .              5,000.00
           To record interest paid on bonds and
           premium amortized by the straight-
           line method.
```

At this time the Premium on Bonds Payable account has a balance of $7,299.79 ($8,110.88 − $811.09) and the book value of the bonds has decreased to $107,299.79 ($100,000 + $7,299.79).

The accrual of interest on December 30, 1983, and the interest payment on March 31, 1984, are computed in the same way as the discount example. The journal entry to record the accrual of interest is as follows:

```
1983
Dec.  31   Interest Expense ($4,188.91 × 3/6). . . . .   2,094.46
           Premium on Bonds Payable
               ($811.09 × 3/6) . . . . . . . . . . . .    405.54
             Interest Payable . . . . . . . . . . . . . .              2,500.00
           To accrue interest at the end of the year.
```

The journal entry to record the interest payment is as follows:

```
1984
Mar.  31   Interest Expense. . . . . . . . . . . . . . .   2,094.45
           Premium on Bonds Payable . . . . . . . . .    405.55
           Interest Payable . . . . . . . . . . . . . . .  2,500.00
             Cash. . . . . . . . . . . . . . . . . . . . .              5,000.00
           To record interest paid on bonds and pre-
           mium amortized by the straight-line method.
```

To summarize the interest expense for each 6-month period, a premium amortization schedule can be prepared as shown in Exhibit 16-4. For simplicity, the accrual of interest at December 31 of each year has been omitted. At the end of the life of the bonds on March 31, 1988, the premium has been completely amortized so that the book value of the bonds is equal to the face value of $100,000.

EXHIBIT 16-4
Bond Premium
Amortization Schedule

		HOMESTAKE COMPANY		
		Bond Premium Amortization Schedule		
		Straight-Line Method		
Date	Cash Paid[a] (credit)	Amortization of Premium on Bonds Payable[b] (debit)	Interest Expense[c] (debit)	Book Value of Bonds[d]
4/1/1983				$108,110.88
9/30/1983	$5,000	$811.09	$4,188.91	107,299.79
3/31/1984	5,000	811.09	4,188.91	106,488.70
9/30/1984	5,000	811.09	4,188.91	105,677.61
3/31/1985	5,000	811.09	4,188.91	104,866.52
9/30/1985	5,000	811.09	4,188.91	104,055.43
3/31/1986	5,000	811.09	4,188.91	103,244.34
9/30/1986	5,000	811.09	4,188.91	102,433.25
3/31/1987	5,000	811.09	4,188.91	101,622.16
9/30/1987	5,000	811.09	4,188.91	100,811.07
3/31/1988	5,000	811.07[e]	4,188.93	100,000.00

[a] Face value × (Annual contract rate ÷ Number of interest payments per year), or $100,000 × (10% ÷ 2).
[b] (Selling price − Face value) ÷ (Number of interest payments per year × Life of the bonds in years), or ($108,110.88 − $100,000) ÷ (2 × 5).
[c] Cash paid − Amortization of premium on bonds payable, or $5,000 − $811.09.
[d] Previous book value − Amortization of premium on bonds payable.
[e] Adjusted for rounding error of $.02.

Because of its simplicity, many companies use the straight-line method to amortize the premium or discount on bonds payable. This is acceptable when the results are not materially different from another method of amortization known as the effective interest method.[1] The effective interest method requires an understanding of present value concepts, discussed next.

PRESENT VALUE AND FUTURE VALUE

Would you rather receive $1 today or $1 next year? The answer to this question should be that you would rather receive $1 today because a dollar held today is worth more than a dollar to be received a year from now. The difference between the two amounts is *interest*, or more generally, there is a *time value of money*. The components of the interest rate were discussed earlier in the chapter; they are the factors that cause money to have a time value.

To illustrate the time value of money suppose that Peter Cameron has $100 on January 1, 1983, and can invest it at 10%. This money will grow over the next three years as shown on the following page:

[1] "Interest on Receivables and Payables," *APB Opinion No. 21* (New York: AICPA, 1971), par. 15.

	Principal Amount at Beginning of the Year	Interest at 10%	Principal Amount at End of the Year
1983	$100	$10.00	$110.00
1984	110	11.00	121.00
1985	121	12.10	133.10

This analysis tells us that the following amounts, given the 10% interest rate and their respective dates, have equivalent values:

— $100 at the beginning of 1983
— $110 at the end of 1983
— $121 at the end of 1984
— $133.10 at the end of 1985

Since these amounts have equivalent values, if you were asked which amount you wanted to receive, you would be indifferent between the four alternatives, given the 10% rate. It is essential to note, however, that the dollar amounts have a time attached to them. Whenever we are considering the time value of money, we must always know the date at which the dollar amount is measured. A dollar received or paid in 1983 is not the same as a dollar received or paid in 1984.

Definitions of Present Value and Future Value

There are two important terms that are widely used whenever the value of money is being considered. **Present value is the value today of a certain number of dollars measured in the future.** It does not matter whether the dollars are paid or received. In the example above, therefore, $100 is the present value at the beginning of 1983 of $133.10 at the end of 1985 when the interest rate is 10%. **Future value is the value at a future date of a certain number of dollars measured today.** Therefore $133.10 at the end of 1985 is the future value of $100 at the beginning of 1983. Again, it does not matter whether the dollars are received or paid.

Although present value and future value are both widely used concepts, present value is a much more useful accounting concept than future value. Therefore the discussion in this chapter concentrates on present value although future value is also discussed.

Simple Interest and Compound Interest

Simple interest was discussed in Chapter 8; remember that simple interest is calculated by the formula:

$$\text{Interest} \ = \ \text{Principal} \ \times \ \text{Rate} \ \times \ \text{Time}$$

Therefore simple interest on $100 for 3 years at 10% would be:

$$\begin{aligned} \text{Interest} \ &= \ \$100 \ \times \ 10\% \ \times \ 3 \text{ years} \\ &= \ \$30 \end{aligned}$$

This interest is different from the interest in our example above, which amounted to $33.10 ($133.10 − $100.00), because the example used compound interest.

Compound interest is interest that accrues on both the principal and past accrued (unpaid) interest. Thus during 1983 interest of 10% is accrued on the principal of $100, making a total of $110 at the end of 1983. In 1984 interest of 10% is accrued on the principal of $100 *and* the 1983 interest of $10, or on a total of $110. The interest amounts to $11 in 1984. In 1985 interest is similarly accrued on the principal of $100 plus the interest for 1983 and 1984 of $21. The interest on the $121 is $12.10. Thus the total compound interest is $33.10 ($10 + $11 + $12.10) compared to the simple interest of $30. Compound interest is the concept that underlies the concepts of present and future value.

Calculations of present and future values are essential in many situations. If a company has an obligation to pay a certain number of dollars in the future, the present value of those dollars should be disclosed as a liability in the balance sheet. Application of this present value concept in accounting for bonds payable and mortgages payable is discussed later in this chapter. Accounting for leases also utilizes present value concepts and is discussed in the next chapter. In addition, present and future values are necessary for many types of investment decisions, such as the acquisition of property, plant, and equipment. These types of decisions are discussed in Chapter 27. To assist these types of accounting disclosures and management decisions, formulas and tables are frequently used.

Formulas and Tables

Instead of preparing a year-by-year calculation of present and future values, a formula or a table may be used. The general relationship between present and future value is as follows:

$$FV = PV(1+i)^n \quad \text{or} \quad PV = \frac{FV}{(1+i)^n}$$

where

PV = Present value
FV = Future value
i = Interest rate
n = Number of periods

Using the same example of 10% and 3 years, if we know the present value of $100 the future value is calculated as follows:

$$
\begin{aligned}
FV &= PV(1+i)^n \\
&= \$100(1 + 0.10)^3 \\
&= \$100(1.331) \\
&= \$133.10
\end{aligned}
$$

Alternatively, if the future value of $133.10 is known the present value is calculated as follows:

$$
\begin{aligned}
PV &= \frac{FV}{(1+i)^n} \\
&= \frac{\$133.10}{(1 + 0.10)^3} \\
&= \frac{\$133.10}{1.331} \\
&= \$100
\end{aligned}
$$

Tables have been developed that simplify the calculation process even more. Table 1 in Appendix B is entitled the Future Value of $1. *Table 1 is used to compute the future value of a single amount when the present value is known.* A future value is computed by using the table as follows:

$$FV = PV \times \text{Future value of \$1 factor}$$

A *factor* is a decimal fraction for a certain time period and rate. Thus each decimal fraction included in Table 1 is a future value factor for a certain time period and rate. If you look up the factor for 10% and 3 periods, you will find that it is 1.331000. Therefore the future value at the end of 3 years of $100 received or paid today using a 10% interest rate is as follows:

$$FV = \$100 \times 1.331000$$
$$= \$133.10$$

Table 2 in Appendix B is entitled the Present Value of $1. *Table 2 is used to compute the present value of a single amount when the future value is known.* A present value is computed by using the table as follows:

$$PV = FV \times \text{Present value of \$1 factor}$$

If you look up the factor in Table 2 for 10% and 3 periods, you will find that it is 0.751315. Therefore the present value of $133.10 received or paid at the end of 3 years, using a 10% interest rate is:

$$PV = \$133.10 \times 0.751315$$
$$= \$100$$

The process of converting a future value to a smaller present value is known as *discounting*. Thus the $133.10 future value is discounted to the $100 present value by multiplying it times the 0.751315 factor.

Tables 1 and 2 are following exactly the same procedures as the formulas. They simply provide the answers that would be obtained by using the formulas for the various rates and time periods. Thus the Future Value of $1 table is based on the formula $(1 + i)^n$ and the Present Value of $1 table is based on the formula $1/(1 + i)^n$.

In summary, the Present Value of $1 table is used to convert (discount) a future value back to the present. Note that all numbers in the table are less than 1.0. The calculation of the present value can be diagrammed as follows:

$$
\begin{array}{ccccc}
\text{Present} & = & \text{Present Value} & \times & \text{Future} \\
\text{Value} & & \text{of \$1 Factor} & & \text{Value}
\end{array}
$$
$$\longleftarrow\!\longrightarrow$$

The Future Value of $1 table is used to convert a present value to a future value. Note that all the numbers in the table are greater than 1.0. The calculation of the future value may be diagrammed as follows:

$$
\begin{array}{ccccc}
\text{Present} & \times & \text{Future Value} & = & \text{Future} \\
\text{Value} & & \text{of \$1 Factor} & & \text{Value}
\end{array}
$$
$$\longmapsto\!\longrightarrow$$

An Annuity In many situations we are not concerned with the present or future value of a single amount as in the above examples, but with an annuity. **An annuity is a series of equal periodic cash flows.** These cash flows may be either received or paid. For example, a 3-year $100 annuity consists of a cash flow of $100 per year for 3 years. In this book we will assume that the first cash flow in an annuity occurs at the *end* of the first time period. Thus if an annual annuity begins on January 1, 1983, the first cash flow occurs on December 31, 1983.

We could compute the present value on January 1, 1983, of a 3-year $100 annuity at 10% by treating it as three separate single amounts and using the factors from Table 2 as follows:

PV of $100 paid or received on Dec. 31, 1983 = $100 × 0.909091 = $ 90.9091

PV of $100 paid or received on Dec. 31, 1984 = $100 × 0.826446 = 82.6446

PV of $100 paid or received on Dec. 31, 1985 = $100 × 0.751315 = 75.1315

PV of $100, 3-year annuity at 10% on Jan. 1, 1983 = $248.6852

This computation can also be illustrated by using a time diagram as follows:

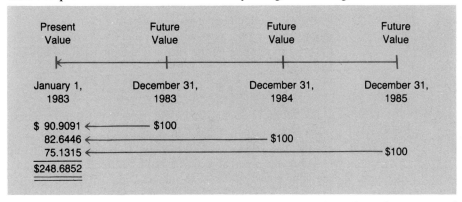

Instead of using Table 2 and completing the numerous calculations shown, use of Table 4 in Appendix B makes the calculation process much simpler. The table is entitled Present Value of Ordinary Annuity of $1 and is developed on the basis of the assumption that the first cash flow occurs at the *end* of the first time period. *Table 4 is used to compute the present value of an annuity*. The present value is computed by using the table as follows:

PV of annuity = Periodic amount of the annuity × Present value of annuity factor

If you look up the factor for 10% and 3 periods in Table 4, you will find that it is 2.486852. Therefore the present value of the annuity of $100 received or paid at the end of each year for 3 years using a 10% interest rate is as follows:

PV of annuity = $100 × 2.486852

= $248.6852

Another way of saying this is that the annuity of $100 received or paid at the end of each year for 3 years is discounted to a present value of $248.6852. This process enables the present value to be computed by a single multiplication rather than three multiplications and an addition. It is important to realize, however, that exactly the same present value concept is involved. The purpose of Table 4 is to simplify the calculations.

Table 3 in Appendix B is entitled Future Value of Ordinary Annuity of $1. *Table 3 is used to compute the future value of an annuity.* The future value is computed by using the table as follows:

> FV of annuity = Periodic amount of the annuity × Future value of annuity factor

The future value of a 3-year annuity of $100 received or paid at the end of each year for 3 years using a 10% interest rate is calculated by looking up the factor for 3 periods at 10%, which is 3.310000:

> FV of annuity = $100 × 3.310000
>   = $331.00

Many electronic calculators have the capacity to compute present and future values. The calculation process follows exactly the same concepts as discussed above. The calculator uses formulas to determine each factor whenever a calculation is made (we have not illustrated the formulas for the annuity calculations), rather than looking up the factor in a table as is usually done when a calculator is not available.

Interest Periods Other Than One Year

It is often necessary to calculate present and future values for situations in which interest periods other than 1 year are used. For example, a savings account may pay 8% interest, compounded quarterly. This means that the interest is 2% each quarter and that the interest accrues each quarter on the principal plus interest of the previous quarters. Thus, in this example, if we are computing a present value or future value for a 3-year period we would look up in the appropriate table the factor for 2% for 12 periods (3 years x 4 quarters) rather than 8% for 3 years. *The general rule is that if there are* n *compounding periods in the year, the interest rate per period is the annual interest rate divided by* n *and the number of interest periods is the number of years multiplied by* n.

To illustrate, suppose that we need to compute the present value of $1,000 to be received at the end of 4 years. The annual interest rate is 10%, but interest accrues semiannually. Therefore the appropriate rate to use is 5% (10% ÷ 2) per period; and there are 8 (4 years × 2) time periods. The calculation (using the factor from Table 2) is as follows:

> Present value = Future value × Present value of $1 factor
>   for 8 periods at 5%
>   = $1,000 × 0.676839
>   = $676.84 (rounded)

In contrast, the present value calculated with annual compounding would be as follows:

$$Present\ value = Future\ value \times Present\ value\ of\ \$1\ factor$$
$$for\ 4\ periods\ at\ 10\%$$
$$= \$1,000 \times 0.683013$$
$$= \$683.01\ (rounded)$$

It should be expected that the semiannual compounding would result in a lower *present value* because of the added interest that will accrue. That is, a smaller present value will accrue to the same future value when interest is compounded more often. Similarly, if the future value is being calculated from a present value, compounding more frequently than once a year will result in a higher future value.

BOND SELLING PRICES AND EFFECTIVE INTEREST METHOD

The selling price of a bond issue may be calculated by a present value computation if the maturity date, the face value, the contract rate, and the yield are known. The selling price is the present value of the cash flows that the company is committed to pay under the terms of the bond issue. The cash flows consist of the semiannual interest payments and the face value at the end of the life of the bonds. The selling price is calculated as follows:

$$Selling\ price\ of\ the\ bond\ issue = Present\ value\ of + Present\ value\ of$$
$$interest\ payments \quad face\ value$$

The present value of the interest payments is computed as follows:

$$Present\ value\ of\ interest\ payments = Periodic\ interest \times Present\ value\ of$$
$$payment \qquad annuity\ factor$$

and

$$Periodic\ interest\ payment = Face\ value\ of\ bonds \times Periodic\ interest\ rate$$

and

$$Periodic\ interest\ rate = Annual\ contract\ rate \div Number\ of\ interest$$
$$payments\ per\ year$$

The present value of the face value is computed as follows:

$$Present\ value\ of\ face\ value = Face\ value \times Present\ value\ of\ \$1\ factor$$

The present value factors in each calculation are based on the yield and the life of the bonds. Recall from our earlier discussion that the yield on the bonds is the market rate of interest when the bonds are issued; it is the return that will be earned by the purchaser of the bonds on the purchase price and is also the cost to the company of the money it borrows. Although bond yields are stated in terms of annual rates, in reality the actual yield is half the annual yield because bonds pay interest semiannually. Thus the semiannual yield is determined as follows:

$$Semiannual\ Yield = Annual\ Yield \div 2$$

Since the yield is stated in terms of a semiannual rate, the periods must also be semiannual as follows:

$$Number\ of\ semiannual\ periods = Life\ of\ the\ bonds\ in\ years \times 2$$

Therefore the cash payments to which the company is committed are discounted at the semiannual yield for the number of semiannual periods in the life of the bonds.

Selling Price Less Than Face Value (Discount)

To illustrate the calculation of the selling price of a bond issue by using present value concepts, consider the Homestake Company example used earlier in the chapter. The bond issue has the following characteristics:

Date of sale	Apr. 1, 1983
Maturity date	Mar. 31, 1988
Face value	$100,000
Contract rate	10%
Interest payment dates	Sept. 30 and Mar. 31

The selling price of the 10% bonds is the present value of the future cash payments to which Homestake is committed. These payments are the face value of $100,000 at the maturity date and the interest payment of $5,000 ($100,000 × 10% × ½) every 6 months.

If the bonds are sold to yield 12%, the cash payments to which Homestake is committed should *not* be discounted at 12% per year for 5 years. They should instead be discounted at 6% per semiannual period for 10 semiannual periods. The present value is calculated as follows:

Present value of semiannual interest payments	=	Semiannual interest payment	×	Present value of annuity factor for 10 periods at 6%
	=	$5,000	×	7.360087 (from Table 4)
	=	$36,800.43		

Present value of face value	=	Face value	×	Present value of $1 factor for 10 periods at 6%
	=	$100,000	×	0.558395 (from Table 2)
	=	$55,839.50		

Selling price of the bonds	=	Present value of semiannual interest payments	+	Present value of face value
	=	$36,800.43	+	$55,839.50
	=	$92,639.93		

In this case the bonds sell at a discount; that is, at a selling price that is *less* than the face value. The discount occurs because the yield is *higher* than the contract rate. The purchasers of the bonds are obtaining a 12% return (6% semiannually) on the $92,639.93 they are lending the company, and the company is borrowing $92,639.93 at a cost of 12% (6% semiannually).

The journal entry to record the issue of the Homestake Company bonds on April 1, 1983 is the same as the one illustrated earlier in the chapter:

```
1983
Apr.  1   Cash . . . . . . . . . . . . . . . . . . .      92,639.93
             Discount on Bonds Payable . . . . . . .       7,360.07
             Bonds Payable . . . . . . . . . . . .                    100,000.00
          Issued 10% bonds to yield 12%.
```

Interest Expense and Interest Payment

The Homestake Company makes its first interest payment of $5,000 on September 30, 1983, as indicated earlier. This amount is *not* the interest expense for the period, however. **The effective interest method is a method of recognizing interest expense in which the expense is based on the amount of money borrowed and the rate at which it is borrowed.** The effective interest method is the preferred method of recognizing interest expense and is an alternative to the straight-line method discussed earlier in the chapter. The two methods are compared later in the chapter. *Under the effective interest method, the interest expense for a period is calculated by multiplying the book value of the bonds at the beginning of the period by the yield per period.* The yield per period is computed by dividing the annual yield by the number of interest periods in the year. For the Homestake Company, the book value at the beginning of the first period is the issuance price and the yield is 6% (12% ÷ 2) per semiannual interest period. The semiannual interest expense is calculated as follows:

$$
\begin{aligned}
\text{Semiannual interest expense} &= \left(\text{Annual yield} \div \begin{array}{c}\text{Number of interest}\\\text{payments per year}\end{array}\right) \times \begin{array}{l}\text{Book value of the}\\\text{bonds at the}\\\text{beginning of the}\\\text{period}\end{array}\\
&= (12\% \div 2) \times (\$100,000 - \$7,360.07)\\
&= 6\% \times \$92,639.93\\
&= \$5,558.40
\end{aligned}
$$

The interest paid of $5,000 is computed in the usual manner by multiplying the face value by the semiannual contract rate. Since the company has an interest expense of $5,558.40 but is only paying interest of $5,000, it is increasing its liability by the difference of $558.40. The company increases its bond liability by amortizing a portion of the discount. Using the effective interest method the amount of the amortization may be expressed as follows:

$$
\begin{aligned}
\text{Discount amortization} &= \begin{array}{l}\text{Semiannual interest}\\\text{expense}\end{array} - \begin{array}{l}\text{Semiannual interest}\\\text{payment}\end{array}\\
&= \$5,558.40 - \$5,000\\
&= \$558.40
\end{aligned}
$$

The amount of the discount amortization is subtracted from (credited to) the Discount on Bonds Payable account, thereby increasing the book value of the liability. The journal entry to record the interest expense, discount amortization, and interest payment using the effective interest method is:

1983			
Sept. 30	Interest Expense.	5,558.40	
	Discount on Bonds Payable.		558.40
	Cash.		5,000.00
	To record interest paid on bonds and interest expense by the effective interest method.		

At this point the Discount on Bonds Payable account has a balance of $6,801.67 ($7,360.07 − $558.40) and the book value of the bonds has increased from $92,639.93 to $93,198.33 ($100,000 − $6,801.67).

On December 31, 1983 (the end of the accounting period), the Homestake Company must recognize the interest expense that has accrued since the last interest payment date (September 30, 1983). The interest expense for these 3 months is determined by computing the interest for 6 months and then allocating this amount proportionately over the 6 months as follows:

$$
\begin{aligned}
\text{Semiannual interest expense} &= \left(\text{Annual yield} \div \frac{\text{Number of interest}}{\text{payments per year}} \right) \times \frac{\text{Book value of}}{\text{the bonds}} \\
&= (12\% \div 2) \times (\$100{,}000 - \$6{,}801.67) \\
&= 6\% \times \$93{,}198.33 \\
&= \$5{,}591.90
\end{aligned}
$$

$$
\begin{aligned}
\text{Interest expense for fraction of period} &= \frac{\text{Semiannual interest}}{\text{expense}} \times \frac{\text{Fraction of period since previous recognition of interest expense}}{} \\
&= \$5{,}591.90 \times 3/6 \\
&= \$2{,}795.95
\end{aligned}
$$

The amount of interest owed at this date is calculated as follows:

$$
\begin{aligned}
\text{Interest payable for fraction of period} &= \frac{\text{Semiannual interest}}{\text{payment}} \times \frac{\text{Fraction of period since previous interest payment}}{} \\
&= \$5{,}000 \times 3/6 \\
&= \$2{,}500
\end{aligned}
$$

The difference between the interest expense and the interest payable is again a reduction in the Discount on Bonds Payable account. The year-end accrual of the interest expense would be recognized as follows:

```
1983
Dec. 31   Interest Expense. . . . . . . . . . . . . . .      2,795.95
              Discount on Bonds Payable. . . . . . .                    295.95
              Interest Payable . . . . . . . . . . . . .                  2,500.00
          To accrue interest at the end of the year.
```

The balance in the Discount on Bonds Payable account is now $6,505.72 ($6,801.67 − $295.95) and the book value of the bonds is $93,494.28. These amounts would be reported on the December 31, 1983, balance sheet as follows:

```
10% Bonds payable, due 3/31/1988 . . . . . . . .    $100,000.00
Less: Discount on bonds payable . . . . . . . . .        6,505.72
                                                     $ 93,494.28
```

The total interest expense of $8,354.35 ($5,558.40 from the first payment on September 30 and $2,795.95 from the December 31 accrual) would be shown on the income statement for 1983 in the Other Revenues and Expenses section.

On March 31, 1984, the second semiannual interest payment of $5,000 occurs. The interest expense to be recognized at this time is the remaining portion of the semiannual interest expense not recognized at December 31, 1983. This expense is calculated as follows:

$$\text{Interest expense} = \text{Semiannual interest expense} \times \text{Fraction of period since previous recognition of interest expense}$$

$$= \$5,591.90 \times 3/6$$
$$= \$2,795.95$$

Therefore the journal entry to record the interest payment is:

```
1984
Mar. 31  Interest Expense. . . . . . . . . . . . . . .    2,795.95
         Interest Payable . . . . . . . . . . . . . . .   2,500.00
             Discount on Bonds Payable. . . . . . .                  295.95
             Cash. . . . . . . . . . . . . . . . . . . .            5,000.00
         To record interest paid on bonds and
         interest expense by the effective interest
         method.
```

To summarize the interest expense each 6-month period, a discount amortization schedule can be prepared as shown in Exhibit 16-5. For simplicity, the accrual of

EXHIBIT 16-5
Bond Discount
Amortization Schedule

HOMESTAKE COMPANY
Bond Discount Amortization Schedule
Effective Interest Method
(10% bonds to yield 12%)

Date	Cash Paid[a] (credit)	Interest Expense[b] (debit)	Amortization of Discount on Bonds Payable[c] (credit)	Book Value of Bonds[d]
4/1/1983				$ 92,639.93
9/30/1983	$5,000	$5,558.40	$558.40	93,198.33
3/31/1984	5,000	5,591.90	591.90	93,790.23
9/30/1984	5,000	5,627.41	627.41	94,417.64
3/31/1985	5,000	5,665.06	665.06	95,082.70
9/30/1985	5,000	5,704.96	704.96	95,787.66
3/31/1986	5,000	5,747.26	747.26	96,534.92
9/30/1986	5,000	5,792.10	792.10	97,327.02
3/31/1987	5,000	5,839.62	839.62	98,166.64
9/30/1987	5,000	5,890.00	890.00	99,056.64
3/31/1988	5,000	5,943.36[e]	943.36	100,000.00

[a] Face value × (Annual contract rate ÷ Number of interest payments per year), or $100,000 × (10% ÷ 2).
[b] (Annual yield ÷ Number of interest payments per year) × Book value of bonds at beginning of period (from previous line); at 9/30/1983, (12% ÷ 2) × $92,639.93.
[c] Interest expense − Cash paid; at 9/30/1983, $5,558.40 − $5,000.00.
[d] Book value of bonds from previous line + Amortization of discount on bonds payable (this is equal to the face value of the bonds payable − the unamortized discount on bonds payable); at 9/30/1983, $92,639.93 + $558.40.
[e] Adjusted for rounding error of $.04.

interest at December 31 of each year has been omitted. At the end of the life of the bonds on March 31, 1988, the discount has been completely amortized so that the book value of the bonds is equal to the face value of $100,000.

Selling Price More Than Face Value (Premium)

As we saw in the above example, a bond may be sold at a price below its face value. A bond may also be sold at a price above its face value, that is, at a premium. This will occur when the yield required by investors is less than the contract rate.

To illustrate a bond sold at a premium consider the same bond issue by the Homestake Company, except that now the yield is 8%, or 4% each 6 months. The selling price of the 10% bonds is computed as follows:

Present value of face value = Face value × Present value of $1 factor
for 10 periods at 4%
= $100,000 × 0.675564
= $67,556.40

Present value of semiannual = Semiannual interest × Present value of annuity
interest payments   payment   factor for 10 periods at 4%
= $5,000 × 8.110896
= $40,554.48

Selling price of the bonds = Present value of + Present value of semiannual
face value   interest payments
= $67,556.40 + $40,554.48
= $108,110.88

As discussed earlier the liability for the bonds is separated into two accounts when the sale is recorded. The face value is recorded in the Bonds Payable account and the excess of the selling price over the face value is recorded in the Premium on Bonds Payable account. The journal entry to record the sale of the bonds on April 1, 1983, is:

```
1983
Apr.   1   Cash . . . . . . . . . . . . . . . . . . . .   108,110.88
              Bonds Payable . . . . . . . . . . . .              100,000.00
              Premium on Bonds Payable  . . . . .                 8,110.88
           Issued 10% bonds to yield 8%.
```

The interest expense using the effective interest method and the related premium amortization are computed in the same way as for a discount as follows:

Semiannual interest = (Annual yield ÷ Number of interest) × Book value of
expense   payments per year   the bonds at
the beginning
of the period

Semiannual interest = (Annual contract ÷ Number of interest) × Face value
payment   rate   payments per year

Premium amortization = Semiannual interest − Semiannual interest
payment   expense

EXHIBIT 16-6
Bond Premium
Amortization Schedule

			Amortization of	
		Interest	Premium on	
	Cash Paid[a]	Expense[b]	Bonds Payable[c]	Book Value
Date	(credit)	(debit)	(debit)	of Bonds[d]
4/1/1983				$108,110.88
9/30/1983	$5,000	$4,324.44	$675.56	107,435.32
3/31/1984	5,000	4,297.41	702.59	106,732.73
9/30/1984	5,000	4,269.31	730.69	106,002.04
3/31/1985	5,000	4,240.08	759.92	105,242.12
9/30/1985	5,000	4,209.68	790.32	104,451.80
3/31/1986	5,000	4,178.07	821.93	103,629.87
9/30/1986	5,000	4,145.19	854.81	102,775.06
3/31/1987	5,000	4,111.00	889.00	101,886.06
9/30/1987	5,000	4,075.44	924.56	100,961.50
3/31/1988	5,000	4,038.50[e]	961.50	100,000.00

HOMESTAKE COMPANY
Bond Premium Amortization Schedule
Effective Interest Method
(10% bonds to yield 8%)

[a] Face value × (Annual contract rate ÷ Number of interest payments per year), or $100,000 × (10% ÷ 2).
[b] (Annual yield ÷ Number of interest payments per year) × Book value of bonds at beginning of period (from previous line); at 9/30/1983, (8% ÷ 2) × $108,110.88.
[c] Cash paid − Interest expense; at 9/30/1983, $5,000 − $4,324.44.
[d] Book value of bonds from previous line − Amortization of premium on bonds payable (this is equal to the face value of the bonds payable + the unamortized premium on bonds payable); at 9/30/1983, $108,110.88 − $675.56.
[e] Adjusted for rounding error of $.04.

A premium amortization schedule may be prepared for these bonds and is shown in Exhibit 16-6. We can see from the exhibit that the entry to record the interest expense on September 30, 1983, would be:

```
1983
Sept. 30  Interest Expense. . . . . . . . . . . . . . .  4,324.44
          Premium on Bonds Payable . . . . . . . . .    675.56
              Cash. . . . . . . . . . . . . . . . . .              5,000.00
          To record interest paid on bonds and
          interest expense by the effective interest
          method.
```

When bonds are sold at a premium the interest expense each period is less than the interest paid. Therefore the company is repaying some of its liability with each interest payment. This is recognized by reducing the amount in the Premium on Bonds Payable account, which in turn reduces the book value of the liability (Bonds Payable plus Premium on Bonds Payable).

At the end of the life of the bonds on March 31, 1988, the premium is completely amortized. At this point the book value of the bonds equals the face value of $100,000.

ADDITIONAL CONSIDERATIONS

Several additional aspects of bonds need to be discussed. Bonds are frequently issued between interest payment dates; bonds are retired either at the maturity date or earlier; some bonds are convertible into common stock; and some bonds require the establishment of sinking funds. Each of these factors is discussed in the following sections.

Bonds Issued Between Interest Payment Dates

As we have seen, the dates on which the company issuing bonds agrees to pay interest are included in the terms of the bond and are printed on the bond certificate. These payments are usually semiannual, and at the end of each semiannual period the company pays a full 6 months interest. A company may issue the bonds between the specified interest dates because of the time that may elapse between the announcement of the bond issue and the actual sale of the bonds. In such a case the purchasers of bonds are entitled to receive interest only for the period the bonds are owned, which on the first interest payment date is the period from the purchase date to the first interest payment date. To reduce record keeping at the time of issuance, the purchasers of the bonds pay accrued interest in addition to the purchase price of the bond. The accrued interest is the interest that has accumulated from the interest payment date preceding the sale of the bonds to the date of the sale of the bonds. At the next interest payment date the company then pays the full 6 months' interest.

To illustrate, suppose that on March 1, 1983, the Lowland Company sells 5-year, 10% bonds with a face value of $24,000 at par value plus accrued interest. The bonds pay interest on June 30 and December 31. Two months have elapsed, therefore, between the interest payment date preceding the sale (December 31) and the date of the sale (March 1). On March 1 accrued interest of $400 ($24,000 $\times$ 10% $\times$ 2/12) is paid by the purchasers of the bonds in addition to the par value of $24,000.

The journal entry to record the sale on March 1 is:

```
1983
Mar.  1   Cash . . . . . . . . . . . . . . . . . . . . . . . . . .   24,400
              Interest Payable . . . . . . . . . . . . . . . . . .            400
              Bonds Payable . . . . . . . . . . . . . . . . . .             24,000
          Issued 10% bonds at par plus accrued
          interest for 2 months.
```

The accrued interest is recorded as a liability because it will be paid on June 30, 1983, when the next semiannual interest payment is made. This payment will be $1,200 ($24,000 $\times$ 10% $\times$ 1/2), although only $800 is the interest expense for the 4 months the bonds have been outstanding while the remaining $400 is the payment of the liability recorded on March 1. The journal entry to record the first semiannual interest payment on June 30, 1983, is:

```
1983
June  30   Interest Expense. . . . . . . . . . . . . . . .        800
           Interest Payable . . . . . . . . . . . . . . . .       400
              Cash. . . . . . . . . . . . . . . . . . . . . .              1,200
                 To record interest paid on bonds.
```

The above sequence of events may be illustrated by the following diagram:

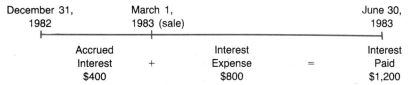

December 31, 1982		March 1, 1983 (sale)		June 30, 1983
Accrued Interest $400	+	Interest Expense $800	=	Interest Paid $1,200

It may seem confusing for a company to charge bond purchasers for accrued interest and then return this accrued interest when the first interest payment is made. The primary purpose for this practice is that if the bonds were sold on different dates to different purchasers and the company did not charge accrued interest, it would have to record separately the date of each sale and calculate the amount of interest it has to pay each purchaser on the first interest payment date. By charging accrued interest at the time of the sale, the company can make a full semiannual interest payment to all purchasers. It should also be noted that the bonds will not be outstanding for the full 5 years, but only for 4 years and 10 months.

Retirement of Bonds at Maturity

As discussed earlier in the chapter, the process of amortizing the discount or premium over the life of the bonds by either the straight-line or effective interest method means that at the maturity date the balance in the Discount or Premium account will have been eliminated. On the maturity date, therefore, the Bonds Payable account is the only account with a remaining balance and reflects the maturity value, which is the amount of cash that must be paid to the holders of the bonds. The journal entry to record the retirement of the bonds of the Homestake Company on March 31, 1988, is:

```
1988
Mar.  31   Bonds Payable. . . . . . . . . . . . . . . .    100,000
              Cash. . . . . . . . . . . . . . . . . . . . . .              100,000
                 Redeemed bonds payable at maturity date.
```

Retirement of Bonds Prior to Maturity

As mentioned earlier in the chapter, bonds may be issued with a call provision that allows a company to retire (*call*) the bonds before they mature by paying an amount to the holders that was specified at the time the bonds were sold. Alternatively, if the bonds are being traded on a bond market the company can purchase the bonds and retire them.

Before accounting for the retirement, the company must first accrue the interest expense and pay the interest for the period since the last interest payment or accrual. This is done by using the method discussed for accruing the interest on December

31, 1983, for the bonds issued by the Homestake Company at a discount or premium. That is, the semiannual interest is calculated in the normal way (for either the straight-line or effective interest method, whichever method the company is using), and this amount is multiplied by the fraction of the 6 months that has passed.

After recognizing the interest expense the company has to account for the retirement of the bonds. When the cash used to retire the bonds is less than the book value of the bonds the company recognizes a *gain* on the retirement. Or, if the cash payment is greater than the book value of the bonds the company recognizes a *loss*. If such gains and losses are material they must be classified as extraordinary items on the income statement (discussed in Chapter 15), even though they do not meet the criteria of being unusual in nature and occurring infrequently.[2]

To illustrate the early retirement of bonds suppose that a company calls bonds with a face value of $10,000 when they have a book value of $9,800 (we will assume that the recording of interest is up to date). The cost to retire the bonds is $10,200. This can be stated as *a call price* of 102 because bond prices are quoted as a percentage of the face value. The face value of $10,000 multiplied by the call price of 102 stated as a fraction gives the cost of retiring the bonds ($10,000 × 1.02 = $10,200). The extraordinary loss on retirement of the bonds is the cost of retiring the bonds minus the book value of the bonds ($10,200 − $9,800). The journal entry to record the retirement is:

Bonds Payable	10,000	
Extraordinary Loss on Retirement of Bonds	400	
Discount on Bonds Payable		200
Cash		10,200

Bonds retired at a call price of 102.

The extraordinary loss would be disclosed, net of applicable income taxes, in the extraordinary items section of the income statement.

Conversion of Bonds

To make a bond issue more attractive to purchasers the bonds may be convertible into common stock. This enables the purchaser to acquire a security that has some features of both bonds and common stock. This is similar to convertible preferred stock discussed in Chapter 14. For example, suppose that the Teague Company sells a $1,000 bond for $1,040 that is convertible into 20 shares of $10 par common stock. At the time of the sale the stock is selling for $35 per share. The common stock price at which conversion becomes attractive is $52 per share ($1,040 ÷ 20 shares), and therefore at the time of the sale of the bond the purchaser owns a security that has the characteristics of a bond. Once the price of the common stock rises above $52 per share, however, the bond price will tend to change in proportion to any change in the stock price. It would be expected to sell for approximately 20

[2] "Reporting Gains and Losses from Extinguishment of Debt." *FASB Statement No. 4* (Stamford, Conn.: FASB, 1975), par. 8.

times the common stock price. Therefore the owner of the bond is able to participate in the rise in the stock price while at the same time having the safety of a bond. A purchaser pays for this privilege, however, because a convertible bond is issued at a lower yield than a nonconvertible bond.

When convertible bonds are issued they are recorded in exactly the same manner as nonconvertible bonds, as discussed earlier. Similarly, the subsequent interest expense and discount or premium amortization are accounted for in the same ways as nonconvertible bonds. When convertible bonds are converted, any accrued interest since the last interest payment date must be recorded and paid. Then the common stock issued is recorded at the book value of the bonds retired. For example, if a $1,000 bond with a book value of $1,020 (we will assume that the recording of interest is up to date) is converted into 20 shares of common stock with a par value of $10 per share, the journal entry is:

```
Bonds Payable . . . . . . . . . . . . . . . . . . . . . . . . . . . .   1,000
Premium on Bonds Payable . . . . . . . . . . . . . . . . . . .      20
    Common Stock, $10 par (20 × $10). . . . . . . . . . . . .              200
    Additional Paid-in Capital
        on Common Stock ($1,020 − $200) . . . . . . . . . . .              820
Conversion of 1 bond into 20 shares of common stock.
```

This procedure is consistent with accounting for the conversion of preferred stock discussed in Chapter 14. The book value of the bonds is replaced by an equivalent amount of contributed capital.

Sinking Fund Many bonds have a sinking fund provision that requires the company issuing the bond to set aside enough cash over a specified period so that sufficient cash will be available at maturity to retire the bonds. This cash is transferred to a sinking fund account. For example, if a company issues $100,000, 20-year bonds, there might be a provision to make an annual payment at the end of each year into a sinking fund starting after 10 years. Therefore the company will make 10 payments into the fund, which must amount to $100,000 at the maturity date of the bonds. If the company can earn 6% on the money it invests in the sinking fund, how much must each annual payment be? This is a future value problem in which we must find the value of a 10-period annuity at 6% that has a future value of $100,000:

$$
\text{Future value of annuity} = \begin{array}{l} \text{Periodic amount of} \\ \text{the annuity} \end{array} \times \begin{array}{l} \text{Future value} \\ \text{of annuity factor} \end{array}
$$

$$
\$100,000 = \begin{array}{l} \text{Periodic amount of} \\ \text{the annuity} \end{array} \times 13.180795 \text{ (from Table 3)}
$$

$$
\text{Periodic amount of the annuity} = \frac{\$100,000}{13.180795}
$$

$$
= \$7,586.80
$$

Therefore the company must put $7,586.80 into the sinking fund at the end of each year for 10 years. The journal entry to record the payment is:

Bond Sinking Fund 7,586.80
    Cash 7,586.80
To record annual sinking fund deposit.

The bond sinking fund is shown as a noncurrent asset in the balance sheet under the category of Long-Term Investments. The cash deposited in the sinking fund will be invested, and the interest or dividends received on these investments will be added (debited) to the Bond Sinking Fund account. These additions, along with the annual deposits, will amount to $100,000 at the maturity date of the bonds. At maturity, the cash from the bond sinking fund is used to retire the bonds.

THE STRAIGHT-LINE AND EFFECTIVE INTEREST METHODS

Accounting principles require the use of the effective interest method unless the results obtained by the straight-line method are not materially different. Since the two methods do not produce material differences for bonds issued at a value close to par, many companies use the straight-line method. The advantage of using the straight-line method is that it is simpler to apply because the same entry is made every semiannual period. It does not lead to a rational measure of interest expense, however, because the expense stays constant even though the book value of the bonds increases (decreases) each period as the discount (premium) is amortized.

In contrast, the effective interest method records an interest expense each semiannual period that is based on the yield and the book value of the bonds. Since the yield represents the interest rate on the money borrowed by the company and the book value is the outstanding balance of the amount borrowed during the period, the interest expense is a rational measure of the cost of borrowing money for the period. The interest expense increases (decreases) as the book value of the bonds increases (decreases) as the discount (premium) is amortized.

In summary, under the straight-line method the amount of the semiannual interest expense is calculated by adding (subtracting) the discount (premium) amortized to the cash paid. Under the effective interest method, the semiannual interest expense is computed by multiplying the semiannual yield times the book value of the bonds and the difference between the interest expense and the cash payment is the amount of the discount or premium amortization.

MORTGAGES PAYABLE

A mortgage payable is a long-term debt for which the lender has a specific claim against an asset of the borrower. For example, most homeowners purchase their homes by issuing a mortgage. That is, they borrow the money from a lender and the lender is assigned a secured claim on the home. Companies also acquire assets through mortgages.

The typical mortgage requires equal monthly payments (an annuity), and these payments are determined according to present value principles as follows:

Monthly payment = Amount borrowed ÷ Present value of annuity factor
based on the interest rate and
the life of the mortgage

Each payment consists of two components: (1) interest expense based on the periodic interest rate and the book value of the loan at the beginning of the period and (2) a portion of the principal balance. These components are calculated as follows:

$$\text{Interest expense} = \text{Periodic interest rate} \times \text{Book value of loan at the beginning of the period}$$

$$\text{Repayment of principal} = \text{Monthly payment} - \text{Interest expense}$$

To illustrate how to account for a mortgage suppose that the Joma Company purchases a building for $100,000. It agrees to pay $20,000 at acquisition and to pay the remainder under the terms of a 30-year mortgage at 12%. The journal entry to record the acquisition is:

Building.	100,000	
Cash		20,000
Mortgage Payable		80,000

Purchased building with $20,000 cash payment
and a 30-year, 12% mortgage.

Since the payments are to be monthly, the annual rate of 12% and time period of 30 years must be converted into their monthly equivalents of 1% and 360 periods. Since this factor is not included in Table 4 of Appendix B, we will assume that it is 97.218331. The monthly payment is computed as follows:

$$\begin{aligned}\text{Monthly payment} &= \text{Amount borrowed} \div \text{Present value of annuity factor} \\ &= \$80,000 \div 97.218331 \\ &= \$822.89\end{aligned}$$

The interest expense for the first month would be calculated as follows:

$$\begin{aligned}\text{Interest expense} &= \text{Periodic interest rate} \times \text{Book value of loan at the beginning of the month} \\ &= 1\% \times \$80,000 \\ &= \$800\end{aligned}$$

The remaining portion of the monthly payment is $22.89 ($822.89 − $800.00) and is the reduction of the principal. The journal entry to record the payment is:

Interest Expense	800.00	
Mortgage Payable	22.89	
Cash		822.89

To record monthly mortgage payment.

The journal entry to record the second monthly payment is:

Interest Expense [1% × ($80,000 − $22.89)]	799.77	
Mortgage Payable	23.12	
Cash		822.89

To record monthly mortgage payment.

Each month the balance in the Mortgage Payable account is reduced so that the balance in the account is eliminated when the final monthly payment is made.

REVIEW
PROBLEM

On January 1, 1983, the Cleese Company sold 6-year, 12% bonds with a face value of $20,000. The bonds were sold for $21,772.64. The bonds pay interest on June 30 and December 31 each year.

Required: 1. If the company uses the straight-line method:
   (a) Prepare a bond premium amortization schedule.
   (b) Prepare journal entries to record the sale and interest expense for the bonds during 1983.
   (c) Show how the bonds would be reported in the balance sheet on December 31, 1983.
2. If the company uses the effective interest method:
   (a) Compute the selling price of the bonds if the yield is 10%.
   (b) Prepare a bond premium amortization schedule.
   (c) Prepare journal entries to record the sale and interest expense for the bonds during 1983.
   (d) Show how the bonds would be reported in the balance sheet on December 31, 1983.

SOLUTION TO
REVIEW
PROBLEM

Requirement 1(a)

CLEESE COMPANY
Bond Premium Amortization Schedule
Straight-Line Method

Date	Cash Paid[a] (credit)	Amortization of Premium on Bonds Payable[b] (debit)	Interest Expense[c] (debit)	Book Value of Bonds[d]
1/1/1983				$21,772.64
6/30/1983	$1,200	$147.72	$1,052.28	21,624.92
12/31/1983	1,200	147.72	1,052.28	21,477.20
6/30/1984	1,200	147.72	1,052.28	21,329.48
12/31/1984	1,200	147.72	1,052.28	21,181.76
6/30/1985	1,200	147.72	1,052.28	21,034.04
12/31/1985	1,200	147.72	1,052.28	20,886.32
6/30/1986	1,200	147.72	1,052.28	20,738.60
12/31/1986	1,200	147.72	1,052.28	20,590.88
6/30/1987	1,200	147.72	1,052.28	20,443.16
12/31/1987	1,200	147.72	1,052.28	20,295.44
6/30/1988	1,200	147.72	1,052.28	20,147.72
12/31/1988	1,200	147.72	1,052.28	20,000.00

[a] $20,000 × (12% ÷ 2).
[b] ($21,772.64 − $20,000) ÷ (2 × 6).
[c] $1,200 − $147.72.
[d] Book value of bonds from previous line − $147.72; at 6/30/1983, $21,772.64 − $147.72.

Requirement 1(b)

1983
Jan. 1 Cash 21,772.64
      Bonds Payable 20,000.00
      Premium on Bonds Payable 1,772.64
      Issued 12% bonds at a premium.

June 30 Interest Expense 1,052.28
      Premium on Bonds Payable 147.72
      Cash 1,200.00
      To record interest paid on bonds and
      premium amortized by the straight-line
      method.

Dec. 31 Interest Expense 1,052.28
      Premium on Bonds Payable 147.72
      Cash 1,200.00
      To record interest paid on bonds and
      premium amortized by the straight-line
      method.

Requirement 1(c)

Noncurrent liabilities
12% Bonds payable, due 12/31/1988 . . . . $20,000.00
Plus: Premium on bonds payable 1,477.20
$21,477.20

Requirement 2(a)

Selling price = Present value of semiannual + Present value of
interest payments   face value
= ($1,200 × 8.863252) + ($20,000 × 0.556837)
= $21,772.64

Note: Each present value factor is for 12 periods (6 years × 2) and 5% (10% ÷ 2).

Requirement 2(b)

CLEESE COMPANY
Bond Premium Amortization Schedule
Effective Interest Method
(12% bonds to yield 10%)

Date	Cash Paid[a] (credit)	Interest Expense[b] (debit)	Amortization of Premium on Bonds Payable[c] (debit)	Book Value of Bonds[d]
1/1/1983				$21,772.64
6/30/1983	$1,200	$1,088.63	$111.37	21,661.27
12/31/1983	1,200	1,083.06	116.94	21,544.33
6/30/1984	1,200	1,077.22	122.78	21,421.55
12/31/1984	1,200	1,071.08	128.92	21,292.63
6/30/1985	1,200	1,064.63	135.37	21,157.26
12/31/1985	1,200	1,057.86	142.14	21,015.12
6/30/1986	1,200	1,050.76	149.24	20,865.88
12/31/1986	1,200	1,043.29	156.71	20,709.17
6/30/1987	1,200	1,035.46	164.54	20,544.63
12/31/1987	1,200	1,027.23	172.77	20,371.86
6/30/1988	1,200	1,018.59	181.41	20,190.45
12/31/1988	1,200	1,009.55[e]	190.45	20,000.00

[a] $20,000 × (12% ÷ 2).
[b] (10% ÷ 2) × Book value of bonds at beginning of period (from previous line); at 6/30/1983, (10% ÷ 2) × $21,772.64.
[c] Cash paid − Interest expense; at 6/30/1983, $1,200 − $1,088.63.
[d] Book value of bonds from previous line − Amortization of premium on bonds payable; at 6/30/1983, $21,772.64 − $111.37.
[e] Adjusted for rounding error of $.03.

Requirement 2(c)

```
1983
Jan.   1   Cash . . . . . . . . . . . . . . . . . . . .   21,772.64
               Bonds Payable . . . . . . . . . . . . .              20,000.00
               Premium on Bonds Payable  . . . . . .                 1,772.64
           Issued 12% bonds to yield 10%.



June 30    Interest Expense  . . . . . . . . . . . .    1,088.63
           Premium on Bonds Payable . . . . . . . .       111.37
               Cash  . . . . . . . . . . . . . . . . . .               1,200.00
           To record interest paid on bonds and
           interest expense by the effective interest
           method.
```

Dec. 31	Interest Expense	1,083.06	
	Premium on Bonds Payable	116.94	
	Cash		1,200.00

To record interest paid on bonds and
interest expense by the effective interest
method.

Requirement 2(d)

Noncurrent liabilities

12% Bonds payable, due 12/31/1988	$20,000.00
Plus: Premium on bonds payable	1,544.33
	$21,544.33

GLOSSARY

Adjunct Account. An account added to another account to determine the book value.

Amortization. The process of writing off the discount, or premium, on bonds payable as an adjustment of interest expense over the life of the bond issue.

Annuity. A series of equal periodic cash flows. The tables in Appendix B used to compute the present or future value of an annuity are prepared on the assumption that the first cash flow occurs at the end of the first time period.

Bonds Payable. A type of note payable in which the issuer (borrower) makes an unconditional promise to pay the holder (lender) the face value at the maturity date and to pay interest periodically at a specified rate on the face value.

Book Value of Bonds Payable. The face value of the bonds less the unamortized discount or plus the unamortized premium.

Callable Bonds. Bonds that are callable by the issuer at a predetermined price. That is, the issuer may require the holder to return the bonds before the maturity date and the issuer pays the predetermined price and interest to date.

Compound Interest. Interest that accrues on both the principal and past accrued interest.

Contract Rate. The rate at which an issuer of a bond pays interest. Also called the *stated rate*, the *face rate*, or the *nominal rate*.

Convertible Bonds. Bonds that are convertible into a predetermined number of shares of common stock.

Coupon Bonds. Unregistered bonds on which interest is claimed by the holder by presenting a coupon to the issuer.

Debenture Bonds. Unsecured bonds. That is, the holder is considered as a general creditor if the issuer fails to pay the interest or principal.

Discount on Bonds Payable. An account in which is recorded the amount by which the book value of the bonds payable is less than the face value.

Effective Interest Method. A method of recognizing interest expense in which the semiannual expense is based on the semiannual yield times the book value of the bonds.

Face Value. The amount of money that the issuer of the bonds will pay on the maturity date. Also called *par value*.

Future Value. The value in the future of a certain number of dollars.

Leverage. The use of borrowing by a company to increase the return to the common stockholders. Also called *trading on equity*.

Maturity Date. The date on which the issuer of a bond agrees to pay the face value to the holder.

Mortgage Bonds. Bonds that are secured with specific property. That is, the holder of the bonds has a priority right to the specific property if the issuer fails to pay the interest or principal.

Mortgage Payable. A long-term debt for which the lender has a specific claim against an asset of the borrower.

Premium on Bonds Payable. An account in which is recorded the amount by which the book value of the bonds payable exceeds the face value.

Present Value. The value today of a certain number of dollars in the future.

Registered Bonds. Bonds for which ownership is registered with the issuer. That is, the issuer maintains a record of the holder of each bond so that payment of interest and principal can be made without such payment being requested by the holder.

Serial Bonds. Bonds issued at one time but portions of which mature at different future dates.

Sinking Fund Bonds. Bonds for which the issuer must pay an agreed amount each period into a sinking fund to be used to retire the bonds at maturity. *Sinking fund* is the term used to describe the account into which the cash is paid.

Straight-Line Method. A method of amortizing a discount or premium on bonds payable by an equal amount each period.

Unamortized Discount (or Premium) on Bonds Payable. The amount of the discount (or premium) that has not yet been amortized.

Yield. The market (or effective) interest rate at which bonds are issued. The rate of return earned by the purchaser of bonds, and the cost of the money borrowed by the issuer.

QUESTIONS

Q16-1 Define the following terms as they relate to bonds: (a) face value; (b) maturity date; and (c) contract rate.

Q16-2 Why would a company issue bonds when it is obliged to pay interest each period instead of issuing stock for which dividend payments are discretionary?

Q16-3 Distinguish between the following types of bonds: (a) debenture and mortgage bonds; (b) registered and coupon bonds; (c) serial bonds and callable bonds.

Q16-4   Why may a bond's contract rate differ from its yield?

Q16-5   What are the factors that affect an interest rate?

Q16-6   Under what condition will a bond be sold at a discount? At a premium?

Q16-7   What type of accounts are the Discount on Bonds Payable account and the Premium on Bonds Payable account? How is each included in the financial statements?

Q16-8   What is meant by the time value of money?

Q16-9   What is the difference between present value and future value?

Q16-10   Explain the difference between simple interest and compound interest.

Q16-11   What is an annuity? Why is an annuity a useful financial concept?

Q16-12   In calculating compound interest, how are the number of periods and the interest rate computed for interest periods other than 1 year?

Q16-13   How does a company record the selling price of bonds issued at par plus accrued interest when the bonds are sold between the interest payment dates?

Q16-14   If a bond is retired prior to its maturity date, under what condition will the issuing company report a loss on its income statement? A gain? Is the loss or gain ordinary or extraordinary?

Q16-15   What are convertible bonds? When can it be expected that conversion will occur?

Q16-16   How is the conversion of bonds into common stock recorded?

Q16-17   What is a sinking fund bond? Why do many bond issues require the establishment of a sinking fund? How is a sinking fund disclosed on the financial statements?

Q16-18   Explain how interest expense is computed under the effective interest and straight-line methods.

Q16-19   What are the two components of each monthly mortgage payment? How is each calculated?

EXERCISES

E16-1   Bonds Sold at Par.   On January 1, 1983, the Miles Company issued 20-year, 8% bonds with a face value of $100,000 at par. Interest is to be paid semiannually on June 30 and December 31.

Required: 1. How much interest expense will be recorded in 1983?
2. What will be the book value of the bonds in the December 31, 1983, balance sheet? Show how this would be disclosed.

E16-2   Straight-Line Method.   Use the same information as in E16-1, except that the company uses the straight-line amortization method and the bonds were issued at 102.

Required: 1. How much interest expense will the Miles Company recognize in 1983?
2. What will be the book value of the bonds in the December 31, 1983, balance sheet? Show how this would be disclosed.

E16-3 **Straight-Line Method.** Use the same information as in E16-1, except that the company uses the straight-line amortization method and the bonds were issued at 99.

Required: 1. How much interest expense will the Miles Company recognize in 1983?
2. What will be the book value of the bonds in the December 31, 1983, balance sheet? Show how this would be disclosed.

E16-4 **Present Value of a Single Sum.** Listed below are amounts to be received or paid in the future:

(a) $1,000 to be received at the end of 3 years; interest rate of 6%.
(b) $5,000 to be received at the end of 6 years; interest rate of 8%.
(c) $10,000 to be paid at the end of 10 years; interest rate of 10%.
(d) $20,000 to be paid at the end of 15 years; interest rate of 5%.
(e) $3,000 to be received at the end of 8 years; interest rate of 6%.

Required: Compute the present value of each amount.

E16-5 **Future Value of a Single Sum.** Listed below are present value amounts, numbers of periods, and interest rates:

(a) $1,000; 3 years; interest rate of 6%.
(b) $5,000; 6 years; interest rate of 8%.
(c) $10,000; 10 years; interest rate of 10%.
(d) $20,000; 15 years; interest rate of 5%.
(e) $3,000; 8 years; interest rate of 6%.

Required: Compute the future value of each amount at the end of the given number of periods.

E16-6 **Present Value of an Annuity.** Listed below are annuities to be received or paid in the future:

(a) A 3-year annuity of $1,000 at 6%.
(b) A 6-year annuity of $5,000 at 8%.
(c) A 10-year annuity of $10,000 at 10%.
(d) A 15-year annuity of $20,000 at 5%.
(e) An 8-year annuity of $3,000 at 6%.

Required: Compute the present value of each annuity.

E16-7 **Future Value of an Annuity.** Use the information in E16-6.

Required: Compute the future value of each annuity.

E16-8 **Bonds Sold at a Discount.** On January 1, 1983, the Loveland Company issued 10-year, 8% bonds with a face value of $100,000. The bonds pay interest semiannually and were issued to yield 10%. The company uses the effective interest method.

Required: 1. What is the selling price of the bonds? What is the amount of the discount?
2. How much interest expense will the Loveland Company record in 1983?
3. What will be the book value of the bonds in the December 31, 1983, balance sheet? Show how this would be disclosed.

E16-9 **Bonds Sold at a Premium.** Use the same information as E16-8, except that the bonds were issued to yield 6%. The company uses the effective interest method.

Required: 1. What is the selling price of the bonds? What is the amount of the premium?
2. How much interest expense will the Loveland Company recognize in 1983?
3. What will be the book value of the bonds in the December 31, 1983, balance sheet? Show how this would be disclosed.

E16-10 Retirement of Bonds at Maturity. Use the same information as E16-8.

Required: Prepare the journal entry to record the retirement of the bonds at their maturity date.

E16-11 Bonds Issued Between Interest Payment Dates. On August 1, 1983, the Linjo Company issued 10-year, 12% bonds with a face value of $30,000 at par plus accrued interest. The bonds pay interest on June 30 and December 31.

Required: 1. How much accrued interest do the purchasers of the bonds pay to the Linjo Company on August 1, 1983?
2. How much cash will Linjo Company receive at the sale?
3. Prepare the journal entry for the Linjo Company to record the payment of interest on December 31, 1983.

E16-12 Retirement of Bonds Before Maturity. The Porter Company has 10% bonds outstanding with a face value of $20,000. The bonds pay interest on June 30 and December 31. On July 1, 1983, when the bonds have a book value of $20,250, the Porter Company calls them at 102.

Required: Prepare the journal entry to record the redemption of the bonds.

E16-13 Conversion of Bonds. The Derek Company issued 10% bonds with a face value of $50,000 at 102 on January 1, 1980. The bonds pay interest every June 30 and December 31. Each $1,000 bond is convertible into 50 shares of $10 par common stock. The bonds have a book value of $50,700 on January 1, 1983. At that time all the bonds are converted.

Required: 1. How many shares of common stock does the company issue upon conversion?
2. Prepare the journal entry to record the conversion.

E16-14 Bond Sinking Fund. The Crawford Company issued 10-year bonds with a face value of $100,000 on January 1, 1983. The terms of the bond issue require the establishment of a sinking fund. The company believes that it can earn a return of 8% on the money invested in the sinking fund.

Required: 1. How much must the company invest in the sinking fund each year if the first payment is made on December 31, 1983?
2. Prepare the journal entry on December 31, 1983, to record the first payment.
3. Where would the sinking fund be disclosed in the financial statements?

E16-15 Mortgage. The Holliday Company purchased a building for $150,000 and paid 20% down. The remainder was financed by a 20-year mortgage at 12%, with payments to be made monthly. The present value of an annuity of 1% for 240 periods is 90.819416.

Required: 1. Compute the amount of the monthly mortgage payment.
2. Prepare journal entries to record the acquisition of the building and to record each of the first two interest payments.

PROBLEMS

Part A

P16-1A Straight-Line Amortization. On January 1, 1983, the Myrtle Company issued 10-year, 8% bonds with a face value of $100,000 at 98. Interest is paid on June 30 and December 31 each year. The company uses the straight-line method of amortization.

Required: 1. Prepare an amortization schedule for the discount or premium.
2. Prepare the journal entries to record all the events for the bonds during 1983.
3. What will be the book value of the bonds on the December 31, 1983, balance sheet? Show how it would be disclosed.
4. What is the interest expense for 1983? Show how it would be disclosed on the 1983 income statement.

P16-2A   Present and Future Values.   Listed below are four independent situations:

(a) Jane Seymour invests $5,000 on January 1, 1983, in a savings account that earns interest at 8% compounded quarterly. How much will be in the account on December 31, 1985?

(b) David Jones wants to put enough money in a fund to pay for his son's college education for 4 years. The fund will pay $2,500 every 6 months, starting September 1, 1983, and it is expected that the fund can be invested to earn 10% compounded semiannually. How much money must be put in the fund on March 1, 1983?

(c) Peter Morgan is saving to buy a house. On December 31, 1983, a relative dies and leaves him $10,000, which he puts into a savings account. He believes he can also put $4,000 per year into the account starting on December 31, 1984. If the savings account pays 6% compounded annually, how much will Peter Morgan have available on January 1, 1989?

(d) Anne Boleyn purchases a 10-year annuity on January 1, 1983, for $100,000. The annuity will pay her an equal amount each year for 10 years. If she wants an 8% return on her investment, how much will each annuity payment be? Assume that the annuity is paid once each year beginning on December 31, 1983.

Required: Using the appropriate present and future value tables in Appendix B, solve each of the above situations.

P16-3A   Effective Interest Method of Amortization.   On February 1, 1983, the Mussel Company issued 10% bonds with a face value of $60,000. Interest on the bonds is paid on July 31 and January 31 each year, and the bonds mature on January 31, 1989. The bonds are sold to yield 8% and the company uses the effective interest method of amortization.

Required: 1. Compute the selling price of the bonds.
2. Prepare an amortization schedule for the premium or discount.
3. Prepare the journal entries to record all the events for the bonds in 1983.
4. Prepare the journal entry to retire the bonds at the maturity date.

P16-4A   Effective Interest Method of Amortization.   Use the same information as P16-3A, except that the bonds were sold to yield 12%.

Required: 1. Compute the selling price of the bonds.
2. Prepare an amortization schedule for the premium or discount.
3. Prepare the journal entries to record all the events for the bonds in 1983.
4. Prepare the journal entry to retire the bonds at the maturity date.

P16-5A   Retirement of Bonds Before Maturity.   On December 31, 1982, the following information appeared in the balance sheet of the Zoom Company:

7% Bonds payable, due December 31, 1988	$50,000
Less: Discount on bonds payable	1,200
	$48,800

Interest is paid on June 30 and December 31. The bonds were originally sold to yield 8%. On January 1, 1983, the Zoom Company retired bonds with a face value of $10,000 by purchasing them at 101 on the bond market. On July 1, 1983, the company called the remaining bonds at 102. The company uses the effective interest method.

Required: 1. Prepare journal entries to record all the events for the bonds during 1983.
2. Prepare a partial income statement for 1983 for the Zoom Company relating to the above information.

P16-6A Conversion of Bonds. At the end of the Robbins Company's fiscal year on June 30, 1983, the balance sheet included the following information:

6% Bonds payable, due June 30, 1988	
(each $1,000 bond is convertible into	
30 shares of $5 par common stock)	$20,000
Add: Premium on bonds payable	500
	$20,500

Interest on the bonds is paid on June 30 and December 31. The company uses the straight-line method of amortization. On August 31, 1983, all the bonds were converted after the company recorded and paid accrued interest on these bonds. At this time the $5 par common stock was selling for $40 per share.

Required: 1. Prepare journal entries to record all the events for the bonds from July 1 through December 31, 1983.
2. Does it appear that the owners of the bonds who converted them made a rational decision? Why or why not?

P16-7A Mortgage. On November 1, 1983, the Williams Company purchased a building for $120,000 and paid 30% down. The remainder was financed by a 25-year mortgage at 12% with payments to be made monthly. The present value of an annuity of 1% for 300 periods is 94.946551. The building has an estimated service life and residual value of 40 years and $20,000, respectively. The company uses the straight-line depreciation method.

Required: 1. Compute the amount of the monthly mortgage payment.
2. Prepare journal entries to record all of the events for the building and the mortgage in 1983.
3. Prepare the required disclosures in the financial statements for 1983.

PROBLEMS

Part B

P16-1B Straight-Line Amortization. On January 1, 1984, the Golden Company sold 5-year, 10% bonds with a face value of $500,000 at 102. Interest is paid on June 30 and December 31 each year. The company uses the straight-line method of amortization.

Required: 1. Prepare an amortization schedule for the discount or premium.
2. Prepare the journal entries to record all of the events for the bonds during 1984.
3. What will be the book value of the bonds on the December 31, 1984, balance sheet? Show how it would be disclosed.
4. What is the interest expense for 1984? Show how it would be disclosed on the 1984 income statement.

P16-2B Present and Future Values. Listed below are four independent situations:

(a) Steve Stunning is saving to build a weight room in his home. On July 1, 1983, he sells his motorcycle for $1,000 and puts the money into his savings account. He believes that he can also put $800 per year into this account starting on July 1, 1984. If the savings account pays 8% compounded annually, how much will Steve have in the account on July 1, 1987?

(b) Laurie Lightly purchases a 20-year annuity on January 1, 1983, for $200,000. The annuity will pay her an equal amount each year for 20 years. If she wants a 6% return on her investment, how much will the annuity payment be each December 31 if the first payment is received on December 31, 1983?

(c) Rhonda Ritz puts $400,000 in a savings account on June 1, 1984. If the account pays 10% interest compounded annually, how much will be in the account on May 31, 1990?

(d) Brian Bright wants to put enough money in a fund to pay for his daughter's college education for four years. The fund will pay $3,000 every 4 months starting September 1, 1983, and the fund will earn 12% compounded every four months. How much money must Brian put in the fund on May 1, 1983?

Required: Using the appropriate present and future value tables in Appendix B, solve each of the above situations.

P16-3B   Effective Interest Method of Amortization.   On August 1, 1983, the Adobe Company issued 16% bonds with a face value of $80,000. Interest on the bonds is paid on July 31 and January 31 each year, and the bonds mature on July 31, 1989. The bonds were sold to yield 12% and the company uses the effective interest method of amortization.

Required: 1. Compute the selling price of the bonds.
2. Prepare an amortization schedule for the premium or discount.
3. Prepare the journal entries to record all the events for the bonds in 1983.
4. Prepare the journal entry to retire the bonds at the maturity date.

P16-4B   Effective Interest Method of Amortization.   Use the same information given in P16-3B, except that the bonds were sold to yield 20%.

Required: 1. Compute the selling price of the bonds.
2. Prepare an amortization schedule for the premium or discount.
3. Prepare the journal entries to record all the events for the bonds in 1983.
4. Prepare the journal entry to retire the bonds at the maturity date.

P16-5B   Retirement of Bonds Before Maturity.   On December 31, 1982, the following information appeared in the balance sheet of the Bix Company:

9% Bonds payable, due December 31, 2000 . . . . . $75,000
Plus: Premium on bonds payable   3,000
$78,000

Interest on the bonds is paid June 30 and December 31. The bonds were originally sold to yield 8%. On July 1, 1983, the Bix Company retired bonds with a face value of $25,000 by purchasing them at 98 on the bond market. On December 31, 1983, the company called the remaining bonds at 101. The company uses the effective interest method.

Required: 1. Prepare journal entries to record all events for the bonds during 1983.
2. Prepare a partial income statement for 1983 for the Bix Company relating to the above information.

P16-6B   Conversion of Bonds.   At the end of the Hoedown Company's fiscal year on April 30, 1983, the balance sheet included the following information:

8% Bonds payable, due April 30, 1988
(each $1,000 bond is convertible into
25 shares of $10 par common stock) $225,000
Less: Discount on bonds payable   5,000
$220,000

Interest on the bonds is paid on April 30 and October 31. The company uses the straight-line method of amortization. On July 1, 1983, all the bonds were converted after the company recorded and paid accrued interest on these bonds. At this time the common stock was selling for $30 per share.

Required: 1. Prepare journal entries to record all the events for the bonds from July 1 through December 31, 1983.
2. Does it appear that the owners who converted their bonds made a rational decision? Why or why not?

P16-7B   Mortgage. On November 1, 1983, the Blossom Company purchased a building for $90,000 and paid 10% down. The remainder was financed by a 15-year mortgage at 15% with payments to be made monthly. The present value of an annuity of 1.25% for 180 periods is 71.449643. The building has an estimated service life and residual value of 30 years and $10,000, respectively. The company uses the straight-line depreciation method.

Required: 1. Compute the amount of the monthly mortgage payment.
2. Prepare journal entries to record all of the events for the building and the mortgage in 1983.
3. Prepare the required disclosures in the financial statements for 1983.

DISCUSSION CASES

C16-1   Financing by Stocks or Bonds. The Underhill Company has been operating at a very stable level, consistently earning a pretax income of $250,000. The company is evaluating the possibility of expanding its operations. It has calculated that it would cost $1 million to build a new plant. It is expected that pretax income would increase by $150,000 as a result of the expansion. The company currently has 100,000 shares of $10 par value common stock outstanding. Its income tax rate is 40%. The company is considering whether to finance the expansion by selling 10% bonds at par or by selling 70,000 shares of common stock to obtain the $1 million.

Required: 1. How much will earnings per share be using each of the alternative methods of financing?
2. Which method of financing would you recommend?

C16-2   Sale of Bonds at a Premium or Discount. At a board meeting of the Temple Company to discuss the issuance of bonds with a face value of $100,000, the following comments were made:

"At current market rates, I think the bonds will sell to yield 10%. Therefore, we should have a contract rate of 11% so that the bonds will sell at a premium. Like anyone else, investors view premiums as favorable, and we should do anything we can to get favorable reactions."

"I agree that the yield will be 10%, but I think we should have a contract rate of 8%, so that the bonds will be sold at a discount. We all know people like to get a good deal, and if they can buy the bonds for less than the face value, I'm sure they will sell very easily."

"If the yield is 10%, we should have a contract rate of 10%. Since we need exactly $100,000 to finance our expansion, that is the best alternative."

Required: Critically evaluate each of the comments.

C16-3   Convertible Bonds. The Brooks Company needs to raise capital of $1 million. It is considering selling 10% debenture bonds, 8% convertible bonds, or $10 par common stock.

Required: Discuss the advantages and disadvantages of each method of financing from the perspective of the company. Include in your discussion an analysis of the effect of each method on the financial statements at the time of the sale of the bonds and the stock, and also in subsequent years.

17 Long-Term Investments and Leases

After reading this chapter, you should understand:

- How the percentage of ownership in the common stock of another company affects the accounting method used for a noncurrent investment
- The lower of cost or market method for noncurrent investments in stock
- The equity method
- Consolidated financial statements
- Accounting for long-term investments in bonds
- The characteristics of a capital lease
- Accounting for a capital lease by the lessee and the lessor
- Accounting for an operating lease

As described in Chapter 7, a company often has excess cash that it invests in current (short-term) marketable securities. In addition, companies also make long-term investments in the stocks and bonds of other companies. These noncurrent investments may be made because they appear to be more profitable than investing in property, plant, and equipment, but it is more likely that they are made for operating reasons. For example, a company can obtain a certain degree of influence on the operations of other companies from which it purchases inventory or to which it sells a product by purchasing common stock of these companies and voting at the stockholders' meeting and being represented on the board of directors. A company also invests in the stock of companies that tend to have a business cycle different from their own. In this way it is hoped that the income earned on the stock will help to offset any declines in the income from the company's own business, and therefore a more level trend of earnings may result.

In other situations a company may buy enough stock to obtain control of another company. That is, it buys more than 50% of the company's common stock. A company may find it easier to grow larger by buying control of other companies than by buying property, plant, and equipment to expand its product lines and sales. A company may also invest in the bonds of other companies, either to acquire a financial relationship with another company or to obtain a safe source of continuing revenue. In this chapter we discuss accounting for these various types of long-term (or noncurrent) investments.

Leasing of assets is becoming an increasingly common method by which a company may obtain the use of assets for its operating activities. In many cases leases result in the recording of an asset and a liability by a company. A discussion of the accounting for leased assets is also included in this chapter.

NONCURRENT INVESTMENTS IN STOCK

Accounting for noncurrent investments in common stock is complex. First, it is important to understand that the accounting method used for a particular investment depends on the ownership interest in the other company measured in terms of the proportion of the common stock owned. **The investor is the company purchasing the stock. The investee is the company whose stock is being purchased.** The ownership interest of the investor company in the investee company and the accounting methods used are as follows:

Ownership Interest in Outstanding Common Stock	Accounting Method Used
Less than 20%	Lower of cost or market
20% to 50%	Equity
More than 50%	Consolidation

The lower of cost or market method is used when less than 20% of the outstanding common stock of the investee company is owned by the investor company. This method is similar to the method discussed for current marketable investments in common stock in Chapter 7. **The equity method is used when it is presumed that the investor company has significant influence over the investee company. Significant influence is presumed to exist when 20% or more of the outstanding common stock is owned by the investor company.** Significant influence, however, can be indicated by other factors, such as representation on the board of directors, participation in the policy-making process, significant intercompany transactions, interchange of managerial personnel, or technological dependency. If the other evidence outweighs the ownership interest, the 20% rule can be ignored. For example, a company with 10% of the common stock might be able to elect 4 of the 10 members of the board of directors, in which case it would be appropriate to use the equity method. In this book we will use the equity method only when the ownership interest is 20% or more. The lower of cost or market and the equity methods are discussed in more detail later in the chapter.

If the ownership interest exceeds 50% of the outstanding common stock, the investor company uses the equity method to account for the investment during the period. Because the investor company has *control* over the investee company however, *consolidated* financial statements must be prepared. This is a very complex area of accounting and will be discussed only briefly in this book.

How the Investment Is Made

Before discussing the various methods of accounting for noncurrent investments in stock, it is important to understand how the investor company acquires the shares of the investee company. In most situations the investor buys the shares on the stock market from existing owners who are willing to sell their shares. This transaction has no direct effect on the investee company whose shares are being purchased and sold, and therefore there is no effect on its financial statements (the investee company does have to record the name and address of the new owners in its stockholders' ledger, however, so that dividend checks and other shareholder information can be correctly mailed).

Occasionally an investor company purchases shares that are being newly issued. In this situation the financial statements of the investee company whose shares are being sold are affected. The issuance of new shares was discussed in Chapter 14. In this chapter it is assumed that the investor company is purchasing shares that are already outstanding. Therefore the transaction has no effect on the financial statements of the investee company whose shares are being purchased.

No matter how the acquisition is made, the investor company records (debits) an asset account for the cost of acquisition, which includes the purchase price, commissions to the stockbroker, and any transfer taxes that are imposed (as discussed in Chapter 7). The title given to the asset account usually varies according to the type of acquisition. When the investment is to be accounted for by the lower of cost or market method, a title such as Noncurrent Marketable Securities — Stocks is used. When the investment is to be accounted for by the equity method, a title such as Investment in XYZ Company is used. For example, if 200 shares of Texaco stock are purchased for $30 per share (and will be accounted for by the lower of cost or market method), the journal entry to record the transaction would be:

```
Noncurrent Marketable Securities—Stocks  . . . . . . . . . . .    6,000
    Cash . . . . . . . . . . . . . . . . . . . . . . . . . . . . .          6,000
Acquired 200 shares of Texaco.
```

Regardless of the title and method of accounting used, the balance of any noncurrent investments in stock account is reported as a noncurrent asset in the long-term investments section of a company's balance sheet.

LOWER OF COST OR MARKET METHOD FOR NONCURRENT MARKETABLE INVESTMENTS IN STOCK

As mentioned above, accounting for noncurrent marketable investments in stock when the ownership interest is less than 20% is very similar to the method used for current marketable investments in stock, which was discussed in Chapter 7. That is, the portfolio of noncurrent marketable investments in stock (investments that will be held for more than 1 year or the operating cycle, whichever is longer) are valued at the lower of the cost of the portfolio or the market value of the portfolio. In contrast to the lower of cost or market method for current marketable securities in which the loss caused by the decline in value is included in the income statement, however, the "loss" caused by a decline in the value of the noncurrent portfolio is included directly as a reduction in stockholders' equity on the balance sheet.[1]

The reason for not including the reduction in market value in the income

---

[1] "Accounting for Certain Marketable Securities." *FASB Statement No. 12* (Stamford, Conn.: FASB, 1975), par. 11.

statement is that, since the investment is to be held for at least a year, there is a reasonable possibility that the decline will be reversed before a sale is made. Including these declines and reversals in the income statement might tend to distort the results of the ongoing operating activities of the company. It seems just as likely, however, that the reader of the financial statements will be confused by the placement of this decline on noncurrent marketable securities in the stockholders' equity section of the balance sheet and the loss on current marketable securities in the income statement.

As discussed in Chapter 7 an Allowance account is used to reduce the cost of the portfolio to market. To determine the necessary balance in the Allowance account, the market value of the portfolio is subtracted from the cost. The amount of the adjustment is determined by comparing the required balance in the Allowance account with the actual balance.

The journal entry to record a decline is (amounts assumed):

Unrealized Decline in Value of Noncurrent Marketable Securities — Stocks	2,000	
Allowance for Decline in Value of Noncurrent Marketable Securities — Stocks		2,000

To record noncurrent marketable securities — stocks at lower of cost or market.

As with the current marketable investments in stock on the balance sheet, the Allowance account balance is subtracted from the cost of the noncurrent marketable investments in stock to report the market value of these securities. The reduction in the value of the securities that is included in stockholders' equity would be reported in the balance sheet in the following manner (amounts assumed):

Stockholders' Equity

Contributed capital		
Common stock, $5 par	$10,000	
Additional paid-in capital	25,000	
Total contributed capital		$35,000
Retained earnings		42,000
Total contributed capital and retained earnings		$77,000
Less: Unrealized decline in value of noncurrent marketable securities — stocks		(2,000)
Total Stockholders' Equity		$75,000

Under the lower of cost or market method applied to either current or noncurrent marketable investments in stock, recoveries in the market value *up to* the cost of the portfolio are recognized. Remember that investments in stock cannot be carried at a value in excess of their cost. For noncurrent marketable investments in stock this recovery of value is not a gain reported in the income statement. Instead the journal entry to recognize this recovery of value would simply be the reverse of the entry used to record the decline. The debit would be to the Allowance account and the credit to the Unrealized Decline account, which therefore has the effect of reducing the amount of the Unrealized Decline included in stockholders' equity on the balance sheet.

To illustrate the application of the lower of cost or market method to noncurrent marketable investments in stock, assume that on January 1, 1982, the Fowles Company purchased the following shares of common stock as a long-term investment (stockbroker's fees and transfer taxes are ignored):

Company	Number of Shares	Cost per Share	Total Cost
RCA	100	$50	$ 5,000
Sears	200	20	4,000
Alcoa	50	70	3,500
			$12,500

The acquisition would be recorded on January 1, 1982, as follows:

```
1982
Jan. 1   Noncurrent Marketable Securities — Stocks  ....   12,500
              Cash . . . . . . . . . . . . . . . . . . . . . . .         12,500
         Acquired shares of RCA, Sears, and Alcoa
         Companies common stock.
```

On December 31, 1982, the securities had the following values:

Company	Number of Shares	Cost per Share	Market Value per Share	Total Cost	Total Market Value
RCA	100	$50	$60	$ 5,000	$ 6,000
Sears	200	20	15	4,000	3,000
Alcoa	50	70	40	3,500	2,000
				$12,500	$11,000

The $1,500 ($12,500 − $11,000) decline in the value of the portfolio of securities is recognized by the following journal entry on December 31, 1982:

```
1982
Dec. 31   Unrealized Decline in Value of Noncurrent
              Marketable Securities — Stocks . . . . . . .   1,500
          Allowance for Decline in Value of Noncurrent
              Marketable Securities — Stocks . . . . . . .           1,500
          To record noncurrent marketable securities —
          stocks at lower of cost or market.
```

Therefore the carrying value of the securities in the balance sheet would be $11,000 as follows:

```
Noncurrent marketable securities — stocks,
    at cost  . . . . . . . . . . . . . . . . . . . . . . .   $12,500
Less: Allowance for decline in value  . . . . . . . . .        1,500
Noncurrent marketable securities — stocks at
    lower of cost or market . . . . . . . . . . . . . . .   $11,000
```

The unrealized decline of $1,500 would be included in the stockholders' equity section of the balance sheet, as illustrated earlier.

On August 10, 1983, the Fowles Company sold the 50 shares of Alcoa (which originally cost $70 per share) for $60 per share. The gain or loss on the sale is measured by the difference between the proceeds from the sale and the *cost* of the securities and therefore is not affected by the balance in the Allowance account. As discussed in Chapter 7, the gain or loss is *not* measured as the difference between the proceeds from the sale and the market value of the securities on the last balance sheet date because individual stocks are not carried at their market value. It is the *total portfolio* that is being carried at the lower of cost or market. Thus there is a loss on the sale of $500 [50 shares × ($70 − $60)], which would be recorded on August 10, 1983, as follows:

```
1983
Aug. 10   Cash . . . . . . . . . . . . . . . . . . . . . . . . . . . .   3,000
              Loss on Sale of Noncurrent Marketable Securities —
                  Stocks . . . . . . . . . . . . . . . . . . . . . . .      500
              Noncurrent Marketable Securities — Stocks  . . .               3,500
          Sold 50 shares of Alcoa Company common stock.
```

The loss would be included in the Other Revenues and Expenses section of the income statement.

On December 31, 1983, the securities owned by the Fowles Company had the following values:

Company	Number of Shares	Cost per share	Market Value per Share	Total Cost	Total Market Value
RCA	100	$50	$40	$5,000	$4,000
Sears	200	20	22	4,000	4,400
				$9,000	$8,400

Before discussing the journal entry required, let us review the entries that have been made in the relevant accounts as shown below:

Noncurrent Marketable Securities — Stocks			Allowance for Decline in Value of Noncurrent Marketable Securities — Stocks	
1/1/82 12,500	8/10/83 3,500		12/31/82 1,500	

Since the Noncurrent Marketable Securities account has a balance of $9,000 ($12,500 − $3,500) and the Allowance account has a balance of $1,500, the book value of the portfolio of noncurrent marketable investments in stock is $7,500.

At December 31, 1983, the $8,400 market value of the portfolio is still less than the $9,000 cost, and therefore the securities should be carried at their market value of $8,400 in the balance sheet. This requires an ending balance in the Allowance account of $600. Since the existing balance is $1,500, this balance has to be reduced by $900 ($1,500 − $600) to $600 by the following journal entry on December 31, 1983:

1983

Dec. 31   Allowance for Decline in Value of Noncurrent
    Marketable Securities — Stocks 900
   Unrealized Decline in Value of Noncurrent Marketable
    Securities — Stocks   900
   To record noncurrent marketable securities — stocks at
   lower of cost or market.

At December 31, 1984, the securities owed by the Fowles Company had the following values:

Company	Number of Shares	Cost per Share	Market Value per Share	Total Cost	Total Market Value
RCA	100	$50	$60	$5,000	$ 6,000
Sears	200	20	25	4,000	5,000
				$9,000	$11,000

The market value of the portfolio now *exceeds* the cost, and therefore the securities should be carried at their cost of $9,000 in the balance sheet. The balance in the Allowance account of $600 has to be eliminated by the following journal entry:

1984

Dec. 31   Allowance for Decline in Value of Noncurrent
    Marketable Securities — Stocks 600
   Unrealized Decline in Value of Noncurrent
    Marketable Securities — Stocks   600
   To record noncurrent marketable securities — stocks at
   lower of cost or market.

The effect of this entry is also to eliminate the balance in the Unrealized Decline account, and therefore the only item that appears in the balance sheet at December 31, 1984, is the cost of the securities.

Revenue from dividends on noncurrent marketable investments in stock is recognized in exactly the same way as for current investments. That is, revenue is recognized as the dividends are declared by the investee. Assuming that dividends are declared by the investee company on July 31, 1984, the investor company would record the transaction as follows (amounts assumed):

1984

July 31   Dividends Receivable 300
   Dividend Revenue   300
   To record declaration of dividends by investee company.

The Dividends Receivable would be listed as a current asset on the balance sheet and would be eliminated when the cash is received. The Dividend Revenue would be included in the Other Revenues and Expenses section of the income statement. For convenience, some companies record dividend revenue when the cash is received.

Evaluation of the Lower of Cost or Market Method

The lower of cost or market method is consistent with the historical cost and conservatism concepts discussed in Chapters 1 and 7, respectively. Many accountants criticize this method, however, because it fails to recognize a gain that can easily be measured. The market value of most investments in stock can be determined by reference to the stock market price at the time the financial statements are being prepared. If this market value is above the cost, then a gain has arisen. Since this gain can be achieved very easily through a sale, many accountants argue that it should be included in the income statement of the period along with a recognition of the market value in the balance sheet. It should be noted that even though the market value is not included in the financial statements, it is disclosed in the footnotes to the financial statements, or parenthetically in the balance sheet.

Those who support the lower of cost or market method suggest that a gain should not be recognized until there is a transaction (the sale of the stock) so that the increase in value can be measured objectively. Supporters also suggest that including the investment at market value would violate the historical cost concept and confuse the users of financial statements by valuing different assets in different ways.

THE EQUITY METHOD

As discussed earlier, the equity method of accounting for noncurrent investments in common stock is used when the investor company has significant influence over the investee company. Significant influence is presumed to exist when the ownership interest is 20% or more of the common stock of the investee.

At this level of ownership there are several reasons why the lower of cost or market method is not appropriate. First, it can be expected that the investment will be for a long period of time and therefore the cost may become outdated. Second, the market value of the shares of the investee company will not necessarily represent a good measure of the total value of the investment. The price of a share on the stock market on any given day is the result of the supply and demand on that day. The sale of over 20% of the shares of a company would almost certainly be at a different market price than the sale of a small quantity of shares. Third, income is not best measured by the dividends received. For example, suppose that an investee company earns $40,000 and pays dividends of $4,000. If an investor company owns 25% of the shares it would receive dividends of $1,000, but this amount does not represent the income accumulation of the investor company in the sense that it is not the best measure of the increase in its wealth. Since the investee has earned $40,000 and the investor owns 25% of the income, the investor should instead recognize income of $10,000.

The equity method uses a different approach for recording the value of the investment and recognizing income than the lower of cost or market method. The investment and the income are accounted for by the investor company as follows:

Investment = Cost + Income − Dividends

Income = Investee's net income × Ownership %

Dividends = Total dividends paid by investee × Ownership %

The journal entry used to record the acquisition is as follows (amounts assumed):

```
Investment in XYZ Company  . . . . . . . . . . . . . . .   20,000
    Cash  . . . . . . . . . . . . . . . . . . . . . . .           20,000
Acquired shares in XYZ Company.
```

The journal entry to record the income of the investor company is as follows (amounts assumed):

```
Investment in XYZ Company  . . . . . . . . . . . . . . .   4,700
    Income from Investment in XYZ Company  . . . . . . .          4,700
To recognize share of XYZ Company's net income.
```

As discussed above, the investor company recognizes as income its share of the investee company's net income. When this income is recognized, the value of the asset is increased by the same amount.

The journal entry to record the receipt of dividends does *not* involve recognition of income, but instead reduces the value of the investment as follows (amounts assumed):

```
Cash (or Dividends Receivable)  . . . . . . . . . . . . .   800
    Investment in XYZ Company  . . . . . . . . . . . . .          800
Dividends received from XYZ Company.
```

When dividends are received from the investee company, the investor company records this receipt as a *reduction* in the book value of the Investment account. The accounting by the investor company parallels the accounting by the investee company. When the investee company earns income there is an increase in its stockholders' equity, and when it pays dividends its stockholders' equity is decreased. The book value of the investor company's Investment account is increased as its share of the investee company's stockholders' equity increases (as income is earned) and is decreased as its share of the investee company's stockholders' equity decreases (as dividends are received). For the investor company to record dividends received as income would involve double counting because the investee company's income out of which the dividends are received has already been recognized as income by the investor company. The receipt of dividends is instead recorded as an increase in a current asset (Cash) along with a decrease in the noncurrent Investment account.

Comprehensive Example

To illustrate the equity method, suppose that the Davis Company purchases 25% of the outstanding common shares of the Bristol Company on January 1, 1983, for $50,000. The investment would be recorded by the Davis Company on this date as follows:

```
1983
Jan. 1   Investment in Bristol Company . . . . . . . . . . .   50,000
             Cash . . . . . . . . . . . . . . . . . . . . . .         50,000
         Acquired 25% of the outstanding common stock of
         Bristol Company.
```

EXHIBIT 17-1
Balance Sheet

BRISTOL COMPANY
Balance Sheet
January 1, 1983

Assets		Liabilities	
Current assets	$120,000	Current liabilities	$ 40,000
Noncurrent assets	280,000	Noncurrent liabilities	160,000
		Total Liabilities . . .	$200,000
		Stockholders' Equity	
		Common stock, no par . . .	$ 30,000
		Retained earnings	170,000
		Total Stockholders' Equity	$200,000
		Total Liabilities and Stockholders' Equity	
Total Assets	$400,000		$400,000

On January 1, 1983, the Bristol Company's condensed balance sheet was as shown in Exhibit 17-1.

At the end of 1983 the Bristol Company reported net income of $60,000 and paid dividends of $20,000. The income from the investment that is included in the Davis Company's income statement is:

$$
\begin{aligned}
\text{Income} &= \text{Investee's net income} \times \text{Ownership \%} \\
&= \$60,000 \times 25\% \\
&= \$15,000
\end{aligned}
$$

The dividends that are received by the Davis Company are:

$$
\begin{aligned}
\text{Dividends} &= \text{Total dividends paid by the investee} \times \text{Ownership \%} \\
&= \$20,000 \times 25\% \\
&= \$5,000
\end{aligned}
$$

The Davis Company would recognize its share of the Bristol Company's net income as follows:

```
1983
Dec. 31   Investment in Bristol Company . . . . . . . . . . .   15,000
              Income from Investment in Bristol Company              15,000
          To recognize 25% of Bristol Company's net
          income.
```

The receipt of the dividends from Bristol Company would be recorded by the Davis Company as follows:

```
Dec. 31   Cash  . . . . . . . . . . . . . . . . . . . . . . . .   5,000
              Investment in Bristol Company  . . . . . . . . .            5,000
          Dividends received from Bristol Company.
```

The book value of the Davis Company's investment at the end of 1983 is:

Cost of investment	$50,000
+ Share of Bristol Company's net income	
(25% × $60,000)	15,000
− Dividends received (25% × $20,000)	(5,000)
Book Value of Investment at Year End	$60,000

In order to further emphasize the rationale of the equity method, consider the balance sheet of the Bristol Company (the investee) after the above events have been recorded. The investment by the Davis Company has no effect on the balance sheet of the Bristol Company because the Davis Company purchased 25% of the *existing* outstanding shares. The earning of income and the payment of dividends by the Bristol Company do affect its balance sheet. By using the basic accounting equation (Assets = Liabilities + Stockholders' Equity) we can examine the effect of these events. For simplicity, we will assume that liabilities remain unchanged. The income and dividends have the following impact on Bristol Company's accounting equation (and balance sheet):

	Assets	=	Liabilities	+	Stockholders' Equity
Earning income	+ $60,000	=	0		+ $60,000
Payment of dividends	− 20,000	=	0		− 20,000
Net Effect	+ $40,000	=	0		+ $40,000

The net effect is an increase in the assets and the stockholders' equity of the Bristol Company of $40,000. The assets of the Bristol Company are now $440,000 ($400,000 at the beginning of the period plus the increase of $40,000) and the liabilities are $200,000 (it is assumed they remain unchanged), and therefore the net assets (stockholders' equity) are $240,000 ($440,000 − $200,000). Since the Davis Company owns 25% of the Bristol Company, it effectively owns 25% of the net assets of the company. The value of this 25% share is $60,000 (25% × $240,000). Note that this is exactly the balance of the Davis Company's account, Investment in Bristol Company.

The fact that the value in the Investment account of the investor company parallels the value of the ownership interest in the net assets (stockholders' equity) of the investee company is the primary justification for the equity method. It should be recognized that the values are *equal* only because the Davis Company made the original purchase of the shares at a cost ($50,000) that was equal to the value of the ownership interest in the net assets of the Bristol Company on January 1, 1983 [25% × ($30,000 common stock + $170,000 retained earnings) or 25% × ($400,000 assets − $200,000 liabilities)]. If the Davis Company had made the purchase for an amount different from $50,000, the value of the Investment in Bristol Company account at year end would not be equal to the ownership interest in the net assets of the Bristol Company. The increase in the value of the Investment account ($10,000), however, would be equal to the Davis Company's share of the increase in the net assets of the Bristol Company (25% × $40,000).

Some accountants and financial analysts criticize the equity method because the investor company recognizes income in excess of the cash received as dividends. They argue that the cash received from dividends is a more useful measure of the investor company's income. This criticism is not consistent with the accrual concept which has such a strong influence on accounting. In accrual accounting, income is recognized in the period in which it is earned and therefore income flows and cash flows are seldom, if ever, equal. The equity method is another example of the recognition of income on the accrual basis. An understanding of the above discussion of the equity method should enable the reader to recognize why generally accepted accounting principles require the use of the equity method when the investor company can exercise significant influence over the investee company.

ACCOUNTING FOR A CONTROLLING INTEREST

When an investor company owns more than 50% of the common stock of another company, the investor has control over the investee. **The parent company is the investor company that owns more than 50% of the outstanding common stock of the investee. The subsidiary company is the investee company that has more than 50% of its outstanding common stock owned by the investor.** The companies remain separate legal entities and maintain separate accounting records during the accounting period. The individual who owns stock in the parent company, however, is interested in financial statements that report the activities of the parent company and all the entities in which the parent company has a controlling interest. At the end of the accounting period, therefore, the results of operations and the ending financial position are accounted for in the parent company's annual report as if the separate legal entities are a single accounting entity. That is, a single set of financial statements is published. They are called consolidated financial statements. **Consolidated financial statements are the financial statements prepared by the parent company that owns more than 50% of the outstanding common stock of the subsidiary company.** The financial statements are the result of bringing together, or consolidating, the financial statements of the separate companies.

For example, the Ford Motor Company's financial statements represent the consolidated results of at least 45 separate companies. The individual who owns shares in Ford does not receive (or want) financial statements that report separately on the activities of each of the 45 companies. Instead a single set of consolidated financial statements is prepared. The separate legal entities are treated as a single accounting entity for financial reporting. Ideally, the investor in Ford should receive a set of financial statements that would be identical to the statements that would be prepared if the entire operations of Ford consisted of only one company. Although the consolidated financial statements are not identical, the principles used to prepare consolidated financial statements ensure that the consolidated financial statements are prepared in such a way that they are essentially the same as if there were only one company.

Consolidated financial statements are prepared when the ownership of a parent company in a subsidiary exceeds 50%.[2] For simplicity, however, we will assume in the following discussion that the parent company owns 100% of the subsidiary. Even when there is 100% ownership, it is common for the subsidiary to continue to exist as a separate legal entity. A major advantage of this continued separate legal identity is that the principle of limited liability applies to each corporation. Thus the parent company is not responsible for the debts of the subsidiary. There may also be other reasons, such as tax advantages, for maintaining the separate legal entities.

In principle the consolidated financial statements are the sum of the financial statements of the separate companies. Thus the assets and liabilities of the separate companies are added together in the consolidated balance sheet, and the revenues and expenses of the separate companies are combined in the consolidated income statement (except for the items discussed below). It is common, however, for the parent and subsidiary to buy and sell from each other and engage in other kinds of intercompany transactions. Since they are separate legal entities, they would record these transactions in their own accounting records. To avoid double counting, certain items that are included in the separate financial statements must be excluded from the consolidated financial statements.

Since each company maintains its own accounting records, there is no set of consolidated financial records. Thus there is no consolidated general journal or consolidated general ledger. The consolidated financial statements are prepared by using a worksheet. The adjusted trial balances of the parent and subsidiaries are listed on the worksheet and certain items are eliminated. **Eliminations are items that must be removed from the investor company's and the investee company's financial statements to avoid double counting in the consolidated financial statements.** The consolidated financial statements are prepared by adding together the adjusted trial balances after the eliminations. The eliminations appear only on the worksheet and do not affect the financial records of the individual companies. Some of the items that must be eliminated are discussed in the following sections.

Investment of the Parent and Stockholders' Equity of the Subsidiary

The parent company accounts for its investment in the subsidiary in its own accounting records by the equity method. Thus the parent company has an asset, Investment in Subsidiary, on its individual balance sheet. This asset represents the ownership of the assets of the subsidiary. When the assets of both companies are combined in the consolidated balance sheet, the Investment account must be eliminated to avoid double counting.

Furthermore, the stockholders' equity of the subsidiary is entirely owned by the parent (assuming 100% ownership). To include the stockholders' equity of both the parent and the subsidiary in the consolidated balance sheet would also result in double counting. Since the consolidated financial statements are prepared for the use of the stockholders of the parent company, the stockholders' equity of the subsidiary is eliminated.

---

[2] There are some exceptions to this rule. Financial subsidiaries and some foreign subsidiaries are not consolidated.

EXHIBIT 17-2   Preparation of Consolidated Balance Sheet

Parent Company and Its Subsidiary
Worksheet for Preparation of Consolidated Balance Sheet
December 31, 1983

	Parent Company	Subsidiary Company	Eliminations Debit	Eliminations Credit	Consolidated Balance Sheet
Cash	$ 70,000	$ 10,000			$ 80,000
Notes receivable	30,000	20,000		(b) 10,000	40,000
Inventory	80,000	30,000			110,000
Investment in subsidiary company	150,000			(a) 150,000	
Property, plant, and equipment (net)	270,000	160,000			430,000
	$600,000	$220,000			$660,000
Notes payable	$ 25,000	$ 20,000	(b) 10,000		$ 35,000
Bonds payable	100,000	50,000			150,000
Common stock, no par	200,000	100,000	(a) 100,000		200,000
Retained earnings	275,000	50,000	(a) 50,000		275,000
	$600,000	$220,000	$160,000	$160,000	$660,000

In summary, to avoid double counting the parent company's Investment account and the subsidiary company's stockholders' equity accounts must not be included (they must be eliminated) in the consolidated balance sheet. To illustrate this process consider the balance sheets of the Parent Company and the Subsidiary Company on December 31, 1983, which are shown in worksheet form[3] in Exhibit 17-2.

On January 1, 1983, the Parent Company had purchased all the common stock of the Subsidiary Company for $130,000 on the stock market, and the Parent Company's investment was recorded at the purchase price. At that time the Subsidiary Company's no-par common stock totaled $100,000 and its retained earnings totaled $30,000. During 1983 the Subsidiary earned income of $20,000 and no dividends were paid. This increased its Retained Earnings to $50,000. Since the Parent Company owns 100% of the common stock of the Subsidiary Company, it recorded its share of the Subsidiary's income (100% × $20,000) in its Investment account (in accordance with the principles described for the equity method), thereby increasing the Investment account balance to $150,000. The $150,000 balance in the Investment account of the Parent Company and the Subsidiary's Common Stock and Retained Earnings balances of $100,000 and $50,000, respectively, must be eliminated from the consolidated financial statements. Therefore the Investment account is reduced (credited) by $150,000 and the Subsidiary's Common Stock and Retained Earnings accounts are reduced (debited) by $100,000

[3] For simplicity, only the ending balance sheets are included in Exhibit 17-2. The adjusted trial balances and income statements are not included because many complexities involving these items are beyond the scope of this book.

and $50,000, respectively. This elimination entry, labeled (a) in Exhibit 17-2, is included only in the worksheet used to prepare the consolidated financial statements. It is not recorded in the accounting system of either company. Two examples of other eliminations are discussed below.

Intercompany Transactions

Parent and subsidiary companies often engage in transactions with each other. **Intercompany transactions are transactions between a parent and a subsidiary company.** These transactions must be eliminated when preparing consolidated financial statements.

INTERCOMPANY LOANS.   One company may loan money to the other, or one company may owe money as a result of a transaction. For example, suppose that in addition to the purchase of the common stock the Parent Company lent $10,000 to the Subsidiary Company. Therefore the Subsidiary Company has a note payable of $10,000 and the Parent Company has a note receivable of $10,000. To avoid double counting both the note payable and the note receivable must be eliminated. This is accomplished by reducing (debiting) the note payable of the Subsidiary Company and reducing (crediting) the note receivable of the Parent Company. This is shown as entry (b) in Exhibit 17-2.

The consolidated balance sheet is prepared by adding together the amounts from the individual balance sheets less the amounts eliminated, as shown in the last column in Exhibit 17-2.

SALES BETWEEN THE PARENT AND SUBSIDIARY.   When a sale is made from one company to another and both companies are included in the consolidated financial statements, the sale must be eliminated from the consolidated income statement. This elimination is required because no sale has occurred for the consolidated entity. It is only when a sale has been made outside the consolidated entity that sales revenue is recognized. Along with the elimination of the sale the cost of the inventory recorded as cost of goods sold by the other company must be eliminated.

For example, suppose that the Parent Company purchases inventory for $5,000 from the Subsidiary Company and sells it to outsiders for $9,000. The Subsidiary Company had originally purchased the inventory for $3,000. On their separate income statements, the two companies would include the following information:

	Parent	Subsidiary
Sales	$9,000	$5,000
Cost of goods sold	5,000	3,000
Gross Profit	$4,000	$2,000

For the consolidated entity, however, the sales to outsiders are only $9,000 and the cost of the goods sold to outsiders is only $3,000. Therefore when the consolidated income statement is prepared by adding together the income statements of the two companies, sales of $5,000 and cost of goods sold of $5,000 must be eliminated to avoid double counting.

Although sales between parent and subsidiary companies are usually the most significant elimination in the consolidated income statement, other eliminations may also be necessary. For example, interest revenue and interest expense on a loan between the companies would also have to be eliminated.

Purchase Price Greater Than the Book Value

In the earlier example the purchase price of $130,000 equaled the book value (net assets) of the Subsidiary Company. It was also assumed that the market value of the net assets was equal to the book value of the net assets. Neither of these conditions typically exists in a real transaction, however. Usually the purchase price exceeds the book value of the net assets of the Subsidiary Company.

In these situations the net assets of the subsidiary included in the consolidated balance sheet must be adjusted to their market value and goodwill must be recorded. It is appropriate to record the net assets at their market values because they represent the purchase prices of those individual assets. **Goodwill is recorded as the difference between the purchase price of the company and the market value of the net assets** (goodwill was discussed in Chapter 12). Remember that the accounting records of the subsidiary are *not* adjusted to record the market values. For example, suppose that in the earlier example the following values existed at the time of acquisition:

Price paid by Parent Company	$200,000
Market value of net assets of Subsidiary Company . .	170,000

Although the book value of the net assets of the Subsidiary Company at the time of acquisition was $130,000 ($100,000 common stock + $30,000 retained earnings), the market value of the net assets of the Subsidiary Company is $170,000 and

**EXHIBIT 17-3
Consolidated Balance Sheet**

PARENT COMPANY AND ITS SUBSIDIARY
Consolidated Balance Sheet
December 31, 1983

Assets		Liabilities	
Current assets		Current liabilities	
Cash	$ 10,000	Notes payable	$ 35,000
Notes receivable	40,000	Noncurrent liabilities	
Inventory	110,000	Bonds payable	150,000
Noncurrent assets		Total Liabilities . . .	$185,000
Property, plant, and			
equipment (net)	470,000	*Stockholders' Equity*	
Goodwill	30,000	Common stock, no par . . .	$200,000
		Retained earnings	275,000
		Total Stockholders' Equity	$475,000
		Total Liabilities and	
Total Assets	$660,000	Stockholders' Equity	$660,000

would be included in the ending consolidated balance sheet. Goodwill of $30,000 would also be recognized and included in the consolidated balance sheet. Goodwill is measured as the difference between the purchase price of $200,000 and the market value of the net assets. It is therefore valued at $30,000 ($200,000 − $170,000). Under these conditions the consolidated balance sheet of Parent Company would be as shown in Exhibit 17-3.

Comparing this balance sheet to the balance sheet shown in Exhibit 17-2, it may be seen that the cash is only $10,000 because the Parent Company would have $70,000 less cash since it paid that much more for the investment in the second example ($200,000 purchase price compared to $130,000). The property, plant, and equipment are $470,000 (instead of the $430,000 shown in Exhibit 17-2), because it is assumed that all of the $40,000 excess of the market value of the net assets above their book value ($170,000 compared to $130,000) is attributable to property, plant, and equipment. In addition, the goodwill of $30,000 is included on the consolidated balance sheet.

Minority Interest All the above examples have assumed that the parent purchased 100% of the common stock of the subsidiary. When the parent buys more than 50% but less than 100% of the stock, consolidated financial statements are prepared by using the same general principles discussed above. In this case, however, the subsidiary has other stockholders who own a minority interest in its net assets. **Minority interest is the ownership of other stockholders when the parent company owns less than 100% of the common stock of the subsidiary company.** The minority interest is included in the consolidated balance sheet. The amount of the minority interest is computed by multiplying the percentage ownership interest of the minority stockholders by the total stockholders' equity of the subsidiary.

To illustrate minority interest, suppose that in the first example the Parent Company purchased 70% of the common stock of the Subsidiary Company for $91,000 (70% × $130,000). The Parent Company would record its $14,000 (70% × $20,000) share of the Subsidiary's net income of $20,000, and therefore its investment account balance on December 31, 1983, would be $105,000 ($91,000 + $14,000 or 70% × $150,000 total stockholders' equity of subsidiary). The minority interest at December 31, 1983, is $45,000 (30% × $150,000). In this case the elimination of the stockholders' equity of the subsidiary at December 31, 1983, can be illustrated in journal entry form as follows (remember this is only recorded on a worksheet):

Common Stock, no par (subsidiary)	100,000	
Retained Earnings (subsidiary)	50,000	
Investment in Subsidiary (parent)		105,000
Minority Interest		45,000

The minority interest is often listed in the stockholders' equity section of the consolidated balance sheet, although it is sometimes listed in a separate section between liabilities and stockholders' equity.

NONCURRENT INVESTMENTS IN BONDS

Just as investor companies invest in the stock of investee companies, they also may invest in the bonds of other companies. Investments in bonds for short periods, current marketable securities, were discussed in Chapter 7. Accounting for non-current investments in bonds, however, does not follow the same principles, but instead parallels the accounting for bonds payable discussed in Chapter 16. A noncurrent investment in bonds is classified as such if management's intent is not to sell the bonds within 1 year or the operating cycle, whichever is longer.

An investor company would purchase the bonds of another company as a noncurrent investment to acquire a relatively safe source of continuing revenue or to establish a financial relationship with another company, perhaps a company whose stock it already owns. Insurance companies and companies with investments in pension funds often purchase bonds for the former reason. Because they can plan their cash payments to the insurance policyholders or the recipients of the pensions over a long period of time, they can plan to hold the bonds until maturity and avoid having to sell the bonds if their market price should become depressed.

Bonds Purchased at a Discount or Premium

Bonds are purchased at the current market price as an investment in order to earn periodic interest revenue and receive the face value on the maturity date. Bonds purchased at a discount or premium (i.e., at an amount below or above face value) are recorded at their acquisition cost, which includes the cost of the bonds, broker's fees, and transfer taxes. The cost is recorded in an Investment in Bonds account, and no separate discount or premium account is usually used.

Even though a separate discount or premium account is not used, the discount or premium (the difference between the purchase price and the face value) is amortized as an adjustment to interest revenue over the remaining life of the bonds. Thus the balance of the Investment account will increase (in the case of a purchase at a discount) or decrease (in the case of a purchase at a premium) over the life of the bonds until the balance equals the face value on the maturity date of the bonds. As with accounting for bonds payable the effective interest method should be used, although the straight-line method is acceptable if the results are not materially different. The related interest revenue is recognized periodically when cash is received and must also be accrued at the end of the accounting period. The interest revenue is included in the Other Revenues and Expenses section in the income statement.

To illustrate the accounting for a bond investment assume that the Wilkens Company purchased bonds issued by the Homestake Company with the following characteristics:

Date of purchase	Apr. 1, 1983
Maturity date	Mar. 31, 1988
Face value	$100,000
Contract rate	10%
Interest payment dates	Sept. 30 and Mar. 31
Yield	12%

Accounting for these bonds by the Homestake Company was discussed in Chapter

16, and it may be useful to refer to that chapter and compare the accounting by the Wilkens Company and the Homestake Company.

The purchase price of the bonds is $92,639.93, as discussed in Chapter 16 (brokerage fees and transfer taxes are ignored in this example).[4] The Wilkens Company records the acquisition on April 1, 1983, as follows:

```
1983
Apr. 1   Investment in Bonds . . . . . . . . . . . . .    92,639.93
           Cash . . . . . . . . . . . . . . . . . . . .                92,639.93
         Purchase of 10% Homestake Company bonds
         to yield 12%.
```

The discount of $7,360.07 ($100,000 − $92,639.93) can be amortized by either the straight-line method or the effective interest method each time the interest revenue is recorded.

Straight-Line Method

When a company uses the straight-line method to amortize a premium or discount for an investment in bonds, the semiannual amortization is computed by dividing the total premium or discount by the number of semiannual periods remaining in the life of the bonds. The semiannual interest receipt is calculated by multiplying the face value times half the annual contract rate. The semiannual premium (discount) amortization is then subtracted from (added to) the semiannual interest receipt to calculate the interest revenue for the semiannual period.

If the Wilkens Company amortizes the discount by using the straight-line method, the discount of $7,360.07 would be amortized evenly over 10 semiannual periods, or $736.01 ($7,360.07 ÷ 10, rounded) each period. Since the interest received on September 30, 1983, is $5,000 [$100,000 × (10% ÷ 2)] the interest revenue is $5,736.01 ($5,000 + $736.01). The receipt of the first interest payment on September 30, 1983, is recorded as follows:

```
1983
Sept. 30   Cash . . . . . . . . . . . . . . . . . . . .     5,000.00
           Investment in Bonds  . . . . . . . . . . . .       736.01
             Interest Revenue . . . . . . . . . . . .                 5,736.01
           To record receipt of interest on investment in
           Homestake Company bonds and discount
           amortization by the straight-line method.
```

When the straight-line method is used, the Wilkens Company recognizes the same amount of interest revenue each 6-month period. At December 31, 1983, however, the Wilkens Company must accrue interest revenue for the last 3 months of the year. The interest revenue is $2,868.00 ($5,736.01 × 3/6). The investment ac-

---

[4] The present value of the bonds is computed as follows:

$$\text{Present value} = \text{Present value of face value} + \text{Present value of interest payments}$$
$$= (\$100,000 \times .558395) + (\$5,000 \times 7.360087)$$
$$= \$55,839.50 + \$36,800.43$$
$$= \$92,639.93$$

count is increased by $368 ($736.01 × 3/6) and the interest receivable is $2,500 ($5,000 × 3/6). The journal entry to accrue the interest on December 31, 1983, is:

```
1983
Dec. 31   Interest Receivable . . . . . . . . . . . . . .   2,500.00
          Investment in Bonds . . . . . . . . . . . . . .     368.00
              Interest Revenue . . . . . . . . . . . . . .              2,868.00
          To accrue interest on investment in Home-
          stake Company bonds.
```

At the end of the year the Investment in Bonds account would be included in the Noncurrent Assets section of the balance sheet at a book value of $93,743.94 ($92,639.93 + $736.01 + $368.00). The $2,500 interest receivable would be included in the Current Assets section of the balance sheet. Interest revenue of $8,604.01 ($5,736.01 + $2,868.00) would be included in the Other Revenues and Expenses section of the 1983 income statement. To facilitate the recording of the interest revenue each period the Wilkens Company could prepare a discount or premium amortization schedule similar to Exhibits 16-3 and 16-4, except that the headings would be labeled Cash Received (debit), Increase (Decrease) in Investment (debit or credit), Interest Revenue (credit), and Book Value of Investment.

The Effective Interest Method

When a company uses the effective interest method to amortize the premium or discount for an investment in bonds, the interest revenue each semiannual period is computed by multiplying the semiannual yield rate by the book value of the investment at the beginning of the period. The semiannual interest receipt is calculated by multiplying half the annual contract rate times the face value of the bonds. The amortization of the discount or premium is the difference between the interest revenue and the interest received. If the Wilkens Company uses the effective interest method to amortize the discount, the interest revenue recognized on September 30, 1983, is $5,558.40 [(12% ÷ 2) × $92,639.93], the cash received is $5,000 [(10% × $\frac{1}{2}$) × $100,000], and the difference of $558.40 is the amortization of the discount that increases the book value of the Investment in Bonds. The journal entry on September 30, 1983, to record the interest revenue is:

```
1983
Sept. 30   Cash . . . . . . . . . . . . . . . . . . . . . .   5,000.00
           Investment in Bonds . . . . . . . . . . . . .        558.40
               Interest Revenue . . . . . . . . . . . . . .              5,558.40
           To record receipt of interest on investment in
           Homestake Company bonds and discount
           amortization by the effective interest method.
```

At December 31, 1983, the Wilkens Company must accrue interest revenue for the last 3 months of the year. The interest revenue is $2,795.95 [(12% ÷ 2) × ($92,639.93 + $558.40) × 3/6]. Since the interest receivable is $2,500

$[(10\% \div 2) \times \$100,000 \times 3/6]$ the increase in the value of the Investment is $\$295.95$ ($\$2,795.95 - \$2,500$). The journal entry to accrue this interest on December 31, 1983, is recorded as follows:

```
1983
Dec. 31   Interest Receivable  . . . . . . . . . . . . . .    2,500.00
          Investment in Bonds . . . . . . . . . . . . .         295.95
              Interest Revenue . . . . . . . . . . . . .                  2,795.95
          To accrue interest on investment in Home-
          stake Company bonds.
```

At the end of the year the Investment account would be included in the Noncurrent Assets section on the balance sheet at a book value of $\$93,494.28$ ($\$92,639.93 + \$558.40 + \$295.95$). The $\$2,500$ interest receivable would be included in the Current Assets on the balance sheet. Interest revenue of $\$8,354.35$ ($\$5,558.40 + \$2,795.95$) would be included in the Other Revenues and Expenses section of the 1983 income statement. Recognition of interest revenue in subsequent years would parallel the recording of the Homestake Company's interest expense. To facilitate the recording of the interest revenue each period the Wilkens Company could prepare a discount or premium amortization schedule similar to Exhibits 16-5 and 16-6, except that the headings would be labeled Cash Received (debit), Interest Revenue (credit), Increase (Decrease) in Investment (debit or credit), and Book Value of Investment.

Under either the effective interest or straight-line methods, the book value of the bonds in the balance sheet will increase (for bonds purchased at a discount) or decrease (for bonds purchased at a premium) until the book value equals the face value on the maturity date. The book value of the bonds under either method is not affected by any changes in the market value of the bonds.

LEASES

A lease is an agreement conveying the right to use property, plant, or equipment without transferring legal ownership of the item. For example, when a company leases a computer from IBM the company acquires the right to use the computer for the period of the lease, but it does not acquire legal ownership. IBM remains the legal owner of the computer. **The lessee is the company that acquires the right to use the property, plant, or equipment. The lessor is the company giving up the use of the property, plant, or equipment.** (For instance, IBM is the lessor in the above example.)

Note that a lease is an agreement conveying the right to use property, plant, and equipment and not an agreement to perform services. For example, if a coal exporting company signs an agreement with a shipping company to use specific ships for a period of time to transport the coal, a lease exists. If the agreement is only for the shipping company to transport an agreed volume of coal on whichever ships it chooses, a lease does not exist. Although this may be a narrow distinction, in the second case there is no agreement conveying the right to use *specific* property. In addition, as discussed below the risks and benefits of ownership of the ships have not been transferred from the shipping company to the coal company.

Before discussing how to account for leases, it is useful to compare leasing an asset to purchasing an asset on credit. For example, if a company purchases a building for use in its operations by issuing a 30-year mortgage, there is no doubt about how the transaction should be recorded. An operating asset, the building, and a noncurrent liability, the mortgage payable, are both recognized. Although the company owns the building, the mortgage company has a legally secured interest in the building to protect its financial interests.

Now suppose that a company leases a building for 30 years for use in its operations. It does not acquire legal ownership of the building but agrees to make lease payments for 30 years. In both the lease and the mortgage situations, the company purchasing the building and the company leasing the building will use the building in their operations and each is committed to make payments for 30 years. Should accountants focus on the legal difference and decide that for a lease there is no asset because there is no legal ownership even though both were acquired for use in operations? Does that mean there is no liability for the lessee despite the 30-year commitment to make lease payments? Or should accountants focus on the economic substance of the transaction and decide that both the purchaser of the building and the lessee of the building have engaged in substantially similar economic transactions to acquire operating assets? If so, the lease should result in the lessee recording both an operating asset and a noncurrent liability.

Accountants have generally concluded that economic substance is more important than legal form. Therefore generally accepted accounting principles require that the lessee record an operating asset and a noncurrent liability for a lease when substantially all the risks and benefits of ownership have been transferred by the lessor to the lessee. The specific criteria used to determine whether the risks and benefits of ownership have been transferred are beyond the scope of this book. A lease is considered to have transferred these risks and benefits, however, if the lessee is expected to acquire ownership of the property, plant, or equipment at the end of the life of the lease, if the lease is for more than 75% of the life of the property, or if the present value of the lease payments exceeds 90% of the fair value of the property.[5] Although these criteria are somewhat arbitrary, the reader should be able to recognize that if *any one* of them is satisfied the lessee has accepted the major risks and benefits of ownership.

A lease is a capital lease if it meets one of the criteria for transfer of the risks and benefits of ownership. A lease is an operating lease if it does not meet any of the criteria for transfer of the risks and benefits of ownership. Accounting for capital and operating leases for both the lessee and the lessor are discussed in the following sections. This discussion has focused only on the basic principles involved because accounting for leases is a very complex area involving numerous rules that are beyond the scope of this book.

---

[5] "Accounting for Leases," *FASB Statement No. 13* (Stamford, Conn.: FASB, 1975), par. 7.

If the lease meets the criteria of a capital lease, the lessee records an operating asset and a noncurrent liability. Both the asset and the liability are valued at the present value of the lease payments agreed to in the lease. Determination of the appropriate interest rate to use in the present value calculation is a complex procedure beyond the scope of this book, and therefore a rate will always be assumed. For example, suppose that the Adams Company enters into a capital lease for a computer from the Binary Company under the following terms:

Inception of lease	Jan. 1, 1983
Life of lease	8 years
Annual lease payments at the end of each year	$5,000
Date of first payment	Dec. 31, 1983
Interest rate	10%

The value at which to record the asset and liability is computed as follows:

$$\text{Present value of lease payments} = \text{Annual payment} \times \text{Present value of annuity factor for 8 periods at 10\%}$$
$$= \$5,000 \times 5.334926$$
$$= \$26,675 \text{ (rounded)}$$

The asset and liability would be recorded by the lessee (Adams Company) on January 1, 1983, as follows:

```
1983
Jan. 1   Leased Property . . . . . . . . . . . . . . . . . . . . .    26,675
              Obligation Under Capital Lease . . . . . . . . . .              26,675
         Acquired computer under lease from Binary
         Company.
```

The leased property is listed in the Property, Plant, and Equipment section of the balance sheet. The portion of the Obligation liability to be paid in the next year is included as a current liability, with the remaining portion classified as a noncurrent liability.

Since the Adams Company has recorded an asset, the cost must be amortized as an expense over its useful life (the term *amortization* is used more commonly than *depreciation* for leased property but the concept is exactly the same). The life of the lease is 8 years, and if it is assumed that straight-line amortization is used with no residual value, the amortization each year is calculated as follows:

$$\text{Annual Amortization} = \frac{\text{Cost of Leased Property} - \text{Estimated Residual Value}}{\text{Estimated Life}}$$
$$= \frac{\$26,675 - \$0}{8}$$
$$= \$3,334 \text{ (rounded)}$$

The Adams Company would record this amortization in the normal manner on December 31, 1983, as follows:

1983

Dec. 31   Amortization Expense   3,334
                Accumulated Amortization: Leased Property . .   3,334
            To record annual amortization on leased computer.

This entry would be repeated for each year of the asset's life. The amortization expense is classified as an operating expense on the income statement. The accumulated amortization is deducted from the Leased Property on the balance sheet to show the remaining book value of the asset.

As in other annuity situations involving compound interest, each $5,000 lease payment consists of a payment of both interest and principal. Every year when the Adams Company records the payment, it must separate the payment into the Interest Expense portion and the portion involving a reduction in the Obligation liability. The procedure used for this purpose is the effective interest method described in the previous chapter, except that if the lease payment is made annually as assumed in this example the *annual* interest rate is used in the interest expense computation.

The interest expense and the reduction in the liability are computed as follows:

$$
\begin{aligned}
\text{Interest expense} &= \text{Interest rate} \times \text{Book value of liability} \\
&= 10\% \times \$26,675 \\
&= \$2,667 \text{ (rounded)}
\end{aligned}
$$

$$
\begin{aligned}
\text{Reduction of liability} &= \text{Cash payment} - \text{Interest expense} \\
&= \$5,000 - \$2,667 \\
&= \$2,333
\end{aligned}
$$

EXHIBIT 17-4
Interest Expense and Amortization Expense for Lessee

Date	Lease Obligation[a]	Interest Expense[b]	Cash Payment[c]	Reduction in Lease Obligation[d]	Amortization Expense[e]	Total Expenses[f]
1/01/1983	$26,675					
12/31/1983	26,675	$2,667	$5,000	$2,333	$3,334	$6,001
12/31/1984	24,342	2,434	5,000	2,566	3,334	5,768
12/31/1985	21,776	2,178	5,000	2,822	3,334	5,512
12/31/1986	18,954	1,895	5,000	3,105	3,334	5,229
12/31/1987	15,849	1,585	5,000	3,415	3,334	4,919
12/31/1988	12,434	1,243	5,000	3,757	3,334	4,577
12/31/1989	8,677	868	5,000	4,132	3,334	4,202
12/31/1990	4,545	455[g]	5,000	4,545	3,337[h]	3,792

[a] Lease obligation from previous line less reduction in lease obligation; at 12/31/84, $26,675 − $2,333.

[b] Interest rate × Lease obligation (rounded); at 12/31/83, 10% × $26,675.

[c] Defined by the lease.

[d] Cash payment − Interest expense; at 12/31/83, $5,000 − $2,667.

[e] (Cost of leased property − Residual value) ÷ Life; ($26,675 − $0) ÷ 8 (rounded).

[f] Interest expense + Amortization expense; at 12/31/83, $2,667 + $3,334.

[g] Adjusted for rounding error of $1.

[h] Adjusted for rounding error of $3.

Therefore the journal entry to record the lease payment by the Adams Company on December 31, 1983, is:

```
1983
Dec. 31   Interest Expense . . . . . . . . . . . . . . . . . . . . .   2,667
          Obligation Under Capital Lease  . . . . . . . . . .   2,333
              Cash . . . . . . . . . . . . . . . . . . . . . . . .              5,000
          To record lease payment for computer.
```

The book value of the liability is now $24,342 ($26,675 − $2,333), and this amount is reported on the balance sheet. The amount payable in the next year ($5,000) is included as a current liability and the remaining portion ($19,342) as a noncurrent liability. The interest expense is included in the Other Revenues and Expenses section of the income statement.

The computation of the interest expense, reduction of the liability, and amortization expense for each of the years of the lease is shown in Exhibit 17-4. The calculation of the interest expense and reduction in liability for 1984 is as follows:

$$\begin{aligned}
1984 \text{ Interest expense} \quad &= \quad \text{Interest rate} \quad \times \quad \text{Book value of liability} \\
&= \quad 10\% \quad \times \quad \$24,342 \\
&= \quad \$2,434 \text{ (rounded)}
\end{aligned}$$

$$\begin{aligned}
1984 \text{ Reduction of liability} \quad &= \quad \text{Cash payment} \quad - \quad \text{Interest expense} \\
&= \quad \$5,000 \quad - \quad \$2,434 \\
&= \quad \$2,566
\end{aligned}$$

This procedure is followed every year for the remaining life of the lease, and the recording of the final lease payment will cause the book value of the liability, Obligation Under Capital Lease, to be reduced to zero.

Lessor Accounting for a Capital Lease

Since the lessee records an asset when there is a capital lease, it is consistent for the lessor to record the sale of the asset. Similarly, since the lessee has recorded the payments to be made as a liability, to be consistent the lessor should record the payments to be received as an asset. Therefore, in summary, a lessor records a capital lease as a sale on credit.

In the above example the Binary Company is the lessor. Since it has agreed to receive a series of lease payments that have a present value of $26,675, that is the value assigned to the asset (the receivable) and the sales revenue. The journal entry of the Binary Company to record the inception of the lease on January 1, 1983, is:

```
1983
Jan. 1   Lease Payments Receivable . . . . . . . . . . . . .   26,675
             Sales  . . . . . . . . . . . . . . . . . . . . . . . .              26,675
         Computer leased to Adams Company.
```

At the same time the Binary Company would record the cost of the computer as an expense (cost of goods sold). For example, if the computer cost $15,000, the Binary Company would also record the following entry:

```
1983
Jan. 1    Cost of Goods Sold . . . . . . . . . . . . . . . . .    15,000
              Inventory  . . . . . . . . . . . . . . . . . . . . . .              15,000
          To record cost of computer leased to Adams
          Company.
```

The Binary Company will receive $5,000 per year for the next 8 years. Each receipt consists of interest revenue and a reduction in the principal. Since the interest rate and the book value of the asset are the same as the interest rate and the book value of the liability for the lessee, the interest revenue for the lessor will be the same as the interest expense for the lessee. In the first year this revenue is $2,667 ($10\% \times \$26,675$). The $2,333 remainder of the $5,000 cash received is a reduction in the receivable account. Therefore the Binary Company would record the following journal entry on December 31, 1983:

```
1983
Dec. 31   Cash  . . . . . . . . . . . . . . . . . . . . . . . .    5,000
              Lease Payments Receivable  . . . . . . . . . .              2,333
              Interest Revenue . . . . . . . . . . . . . . . .              2,667
          To record cash received and interest earned on the
          leased computer.
```

In each subsequent period Interest Revenue will be calculated by multiplying the interest rate times the book value of the asset [$10\% \times (\$26,675 - \$2,333) = \$2,434$ in 1984], and the Lease Payments Receivable account will be reduced by the difference between the cash received and the interest revenue ($5,000 - \$2,434 = \$2,566$ in 1984).

The Lease Payments Receivable account is listed as an asset on the balance sheet. The amount receivable in the next year is included as a current asset and the remaining portion as a noncurrent asset. The interest revenue is included in the Other Revenues and Expenses section of the income statement.

Operating Lease   When a lease does not meet any of the criteria for a capital lease, it is classified as an operating lease. The lessee does not record an operating asset or a noncurrent liability, and the lessor does not record the sale or a noncurrent receivable.

If the lease of the computer was considered an operating lease, the Adams Company would record nothing at the inception of the lease. When the payment is made each December 31, the company would record the payment as an expense, commonly called Rent Expense, because the lease is being accounted for as a rental. The payment on December 31, 1983 (and each successive year) would be recorded as follows:

```
1983
Dec. 31   Rent Expense . . . . . . . . . . . . . . . . . . . .    5,000
              Cash . . . . . . . . . . . . . . . . . . . . . . . .              5,000
          Lease payment for computer.
```

The rent expense is included as an operating expense in the income statement.

The Binary Company would record the receipt as rent revenue as follows:

```
1983
Dec. 31   Cash  . . . . . . . . . . . . . . . . . . . . . . . .    5,000
              Rent Revenue  . . . . . . . . . . . . . . . .            5,000
          Received lease payment for computer.
```

When an asset is leased to another company under an *operating* lease, it is desirable for the lessor to classify the asset separately in the balance sheet under a caption such as Property Leased to Others, and therefore the following journal entry would be made by the Binary Company on January 1, 1983:

```
1983
Jan. 1    Property Leased to Others  . . . . . . . . . . . .   15,000
              Inventory  . . . . . . . . . . . . . . . . . . . . .          15,000
          Computer leased to Adams Company under
          operating lease.
```

In addition, the Binary Company would depreciate the computer since it is now included as an operating asset on its balance sheet. If it is assumed that the life of the computer is 8 years with no residual value and straight-line depreciation is used, the Binary Company would record depreciation of $1,875 ($15,000 ÷ 8) on December 31 (and each successive year) as follows:

```
1983
Dec. 31   Depreciation Expense . . . . . . . . . . . . . . .    1,875
              Accumulated Depreciation . . . . . . . . . . .            1,875
          To record depreciation on computer leased to
          Adams Company.
```

If it is assumed that the Binary Company is in the business of leasing, the rent revenue and the depreciation expense would both be included in operating income in the income statement.

Effects of Capital and Operating Leases on the Financial Statements

As a summary of accounting for capital and operating leases it is useful to emphasize the effects of the two types of leases on the financial statements. These effects are shown in Exhibit 17-5.

A review of the difference in the financial statement effects illustrated in Exhibit 17-5 should indicate to the reader the meaning of the term *off-balance sheet financing*. When the lease is classified as an operating lease, the lessee has obtained the use of the equipment without paying cash for it at the time of acquisition or showing a liability for future payments. Thus the equipment has been acquired by using financing that does not appear on the balance sheet.

Off-Balance Sheet Financing

In recent years there has been an increasing trend to structure transactions in such a way that a liability does not appear on the balance sheet. This is considered desirable by the company acquiring the asset because many financial analysts and banks consider the amount of the liabilities in proportion to the total assets to be a useful indicator of the financial stability of the company. Therefore keeping the

EXHIBIT 17-5
Effects of
Leases on the
Financial Statements

Capital Lease

Lessee	Lessor
Income Statement	*Income Statement*
Operating Expenses:	Revenues:
Amortization expense	Sales revenue (in the year of inception of the lease)
Other Revenues and Expenses:	Other Revenues and Expenses:
Interest expense	Interest revenue
Balance Sheet	*Balance Sheet*
Property, Plant, and Equipment:	Current Assets:
Leased property	Lease payments receivable (receivable within 1 year)
Less: Accumulated amortization	Noncurrent Assets:
Current Liabilities:	Lease payments receivable (receivable after 1 year)
Obligation under capital lease (payable within 1 year)	
Noncurrent Liabilities:	
Obligation under capital lease (payable after 1 year)	

Operating Lease

Lessee	Lessor
Income Statement	*Income Statement*
Operating Expenses:	Revenues:
Rent expense	Rent revenue
	Operating Expenses:
	Depreciation expense
Balance Sheet	*Balance Sheet*
No asset or liability	Noncurrent Assets:
	Property leased to others
	Less: Accumulated depreciation

liabilities lower will reflect favorably on the company. This is discussed further in Chapter 19. Many accountants and financial analysts, however, consider off-balance sheet financing to be undesirable because the substance of the transaction is ignored. Recently, the Financial Accounting Standards Board has increased the disclosures for companies that use off-balance sheet financing. The disclosures are included in the footnotes to each company's financial statements.

REVIEW PROBLEM

On January 1, 1983, the Simone Company was involved in the following transactions:

1. Purchased 40% of the outstanding common stock of the Holday Company for $150,000. The book value of the Holday Company net assets on this date was $375,000.

2. Signed a 6-year lease for a machine and agreed to pay $8,000 per year with the first payment to be made on December 31, 1983. The interest rate is 12% and the lease is a capital lease. The machine has no expected residual value at the end of the lease.

At the end of 1983 the Holday Company reported net income of $60,000 and paid dividends of $25,000.

Required: 1. Prepare all the necessary journal entries for 1983 based on the above information.
2. Prepare the relevant sections of the Simone Company's financial statements for 1983.

**SOLUTION TO
REVIEW
PROBLEM**

Requirement 1:

1983
Jan. 1

| Investment in Holday Company .... | 150,000 | |
| Cash .... | | 150,000 |

Purchased 40% of the common stock of Holday Company.

1

| Leased Property .... | 32,891[a] | |
| Obligation Under Capital Lease ...... | | 32,891 |

Signed a 6-year lease for a machine.

[a] $8,000 × 4.111407 (rounded)

Dec. 31

| Investment in Holday Company .... | 24,000[a] | |
| Income from Investment in Holday Company .... | | 24,000 |

To recognize 40% of Holday Company's net income.

[a] 40% × $60,000

31

| Cash .... | 10,000[a] | |
| Investment in Holday Company ...... | | 10,000 |

Dividends received from Holday Company.

[a] 40% × $25,000

31

Interest Expense	3,947[a]	
Obligation Under Capital Lease	4,053[b]	
Cash		8,000

To record lease payment for machine.

[a] 12% × $32,891 (rounded)
[b] $8,000 − $3,947

31	Amortization Expense	5,482[a]	
	Accumulated Amortization:		
	Leased Property		5,482

To record annual amortization on leased machine.

[a] ($32,891 − $0) ÷ 6 (rounded)

Requirement 2:

SIMONE COMPANY
Partial Income Statement
For Year Ended December 31, 1983

Operating Expenses:	
Amortization expense	$ (5,482)
Other revenues and expenses:	
Interest expense	$ (3,947)
Income from Investment in Holday Company	24,000

SIMONE COMPANY
Partial Balance Sheet
December 31, 1983

Long-term investments:		
Investment in Holday Company		$164,000[a]
Property, plant, and equipment:		
Leased property	$32,891	
Less: Accumulated amortization	5,482	27,409
Current liabilities:		
Obligation under capital lease		8,000
Noncurrent liabilities:		
Obligation under capital lease		20,838[b]

[a] $150,000 + $24,000 − $10,000
[b] $32,891 − $4,053 − $8,000 (current portion of the liability)

GLOSSARY

Consolidated Financial Statements.   Financial statements prepared by an investor company (the parent) that owns more than 50% of the outstanding common stock of an investee company (the subsidiary). The financial statements of each company are combined into consolidated financial statements.

Capital Lease.   A lease in which substantially all the risks and benefits of ownership are considered to have been transferred from the lessor to the lessee and which is recorded as the acquisition of an asset by the lessee and the sale of an asset by the lessor.

Eliminations.   Items that must be removed from the investor company's and investee company's financial statements to prevent double counting in a set of consolidated financial statements.

Equity Method.   A method of accounting for a long-term investment in the common stock of an investee company that is used when the investor company has significant influence over the investee (e.g., 20% or more ownership). The investor company recognizes income based on the percentage ownership in the investee.

Intercompany Transactions. Transactions between a parent and subsidiary company. These transactions must be eliminated when consolidated financial statements are prepared.

Investee Company. The company whose common stock has been purchased by another company (the investor).

Investor Company. The company that has acquired the common stock of another company (the investee).

Lower of Cost or Market Method. A method of accounting for an investment in the common stock of an investee company that is used when the investor does not have significant influence over the investee (e.g., less than 20% ownership). The portfolio of noncurrent investments in stocks is reported at the lower of cost or the aggregate market value of the portfolio on the balance sheet date.

Lease. An agreement conveying the right to use property, plant, or equipment (without passage of legal title).

Lease Payments Receivable. An asset recognized by the lessor of a capital lease. It is recorded at the present value of the remaining lease payments to be received.

Leased Property. An asset recognized by the lessee of a capital lease. It is reported at the present value of the total lease payments, less the accumulated amortization. Included in Property, Plant, and Equipment in the balance sheet.

Minority Interest. The ownership interest of other stockholders when the parent company owns less than 100% of the common stock of the subsidiary company. Included in a consolidated balance sheet.

Obligation Under Capital Lease. A liability recognized by the lessee under a capital lease. It is recorded at the present value of the remaining lease payments.

Operating Lease. A lease in which substantially all the risks and benefits of ownership have not been transferred from the lessor to the lessee.

Parent. The investor company that owns more than 50% of the outstanding common stock of the investee (subsidiary) company.

Significant Influence. The criterion that must exist for the equity method of accounting to be used. Significant influence is presumed to exist when the investor owns 20% or more of the outstanding common stock of the investee.

Subsidiary. The investee company that has more than 50% of its outstanding common stock owned by the investor (parent) company.

QUESTIONS

Q17-1 Why may a company make a long-term investment in the stock of another company rather than a short-term investment in the same stock?

Q17-2 Define the terms investor company and investee company.

Q17-3 What are the three methods that may be used to account for a noncurrent investment in the common stock of another company? When is each used?

Q17-4 What characteristics may be used to indicate that the investor company has significant influence over the investee company?

Q17-5 An investor may purchase shares on the stock market or from the investee company itself. How does each of these methods of acquisition affect the investee company's financial statements?

Q17-6 When the lower of cost or market method is used for noncurrent marketable investments in stock, how is a decline in the value of the securities included in the financial statements?

Q17-7 Why do some accountants criticize the lower of cost or market method?

Q17-8 Why is the equity method considered to be a better accounting method than the lower of cost or market method for certain types of investments?

Q17-9 When the equity method is used, how does the investor company record the value of its investment? How does the investor company record the income earned on its investment?

Q17-10 When the equity method is used, what is the relationship between the change in the balance of the investor company's investment account and the change in the balance sheet of the investee company?

Q17-11 When a consolidated balance sheet is prepared, why is it necessary to eliminate certain items? Give two examples of items that might be eliminated.

Q17-12 When a consolidated income statement is prepared, why is it necessary to eliminate certain items? Give two examples of items that might be eliminated.

Q17-13 What is minority interest? Where would it appear in a consolidated balance sheet? How is it computed?

Q17-14 Why may a company make a long-term investment in the bonds of another company?

Q17-15 How does the recording of an investment in bonds differ from the recording of bonds payable?

Q17-16 What are the two methods by which a premium or discount on an investment in bonds may be amortized? Explain how interest revenue is calculated for each method.

Q17-17 Define a lease. Under what conditions is a lease considered a capital lease? An operating lease?

Q17-18 If ABC Company leases a machine from the XYZ Company, which company is the lessee? The lessor?

Q17-19 If there is a capital lease for a building, does the lessee or the lessor include the building and amortization (depreciation) expense in its financial statements?

Q17-20 If there is a capital lease, how does the lessee compute its interest expense? How does the lessor compute its interest revenue? How does the lessee compute the reduction in its liability? How does the lessor compute the reduction in its receivable?

Q17-21 What is off-balance sheet financing? Why do some companies find such financing attractive?

EXERCISES

E17-1 **Lower of Cost or Market Method.** On September 15, 1983, the Morton Corporation purchased shares of common stock (all less than 20% of the outstanding stock) in three companies as a long-term investment. No dividends were declared or received on any of the shares during 1983. The costs and the market values on December 31, 1983, were as follows:

	Number of Shares	Cost per Share	Market Value per Share
Moses Company	100	$20	$23
Upchurch Company	200	40	41
Jensen Company	500	10	8

Required: Show all of the items that will appear in the Morton Corporation's financial statements in 1983 relating to the investment.

E17-2 Lower of Cost or Market Method. Use the same information as in E17-1. Assume that the Morton Corporation sold the shares of the Jensen Company on December 10, 1984, for $7 per share.

Required:
1. How much is the gain or loss that is recognized on the sale?
2. If the prices of the shares in the other two companies have not changed since December 31, 1983, show all of the items that will appear in the Morton Corporation's 1984 financial statements relating to the investment.

E17-3 Equity Method. On January 1, 1983, the Jackson Company purchased 10,000 shares of the Rizzo Company, which represented 40% of its outstanding common stock. On that date the book value of the net assets of the Jackson Company was $125,000. The total cost of the shares was $50,000. At the end of 1983 the Rizzo Company reported net income of $30,000 and paid total dividends of $12,000.

Required:
1. How much does the Jackson Company recognize as income for 1983?
2. What is the book value of the investment reported in the balance sheet of the Jackson Company on December 31, 1983?

E17-4 Equity Method. On January 1, 1983, the Foley Company purchased 20,000 shares of the Preston Company for $100,000. This represents 25% of the Preston Company's outstanding shares. On that date the book value of the net assets of the Preston Company was $400,000. On December 31, 1983, the Foley Company reported a balance in its investment account of $120,000. The Preston Company did not pay dividends during 1983.

Required:
1. How much did the Foley Company report as 1983 income on its investment?
2. What was the total net income of the Preston Company during 1983?

E17-5 Investment in Bonds and the Straight-Line Method. On January 1, 1983, the Porter Company purchased 12%, 20-year bonds with a face value of $100,000 for $97,500. Interest is paid on June 30 and December 31. The company uses the straight-line amortization method.

Required:
1. Compute the interest revenue recorded during 1983.
2. What would be the balance of the Investment in Bonds account on the Porter Company's December 31, 1983, balance sheet?

E17-6 Investment in Bonds and the Effective Interest Method. On January 1, 1983, the Robinson Company purchased 10%, 10-year bonds with a face value of $100,000 for $113,590.33. At this price the bonds yield 8%. Interest on the bonds is paid on June 30 and December 31. The company uses the effective interest method of amortization.

Required:
1. Compute the interest revenue recorded during 1983.
2. What would be the balance of the Investment in Bonds account on the Robinson Company's December 31, 1983, balance sheet?

E17-7   Consolidated Balance Sheet.   On January 1, 1983, the Kyle Company had total assets of $300,000, including cash of $20,000, a note receivable of $30,000, inventory of $80,000, property, plant, and equipment of $120,000, and investment in the Swensen Company of $50,000; liabilities of $200,000; and stockholders' equity of $100,000. The Swensen Company had assets of $120,000, consisting of cash of $10,000, inventory of $40,000, and property, plant, and equipment of $70,000; liabilities of $70,000; and stockholders' equity of $50,000. The Kyle Company owns 100% of the outstanding common stock of the Swensen Company.

Required: Prepare a consolidated balance sheet on January 1, 1983, for the Kyle Company and its subsidiary.

E17-8   Consolidated Income Statement.   During 1983 the Merman Company had sales of $50,000, cost of goods sold of $20,000, and operating expenses of $18,000. During 1983 the Harrison Company had sales of $40,000, cost of goods sold of $16,000, and operating expenses of $12,000. The Merman Company owns 100% of the outstanding common stock of the Harrison Company. Included in the above sales were goods costing the Harrison Company $6,000 which it sold to the Merman Company for $9,000. The Merman Company has resold the goods to its outside customers.

Required: Prepare a consolidated income statement for the Merman Company and its subsidiary for 1983.

E17-9   Minority Interest.   On January 1, 1983, the Norel Company purchased 80% of the common stock of the Weir Company for $96,000. At that date the Weir Company had common stock of $50,000 and retained earnings of $70,000.

Required: 1. How much is the minority interest on the January 1, 1983, consolidated balance sheet?
2. Prepare the necessary elimination entry for the worksheet in general journal form.

E17-10   Expense and Income from Capital Lease.   On January 1, 1983, the Thompson Company leased a computer from the Hexad Company. The lease was a capital lease, and the asset and liability were recorded by the Thompson Company at $84,000 based on a 10% interest rate and a 12-year life. The lease payment of $12,328 is made at the end of each year. The company uses the straight-line amortization (depreciation) method for the leased asset and no residual value is expected.

Required: 1. What is the interest expense and the amortization expense for the Thompson Company in 1983?
2. How much income from the lease would the Hexad Company recognize in 1983 if the cost of the computer to it was $70,000? Show your calculations.

E17-11   Operating Lease.   Using the information in E17-10 assume the lease was classified as an operating lease.

Required: 1. How much expense due to the lease will the Thompson Company recognize in 1983?
2. How much income from the lease will the Hexad Company recognize in 1983?
3. On which company's balance sheet will the computer be recorded at the end of 1983? Why?

E17-12   Capital Lease — Lessee.   On January 1, 1983, the Eton Company leased a Rolls Royce from Elite Cars for the president's use. The lease specified that $20,000 was to be paid at the end of each year for 5 years. The lease was classified as a capital lease. The interest rate is 12%. The straight-line amortization (depreciation) method and a zero residual value are used.

Required: 1. Show how the leased asset would be reported on the balance sheet of the Eton Company at December 31, 1983.
2. What is the amount of the liability on the balance sheet of the Eton Company at December 31, 1983?

E17-13   Operating Lease — Lessee and Lessor.   On January 1, 1983, the Meyers Company leased a jet from the Harris Aviation Company. The jet cost the Harris Aviation Company $400,000 to build. The company uses the straight-line amortization (depreciation) method with an estimated life of 10 years and an estimated residual value of $50,000. The lease is for 8 years and requires a payment of $100,000 on December 31 each year. The lease is classified as an operating lease.

Required: 1. Prepare the journal entry to record the lease for the Meyers Company during 1983.
2. Prepare a partial income statement for 1983 for the Meyers Company.
3. Prepare journal entries to record the lease for the Harris Aviation Company during 1983.
4. Prepare a partial income statement for 1983 and a partial balance sheet at December 31, 1983, for the Harris Aviation Company.

PROBLEMS

Part A

P17-1A   Lower of Cost or Market.   The Prestridge Corporation uses the lower of cost or market method to account for its noncurrent investments in common stock. The following information is available for its noncurrent investment account:

January 1, 1983. Purchased common stock as follows:
   Wright Company, 700 shares for $20 per share
   Armstrong Company, 500 shares for $30 per share
   Keyworth Company, 900 shares for $15 per share

December 31, 1983.

	Cost per Share	Market Value per Share	Dividends Received per Share
Wright Company	$20	$19	$1
Armstrong Company	30	28	2
Keyworth Company	15	16	1

June 10, 1984. Sold 500 shares of Wright Company for $19 per share.

August 15, 1984. Sold 300 shares of Keyworth Company for $17 per share.

December 31, 1984.

	Cost per Share	Market Value per Share	Dividends Received per Share
Wright Company	$20	$21	$1
Armstrong Company	30	35	2
Keyworth Company	15	17	1

Required: 1. Prepare journal entries to record the above events for the Prestridge Corporation. The corporation records dividend revenue when the cash is received.
2. Prepare partial income statements for 1983 and 1984 and also partial balance sheets at December 31, 1983, and December 31, 1984, relating to the above events for the Prestridge Corporation.

P17-2A **Equity Method.** The Carter Company purchased, on the stock market, 40,000 of the 160,000 outstanding shares of the Chavous Company on January 1, 1983, for $200,000. The condensed balance sheet of the Chavous Company on January 1, 1983, is as follows:

CHAVOUS COMPANY
Balance Sheet
January 1, 1983

Assets		*Liabilities*	
Current assets	$ 400,000	Current liabilities	$ 100,000
Noncurrent assets	800,000	Noncurrent liabilities . . .	300,000
		Total Liabilities	$ 400,000
		Stockholders' Equity	
		Common stock, no par . .	$ 350,000
		Retained earnings	450,000
		Total Stockholders' Equity	$ 800,000
		Total Liabilities and	
Total Assets	$1,200,000	Stockholders' Equity . . .	$1,200,000

At the end of 1983 the Chavous Company reported net income of $200,000 and paid dividends of $50,000.

Required: 1. Prepare journal entries to record the above events in 1983 for the Carter Company.
2. Prepare a partial income statement for 1983 and a partial balance sheet at December 31, 1983, for the Carter Company relating to the above events.
3. Assuming that noncurrent assets decreased by $50,000 and liabilities and common stock are unchanged, prepare a condensed balance sheet for the Chavous Company at December 31, 1983.
4. What is the relationship between the change in the balance of the Investment account of the Carter Company since the purchase of the investment and the change in the balance sheet of the Chavous Company?

P17-3A **Investments in Bonds and the Straight-Line Method.** On January 1, 1983, the Andrews Company purchased noncurrent investments in the bonds of two companies:

	Damar	Ackerman
Cost	$78,000	$65,000
Face value	$80,000	$60,000
Maturity date	Dec. 31, 1990	Dec. 31, 1988
Contract rate	10%	12%

Both bonds pay interest on June 30 and December 31. The company uses the straight-line method to amortize any premiums or discounts in regard to the investments in bonds.

Required: 1. Prepare journal entries for the Andrews Company to record all the events for the investments in 1983.
2. Show how the balance of the Investments account would be reported on the December 31, 1983, balance sheet of the Andrews Company.

P17-4A **Investments in Bonds and the Effective Interest Method.** On January 1, 1983, the Nairne Company purchased noncurrent investments in the bonds of two companies:

	Simon Company	Fraser Company
Face value	$50,000	$30,000
Maturity date	Dec. 31, 1988	Dec. 31, 1992
Contract rate	9%	7%
Yield	8%	8%

Both bonds pay interest on June 30 and December 31. The company uses the effective interest method to amortize any premiums or discounts in regard to the investments in bonds.

Required: 1. Compute the purchase price of each bond issue.
2. Prepare journal entries for the Nairne Company to record all the events for the investments during 1983.
3. Compute the book value of each investment at December 31, 1983.

P17-5A Consolidation. On June 30, 1983, the Milo Company purchased 100% of the common stock of the Alpha Company. In addition, on the same date the Alpha Company borrowed $20,000 from the Milo Company by issuing a note. After these transactions the balance sheet accounts of the two companies on June 30, 1983, were as follows:

Assets	Milo Company	Alpha Company
Cash	$ 12,000	$ 9,000
Accounts receivable	30,000	8,000
Notes receivable	50,000	30,000
Inventory	80,000	40,000
Investment in Alpha Company	70,000	–
Property, plant, and equipment (net)	120,000	80,000
Total Assets	$362,000	$167,000

Liabilities and Stockholders' Equity		
Accounts payable	$ 62,000	$ 27,000
Notes payable	60,000	70,000
Common stock, no par	100,000	40,000
Retained earnings	140,000	30,000
Total Liabilities and Stockholders' Equity	$362,000	$167,000

Required: Prepare the consolidated balance sheet for the Milo Company and its subsidiary at June 30, 1983.

P17-6A Capital Lease — Lessee. On January 1, 1983, the Odoms Company leased a building from the Weese Development Company. The lease is for 20 years and requires a payment of $10,000 on December 31 of each year. An interest rate of 10% is used and the lease is classified as a capital lease. The company uses the straight-line amortization (depreciation) method and no residual value is expected.

Required: 1. Prepare the journal entries to record the lease for the Odoms Company during 1983.
2. Prepare a partial income statement for 1983 and a partial balance sheet at December 31, 1983, for the Odoms Company relating to the lease.

P17-7A Capital Lease — Lessor. Use the information in P17-6A. The building cost the Weese Development Company $50,000 to construct.

Required: 1. Prepare journal entries to record the lease for the Weese Development Company during 1983.
2. Prepare a partial income statement for 1983 and a partial balance sheet at December 31, 1983, for the Weese Development Company relating to the lease.

PROBLEMS

Part B

P17-1B **Lower of Cost or Market.** The Adams Corporation uses the lower of cost or market method to account for its noncurrent investments in common stock. The following information is available for its noncurrent investment account:

March 21, 1983. Purchased common stock as follows:
Stephens Company, 300 shares for $30 per share
Wheaton Company, 800 shares for $15 per share
White Company, 500 shares for $20 per share

December 31, 1983.

	Cost per Share	Market Value per Share	Dividends Received per Share
Stephens Company	$30	$32	$2
Wheaton Company	15	13	1
White Company	20	17	1

July 2, 1984. Sold 150 shares of Stephens Company stock for $33 per share.

September 9, 1984. Sold 400 shares of White Company stock for $16 per share.

December 31, 1984.

	Cost per Share	Market Value per Share	Dividends Received per Share
Stephens Company	$30	$31	$2
Wheaton Company	15	14	1
White Company	20	16	1

Required: 1. Prepare journal entries to record the above events for the Adams Corporation. The corporation records dividend revenue when the cash is received.
2. Prepare partial income statements for 1983 and 1984 and partial balance sheets at December 31, 1983, and December 31, 1984, relating to the above events for the Adams Corporation.

P17-2B **Equity Method.** The Wild Company purchased, on the stock market, 75,000 of the 225,000 outstanding shares of the Dynan Company on January 1, 1983, for $300,000. The condensed balance sheet of the Dynan Company on January 1, 1983, is as follows:

DYNAN COMPANY
Balance Sheet
January 1, 1983

Assets		Liabilities	
Current assets	$ 600,000	Current liabilities	$ 200,000
Noncurrent assets	900,000	Noncurrent liabilities . . .	400,000
		Total Liabilities	$ 600,000
		Stockholders' Equity	
		Common stock, no par . .	$ 400,000
		Retained earnings	500,000
		Total Stockholders' Equity	$ 900,000
		Total Liabilities and	
Total Assets	$1,500,000	Stockholders' Equity . . .	$1,500,000

At the end of 1983 the Dynan Company reported net income of $300,000 and paid dividends of $60,000.

Required: 1. Prepare journal entries to record the above events in 1983 for the Wild Company.
2. Prepare a partial income statement for 1983 and a partial balance sheet at December 31, 1983, for the Wild Company relating to the above events.
3. Assuming that noncurrent assets increased by $100,000 and that liabilities and common stock are unchanged, prepare a condensed balance sheet for the Dynan Company at December 31, 1983.
4. What is the relationship between the change in the balance of the Investment account of the Wild Company since the purchase of the investment and the change in the balance sheet of the Dynan Company?

P17-3B **Investments in Bonds and the Straight-Line Method.** On January 1, 1983, the Gooch Company purchased noncurrent investments in the bonds of two companies:

	Tanner	*Carew*
Cost	$46,000	$92,000
Face value	$50,000	$90,000
Maturity date	Dec. 31, 1989	Dec. 31, 1994
Contract rate	12%	11%

Both bonds pay interest on June 30 and December 31. The company uses the straight-line method to amortize any premium or discount in regard to the investments in bonds.

Required: 1. Prepare journal entries for the Gooch Company to record all of the events for the investments during 1983.
2. Show how the balance of the Investments account would be reported on the December 31, 1983, balance sheet of the Gooch Company.

P17-4B **Investments in Bonds and the Effective Interest Method.** On January 1, 1983, the Winfrey Company purchased noncurrent investments in the bonds of two companies:

	Bates Company	*Clevett Company*
Face value	$80,000	$60,000
Maturity date	Dec. 31, 1987	Dec. 31, 1992
Contract rate	9%	11%
Yield	10%	10%

Both bonds pay interest on June 30 and December 31. The company uses the effective interest method to amortize any premium or discount in regard to the investments in bonds.

Required: 1. Compute the purchase price of each bond issue.
2. Prepare journal entries for the Winfrey Company to record all of the events for the investments during 1983.
3. Compute the book value of each investment at December 31, 1983.

P17-5B **Consolidation.** On January 1, 1983, the Bashor Company purchased 100% of the common stock of the Cohen Company. It paid $110,000, which was equal to the book value of the Cohen Company at that time. During the year the Cohen Company earned income of $30,000 and no dividends were paid. In addition, the Bashor Company sold goods costing $10,000 to the Cohen Company for $15,000 on account. The account has not yet been paid. The Cohen Company sold these goods to its outside customers for $25,000 cash. At December 31, 1983, the balance sheets of the two companies were as follows:

Assets	Bashor Company	Cohen Company
Cash	$ 30,000	$ 14,000
Accounts receivable	52,000	21,000
Notes receivable	43,000	13,000
Inventory	90,000	52,000
Investment in Cohen Company	140,000	–
Property and equipment (net)	100,000	75,000
Total Assets	$455,000	$175,000

Liabilities and Stockholders' Equity		
Accounts payable	$ 75,000	$ 20,000
Notes payable	35,000	15,000
Common stock, no par	120,000	60,000
Retained earnings	225,000	80,000
Total Liabilities and Stockholders' Equity . . .	$455,000	$175,000

Required:　1. Develop a worksheet for the preparation of a consolidated balance sheet for the Bashor Company and its subsidiary on December 31, 1983.

2. What items would be eliminated on a consolidated income statement for 1983?

P17-6B　Capital Lease — Lessee.　On January 1, 1983, the Ventrello Company leased a jet from the Cate Aviation Company. The lease is for 8 years and requires a payment of $200,000 on December 31 each year. The lease is classified as a capital lease and the interest rate is 12%. The company uses the straight-line amortization (depreciation) method and no residual value is expected.

Required:　1. Prepare journal entries to record the lease for the Ventrello Company during 1983.

2. Prepare a partial income statement for 1983 and a partial balance sheet at December 31, 1983, for the Ventrello Company in regard to the lease.

P17-7B　Capital Lease — Lessor.　Use the information in P17-6B. The jet cost the Cate Aviation Company $400,000 to build.

Required:　1. Prepare journal entries to record the lease for the Cate Aviation Company during 1983.

2. Prepare a partial income statement for 1983 and a partial balance sheet at December 31, 1983, for the Cate Aviation Company in regard to the lease.

DISCUSSION CASES

C17-1　Investments in Common Stock.　When a company buys common stock of another company the acquisition can be accounted for under one of four alternative methods: lower of cost or market with the loss on the decline in market value included in the income statement; lower of cost or market with the "loss" included in stockholders' equity; the equity method; or consolidation. Each method results in different amounts appearing in various sections of the financial statements.

Required:　1. In what situation is each of the four methods used?

2. Explain how the results of the four methods appear on the financial statements.

3. Explain the justification for requiring the use of each of the four different methods from the perspective of the user of the financial statements.

C17-2 **Leasing.** The Byrne Company is planning to acquire some office machinery. It is considering three different methods of acquiring the machinery, which has a 6-year life and no residual value.

(a) Buy the machinery for $50,000, pay $10,000 down, and borrow the balance from a bank at 10% for 6 years. Interest is to be paid on December 31 each year.
(b) Lease the machinery under a 6-year lease, which would be classified as a capital lease. The lease would require a payment of $15,000 at the end of each year. There is no option to buy the machinery included in the lease.
(c) Lease the machinery under a 1-year lease, which would be classified as an operating lease. The company intends to renew the lease each year for 6 years. The lease payment, which is due when the lease is signed, is $15,000.

Required: 1. Prepare an analysis (using assumptions that you think are appropriate) of the cash flows the company would pay over the 6 years under each alternative.
2. Explain how each of the alternatives would affect the financial statements.
3. Which alternative would you recommend?

18 | Statement of Changes in Financial Position

After reading this chapter, you should understand:

- The need for a statement of changes in financial position
- The uses of the statement
- How to prepare the statement
- The differences between net income and sources of funds from operations
- The differences between working capital and cash provided by operations
- The items included in the sources of financial resources
- The items included in the uses of financial resources
- The investing and financing transactions not affecting working capital or cash

Throughout this textbook we have studied two major financial statements: the income statement, which summarizes the results of the operating activities of a company during the accounting period, and the balance sheet, which shows the financial position of the company at a specific time in the accounting period. A vital link between the company's activities and the information reported to the users of accounting information is missing. A financial statement is needed to report the results of a company's financing and investing activities during the accounting period. This statement should report such items as how much working capital was increased because of operations, what proceeds were received from the issuance of stocks or bonds, and how the acquisition of equipment was financed. This financial statement, known as the statement of changes in financial position, is the subject of this chapter.

BACKGROUND AND CURRENT REPORTING REQUIREMENTS

Companies have prepared versions of the statement of changes in financial position for a long time. These reports were mainly used to assist the managers of the business in day-to-day operations, however. These statements were referred to by many names, including the "sources and uses statement," the "working capital flow statement," the "cash flow statement," and the "funds statement." This last term is still commonly used today. When defining the "funds" used in financing and investing activities, some companies reported on the sources and uses of cash, others on working capital (current assets minus current liabilities), and still others on a combination of cash and marketable securities. Until 1971 companies were not required to include such a statement in reports prepared for external users. In that year the Accounting Principles Board required that a statement of changes in financial position be shown whenever a balance sheet or income statement is issued.[1]

A statement of changes in financial position is a financial statement that shows the results of the financing and investing activities of a company, includ-

EXHIBIT 18-1
Statement of
Changes in
Financial Position

RAINEY CORPORATION
Statement of Changes in Financial Position
For Year Ended December 31, 1983

Sources of Working Capital

Sources from Operations:		
Net income	$10,000	
Add: Items not requiring working capital		
Depreciation expense	2,000	
Working capital provided by operations		$12,000
Other Sources of Working Capital:		
Issuance of common stock		6,000
Total Sources of Working Capital		$18,000

Uses of Working Capital

Purchase of equipment	$ 8,000	
For dividends	7,000	
Total Uses of Working Capital		15,000
Increase in Working Capital		$ 3,000

Schedule of Changes in Working Capital Accounts

	Balances		
Accounts	1/1/1983	12/31/1983	Change
Cash	$11,000	$10,000	$(1,000)
Accounts receivable	16,000	24,200	8,200
Current Assets	$27,000	$34,200	$ 7,200
Accounts payable	$16,000	$20,300	$ 4,300
Wages payable	500	400	(100)
Current Liabilities	$16,500	$20,700	$ 4,200
Working Capital	$10,500	$13,500	$ 3,000

[1] "Reporting Changes in Financial Position," *APB Opinion No. 19* (New York: AICPA, 1971), par. 7.

ing the extent to which funds were increased by operations, during an accounting period. This information is very important to financial statement users, particularly owners and creditors, in making economic decisions. It is important, therefore, to have an agreement about what to include in the statement. The statement should clearly show:

1. The *working capital* or *cash* provided or used in the company's *operations* during an accounting period.
2. The results of the other important financing and investing activities during the period, regardless of whether working capital or cash was affected.

As we will see, most of the important financing and investing activities do affect cash or working capital; we will discuss those activities that do not in a later part of this chapter.

Most companies use working capital (current assets less current liabilities) instead of cash as their concept of funds from operations. It is useful to understand why this is so. Recall that when a company makes a sale, inventory is reduced. When the sale is made on credit, accounts receivable is increased and later the account is collected. When the company purchases inventory, it may incur a liability (accounts payable) that it will pay at a later date. These examples show that the components of working capital (e.g., inventory, accounts receivable, and accounts payable) are involved more directly in a company's operations than cash. Since the working capital concept of funds from operations is most often used, we mainly study this concept in this chapter.

Exhibit 18-1 shows a typical statement of changes in financial position using the working capital concept of funds. An overview of this statement is presented in the next section.

OVERVIEW OF STATEMENT OF CHANGES IN FINANCIAL POSITION

A company cannot continue operating unless it has sufficient funds to do so. The Financial Accounting Standards Board recently stated that financial reporting should provide useful information about a company's sources and uses of funds. This includes information about how it obtains and spends cash, about its borrowing and repayments, about its capital transactions including cash dividends, and about other items that may affect its solvency. The Board also stated that a company's receivables, payables, and inventory (i.e., items of working capital) are the links between its operations and its cash inflows and outflows and that information about these relationships may be useful in understanding the operations of the company.[2]

The statement of changes in financial position, whether prepared on the basis of working capital or cash, is intended to provide useful information to external users about the above items. Owners, potential investors, and creditors may use the information in the statement to evaluate how effectively the management of the

---

[2] "Objectives of Financial Reporting by Business Enterprises," *FASB Statement of Financial Accounting Concepts No. 1* (Stamford, Conn.: FASB, 1978), par. 45 and 49.

company obtains and uses its financial resources. To help in such an evaluation, the statement of changes in financial position is divided into two sections, a "sources" section and a "uses" section.

It is unlikely that a company will continue to be successful unless it is able to obtain most of its working capital (or cash) from its operations. This occurs when the funds received from selling goods or services exceed the funds needed to provide the goods or services. One part of the sources section in the statement, therefore, is *sources from operations*. Exhibit 18-1 shows that the Rainey Corporation provided $12,000 of its working capital from operations during 1983. (How this figure of $12,000 was determined is discussed later in the chapter.) Owners, potential investors, and creditors can compare a company's sources of working capital (or cash) from operations for a given year with the same information from previous years in order to detect favorable or unfavorable *trends* in the company's funding activities. This information can also be compared with the same information from other companies for the same purpose.

In addition, a company obtains working capital (or cash) from activities other than operations. These activities are sometimes referred to as *financing activities* and the results are reported in the sources section as *other sources*. Exhibit 18-1 shows that the Rainey Corporation obtained $6,000 of working capital by issuing common stock during 1983. It also shows that the total sources of working capital were $18,000 for 1983. By reviewing the other sources, owners, potential investors, and creditors can see how (in addition to operations) a company obtained its working capital. They can also compare the percentage of sources provided by operations (67% in Exhibit 18-1, $12,000 ÷ $18,000) and the sources provided by other financing activities (33% in Exhibit 18-1, $6,000 ÷ $18,000) for a company in a given year to the percentages of other years to see whether any important changes have occurred. A comparison of these percentages to the same information for other companies can reveal, for instance, whether the company is obtaining a greater percentage of its sources of funds from financing activities other than operations.

A company uses its funds in a variety of activities, which are sometimes called *investing activities*. The results of a company's investing activities are shown in the *uses* section of the statement of changes in financial position. In Exhibit 18-1 it can be seen that the Rainey Corporation used $15,000 of working capital in 1983, consisting of $8,000 for the purchase of equipment and $7,000 for dividends. The company's working capital increased by $3,000 during the year because the total sources ($18,000) exceeded the total uses. By reviewing the various uses of a company's funds and comparing them to the sources of funds, owners, potential owners, and creditors can evaluate the likelihood of future cash dividends as well as the need for additional financial resources to finance existing operations or the expansion of operations. They can also evaluate the ability of the company to pay current obligations, make continual interest payments, and to pay off long-term bonds when they reach their maturity date.

Management, too, as internal users are able to use the information in the statement of changes in financial position in much the same way as external users. They can determine whether sources from operations are large enough to finance existing operations, whether excess sources from operations may be sufficient to finance expansion projects, or whether additional capital must be obtained from external sources. As we will see in Chapter 24, management uses a form of the statement of changes in financial position in the budgeting process.

The information in the statement of changes in financial position, combined with the information from the income statement and balance sheet, provides useful information to both external and internal users for many economic decisions. The preparation of this statement is explained in the remainder of this chapter.

WORKING CAPITAL INFLOWS AND OUTFLOWS

Before discussing how to prepare the statement of changes in financial position, it is helpful to understand the main inflows (sources) and outflows (uses) of working capital from a company's financing and investing activities during an accounting period. These flows of working capital are shown in Exhibit 18-2.

In studying Exhibit 18-2, we see that the sources (inflows) and uses (outflows) of working capital can be grouped into several major categories.

Sources of Working Capital

There are three categories of sources of working capital:

1. *Decreases in Noncurrent Assets.*   The sale or other disposal of noncurrent

**EXHIBIT 18-2
Major Inflows and
Outflows of
Working Capital**

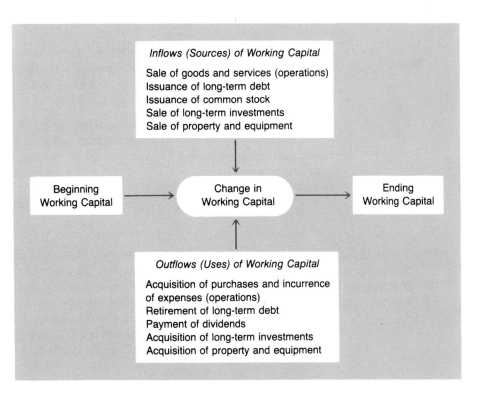

assets (e.g., the sale of land) results in an inflow (source) of working capital because current assets (cash, short-term receivables) are received in exchange for the noncurrent assets (land).

2. *Increases in Noncurrent Liabilities.* The issuance of long-term liabilities (e.g., bonds or a long-term note payable) causes an inflow of working capital because a current asset (cash) is received in exchange for the noncurrent liability (e.g., bonds).

3. *Increases in Owners' Equity.* Owners' equity increases mainly because of net income *and* additional investments by the owners. Additional investments (e.g., the issuance of common stock to stockholders) result in an inflow of working capital (cash or subscriptions receivable). Net income is slightly more complicated because, during operations, both inflows and outflows of working capital from operations are usually combined and entitled Sources of Working Capital from Operations (this is discussed later).

Uses of Working Capital

There are also three categories of uses of working capital.

1. *Increases in Noncurrent Assets.* The acquisition of noncurrent assets (e.g., equipment) results in an outflow of working capital (e.g., decrease in cash or increase in current payables).

2. *Decreases in Noncurrent Liabilities.* The payment of long-term liabilities (e.g., the retirement of bonds) results in an outflow of working capital because the decrease in long-term liabilities (bonds) is accompanied by a decrease in a current asset (cash).

3. *Decreases in Owners' Equity.* Owners' equity may decrease as a result of several transactions. Two common transactions are withdrawals by owners (e.g., dividends) and the acquisition of treasury stock. In each case a decrease in owners' equity is accompanied by an outflow of working capital.

To summarize, inflows (sources) of working capital are the result of decreases in noncurrent assets and increases in noncurrent liabilities and/or in owners' equity during an accounting period. Outflows (uses) of working capital are the result of increases in noncurrent assets and decreases in noncurrent liabilities and/or in owners' equity during the period. The difference between the inflows and outflows is the change in working capital during the accounting period.

Working Capital Provided by Operations

As indicated earlier, one part of the statement of changes in financial position is the sources of working capital from operations. To report these sources, the outflows of working capital for expenses must be subtracted from the inflows of working capital from revenues. This information may be obtained from the company's income statement for the current period. The net income (revenues minus expenses) for the period, however, may *not* be the sources of working capital from operations. This is because the net income is likely to include some expenses, such as depreciation, that did not require the outflow of working capital. Thus net income must be adjusted for any nonworking capital transactions (e.g., depreciation) to determine the sources of working capital from operations. For example, suppose that the Rainey Corporation presents the following income statement information for the year ended December 31, 1983:

Sales (cash and accounts receivable)		$32,000
Less:		
Salaries expense (cash and wages payable)	$ 9,000	
Depreciation expense	2,000	
Other expenses (cash)	11,000	22,000
Net Income		$10,000

One possible way of disclosing the working capital from operations is to list each revenue and expense that resulted in an inflow or outflow of working capital as follows:

Operating items increasing working capital	
Sales	$32,000
Less: Operating items decreasing working capital	
Salaries expense	(9,000)
Other expenses	(11,000)
Working capital provided by operations	$12,000

Note that depreciation expense was *not* deducted because it did not decrease working capital (i.e., the journal entry to record the depreciation involved a credit to accumulated depreciation, which is not a current asset or current liability).

A more common approach to reporting the working capital from operations is to begin with net income and *eliminate* the items not affecting working capital, as follows:

Sources from Operations:	
Net income	$10,000
Add: Items not requiring working capital	
Depreciation expense	2,000
Working capital provided by operations	$12,000

It is important to understand that depreciation is *not* a source of funds; the expense was added back to net income because it did not result in an outflow of working capital. Note that by using either method the result is the same; working capital provided by operations is $12,000. As mentioned, the second approach is much more common and was used by Rainey Corporation in its statement of changes in financial position shown in Exhibit 18-1.

Other items may also be included in net income but may not have resulted in an inflow or outflow of working capital. These items must be eliminated (added back or subtracted) from net income to determine the sources of working capital from operations. Exhibit 18-3 lists the more common items and summarizes the adjustments to net income. These adjustments are explained in more detail in the comprehensive example later in the chapter.

**EXHIBIT 18-3
Adjustments to
Net Income to
Convert to Sources
of Working Capital
from Operations**

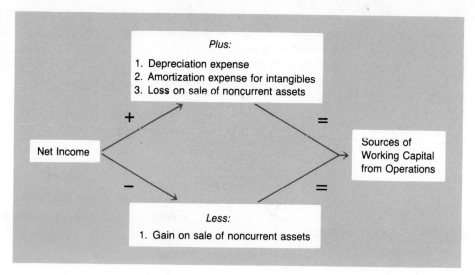

PROCEDURES FOR PREPARATION OF STATEMENT

When beginning to prepare the statement of changes in financial position for a company, it is helpful to remember that (1) the statement is used to show the results (dollar amounts of sources and uses) of the company's financing and investing activities, and (2) sources from operations should be clearly disclosed. It is also helpful to recall the three categories of sources and uses of working capital, because the preparation of the statement involves an analysis of transactions affecting these categories.

Information Requirements

When preparing the statement of changes in financial position, it is necessary to analyze the changes in the noncurrent assets, the noncurrent liabilities, and the owners' equity accounts (including the impact of net income). The analysis is normally prepared on a 5-column worksheet (see Exhibit 18-6). Information from the following financial statements of the current period is required for this analysis:

1. The beginning and ending balance sheets.
2. The income statement.
3. The retained earnings statement (or in the case of a sole proprietorship or partnership, the statement of changes in owner's equity and statement of changes in partners' equity, respectively).
4. Other supplemental information concerning the reasons for the changes in the noncurrent accounts.

Steps in Preparation

After gathering the above information several steps must be completed to prepare the statement of changes in financial position. These steps are summarized below, after which a comprehensive example is used to explain each step.

Step 1: Compute the beginning and ending working capital and the change in working capital for the period. Using the beginning and ending balance sheets, prepare a schedule that lists the beginning and ending balance and change in each current asset and current liability. Include the beginning balance, ending balance, and change in working capital (see Exhibit 18-5). Enter the title "Working Capital" on the 5-column worksheet (see Exhibit 18-6) and in the first three columns list the beginning working capital, the ending working capital, and the change in working capital, respectively.

Step 2: Enter the titles of all the noncurrent accounts (from the balance sheet) on the worksheet and list each beginning account balance, ending account balance, and the change in the account balance directly below the working capital information. The accounts with debit balances are listed first, followed by the accounts with credit balances (see Exhibit 18-6).

Step 3: Directly below these noncurrent accounts add the following headings:

A. Sources from Operations[3]
B. Other Sources of Working Capital
C. Sources Not Affecting Working Capital
D. Uses of Working Capital
E. Uses Not Affecting Working Capital

Leave sufficient room (about six lines) below each heading so that each source and use may be listed where appropriate.

Step 4: Account for all the changes in the noncurrent accounts that occurred during the current period. *Reconstruct* the journal entries that caused the changes in the noncurrent accounts directly on the worksheet,[4] making certain modifications to show the sources and uses of working capital. Use the following general rules.

A. Start with net income. The net income is a summary of all the journal entries from operations affecting current assets or current liabilities and retained earnings (in the case of a corporation). Consequently, the proper entry on the worksheet to show the net income as a source of working capital and to explain the impact upon retained earnings is a debit to Sources from Operations: Net Income and a credit to Retained Earnings.[5] This entry (and later entries in this section) is illustrated in general journal form below (the

---

[3] *APB Opinion No. 19* also requires the disclosure of sources from extraordinary items (discussed in Chapter 15). A later *Opinion*, however, reduced the likelihood of reporting these items, and therefore they are not considered further in this chapter.

[4] Remember that the actual journal entries that caused the changes have already been made and posted to the accounts. In this step we are simply reconstructing the journal entries on the worksheet to prepare the statement of changes in financial position.

[5] The entry to show a net loss would involve a debit to Retained Earnings and a credit to Sources from Operations: Net Loss. Any adjustments for items not affecting working capital from operations such as in Step 4B(2) would be made as usual.

amounts shown are from the comprehensive example, which is discussed later):

Sources from Operations: Net Income   4,300
   Retained Earnings   4,300

B. Account for the other changes in the noncurrent accounts. Review each noncurrent account and determine the journal entry responsible for its change. Make this entry on the worksheet with the following changes:

(1) If the entry affects a current asset or current liability, replace the debit to the current asset or current liability with the heading Other Sources of Working Capital (and list the specific source). Replace the credit to any current asset or current liability with the heading Uses of Working Capital (and list the specific use). For example:

Other Sources of Working Capital: Issuance of Bonds   4,000
   Bonds Payable   4,000

(2) If the entry affects a nonworking capital income statement item (e.g., depreciation, gains, or losses) replace the debit or credit to this non-working capital item with the heading Sources from Operations (and list the specific adjustment). For example:

Sources from Operations: Depreciation Expense   700
   Accumulated Depreciation   700

(3) If the entry does not affect a current asset or current liability, it is a "combined financing and investing transaction." For this type of trans-action, create "expanded" entries on the worksheet to record both the source and use of financial resources. For example, if common stock was exchanged for land, the following two worksheet entries would be made:

Sources Not Affecting Working Capital:
   Issuance of Common Stock for Land   2,000
   Common Stock, $10 par   500
   Additional Paid-in Capital   1,500

Land   2,000
   Uses Not Affecting Working Capital:
   Acquisition of Land by Issuance of Common Stock . . .   2,000

The first entry shows the financing (source) aspect of the exchange while the second entry shows the investing (use) aspect. These types of transactions are not common but are required to be disclosed on the statement of changes in financial position.

Step 5: Make a final worksheet entry to record the change in working capital. The worksheet entries must account for all the changes in the noncurrent accounts recorded in Step 2. The difference between the total sources and uses must be equal to the Working Capital account change. A final entry to record an increase in working capital would be made as follows:

Working Capital	3,100	
Increase in Working Capital		3,100

For a decrease in working capital, an opposite entry (a debit to Decrease in Working Capital and a credit to Working Capital) would be made.

Step 6: Prepare the statement of changes in financial position. Use the information developed in the lower portion of the worksheet. Under the major headings list the various sources and uses. Subtract the total uses from the total sources to determine the change in working capital. Below the change in working capital include the schedule of changes in the working capital accounts from Step 1.

Several observations should be made at this point. First, other than usually starting with net income, there is no particular order in which the worksheet entries are reconstructed. You should develop a method so that you can account for all the changes in the noncurrent accounts in an orderly way. Second, you may have to make more than one worksheet entry to account for the change in an account. For instance, the change in the Land account may be the result of both a sale and purchase of land. Third, remember that these worksheet entries are *not* posted to any accounts. They are recorded on the worksheet for only one purpose, that is, to help in preparing the statement of changes in financial position.

Finally, you do not always have to prepare a worksheet. The investing and financing transactions of some companies are simple, and the sources and uses of working capital can be determined by simply reviewing the income statement and the changes in the balance sheet accounts. Other working papers may also be used. For instance, instead of preparing a worksheet, T-accounts may be used. In this case the change in working capital and in each noncurrent account is entered in separate T-accounts. The major sources and uses are also set up as T-accounts. The reconstructed journal entries are then recorded directly in the T-accounts. Because the worksheet is a more efficient way of preparing the information, it is the method used in this book.

COMPREHENSIVE EXAMPLE (WORKING CAPITAL BASIS)

It is easier to understand the process of preparing the statement of changes in financial position by studying an example, as shown below. The example includes a detailed discussion of each step presented earlier. As you study this example it will be helpful to reread these steps. The condensed information in Exhibit 18-4 is used in the example.

Step 1: Schedule of Changes in Working Capital Accounts

Step 1 involves completion of a schedule that computes the change in working capital by analyzing the change in the account balances of the current assets and current liabilities. This schedule is shown in Exhibit 18-5.

In Exhibit 18-5 the beginning balance, ending balance, and change in each individual current asset and current liability are listed. Beginning total current

EXHIBIT 18-4
Condensed Financial
Information

SYMES COMPANY
Condensed Financial Information

1. Balance sheet information:

	Balances	
Accounts	*1/1/1983*	*12/31/1983*
Cash	$ 500	$ 1,500
Accounts receivable	1,400	1,000
Inventory	2,000	3,800
Land	5,200	7,200
Equipment	23,700	28,200
Accumulated depreciation	(1,000)	(1,300)
	$31,800	$40,400
Accounts payable	$ 2,100	$ 1,200
Salaries payable	400	600
Bonds payable	–0–	4,000
Common stock, $10 par	8,000	8,500
Additional paid-in capital	16,000	17,500
Retained earnings	5,300	8,600
	$31,800	$40,400

2. Income statement information:

Sales		$7,000
Operating expenses:		
Depreciation expense	$ 700	
Other operating expenses	2,200	2,900
Operating income		$ 4,100
Other revenues:		
Gain on sale of equipment		200
Net Income		$ 4,300

3. Retained earnings information:

Beginning retained earnings	$ 5,300
Add: Net income	4,300
	$ 9,600
Less: Dividends	(1,000)
Ending retained earnings	$ 8,600

4. Supplemental information for 1983 (including data from the income statement and retained earnings statement above and from a review of the transactions affecting various accounts during the year).
   (a) Net income is $4,300.
   (b) Dividends declared and paid are $1,000.
   (c) Equipment was purchased at a cost of $5,600.
   (d) Ten-year bonds payable with a face value of $4,000 were issued for $4,000.
   (e) Depreciation expense for the year is $700.
   (f) Land was acquired through the issuance of 50 shares of $10 par common stock when the stock was selling at a market price of $40 per share.
   (g) Equipment with a cost of $1,100 and a book value of $700 was sold for $900.

EXHIBIT 18-5
Schedule of Changes
in Working Capital
Accounts

SYMES COMPANY				
Schedule of Changes in Working Capital Accounts				
For Year Ended December 31, 1983				
		Balances		
Accounts		*1/1/1983*	*12/31/1983*	*Change*
Cash		$ 500	$1,500	$1,000
Accounts receivable		1,400	1,000	(400)
Inventory		2,000	3,800	1,800
Current Assets		$3,900	$6,300	$2,400
Accounts payable		$2,100	$1,200	$ (900)
Salaries payable		400	600	200
Current Liabilities		$2,500	$1,800	$ (700)
Working Capital		$1,400	$4,500	$3,100

liabilities are subtracted from beginning total current assets to determine beginning working capital of $1,400. Similarly, ending working capital is computed to be $4,500. The change (increase) in working capital is $3,100 ($4,500 − $1,400). The beginning working capital, ending working capital, and change in working capital are listed on the first line of the worksheet in Exhibit 18-6.

Steps 2 and 3:
Setting Up the
Worksheet

In Step 2 the noncurrent accounts, their beginning and ending balances, and changes are listed on the worksheet directly below the working capital information. In Step 3 the major headings, Sources from Operations, Other Sources of Working Capital, Sources Not Affecting Working Capital, Uses of Working Capital, and Uses Not Affecting Working Capital, are then listed on the worksheet. Enough space is left under each heading so that the sources and uses may be listed accordingly. These accounts and headings are shown in Exhibit 18-6.

Step 4:
Completion of the
Worksheet

The worksheet entries to account for the changes in the noncurrent accounts are entered directly on the worksheet in Step 4, as shown in Exhibit 18-6. To explain them better, however, each of the entries listed in Exhibit 18-6 is also presented in journal entry *form* below.[6] The entries are listed (a) through (h) to correspond to the supplemental information presented in Exhibit 18-4. You should review each entry and explanation and then trace the entry back to the corresponding entry on the worksheet.

The usual procedure is to start with the net income figure — which is itself a summary amount mainly including the inflows and outflows of working capital for operations. Net income caused an increase in both working capital and retained earnings. To record the impact of net income on working capital and retained earnings, the entry on the following page is made on the worksheet:

---

[6] It is important to remember that these journal entries are *not* posted to the accounts. See footnote 4.

EXHIBIT 18-6   Worksheet (Working Capital Basis)

SYMES COMPANY
Worksheet for Statement of Changes in Financial Position
For Year Ended December 31, 1983

Account Titles	Balances 1/1/1983	Balances 12/31/1983	Change	Worksheet Entries Debit	Worksheet Entries Credit
Debits					
Working Capital	1,400	$ 4,500	$3,100	(h) $3,100	
Noncurrent Accounts:					
Land	5,200	7,200	2,000	(f-2) 2,000	
Equipment	23,700	28,200	4,500	(c) 5,600	(g) $ 1,100
Totals	$30,300	$39,900	$9,600		
Credits					
Accumulated depreciation	$ 1,000	$ 1,300	$ 300	(g) 400	(e) 700
Bonds payable	–0–	4,000	4,000		(d) 4,000
Common stock, $10 par	8,000	8,500	500		(f-1) 500
Additional paid-in capital	16,000	17,500	1,500		(f-1) 1,500
Retained earnings	5,300	8,600	3,300	(b) 1,000	(a) 4,300
Totals	$30,300	$39,900	$9,600	$12,100	$12,100

	Debit	Credit
Sources from Operations		
Net income	(a) $ 4,300	
Add: Depreciation expense	(e) 700	
Less: Gain on sale of equipment		(g) $ 200
Other Sources of Working Capital		
Issuance of bonds	(d) 4,000	
Sale of equipment	(g) 900	
Sources Not Affecting Working Capital		
Issuance of common stock for land	(f-1) 2,000	
Uses of Working Capital		
For dividends		(b) 1,000
Purchase of equipment		(c) 5,600
Uses Not Affecting Working Capital		
Acquisition of land by issuance of common stock		(f-2) 2,000
Increase in Working Capital		(h) 3,100
Totals	$11,900	$11,900

(a) Sources from Operations: Net Income   4,300
        Retained Earnings   4,300

Retained earnings and working capital were reduced by the declaration and payment of cash dividends (e.g., a debit to Retained Earnings and a credit to Cash).

The following worksheet entry accounts for the decrease in retained earnings as well as the use of working capital for dividends (note that the credit to the current asset Cash is replaced with the heading, Uses of Working Capital: For Dividends):

(b) Retained Earnings	1,000	
Uses of Working Capital: For Dividends		1,000

The increase in Retained Earnings of $4,300 resulting from net income, reduced by the decrease of $1,000 because of dividends, accounts for the $3,300 change in Retained Earnings.

The purchase of the new equipment required the use of working capital (e.g., a debit to Equipment and a credit to Cash). The worksheet entry to record the purchase is shown below (note that the credit to the current asset Cash is replaced with the caption, Uses of Working Capital: Purchase of Equipment):

(c) Equipment	5,600	
Uses of Working Capital: Purchase of Equipment		5,600

The issuance of the long-term bonds caused an increase in Bonds Payable and an inflow of working capital that was not related to operations (e.g., debit to Cash and credit to Bonds Payable). The worksheet entry to record the issuance is shown below (the debit to the current asset Cash is replaced by the caption, Other Sources of Working Capital: Issuance of Bonds):

(d) Other Sources of Working Capital: Issuance of Bonds . . .	4,000	
Bonds Payable		4,000

During the year Depreciation Expense was increased (debited) for $700, and this amount was shown as a deduction to determine net income. The noncurrent account, Accumulated Depreciation, was also increased (credited) for $700. Although the depreciation expense reduced net income, there was no outflow of working capital from operations. Therefore this depreciation deduction must be *added back* to net income to show correctly the working capital provided by operations. To do this, as well as to show the increase in the Accumulated Depreciation account, the following worksheet entry is made:

(e) Sources from Operations: Depreciation Expense	700	
Accumulated Depreciation		700

It should be remembered that depreciation is *not* a source of funds! It is added back to net income because when depreciation was originally deducted in computing the amount of net income, there was no corresponding outflow of working capital.

When the company issued shares of its common stock in exchange for land, the exchange was recorded at the market price of the 50 shares of stock. At that time the Land account was increased (debited) by $2,000, the Common-Stock, $10 par account was increased (credited) for the par value of $500, and the Additional Paid-in Capital account was increased (credited) for the excess of market value over par value, $1,500. Although this transaction did not affect working capital, it did involve both financing and investing activities. The company invested in land and financed this investment by the issuance of common stock. Both the financing and the investing information should be disclosed on the statement of changes in financial position. To do so, the original transaction is "expanded" into two transactions, a *sources* (financing) transaction and a *uses* (investing) transaction, which are recorded on the worksheet as follows:

(f-1) Sources Not Affecting Working Capital:		
Issuance of Common Stock for Land	2,000	
Common Stock, $10 par		500
Additional Paid-in Capital		1,500

(f-2) Land	2,000	
Uses Not Affecting Working Capital: Acquisition		
of Land by Issuance of Common Stock		2,000

The recording of these expanded entries on the worksheet accounts for the changes in the Land, Common Stock, and Additional Paid-in Capital accounts and shows both the investing and financing parts of the original transaction.

When the company sold the equipment it recorded an increase (debit) in Cash of $900, a decrease (debit) in Accumulated Depreciation for $400, and a decrease (credit) in Equipment for $1,100. Since the proceeds were more than the book value, it also recorded (credited) a Gain on Sale of Equipment of $200. As shown on the income statement, this gain caused net income to increase even though there was no inflow of working capital *from operations*. In preparing the worksheet entry for this financing transaction, two modifications must be made: (1) instead of debiting Cash, the caption, Other Sources of Working Capital: Sale of Equipment, must be debited for the $900 proceeds, and (2) instead of crediting the Gain account, the caption, Sources from Operations: Gain on Sale of Equipment, must be *credited* to *deduct* the gain from net income in order to avoid double counting and to show correctly the working capital provided by operations.[7] The worksheet entry would appear as follows:

(g) Other Sources of Working Capital: Sale of Equipment . . .	900	
Accumulated Depreciation	400	
Sources from Operations: Gain on Sale of Equipment .		200
Equipment		1,100

After recording this worksheet entry and combining it with the entry from item (e), it may be seen that the $300 change (increase) in Accumulated Depreciation has now been accounted for. In addition, combining the results of this worksheet entry

---

[7] If the equipment had been sold at a loss, the loss would have decreased net income even though there was no outflow of working capital from operations. In this case the worksheet entry would be modified as discussed, except instead of debiting the Loss account, the caption, Sources from Operations: Loss on Sale of Equipment, must be debited to *add back* the loss to net income in a manner similar to depreciation expense.

with the results of the entry for item (c) accounts for the $4,500 change (increase) in the Equipment account. It is often necessary to record the results of two (or more) unrelated transactions before accounting for the change in an account.

Step 5:
Final Worksheet
Entry

In Step 5 a double check of the debit and credit entries on the worksheet shows that all the changes in the noncurrent accounts have been accounted for. A final worksheet entry is made to record the increase in working capital and to bring the debit and credit columns into balance. It is recorded as shown below:

(h) Working Capital   3,100
         Increase in Working Capital   3,100

Step 6:
Preparation of
Statement

When the worksheet is complete the statement of changes in financial position is prepared (Step 6). This statement is shown in Exhibit 18-7. The information developed in the lower portion of the worksheet (Exhibit 18-6) is used to list the sources and uses, beginning with sources from operations. The total uses of $8,600 are subtracted from the total sources of $11,700 to determine the $3,100 increase in working capital. To complete the statement, the schedule of changes in the working capital accounts (prepared in Step 1 on Exhibit 18-5) is included below the increase in working capital figure. Because the company engaged in a financing and investing transaction not involving working capital (the exchange of common stock for land), the headings Sources of Financial Resources and Uses of Financial Resources (rather than Sources of and Uses of Working Capital) are used for the related totals because they are more descriptive.

After studying the six steps and the completed worksheet of the comprehensive example you should be well on your way to understanding the procedures involved in preparing the statement of changes in financial position. Not all the possible financing and investing transactions were included in this example. Additional transactions are shown in the review problem at the end of this chapter.

CASH SOURCES
FROM
OPERATIONS

Differences in
Sources from
Operations (Cash)

Most companies use working capital for the sources from operations section of their statement of changes in financial position. A few companies use cash, however.[8] This involves computing the sources from operations on a cash basis instead of a working capital basis, and showing the change in cash instead of the change in working capital as the final amount of the statement. For all practical purposes, the rest of the statement is the same under either approach. Once you understand the development of the worksheet and statement under a working capital basis, the shift to a cash basis is not difficult.

When the cash basis is used only slight modifications must be made, and it is necessary to include one additional step, in the set of steps shown earlier. Since the final amount on the statement is the change in cash, Step 1 involves listing on the

---

[8] As we will see in Chapter 24, most companies use cash sources from operations for their *internal* reporting for planning and control purposes, even though they may report sources of working capital from operations in their statement of changes in financial position.

EXHIBIT 18-7
Statement of
Changes in
Financial Position

SYMES COMPANY
Statement of Changes in Financial Position
For Year Ended December 31, 1983

Sources of Financial Resources

Sources from Operations:

Net income	$4,300	
Add: Items not requiring working capital		
Depreciation expense	700	
Less: Items not providing working capital		
Gain on sale of equipment	(200)	
Working capital provided by operations		$ 4,800

Other Sources of Working Capital:

Issuance of bonds	4,000
Sale of equipment	900

Sources Not Affecting Working Capital:

Issuance of common stock for land	2,000
Total Sources of Financial Resources	$11,700

Uses of Financial Resources

Uses of Working Capital:

For dividends	$1,000	
Purchase of equipment	5,600	

Uses Not Affecting Working Capital:

Acquisition of land by issuance of common stock	2,000	
Total Uses of Financial Resources		8,600

Increase in Working Capital	$ 3,100

Schedule of Changes in Working Capital Accounts

	Balances		
Accounts	1/1/1983	12/31/1983	Change
Cash	$ 500	$1,500	$1,000
Accounts receivable	1,400	1,000	(400)
Inventory	2,000	3,800	1,800
Current Assets	$3,900	$6,300	$2,400
Accounts payable	$2,100	$1,200	$ (900)
Salaries payable	400	600	200
Current Liabilities	$2,500	$1,800	$ (700)
Working Capital	$1,400	$4,500	$3,100

worksheet the beginning and ending balance and the change in the *Cash* account (instead of working capital). The rest of the steps are similar to the steps shown earlier except that the causes (the sources and uses) of the change in the Cash account are determined by analyzing the changes in the *noncash* (instead of only the noncurrent) balance sheet accounts. Thus an extra step must be completed, which involves an analysis of the changes in all the current assets (except cash) and the current liabilities.

This step is completed *in addition to* the usual analysis of the noncurrent accounts. Instead of including a separate schedule that summarizes the changes in the current assets and current liabilities as the lower portion of the statement (as was done in the working capital approach on Exhibit 18-7), the change in each current asset (except cash) and current liability is listed on the worksheet. A worksheet entry is then made to account for the impact of each change upon *cash*. Since the changes in the current assets and current liabilities are part of the company's *operating cycle*, the impacts of these changes on cash are listed directly in the statement of changes in financial position as *adjustments to sources from operations*.

Before going through a comprehensive example, it is useful to understand the relationship between the sales revenues, expenses, and cash flows within a company's operating cycle. The company initially purchases inventory for cash or on account. To make cash or credit sales it incurs selling expenses and either pays cash or incurs current liabilities. Finally, the company collects its accounts receivable, converting them back into cash, incurring related general and administrative expenses (both cash and noncash in nature) and completing the operating cycle. These revenues, expenses, and related cash flows in the operating cycle are depicted in Exhibit 18-8.

As seen in Exhibit 18-8 each phase of the operating cycle has an impact on both net income and the company's cash flows for operations. The impact is not likely

EXHIBIT 18-8
Operating Cycle:
Revenues, Expenses,
and Related
Cash Flows

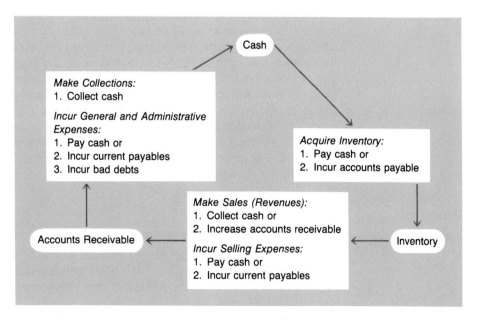

EXHIBIT 18-9
Adjustments to Net
Income to Convert to
Cash Sources from
Operations

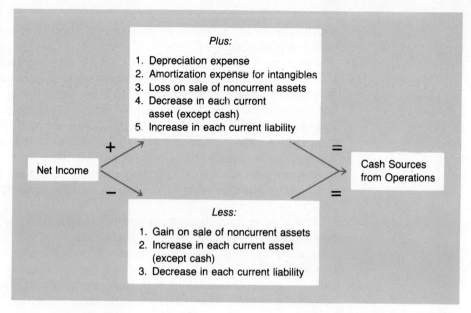

Plus:
1. Depreciation expense
2. Amortization expense for intangibles
3. Loss on sale of noncurrent assets
4. Decrease in each current
   asset (except cash)
5. Increase in each current liability

Net Income

Cash Sources
from Operations

Less:
1. Gain on sale of noncurrent assets
2. Increase in each current asset
   (except cash)
3. Decrease in each current liability

to be the same for both items, however, because of differences in the recognition of net income and the timing of the cash flows. For instance, when a credit sale is made both sales revenues and an accounts receivable are increased but no inflow of cash is received. Later, when the accounts receivable is collected no sales revenue is recognized but a cash inflow occurs. In addition, when inventory is purchased for cash an outflow of cash occurs but no expense is recorded. A purchase on account involves no immediate expense or cash payment although a later cash outflow occurs. The expense is recorded (as cost of goods sold) when the inventory is sold even though no cash outflow occurs at that time. The additional step of making worksheet entries for the changes in the current assets and current liabilities is needed to adjust for these differences. The objective of the additional step is to convert the net income computed on an accrual basis to sources from operations computed on a cash basis. Thus every change in a current asset (except cash) or in a current liability is treated in the worksheet entries as an adjustment to net income. The proper adjustments to net income to convert it to cash sources from operations are shown in Exhibit 18-9.

Comprehensive
Example
(Cash Basis)

With this background in mind we can prepare the worksheet for the statement of changes in financial position of the Symes Company on a cash basis instead of a working capital basis. The condensed financial information was presented in Exhibit 18-4. A worksheet on a cash basis is presented in Exhibit 18-10. Preparation of the worksheet involves the following steps. First, the Cash account title, the

EXHIBIT 18-10   Worksheet (Cash Basis)

SYMES COMPANY
Worksheet for Statement of Changes in Financial Position
For Year Ended December 31, 1983

Account Titles	Balances 1/1/1983	Balances 12/31/1983	Change	Worksheet Entries Debit	Worksheet Entries Credit
Debits					
Cash	$ 500	$ 1,500	$1,000	(l) $1,000	
Noncash Accounts:					
Accounts receivable	1,400	1,000	(400)		(h) $ 400
Inventory	2,000	3,800	1,800	(i) 1,800	
Land	5,200	7,200	2,000	(f-2) 2,000	
Equipment	23,700	28,200	4,500	(c) 5,600	(g) 1,100
Totals	$32,800	$41,700	$8,900		
Credits					
Accumulated depreciation	$ 1,000	$ 1,300	$ 300	(g) 400	(e) 700
Accounts payable	2,100	1,200	(900)	(j) 900	
Salaries payable	400	600	200		(k) 200
Bonds payable	–0–	4,000	4,000		(d) 4,000
Common stock, $10 par	8,000	8,500	500		(f-1) 500
Additional paid-in capital	16,000	17,500	1,500		(f-1) 1,500
Retained earnings	5,300	8,600	3,300	(b) 1,000	(a) 4,300
Totals	$32,800	$41,700	$8,900	$12,700	$12,700

Cash Sources from Operations				
Net income			(a) $ 4,300	
Add: Depreciation expense			(e) 700	
Decrease in accounts receivable			(h) 400	
Increase in salaries payable			(k) 200	
Less: Gain on sale of equipment				(g) $ 200
Increase in inventory				(i) 1,800
Decrease in accounts payable				(j) 900
Other Sources of Cash				
Issuance of bonds			(d) 4,000	
Sale of equipment			(g) 900	
Sources Not Affecting Cash				
Issuance of common stock for land			(f-1) 2,000	
Uses of Cash				
For dividends				(b) 1,000
Purchase of equipment				(c) 5,600
Uses Not Affecting Cash				
Acquisition of land by issuance of common stock				(f-2) 2,000
Increase in Cash				(l) 1,000
Totals				$12,500	$12,500

beginning and ending balances, and the change in the account are listed on the first line of the worksheet. Next, each noncash account, its beginning and ending balance, and the change in the account are listed on the worksheet. These items include the current assets (except cash) and the current liabilities along with the noncurrent accounts. Again, accounts with debit balances are listed first, followed by accounts with credit balances.

The analysis begins with a worksheet entry to record net income as the initial cash source from operations and continues until all the changes in the *non*current assets, *non*current liabilities, and owners' equity accounts have been accounted for. Up to this point the worksheet entries are identical to the entries made for the working capital approach (except for the changes in terminology). These are entries (a) through (g) in Exhibit 18-10. Since they were explained earlier the discussion is not repeated here.

The procedure now turns to an analysis of the changes in the current assets (except cash) and current liabilities. The related worksheet entries are labeled (h) through (k) in Exhibit 18-10. To explain these entries better they are also shown in journal entry *form* below.

The Accounts Receivable decreased $400 during the year. This is because cash collections exceeded credit sales by this amount. To show the additional cash inflow from operations, the following worksheet entry is made:

(h) Cash Sources from Operations: Decrease
     in Accounts Receivable 400
     Accounts Receivable   400

Inventory increased by $1,800 during the year, indicating that purchases exceeded the cost of goods sold. To show the additional operating cash outflow due to the purchase of inventory, sources from operations must be decreased. The following worksheet entry is made:

(i) Inventory 1,800
     Cash Sources from Operations:
       Increase in Inventory   1,800

Accounts Payable decreased by $900 during the year, indicating that cash payments for operations exceeded expenses. This additional cash outflow for operations must be shown as a decrease in sources from operations, as follows:

(j) Accounts Payable 900
     Cash Sources from Operations:
       Decrease in Accounts Payable   900

Salaries Payable increased by $200 during the year, indicating that less cash was paid than that shown as salaries expense for the year. To adjust net income to show higher cash sources from operations, the following worksheet entry is made:

(k) Cash Sources from Operations: Increase in
  Salaries Payable 200
  Salaries Payable 200

At this point a double check should be made to determine that all the changes in the noncash accounts have been accounted for. The final entry (l) is made to record the increase in cash (the final amount on the statement of changes in financial position) and to bring the worksheet debit and credit columns into balance. The following worksheet entry is made:

(l) Cash 1,000
  Increase in Cash 1,000

The worksheet may now be used to prepare the statement of changes in financial position (shown in Exhibit 18-11). Again, this worksheet approach is very efficient

EXHIBIT 18-11
Statement of Changes in Financial Position

SYMES COMPANY
Statement of Changes in Financial Position
For Year Ended December 31, 1983

Sources of Financial Resources

Cash Sources from Operations:
Net income	$4,300	
Add: Items not requiring cash outflow		
Depreciation expense	700	
Decrease in accounts receivable	400	
Increase in salaries payable	200	
Less: Items not providing cash		
Gain on sale of equipment	(200)	
Increase in inventories	(1,800)	
Decrease in accounts payable	(900)	
Cash provided by operations		$2,700
Other Sources of Cash:		
Issuance of bonds		4,000
Sale of equipment		900
Sources Not Affecting Cash:		
Issuance of common stock for land		2,000
Total Sources of Financial Resources		$9,600

Uses of Financial Resources

Uses of Cash:		
For dividends	$1,000	
Purchase of equipment	5,600	
Uses Not Affecting Cash:		
Acquisition of land by issuance of common stock	2,000	
Total Uses of Financial Resources		8,600
Increase in Cash		$1,000

because the lower portion of the worksheet is nearly identical to the statement. Note that since the changes in the current assets (except cash) and the current liabilities are listed directly on the statement, it is not necessary to prepare a schedule of these changes (as was required in the working capital approach). Also note, except for the sources from operations, the similarity between the statement of changes in financial position prepared on a cash basis (Exhibit 18-11) and the statement prepared on a working capital basis (Exhibit 18-7). Finally, note that because the company engaged in a financing and investing transaction not involving cash, the headings Sources of Financial Resources and Uses of Financial Resources (rather than Sources of and Uses of Cash) are used for the related totals because they are more descriptive.

REVIEW PROBLEM

LAMB COMPANY
Condensed Financial Information

1. Balance sheet information:

| | Balances | |
Accounts	1/1/1983	12/31/1983
Cash	$ 800	$ 2,000
Accounts receivable	1,200	2,200
Inventory	3,200	4,300
Land	4,800	3,800
Machinery	14,500	17,500
Accumulated depreciation	(1,400)	(1,800)
Patents (net)	2,300	2,200
	$25,400	$30,200
Accounts payable	$ 2,300	$ 1,700
Bonds payable	2,000	–0–
Note payable (long-term)	–0–	3,000
Common stock, $5 par	6,000	6,500
Additional paid-in capital	11,000	12,300
Retained earnings	4,100	6,700
	$25,400	$30,200

2. Income statement information:

Revenues		$5,000
Expenses:		
Depreciation expense	$ 400	
Patent amortization expense	100	
Other operating expenses	1,000	1,500
Operating income		$3,500
Other items:		
Loss on sale of land		(300)
Net Income		$3,200

3. Retained earnings information:

Beginning retained earnings	$4,100
Add: Net income	3,200
	$7,300
Less: Dividends	(600)
Ending retained earnings	$6,700

4. Supplemental information for 1983 (including data from the above items).
   (a) Net income is $3,200.
   (b) Dividends declared and paid are $600.
   (c) One hundred shares of $5 par common stock were issued for $18 per share.
   (d) Bonds payable with a book value of $2,000 were retired for $2,000.
   (e) Depreciation expense for the year is $400.
   (f) Patent amortization expense for the year is $100. No patents were sold or acquired during the year.
   (g) Machinery with a value of $3,000 was acquired through the issuance of a long-term note.
   (h) Land at a cost of $1,000 was sold for $700.

Required: Prepare (1) a worksheet and (2) a statement of changes in financial position. Use a working capital basis.

SOLUTION TO REVIEW PROBLEM

Requirement 1:

LAMB COMPANY
Worksheet for Statement of Changes in Financial Position
For Year Ended December 31, 1983

Account Titles	Balances 1/1/1983	Balances 12/31/1983	Change	Worksheet Entries Debit	Worksheet Entries Credit
Debits					
Working Capital	$ 2,900	$ 6,800	$3,900	(i) $3,900	
Noncurrent Accounts:					
Land	4,800	3,800	(1,000)		(h) $1,000
Machinery	14,500	17,500	3,000	(g-2) 3,000	
Patents (net)	2,300	2,200	(100)		(f) 100
Totals	$24,500	$30,300	$5,800		
Credits					
Accumulated depreciation	$ 1,400	$ 1,800	$ 400		(e) 400
Bonds payable	2,000	–0–	(2,000)	(d) 2,000	
Note payable (long-term)	–0–	3,000	3,000		(g-1) 3,000
Common stock, $5 par	6,000	6,500	500		(c) 500
Additional paid-in capital	11,000	12,300	1,300		(c) 1,300
Retained earnings	4,100	6,700	2,600	(b) 600	(a) 3,200
Totals	$24,500	$30,300	$5,800	$9,500	$9,500

	Debit	Credit
Sources from Operations		
Net income	(a) $3,200	
Add: Depreciation expense	(e) 400	
Patent amortization expense	(f) 100	
Loss on sale of land	(h) 300	
Other Sources of Working Capital		
Issuance of common stock	(c) 1,800	
Sale of land	(h) 700	
Sources Not Affecting Working Capital		
Issuance of note payable for machinery	(g-1) 3,000	
Uses of Working Capital		
For dividends		(b) $ 600
Retirement of bonds payable		(d) 2,000
Uses Not Affecting Working Capital		
Acquisition of machinery by issuance of note payable		(g-2) 3,000
Increase in Working Capital		(i) 3,900
Totals	$9,500	$9,500

Requirement 2:

LAMB COMPANY
Statement of Changes in Financial Position
For Year Ended December 31, 1983

Sources of Financial Resources

Sources from Operations:

Net income	$3,200	
Add: Items not requiring working capital		
Depreciation expense	400	
Patent amortization expense	100	
Loss on sale of land	300	
Working capital provided by operations		$4,000

Other Sources of Working Capital:

Issuance of common stock		1,800
Sale of land		700

Sources Not Affecting Working Capital:

Issuance of note payable for machinery		3,000
Total Sources of Financial Resources		$9,500

Uses of Financial Resources

Uses of Working Capital:

For dividends	$ 600	
Retirement of bonds payable	2,000	

Uses Not Affecting Working Capital:

Acquisition of machinery by issuance of note payable	3,000	
Total Uses of Financial Resources		5,600
Increase in Working Capital		$3,900

Schedule of Changes in Working Capital Accounts

Accounts	Balances		Change
	1/1/1983	*12/31/1983*	*Change*
Cash	$ 800	$2,000	$1,200
Accounts receivable	1,200	2,200	1,000
Inventory	3,200	4,300	1,100
Current Assets	$5,200	$8,500	$3,300
Accounts payable	$2,300	$1,700	$ (600)
Current Liabilities	$2,300	$1,700	$ (600)
Working Capital	$2,900	$6,800	$3,900

GLOSSARY

Cash Provided by Operations.   A major source of financial resources on a statement of changes in financial position prepared on a cash basis. The amount is computed by adding back to net income the items on the income statement that did not result in an outflow of cash and subtracting the items on the income statement that did not provide an inflow of cash.

Schedule of Changes in Working Capital.   A schedule that lists the beginning and ending balance and change in each current asset and current liability. It also shows the beginning and ending working capital and the change in working capital. This schedule is part of the statement of changes in financial position (working capital basis) and is shown at the bottom of the statement.

Sources Not Affecting Working Capital (or Cash).   A section of a company's statement of changes in financial position that reports any financing activities that did not involve working capital (or cash).

Sources of Working Capital.   A section of a company's statement of changes in financial position that reports the items causing increases in working capital.

Statement of Changes in Financial Position.   A financial statement used to report the results of a company's financing and investing activities during the accounting period. The results are usually shown as sources and uses of working capital, although some companies show the results as sources and uses of cash.

Uses Not Affecting Working Capital (or Cash).   A section of the statement of changes in financial position that reports any investing activities of a company that did not involve working capital (or cash).

Uses of Working Capital.   A section of the statement of changes in financial position that reports the items causing decreases in working capital.

Working Capital.   Current assets (e.g., cash, receivables, short-term marketable securities, inventory, and prepaid items) less current liabilities.

Working Capital Provided by Operations.   A major source of financial resources on a statement of changes in financial position prepared on a working capital basis. The amount is computed by adding back to net income the items on the income statement that did not result in an outflow of working capital and subtracting the items that did not provide an inflow of working capital.

QUESTIONS

Q18-1   What is a statement of changes in financial position? What information does it provide?

Q18-2   What are the five major headings on a statement of changes in financial position (working capital basis)?

Q18-3   What concept of "funds" is most commonly used in the sources from operations section of a statement of changes in financial position? Why?

Q18-4   What is usually the most important source of working capital or cash on the statement of changes in financial position? Why do you think this is the case?

Q18-5   What are the most common adjustments to net income to determine the sources from operations on the working capital basis? What additional adjustments must be made to determine cash sources from operations?

Q18-6   Which changes in balance sheet accounts result in sources of working capital? Give an example of each.

Q18-7   Which changes in balance sheet accounts result in uses of working capital? Give an example of each.

Q18-8   What is a "source not affecting working capital"? Give an example.

Q18-9   What is a "use not affecting working capital"? Give an example.

Q18-10 List and briefly describe the steps necessary to develop the information for the statement of changes in financial position (working capital basis).

Q18-11 What modifications in the steps and what additional step must be made to the answer in Q18-10 to develop the information for the statement of changes in financial position (cash basis)?

Q18-12 Indicate how each of the following items would be reported on a statement of changes in financial position (working capital basis):

(a) Purchase of land.
(b) Sale of used equipment at a loss.
(c) Depreciation expense.
(d) Sale of common stock.
(e) Issuance of common stock in exchange for a building.

Q18-13 Indicate how each of the following items would be reported on a statement of changes in financial position (cash basis):

(a) Purchase of equipment.
(b) Sale of land at a gain.
(c) Patent amortization expense.
(d) Sale of preferred stock.
(e) Issuance of common stock in exchange for land.

Q18-14 How would (a) the payment of accounts payable and (b) the payment of dividends by a company be reported on the company's statement of changes in financial position (cash basis)? If your answers to (a) and (b) are different, why are they different?

EXERCISES   **E18-1   Impact on Statement.**   Below are several transactions of a company.

(a) Purchase of machinery for $5,000.
(b) Declaration and payment of 60¢ per share dividend on 8,000 shares of common stock.
(c) Issuance of $10,000, 5-year bonds at face value.
(d) Depreciation expense of $4,000.
(e) Sale of equipment for $3,000. The equipment had originally cost $6,000 and had a book value of $2,200 at the time of sale.
(f) Purchase of a $7,000 machine by issuance of a 2-year note payable for the same amount.

Required: Indicate how (and the amount) each of the above transactions would be reported on the company's statement of changes in financial position (working capital basis).

E18-2 Working Capital Schedule. Below are the current assets and current liabilities of the Ebert Company as of the beginning and end of the year:

Accounts	Beginning Balance Debit (credit)	Ending Balance Debit (credit)
Cash	$ 2,000	$ 2,200
Accounts receivable	9,600	8,900
Notes receivable (short-term)	4,700	4,500
Marketable securities	3,500	4,000
Inventory	8,700	9,800
Prepaid insurance	1,100	900
Accounts payable	(7,500)	(7,800)
Notes payable (short-term)	(6,600)	(5,400)
Wages payable	(1,200)	(1,500)
Unearned rent	(800)	(600)

Required: Prepare a schedule of changes in working capital accounts for the Ebert Company.

E18-3 Sources from Operations (Working Capital). Listed below are accounting items taken from the records of the Wilson Company for 1983:

(a) Net income, $10,000.
(b) Purchase of land, $4,000.
(c) Increase in accounts receivable, $1,800.
(d) Depreciation expense, $2,000.
(e) Gain on sale of equipment, $700.
(f) Issuance of $8,000 bonds at face value.
(g) Increase in accounts payable, $3,100.
(h) Patent amortization expense, $1,300.
(i) Decrease in inventory, $1,000.
(j) Loss on sale of land, $500.
(k) Decrease in wages payable, $300.
(l) Declaration and payment of dividends, $3,400.

Required: Prepare the sources from operations section of the Wilson Company's statement of changes in financial position for 1983 using a working capital basis.

E18-4 Cash Sources from Operations. Refer to the items listed in E18-3.

Required: Prepare the cash sources from operations section of the statement of changes in financial position for 1983.

E18-5 Funds Statement. Listed below are several items involving the sources and uses of working capital of the Rocky Company for 1983:

(a) Net income, $18,000.
(b) Dividends of $8,000 were declared and paid.
(c) Ten-year, $5,000 bonds payable were issued at face value.
(d) Depreciation expense, $6,000.
(e) Building was acquired at a cost of $15,000.
(f) Common stock was issued for $7,000.

Required: Without using a worksheet, prepare a statement of changes in financial position for 1983 (a schedule of changes in working capital is not necessary).

E18-6 Funds Statement (Working Capital). The following changes occurred in the balance sheet accounts of the Frye Company during 1983:

	Changes for 1983	
Accounts	Debit	Credit
Working capital		$ 1,000
Land	$ 6,000	
Buildings and equipment	13,000	
Accumulated depreciation		5,000
Bonds payable		4,000
Common stock, no par		2,000
Retained earnings		7,000
	$19,000	$19,000

Additional Information for 1983:
1. Net income for 1983 was $15,000. Included in net income was depreciation expense of $5,000.
2. Land that had been acquired in 1980 at a cost of $3,000 was sold for $3,000.
3. Additional land was purchased for $9,000.
4. Buildings and equipment were purchased at a cost of $13,000.
5. Two hundred shares of common stock were sold for $10 per share.
6. Ten-year, $4,000 bonds were issued at face value.
7. Dividends of $8,000 were declared and paid.

Required: 1. Prepare a 1983 statement of changes in financial position (working capital basis) for the Frye Company without using a worksheet. A schedule of changes in working capital is not necessary.
   2. What do you observe about the amount of the total uses of working capital in comparison to the working capital provided by operations?

E18-7   Funds Statement (Working Capital).   The following changes in account balances for 1983 were taken from the accounting records of the Ment Company:

	Changes for 1983	
Accounts	Debit	Credit
Current assets	$ 5,000	
Land	3,000	
Plant and equipment	7,200	
Accumulated depreciation		$ 1,500
Current liabilities		3,500
Bonds payable		2,000
Common stock, no par		1,400
Retained earnings		6,800
	$15,200	$15,200

Additional Information for 1983:
1. Net income was $9,000.
2. Dividends declared and paid totaled $2,200.
3. Plant and equipment were purchased at a cost of $7,200. No plant and equipment were sold during the year.
4. Land was purchased at a cost of $3,000.
5. One hundred shares of common stock were sold for $14 per share.
6. Five-year, $2,000 bonds were issued at face value.

Required: 1. Prepare a statement of changes in financial position (working capital basis) for 1983 without using a worksheet. A schedule of changes in working capital is not necessary.
   2. What would have happened to working capital if the company did not have any "other sources of working capital"?

E18-8 Funds Statement (Working Capital and Cash). Listed below are the beginning and ending balance sheet accounts of the Anita Company for 1983:

Accounts	1/1/1983	12/31/1983
Cash	$ 2,000	$ 3,500
Accounts receivable	4,000	7,000
Inventory	7,000	6,500
Land	6,000	10,000
Equipment	30,000	30,000
Accumulated depreciation	(10,000)	(11,000)
Totals	$39,000	$46,000
Accounts payable	$ 2,000	$ 1,500
Bonds payable	-0-	2,000
Common stock, no par	17,000	20,000
Retained earnings	20,000	22,500
Totals	$39,000	$46,000

Additional Information for 1983:

1. Net income was $5,000. Included in net income was depreciation expense of $1,000.
2. Dividends were $2,500.
3. Land was purchased for $4,000.
4. Ten-year, $2,000 bonds payable were issued at face value.
5. Two hundred shares of no par common stock were issued for $15 per share.

Required: 1. Without using a worksheet, (a) prepare a statement of changes in financial position (working capital basis) for 1983 and (b) prepare a statement of changes in financial position (cash basis) for 1983.

2. Briefly describe the differences in format (if any) between your two statements.

E18-9 Funds Statement (Cash Basis). The beginning and ending balance sheet accounts of the Tyler Company for 1983 are shown below:

Accounts	1/1/1983	12/31/1983
Cash	$ 3,000	$ 5,000
Accounts receivable	5,000	4,500
Inventory	6,000	7,100
Property and equipment	70,000	70,000
Accumulated depreciation	(12,000)	(13,600)
Totals	$72,000	$73,000
Accounts payable	$ 4,000	$ 2,500
Common stock, $5 par	12,000	12,250
Additional paid-in capital	36,000	36,750
Retained earnings	20,000	21,500
Totals	$72,000	$73,000

Additional Information for 1983:

1. Net income was $6,000, including depreciation expense of $1,600.
2. Fifty shares of common stock were issued for $20 per share.
3. Dividends of $4,500 were declared and paid.

Required: 1. Prepare a statement of changes in financial position (cash basis) for 1983. A worksheet is not required.

2. Briefly describe the differences in format between this statement and a statement prepared on a working capital basis.

E18-10 **Ending Balance Sheet.** The following beginning balance sheet and the statement of changes in financial position for 1983 are available for the Wolfe Company:

WOLFE COMPANY
Balance Sheet
January 1, 1983

Assets

Cash	$ 1,000
Accounts receivable	6,000
Land	9,000
Equipment	22,000
Accumulated depreciation	(7,000)
Total Assets	$31,000

Liabilities and Stockholders' Equity

Accounts payable	$ 3,000
Bonds payable	5,000
Total Liabilities	$ 8,000
Common stock, no par	$11,000
Retained earnings	12,000
Total Stockholders' Equity	$23,000
Total Liabilities and Stockholders' Equity	$31,000

WOLFE COMPANY
Statement of Changes in Financial Position
For Year Ended December 31, 1983

Sources from Operations:		
Net income	$7,500	
Add: Depreciation expense	1,700	
Working capital provided by operations		$ 9,200
Other Sources of Working Capital:		
Issuance of common stock		2,000
Total Sources of Working Capital		$11,200
Uses of Working Capital:		
Purchase of land	$2,200	
For dividends	3,000	
Retirement of bonds	5,000	
Total Uses of Working Capital		10,200
Increase in Working Capital		$ 1,000

Schedule of Changes in Working Capital Accounts

	Balances		
	1/1/1983	*12/31/1983*	*Change*
Cash	$1,000	$1,400	$ 400
Accounts receivable	6,000	6,800	800
Current Assets	$7,000	$8,200	$1,200
Accounts payable	3,000	3,200	200
Current Liabilities	$3,000	$3,200	$ 200
Working Capital	$4,000	$5,000	$1,000

Required: Based on the above information prepare a balance sheet as of December 31, 1983, for the Wolfe Company. Hint: Combine the information from the statement of changes in financial position with the information from the beginning balance sheet to determine the ending account balances.

E18-11   Funds Statement (Working Capital).   Below are the beginning and ending balance sheet accounts of the Henley Corporation for 1983:

Accounts	Beginning of 1983	End of 1983
Working capital	$ 9,000	$12,600
Land	12,000	8,000
Equipment	30,000	45,000
Accumulated depreciation	(8,000)	(10,600)
Totals	$43,000	$55,000
Bonds payable (due 1989)	$ -0-	$ 4,000
Common stock, $10 par	10,000	11,000
Additional paid-in capital	18,000	19,000
Retained earnings	15,000	21,000
Totals	$43,000	$55,000

Additional Information for 1983:
1. Net income was $8,000.
2. Depreciation expense was $2,600.
3. Cash dividends declared and paid were $2,000.
4. Land that originally cost $4,000 was sold for $5,200.
5. Equipment was purchased at a cost of $15,000.
6. Ten-year, $4,000 bonds payable were issued at face value.
7. One hundred shares of common stock were sold for $20 per share.

Required: 1. Prepare a statement of changes in financial position (working capital basis) for 1983 without using a worksheet. A schedule of changes in working capital is not necessary.
2. What do you notice about the amounts of the sources in comparison to the uses of working capital?

PROBLEMS
Part A

P18-1A   Funds Statement.   Below is a list of accounting information of the Bartle Company for 1983:

(a) Net income, $20,000.
(b) Equipment was acquired at a cost of $12,000.
(c) Dividends of $5,000 were declared and paid.
(d) Three hundred shares of $10 par common stock were issued for $20 per share.
(e) Depreciation expense, $8,200.
(f) Twenty-year, $8,000 bonds payable were issued at face value.
(g) Land was acquired in exchange for 100 shares of $10 par common stock when the stock was selling for $22 per share.
(h) Patent amortization expense, $2,600.
(i) Land with a cost of $800 was sold for $1,000.
(j) A building was acquired at a cost of $30,000.

Required: 1. Based on the above information prepare a statement of changes in financial position (working capital basis) for 1983. A schedule of changes in working capital is not necessary.
2. What brief observations can you make about the amounts of the sources as compared to the uses of working capital?

P18-2A   Worksheet.   The following partially completed worksheet has been prepared for the Voss Company for the year ended December 31, 1983:

Account Titles	Balances			Worksheet Entries	
	1/1/1983	12/31/1983	Change	Debit	Credit
Debits					
Working Capital	$ 4,000	$11,400	$ 7,400		
Noncurrent Accounts:					
Investments (long-term)	2,100	7,300	5,200		
Land	12,300	15,800	3,500		
Equipment	42,000	50,000	8,000		
Patents (net)	14,400	12,800	(1,600)		
Totals	$74,800	$97,300	$22,500		
Credits					
Accumulated depreciation	$17,300	$20,000	$ 2,700		
Bonds payable (due 12/31/93)	–0–	6,000	6,000		
Common stock, $10 par	12,000	14,000	2,000		
Additional paid-in capital	20,000	26,000	6,000		
Retained earnings	25,500	31,300	5,800		
Totals	$74,800	$97,300	$22,500		
Sources from Operations					
Net income					
Other Sources of Working Capital					
Sources Not Affecting Working Capital					
Uses of Working Capital					
Uses Not Affecting Working Capital					

Additional information for 1983:
1. Net income was $9,800, which included depreciation expense of $2,700 and patent amortization expense of $1,600.
2. Dividends declared and paid totaled $4,000.
3. Land that cost $4,400 was sold for $3,000.
4. Additional land was purchased at a cost of $7,900.
5. Ten-year bonds were issued at their face value of $6,000.
6. Long-term investments were purchased at a cost of $5,200.
7. Two-hundred shares of $10 par common stock were issued in exchange for equipment valued at $8,000.

Required: Complete the worksheet on the basis of the above information.

P18-3A Working Capital Schedule. Below is an alphabetical list of the beginning and ending balance sheet accounts of the Natton Company for 1983:

Accounts	Beginning Balance Debit	Beginning Balance Credit	Ending Balance Debit	Ending Balance Credit
Accounts payable		$ 7,100		$ 8,900
Accounts receivable	$ 6,200		$ 9,100	
Accumulated depreciation		32,000		36,000
Additional paid-in capital		24,000		24,000
Buildings and equipment	80,000		89,000	
Cash	1,100		1,900	
Common stock		16,000		16,000
Current income taxes payable . .		3,600		3,800
Dividends payable		2,000		2,700
Interest payable (due 7/1/1984) . .		–0–		500
Inventory	14,300		16,700	
Land	10,000		10,000	
Marketable securities (current) . .	7,500		7,000	
Note payable (due 7/1/1988) . . .		5,000		5,000
Note receivable (due 3/1/1984) . .	–0–		5,000	
Prepaid insurance	1,300		1,000	
Retained earnings		27,500		40,500
Unearned rent		1,800		1,200
Wages payable		1,400		1,100
Totals	$120,400	$120,400	$139,700	$139,700

Required: In proper form, prepare a schedule of changes in working capital accounts in 1983 for the Natton Company.

P18-4A Funds Statement (Working Capital). The following changes in account balances for 1983 were taken from the records of the Ryan Company:

Accounts	Changes for 1983 Debit	Changes for 1983 Credit
Working capital	$ 8,400	
Land	3,300	
Buildings and equipment	25,000	
Accumulated depreciation		$ 4,500
Patents (net)		1,500
Bonds payable	9,000	
Note payable (due 12/31/1985)		25,000
Common stock, $5 par		2,000
Additional paid-in capital		6,000
Retained earnings		6,700
	$45,700	$45,700

Additional Information for 1983:
1. Net income was $13,000. Included in net income was depreciation expense of $4,500 and patent amortization expense of $1,500.
2. Dividends of $6,300 were declared and paid.
3. Four hundred shares of $5 par common stock were sold for $20 per share.
4. A building worth $25,000 was acquired by issuing a long-term note for the same amount.
5. Land was purchased at a cost of $7,200.
6. Bonds payable with a book value of $9,000 were retired for $9,000.
7. Land that had originally cost $3,900 was sold for $5,900.

Required:
1. Prepare a worksheet (working capital basis) for the 1983 statement of changes in financial position (put the debit and credit changes in the third amount column, do not complete the first two amount columns).
2. Prepare the statement of changes in financial position.
3. In your answer to Requirement 2, what do you notice about the amounts of the sources and uses *not* affecting working capital as compared to the other sources and uses?

P18-5A Worksheet and Funds Statement (Cash Basis). The following is a list of increases and decreases that occurred in the balance sheet accounts of the Pierce Company for 1983:

Accounts	Increase (decrease)
Cash	$ 5,000
Accounts receivable	(1,000)
Inventory	4,900
Prepaid insurance	700
Land	3,900
Buildings and equipment	15,800
Accumulated depreciation	5,100
Accounts payable	2,300
Other current payables	(600)
Bonds payable	6,000
Common stock, $10 par	5,000
Additional paid-in capital	3,500
Retained earnings	8,000

Additional Information for 1983:
1. Net income was $17,200, which included $5,100 of depreciation.
2. Dividends of $9,200 were declared and paid.
3. Land and equipment were purchased at $7,900 and $15,800, respectively.
4. Long-term bonds were issued at their face value of $6,000.
5. Five hundred shares of $10 par common stock were issued at $17 per share.
6. Land that had cost $4,000 was sold for $2,600.

Required:
1. Prepare a worksheet (cash basis) for the 1983 statement of changes in financial position (put the increases and decreases in the third amount column, do not complete the first two amount columns.)
2. Prepare the statement of changes in financial position for 1983.
3. Briefly describe the differences in format between the statement prepared in Requirement 2 and the statement prepared on a working capital basis.

P18-6A   Complex Worksheet and Funds Statement (Working Capital).   Below are the comparative condensed balance sheets and the condensed income statement of the McVey Company for 1983:

McVEY COMPANY
Comparative Balance Sheets

	January 1, 1983	December 31, 1983
Cash	$ 3,200	$ 6,900
Accounts receivable	6,800	11,600
Inventory	8,000	7,800
Land	9,200	15,200
Buildings	75,100	100,300
Accumulated depreciation: buildings	(26,700)	(30,600)
Equipment	33,900	34,600
Accumulated depreciation: equipment	(10,300)	(11,100)
Patents (net)	8,500	7,800
Total Assets	$107,700	$142,500
Accounts payable	$ 11,000	$ 17,500
Accrued current payables	700	500
Bonds payable (due 12/31/1993)	–0–	9,000
Premium on bonds payable	–0–	400
Common stock, $10 par	22,000	27,500
Additional paid-in capital	31,000	38,100
Retained earnings	43,000	49,500
Total Liabilities and Stockholders' Equity	$107,700	$142,500

McVEY COMPANY
Income Statement
For Year Ended December 31, 1983

Sales	$72,000
Cost of goods sold	(43,200)
Depreciation expense: buildings	(3,900)
Depreciation expense: equipment	(2,100)
Patent amortization expense	(700)
Other operating expenses	(8,300)
Operating income	$13,800
Loss on sale of equipment	(1,500)
Net Income	$12,300

Additional Information for 1983:
1. Dividends declared and paid total $5,800.
2. Three hundred shares of $10 par common stock were sold for $22 per share.
3. Equipment and a building were purchased for $8,700 and $25,200 respectively.
4. Equipment with a cost of $8,000 and accumulated depreciation of $1,300 was sold for $5,200.
5. Ten-year bonds payable with a face value of $9,000 were issued for $9,400 on December 31, 1983. (Hint: Record the issuance of the bonds at a premium in the usual manner.)
6. Two hundred and fifty shares of $10 par common stock with a current market value of $24 per share were issued in exchange for land.

Required: 1. Prepare a worksheet for a 1983 statement of changes in financial position (working capital basis).
2. Prepare the statement of changes in financial position for 1983.

PROBLEMS

Part B

P18-1B Sources from Operations. Below is a list of accounting information taken from the records of the Fox Corporation for 1983:

(a) Issuance of common stock, $25,000.
(b) Loss on sale of equipment, $3,700.
(c) Purchase of land, $22,000.
(d) Decrease in accounts receivable, $8,700.
(e) Depreciation expense, $18,000.
(f) Increase in inventory, $7,300.
(g) Gain on sale of land, $4,900.
(h) Decrease in accounts payable, $5,500.
(i) Increase in short-term marketable securities, $2,400.
(j) Increase in salaries payable, $900.
(k) Issuance of long-term note payable, $6,000.
(l) Decrease in unearned rent revenue, $500.
(m) Declaration and payment of dividends, $19,000.
(n) Decrease in prepaid rent, $1,100.
(o) Net income, $40,000.
(p) Patent amortization expense, $4,200.

Required: Using the above information prepare the sources from operations section of the statement of changes in financial position on (1) a working capital basis and (2) a cash basis.

P18-2B Funds Statement (Working Capital). The following is a list of increases in the balance sheet accounts of the Johnson Company for 1983:

Accounts	Increase
Current assets	$ 9,000
Land	2,000
Buildings	20,000
Equipment	11,000
Accumulated depreciation	5,000
Current liabilities	4,000
Mortgage payable (20-year)	20,000
Common stock, $2 par	1,400
Additional paid-in capital	5,600
Retained earnings	6,000

Additional Information for 1983:
1. The company earned net income of $16,000, which included depreciation expense of $5,000.
2. Dividends declared and paid amounted to $10,000.
3. A building worth $20,000 was acquired at year end by issuing a 20-year, $20,000 mortgage.
4. Equipment and land were purchased for $11,000 and $8,000, respectively.
5. Seven hundred shares of $2 par common stock were issued for $10 per share.
6. Land that had cost $6,000 was sold for $4,800.

Required: 1. Prepare a worksheet (working capital basis) for the 1983 statement of changes in financial position (put the increases in the third amount column, do not complete the first two amount columns).
2. Prepare the statement of changes in financial position for 1983.
3. Briefly describe the differences in format between the statement prepared in Requirement 2 and the statement prepared on a cash basis.

P18-3B Worksheet. Below is a partially completed worksheet of the Schumm Company for the year ended December 31, 1983:

Account Titles	Balances 1/1/1983	12/31/1983	Change	Worksheet Entries Debit	Credit
Debits					
Working Capital	$ 3,000	$ 8,000	$ 5,000		
Noncurrent Accounts:					
Land	6,200	14,300	8,100		
Buildings and equipment	55,000	100,000	45,000		
Copyrights (net)	11,800	9,800	(2,000)		
Totals	$76,000	$132,100	$56,100		
Credits					
Accumulated depreciation	$12,100	$ 15,600	$ 3,500		
Bonds payable (due 12/31/1988)	–0–	8,000	8,000		
Premium on bonds payable	–0–	200	200		
Mortgage payable	–0–	30,000	30,000		
Common stock, $5 par	10,000	12,500	2,500		
Additional paid-in capital	20,000	27,500	7,500		
Retained earnings	33,900	38,300	4,400		
Totals	$76,000	$132,100	$56,100		
Sources from Operations Net income					
Other Sources of Working Capital					
Sources Not Affecting Working Capital					
Uses of Working Capital					
Uses Not Affecting Working Capital					

Additional Information for 1983:
1. Net income was $11,200, which included depreciation expense of $3,500 and copyright amortization expense of $2,000.
2. Dividends declared and paid were $6,800.
3. Land that cost $4,000 was sold for $5,700.
4. Equipment and land were purchased at costs of $15,000 and $12,100, respectively.
5. Five hundred shares of $5 par common stock were issued for $20 per share.
6. Five-year bonds with an $8,000 face value were issued for $8,200 on December 31, 1983. (Hint: Record the issuance of the bonds at a premium in the usual manner.)
7. On December 28, 1983, a building with a value of $30,000 was acquired by issuing a 10-year mortgage for the same amount.

Required: Complete the worksheet on the basis of the above information.

P18-4B **Complex Worksheet and Funds Statement (Working Capital).** Presented below are condensed balance sheets, a condensed income statement, and the retained earnings statement of the Fite Company for 1983:

FITE COMPANY
Comparative Balance Sheets

	1/1/1983	12/31/1983
Cash	$ 2,700	$ 2,900
Receivables (short-term)	7,100	9,600
Inventory	8,200	7,700
Land	10,100	18,700
Buildings and machinery	105,300	135,300
Accumulated depreciation	(42,400)	(45,000)
Copyrights (net)	9,400	8,000
Total Assets	$100,400	$137,200
Accounts payable	$ 8,100	$ 9,200
Salaries payable	1,300	1,000
Note payable (due 12/31/1988)	-0-	8,600
Bonds payable	-0-	10,000
Common stock, $5 par	25,000	30,000
Additional paid-in capital	29,000	36,000
Retained earnings	38,000	45,600
Treasury stock (at cost)	(1,000)	(3,200)
Total Liabilities and Stockholders' Equity	$100,400	$137,200

FITE COMPANY
Income Statement
For Year Ended December 31, 1983

Sales	$81,000
Cost of goods sold	(48,500)
Depreciation expense	(6,800)
Copyright amortization expense	(1,400)
Other expenses	(12,300)
Operating income	$12,000
Gain on sale of machinery . .	1,700
Net Income	$13,700

FITE COMPANY
Retained Earnings Statement
For Year Ended December 31, 1983

Beginning retained earnings	$38,000
Add: Net income	13,700
	$51,700
Less: Cash dividends	(6,100)
Ending Retained Earnings . .	$45,600

Additional Information for 1983:

1. Long-term bonds were issued at their face value of $10,000.
2. A building was purchased at a cost of $42,200.
3. Machinery with a cost of $12,200 and accumulated depreciation of $4,200 was sold for $9,700.
4. One thousand shares of $5 par common stock were issued for $12 per share.
5. On December 31, 1983, a 5-year note for $8,600 was issued in exchange for an acre of land.
6. Two hundred shares of the company's common stock were reacquired as treasury stock for $11 per share.

Required: 1. Prepare a worksheet for the 1983 statement of changes in financial position (working capital basis).

2. Prepare the statement of changes in financial position for 1983.

P18-5B   Complex Worksheet and Funds Statement (Cash). Review the information presented in P18-4B for the Fite Company.

Required: 1. Prepare a worksheet for a 1983 statement of changes in financial position (*cash* basis).
2. Prepare the statement of changes in financial position for 1983.

P18-6B   Funds Statement. A list of selected accounting information of the Topps Company for 1983 is presented below:

(a) Copyright amortization expense was $3,200.
(b) Machinery was purchased for $13,300.
(c) Bonds payable with a face value and book value of $10,000 were retired for $10,000.
(d) Depreciation expense was $9,800.
(e) Six hundred shares of $5 par common stock were issued for $15 per share.
(f) A building valued at $32,000 was acquired by issuing 2,000 shares of $5 par common stock. The stock was selling for $16 per share.
(g) Net income was $28,000.
(h) Dividends declared and paid were $15,000.
(i) Equipment with a cost of $11,000 and a book value of $4,500 was sold for $8,500.
(j) Land was purchased at a cost of $7,200.

Required: 1. Based on the above information prepare a statement of changes in financial position (working capital basis) for 1983. A schedule of changes in working capital is not necessary.
2. What observations can you make about the amounts of the sources as compared to the uses of working capital?

DISCUSSION CASES

C18-1   Erroneous Statement. The president of Tide Corporation has come to your bank for a loan. He states: "Each of the last three years our working capital has gone down. This year we need to increase our working capital by $6,000. We have never borrowed any money on a long-term basis and are reluctant to do so. However, we definitely need to purchase some new, more advanced equipment to replace the old equipment we are selling this year. We also want to acquire some treasury stock because it would be a good investment. We also would like to pay dividends of 50% of net income instead of our usual 40%. Given our expected net income and the money we will receive from our depreciation expense and the gain on the sale of the old equipment, I estimate we will have to borrow $11,000, based on the following schedule."

Schedule of Working Capital

Inflows of working capital:		
Sources from net income		$20,000
Other sources:		
Depreciation expense		4,000
Gain on sale of old equipment		3,000
Proceeds from sale of old equipment		8,000
Bank loan (estimated)		11,000
Total inflows		$46,000
Outflows of working capital:		
Purchase equipment	$30,000	
Pay dividends (50% of net income)	10,000	
Total outflows		40,000
Increase in Working Capital		$ 6,000

The president explains that the $5,000 expected cost of acquiring the treasury stock was not included because it would involve only a transaction between the corporation and the existing stockholders and would be of no interest to "outsiders." He also states that "if his figures are off a little bit," the most the corporation wants to borrow is $15,000. You determine that the amounts he has listed for each item (except the bank loan) are accurate.

Required: 1. Prepare a statement of changes in financial position for the Tide Corporation that shows the necessary bank loan in order to increase working capital by $6,000.
2. Explain to the president why his $11,000 estimate of the bank loan is incorrect.
3. Suggest ways to reduce the necessary bank loan and still increase working capital.

C18-2   Outline and Discussion.   A friend of yours is having difficulty understanding the statement of changes in financial position and has asked for your assistance. Prepare an outline (including all the possible major headings) of the statement (use a working capital basis). Present examples of financing or investing transactions that would be disclosed under each major heading. Finally, discuss the financial information that is disclosed in the statement of changes in financial position that is not disclosed in the income statement or balance sheet.

19 | Analysis of Financial Statements

After reading this chapter, you should understand:

- The difference between intracompany and intercompany comparisons
- Segment reporting
- Interim financial statements
- Horizontal analysis
- Vertical analysis
- How to compute stockholder and company profitability ratios, solvency ratios, activity ratios, and stability ratios
- The uses of segment reports, interim financial reports, and horizontal, vertical, and ratio analyses

A company's financial statements are intended to summarize the results of its operations and its ending financial position. The information in the statements is studied and related to other information by external users for several reasons. Current stockholders, for example, are concerned about their investment income, as well as about the company's overall profitability and stability. Some potential investors are interested in "solid" companies, that is, companies whose financial statements indicate stable earnings and dividends with little growth in operations. Others prefer companies whose financial statements indicate a trend for rapid growth in different lines of business. Short-term creditors are interested in a company's short-run solvency — its ability to pay current obligations as they become due. Long-term creditors are concerned about the safety of their interest income and the company's ability to continue its earnings and cash flows to meet its financial commitments. And these are only a few of the users, and uses, of financial statements.

Companies prepare their financial statements on an annual basis (many also prepare statements on a shorter basis, for instance, quarterly). These companies often include certain supplementary schedules and analyses with their annual financial statements. Additional analyses of the financial statement information may be made by the external users of the information, such as lending institutions, current and potential stockholders, and other groups. Whether a person is an accountant who prepares the financial statement information for the company or an external user who uses the information in decision making, it is necessary to understand the content, uses, and limitations of these analyses.

The purpose of this chapter is to discuss the various types of financial analyses that might be made and reported in addition to the financial statements. They include: (1) reports on the results of business segments, (2) interim financial reports, (3) horizontal and vertical percentage analyses, and (4) ratio analyses.

FINANCIAL ANALYSIS COMPARISONS

Before discussing the various financial analyses it is helpful to review how this information is used. Recall from Chapter 1 that decision making consists of several stages, including recognition of the problem, identification of the alternatives, evaluation of the alternatives, and the decision itself. Financial accounting information is especially useful in the evaluation stage for external users. In this stage external users study the various data of importance to them in financial reports in order to evaluate the data and make their decisions. They usually make comparisons within the same or related industries. These comparisons are important in financial analysis.

Intracompany Comparisons

One method of evaluating the results of a company's current operations and its financial position is to compare them with the company's past results. These are referred to as intracompany comparisons. **Intracompany comparisons are comparisons *within* the company.** Important in these comparisons is the evidence of *trends* — indications that a company's performance is stable, is improving, or is declining, not only in the short run but also in the longer run. Most companies now present at least 2 years of comparable data in their financial statements. That is, they include the current and previous year's income statements, balance sheets, and statements of changes in financial position. Many companies also include 5- , 10- , or 15-year summaries of key data from these financial statements.

An important point to remember when preparing and using financial analysis information in these comparisons is to be consistent over time. Whether business segment information, interim data, percentage analyses, or ratios are prepared, each year's information should be presented in a similar manner so that valid comparisons and reliable trends may be obtained. When making these comparisons, consideration should be given to how changes in the general, regional, or industry economy might have affected the company's results from year to year.

Intercompany Comparisons

A second method of evaluation involves the use of intercompany comparisons. **Intercompany comparisons are comparisons of a company's performance with that of competing companies, with the industry as a whole, or with the results in related industries.** Intercompany comparisons may be made for a single period or for several past periods. Competing companies' financial information may be obtained from their financial statements. Information on the performance of the industry as a whole or of related industries may be based on financial information provided by such financial analysis companies as Moody's Investors Service, Standard and Poor's, Dun and Bradstreet, and Robert Morris and Associates, available in most college and public libraries. These companies not only provide information from annual reports but also publish monthly and quarterly updates and supplements. Other organizations and trade associations provide similar information.

Anyone preparing or using financial analysis information in intercompany comparisons must be concerned with the consistency of data across companies. For instance, they should take into consideration the impact of different generally acceptable accounting practices (e.g., LIFO versus FIFO for inventories, or accelerated versus straight-line depreciation for property and equipment) upon the results. When making these comparisons, the impact of changes in the general, regional, or industry economy should be considered.

SEGMENT REPORTING

Many financial statements of large corporations with several subsidiaries and divisions are prepared on a *consolidated* basis. That is, the accounting results of the various segments are combined into a set of financial statements for the entire economic entity. Consolidated financial statements were briefly discussed in Chapter 17. Although investors and creditors think that consolidated financial statements are important in evaluating the overall performance of each corporation, they also like to know information about the corporation's operating segments. These users feel that evaluations of the operations and assets of the separate segments of each corporation are useful in their decision making.

Because of the need for such data, accounting principles require that a company's financial statements include information about its operations in different industries.[1] The required information, how it is prepared, and the way it is reported are discussed below.

Information to be Reported

Company operations are reported by *segments*. **An industry segment is a component (e.g., department, division, or subsidiary) of a company that provides a product or service to customers for a profit.** To determine its industry segments, a company might consider its products (e.g., appliances, chemicals), its geographic sales territories (e.g., East Coast, Midwest), or its methods of sales (e.g., discount stores, department stores). For instance, the DuPont Corporation reports its segment information by products, showing certain information separately for its chemicals, plastics, fibers, and specialty products segments.

A company need not report separate financial information about all of its industry segments, however. Only information about a company's reportable industry segments must be separately reported. **A reportable industry segment has revenues, operating profits, or identifiable assets that are 10% or more of the**

---

[1] Other information, including information related to a company's foreign operations, export sales, and major customers, is also required to be reported, but it is beyond the scope of this textbook.

company's total revenues, operating profits, or identifiable assets.[2] Certain financial information must be reported separately for each reportable industry segment. This information includes:

1. *Revenues.* The revenues of a reportable industry segment include revenues from sales to customers.[3] *Excluded* from segment revenues are *general corporate revenues* (i.e., revenues earned by the company as a whole, such as interest revenue).

2. *Operating Profit.* The operating profit of a reportable industry segment is its revenues minus its segment expenses. Included in segment expenses are cost of goods sold, selling expenses, and general and administrative expenses. *Excluded* from segment expenses are *general corporate expenses* (i.e., expenses incurred by the company as a whole, such as interest expense) and *income taxes*. Thus the operating profit is reported *before income taxes*.

3. *Identifiable Assets.* The identifiable assets of a reportable industry segment are the assets that are used by the segment. *Excluded* from identifiable assets are *general corporate assets* (i.e., assets used only for general corporate purposes, such as marketable securities).

This same information is also reported for the rest of the company's industry segments. That is, the remaining other industry segments are combined and their combined revenues, operating profits, and identifiable assets are reported.

Preparation and Reporting of Segment Information

The revenues, operating profits, and assets of the reportable industry segments and the combined remaining segments are reported in a schedule accompanying the financial statements. On the schedule the revenues listed for the reportable industry segments and the other combined industry segments must sum to the total sales revenue reported in the company's income statement; the operating profit of the segments (plus or minus any general corporate revenues and expenses) must sum to the income before income taxes; and the identifiable assets (plus any general corporate assets) of the segments must sum to the company's total assets. Any general corporate revenues, expenses, and assets should be separately identified in the schedule.

On the schedule the revenues for the segments and in total are listed first. The segment expenses (cost of goods sold, selling expenses, and general and administrative expenses) are deducted from the revenues to determine the operating profit of each segment and in total. Any general corporate revenues and expenses are added to or subtracted from the *total* operating profit to arrive at the income before income taxes, as reported on the income statement. Finally, the identifiable assets

---

[2] "Financial Reporting for Segments of a Business Enterprise," *FASB Statement No. 14* (Stamford, Conn.: Conn.: FASB, 1976), par. 1.

[3] Intersegment sales (e.g., sales by one department to another department within the company) are also included in revenues. These types of sales are a concern of *consolidation* accounting, however, and are not considered further in this chapter.

**EXHIBIT 19-1
Income Statement**

**BAXTER CORPORATION
Income Statement
For Year Ended December 31, 1983**

Sales		$100,000
Cost of goods sold		60,000
Gross profit		$ 40,000
Operating expenses		
Selling expenses	$ 8,000	
General and administrative expenses	13,000	
Total operating expenses		21,000
Operating income		$ 19,000
Other revenues and expenses		
Interest revenue	$ 1,300	
Interest expense	(300)	1,000
Income before income taxes		$ 20,000
Income tax expense		8,000
Net Income		$ 12,000

are listed for each segment and in total. Any general corporate assets are added to the *total* identifiable assets to arrive at the company's total assets, as reported on its ending balance sheet.

ILLUSTRATION. To illustrate, suppose that the Baxter Corporation presents the income statement shown in Exhibit 19-1.

The Baxter Corporation has two reportable segments, A and B. Its several other segments are to be combined for reporting purposes. The company has total assets of $150,000 on December 31, 1983. Of the total assets, $4,000 are general corporate assets. The sales, expenses, and *remaining* assets are assigned to the segments according to the following amounts:

	Amounts Identified with		
	Segment A	*Segment B*	*Other Segments*
Sales	$30,000	$50,000	$20,000
Cost of goods sold	17,000	32,000	11,000
Selling expenses	2,000	4,400	1,600
General and administrative expenses . . .	4,200	6,000	2,800
Identifiable assets	46,000	70,000	30,000

The schedule that the Baxter Corporation would use to report its segment information is shown in Exhibit 19-2.

In Exhibit 19-2 the revenues are listed first and total $100,000, the amount of sales reported in Exhibit 19-1. The expenses of each segment are listed next and subtracted from the revenues to determine the operating profit of each segment. Reportable

EXHIBIT 19-2
Industry Segment
Financial Information

BAXTER CORPORATION
Industry Segment Financial Information
For Year Ended December 31, 1983

	Reportable Industry Segments		Other Industry Segments	Totals
	A	B		
Revenues (sales)	$30,000	$50,000	$20,000	$100,000
Segment expenses:				
Cost of goods sold	$17,000	$32,000	$11,000	$ 60,000
Selling expenses	2,000	4,400	1,600	8,000
General and administrative				
expenses	4,200	6,000	2,800	13,000
Total segment expenses	$23,200	$42,400	$15,400	$ 81,000
Operating profit	$ 6,800	$ 7,600	$ 4,600	$ 19,000
Interest revenue				1,300
Interest expense				(300)
Income before income taxes				$ 20,000
Identifiable assets	$46,000	$70,000	$30,000	$146,000
General corporate assets				4,000
Total assets				$150,000

industry segments A and B earned operating profits of $6,800 and $7,600, respectively, while the other industry segments earned a combined operating profit of $4,600. The $1,300 interest revenue is added to and the $300 interest expense is subtracted from the $19,000 total operating profit to obtain the $20,000 income before income taxes listed in Exhibit 19-1. The identifiable assets are allocated to each segment, and the $146,000 total identifiable assets are then added to the $4,000 general corporate assets to reconcile with the $150,000 total assets.

Uses of Segment Information

The reporting of segment information by companies provides useful information for investors and creditors. Intracompany comparisons of revenues and operating profits of each reportable industry segment can be made. These comparisons can show how well one segment is performing as compared to another segment. For instance, comparisons can be made of each segment's operating profits to its sales and to its identifiable assets to see how well each segment is using its resources (e.g., in Exhibit 19-2 Segment A earned an operating profit of $6,800 using assets of $46,000, or a 15% "return" on the resources used by this segment, while Segment B earned $7,600 using $70,000 assets, only an 11% return). Or the results of one segment for several years can be compared to identify any trends in its operating performance. Intercompany comparisons can also be made, although care must be taken to be sure that each company has identified its reportable industry segments in the same manner. If not, valid comparisons cannot be made because there is a lack of *comparability*. Later in the chapter we use certain ratios to make these comparisons easier.

INTERIM FINANCIAL STATEMENTS

External users often want more frequent accounting information than is provided in a company's annual financial statements. As a result, interim reports called interim financial statements are prepared. **Interim financial statements are reports for periods of less than a year.** Interim financial statements are normally issued four times a year. Hence the term *quarterly report* is often used for these interim statements. Accounting principles have been established for interim financial statements. Basically, each interim (quarterly) period is considered to be part of the annual accounting period. Thus all adjustments made at the end of each interim period must consider the impact on the operating results for the rest of the annual period. Certain principles are modified, however, so that the results will be more useful.

Principles of Interim Reporting

The accounting principles for interim financial statements apply primarily to income statement items. They are summarized below:

REVENUES. Revenues should be recognized during an interim period in the same manner as during the annual accounting period. If revenues are subject to seasonal variations (e.g., toy sales), the company should report the seasonal nature of its activities.

COST OF GOODS SOLD. Companies that use a periodic inventory system may use the *gross profit method* or *retail inventory method* (discussed in Chapter 9) to estimate their interim inventory. The method used should be disclosed. The company should also report any adjustments that must be made at the end of the year because of a difference between the estimated ending inventory and the annual physical inventory.

EXPENSES. Expenses that affect the operating activities of more than one interim period should be allocated among the interim periods. This allocation should be based on, say, the time expired or some activity related to the periods. For instance, prepaid insurance might be allocated as insurance expense based on the months expired in each interim period. Or depreciation expense might be based on the units produced in each interim period. Expenses such as utilities, interest, and rent that affect only one interim period should be assigned *only* to that period. Gains and losses on the sale of land or equipment, for example, should also be recognized in the interim period when they occur.

INCOME TAXES. Income tax expense for each interim period should be based on the income tax rate applicable for the entire year. In this chapter we continue our assumption that a 40% income tax rate is applicable to interim income before income taxes.

EXTRAORDINARY ITEMS AND DISPOSALS OF BUSINESS SEGMENTS. Extraordinary items (net of income taxes) and the results from the disposal of a business segment (net of income taxes) should be disclosed in the interim period during which the events occur.

EARNINGS PER SHARE. Earnings per share should be computed for each interim period and reported on the face of the interim income statement. A breakdown of earnings per share related to continuing income, the disposal of a business segment, and extraordinary items should also be disclosed.

INTERIM INCOME. The income for the current interim period is reported in that interim income statement. In addition, current *year-to-date* (i.e., from the beginning of the year until the end of the interim period) income information is also provided. Thus in the second quarter of a company's fiscal year, the company prepares an income statement for the second quarter as well as an income statement for the first 6 months of the year. These income statements are shown beside each other.

Preparation and Disclosure of Interim Financial Statements

The accounting procedures involved in preparing the interim financial statements are similar to those for annual statements. A worksheet is typically used. A trial balance of the year-to-date account balances is listed on the worksheet. Year-to-date adjusting entries are recorded on the worksheet, after which the worksheet is completed and the year-to-date financial statements are prepared. The interim accounting procedures are different in several ways from those completed at the end of the year, however.

First, for companies using a periodic inventory system, the ending inventory for the interim financial statements is usually determined by using an estimate instead of taking a physical inventory. The gross profit method or retail inventory method is typically used to estimate the ending interim inventory. Second, the adjusting entries required at the end of the interim period to bring the accounts up to date are usually prepared only on the worksheet and are not entered into the accounts. Only at the end of the year are the annual adjusting entries journalized and posted to the accounts. Finally, the accounts are not closed at the end of each interim period. In an interim period after the first period, care must be taken therefore *not* to include amounts from previous interim periods in the revenues and expenses on the current interim income statement. To avoid this problem, companies usually prepare the interim income statement on a year-to-date basis and then deduct out the income statement results from any previous interim periods. For example, at the end of 6 months a company must report an income statement for the second quarter (as well as for 6 months). To do so the company prepares an income statement for 6 months from the worksheet and then deducts out (subtracts) the first-quarter income statement results to determine the second-quarter income statement.

**EXHIBIT 19-3
Interim Income
Statement**

BAKER CORPORATION
Income Statement
For First Quarter Ended March 31, 1983

Sales (net)		$8,000
Cost of goods sold		
Inventory (1/1/1983)	$2,100	
Purchases (net)	5,100	
Cost of goods available for sale	$7,200	
Less: Inventory (3/31/1983, estimated)	2,400	
Cost of goods sold		4,800
Gross profit		$3,200
Operating expenses		
Selling expenses	$1,000	
General and administrative expenses	1,200	
Total operating expenses		2,200
Income before income taxes		$1,000
Income tax expense		400
Net Income		$ 600
Earnings per share (2,000 shares)		$ .30

ILLUSTRATION. Suppose that the Baker Corporation reported the income statement shown in Exhibit 19-3 at the end of its first quarter of 1983. The corporation is now preparing its interim income statements for the second quarter and first 6 months of 1983. The worksheet used for these income statements is shown in Exhibit 19-4.

In studying Exhibit 19-4 several items are important. Adjusting entry (a) is for one-half of the yearly depreciation expense on the property and equipment, based on straight-line depreciation over a 20-year estimated life (no residual value). The depreciation is allocated one-third to selling expenses and two-thirds to general and administrative expenses and is recorded directly in these *control* accounts on the worksheet. Adjusting entry (b) is for interest on a $2,000, 12% note receivable issued April 1, 1983. The note was outstanding for only 3 months, and therefore interest of $60 ($2,000 × 0.12 × 3/12) is accrued. Adjusting entry (c) is for the year-to-date income tax expense and income taxes payable. The income tax expense for the 6 months is $1,000, computed by multiplying the 40% income tax rate times the $2,500 income before income taxes (shown in Exhibit 19-5).[4]

[4] As may be seen, the income before income taxes must be known *before* preparing the income tax expense adjusting entry on the worksheet. The income before income taxes is normally not known until *after* the adjusting entries are recorded and the worksheets completed. This complexity is beyond the scope of this textbook. To simplify any homework requiring preparation of a worksheet, the year-to-date income tax expense is always provided.

EXHIBIT 19-4   Interim Worksheet

		BAKER CORPORATION Interim Worksheet For Six Months Ended June 30, 1983			
	Trial Balance		Adjustments		
Account Titles	Debit	Credit	Debit		Credit	
Cash	3,200					
Accounts receivable	1,900					
Inventory (1/1/1983)	2,100					
Note receivable (due 4/1/1984)	2,000					
Property and equipment	6,000					
Accumulated depreciation		1,200			(a)	150
Accounts payable		1,800				
Common stock, no par		4,000				
Retained earnings (1/1/1983)		6,110				
Sales (net)		18,000				
Purchases (net)	11,300					
Selling expenses	2,110		(a)	50		
General and administrative expenses	2,500		(a)	100		
Totals	31,110	31,110				
Interest receivable			(b)	60		
Interest revenue					(b)	60
Income tax expense			(c)	1,000		
Income taxes payable					(c)	1,000
			1,210		1,210	
Inventory (6/30/1983, estimated)[d]						
Net Income						

Explanations:
(a) Depreciation = $6,000 \div 20$ years $\times \frac{1}{2}$ year = $150, of which $\frac{1}{3}$ is selling and $\frac{2}{3}$ is general and administrative expense.
(b) Interest = $2,000 \times 0.12 \times \frac{1}{4}$ year = $60.
(c) Income taxes = ($18,000 + $60 + $2,600 − $2,100 − $11,300 − $2,160 − $2,600) income before income taxes $\times 0.40$ = $1,000.
(d) $7,200 gross profit = $0.40 \times $18,000 net sales. $10,800 cost of goods sold = $18,000 net sales − $7,200 gross profit. $2,600 ending inventory = $2,100 beginning inventory + $11,300 net purchases − $10,800 cost of goods sold.

Adjusted Trial Balance		Income Statement		Balance Sheet	
Debit	Credit	Debit	Credit	Debit	Credit
3,200				3,200	
1,900				1,900	
2,100		2,100			
2,000				2,000	
6,000				6,000	
	1,350				1,350
	1,800				1,800
	4,000				4,000
	6,110				6,110
	18,000		18,000		
11,300		11,300			
2,160		2,160			
2,600		2,600			
60				60	
	60		60		
1,000		1,000			
	1,000				1,000
32,320	32,320				
			2,600	2,600	
		19,160	20,660	15,760	14,260
		1,500			1,500
		20,660	20,660	15,760	15,760

The $2,600 ending inventory on June 30, 1983, is estimated by using the gross profit method instead of taking a physical inventory, as follows. Based on experience, Baker Corporation estimates its gross profit is 40% of net sales, or $7,200 ($18,000 × 0.40). Cost of goods sold is estimated to be $10,800 ($18,000 net sales less $7,200 gross profit). Finally, the $2,600 ending inventory is found by deducting the $10,800 cost of goods sold from the cost of goods available for sale ($2,100 beginning inventory plus $11,300 net purchases).

The $1,500 net income for the 6 months brings the income statement and balance sheet debit and credit columns into balance and the worksheet is complete. Upon completion of the worksheet the income statement and balance sheet are prepared; they are shown in Exhibits 19-5 and 19-6. Note that, with the exception of the inventories, the income statement results for the *second* quarter of 1983 were determined by subtracting the first quarter results (Exhibit 19-3) from the 6-months income statement. The beginning inventory of the second quarter ($2,400) is the ending inventory of the first quarter. The ending inventory is the same for both the second quarter and the 6 months.

EXHIBIT 19-5
Income Statement

BAKER CORPORATION
Income Statements

	For Periods	
	Apr. 1–June 30, 1983	Jan. 1–June 30, 1983
Sales (net)	$10,000	$18,000
Cost of goods sold		
Inventory (beginning)	$2,400	$ 2,100
Purchases (net)	6,200	11,300
Cost of goods available for sale	$8,600	$13,400
Less: Ending inventory (estimated)	2,600	2,600
Cost of goods sold	6,000	10,800
Gross profit	$ 4,000	$ 7,200
Operating expenses		
Selling expenses	$1,160	$ 2,160
General and administrative expenses	1,400	2,600
Total operating expenses	2,560	4,760
Operating income	$ 1,440	$ 2,440
Other revenues		
Interest revenue	60	60
Income before income taxes	$ 1,500	$ 2,500
Income tax expense	600	1,000
Net Income	$ 900	$ 1,500
Earnings per share (2,000 shares)	$ .45	$ .75

EXHIBIT 19-6
Balance Sheet

BAKER CORPORATION
Balance Sheet
June 30, 1983

Assets

Current assets
Cash	$3,200	
Accounts receivable	1,900	
Note receivable	2,000	
Interest receivable	60	
Inventory	2,600	
Total current assets		$ 9,760
Property and equipment	$6,000	
Less: Accumulated depreciation	(1,350)	4,650
Total Assets		$14,410

Liabilities

Current liabilities
Accounts payable	$1,800	
Income taxes payable	1,000	
Total Liabilities		$ 2,800

Stockholders' Equity

Common stock, no par	$4,000	
Retained earnings	7,610[a]	
Total Stockholders' Equity		11,610
Total Liabilities and Stockholders' Equity		$14,410

[a] $6,110 beginning retained earnings + $1,500 net income − $0 dividends.

Uses of Interim Financial Statements

Interim reports provide more timely information for external users in decision making than annual reports. The same intercompany and intracompany comparisons can be made with interim financial statements as are made with annual financial statements, although on a more frequent basis. For instance, trends in a company's sales, operating expenses, and earnings over time can be quickly detected in interim reports. Or for seasonal industries, the current sales and earnings of a company can be compared either to its own past results or to the results of other companies in the interim "peak sales" periods and in the "low-volume" interim periods to identify differences in operating activities. For instance, Eastman Kodak Company reported sales and net earnings of $3,107.7 million and $404.8 million in the fourth quarter of 1980, respectively, as compared to $2,137.1 million sales and $193.0 million net earnings for the first quarter. It is likely that these increases were due, in part, to the greater demand for photographic equipment around Christmas. Managers, as internal users, can also use interim financial statement information in their planning and control functions, as discussed in Chapter 24.

PERCENTAGE ANALYSES

The evaluation of current operating results and the comparison of a company's operating results and financial position across several accounting periods or with other companies may be improved by converting the monetary relationships within the financial statements to percentage relationships. The three types of analyses that use percentage relationships are referred to as horizontal analysis, vertical analysis, and ratio analysis. The first two types are discussed in this section; ratio analysis is discussed in the following section.

Horizontal Analysis

Horizontal analysis shows the changes in a company's operating results *over time* in percentages as well as in dollar amounts. Horizontal analysis is usually done for each item on the income statement. It is less often used for balance sheet comparisons. Two years of income statement data are usually shown in dollars. The earlier year is used as the base year, and the amount of change in each item on the income statement is expressed as a *percentage* of that item's base year amount. That is, the percentage change in each item is computed by dividing the dollar amount of the change by the base year dollar amount of the item.

Exhibit 19-7 shows a horizontal analysis of the 1982 and 1983 income statements of the Trumbell Company. Note that the 10.0% increase in sales is computed

EXHIBIT 19-7
Horizontal Analysis of Income Statements

TRUMBELL COMPANY
Comparative Income Statements
(Horizontal Analysis)

	For Years Ended December 31		Year-to-Year Increase (Decrease) 1982 to 1983	
	1983	1982	Amount	Percent
Sales	$110,000	$100,000	$10,000	10.0%
Sales returns	9,200	10,000	(800)	(8.0)
Sales (net)	$100,800	$ 90,000	$10,800	12.0
Cost of goods sold	69,000	60,000	9,000	15.0
Gross profit	$ 31,800	$ 30,000	$ 1,800	6.0
Selling expenses	9,000	8,000	1,000	12.5
General expenses	10,800	11,400	(600)	(5.3)
Interest expense	1,000	600	400	66.7
Total expenses	$ 20,800	$ 20,000	$ 800	4.0
Income before income taxes	$ 11,000	$ 10,000	$ 1,000	10.0
Income tax expense	4,400	4,000	400	10.0
Net Income	$ 6,600	$ 6,000	$ 600	10.0
Number of common shares	3,500	3,000	500	16.7
Earnings per share[a]	$ 1.63	$ 1.70	$ (.07)	(4.1)

[a] Earnings per share = $\frac{\text{Net income } - \text{ Preferred dividends (\$900)}}{\text{Average common shares outstanding}}$

by dividing the $10,000 increase ($110,000 in 1983 compared to $100,000 in 1982) by the $100,000 sales for 1982. The other percentage changes are computed in a similar way.

Several observations can be made by analyzing the horizontal percentage changes that are not readily apparent from the absolute dollar amounts. First, net income has increased by the same percentage (10.0) as sales. Cost of goods sold, however, increased at a greater percentage (15.0), resulting in gross profit increasing by only 6.0%. Selling expenses also increased by 12.5%, which was more than the increase in revenues. Only by a *reduction* of 5.3% in general expenses was the company able to increase its net income at the same rate as sales. Even though net income increased by 10.0%, earnings per share *decreased* by 4.1% because the percentage increase in the number of common shares outstanding was greater than the percentage increase in net income.

Whenever horizontal analysis is used care must be taken in computing and evaluating percentage changes. If a base figure is zero, although an *amount* of the change may be shown, *no percentage* change may be validly expressed. Furthermore, if horizontal changes are shown as percentages, no addition or subtraction of the percentages can be made because the percentage changes result from the use of a different base for each item. Finally, for items of small base amounts (such as interest expense in Exhibit 19-7) a small dollar change may result in a very high percentage change. This may lead users to attach more importance to the item than they should.

Vertical Analysis

Vertical analysis shows the items on the financial statements of a given *period* or *date* in percentages as well as in dollar amounts. When vertical analysis is used for comparisons of financial statements from several periods, trends or changes in the relationships between items are more easily identified. **Financial statements expressed only in percentages are referred to as common-size statements.**

Vertical analysis may be used for the income statement or balance sheet. In the income statement, net sales usually are shown as 100% and all the other items are expressed as a percentage of sales. That is, the dollar amount of each item is divided by the dollar amount of net sales to determine the percentage. On the balance sheet, total assets and total liabilities and stockholders' equity are shown as 100%.

Vertical analyses for the Trumbell Company are shown in Exhibits 19-8 and 19-9. Note in Exhibit 19-8 that the 66.7% cost of goods sold in 1982 is computed by dividing the $60,000 cost of goods sold by the $90,000 net sales. In Exhibit 19-9 the 8.6% inventory in 1983 is computed by dividing the $8,200 inventory by the $95,000 total assets. The other percentages are computed in a similar way.

The vertical percentage changes from the 1982 to the 1983 income statement in Exhibit 19-8 reveal that although net income has increased in dollars, it has decreased slightly as a percentage of net sales. This is primarily due to the increase in cost of goods sold as a percent of 1983 sales being offset by a decrease in general expenses as a percent of 1983 sales, while the percentage of selling expenses to 1983 sales remained unchanged as compared to 1982. The vertical analyses of the

EXHIBIT 19-8
Vertical Analysis of
Income Statements

TRUMBELL COMPANY
Comparative Income Statements
For Years Ended December 31, 1982, and 1983
(Vertical Analysis)

	1983		1982	
	Amount	*Percent*	*Amount*	*Percent*
Sales	$110,000	109.1%	$100,000	111.1%
Sales returns	9,200	9.1	10,000	11.1
Sales (net)[a]	$100,800	100.0	$ 90,000	100.0
Cost of goods sold	69,000	68.5	60,000	66.7
Gross profit	$ 31,800	31.5	$ 30,000	33.3
Selling expenses	9,000	8.9	8,000	8.9
General expenses	10,800	10.7	11,400	12.7
Interest expense	1,000	1.0	600	.6
Total expenses	$ 20,800	20.6	$ 20,000	22.2
Income before income taxes	$ 11,000	10.9	$ 10,000	11.1
Income tax expense	4,400	4.4	4,000	4.4
Net Income	$ 6,600	6.5	$ 6,000	6.7
Number of common shares	3,500		3,000	
Earnings per share	$ 1.63		$ 1.70	

[a] Seventy percent of the net sales were credit sales (used in the ratio analysis discussed later).

ending 1982 and 1983 balance sheets in Exhibit 19-9 reveal a shift in the percentage composition of total assets from 1982 to 1983. The percentage of the more liquid current assets has decreased and the percentage of noncurrent assets has increased. The percentage composition of "equities" has also changed. As compared to 1982, the 1983 creditor equities (total liabilities) have increased while the preferred stockholders' equities have decreased and the common stockholders' equities have remained about the same.

Both vertical and horizontal analysis may be used to a limited extent in analyzing interim reports and reports of the results of business segments. Vertical and horizontal analyses are also used in conjunction with ratio analysis.

RATIO ANALYSIS

Another form of percentage analysis involves the use of ratios. **Ratios are computations in which one (or more than one) item on the financial statements is divided by another related item or items.** Ratios are often used to evaluate the financial success of a company. Many ratios have become standardized; they are considered to be useful indicators of financial success (or lack of success) and are routinely computed and published on a company and industry basis by the financial analysis companies mentioned earlier. These ratios become "benchmarks" against

**EXHIBIT 19-9
Vertical Analysis of
Balance Sheets**

TRUMBELL COMPANY
Comparative Balance Sheets
December 31, 1983, and December 31, 1984
(Vertical Analysis)

	1984		1983	
	Amount	Percent	Amount	Percent
Cash	$ 2,000	2.1%	$ 2,200	2.7%
Marketable securities (short-term)	2,900	3.0	2,700	3.4
Accounts receivable (net)	6,900	7.3	6,300	7.9
Inventory	8,200	8.6	7,800	9.8
Prepaid items	1,000	1.1	1,200	1.5
Total current assets	$21,000	22.1	$20,200	25.3
Noncurrent assets (net)	74,000	77.9	59,800	74.7
Total Assets	$95,000	100.0	$80,000	100.0
Current liabilities	$10,000	10.5	$ 9,000	11.2
Long-term liabilities (8%)	12,500	13.2	7,500	9.4
Total Liabilities	$22,500	23.7	$16,500	20.6
Preferred stock, 6%, $100 par	$15,000	15.8	$15,000	18.8
Common stock, $5 par[a]	17,500	18.4	15,000	18.8
Additional paid-in capital	17,800	18.7	12,800	16.0
Retained earnings[b]	22,200	23.4	20,700	25.8
Total Stockholders' Equity	$72,500	76.3	$63,500	79.4
Total Liabilities and Stockholders' Equity	$95,000	100.0	$80,000	100.0

[a] December 31, 1984, market price is $20.00 per share.

[b] Retained earnings in 1984 were reduced by dividends of $6 per share on the preferred stock and $1.20 per share on the common stock.

which to compare a company's results to evaluate its effectiveness. The ratios are used by different external users in intracompany and intercompany comparisons for numerous economic decisions. Other ratios are developed by individual users or user groups for their own specific needs.

It is safe to say that more than 30 different ratios or variations of ratios have been discussed in the financial analysis literature. We shall study only the main standard ratios, however. They are classified into five groups: (1) stockholder profitability ratios, (2) company profitability ratios, (3) solvency ratios, (4) activity ratios, and (5) stability ratios. We discuss the use of each ratio and its computation in the following sections. The 1984 data for computing each of these ratios is included in Exhibits 19-8 and 19-9 for the Trumbell Company. Since the numbers used in each calculation are not discussed in the text, you should study these exhibits to identify the information used for each ratio.

For certain ratios an *average* figure is used for the denominator of the ratio. This is because the numerator is an amount flowing into or out of the company (e.g., net income, net credit sales, cost of goods sold) during the accounting period. In these cases the denominator should be expressed as an average amount for the accounting period (e.g., average total assets, average stockholders' equity, average inventory). A simple, unweighted average is usually calculated for the denominator by summing the beginning balance and the ending balance of the item for the period and dividing the result by 2 (e.g., beginning inventory plus ending inventory, divided by 2). Occasionally, only an ending (or a beginning) balance of an item is known, in which case no average can be computed. The ending amount must then be used even though it results in a less accurate ratio.

Stockholder Profitability Ratios

Stockholder profitability ratios have been developed to serve as indicators of how effective a company has been (or will be) in meeting the profit objectives of its owners. Several stockholder profitability ratios have been developed; they are shown in Exhibit 19-10, along with the calculations for the Trumbell Company. Each of these ratios is discussed below.

EARNINGS PER SHARE. The earnings per share information is probably the most frequently cited ratio in a financial analysis. It is considered so important that it is a required disclosure on the face of the income statement. As its name indicates, it shows the amount of a company's earnings for each share of common stock held by stockholders. Earnings per share information is used to evaluate a company's past, current, and potential earnings performance. Because this ratio involves only common stockholders' earnings, in the numerator the net income is reduced by the amount of preferred dividends. The denominator is based on a weighted average of the common shares outstanding, as discussed in Chapter 15.

PRICE/EARNINGS. Although it is not exactly a stockholder profitability ratio, actual and potential stockholders use the price/earnings ratio to evaluate how attractive an investment is in a company's common stock. A higher price/earnings ratio as compared to other companies may indicate that investors see a good chance that the company will expand. Care must be taken, however, that the comparison is made

**EXHIBIT 19-10
Stockholder
Profitability
Ratios**

Ratio	Formula	Calculations (1983)
1. Earnings per Share	$\dfrac{\text{Net Income} - \text{Preferred Dividends}}{\text{Average Common Shares Outstanding}}$	$\dfrac{\$6,600 - \$900}{3,500} = \$1.63$
2. Price/Earnings	$\dfrac{\text{Ending Market Price per Common Share}}{\text{Earnings per Share}}$	$\dfrac{\$20.00}{\$1.63} = 12.3 \text{ times}$
3. Dividend Yield	$\dfrac{\text{Dividends per Common Share}}{\text{Ending Market Price per Common Share}}$	$\dfrac{\$1.20}{\$20.00} = 6.0\%$

to other "similar" companies. The price/earnings ratio for companies in certain "growth" industries, such as the electronics industry, will be much higher than for, say, companies in the automobile or steel industries. Interpretation of the ratio is also affected by investors' evaluations of the company's quality and trend of earnings, relative risk, use of alternative accounting methods, and economic and other factors.

DIVIDEND YIELD.   The market value of common stock is the value a stockholder must forego to continue owning the security. Stockholders are interested in their individual rates of return based on the actual dividends received as compared with the ending market price of the stock. The dividend yield provides this information. The return from an investment, however, also includes the change in the market price of the stock held during the accounting period. Thus the dividend yield is often combined with the percentage change in the market price of the stock to determine the total annual percentage return on the stockholders' investment.

Company Profitability Ratios   Company profitability ratios are used as indicators of how efficient a company has been in meeting its overall profit objectives, especially in relation to the resources invested. Several overall company profitability ratios are shown in Exhibit 19-11, along with the calculations for the Trumbell Company. Each is discussed below.

PROFIT MARGIN.   The relationship of net income to net sales is commonly used to evaluate a company's efficiency in controlling costs and expenses in relation to sales. That is, the lower a company's expenses relative to sales, the higher the sales dollars remaining for other activities. Extraordinary gains or losses and results of disposals of discontinued segments are typically excluded from the numerator because they are the results of events not directly related to ongoing sales or

EXHIBIT 19-11   Company Profitability Ratios

Ratio	Formula	Calculations (1983)
1. Profit Margin	$\dfrac{\text{Net Income}}{\text{Net Sales}}$	$\dfrac{\$6,600}{\$100,800} = 6.5\%$
2. Return on Total Assets	$\dfrac{\text{Net Income} + \text{Interest Expense (net of tax)}}{\text{Average Total Assets}}$	$\dfrac{\$6,600 + (\$1,000 \times 0.6)}{\dfrac{\$95,000 + \$80,000}{2}} = 8.2\%$
3. Return on Stockholders' Equity	$\dfrac{\text{Net Income}}{\text{Average Stockholders' Equity}}$	$\dfrac{\$6,600}{\dfrac{\$72,500 + \$63,500}{2}} = 9.7\%$

expenses. The reporting of industry segment information discussed earlier in the chapter permits a variation of this ratio to be computed for the main segments of a company. For each segment, the profit margin *before* income taxes can be computed by dividing the segment's operating profit by its revenues (sales). A weakness of the ratio is that it does not consider the investment (the total assets or stockholders' equity) required to make the sales and income. A "return on investment" (either total assets or stockholders' equity) overcomes this weakness.

RETURN ON TOTAL ASSETS.   The management of a company has the responsibility to use the company's assets to earn a satisfactory profit. The amount of net income earned in relation to total assets is an indicator of a company's efficiency in the use of its economic resources. When comparing the return on total assets of one company to the return on total assets of another company, consideration should be given to the age of the assets of each company. With increasing prices today, a company utilizing recently purchased assets (at higher prices) will show a lower return on these assets. Extraordinary items and results of disposals of discontinued segments are typically excluded from the numerator because they are the result of infrequent events not directly related to the ongoing economic resources used in a company's operations. Interest expense (after taxes)[5] is added back to net income because it is a financial cost paid to creditors to acquire the assets and not an expense of making sales. Since net income is earned over the entire period, the *average* total assets (beginning plus ending assets divided by 2) for the period are used as the denominator. Reporting the results of industry segments permits the computation of a variation of this ratio for the main segments of a company. For each segment the *pretax* return on *identifiable* assets can be computed by dividing the segment's operating profit by its identifiable assets.

RETURN ON STOCKHOLDERS' EQUITY.   Total assets are financed (provided) by both creditors and owners (stockholders). The management of a company not only has the responsibility of efficiently using the company's assets to earn income, but also to earn a satisfactory return for its stockholders on their equity (investment). Net income may also be divided by stockholders' equity to show the return on the owners' equity. When this return is higher than the return on total assets, the company has favorable financial leverage (i.e., it is trading on the equity, discussed in Chapter 16 and later in this chapter, in regard to the debt ratio). A weakness of both ratios, however, is that they do not consider the current values of the assets or investments because both are shown in the financial statements based on historical cost dollar amounts. Extraordinary items and results of disposals of discon-

---

[5] After-tax interest expense is usually computed by multiplying the pretax interest expense by 1 minus the income tax rate. For the Trumbell Company it is assumed that the income tax rate is 40%, and therefore the $1,000 pretax interest expense is multiplied by 60% $(1 - 0.40)$ to determine the after-tax results.

EXHIBIT 19-12
Solvency Ratios

Ratio	Formula	Calculations (1983)
1. Current	$\dfrac{\text{Current Assets}}{\text{Current Liabilities}}$	$\dfrac{\$21,000}{\$10,000} = 2.1 \text{ to } 1$
2. Acid-Test	$\dfrac{\text{Quick Assets}}{\text{Current Liabilities}}$	$\dfrac{\$11,800}{\$10,000} = 1.2 \text{ to } 1$

tinued segments are not included in the numerator (for the reason cited earlier) and *average* stockholders' equity is usually used for the denominator.

Solvency Ratios Solvency ratios are used to evaluate a company's liquidity. They provide an indication of a company's ability to meet its current debts. These ratios generally involve all or most of the components of a company's working capital, its current assets less its current liabilities. Current assets include cash, short-term marketable securities, receivables, inventory, and prepaid items. Among current liabilities are items such as accounts payable incurred for goods or services, accruals for wages, taxes, and interest payable, short-term notes payable, and advance collections of unearned revenues. The common solvency ratios are shown in Exhibit 19-12, along with the calculations for the Trumbell Company. Each is discussed below.

CURRENT RATIO. The current ratio is probably the most commonly used indicator of a company's short-run solvency. This ratio is sometimes referred to as the working capital ratio. It is considered to be a better indicator of a company's current debt-paying ability than simply using working capital. This is because working capital shows only the absolute difference between a company's current assets and its current liabilities. By computing the current ratio the relative relationship between the current assets and current liabilities is known, and therefore comparisons of different sized companies may be made. In the past, as a "rule of thumb," a 2.0 current ratio was considered satisfactory. Today, however, more attention is given to (1) industry practices, (2) the length of a company's operating cycle, and (3) the mix of the current assets. Too *high* a current ratio as compared to similar companies in the same industry may indicate inefficient management of current assets. The shorter a company's operating cycle, the less likely it will need a large amount of working capital or as high a current ratio to operate efficiently. (A company's operating cycle is evaluated by the use of activity ratios, discussed in the next section.) The proportion of different items that make up the total current assets is called the *mix* of the current assets. This mix has an effect upon how quickly the current assets can be converted into cash. As an extreme, a high proportion of prepaid items within current assets may indicate a weak liquidity position since prepaid assets are consumed in the operating cycle instead of being converted back into cash. The mix of a company's current assets and the impact upon its solvency are considered in the acid-test ratio.

ACID-TEST RATIO.   The acid-test or *quick* ratio is a more severe (and more accurate) test of a company's short-term debt-paying abilities. In this ratio only the current assets that may be easily converted into cash are used in the calculation. These assets are referred to as quick assets, and they generally consist of cash, short-term marketable securities, accounts receivable, and short-term notes receivable. Inventory is excluded because it is frequently sold on credit, which means it cannot be quickly converted into cash. Prepaid items are excluded because they are not convertible into cash. Since short-term marketable securities are shown on a company's balance sheet at their lower of cost or market value, if the market value of these securities is *higher* than cost this market value should be included (instead of cost) in the computation. The acid-test ratio highlights potential solvency problems resulting from a poor mix of current assets. For instance, the use of this ratio usually shows the lower liquidity of a company with a high investment in inventory that would not be revealed in the current ratio. Care must be taken when thinking about which assets to include, however. Even though inventory is usually not included in the numerator of the acid-test ratio, sometimes inventory is, in fact, more liquid than certain receivables. This may be the case when a company makes a high percentage of its sales for cash. A quick ratio of 1.0 has been used as a general rule of thumb. Today, however, more attention is given to industry practices and the company's typical operations.

Activity Ratios   Activity ratios are used to give a general idea of the length of the segments of a company's operating cycle so that the liquidity of selected current assets may be evaluated. A company's operating cycle is the length of time it takes to invest in inventory, make credit sales, and convert the receivables into cash. The ratios also

EXHIBIT 19-13   Activity Ratios

Ratio	Formula	Calculations (1983)
1. Inventory Turnover	$\dfrac{\text{Cost of Goods Sold}}{\text{Average Inventory}}$	$\dfrac{\$69,000}{\dfrac{\$8,200 + \$7,800}{2}} = $ 8.6 times or 35 days[a]
2. Accounts Receivable Turnover	$\dfrac{\text{Net Credit Sales}}{\text{Average Net Accounts Receivable}}$	$\dfrac{\$100,800 \times 0.70}{\dfrac{\$6,900 + \$6,300}{2}} = $ 10.7 times or 28 days[a]

[a] 300-day business year.

indicate the efficiency with which the company uses its short-term economic resources. The two common activity ratios are shown in Exhibit 19-13, along with the calculations for the Trumbell Company. Each is subsequently discussed.

INVENTORY TURNOVER.   Inventory is purchased, sold, and replaced as part of a company's normal operations during its accounting period. Dividing a company's cost of goods sold for the period by its average inventory shows the number of times the inventory is *turned over* or sold during that period. As a general rule, the higher the inventory turnover, the more efficient the company is in its operations and the lesser the amount of investment that must be tied up in inventory. A company with a higher turnover is usually using its purchasing, receiving, and sales departments more efficiently. It is also minimizing the chance of having obsolete inventory. The lesser amount needed for investment in inventory means that the company either needs less capital or can invest its capital in other earnings activities.

Too high an inventory turnover, however, may indicate lost sales because there was not enough inventory on hand. Furthermore, when a comparison is made of one company to another, both companies should be using similar inventory costing methods. In periods of rising prices, no valid comparison of inventory turnovers can be made when one company is using FIFO and the other company is using LIFO. This is because the company using LIFO will show a higher cost of goods sold and lower inventory than the FIFO company, even though their operations are similar. The inventory turnover is frequently divided into the number of operating days in a *business year* (companies conduct their business on a 7-day, 6-day, or 5-day work week, resulting in a business year of 365, 300, or 250, depending on the industry) so that the inventory segment of the operating cycle may be shown in days.

ACCOUNTS RECEIVABLE TURNOVER.   Once inventory has been sold on credit, the company must collect the receivables to complete its operating cycle. Dividing net credit sales by average net accounts receivable shows how many times the average receivables are *turned over* or collected each period. The accounts receivable turnover is a measure of the efficiency with which the company collects its receivables and converts them back into cash. As a general rule, the higher the turnover the better, because the company has less resources tied up in receivables, collects these resources at a faster pace, and usually has fewer uncollectible accounts. The amount of net *credit* sales is the appropriate figure to use in the accounts receivable turnover. Most companies report only total sales without giving a breakdown of credit and cash sales, however. In this case net sales may be used in the ratio.

A comparison of a company's accounts receivable turnover to the days in its typical credit terms gives an indication of how aggressively the company's credit department collects overdue accounts. When comparing the accounts receivable turnovers of different companies, consideration also should be given to the length of each company's credit terms. Companies operating in industries where the typical credit terms are 30 days are likely to have shorter turnovers of receivables

EXHIBIT 19-14   Stability Ratios

Ratios	Formula	Calculations (1983)	
1. Debt	$\dfrac{\text{Total Liabilities}}{\text{Total Assets}}$	$\dfrac{\$22,500}{\$95,000}$	= 23.7%
2. Times Interest Earned	$\dfrac{\text{Pretax Operating Income}}{\text{Interest Expense}}$	$\dfrac{\$11,000 + \$1,000}{\$1,000}$	= 12 times
3. Book Value per Common Share	$\dfrac{\text{Common Stockholders' Equity}}{\text{Outstanding Common Shares}}$	$\dfrac{\$72,500 - (\$100 \times 150)}{3,500}$	= $16.43 per Common Share

than companies with 60-day credit terms. The accounts receivable turnover is often divided into the business year (365, 300, or 250) to show the average collection period (in days). Then the days in the inventory turnover may be added to the average collection period for an approximation of the days in the company's operating cycle. The Trumbell Company's operating cycle is approximately 63 days (a 35-day inventory turnover plus a 28-day accounts receivable turnover).

Stability Ratios

Stability ratios are used to indicate the long-run solvency and stability of the company. They provide evidence of the safety of the investments in the company by long-term bondholders and stockholders. Several stability ratios are shown in Exhibit 19-14, along with the calculations for the Trumbell Company. Each is discussed below.

DEBT RATIO. The debt ratio shows the percentage of total assets contributed by creditors. This ratio is subtracted from 100% to show the percentage of total assets (i.e., equity ratio) contributed by stockholders.[6] The desired relationship (or *mix*) between the debt and equity ratios depends on the industry. In general, creditors prefer to see a lower debt ratio because if business declines it is more likely that the company will be able to pay its interest costs. Up to a point, stockholders prefer a higher debt ratio, especially when the company is favorably *trading on the equity* or applying favorable *financial leverage*. This occurs when the company borrows money from creditors at an interest rate (net of income taxes) that is lower than the return the company can earn in its operations (discussed in Chapter 16). A very high debt ratio, however, is usually a disadvantage when a company wants to attract additional capital. Investors in both long-term bonds and stocks usually feel that a highly leveraged company is not a very stable or attractive investment.

[6] Total liabilities are sometimes divided by total stockholders' equity to determine the *debt/equity* ratio.

TIMES INTEREST EARNED. The times interest earned ratio (sometimes called the *interest coverage* ratio) is used to show the ability of a company to cover its interest obligations through its annual earnings. It is a measure of the safety of creditors' (especially long-term) investments in the company. As a general rule, the higher the ratio, the better able is the company to meet its interest obligations. While interest obligations are legal commitments, it is also true that continued interest payments are endangered by low earnings over an extended period of time. Because both earnings and interest expense are based on accrual accounting, the times interest earned ratio is slightly inaccurate, since it should include only cash outflows for interest and cash inflows from earnings. Such refinements are not usually made to this ratio, however.

The numerator of the times interest earned ratio is usually pretax operating income; that is, income before income taxes, to which interest expense is added back. When a company reports income from continuing operations along with the results of discontinued operations and extraordinary gains and losses, interest expense is added back to pretax income from continuing operations to get pretax operating income. Extraordinary gains and losses and results of disposals of discontinued segments are not included because they generally do not affect the long-run interest-paying ability of a company.

BOOK VALUE. The book value per common share shows the net assets per share of common stock. It is sometimes called the *liquidation* value per share (liquidation occurs when a company ceases to operate, sells all its assets, and pays off its debts). Although book value is frequently computed, for several reasons it is actually not very useful for showing a company's financial stability. First, most companies are ongoing businesses so that a liquidation value is not important. Second, even if a liquidation value were important, the book value is based on assets recorded primarily at historical costs and not at current liquidation selling prices. Third, what is important in evaluating a company's stability is the market value per share of its common stock. Since book value is based on historical costs, it also has no direct relationship to a common stock's market value.

When book value per share is computed and the company has both preferred and common stock outstanding, it is necessary to determine the stockholders' equity belonging to the common stockholders. Of the total stockholders' equity, preferred stock is usually allocated its par value. When preferred dividends are cumulative and in arrears, a portion of retained earnings equal to the dividends in arrears is also assigned as preferred stockholders' equity. The remaining amount of stockholders' equity is then assigned as common stockholders' equity. The book value per common share is computed by dividing the number of common shares outstanding into this remaining stockholders' equity.

Summary Only the primary standard ratios were identified and discussed in this section. Exhibit 19-15 summarizes these ratios and their computations.

EXHIBIT 19-15
Summary of Ratios

Ratio	Formula
Stockholder Profitability Ratios	
1. Earnings per Share	$\dfrac{\text{Net Income} - \text{Preferred Dividends}}{\text{Average Common Shares Outstanding}}$
2. Price/Earnings	$\dfrac{\text{Ending Market Price per Common Share}}{\text{Earnings per Share}}$
3. Dividend Yield	$\dfrac{\text{Dividends per Common Share}}{\text{Ending Market Price per Common Share}}$
Company Profitability Ratios	
1. Profit Margin	$\dfrac{\text{Net Income}}{\text{Net Sales}}$
2. Return on Total Assets	$\dfrac{\text{Net Income} + \text{Interest Expense (net of tax)}}{\text{Average Total Assets}}$
3. Return on Stockholders' Equity	$\dfrac{\text{Net Income}}{\text{Average Stockholders' Equity}}$
Solvency Ratios	
1. Current	$\dfrac{\text{Current Assets}}{\text{Current Liabilities}}$
2. Acid-Test	$\dfrac{\text{Quick Assets}}{\text{Current Liabilities}}$
Activity Ratios	
1. Inventory Turnover	$\dfrac{\text{Cost of Goods Sold}}{\text{Average Inventory}}$
2. Accounts Receivable Turnover	$\dfrac{\text{Net Credit Sales}}{\text{Average Net Accounts Receivable}}$
Stability Ratios	
1. Debt	$\dfrac{\text{Total Liabilities}}{\text{Total Assets}}$
2. Times Interest Earned	$\dfrac{\text{Pretax Operating Income}}{\text{Interest Expense}}$
3. Book Value per Common Share	$\dfrac{\text{Common Stockholders' Equity}}{\text{Outstanding Common Shares}}$

REVIEW PROBLEM

Davis Diversified Corporation operates in several different industries. On the following page is a condensed 1983 income statement of the entire company for the year ended December 31, 1983.

DAVIS DIVERSIFIED CORPORATION
Income Statement
For Year Ended December 31, 1983

Sales	$100,000
Less: Cost of goods sold	60,000
Gross profit	$ 40,000
Less: Selling and general expenses	25,000
Income before income taxes	$ 15,000
Income tax expense	6,000
Net Income	$ 9,000

The company has two reportable industry segments, L and M. On December 31, 1983, the company has $116,000 total assets. Of these total assets, $11,000 are general corporate assets. The remaining assets and the sales and operating expenses are assigned to segments according to the following percentages:

	Segment L	Segment M	Other Segments
Sales	46%	34%	20%
Cost of goods sold	43	36	21
Selling and general expenses	50	33	17
Identifiable assets	48	30	22

Required: Based on the above information prepare a schedule that reports the 1983 segment financial information for Davis Diversified Corporation.

SOLUTION TO REVIEW PROBLEM

DAVIS DIVERSIFIED CORPORATION
Industry Segment Financial Information
For Year Ended December 31, 1983

	Reportable Industry Segments		Other Industry Segments	Totals
	L	M		
Revenues (sales)	$46,000[a]	$34,000	$20,000	$100,000
Segment expenses:				
Cost of goods sold	$25,800	$21,600[b]	$12,600	$ 60,000
Selling and general expenses	12,500	8,250	4,250[c]	25,000
Total segment expenses	$38,300	$29,850	$16,850	$ 85,000
Operating profit (and income before income taxes)	$ 7,700	$ 4,150	$ 3,150	$ 15,000
Identifiable assets	$50,400	$31,500	$23,100	$105,000
General corporate assets				11,000
Total assets				$116,000

[a] $100,000 × 0.46.
[b] $ 60,000 × 0.36.
[c] $ 25,000 × 0.17.

GLOSSARY **Common-Size Statements.** Financial statements that are expressed only in percentages.

Horizontal Analysis. Shows the changes in a company's operating results *over time* in percentages as well as in dollar amounts.

General Corporate Assets. Assets used only for general corporate purposes. Not included in identifiable assets of industry segments for segment reporting. Example is marketable securities.

General Corporate Revenues and Expenses. Revenues earned and expenses incurred by a company as a whole. Not included in the operating profits of industry segments for segment reporting. Examples are interest revenue and interest expense.

Industry Segment. Department, division, or subsidiary of a company that provides a product or service to customers for a profit.

Intercompany Comparisons. Comparisons of a company's operating results and financial position with those of competing companies.

Interim Financial Statements. Financial statements for periods of less than a year; usually issued quarterly. Also called *interim reports* or *quarterly reports*.

Intracompany Comparisons. Comparisons of a company's current operating results and financial position with its past results.

Ratio. Computation in which one (or more than one) item on the financial statements is divided by another related item or items.

Reportable Industry Segment. Industry segment that has revenues, operating profits, or identifiable assets that are 10% or more of the company's total revenues, operating profits, or identifiable assets.

Vertical Analysis. Shows the items on a financial statement for a given *period* or *date* in percentages as well as in dollar amounts.

QUESTIONS **Q19-1** What two types of comparisons are often made by external users in their financial decision making? What points should be remembered when making these comparisons?

Q19-2 Why do financial statement users desire financial information about the segments of a company?

Q19-3 Briefly define the terms (a) revenues, (b) operating profit, and (c) identifiable assets as they apply to reportable industry segments. What items are excluded from each?

Q19-4 What are interim financial statements? How often are they usually issued?

Q19-5 What specific principles may be used by a company using the periodic inventory system in reporting cost of goods sold and inventory in its interim financial statements?

Q19-6 What principles should be used in accounting for expenses during an interim period?

Q19-7   Briefly explain how the accounting procedures for preparing interim financial statements are (a) similar to and (b) dissimilar from those used in preparing annual financial statements.

Q19-8   What is a horizontal analysis and how is it prepared?

Q19-9   What is a vertical analysis and how does it differ from a horizontal analysis?

Q19-10   What are ratios and for what are they used?

Q19-11   Briefly describe how each of the stockholder profitability ratios is computed.

Q19-12   Briefly describe how each of the company profitability ratios is computed.

Q19-13   Which financial ratios may be used to evaluate the efficiency of a company's reportable industry segments?

Q19-14   Briefly describe how each of the solvency ratios is computed.

Q19-15   Briefly describe how each of the activity ratios is computed.

Q19-16   Briefly describe how each of the stability ratios is computed.

EXERCISES   **E19-1   Segment Reporting.**   Mory Conglomerate Company has total assets of $140,000 at the end of 1983 and lists the following condensed income statement for 1983.

MORY CONGLOMERATE COMPANY
Income Statement
For Year Ended December 31, 1983

Sales	$90,000
Operating expenses	60,000
Income before income taxes	$30,000
Income tax expense	12,000
Net Income	$18,000

The company has two reportable industry segments, A and B, and has developed the information listed below:

	Segments		Other	
	A	B	Segments	Total
Sales	$42,000	$28,000	$20,000	$90,000
Operating expenses	28,000	19,000	13,000	60,000

All assets are identifiable assets and are assigned to the segments as follows: $67,000 to Segment A; $44,000 to Segment B; and $29,000 to the other segments.

Required: Prepare a schedule to report on the 1983 revenues, operating profits, and identifiable assets of Segments A and B and the other industry segments of the Mory Conglomerate Company.

E19-2   Determination of Reportable Industry Segments. In preparing its segment reporting schedule, the Loxer Diversified Company has developed the information listed below for each of its five segments:

| | Segments | | | | | |
	1	2	3	4	5	Totals
Sales	$3,520	$3,000	$3,880	$25,800	$3,800	$40,000
Operating expenses	2,200	1,800	1,700	15,480	2,820	24,000
Identifiable assets	6,300	7,500	6,200	40,000	5,000	65,000

Required: Using the reportable industry segment definition from the text (e.g., the percentage of revenues, operating profits, or identifiable assets rule) prepare a schedule to determine which of the above segments are reportable industry segments and which should be combined for segment reporting. Justify your conclusions.

E19-3   Interim Reporting. The Campbell Company prepares quarterly and year-to-date interim reports. Shown below is its interim income statement for the quarter ended March 31, 1983:

CAMPBELL COMPANY
Income Statement
For First Quarter Ended March 31, 1983

Sales (net)		$80,000
Cost of goods sold		44,000
Gross profit		$36,000
Operating expenses		
Selling expenses	$11,500	
General expenses	10,800	22,300
Operating income		$13,700
Other revenues and expenses		
Interest revenue	$ 300	
Interest expense	(500)	200
Income before income taxes		$13,500
Income tax expense		5,400
Net Income		$ 8,100
Earnings per share (10,000 shares)		$ .81

On June 30, 1983, the company accountant completed a worksheet in preparation for developing the year-to-date (i.e., 6-month) interim income statement. Below are the accounts and amounts listed in the income statement debit and credit columns of this worksheet:

	Debit	Credit
Sales (net)		170,000
Interest revenue		750
Cost of goods sold	95,000	
Selling expenses	25,000	
General expenses	19,000	
Interest expense	1,050	
Income tax expense	12,280	

In addition, 10,000 shares of common stock have been outstanding for the entire 6 months.

Required: Based on the above information for the Campbell Company, prepare:
1. A year-to-date interim income statement for the first 6 months of 1983.
2. An interim income statement for the second quarter of 1983.

E19-4   Segment Reporting. York Company has two reportable industry segments, A and B. A 1983 condensed income statement for the entire company is presented below:

YORK COMPANY
Income Statement
For Year Ended December 31, 1983

Sales	$80,000
Cost of goods sold	50,000
Gross profit	$30,000
Operating expenses	22,000
Income before income taxes	$ 8,000
Income tax expense	3,200
Net Income	$ 4,800

Additional Information:
1. Sales are made as follows: Segment A, $48,000; Segment B, $20,000; other segments, $12,000 of the total.
2. Cost of goods sold for each segment is as follows: Segment A, $30,000; Segment B, $12,500; other segments, $7,500.
3. Operating expenses are identified with the segments as follows: Segment A, $12,000; Segment B, $6,000; other segments, $4,000.
4. The company has $110,000 total assets as of December 31, 1983. All assets are identifiable assets and are assigned to the segments as follows: Segment A, $49,500; Segment B, $38,500; other segments, $22,000.

Required: Prepare a schedule that reports on the 1983 revenues, operating profits, and identifiable assets of Segments A and B and the other segments of the York Company.

E19-5   Interim Reporting, Gross Profit Method. The Jolsh Corporation listed the following items on its interim worksheet for the second quarter, ended June 30, 1983:

Inventory (beginning)	$ 4,000
Purchases	22,000
Sales	28,000
Sales returns and allowances	3,000

Based on experience Jolsh Corporation estimates its gross profit is 30% of net sales.

Required: 1. Compute the estimated cost of goods sold of the Jolsh Corporation for the second quarter of 1983 using the gross profit method.
2. Based on your answer to Requirement 1, compute the estimated ending inventory on June 30, 1983.

E19-6 Interim Reporting. The Doley Corporation showed the following income statement for the first 6 months of 1983:

DOLEY CORPORATION
Income Statement

	Jan. 1–June 30, 1983	Percent Applicable to Jan. 1–Mar. 31, 1983
Sales (net)	$25,000	40%
Cost of goods sold		
Inventory (beginning)	$ 5,000	–
Purchases (net)	15,000	35
Cost of goods available for sale	$20,000	
Less: Ending inventory (estimated)	4,800[a]	–
Cost of goods sold	15,200	
Gross profit	$ 9,800	
Operating expenses		
Selling expenses	$ 3,100	42
General and administrative expenses	3,250	46
Total operating expenses	6,350	
Operating income	$ 3,450	
Other revenues		
Interest revenue	100	50
Income before income taxes	$ 3,550	
Income tax expense	1,420[b]	
Net Income	$ 2,130	

[a] The estimated ending inventory on March 31, 1983, was $4,547.
[b] Assume a 40% tax rate for the first and second quarters.

Required: Prepare an income statement for the second quarter of 1983. Assume that 1,000 shares of common stock have been outstanding for the entire 6 months.

E19-7 Horizontal Analysis. The Clovland Company presents the following condensed comparative income statements for 1982 and 1983:

CLOVLAND COMPANY
Comparative Income Statements

	For Years Ended December 31	
	1983	1982
Sales (net)	$110,000	$90,000
Cost of goods sold	62,000	45,000
Gross profit	$ 48,000	$45,000
Operating expenses	22,000	20,000
Income before income taxes	$ 26,000	$25,000
Income tax expense	10,400	10,000
Net Income	$ 15,600	$15,000
Number of common shares	7,000	7,500
Earnings per share	$2.23	$2.00

Required: Based on the above information prepare a horizontal analysis for the years 1982 and 1983. Calculate the profit margin for the company for the 2 years. What is this ratio generally used for and what does it indicate about the Clovland Company?

E19-8 Horizontal Analysis. The Taboue Corporation showed the following information for the years 1982 and 1983:

TABOUE CORPORATION
Comparative Income Statements

	For Years Ended December 31		Year-to-Year Increase (decrease) 1982 to 1983	
	1983	*1982*	*Amount*	*Percent*
Sales (net)	$65,000	$60,000	$ (a)	(b) %
Cost of goods sold	(c)	33,600	(d)	(e)
Gross profit	$27,950	$26,400	$ (f)	(g)
Operating expenses	19,050	(h)	400	(i)
Income before income taxes	$ 8,900	$ (j)	$1,150	(k)
Income tax expense	3,560	3,100	(l)	(m)
Net Income	$ (n)	$ 4,650	$ (o)	(p)
Number of common shares	2,700	(q)	(r)	17.4
Earnings per share	$ 1.98	$ 2.02	$ (s)	(t)

Required: Determine the appropriate percentages and amounts for the blanks lettered (a) through (t). Round to the nearest tenth of a percent. Briefly comment on what your analysis reveals.

E19-9 Vertical Analysis. The Cooke Company presents the following condensed balance sheet information for 1983:

COOKE COMPANY
Balance Sheet
December 31, 1983

Cash	$ 1,500
Accounts receivable	3,500
Inventory	5,500
Long-term investments	10,000
Property and equipment (net)	39,500
Total Assets	$60,000
Current liabilities	$ 5,000
Bonds payable, 8%	20,000
Total Liabilities	$25,000
Common stock, $2 par	$ 6,000
Additional paid-in capital	9,000
Retained earnings	20,000
Total Stockholders' Equity	$35,000
Total Liabilities and Stockholders' Equity	$60,000

Required: Based on the above information prepare a vertical analysis of the Cooke Company balance sheet for 1983. Round to the nearest tenth of a percent. What is the company's current ratio? Based on the "rule of thumb" is it satisfactory?

E19-10   Vertical Analysis. The Anton Company presents the following condensed income statement for 1983:

ANTON COMPANY
Income Statement
For Year Ended December 31, 1983

Sales (net)	$135,000
Cost of goods sold	75,000
Gross profit	$ 60,000
Operating expenses	33,750
Income before income taxes	$ 26,250
Income tax expense	10,500
Net Income	$ 15,750
Earnings per share	$3.00

In addition, the average inventory for 1983 was $10,000.

Required: Based on the above information prepare a vertical analysis of the income statement for 1983. What is the company's inventory turnover and what does this ratio tell us about a company?

E19-11   Ratio Analysis. The Tomor Company listed the following items as of December 31, 1983:

Net income	$ 10,000
Current assets	$ 14,000
Average stockholders' equity	$ 70,000
Cost of goods sold	$ 75,000
Total liabilities	$ 25,000
Preferred dividends paid	$ 1,000
Net sales	$100,000
Current liabilities	$ 6,000
Average inventory	$ 10,000
Total assets	$100,000
Ending market price per common share . . .	$ 24
Average common shares outstanding	3,000 shares

The company uses a 300-day business year.

Required: Based on the information given above determine the following ratios for the Tomor Company:
1. Earnings per share
2. Price/earnings
3. Profit margin
4. Return on stockholders' equity
5. Current
6. Inventory turnover (in days)
7. Debt

E19-12 Ratio Analysis. Shown below are six ratios partially completed for the Yarby Company (assume a 40% income tax rate):

$$\text{Acid-Test} \quad \frac{(a)}{\$14,000} = 1.5$$

$$\text{Accounts Receivable Turnover} \quad \frac{\$68,000}{(b)} = 8.5 \text{ times}$$

$$\text{Times Interest Earned} \quad \frac{\$18,000}{(c)} = 9 \text{ times}$$

$$\text{Dividend Yield} \quad \frac{(d)}{\$18.00} = 5\tfrac{1}{2}\%$$

$$\text{Return on Total Assets} \quad \frac{(e) + (\$2,000 \times 0.6)}{\$100,000} = 12\%$$

$$\text{Book Value per Common Share} \quad \frac{\$74,250}{(f)} = \$14.85 \text{ per common share}$$

Required: Determine the names and correct amounts for the blanks lettered (a) through (f). All the necessary information is provided.

PROBLEMS

Part A

P19-1A Segment Reporting. The Doxy Diversified Company has total assets of $124,000 at the end of 1983 and the following condensed income statement for 1983:

DOXY DIVERSIFIED COMPANY
Income Statement
For Year Ended December 31, 1983

Sales	$80,000
Operating expenses	57,600
Income before income taxes	$22,400
Income tax expense (40%)	8,960
Net Income	$13,440

The company has two reportable industry segments, A and B, and has developed the information listed below to prepare its segmental reporting schedule:

	Segments			
	A	B	Other	Totals
Sales	$51,360	$14,460	$14,180	$ 80,000
Operating expenses	36,780	10,400	10,420	57,600
Identifiable assets	70,320	22,720	21,960	124,000[a]

[a] Of the $124,000 total assets $9,000 are general corporate assets.

Required: 1. Based on the above information prepare a schedule that reports on the 1983 revenues, operating profits, and identifiable assets of Segments A and B and the other segments of the Doxy Diversified Company.
2. Compute the profit margin *before* income taxes for Segments A and B, and for the other segments. What do these ratio results reveal?

P19-2A   Interim Worksheet. The Boonel Company prepared the following trial balance for the period ended March 31, 1983:

Account Titles	Debits	Credits
Cash	$ 1,000	
Accounts receivable (net)	4,400	
Inventory (1-1-1983)	5,000	
Prepaid insurance	4,800	
Note receivable (due 1-1-1985)	6,000	
Land	3,000	
Buildings and equipment	54,000	
Accumulated depreciation		$ 18,000
Accounts payable		9,100
Common stock, $1 par		6,600
Additional paid-in capital		12,400
Retained earnings (1-1-1983)		22,450
Sales (net)		50,000
Purchases (net)	30,000	
Selling expenses	6,000	
General and administrative expenses	4,350	
Totals	$118,550	$118,550

Additional Information:

1. The company uses the gross profit method to determine interim inventory. Historical gross profit has averaged 44% of net sales.
2. The buildings and equipment have an estimated life of 15 years with no residual value. One-half of the depreciation expense is recognized as a selling expense and one-half as a general and administrative expense. The company uses straight-line depreciation.
3. The note receivable was issued on January 1, 1983, and carries an annual interest rate of 10%.
4. On January 1, 1983, the company had purchased a 3-year insurance policy for $4,800.
5. Year-to-date income tax expense amounts to $4,200 on March 31, 1983, and will be paid in early 1984.
6. No common stock has been issued or retired in 1983.

Required: On the basis of the above information prepare an interim worksheet for the first quarter ended March 31, 1983.

P19-3A   Segment Reporting. The Slotter Conglomerate Company does business in several different industries. A 1983 condensed income statement for the entire company is presented below:

SLOTTER CONGLOMERATE COMPANY
Income Statement
For Year Ended December 31, 1983

Sales		$150,000
Operating expenses		
Cost of goods sold	$70,000	
Selling expenses	15,000	
General and administrative expenses	30,000	115,000
Operating profit		$ 35,000
Interest revenue		1,500
Income before income taxes		$ 36,500
Income tax expense (40%)		14,600
Net Income		$ 21,900

Slotter has two reportable industry segments, X and Y. No other segment contributes 10% or more of the company's activities. As of December 31, 1983, the company had assets totaling $530,000. An analysis reveals that $30,000 of the total assets are related to general corporate activities. The remaining assets and the sales and expenses are assigned to segment activities according to the following percentages:

	Percent Identified with		
	Segment X	Segment Y	Other Segments
Sales	40%	45%	15%
Cost of goods sold	36	50	14
Selling expenses	40	40	20
General and administrative			
expenses	35	40	25
Identifiable assets (exclusive of			
general corporate assets)	30	50	20

Required: 1. Prepare a schedule that reports the Slotter Conglomerate Company's industry segment financial information for the year ended December 31, 1983.
2. Compute the *pretax* return on *identifiable* assets for Segments X and Y, and for the other segments. What do these ratio results reveal?

P19-4A   Horizontal Analysis and Ratios.   The Shulz Company presents the following comparative income statements for 1982 and 1983:

SHULZ COMPANY
Comparative Income Statements

	For Years Ended December 31,	
	1983	1982
Sales (net)	$100,000	$85,000
Cost of goods sold	55,000	45,000
Gross profit	$ 45,000	$40,000
Selling expenses	12,000	10,000
General expenses	8,000	8,000
Operating income	$ 25,000	$22,000
Interest revenue	500	200
Interest expense	1,000	500
Income before income taxes	$ 24,500	$21,700
Income tax expense	9,800	8,680
Net Income	$ 14,700	$13,020
Average number of common shares	6,000	5,000

Additional Information:
1. There were no shares of preferred stock outstanding in 1982 or 1983.
2. As of December 31, 1983, the company's common stock had a market price of $12.50 per share. The market price on December 31, 1982, was $15.00 per share.
3. Dividends in the amount of $6,000 and $7,500 were paid to common stockholders in 1983 and 1982, respectively.

Required: 1. Prepare a horizontal analysis for the Shulz Company for 1982 and 1983.

2. Compute the following ratios for the company for 1982 and 1983:
   (a) Earnings per share
   (b) Price/earnings
   (c) Profit margin
   (d) Dividend yield
   (e) Times interest earned
3. Briefly discuss any important changes in operating results revealed by your horizontal and ratio analyses.

P19-5A Vertical Analysis and Ratios. The Koeppen Company operates a high-volume retail outlet. Presented below are comparative financial statements for the company for 1982 and 1983.

KOEPPEN COMPANY
Comparative Income Statements

	For Years Ended December 31,	
	1983	1982
Sales	$180,000	$150,000
Cost of goods sold	108,000	85,500
Gross profit	$ 72,000	$ 64,500
Operating expenses	44,600	37,300
Income before income taxes	$ 27,400	$ 27,200
Income tax expense (40%)	10,960	10,880
Net Income	$ 16,440	$ 16,320
Earnings per share (6,000 shares)	$2.74	$2.72

KOEPPEN COMPANY
Comparative Balance Sheets

	December 31,	
	1983	1982
Cash	$ 4,200	$ 3,000
Marketable securities (short-term)	2,000	2,100
Accounts receivable (net)	8,600	6,400
Inventory	11,300	9,700
Noncurrent assets (net)	129,900	118,800
Total Assets	$156,000	$140,000
Current liabilities	$ 13,000	$ 12,400
Long-term liabilities (10%)	40,000	35,000
Total Liabilities	$ 53,000	$ 47,400
Common stock, $3 par	$ 18,000	$ 18,000
Additional paid-in capital	30,000	30,000
Retained earnings	55,000	44,600
Total Stockholders' Equity	$103,000	$ 92,600
Total Liabilities and Stockholders' Equity	$156,000	$140,000

Additional Information:
1. At the beginning of 1982 the company had outstanding accounts receivable (net) of $7,600.
2. On January 1, 1982, the inventory totaled $10,100.
3. The beginning balance of stockholders' equity for 1982 was $85,400.
4. Sixty percent of the company's sales were on credit.

Required: 1. Prepare vertical analyses of the Koeppen Company income statements and balance sheets for 1982 and 1983.
   2. Compute the following ratios for 1982 and 1983:
      (a) Current
      (b) Inventory turnover (in days, assuming a 300-day business year)
      (c) Accounts receivable turnover (in days, assuming a 300-day business year)
      (d) Return on stockholders' equity.
   3. Briefly discuss any important changes revealed by your vertical and ratio analyses.

P19-6A   Ratios.   The Lobe Company presents the following condensed income statement for 1983 and condensed December 31, 1983, balance sheet.

LOBE COMPANY
Income Statement
For Year Ended December 31, 1983

Sales (net)		$400,500
Less: Cost of goods sold	$240,000	
Operating expenses	88,950	
Interest expense	11,550	
Income taxes	24,000	
Total expenses		364,500
Net Income		$ 36,000

LOBE COMPANY
Balance Sheet
December 31, 1983

Cash	$ 7,500
Marketable securities (short-term)	15,000
Accounts receivable (net)	23,000
Inventory	86,500
Long-term investments	45,000
Property and equipment (net)	423,000
Total Assets	$600,000
Current liabilities	$ 60,000
Bonds payable, 7%	190,000
Common stock, $10 par	200,000
Additional paid-in capital	67,500
Retained earnings	82,500
Total Liabilities and Stockholders' Equity	$600,000

Additional Information:

1. Common stock was outstanding the entire year and dividends of $1.50 per share were declared and paid in 1983. The common stock is selling for $22.00 per share on December 31, 1983.
2. Credit sales for the year totaled $300,375.
3. Average net accounts receivable for the year were $34,500.
4. Average stockholders' equity for the year was $347,000.
5. The company operates on a 365-day business year.

Required: On the basis of the above information compute the following ratios for the Lobe Company:

1. Earnings per share
2. Dividend yield
3. Return on stockholders' equity
4. Current
5. Acid-test
6. Accounts receivable turnover (in days)
7. Times interest earned
8. Book value per common share

On the basis of applicable "rules of thumb," what information is revealed by the acid-test ratio for the company that is not disclosed by its current ratio?

P19-7A   Interim Reporting.   The Ziegler Corporation presented the following interim income statement for the first quarter of 1983:

ZIEGLER CORPORATION
Income Statement
For First Quarter Ended March 31, 1983

Sales (net)		$320,000
Cost of goods sold		
Inventory (1-1-1983)	$ 38,400	
Purchases (net)	192,000	
Cost of goods available for sale	$230,400	
Less: Inventory (3-31-1983, estimated)	54,400	
Cost of goods sold		176,000
Gross profit		$144,000
Operating expenses		
Selling expenses	$ 52,000	
General and administrative expenses	32,000	
Total operating expenses		84,000
Income before income taxes		$ 60,000
Income tax expense		24,000
Net Income		$ 36,000
Earnings per share (12,000 shares)		$3.00

On June 30, 1983, the accounting department prepared a worksheet that included the following adjusted trial balance:

Account Titles	Debits	Credits
Cash	$ 54,400	
Accounts receivable	32,300	
Notes receivable (due 12-31-1983)	16,000	
Inventory (1-1-1983)	38,400	
Property and equipment	100,000	
Accumulated depreciation		$ 22,500
Accounts payable		16,000
Common stock, no par		56,000
Retained earnings		22,600
Sales (net)		600,000
Purchases (net)	320,000	
Selling expenses	97,500	
General and administrative expenses	58,500	
Interest receivable	400	
Interest revenue		400
Income tax expense	45,760	
Income taxes payable		45,760
Totals	$763,260	$763,260

The company uses the gross profit method to estimate its interim inventory. Historical gross profit has averaged 45% of net sales. No common stock has been issued or retired in 1983.

Required: 1. Prepare interim income statements for the periods April 1–June 30, 1983, and January 1–June 30, 1983.

2. Prepare a June 30, 1983, interim balance sheet (report form).

3. For both the first quarter (January 1–March 31, 1983) and the second quarter (April 1–June 30, 1983) compute the following ratios: (a) earnings per share, (b) inventory turnover, and (c) profit margin. What do your ratio results reveal?

PROBLEMS

Part B

P19-1B Segment Reporting.   Steinoff Industries has total assets of $186,000 at the end of 1983 and the following condensed income statement for 1983:

STEINOFF INDUSTRIES
Income Statement
For Year Ended December 31, 1983

Sales	$120,000
Operating expenses	86,400
Income before income taxes	$ 33,600
Income tax expense (40%)	13,440
Net Income	$ 20,160

The company has two reportable industry segments, Q and R, and has developed the following information in preparing its segmental reporting schedule:

	Segments			
	Q	R	Other	Totals
Sales	$ 77,040	$28,920	$14,040	$120,000
Operating expenses	55,170	20,800	10,430	86,400
Identifiable assets	110,000	29,040	31,960	186,000[a]

[a] $15,000 of the $186,000 total assets are general corporate assets.

Required: 1. On the basis of the above information prepare a schedule that reports on the 1983 revenues, operating profits, and identifiable assets of Segments Q and R, and the other segments of Steinoff Industries.
2. Compute the *pretax* return on *identifiable* assets for Segments Q and R, and for the other segments. What do these ratio results reveal?

P19-2B   Interim Reporting.   The Renax Company prepared the following interim income statement for the first quarter of 1983:

RENAX COMPANY
Income Statement
For First Quarter Ended March 31, 1983

Sales (net)		$480,000
Cost of goods sold		
Inventory (1-1-1983)	$ 57,600	
Purchases (net)	288,000	
Cost of goods available for sale	$345,600	
Less: Inventory (3-31-1983, estimated)	81,600	
Cost of goods sold		264,000
Gross profit		$216,000
Operating expenses		
Selling expenses	$ 78,000	
General and administrative expenses	48,000	
Total operating expenses		126,000
Income before income taxes		$ 90,000
Income tax expense		36,000
Net Income		$ 54,000
Earnings per share (22,000 shares)		$2.45

The accounting department prepared the following adjusted trial balance on June 30, 1983, the end of the second quarter:

Account Titles	Debits	Credits
Cash	$ 81,600	
Accounts receivable	48,450	
Notes receivable (due 12-31-1983)	24,000	
Inventory (1-1-1983)	57,600	
Property and equipment	150,000	
Accumulated depreciation		$ 33,750
Accounts payable		24,000
Common stock, no par		84,000
Retained earnings		33,900
Sales (net)		900,000
Purchases (net)	480,000	
Selling expenses	146,250	
General and administrative expenses	87,750	
Interest receivable	600	
Interest revenue		600
Income tax expense	68,640	
Income taxes payable		68,640
Totals	$1,144,890	$1,144,890

No common stock has been issued or retired in 1983. The company uses the gross profit method to estimate its interim inventory. Historical gross profit has averaged 45% of net sales.

Required:
1. Prepare interim income statements for the periods April 1–June 30, 1983, and January 1–June 30, 1983.
2. Prepare a June 30, 1983, interim balance sheet (account form).
3. For both the first quarter (January 1–March 31, 1983) and the second quarter (April 1–June 30, 1983) compute the following ratios: (a) earnings per share, (b) inventory turnover, and (c) profit margin. What do your ratio results reveal?

P19-3B Segment Reporting. The Walters Company does business in several different industries. A 1983 condensed income statement for the entire company is presented below:

WALTERS COMPANY
Income Statement
For Year Ended December 31, 1983

Sales		$75,000
Cost of goods sold		35,000
Gross profit		$40,000
Selling expenses	$ 7,500	
General and administrative expenses	15,000	22,500
Operating profit		$17,500
Interest revenue		950
Income before income taxes		$18,450
Income tax expense		7,380
Net Income		$11,070

Walters has two reportable industry segments, 1 and 2. No other segment contributes 10% or more of the company's activities. As of December 31, 1983, the company had assets totaling $300,000. An analysis reveals that $15,000 of the total assets are related to general corporate activities. The remaining assets and the sales and expenses are assigned to the segments according to the following percentages:

	Percent Identified with		
	Segment 1	Segment 2	Other Segments
Sales	50%	35%	15%
Cost of goods sold	42	40	18
Selling expenses	45	40	15
General and administrative expenses	40	40	20
Identifiable assets (exclusive) of general corporate assets)	52	38	10

Required:
1. Prepare a schedule that reports the Walters Company's industry segment financial information for the year ended December 31, 1983.
2. Compute the profit margin *before* income taxes for Segments 1 and 2, and for the other segments. What do these ratio results reveal?

P19-4B **Interim Worksheet.** The Easex Corporation presented the following trial balance for the quarter ended March 31, 1983:

Account Titles	Debits	Credits
Cash	$ 14,000	
Accounts receivable	8,800	
Inventory (1-1-1983)	10,000	
Prepaid insurance	9,600	
Land	16,000	
Buildings and equipment	108,000	
Accumulated depreciation		$ 36,000
Accounts payable		28,200
Common stock, $1 par		13,200
Additional paid-in capital		24,800
Retained earnings (1-1-1983)		44,900
Sales (net)		100,000
Purchases (net)	60,000	
Selling expenses	12,000	
General and administrative expenses	8,700	
Totals	$247,100	$247,100

Additional Information:

1. The company uses the gross profit method to determine interim inventory. Historical gross profit has averaged 45% of net sales.
2. On January 1, 1983, the company purchased a 4-year insurance policy for $9,600.
3. No common stock has been issued or retired in 1983.
4. Year-to-date income tax expense amounts to $8,760 on March 31, 1983, and will be paid in early 1984.
5. The buildings and equipment have an estimated life of 15 years with no residual value. The company uses straight-line depreciation; it records one-third of the depreciation as a selling expense and the remainder as a general and administrative expense.

Required: On the basis of the above information prepare an interim worksheet for the first quarter ended March 31, 1983.

P19-5B **Vertical Analysis and Ratios.** The Tuscumber Company presented the following comparative financial statements for 1982 and 1983.

TUSCUMBER COMPANY
Comparative Income Statements

	For Years Ended December 31,	
	1983	1982
Sales	$200,000	$185,000
Cost of goods sold	130,000	134,000
Gross profit	$ 70,000	$ 51,000
Operating expenses	52,400	39,600
Income before income taxes	$ 17,600	$ 11,400
Income tax expense	7,040	4,560
Net Income	$ 10,560	$ 6,840
Earnings per share (6,000 shares)	$1.76	$1.14

TUSCUMBER COMPANY
Comparative Balance Sheets

	December 31,	
	1983	*1982*
Cash	$ 12,000	$ 10,500
Marketable securities (short-term)	8,000	8,300
Accounts receivable (net)	10,400	13,300
Inventory	17,600	12,000
Noncurrent assets (net)	106,000	105,900
Total Assets	$154,000	$150,000
Current liabilities	$ 25,100	$ 34,700
Long-term liabilities (12%)	52,300	47,300
Total Liabilities	$ 77,400	$ 82,000
Common stock, $3 par	$ 18,000	$ 18,000
Additional paid-in capital	20,000	20,000
Retained earnings	38,600	30,000
Total Stockholders' Equity	$ 76,600	$ 68,000
Total Liabilities and Stockholders' Equity	$154,000	$150,000

Additional Information:
1. At the beginning of 1982 the company had outstanding accounts receivable (net) of $11,600.
2. On January 1, 1982, the inventory totaled $18,000.
3. The beginning balance of stockholders' equity for 1982 was $64,000.
4. Seventy percent of the company's sales were on credit.

Required: 1. Prepare a vertical analysis of the Tuscumber Company income statements and balance sheets for 1982 and 1983.
        2. Compute the following ratios for 1982 and 1983:
          (a) Current
          (b) Inventory turnover (in days, assuming a 300-day business year)
          (c) Accounts receivable turnover (in days, assuming a 300-day business year)
          (d) Return on stockholders' equity.
        3. Briefly discuss any important changes revealed by your vertical and ratio analyses.

P19-6B   Ratios.   Below is a condensed income statement for 1983 and a December 31, 1983, balance sheet for the Mea Company:

MEA COMPANY
Income Statement
For Year Ended December 31, 1983

Sales (net)	$152,200
Cost of goods sold	91,300
Gross profit	$ 60,900
Operating expenses	40,433
Interest expense	2,800
Income before income taxes	$ 17,667
Income taxes	7,067
Net Income	$ 10,600

MEA COMPANY
Balance Sheet
December 31, 1983

Cash	$ 3,000
Marketable securities (short-term)	2,100
Accounts receivable (net)	6,350
Inventory	9,650
Property and equipment (net)	97,900
Total Assets	$119,000
Current liabilities	$ 12,400
Bonds payable, 8%	35,000
Common stock, $10 par	40,250
Additional paid-in capital	12,000
Retained earnings	19,350
Total Liabilities and Stockholders' Equity	$119,000

Additional Information:
1. The common stock was outstanding the entire year and is selling for $18 per share at year end.
2. On January 1, 1983, the inventory was $10,750, the total assets were $112,000, and the total stockholders' equity was $65,400.
3. The company operates on a 300-day business year and is subject to a 40% income tax rate.

Required: Compute the following ratios for the Mea Company:
1. Price/earnings
2. Profit margin
3. Return on total assets
4. Return on stockholders' equity
5. Current
6. Inventory turnover (in days)
7. Debt
Is the company favorably "trading on its equity"? Explain.

P19-7B   Horizontal Analysis and Ratios. Howale Corporation presented the following comparative income statements for 1982 and 1983:

HOWALE CORPORATION
Comparative Income Statements

	For Years Ended December 31,	
	1983	*1982*
Sales (net)	$250,000	$262,000
Cost of goods sold	150,000	129,400
Gross profit	$100,000	$132,600
Selling expenses	28,000	25,500
General expenses	23,500	21,000
Operating income	$ 48,500	$ 86,100
Interest revenue	500	400
Interest expense	1,500	500
Income before income taxes	$ 47,500	$ 86,000
Income tax expense	19,000	34,400
Net Income	$ 28,500	$ 51,600
Average number of common shares	16,000	15,000

Additional Information:

1. Dividends in the amounts of $20,000 and $53,000 were paid to common stockholders in 1983 and 1982, respectively.
2. There were no preferred shares outstanding in either year.
3. As of December 31, 1983, the company's common stock had a market price of $14.00 per share. On December 31, 1982, the stock had a market price of $29.50 per share.

Required:
1. Prepare a horizontal analysis for the Howale Corporation for 1982 and 1983.
2. Compute the following ratios for the company for 1982 and 1983:
   (a) Earnings per share
   (b) Price/earnings
   (c) Profit margin
   (d) Dividend yield
3. Briefly discuss any important changes in operating results revealed by your horizontal and ratio analyses.

DISCUSSION CASES

19-1 Royal Crown Companies, Inc. (in Appendix). Review the financial statements and related financial information of the Royal Crown Companies, Inc. in Appendix A.

Required: Answer the following questions (a) through (p). Indicate the page number of Appendix A where you located the information for your answer.

(a) What are the four reportable industry segments of the company?
(b) What was the company's net sales in 1980? In 1979? What was the company's gross profit rate in 1980? In 1979?
(c) What was the amount of the company's "provision for doubtful accounts" (bad debt expense) for 1980 and in what category of expenses was it included?
(d) In what year did the company have "unusual write-offs and losses," and what was the total amount? What were the reasons for these items?
(e) What was the net income for 1980? For 1979? What were the earnings per share for 1980? For 1979?
(f) What was the rate of return on *ending* stockholders' equity for 1980? For 1979? What was the dividend yield for 1980? For 1979?
(g) Briefly summarize the company's explanation of the percent changes in the factors that caused the decrease in net income from 1979 to 1980.
(h) What was the working capital at the end of 1980? At the end of 1979? What was the current ratio for 1980? For 1979?
(i) How much working capital was provided by operations during 1980? During 1979? What was the amount of the largest "application of working capital" in 1980 and what was it for? How does this compare to 1979?
(j) Briefly discuss the company's explanation of the reasons for its decrease in liquidity from 1979 to 1980. What actions does the company plan to take to strengthen its liquidity position?
(k) Into what three categories does the company classify its depreciable property, plant, and equipment? What depreciation method is used by the company? What is the estimated useful life range for each category?
(l) What types of items does the company lease from other companies? Over what periods does the company lease these items? What is the book value of these items on December 31, 1980?
(m) How many shares of preferred stock is the company authorized to issue? How many shares has it issued on December 31, 1980? How many shares of common stock is the company authorized to issue? How many shares has it issued on December 31, 1980?

(n) What was the operating profit of each reportable industry segment during 1980? What was the pre-tax return on ending identifiable assets for each segment in 1980?

(o) What were the net sales and gross profit during each of the 4 quarters of 1980?

(p) What do you think was a primary reason for the highest quarterly sales occurring in the third quarter of 1980?

C19-2 Intra- and Intercompany Comparisons. A classmate of yours asks, "What is the difference between 'intra' and 'inter' company comparisons? I always thought they meant the same thing because they sound so much alike. Now I'm not so sure. And what information is compared? It seems to me that if each company presents annual financial statements, surely this is enough information for comparison. But now I am told that segment reports, interim financial reports, and horizontal, vertical, and ratio analyses are used for comparisons. What are these analyses anyway? It seems like a lot of extra work to prepare them when the only information investors and creditors are interested in is a company's annual earnings and its financial position at the end of the year."

Required: Write a brief report to your friend: (1) explaining the differences between intra-company and intercompany comparisons; (2) describing segment reports, interim financial reports, and horizontal, vertical, and ratio analyses; and (3) discussing how the analyses in Requirement 2 are useful for the comparisons in Requirement 1.

20 | Accounting for Changing Prices

After reading this chapter, you should understand:

- General price–level changes and the constant dollar adjustment process
- Specific price changes and the current cost adjustment process
- How to prepare constant dollar financial statements
- The nature of a purchasing power gain or loss on net monetary items
- How to prepare current cost financial statements
- The nature of holding gains and losses
- The companies that are required to prepare supplementary disclosures of the effect of changing prices
- The supplementary disclosure requirements

For many years accountants have discussed methods by which financial statements could reflect the effects of changing prices. In this chapter the two methods that have received the most support in recent years are discussed. Certain companies are required to include with their financial statements supplementary information on the effects of changing prices. These requirements are also discussed in this chapter.

ALTERNATIVE MEASURES OF INCOME WHEN PRICES CHANGE

Suppose that a company purchased land at the beginning of 1983 for $50,000. A year later, after there has been inflation of 10%, the land is sold for $65,000. What is the profit on the sale of the land? There are three different answers depending on how profit is measured. Before we discuss the three alternatives, however, we should have a clear understanding of what is meant by the term *profit* or *income*.

A common definition of income in economics is that income is the amount that could be paid to the owners of the company during a period of time and still enable the company to be as well off at the end of the period as it was at the beginning. The issue is the measurement of the wealth at the beginning and the end of the period.

One answer to the earlier question is that the profit is $15,000. This is the answer if profit is measured according to the generally accepted accounting principles developed in this book. In this case profit is being measured as the difference between the dollars received from the sale and the historical dollars used to acquire the item being sold. The wealth at the beginning of the period is measured as the *nominal* dollars used to acquire the land, and therefore the profit of $15,000 is the increase in the nominal dollars during the period. **Nominal dollars are dollars that have not been adjusted to reflect changes in prices.** Nominal dollars are used in the historical cost financial statements that have been discussed throughout this book.

A second answer is that the profit is $10,000. This is the answer if the wealth at the beginning of the period is measured in terms of the purchasing power at the end of the period of the dollars that were originally used to buy the land. **Purchasing power is the measure of the ability of dollars to purchase goods and services.** Since the land cost $50,000 and there has been inflation of 10% since the purchase, the $50,000 historical dollars have the same value, or purchasing power, as $55,000 at the end of the period. Therefore the purchasing power of the owner of the land has increased by $10,000 ($65,000 − $55,000). This is the measure of profit when the wealth at the beginning of the period is measured in terms of the purchasing power of the dollars at the end of the period, or more generally, when profit is measured in terms of constant dollars. **Constant dollars are historical (nominal) dollars that have been adjusted for changes in the general purchasing power.**

A third answer is that the profit is zero. If it is accepted that the owner of the land needs to replace it with land of equivalent capacity (e.g., size and location), there is no profit because the $65,000 obtained from the sale is needed to replace the land. An identical piece of land of the same size and location would, of course, cost $65,000 and therefore there is no profit. This is the measure of profit when the wealth at the beginning of the period is measured in terms of the current cost of the item being sold. **Current cost is the amount that would have to be paid in the current period to purchase an identical, or similar, item.**

As we will see later in the chapter, the financial statements of certain companies must include the disclosure of selected information prepared according to constant dollar and current cost principles. Before discussing these particular disclosures, it is useful to examine additional characteristics of these two alternative methods of measurement.

The Nature of Price Changes

As all of us are aware the price of virtually everything that is bought and sold changes each year. In recent times most of the price changes have been increases rather than decreases. It can easily be seen, however, that some prices rise much faster than others. The prices of energy and housing have tended to rise much more than most other items, whereas the prices of computers and calculators have tended to rise much less rapidly, or even fall.

A price change is either a specific price change or a general price change. **A specific price change is the measure of the change in the price of a *particular* good or service.** Examples are the price changes in such items as a gallon of regular gas or a pound of lean hamburger. Current cost accounting is based upon changes in specific prices. **A general price change is the weighted average of the changes** in the individual prices of a *group* of goods and services. This measure of the change in prices indicates the general inflation rate and therefore the change in the purchasing power of the dollar. **A general price–level index is a measure of general price changes over a period of time stated as an index rather than in dollar amounts.** Constant dollar accounting is based on changes in the general price level as measured by a general price–level index.

To illustrate the difference between the two concepts of price changes further, consider a general price–level (GPL) index made up of four individual items. To simplify the illustration we are including only four items, whereas the available indexes (discussed below) include thousands of items. The items are included in the index by using weighting factors that reflect average buying patterns. For example, if the average household spends 1% of its income on hamburger, the price of hamburger will be assigned a weighting factor of 1% when the index is computed. The changes in the prices of the four items are as follows:

Item	Price per Unit in 1983	Weighting Factor	Weighted Price per Unit in 1983
A	$ 2.00	40%	$0.80
B	5.00	30	1.50
C	10.00	20	2.00
D	40.00	10	4.00
Total		100%	$8.30

In 1984 the prices of the individual items are:

Item	Price per Unit in 1984	Weighting Factor	Weighted Price per Unit in 1984
A	$ 3.00	40%	$1.20
B	6.00	30	1.80
C	12.00	20	2.40
D	40.00	10	4.00
Total		100%	$9.40

The change in prices between 1983 and 1984 may be summarized as follows:

Percent Change in Prices

Item		
A	50%	($3.00 ÷ $2.00 = 1.50)
B	20	($6.00 ÷ $5.00 = 1.20)
C	20	($12.00 ÷ $10.00 = 1.20)
D	0	($40.00 ÷ $40.00 = 1.00)
Overall	13.25%	($9.40 ÷ $8.30 = 1.1325)

The prices of individual items, that is, the specific prices, have increased in the range from zero (Item D) to 50% (Item A), whereas the general price change indicates an average increase of 13.25% [($9.40 − $8.30) ÷ $8.30].

Although this is a very simple measure of the change in the general price level, it is possible to use it to develop a general price–level index. If the price of the items in 1983 is assigned an index number of 100, the general price level in 1984 has an index of 113.25:

$$\text{GPL index in 1984} = \frac{\text{Weighted average prices in 1984}}{\text{Weighted average prices in 1983}} \times \text{Index in 1983}$$

$$= \frac{\$9.40}{\$8.30} \times 100$$

$$= 113.25$$

To illustrate the index concept further, suppose that in 1985 the total weighted average price per unit for the four items is $10.20. The index in 1985 would be:

$$\text{GPL index in 1985} = \frac{\text{Weighted average prices in 1985}}{\text{Weighted average prices in 1983}} \times \text{Index in 1983}$$

$$= \frac{\$10.20}{\$\ 8.30} \times 100$$

$$= 122.89$$

Alternatively, the index in 1985 could be calculated as follows:

$$\text{GPL index in 1985} = \frac{\text{Weighted average prices in 1985}}{\text{Weighted average prices in 1984}} \times \text{Index in 1984}$$

$$= \frac{\$10.20}{\$\ 9.40} \times 113.25$$

$$= 122.89$$

A *specific* price–level index of a particular item can be developed in the same way as the general price–level index, based on a comparison of the specific prices of an individual item in each year. For example, the price of Item A has risen from $2.00 in 1983 to $3.00 in 1984. If the price of $2.00 in 1983 is assigned an index number of 100, the specific price–level index for Item A in 1984 is 150 [($3.00 ÷ $2.00) × 100].

Available Price–Level Indexes

Numerous price–level indexes are developed by various groups and are publicly available. The largest developer of price–level indexes is the federal government, which publishes over 2,700 different indexes. Most of them are specific price–level indexes, although many of them measure the change in the general price level. Of the latter type, there are three indexes that are widely publicized — the Wholesale Price Index, the Gross National Product Implicit Price Deflator, and the Consumer Price Index. The Consumer Price Index is prepared for various types of consumers. **The Consumer Price Index for All Urban Consumers (CPI–U) is required for the constant dollar supplementary disclosures discussed later in the chapter.** We use the CPI–U as the general price–level index throughout this chapter.

COMPREHEN-SIVELY RESTATED FINANCIAL STATEMENTS

In the introductory paragraphs to this chapter the basic principles underlying the historical cost, constant dollar, and current cost methods of accounting were discussed. To illustrate these three alternatives further, consider the following example of a series of simplified events for a corporation. In this example we use a corporation because all the companies required to make disclosures of the effects of changing prices (discussed later in the chapter) are corporations. Some of the situations and amounts discussed are very simple so that the reader can more easily focus on the concepts and not be distracted by complex arithmetic. A more complex example is included as a review problem at the end of the chapter. A study of that problem will assist in the solution of homework problems.

1. The Triad Company was formed by selling no par common stock for $100 when the CPI–U index was 100.
2. The company purchased a building for $30 with a 2-year life and no residual value when the CPI–U index was 100.
3. The company purchased three units of inventory for $10, $12, and $14 each when the CPI–U index was 100, 110, and 120 respectively.
4. The company sold two units of inventory for $30 each when the CPI–U index was 110. A FIFO cost flow assumption is used.
5. The average CPI–U index for the year was 110.
6. The current cost at year end was $14 for the inventory and $40 for the building. The CPI–U index at year end was 120.
7. Income taxes are disregarded.

Historical Cost Financial Statements

The income statement and ending balance sheet prepared under the three alternatives are presented in Exhibits 20-1 and 20-2. In Exhibit 20-1 the historical cost (or nominal dollar) net income is $23 because sales are $60, the cost of goods sold on a FIFO basis is $22, and the depreciation expense, computed on a straight-line

EXHIBIT 20-1 Income Statement

TRIAD COMPANY
Income Statement
For Current Year

	Historical Cost	Constant Dollars	Current Cost
Sales revenue	$60[a]	$60.00[d]	$60.00[g]
Cost of goods sold	(22)[b]	(23.00)[e]	(24.00)[h]
Depreciation expense	(15)[c]	(16.50)[f]	(17.50)[i]
Net Income	$23	$20.50	$18.50

[a] 2 units × $30.
[b] Since a FIFO cost flow assumption is used, the cost of the first two units ($10 + $12) is included in the cost of goods sold.
[c] (Cost − Residual value) ÷ Life = ($30 − $0) ÷ 2.
[d] It is assumed that the sales were made at the average general price level for the year, or $60 × $\frac{110}{110}$ = $60.
[e] $\left(\$10 \times \frac{110}{100}\right) + \left(\$12 \times \frac{110}{110}\right)$ = $23.
[f] $\$15 \times \frac{110}{100}$.
[g] The sales revenue does not require adjusting.
[h] Average current cost × Number of units sold = $\frac{\$14 + \$10}{2} \times 2$.
[i] (Average current cost − Residual value) ÷ Life = $\left(\frac{\$40 + \$30}{2} - \$0\right) \div 2$.

EXHIBIT 20-2
Ending Balance Sheet

TRIAD COMPANY
Balance Sheet
At End of Current Year

	Historical Cost	Constant Dollars	Current Cost
Cash	$ 94[a]	$ 86.17[d]	$ 94[a]
Inventory	14[b]	12.83[e]	14[j]
Building			
Cost	30	33.00[f]	40[k]
Less: Accumulated depreciation	(15)	(16.50)[g]	(20)[l]
Total Assets	$123	$115.50	$128
Common stock, no par	$100	$110.00[h]	$100
Retained earnings[c]	23	5.50[i]	28[m]
Total Liabilities and Stockholders' Equity	$123	$115.50	$128

[a] $100 (sale of common stock) − $30 (building) − $36 (inventory) + $60 (sales).
[b] Since a FIFO cost flow assumption is used, the cost of the last unit purchased is included in inventory.
[c] Since the beginning retained earnings is assumed to be zero and no dividends are paid, the retained earnings in the ending balance sheet is equal to the net income adjusted for the items shown in footnotes i and m.
[d] $94 × (110 ÷ 120).
[e] $14 × (110 ÷ 120).
[f] $30 × (110 ÷ 100).
[g] $15 × (110 ÷ 100).
[h] $100 × (110 ÷ 100).
[i] Net income ($20.50) − Purchasing power loss ($15.00).
[j] 1 unit × Ending current cost of $14.
[k] Current cost at year end.
[l] (Current cost − Residual value) ÷ Life = ($40 − $0) ÷ 2 = $20.
[m] Net income ($18.50) + Holding gains ($9.50).

basis, is $15. In Exhibit 20-2 the total assets, measured on a historical cost (nominal dollar) basis, are $123, consisting of cash of $94, inventory of $14, and the building with a book value of $15. In this simple example there are no liabilities. Common stock is $100 and the retained earnings are equal to the net income of the period because there were no beginning retained earnings or dividends paid during the year. The remaining items in the exhibits expressed in constant dollars and current costs are discussed in the next section.

Constant Dollar Financial Statements

The underlying principle of constant dollar financial statements is to adjust historical costs into dollars of constant purchasing power. The general formula for this adjustment is:

$$\text{Constant dollars} = \text{Historical dollars} \times \frac{\text{General price-level index in current period}}{\text{General price-level index at time of historical cost transaction}}$$

For example, in the illustration used at the beginning of the chapter the land was purchased for $50,000 and there was inflation of 10%, which is equivalent to a general price–level index increasing from, for example, 150 to 165 (150 × 1.10 = 165). Therefore the cost of the land in constant dollars is measured by:

$$\text{Constant dollar cost of land} = \$50,000 \times \frac{165}{150}$$
$$= \$55,000$$

This approach has been used to calculate the constant dollar amount of the sales, cost of goods sold, depreciation expense, cash, inventory, building, accumulated depreciation, and common stock for the Triad Company. The amount in the retained earnings account is calculated differently, as is discussed later. In this example the price–level index in the current period that is used for the numerator of the general price–level calculation is the *average* index for the current period, or 110. The computations of the constant dollar income statement items in Exhibit 20-1 are discussed below.

SALES. The sales were made when the CPI–U index was 110 and therefore do not need adjusting. Alternatively, the formula for the adjustment could be used as follows:

$$\$60 \times \frac{110}{110} = \$60 \text{ Sales}$$

COST OF GOODS SOLD. Under the FIFO cost flow assumption the cost of goods sold included units with historical costs of $10 and $12, which were purchased when the CPI–U index was 100 and 110, respectively. The cost of goods sold is adjusted as follows:

$$\left(\$10 \times \frac{110}{100}\right) + \left(12 \times \frac{110}{110}\right) = \$23 \text{ Cost of goods sold}$$

Note that if the average cost flow assumption had been used, the average historical cost per unit would be $12 [($10 + $12 + $14) ÷ 3] and the cost of goods sold on a historical cost basis would be $24 (2 units × $12). It would be typical to assume that the cost of goods sold on an average cost basis was measured in terms of the average price level for the year and therefore would not need adjusting. The constant dollar cost of goods sold would be $24 [$24 × (110 ÷ 110)].

DEPRECIATION EXPENSE. For historical cost depreciation expense the original cost of the asset is depreciated over its expected life (2 years in this example), and therefore depreciation expense is measured in terms of the historical dollars at the time of acquisition of the asset and not in constant dollars. Thus the historical cost depreciation of $15 is measured in terms of a CPI–U index of 100 and needs to be adjusted as follows:

$$\$15 \times \frac{110}{100} = \$16.50 \text{ Depreciation expense}$$

Other expenses included in the income statement (such as selling expenses, general and administrative expenses, and income tax expense) are typically assumed to occur at the average price level for the year and therefore do not need adjusting. The computations of the constant dollar balance sheet items in Exhibit 20-2 are discussed below.

CASH. The cash in the historical cost balance sheet is measured in terms of the CPI–U index at that time, which is the year-end index of 120. Therefore the cash needs to be adjusted to the average price level of the year as follows:

$$\$94 \times \frac{110}{120} = \$86.17 \text{ Cash}$$

Other "monetary" assets (defined later), such as accounts receivable, would be adjusted to the average price level by using the same adjustment factor.

INVENTORY. Under the FIFO cost flow assumption the unit in the ending inventory cost \$14; it was purchased when the index was 120 and is adjusted as follows:

$$\$14 \times \frac{110}{120} = \$12.83 \text{ Inventory}$$

BUILDING AND ACCUMULATED DEPRECIATION. The building was purchased for \$30 and accumulated depreciation of \$15 has been recorded. Since both of these amounts are measured in terms of the CPI–U index of 100, they have to be adjusted as follows:

$$\text{Building} \quad \$30 \times \frac{110}{100} = \$33.00$$

$$\text{Accumulated depreciation} \quad (\$15) \times \frac{110}{100} = (\$16.50)$$

The Triad Company has no "monetary" liabilities (defined later), but if they did these monetary liabilities would be adjusted in the same way as cash. That is, they are included in the historical cost balance sheet at the price level of the end of the year, and they must be adjusted to the average price level.

COMMON STOCK. The common stock was sold when the CPI–U index was 100 and therefore is adjusted as follows:

$$\$100 \times \frac{110}{100} = \$110 \text{ Common stock}$$

PURCHASING POWER GAIN OR LOSS ON NET MONETARY ITEMS. During a period of inflation, holding cash results in a loss of purchasing power. For example, \$10 cash when hamburger is \$2 per pound enables you to buy 5 pounds of hamburger. When the price of hamburger rises to \$2.50 per pound, \$10 will buy only 4 pounds of hamburger. Therefore holding the \$10 cash during the period of inflation has resulted in the loss of purchasing power of 1 pound of hamburger. This loss is 25% of the purchasing power needed to buy 4 pounds of hamburger at the end of the period (1 pound ÷ 4 pounds = 0.25). This loss can also be measured as 25% of the cash held or $2.50 ($10 × 0.25 = $2.50). This can be seen by noting that at the end of the period it takes $12.50 (or an increase of 25%) to buy 5 pounds of hamburger. More generally, *the purchasing power of cash declines as inflation in the prices of all goods and services occurs.* When constant dollar financial statements are prepared this loss of general purchasing power must be recognized.

Cash is only one monetary asset. There are several monetary assets (and liabilities) that a company can own (or owe). **A monetary asset is money or a claim to receive a fixed amount of money in the future.** The principal monetary assets are cash, accounts receivable, and notes receivable. Holding monetary *assets* during a period of inflation results in a purchasing power *loss*. **A monetary liability is an obligation to repay a fixed amount of money in the future.** Principal monetary liabilities include accounts payable, notes payable, and bonds payable. Holding a monetary *liability* during a period of inflation results in a purchasing power *gain* because inflation reduces the purchasing power of the dollars needed to repay these liabilities. The reduction in the purchasing power owed results in a purchasing power gain. **Net monetary items are monetary assets less monetary liabilities.** The purchasing power gain or loss is the combined gain or loss in purchasing power that occurs when net monetary items are held during a period in which the general price level changes. The computation of the purchasing power gain or loss is made more complex because the net monetary items are changed during the period by some of a company's transactions.

In the Triad Company example cash is the only monetary item. The cash balance has decreased from $100 to $94 during the period, however. The company has incurred a purchasing power loss that is computed as follows. First, all the cash transactions are adjusted to the constant purchasing power represented by the average CPI-U index of 110 as shown below:

	Historical Amount		Adjustment		Constant Dollar Amount
Beginning net monetary items . .	$100	×	$\dfrac{110}{100}$	=	$110.00
Sales	60	×	$\dfrac{110}{110}$	=	60.00
Purchase of building	(30)	×	$\dfrac{110}{100}$	=	(33.00)
Purchases of inventory	(10)	×	$\dfrac{110}{100}$	=	(11.00)
	(12)	×	$\dfrac{110}{110}$	=	(12.00)
	(14)	×	$\dfrac{110}{120}$	=	(12.83)
Ending Net Monetary Items . . .	$ 94				$101.17

The historical beginning net monetary items (cash) of $100 are measured in beginning-of-the-year purchasing power (CPI–U = 100), whereas the constant dollar amount is measured in average purchasing power (CPI–U = 110). Therefore the beginning balance of $100 must be adjusted to the average purchasing power of the period (i.e., constant dollar amount) by multiplying times an adjustment factor of 110/100. The sales during the year caused an increase in net monetary items while the payments for the purchases of the building and inventory caused a decrease in net monetary items. Each is adjusted to the average purchasing power of the period from the general price level at the time the cash was received or paid by multiplying times the appropriate adjustment factor. The ending net monetary items at historical cost and at constant dollars are computed by adding or subtracting the inflows or outflows.

The historical ending net monetary items of $94 are measured in year-end purchasing power (CPI–U = 120), whereas the constant dollar amount of $101.17 is measured in average purchasing power (CPI–U = 110). To complete the computation of the purchasing power loss, the historical ending balance of $94 must be adjusted to the average purchasing power of the period. The purchasing power loss (measured in terms of the average purchasing power of the period) is computed by comparing the constant dollar ending balance to the adjusted historical ending balance as shown below:

Constant dollar ending balance	$101.17
Historical ending balance adjusted to average price level $\left(\$94 \times \dfrac{110}{120}\right)$	86.17
Purchasing Power Loss (at average price level)	$ 15.00

The constant dollar ending balance of $101.17 is the average purchasing power that the company's cash balance *should have had*. Since the ending cash balance of $94 had only an average purchasing power of $86.17, there has been a purchasing power loss of $15. If the company had held net monetary liabilities instead of net monetary assets, there would have been a purchasing power gain. Usually all of these computations are shown on a single schedule entitled *schedule to compute purchasing power gain or loss*.

If the company had held monetary liabilities and monetary assets other than cash, the beginning net monetary items (monetary assets less monetary liabilities) would be computed in a separate schedule. This amount would be included as the beginning balance and adjusted to the constant dollar amount. The changes in the net monetary items during the period would be recorded in the same way as shown in the example above and also adjusted to the constant dollar amount. The resulting ending balance of net monetary items in the *historical amount* column would be adjusted to the constant dollar amount and subtracted from the ending balance of the *constant dollar amount* column to determine the purchasing power gain or loss.

There is disagreement among accountants about whether the purchasing power gain or loss should be included in the computation of constant dollar net income.

In this example the loss has been *excluded* from net income but has been *deducted* from retained earnings.

RETAINED EARNINGS.   Since there was no beginning balance of retained earnings and no dividends were paid, the amount in the balance sheet ($5.50) is the net income for the period ($20.50) less the purchasing power loss ($15.00). Examples of adjustments to additional items not included in the above example are included in the review problem at the end of the chapter.

Current Cost Financial Statements   The current cost financial statements include the current cost of each item. The current cost of an item is the amount it would cost to acquire the item in the current period. Because the income statement is a report on the performance of the company for an entire period, *average* current costs for the period are used in the income statement. The balance sheet, in contrast, is a report of the financial position at year end, and therefore *year-end* current costs are used in the balance sheet. The computations of the current cost income statement items in Exhibit 20-1 are discussed below.

SALES.   Sales are typically not adjusted because it is assumed that they are made at the average prices for the period.

COST OF GOODS SOLD.   Cost of goods sold is computed by multiplying the number of units sold by the average current cost for the period. In this example two units are sold during the period, and they are included in the income statement at the average current cost for the period, which is based on the beginning ($10) and ending ($14) current costs for the period. The computation of the $24 cost of goods sold is as follows:

$$\text{Cost of goods sold} = \text{Units sold} \times \text{Average current cost per unit}$$
$$= 2 \times \frac{\$10 + \$14}{2}$$
$$= \$24$$

DEPRECIATION EXPENSE.   The depreciation expense is based on the average current cost of the building as follows:

$$\text{Depreciation expense} = \frac{\text{Average current cost} - \text{Residual value}}{\text{Life}}$$
$$= \frac{\left(\dfrac{\$30 + \$40}{2}\right) - \$0}{2}$$
$$= \$17.50$$

Other expenses typically included in the income statement (such as selling expenses, general and administrative expenses, and income tax expense) are assumed to occur at the average cost for the year and therefore do not need adjusting. The computations of the current cost balance sheet items in Exhibit 20-2 are discussed below.

CASH.   Cash does not need adjustment because it is already stated in terms of its value at the end of the year. Similarly, all other monetary assets and monetary liabilities are not adjusted.

INVENTORY.   The inventory in the balance sheet is valued at the current cost of the units in the inventory at year end. In our example the ending inventory of $14 is computed as follows:

$$\text{Ending inventory} = \text{Number of units} \times \text{Ending current cost}$$
$$= 1 \times \$14$$
$$= \$14$$

BUILDING AND ACCUMULATED DEPRECIATION.   The building is valued at the current cost at year end ($40) less accumulated depreciation based on this year-end value. Since the life of the building is half over, the accumulated depreciation is half the current cost:

$$\text{Building} = \$40$$

$$\text{Accumulated depreciation} = \left(\begin{array}{c} \text{Current cost at the} \\ \text{end of the period} \end{array} - \begin{array}{c} \text{Residual} \\ \text{value} \end{array} \right) \times \frac{\text{Number of years owned}}{\text{Life}}$$

$$= (\$40 - \$0) \times \frac{1}{2}$$

$$= \$20$$

COMMON STOCK.   The common stock is not adjusted because there is no reliable measure of the amount for which all the common stock outstanding could be sold in the current period.

HOLDING GAINS AND LOSSES.   When current cost financial statements are being prepared holding gains and losses arise. **A holding gain (loss) is the increase (decrease) in the current cost of a nonmonetary asset during the period. A realized holding gain (loss) is a gain (loss) that has been recognized on an item that has been included in the historical cost income statement. An unrealized holding gain (loss) is a gain (loss) on an item that has not yet been recognized in the historical cost income statement.** In general, the realized and unrealized holding gains (losses) are measured as follows:

Realized holding gain (loss)   =   Current cost expense   −   Historical cost expense
Unrealized holding gain (loss)   =   Current cost asset value   −   Historical cost asset value

In the Triad Company example holding gains arise on the inventory and the building. Therefore the realized and unrealized holding gains are calculated as follows:

Realized holding gain (inventory)	=	Current cost of the cost of goods sold	−	Historical cost of the cost of goods sold
	=	$24	−	$22
	=	$2		

Realized holding gain (building)	=	Current cost depreciation expense	−	Historical cost depreciation expense
	=	$17.50	−	$15.00
	=	$2.50		

Unrealized holding gain (inventory)	=	Current cost of inventory	−	Historical cost of inventory
	=	$14	−	$14
	=	$0		

Unrealized holding gain (building)	=	Net current cost of building	−	Net historical cost of building
	=	($40 − $20)	−	($30 − $15)
	=	$5		

The total holding gains are $9.50 ($2 + $2.50 + $0 + $5). There is disagreement among accountants about whether holding gains and losses should be included in income. In this example the holding gains are *excluded* from income, but they are *added* to retained earnings. No matter how holding gains and losses are included in financial statements it is important to recognize the nature of these gains. They result simply from the rise in price of the respective assets, and they do not increase the wealth of the company if it is agreed that the assets will have to be replaced at the higher cost. It is difficult to argue that the company is better off because it will have to replace assets at the higher cost.

RETAINED EARNINGS.   Since there is no beginning balance of retained earnings and no dividends were paid, the amount in the balance sheet is the net income for the period ($18.50) plus the holding gain ($9.50), or $28. Examples of the adjustments to additional items not included in the above example are included in the review problem at the end of the chapter.

SUPPLEMENTARY DISCLOSURE REQUIREMENTS

The above illustration of the preparation of comprehensive constant dollar and current cost financial statements was based on very simple historical cost financial statements. In practice, however, financial statements are much more complex. No companies are required to prepare *comprehensively* adjusted financial statements. Selected companies (beginning in 1979), however, are *required* to make certain supplementary disclosures in their financial statements of the effects of changing prices.[1] These supplemental disclosures are made in the footnotes to the financial statements. These disclosure requirements have been developed to assist users of financial statements to understand the impact of changing prices and to reduce the limitations of historical cost financial statements, which ignore such changes.

The following companies are required to present the disclosures in their financial statements:

1. Companies with $1 billion of assets (*after* deducting accumulated depreciation).
2. Companies with $125 million of inventories and property, plant, and equipment (*before* deducting accumulated depreciation).

Approximately 1,500 companies meet these criteria and therefore began making the following required disclosures in their 1979 annual reports:

1. For the current year:
   A. *Constant dollar*
      (1) Income from continuing operations.
      (2) Purchasing power gain or loss on net monetary items (excluded from income from continuing operations).
   B. *Current cost*
      (1) Income from continuing operations.
      (2) Current cost amounts of inventory and property, plant, and equipment at the end of the current fiscal year.
      (3) Increases or decreases in the current cost amounts (i.e., holding gains and losses) of inventory and property, plant, and equipment, net of inflation (excluded from income from continuing operations).
2. A 5-year summary of selected data. The required disclosures and the alternative methods of computing them are discussed in the appendix to this chapter.

To illustrate the relationship between the basic financial statements and the selected disclosures for the current year listed above, consider the Colonial Company's historical cost income statement and balance sheet in Exhibit 20-3 along with the additional information. The required supplementary disclosures as well as information that helps to relate the supplementary disclosures to the historical cost income statement are shown in Exhibit 20-4. This exhibit would be included in the footnotes to the financial statements. Each of the supplementary disclosures is discussed in the following sections.

Income from Continuing Operations

Income from continuing operations is disclosed under both the constant dollar and current cost bases. In this example income from continuing operations is the same as net income because there are no gains or losses from discontinued operations or extraordinary items. The only two items that are typically adjusted to compute income from continuing operations under both the constant dollar and current cost bases are the cost of goods sold and depreciation expense. The other items are not

---

[1] "Financial Reporting and Changing Prices," *FASB Statement No. 33* (Stamford, Conn.: FASB, 1979).

EXHIBIT 20-3
Historical Cost
Income Statement
and Balance Sheet

COLONIAL COMPANY
Income Statement
For Year Ended December 31, 1983

Sales		$300,000
Cost of goods sold		
Inventory, December 31, 1982	$ 40,000	
Purchases	132,000	
Inventory, December 31, 1983	(60,000)	
Cost of goods sold		112,000
Gross profit		$188,000
Operating expenses		
Depreciation expense	$ 50,000	
Selling and administrative expenses	80,000	
Total operating expenses		130,000
Income before income taxes		$ 58,000
Income tax expense (at 40%)		23,200
Net Income		$ 34,800

COLONIAL COMPANY
Balance Sheets

	December 31, 1982	December 31, 1983
Cash	$ 20,000	$ 59,800
Accounts receivable	50,000	80,000
Inventory	40,000	60,000
Equipment	400,000	400,000
Less: Accumulated depreciation	(150,000)	(200,000)
Total Assets	$360,000	$399,800
Accounts payable	$ 40,000	$ 45,000
Bonds payable	150,000	150,000
Common stock, no par	100,000	100,000
Retained earnings	70,000	104,800
Total Liabilities and		
Stockholders' Equity	$360,000	$399,800

Additional information:

CPI–U index: December 1982:   260
                  Average   1983:   273
                  December 1983:   286

Inventory: The company uses the FIFO cost flow assumption
             Beginning inventory: 10,000 units at $4 each = $40,000; CPI–U = 255
             Ending inventory: 12,000 units at $5 each = $60,000; CPI–U = 280
             Purchases during the year: 30,000 units at $4.40 each; CPI–U = 273
             Average current cost during the year: $4.75 per unit
             Current cost at the end of the year: $5.25 per unit
             Current cost at the beginning of the year: $4.10 per unit

Equipment: Purchased January 1, 1980; CPI–U = 210
             Residual value: Zero
             Estimated life: 8 years
             Depreciation method: Straight line
             Current cost, December 31, 1982: $500,000
             Current cost, December 31, 1983: $650,000

EXHIBIT 20-4
Supplementary
Disclosure of the
Effects of
Changing Prices

COLONIAL COMPANY
Supplementary Disclosure of the Effects of Changing Prices
For Year Ended December 31, 1983

	As Reported in the Historical Cost Income Statement	Adjusted for General Inflation (constant dollars)	Adjusted for Changes in Specific Prices (current costs)
Sales	$300,000	$300,000	$300,000
Cost of goods sold	(112,000)	(116,324)	(133,000)
Depreciation expense	(50,000)	(65,000)	(71,875)
Selling and administrative expenses	(80,000)	(80,000)	(80,000)
Income tax expense	(23,200)	(23,200)	(23,200)
Income (loss) from continuing operations	$ 34,800	$ 15,476	($ 8,075)
Gain from increase in purchasing power of net monetary items		$ 8,509	

	Inventory	Property, Plant, and Equipment
Current cost:		
Specific price (current cost) at year end	$63,000	$325,000
Increases or decreases in current costs:		
Increase in specific prices	$22,000	$ 12,500
Effect of increase in general price level	2,000	1,136
Excess of increase in specific prices over increase in the general price level	$20,000	$ 11,364

adjusted because it is assumed that they are already at the average current cost for the period and are measured in average-for-the-year dollars.

CONSTANT DOLLAR ADJUSTMENTS.   For the *constant dollar* income from continuing operations the following adjustments are made:

Cost of Goods Sold (Constant Dollars)

	Historical Cost		Adjustment		Constant Dollars
Beginning inventory	$ 40,000	×	$\frac{273}{255}$	=	$ 42,824
Purchases	132,000	×	$\frac{273}{273}$	=	132,000
Ending inventory	(60,000)	×	$\frac{273}{280}$	=	(58,500)
Cost of Goods Sold	$112,000				$116,324

Depreciation Expense (Constant Dollars)

Constant dollar depreciation   =   Historical cost depreciation   ×   Adjustment factor
expense   expense

$$= \$50{,}000 \ \times \ \frac{273}{210}$$

$$= \$65{,}000$$

The disclosure of income from continuing operations on a constant dollar basis of $15,476 is shown in Exhibit 20-4.

CURRENT COST ADJUSTMENTS.   For the *current cost* income from continuing operations the following adjustments are made:

Cost of Goods Sold (Current Cost)

Units sold   =   Units in beginning   +   Units purchased   −   Units in ending
                   inventory   inventory

       =   10,000   +   30,000   −   12,000

       =   28,000

Average current cost of goods sold   =   Units sold   ×   Average current
                                                          cost per unit

                  =   28,000   × $4.75

                  = $133,000

Depreciation Expense (Current Cost)

Current cost depreciation   =   (Average current cost   −   Residual value)   ÷   Life
expense

$$= \left(\frac{\$500{,}000 \ + \ \$650{,}000}{2} - \$0 \right) \div 8$$

$$= \$71{,}875$$

The disclosure of the loss from continuing operations on a current cost basis of $8,075 is shown in Exhibit 20-4.

Purchasing Power Gain or Loss on Net Monetary Items   Instead of analyzing each individual cash flow as we did in the example earlier in the chapter, a simplified method of calculating the purchasing power gain or loss on net monetary items is usually used. The beginning and ending historical cost net monetary items (monetary assets minus monetary liabilities) are calculated, and the net increase or decrease is the difference between the two amounts. The beginning net monetary items are adjusted to the average price level (i.e., to constant dollars). The net increase or decrease for the year is assumed to have occurred at the average price level for the year so that no adjustment is necessary to express it in terms of the constant dollar amount. This is in contrast to our earlier example where the amount and timing of *each* change in the net monetary items was adjusted by multiplying it times an appropriate adjustment factor. The balance of the beginning net monetary items (in constant dollars) is added to the increase in net monetary items to determine the balance of the ending net monetary items (in constant dollars). The balance of the ending net monetary items (at historical cost) is computed in a similar way and then adjusted to the average price level. The purchasing power gain or loss is calculated by deducting the historical ending net monetary items (adjusted to the average price level) from the constant dollar ending net monetary items.

In the Colonial Company example the beginning and ending net monetary items are both negative; that is, monetary liabilities exceed monetary assets. When this occurs the net monetary items are called *net monetary liabilities*. When monetary assets exceed monetary liabilities, the net monetary items are called *net monetary assets*. In our example the net monetary liabilities are calculated in a schedule as follows:

Schedule of Net Monetary Items

	December 31, 1982 (beginning)	December 31, 1983 (ending)
Cash	$ 20,000	$ 59,800
Accounts receivable	50,000	80,000
Less: Accounts payable	(40,000)	(45,000)
Bonds payable	(150,000)	(150,000)
Net Monetary Items	($120,000)	($ 55,200)

The decrease in the net monetary liabilities (or an increase in net monetary items) is $64,800 ($120,000 − $55,200) and is assumed to occur at the average price level for the year. Since the company has held net monetary liabilities, there is a purchasing power *gain* calculated as follows:

Schedule to Compute Purchasing Power Gain or Loss

	Historical Cost	Adjustment	Constant Dollars
Beginning net monetary items	($120,000)	$\frac{273}{260}$	($126,000)
Increase in net monetary items	64,800		64,800
Ending net monetary items unadjusted	($ 55,200)		
Constant dollar ending balance (at average price level)			($ 61,200)
Historical ending balance adjusted to average price level $\left[(\$55,200) \times \frac{273}{286} \right]$			(52,691)
Purchasing power gain (at average price level)			($ 8,509)

The historical cost measure of the ending net monetary *liabilities* is $55,200, which is adjusted to a constant dollar amount of $52,691. The constant dollar measure of the ending net monetary *liabilities*, giving consideration to the changes that have occurred during the year, is $61,200. Therefore the company has a purchasing power *gain* of $8,509 ($61,200 − $52,691), as shown above. The disclosure of the purchasing power gain is shown in Exhibit 20-4.

Current Cost at the End of the Current Fiscal Year

The current cost of the inventory and property, plant, and equipment at the end of the current fiscal year must be disclosed. The inventory at the end of 1983 consists of 12,000 units. The current cost of the inventory at the end of the year is $5.25 per unit, and therefore the total current cost is $63,000 (12,000 × $5.25), as shown in Exhibit 20-4.

The equipment at the end of 1983 is shown at the current cost at the year end ($650,000) less the accumulated depreciation based on that current cost. The equipment was purchased on January 1, 1980, and has an 8-year life. Therefore at the end of 1983 it is one-half (4 ÷ 8) depreciated. The current cost is $325,000 [$650,000 − ($650,000 × 1/2)], as shown in Exhibit 20-4.[2]

Increases or Decreases in the Current Cost, Net of Inflation

The increases or decreases in the current cost of the inventory and property, plant, and equipment, net of inflation must be disclosed. The beginning current cost of the inventory and property, plant, and equipment are computed in the same way as above:

$$
\begin{aligned}
\text{Current cost of beginning inventory} &= \text{Units} \times \text{Current cost per unit} \\
&= 10{,}000 \times \$4.10 \\
&= \$41{,}000
\end{aligned}
$$

$$
\begin{aligned}
\text{Current cost of equipment} &= \text{Beginning current cost} - \text{Accumulated depreciation} \\
&= \$500{,}000 - (\$500{,}000 \times 3/8) \\
&= \$500{,}000 - \$187{,}500 \\
&= \$312{,}500
\end{aligned}
$$

Therefore the increase and decrease in the current cost of the inventory and equipment are calculated as follows:

Inventory

$$
\begin{aligned}
\text{Increase} &= \text{Ending current cost} - \text{Beginning current cost} \\
&= \$63{,}000 \text{ (calculated earlier)} - \$41{,}000 \\
&= \$22{,}000
\end{aligned}
$$

Equipment

$$
\begin{aligned}
\text{Increase} &= \text{Ending current cost} - \text{Beginning current cost} \\
&= \$325{,}000 \text{ (calculated earlier)} - \$312{,}500 \\
&= \$12{,}500
\end{aligned}
$$

The $22,000 and $12,500 increases in the current costs of the inventory and the equipment are shown in Exhibit 20-4.

The *specific* methods by which each increase and decrease is measured *net of*

[2] The accumulated depreciation included in the current cost disclosures is *not* the sum of the current cost depreciation expense calculated each year of the asset's life. The accumulated depreciation is based on the current cost of the asset at the end of the particular year and the length of time the asset has been owned, whereas the depreciation expense each year is based on the average current cost for that year.

inflation will not be discussed because these methods can be complex. A simplified measurement, however, involves adjustment of the increase or decrease based on the change in the general price–level index. Since inflation during 1983 was 10% (the ending CPI–U of 286 ÷ the beginning CPI–U of 260 = 1.10) the increase in the current cost of the inventory ($22,000) could be divided by 1.10 to indicate the increase expressed in constant dollars ($20,000). The difference between the unadjusted increase and the adjusted increase shows the amount by which the current cost has increased or decreased over and above the effect of general inflation as follows:

Increase in current cost of inventory	$22,000
Increase in current cost in constant dollars	20,000
Inflation Component	$ 2,000

Similar calculations for equipment would result in the following information:

Increase in current cost of property, plant, and equipment	$12,500
Increase in current cost in constant dollars ($12,500 ÷ 1.10)	11,364
Inflation Component	$ 1,136

The increase in the current cost of the inventory and equipment is shown both before and after inflation, as illustrated in Exhibit 20-4.

METHODS OF COMPUTING CURRENT COST

As we have seen, the method of computing the constant dollar supplementary disclosures is clearly defined because the CPI–U index must be used, and this index is prepared by the federal government.

The method of computing the current cost supplementary disclosures, in contrast, is much less well defined. There are three basic methods of finding the current cost of inventory and property, plant, and equipment.[3]

Direct Pricing

The current cost of the asset is determined directly by using the most recent invoice price, a supplier's price list or other quotations or estimates, or by using standard manufacturing costs (discussed later in the book). This is an appropriate measurement technique for assets that are frequently purchased or manufactured or that have an established market price, such as inventory and office equipment.

Functional or Unit Pricing

The current cost is calculated by estimating the construction (or acquisition) cost per unit (such as per square foot of building space) and multiplying this figure by the number of units in the asset. For example, if a company owns a building with 5,000 square feet and current construction costs are $100 per square foot, the current cost of the building would be $500,000.

---

[3] FASB Statement No. 33, *op. cit.*, par. 60.

Specific Price Index

The current cost is calculated by adjusting the historical cost by a specific price index appropriate to the asset. Since the federal government publishes more than 2,700 price indexes, it should be possible to find an index that is appropriate for each particular asset, or component of an asset. The adjustment process is the same as that used for a general price index:

$$\text{Current cost} = \text{Historical dollars} \times \frac{\text{Specific price index in current period}}{\text{Specific price index at time of historical cost transaction}}$$

The second two methods are more likely to be appropriate for property, plant, and equipment. Since any of the methods may be used for any asset, however, and the second two methods do not necessarily result in accurate measures of current cost, there is likely to be much variation in the current cost figures published by companies. This potential variation is one of the major criticisms of the supplementary current cost disclosures.

COMPARISON OF THE ALTERNATIVES

As can be seen from the various examples in the chapter, income and asset values can vary significantly under the historical cost, constant dollar, and current cost alternatives. To illustrate the significant differences in net income as a result of using the constant dollar and current cost approaches, Exhibits 20-5 and 20-6 summarize the differences reported for selected industries in 1981. For example, the average income of the companies in the chemical industry using the constant dollar and current cost methods was only 44% and 48%, respectively, of the historical cost income. The financial performance of companies was also affected

EXHIBIT 20-5
Inflation-Adjusted Income as Percent of 1980 Historical Cost Income

Industry	Using Constant Dollar Method	Using Current Cost Method
Aerospace	79%	80%
Beverages	70	64
Chemicals	44	48
Electrical and electronics	61	69
Food processing	43	52
General machinery	68	71
Metals and mining	59	49
Natural resources (fuel)	65	44
Office equipment	61	87
Paper and forest products	27	22
Publishing and broadcasting	76	77
Textiles and apparel	39	51
All-industry average	48	43

Source: Business Week, May 4, 1981.

**EXHIBIT 20-6   Inflation's Impact on Measures of Financial Performance
Average Compound Growth Rate 1976–80**

	Growth in Profits		Growth in Sales		Growth in Dividends	
	Historical Cost	Constant Dollar	Historical Cost	Constant Dollar	Historical Cost	Constant Dollar
Aerospace	29%	17%	21%	9%	37%	22%
Beverages	11	1	16	6	3	–8
Chemicals	10	0	14	4	13	2
Electrical	16	6	14	4	16	5
Food processing	10	1	12	3	13	3
General machinery	21	10	18	7	18	7
Metals and mining	58	37	19	8	21	9
Natural resources (fuel)	32	18	23	11	23	10
Office equipment	13	3	15	4	35	22
Paper and forest products	9	0	11	2	14	3
Publishing and broadcasting	15	5	18	7	22	12
Textiles and apparel	10	0	10	1	13	3
All-industry average	14	4	16	5	15	5

Source: Business Week, May 4, 1981.

as shown in Exhibit 20-6. For example, all industrial companies showed a growth in profits on a historical cost basis of 14%, whereas the growth was only 4% when profits were measured on a constant dollar basis.

As has been explained throughout this chapter the three methods are based on different concepts. The historical cost method is based on nominal dollars, the constant dollar method is based on constant purchasing power, and the current cost method is based on productive capacity. Since the methods are alternatives, and *not* substitutes, for each other it is impossible to state that one is the best. The user of the information needs to understand the meaning of the information presented under each alternative and therefore decide which method yields the most useful information for any particular purpose.

The historical cost method has the advantage of being the most objective and widely understood method. It is also the most conservative in terms of the balance sheet valuations, but as we have seen, it does not necessarily produce the most conservative, or lowest, measure of income during periods of inflation. It is difficult to see that it best satisfies the needs of users of financial statements, however. The user has no assurance that the purchasing power of a company's capital is being maintained or that the company can continue to operate at the same level of capacity.

To ensure that the company maintains the purchasing power of its capital would probably be considered desirable by most stockholders. They contributed a certain number of dollars to the company when they invested in the company, and they are more concerned about the purchasing power of these dollars than about the number of dollars originally contributed. Constant dollar financial statements ensure that the purchasing power of the capital is maintained before income is earned. In addition, the value of the assets is reported in terms of constant dollars, and therefore this value is more comparable than the historical cost value. Remember that a historical cost balance sheet includes costs incurred at many different times, and therefore these costs are very difficult, if not impossible, to compare. When the assets are measured in constant dollars, these historical costs have all been converted to dollars of the same purchasing power and for this reason are more comparable.

A company needs specific assets to conduct its operations, and it is possible that the company could be maintaining the general purchasing power of its capital but not its ability to replace these assets. This would arise when the costs of the particular assets that the company is using rise faster than the general price level. Use of the current cost concept ensures that the operating capability of the company is maintained before income is earned. In addition, the current value of the assets reported in the balance sheet represents the value of these assets at that particular time, which many users of financial statements consider to be the most useful valuation.

When the three alternatives are compared many accountants argue that the current cost method of preparing financial statements is conceptually the most desirable, and therefore it is much more relevant to the users of financial statements. It must be recognized that the numbers may be less precise than the numbers produced under the historical cost or constant dollar methods. It is very difficult to evaluate a tradeoff between relevance and precision, but as increased experience with current cost information is acquired, the accuracy of the information should be improved.

CHAPTER APPENDIX **The Five-Year Summary Included in the Supplementary Disclosures on the Effects of Changing Prices**

In addition to the supplementary disclosures required by selected companies for the current year, a 5-year summary of the following information is required:

1. Net sales and other operating revenues.
2. Income from continuing operations under both the constant dollar and current cost bases (including amounts for earnings per share).
3. Net assets at year end, under both the constant dollar and current cost bases.
4. Increases or decreases in the current cost amounts of inventory and property, plant, and equipment, net of inflation.
5. Purchasing power gain or loss on net monetary items.
6. Cash dividends declared and market price at year end, per common share.

To illustrate the 5-year summary, we continue our example of the Colonial Company discussed earlier. The data as *originally* reported in *each* of the 5 years

EXHIBIT 20-7   Data for Five-Year Summary

COLONIAL COMPANY
Data for 5-Year Summary
as Originally Reported

	1983	1982	1981	1980	1979
Net sales and other operating revenues	$300,000[a]	$280,000	$250,000	$200,000	$180,000
Income from continuing operations:					
Constant dollars	15,476[a]	27,650	42,800	55,000	38,000
Earnings per share[b]	1.55	2.77	4.28	5.50	3.80
Current cost	(8,075)[a]	5,420	27,618	45,000	42,300
Earnings per share[b]	(0.81)	0.54	2.76	4.50	4.23
Net assets at year end:					
Constant dollars	265,809[c]	200,400	193,000	186,000	150,800
Current cost	332,800[d]	210,000	200,000	190,000	145,000
Increase or decrease in the current cost amount of					
inventory, net of inflation	20,000[a]	18,000	16,000	15,000	12,000
Increase or decrease in the current cost amount of property,					
plant, and equipment, net of inflation	11,364[a]	(18,000)	20,000	33,000	(8,000)
Purchasing power loss on net monetary items	8,509[a]	3,000	2,750	4,120	2,300
Cash dividends declared per share	–	1.00	1.00	1.00	1.00
Market price of common stock at year end	17	12	15	18	12

All amounts are assumed except for those calculated in the footnotes below.
  [a] Calculated in earlier analysis.
  [b] Assuming 10,000 shares outstanding.

[c] Cash $\left(\$59,800 \times \dfrac{273}{286}\right)$ + Accounts receivable $\left(\$80,000 \times \dfrac{273}{286}\right)$ + Inventory $\left(\$60,000 \times \dfrac{273}{280}\right)$ +

Equipment $\left(\$400,000 \times \dfrac{273}{210} - \$200,000 \times \dfrac{273}{210}\right)$ − Accounts payable $\left(\$45,000 \times \dfrac{273}{286}\right)$ − Bonds

payable $\left(\$150,000 \times \dfrac{273}{286}\right)$.

[d] Cash ($59,800) + Accounts receivable ($80,000) + Inventory (12,000 × $5.25 = $63,000) +
Equipment ($325,000) − Accounts payable ($45,000) − Bonds payable ($150,000).

Additional Information:
CPI–U Index: Average 1983 = 273
             Average 1982 = 250
             Average 1981 = 235
             Average 1980 = 220
             Average 1979 = 200
                     1967 = 100

is shown in Exhibit 20-7. Some of this information is taken from the historical cost financial statements (item 1 on the previous page), some from the supplementary disclosures of the effects of changing prices (items 2, 3, 4, and 5), and some of it is additional data (item 6). Since the data for each year are measured in terms of dollars of that year, each year's figures are measured in terms of different purchasing powers. Therefore the 5-year summary is adjusted to dollars of constant purchasing power so that a realistic comparison of the data can be made. There are two alternatives for the value of the CPI–U index that may be used for adjusting the 5-year summary. Either alternative may be chosen by the company. These methods are briefly discussed below.

EXHIBIT 20-8   Five-Year Summary

COLONIAL COMPANY
Five-Year Summary in Constant Dollars
(average 1983 dollars CPI–U = 273)

	1983[a]	1982[b]	1981[c]	1980[d]	1979[e]
Net sales and other operating revenues	$300,000	$305,760	$290,426	$248,182	$245,700
Income from continuing operations:					
Constant dollars	15,476	30,194	49,721	68,250	51,870
Earnings per share	1.55	3.02	4.97	6.83	5.19
Current cost	(8,075)	5,919	32,084	55,841	57,740
Earnings per share	(0.81)	0.59	3.21	5.58	5.77
Net assets at year end:					
Constant dollars	265,809	218,837	224,209	230,809	205,842
Current cost	332,800	229,320	232,340	235,773	197,925
Increase or decrease in the current cost amount of					
inventory, net of inflation	20,000	19,656	18,587	18,614	16,380
Increase or decrease in the current cost amount of property,					
plant, and equipment, net of inflation	11,364	(19,656)	23,234	40,950	(10,920)
Purchasing power loss on net monetary items	8,509	3,276	3,195	5,113	3,140
Cash dividends declared per share	–	1.09	1.16	1.24	1.37
Market price of common stock at year end	17.00	13.10	17.43	22.34	16.38

[a] Exhibit 20-7 data for 1983.

[b] Exhibit 20-7 data for 1982 $\times \dfrac{273}{250}$.

[c] Exhibit 20-7 data for 1981 $\times \dfrac{273}{235}$.

[d] Exhibit 20-7 data for 1980 $\times \dfrac{273}{220}$.

[e] Exhibit 20-7 data for 1979 $\times \dfrac{273}{200}$.

Average Index for the Current Year

All the dollar amounts from the different years may be adjusted to the average CPI–U index for the current year (273 as shown in Exhibit 20-7 for this example). If this alternative is used the dollars from each past year are adjusted forward to the purchasing power of the current period. Therefore the dollar amounts in the 5-year summary are larger (assuming inflation) than when they were originally measured and reported in the financial statements of past years. The 5-year summary of Exhibit 20-7 adjusted to the average index for the current year (1983) is illustrated in Exhibit 20-8.

Base Period Index

The second alternative is to adjust all the historical dollars to the CPI–U index of the base period. **The base period is the year for which the index value is 100.** For the CPI–U index the base period is 1967, and it is usually written as 1967 = 100. If this alternative is used the historical dollars in the 5-year summary are adjusted back to the purchasing power of 1967. Therefore each dollar amount in the 5-year summary is smaller than when it was originally measured (assuming inflation) and reported in the financial statements for the particular year.

To illustrate this alternative consider the net sales and other operating revenues from Exhibit 20-7. Each of these items would be adjusted to the 1967 base index of 100 as follows:

1983	$300,000	×	100/273	=	$109,890
1982	$280,000	×	100/250	=	$112,000
1981	$250,000	×	100/235	=	$106,383
1980	$200,000	×	100/220	=	$90,909
1979	$180,000	×	100/200	=	$90,000

The adjusted amounts would be reported in the 5-year summary, and each of the other items in the 5-year summary would be adjusted in the same way.

Understanding the Two Alternatives

A comparison of the two alternative presentations of "net sales and other operating revenues" should provide an understanding of the differences between the two methods. As another example consider the disclosure of the market price of the common stock at year end. The market price in 1979 was $12. At that time the CPI–U index was 200, whereas in 1983 it is 273. Therefore the $12 in 1979 has an equivalent purchasing power of $16.38 [$12 × (273 ÷ 200)] in 1983 as disclosed in Exhibit 20-8. On the other hand, the base year index was 100 in 1967 and thus the $12 in 1979 has an equivalent purchasing power of $6 [$12 × (100 ÷ 200)] in 1967.

REVIEW PROBLEM

The historical cost financial statements of the Burke Company for 1983 are shown below:

BURKE COMPANY
Income Statement
For Year Ended December 31, 1983

Sales		$150,000
Cost of goods sold		
Beginning inventory	$ 30,000	
Purchases	74,000	
Cost of goods available for sale	$104,000	
Less: Ending inventory	40,000	
Cost of goods sold		64,000
Gross profit		$ 86,000
Operating expenses		
Depreciation expense	$ 10,000	
Selling expenses	16,000	
General and administrative expenses	24,000	
Total operating expenses		50,000
Net Income		$ 36,000

BURKE COMPANY
Balance Sheets

	December 31, 1982	December 31, 1983
Cash	$ 5,000	$ 10,000
Accounts receivable	10,000	15,000
Inventory	30,000	40,000
Property and equipment	90,000	90,000
Less: Accumulated depreciation	(20,000)	(30,000)
Total Assets	$115,000	$125,000
Accounts payable	$ 30,000	$ 4,000
Bonds payable	25,000	25,000
Common stock, no par	20,000	20,000
Retained earnings	40,000	76,000
Total Liabilities and Stockholders' Equity	$115,000	$125,000

The following additional information for 1983 is available:

1. Sales, selling expenses, and general and administrative expenses occurred evenly throughout the year. Income taxes are ignored.
2. The inventory was valued on a FIFO cost flow assumption. The December 31, 1982, inventory consisted of 10,000 units purchased at $3 each in September 1982. The December 31, 1983, inventory consisted of 10,000 units purchased at $4 each in September 1983. Purchases of 20,000 units at a cost of $3.70 each were made. These purchases were at the average general price level for the year. The current cost of the inventory was as follows:

   December 1982 $3.30 per unit
   Average 1983   3.80 per unit
   December 1983   4.30 per unit

3. The property and equipment included the following items:

Item	Cost	Date of Purchase	Current Cost of Equivalent New Assets		Depreciation Life	Depreciation Method
			December 1982	December 1983		
Land	$10,000	January 1969	$40,000	$44,000	–	–
Building	80,000	January 1981	90,000	96,000	8 years	Straight line (no residual value)

4. The common stock was sold when the company was formed in January 1969.
5. The CPI–U index was as follows:

   January 1969 110
   January 1981 240
   September 1982 254
   December 1982 260
   Average 1983 275
   September 1983 282
   December 1983 290

6. Net monetary items were affected by sales, purchases, selling expenses, and general and administrative expenses.

Required: Compute the following (round each amount to the nearest dollar):
1. Prepare in terms of the average CPI–U for 1983:
    (a) a comprehensively adjusted income statement for 1983
    (b) a schedule of net monetary items and a schedule to compute the purchasing power gain or loss for 1983
    (c) a comprehensively adjusted balance sheet. (Hint: Use the retained earnings as a balancing amount.)
2. Prepare a comprehensively adjusted current cost income statement for 1983 in terms of the average current cost for the year. Do not compute holding gains or losses.
3. Prepare comprehensively adjusted current cost balance sheets in terms of the current cost at the end of 1982 and 1983. (Hint: Use the retained earnings as a balancing amount.)

SOLUTION TO REVIEW PROBLEM

Requirement 1:

(a)

BURKE COMPANY
Income Statement
For Year Ended December 31, 1983

Sales		$150,000[a]
Cost of goods sold		
Beginning inventory	$ 32,480[b]	
Purchases	74,000[a]	
Cost of goods available for sale	$106,480	
Less: Ending inventory	39,007[c]	
Cost of goods sold		67,473[d]
Gross profit		$ 82,527
Operating expenses		
Depreciation expense	$ 11,458[e]	
Selling expenses	16,000[a]	
General and administrative expenses	24,000[a]	
Total operating expenses		51,458
Net Income		$ 31,069

[a] No adjustment because the item occurred evenly throughout the year.
[b] $30,000 × 275/254.
[c] $40,000 × 275/282.
[d] Note that if the average cost flow assumption was used, the cost of goods sold on a historical cost basis would have been 20,000 × $3.60 [(10,000 × $3.00 + 20,000 × $3.70 + 10,000 × $4.00) ÷ (10,000 + 20,000 + 10,000)] and no adjustment would have been necessary.
[e] $10,000 × 275/240.

(b)
Schedule of Net Monetary Items

	December 31, 1982 (beginning)	December 31, 1983 (ending)
Cash	$ 5,000	$10,000
Accounts receivable	10,000	15,000
Less: Accounts payable	(30,000)	(4,000)
Bonds payable	(25,000)	(25,000)
Net Monetary Items	($40,000)	($ 4,000)

Schedule to Compute Purchasing Power Gain or Loss for 1983

	Historical Amount	Adjustments	Constant Dollar Amounts
Beginning net monetary items	($40,000)	275/260	($42,308)
Sales	150,000	275/275	150,000
Purchases	(74,000)	275/275	(74,000)
Selling expenses	(16,000)	275/275	(16,000)
General and administrative expenses	(24,000)	275/275	(24,000)
Ending net monetary items	($ 4,000)		
Constant dollar ending balance (at average price level)			($ 6,308)
Historical ending balance adjusted to average price level ($4,000 × 275/290)			(3,793)
Purchasing Power Gain for 1983 (at average price level)			($ 2,515)

(c)
BURKE COMPANY
Balance Sheets

	December 31, 1982	December 31, 1983
Cash	$ 5,288[a]	$ 9,483[j]
Accounts receivable	10,577[b]	14,224[k]
Inventory	32,480[c]	39,007[l]
Property and equipment	116,667[d]	116,667[d]
Less: Accumulated depreciation	(22,917)[e]	(34,375)[m]
Total Assets	$142,095	$145,006
Accounts payable	$ 31,731[f]	$ 3,793[n]
Bonds payable	26,442[g]	23,707[o]
Common stock, no par	50,000[h]	50,000[h]
Retained earnings	33,922[i]	67,506[i]
Total Liabilities and Stockholders' Equity	$142,095	$145,006

[a] $5,000 × 275/260.
[b] $10,000 × 275/260.
[c] $30,000 × 275/254.
[d] $80,000 × 275/240 + $10,000 × 275/110.
[e] $20,000 × 275/240.
[f] $30,000 × 275/260.
[g] $25,000 × 275/260.
[h] $20,000 × 275/110.

[i] Balancing amount.
[j] $10,000 × 275/290.
[k] $15,000 × 275/290.
[l] $40,000 × 275/282.
[m] $30,000 × 275/240.
[n] $4,000 × 275/290.
[o] $25,000 × 275/290.

Requirement 2:

BURKE COMPANY
Income Statement
For Year Ended December 31, 1983

Sales		$150,000[a]
Cost of goods sold		76,000[b]
Gross profit		$ 74,000
Operating expenses		
Depreciation expense	$11,625[c]	
Selling expenses	16,000[a]	
General and administrative expenses	24,000[a]	
Total operating expenses		51,625
Net Income		$ 22,375

[a] No adjustment because the item occurred evenly throughout the year.
[b] 20,000 units × $3.80.
[c] [($96,000 + $90,000) ÷ 2] ÷ 8.

Requirement 3:

BURKE COMPANY
Balance Sheets

	December 31, 1982	December 31, 1983
Cash	$ 5,000[a]	$ 10,000[a]
Accounts receivable	10,000[a]	15,000[a]
Inventory	33,000[b]	43,000[g]
Property and equipment	130,000[c]	140,000[c]
Less: Accumulated depreciation	(22,500)[d]	(36,000)[h]
Total Assets	$155,500	$172,000
Accounts payable	$ 30,000[a]	$ 4,000[a]
Bonds payable	25,000[a]	25,000[a]
Common stock, no par	20,000[e]	20,000[e]
Retained earnings	80,500[f]	123,000[f]
Total Liabilities and Stockholders' Equity	$155,500	$172,000

[a] No adjustment because the item is at the current cost at the end of the year.
[b] 10,000 units × $3.30.
[c] Amount given in original information.
[d] [$90,000 × (2 years old ÷ 8-year life)].
[e] Not adjusted because no reliable measure is available.
[f] Balancing amount.
[g] 10,000 units × $4.30 per unit.
[h] [$96,000 × (3 years old ÷ 8-year life)].

GLOSSARY

Constant Dollars. Dollars that have been adjusted for changes in the general price level. That is, each dollar is expressed in the same purchasing power.

Current Cost. The amount it would cost to acquire an item in the current period.

General Price–Level Change. The weighted average of the changes in the individual prices of a group of goods and services. The measure of the general price change used for supplementary disclosures is the Consumer Price Index for All Urban Consumers (CPI–U).

Holding Gain (Loss).   The increase (decrease) in the current cost of an item. A realized holding gain (loss) is a gain (loss) on an item that has been included in the historical cost income statement. An unrealized holding gain (loss) is a gain (loss) on an item that has not yet been recognized in the historical cost income statement.

Monetary Asset.   Money or a claim to receive a fixed amount of money in the future.

Monetary Liability.   An obligation to repay a fixed amount of money in the future.

Net Monetary Items.   Monetary assets less monetary liabilities. When monetary assets exceed monetary liabilities, net monetary items are referred to as net monetary assets. When monetary liabilities exceed monetary assets, net monetary items are referred to as net monetary liabilities.

Nominal Dollars.   Dollars that have not been adjusted for changes in prices. Nominal dollars are the dollars used in historical cost financial statements.

Purchasing Power.   A measure of the ability of a certain number of dollars to purchase goods and services.

Purchasing Power Gain or Loss on Net Monetary Items.   The gain or loss in purchasing power that occurs when net monetary items are held during a period in which the general price level changes. A loss (gain) results when net monetary assets (liabilities) are held during a period of inflation.

Specific Price Change.   A change in the price of a particular good or service.

QUESTIONS

Q20-1   Define the following terms: (a) nominal dollars; (b) constant dollars; and (c) current cost. Which measure adjusts for the changing purchasing power of the dollar?

Q20-2   Explain the difference between a general and a specific price change.

Q20-3   Which general price-level index is required for supplementary disclosures of the effect of changing prices in the annual reports issued by selected corporations?

Q20-4   Describe how historical costs are adjusted to constant dollars.

Q20-5   Define monetary assets and monetary liabilities. Give two examples of each.

Q20-6   During a period of inflation does holding net monetary assets result in a purchasing power gain or loss? Why?

Q20-7   Is the base year of a price index significant to accountants? Why or why not?

Q20-8   What is a holding gain? Distinguish between a realized and an unrealized holding gain.

Q20-9   Why is a current cost income statement prepared in terms of the average current costs for the year, whereas a current cost balance sheet is prepared in terms of the current costs at the end of the year?

Q20-10   Which companies are required to include supplementary disclosures of the effect of changing prices in their annual financial statements?

Q20-11 What methods may be used to determine the current cost of inventory, and property, plant, and equipment? Give an example of an asset for which each method is appropriate.

Q20-12 When supplementary information about the effects of changing prices is disclosed, what information about the current year must be included?

Q20-13 *Appendix.* When supplementary information about the effects of changing prices is disclosed, what information must be included in the 5-year summary?

Q20-14 *Appendix.* When a 5-year summary is presented it must be stated in constant dollars. What are the two alternatives for the value of the CPI–U index which may be used for adjusting the 5-year summary?

EXERCISES

E20-1   Income Measurement. A company purchased land for $19,000. Three years later the current cost of the land is $30,000. During the 3 years the general price level rose from 120 to 150.

Required: 1. If the company sells the land how much income would be computed at the time of the sale under each of the following concepts:
   (a) Historical cost.
   (b) Constant dollars.
   (c) Current cost.
   2. What is the concept of income used in each of the alternatives?

E20-2   General Price–Level Index. January 1980 is the base period for a general price–level index. For simplicity, it will be assumed that the price index includes only five items. The prices of the items in January 1980, January 1983, and January 1984 are given below:

Item	Price in January 1980	Price in January 1983	Price in January 1984
A	$ 3.00	$ 3.60	$ 4.00
B	5.00	5.40	5.20
C	8.00	9.10	10.00
D	20.00	23.00	23.00
E	50.00	58.00	60.00

The five items are assigned weighting factors of 30%, 25%, 20%, 15%, and 10%, respectively.

Required: 1. What is the general price–level index in January 1983 and in January 1984?
   2. What is the percentage change in the weighted average prices between January 1983 and January 1984?
   3. What would be the general price–level index in each of the three years if January 1983 was the base period?
   4. What is the purpose of the weighting factors? (Hint: Compute the general price–level index in January 1983, using January 1980 as the base period, if no weighting factors are used in either year.)

E20-3   Specific Price–Level Indexes. Use the information in E20-2.

Required: Compute a specific price–level index for each of the five items if January 1980 is the base period for each index.

E20-4 Constant Dollar Income Statement. The Abaco Company is preparing a comprehensively adjusted constant dollar income statement for the year at the average CPI–U index of 132. Below are listed the historical cost amounts and the index when the amount was recorded:

	Amount	Index
Sales	$80,000	132
Cost of goods sold	30,000	–
Depreciation expense	10,000	–
Selling expenses	12,000	132
Administrative expenses	15,000	132

The depreciation expense was calculated on a straight-line basis for assets purchased when the index was 110. The cost of goods sold was calculated on a FIFO basis. It included inventory that was purchased for $20,000 when the index was 128 and for $10,000 when the index was 130. The CPI–U index at the end of the year is 136.

Required: Prepare a comprehensively adjusted constant dollar income statement for the Abaco Company using the average CPI–U index. Round each amount to the nearest dollar.

E20-5 Constant Dollar Balance Sheet. The Marsh Company is preparing a comprehensively adjusted constant dollar balance sheet at the end of the year in terms of the average CPI–U index for the year of 132. The CPI–U index at the end of the year is 136. Below are listed the historical cost amounts in the various balance sheet accounts and the index when the amount was recorded:

	Amount	Index
Cash	$10,000	136
Accounts receivable	15,000	136
Inventory	26,000	–
Machinery	37,000	110
Accumulated depreciation: machinery	12,000	–
Accounts payable	20,000	136
Common stock, no par	30,000	100
Retained earnings	26,000	–

The machinery is being depreciated on a straight-line basis with no residual value. The company used the FIFO inventory method and the ending inventory for the year included units that had cost $15,000 when the index was 134 and $11,000 when the index was 135.

Required: Prepare a comprehensively adjusted constant dollar balance sheet for the Marsh Company using the average CPI–U index. Round each amount to the nearest dollar. (Hint: Use the retained earnings as a balancing amount.)

E20-6 Purchasing Power Gain or Loss. The Shire Company had the following beginning and ending historical cost balances for the current year in selected accounts:

	Beginning Balance	Ending Balance
Cash	$ 6,000	$ 8,000
Accounts receivable	27,000	28,000
Inventory	35,000	38,000
Accounts payable	9,000	11,000
Bonds payable	20,000	20,000

The beginning, average, and ending CPI–U index for the year was 140, 148, and 155, respectively.

Required: Prepare (a) a schedule of net monetary items and (b) a schedule to compute the purchasing power gain or loss for the year. In part (b) use the method that assumes that the increase or decrease in all the net monetary items during the year occurred at the average price level for the year. Round each amount to the nearest dollar.

E20-7   Purchasing Power Gain or Loss.   At the beginning of the year the Baker Company had net monetary assets of $40,000. At the end of the year the net monetary assets were $50,000. During the year the following transactions affected the net monetary assets:

(a) Sales of $100,000, which occurred evenly throughout the year.
(b) Purchases of inventory of $40,000, which occurred when the CPI–U index was 120.
(c) Payment of wages of $30,000, which occurred evenly throughout the year.
(d) Purchase of a building for $20,000, which occurred when the CPI–U index was 126.

The beginning, average, and ending CPI–U indexes for the year were 118, 124, and 130, respectively.

Required: Prepare a schedule to compute the purchasing power gain or loss for the year at the average price level. Use the method that requires an analysis of the time at which each increase or decrease in net monetary items occurred. Round each amount to the nearest dollar.

E20-8   Current Cost Income Statement.   The Powell Company is preparing a comprehensively adjusted current cost income statement using average current costs for the current year. The following items are the historical cost amounts in selected accounts:

Sales	$90,000
Cost of goods sold	40,000
Depreciation expense	12,000
Selling expenses	16,000
Administrative expenses	18,000

The cost of goods sold consisted of 10,000 units at $4 each. The cost of the inventory at the beginning of the year was $3.80 per unit and rose by 20% during the year. Selling and administrative expenses were incurred at average costs for the year. The depreciation was calculated by using straight-line depreciation on an asset that cost $60,000, with a 5-year life and no expected residual value. The cost of an equivalent asset at the beginning of the year was $80,000 and rose by 15% during the year.

Required: Prepare a comprehensively adjusted current cost income statement for the current year.

E20-9   Current Cost Balance Sheet.   The Erikson Company is preparing a comprehensively adjusted current cost balance sheet using ending current costs for the period. The following items are the historical cost amounts in selected accounts:

Cash	$ 8,000
Marketable securities	11,000
Inventory	16,000
Machinery	40,000
Accumulated depreciation: machinery	5,000

The following additional information is available:
1. The market value of the marketable securities at the end of the year is $9,000.
2. The inventory consists of 10,000 units purchased at an average cost of $1.60 per unit. The current cost of the inventory at the beginning and end of the year was $1.50 and $1.70 per unit, respectively.
3. The machinery was purchased at the beginning of the year and is being depreciated on a straight-line basis over an expected life of 8 years with no residual value. At year end the current cost is $48,000.

Required: At what amount should each item be included in the current cost balance sheet of the Erikson Company?

E20-10   Appendix: The Five-Year Summary Included in the Supplementary Disclosures.   The following selected items were prepared by the accountants for the Clark Company for inclusion in the 5-year summary prepared as part of the supplementary disclosures of the effects of changing prices. Selected data reported in each year's financial statements are as follows:

	1983	1982	1981	1980	1979
Net sales and other operating revenues	$98,000	$90,000	$76,000	$78,000	$70,000
Income from continuing operations — constant dollars	24,000	26,000	22,000	17,000	18,000
Income from continuing operations — current cost	16,000	18,000	13,000	11,000	14,000

The average CPI–U index for each year is: 1983 = 300, 1982 = 290, 1981 = 283, 1980 = 278, 1979 = 274.

Required: 1. Prepare a 5-year summary of the above items for the Clark Company in terms of the average index for 1983. Round each amount to the nearest dollar.
2. Compute the "net sales and other operating revenues" in terms of the 1967 base year index of 100. Round each amount to the nearest dollar.

PROBLEMS

Part A

P20-1A   Current Cost Financial Statements.   Use the historical cost financial statements for the Newport Company in P20-2A. The following additional information is available:
1. Sales and other operating expenses occurred evenly throughout the year.
2. The ending inventory each year included 10,000 units. The cost of goods sold in 1983 was composed of 20,000 units. The current cost of the inventory was as follows:

December 1982	$2.35 per unit
Average 1983	2.60 per unit
December 1983	2.90 per unit

3. The property and equipment includes the following items:

Item	Cost	Current Cost of Equivalent New Assets December 1982	Current Cost of Equivalent New Assets December 1983	Depreciable Life
Land	$20,000	$50,000	$55,000	–
Building	60,000	80,000	90,000	10 years (no residual value)

Required: 1. Prepare a comprehensively adjusted current cost income statement in terms of the average current costs for the year. Ignore income taxes and holding gains or losses.
2. Prepare a current cost balance sheet at December 31, 1983, in terms of the current costs at that time. (Hint: Use the retained earnings as a balancing amount in the balance sheet.)

P20-2A   Constant Dollar Financial Statements.   The historical cost financial statements of the Newport Company are shown on the following page:

NEWPORT COMPANY
Income Statement
For Year Ended December 31, 1983

Sales		$82,000
Cost of goods sold		
Beginning inventory	$23,000	
Purchases	55,000	
Cost of goods available for sale	$78,000	
Less: Ending inventory	28,000	
Cost of goods sold		50,000
Gross profit		$32,000
Operating expenses		
Depreciation expense	$ 6,000	
Other operating expenses	16,000	
Total operating expenses		22,000
Net Income		$10,000

NEWPORT COMPANY
Balance Sheets

	December 31, 1982	December 31, 1983
Cash	$ 12,000	$ 15,000
Accounts receivable	16,000	22,000
Inventory	23,000	28,000
Property and equipment	80,000	80,000
Less: Accumulated depreciation	(24,000)	(30,000)
Total Assets	$107,000	$115,000
Accounts payable	$ 5,000	$ 3,000
Bonds payable	16,000	16,000
Common stock, no par	40,000	40,000
Retained earnings	46,000	56,000
Total Liabilities and Stockholders' Equity	$107,000	$115,000

The following additional Information is available:
1. Sales and other operating expenses occurred evenly throughout the year.
2. Inventory is valued on a FIFO cost flow assumption. Ending inventory each year was purchased in September of that year. Purchases were made at the average price level for the year.
3. The property and equipment consists of land that was purchased for $20,000 in January 1975 and a building that cost $60,000 on January 1, 1979 and is being depreciated using the straight-line method over a 10-year life with no residual value.
4. The common stock was sold when the company was formed in January 1975.
5. The CPI–U index was as follows:

January 1975	150
January 1979	210
September 1982	270
December 1982	275
January 1983	280
Average for 1983	285
September 1983	295
December 1983	300

6. Net monetary items were affected by sales, purchases, and other operating expenses.

Required: Prepare (a) a comprehensively adjusted income statement for 1983, (b) a schedule of net monetary items and a schedule to compute the purchasing power gain or loss, and (c) a balance sheet at December 31, 1983, all in terms of the average index for 1983. Ignore income taxes. Round each amount to the nearest dollar. (Hint: In the balance sheet, use the retained earnings as a balancing amount.)

P20-3A Appendix: Five-Year Summary. The Young Company has been required to report supplementary information on the effects of changing prices for the last 5 years. Below is the information that has been reported each year over the last 5 years:

	1983	1982	1981	1980	1979
Net sales and other operating revenues	$200,000	$220,000	$180,000	$160,000	$120,000
Income from continuing operations:					
Constant dollars	42,670	56,800	40,100	32,000	26,500
Earnings per share	4.27	5.68	4.01	3.20	2.65
Current cost	27,650	42,500	36,000	35,000	21,500
Earnings per share	2.77	4.25	3.60	3.50	2.15
Net assets at year end:					
Constant dollars	560,000	540,000	480,000	385,000	290,000
Current cost	590,000	570,000	520,000	450,000	370,000
Increase or decrease in the current cost amount of inventory, net of inflation	29,000	24,500	21,750	18,420	19,600
Increase or decrease in the current cost amount of property, plant, and equipment, net of inflation	32,000	60,000	48,000	41,200	40,100
Purchasing power loss on net monetary items . . . . : .	6,050	4,100	8,000	4,200	3,750
Cash dividends declared per share	2.00	1.50	1.50	1.25	1.25
Market price of common stock at year end	21	26	22	19	18
Average CPI–U index	290	270	250	235	210

Required: 1. Prepare a 5-year summary of supplemental disclosures in terms of the average CPI–U index for 1983. Round each amount to the nearest dollar except for the earnings per share, the cash dividends per share, and the market price per share.
2. Compute the "net sales and other operating revenues" in terms of the 1967 base year CPI–U index of 100. Round each amount to the nearest dollar.

P20-4A Constant Dollar Supplementary Information. The historical cost financial statements of the Chandler Company are shown below and on the following page:

CHANDLER COMPANY
Income Statement
For Year Ended December 31, 1983

Sales		$120,000
Cost of goods sold		
Inventory, December 31, 1982	$20,000	
Purchases	63,000	
Cost of goods available for sale	$83,000	
Less: Inventory, December 31, 1983	25,000	
Cost of goods sold		58,000
Gross profit		$ 62,000
Operating expenses		
Depreciation expense	$12,000	
Selling and administrative expenses	20,000	
Total operating expenses		32,000
Income before income taxes		$ 30,000
Income tax expense		12,000
Net Income		$ 18,000

CHANDLER COMPANY
Balance Sheets

	December 31, 1983	December 31, 1984
Cash	$ 22,000	$ 35,000
Accounts receivable	30,000	38,000
Inventory	20,000	25,000
Equipment	96,000	96,000
Less: Accumulated depreciation	(48,000)	(60,000)
Total Assets	$120,000	$134,000
Accounts payable	$ 18,000	$ 14,000
Bonds payable	30,000	30,000
Common stock, no par	50,000	50,000
Retained earnings	22,000	40,000
Total Liabilities and Stockholders' Equity	$120,000	$134,000

The following additional information is available:

1. Inventory: The company uses the FIFO cost flow assumption.
   Inventory, December 31, 1983: purchased October 1983.
   Inventory, December 31, 1984: purchased August 1984.
   Purchases were made evenly throughout the year.
2. Equipment: The equipment was purchased on January 1, 1980. Straight-line depreciation is used with no residual value and an estimated life of 8 years.
3. CPI–U index:

January 1980	200
October 1983	240
December 1983	255
Average for 1984	265
August 1984	270
December 1984	280

Required: Prepare a schedule that would be included in the footnotes to the financial statements of the Chandler Company to report the 1984 supplementary disclosures under the *constant dollar* basis that are required for selected companies. Include the related historical cost information for income from continuing operations. Round each amount to the nearest dollar.

P20-5A   Current Cost Supplementary Information. Use the historical cost financial statements for the Chandler Company in P20-4A. The following additional information is available:

1. Inventory: The company uses the FIFO cost flow assumption.
   Inventory, December 31, 1983: 10,000 units purchased at $2.00 each.
   Inventory, December 31, 1984: 10,000 units purchased at $2.50 each.
   Purchases: 30,000 units at $2.10 each.
   Average current cost for the year is $2.30 per unit.
   Current cost at the beginning of the year is $2.05 per unit.
   Current cost at the end of the year is $2.55 per unit.
2. Equipment: Purchased on January 1, 1980.
   Depreciation method: straight line
   Residual value: zero
   Estimated life: 8 years
   Current cost, December 1983: $150,000
   Current cost, December 1984: $210,000

Required: Prepare a schedule that would be included in the footnotes to the financial statements of the Chandler Company to report the 1983 supplementary disclosures under the current cost basis that are required for selected companies. Round each amount to the nearest dollar. Include the related historical cost information for income from continuing operations. (Use the appropriate CPI–U indexes from P20-4A to determine the change in the general price–level index.)

PROBLEMS

Part B

P20-1B Constant Dollar Financial Statements. The historical cost financial statements of the Basin Company are shown below:

BASIN COMPANY
Income Statement
For Year Ended December 31, 1983

Sales		$153,000
Cost of goods sold		
Beginning inventory	$ 41,000	
Purchases	101,000	
Cost of goods available for sale	$142,000	
Less: Ending inventory	70,000	
Cost of goods sold		72,000
Gross profit		$ 81,000
Operating expenses		
Depreciation expense	$ 20,000	
Other operating expenses	34,000	
Total operating expenses		54,000
Net Income		$ 27,000

BASIN COMPANY
Balance Sheets

	December 31, 1982	December 31, 1983
Cash	$ 23,000	$ 47,000
Accounts receivable	36,000	50,000
Inventory	41,000	70,000
Property and equipment	200,000	200,000
Less: Accumulated depreciation	(80,000)	(100,000)
Total Assets	$220,000	$267,000
Accounts payable	$ 12,000	$ 32,000
Bonds payable	70,000	70,000
Common stock, no par	50,000	50,000
Retained earnings	88,000	115,000
Total Liabilities and		
Stockholders' Equity	$220,000	$267,000

The following additional information is available:
1. Sales and other operating expenses occurred evenly throughout the year.
2. The inventory is valued on a FIFO cost flow assumption. The ending inventory each year was purchased in October of that year. Purchases were made at the average price level for 1983.
3. The property and equipment consist of land that was purchased for $60,000 in May 1974 and

a machine that cost $140,000 on January 1, 1979 and is being depreciated using the straight-line method over a 7-year life with no residual value.

4. The common stock was sold when the company was formed in May 1974.
5. The CPI–U index was as follows:

May 1974	110
January 1979	190
October 1982	260
December 1982	270
January 1983	275
Average for 1983	280
October 1983	290
December 1983	295

6. The net monetary items were affected by the sales, the purchases, and the other operating expenses.

Required: Prepare (a) a comprehensively adjusted income statement for 1983, (b) a schedule of net monetary items and a schedule to compute the purchasing power gain or loss for 1983, and (c) a balance sheet at December 31, 1983, all in terms of the average CPI–U index for 1983. Ignore income taxes. Round each amount to the nearest dollar. (Hint: In the balance sheet use the retained earnings as a balancing amount.)

P20-2B   Current Cost Financial Statements.   Use the historical cost financial statements for the Basin Company in P20-1B. The following additional information is available for the company;
1. Sales and other operating expenses occurred evenly throughout the year.
2. The ending inventory for 1982 and 1983 included 5,000 units and 7,000 units, respectively. The cost of goods sold in 1983 was composed of 8,000 units. The current cost of the inventory was as follows:

December 1982	$ 8.50 per unit
Average 1983	9.70 per unit
December 1983	10.30 per unit

3. The property and equipment includes the following items:

		Current Cost of Equivalent New Asset		Depreciable
Item	Cost	December 31, 1982	December 31, 1983	Life
Land	$ 60,000	$ 90,000	$100,000	–
Building	140,000	180,000	200,000	7 years (no residual value)

Required: 1. Prepare a comprehensively adjusted current cost income statement in terms of the average current costs for the year. Ignore income taxes and holding gains or losses.
2. Prepare a current cost balance sheet at December 31, 1983, in terms of the current costs at that time. (Hint: Use the retained earnings as a balancing amount in the balance sheet.)

P20-3B   Constant Dollar Supplementary Information.   The historical cost financial statements of the Barnes Company are shown on the following page:

BARNES COMPANY
Income Statement
For Year Ended December 31, 1984

Sales		$210,000
Cost of goods sold		
Inventory, December 31, 1983	$ 35,000	
Purchases	110,000	
Cost of goods available for sale	$145,000	
Less: Inventory, December 31, 1984	40,000	
Cost of goods sold		105,000
Gross profit		$105,000
Operating expenses		
Depreciation expense	$ 10,000	
Selling and administrative expenses	47,000	
Total operating expenses		57,000
Income before income taxes		$ 48,000
Income tax expense		19,200
Net Income		$ 28,800

BARNES COMPANY
Balance Sheets

	December 31, 1983	December 31, 1984
Cash	$ 41,000	$ 56,000
Accounts receivable	54,000	68,000
Inventory	35,000	40,000
Equipment	90,000	90,000
Less: Accumulated depreciation	(30,000)	(40,000)
Total Assets	$190,000	$214,000
Accounts payable	$ 24,000	$ 15,000
Bonds payable	36,000	36,000
Common stock, no par	75,000	75,000
Retained earnings	55,000	88,000
Total Liabilities and		
Stockholders' Equity	$190,000	$214,000

The following additional information is available:
1. Inventory: The company uses the FIFO cost flow assumption.
       Inventory, December 31, 1983: purchased September 1983.
       Inventory, December 31, 1984: purchased November 1984.
   Purchases were made evenly throughout the year.
2. Equipment: Purchased on January 1, 1982
       Depreciation method: straight line
       Residual value: zero
       Estimated life: 9 years
3. CPI–U index:

January 1982	220
September 1983	250
December 1983	270
Average for 1984	280
November 1984	285
December 1984	290

Required: Prepare a schedule that would be included in the footnotes to the financial statements of the Barnes Company to report the 1984 supplementary disclosures under the *constant dollar* basis that are required for selected companies. Include the related historical cost information for income from continuing operations. Round each amount to the nearest dollar.

P20-4B   Current Cost Supplementary Information.   Use the historical cost financial statements for the Barnes Company in P20-3B. The following additional information is available:

1. Inventory: The company uses the FIFO cost flow assumption.
    Inventory, December 31, 1983: 5,000 units at $7.00 each.
    Inventory, December 31, 1984: 5,000 units at $8.00 each.
    Purchases: 14,765 units at $7.45 each.
    Average current cost for the year is $7.65 per unit.
    Current cost at the beginning of the year is $7.10 per unit.
    Current cost at the end of the year is $8.20 per unit.
2. Equipment: Purchased on January 1, 1982
    Depreciation method: straight line
    Residual value: zero
    Estimated life: 9 years
    Current cost, December 1983: $120,000
    Current cost, December 1984: $170,000

Required: Prepare a schedule that would be included in the footnotes to the financial statements of the Barnes Company to report the 1984 supplementary disclosures under the *current cost* basis that are required for selected companies. Round each amount to the nearest dollar. Include the related historical cost information for income from continuing operations. (Use the appropriate CPI–U indexes from P20-3B to determine the change in the general price–level index.)

20-5B   Appendix: Five-Year Summary.   The Vento Company has been required to report supplementary information on the effects of changing prices for the last 5 years. Below is the information that has been reported each year over the last 5 years.

	1984	1983	1982	1981	1980
Net sales and other operating revenues	$400,000	$440,000	$375,000	$340,000	$310,000
Income from continuing operations:					
Constant dollars	85,210	96,150	78,500	69,000	56,290
Earnings per share	8.52	9.61	7.85	6.90	5.63
Current cost	51,000	57,900	48,250	39,100	30,400
Earnings per share	5.10	5.79	4.82	3.91	3.04
Net assets at year end:					
Constant dollars	1,200,000	900,000	750,000	620,000	540,000
Current cost	1,500,000	950,000	795,000	660,000	600,000
Increase or decrease in the current cost amount of inventory, net of inflation	52,000	47,500	40,250	34,900	30,000
Increase or decrease in the current cost amount of property, plant, and equipment, net of inflation	58,400	70,300	67,600	60,100	57,600
Purchasing power loss on net monetary items	10,500	8,400	7,600	12,500	9,750
Cash dividends declared per share	4.00	3.00	3.00	2.50	2.50
Market price of common stock at year end	42	52	44	38	36
Average CPI–U index	300	285	275	270	265

Required: 1. Prepare a 5-year summary of supplemental disclosures in terms of the 1967 base year CPI–U index of 100. Round each amount to the nearest dollar except for the earnings per share, the cash dividends per share, and the market price per share.

                 2. Compute the "net sales and other operating revenues" in terms of the average CPI–U index for 1983. Round each amount to the nearest dollar.

DISCUSSION CASES

C20-1   **Alternative Income Concepts.**   Alan Pierce owns and operates a small company. He has heard about the supplementary disclosures required by large companies and is interested in having the same disclosures prepared for his company. During a meeting to discuss the disclosures, he makes the following comments:

1. "I understand these alternatives are measuring different types of income because they assume different things about how to measure wealth. I don't understand how that can be, because I invested $50,000 in my business 5 years ago and nobody can change that."

2. "This purchasing power loss is very strange. How can I have a loss when I haven't paid money out, sold something, or had a debit or credit in the accounting system?"

3. "How can it be useful to know the current cost of the building when I have no intention of replacing the building for at least 10 years?"

4. "Net income, after income taxes at 40%, this year was $20,000. Dividends paid by the company to me were $15,000. I thought that the company was $5,000 better off. Now you say that the current cost income before income taxes is $12,000. I still have to pay the taxes, but the company seems to be heading for trouble. . . ."

Required: Prepare a response to each comment made by Mr. Pierce.

C20-2   **Measuring Current Cost.**   A company is preparing its supplementary disclosures on the effects of changing prices. The accountant who has been assigned the task of calculating the current cost of the assets has come to you for help.

"For example," she says, "think about the building we're sitting in. The company paid $60,000 for it when it was brand new 3 years ago. I can go to a real estate agency and find out what they think it's worth. But they're always optimistic. I could go to a builder and ask what it would cost to build today. But they don't build them quite the same way today; different materials, better insulation, and so on. I could look up a government-prepared index for building prices, but that's only an overall average. Or I could apply functional pricing. This building has 2,000 square feet, and I could find out the cost per square foot to build now. But that wouldn't be the same building, and what about all of the improvements the company has made. What should I do?"

Required: Clearly describe the alternative methods of calculating current costs. Describe the advantages and disadvantages of each method in the context of a building. How would you recommend the current cost of the building be determined?

PART 5 | MANAGERIAL ACCOUNTING FOR BUSINESS ENTITIES

21 Financial Statements of Manufacturing Companies

After reading this chapter, you should understand:

- The differences between merchandising and manufacturing companies
- The three elements of cost for a manufacturing company
- The recording and closing process for a manufacturing company using the periodic inventory system
- The cost of goods manufactured statement
- The differences between the financial statements for manufacturing and merchandising companies
- The use of a worksheet by a manufacturing company

In the previous chapters of this book many aspects of accounting and financial statement presentation have been discussed. Most of the discussions apply equally to merchandising and manufacturing companies. When there has been a difference in the accounting practices, however, we discussed accounting for a merchandising company, leaving the discussion of manufacturing companies to this chapter.

In this chapter the elements of manufacturing costs and the related inventory accounts are introduced. The recording and closing entries are explained and illustrated as are the financial statements prepared by a manufacturing company. In the last section of the chapter the modifications that a manufacturing company makes to the worksheet prepared at the end of the period are illustrated. The use of the *periodic* inventory system is assumed in this chapter.

MERCHAN-DISING AND MANUFACTURING COMPANIES

The basic difference between merchandising and manufacturing companies is that a merchandising company buys products that are physically ready for sale and sells these products to the customer. A manufacturing company, in contrast, makes the products from direct materials and then sells these products to the retailer. For example, a furniture retailing store sells furniture that it has purchased from a furniture manufacturer. A furniture manufacturer purchases wood, glue, screws, and upholstery to make furniture, which it then sells to furniture retailing stores.

This difference in the physical activities of the two types of company does not alter the basic accounting principles used, but it does alter the way in which the principles are applied. The major difference is in accounting for inventories. A manufacturing company uses three inventory accounts, one for the direct materials inventory, one for the goods in process inventory, and one for the finished goods inventory. As a result the computation of the cost of a company's inventories and the cost of the products it sells is more complex. A manufacturing company, in essence, "attaches" manufacturing costs to the units produced during the period. When units of the product are sold the manufacturing costs associated with them are the cost of the goods sold. Manufacturing costs associated with units that have not been sold are the cost of the ending inventory.

THREE ELEMENTS OF MANUFACTURING COST

In a simple manufacturing process there are three elements associated with the cost of manufacturing a product. The three elements are direct materials cost, direct labor cost, and factory overhead cost. The relationships between the elements are illustrated in Exhibit 21-1. Direct materials cost, direct labor cost, and fixed overhead cost are discussed in this section. The accounts that are used by a manufacturing company to record the costs of each of these three elements are discussed in the following section.

Raw Materials Cost

Raw materials include both direct materials and indirect materials. Direct materials are the raw materials that physically become part of a manufactured product. In other words, they are the materials from which the product is made. Direct materials include materials acquired from natural sources, such as the wood used by the furniture manufacturer, and also products purchased from other companies, such as the fittings and the upholstery used by the furniture manufacturer.

Indirect materials are the raw materials that do not physically become part of a manufactured product but which are necessary for the successful operation of the manufacturing process. Indirect materials may also be called *factory supplies* or *manufacturing supplies*. For example, the lubricating oil for the machines used to make the furniture would be included in this category. To simplify the procedures discussed in this chapter, we assume that indirect materials are purchased as needed, and thus no indirect materials inventory exists.

EXHIBIT 21-1 Flow of Manufacturing Costs for a Manufacturing Company

Raw Materials Storeroom	Factory	Finished Goods Storeroom
Beginning Direct Materials Inventory	Beginning Goods in Process Inventory	Beginning Finished Goods Inventory
+ Direct Materials Purchases	+ Direct Materials Used	+ Cost of Goods Manufactured
− Ending Direct Materials Inventory	+ Direct Labor	− Ending Finished Goods Inventory
= Cost of Direct Materials Used	+ Factory Overhead	= Cost of Goods Sold
	− Ending Goods in Process Inventory	
	= Cost of Goods Manufactured	

It may sometimes be difficult to determine whether an item is a direct or indirect material. The decision is made by considering whether the item is directly *traceable* to the product or whether its cost is a *significant* amount. For example, the varnish used by a furniture manufacturer is technically a direct material because it is incorporated into the finished product. It is likely to be treated as an indirect material, however, because it is difficult to trace specific quantities of varnish to each piece of furniture and the dollar amount is unlikely to be significant. These issues are discussed further in Chapter 22.

Since direct materials physically become part of the finished product, the cost of the direct materials *used* should be included in the cost of the finished product as one of the three elements of manufacturing cost. Since the indirect materials do not become part of the product, it is difficult to associate their cost with specific product units. As a result they are normally included in *factory overhead*, which is treated as a separate cost element as discussed later.

Direct Labor Cost

In the production process employees convert, or assemble, the direct materials into a finished product. **Direct labor is the labor of the employees who work with the direct materials to convert or assemble them into the finished product.** For example, the labor of the employees who prepare the wood for use in the furniture, assemble the furniture, and attach the upholstery would all be included in direct labor. The cost of direct labor is the wages earned by these employees. The wages *paid* to the employees are the wages earned less the payroll deductions withheld by the company such as federal and state income taxes. The additional costs of payroll taxes, pensions, and other fringe benefits associated with the employees are usually included in indirect labor (and therefore factory overhead) even though they may be related to the direct labor cost.

Indirect labor is the labor of the employees who are involved in the operation of the production process but who do not convert or assemble the direct materials into the finished product. For example, the labor of employees involved in the supervision of the production and the maintenance of the production equipment would be included in indirect labor. The same problem that exists for distinguishing between direct and indirect materials also exists for the costs of direct and indirect labor. Again, the criteria of traceability and the significance of the dollar amount are used.

Since both direct labor and indirect labor are involved in the production of the product, the cost of both elements should be included in the cost of the finished product. Direct labor is accounted for as a separate element of manufacturing cost, whereas the cost of indirect labor is included in factory overhead.

Factory Overhead Cost

Factory overhead includes all the items that are necessary for the manufacture of the product, except for direct materials and direct labor. Factory overhead is often called *manufacturing overhead*. Although factory overhead items are necessary for the manufacture of the product, they cannot be traced directly to each unit produced. Examples of factory overhead include indirect materials and indirect labor discussed above, repairs and maintenance, utilities used in the manufacturing process, insurance and property taxes on the manufacturing facilities, the payroll taxes, pensions, and other fringe benefits incurred for all employees whose labor effort is included in direct or indirect labor, and depreciation on manufacturing facilities.

The costs of these factory overhead items are included in the cost of the finished product. Although a large number and wide variety of different manufacturing costs are part of factory overhead, they are normally treated as a single cost element included in the total manufacturing cost for the period. This process is discussed later in the chapter.

The extra cost associated with *overtime* work, including the overtime premium paid to direct labor, should also be included in factory overhead cost. This is desirable because the need to work overtime is usually caused by the total production activity and not the manufacture of a particular unit that happened to be made during an overtime period. Including the overtime cost in direct labor would result in a higher cost being attached to a unit produced during overtime than an identical unit produced during regular working hours.

Factory overhead does not include selling expenses, general and administrative expenses, or other revenues and expenses that have been discussed earlier in the book. These items are treated in exactly the same way for manufacturing companies as they are for merchandising companies.

DIFFERENCES IN COST OF GOODS SOLD

Since direct materials, direct labor, and factory overhead are all included in the cost of the products manufactured, an income statement for a manufacturing company includes more items than for a merchandising company. To provide a comparison between the two kinds of companies, the cost of goods sold section of the income statements for the current year of the Quality Retail Company and the Perfection Manufacturing Company are presented in Exhibit 21-2. The comparison clearly shows the additional components of cost that are included in the cost of goods sold for a manufacturing company.

The cost of goods sold for a merchandising company is calculated by adding the beginning inventory and the net purchases (to give the cost of goods available for sale) and subtracting the ending inventory as illustrated in the first part of Exhibit 21-2. In contrast, as illustrated in the second part of Exhibit 21-2, the cost of goods sold for a manufacturing company includes the three elements of manufacturing cost discussed above. Since we assume use of the periodic inventory system the cost of goods sold for a manufacturing company is computed in several steps. First, the cost of direct materials used during the period and the total manufacturing cost for the period are computed as follows:

Cost of direct materials used	=	Beginning direct materials inventory	+	Direct materials purchases (net)	−	Ending direct materials inventory

Total manufacturing cost	=	Cost of direct materials used	+	Cost of direct labor	+	Factory overhead cost

EXHIBIT 21-2
Differences in Cost
of Goods Sold

The Cost of Goods Sold Section of the Income Statement
for a Merchandising Company and a Manufacturing Company

QUALITY RETAIL COMPANY
Partial Income Statement
For Current Year

Cost of goods sold	
Beginning inventory	$ 43,000
Purchases (net)	63,000
Cost of goods available for sale	$106,000
Less: Ending inventory	54,000
Cost of goods sold	$ 52,000

PERFECTION MANUFACTURING COMPANY
Partial Income Statement
For Current Year

Cost of goods sold			
Beginning finished goods inventory			$ 20,000
Beginning goods in process inventory		$14,000	
Beginning direct materials inventory	$19,000		
Direct materials purchases (net)	24,000		
Direct materials available for use	$43,000		
Less: Ending direct materials inventory	21,000		
Direct materials used	$22,000		
Direct labor	20,000		
Factory overhead	18,000		
Total manufacturing cost		60,000	
Cost of goods in process during the period		$74,000	
Less: Ending goods in process inventory		17,000	
Cost of goods manufactured			57,000
Cost of goods available for sale			$ 77,000
Less: Ending finished goods inventory			16,000
Cost of goods sold			$ 61,000

Using the amounts from Exhibit 21-2 the two costs are:

Cost of direct materials used = $19,000 + $24,000 − $21,000
  = $22,000

Total manufacturing cost = $22,000 + $20,000 + $18,000
  = $60,000

The cost of goods manufactured must be computed next. **The cost of goods manufactured during the period is the cost of the units that were completed during the period and were ready for sale.** The total manufacturing cost and the cost of goods manufactured are different when a manufacturing company has a beginning or ending inventory of partially completed units (called the goods in process inventory and discussed later). The cost of goods manufactured during the period is calculated as follows:

Cost of goods manufactured	=	Beginning goods in process inventory	+	Total manufacturing costs	−	Ending goods in process inventory

Finally, the cost of goods sold is computed as follows:

Cost of goods sold	=	Beginning finished goods inventory	+	Cost of goods manufactured	−	Ending finished goods inventory

Using the amounts from Exhibit 21-2 the costs of goods manufactured and sold are:

$$\text{Cost of goods manufactured} = \$14,000 + \$60,000 - \$17,000$$
$$= \$57,000$$

$$\text{Cost of goods sold} = \$20,000 + \$57,000 - \$16,000$$
$$= \$61,000$$

It can be seen that the relationship between the cost of goods manufactured and the cost of goods sold for a manufacturing company is similar to the relationship between the purchases and the cost of goods sold for a merchandising company. The cost of goods sold for a manufacturing company is the beginning finished goods inventory plus the cost of goods manufactured minus the ending finished goods inventory. In contrast, the cost of goods sold for a merchandising company is the beginning merchandise inventory plus the cost of purchases minus the ending merchandise inventory.

In the next section each step of the process of accumulating manufacturing costs is illustrated using general journal entries. The amounts used in the examples are consistent with the information for the Perfection Manufacturing Company given in Exhibit 21-2. It should be recognized that the form of presentation illustrated in Exhibit 21-2 for a manufacturing company is somewhat artificial. On the one hand, reports developed for use by the management of an actual company contain more detail. The cost of goods manufactured statement in particular, which is discussed later in the chapter, provides extra detail. On the other hand, the income statement included in the financial statements of a company's annual report is likely to include only the one item, cost of goods sold, without additional explanatory detail. In such cases the income statements of a manufacturing and a merchandising company appear to be identical even though the components of the cost of goods sold amounts are very different.

ACCOUNTING FOR MANUFACTURING COSTS

A manufacturing company can use either a periodic or perpetual inventory system. In this chapter we illustrate only the periodic inventory system and the related accounts and closing procedures. The perpetual system is discussed in Chapter 22. In a periodic inventory system some accounts and accounting procedures are used by a manufacturing company that are not used by a merchandising company, and other accounts and procedures are used in different ways. These accounts and procedures are discussed below. The accounts and illustrations used throughout this chapter are presented in a general journal and general ledger format that is consistent with the basic practices followed by all manufacturing companies. Companies often modify these accounting practices, however, as they develop accounting systems suitable for their particular needs. The two basic types of cost accounting systems, the job order cost system and the process cost system, are discussed in Chapter 22. A basic understanding of the principles discussed in this chapter are necessary for a proper understanding of this later material.

Overview of the Periodic Inventory System

As mentioned earlier a manufacturing company has three elements of manufacturing cost—direct materials, direct labor, and factory overhead. It also has three related inventory accounts—Direct Materials Inventory, Goods in Process Inventory, and Finished Goods Inventory. When a periodic inventory system is used the actual costs of direct materials, direct labor, and factory overhead are recorded in temporary manufacturing accounts during the accounting period, which is similar to the method used for purchases by a merchandising company. In addition, each of the three inventory accounts contains the respective beginning inventory throughout the accounting period. This is also similar to the merchandise inventory of a merchandising company.

At the end of a manufacturing company's accounting period, the temporary manufacturing accounts and the three beginning inventories are closed in the closing entries. The three ending inventories are also recorded in the closing entries. These closing entries are somewhat similar to the entries of a merchandising company but they are more complex. Because of the several manufacturing accounts and additional inventory accounts, a Manufacturing Summary closing account is used by a manufacturing company in addition to a Cost of Goods Sold closing account and an Income Summary account. The Manufacturing Summary account is used to accumulate all the costs included in cost of goods manufactured. It is then closed to the Cost of Goods Sold account. The relationship between the three inventory accounts and the temporary manufacturing accounts in a periodic inventory system is briefly discussed below.

The Direct Materials Inventory account remains unchanged throughout the accounting period because purchases of direct materials are recorded (debited to) the Direct Materials Purchases account. At the end of the period the Direct Materials Inventory account and the Direct Materials Purchases account are closed to the Manufacturing Summary account. These entries have the effect of transferring the cost of direct materials available for use (the beginning inventory and the purchases) as a debit balance to the Manufacturing Summary account. Another closing entry records (debits) the ending direct materials inventory in the Direct Materials Inventory account and credits the same amount to the Manufacturing Summary account. The net effect of the two closing entries is to record the cost of the direct materials used in the Manufacturing Summary account.

The Goods in Process inventory account remains unchanged during the accounting period because the other two elements of manufacturing cost incurred during the period, direct labor and factory overhead, are recorded in separate temporary accounts during the period. These accounts are entitled Direct Labor and Factory Overhead. At the end of the period, the Direct Labor account, the Factory Overhead account, and the Goods in Process Inventory account (containing the beginning inventory) are closed to the Manufacturing Summary account. Another closing entry records (debits) the ending inventory in the Goods in Process Inventory account and credits the same amount to the Manufacturing Summary account. The Manufacturing Summary account now includes the cost of goods manufactured during the period.

The Finished Goods Inventory account remains unchanged during the period because, as we have seen, the cost of goods manufactured is calculated only during the recording of the closing entries. In addition, in a periodic system the cost of goods sold is not recorded as each sale is made. The Manufacturing Summary account (containing the cost of goods manufactured) and the Finished Goods Inventory account (containing the beginning inventory) are closed to the Cost of Goods Sold closing account. Another closing entry records (debits) the ending inventory in the Finished Goods Inventory account and credits the same amount to the Cost of Goods Sold account. The Cost of Goods Sold account now includes the cost of goods sold for the period. The Cost of Goods Sold account is then closed to the Income Summary account in the usual manner. This journalizing and closing process parallels the cost flow diagram shown in Exhibit 21-1.

In order to illustrate the relationship between recording the manufacturing costs incurred during the period and the accounting for the three inventory accounts in the closing entries at the end of the period, each of the elements of manufacturing cost (direct materials, direct labor, and factory overhead) is discussed separately in the next section. Examples are provided based on the information in Exhibit 21-2. An illustration is presented later in the chapter, in which the journal entries prepared by a typical manufacturing company during its accounting period are presented in chronological order.

Accounting for Direct Materials Used

DIRECT MATERIALS PURCHASES. The Direct Materials Purchases account is used to record the cost of all the purchases of direct materials during the period. A single control account is typically included in the general ledger, and each type of material purchased is recorded in a subsidiary ledger under titles such as Direct Materials Purchases — Wood, Direct Materials Purchases — Fittings, and Direct Materials Purchases — Upholstery. In the illustrations in the remainder of the chapter, for simplicity we use a single Direct Materials Purchases account without a subsidiary ledger. The purchase of direct materials during the accounting period would be recorded as shown below (using data consistent with Exhibit 21-2):

```
Direct Materials Purchases. . . . . . . . . . . . . . . . . . .    24,000
    Cash (or Accounts Payable) . . . . . . . . . . . . . . .              24,000
To record the purchase of direct materials.
```

DIRECT MATERIALS INVENTORY. **The Direct Materials Inventory account is used to record the cost of the remaining unused direct materials at the end of each period.** As with the direct materials purchases account, a single control account is usually included in the general ledger and a subsidiary ledger is used for recording each type of direct material inventory. Again, for simplicity, we use only one direct materials inventory account without a subsidiary ledger in this chapter.

As discussed earlier, in a periodic inventory system the Direct Materials Inventory account contains the beginning inventory balance (i.e., the ending balance from the previous period) throughout the period. During the closing process at the end of the period, this beginning inventory is removed from the account and replaced by the ending inventory. This ending inventory is determined by a physical count.

CLOSING PROCEDURE. The ending balance of the Direct Materials Purchases account and the beginning balance of the Direct Materials Inventory are closed to the Manufacturing Summary account at the end of the period as follows:

```
Manufacturing Summary . . . . . . . . . . . . . . . . . . . . .   43,000
    Direct Materials Purchases . . . . . . . . . . . . . . . . .           24,000
    Direct Materials Inventory. . . . . . . . . . . . . . . . . .           19,000
To close the beginning direct materials inventory and direct
materials purchases.
```

This journal entry transfers to the Manufacturing Summary account the $19,000 beginning balance of the Direct Materials Inventory account and the $24,000 balance recorded in the Direct Materials Purchases account during the period. After the closing entry both direct materials accounts have zero balances, and the Manufacturing Summary account now includes a debit balance equal to the cost of direct materials available for use. The cost of the ending direct materials inventory is recorded as follows:

```
Direct Materials Inventory . . . . . . . . . . . . . . . . . . .   21,000
    Manufacturing Summary . . . . . . . . . . . . . . . . . .              21,000
To record the ending direct materials inventory.
```

The Direct Materials Inventory account now includes the ending inventory of $21,000, which will be the beginning inventory of the next period. The effect of these two entries to the Manufacturing Summary account is to record the cost of the direct materials used of $22,000 ($19,000 + $24,000 − $21,000) as a net debit in the Manufacturing Summary account ($43,000 debit − $21,000 credit).

Accounting for Direct Labor

DIRECT LABOR. The costs of direct labor are recorded (debited) in the Direct Labor account during the accounting period as follows (using assumed amounts for federal income taxes payable and social security taxes payable):

Direct Labor	20,000	
Cash		15,000
Federal Income Taxes Payable		3,800
Social Security Taxes Payable		1,200
To record the payment of factory payroll.		

CLOSING PROCEDURE. The Direct Labor account is closed to the Manufacturing Summary account at the end of the period as follows:

Manufacturing Summary	20,000	
Direct Labor		20,000
To close the direct labor account.		

The effect of this journal entry is that the Direct Labor account now has a zero balance and the Manufacturing Summary account now includes two elements of manufacturing cost for the period, the cost of the direct materials used and the cost of direct labor.

Accounting for Factory Overhead

FACTORY OVERHEAD. A factory overhead account is used to record the costs of the factory overhead items incurred during the period. A single control account is typically included in the general ledger, and each type of factory overhead cost is recorded in a subsidiary ledger. (For simplicity, we do not illustrate the subsidiary ledger.) All factory overhead costs are recorded as increases (debits) in the Factory Overhead account when they are incurred and as credits to various accounts depending on the nature of the cost (examples are given later in the chapter). For example, if it is assumed that factory overhead costs are all paid in cash, the following journal entry would be recorded during the accounting period:

Factory Overhead	18,000	
Cash		18,000
To record factory overhead costs incurred.		

CLOSING PROCEDURE. The Factory Overhead account is closed to the Manufacturing Summary account at the end of the period as follows:

Manufacturing Summary	18,000	
Factory Overhead		18,000
To close the factory overhead account.		

After closing the Direct Materials, Direct Labor, and Factory Overhead accounts, the Manufacturing Summary account contains the total manufacturing costs for the period of $60,000 ($22,000 + $20,000 + $18,000).

**Goods in
Process Inventory
Account**

The Goods in Process Inventory account is used to record the cost of the partially completed units that are in the production process at the end of each period. This account is often called the *Work in Process Inventory* account. The ending inventory balance is determined by a physical count of the partially completed units. Until the physical count is made the Goods in Process Inventory account contains the beginning inventory balance (i.e., the ending balance from the previous period). In the physical count the costs of the direct materials, direct labor, and factory overhead associated with the incomplete units are calculated, and the total cost is included as the cost of the ending goods in process inventory. This process is explained in more detail in Chapter 22. A separate record of the goods in process inventory should be maintained for each type of product being manufactured.

CLOSING PROCEDURE. The beginning Goods in Process Inventory account is closed to the Manufacturing Summary account at the end of the period as follows:

Manufacturing Summary	14,000	
Goods in Process Inventory		14,000
To close the beginning goods in process inventory.		

This journal entry transfers the $14,000 beginning balance of the Goods in Process Inventory account to the Manufacturing Summary account so that the inventory account has a zero balance. The cost of the ending goods in process inventory, as determined by a physical count, is recorded as follows:

Goods in Process Inventory	17,000	
Manufacturing Summary		17,000
To record the ending goods in process inventory.		

The Goods in Process Inventory account now includes the ending inventory of $17,000, which will be the beginning inventory of the next period. The Manufacturing Summary account now includes the cost of goods manufactured (see Exhibit 21-2) for the period ($57,000) based on the beginning goods in process inventory, plus the total manufacturing costs for the period, minus the ending goods in process inventory ($14,000 + $60,000 − $17,000).

**The Finished
Goods Inventory
Account**

The Finished Goods Inventory account is used to record the cost of the units that have finished the production process and are ready for sale but have not been sold at the end of the accounting period. In a periodic inventory system the ending finished goods inventory is determined by a physical count. Thus during the period the Finished Goods Inventory account contains the beginning inventory balance (i.e., the ending inventory from the previous period). Again, a separate record of each type of product included in the finished goods inventory should be maintained in a subsidiary ledger. At the end of the accounting period the beginning finished goods inventory is transferred to the Cost of Goods Sold account and replaced by the ending finished goods inventory in the closing entries, as discussed below.

Recording the Cost of Goods Sold

The Manufacturing Summary account is closed at the end of the period after it contains all the elements of the cost of goods manufactured for the period. Because cost of goods sold is such a significant operating expense, a manufacturing company that uses a periodic inventory system uses a Cost of Goods Sold closing account in addition to the Income Summary account. (A company using a perpetual inventory system would use a Cost of Goods Sold account to record the cost of each sale as it is made.) The accounts used to compute cost of goods sold are first closed to the Cost of Goods Sold account and the balance of the Cost of Goods Sold account is then closed to the Income Summary account. The accounts used to compute the cost of goods sold are the beginning and ending balances in the Finished Goods Inventory account and the cost of goods manufactured, which is the balance in the Manufacturing Summary account. Based on the costs accumulated in our example, the closing entries are as follows:

Cost of Goods Sold.	57,000	
Manufacturing Summary		57,000
To close the manufacturing summary account.		

This entry transfers the cost of goods manufactured of $57,000 to the Cost of Goods Sold closing account. Another closing entry is necessary to close the beginning finished goods inventory as follows:

Cost of Goods Sold.	20,000	
Finished Goods Inventory.		20,000
To close the beginning finished goods inventory.		

This journal entry transfers the beginning finished goods inventory of $20,000 to the Cost of Goods Sold account so that the inventory account now has a balance of zero. After these two closing entries, the Cost of Goods Sold account includes the cost of goods available for sale of $77,000 (the beginning finished goods inventory of $20,000 plus the cost of goods manufactured of $57,000). Another closing entry is necessary to record the ending finished goods inventory, which is as follows:

Finished Goods Inventory	16,000	
Cost of Goods Sold		16,000
To record the ending finished goods inventory.		

The Finished Goods Inventory account now includes the ending inventory of $16,000, which will be the beginning inventory of the next period. The Cost of Goods Sold account now includes the cost of goods sold for the period of $61,000 ($77,000 debit balance − $16,000 credit balance) as shown in Exhibit 21-2. The Cost of Goods Sold account is then closed to the Income Summary account as follows:

Income Summary	61,000	
Cost of Goods Sold		61,000
To close the cost of goods sold.		

In an actual situation the Cost of Goods Sold account would be closed with all the other revenue and expense accounts in exactly the same way as discussed for merchandising companies in Chapter 5.

RECORDING MANUFACTURING COSTS IN CHRONOLOGICAL ORDER

In the previous discussion we presented simple journal entries to illustrate the accounting for each element of manufacturing cost, using a periodic inventory system. To explain the various relationships we showed the journal entry to record each cost and the closing entry at the same time. In reality, however, manufacturing as well as nonmanufacturing costs and revenues are recorded throughout the accounting period. In addition, all the closing entries are prepared at the end of the accounting period. In this section we present a more comprehensive example and show how each item is recorded in chronological order during the period. Sales are recorded throughout the period in exactly the same way as for a merchandising company. As purchases of direct materials are made during the period they are recorded in the Direct Materials Purchases account. The other two elements of manufacturing cost, direct labor and factory overhead, are recorded in their respective accounts when they are incurred. Selling expenses and general and administrative expenses are also recorded as they are incurred. At the end of the period adjusting entries are needed for such items as wages payable, accumulated depreciation, and prepaid insurance.

The basic information for the comprehensive example involving the 1983 transactions of the Elm Company is shown in Exhibit 21-3. The beginning and ending inventories of direct materials, goods in process, and finished goods are provided. In addition, the costs incurred during the year and the cash payments made during the year are listed. The 1983 transactions are recorded in summarized general journal entries in the following sections. The number preceding each journal entry is used to cross-reference the posting to the ledger accounts, which is illustrated later in the chapter in Exhibit 21-4. It is assumed that the Elm Company uses a periodic inventory system.

Recording Costs and Revenues During the Accounting Period

The direct materials purchases were $40,000 of which $38,000 was paid in cash. The summary journal entry to record the acquisition of direct materials during the accounting period is:

(1) Direct Materials Purchases.	40,000	
Cash.		38,000
Accounts Payable		2,000

To record purchase of direct materials.

During 1983 total factory labor was $80,000, $60,000 of which was for direct labor and $20,000 for indirect labor. Total cash payments to employees for this labor were $61,000 ($45,000 + $16,000). The remaining $19,000 consisted of federal income taxes of $13,640 ($10,980 + $2,660) and social security taxes of $5,360 ($4,020 + $1,340), which were withheld from the employees' paychecks (payroll taxes incurred by the employer are ignored in this example). Since indirect

EXHIBIT 21-3
Elm Company
Relevant Data for
1983

Beginning inventories	
Direct materials	$ 10,000
Goods in process	12,000
Finished goods	7,000
Manufacturing costs incurred during the year	
Direct materials purchases	$ 40,000
Direct labor	60,000
Indirect labor	20,000
Factory supplies	5,000
Repairs	2,000
Maintenance	1,000
Utilities	3,000
Insurance (paid for in previous period)	4,000
Depreciation on machinery	8,000
Selling and general and administrative expenses incurred during the year	
Depreciation on selling equipment	$ 3,000
Depreciation on office equipment	5,000
Other selling expenses	13,000
Other general and administrative expenses	19,000
Cash payments during the year	
Direct materials purchases	$ 38,000
Direct labor (federal income taxes withheld $10,980, social security taxes withheld $4,020)	45,000
Indirect labor (federal income taxes withheld $2,660, social security taxes withheld $1,340)	16,000
Factory supplies	5,000
Repairs	2,000
Maintenance	1,000
Utilities	3,000
Selling expenses	13,000
General and administrative expenses	19,000
Sales (all on account)	$200,000
Ending inventories	
Direct materials	$ 11,000
Goods in process	14,000
Finished goods	6,000

labor is part of factory overhead, the summary journal entry to record the payment of the factory labor cost is:

(2)	Direct Labor	60,000	
	Factory Overhead	20,000	
	Cash		61,000
	Federal Income Taxes Payable		13,640
	Social Security Taxes Payable		5,360
	To record payment of factory payroll.		

If the last wage payment of the year did not take place on the last day of the year, some of the wages earned by the employees would not have been paid to them. For example, suppose that the company had paid only $59,000 in wages and owed the employees $2,000 for wages earned since the last wage payment date. The summary journal entry would be the same as the entry above except that the credit to cash would be only $59,000 and wages payable would be recorded (credited) for $2,000.

In the example earlier in the chapter we assumed that all factory overhead costs were paid in cash, but this is not the usual case. One of the factory overhead costs that is not paid in cash is the depreciation on the property, plant, and equipment used to produce the product. Depreciation on assets which are *not* part of the manufacturing process is included as an expense of the period as discussed in Chapter 11. Depreciation on assets which *are* used in the manufacturing process is included in the manufacturing costs of the period as part of the factory overhead costs. Usually depreciation is recorded at the end of the period by an adjusting entry. The journal entry to record the depreciation on an asset used in the manufacturing process is an increase (debit) to Factory Overhead and an increase (credit) to Accumulated Depreciation. Because depreciation on assets used in the manufacturing process is included in factory overhead, it is included as an expense (as a component of cost of goods sold) only as the units are sold. For example, suppose that the depreciation on factory machinery is $10,000 in one period. Since this cost is included in the factory overhead, it is also included in the cost of goods manufactured during the period. If *none* of the units manufactured during the current period is sold in the period, however, none of the $10,000 would be included in the income statement. Alternatively, if all of the units are sold the entire $10,000 would be included as part of the cost of goods sold. Note that this is depreciation only on the assets used in the production process. Depreciation on assets used in selling and administration is shown as depreciation expense in the period incurred, just as for a merchandising company.

Some of the other factory overhead costs are also recognized through adjusting entries at the end of the period because the cash payment does not occur at the same time as the item is included in factory overhead. For example, the payment in advance for insurance on the assets used in manufacturing would be recorded as an asset, prepaid insurance. The cost of the insurance for the current period would be included as part of factory overhead by a year-end adjusting entry. Another example of an item that would be included in factory overhead through an adjusting entry is the cost of utilities for manufacturing activities that has been incurred but has not yet been paid. As with depreciation the insurance and utility costs related to manufacturing are included in factory overhead by a manufacturing company, whereas the similar costs for merchandising activities would be expensed directly by a merchandising company.

To return to the Elm Company example, the factory overhead costs for 1983 include indirect labor (recorded earlier as part of payroll), and factory supplies of $5,000, repairs of $2,000, maintenance of $1,000, and utilities of $3,000, all of which were paid in cash. Insurance of $4,000, which had been paid for in a prior period, and depreciation on machinery of $8,000 also must be included in factory overhead. The summary journal entry to record these costs during the accounting period is:

```
(3)  Factory Overhead . . . . . . . . . . . . . . . . . . . . .        23,000
         Cash ($5,000 + $2,000 + $1,000 + $3,000) . . . .                      11,000
         Prepaid Insurance . . . . . . . . . . . . . . . . . .                   4,000
         Accumulated Depreciation:  Machinery . . . . . . .                      8,000
     To record factory overhead costs incurred.
```

These costs would also be recorded in a factory overhead subsidiary ledger (which is not illustrated) so that they could be reported individually in the cost of goods manufactured statement (shown later in Exhibit 21-5).

During the year the company incurred selling expenses of $16,000; $13,000 was paid in cash and $3,000 was for depreciation on selling equipment. The company also incurred general and administrative expenses of $24,000; $19,000 was paid in cash and $5,000 was for depreciation on office equipment. The summary journal entry to record these costs during the accounting period is:

```
(4)  Selling Expenses . . . . . . . . . . . . . . . . . . . . .       16,000
     General and Administrative Expenses. . . . . . . . . .           24,000
         Cash ($13,000 + $19,000) . . . . . . . . . . . . . .                   32,000
         Accumulated Depreciation:  Selling Equipment . .                        3,000
         Accumulated Depreciation:  Office Equipment . . .                        5,000
     To record selling and general and administrative
     expenses.
```

The summary journal entry to record the sales during the year is:

```
(5)  Accounts Receivable . . . . . . . . . . . . . . . . . . . .      200,000
         Sales . . . . . . . . . . . . . . . . . . . . . . . . . .              200,000
     To record sales.
```

Closing Entries at the End of the Accounting Period

At the end of the accounting period the various manufacturing costs and the beginning inventory of direct materials and goods in process would be closed to the Manufacturing Summary account. This is typically done in a compound entry as follows:

```
(6)  Manufacturing Summary . . . . . . . . . . . . . . . . . .      165,000
         Direct Materials Inventory . . . . . . . . . . . . . . .               10,000
         Goods in Process Inventory. . . . . . . . . . . . . .                  12,000
         Direct Material Purchases. . . . . . . . . . . . . . .                 40,000
         Direct Labor . . . . . . . . . . . . . . . . . . . . . .               60,000
         Factory Overhead ($20,000 + $23,000). . . . . . . .                    43,000
     To close the beginning inventories and manufacturing
     accounts with debit balances.
```

The ending direct materials and goods in process are recorded as follows:

(7) Direct Materials Inventory.   11,000
     Goods in Process Inventory   14,000
         Manufacturing Summary   25,000

To record the ending direct materials and goods in
process inventories.

Note that the difference between the two entries to the Manufacturing Summary
account is equal to the cost of goods manufactured of $140,000 ($165,000 −
$25,000) shown in Exhibit 21-5 (discussed later).

The Manufacturing Summary account is next closed to the Cost of Goods Sold
account along with the beginning finished goods inventory as follows:

(8) Cost of Goods Sold   147,000
         Manufacturing Summary   140,000
         Finished Goods Inventory   7,000

To close the manufacturing summary account and the
beginning finished goods inventory.

The journal entry to record the ending inventory of finished goods is:

(9) Finished Goods Inventory   6,000
         Cost of Goods Sold   6,000

To record the ending finished goods inventory.

Since the beginning finished goods inventory was $7,000, the cost of goods
manufactured $140,000, and the ending finished goods inventory $6,000, the cost
of goods sold is $141,000 ($7,000 + $140,000 − $6,000). This is the balance in
the Cost of Goods Sold account after the above closing entries, as shown in Exhibit
21-4 (discussed later). The Cost of Goods Sold account is closed to the Income
Summary account along with the other expenses as follows:

(10) Income Summary   181,000
         Cost of Goods Sold   141,000
         Selling Expenses   16,000
         General and Administrative Expenses   24,000

To close the cost of goods sold account and
other expense accounts.

The sales revenues would be closed to the Income Summary account as follows:

(11) Sales   200,000
         Income Summary   200,000

To close the sales account.

Thus the Income Summary account would have a credit balance of $19,000
($200,000 − $181,000) representing the net income for 1983. The Income Sum-

mary account would then be closed to a permanent owners' equity account. If we assume that the Elm Company is a corporation, the $19,000 net income (disregarding income taxes) would be closed to retained earnings as follows:

(12)   Income Summary   19,000
          Retained Earnings   19,000
       To close the income summary account and transfer the
       net income to retained earnings.

Ledger Accounts

The postings to the ledger accounts as a result of the summary journal entries prepared for the Elm Company example are illustrated on the lower right side of Exhibit 21-4. The 12 journal entries are repeated for comparison purposes on the left side and upper right side. The debit and credit portions are cross-referenced by the number to the left of each posting entry. The journal entries are numbered by the order in which they were discussed in the chapter. So that the manufacturing costs can be emphasized, the credit postings for the direct material purchases, direct labor, factory overhead, selling expenses, general and administrative expenses, and the beginning balance of retained earnings have been omitted.

FINANCIAL STATEMENTS OF A MANUFACTURING COMPANY

There are several differences between the financial statements prepared by a manufacturing company and those of a merchandising company. They include an extra statement entitled the *cost of goods manufactured statement*, as well as modifications to the income statement and the balance sheet. Each of these differences is discussed below.

The Cost of Goods Manufactured Statement

The cost of goods manufactured statement summarizes the costs of each component of the cost of goods manufactured during the period. The statement for the Elm Company for 1983 is shown in Exhibit 21-5. As mentioned earlier in the chapter, this statement is primarily prepared for the internal use of management and is rarely included in the published financial statements. The statement simply lists in statement format the information that was recorded in the journal entries.

The cost of goods manufactured statement summarizes the costs of all the elements in the manufacturing process, which is therefore the information contained in the Manufacturing Summary account. The beginning direct materials inventory, plus the direct materials purchases and minus the ending direct materials inventory, indicates the cost of the direct materials used in the production during the year. To this cost is added the direct labor and the factory overhead costs to give the total manufacturing costs for the year. These total manufacturing costs plus the beginning goods in process give the total cost of goods in process during the year. The cost of goods manufactured (the cost of the units completed during the year) is obtained by subtracting the ending goods in process inventory from the total cost of goods in process.

The format of this statement should be compared with the format shown for the Perfection Manufacturing Company in Exhibit 21-2. The two formats should be reviewed, for then it can be seen that they both include the same type of information.

Modifications to the Income Statement

The income statement for a manufacturing company is similar to that of a merchandising company, except that the cost of goods sold section includes the cost of goods manufactured rather than the cost of purchases. The 1983 income statement for the Elm Company (disregarding income taxes) is shown in Exhibit 21-6. Note that the cost of goods manufactured of $140,000, as computed in Exhibit 21-5, is included in the calculation of the cost of goods sold in Exhibit 21-6. Often this detail is omitted from the income statement included in the published financial statements, with only the cost of goods sold being reported. In these situations the income statements of merchandising and manufacturing companies are not different in format. With the exception of the cost of goods sold section the income statement is the same as for a merchandising company.

Modifications to the Balance Sheet

The balance sheet of a manufacturing company has two distinguishing features as compared to that of a merchandising company. First, there are three categories of inventory that are reported in the balance sheet. The inventory section of the current assets in the balance sheet of the Elm Company at December 31, 1983, is as follows:

Inventories	
Direct materials	$11,000
Goods in process	14,000
Finished goods	6,000
Total inventories	$31,000

Note that the direct materials, goods in process, and finished goods inventory figures are the December 31, 1983, account balances shown in Exhibit 21-4. We have not discussed the application of alternative cost flow assumptions, such as FIFO, average cost, and LIFO, to a manufacturing company, but this would be done using the principles discussed in Chapter 9.

The second distinguishing feature involves noncurrent assets. A manufacturing company generally uses the title, "Property, Plant, and Equipment," rather than "Property and Equipment," which is more typical for a merchandising company. This section shows the cost, accumulated depreciation, and book value of the physical manufacturing facilities as well as the same information for the physical assets used in nonmanufacturing activities.

EXHIBIT 21-4
Journal Entries and
Ledger Accounts for
Elm Company

(1)	Direct Materials Purchases	40,000
	Cash	
	Accounts Payable	
	To record the purchase of direct materials.	

(1) Direct Materials Purchases 40,000
    Cash 38,000
    Accounts Payable 2,000
To record the purchase of direct materials.

(2) Direct Labor 60,000
    Factory Overhead 20,000
    Cash 61,000
    Federal Income Taxes Payable 13,640
    Social Security Taxes Payable 5,360
To record the payment of factory payroll.

(3) Factory Overhead 23,000
    Cash 11,000
    Prepaid Insurance 4,000
    Accumulated Depreciation: Machinery 8,000
To record factory overhead costs incurred.

(4) Selling Expenses 16,000
    General and Administrative Expenses 24,000
    Cash 32,000
    Accumulated Depreciation: Selling Equipment 3,000
    Accumulated Depreciation: Office Equipment 5,000
To record selling and general and administrative
expenses.

(5) Accounts Receivable 200,000
    Sales 200,000
To record sales.

(6) Manufacturing Summary 165,000
    Direct Materials Inventory 10,000
    Goods in Process Inventory 12,000
    Direct Materials Purchases 40,000
    Direct Labor 60,000
    Factory Overhead 43,000
To close the beginning inventories and manufacturing
accounts with debit balances.

(7) Direct Materials Inventory 11,000
    Goods in Process Inventory 14,000
    Manufacturing Summary 25,000
To record the ending direct materials and goods in process
inventories.

(8) Cost of Goods Sold 147,000
    Manufacturing Summary 140,000
    Finished Goods Inventory 7,000
To close the manufacturing summary account and
the beginning finished goods inventory.

(9) Finished Goods Inventory 6,000
    Cost of Goods Sold 6,000
To record the ending finished goods inventory.

(10)	Income Summary	181,000	
	Cost of Goods Sold		141,000
	Selling Expenses		16,000
	General and Administrative Expenses		24,000

To close the cost of goods sold account and other expense accounts.

| (11) | Sales | 200,000 | |
| | Income Summary | | 200,000 |

To close the sales account.

| (12) | Income Summary | 19,000 | |
| | Retained Earnings | | 19,000 |

To close the income summary account and transfer the net income to retained earnings.

Direct Materials Inventory

| Balance 1/1/83 | 10,000 | (6) | 10,000 |
| (7) Balance 12/31/83 | 11,000 | | |

Goods in Process Inventory

| Balance 1/1/83 | 12,000 | (6) | 12,000 |
| (7) Balance 12/31/83 | 14,000 | | |

Finished Goods Inventory

| Balance 1/1/83 | 7,000 | (8) | 7,000 |
| (9) Balance 12/31/83 | 6,000 | | |

Direct Materials Purchases

| (1) | 40,000 | (6) | 40,000 |

Direct Labor

| (2) | 60,000 | (6) | 60,000 |

Factory Overhead

| (2) | 20,000 | (6) | 43,000 |
| (3) | 23,000 | | |

Manufacturing Summary

| (6) | 165,000 | (7) | 25,000 |
| | | (8) | 140,000 |

Cost of Goods Sold

| (8) | 147,000 | (9) | 6,000 |
| | | (10) | 141,000 |

Income Summary

| (10) | 181,000 | (11) | 200,000 |
| (12) | 19,000 | | |

Selling Expenses

| (4) | 16,000 | (10) | 16,000 |

General and Administrative Expenses

| (4) | 24,000 | (10) | 24,000 |

Retained Earnings

| | | (12) | 19,000 |

Accounts Receivable

| (5) | 200,000 | | |

Sales

| (11) | 200,000 | (5) | 200,000 |

Notes: (a) Each entry is referenced by a number that indicates the related journal entry.

(b) The credit postings for the direct materials purchases, direct labor, factory overhead, selling, general and administrative expenses, and the beginning balance of retained earnings are omitted for simplicity.

EXHIBIT 21-5
Cost of Goods
Manufactured
Statement

ELM COMPANY
Cost of Goods Manufactured Statement
For Year Ended December 31, 1983

Direct materials		
Direct materials inventory, January 1, 1983	$10,000	
Direct materials purchases	40,000	
Direct materials available for use	$50,000	
Less: Direct materials inventory, December 31, 1983	11,000	
Direct materials used		$ 39,000
Direct labor		60,000
Factory overhead costs		
Indirect labor	$20,000	
Factory supplies	5,000	
Repairs	2,000	
Maintenance	1,000	
Utilities	3,000	
Insurance	4,000	
Depreciation on machinery	8,000	
Total factory overhead costs		43,000
Total manufacturing costs		$142,000
Add: Goods in process inventory, January 1, 1983		12,000
Cost of goods in process during 1983		$154,000
Less: Goods in process inventory, December 31, 1983		14,000
Cost of Goods Manufactured		$140,000

EXHIBIT 21-6
Income Statement

ELM COMPANY
Income Statement
For Year Ended December 31, 1983

Sales		$200,000
Cost of goods sold		
Finished goods inventory, January 1, 1983	$ 7,000	
Cost of goods manufactured	140,000	
Cost of goods available for sale	$147,000	
Less: Finished goods inventory, December 31, 1983	6,000	
Cost of goods sold		141,000
Gross profit		$ 59,000
Operating expenses		
Selling expenses	$ 16,000	
General and administrative expenses	24,000	
Total operating expenses		40,000
Net Income		$ 19,000

The worksheet of a manufacturing company is similar in many respects to that of a merchandising company (illustrated in Chapter 5). A trial balance, adjusting entries, and an adjusted trial balance are prepared in the usual way. The worksheet of a manufacturing company, however, must be modified in several ways. The primary modification is the inclusion of a Manufacturing Statement debit and credit column to accumulate the cost of goods manufactured. A partial worksheet using the numerical information for the Elm Company is shown in Exhibit 21-7.

Since the Elm Company uses the periodic inventory system the adjusted trial balance contains the beginning balances in the three inventory accounts. The beginning balances in the direct materials inventory ($10,000) and the goods in process inventory ($12,000) accounts are carried to the debit column of the manufacturing statement. The balances of the direct materials purchases ($40,000), the direct labor ($60,000), and the factory overhead ($43,000) accounts are also carried to the debit column. The ending direct materials inventory ($11,000) and the ending goods in process inventory ($14,000) are recorded in the credit column of the manufacturing statement and the debit column of the balance sheet. The total of the manufacturing statement debit column minus the total of the credit column is the cost of goods manufactured ($140,000), which is then transferred to the income statement debit column. The beginning finished goods inventory ($7,000) is carried from the adjusted trial balance to the income statement debit column. The

EXHIBIT 21-7   Partial Worksheet

	ELM COMPANY Partial Worksheet For Year Ended December 31, 1983							
	Adjusted Trial Balance		Manufacturing Statement		Income Statement		Balance Sheet	
Account Titles	Debit	Credit	Debit	Credit	Debit	Credit	Debit	Credit
Direct materials inventory, beginning	10,000		10,000					
Goods in process inventory, beginning	12,000		12,000					
Finished goods inventory, beginning	7,000				7,000			
Direct materials purchases	40,000		40,000					
Direct labor	60,000		60,000					
Factory overhead	43,000		43,000					
Direct materials inventory, ending				11,000			11,000	
Goods in process inventory, ending				14,000			14,000	
Finished goods inventory, ending						6,000	6,000	
			165,000	25,000				
Cost of goods manufactured				140,000	140,000			
			165,000	165,000				

ending finished goods inventory is recorded in the income statement credit column and the balance sheet debit column.

The remaining steps to complete the worksheet (not illustrated in Exhibit 21-7) are the same as those discussed for a merchandising company. That is, the non-manufacturing amounts from the adjusted trial balance are entered in the appropriate income statement and balance sheet debit and credit columns. The difference between the income statement debit and credit columns (including the cost of the goods manufactured) is the net income of the period, which is transferred to the balance sheet credit column to complete the worksheet.

REVIEW PROBLEM

On December 31, 1983, the Tader Company had the following alphabetical list of balances in selected accounts. These balances represent the amounts in the accounts after the adjusting entries have been made, but before the closing entries are recorded. The company uses the periodic inventory system.

Direct labor	$ 60,000
Direct materials purchases	90,000
Factory overhead	126,000
General and administrative expenses	92,000
Inventories	
Direct materials	47,000
Goods in process	35,000
Finished goods	41,000
Sales	500,000
Selling expenses	36,000

The ending inventories determined by a physical count are as follows:

Direct materials	$55,000
Goods in process	42,000
Finished goods	38,000

Required:
1. Prepare closing entries. Close the net income or loss to the R. Tader, Capital account.
2. Prepare a cost of goods manufactured statement and an income statement for 1983.

SOLUTION TO REVIEW PROBLEM

Requirement 1:

Manufacturing Summary	358,000	
Direct Materials Inventory		47,000
Goods in Process Inventory		35,000
Direct Materials Purchases		90,000
Direct Labor		60,000
Factory Overhead		126,000

To close the beginning inventories and manufacturing accounts with debit balances.

Direct Materials Inventory	55,000	
Goods in Process Inventory	42,000	
Manufacturing Summary		97,000

To record the ending direct materials and goods in
process inventories.

Cost of Goods Sold	302,000	
Manufacturing Summary		261,000
Finished Goods Inventory		41,000

To close the manufacturing summary account and the
beginning finished goods inventory.

Finished Goods Inventory	38,000	
Cost of Goods Sold		38,000

To record the ending finished goods inventory.

Income Summary	392,000	
Cost of Goods Sold		264,000
Selling Expenses		36,000
General and Administrative Expenses		92,000

To close the cost of goods sold account and other
expense accounts.

Sales	500,000	
Income Summary		500,000

To close the sales account.

Income Summary	108,000	
R. Tader, Capital		108,000

To close the income summary account and transfer
net income to owner's capital account.

Requirement 2:

TADER COMPANY
Cost of Goods Manufactured Statement
For Year Ended December 31, 1983

Direct materials		
Direct materials inventory, January 1, 1983	$ 47,000	
Direct materials purchases	90,000	
Direct materials available for use	$137,000	
Less: Direct materials inventory, December 31, 1983	55,000	
Direct materials used		$ 82,000
Direct labor		60,000
Factory overhead		126,000
Total manufacturing costs		$268,000
Add: Goods in process inventory, January 1, 1983		35,000
Cost of goods in process during 1983		$303,000
Less: Goods in process inventory, December 31, 1983		42,000
Cost of Goods Manufactured		$261,000

TADER COMPANY
Income Statement
For Year Ended December 31, 1983

Sales		$500,000
Cost of goods sold		
Finished goods inventory, January 1, 1983	$ 41,000	
Cost of goods manufactured	261,000	
Cost of goods available for sale	$302,000	
Less: Finished goods inventory, December 31, 1983	38,000	
Cost of goods sold		264,000
Gross profit		$236,000
Operating expenses		
Selling expenses	$ 36,000	
General and administrative expenses	92,000	
Total operating expenses		$128,000
Net Income		$108,000

GLOSSARY

Cost of Goods Manufactured.   The cost of the units that were completed during the period and were ready for sale.

Cost of Goods Manufactured Statement.   A statement summarizing the cost of each component of the cost of goods manufactured during the period. An internal statement that is rarely included in the published financial statements.

Direct Labor.   The labor of the employees who work with the direct materials to convert or assemble them into the finished product.

Direct Materials.   The raw materials that physically become part of a manufactured product.

Direct Materials Inventory.   The account used to record the inventory of direct materials on hand at the end of the accounting period. The balance in the account is the beginning inventory of the next period, and in a periodic system it remains in the account throughout that period.

Factory Overhead.   The items that are necessary for the manufacture of a product, except for direct materials and direct labor. For example, included are indirect materials, indirect labor, repairs and maintenance, utilities, insurance, property taxes, and depreciation relating to the manufacturing activity. Also called *manufacturing overhead.*

Finished Goods Inventory.   The account used to record the cost of the units that have finished the production process but have not been sold at the end of the accounting period.

Goods in Process Inventory.   The account used to record the costs of partially completed products in the production process at the end of the period. Direct materials, direct labor, and factory overhead costs associated with incomplete units of the product are the cost components included in the ending goods in process inventory. Also called *work in process* inventory.

Indirect Labor. The labor of the employees who are involved in the operation of the production process but who do not convert or assemble the direct materials into the finished product. For example, the labor of employees involved in the supervision of production and the maintenance of the production equipment would be included in indirect labor.

Indirect Materials. The materials that are not directly incorporated into the product during the manufacturing process but which are necessary for the successful operation of the process. For example, lubricating oil used in production machinery would be included in indirect materials. Also called *factory supplies* or *manufacturing supplies*.

Raw Materials. Direct materials and indirect materials.

QUESTIONS

Q21-1 What is the basic difference between a merchandising and a manufacturing company? Does this difference result in different accounting principles being used? Explain.

Q21-2 What are the three elements included in the cost of manufacturing a product? Describe the items that are typically included in each.

Q21-3 Distinguish between (a) direct materials and indirect materials; (b) direct labor and indirect labor; and (c) factory overhead and manufacturing overhead.

Q21-4 What are the three types of inventory accounts used by a manufacturing company? Describe the costs that are typically included in each when a company uses a periodic inventory system.

Q21-5 What is the purpose of the Manufacturing Summary account? What items are included in the account?

Q21-6 Is depreciation on assets used in manufacturing shown as a separate expense directly on the income statement? If not, how is the depreciation included in the income statement?

Q21-7 Summarize how total manufacturing costs are accounted for by a typical manufacturing company using the periodic inventory system.

Q21-8 When are the costs incurred during manufacturing reported as an expense on the income statement under a periodic inventory system? How are they reported?

Q21-9 What is the purpose of the Cost of Goods Sold closing account for a manufacturing company? What items are included in the account?

Q21-10 What information is included in a cost of goods manufactured statement?

Q21-11 How does the income statement of a manufacturing company differ from the income statement of a merchandising company?

Q21-12 How does the balance sheet of a manufacturing company differ from the balance sheet of a merchandising company?

Q21-13 How does the worksheet of a manufacturing company differ from the worksheet of a merchandising company?

E21-1   Classification of Costs.   Below is a list of costs incurred by a company producing billiard tables:

(a) The cost of the wood used for the frame
(b) The wages earned by the foreman who supervises the manufacturing process
(c) The cost of the cloth used to cover the table
(d) The salary earned by a salesperson
(e) The commission earned by a salesperson
(f) The cost of the tools used by the employees who build the tables
(g) The wages earned by the employees who build the tables
(h) The cost of the sandpaper used to smooth the wood
(i) The cost of the varnish used to finish the wood
(j) The wages earned by the manager who supervises all the production departments

Required: Classify each cost according to whether it would be included in direct materials, direct labor, factory overhead, or another account.

E21-2   Classification of Costs.   Each of the following costs was computed or known at the end of the period before closing entries were made.

(a) The cost of the units in the warehouse awaiting sale at the beginning of the period
(b) The cost of completed units shipped by the company FOB destination
(c) The cost of partially completed units still in the manufacturing process
(d) The cost of the inventory of direct materials at the beginning of the period
(e) The cost of completed units shipped by the company FOB shipping point

Required: Classify each cost according to which account, if any, it would be recorded in before closing entries are made. Indicate how it would be included in the closing entries.

E21-3   Direct Material Costs.   On January 1 the direct materials inventory was $20,000. The direct materials purchases during the year were $70,000, of which $65,000 was paid for. The December 31 direct materials inventory was $30,000.

Required: Prepare summary journal entries, including closing entries to the manufacturing summary account, to record the above events.

E21-4   Direct Labor Costs.   During the year direct labor and indirect labor at a total cost of $50,000 and $40,000, respectively, were incurred. Payments to employees totaled $65,000. Social security taxes withheld were $6,030 and federal income taxes withheld were $18,970. The withheld taxes have not been remitted to the government.

Required: Prepare summary journal entries, including closing entries to the manufacturing summary account, to record the above events.

E21-5   Factory Overhead Costs.   Factory overhead costs for the year include factory supplies of $7,000, indirect labor of $22,000, utilities of $14,000, depreciation of $8,000, and insurance of $1,000. The supplies and utilities were paid in cash. Social security taxes of $1,474 and federal income taxes of $3,200 were withheld from the wages of the indirect labor; the remainder was paid in cash. The withheld taxes have not been remitted to the government. The insurance was paid for in a previous period.

Required: Prepare summary journal entries, including closing entries to the manufacturing summary account, to record the above events.

E21-6 The Cost of Finished Goods. For the Bas Company at the beginning of 1983 the direct materials inventory was $10,000, the goods in process inventory was $12,000, and the finished goods inventory was $18,000. The manufacturing costs incurred (and paid in cash) during the year included direct materials purchases of $18,000, direct labor of $35,000, and factory overhead of $25,000. The ending direct materials inventory was $11,000, the ending goods in process inventory was $19,000, and the ending finished goods inventory was $31,000.

Required: 1. Prepare summary journal entries, including closing entries through the closing of the Cost of Goods Sold account, to record the above events.

                 2. Prepare (a) a cost of goods manufactured statement for 1983 and (b) the cost of goods sold section of the income statement for 1983.

E21-7 General Ledger Accounts. Use the information in E21-3, E21-4, and E21-5.

Required: Record the information in general ledger accounts (including closing entries) without first preparing journal entries.

E21-8 General Ledger Accounts. Use the information in E21-6.

Required: Record the information in general ledger accounts (including closing entries) without first preparing journal entries.

E21-9 Financial Statements. The following information is for the Halley Company for March, 1983:

Goods in process inventory, March 1	$ 29,000
Goods in process inventory, March 31	37,000
Finished goods inventory, March 1	48,000
Finished goods inventory, March 31	41,000
Direct materials used	42,000
Direct labor	67,000
Cost of goods manufactured	154,000

Required: 1. Compute the factory overhead for March.

                 2. Prepare a cost of goods manufactured statement for March.

                 3. Prepare the cost of goods sold section of the March income statement.

E21-10 Closing Entries. The following are the amounts in selected accounts of the James Corporation before closing entries have been prepared:

Direct materials inventory	$ 10,000
Goods in process inventory	15,000
Finished goods inventory	14,000
Direct labor	50,000
Direct materials purchases	28,000
Factory overhead	45,000
Selling, general, and administrative expenses	35,000
Sales	200,000

The ending inventories determined by a physical count were as follows:

Direct materials	$ 8,000
Goods in process	13,000
Finished goods	18,000

Required: Prepare all the necessary closing entries (disregard income taxes).

E21-11 Financial Statements. The following information is taken from the accounting records of the Gentry Company for 1983:

Direct materials inventory, January 1	$ 15,000
Direct materials inventory, December 31	22,000
Goods in process inventory, January 1	25,000
Goods in process inventory, December 31	36,000
Finished goods inventory, January 1	27,000
Finished goods inventory, December 31	21,000
Direct materials purchases	60,000
Direct labor	80,000
Factory overhead	92,000
Sales	300,000

Required: Prepare the following:
1. The cost of goods manufactured statement for 1983.
2. A partial income statement for 1983 (through gross profit).
3. A partial balance sheet at December 31, 1983.

E21-12 Worksheet. Use the information in E21-11.

Required: Prepare a partial worksheet through cost of goods manufactured at the end of 1983.

PROBLEMS

Part A

P21-1A Financial Statements. The following information was taken from the accounting records of the Marino Company at the end of 1983:

Advertising expense	$ 5,000
Depreciation expense: Machinery	7,500
Depreciation expense: Office equipment	3,100
Direct labor	46,000
Direct materials purchases	40,000
Factory supplies used	13,200
Indirect labor	35,000
Inventories:	
Direct materials, January 1	22,000
Direct materials, December 31	24,000
Goods in process, January 1	26,000
Goods in process, December 31	25,000
Finished goods, January 1	19,000
Finished goods, December 31	16,000
Miscellaneous factory expenses	1,700
Factory supervisor's salary	21,400
Office salaries	43,000
Purchases discounts taken on direct materials purchases	300
Rent expense, machinery	1,900
Rent expense, office equipment	1,600
Repairs and maintenance, machinery	1,400
Sales	298,000
Sales returns	1,500
Sales salaries	32,000
Utilities for factory	21,800
Utilities for office	7,700

Required: Prepare a cost of goods manufactured statement and properly classified income statement for 1983.

P21-2A Recording Manufacturing Costs. The following information for the Metro Corporation, which uses the periodic inventory system, is available for 1983:

Beginning inventories	
Direct materials	$ 27,000
Goods in process	43,000
Finished goods	75,000
Manufacturing costs incurred during the year	
Direct materials purchases	$ 90,000
Direct labor	73,000
Factory supplies	8,000
Indirect labor	22,000
Repairs	16,000
Maintenance	5,000
Utilities	21,000
Insurance (paid in previous period)	2,000
Depreciation on machinery	12,000
Selling and general and administrative expenses incurred during the year	
Depreciation on selling equipment	$ 2,000
Depreciation on office equipment	4,000
Other selling expenses	16,000
Other general and administrative expenses	21,000
Cash payments during the year	
Direct materials purchases	$ 82,000
Direct labor (federal income taxes withheld, $14,609;	
social security taxes withheld, $4,891)	53,500
Factory supplies	8,000
Indirect labor (federal income taxes withheld, $3,926;	
social security taxes withheld, $1,474)	16,600
Repairs	16,000
Maintenance	5,000
Utilities	19,000
Selling expenses	16,000
General and administrative expenses	21,000
Sales (all on account)	$350,000
Ending inventories	
Direct materials	$ 30,000
Goods in process	42,000
Finished goods	71,000

Required: Prepare summary journal entries, including closing entries, for the Metro Corporation for 1983 (disregard corporate income taxes).

P21-3A Financial Statements. Use the information in P21-2A.

Required: Prepare a cost of goods manufactured statement and an income statement of the Metro Corporation for 1983.

P21-4A Comprehensive Problem. The Baldwin Corporation obtained the following information from its accounting records on December 31, 1983, before adjusting entries or closing entries were prepared. The company uses the periodic inventory system.

Cash	$ 26,000
Accounts receivable	15,000
Allowance for uncollectible accounts	3,000
Prepaid insurance on factory machinery	12,000
Direct materials inventory	20,000
Goods in process inventory	27,000
Finished goods inventory	46,000
Direct materials purchases	52,000
Machinery	84,000
Accumulated depreciation: Machinery	36,000
Office building	160,000
Accumulated depreciation: Office building	40,000
Accounts payable	13,100
Common stock, $10 par	100,000
Additional paid-in capital	44,000
Bonds payable	40,000
Retained earnings	41,502
Sales (net)	275,000
Direct labor	45,000
Factory overhead	58,000
Selling expenses	20,000
Administrative expenses	35,000
Social security taxes payable	1,250
Federal income taxes payable	6,148

Additional Information for 1983:
1. Bad debt expense is $2,000.
2. Insurance worth $2,000 on the factory machinery remained in effect for next year.
3. On December 31, 1983, a physical count determined that the direct materials, goods in process, and finished goods inventories were $25,000, $32,000, and $40,000, respectively.
4. Depreciation on the machinery and the office building was $12,000 and $8,000, respectively.
5. Direct labor earned by employees but not yet paid at the end of the year amounted to $2,500. Federal income taxes and social security taxes on these wages were $125 and $470, respectively.

Required: 1. Prepare adjusting entries at the end of 1983.
2. Prepare closing entries at the end of 1983 (disregard corporate income taxes).
3. Prepare the cost of goods manufactured statement for 1983, the income statement for 1983, and the balance sheet at December 31, 1983.

P21-5A Manufacturing Costs. At the beginning of 1983 the Petrie Company had beginning inventories of direct materials, goods in process, and finished goods of $8,000, $25,000 and $21,000, respectively. Selected general ledger accounts for the year included the following partial entries:

Cash		
Insurance	6,000	
Direct materials	20,000	
Direct labor	42,000	
Indirect labor	37,000	
Supplies	8,000	
Utilities	7,000	

Accounts Payable (for Direct Materials)		
20,000	Bal. 1/1/83	5,000
		27,000

Federal Income Taxes Payable		
Direct labor	8,400	
Indirect labor	7,800	

Utilities Payable		
	Bal. 1/1/83	–0–
		1,000
	Bal. 12/31/83	1,000

Social Security Taxes Payable		
	Direct labor	2,814
	Indirect labor	2,479

The direct materials used during the year were $21,000. The ending inventories of goods in process and finished goods were $27,000 and $32,000, respectively. A 2-year insurance policy on the factory was purchased on January 1.

Required: 1. Reconstruct the summary journal entries that were made during 1983, including closing entries (through to the closing of the Cost of Goods Sold account).

2. Prepare a cost of goods manufactured statement for 1983.

PROBLEMS

Part B

P21-1B Financial Statements. The following information was taken from the accounting records of the Petty Company at the end of 1983:

Advertising expense	$ 4,500
Depreciation expense: Machinery	3,400
Depreciation expense: Office equipment	2,000
Direct labor	28,000
Factory supplies used	4,100
Indirect labor	26,500
Inventories:	
Direct materials, January 1	34,000
Direct materials, December 31	35,000
Goods in process, January 1	37,000
Goods in process, December 31	36,000
Finished goods, January 1	31,000
Finished goods, December 31	28,000
Miscellaneous factory expenses	2,500
Manufacturing supervisor's salary	22,700
Office salaries	44,000
Purchases discounts taken on direct materials purchases	1,200
Direct materials purchases	62,000
Rent expense, machinery	1,800
Rent expense, office equipment	1,300
Repairs and maintenance on machinery	1,100
Sales	300,000
Sales returns	2,700
Sales salaries	43,400
Utilities for factory	12,900
Utilities for office	11,300

Required: Prepare a cost of goods manufactured statement and properly classified income statement for 1983.

P21-2B Recording Manufacturing Costs. The following information for the Sage Corporation, which uses the periodic inventory system, is available for 1983:

Beginning inventories	
Direct materials	$ 13,000
Goods in process	24,000
Finished goods	37,000
Manufacturing costs incurred during the year	
Direct materials purchases	$ 75,000
Direct labor	68,000
Factory supplies	4,500
Indirect labor	16,000
Repairs	12,000
Maintenance	3,000
Utilities	15,000
Insurance (paid in previous period)	1,000
Depreciation on machinery	9,000
Selling and administrative expenses incurred during the year	
Depreciation on selling equipment	$ 900
Depreciation on office equipment	1,500
Other selling expenses	10,000
Other administrative expenses	11,000
Cash payments during the year	
Direct materials purchases	$ 70,000
Direct labor (federal income taxes withheld, $7,315;	
social security taxes withheld, $2,495)	58,190
Factory supplies	4,500
Indirect labor (federal income taxes withheld, $1,577;	
social security taxes withheld, $643)	13,780
Repairs	10,000
Maintenance	3,000
Utilities	15,000
Selling expenses	10,000
Administrative expenses	11,000
Sales (all on account)	$300,000
Ending inventories	
Diroct materials	$ 16,000
Goods in process	26,000
Finished goods	33,000

Required: Prepare summary journal entries, including closing entries, for the Sage Corporation for 1983 (disregard corporate income taxes).

P21-3B Financial Statements. Use the information in P21-2B.

Required: Prepare a cost of goods manufactured statement and an income statement of the Sage Corporation for 1983.

P21-4B   Comprehensive Problem.   The Fenner Corporation obtained the following informa-tion from its accounting records on December 31, 1983, before adjusting entries or closing entries were prepared. The company uses the periodic inventory system.

Cash	$ 75,000
Accounts receivable	45,000
Allowance for uncollectible accounts	9,000
Prepaid insurance on factory machinery	36,000
Direct materials inventory	60,000
Goods in process inventory	84,000
Finished goods inventory	132,000
Direct materials purchases	160,000
Machinery	232,000
Accumulated depreciation: Machinery	110,000
Office building	440,000
Accumulated depreciation: Office building	120,000
Accounts payable	75,000
Common stock, $5 par	150,000
Additional paid-in capital	55,000
Bonds payable	300,000
Retained earnings	61,700
Sales	850,000
Direct labor	140,000
Factory overhead	174,000
Selling expenses	57,000
Administrative expenses	105,000
Federal income taxes payable	6,200
Social security taxes payable	3,100

Additional Information for 1983:
1. Bad debt expense is $6,000.
2. Insurance worth $12,000 on the factory remains in effect for the next year.
3. On December 31, 1983, a physical count determined that the direct materials, goods in process, and finished goods inventories were $75,000, $96,000, and $120,000, respectively.
4. Depreciation on the machinery and the office building were $36,000 and $24,000, respectively.
5. Direct labor earned by employees but not yet paid amounted to $8,000. Federal income taxes and social security taxes on these wages were $1,570 and $450, respectively.

Required: 1. Prepare adjusting entries at the end of 1983.
  2. Prepare closing entries at the end of 1983 (disregard corporate income taxes)
  3. Prepare the cost of goods manufactured for 1983, the income statement for 1983, and the balance sheet at December 31, 1983.

P21-5B **Manufacturing Costs.** At the beginning of 1983 the Ackerman Company had beginning inventories of direct materials, goods in process, and finished goods of $14,000, $46,000, and $39,000, respectively. Selected general ledger accounts for the year included the following partial entries:

Cash		
Insurance	9,000	
Direct materials	37,000	
Direct labor	76,000	
Indirect labor	68,000	
Supplies	13,000	
Utilities	11,000	

Federal Income Taxes Payable		
	Direct labor	17,000
	Indirect labor	15,400

Utilities Payable		
	Bal. 1/1/83	–0–
		2,000
	Bal. 12/31/81	2,000

Accounts Payable (for Direct Materials)		
37,000	Bal. 1/1/83	8,000
		47,000

Social Security Taxes Payable		
	Direct labor	4,750
	Indirect labor	4,200

The direct materials used during the year were $40,000. The ending inventories of goods in process and finished goods were $52,000 and $61,000, respectively. A 3-year insurance policy on the factory was purchased on January 1.

Required: 1. Reconstruct the summary journal entries that were made during 1983, including closing entries (through to the closing of the Cost of Goods Sold account).
2. Prepare a cost of goods manufactured statement for 1983.

DISCUSSION CASES

C21-1 **Loss of Accounting Records.** On June 30, 1983, a fire destroyed some of the accounting records of the Watkins Manufacturing Company. The following amounts were obtained from the accounting records that were not destroyed:

Costs incurred, January 1 to June 30
Direct materials purchases . . . . $ 30,000
Direct labor 40,000
Factory overhead 55,000
Sales, January 1 to June 30 . . . . $120,000

The company took a physical inventory immediately after the fire and found that the inventory amounts were:

Direct materials $16,000
Goods in process 27,000
Finished goods 34,000

David Watkins, the owner of the company, believed that the gross profit ratio of the company in the past had been 40% and he had no reason to believe that the ratio had changed. Some of the records that were not destroyed showed that direct labor was usually twice the amount of the direct materials used in production. The company also tried to maintain a direct materials inventory at the end of the year that was half the cost of the goods in process inventory at the time.

Required: Prepare a cost of goods manufactured statement and an income statement (through the calculation of gross profit) for January 1 to June 30, 1983.

C21-2 Pricing Policy. Fred Fast operates Friendly Motors, a car restoration company. Fred took an accounting class in college many years ago, and he can still remember the professor saying, "If you don't cover all your costs, you can't make a profit." Fred is fairly conservative, and therefore at the beginning of each month he estimates the number of cars he can expect to restore during the month. He then estimates his factory overhead costs and, by dividing the costs by the expected restorations, he determines the factory overhead costs per restoration. By adding this figure to the amount of labor and materials that he estimates will be used in each restoration, he calculates the lowest price that he can charge for each restoration (ignore other expenses). If Fred has a good month and it appears that the number of restorations will exceed his estimate, he is willing to lower his price. Although he is not sure, he thinks that in these successful months his revenues actually increase in the last few days of the month.

Required: Discuss the appropriateness of Fred's pricing policy. Is there an alternative policy that would be preferable?

22 Cost Accounting Systems for Product Costing

After reading this chapter, you should understand:

- The reasons for recording actual manufacturing costs
- The basic structure of cost accounting systems
- The use of perpetual inventory systems and subsidiary ledgers for Raw Materials Inventory, Goods in Process Inventory, and Finished Goods Inventory accounts
- How manufacturing costs are applied to units in a job order costing system
- The use of predetermined factory overhead rates
- How manufacturing costs are applied to units in a process costing system

In Chapter 21 we introduced some of the unique aspects of accounting for the operations of a manufacturing company. We explained how three inventory accounts, one for direct materials, another for goods in process, and a third for finished goods, could be used to account for the costs of manufacturing a product. These manufacturing costs include direct materials, direct labor, and factory overhead. Manufacturing costs become expenses in the income statement only when the units of manufactured product are sold. They are deducted as cost of goods sold from sales revenue to compute the gross profit for the period. If units of manufactured product are not sold, the related costs are included in the balance sheet as ending inventory. Selling expenses and general and administrative expenses are not included in cost of goods sold or in inventory but are deducted from gross profit in the income statement as expenses of the period in which they are incurred.

In this chapter we introduce two kinds of cost accounting systems commonly used to assign manufacturing costs to units of manufactured product. These systems are called job order costing and process costing. Adoption of a job order or process cost accounting system is the only practical way for manufacturing companies to obtain timely information necessary for the following five activities:

1. Preparing financial statements.
2. Planning the company's manufacturing operations.
3. Deciding what products to manufacture, what operations to use in their production, how many units of each to produce, and perhaps even what selling prices to charge for them.

4. Evaluating the performance of manufacturing operations, departments, and individual employees.
5. Maintaining control over manufacturing costs and discovering ways to reduce costs and improve efficiency.

Although our discussion centers on accounting systems for manufacturing operations, many of the ideas and procedures described could be modified to develop cost accounting systems for nonmanufacturing operations. Hospitals, governmental organizations, airlines, banks, and social service agencies can also use cost accounting systems.

THE STRUCTURE OF COST ACCOUNTING SYSTEMS

Costs are incurred as goods and services are acquired by a manufacturing company. A system of accounts can easily show the amount of cost incurred for each of many *inputs* to the company's operations. Expense accounts for rent, utilities, and employee wages, as well as asset accounts for land, manufacturing equipment, prepaid insurance, and raw materials inventory,[1] are used for this purpose.

The task of the cost accounting system is to reclassify the costs incurred in order to show their association with *activities* performed and the product *output* of those activities. To accomplish this, most cost accounting systems use the recording and reporting procedures described in the early chapters of this book. Journals and general ledgers, control accounts and supporting subsidiary ledgers, worksheets, and a variety of reporting forms are used by managerial accountants to record, analyze, and report the cost information needed by their companies. We begin by describing the structure of the ledger and the kinds of entries necessary to associate manufacturing costs with units of product output.

Ledger Accounts and Cost Flows

THE PERPETUAL INVENTORY METHOD. In Chapter 21 we used a periodic inventory system to explain more thoroughly the components of manufacturing cost and the inventory accounts of manufacturing companies. Most cost accounting systems, however, use a perpetual inventory system to record Raw Materials Inventory, Goods in Process Inventory, and Finished Goods Inventory, and for this reason we use a perpetual inventory system in this chapter. As described in Chapter 9, in a perpetual inventory system a continuous record is kept of the balance of an inventory account. For a merchandising company this involves increasing (debiting) the inventory account for the cost of all merchandise purchases and decreasing (crediting) this account for the cost of merchandise sold. If an item is purchased on account for $100, the journal entry to record the purchase would be:

---

[1] In Chapter 21 we explained that raw materials includes both direct and indirect materials. To simplify the discussion in that chapter we assumed that no inventory of indirect materials existed; we therefore used an account entitled Direct Materials Inventory. In this chapter to account for the more usual case where a company does have an inventory of indirect materials, we use a Raw Materials Inventory account for both direct and indirect materials.

```
Inventory  . . . . . . . . . . . . . . . . . . . . . . . . . . . . . . .  100
    Accounts Payable . . . . . . . . . . . . . . . . . . . . . . . . .       100
To record purchase of merchandise.
```

If the item is sold on account for $160 two journal entries would be made, one to record the revenue from the sale and one to record the cost of merchandise (goods) sold. These journal entries are as follows:

```
Accounts Receivable . . . . . . . . . . . . . . . . . . . . . . . .  160
    Sales . . . . . . . . . . . . . . . . . . . . . . . . . . . . . . . .       160
To record revenue from the sale of merchandise.

Cost of Goods Sold  . . . . . . . . . . . . . . . . . . . . . . . .  100
    Inventory . . . . . . . . . . . . . . . . . . . . . . . . . . . . . .       100
To record the cost of merchandise sold.
```

For a manufacturing company the perpetual system is used for all three inventory accounts. The Raw Materials Inventory is increased by the cost of raw materials purchased and decreased by the cost of raw materials used in production. The Goods in Process Inventory is increased by the cost of direct materials, direct labor, and factory overhead used in production and decreased by the cost of units completed. The Finished Goods Inventory is increased by the cost of units completed and decreased by the cost of units sold.

When a manufacturing company uses a perpetual inventory system it knows its inventory balances and cost of goods sold as soon as its journal entries are posted to the inventory accounts. This system is in contrast to the periodic inventory system in which the inventory balances and cost of goods sold are known only after closing entries are made at the end of an accounting period. We carefully explain and illustrate the journal entries used by a manufacturing company with a perpetual inventory system as we discuss how cost accounting systems work.

THE FLOW OF MANUFACTURING COSTS.   When a perpetual inventory system is used by a manufacturing company, manufacturing costs almost seem as if they flow through the accounts, entering the system as they are incurred and then flowing into the Goods in Process Inventory account, where they are assigned to specific units of product as manufacturing operations take place. **Cost application is the assignment of manufacturing costs to specific units of product.** Direct materials, direct labor, and factory overhead costs are "applied" by debiting them to one or more Goods in Process Inventory accounts set up to show the costs incurred to produce a unit or group of units.

Exhibit 22-1 provides a description of the basic manufacturing cost flows through the general ledger accounts. In this exhibit the cost flows are shown by arrows. Each arrow from the credit side of one account to the debit side of another account represents a journal entry transferring costs from one account to the next. Notice how direct materials, direct labor, and factory overhead costs all flow into the Goods in Process Inventory account where they are applied to units of product.

EXHIBIT 22-1   Basic Manufacturing Cost Flows in a Cost Accounting System

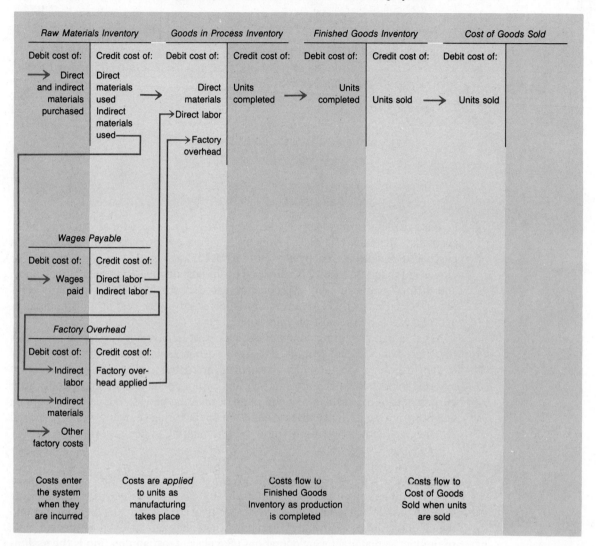

Note in Exhibit 22-1 that the costs of both direct and indirect materials are recorded in a single inventory account, Raw Materials Inventory, when they are purchased. We do *not* use a separate inventory account for direct materials in this chapter, nor do we use a Direct Materials Purchases account. The cost of direct materials *used* is applied directly to Goods in Process Inventory. Indirect materials are added to Factory Overhead, however. Similarly, while the costs of direct labor are applied directly to Goods in Process Inventory, the costs of indirect labor are added to Factory Overhead. Since we are using a perpetual inventory system in this chapter, we do not need a Direct Labor account as was used in Chapter 21.

We now explain the fundamental procedures required by job order costing and process costing systems. The procedures of these systems produce cost flows through the accounts as pictured in Exhibit 22-1. Because job order costing is easier to understand, it is discussed first.

JOB ORDER COSTING

Some manufacturing companies produce many different products in a wide variety of sizes and colors or with other unique features that might be requested by specific customers. For example, in furniture manufacturing, sofas might be produced in several styles with many upholstery options. Tables, chairs, dressers, and cabinets may vary as to style, wood used, and type of finish.

When one or many units of a particular kind and style are needed, the required units are processed together by sending them through the necessary manufacturing operations until they are finished. **A job order is a group of similar units being processed together.** Job orders are often started as a result of purchase orders for particular items from specific customers.

In job order manufacturing, production departments such as machine shops or assembly and finishing departments may perform manufacturing operations on hundreds of different job orders in a month's time. Also, the individual job orders may require processing in several production departments. This presents a problem for the cost accounting system, which is to determine how much of the manufacturing cost incurred in each of the several departments to apply to each of the many job orders on which those departments have worked. The cost accounting system best suited for this situation is known as a job order cost accounting system. **A job order cost accounting system is a cost accounting system in which a Goods in Process Inventory subsidiary account is kept for each job order so that the costs for each job order can be accumulated separately.**

In a job order cost system the individual job order is the key to product costing. Direct materials, direct labor, and factory overhead costs are accumulated in inventory accounts set up for each specific job order. These individual job order accounts are *not* part of the general ledger, however. Instead, a *subsidiary* ledger is used for these inventory accounts and a Goods in Process Inventory *control* account is listed in the general ledger. This is similar to the use of an accounts receivable subsidiary ledger for individual customers and an Accounts Receivable control account.

As work is done on a particular job order, the costs are applied (debited) to the account for this job order in the subsidiary ledger and to the Goods in Process Inventory control account. When a job order is completed, the total costs that have been applied to it are then taken out of the Goods in Process Inventory control account (and the subsidiary ledger) and added (debited) to the Finished Goods Inventory account.

Job Order Cost Sheets

Job order cost sheets are the subsidiary goods in process inventory ledger accounts in which the manufacturing costs for individual job orders are recorded. They are designed in a convenient form for recording the manufacturing costs as they are applied to the job order and for showing other important informa-

EXHIBIT 22-2
A Job Order
Cost Sheet

Job Order Cost Sheet

Product Description _Walnut Cabinets_   Job Order Number ___101___

Notes _Rush order! Six units to be shipped_   Units Required ___10___

to Batterson Furniture Store by March 15   Date Started _March 9_

Four units to replenish finished goods inventory   Date Completed _March 12_

Date	Direct Materials		Direct Labor		Factory Overhead Applied
	Requisition Number	Cost	Labor Ticket Number	Cost	
3-9	513	$1,100	380	$40.00	
	516	450	381	31.50	
3-11			400	37.50	
			401	21.00	
			402	35.00	
3-12	541	200	413	9.00	40 hours @ $2.40 = 96

Summary of Costs

Direct Materials	$1,750
Direct Labor	174
Factory Overhead	96
Total Job Cost	$2,020
Units	10
Cost per Unit	$202.00

tion relating to the job, such as the number of units in the job, the dates it was started and completed, and so on. Exhibit 22-2 shows an example of a job order cost sheet for a job order completed by a furniture manufacturer on March 12.

Note in Exhibit 22-2 the separate columns used to record the direct materials, direct labor, and factory overhead costs applied to this job and the summary of these costs made after the job was finished. In the following discussion of how manufacturing costs are applied to job orders, we use illustrations that relate to the March 12 entries highlighted on the job order cost sheet in Exhibit 22-2.

Application of Raw Materials Cost

When raw materials are purchased they are placed in the raw materials storeroom, and their cost is recorded in the Raw Materials Inventory account in the general ledger. For example, the purchase of raw materials costing $30,000 on account by the furniture manufacturer would be recorded by a journal entry as follows:

Raw Materials Inventory 30,000
   Accounts Payable 30,000
To record the purchase of raw materials on account. .

Note in this journal entry that the cost of raw materials purchased is added directly to the Raw Materials Inventory account. The Raw Materials Inventory account in the general ledger is a control account supported by a subsidiary raw materials ledger in which separate subsidiary accounts show the receipts, issues, and current balance for each individual raw material item.

All raw materials kept in the storeroom are the responsibility of the storekeeper. The storekeeper may not issue raw materials for use in the factory without a written authorization form, which is known as a raw materials requisition. **A raw materials requisition is a source document requesting a certain number of units of a particular raw material for a specific factory use.** When it is signed by a foreman, production supervisor, or other authorized individual, the raw materials requisition gives the storekeeper permission to issue the raw materials. Exhibit 22-3 shows an example of a raw materials requisition.

On a raw materials requisition form such as the form shown in Exhibit 22-3, the foreman fills in the item number, description, and quantity of raw materials requested. The reason for using the raw materials is also specified and the requisition is then signed. Costs are assigned to the requisition in the accounting department as discussed later.

Recall from Chapter 21 that raw materials include both direct materials and indirect materials. Direct materials were defined as raw materials that physically become part of a manufactured product. Wood, upholstery material, and fittings

EXHIBIT 22-3
Raw Materials
Requisition Form

Raw Materials Requisition
541

Item No.	Description	Quantity	Cost per Unit	Cost
885	Brass fittings	50	$ 4	$200

Requested for Job Order # _101_
or general factory use _____
by _G Jones_ Date _3-12_

Issued by _T. Hall_
Date _March 12_
Received by _G. Jones_ Date _3-12_

were given as examples of direct materials used in furniture manufacturing. The quantity and cost of direct materials used for specific job orders are easily traced to those job orders on the basis of the raw materials requisitions, and in this way direct materials cost can be applied directly to the specific job orders. Note that the raw materials requisition shown in Exhibit 22-3 is for direct materials to be used on job order number 101 and gives the information needed (requisition number 541, cost $200, and job order number 101) for the March 12 entry for direct materials on the job order cost sheet shown in Exhibit 22-2. Thus this raw materials requisition is used to trace the $200 direct materials cost to that job.

In Chapter 21 indirect materials were defined as raw materials that do not physically become part of a manufactured product, such as lubricating oil used for machinery. In practice, however, many inexpensive raw materials that actually become part of the units being produced are treated as indirect materials. This is particularly true in job order costing. The reason is that it makes little sense to spend the time and effort necessary to measure the small amounts of such raw materials used on specific job orders so that their cost can be applied directly. Thus the cost of glue, staples, screws, stain, and lacquer used in furniture manufacturing would normally not be applied directly to individual job orders. Such commonly used and inexpensive raw materials would be issued for general factory use and not for specific jobs. This would be indicated on the raw materials requisition.

After the raw materials are issued, a copy of each raw materials requisition form is sent to the accounting department. There, costs are assigned to each requisition form and the raw materials requisitions for direct materials are separated from those for indirect materials. The requisitions are then used to apply (debit) *direct* materials costs to specific job order cost sheets in the subsidiary goods in process ledger and increase (debit) the Goods in Process Inventory control account in the general ledger for the total direct materials cost applied. The total cost of *indirect* materials used is added (debited) to the Factory Overhead account to be applied to job orders along with other indirect manufacturing costs, as is discussed later. The requisitions are also used to decrease (credit) the Raw Materials Inventory control account by the total cost of all raw materials issued and the individual accounts in the subsidiary raw materials ledger by the cost of each individual raw material issued.

For example, a day's raw materials requisitions might total $14,500 for direct materials and $89 for indirect materials. Exhibit 22-4 shows a summary of these requisitions arranged by job order number. The journal entry to record the issuing of these materials would be as follows:

Goods in Process Inventory	14,500	
Factory Overhead	89	
Raw Materials Inventory		14,589

To record the issue of raw materials.

The $14,500 debit to Goods in Process Inventory would be supported by recording appropriate amounts on individual job order cost sheets in the subsidiary goods in process ledger totaling $14,500. Recording the $200 cost of brass fittings from requisition number 541 on the job cost sheet in Exhibit 22-2 is one example of these

EXHIBIT 22-4
Raw Materials
Requisition Summary

Raw Materials Requisition Summary				
Job Order Number	Requisition Number	Department	Amount	Job Order Total
101	541	4	$ 200	$ 200
102	543	3	4,600	
102	544	4	2,100	6,700
103	542	2	4,150	
103	546	3	450	4,600
104	540	2	3,000	3,000
			Total Direct	$14,500
Indirect Material				
	545	4	$40	
	547	3	49	
			Total Indirect	89
Summary for Period 3-12			Total Raw Materials	$14,589
Notes:				

supporting entries. The credit of $14,589 to Raw Materials Inventory would be supported by credits to the individual raw materials accounts in the subsidiary raw materials ledger.

Sometimes not all of the direct materials issued for a particular job order are used. When they are returned to the storeroom, the storekeeper again accepts responsibility for these materials and issues a *raw materials credit memo* showing the type, amount, and cost of direct materials returned and the job order to be credited. A copy of this memo is sent to the accounting department, where a journal entry is made crediting the Goods in Process Inventory control account (and the specific job order cost sheet) and debiting the Raw Materials Inventory control account (and the specific raw materials subsidiary ledger accounts) for the cost of the returned materials.

Application of Factory Labor Costs

Factory labor costs are also applied both directly and indirectly to jobs in a job order cost system. Recall that in Chapter 21 direct labor was defined as the labor of employees who work with the raw materials to convert or assemble them into the finished product. The wages earned by machine operators and craftsmen performing hand labor directly on the sofas, chairs, tables, and so on, are direct labor costs of furniture manufacturing. These direct labor costs can be traced directly to specific job orders on the basis of labor tickets kept by the workers showing the

EXHIBIT 22-5
Labor Ticket

Labor Ticket

#413

Date _March 12_   Employee Number _2·3-195_

Operation _Attach brass fittings_   Department Number _4_

Started _3:00_   Job Order Number _101_

Completed _5:00_   Verified by _cfm_

Time	Rate	Amount
2 hours	$4.50	$9.00

amount of time spent on each specific job. **A labor ticket is a source document showing the amount of direct labor time and cost to charge to a job order.** Exhibit 22-5 shows a sample labor ticket. Note that the $9 cost on this labor ticket is recorded on the job order cost sheet for job order number 101 shown in Exhibit 22-2.

These labor tickets are used to apply direct labor costs to jobs in the same way that raw materials requisitions are used in applying direct materials costs. The time spent on a specific job order multiplied by the worker's hourly wage rate gives the direct labor cost to be applied to that particular job for the manufacturing operation performed. Labor tickets can be sorted and summarized by job order, employee, department, or time period involved to provide information for payroll records and application of labor costs.

Direct labor costs are applied to manufactured products by debiting the Goods in Process Inventory account (and the job cost sheet of the specific jobs) and crediting the Wages Payable account. This direct application of labor cost to specific job orders, however, is only for work done on those job orders. Wages paid to the same workers for the time they spend cleaning and oiling machinery, waiting for work to do between jobs, or making equipment adjustments are normally applied *indirectly* to job orders along with indirect labor costs. Overtime premiums, the employer's share of payroll taxes, and the cost of fringe benefits such as vacation pay are normally also applied with indirect labor.

In Chapter 21 indirect labor was defined as the labor of the employees who are needed for the operation of the production process but who do not convert or assemble the direct materials into the finished product. Thus wages paid for supervision, maintenance, materials handling, storekeeping, inspecting, and so on, are applied *indirectly* to jobs through the application of factory overhead. When indirect labor costs are incurred, the Factory Overhead account is debited and the Wages Payable account is credited.

The journal entry to record direct and indirect labor costs is similar to the journal entry made to record direct and indirect materials cost. For example, suppose payroll records show that wages and salaries of factory personnel for a month total

$48,000. If a summary of labor tickets shows that only $31,000 is for direct labor on specific job orders, the journal entry to record these costs would be:

Goods in Process Inventory	31,000	
Factory Overhead	17,000	
Wages Payable		48,000

To record direct and indirect labor costs incurred.

The $31,000 debit is to the Goods in Process Inventory control account in the general ledger. The labor tickets would also be used to determine the amounts (totaling $31,000) that would be applied to the individual job order cost sheets in the subsidiary goods in process ledger. The $9 entry for job order number 101 (Exhibit 22-2) based on labor ticket number 413 in Exhibit 22-5 is an example of applying direct labor cost to an individual job order cost sheet.

Application of Factory Overhead Costs

The amount of direct materials cost applied to a particular job order is the specific direct materials cost incurred because the job order was manufactured. This amount is traced to the job order with information from raw materials requisitions. Similarly, the amount of direct labor cost applied to a job order is the specific direct labor cost incurred because the job order was manufactured. This direct labor cost is traced to each job order through information recorded on labor tickets. Note that direct materials costs and direct labor costs are costs incurred because of specific manufacturing activities performed on specific job orders, and they can be easily traced to the particular job orders.

Factory overhead costs are quite different, however, and as a result, the manner in which they are applied must also be different. Factory overhead includes a wide variety of costs. It includes depreciation, insurance and property taxes on factory plant and equipment, utility costs, supplies, indirect labor costs, and indirect materials costs. Almost all factory overhead costs are incurred for the general benefit of manufacturing activity and not specifically because of individual job orders. For example, no individual job can be considered the cause for incurring depreciation on a factory building, although all jobs, of course, benefit from that cost being incurred.

Because all job orders share the benefit of the resources and services obtained by incurring factory overhead costs, these costs are also applied to the job orders. Individual factory overhead costs, however, cannot be applied directly to a job order in the way that direct labor and direct materials costs are applied. All factory overhead costs are instead added together and applied *indirectly* by assigning amounts to job orders in proportion to the amount of manufacturing activity devoted to each job order. For this purpose, manufacturing activity might be measured by direct labor hours, machine hours, or direct labor cost used on each job. If direct labor hours are used, for example, a job requiring 10 hours of direct labor would have twice as much factory overhead applied to it as another job requiring 5 hours of direct labor.

This procedure does not apply to each job order the exact amount of factory overhead resulting because that job order was manufactured. The procedure applies factory overhead cost roughly in proportion to the benefits received by the individual job orders, however, which is a desirable and reasonable result.

PREDETERMINED OVERHEAD RATES. In order to use a perpetual inventory system with a goods in process inventory, it is necessary to apply factory overhead costs to individual job orders when manufacturing operations take place or at the time job orders are completed. Therefore an overhead *rate* (cost per direct labor hour, machine hour, or direct labor dollar) is set at the beginning of the year. Such a rate is called a predetermined overhead rate. **A predetermined overhead rate is an overhead rate determined at the beginning of a year by dividing the year's expected factory overhead by the expected volume of activity.** For example, suppose that a company wished to apply factory overhead costs to job orders based on the number of direct labor hours (DLH) worked on each job order. If it expects $120,000 of factory overhead costs to be incurred during the year and expects 50,000 direct labor hours to be worked, the predetermined overhead rate would be as follows:

$$\text{Predetermined overhead rate} = \frac{\text{Expected factory overhead cost for the year}}{\text{Expected direct labor hours for the year}}$$

$$= \frac{\$120,000}{50,000 \text{ DLH}}$$

$$= \$2.40/\text{DLH}$$

Having established this rate at the beginning of the year, the company uses it to apply factory overhead costs throughout the whole year. A job order requiring 10 hours of direct labor would have $24 (10 DLH × $2.40/DLH) applied whether it was produced in January or December. Another job order requiring 40 direct labor hours would have four times as much factory overhead cost applied (40 DLH × $2.40/DLH = $96) as the job order requiring 10 hours of direct labor effort.

As factory overhead costs are incurred they are added (debited) to the factory overhead account. A month's cost might be recorded with the following summary journal entry (amounts assumed):

Factory Overhead	5,700	
Accounts Payable		1,700
Accumulated Depreciation: Factory Building		2,100
Accumulated Depreciation: Factory Equipment		1,600
Prepaid Insurance		300

To record factory overhead incurred.

The journal entry to apply factory overhead to a job order requiring 40 direct labor hours during the month (assuming a predetermined overhead rate of $2.40 per DLH) would be:

Goods in Process Inventory	96	
Factory Overhead		96

To apply factory overhead.

The $96 debit to Goods in Process Inventory increases the balance of that control account in the general ledger. The overhead cost is also applied to the specific job order by recording the $96 in the factory overhead column of that job order cost sheet, as shown in Exhibit 22-2.

OVERAPPLIED AND UNDERAPPLIED OVERHEAD. By using a predetermined overhead rate, the managerial accountant does not have to wait until the end of the year when the *actual* total factory overhead cost incurred is known before applying that cost to job orders. The actual factory overhead, however, may not be equal to the expected factory overhead for the year, or the number of direct labor hours actually worked may be different from the expected number of hours. In both cases the total factory overhead *applied* to all job orders manufactured during a year does not equal the total factory overhead *incurred*. When this happens a balance remains in the Factory Overhead account at the end of the year.

If more factory overhead cost is incurred than is applied during the year, at the end of the year the total of the debits in the Factory Overhead account exceeds the total of the credits and factory overhead is "underapplied" by the amount of the debit balance. If more factory overhead is applied than is incurred, a credit balance exists in the Factory Overhead account at the end of the year and factory overhead is "overapplied." Managerial accountants can often estimate factory overhead costs and activity levels quite accurately. As a result of this accuracy the amount by which factory overhead is overapplied or underapplied is seldom very large and the balance of the Factory Overhead account is closed at year end to the Cost of Goods Sold account.

For example, suppose for the company which just computed its predetermined overhead rate to be $2.40 per direct labor hour ($120,000 ÷ 50,000 DLH) that 53,000 direct labor hours were actually worked and $126,000 of factory overhead costs were actually incurred. Throughout the year this company would record total debits in its Factory Overhead account of $126,000 (the total actually incurred). The company, however, would have applied factory overhead at a predetermined overhead rate of $2.40 on each direct labor hour worked. As a result, the total amount applied at the end of the year (the total credits to the Factory Overhead account) is $127,200 (53,000 DLH × $2.40/DLH). Thus factory overhead would be *overapplied* by $1,200 ($127,200 applied − $126,000 incurred), and the Factory Overhead account would have a credit balance of that amount at the end of the year. This balance would be closed at the end of the year to Cost of Goods Sold with the following journal entry:

Factory Overhead	1,200	
Cost of Goods Sold		1,200

To close overapplied factory overhead to cost of goods sold.

Note that the credit to Cost of Goods Sold reduces its balance. This is reasonable because when factory overhead is overapplied, more than the actual total of factory overhead has been added to the Goods in Process Inventory account. This excess flows to Finished Goods Inventory as units are completed and to Cost of Goods Sold as completed units are sold. Thus when factory overhead is overapplied, the Cost of Goods Sold account balance is overstated. The credit to that account offsets this overstatement. Similarly, if factory overhead had been underapplied (i.e., the Factory Overhead account has a debit balance at year-end), the Cost of Goods Sold account balance would be understated and the closing entry would correct for this understatement with a *debit* to the Cost of Goods Sold account (and a credit to Factory Overhead).

Recording the Completion of Job Orders

When a job order is completed it is removed from the factory and taken to the finished goods storeroom. Its cost, calculated on the job order cost sheet, is transferred from the Goods in Process Inventory account into the Finished Goods Inventory account. For example, completion of the job order having the job order cost sheet shown in Exhibit 22-2 would be recorded with the following journal entry:

Finished Goods Inventory	2,020	
Goods in Process Inventory		2,020

To record transfer of completed goods to finished goods inventory.

The job order cost sheet of the completed job order would be removed from the goods in process subsidiary ledger. If the company involved also keeps a subsidiary finished goods ledger, the costs of the completed job order would be added to an account in that ledger. Each unit of the completed job order would be assigned the *cost per unit* calculated on the job cost sheet (see Exhibit 22-2).

Recording the Sale of Finished Goods

When a perpetual inventory system is used for the finished goods inventory, two entries are required to record a sale. First, an entry would be made to record the revenue from the sale. If the six units from the completed job order with the job order cost sheet shown in Exhibit 22-2 had been sold to the Batterson Furniture Store on credit at a price of $2,500, the journal entry to record the revenue from this sale would be:

Accounts Receivable	2,500	
Sales		2,500

To record revenue from the sale of finished goods.

Second, the cost of the units that are sold is transferred from the Finished Goods Inventory account to the Cost of Goods Sold account. For example, the cost of the six units delivered to the Batterson Furniture Store would be transferred to cost of goods sold by the following journal entry:

```
Cost of Goods Sold  . . . . . . . . . . . . . . . . . . . . . . .    1,212
    Finished Goods Inventory  . . . . . . . . . . . . . . . . . .              1,212
To record the cost of goods sold (6 units @ $202.00 per unit).
```

COMPREHENSIVE EXAMPLE OF JOB ORDER COSTING

We have discussed the basic procedures needed for a job order costing system. We have illustrated important source documents and described the kinds of journal entries necessary for applying manufacturing costs to job orders and for recording the completion of those job orders and the sale of units from them. We now conclude the discussion with a comprehensive illustration of job order costing procedures.

The Problem

The Weber Diary Company is a small custom printing shop and book bindery specializing in diaries, address books, calendars, appointment books, note pads, and so on, which are usually printed with the customer's name on the front cover. These items are used by most of Weber's customers as promotional materials. April's transactions are summarized below:

(a) The company worked on five jobs during April. Job order 41 was in process at the beginning of April. Costs applied prior to April 1 were direct materials $2,050, direct labor $120, and factory overhead $180. Job orders 42–45 were started during April.

(b) Raw materials purchased on account and taken to the storeroom:

Paper	$12,600
Covers	1,150
Binding materials	450
Inks	300
Total raw materials purchases	$14,500

(c) The raw materials requisition summary for the month showed direct and indirect materials issued as follows:

Direct materials for		
Job order 42	$ 300	
Job order 43	1,200	
Job order 44	4,600	
Job order 45	2,340	$8,440
Indirect materials		210
Total raw materials issued		$8,650

(d) A summary of the month's labor tickets showed:

Direct labor for		
Job order 41 (180 hours)	$ 720	
Job order 42 (25 hours)	100	
Job order 43 (60 hours)	255	
Job order 44 (300 hours)	1,275	
Job order 45 (200 hours)	840	$3,190
Indirect labor		1,640
Total factory labor		$4,830

(e) Excess binding materials costing $25, which were issued for use in job order 44, were returned to the storeroom.

(f) The month's factory overhead costs incurred in addition to indirect materials and indirect labor were:

Rent on factory building (paid monthly)	$1,000
Depreciation on factory equipment	1,100
Utilities (paid monthly)	350
Property taxes on factory assets (to be paid in December)	160
Insurance (prepaid)	110
Total	$2,720

(g) Factory overhead is applied at a predetermined overhead rate of $6 per direct labor hour.

(h) Job orders 41, 42, 43, and 44 were completed and transferred to finished goods inventory.

(i) All of the units in job orders 41, 42, and 43 were shipped to customers. Of the 10,000 units produced in job order 44, 1,200 were shipped to customers; the remaining units are in finished goods inventory. Sales revenue totaled $13,850.

Required:

1. Set up the subsidiary goods in process ledger, recording the costs applied to the various job orders during the month, computing the total costs of each completed job order, and determining the goods in process inventory at the end of April.

2. Prepare summary journal entries necessary to record the month's transactions.

3. Calculate the amount by which factory overhead was overapplied or underapplied during April.

The Solution

1. The subsidiary goods in process ledger is used to determine the cost of manufacturing individual job orders. The subsidiary goods in process ledger of Weber Diary is presented below. It shows the direct materials, direct labor, and factory overhead costs applied to each individual job order on which the company worked during April. Note that job order number 41 was the only job order in process on April 1. The total of the costs that had been applied to it in March ($2,350) would be the balance in the Goods in Process Inventory control account on April 1.

Subsidiary Goods in Process Ledger (job order cost sheets)

	Job order 41	Job order 42	Job order 43	Job order 44	Job order 45
Applied in March:					
Direct materials	$2,050				
Direct labor	120				
Factory overhead	180				
Total	$2,350				
Applied in April:					
Direct materials		$300	$1,200	$4,600	$2,340
				(25)	
Direct labor	$ 720	100	255	1,275	840
Factory overhead	1,080[a]	150	360	1,800	1,200
Total job order costs	$4,150	$550	$1,815	$7,650	$4,380

Completed job orders
Total cost applied = $14,165

Ending Goods
in Process
Inventory
Balance

[a] 180 direct labor hours [from item (d)] × $6.00 per hour.

The costs shown on the job order cost sheets as being applied in April to the job orders come from the information listed in items (c), (d), (e), and (g) of the summary of transactions. Direct materials costs are applied on the basis of the raw materials requisition summary (item c). Note that some direct materials issued for job order number 44 were returned to the storeroom (item e) and that $25 of direct materials cost is removed from that job order.

Direct labor costs are applied to the job orders on the basis of the summary of labor tickets (item d). To determine the amount of factory overhead to be applied to each job order, Weber's predetermined overhead rate of $6 per direct labor hour (given in item g) is multiplied by the number of direct labor hours devoted to each job order, which is given in the summary of work tickets (item d). For example, the $1,080 of factory overhead applied to job order number 41 was computed by multiplying 180 direct labor hours times the $6 per hour predetermined factory overhead rate.

Note that the $14,165 total cost of completed job orders (41, 42, 43, and 44) is easily determined by adding the cost totals of their job cost sheets. This is the cost of the job orders completed in April transferred from Goods in Process Inventory to Finished Goods Inventory in Requirement 2. The only job order not completed is job order 45. The total cost applied to job order 45 ($4,380) is the balance of Weber's ending Goods in Process Inventory account on April 30.

2. The journal entries that Weber Diary would make for the summarized transactions are shown below. The entries are presented in the order listed in the transaction summary. Note that no entry is required for the information given

as item (a) in the transaction summary. Entries related to that information have already been made by Weber (in March).

Journal entries:

(b)   *Raw Materials Purchases*

Raw Materials Inventory	14,500	
Accounts Payable		14,500

To record the purchase of raw materials on account.

(c)   *Issue of Raw Materials*

Goods in Process Inventory	8,440	
Factory Overhead	210	
Raw Materials Inventory		8,650

To record the issue of raw materials.

(d)   *Factory Labor Usage*

Goods in Process Inventory	3,190	
Factory Overhead	1,640	
Wages Payable		4,830

To record direct and indirect labor costs incurred.

(e)   *Return of Direct Materials*

Raw Materials Inventory	25	
Goods in Process Inventory		25

To record the return of direct materials to the storeroom.

(f)   *Factory Overhead Incurred*

Factory Overhead	2,720	
Accumulated Depreciation: Factory Equipment		1,100
Property Taxes Payable		160
Prepaid Insurance		110
Cash		1,350

To record factory overhead incurred.

(g)   *Factory Overhead Application*

Goods in Process Inventory	4,590	
Factory Overhead		4,590

To apply factory overhead (765 DLH $\times$ $6/DLH).

(h)   *Completion of Job Orders*

Finished Goods Inventory   14,165
    Goods in Process Inventory . . . .   14,165[a]

To record the transfer of completed goods to finished goods
inventory.

[a]Job order 41	$ 4,150
Job order 42	550
Job order 43	1,815
Job order 44	7,650
	$14,165

(i)   *Sale of Finished Goods*

Accounts Receivable   13,850
    Sales   13,850

To record revenue from the sale of finished goods.

Cost of Goods Sold . . . .   7,433[a]
    Finished Goods Inventory   7,433

To record the cost of goods sold.

[a]Job order 41	$4,150
Job order 42	550
Job order 43	1,815
Job order 44	918 (1,200 units @ $.765* per unit)
	$7,433

*$.765 = $7,650 ÷ 10,000 units.

3. Weber Diary overapplied its factory overhead during April. The amount of
   overapplied factory overhead is computed by subtracting factory overhead incurred from factory overhead applied. In the computation of overapplied factory
   overhead shown below, note the inclusion of indirect materials and labor with
   other factory overhead costs incurred during April.

Factory overhead applied (765 DLH × $6)		$4,590
Factory overhead incurred:		
Indirect materials	$ 210	
Indirect labor	1,640	
Other	2,720	4,570
Overapplied factory overhead (for April)		$ 20

PROCESS COSTING

Recall that the job order costing system discussed in the previous section is well
suited for a company producing a variety of products in small quantities to customers' orders and where each of several manufacturing departments works on many

products. In some industries, however, companies produce large volumes of identical units of few products. In many cases the nature of the products or the high demand for each requires the company to organize manufacturing operations of each product *separately* to obtain smooth, continuous, and efficient production. That is, each manufacturing process is devoted to a single product, such as bricks, sugar, or baseballs.

Sometimes only one process is needed to produce a product, and at other times, several manufacturing processes are needed to produce one product. In these cases the operations or processes are normally arranged so that the units flow from one to another continuously as each stage of their production is completed. In each process, however, only one product is worked on and the manufacturing operations are performed on large quantities of identical units of that product continuously over long periods of time. Examples of such manufacturing can be found in the production of paper, flour, some chemicals, and many other products.

The cost accounting system best suited to apply manufacturing costs to units of a product manufactured in this way is the process cost accounting system. **A process cost accounting system is a cost accounting system that sets up a Goods in Process Inventory account for each manufacturing process to accumulate the costs to be applied to the units produced in that process.** That is, a process cost accounting system uses manufacturing *processes* as the points of cost accumulation. As manufacturing takes place, direct materials, direct labor, and factory overhead costs incurred in a process are added (debited) to a Goods in Process Inventory account set up for that process. Since only one product is being produced continuously in the process, these accumulated manufacturing costs are applied to the units of that product. This is usually done at the end of each month.

Single Process Manufacturing

Sometimes a product is manufactured completely in a single process. For example, a cleaning solvent might be manufactured by mixing several chemicals in a single mixing process. All the manufacturing costs incurred during a month in that process are applied to the units manufactured in the process during the month. This includes the cost of the direct materials used in the process and the direct labor cost incurred. It also includes the factory overhead cost applied using a predetermined overhead rate as described in the job order costing section of this chapter.

As these costs are incurred, they are recorded in the same way as in job order costing except that they are added (debited) to the Goods in Process Inventory account for the *process* rather than to individual job order cost sheets. A company that has many manufacturing processes could set up a subsidiary goods in process ledger with an account for each process; it would then include a single Goods in Process Inventory control account in its general ledger. A company does not normally have many processes, however. In this situation the Goods in Process Inventory account for *each* process is put in the general ledger. In our discussion we assume this to be the case.

NO BEGINNING OR ENDING GOODS IN PROCESS INVENTORIES. The simplest process costing situation is when a process has no inventory of unfinished units at either the beginning or the end of a month. In this case all of the units manufactured during a month have to be started and completed during the month. Each unit completed would be assigned the *average* unit cost of direct materials, direct labor, and factory overhead.

In process costing, the direct labor cost and factory overhead cost are often added together and assigned to units as a single cost element called processing cost in order to simplify computations. This is a common practice and we use it throughout this chapter. **Processing cost is the sum of direct labor and factory overhead costs.** Direct materials costs are assigned separately. Thus our discussion of single process manufacturing involves assigning two cost elements to units, direct materials cost and processing cost.

For example, suppose that a company produces 1,500 units of a product during April in a single process. There are no unfinished units at the beginning or at the end of April. During the month a total of $7,500 ($3,000 of direct materials, $2,000 of direct labor, and $2,500 of factory overhead) was recorded (debited) in the Goods in Process Inventory account. These costs are treated as two cost elements, $3,000 of direct materials and $4,500 ($2,000 + $2,500) of processing cost, and are assigned to the 1,500 units as shown below:

Average Costs per Unit

	Total Costs Accumulated in Goods in Process Inventory		Units		Average Costs per Unit
Direct materials	$3,000	÷	1,500	=	$2.00
Processing	4,500[a]	÷	1,500	=	3.00
Total	$7,500				

[a] $2,000 direct labor + $2,500 factory overhead.

Costs Assigned

To units completed and transferred to finished goods inventory		
Direct materials	1,500 units @ $2.00	=	$3,000
Processing	1,500 units @ $3.00	=	4,500
Total costs assigned			$7,500

The journal entry made to remove the cost of completed units from the Goods in Process Inventory account would be as follows:

Finished Goods Inventory	7,500	
Goods in Process Inventory		7,500

To record the transfer of completed units to finished goods inventory.

Each completed unit would be assigned the same amount of cost ($2.00 per unit average direct materials cost plus $3.00 per unit average processing cost). Since $7,500 was debited to Goods in Process Inventory as direct materials and processing costs were incurred, the above journal entry reduces this inventory account balance to zero. The computations shown may seem more complicated than are necessary for this simple example. It is important to note the steps used in these computations, however. With some modification the same steps can be used to handle much more complex situations. The three steps are to (1) compute the total for each cost element (direct materials and processing costs), (2) compute the average direct materials cost per unit and the average processing cost per unit, and (3) assign the total cost to the units by multiplying the number of units times the average unit costs. We now discuss the modification to these steps when a process contains unfinished units at the end of a month.

ENDING GOODS IN PROCESS INVENTORIES.   Because the manufacture of a product takes time, we often find units in a particular process at the end of a month that are only partially completed. That is, the process has an ending inventory of goods in process. When this occurs the cost assignment procedure must be modified so that costs are assigned to units completed and transferred out of the process *and* to unfinished units left in the process.[2] The modification involves counting the unfinished units as well as the units that have been completed and transferred, computing the average per unit costs for all units counted, and assigning costs to all units.

It is usually easy to count the physical units of a process regardless of whether they are completed or unfinished. The reason for counting units, however, is to compute an average cost per unit for direct materials and processing so that each average cost can be used in assigning those costs to the units involved. In order for the costs assigned to units to be reasonable, unfinished units are counted differently from completed units.

Each *completed* unit is counted as a whole unit. Each unfinished unit is counted as a part of a whole unit, however, the part being the estimated percent that the unit is complete. For example, a unit 80 percent complete is counted as 80 percent of a whole unit. Unfinished units are not normally examined individually, but the average percentage of completion is instead estimated for all unfinished units as a group. The unfinished units are then counted by multiplying the total number of physical units by their average percentage of completion. Thus, 10 units that are 40 percent complete would be counted as 4 (10 × 40%) whole units, 300 units 80 percent complete would be counted as 240 (300 × 80%) whole units, and so on.

When physical units in a process are counted this way they are called equivalent units. **The number of equivalent units in a group of physical units is the total number of physical units multiplied times their average percentage of completion.** A group of 500 completed units that are 100 percent complete would be

---

[2] To simplify this introductory discussion, we are ignoring the possibility that a third group of units, that is, lost or spoiled units, might also result from the month's operations. Accounting for the costs of spoilage or lost units is very complex and is not discussed in this book.

counted as 500 (500 × 100%) equivalent units, whereas a group of 500 unfinished units that are 40 percent complete would be counted as 200 (500 × 40%) equivalent units. The reason why such equivalent unit computations are useful is that it is usually fair to assume that the cost incurred to bring 500 units to 40 percent of completion is the same as would be incurred to complete 200 whole units. Using equivalent units to compute per unit costs allows those costs to be assigned to completed units and to unfinished units in approximately the amounts incurred for each group.

Equivalent units are counted separately for direct materials cost and processing cost because *unfinished* units may be at different stages of completion for each cost. Direct materials, for example, are often added completely to a process at the beginning of processing, whereas processing normally takes place uniformly as the direct materials are converted or assembled into units of product. In this case all physical units in the process are 100 percent complete with regard to direct materials even though their processing may be only 10 percent complete.

In this chapter we always make equivalent unit computations separately for direct materials and for processing. To simplify these computations, we assume that direct materials are always added at the beginning of processing so that both completed and unfinished units are always 100 percent complete with regard to direct materials. We also assume that processing takes place uniformly. Thus while *completed* units are 100 percent complete with regard to processing, *unfinished* units are always less than 100 percent processed.

The following example illustrates the use of equivalent unit computations in assigning direct materials and processing costs when the process has no beginning inventory but has an ending inventory of unfinished units. The Bristol Company produces product X in a single process. During January a total of $12,400 has been incurred in that process. These costs have been added (debited) to the Goods in Process Inventory account. Direct materials are added at the beginning of processing while processing takes place uniformly. Information from the operations of the process during January are shown below:

Total Costs Accumulated in Goods in Process Inventory (all added during January)		Production Information (physical units)	
Direct materials	$ 7,000	Completed and transferred . .	1,000
Processing	5,400	Ending inventory	
		(50% processed)	400
Total	$12,400	Total	1,400

Since 400 unfinished units are in this process at the end of January, the direct materials and processing costs incurred must be assigned to those units as well as to units completed and transferred out of the process. In order to compute the costs per unit, we must count the equivalent units for direct materials and processing. This is shown in the schedule on the following page:

	Physical Units	Equivalent Units for Direct Materials	Equivalent Units for Processing
Completed and transferred	1,000	1,000	1,000
Ending inventory (50% processed)	400	400	200[a]
Total	1,400	1,400	1,200

[a] 400 × 50%

Notice that in the computation of equivalent units for both direct materials and processing, each of the 1,000 *completed* units is counted as a full equivalent unit. The ending inventory of 400 *unfinished* units, however, is counted as only 200 equivalent units for processing because processing of those units is only 50 percent complete. Each unfinished unit is counted as a full equivalent unit for direct materials, however. This is because direct materials are added at the beginning of processing. Thus although the unfinished units are only 50 percent processed, they are 100 percent complete with regard to direct materials. The total of 1,400 equivalent units for direct materials is used to compute the average direct materials cost per equivalent unit, and the total of 1,200 equivalent units for processing is used to compute the average processing cost per equivalent unit. These computations are shown in the schedule below:

Average Costs per Unit

	Total Costs Accumulated in Goods in Process Inventory		Equivalent Units		Average Cost per Equivalent Unit
Direct materials	$ 7,000	÷	1,400	=	$5.00
Processing	5,400	÷	1,200	=	4.50
Total	$12,400				

Direct materials costs and processing costs can now be assigned separately to completed units and unfinished units based on the average costs per equivalent unit. This is done for each group of units (both completed and unfinished units) by multiplying the average costs per equivalent unit times the number of equivalent units in the group. These computations are shown in the schedule below:

Costs Assigned

To units completed and transferred to finished goods inventory
Direct materials	1,000 equivalent units @ $5.00	=	$5,000		
Processing	1,000 equivalent units @ $4.50	=	4,500	$ 9,500

To ending (Jan. 31) goods in process inventory (unfinished units)
Direct materials	400 equivalent units @ $5.00	=	$2,000		
Processing	200 equivalent units @ $4.50	=	900	2,900
Total costs assigned					$12,400

Notice in this computation that the total costs assigned ($12,400) equal the total costs that were accumulated in the process. On the basis of this cost assignment a journal entry would be made to transfer the costs of the completed units from the Goods in Process Inventory account to the Finished Goods Inventory account. This journal entry would be:

Finished Goods Inventory   9,500
    Goods in Process Inventory   9,500
To record the transfer of units completed in January to
finished goods inventory.

Recall that $12,400 had been added (debited) to the Goods in Process Inventory account in January. After the above entry is made to transfer the $9,500 cost of completed units to the Finished Goods Inventory, the ending balance of the Goods in Process Inventory account for this process is $2,900, the amount of cost assigned to the unfinished units. January's ending inventory becomes February's beginning inventory for this process. We now discuss a further modification of the steps used in assigning process costs to handle beginning goods in process inventories.

BEGINNING AND ENDING GOODS IN PROCESS INVENTORIES. When partially completed units are in a process at the beginning of a month, the Goods in Process Inventory account for that process has a beginning debit balance equal to the cost assigned to those units at the end of the previous month. Additional costs incurred during the month increase this balance. Thus at the end of the month the total cost accumulated in the Goods in Process Inventory account consists of (1) the beginning inventory balance and (2) additional costs added during the current month.

To determine the amount of the total cost to assign to completed units transferred out of the process (and to unfinished units still in the process at the end of the month) several methods can be used. These methods are based on the commonly used inventory flow assumptions, the LIFO, FIFO, and average cost methods. Because of its widespread use and simplicity we discuss the average cost method. The average cost method assigns the total costs of direct materials and processing separately to units at *average* costs per equivalent unit. These average costs per equivalent unit are computed by making a small modification in one of the steps previously discussed. This modification is simple and involves computing the total for each cost element by adding the amount in the beginning inventory to the amount incurred during the month. The rest of the steps are the same.

To illustrate the procedure, we continue the example of the Bristol Company by determining its cost assignment in February. Recall that our previous computations assigned direct materials costs of $2,000 and processing costs of $900 to January's ending inventory (February's beginning inventory) of goods in process. During February $11,908 of additional costs ($6,000 direct materials and $5,908 processing) are incurred in the process and added (debited) to the Goods in Process Inventory account bringing the balance to $14,808 ($2,900 + $11,908). Information from the operations of the process during February is shown on the following page:

Cost Information		Production Information (physical units)	
Costs in beginning inventory (Feb. 1)		Beginning inventory	
Direct materials	$ 2,000	(50% processed)	400
Processing	900	Added in February	1,200
Costs added during February		Total	1,600
Direct materials	6,000		
Processing	5,908	Completed and transferred . .	1,300
Total	$14,808	Ending inventory	
		(60% processed)	300
		Total	1,600

The total of $14,808 ($2,000 + $6,000 for direct materials, and $900 + $5,908 for processing) must be assigned to units for February. All of the computations needed to assign the $14,808 total costs accumulated in the Goods in Process Inventory account of the Bristol Company at the end of February are shown in Exhibit 22-6. These computations illustrate the steps needed to assign process costs to units when there are both beginning and ending goods in process inventories.

Note in Exhibit 22-6 that the computations do not differ a great deal from those used in the example presented for a process without inventories. We still follow the three basic steps, to (1) separately compute the total costs of direct materials and processing, (2) compute the average cost per (equivalent) unit for direct materials and processing, and (3) assign the total cost to the units by multiplying the average costs per equivalent unit times the number of equivalent units. On the basis of the cost assignment shown in Exhibit 22-6, the Bristol Company would make a journal entry to transfer the costs of the completed units from the Goods in Process Inventory account to the Finished Goods Inventory account. This journal entry would be as follows:

Finished Goods Inventory   12,480
    Goods in Process Inventory   12,480
To record the transfer of units completed in February to finished goods Inventory.

After this journal entry is made the ending (February 28) balance of the Goods in Process Inventory account for this process is $2,328 ($2,900 beginning balance + $11,908 added − $12,480 transferred out), which is the amount of cost assigned to the unfinished units.

Multiple Process Manufacturing

The manufacturing of some products involves more than one process. In these cases the units transferred out of a process may not be ready for sale, but they may instead require further processing in another process. Very little modification of the steps we have illustrated for assigning process costs in single process manufacturing is necessary to handle this situation.

Exhibit 22-7 shows three diagrams of simple arrangements for multiple process manufacturing. These and many more complex arrangements are commonly used

EXHIBIT 22-6   Process Cost Assignment

THE BRISTOL COMPANY
Process Cost Assignment (February)

Equivalent Unit Computations

	Physical Units	Equivalent Units for Direct Materials	Equivalent Units for Processing
Completed and transferred	1,300	1,300	1,300
Ending inventory (60% processed)	300	300	180[a]
Total	1,600	1,600	1,480

[a] 300 × 60%

Computations of Average Costs per Equivalent Unit

	Costs in Beginning Inventory	+	Costs Added During February	=	Total Costs Accumulated	÷	Equivalent Units	=	Average Costs per Equivalent Unit
Direct materials	$2,000		$ 6,000		$ 8,000	÷	1,600	=	$5.00
Processing	900		5,908		6,808	÷	1,480	=	4.60
Total	$2,900		$11,908		$14,808				

Computations of Costs Assigned

To units completed and transferred to finished goods inventory

Direct materials	1,300 equivalent units @ $5.00	=	$6,500
Processing	1,300 equivalent units @ $4.60	=	5,980	$12,480

To ending (Feb. 28) goods in process inventory

Direct materials	300 equivalent units @ $5.00	=	$1,500
Processing	180 equivalent units @ $4.60	=	828	2,328
Total costs assigned			$14,808

in the manufacture of a wide variety of products. The arrows in these diagrams show the flow of *units* from one process to the next until all necessary processing is completed and the units have been converted into finished goods. With the accounting procedures used in these multiple process situations, manufacturing *costs* flow from one Goods in Process Inventory account to the next in a manner corresponding to the flow of units through the processes. When all necessary processing has been completed, all costs assigned to the units are removed from the last process and transferred to the Finished Goods Inventory account. In the discussion to follow, we describe accounting procedures used to assign costs to units flowing through two processes as shown in the first of the three diagrams in Exhibit 22-7.

**EXHIBIT 22-7
Flow of Units
Through Multiple
Manufacturing
Processes**

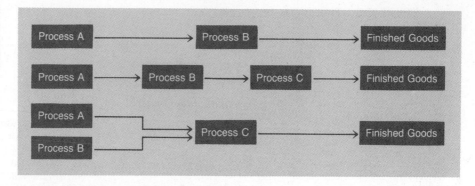

Consider the case of a product that requires processing in two processes, first in process A and then in process B. No modification of the cost assignment procedure is necessary for the cost assignment in process A. The journal entry made to transfer the costs of the completed units out of the Goods in Process Inventory account for process A, however, differs from that made in the single process case. In the single process case, completed units are finished goods. In this case, however, the completed units from process A are transferred into process B, becoming goods in process in process B. Therefore the costs assigned to the completed units from process A are transferred to the Goods in Process Inventory account for process B. For example, if $1,200 of cost is assigned to units transferred from process A to process B, the entry would be:

Goods in Process Inventory: Process B   1,200
    Goods in Process Inventory: Process A   1,200
To record the transfer of units completed in process A
to process B.

Only one modification is required in the steps needed to assign process B costs. Since the costs of units transferred from process A to process B are added (debited) to the Goods in Process Inventory: Process B account, they must be treated separately as an additional cost element in process B. That is, process B now has processing costs, costs transferred in from process A, and perhaps direct materials costs (if new direct materials are also added in process B). Although the costs transferred from process A consist of direct materials and processing costs in process A, they are treated in process B as a single cost element that is called *prior production cost*.

In the assignment of process B costs, this element of cost from prior production is treated separately from processing and direct materials cost. Prior production costs are recorded separately in the Goods in Process Inventory: Process B account. In addition, a separate equivalent units computation is made for prior production costs. Finally, prior production costs are assigned to completed and unfinished units of process B separately from the other cost elements. In this chapter we assume that prior production, like direct materials, is always added at the beginning of processing. The treatment of prior production costs is illustrated in the example discussed below.

EXAMPLE OF MULTIPLE PROCESSES. The Philadelphia Paint Company produces an exterior house paint in two processes. In process A several different oils are blended and mixed with other direct materials. This production process provides a standard paint mixture that is transferred directly to process B when completed.

In process B the standard paint mixture is added at the beginning of processing along with a new direct material, Chemical X, which is added to reduce the paint's tendency to crack and peel. The mixture is stirred, heated slightly, and cooled uniformly. Completed paint is transferred to finished goods.

Cost and production information from June's operations in process B are shown below:

Cost Information		*Production Information* *(physical units)*	
Costs in beginning inventory (June 1)		Beginning inventory	
Prior production	$ 8,700	(80% processed)	2,000
Direct materials	3,000	Added in June	51,000
Processing	720	Total	53,000
Costs added during June			
Prior production	229,800	Completed and transferred . .	50,000
Direct materials	76,500	Ending inventory	
Processing	19,520	(20% processed)	3,000
Total	$338,240	Total	53,000

The beginning balance of the Goods in Process: Process B account is $12,420 ($8,700 prior production costs, $3,000 direct materials cost, and $720 processing costs), which was assigned to unfinished units at the end of the previous month (May). Additional costs of $325,820 ($229,800 + $76,500 + $19,520) were added (debited) to the account during June, bringing its balance to a total of $338,240. The computations needed to assign the $338,240 total manufacturing costs accumulated in the Goods in Process Inventory: Process B account to the units completed and transferred to finished goods and to the unfinished units in process B at the end of June are shown in the schedules in Exhibit 22-8. In this exhibit three elements of manufacturing cost are assigned to units. The first, prior production, is the cost of the standard paint mixture transferred into process B from process A. The second cost element, direct materials, is the cost of Chemical X, which was stirred into the standard paint mixture in process B. The third, processing, is the direct labor and factory overhead cost incurred to stir, heat, and cool the mixture.

Notice in Exhibit 22-8 how prior production costs, direct materials costs, and processing costs are treated separately. Total equivalent units are counted for each cost and used to compute the costs per equivalent unit. Note that the total equivalent units for prior production and direct materials are both equal to the total physical units. This is because both the standard paint mixture and Chemical X are added

EXHIBIT 22-8   Cost Assignment Computations

THE PHILADELPHIA PAINT COMPANY
Cost Assignment Computations: Process B

Equivalent Unit Computations

| | | | Equivalent Units for | |
	Physical Units	Prior Production	Direct Materials (Chemical X)	Processing
Completed and transferred	50,000	50,000	50,000	50,000
Ending inventory (20% processed)	3,000	3,000	3,000	600[a]
Total	53,000	53,000	53,000	50,600

[a] 3,000 × 20%

Computations of Average Costs per Equivalent Unit

	Costs in Beginning Inventory	+	Costs Added During June	=	Total Costs Accumulated		Equivalent Units		Average Costs per Equivalent Unit
Prior production	$ 8,700		$229,800		$238,500	÷	53,000	=	$4.50
Direct materials	3,000		76,500		79,500	÷	53,000	=	1.50
Processing	720		19,520		20,240	÷	50,600	=	.40
Total	$12,420		$325,820		$338,240				

Computations of Costs Assigned

To units completed and transferred from process B to finished goods inventory

Prior production	50,000 equivalent units @ $4.50 = $225,000	
Direct materials	50,000 equivalent units @ $1.50 = 75,000	
Processing	50,000 equivalent units @ .40 = 20,000	$320,000

To ending (June 30) goods in process B inventory

Prior production	3,000 equivalent units @ $4.50 = $ 13,500	
Direct materials	3,000 equivalent units @ $1.50 = 4,500	
Processing	600 equivalent units @ $ .40 = 240	18,240
Total costs assigned		$338,240

at the beginning of processing. Thus all units (completed and unfinished) are 100 percent complete with regard to these elements. Equivalent units for processing differ because processing is not complete for the unfinished units.

Notice also that assignment of costs to units involves multiplying the equivalent units for prior production, direct materials, and processing in each group (completed and unfinished) by the average costs per equivalent unit. As in previous examples the total cost assigned equals the total cost that had accumulated in the account ($338,240).

On the basis of the cost assignment shown in Exhibit 22-8, the Philadelphia Paint Company would make a journal entry to transfer the cost of units completed in process B during June to the Finished Goods Inventory account. This journal entry would be:

Finished Goods Inventory	320,000	
Goods in Process Inventory: Process B		320,000

To record the transfer of units completed in process B during June to finished goods inventory.

After this journal entry is made the ending (June 30) balance of the Goods in Process Inventory: Process B account is $18,240 ($12,420 beginning balance + $325,820 added − $320,000 transferred out), which is the amount of cost assigned to the unfinished units.

CHOOSING WHICH COST ACCOUNTING SYSTEM TO USE

A company chooses the cost accounting system (job order costing or process costing) that best meets its particular needs. A company needs accurate product costing information for financial statements. It also needs information from its cost accounting system to aid in planning and controlling its operations and for a variety of decisions that have to be made. A cost accounting system can be expensive to operate, however. Thus a company must also consider how much it will cost to obtain the information it wants. Both the ability of a particular cost accounting system to provide needed information and the cost of operating that system depend largely on the way the company organizes its manufacturing operations and the nature and variety of the products it produces.

Developing an efficient cost accounting system that can provide the management of a company with the information it needs is important. In the remaining chapters of this book we discuss how information gathered in a cost accounting system can be used for planning, controlling, and decision making.

REVIEW PROBLEM

Below are listed eight items of information summarizing the transactions of the E. S. Manufacturing Company for the month of May:

(a) Raw materials of $26,500 were purchased on account.
(b) Raw materials issued for production totaled $22,000. Of this total, $21,500 was direct materials and $500 indirect materials.
(c) Factory labor records showed that 3,230 direct labor hours @ $4.50 per hour were worked and that indirect labor cost totaled $2,150.
(d) Direct materials costing $95 were returned to the raw materials storeroom.
(e) Factory overhead, other than indirect materials and indirect labor, amounted to $26,400 as follows:

Depreciation on plant and equipment	$18,000
Insurance (premium was paid earlier in the year) . . .	1,000
Property taxes (to be paid in December)	1,400
Other factory overhead costs (assume all	
paid in cash)	6,000
Total	$26,400

(f) Factory overhead is applied by the company at a predetermined overhead rate of $2.00 per direct labor *dollar*.

(g) Units completed had $65,000 of manufacturing cost assigned to them.

(h) Units costing $57,000 were sold for $90,000 on account.

Required: 1. Prepare journal entries to record the transactions of the E. S. Manufacturing Company.

2. Assume that inventory balances on May 1 were:

Raw Materials Inventory	$ 5,000
Goods in Process Inventory	10,000
Finished Goods Inventory	15,000

Set up the necessary T accounts, enter the beginning inventory balances (other accounts also have balances, but they are being ignored to simplify the problem), and post the journal entries from Requirement 1.

3. Calculate the amount of overapplied or underapplied overhead for May.

**SOLUTION TO
REVIEW
PROBLEM**

1. Journal entries:

(a)   *Raw Materials Purchases*

Raw Materials Inventory	26,500	
Accounts Payable		26,500

To record the purchase of raw materials on account.

(b)   *Issue of Raw Materials*

Goods in Process Inventory	21,500	
Factory Overhead	500	
Raw Materials Inventory		22,000

To record the issue of raw materials.

(c) *Factory Labor Usage*

Goods in Process Inventory . . . . 14,535[a]
Factory Overhead 2,150
    Wages Payable 16,685
To record direct and indirect labor costs incurred.

  [a] 3,230 hours @ $4.50 = $14,535.

(d) *Return of Direct Materials*

Raw Materials Inventory 95
    Goods in Process Inventory 95
To record the return of direct materials to the storeroom.

(e) *Factory Overhead Incurred*

Factory Overhead 26,400
    Accumulated Depreciation: Plant and Equipment 18,000
    Prepaid Insurance 1,000
    Property Taxes Payable 1,400
    Cash 6,000
To record factory overhead incurred.

(f) *Factory Overhead Application*

Goods in Process Inventory . . . . 29,070[a]
    Factory Overhead 29,070
To apply factory overhead.

  [a] $14,535 direct labor dollars × $2.00 overhead per direct labor dollar.

(g) *Completion of Production*

Finished Goods Inventory 65,000
    Goods in Process Inventory 65,000
To record the transfer of completed goods to finished
goods inventory.

(h) *Sale of Finished Goods*

Accounts Receivable 90,000
    Sales 90,000
To record the revenue from the sale of finished goods.

Cost of Goods Sold 57,000
    Finished Goods Inventory 57,000
To record the cost of goods sold.

2. Posting journal entries to the general ledger:

Raw Materials Inventory			
Balance			
(May 1) 5,000		(b)	22,000
(a) 26,500			
(d) 95			

Goods in Process Inventory			
Balance			
(May 1) 10,000		(d)	95
(b) 21,500		(g)	65,000
(c) 14,535			
(f) 29,070			

Finished Goods Inventory			
Balance			
(May 1) 15,000		(h)	57,000
(g) 65,000			

Cost of Goods Sold	
(h) 57,000	

Wages Payable	
	(c) 16,685

Factory Overhead			
(b)	500	(f)	29,070
(c)	2,150		
(e)	26,400		

Sales	
	(h) 90,000

Accounts Receivable	
(h) 90,000	

Accounts Payable	
	(a) 26,500

Cash	
	(e) 6,000

Prepaid Insurance	
	(e) 1,000

Accumulated Depreciation: Plant and Equipment	
	(e) 18,000

Property Taxes Payable	
	(e) 1,400

3. Calculation of overapplied factory overhead:

Factory overhead applied ($14,535 × $2.00 per direct labor dollar)		$29,070
Factory overhead incurred:		
Indirect materials	$ 500	
Indirect labor	2,150	
Other factory overhead costs	26,400	29,050
Overapplied factory overhead		$ 20

GLOSSARY

Cost Application. The assignment of manufacturing costs to specific units of product.

Equivalent Units. The number of physical units in a group multiplied times their average percentage of completion.

Job Order. A group of identical units being manufactured together, often in response to a specific customer order.

Job Order Cost Accounting System. A cost accounting system that accumulates manufacturing costs separately for each job order. The cost per unit for each job order is computed by dividing the total costs on the job order cost sheet by the number of units produced in that job.

Job Order Cost Sheets. Subsidiary goods in process inventory ledger accounts established to accumulate manufacturing costs separately for each job order.

Labor Ticket. A source document showing the amount of direct labor time and cost to charge to a job order.

Overapplied Overhead. The amount by which factory overhead applied exceeds the amount of factory overhead incurred for a period.

Predetermined Overhead Rate. The rate by which factory overhead is applied to production. It is computed by dividing expected factory overhead costs by the expected activity level of manufacturing operations (usually measured by direct labor hours, machine hours, or direct labor cost).

Process Cost Accounting System. A cost accounting system that accumulates manufacturing costs for each production process. The average cost per unit for the process is computed for each cost element by dividing the total costs of that element by the total related equivalent units.

Processing Cost. The total of direct labor and factory overhead costs, which is treated as a single cost element in process costing.

Raw Materials Credit Memo. A source document showing the type, amount, and cost of previously issued raw materials returned to the storeroom.

Raw Materials Requisition. A source document requesting a specific number of units of a particular raw material to be issued from the storeroom.

Underapplied Overhead. The amount by which factory overhead incurred exceeds the factory overhead applied for a period.

QUESTIONS

Q22-1 Describe the type of manufacturing company for which a job order cost accounting system is best suited.

Q22-2 What is a perpetual inventory system?

Q22-3 What is the purpose of using a subsidiary ledger of job order cost sheets to support the Goods in Process Inventory control account in a job order system?

Q22-4 What is meant by cost application?

Q22-5 Discuss the purposes of the raw materials requisition.

Q22-6 What purpose does a raw materials credit memo serve?

Q22-7 Distinguish between indirect materials and direct materials.

Q22-8 What purpose do labor tickets serve?

Q22-9 Distinguish between direct labor and indirect labor.

Q22-10 Why are factory overhead costs not applied directly to job orders?

Q22-11 Why are factory overhead rates normally predetermined?

Q22-12 Under what conditions is factory overhead overapplied?

Q22-13 Under what conditions is factory overhead underapplied? Discuss how the journal entry closing underapplied overhead to Cost of Goods Sold changes the Cost of Goods Sold balance. Why is the change desirable?

Q22-14 Describe the subsidiary ledgers that support the three inventory control accounts in the general ledger of a manufacturing company.

Q22-15 Describe the type of manufacturing company for which a process cost accounting system is best suited.

Q22-16 In a process cost accounting system, what are processing costs?

Q22-17 In a process cost accounting system, what are prior production costs?

Q22-18 How are the equivalent units for processing determined for a group of units?

Q22-19 Why do equivalent unit computations have to be made for each cost element in a process in order to properly apply the costs accumulated in the Goods in Process Inventory account?

EXERCISES

E22-1 Journal Entries for Raw Materials Costs. During May, $21,500 of raw materials were purchased on account by the Ramo Corporation. The raw materials requisition summary for May showed that raw materials were issued as follows:

Direct materials for

Job order 101	$6,435	
Job order 102	2,120	
Job order 104	3,750	
Job order 105	1,910	
Total direct materials		$14,215
Indirect materials		420
Total raw materials issued		$14,635

Required: 1. Prepare the journal entry needed to record the purchase of raw materials in May.
2. Prepare the journal entry needed to record the issue of raw materials in May.

E22-2 Journal Entries for Labor Costs. The Ramo Corporation summarized its labor tickets for May as follows:

Direct labor for

Job order 101 (275 hours) . . .	$1,512.50	
Job order 102 (290 hours) . . .	1,465.00	
Job order 104 (210 hours) . . .	1,102.50	
Job order 105 (70 hours) . . .	350.00	
Total direct labor (845 hours) . . .		$4,430.00
Total indirect labor		2,100.00
Total direct and indirect labor .		$6,530.00

Required: Prepare the journal entry to record the direct and indirect labor costs of the Ramo Corporation for May.

E22-3 Predetermined Overhead Rates. The Ramo Corporation sets its predetermined overhead rate based on the year's expected factory overhead cost and either the year's expected direct labor hours or direct labor cost (dollars). Ramo's expected factory overhead cost totals $96,000. Expected direct labor hours are 12,000 and expected direct labor cost is $64,000.

Required:
1. Compute Ramo's predetermined overhead rate per direct labor hour.
2. Compute Ramo's predetermined overhead rate per direct labor dollar.
3. Refer to E22-2. Compute the total amount of factory overhead that would be applied to job orders in May using the predetermined overhead rate per direct labor *hour* and prepare the journal entry needed to record this application.
4. Refer to E22-2. Compute the total amount of factory overhead that would be applied to jobs in May using the predetermined overhead rate per direct labor *dollar*.

E22-4 **Overapplied and Underapplied Overhead.** Harmon Metal Products computed its predetermined overhead rate to be $12.50 per machine hour by dividing its expected factory overhead costs of $125,000 by 10,000 expected machine hours for the year.

Required:
1. Compute the overapplied or underapplied overhead if actual factory overhead costs amount to $130,000 and total actual machine hours are 10,100 for the year. Prepare the journal entry needed to close the Factory Overhead account balance at the end of the year to the Cost of Goods Sold account.
2. Compute the overapplied or underapplied overhead if actual factory overhead amounts to $121,000 and total actual machine hours are 9,900 for the year. Prepare the journal entry needed to close the Factory Overhead account balance at the end of the year to the Cost of Goods Sold account.

E22-5 **Recording Completion and Sale of Job Orders.** The Contemporary Products Company records show the following cost totals (and units) on the job order cost sheets of its subsidiary goods in process ledger at the end of July:

Job order 16 . . . . $10,500 (300 units)
Job order 17 . . . . 40,250 (1,100 units)
Job order 18 . . . . 2,697 (40 units)
Job order 19 . . . . 10,750 (250 units)
Job order 20 . . . . 52,000 (2,000 units)

Job orders 16, 17, 18, and 20 were completed during the last week of July. Job orders 17 and 18 were sold completely and 400 units out of job order 20 were sold during the last week of July. Cash was received for the total of these sales in the amount of $105,000.

Required:
1. Prepare the journal entry needed to record the completion of job orders during the last week of July.
2. Prepare the journal entries needed to record the sales that occurred during the last week of July.

E22-6 **Equivalent Units for Processing.** The May Company uses process costing for a single product produced in process B.

Required: Compute the number of equivalent units for processing in each of the following five groups of units.
1. 600 completed units.
2. 500 units ($\frac{1}{2}$ processed).
3. 900 units ($\frac{1}{3}$ processed).
4. 200 units (20% processed) and 400 units (25% processed).
5. 300 completed units and 100 units (75% processed).

E22-7 **Equivalent Units for Direct Materials.** Refer to E22-6.

Required: Compute the number of equivalent units for direct materials for each of the five groups of units assuming direct materials are added to process B at the beginning of processing.

E22-8   All Job Order Costing Entries. Wonnote Manufacturing worked on a single job order during the entire month of August. The job was started at the beginning of the month and completed and sold at the end of the month. The following events took place during the month:

(a) Raw materials of $13,000 were purchased on account.
(b) Raw materials issued were $16,000 direct, $450 indirect.
(c) A total of 1,056 direct labor hours @ $5.00 per hour were worked. Indirect labor cost was $2,000.
(d) Direct materials costing $120 were returned to the storeroom.
(e) Factory overhead, other than indirect labor and materials, amounted to $23,500 as follows:

Depreciation on plant and equipment	$10,500
Insurance (prepaid earlier in the year)	2,500
Property taxes (to be paid in December)	1,500
Other factory overhead (all cash payments)	9,000
Total	$23,500

(f) Factory overhead is applied by the company at a predetermined overhead rate of $30 per direct labor hour.
(g) The job order was sold for $95,000 on account.

Required: Prepare the journal entries required to record the above events for Wonnote Manufacturing.

E22-9   Single Process, No Beginning Inventory. Northern Industries produces a single product in process A that has no beginning inventory in May. Costs accumulated in the Goods in Process Inventory account at the end of May are as follows:

Direct materials	$2,450
Processing	3,900
Total	$6,350

A total of 500 units were completed and transferred to the finished goods inventory during May. At the end of May, 200 unfinished units were still in process. They were 100% complete as to direct materials, but only 50% complete as to processing.

Required: 1. Prepare the schedules needed to assign the total direct materials and processing costs to the completed units and the ending inventory of unfinished units.
2. Prepare the journal entry needed to transfer the costs of the completed units from the Goods in Process Inventory to the Finished Goods Inventory.

E22-10   Single Process, No Beginning Inventory. Apollo Industries produces a single product in process A. There is no inventory in process A at the beginning of September. Direct materials are added in process A at the beginning of processing. Twelve hundred units were completed and transferred from process A to the finished goods inventory. Five hundred units, 80% processed, remained in process A at the end of September. Costs incurred in process A during September were as follows:

Direct materials	$3,060
Direct labor	1,280
Factory overhead	2,560
Total	$6,900

Required: 1. Prepare the schedules needed to assign the direct materials and processing costs incurred in process A to the completed units and to the unfinished units.
2. Prepare the journal entry needed to transfer the costs of the completed units from the Goods in Process Inventory account to the Finished Goods Inventory account.

E22-11 Single Process, Beginning Inventory. Greyson Grinding Company produces product X in a grinding process. This process had an inventory at the beginning of February to which the following costs had been assigned:

Direct materials	$5,600
Processing	980
Total beginning Goods in Process Inventory balance	$6,580

Additional costs added to the Goods in Process Inventory account during February were:

Direct materials	$20,650
Direct labor	18,080
Factory overhead	36,160
Total	$74,890

Direct materials are added at the beginning of processing. A total of 20,000 units of product X were completed and transferred to the finished goods inventory during February and 5,000 units of product X were unfinished at the end of February. The unfinished units were 40% processed.

Required: 1. Prepare the schedules needed to assign the total costs accumulated in the Goods in Process Inventory account at the end of February to the completed and the unfinished units.
2. Prepare the journal entry needed to transfer the costs of the completed units from the Goods in Process Inventory account to the Finished Goods Inventory account.

PROBLEMS

Part A

P22-1A Job Order Costing. The Colure Tool Company builds equipment to customer order. Costs of individual job orders are accumulated on job order cost sheets. On March 31 two job orders were in process with costs applied as shown below:

	Job order 101	Job order 102
Direct materials	$ 9,000	$11,600
Direct labor	6,500	7,700
Factory overhead applied	3,900	4,620
Total	$19,400	$23,920

During the month of April two additional orders were received. Production data for April are summarized below.

(a) Requisitions for raw materials were:

Job order 103	$6,200
Job order 104	7,500
Indirect	1,300
Total	$15,000

(b) Labor tickets totaled $14,000. Of this total, $12,300 was applied to job orders as follows (the rest was indirect labor):

Job order 101	$ 1,200
Job order 102	800
Job order 103	4,500
Job order 104	5,800
Total	$12,300

(c) Factory overhead costs incurred during the month, other than indirect materials and labor, totaled $4,500 (all paid in cash).

(d) Factory overhead cost is applied to job orders at a predetermined overhead rate of 60% of direct labor costs ($.60 per direct labor dollar applied).

(e) Job orders 101, 102, and 104 were completed and delivered to customers during April for a total price of $120,000 (on account).

Required: 1. Compute the cost of finished job orders delivered to customers.
2. Compute the balance of the Goods in Process Inventory account (after the cost of completed job orders has been transferred) at the end of April.
3. Prepare the journal entries needed to record the above information for April.
4. By how much was factory overhead overapplied or underapplied during April?

P22-2A Job Order Costing. The Bonanza Company manufactures several models of cartwheels. The company uses a job order cost system. Factory overhead is applied to job orders using a predetermined overhead rate based on direct labor cost. On January 1 it was estimated that $300,000 of direct labor cost and $150,000 of factory overhead cost would be incurred during the year. The following information relates to the company's operations during January:

	Balances	
Inventory Accounts	*January 1*	*January 31*
Raw Materials Inventory (all direct materials)	$10,000	$14,000
Goods in Process Inventory	10,500[b]	?[a]
Finished Goods Inventory	5,000	3,000

[a] To be computed.
[b] This cost relates entirely to job order 201, which was the only job order in process on January 1.

(a) During January two additional job orders were started and direct materials costs were applied as follows:

Job order 201	$ 1,000
Job order 202	7,000
Job order 203	4,000
Total direct materials costs	$12,000

(b) During January direct labor costs were applied as follows:

Job order 201	$ 2,000
Job order 202	12,000
Job order 203	10,000
Total direct labor costs	$24,000

(c) Factory overhead costs were applied to job orders at the rate set on January 1.

(d) Job orders 201 and 202 were completed during January and transferred to finished goods inventory.

(e) Direct materials were purchased on account during January (cost to be computed).

(f) Bonanza received $60,000 cash for finished goods that were sold during January.

Required: 1. Compute the cost of direct materials purchased in January.
2. Set up job order cost sheets and apply the manufacturing costs to each.
3. Compute the balance of the Goods in Process Inventory account on January 31.
4. Compute the cost of the completed job orders transferred to finished goods during January.
5. Compute the cost of the goods that were sold during January.
6. Prepare the journal entries (for which you have enough information) needed to record the events related to January's operations.

P22-3A Job Order Costing, Journal Entries. Bahama Textiles started and completed two job orders during December, job order 40 and job order 41. The following events took place during the month:

(a) Raw materials costing $89,000 were purchased on account.
(b) Raw materials were issued as follows:

Job order 40	$41,000
Job order 41	35,924
Indirect	150
Total	$77,074

(c) Labor costs incurred were:

Job order 40 (7,040 hours)	$26,400
Job order 41 (6,336 hours)	23,760
Indirect	7,350
Total	$57,510

(d) Direct materials costing $640 previously applied to job order 40 were returned to the storeroom.
(e) Factory overhead costs were applied to job orders at a predetermined overhead rate of $6.00 per direct labor hour.
(f) Both job orders were completed. Job order 40 contained 50,000 units and job order 41 contained 10,000 units.
(g) Fifteen thousand units were sold from job order 40 for a total of $45,750 and 7,000 units were sold from job order 41 for a total of $84,000. All sales were on account.
(h) In December $90,000 of factory overhead costs were incurred ($40,000 was depreciation; the rest were factory costs paid in cash) in addition to indirect materials and indirect labor, bringing the total for the year to $1,045,000. A total of $1,080,000 of factory overhead cost had been applied by the end of December.

Required: 1. Set up job order cost sheets for job orders 40 and 41 and record on them the information from the above events.
2. Prepare the journal entries required to record the above events for Bahama Textiles for December.

P22-4A Single Process, Two Months. ERIC Industries manufactures product X in process A. Direct materials are added at the beginning of processing. Cost and production information for the months of July and August are shown below:

Cost Information	July	August
Costs in beginning inventory		
Direct materials	$ 11,600	?[a]
Processing	2,350	?[a]
Costs added during the month		
Direct materials	72,400	$84,900
Processing	22,450	29,640
Total	$108,800	?[a]

Production Information (physical units)	July	August
Beginning inventory		
(60% processed)	100	200
Added during the month	600	700
Total	700	900
Completed and transferred	500	800
Ending inventory		
July (60% processed)	200	
August (20% processed)		100
Total	700	900

[a] To be computed.

Required: 1. Prepare the schedules needed to assign the total costs accumulated in the Goods in Process Inventory account for process A at the end of July to the completed and unfinished units. Repeat for the month of August.
2. Prepare the journal entries needed to transfer the costs of the completed units from the Goods In Process Inventory account for process A to the Finished Goods Inventory account at the end of July and August.

P22-5A   Two Processes.   The Genuine Products Company manufactures "antique tables" in two processes. First, direct materials are added at the beginning of an assembly process in which the tables are assembled with precut and finished tops and legs. Completed tables are then transferred into an "aging" process in which they are nicked, scratched, and water spotted by two skilled craftsmen. No new direct materials are added in the aging process. At the end of the aging process, tables are transferred to finished goods inventory. Cost and production information for the two processes during the month of March are shown below:

Cost Information	Assembly	Aging	Production Information (physical units)	Assembly	Aging
Beginning inventory costs:			Beginning inventory		
Prior production	–	$2,068	(50% processed)	20	
Direct materials	$ 700	–	(10% processed)		40
Processing	215	46	Added	400	390
Costs added during March:			Total	420	430
Prior production	–	?ª			
Direct materials	14,000	–	Completed and transferred	390	415
Processing	8,290	4,970	Ending inventory		
			(50% processed)	30	
			(20% processed)		15
Total	$23,205	?ª	Total	420	430

ª To be computed.

Required: 1. Prepare the schedules needed to assign the total costs accumulated in each of the two Goods in Process Inventory accounts at the end of March to the completed and unfinished units.
2. Prepare the journal entries needed to transfer the costs of the completed units out of the two Goods in Process Inventory accounts at the end of March.

P22-6A   Two Processes.   The Granzin Chemical Company manufactures industrial chemicals. One of its products is produced in two processes, distilling and blending. Direct material X is added at the beginning of the distilling process. When completely distilled, it is piped into the blending process. In the blending process the distilled chemical is added at the beginning of processing to direct material Y and thoroughly mixed. The mixture is then piped into large tanks (finished goods inventory) to await sale. Cost and production information for the two processes are shown below for the month of October:

Cost Information				Production Information (physical units)		
	Distilling	Blending			Distilling	Blending
Beginning inventory costs:				Beginning inventory		
Prior production	–	$ 7,250		(50% processed)	10,000	
Direct materials	$ 2,950	1,000		(20% processed)		20,000
Processing	495	980		Added	60,000	55,000
Costs added during October:				Total	70,000	75,000
Prior production	–	?ª				
Direct materials	18,050	2,750		Completed and transferred	55,000	65,000
Processing	5,755	17,270		Ending inventory		
				(50% processed)	15,000	
				(80% processed)		10,000
Total	$27,250	?ª		Total	70,000	75,000

ª To be computed.

Required:

1. Prepare the schedules needed to assign the total costs accumulated in each of the two Goods in Process Inventory accounts at the end of October to the completed and unfinished units.
2. Prepare the journal entries needed to transfer the costs of the completed units out of the two Goods in Process Inventory accounts at the end of October.

PROBLEMS

Part B

P22-1B Job Order Costing. The Columbia Tools Company started and completed two jobs during December, job order 66 and job order 67. The following events took place during the month:

(a) Raw materials costing $43,000 were purchased on account.

(b) Raw materials were issued as follows:

Job order 66	$20,000
Job order 67	17,500
Indirect	200
Total raw materials issued	$37,700

(c) Labor costs incurred were:

Job order 66 (350 hours)	$1,925
Job order 67 (290 hours)	1,595
Indirect	600
Total factory labor costs	$4,120

(d) Direct materials costing $100, which were previously applied to job order 67, were returned to the storeroom.

(e) Factory overhead costs were applied to job orders at a predetermined overhead rate of $12 per direct labor hour.

(f) Both job orders were completed. Job order 66 contained 100 units and job order 67 contained 200 units.

(g) Forty-five units from job order 66 were sold and all 200 units of job order 67 were sold. The total selling price of all units amounted to $60,000. All sales were for cash.

(h) In December, $10,000 of factory overhead costs were incurred ($6,000 was depreciation; the rest were other indirect factory costs paid in cash) in addition to indirect materials and indirect labor, bringing the total for the year to $95,000. A total of $88,000 of factory overhead had been applied by the end of December.

Required: 1. Set up job cost sheets for job orders 66 and 67 and record on them the information from the above events.
2. Prepare the journal entries required to record the above events for the Columbia Tools Company.

P22-2B   Job Order Costing.

Brandywine Company is a custom cabinet builder that uses a job order cost system. Costs of individual job orders are accumulated on job order cost sheets. When an order is completed the cabinets are installed for the customer. No finished goods inventory is kept, and the company does not use a Finished Goods Inventory account. On March 31 two job orders were in process with costs applied as shown below:

	Job Order 16	Job Order 17
Direct materials	$1,200	$1,700
Direct labor	1,250	1,600
Factory overhead applied	375	480
Total	$2,825	$3,780

During the month of April two additional orders were received. Production data for April are summarized below:

(a) Raw materials were used as follows:

Job order 18	$ 900
Job order 19	2,100
Indirect	45
Total raw materials issued	$3,045

(b) Labor costs totaled $5,700. Of this total $5,500 was applied to job orders as follows (the rest was indirect):

Job order 16	$ 600
Job order 17	750
Job order 18	1,250
Job order 19	2,900
Total direct labor costs	$5,500

(c) Factory overhead costs incurred during the month, other than indirect materials and labor, totaled $1,380 (all paid in cash).
(d) Factory overhead cost is applied to job orders at a predetermined overhead rate of 30% of direct labor costs ($.30 per direct labor dollar applied).
(e) Job orders 16, 17, and 19 were completed and installed for customers during April for a total price of $20,000 cash.

Required: 1. Compute the cost of the finished cabinets installed for customers.
2. Compute the balance of the Goods in Process Inventory account at the end of April (after the cost of completed job orders have been removed).
3. Prepare the journal entries needed to record the above events for April.
4. By how much was factory overhead overapplied or underapplied during April?

P22-3B   Job Order Costing.

The Bradley Company manufactures several different products. The company uses a job order cost system. Factory overhead is applied to job orders using a predetermined overhead rate based on direct labor cost. This year's expected factory overhead cost totals $450,000 while expected direct labor cost is $300,000. The following information is from the company's operations during May:

	Balances	
Inventory Accounts	May 1	May 31
Raw Materials Inventory (all direct materials)	$35,000	$30,000
Goods in Process Inventory	20,600[b]	?[a]
Finished Goods Inventory	40,000	48,000

[a] To be computed.

[b] This cost relates entirely to job order 401, which was the only job order in process on May 1. Two additional job orders, 402 and 403, were started during May.

(a) During May direct materials costs were applied as follows:

Job order 401	$ 2,100
Job order 402	20,500
Job order 403	8,000
Total direct materials costs	$30,600

(b) During May labor costs were incurred as shown below:

Job order 401	$ 3,000
Job order 402	16,000
Job order 403	9,000
Indirect	4,000
Total factory labor costs	$32,000

(c) Factory overhead costs were applied to job orders at the predetermined rate.

(d) Job orders 401 and 402 were completed during May and transferred to finished goods inventory.

(e) Direct materials were purchased on account (cost to be computed).

(f) Bradley sold finished goods on account for a selling price of $130,000 during May.

Required: 1. Compute the cost of direct materials purchased during May.
2. Set up job order cost sheets and show the costs applied to each.
3. Compute the balance of the Goods in Process Inventory account on May 31.
4. Compute the cost of completed job orders transferred to finished goods during May.
5. Compute the cost of the goods that were sold during May.
6. Prepare the journal entries (for which you have enough information) needed to record the events of May's operations for the Bradley Company.

P22-4B Single Process, Two Months. The Hausam Company manufactures product Y in process A. Direct materials are added at the beginning of processing. Cost and production information for the months of April and May are shown below:

Cost Information			Production Information (physical units)		
	April	May		April	May
Costs in beginning inventory:			Beginning inventory		
Direct materials	$ 23,200	?[a]	(60% processed)	200	400
Processing	4,700	?[a]	Added during the month	1,200	1,400
Costs added during the month:			Total	1,400	1,800
Direct materials	144,800	$167,100			
Processing	44,900	60,920	Completed and transferred	1,000	1,600
			Ending inventory		
			April (60% processed)	400	
			May (20% processed)		200
Total	$217,600	?[a]	Total	1,400	1,800

[a] To be computed.

Required: 1. Prepare the schedules needed to assign the total costs accumulated in the Goods in Process Inventory account for process A at the end of April to the completed and unfinished units. Repeat for the month of May.
2. Prepare the journal entries needed to transfer the costs of the completed units from the Goods in Process Inventory account for process A to the Finished Goods Inventory account at the end of April and May.

P22-5B Two Processes. Barthol Iron Works manufactures a product in two processes. Iron is added at the beginning of the melting process along with several secret ingredients. In melting, processing is complete when molten iron is thoroughly mixed with the other direct materials. The mixture is then transferred to the casting process in which it is poured into molds. There the iron mixture is quickly cooled and removed from the molds. Rough edges are removed to complete the processing of the product. Completed units are then transferred to the finished goods inventory. No new direct materials are added in the casting process. Cost and production information for the two processes during the month of May are shown below:

Cost Information	Melting	Casting	Production Information (physical units)	Melting	Casting
Beginning inventory costs:			Beginning inventory		
Prior production	–	$4,136	(50% processed)	400	
Direct materials	$ 1,400	–	(10% processed)		800
Processing	430	92	Added	8,000	7,800
Costs added during May:			Total	8,400	8,600
Prior production	–	?a			
Direct materials	28,000	–	Completed and transferred	7,800	8,300
Processing	16,580	9,940	Ending inventory		
			(50% processed)	600	
			(20% processed)		300
Total	$46,410	?a	Total	8,400	8,600

a To be computed.

Required: 1. Prepare the schedules needed to assign the total costs accumulated in each of the two Goods in Process Inventory accounts at the end of May to the completed and unfinished units.
2. Prepare the journal entries needed to transfer the costs of the completed units out of the two Goods in Process Inventory accounts at the end of May.

P22-6B Two Processes. The Howard Distilling Company makes alcoholic beverages. One of its products is produced in two processes, distilling and blending. Direct material X is added at the beginning of the distilling process. When distilling is complete the distilled liquid is taken to the blending process. In the blending process, the distilled liquid is added to direct material Y at the beginning of processing and the mixture is stirred until thoroughly blended. The mixture is then piped into huge barrels (finished goods inventory) to await sale. Cost and production information for the two processes are shown below for the month of June:

Cost Information				Production Information (physical units — gallons)		
	Distilling	Blending			Distilling	Blending
Beginning inventory costs:				Beginning inventory		
Prior production	–	$29,000		(50% processed)	20,000	
Direct materials	$ 11,800	4,000		(20% processed)		40,000
Processing	1,980	3,920		Added	120,000	110,000
Costs added during June:				Total	140,000	150,000
Prior production	–	?ª				
Direct materials	75,000	11,000		Completed and transferred . . .	110,000	130,000
Processing	20,520	69,080		Ending inventory		
				(50% processed)	30,000	
				(80% processed)		20,000
Total	$109,300	?ª		Total	140,000	150,000

ª To be computed.

Required:
1. Prepare the schedules needed to assign the total costs accumulated in each of the two Goods in Process Inventory accounts at the end of June to the completed and unfinished units.
2. Prepare the journal entries needed to transfer the costs of the completed units out of the two Goods in Process Inventory accounts at the end of June.

DISCUSSION CASES

C22-1 Choice of Costing System. The Baker Machine Company operates a small machine shop with lathes, drill presses, and other metal-working equipment. Baker does machining to customer order. The company grinds valves, cuts, drills, and bends sheet metal, and welds. A large portion of the company's business is fabrication of machine parts for machine repair work by other companies in the vicinity. The company also often repairs brush hogs and other equipment for local farmers.

Required: What kind of cost accounting system is best suited for the Baker Machine Company? Outline the features of the system chosen and discuss why each is useful to Baker.

C22-2 Choice of Costing System. Carver Chemicals Company operates a large plant in the Midwest. It manufactures several common acids that are in high demand. In fact, several of its acid departments operate 24 hours per day, 7 days a week. Equipment in most of Carver's departments is specialized. For example, mixing vats and piping are lined for sulphuric acid production. This is not necessary for several other chemicals produced by the company. Carver keeps a huge storage warehouse near the factory to hold finished chemicals because demand fluctuates greatly and, in some months, exceeds the company's production capability.

Required: What kind of cost accounting system is best suited for Carver Chemicals? Outline the features of the system chosen and discuss how the system should be set up by Carver.

23

Cost-Volume-Profit Planning and Analysis

After reading this chapter, you should understand:

- The importance of managerial accounting to management's planning and controlling functions
- The uses of cost estimation
- The behavior of fixed, variable, and mixed costs
- The use of the high–low method of estimating costs from past cost data
- The graphical and computational analysis of relationships between costs, profits, and sales volume

Most of our discussion in the previous 22 chapters of this book has been oriented toward developing your understanding of the systems and procedures of financial accounting; that is, the systems and procedures that support the preparation of financial statements. Financial statements provide a useful presentation of accounting information for *external* use by investors, creditors, governmental agencies, and so on. They are also of limited value for *internal* use by the management of a company. A company's management, however, often has need for other forms of analysis and presentation of accounting information. Accountants have responded to this need by developing managerial accounting. **Managerial accounting is the specialized set of concepts, analysis techniques, and reporting forms used to supply accounting information to management for decision making.** The specialist in this area is called a *managerial accountant*.

In this chapter we outline some of the functions of management that give rise to these additional information needs and present one of the most basic and commonly used forms of analysis of accounting information, cost–volume–profit analysis. In the chapters to follow, we introduce several additional types of analysis that form important parts of managerial accounting.

MANAGEMENT FUNCTIONS

The operations of a company can be described in basic terms as *individuals* using *resources* to perform *activities* directed at accomplishing *goals*. The success of these operations depends upon the performance of several important functions by the company's management. Managerial accounting is valuable because it helps management perform these functions. The functions consist of planning and controlling. They are discussed in the following sections.

Planning

Planning is the process by which management determines the activities that must be performed and the types and amounts of resources that must be provided for the company to accomplish its goals. The planning process consists of three parts: goal setting, organizing, and scheduling.

SETTING COMPANY GOALS.   The first part of planning is goal setting. Goal setting specifies the purpose for the company's existence and the objectives it hopes to accomplish. Starting with one or perhaps two broad overall goals, most companies develop a set of supporting subgoals that must be reached in order to accomplish the broad goals. Many more layers of subgoals may be set, with each new layer being more specific in nature and supporting the goals of the previous layer. **The set of goals and supporting subgoals of a company is called a goal structure.**

Exhibit 23-1 presents a partial description of a manufacturing company's goal structure. The arrows show supporting relationships among the goals. Notice that the goals near the top of the exhibit are very broad, but that the subgoals farther down the structure are more specific and begin to suggest particular kinds of activities. The goal structure described in this exhibit is not complete. Many additional subgoals must be determined before the company has a clear indication of all of the activities it needs to perform.

The process of establishing such a goal structure and expanding it to include more and more specific objectives enables management to see the nature and relative importance of the various activities that have to be performed. All activities that need to be performed must ultimately be identified, and specific objectives to be accomplished by each activity must be set. In addition, an organization must be developed that can aid in the performance of the required activities.

ORGANIZING.   The second part of the planning process involves organizing the company's activities. The work that needs to be done must be assigned to the individuals employed by the company. **Organizing means establishing logical working relationships between employees, and between the jobs they are assigned, so that the company's required activities can be performed.**

Most large companies organize by establishing departments such as manufacturing, personnel, engineering, accounting, sales or marketing, and so on, to perform the necessary activities. A department manager in charge of each department is assigned the responsibility of seeing that the work is done. The department manager directs or supervises the work of the other employees in the

EXHIBIT 23-1 A Sample Company's Goal Structure

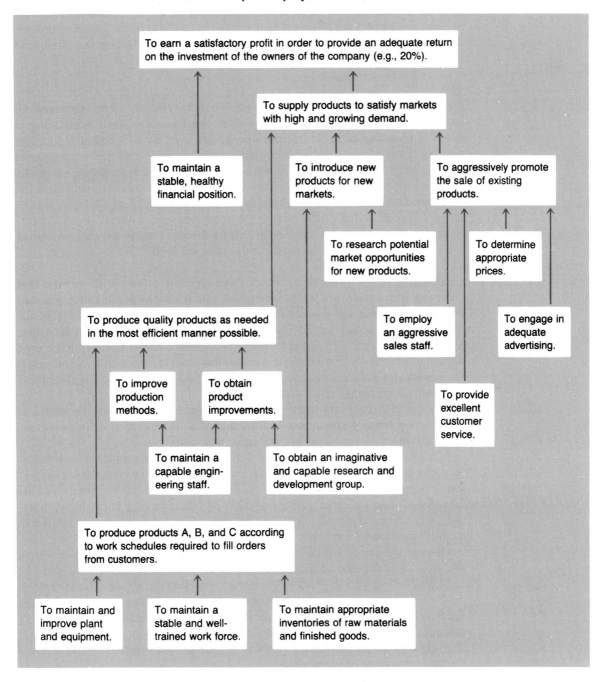

department, makes day-to-day decisions to keep the department running smoothly, and coordinates the activities of the department with those of other departments.

Goal setting and organizing together make up a phase of the planning process that is often called *long-range planning*, because decisions made in this phase tend to affect a company's operations over long periods of time.

SCHEDULING. The third part of the planning process is scheduling. Once the activities necessary to accomplish company goals have been identified and the company has been organized, specific work schedules must be developed. **Scheduling is detailed planning of departmental operations over time.** Scheduling specifies what work must be accomplished within each department over the coming weeks and months and, consequently, is often referred to as *short-range planning*. Its purpose is to help departmental activities to run smoothly and continuously so that they can contribute to reaching the company goals. Scheduling also aids coordination between activities that may be vital to their effectiveness. For example, production activity must be planned in relation to sales activity and the purchase of raw materials must be coordinated with production needs.

Controlling

Controlling is the process by which management attempts to ensure that company employees are using resources efficiently in performing planned activities and that those activities are effective in attaining company goals. Controlling, then, requires the evaluation of performance of planned activities. Such evaluations are normally obtained by comparing actual results being achieved with planned results. Performance evaluations provide information to managers responsible for various activities. This information helps them recognize where deviations from plans are occurring.

Deviations from plans occur because of unexpected problems. **Feedback is information from performance evaluations of an activity that draws management attention to problems occurring in that activity.**

Some problems are easily recognized. Rapid feedback allows these problems to be corrected quickly. For example, an experienced machine operator may detect erratic behavior in his machine, which can then be adjusted quickly before a costly breakdown occurs or before a large number of defective units is produced. Similarly, a production foreman might see a new employee using improper or inefficient methods that can be improved with a little instruction.

Other problems are difficult to identify, however. They may require observation and analysis of operating data from an activity over a long period of time, often by an individual not directly involved in the activity. Feedback cannot be as rapid in these cases because of the length of time needed to observe and to analyze the activity. For example, another machine may never display erratic behavior but may gradually become out of adjustment. An analysis by the managerial accountant showing abnormally high direct materials and direct labor costs might be required for this problem to be recognized.

Again, adjusting the machine might correct the problem, bringing future material and labor costs in line with plans. On the other hand, it might not be possible to adjust the machine. In this case plans might have to be revised. A new machine might have to be purchased and production schedules adjusted accordingly. The relationships between planning and controlling of activity performance are shown in Exhibit 23-2.

From Exhibit 23-2 you can see that planning and controlling go hand in hand. The best performance evaluation procedures compare the actual results achieved by an activity with planned results. Here detailed plans become a basic part of the control process. At the same time control through performance evaluation often leads to the need for revising plans.

THE ROLE OF MANAGERIAL ACCOUNTING

Managerial accounting can play an important role in planning and controlling by providing needed information. As management plans the various activities needed to meet its goals, many decisions must be made about the number of employees and amounts of resources to commit to each activity. Managerial accounting can provide cost analyses to estimate the cost of performing these activities. It can provide information needed to make specific operating decisions and can describe the financial impact of all decisions affecting the coming months or years so that plans can be changed if goals are not expected to be met.

Managerial accounting can also provide important information for the control process. Reports comparing actual versus planned cost levels in various activities can be used to pinpoint problem areas that require attention. When problems do occur and there are alternative ways to correct them, managerial accounting can often provide information to aid in the control decision.

In order to provide the kinds of information that will be helpful to management

**EXHIBIT 23-2
Planning and
Controlling Activity
Performance**

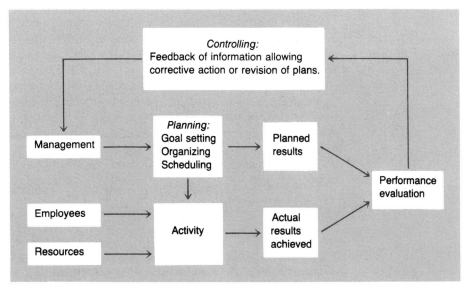

in making its planning and controlling decisions, the managerial accountant must often estimate costs. The reason for this is that decision making requires choosing between alternative courses of action. Providing estimates of the cost of following these alternatives enables management to see their financial consequences. Therefore we must first introduce some of the basic ideas of cost estimation before proceeding to more involved techniques used by the managerial accountant.

COST ESTIMATION

Estimating costs is not always easy because costs are influenced by many factors. To make cost estimates sufficiently accurate to be useful requires a careful analysis of how costs are affected by the various factors. Usually the first and often the only factor studied in such analyses is the level of activity (volume) of the operation for which the cost is incurred.[1] For example, the number of units produced or the number of direct labor hours worked might be used as measures of the volume of a manufacturing operation; the number of units sold might be used to measure the volume of a sales department. Volume is such an important factor, however, that even simple analyses based on this single factor can often produce useful cost estimates. We now describe three basic cost behavior patterns that can be used to describe the majority of all costs. As the examples are given, cost equations that are helpful in making cost estimates are presented.

Fixed Costs

Fixed costs are costs that are not affected by changes in the volume of an operation. For example, consider the $40,000 straight-line depreciation cost on the factory building of Lures Unlimited, a company manufacturing fishing lures of a particular new design. The production volume is measured by the number of lures produced. This depreciation cost would not change because of the number of lures produced. It is a fixed cost. If we drew a graph of the relationship between the depreciation cost and the volume of production, it would look like the graph in Exhibit 23-3.

Note in Exhibit 23-3 that a fixed cost appears as a straight horizontal line on the graph indicating that the cost is expected to be the same (fixed) regardless of the volume. It is important not to be misled about the nature of fixed costs. Fixed costs are not "fixed" in the sense that they cannot change from one period to the next. The company could certainly expand the size of its factory by purchasing more assets so that next year the depreciation cost would be higher. To be classified as fixed, a cost must only remain constant for a period in relation to the volume attained in that period. That is, a fixed cost is not influenced by volume changes in the period.

The cost equation describing the fixed cost line in Exhibit 23-3 is simply

$$\text{Total annual depreciation cost} \quad = \quad \$40,000$$

Depreciation on factory and office equipment, rent on warehouse facilities, and

---

[1] The level of activity of an operation is commonly referred to as its *volume*. We use this terminology throughout this chapter and later when it is useful to do so.

EXHIBIT 23-3
Fixed Cost Behavior

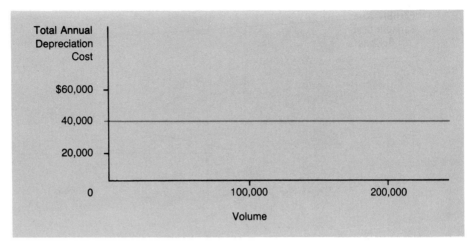

managers' salaries are additional examples of costs that are normally fixed. It should be noted that the total of several fixed costs would also be fixed.

Fixed costs are sometimes stated as a dollar amount per unit. The fixed cost per unit is computed by dividing fixed costs in total by the volume in units. It is important to note, in order to avoid confusion later, that fixed costs *per unit* decrease as volume increases. This is because their fixed total is being divided by an increasing number of units. For example, if Lures Unlimited produced 100,000 lures, depreciation cost per lure would be $.40 ($40,000 ÷ 100,000 lures). If 200,000 lures were produced, depreciation cost per lure would be only $.20 ($40,000 ÷ 200,000 lures). While fixed cost per unit computations are useful for some purposes, they can be very misleading for others because of this fact.

Variable Costs   **A variable cost is a cost that varies in total directly in proportion to the volume of an operation.** For example, consider now the cost of the wood used to form the body of the lures made by Lures Unlimited. Suppose the company purchases pine dowel in 6-foot lengths for $1.00 and can produce 25 lures from each 6-foot piece. The cost of the wood would be $.04 per lure ($1.00 ÷ 25 lures), causing the total cost of this direct material to vary in proportion to the number of lures produced. That is, if Lures Unlimited produces 100,000 lures, for example, the total cost of the wood used is $4,000 (100,000 lures × $.04 per lure). If the volume doubles to 200,000 lures, the total wood cost also doubles to $8,000 (200,000 lures × $.04 per lure). It is important to recognize that the reason why total variable cost increases in proportion to volume is that the variable cost *per unit* is constant.

Exhibit 23-4 shows the variable cost behavior of wood used by Lures Unlimited. Note that a variable cost is described by a straight line sloping upward from the origin of the graph. The slope of the line is the rate at which the total of the variable cost increases, the constant variable cost per unit of volume. For the fishing lures,

EXHIBIT 23-4
Variable Cost
Behavior

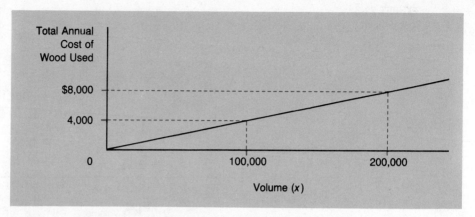

the total variable cost of wood for the bodies of the lures increases at a rate of $.04 per lure.

The cost equation describing the variable cost line in Exhibit 23-4 would be:

$$\text{Total cost of wood used} \quad = \quad \$.04\, x$$

where:

$$x \;=\; \text{number of lures produced per year}$$

It should be noted that the sum of several variable costs is also variable, with a rate per unit of volume equal to the sum of the individual variable cost rates. For example, if hooks cost $.10 per lure and the blade and swivel $.12, the total direct materials cost *per lure* (wood, hooks, blade and swivel) would be $.26 ($.04 + $.10 + $.12), and the cost equation for the total direct materials cost would be:

$$\text{Total direct materials cost} \quad = \quad \$.26\, x$$

Mixed Costs   **Mixed costs are costs that behave as the sum of a fixed cost and a variable cost would behave.** That is, they have a fixed cost component and a variable cost component. Mixed costs are sometimes called *semivariable costs*. To illustrate a mixed cost, suppose that the local power company charges Lures Unlimited a constant amount, say $.10, per kilowatt hour (kwh) for electricity used. If the amount of electricity used for factory lighting tends to remain constant regardless of the volume of production, say at 30,000 kwh, the power cost for this use would be fixed at $3,000. The amount of electricity required by the saws, lathes, and drill presses used in production, however, is directly proportional to the number of lures produced. The power cost for this use would therefore vary in proportion to the number of lures produced. Suppose for the sake of illustration that we know it takes .1 kwh of electricity for each lure produced. Total power cost would be a mixed cost because it would equal the sum of a fixed component of $3,000 (from its use for factory lighting) and a variable component (from machine use) that increases at a rate of $.01 per lure produced ($.10 per kwh × .1 kwh per lure).

The cost equation describing this power cost would be:

$$\text{Power cost} = \$3,000 + \$.01\,x$$

where:

$$x = \text{the number of lures produced per year}$$

Thus at a production volume of 100,000 lures, power cost would be:

$$\text{Power cost} = \$3,000 + \$.01\,(100,000) = \$4,000$$

At a production volume of 200,000 lures, power cost would be:

$$\text{Power cost} = \$3,000 + \$.01\,(200,000) = \$5,000$$

Exhibit 23-5 shows a graph of the mixed cost just described. In this exhibit we see that a mixed cost increases in a straight line (at a constant rate equal to the rate of its variable component) as volume increases. Notice, however, that it cuts the vertical (cost) axis above the origin at an amount equal to its fixed component.

The fixed and variable components of mixed costs are often separated and treated independently. Fixed components of mixed costs are grouped with (and treated as) fixed costs and variable components are treated as variable costs.

The Relevant Range

Each time the managerial accountant prepares an analysis that involves cost estimates to provide information for a management decision, the requirements of the decision determine a range of volumes over which the estimates must be especially accurate. For example, if a manufacturing company expects to produce between 100,000 and 200,000 units each year and wants to decide whether or not to change its manufacturing process, cost estimates for the existing process and the alternative process over that specific range would be useful in making the decision. It would not be helpful to know which process would be less expensive to operate when producing below 100,000 units, nor would the company care about comparing

EXHIBIT 23-5
Mixed Cost Behavior

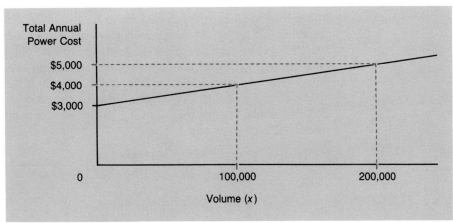

manufacturing costs for volumes above 200,000 units. Only the range of volumes from 100,000 to 200,000 is relevant (useful) to the decision.

The relevant range is the range of volumes over which cost estimates are needed for a particular use. The relevant range concept is extremely important because it focuses the attention of the managerial accountant on the range of volumes in which cost estimates must be accurate. Cost behavior patterns outside of the relevant range can be ignored.

Some costs do not precisely fit the fixed, variable, or mixed cost behavior patterns we described. They may vary, but not in a straight line over all possible volumes. Or they may be fixed over a wide range of volumes, but increase abruptly to a higher amount if the upper limit of that volume range is exceeded. The managerial accountant, however, must determine only how they behave within the relevant range, and in most cases, these costs fit one of the three common behavior patterns.

We now briefly consider two methods commonly used by managerial accountants to obtain the cost equations needed to make cost estimates.

Determining the Cost Equations

THE ENGINEERING APPROACH. One approach to determining the cost equation for a particular cost is to study the prices of the goods or services being acquired and the physical relationships between the use of those goods or services and the volume of the operation being analyzed. For example, this approach might have been used to gather the information with which we determined the power cost equation for Lures Unlimited. Recall that we assumed that lighting would require 30,000 kwh and that the cutting, shaping, and drilling operations would require .1 kwh for each lure produced. These are the kinds of physical relationships that would be studied in the engineering approach. With these engineering estimates and knowledge that the price of electricity is $.10 per kwh, the company could determine its power cost equation as we illustrated. Sometimes these physical relationships are difficult to determine, however, and another approach is needed.

THE STUDY OF PAST COSTS. The second approach involves the study of past costs. The first step in this approach is to gather data showing the amount of the cost and the volume of operations during each of several past periods. The pair of values (a cost and volume) from each period determines a data point, which is then plotted on a graph. Plotting all the points on the same graph results in a pattern of data points called a *scatter diagram*. The scatter diagram is useful because it shows a "picture" of the behavior of the cost being estimated.

To illustrate, assume the following past power cost and volume data from the records of Lures Unlimited:

Year	Power Cost	Volume
1	$3,400	40,000
2	$3,800	80,000
3	$4,200	120,000
4	$4,000	100,000

EXHIBIT 23-6
Scatter Diagram for
Power Costs

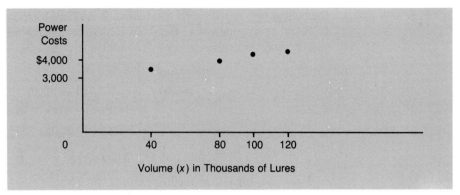

The scatter diagram for these data would appear as the diagram in Exhibit 23-6. The "picture" from this scatter diagram suggests that the points lie along a straight line that would intersect the vertical axis above the origin of the graph. That is, power cost seems to follow the behavior pattern of a mixed cost. As this seems reasonable, we assume a mixed behavior pattern for power cost having the following equation:

$$\text{Power cost} \ = \ F \ + \ vx$$

where:

F = the fixed component

v = the rate at which the variable component increases per unit of volume

x = the volume

The task remaining is to estimate F and v so that we have a useful equation for estimating power cost. Several procedures are available for estimating F and v. One procedure often used is called the high–low method.

THE HIGH–LOW METHOD. **The high–low method involves determining the equation of the straight line through the data points associated with the highest and lowest activity levels experienced.** The high–low method starts by estimating v, the rate at which the cost increases per unit of volume (the slope of the line). This is done by dividing the change in cost between the high and low volume points by the change in volume between them (v = cost change/volume change). The computation of v for the power cost equation would be as follows:

	Power Cost	Volume
High volume	$4,200	120,000 lures
Low volume	3,400	40,000 lures
Change	$ 800	80,000 lures

$$v \ = \ \frac{\text{Cost change}}{\text{Volume change}} \ = \ \frac{\$800}{80,000 \text{ lures}} \ = \ \$.01 \text{ per lure}$$

Having determined v, we estimate the total of the variable component at either the high or low activity level and subtract it from the total cost observed at that level to obtain an estimate of F, the fixed component. Using the data from the highest activity level we compute:

$$
\begin{aligned}
\text{Power cost} &= F + vx \\
\$4,200 &= F + \$.01\,(120,000) \\
F &= \$4,200 - \$.01\,(120,000) \\
F &= \$4,200 - \$1,200 \\
F &= \underline{\underline{\$3,000}}
\end{aligned}
$$

Thus the high–low method results in obtaining a cost equation (power cost = \$3,000 + \$.01x) that Lures Unlimited can use to estimate its total annual power cost.

It is important to be careful when using past cost data to study cost behavior patterns. The managerial accountant making the analysis should be able to answer *yes* to three important questions before using a cost equation calculated as shown above.

1. Were conditions essentially the same during the periods from which the data were obtained?
2. Will those previous conditions continue unchanged in the future so that cost behavior patterns will remain the same?
3. Does the derived cost pattern make sense?

Similar conditions must have been present during the periods from which the data were obtained so that distortions due to abnormal conditions are not present in the data. Suppose, for example, that during one of the four years from which we obtained the power cost data just analyzed, a natural gas shortage caused the factory to switch to more expensive electrical heat for one of the winter months. If that year happened to be the high or low activity year, the high–low method would produce an inaccurate cost equation because of the abnormally high power cost during that year.

The conditions experienced during the period of data collection must be expected to continue into the future so that cost behavior patterns will not be changing. For example, if the power company changes its price per kilowatt hour or plant expansion increases lighting requirements, the cost equation representing future power cost behavior will be different from that of the past. Again, past data analysis will produce misleading results.

As a final check, the managerial accountant should always ask if the derived cost pattern makes sense. Using the high–low method to estimate the relationship between four years of double-declining balance depreciation cost and the volumes experienced during those years would be misleading, for example. The amount of depreciation cost in any one year depends entirely upon the depreciable cost of the asset involved, the life of the asset, and the year that is being considered. It has nothing to do with the volume in that year.

Now that you have an understanding of the basics of cost estimation we can turn our attention to Cost–Volume–Profit Analysis, one of the simplest yet most useful of the analytic tools used by the managerial accountant to supply planning information to management.

COST–VOLUME–PROFIT ANALYSIS

One of the most common forms of analysis in which cost estimates are used is Cost–Volume–Profit (C–V–P) Analysis. **Cost–Volume–Profit Analysis is an analysis of the effects on profit of changes in sales volume, selling prices of products, variable manufacturing and selling costs per unit, and total fixed costs.** C–V–P analysis is sometimes called *break-even analysis*. It is used to gain an understanding of the profit impact of plans that are being made. This understanding can produce more informed decisions during the planning process.

C–V–P Analysis is based on a simple profit computation that relies upon knowledge of the behavior of costs. As will be shown, this profit computation can be expressed in the form of an equation. The equation can then be used to make quick calculations of the profit impact of changes in selling prices, sales volume, and variable and fixed costs. The relationships between cost, sales volume, and profit can also be graphed, which provides a convenient form for presentation of the analysis to a company's managers.

The Profit Computation

We begin our discussion of C–V–P Analysis by examining a profit computation for the Moran Manufacturing Company, which produces a single product, riding lawn mowers. The company produces for customer order and never has an inventory of finished or partially completed mowers at year end. The profit computation for 1983 appears in Exhibit 23-7.

In Exhibit 23-7 note that Moran first calculates its sales revenue ($800,000) by multiplying the number of mowers sold (1,000) by the selling price per mower ($800). Total variable costs of manufacturing and selling the 1,000 mowers are calculated next. The total variable manufacturing costs of the mowers sold ($250,000) are found by multiplying the number of mowers sold (1,000) times the

EXHIBIT 23-7
Profit Computation for 1983

MORAN MANUFACTURING COMPANY Profit Computation for 1983		
Sales revenue (1,000 mowers @ $800 per mower)		$800,000
Less variable cost:		
Variable manufacturing cost (1,000 mowers @ $250 per mower)	$250,000	
Variable selling cost (1,000 mowers @ $70 per mower) . . .	70,000	320,000
Contribution margin		$480,000
Less fixed cost:		
Fixed manufacturing cost	$300,000	
Fixed selling and administrative cost	60,000	360,000
Profit		$120,000

variable manufacturing cost per mower ($250). Total variable selling costs are calculated to be $70,000 (1,000 mowers × $70 per mower) by a similar computation. The total variable costs of $320,000 ($250,000 manufacturing + $70,000 selling) are then subtracted from total sales revenue. The difference, $480,000 ($800,000 − $320,000) is called the total contribution margin.

The total contribution margin is the difference between total sales revenue and total variable costs. Profit is computed by subtracting total fixed costs incurred during the year from the total contribution margin. In Exhibit 23-7 Moran's profit is $120,000 ($480,000 total contribution margin − $360,000 total fixed costs).[2] This simple form of profit computation is widely used by companies for profit reports prepared for management. We shall see that the computation of the total contribution margin is the key to understanding the relationship between profit and sales volume.

It is important to note that this profit computation is different from the computation normally found in a published income statement. In an income statement prepared for external users we would first deduct all manufacturing costs associated with the goods sold during the year from sales revenue to determine gross profit. We would next deduct all selling and general and administrative expenses incurred during the year to compute net income (profit). No distinction would normally be made between fixed costs and variable costs in income statements prepared for external users. Thus this form of profit computation would be used for internal reporting but would be modified for external reporting.

The Profit Computation in Equation Form

In the simple profit computation we have just described, profit equals total sales revenue minus total variable cost minus total fixed cost. We can write this computation in the form of an equation. The equation is as follows:

Profit   =   Total sales revenue   −   Total variable cost   −   Total fixed cost

Since total sales revenue minus total variable cost equals total contribution margin, the profit equation can also be written as:

Profit   =   Total contribution margin   −   Total fixed cost

In order to make these equations useful in an analysis of cost, sales volume, and profit relationships, we must consider the behavior of total sales revenue, total variable cost, total contribution margin, and total fixed cost as sales volume varies. In the following discussion the cost and revenue information from the profit computation in Exhibit 23-7 is used.

TOTAL SALES REVENUE.   Total sales revenue in the profit computation equals selling price per unit times the number of units sold (unit sales volume). As long as the selling price per unit remains constant, total sales revenue varies in proportion to unit sales volume. For example, recall that the selling price of Moran's riding

---

[2]Income taxes are not considered in this discussion.

mower is $800 per unit. If Moran sells 500 mowers its total sales revenue is $400,000 ($800 per unit × 500 units). If Moran sells 1,000 mowers its total sales revenue is $800,000 ($800 per unit × 1,000 units). If we use x to stand for unit sales volume, total sales revenue for Moran equals $800 x.

TOTAL VARIABLE COST. Total variable cost in the profit computation equals the variable cost per unit times the number of units sold (unit sales volume). As long as the variable cost per unit remains constant, total variable cost varies in proportion to unit sales volume (just as total sales revenue does).[3] For example, recall from Exhibit 23-7 that Moran's variable cost per mower is $320 ($250 manufacturing + $70 selling). If Moran sells 500 mowers its total variable cost is $160,000 ($320 per unit × 500 units). If 1,000 mowers are sold total variable cost amounts to $320,000 ($320 per unit × 1,000 units). If we use x to stand for unit sales volume, the total variable cost in Moran's profit computation equals $320 x.

TOTAL CONTRIBUTION MARGIN. Total contribution margin equals total sales revenue minus total variable cost. Recall that total sales revenue and total variable cost both vary directly in proportion to unit sales volume. As a result total contribution margin, which is the difference between total sales revenue and total variable cost, also varies in proportion to unit sales volume. This is because the contribution margin *per unit*, which equals the selling price minus the variable cost per unit, is constant. For Moran the contribution margin per unit is $480 (that is, $800 selling price per unit − $320 variable cost per unit). At a sales volume of 500 mowers Moran's total contribution margin is $240,000 ($480 per unit × 500 units). At a sales volume of 1,000 mowers Moran's total contribution margin is $480,000 ($480 per unit × 1,000 units). If we use x to stand for unit sales volume, Moran's total contribution margin equals $480 x. The two graphs in Exhibit 23-8 show the variable behavior of total sales revenue, total variable cost, and total contribution margin for the Moran Manufacturing Company.

In graph (a) of Exhibit 23-8 total sales revenue increases at a rate of $800 per unit sold (the selling price per unit) while total variable cost increases at a rate of $320 per unit (the variable cost per unit). It is easy to see that total sales revenue is increasing faster (its line is steeper) than total variable cost as the number of units sold increases. Thus the vertical distance between the total sales revenue line and the total variable cost line, which represents total contribution margin, increases steadily as unit sales volume increases.

The steady increase in total contribution margin is even more clearly shown in graph (b) of Exhibit 23-8. In this graph total contribution margin at each unit sales volume is given directly by the height of the line drawn on the graph. Total contribution margin increases at a rate of $480 per unit sold.

---

[3] In this chapter we assume that selling price and variable cost *per unit* remain constant at all volumes within the relevant range. Any changes in selling price or variable cost per unit considered in this book are the result of a management decision for a period, not volume changes within the period.

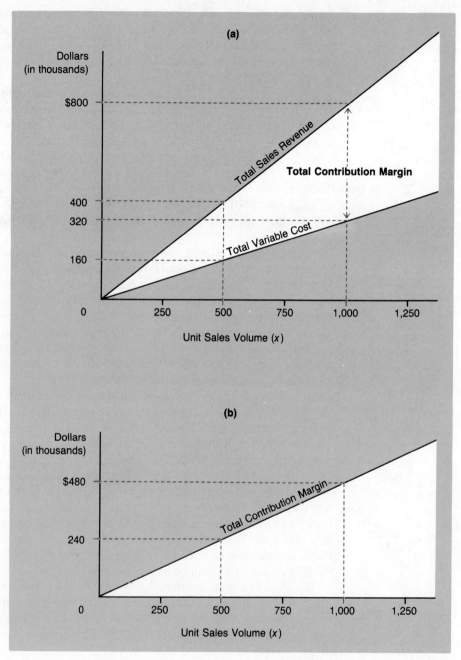

TOTAL FIXED COST. The total fixed cost in the profit computation does not vary with changes in sales volume as do total sales revenue and total variable cost. Total fixed cost remains constant. For the Moran Manufacturing Company, total fixed cost is $360,000 ($300,000 fixed manufacturing cost plus $60,000 fixed selling cost).

THE PROFIT EQUATION.   Now that we understand the behavior of total sales revenue, total variable cost, and total fixed cost in the profit computation, we can write the profit equation for the Moran Manufacturing Company as shown below:

$$\text{Profit} = \$800\,x - \$320\,x - \$360{,}000$$

or in words,

$$\text{Profit} = \left(\begin{array}{c}\text{Selling}\\\text{price}\\\text{per unit}\end{array} \times \begin{array}{c}\text{Unit}\\\text{sales}\\\text{volume}\end{array}\right) - \left(\begin{array}{c}\text{Variable}\\\text{cost}\\\text{per unit}\end{array} \times \begin{array}{c}\text{Unit}\\\text{sales}\\\text{volume}\end{array}\right) - \begin{array}{c}\text{Total}\\\text{fixed}\\\text{cost}\end{array}$$

Subtracting total variable cost from total sales revenue to obtain total contribution margin, Moran's profit equation can also be written as:

$$\text{Profit} = \$480\,x - \$360{,}000$$

or in words,

$$\text{Profit} = \left(\begin{array}{c}\text{Contribution}\\\text{margin}\\\text{per unit}\end{array} \times \begin{array}{c}\text{Unit}\\\text{sales}\\\text{volume}\end{array}\right) - \begin{array}{c}\text{Total}\\\text{fixed}\\\text{cost}\end{array}$$

The relationship between costs, profit, and unit sales volume are given by these equations. These relationships can also be shown graphically as in Exhibit 23-9. The two graphs shown in this exhibit correspond to the two graphs in Exhibit 23-8. The addition of one more line to each graph in Exhibit 23-8 to bring fixed costs into the analysis produces the graphs in Exhibit 23-9. On these graphs profit (or loss) can be seen in relation to unit sales volume.

In graph (a) of Exhibit 23-9 we have drawn an additional line showing the amount of total cost that would be deducted in the profit computation as unit sales volume increases. Note that this total cost line has the same slope as the variable cost line but is precisely $360,000 above it at all unit sales volumes because of the addition of $360,000 of fixed costs. Note also in graph (a) that the vertical distance between total sales revenue and total cost represents profit (when total sales revenue is above total cost) or loss (when total sales revenue is below total cost).

Graph (a) of Exhibit 23-9 shows that when 750 riding mowers are sold Moran has a profit of $0. **The break-even point is the sales volume at which zero profit occurs.** At the break-even point, total sales revenue is equal to total cost. When unit sales volume is greater than the break-even point the total sales revenue is larger than the total cost, resulting in a profit. When unit sales volume is less than the break-even point the total sales revenue is less than the total cost, resulting in a loss.

The relationship between profit (or loss) and sales volume is also shown in graph (b) of Exhibit 23-9. In graph (b) two lines are drawn. One represents the total contribution margin while the other represents the total fixed cost for the Moran Manufacturing Company. Note that the vertical distance between these lines represents profit or loss. This is because profit is computed as the total contribution margin minus total fixed cost. Note that the break-even point is also shown on this graph as the unit sales volume (750 units) producing zero profit. Above the break-even unit sales volume the total contribution margin is greater than the total fixed cost, resulting in a profit. Below the break-even unit sales volume the total contribution margin is less than the total fixed cost, resulting in a loss.

**EXHIBIT 23-9
Cost–Unit Sales
Volume–Profit
Relationships for the
Moran Manufacturing
Company**

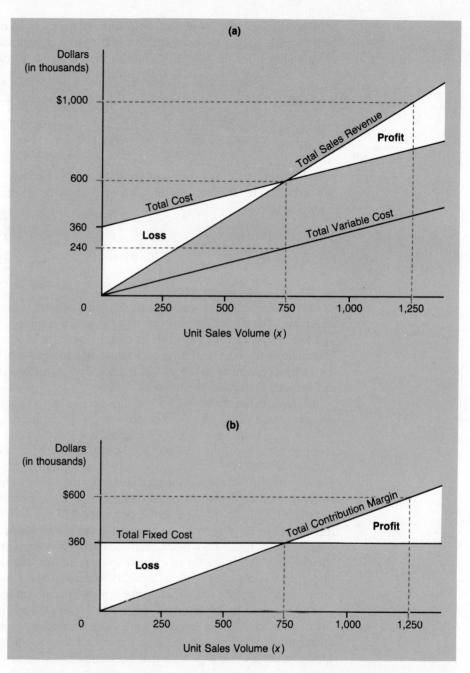

Computations Using the Profit Equation

Graphs are very helpful in presenting cost, sales volume, and profit relationships to a company's managers. Questions related to these relationships, however, are more easily answered using computations based on the profit equations. Three basic questions occur frequently in C–V–P analysis. They are:

1. How much profit will be earned at a given unit sales volume?
2. How many units must be sold to break even?

3. How many units must be sold to earn a given amount of profit? (The given amount is usually a desired profit that the company uses as a goal.)

Recall that the profit equations are:

$$
\text{Profit} = \left(\begin{array}{c} \text{Selling} \\ \text{price} \\ \text{per unit} \end{array} \times \begin{array}{c} \text{Unit} \\ \text{sales} \\ \text{volume} \end{array} \right) - \left(\begin{array}{c} \text{Variable} \\ \text{cost} \\ \text{per unit} \end{array} \times \begin{array}{c} \text{Unit} \\ \text{sales} \\ \text{volume} \end{array} \right) - \begin{array}{c} \text{Total} \\ \text{fixed} \\ \text{cost} \end{array}
$$

and

$$
\text{Profit} = \left(\begin{array}{c} \text{Contribution} \\ \text{margin} \\ \text{per unit} \end{array} \times \begin{array}{c} \text{Unit} \\ \text{sales} \\ \text{volume} \end{array} \right) - \begin{array}{c} \text{Total} \\ \text{fixed} \\ \text{cost} \end{array}
$$

We use these equations to answer the three questions.

ESTIMATING PROFIT AT A GIVEN UNIT SALES VOLUME. Suppose that the Moran Manufacturing Company wants to estimate its profit if 1,200 riding mowers are sold (i.e., at unit sales volume of 1,200). Recall that Moran sells its mowers for $800 per mower and incurs $320 of variable cost for each mower sold. Its contribution margin per unit is $480 ($800 − $320). Moran's fixed costs total $360,000. Moran can estimate its profit when 1,200 mowers are sold by using the first of the two profit equations as follows:

$$
\begin{aligned}
\text{Profit} &= (\$800 \times 1,200) - (\$320 \times 1,200) - \$360,000 \\
&= \$960,000 - \$384,000 - \$360,000 \\
&= \underline{\underline{\$216,000}}
\end{aligned}
$$

Or Moran can use the second of the profit equations as follows:

$$
\begin{aligned}
\text{Profit} &= (\$480 \times 1,200) - \$360,000 \\
&= \$576,000 - \$360,000 \\
&= \underline{\underline{\$216,000}}
\end{aligned}
$$

FINDING THE BREAK-EVEN POINT. The break-even point is the sales volume that results in zero profit. This occurs when total sales revenue equals total cost (total variable cost plus total fixed cost). Stated another way, the break-even point is the sales volume at which total contribution margin equals total fixed cost. Letting x stand for unit sales volume, Moran breaks even when:

$$
\begin{aligned}
\text{Total sales revenue} &= \text{Total variable cost} + \text{Total fixed cost} \\
\$800x &= \$320x + \$360,000
\end{aligned}
$$

Solving for x gives the break-even point.

$$
\begin{aligned}
\$800x &= \$320x + \$360,000 \\
(\$800 - \$320)x &= \$360,000 \\
\$480x &= \$360,000 \\
x &= \frac{\$360,000}{\$480 \text{ (per mower)}} \\
x &= \underline{\underline{750 \text{ mowers}}}
\end{aligned}
$$

Thus the break-even point expressed as a unit sales volume (750 mowers) is found by dividing total fixed cost ($360,000) by the contribution margin per unit ($480). This may be written in equation form as follows:

$$\text{Break-even point (in units)} = \frac{\text{Total fixed cost}}{\text{Contribution margin per unit}}$$

The break-even unit sales volume of 750 riding lawn mowers computed for the Moran Manufacturing Company can be verified by the following profit computation:

Total sales revenue (750 mowers @ $800 per mower)	$600,000
Less: Total variable cost (750 mowers @ $320 per mower)	240,000
Total contribution margin (750 mowers @ $480 per mower)	$360,000
Less: Total fixed cost	360,000
Profit	$ 0

Note in this computation that total sales revenue ($600,000) equals total cost ($240,000 variable + $360,000 fixed). Also note that total contribution margin equals total fixed cost ($360,000).

FINDING THE UNIT SALES VOLUME REQUIRED TO EARN A GIVEN AMOUNT OF PROFIT. Finding the break-even point gives a company useful information. Most companies are not interested in earning zero profit, however. They want to earn a high enough profit to satisfy their goals. Profit goals are often stated at amounts that result in a satisfactory rate of return on average total assets devoted to company operations. The rate of return on average total assets is the ratio of profit to average total assets. It is computed by dividing profit by the average cost of all assets used by the company to earn that profit during the period. For example, if the Moran Manufacturing Company has average total assets of $1,200,000, profit of $180,000 produces a rate of return of 15% ($180,000 ÷ $1,200,000).

Suppose Moran's goal is to earn a 20% rate of return on average total assets of $1,200,000. This would require profit of $240,000 (20% × $1,200,000). How many riding mowers must Moran sell to earn $240,000 profit?

We know that total contribution margin minus total fixed cost equals profit. Thus total contribution margin equals total fixed cost plus profit. This is clearly shown in graph (b) of Exhibit 23-9 and can be stated as follows:

$$\left(\begin{array}{c}\text{Contribution}\\\text{margin per unit}\end{array} \times \begin{array}{c}\text{Unit sales}\\\text{volume}\end{array}\right) = \text{Total fixed cost} + \text{Profit}$$

Thus the unit sales volume that produces a given (desired) amount of profit is computed as shown below:

$$\begin{array}{c}\text{Unit sales volume to}\\\text{earn a desired profit}\end{array} = \frac{\text{Total fixed cost} + \text{Desired profit}}{\text{Contribution margin per unit}}$$

Letting x stand for unit sales volume, Moran would compute the unit sales volume needed to earn $240,000 profit as:

$$x = \frac{\$360,000 + \$240,000}{\$480 \text{ per mower}}$$

$$x = 1,250 \text{ mowers}$$

Selling 1,250 mowers results in a profit of $240,000 for Moran. This is verified by the profit computation shown below:

Total sales revenue (1,250 mowers @ $800 per mower)	$1,000,000
Less: Total variable cost (1,250 mowers @ $320 per mower)	400,000
Total contribution margin (1,250 mowers @ $480 per mower)	$ 600,000
Less: Total fixed cost	360,000
Profit	$ 240,000

Note that $600,000 of contribution margin must be earned to obtain a profit of $240,000.

Contribution Margin Percent

In the preceding discussion sales volume was expressed in units. However, sales volume can also be expressed in dollars. When the selling price and variable cost per unit of a product are constant, total variable cost is a constant *percent* of total sales revenue (sales volume in dollars). For example, since the Moran Manufacturing Company incurs $320 of variable cost to manufacture and sell each riding lawn mower sold for $800, the variable cost is 40% ($320 ÷ $800) of the mower's selling price. Moran's total variable cost at a sales volume of 500 mowers is $160,000 (500 × $320), and its total sales revenue at that volume is $400,000 (500 × $800). Thus at a sales volume of 500 units, total variable cost is 40% ($160,000 ÷ $400,000) of total sales revenue. This can also be observed in the profit computation in Exhibit 23-7, in which total variable cost ($320,000) is 40% of total sales revenue ($800,000) at a sales volume of 1,000 mowers.

The total contribution margin is also a constant percent of total sales revenue. For Moran, since sales are 100% and variable cost 40% of sales revenue, total contribution margin is always 60% (100% − 40%) of sales revenue. This is true for each unit ($480 ÷ $800 = 60%) and must therefore be true for any total number of units. In Exhibit 23-7, for example, Moran's total contribution margin ($480,000) is 60% of its total sales revenue ($800,000) at a sales volume of 1,000 units. A decision to change the selling price or variable cost per unit in the next period (to be discussed later), however, would change the contribution margin percent for the next period.

When sales volume is expressed in dollars instead of units, the contribution margin percent is used in place of the contribution margin per unit. Profit can be expressed by the following equation:

$$\text{Profit} = \left(\begin{array}{ccc} \text{Contribution} & & \text{Dollar} \\ \text{margin} & \times & \text{sales} \\ \text{percent} & & \text{volume} \end{array} \right) - \text{Total fixed cost}$$

Each of the computations described in the previous section to answer the three basic questions of Cost–Volume–Profit Analysis can also be made when sales volume is measured in dollars. Using the profit equation above, for example, Moran could estimate its profit at a given sales volume of $900,000 as follows:

$$
\begin{aligned}
\text{Profit} &= (60\% \times \$900,000) & - \quad \$360,000 \\
&= \$540,000 & - \quad \$360,000 \\
&= \$180,000
\end{aligned}
$$

Similarly, to find the break-even point (in sales dollars) the computation would be:

$$
\frac{\text{Break-even point}}{\text{(in dollars)}} = \frac{\text{Total fixed cost}}{\text{Contribution margin percent}}
$$

Moran's computation would be:

$$
\text{Break-even point (in dollars)} = \frac{\$360,000}{60\%} = \$600,000
$$

Since each mower is sold for $800 the break-even point determined in sales dollars for Moran is consistent with the break-even point in units computed earlier (750 mowers @ $800 per mower = $600,000).

To find the dollar sales volume required to earn a desired amount of profit, the computation would be:

$$
\text{Dollar sales volume to earn a desired profit} = \frac{\text{Total fixed cost} + \text{Desired profit}}{\text{Contribution margin percent}}
$$

Thus for Moran to earn $240,000 of profit would require a dollar sales volume of $1,000,000. The computation would be:

$$
\begin{aligned}
\text{Dollar sales volume to earn \$240,000 profit} &= \frac{\$360,000 + \$240,000}{60\%} \\
&= \frac{\$600,000}{60\%} \\
&= \$1,000,000
\end{aligned}
$$

This sales volume expressed in dollars to earn a $240,000 profit is consistent with the 1,250 units of sales volume (1,250 × $800 = $1 million) computed earlier.

There is little need to perform Cost–Volume–Profit Analysis with sales volume measured in dollars when a company sells only one product. Representing sales volume by units of that product is easier; however, most companies sell several products. When these companies perform a C–V–P Analysis of their overall operations, it is usually more understandable to measure sales volume in dollars. We measure sales volume in dollars later in our discussion of multiproduct C–V–P Analysis.

Using C–V–P Analysis in Planning

C–V–P Analysis is useful in planning because it shows the potential profit impact of alternative plans. Thus the analysis can help management make its planning decisions. Many of the important ideas developed from this chapter are useful in later chapters, particularly Chapter 26, which deals with short-term decision making. In the following discussion we illustrate how C–V–P Analysis can show the potential profit impact of alternative plans.

Although the Moran Manufacturing Company sold only 1,000 riding mowers and earned $120,000 in 1983 (see Exhibit 23-7), suppose that the company believes that during 1984 it will be able to sell 1,250 mowers solely because of increased demand. At that unit sales volume, profit is expected to be $240,000 [($480 contribution margin per unit × 1,250 units) − $360,000 total fixed cost]. Moran's management, however, is considering three alternative plans (only one of which will be followed) that it believes may allow even more than $240,000 to be earned. These plans are as follows:

1. Raise the selling price of the mowers to $920 per mower. With this alternative, variable cost per unit and total fixed cost do not change.
2. Purchase higher quality engines for the mowers, thus increasing the variable manufacturing cost per mower by $80. This alternative is being considered because quality improvement often increases unit sales volume. With this alternative, neither the selling price per unit nor the total fixed cost changes.
3. Increase total fixed cost by spending $96,000 more on advertising. With this alternative, the selling price per unit and the variable cost per unit do not change.

CHANGING SELLING PRICES.   Plans that involve changing the selling price of a product can have a great impact on profit. Total sales revenue can change because of the price change alone, but it can also change if the unit sales volume is affected. If unit sales volume is affected, however, total variable cost also changes. Graphs of the cost, volume, and profit relationships can be used to show the potential profit impact of these changes.

In Exhibit 23-10, graph (b) of Exhibit 23-9 has been redrawn and a new line has been added, showing the total contribution margin that would be earned if Moran increased the selling price of its mower to $920 while not changing the variable cost

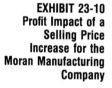

EXHIBIT 23-10
Profit Impact of a
Selling Price
Increase for the
Moran Manufacturing
Company

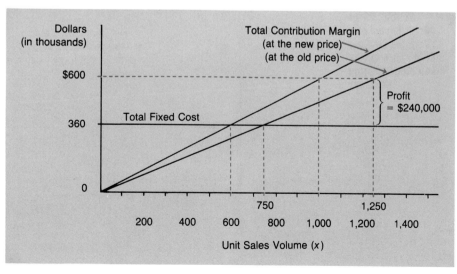

per unit. This new price would increase the contribution margin per unit to $600 ($920 selling price per unit − $320 variable cost per unit). Note that the new line shows total contribution margin increasing faster (the line is steeper) than it did before. The fixed cost line has not changed.

Note in Exhibit 23-10 that Moran can break even by selling only 600 units at the new price of $920 per unit. That is, Moran's break-even point is reduced from 750 units to 600 units by the increase in selling price. In fact, fewer units would have to be sold at the new price of $920 than at the old price of $800 to earn any given level of profit. For example, Exhibit 23-10 shows that if Moran desires to earn $240,000 profit, which requires $600,000 of total contribution margin ($600,000 total contribution margin − $360,000 total fixed costs = $240,000 profit), it has to sell only 1,000 mowers at the $920 selling price as compared to 1,250 mowers at the $800 selling price. Thus if the unit sales volume can be kept above 1,000 mowers after the price increase, Moran would earn more than $240,000 in 1984.

If Moran's plan had called for decreasing the selling price of its mowers, each of the effects described above would be reversed. Decreasing the selling price of a product *reduces* its contribution margin per unit and *increases* the unit sales volume required to break even or to attain any given desired level of profit.

CHANGING VARIABLE COST PER UNIT.   Plans sometimes result in changes in variable cost per unit. Alternative 2 being considered by Moran, for example, would increase variable manufacturing cost per unit by $80 while the selling price per unit and the total fixed cost would not change. This plan would *increase* variable cost per unit to $400 ($320 + $80) and *decrease* the contribution margin per unit to $400 ($800 selling price − $400 variable cost per unit). The potential profit effects of this alternative are pictured in Exhibit 23-11. In this exhibit graph (b) of Exhibit 23-9 has been redrawn with a new line added to show the total contribution margin

EXHIBIT 23-11
Profit Impact of a
Variable Cost per
Unit Increase for the
Moran Manufacturing
Company

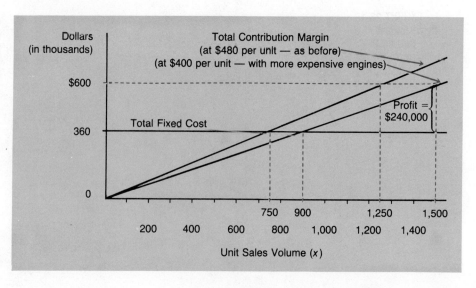

that would be earned if Moran used the more expensive engine in its mowers. Note that the new line shows total contribution margin increasing more slowly (the new line is not as steep) than it did before. The fixed cost line has not changed.

Note in Exhibit 23-11 that Moran must sell 900 riding lawn mowers to break even if variable cost per unit is increased by $80. In fact, more mowers would have to be sold than before the variable cost increase to earn any given level of profit. For example, note in the exhibit that after the variable cost per unit increase, Moran must now sell 1,500 mowers to earn $600,000 total contribution margin and thus earn $240,000 profit. When the contribution margin per unit was $480, it was necessary to sell only 1,250 mowers to earn $240,000 profit. Thus if Moran can sell more than 1,500 mowers because of the higher quality engines, its profit would exceed $240,000.

Plans that result in decreases in variable cost per unit would create effects the reverse of the effects described above. If Moran had *decreased* its variable cost per unit, its contribution margin per unit would have *increased* and fewer riding mowers would have to be sold than before to earn any given amount of profit.

CHANGING FIXED COSTS. Plans that increase or decrease total fixed costs also affect profit. **Discretionary fixed costs are fixed costs that can be changed quickly by the decisions of management.** Advertising is a good example of a discretionary fixed cost. The amount of advertising cost incurred for a period can often be increased or decreased at the discretion of management. Another example is research and development costs. Although advertising and research and development costs can often be increased or decreased rather quickly by management decisions, these decisions must be made carefully because they may affect the company's profit for many years in the future.

Not all fixed costs can be changed quickly, however. Some fixed costs must be incurred to maintain a company's ability to operate. Depreciation on factory and office buildings and equipment, as well as salaries of top management, may be difficult to change (especially to decrease) by substantial amounts. **Committed fixed costs are fixed costs that cannot be changed quickly by management's decisions.** Committed fixed costs must be incurred period after period in about the same amounts because of commitments the company has made by previous decisions. Drastic changes in company operations over several years may be required to affect certain committed fixed costs.

The third alternative being considered by the Moran Manufacturing Company is to increase its advertising cost. This would increase Moran's total fixed cost while its selling price and variable cost per unit would remain unchanged. The potential profit effects of this alternative are shown in Exhibit 23-12. In this exhibit graph (b) of Exhibit 23-9 has been redrawn, adding a new line to show the increased amount of total fixed cost. The total contribution margin line has not changed.

Exhibit 23-12 shows that if Moran increased its advertising cost by $96,000, the profit earned at any given unit sales volume would be $96,000 lower than before. As a result of increasing fixed costs by $96,000, the break-even point is increased by 200 units (from 750 to 950). Increasing the total fixed cost increases the unit sales volume required to earn any given level of profit. Note that if Moran increased

EXHIBIT 23-12
Profit Impact of a
Fixed Cost Increase
for the Moran
Manufacturing
Company

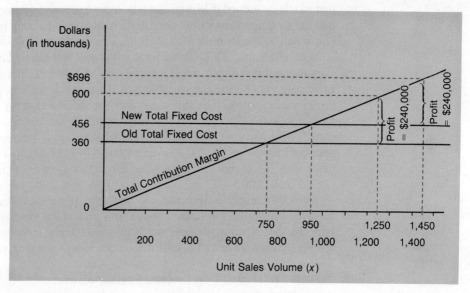

advertising cost by $96,000, it would have to sell 1,450 mowers to earn the $240,000 desired profit which could have been earned by selling 1,250 mowers before the change. If Moran is able to sell more than 1,450 mowers as a result of the increased advertising, however, more than $240,000 profit would be earned.

If fixed costs had been decreased the profit effects would be the reverse of the effects shown in Exhibit 23-12. The break-even point would be reduced and the unit sales volume required to earn any given level of profit would decrease.

Notice that the C–V–P Analysis for these three alternatives does *not* provide enough information for Moran to make a decision. Each of the alternatives is likely to affect the number of mowers Moran can sell. Thus before a decision can be made Moran would have to estimate the probable unit sales volume for each alternative. For whatever sales volume Moran expects, however, the analysis can provide a profit estimate. The alternative resulting in the greatest profit improvement over $240,000 would be chosen.

MULTIPRODUCT COST–VOLUME–PROFIT ANALYSIS

In previous sections of this chapter we discussed C–V–P Analysis for a company with *one* product. In this section we discuss the use of Cost–Volume–Profit Analysis for a company that sells more than one product. We use an example involving two products in order to keep the computations simple. The procedure described can be used with any number of products, however.

Most companies sell more than one product. This does not mean that the single product analysis we have just described is not useful, however. A single product analysis can be applied to study the profit–volume relationship of any one of a company's products as long as the company can separate costs and sales revenues of that product from those caused by the production and sales of other products. The single product form of analysis can also be applied in a multiproduct situation to any group of the company's products, assuming the product mix is known. **The product mix is the number of units of each product sold relative to the total units sold.** For example, a company might sell three units of product X for every unit of product Y sold. As long as the company sells product X and Y in those proportions (75% product X, 25% product Y), it is said to have the same product mix.

Suppose that the Jersey Company produces and sells two products, product A and product B. A unit of product A sells for $10, requires $8 of variable cost, and earns a contribution margin of $2 (20% of sales dollars from product A). A unit of product B sells for $5, requires $1 of variable cost, and earns a contribution margin of $4 (80% of sales dollars from product B). A computation of the contribution margin earned by Jersey last year from product A, from product B, and in total is shown below:

	Product A	Product B	Total
Sales (units)	10,000	10,000	20,000
Sales revenue	$100,000	$50,000	$150,000
Less variable costs	80,000	10,000	90,000
Contribution margin	$ 20,000	$40,000	$ 60,000
Contribution margin percent	(20%)	(80%)	(40%)

In this computation the total unit sales is 20,000, of which 10,000 are of product A and 10,000 are of product B. Therefore, the product mix is 50% product A and 50% product B. Note that at the product mix experienced by Jersey, the total contribution margin from both products ($60,000) is 40% of total sales revenue ($150,000). No matter how many total units are sold, as long as the product mix is 50% product A and 50% product B, Jersey's contribution margin percent for all sales is 40%. That is, the "average" sales dollar earns $.40 of contribution margin.

This contribution margin percent for all sales (40%) is a *weighted average* of the contribution margin percents for products A and B. The "weights" used to compute this weighted average are the proportions of total sales *dollars* from the sale of each product. Note that at last year's product mix, two-thirds ($100,000 ÷ $150,000) of Jersey's sales dollars are from sales of product A (having a contribution margin of 20% of sales dollars) while the remaining one-third of its sales dollars are from sales of product B (having a contribution margin percent of 80%). The weighted average contribution margin percent can be computed as shown below:

$$
\begin{aligned}
\text{Weighted average contribution margin percent} &= \left(\begin{array}{l} \text{Proportion of sales} \\ \text{dollars from} \\ \text{product A} \end{array} \times \begin{array}{l} \text{Product A's} \\ \text{contribution margin} \\ \text{percent} \end{array} \right) + \\
&\quad \left(\begin{array}{l} \text{Proportion of sales} \\ \text{dollars from} \\ \text{product B} \end{array} \times \begin{array}{l} \text{Product B's} \\ \text{contribution margin} \\ \text{percent} \end{array} \right) \\
&= (2/3 \times 20\%) + (1/3 \times 80\%) \\
&= 13.33\% + 26.67\% \\
&= 40\%
\end{aligned}
$$

Jersey can use this weighted average contribution margin percent to perform a C–V–P Analysis for its two products. For instance, assume that Jersey's fixed cost totals $80,000 per year. Jersey could compute its break-even point (in sales dollars) as shown below:

$$\text{Break-even point (in dollars)} = \frac{\text{Total fixed cost}}{\text{Weighted average contribution margin percent}}$$

$$= \frac{\$80,000}{40\%}$$

$$= \$200,000$$

Or Jersey could estimate profit at a total sales volume (in dollars) of $250,000 by computing the following:

$$\text{Profit} = \left(\begin{array}{c}\text{Weighted average} \\ \text{contribution margin} \times \text{Dollar sales volume} \\ \text{percent}\end{array}\right) - \text{Total fixed cost}$$

$$= (40\% \times \$250,000) - \$80,000$$
$$= \$100,000 - \$80,000$$
$$= \$20,000$$

Jersey could also compute the total dollar sales volume needed to earn a desired amount of profit. Suppose that the company wanted to earn $30,000 profit. The computation would be as follows:

$$\text{Dollars sales volume needed to earn a desired profit} = \frac{\text{Total fixed cost} + \text{Desired profit}}{\text{Weighted average contribution margin percent}}$$

$$\text{Dollar sales volume needed to earn \$30,000 profit} = \frac{\$80,000 \text{ fixed cost} + \$30,000 \text{ desired profit}}{40\%}$$

$$= \$275,000$$

These computations would be misleading, however, if Jersey's product mix did not remain 50% product A and 50% product B. When a company's products have different contribution margin percents, a change in product mix changes the weighted average contribution margin percent for the company's total sales.

Suppose, for example, that sales of product A increase relative to product B so that Jersey sells two units of product A for each unit of product B. Since product A sells for $10 per unit and product B sells for $5 per unit, $20 of sales revenue are earned by two units of product A for each $5 of sales revenue earned by one unit of product B. Thus four-fifths [$20 ÷ ($20 + $5)] of all sales dollars are from sales of product A, while one-fifth [$5 ÷ ($20 + $5)] of all sales dollars are from sales of product B. The new weighted average contribution margin percent is as follows:

$$(4/5 \times 20\%) + (1/5 \times 80\%) = 16\% + 16\% = 32\%$$

Thus the computations using the 40% weighted average are no longer appropriate for the new product mix. With the new product mix, for example, total dollar sales volume would have to be $250,000 ($80,000 total fixed cost ÷ 32%) for Jersey to break even.

ASSUMPTIONS OF COST-VOLUME–PROFIT ANALYSIS

There are two basic assumptions required by the C–V–P Analysis described in this chapter to make it useful for management planning. They are:

1. All costs can be separated into two categories (costs that are fixed and costs that are variable) and estimated with some degree of accuracy for the planning period.
2. The total cost and total revenue lines are approximately linear (straight), at least within the sales volume range that is relevant to the intended use of the analysis.

You should recognize, however, that several conditions are necessary for each assumption to be satisfied. The first assumption, for example, requires a well-developed cost accounting system that can provide sufficient data to judge the behavior patterns of various costs and, when necessary, to separate fixed and variable components of mixed costs. In addition, the cost behavior patterns must be fairly stable so that fixed costs of one period, for example, do not become variable costs during the next period.

Similarly, the second assumption requires the selling price per unit to be known and constant so that total sales revenue can be represented by a straight line as volume increases. For total cost to increase linearly requires total fixed cost to remain constant (in total) and variable cost to remain constant *per unit* as sales volume increases. For variable cost to remain constant per unit, approximately the same amount of effort and use of resources must be required to produce and sell, say the five-hundredth unit, as it does the thousandth unit. In addition, for the multiproduct analysis the product mix must be known and constant for the second assumption to be satisfied.

These two assumptions may seem difficult to satisfy. In practice, however, the necessary conditions are often met and many companies find the C–V–P Analysis described in this chapter very helpful in planning their future activities.

SUMMARY OF C–V–P ANALYSIS COMPUTATIONS

Exhibit 23-13 summarizes the computations used in our discussion of C–V–P Analysis. These computations are presented as equations that can be used to answer the basic questions that occur frequently in C–V–P Analysis. Equations to compute profit, the break-even point, or the sales volume to earn a desired profit are shown in each form discussed in this chapter.

**EXHIBIT 23-13
Summary of
Cost–Volume–Profit
Computations**

To Determine	Computation

Profit (for a given unit sales volume) $= \left(\begin{array}{c}\text{Selling}\\ \text{price per} \times \text{Unit sales}\\ \text{unit}\quad\text{volume}\end{array}\right) - \left(\begin{array}{c}\text{Variable}\\ \text{cost} \times \text{Unit sales}\\ \text{per unit}\quad\text{volume}\end{array}\right) - \begin{array}{c}\text{Total}\\ \text{fixed}\\ \text{cost}\end{array}$

or

$= \left(\begin{array}{c}\text{Contribution}\\ \text{margin per} \times \text{Unit sales}\\ \text{unit}\quad\text{volume}\end{array}\right) - \text{Total fixed cost}$

Profit (for a given dollar sales volume) $= \left(\begin{array}{c}\text{Contribution}\\ \text{margin} \times \text{Dollar sales}\\ \text{percent}\quad\text{volume}\end{array}\right) - \text{Total fixed cost}$

Profit (on several products) $= \left(\begin{array}{c}\text{Weighted average}\\ \text{contribution margin} \times \text{Dollar sales}\\ \text{percent}\quad\text{volume}\end{array}\right) - \text{Total fixed cost}$

Break-even point (in units) $= \dfrac{\text{Total fixed cost}}{\text{Contribution margin per unit}}$

Break-even point (in dollars) $= \dfrac{\text{Total fixed cost}}{\text{Contribution margin percent}}$

Break-even point (in total sales dollars for several products) $= \dfrac{\text{Total fixed cost}}{\text{Weighted average contribution margin percent}}$

Unit sales volume required to earn a desired profit $= \dfrac{\text{Total fixed cost} + \text{Desired profit}}{\text{Contribution margin per unit}}$

Dollar sales volume required to earn a desired profit $= \dfrac{\text{Total fixed cost} + \text{Desired profit}}{\text{Contribution margin percent}}$

Total dollar sales volume (from several products) required to earn a desired profit $= \dfrac{\text{Total fixed cost} + \text{Desired profit}}{\text{Weighted average contribution margin percent}}$

Weighted average contribution margin percent (for two products, A and B) $= \left(\begin{array}{c}\text{Proportion}\\ \text{of sales dollars} \times \text{Product A's}\\ \text{from product A}\quad\text{contribution}\\ \text{margin percent}\end{array}\right) +$

$\left(\begin{array}{c}\text{Proportion}\\ \text{of sales dollars} \times \text{Product B's}\\ \text{from product B}\quad\text{contribution}\\ \text{margin percent}\end{array}\right)$

REVIEW PROBLEM

The Campcraft Company is a small manufacturer of camping trailers. The company manufactures only one model and sells the units for $2,500 each. The variable costs of manufacturing and selling each trailer total $1,600. Total fixed cost amounts to $180,000 per year.

Required:
1. Compute the company's contribution margin per unit.
2. Compute the company's profit (or loss) at a sales volume of 160 units.
3. Compute the number of units that must be sold for the company to break even.
4. Compute the number of units that must be sold for the company to earn a profit of $31,500.
5. Compute the company's contribution margin percent.
6. Compute the company's profit (or loss) at a dollar sales volume of $540,000.
7. What dollar sales volume is required for the company to break even?
8. What dollar sales volume is required for the company to earn a profit of $72,000?

SOLUTION TO REVIEW PROBLEM

1. Contribution margin = Selling price − Variable cost
   per unit   per unit   per unit

   = $2,500 − $1,600 = $900

2. Profit (at 160 units) = $\left(\begin{array}{c} \text{Contribution} \\ \text{margin per} \\ \text{unit} \end{array} \times \begin{array}{c} \text{Unit} \\ \text{sales} \\ \text{volume} \end{array} \right)$ − Total fixed cost

   = ($900 × 160) − $180,000
   = $144,000 − $180,000
   = ($36,000) loss

3. Break-even point (in units) = $\dfrac{\text{Total fixed cost}}{\text{Contribution margin per unit}}$

   = $\dfrac{\$180,000}{\$900}$ = 200 units

4. Unit sales volume required to earn profit of $31,500 = $\dfrac{\text{Total fixed cost} + \text{Desired profit}}{\text{Contribution margin per unit}}$

   = $\dfrac{\$180,000 + \$31,500}{\$900}$ = 235 units

5. Contribution margin percent = $\dfrac{\text{Contribution margin per unit}}{\text{Selling price per unit}}$

   = $\dfrac{\$900}{\$2,500}$ = 36%

6. Profit (at \$540,000 sales) $= \begin{pmatrix} \text{Contribution} & \text{Dollar} \\ \text{margin} & \times \text{ sales} \\ \text{percent} & \text{volume} \end{pmatrix} -$ Total fixed cost

$$= (36\% \times \$540,000) - \$180,000$$
$$= \$194,400 - \$180,000$$
$$= \$14,400$$

7. Break-even point (in dollars) $= \dfrac{\text{Total fixed cost}}{\text{Contribution margin percent}}$

$$= \frac{\$180,000}{36\%} = \$500,000$$

8. Dollar sales volume required to earn profit of \$72,000 $= \dfrac{\text{Total fixed cost} + \text{Desired profit}}{\text{Contribution margin percent}}$

$$= \frac{\$180,000 + \$72,000}{36\%}$$
$$= \$700,000$$

GLOSSARY

Break-Even Point. The sales volume (in units or dollars) at which total sales revenue equals total cost so that a company's profit is zero.

Committed Fixed Costs. Fixed costs that cannot be changed (especially not decreased) quickly by management decisions.

Contribution Margin. The difference between total sales revenue and total variable costs. In C–V–P Analysis the contribution margin is often computed *per unit* of product sold, or as a *percent* of sales dollars.

Controlling. The process by which management attempts to ensure that employees are using company resources efficiently in performing planned activities and that those activities are effective in attaining company goals.

Cost Behavior. The manner in which a cost is affected by changes in the volume of activity of the operation in which it is incurred.

Cost–Volume–Profit Analysis. An analysis of the relationships between costs, revenue, and profit as sales volume varies. Also called *break-even analysis*.

Discretionary Fixed Costs. Fixed costs that can be quickly changed by management decisions.

Feedback. Information from the performance evaluation of an activity that draws management's attention to problems occurring in that activity.

Fixed Cost. A cost not affected in total by changes in volume.

Goal Structure. The set of goals and supporting subgoals determined by a company during long-range planning to describe its objectives and to suggest the activities that are necessary to accomplish them.

High–Low Method. A procedure for separating the fixed and variable components of a mixed cost.

Mixed Cost. A cost that has a fixed component and a variable component. Also called *semivariable cost*.

Organizing. The process of establishing working relationships between managers and employees and assigning them specific jobs so that the company's activities can be performed.

Performance Evaluation. A basic form of control in which actual performance is judged against planned performance in order to identify problems or unexpected conditions interfering with the efficiency and effectiveness of operations.

Planning. The process by which management determines the activities that must be performed and the types and amounts of resources that must be provided for the company to accomplish its goals.

Product Mix. The number of units of each product sold relative to total units.

Relevant Range. The range of volume that has to be considered for the intended use of a cost, revenue, or profit analysis.

Scatter Diagram. The diagram obtained by plotting cost and volume data points on a graph.

Scheduling. Detailed short-range planning of a company's activities through time.

Variable Cost. A cost that is constant *per unit* of volume so that the total varies directly in proportion to volume.

QUESTIONS

Q23-1   Briefly describe the three parts of planning.

Q23-2   How are short-range and long-range planning related?

Q23-3   The Brandon Company has identified two goals: (a) to produce the highest quality computers on the market, and (b) to earn a reasonable profit for the company's owners. Does goal (a) support goal (b) or is it in conflict with it? Discuss.

Q23-4   How are planning and controlling related?

Q23-5   How can managerial accounting be helpful in planning?

Q23-6   How can managerial accounting be helpful in controlling?

Q23-7   What is meant by cost behavior?

Q23-8   Why is it useful to study the behavior of costs?

Q23-9   How can accurate and detailed records of past costs be helpful in estimating future costs?

Q23-10   Define fixed costs.

Q23-11   Give two examples of costs that might be fixed under one set of conditions and variable under another. For each example, discuss what conditions must be different for the cost to change its behavior pattern.

Q23-12 "Last year the plant manager earned $24,000. This year he earned $26,000. Next year he may earn $30,000. How can his salary be a fixed cost?" Discuss.

Q23-13 Define variable cost.

Q23-14 Why do total variable costs increase directly in proportion to volume?

Q23-15 Why do fixed costs *per unit of volume* decrease as volume increases?

Q23-16 Define mixed cost.

Q23-17 Do mixed costs *per unit of volume* increase, remain constant, or decrease as volume increases? Discuss.

Q23-18 When is cost estimation useful in controlling?

Q23-19 Define total contribution margin and discuss why it is useful to compute the contribution margin *per unit* and the contribution margin *percent*.

Q23-20 Explain why total contribution margin varies directly in proportion to sales volume.

Q23-21 "When a company sells one product it has one break-even point, when it sells two products it has two break-even points." Discuss.

Q23-22 Why does the number of units a company has to sell to earn a desired amount of profit equal: (Total fixed cost + Desired profit) ÷ Contribution margin per unit?

EXERCISES

E23-1 Cost Behavior. A company incurs three costs, A, B, and C, in manufacturing a product. The volume of the company's manufacturing activity is measured in units of product, (x). Below are the cost equations for the three costs:

$$\text{Cost A} = \$2.00\ x$$
$$\text{Cost B} = \$500 + \$.30\ x$$
$$\text{Cost C} = \$1,000$$

Required:
1. Which cost is the fixed cost? Variable cost? Mixed cost?
2. Compute cost A, cost B, and cost C at the following number of units:
   (a) 200 units
   (b) 400 units
   (c) 600 units
   (d) 800 units
   (e) 1,000 units
3. Graph cost A, cost B, and cost C on the same graph as volume varies from 0 to 1,000 units.

E23-2 Cost Behavior. Refer to the three cost equations in E23-1.

Required:
1. Compute the cost *per unit* for cost A, cost B, and cost C at the following number of units:
   (a) 200 units
   (b) 400 units
   (c) 600 units
   (d) 800 units
   (e) 1,000 units
2. Graph each of the three costs *per unit* on the same graph as volume varies from 200 to 1,000 units.

E23-3 Cost Behavior (Engineering Approach). Western Brands produces western clothing. One product, a western-style tie, is manufactured from a thin 36-inch strip of leather $\frac{1}{4}$-inch wide and four fancy brass rings. The leather strip is threaded through two of the rings, which, together, act as a clasp. The remaining two rings are sewn onto the ends of the leather strip.

Leather strips are purchased in 72-inch lengths that are 2 inches wide for $3.20 each and are cut to $\frac{1}{4}$-inch widths and then cut again to 36-inch lengths. Brass rings cost $6.00 per dozen.

Required: 1. Compute the cost *per unit* (per tie) of the:
   (a) Leather strip
   (b) Brass rings
   (c) Total direct materials
2. Write out the cost equations in terms of ties produced for the *total* cost of:
   (a) Leather strip
   (b) Brass rings
   (c) Total direct materials
3. Estimate the *total* direct materials cost to produce 400 ties.

E23-4 Cost Behavior. Dalco has estimated its factory overhead costs for next year at two volumes, 1,500 and 2,000 units. These estimates are shown below:

	Factory Overhead Costs	
	1,500 units	*2,000 units*
Depreciation on factory equipment	$ 35,000	$ 35,000
Rent	60,000	60,000
Supervisory salaries	45,000	45,000
Maintenance on equipment	19,500	21,000
Utilities	10,500	14,000
Supplies	7,500	10,000
Total	$177,500	$185,000

Each of the individual cost items is a fixed, variable, or mixed cost.

Required: 1. Determine the cost equation for each of the individual cost items and for total factory overhead.
2. Estimate total factory overhead cost at 1,800 units.

E23-5 Cost Behavior. The Brickhouse Company is planning to lease an automobile for the sales manager of its northern sales territory. The leasing company is willing to lease the car under three alternative plans:

Plan A — Brickhouse would pay $.34 per mile and buy its own gas.

Plan B — Brickhouse would pay $320 per month plus $.10 per mile and buy its own gas.

Plan C — Brickhouse would pay $960 per month and the leasing company would pay for all gas.

The leasing company will pay for all repairs and maintenance, insurance, license fees, and so on. Gas is expected to cost $.06 per mile.

Required: Using miles driven as the units of volume:
   1. Write out the cost equation for the cost of operating the sales manager's automobile under each of the three plans.
   2. Graph the three cost equations on the same graph (put cost on the vertical axis and miles driven per month on the horizontal axis).
   3. At what mileage per month would the cost of Plan A equal the cost of Plan B?
   4. At what mileage per month would the cost of Plan B equal the cost of Plan C?
   5. Compute the cost under each of the three plans of driving 3,500 miles per month.

E23-6 **The High–Low Method.** The utility costs and production levels of a company for the last four months were as follows:

Month	Cost	Production Level (units)
1	$1,340	2,000
2	1,600	2,600
3	1,940	3,500
4	1,680	2,900

Required: Assuming the utility cost to be a mixed cost, use the high–low method with the data given to determine its cost equation. What utility cost would be expected during month 5 if 3,100 units are produced?

E23-7 **C–V–P Analysis.** Morelco produces a single product that sells for $8 per unit. Variable cost is $6 per unit and fixed cost totals $30,000 per year.

Required: 1. Draw one graph showing Morelco's total revenue, total variable cost, and total cost as volume varies. Locate the break-even point on the graph.
2. Write out Morelco's profit equation in terms of units sold.
3. Compute Morelco's break-even point in units.
4. Write out Morelco's profit equation in terms of sales dollars.
5. Compute Morelco's break-even point in sales dollars.

E23-8 **C–V–P Analysis — Volume in Sales Units.** The Mallory Motors Company manufactures small electric motors that sell for $1.50 per motor. Variable cost is $1.20 per unit and fixed cost totals $60,000 per year.

Required: 1. Write out Mallory's profit equation in terms of motors sold.
2. Draw a graph of Mallory's total contribution margin and total fixed cost as volume varies. Locate the break-even point on this graph.
3. Compute Mallory's break-even point in units.
4. What total profit would Mallory expect if it sold 500,000 motors?
5. How many motors would Mallory have to sell to earn $50,000 of profit?

E23-9 **C–V–P Analysis — Volume in Sales Dollars.** Refer to E23-8.

Required: 1. Compute Mallory's contribution margin percent.
2. Compute Mallory's break-even point in sales dollars.
3. What total profit (loss) would Mallory have if its total sales revenue amounted to $230,000?
4. How much would total dollar sales volume have to be for Mallory to earn $40,000 of profit?

E23-10 **Changing Fixed Costs.** This year Babco's fixed cost totals $100,000. The company sells a single product for $8 per unit. Variable cost per unit is $6.

Required: 1. Compute the break-even point in units.
2. Compute the number of units required to earn a profit of $20,000.
3. If total fixed cost increases to $120,000 next year:
    (a) What will Babco's break-even point be in units?
    (b) What profit (or loss) will Babco have if 50,000 units are sold?
    (c) How many units will Babco have to sell to earn a profit of $20,000?

E23-11 C–V–P Analysis at Different Selling Prices. The Cardiff Corporation produces a single product currently selling for $40 per unit. Total fixed cost amounts to $360,000 per year and variable cost per unit is $30.

Required: 1. Compute the following amounts for the Cardiff Corporation:
    (a) Contribution margin per unit
    (b) Break-even point in units
    (c) Contribution margin percent
    (d) Break-even point in sales dollars
    (e) The number of units that must be sold to earn $30,000 of profit
    (f) The sales volume (in dollars) required to earn $60,000 of profit
2. Repeat all computations in Requirement 1 above assuming Cardiff decides to increase its selling price per unit to $45. Assume that total fixed cost and variable cost per unit remain the same.

E23-12 Multiproduct C–V–P Analysis. The Gamma Company manufactures two products. Product X has a contribution margin of $6 per unit while product Y has a contribution margin of $3 per unit. Total fixed cost is currently $450,000. Gamma expects to sell two units of product X for each unit of Y sold. Both products sell for $10 per unit.

Required: 1. Compute the weighted average contribution margin percent.
2. At the present product mix, what total dollar sales volume is required for the Gamma Company to earn a profit of $150,000?

PROBLEMS

Part A

P23-1A Computation of Profit — Price and Fixed Cost Changes. The Brandon Company sells a single product. The company's profit computation for last year is shown below:

Sales revenue (10,000 units @ $20)		$200,000
Less variable costs:		
Variable manufacturing cost	$55,000	
Variable selling cost	25,000	80,000
Contribution margin		$120,000
Less fixed costs:		
Fixed manufacturing cost	$50,000	
Fixed selling and administrative cost	30,000	80,000
Profit		$ 40,000

Brandon has decided to increase the price of its product to $24 per unit. The company believes that if it increases fixed advertising (selling) cost by $16,000, sales volume next year will be 9,000 units. Variable cost per unit will be unchanged.

Required: 1. Using the format above, show the computation of expected profit for Brandon's operations next year.
2. How many units would Brandon have to sell to earn as much profit next year as it did last year?
3. Does Brandon's decision seem wise? Explain.

P23-2A C–V–P Analysis — Selling Price and Fixed Cost Changes. The Romeo Company produces a single product that it currently sells for $8 per unit. The variable cost per unit of this product is $6. Romeo's fixed cost totals $20,000.

Required: 1. Compute the following amounts for the Romeo Company:

(a) Contribution margin per unit

(b) Break-even point in units

(c) Contribution margin percent

(d) Break-even point in sales dollars

(e) The profit that Romeo will earn at a sales volume of 25,000 units

(f) The number of units that Romeo must sell to earn a profit of $16,000.

2. Repeat all computations in Requirement 1, assuming Romeo *increases* the selling price of its product to $10 and *decreases* its total fixed cost to $16,000. Variable cost per unit remains unchanged.

3. Draw a graph with four lines to show the following:

(a) Total contribution margin earned at unit sales volumes from 0 to 18,000 when the selling price is $8 per unit

'(b) Total contribution margin earned at unit sales volumes from 0 to 18,000 when the selling price is $10 per unit

(c) Romeo's fixed cost total of $20,000

(d) Romeo's fixed cost total of $16,000

(e) Romeo's break-even point in units before and after the selling price and fixed cost changes.

P23-3A   Single Product C–V–P Analysis — Changing Cost Behavior.   The Vendit Company operates and services cigarette vending machines placed in gas stations, motels, and restaurants. Vendit rents 200 machines from the manufacturer. It also rents the space occupied by the machines at each location where they are placed. Luca Pacioli, the company's owner, has two employees who service the machines. Monthly fixed costs for the company are as follows:

Machine rental	200 machines @ $50 per month	$10,000
Space rental	200 locations @ $30 per month	6,000
Employee wages	2 employees @ $600 per month	1,200
Other fixed costs	. . . .	800
Total	. . . .	$18,000

Currently Vendit's only variable costs are the costs of the cigarettes, which are purchased for $.55 per pack. These cigarettes are sold for $.85 per pack.

Required: 1. (a) What is the monthly break-even point (in packs sold)?

(b) Compute Vendit's monthly profit at monthly sales volumes of 52,000, 56,000, 64,000, and 68,000 packs, respectively.

2. Suppose Luca Pacioli could arrange to pay $.10 per pack sold at each location to rent the space occupied by the machines instead of the $30 fixed rent per month. Repeat all computations required in Requirement 1.

3. Would it be desirable for Luca Pacioli to try to change his space rental from a fixed cost ($30 per location) to a variable cost ($.10 per pack sold)? Discuss.

P23-4A   Cost Estimation, Single Product C–V–P Analysis.   Gaylord Enterprises has just begun operations to produce a single product. The product requires 2 pounds of direct materials costing $4 per pound and 3 hours of direct labor at $5 per hour. Factory overhead costs have been estimated at two production volumes as shown below:

Production volume	*Factory overhead costs*
16,000 units	$230,000
32,000 units	310,000

Fixed selling, general, and administrative costs amount to $90,000. The only nonmanufacturing cost that is variable is a sales commission paid to sales personnel. Sales personnel are paid a commission amounting to 5% of the sales revenue from their territory. The company plans to sell its product for $40 per unit.

Required:
1. Write out the equation for Gaylord's profit with x as the number of units sold.
2. Graph Gaylord's total fixed cost and total contribution margin (with dollars on the vertical axis and the number of units sold on the horizontal axis). Locate the break-even point on the graph.
3. Compute Gaylord's break-even point in units.
4. Gaylord expects to sell 20,000 units. How much profit should it expect?
5. What profit (loss) would Gaylord expect if lowering the price of its product to $38 per unit would increase the number of units sold to 24,000?
6. Does the price reduction seem advisable for Gaylord? Explain.

P23-5A   Multiproduct C–V–P Analysis. Greco Manufacturing produces two products. Product A requires $3 per unit of variable cost and sells for $5. Product B has variable cost of $5 per unit and sells for $10. Total fixed costs amount to $63,750.
   This year Greco sold a total of 35,000 units, 5,000 of which were units of product B.
   Greco believes that consumer tastes will shift dramatically next year. Although it expects total *dollar* sales volume will be the same as this year, the product mix will change so that one-third of the units sold will be units of product B.

Required:
1. Compute Greco's profit for *this* year.
2. At what dollar sales volume would Greco have broken even for *this* year?
3. Compute Greco's expected profit for *next* year assuming total dollar sales volume does not change.
4. Why does Greco expect more profit next year than it earned this year when the total dollar sales volume is expected to be the same? Explain.

P23-6A   Multiproduct C–V–P Analysis. The Brady Company expects to operate at a loss next year on its two products as shown below:

	Commons	Specials	Total
Production and sales (units)	100,000	20,000	120,000
Sales revenue	$200,000	$100,000	$300,000
Variable costs	140,000	40,000	180,000
Contribution margin	$ 60,000	$ 60,000	$120,000
Less: Fixed costs			168,000
Profit (loss)			($ 48,000)

The company has two plans that it believes will improve its profit (reduce its loss) next year:

Plan A — To spend $42,000 on an advertising plan to increase the number of *Specials* sold without affecting the number of *Commons* sold.

Plan B — To reduce the selling price of *Specials* from $5 per unit to $4 per unit. This plan is expected to change the product mix so that one *Special* is sold for every two *Commons*.

Required:
1. If *neither* of the two plans is followed, so that Brady's product mix is one *Special* sold for each five *Commons* sold, what must total dollar sales volume be for the company to break even?
2. If Brady follows plan A, how many *Specials* must be sold next year for the company to break even? (The number of *Commons* sold will still be 100,000.)
3. If Brady follows plan B, what total dollar sales volume is required for the company to break even?
4. Compare your answers to Requirements 1 and 3. Explain the result obtained from this comparison.

P23-7A Single Product Break-even Analysis. The Ferguson Manufacturing Company produces a small platform scale for weighing livestock. This scale sells for $1,000. A recent cost analysis shows that Ferguson's cost structure for the coming year is as follows:

Variable cost per unit:

Manufacturing	$ 450
Selling	50

Total annual fixed costs:

Manufacturing	$100,000
Selling and administrative	140,000

Required:
1. Draw a graph that clearly shows total variable cost, total cost, total sales revenue, and total contribution margin as unit sales volume increases. Locate the break-even point on the graph.
2. Compute the break-even point in units.
3. How many units must Ferguson sell to earn $60,000 of profit per year?
4. How much profit would be earned at a sales volume of $700,000?
5. Bob Ferguson, the owner of Ferguson Manufacturing Company, is considering traveling a circuit of county and state fairs around the Midwest each summer to demonstrate the scale, distribute information, and obtain sales contracts. He estimates that this will cost about $12,000 per year. How many additional scales must the company sell per year as a result of this effort to make it worthwhile?

PROBLEMS

Part B

P23-1B Computation of Profit — Price and Fixed Cost Changes. The Truman Company sells a single product. The company's profit computation for last year is shown below:

Sales revenue (20,000 units @ $20)		$400,000
Less variable costs:		
Variable manufacturing cost	$155,000	
Variable selling cost	25,000	180,000
Contribution margin		$220,000
Less fixed costs:		
Fixed manufacturing cost	$150,000	
Fixed selling and administrative cost	30,000	180,000
Profit		$ 40,000

Truman has decided to increase the price of its product to $24 per unit. The company believes that if it increases fixed advertising (selling) cost by $30,000, sales volume next year will be 16,000 units. Variable cost per unit will be unchanged.

Required:
1. Using the format above, show the computation of expected profit for Truman's operations next year.
2. How many units would Truman have to sell to earn as much profit next year as it did last year?
3. Does Truman's decision seem wise? Explain.

P23-2B C–V–P Analysis — Selling Price and Fixed Cost Changes. The Joliet Company produces a single product that it currently sells for $200 per unit. The variable cost per unit of this product is $120. Joliet's fixed cost totals $12,000.

Required:
1. Compute the following amounts for the Joliet Company:

  (a) Contribution margin per unit
  (b) Break-even point in units
  (c) Contribution margin percent
  (d) Break-even point in sales dollars
  (e) The profit that Joliet will earn at a sales volume of 200 units
  (f) The number of units that Joliet must sell to earn a profit of $24,000
2. Repeat all computations in Requirement 1, assuming the Joliet Company *decreases* its selling price to $180 per unit and *increases* its total fixed cost to $15,000. Variable cost per unit remains unchanged.
3. Draw a graph with four lines to show the following:
  (a) Total contribution margin earned at unit sales volumes from 0 to 650 units when the selling price is $200 per unit
  (b) Total contribution margin earned at unit sales volumes from 0 to 650 units when the selling price is $180 per unit
  (c) Joliet's fixed cost total of $12,000
  (d) Joliet's fixed cost total of $15,000
  (e) Joliet's break-even point in units before and after the selling price and fixed cost changes

P23-3B Single Product C–V–P Analysis — Changing Cost Behavior. The Sweety Company operates and services candy bar vending machines placed in gas stations, motels, and restaurants. Sweety rents 400 machines from the manufacturer. It also rents the space occupied by the machines at each location where they are placed. Dee Kaye, the company's owner, has two employees who service the machines. Monthly fixed costs for the company are as follows:

Machine rental	400 machines @ $40 per month	$16,000
Space rental	400 locations @ $15 per month	6,000
Employee wages	2 employees @ $600 per month	1,200
Other fixed costs	. . . .	800
Total	. . . .	$24,000

Currently Sweety's only variable costs are the costs of the candy bars, which are purchased for $.10 per bar. These candy bars are sold for $.30 per bar.

Required: 1. (a) What is the monthly break-even point (in bars sold)?
       (b) Compute Sweety's monthly profit at monthly sales volumes of 100,000, 110,000, 130,000, and 140,000 bars, respectively.
    2. Suppose Dee Kaye could arrange to pay $.05 per bar sold at each location to rent the space occupied by the machines instead of the $15 fixed rent per month. Repeat all computations in Requirement 1.
    3. Would it be desirable for Dee Kaye to try to change her space rental from a fixed cost ($15 per location) to a variable cost ($.05 per bar sold)? Discuss.

P23-4B Single Product Break-even Analysis. The Farragut Manufacturing Company produces heavy duty wheelbarrows. These wheelbarrows sell for $80 each. A recent cost analysis shows that Farragut's cost structure for the coming year is as follows:

Variable cost per unit:		
Manufacturing	$	45
Selling		5
Total annual fixed cost:		
Manufacturing	$80,000	
Selling and administrative	40,000	

Required: 1. Draw a graph that clearly shows total variable cost, total cost, total sales revenue, and total contribution margin as unit sales volume increases. Locate the break-even point on the graph.
2. Compute the break-even point in units.
3. How many units must Farragut sell to earn $60,000 of profit per year?
4. How much profit would be earned at a sales volume of $400,000?
5. Farragut is considering hiring a sales representative. Travel expenses and salary for this new employee will total $36,000 per year. How many additional wheelbarrows must be sold each year as a result of the sales representative's efforts to make hiring this new employee worthwhile for the company?

P23-5B   Multiproduct C–V–P Analysis. Bingo Manufacturing produces two products. Product A requires $3 per unit of variable costs and sells for $4. Product B has variable costs of $5 per unit and sells for $8. Total fixed costs amount to $36,000.

This year Bingo sold 14,400 units of product A and 9,600 units of product B.

Next year Bingo believes that three-fourths of the units it sells will be units of product A. Total dollar sales volume is expected to remain the same as this year, however.

Required: 1. Compute Bingo's profit for *this* year.
2. What total dollar sales volume will be required *next* year for Bingo to break even?
3. Compute Bingo's expected profit for *next* year assuming total dollar sales volume is the same as this year.
4. Why does Bingo expect less profit for *next* year than it earned this year when total dollar sales volume is expected to be the same? Explain.

P23-6B   Multiproduct C–V–P Analysis. The Gerson Company expects to operate at a loss next year on its two products as shown below:

	Blues	Reds	Total
Production and sales (units)	10,000	20,000	30,000
Sales revenue	$200,000	$100,000	$300,000
Variable costs	140,000	40,000	180,000
Contribution margin	$ 60,000	$ 60,000	$120,000
Less: Fixed costs			150,000
Profit (loss)			($ 30,000)

The company has two plans that it believes will improve its profit (reduce its loss) next year.

Plan A — To spend $32,400 on an advertising plan to increase the number of *Blues* sold without affecting the number of *Reds* sold.

Plan B — To spend $32,400 on an advertising plan to increase the *total* number of units sold and to change the product mix so that one *Blue* is sold for every four *Reds* sold.

Required: 1. If neither of the two plans is followed, so that Gerson's product mix is one *Blue* sold for each two *Reds* sold, what total dollar sales volume is required for the company to break even?
2. If Gerson follows plan A, how many additional *Blues* must be sold for the company to break even? (The number of *Reds* sold will still be 20,000.)
3. If Gerson follows plan B, what total dollar sales volume will be required for the company to break even?
4. Compare your answers to Requirements 1 and 3. Explain why total dollar sales volume required to break even with plan B must be greater than it is if neither plan is followed even though plan B increases the weighted average contribution margin percent.

P23-7B **Cost Estimation, Single Product C–V–P Analysis.** Barnard Enterprises has just begun operations to produce a single product. The product requires 2 pounds of direct materials costing $5 per pound and 3 hours of direct labor at $4 per hour. Factory overhead costs have been estimated at two production volumes as shown below:

Production volume	Factory overhead costs
16,000 units	$236,000
32,000 units	332,000

Fixed selling, general, and administrative costs amount to $64,000. The only nonmanufacturing cost that is variable is a sales commission paid to sales personnel. Sales personnel are paid a commission amounting to 10% of the sales revenue from their territory. The company plans to sell its product for $50 per unit.

Required:
1. Write out the equation for Barnard's profit with x as the number of units sold.
2. Graph Barnard's total fixed cost and total contribution margin with dollars on the vertical axis and the number of units sold on the horizontal axis. Locate the break-even point on the graph.
3. Compute Barnard's break-even point in units.
4. Barnard expects to sell 15,000 units. How much profit should it expect?
5. What profit (loss) would Barnard expect if increasing the price of its product to $60 per unit would decrease the number of units sold to 12,000?
6. Does the price increase seem advisable for Barnard? Explain.

DISCUSSION CASES

C23-1 **C–V–P Analysis for a Bus Company.** The Miniola Hills Bus Company owns 10 buses. Last year, the company lost $102,000 as shown below:

Revenue from riders (496,000 @ $.50)		$248,000
Less operating costs:		
Depreciation on buses	$100,000	
Garage rent	20,000	
Licenses, fees, and insurance	40,000	
Maintenance	15,000	
Driver's salaries	65,000	
Tires	20,000	
Gasoline and oil	90,000	350,000
Profit (loss)		($102,000)

The company's buses made a total of 80 trips per day on 310 days last year. A total of 350,000 miles were driven.

Another year like last year would put the company out of business. Management is trying hard to improve the company's profitability. It is considering the following two plans for the coming year:

Plan A — To change the bus routes and reduce the number of trips to 60 per day in order to reduce the number of miles driven.

Plan B — To sell bus tokens (5 for $2.00) and student passes ($2.50 to ride all week) in order to increase the number of riders.

Required: Prepare a report discussing the effect that each of these plans might have on the costs and revenues of the bus company.

C23-2 Cost, Price, and Volume Changes for a Brewery. Schleuter Brewery has operated in a small midwestern city for over 60 years. Although it is very popular locally, Schleuter beer has never been sold out of state. The brewery is currently capable of producing over 3 million cases of beer per year. Average production has been about 1.2 million cases per year over the last 3 or 4 years. Schleuter has all of the modern equipment and labor skill needed to operate as efficiently as any brewery in the country. Its beer is currently priced about the same as the national brands, but it could be reduced quite a bit and still leave a healthy contribution margin.

Increasing the volume of sales seems to be the key to improved profitability for the company. The following two plans have been suggested:

Plan A — Reduce the price in order to increase unit sales volume locally.

Plan B — Expand the company's advertising program and attempt to increase unit sales volume by selling beer in one or two neighboring states. The price of Schleuter beer would not be changed under this plan.

Required: Discuss the cost and revenue effects of these two plans for increasing unit sales volume.

24 Budgeting

After reading this chapter, you should understand:

- The value of budgeting in planning and controlling
- The nature of the budget schedules that form the master budget
- The relationships between the budget schedules that form the master budget
- How to prepare a set of projected financial statements
- The use of a "flexible" manufacturing cost budget in evaluating the performance of manufacturing activities

In Chapter 23 we introduced the idea that the major functions of a company's management are to plan the company's future activities and to control those activities so that its goals can be accomplished. We also introduced Cost–Volume–Profit Analysis, one of the simplest and most often used forms of analysis provided by managerial accounting to aid in the planning process. In that chapter we discussed that the value of C–V–P Analysis comes from its ability to assist management in making certain types of planning decisions by describing the profit impact of decision alternatives.

In this chapter we introduce budgeting, another important aid to the planning process. **Budgeting is the process of quantifying the plans of management to give a financial description of a company's various activities.** C–V–P Analysis provides a narrow focus on profitability, normally avoids detail by making simplifying assumptions, and is often used to describe the effects of individual planning decisions. Budgeting, in contrast, provides a broad perspective on any or all financial results of plans, attempts to maintain as much detail as is useful, and shows the collective effects of all planning decisions.

AN OVERVIEW OF THE BUDGETING PROCESS

The Purposes of Budgeting

Budgeting is so important to the planning of modern businesses and its use is so widespread that the term *budgeting* is often used as a synonym for planning. While such use may not be quite accurate it is certainly understandable. For companies that take planning seriously, budgeting is usually highly developed as an integral part of the planning process. But budgeting is also an integral part of the control process for most of the same companies.

Budgeting offers a framework within which to describe a set of plans. All business organizations (and many nonbusiness organizations) are economic entities that survive or fail on the financial results of their activities. It is only natural that a description of the financial impact of the plans for those activities would be useful. The contributions of budgeting to planning and controlling are highly interrelated and result from the ability of budgeting to describe company activities. Budgeting provides:

1. A way to add discipline to the planning process
2. An opportunity to recognize and avoid potential problems
3. A means of communicating plans throughout the organization
4. A basis for the evaluation of performance
5. A method of motivating employees

PROVIDING DISCIPLINE.   Budgeting adds discipline to the planning process. Planning is much more beneficial when it is complete and detailed, when all of the consequences of planning decisions are carefully considered. Budgeting imposes this kind of thoroughness on the planning process. Furthermore, budgets must be periodically revised and updated, which forces plans to be systematically reconsidered at regular intervals so they can be improved.

RECOGNIZING POTENTIAL PROBLEMS.   In the process of describing a company's plans in detail within the budgeting framework, it is often possible to uncover potential problems before they occur or to spot omissions or inconsistencies in the plans. For example, plans may call for sales in excess of normal production capability during a particular month. By recognizing this problem, management can consider the advisability of producing extra inventories prior to the beginning of that month, scheduling overtime work during the month, or increasing production capability to obtain the extra units needed for sale. If one of these alternatives is chosen, the budget can be adjusted to incorporate the new plans. Otherwise the planned sales level must be reduced.

It may also be possible to observe that plans call for a greater commitment of resources for certain activities than is justified by their importance in attaining company goals. Such discoveries allow a rethinking of plans, which can increase the chances that performance objectives for company activities will be met.

COMMUNICATING PLANS.   Budgeting provides a means for communicating company plans for various activities to department managers who are responsible for their performance. It allows the goals of the company to be specified in terms of the desired outcomes of each activity. This helps the employees of the company know what is expected of them and to understand the importance of their activities to the company's success. Budgeting also provides a means of communicating the amount of resources the company can make available for each department's operations.

Many companies engage in participative budgeting. **Participative budgeting is budgeting in which department managers participate with top management in the planning decisions that determine performance objectives and resource commitments for the activities of their departments**. Top company management would typically approach such decisions with performance objectives for each department and information about the availability of resources. Department managers, on the other hand, would supply information on the resource requirements needed by their departments to meet those objectives. Participative budgeting aids in making planning decisions through this exchange of information. It helps the two sets of managers arrive at mutually satisfactory decisions, and it ensures that all affected parties are aware of the decisions that have been made.

Budgeting in most large companies is the responsibility of a *budget committee*, which is usually composed of key management personnel such as production, sales, research and development, and financial vice-presidents, the chief accountant, and perhaps others. The activities of this committee can improve a company's chances for effective participative budgeting by bringing department managers and others affected by the budget together to gather information, settle differences, and make decisions.

EVALUATING PERFORMANCE. Budgets are also used as a basis for evaluating the actual performance of activities. Periodic comparisons between planned and actual performance can be used to measure progress toward goals and to evaluate the efficiency of resource use. Such comparisons enable a company's management to employ the principle known as management by exception. **Management by exception is the principle that management should direct its attention to activities where performance seems unusual and leave alone the activities that are operating as planned**. Management by exception attempts to save managerial time and effort by focusing on activities where differences between planned and actual results (*exceptions*) are noted, the assumption being that these activities provide the greatest opportunity for performance improvement.

MOTIVATING EMPLOYEES. Budgets are useful in motivating employees. If a company's employees recognize that budget objectives for the activities they perform are fair and attainable, they tend to accept them as personal goals and be motivated to achieve them. They welcome feedback from performance evaluations and find satisfaction in knowing their work is meaningful and their performance is good. Motivation is reinforced when performance evaluations are used to provide recognition by others of work well done and to justify promotions or pay raises. Unfortunately, budgets are occasionally used unwisely to punish employees rather than to encourage them and help them improve their job performance. The potential motivational benefits of budgeting can be easily lost through improper use.

**EXHIBIT 24-1
Interrelationships
Among Budget
Schedules in the
Master Budget**

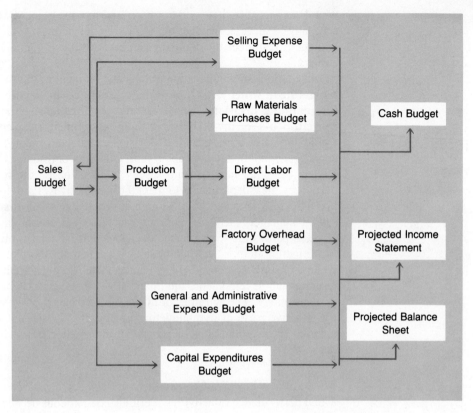

The Budgeting Framework

The basic framework for the description of a company's plans in terms of their financial impact is determined by the form and content of its master budget. **A master budget is a set of interrelated schedules (or budgets) showing the relationships between (1) goals to be accomplished, (2) activities to be performed, (3) resources to be used, and (4) expected financial results**. The form and content of the individual schedules that make up the master budget for two companies may differ because of the industry in which they operate, the number of products they sell, and the size and complexity of their manufacturing and nonmanufacturing operations. Many similarities would also exist, however, because the relationships being described between goals, activities, resources, and results are essentially the same.

A master budget for a manufacturing company usually includes the following budget schedules:

1. Sales budget
2. Production budget
3. Raw materials purchases budget
4. Direct labor budget

5. Factory overhead budget
6. Selling expense budget
7. General and administrative expenses budget
8. Capital expenditures budget
9. Cash budget
10. Projected income statement
11. Projected balance sheet

Exhibit 24-1 depicts a master budget composed of the 11 schedules listed and shows the important relationships (by arrows) among the schedules.

The nature and purpose of these budget schedules are discussed in turn and illustrated to provide an understanding of the manner in which a company's activities can be described. The illustrations presented are simplified to emphasize the construction of the schedules and their relationships. Budget schedules of large companies can be extremely complex and must contain a great amount of detail to be useful. Often, however, simplified summaries of these detailed schedules are prepared that closely resemble the illustrated budget schedules in this chapter. These illustrations should be studied carefully to understand the logic behind the construction of the budget schedules and the relationships between them.

MASTER BUDGET SCHEDULES

All of the budget schedules to be discussed are illustrated with data from the Tike Toy Company, maker of an educational toy for infants. This company began its operations on January 1, 1982, and still manufactures and sells only one product. Exhibit 24-2 shows the balance sheet of the Tike Toy Company prepared as of September 30, 1983.

All of the budget schedules illustrated describe the company's operations for the last three months of 1983. The finished goods inventory shown on Tike's balance sheet is higher than the amount carried at other times of the year. The company anticipates sales far in excess of its ability to produce its product just prior to Christmas and has increased this inventory gradually over the last several months. At the beginning of August Tike borrowed $20,000 from a local bank to help finance this inventory increase. The bank charges 1% interest per month on the face value of the note to be paid when the note is repaid. Interest payable on the note at the balance sheet date is $400 (1% × $20,000 × 2 months).

The Sales Budget

Virtually all of the budget schedules are affected by the sales budget. This is because sales activity usually creates the need for other activities, for example, production. In addition, the amount of cash eventually collected from sales determines to a large extent the amount of resources that can be made available for the performance of the other activities.

The sales budget is a schedule showing the number of units expected to be sold, the sales revenue to be earned, and the cash receipts expected to result from sales each budget period. It is normally prepared to show sales expected by month or quarter, for a year or more into the future.

EXHIBIT 24-2
Balance Sheet

TIKE TOY COMPANY
Balance Sheet
September 30, 1983

Assets

Current assets			
Cash		$ 12,800	
Accounts receivable		10,000	
Raw materials inventory		4,800	
Finished goods inventory		55,800	
Prepaid insurance		9,000	$ 92,400
Property, plant, and equipment			
Plant and equipment	$300,000		
Less: Accumulated depreciation	(52,500)	$247,500	
Office buildings and equipment	$180,000		
Less: Accumulated depreciation	(31,500)	148,500	396,000
Total Assets			$488,400

Liabilities and Stockholders' Equity

Current liabilities			
Accounts payable		$ 2,400	
Property taxes payable		13,500	
Note payable to bank		20,000	
Interest payable on bank note		400	
Total Liabilities			$ 36,300
Stockholders' equity			
Common stock, no par		$400,000	
Retained earnings		52,100	
Total Stockholders' Equity			452,100
Total Liabilities and Stockholders' Equity . . .			$488,400

Estimates of the number of units to be sold are made on the basis of information from several sources. Past sales trends studied in relation to general economic and industry conditions provide perspective for sales estimates. Sales personnel are often able to give useful information as to purchasing plans of major customers or customer groups in their sales territories. Sales managers and advertising specialists contribute information regarding the expected effects of alternative advertising plans in relation to the expected behavior of the company's competitors. Decisions about the prices of the company's products must also be considered in relation to sales promotion policy because prices can have a great impact on the number of units sold.

The sales budget shows the sales revenue for each budget period. This information is useful in preparing the projected income statement. It also shows the cash receipts from sales expected in each budget period. If all sales are cash sales, the cash received each budget period exactly equals the sales revenue of that period. For most companies, however, a substantial portion of their sales are on account.

Consequently, cash receipts tend to be delayed as the company waits for accounts receivable to be collected.

The credit granting policy of a company can have a great impact on the period of delay between sale and receipt of cash. Most companies spend considerable time and effort studying the paying habits of their customers and deciding on an appropriate credit granting policy. They try to reduce the period of delay and the risk of creating uncollectible accounts without discouraging sales.

In the illustration of the sales budget that follows, we have adopted a simplified sales–cash receipt pattern. We have assumed credit terms of n/10. That is, customers are assumed to pay 10 days after purchase with no cash discount, and no accounts become uncollectible. This results in two-thirds of each month's sales revenue being collected in the month of sale and the remaining one-third being collected in the following month. You should realize, however, that the reliability of estimates of cash receipts from sales normally depends on a careful study of a company's past experience with accounts receivable collections. Exhibit 24-3 shows the sales budget of the Tike Toy Company for the last quarter of 1983.

Notice in the sales budget that budgeted sales are shown for each month in units and in dollars of sales revenue and that these monthly sales figures are added to show the fourth quarter totals. Monthly sales differences during the quarter reflect anticipated increases as Christmas is approached. Unit sales information is important in constructing the company's production budget (Exhibit 24-4). The sales

EXHIBIT 24-3
Sales Budget

TIKE TOY COMPANY
Sales Budget
Fourth Quarter 1983

	October	November	December	Quarter
Budgeted sales (units)	9,000	21,000	15,000	45,000
Budgeted selling price per unit	$5	$5	$5	$5
Budgeted sales revenue	$45,000	$105,000	$75,000	$225,000
Expected cash receipts:				
From September sales	$10,000[a]			$ 10,000
From October sales	30,000[b]	$ 15,000[b]		45,000
From November sales		70,000	$35,000	105,000
From December sales			50,000[c]	50,000
Total cash receipts	$40,000	$ 85,000	$85,000	$210,000

[a] This receipt of cash from September sales represents a collection of the $10,000 of Accounts Receivable appearing on the September 30 balance sheet.
[b] The company estimates that two-thirds of each month's sales revenue result in cash receipts during the same month. The remaining one-third is collected during the following month.
[c] The $25,000 of December sales not expected to be collected during December appears as Accounts Receivable on the projected balance sheet the company prepares as of December 31, 1983.

revenue total for the quarter is used in the company's projected quarterly income statement (Exhibit 24-11).

The monthly sales revenue figures are also used to estimate expected cash receipts from sales. Notice that expected cash receipts each month differ from the corresponding sales revenue figures. This is because Tike's customers buy on account and pay later. In the cash receipts section of the sales budget, we have assumed that two-thirds of each month's sales result in cash receipts during the same month and that the remaining one-third is received the following month. This is approximately the pattern that would result if, on the average, customers paid their accounts after 10 days.

The Production Budget

The production budget is a schedule showing the production (in units) for each budget period needed to satisfy expected sales estimates from the sales budget and to meet desired finished goods inventory levels. These required production figures form the basis for estimating the expenses that will be incurred by manufacturing activity. The desired ending finished goods inventory for the budget period is used in estimating the related costs that appear on the projected balance sheet as of the end of the budget period.

The inventory level decisions reflected in the production budget are extremely important. Carrying inventories is expensive. There are costs associated with keeping the company's money invested in inventory, with inventory storage and handling, and with insurance, taxes, and the risk of theft, damage, or obsolescence. On the other hand, it can also be very expensive not to carry inventory. Costs can arise from maintaining excessive production facilities to meet peak production requirements, working overtime to fill rush orders, or losing sales because orders cannot be met. Every company must plan its inventory levels with both the costs of carrying and not carrying inventory in mind, trying to keep the combined total at the lowest possible amount.

Exhibit 24-4 presents the production budget for the Tike Toy Company. This budget is expressed entirely in units. The desired ending inventory levels are assumed. If the company had desired to maintain a constant inventory level through

EXHIBIT 24-4
Production Budget

TIKE TOY COMPANY
Production Budget
Fourth Quarter 1983

	October	November	December	Quarter
Budgeted sales (units)	9,000	21,000	15,000	45,000
Add: Desired ending inventory of finished units	19,000	10,000	5,000	5,000
Total units required	28,000	31,000	20,000	50,000
Less: Beginning inventory of finished units	18,000	19,000	10,000	18,000
Budgeted production (units)	10,000	12,000	10,000	32,000

the quarter, production would have had to increase along with sales. The inventory levels assumed reflect the company's policy of entering the fourth quarter with a large inventory, which was increased gradually through the summer months so that production can remain fairly constant while sales increase before Christmas.

Notice that for each time period (month or quarter) the company is required to have available the sum of budgeted sales and desired ending inventory. This total must come from the period's beginning inventory or its production. Thus, for each period, subtracting the beginning inventory from the total units required gives the necessary production for that period.

Notice also the relationship between the numbers in the monthly and quarterly computations. Budgeted sales for the quarter equal the sum of the budgeted sales figures for the 3 months. Similarly, budgeted production for the quarter equals the sum of the three monthly production requirements. The desired ending and beginning inventories for the quarter, however, are simply the desired ending inventory for the *last* month of the quarter and the beginning inventory for the *first* month of the quarter, respectively. The quarter's total requirement is the quarter's budgeted sales plus its desired ending inventory. Finally, note that each month's ending inventory is the following month's beginning inventory.

The Raw Materials Purchases Budget

The raw materials purchases budget is a schedule that shows the number of raw material units that must be purchased each budget period to meet production and ending raw materials inventory requirements, the costs related to those purchases, and the expected cash payments that result from those purchases. A separate schedule would normally be prepared for each direct material while less expensive indirect material items might be grouped. The raw materials purchases budget illustrated in this chapter is for one item of *direct* materials.

Raw materials purchase requirements are first computed on this budget in raw material units (e.g., pounds, gallons, or pieces). Suppose that raw materials are purchased by the pound. The total raw materials requirement is the expected number of pounds needed for production (the usage requirement) plus the number of pounds desired for the ending inventory of raw materials (the inventory requirement). If the total requirement is greater than the beginning inventory, the company must purchase more raw materials in order to satisfy this requirement. The number of pounds of raw materials that must be purchased (the purchase requirement) is computed by subtracting the number of pounds in the beginning inventory from the total requirement.

The usage requirement in this computation is determined for each budget period by multiplying budgeted production times the expected number of pounds of raw materials needed to produce each unit of product. The number of pounds needed per unit would normally be estimated on the basis of engineering studies and production data from previous periods. The ending raw materials inventory requirements used in this budget are the result of management decisions based on the same kinds of cost considerations (costs of carrying versus cost of not carrying) that determine the desired finished goods inventory levels appearing in the production budget.

Expected raw materials purchase prices are used to convert unit purchase requirements into dollar purchase requirements. These dollar purchase requirements are then used to determine the timing of cash payments for raw materials purchases. This determination requires a review of the company's payment policy when dealing with its raw materials suppliers. If a company pays cash for raw material A, for example, its cash payments for purchases of raw material A equal the dollar purchase requirements each period. On the other hand, if the company always pays for raw material B on the thirtieth day after purchase, the cash payments for purchases of raw material B each month approximately equal the dollar purchase requirement for the previous month.

Exhibit 24-5 shows the raw materials purchases budget of the Tike Toy Company for the fourth quarter of 1983. In this exhibit we have assumed that (1) Tike produces its single product from a single raw (direct) material known as CQ40; (2) it requires one-half pound of this material to produce a unit of product; (3) raw material CQ40 costs $.60 per pound; and (4) Tike always pays its supplier 30 days after the purchase with no cash discount.

Note how the raw materials purchases budget in Exhibit 24-5 is developed. The raw materials usage requirement for each month is derived from the production

EXHIBIT 24-5   Raw Materials Purchases Budget

TIKE TOY COMPANY
Raw Materials Purchases Budget for Direct Material CQ40
Fourth Quarter 1983

	October	November	December	Quarter
Budgeted production (product units)	10,000	12,000	10,000	32,000
Expected raw materials usage per unit (pounds per unit of product)	$\frac{1}{2}$	$\frac{1}{2}$	$\frac{1}{2}$	$\frac{1}{2}$
Raw materials usage requirement (pounds)	5,000 lbs.	6,000 lbs.	5,000 lbs.	16,000 lbs.
Add: Desired ending inventory of raw materials (pounds)	6,000	7,000	3,000	3,000
Total raw materials requirement (pounds)	11,000	13,000	8,000	19,000
Less: Beginning raw materials inventory (pounds)	8,000	6,000	7,000	8,000
Raw materials purchase requirement	3,000 lbs.	7,000 lbs.	1,000 lbs.	11,000 lbs.
Raw materials price per pound	$.60	$.60	$.60	$.60
Raw materials purchase cost	$1,800	$4,200	$ 600[c]	$6,600
Cash payments for purchases	$2,400[a]	$1,800[b]	$4,200	$8,400

[a] This $2,400 represents payment of Accounts Payable (from September purchases) appearing on the September 30 balance sheet.

[b] October raw materials purchases are to be paid in November.

[c] Raw materials purchase cost of $600 for December will not be paid until January, 1984. Thus Accounts Payable of $600 will appear on the projected balance sheet as of December 31, 1983.

requirement (computed in the production budget of Exhibit 24-4) by multiplying the month's unit production by the amount of raw material required (one-half pound) per unit. The raw materials purchase requirement is determined by adding the desired ending raw materials inventory to the raw materials usage to determine the total raw materials required and subtracting the beginning raw materials inventory. The purchase requirement is then converted to dollars using the expected purchase price of $.60 per pound.

Note also that the cash payments for purchases lag 1 month behind the actual purchases. This is because we have assumed the company pays its supplier 30 days after purchase. As a result the payment in October ($2,400) is for the September purchases. That is, it represents payment of the $2,400 of Accounts Payable appearing on the company's balance sheet for September 30, 1983 (Exhibit 24-2). Similarly, December purchases ($600) will not be paid until January 1984, and therefore this amount appears as the Accounts Payable balance on the balance sheet for the Tike Toy Company projected for December 31, 1983 (Exhibit 24-12).

The Direct Labor Budget

The direct labor budget is a schedule that shows the hours and cost of direct labor required to meet the production budget and the expected cash payments for direct labor during each budget period. The total hours of labor time required in each budget period is computed by multiplying the budgeted production by the expected number of hours of labor needed to produce each unit of product. These total labor hour requirements are useful in anticipating the number of workers needed at various times of the year so that hiring and training plans can be made and costly overtime or production delays can be avoided.

Labor cost is computed by multiplying the total labor hour requirements by the expected wage rate. Cash payments for direct labor are also shown in the direct labor budget. The cash payment each budget period is computed by adding the wages payable (for direct labor) at the beginning of the period to the period's direct labor cost and then subtracting the wages payable (for direct labor) at the end of the budget period.

A simple direct labor budget for the Tike Toy Company is shown in Exhibit 24-6. In the budget we have assumed that each unit of product requires one-fourth hour of direct labor time and that all laborers are paid $5 per hour. Beginning and ending wages payable figures (for direct labor) have been assumed to simplify the illustration.

Notice that the computation of budgeted direct labor cost in Exhibit 24-6 is based on budgeted production (from the production budget in Exhibit 24-4) and that the total for the quarter is simply the sum of the amounts for the 3 months. Also notice that the total cash payment for the quarter is the sum of the cash payments for the 3 months. Furthermore, the cash payment for direct labor for the quarter ($40,000) is equal to the direct labor cost for the quarter. This occurs because the quarter's beginning and ending wages payable balances are equal (zero in the exhibit). The cash payments and costs for direct labor, however, are not the same during any of the 3 months because of the changing wages payable balance.

EXHIBIT 24-6   Direct Labor Budget

	October	November	December	Quarter
TIKE TOY COMPANY				
Direct Labor Budget				
Fourth Quarter 1983				
Budgeted production (units)	10,000	12,000	10,000	32,000
Direct labor time per unit (hours per unit)	$\frac{1}{4}$	$\frac{1}{4}$	$\frac{1}{4}$	$\frac{1}{4}$
Direct labor hours required	2,500 hrs.	3,000 hrs.	2,500 hrs.	8,000 hrs.
Labor rate per hour	$5	$5	$5	$5
Budgeted labor cost	$12,500	$15,000	$12,500	$40,000
Add: Beginning wages payable balance	–0–	500	1,000	–0–
Less: Ending wages payable balance	(500)	(1,000)	–0–	–0–
Cash payments for direct labor	$12,000	$14,500	$13,500	$40,000

The Factory Overhead Budget

The factory overhead budget is a schedule showing estimates of all factory overhead costs and their related cash payments for each budget period. These factory overhead cost estimates are based on the production budget and studies of the behavior of the various overhead costs as discussed in Chapter 23. The budget is used to provide estimates for the cost of goods manufactured section of the projected income statement (Exhibit 24-11) as well as estimates of cash payments for the cash budget (Exhibit 24-10).

Exhibit 24-7 shows the factory overhead budget for the Tike Toy Company. Fixed and variable overhead costs have been separated on this budget. We assume that all factory overhead costs are paid in the month incurred, except depreciation, of course. No cash payment is required for depreciation cost.

Several items in Exhibit 24-7 are noteworthy. The first and most obvious is that fixed and variable overhead costs have been separated. Notice that fixed costs are the same in each month's budget, whereas, in contrast, variable costs have fluctuated. Close examination reveals, in fact, that the variable cost totals for each month have varied directly in proportion to changes in budgeted production levels. The constant rates per unit of product for these costs are shown in parentheses in the variable costs section of the budget.

Cash payments related to overhead items are also shown in the factory overhead budget. We have assumed that the company's policy is to pay factory overhead costs, except for depreciation, in the period in which they are incurred.

Depreciation is an allocation of the difference between the original cost and residual value of plant and equipment to the periods of their use. There are cash flows associated with owning plant and equipment, but they are the outflows associated with plant and equipment purchases (in the years of purchase) and the inflows associated with disposal (in the years of disposal) and they do not correspond in any period (except by chance) to the depreciation *expense*.

EXHIBIT 24-7   Factory Overhead Budget

TIKE TOY COMPANY
Factory Overhead Budget
Fourth Quarter 1983

	October	November	December	Quarter
Budgeted production (units)	10,000	12,000	10,000	32,000
Variable overhead costs (rate):				
Utilities ($.20 per unit)	$ 2,000	$ 2,400	$ 2,000	$ 6,400
Supplies ($.05 per unit)	500	600	500	1,600
Other variable costs ($.075 per unit)	750	900	750	2,400
Total variable costs ($.325 per unit)	$ 3,250	$ 3,900	$ 3,250	$10,400
Fixed overhead costs:				
Supervisory salaries	$ 4,000	$ 4,000	$ 4,000	$12,000
Depreciation of plant and equipment	2,500	2,500	2,500	7,500
Other fixed costs	5,500	5,500	5,500	16,500
Total fixed costs	$12,000	$12,000	$12,000	$36,000
Total factory overhead costs	$15,250	$15,900	$15,250	$46,400
Less: Depreciation of plant and equipment	$ 2,500	$ 2,500	$ 2,500	$ 7,500
Cash payments for factory overhead costs	$12,750	$13,400	$12,750	$38,900

There are no purchases or disposals of factory plant and equipment by the Tike Toy Company during the budget period, and consequently there are no associated cash flows. Note that we have simply subtracted the depreciation expense, which involves no corresponding cash flow, from the total factory overhead costs to determine the total cash payments for factory overhead.

The Selling Expense Budget

The selling expense budget shows the expenses associated with sales activity and the related cash payments. This budget is often very similar in appearance to the factory overhead budget. Understanding cost behavior patterns is just as important in budgeting selling expenses as it is in budgeting factory overhead costs. In contrast to variable overhead costs, which vary directly in proportion to the number of units *produced*, variable selling expenses vary directly in proportion to the number of units *sold*.

In addition to distinguishing between fixed and variable selling expenses, the selling expense budget often shows *sales determined expenses* separately from *sales determining expenses*. **Sales determined expenses are selling expenses that are necessary to support the volume of sales budgeted.** They are estimated *after* the sales budget has been set with reference to the supporting activities that are required. Shipping expenses are an example of sales determined expenses. **Sales determining expenses are selling expenses incurred because of their expected impact on the sales volume.** They are not estimated after the sales budget is set but are determined instead by management decision as the sales budget is being prepared. Advertising expenses are a good example of sales determining expenses.

CHAPTER 24

EXHIBIT 24-8 Selling Expense Budget

TIKE TOY COMPANY
Selling Expense Budget
Fourth Quarter 1983

	October	November	December	Quarter
Budgeted sales (units)	9,000	21,000	15,000	45,000
Sales determining expenses:				
Advertising	$ 3,000	$ 3,000	$ 1,000	$ 7,000
Sales salaries	5,500	5,500	5,500	16,500
Other promotional efforts	1,000	–	–	1,000
Sales determined expenses:				
Shipping (variable at $.30 per unit sold)	2,700	6,300	4,500	13,500
Total selling expenses	$12,200	$14,800	$11,000	$38,000
Cash payments for selling expenses[a]	$12,200	$14,800	$11,000	$38,000

[a] Cash payments for selling expenses are assumed to occur in the month of the expense.

Companies often spend a large amount of time and effort studying the factors that affect the sales volumes of their various products. They try to plan strategies to take advantage of those factors. Their decisions regarding sales determining expenses are influenced by general business and industry conditions, actions of competitors, and company policy.

A schedule of cash payments by budget period is also shown as part of the selling expense budget. Cash payments are determined from payment policies for the individual expenses.

Exhibit 24-8 shows the sales expense budget for the Tike Toy Company for the last quarter of 1983. The budgeted sales (units) are taken from Exhibit 24-3. You should notice that the distinction between sales determining and sales determined expenses is highlighted in this budget. You should also notice that the shipping expenses are the only variable selling expenses in this budget. They vary with sales volume at a rate of $.30 per unit sold. We have assumed that the Tike Toy Company pays for its selling expenses in the month in which they are incurred. As a result cash payments are the same as total selling expenses each month.

The General and Administrative Expenses Budget

The general and administrative expenses budget is a schedule showing estimates of all expenses from activities other than manufacturing and selling and the cash payments related to those expenses. In this budget the expenses are often grouped and described in terms of the specific administrative activity or function for which they are incurred. For example, expenses related to accounting, research and development, and legal activities might be shown separately. Such groupings are useful because preparation of the budget in terms of specific administrative activities provides an opportunity to review the commitment of resources to those activities during the planning process. It also provides a standard of comparison against which actual costs incurred in those activities can be evaluated. As with previous expense budgets the cash payments for general and administrative expenses are also shown on the budget. These amounts are determined from payment policies for various expense items.

Exhibit 24-9 presents the general and administrative expenses budget for the Tike Toy Company. Expenses have been grouped in terms of two basic administrative functions and a general or miscellaneous category.

We have assumed that the Tike Toy Company pays accounting and clerical expenses as well as administrative salaries in the month in which they are incurred. Separate consideration must be given to each of the general expenses in this budget, however. The company carries insurance that was prepaid for 3 years when it began operations. The amount paid in January 1982 was $21,600. This resulted in a monthly insurance expense of $600 ($21,600 ÷ 36) and a Prepaid Insurance balance on its September 30, 1983, balance sheet of $9,000 (see Exhibit 24-2). As a result no cash payment is necessary for insurance during the fourth quarter of 1983. The balance of Prepaid Insurance is $1,800 lower on the projected balance sheet for December 31, 1983 (Exhibit 24-12) than it was on the September 30, 1983, balance sheet (Exhibit 24-2).

Depreciation of office buildings and equipment amounts to $1,500 per month, although no monthly cash payments are required. The balance of Accumulated

EXHIBIT 24-9   General and Administrative Expenses Budget

TIKE TOY COMPANY				
General and Administrative Expenses Budget				
Fourth Quarter 1983				
	October	*November*	*December*	*Quarter*
Accounting and clerical expenses	$ 4,100	$ 4,200	$ 4,100	$12,400
Administrative salaries	4,000	4,000	4,000	12,000
General expenses:				
Insurance[a]	600	600	600	1,800
Property taxes[b]	1,500	1,500	1,500	4,500
Depreciation of office buildings and equipment[c]	1,500	1,500	1,500	4,500
Total expenses	$11,700	$11,800	$11,700	$35,200
Schedule of cash payments:				
Accounting and clerical expenses	$ 4,100	$ 4,200	$ 4,100	$12,400
Administrative salaries	4,000	4,000	4,000	12,000
Property taxes			18,000	18,000
Total cash payments	$ 8,100	$ 8,200	$26,100	$42,400

[a] The $600 per month insurance expense equals the monthly reduction in the Prepaid Insurance account (1/36 times the 3-year premium of $21,600). Because the insurance was prepaid, no cash payment is necessary during the fourth quarter.
[b] Property taxes accrue at a rate of $1,500 per month. Property taxes for the full year are paid in December, however.
[c] Depreciation of office buildings and equipment amounts to $1,500 per month. No monthly cash payments are required, however.

Depreciation: Office Buildings and Equipment increases by $4,500, the total depreciation expense during the quarter (from $31,500 on the September 30 balance sheet in Exhibit 24-2 to $36,000 on the December 31 balance sheet in Exhibit 24-12).

Although Tike records $1,500 of property tax expense each month, the entire $18,000 payment for property taxes for each year is made in December. Thus the cash payment for property taxes represents the payment of the $4,500 property tax for the fourth quarter shown on this budget plus the payment of the $13,500 property taxes payable on the September 30 balance sheet in Exhibit 24-2.

The Capital Expenditures Budget

Adding to plant and equipment, replacing old machinery, and remodeling or relocating office facilities may involve large expenditures of cash. Such expenditures often result from commitments to major programs or projects that may require several years to produce benefits for a company. It is important that these commitments not be made without a thorough and objective evaluation of their effect on company operations.

It is also important that the projects to be undertaken are planned carefully so they will not interfere with the company's current operations. Such planning is aided by the capital expenditures budget. **The capital expenditures budget is a set of schedules that details the expected effects on other master budget schedules of each new project to be undertaken.** Information gathered during project evaluations would be used to show (1) the expected timing of cash receipts and payments that affect the cash budget, (2) the cost of assets to be acquired that affect the projected balance sheet, and (3) the increases and decreases in factory overhead costs, selling expenses, general and administrative expenses, and perhaps sales, all of which affect the budgets for those items as well as the projected income statement.

An adequate illustration of a capital expenditures budget would unnecessarily complicate our elementary discussion of the other budgets. We therefore assume that the Tike Toy Company has budgeted no capital expenditures for the fourth quarter of 1983. The evaluation of proposals to invest company resources in long-term projects is important, however, and is discussed in Chapter 27.

The Cash Budget

The cash budget is a schedule showing the effect of the cash receipts and payments of each budget period on a company's cash balance. The cash budget is extremely important because it helps management avoid the problem of having too little cash available to pay bills as they come due. It also helps the company avoid accumulating excessive cash balances. Idle cash is not productive. Cash earns the company nothing unless it is invested internally in profitable company projects or externally in government or business securities. By projecting the effects of planned operations on the company's cash balance, the cash budget can help management anticipate the approach of cash shortages or excesses in time to avoid them.

The cash budget has two major sections, the *operations* section and the *financing* section. The operations section summarizes the cash receipts (inflows) and payments (outflows) that are expected to result from planned operations. This section shows the net cash inflow (excess of operating receipts over operating payments) or net cash outflow (excess of payments over receipts) for each budget period. When the expected net cash inflow from operations is added to (or net outflow deducted from) the period's beginning cash balance, the result is the anticipated ending cash balance from operations.

If the anticipated ending cash balance from operations is too low, the company can arrange to borrow more cash. If the balance is too high, the company may arrange to invest some of its cash or to repay loans taken in previous periods. These additional cash flows, which are planned as a result of financing decisions, are shown in the second major section of the cash budget, the financing section. After adding the net financing inflows to (or deducting the net financing outflows from) the anticipated cash balance from operations (before financing transactions), the budgeted ending cash balance for the period is determined. This ending cash balance would be used as the cash balance for the projected balance sheet at the end of the period. This balance also becomes the budgeted beginning cash balance for the next budget period as the computation and decision process is repeated.

Exhibit 24-10 shows the cash budget of the Tike Toy Company for the last quarter of 1983. Notice that, except for the cash payment for income taxes, the operations section of the cash budget merely summarizes receipts and payments computed in the company's previous budgets. The payment of income taxes must be based on the company's projected income statement. We are assuming that the Tike Toy Company pays income taxes at the end of each quarter for the income earned during the quarter. Thus its fourth quarter income taxes are paid in December.

In Exhibit 24-10 there is a net cash *outflow* from operations in October of $7,450. This would reduce the beginning cash balance of $12,800 to $5,350. The Tike Toy Company management has adopted a policy of not allowing its cash balance to drop below $9,000 at the end of any month, however. Therefore the company must borrow cash to satisfy this policy.

We assume that the company has made arrangements for borrowing small amounts of cash in thousand-dollar increments from a local bank at a simple interest rate of 1% per month on the loan balance at the beginning of the month. All loans are taken at the *beginning* of the month and repayments, when made, occur at the *end* of the month. Interest is paid at the time of repayment. To meet its minimum cash balance policy the company must borrow $4,000 at the beginning of October, raising the ending cash balance to $9,350 for October. This $9,350 becomes November's beginning cash balance. When this beginning balance is added to the $32,300 net cash *inflow* from November's operations, the company anticipates an ending cash balance of $41,650 for November.

Observing that December will also have a net cash inflow from operations, Tike plans to repay its entire loan plus interest at the end of November. At that time it will repay October's $4,000 loan as well as the $20,000 previously borrowed (see the company's September 30, 1983, balance sheet). The $880 of interest to be paid

EXHIBIT 24-10   Cash Budget

TIKE TOY COMPANY
Cash Budget
Fourth Quarter 1983

	October	November	December	Quarter
Cash flow from operations:				
Cash receipts from sales[a]	$40,000	$85,000	$85,000	$210,000
Cash payments for:				
Raw materials purchases[b]	$ 2,400	$ 1,800	$ 4,200	$ 8,400
Direct labor[c]	12,000	14,500	13,500	40,000
Factory overhead[d]	12,750	13,400	12,750	38,900
Selling expenses[e]	12,200	14,800	11,000	38,000
General and administrative expenses[f]	8,100	8,200	26,100	42,400
Income taxes[g]	–	–	5,808	5,808
Total payments	$47,450	$52,700	$73,358	$173,508
Net cash inflow (outflow) from operations	($7,450)	$32,300	$11,642	$ 36,492
Add: Beginning cash balance	12,800	9,350	16,770	12,800
Anticipated ending cash balance from operations	$ 5,350	$41,650	$28,412	$ 49,292
Cash flow from financing transactions:				
Add: Borrowing	$ 4,000	–	–	$ 4,000
Less: Repayment	–	($24,000)	–	(24,000)
Interest	–	(880)	–	(880)
Net cash flow from financing	$ 4,000	($24,880)	–	($20,880)
Ending cash balance	$ 9,350	$16,770	$28,412	$ 28,412

[a] From Exhibit 24-3.
[b] From Exhibit 24-5.
[c] From Exhibit 24-6.
[d] From Exhibit 24-7.
[e] From Exhibit 24-8.
[f] From Exhibit 24-9.
[g] From Exhibit 24-11.

at the end of November is the sum of $400 interest payable as of September 30 plus $480 on the $24,000 total loan balance carried through October and November.

December's $28,412 ending cash balance will appear on the company's projected balance sheet for December 31, 1983.

The Projected Income Statement

A projected income statement is an income statement showing a company's expected revenues and expenses during the budget period, assuming all plans are followed. It is a very important budget schedule because it provides a measure of a company's profitability if plans are followed and conditions expected are experienced. If the expected net income during the budget period seems unsatisfactory to a company, it may attempt to revise its plans in hopes of increasing the net income.

EXHIBIT 24-11   Projected Income Statement

TIKE TOY COMPANY
Projected Income Statement
Fourth Quarter 1983

Sales		$225,000[a]
Cost of goods sold		
Beginning finished goods inventory (18,000 units at $3.10)	$ 55,800[b]	
Add: Cost of goods manufactured (32,000 units)		
Direct materials used (16,000 pounds at $.60) . . . . $ 9,600[c]		
Direct labor . . . . 40,000[d]		
Factory overhead . . . . 46,400[e]		
Total cost of goods manufactured	96,000	
Cost of finished goods available for sale (50,000 units)	$151,800	
Less: Ending finished goods inventory (5,000 units at $3.00)	15,000[f]	
Cost of goods sold		136,800
Gross profit		$ 88,200
Operating expenses		
Selling expenses	$ 38,000[g]	
General and administrative expenses	35,200[h]	
Total operating expenses		73,200
Operating income		$ 15,000
Other revenues and expenses		
Interest expense		480[i]
Income before income taxes		$ 14,520
Income tax expense		5,808[j]
Net Income		$ 8,712

[a] From Exhibit 24-3.
[b] From Exhibit 24-2.
[c] From Exhibit 24-5.
[d] From Exhibit 24-6.
[e] From Exhibit 24-7.
[f] Finished goods manufactured during the fourth quarter are expected to cost $3.00 per unit ($96,000 ÷ 32,000 units). Notice that the company is using a FIFO inventory flow assumption for finished goods inventories.
[g] From Exhibit 24-8.
[h] From Exhibit 24-9.
[i] Interest expense is $480 (1% × $24,000 × 2 months). Although $880 of interest was paid to the bank at the end of November, $400 of it was an expense of the previous quarter.
[j] Income tax expense has been estimated based on a 40% income tax rate.

Exhibit 24-11 shows the projected income statement for the Tike Toy Company for the fourth quarter of 1983. The company actually has enough information to construct projected income statements for each month of this fourth quarter as well as for the whole quarter but has chosen not to do so.

Notice that the revenues and most of the expenses appearing in the projected income statement (Exhibit 24-11) have been computed in previous budget schedules. Cost of goods sold is computed using the beginning finished goods inventory

EXHIBIT 24-12   Projected Balance Sheet

TIKE TOY COMPANY
Projected Balance Sheet
December 31, 1983

Assets

Current assets
Cash		$ 28,412[a]	
Accounts receivable		25,000[b]	
Raw materials inventory		1,800[c]	
Finished goods inventory		15,000[d]	
Prepaid insurance		7,200[e]	$ 77,412

Property, plant, and equipment
Plant and equipment	$300,000		
Less: Accumulated depreciation	(60,000)[f]	$240,000	
Office buildings and equipment	$180,000		
Less: Accumulated depreciation	(36,000)[g]	144,000	384,000
Total Assets			$461,412

Liabilities and Stockholders' Equity

Current liabilities
Accounts payable			$ 600[h]

Stockholders' equity
Common stock, no par		$400,000	
Retained earnings		60,812[i]	460,812
Total Liabilities and Stockholders' Equity			$461,412

[a] From Exhibit 24-10.
[b] From Exhibit 24-3.
[c] From Exhibit 24-5 (3,000 units @ $.60).
[d] From Exhibit 24-11.
[e] The $9,000 balance appearing on the September 30, 1983, balance sheet has been reduced by the $1,800 of insurance expense recorded as general and administrative expenses in Exhibit 24-9.
[f] From Exhibits 24-2 and 24-7.
[g] From Exhibits 24-2 and 24-9.
[h] From Exhibit 24-5. This liability arose from December's raw materials purchases.
[i] This is the sum of $52,100 shown as the September 30 balance of retained earnings in Exhibit 24-2, and Tike's net income of $8,712 shown in Exhibit 24-11. We have assumed that no dividends were paid.

from the September 30, 1983, balance sheet, direct materials *used*, direct labor, and factory overhead from the budget schedules, and use of the FIFO cost flow assumption. Fifty thousand units were available for sale, but only 45,000 were sold. The ending inventory of 5,000 units is assigned the fourth quarter's average manufacturing cost ($3) per unit. Notice also that the interest expense is only $480. The $880 of interest to be paid in November represents payment of $480 interest expense for the fourth quarter plus $400 of interest payable as of September 30.

The income tax expense has been estimated from the expected income before income taxes and the expected 40% income tax rate. The amount of the income tax expense for the fourth quarter ($5,808) also appears in the cash budget for the fourth quarter (Exhibit 24-10). This is because the Tike Toy Company pays income taxes quarterly at the end of the quarter in which income is earned.[1]

The Projected Balance Sheet

The projected balance sheet is a statement of a company's expected financial position at the end of a budget period assuming that all plans are followed. Exhibit 24-12 shows the projected balance sheet of the Tike Toy Company at the end of the fourth quarter of 1983.

You should notice that all of the figures appearing on the December 31, 1983, balance sheet of the Tike Toy Company are determined from previous budget schedules. This projected balance sheet completes the financial description of Tike's fourth quarter plans.

EXCEPTION REPORTING FOR RESPONSIBILITY CENTERS

The budget schedules just discussed as elements of the master budget were constructed as planning budgets to provide a financial description of a company's plans. In addition, the information contained in these budgets can also be used as a basis for performance evaluations. That is, after the budget period has passed, actual costs, revenues, and profit can be compared with expected costs, revenues, and profit appearing in the budget to see how closely the plans were followed.

Large companies usually separate their operations into distinct responsibility centers for performance evaluation. A **responsibility center is an identifiable portion or segment of a company's operations, the activities of which are the responsibility of a particular individual.** Depending upon the decision-making authority of that individual, a responsibility center may be evaluated as a *cost center*, a *profit center*, or an *investment center*.

A cost center is a responsibility center in which the individual who is responsible for its activities (the cost center manager) can control only the level of costs incurred. The cost center manager has no influence over the amount of revenue ultimately received by the company or the level of investment in property, plant, and equipment devoted to operations. Because of this factor, a cost center and its manager are evaluated by a comparison of budgeted costs with actual costs. For example, a small machine shop in a large manufacturing company might be evaluated as a cost center because its foreman, the cost center manager, has no authority to influence the amount of revenue earned by (or the level of investment made in) the machine shop although the foreman's decisions affect costs incurred daily.

A profit center is a responsibility center in which the manager has decision-making authority over both costs and revenues. Profit centers can be evaluated by comparing budgeted profit with actual profit. Decisions affecting revenues, such as which orders to accept and which prices to charge, affect profit. Decisions

---

[1] In Chapter 15, for simplicity, we assumed that income tax expense at a rate of 40% would be paid in the year following the year in which it was incurred. Many companies actually pay income taxes quarterly in the quarter in which income is earned. We have assumed that the Tike Toy Company pays its income taxes quarterly, as income is earned, at a 40% tax rate. We make a similar assumption for all homework.

affecting costs also affect profit. Profit, therefore becomes a convenient summary measure upon which to base the evaluation of the performance of a manager who can control both costs and revenues by the decisions the manager makes.

An investment center is a responsibility center in which the manager has decision-making authority over costs, revenues, and the level of investment in property, plant, and equipment related to its operations. The performance of investment centers is sometimes evaluated by judging decisions that affect the center's investment in plant and equipment separately from decisions that affect costs and revenues. More often, however, their evaluation uses some comprehensive measure affected by all decisions made. The ratio of profit earned by the center to average investment in the center, which is sometimes called *return on average investment*, is a commonly used measure for investment center performance evaluation. In the next section of this chapter we discuss the use of flexible budgets and budget information in the performance evaluation of cost centers.

FLEXIBLE BUDGETS

Performance evaluation of profit and investment centers is beyond the scope of this book. Cost center performance evaluation is so basic and important, however, that it deserves further discussion. Therefore in this section of the chapter we briefly describe the *flexible budget*, which is useful in maintaining control over cost centers. **A flexible budget is a cost or expense budget that shows expected costs or expenses at various activity levels.** Flexible budgets are more meaningful when the budgeted costs are prepared to show the amounts expected at the actual activity level attained. That is, for example, it would be more meaningful to compare the actual sales determined expenses incurred in selling 100 units of a product during a period to the expenses expected at a sales level of 100 units than to expenses expected at a sales level of 200 units, which was budgeted before the period began.

Flexible budget preparation requires a good understanding of cost behavior. The most convenient format for expressing flexible budgets is a form in which the budget for each cost item is expressed as a cost equation. When it is expressed in this form the budget for a particular cost or group of costs can be prepared for any volume of activity desired. After determining the relevant volume of activity and adjusting budgeted costs to that volume, for reporting purposes, the cost budget is usually stated as a table of expected costs. In this table variable costs and variable components of mixed costs are normally grouped and shown separately from fixed costs and fixed components of mixed costs. The value of flexible budgets is illustrated using data from the Tike Toy Company.

Suppose that the president of the Tike Toy Company is trying to evaluate the performance of the company's manufacturing operations for the month of October 1983, which we now assume has just passed. The performance evaluation is to be based on a comparison of actual and budgeted manufacturing costs for October. In this comparison the president wants to include the cost of direct materials, direct labor, and factory overhead.[2] Assuming the actual costs which are shown in Exhibit

---

[2] For the sake of simplicity we are treating Tike's entire manufacturing operation as a single cost center. Manufacturing operations are often broken into a large number of cost centers to improve control.

24-13, the president prepares the *erroneous* report shown in that exhibit. During October the company actually produced *11,000* units instead of the 10,000 budgeted earlier.

As you might expect from looking at Exhibit 24-13, the president was not pleased. With only two exceptions every actual cost exceeded the October budget. But the president would be mistaken in believing that the manufacturing costs had not been kept under control.

The problem with the president's report is that it compares actual costs incurred in October while producing *11,000* units of the product with October's original planning budget, which was based on the budgeted production of only *10,000* units. That is, since the production budget (Exhibit 24-4) called for the production of 10,000 units in October, the direct materials cost, direct labor cost, and factory overhead costs were estimated for that production level. The result is the misleading comparison in Exhibit 24-13.

We can adjust October's budget to show the costs expected to be incurred in producing 11,000 units in order to make a meaningful cost comparison, however. October's budget can be adjusted (made flexible) because we have information about the behavior of the manufacturing costs involved.

Recall that in the raw materials purchases budget (Exhibit 24-5) we assumed that each unit of product would require one-half pound of direct material CQ40 costing $.60 per pound. Thus each unit of product requires $.30 of direct material cost. Similarly, each unit of product (Exhibit 24-6) requires $1.25 of direct labor cost (one-fourth hour at $5.00 per hour). The variable factory overhead cost rates per

EXHIBIT 24-13
Manufacturing Cost
Report

TIKE TOY COMPANY
Manufacturing Cost Report
October 1983

	Actual Costs	Original October Budget	Excess of Actual Cost Over Budget
Production (units)	11,000 units	10,000 units	
Direct materials (CQ40) . .	$ 3,200	$ 3,000 ($.30/unit)	$ 200
Direct labor	13,600	12,500 ($1.25/unit)	1,100
Factory overhead			
Variable:			
Utilities	2,160	2,000 ($.20/unit)	160
Supplies	540	500 ($.05/unit)	40
Other	830	750 ($.075/unit)	80
Fixed:			
Supervisory salaries	4,000	4,000	–
Depreciation	2,500	2,500	–
Other	5,550	5,500	50
Total manufacturing costs .	$32,380	$30,750[a]	$1,630

[a] The budgeted amounts were determined from the budget schedules in Exhibits 24-5, 24-6, and 24-7.

EXHIBIT 24-14
Revised
Manufacturing Cost
Report

TIKE TOY COMPANY Revised Manufacturing Cost Report October 1983			
	Actual Costs	Manufacturing Cost Budgeted at October's Actual Production Volume	Excess of Actual Cost Over Budget
Production (units)	11,000 units	11,000 units	
Direct materials (CQ40) . .	$ 3,200	$ 3,300 ($.30/unit)	($100)
Direct labor	13,600	13,750 ($1.25/unit)	(150)
Factory overhead			
Variable:			
Utilities	2,160	2,200 ($.20/unit)	(40)
Supplies	540	550 ($.05/unit)	(10)
Other	830	825 ($.075/unit)	5
Fixed:			
Supervisory salaries	4,000	4,000	–
Depreciation	2,500	2,500	–
Other	5,550	5,500	50
Total manufacturing costs .	$32,380	$32,625	($245)

unit of product manufactured are shown on the factory overhead budget in Exhibit 24-7. Fixed factory overhead costs would not be adjusted because they are not expected to vary with the volume of production activity. Variable manufacturing costs do vary with the volume of production activity, however, and must be adjusted. The flexible budget for manufacturing costs is shown for October's actual production level of 11,000 units of product in Exhibit 24-14. In relation to October's actual costs, it provides a useful cost comparison for evaluating the performance of October's manufacturing activity.

Notice in Exhibit 24-14 that the restatement of the Tike Toy Company's manufacturing cost budget to show costs expected at October's actual production level of 11,000 units required adjustment of only the variable manufacturing costs. The fixed costs are expected to be the same at either 10,000 or 11,000 units of production. Note also how the cost comparison presents a very different picture of performance. The revised manufacturing cost report shows total actual costs to be *lower* than total expected costs by $245.

The idea of basing cost comparisons used for evaluating cost centers on flexible budgets adjusted to show the expected costs at the *actual* activity level attained is an important one. The flexible budget makes the differences computed between actual and budgeted cost for cost centers meaningful. These differences suggest possible areas of the cost center's operation that may be in need of attention, such as an inexperienced worker using direct materials inefficiently or a machine needing replacement. Cost center evaluation using a flexible budget in comparison with actual costs facilitates use of the management by exception principle.

Resoundo Sound Systems manufactures high-quality loudspeakers that are sold to manufacturers of stereo equipment. Assume the following:

(a) Budgeted sales for the first 4 months of the year are

January	60,000 speakers
February	80,000 speakers
March	100,000 speakers
April	80,000 speakers

(b) The company sells its loudspeakers for $70 per unit and expects one-half of each month's sales revenue to be received in the month of sale and the other half to be received in the month following sale.

(c) On January 1, 15,000 speakers are in finished goods inventory. The company wants the number of speakers in its beginning finished goods inventory each month to equal 25% of the month's budgeted sales (in units).

(d) The Accounts Receivable account has a balance of $4,000,000 on January 1.

(e) Eight feet of expensive audio cable is used in the manufacture of each speaker. On January 1 the company has 104,000 feet of this cable in its raw materials inventory. The amount of cable in inventory at the beginning of each month should be 20% of the month's usage requirement.

(f) The company pays $.40 per foot for audio cable in the month following purchase. December's purchases were 900,000 feet at $.40 per foot.

Required: 1. Prepare a sales budget for the first *4* months of the year.
2. Prepare a production budget for the first *3* months of the year.
3. Prepare a raw materials purchases budget for audio cable for the months of January and February.

SOLUTION TO
REVIEW
PROBLEM   1.

RESOUNDO SOUND SYSTEMS
Sales Budget

	January	February	March	April
Budgeted sales (units)	60,000	80,000	100,000	80,000
Budgeted selling price per unit	$70	$70	$70	$70
Budgeted sales revenue	$4,200,000	$5,600,000	$7,000,000	$5,600,000
Expected cash receipts:				
From December sales	$4,000,000			
From January sales	2,100,000	$2,100,000		
From February sales		2,800,000	$2,800,000	
From March sales			3,500,000	$3,500,000
From April sales				2,800,000
Total cash receipts	$6,100,000	$4,900,000	$6,300,000	$6,300,000

2.   **Production Budget**

	January	February	March
Budget sales (units)	60,000	80,000	100,000
Add: Desired ending inventory of finished units	20,000	25,000	20,000[a]
Total units required	80,000	105,000	120,000
Less: Beginning inventory of finished units	15,000	20,000	25,000
Budgeted production (units)	65,000	85,000	95,000

[a] April budgeted sales, 80,000 × 25%.

3.   **Raw Materials Purchases Budget**
                              (for audio cable)

	January	February	March
Budgeted production (speakers)	65,000	85,000	95,000
Expected usage of audio cable per speaker (feet)	8	8	8
Audio cable usage requirements (feet)	520,000	680,000	760,000
Add: Desired ending inventory of audio cable (feet)	136,000	152,000[b]	
Total audio cable requirements (feet)	656,000	832,000	
Less: Beginning inventory of audio cable (feet)	104,000	136,000	
Purchase requirement for audio cable (feet)	552,000	696,000	
Price per foot	$.40	$.40	
Purchase cost of audio cable	$220,800	$278,400	
Cash payments for purchases	$360,000[a]	$220,800	

[a] From December purchases, 900,000 feet × $.40.
[b] March usage requirements, 760,000 × 20%.

GLOSSARY

Budgeting. The process of quantifying a set of plans into a financial description of the activities involved.

Capital Expenditures Budget. A set of schedules that shows the effects on other master budget schedules of new projects to be undertaken during the budget period, such as acquiring additional plant and equipment.

Cash Budget. A schedule showing the effect of cash receipts and payments from operations and financing transactions on the cash balance during a budget period.

Cost Center. A responsibility center in which the manager has the authority to make decisions affecting costs incurred by the center but not revenues earned or investment in plant and equipment used in the center's operations.

Direct Labor Budget. A budget schedule based on the production budget that shows the hours required, costs, and the cash payments for direct labor.

Factory Overhead Budget. A budget schedule based on the production budget that shows estimated factory overhead costs and their related cash payments.

Flexible Budget. A cost or expense budget that shows expected costs or expenses at various activity levels.

General and Administrative Expenses Budget. A budget schedule showing the expenses and the cash payments related to general and administrative activities.

Investment Center. A responsibility center in which the manager has the authority to make decisions affecting costs incurred, revenues earned, and investment in plant and equipment used in the center's operations.

Management by Exception. The principle of directing management attention to activities that are not operating as planned while leaving alone activities that are operating as planned.

Master Budget. A set of interrelated budget schedules that provides the framework for the financial description of an organization's planned activities.

Participative Budgeting. A budgeting procedure in which department managers participate in the planning decisions that determine performance objectives and resource commitments for the activities of their departments.

Production Budget. A budget schedule based on the sales budget that shows the production levels (in units) needed to satisfy expected sales and to meet desired ending finished goods inventory levels.

Profit Center. A responsibility center in which a manager has the authority to make decisions affecting costs incurred and revenues earned by the center's operations.

Projected Balance Sheet. A balance sheet prepared for the *end* of a budget period based on a company's expected asset, liability, and stockholders' equity account balances.

Projected Income Statement. An income statement showing a company's expected revenues and expenses resulting from plans for the budget period.

Raw Materials Purchases Budget. A budget schedule based on the production budget that shows the number of raw materials units to be purchased to meet usage and ending raw materials inventory requirements, the costs of those purchases, and the cash payments resulting from those purchases.

Responsibility Center. An identifiable portion or segment of an organization, the activities of which are the responsibility of a particular individual.

Sales Budget. A budget schedule showing the number of units expected to be sold, the sales revenue earned, and the cash receipts resulting from sales during each budget period.

Sales Determined Expenses. Selling expenses that are incurred to support the activity necessary to meet the requirements of the sales budget.

Sales Determining Expenses. Selling expenses that are determined by management decisions at the time of the establishment of the sales budget because of their impact on the sales level.

Selling Expense Budget. A budget schedule showing the expenses and cash payments from selling activities.

QUESTIONS

Q24-1   List five ways in which budgeting is helpful in planning and controlling.

Q24-2   How does the budgeting process add discipline to management planning?

Q24-3   In what ways does budgeting help to communicate management plans throughout a company?

Q24-4   Explain the purpose behind the principle of management by exception.

Q24-5   What is the master budget?

Q24-6   Why is the sales budget usually prepared before most of the other budget schedules in the master budget?

Q24-7   Explain the importance of inventory level decisions in the production budget and the raw materials purchases budget.

Q24-8   List four costs that should be considered when setting desired ending finished goods inventory levels in a production budget.

Q24-9   Describe the relationship between the production budget, the raw materials purchases budget, the direct labor budget, and the factory overhead budget.

Q24-10   Distinguish between sales determined and sales determining expenses in a selling expense budget.

Q24-11   Why must the selling expense budget be prepared, at least partially, at the same time the sales budget is prepared?

Q24-12   How do variable selling expenses differ from variable manufacturing costs?

Q24-13   Why are cash payments for a particular cost or expense item sometimes different in amount for a budget period than the amount of the cost or expense itself?

Q24-14   Why does the monthly depreciation cost shown in a factory overhead budget not require a cash payment during the month?

Q24-15   Discuss the purposes of the cash budget.

Q24-16   What is a projected balance sheet?

Q24-17   Discuss the importance of the projected income statement to management planning.

Q24-18   List and describe the differences between the three types of responsibility centers.

Q24-19   What makes a flexible budget "flexible?"

EXERCISES

E24-1   Production Budget.   The sales budget of the Grace Company shows estimated sales to be 30,000 units in October, 40,000 in November, 60,000 in December, and 30,000 in January. The company's policy is to end each month with an inventory of finished goods on hand equal to 40% of the following month's estimated sales.

Required: Prepare a production budget for the last 3 months of the year.

E24-2 Production Budget. Using the sales budget figures for the Grace Company given in E24-1, respond to the following independent requirements.

Required: 1. Prepare a production budget for the last 3 months of the year assuming that Grace wants to have 10,000 units in finished goods inventory at the end of each month.
2. Prepare a production budget for the last 3 months of the year so that production is the same each month. Assume that Grace has a beginning finished goods inventory in October of 10,000 units and wants to have an ending finished goods inventory in December of 15,000 units.

E24-3 Sales Budget. Butler Industries produces a single product that it sells for $6 per unit. Sales estimates (in units) for the last 4 months of the year are:

	Units
September	20,000
October	25,000
November	40,000
December	30,000

All of Butler's sales are on account and Accounts Receivable are expected to be collected 15 days after sale. No cash discounts are given. Assume that all months have 30 days.

Required: Prepare a sales budget for the last 3 months of the year, including estimated cash receipts from collections of Accounts Receivable.

E24-4 Raw Materials Purchases Budget. The production budget of the Merita Metals Company shows budgeted production (in units) for December and the first 4 months of next year at:

	Units
December	5,000
January	3,000
February	10,000
March	15,000
April	5,000

Each unit of this product requires 5 pounds of Material X costing $3.00 per pound. The company buys this material on account, paying in the month following purchase. No cash discounts are taken.

Required: Prepare a raw materials purchases budget for the direct materials needed in the first 3 months of next year for each of the following two *independent* situations:
1. The company's policy is to have raw materials inventory at the end of each month equal to 20% of the following month's usage requirement.
2. The company's policy is to keep raw materials inventory at the end of each month to a minimum, but without letting it fall below 5,000 pounds. Assume that the December 1 raw materials inventory has 5,000 pounds of raw materials and that the company's only supplier is willing to sell a maximum of 60,000 pounds of Material X to the company per month.

E24-5 Direct Labor Budget. Refer to E24-4. Merita Metals uses 2 direct labor hours to produce one unit of product. The direct labor rate is $5 per hour. Three-fourths of each month's wages are paid in the month earned. One-fourth is paid in the following month.

Required: Prepare a direct labor budget for the company for the first 3 months of next year.

E24-6 Estimating Cash Receipts from Sales. The Wankle Radio Company has estimated that sales for 1984 will be as follows:

	Sales Revenue
First quarter	$459,000
Second quarter	405,000
Third quarter	600,000
Fourth quarter	500,000

The company expects one-third of its sales each quarter to be cash sales. The remaining sales are to be on account. No cash discounts are given. The company's experience with collections on Accounts Receivable suggests that seven-ninths of the Accounts Receivable generated each quarter are collected in the same quarter. The remaining two-ninths are collected in the following quarter. The Accounts Receivable balance on December 31, 1983, is expected to be $92,000.

Required: Estimate the cash receipts expected during each of the first and second quarters of 1984 and the balance of Accounts Receivable that would appear on the projected balance sheet prepared for June 30, 1984.

E24-7 Factory Overhead Budget. Heidico Manufacturing is preparing its factory overhead budget for the coming year. Variable factory overhead costs include utilities ($.10 per unit), supplies ($.05 per unit), and other variable costs ($.12 per unit). Fixed factory overhead costs include supervisory salaries ($6,000 per month), depreciation of plant and equipment ($3,500 per month), and other fixed costs ($9,000 per month). Cash payments for factory overhead costs are made in the same month these costs are incurred (except for depreciation).

Required: Prepare a factory overhead budget for a month in which 25,000 units are planned to be produced.

E24-8 Factory Overhead Budget. F. Sor and Company has prepared the factory overhead budget for the first quarter of the year as shown below:

	January	February	March	Quarter
Budgeted production (units)	5,000	8,000	9,000	22,000
Variable overhead costs:				
Supplies	$ 300			
Utilities	200			
Other	650			
Total variable costs	$ 1,150			
Fixed overhead costs:				
Supervisory salaries	$ 1,800			
Depreciation of plant and equipment	6,000			
Other	6,200			
Total fixed costs	$14,000			
Total factory overhead costs	$15,150			

December's factory overhead budget showed total factory overhead costs of $18,500 (including depreciation of $6,000). No changes in monthly fixed costs are expected, except that the production supervisor will receive a $100 per month raise in salary starting March 1. Assume factory overhead costs are paid in the month after they are incurred (except for depreciation).

Required: Complete the factory overhead budget for this company for the first quarter of the year, including budgeted *monthly* cash payments for factory overhead costs.

E24-9   Selling Expense Budget.   Blanchar Business Machines estimates its monthly selling expenses as follows:

Advertising	$15,000 per month
Sales salaries	18,000 per month
Sales calls on customers	40 per unit
Commissions paid to sales personnel . . .	50 per unit
Delivery	20 per unit

Assume that selling expenses are paid in the month after they are incurred. Based on current plans of Blanchar's sales department, monthly sales estimates are: March — 70 units, April — 90 units, May — 100 units, June — 80 units.

Required: Prepare a selling expense budget for the *second* quarter for Blanchar Business Machines.

E24-10   Cash Budget.   Hudek Construction Company builds houses. Currently two houses are completed. The first is priced at $85,000; the second at $100,000. The company pays 10% of the selling price to the realtor when a house is sold.

Two additional houses are under construction. Linda Hudek, the owner, estimates that in May the company will pay $13,000 to workers, $32,000 for raw materials, and $60,000 to other companies for work she has subcontracted. The bank will make a construction loan to the company of $50,000 at 18% per year on May 1 if the company needs it. Interest would be paid at the end of each month on that loan. If this loan is not made, the company will not be able to borrow cash until June 15. On April 30 the company has $25,000 cash on hand.

Required: Prepare two cash budgets (for May) for Hudek Construction, one assuming the company expects to sell *both* houses and the other assuming it expects to sell only the $85,000 house.

E24-11   Flexible Budget for Manufacturing Costs.   The Booneville Manufacturing Company budgeted its manufacturing costs for August at a production level of 10,000 units, although 12,000 units were actually produced. Budgeted and actual costs are shown below:

	Actual	Original August Budget
Units manufactured	12,000	10,000
Direct materials	$ 4,100	$ 3,300
Direct labor	6,450	5,500
Factory overhead		
Variable:		
Utilities	425	360
Supplies	135	105
Other	350	285
Fixed:		
Supervisory salaries	2,900	2,900
Depreciation	1,000	1,000
Other	540	600
Total manufacturing costs	$15,900	$14,050

Required: Prepare a manufacturing cost report comparing August's actual costs with a revised budget based on the actual production level for August.

E24-12 Projected Income Statement. The Hollerbach Company produces a single product that it sells for $500 per unit. The company produces to customer order and does not carry an inventory. The following expenses are expected next year based on an estimate of 1,000 units sold:

Direct materials	$130,000
Direct labor	60,000
Factory overhead	
Variable	35,000
Fixed	80,000
Selling, general and administrative	
(assume all fixed)	100,000
Total	$405,000

Assume the company is subject to a corporate income tax rate of 40%.

Required: Prepare a projected income statement for the company based on a revised sales estimate of 800 units.

PROBLEMS

Part A

P24-1A Sales Budget. National Electric has just begun manufacturing burglar alarm systems. The sales estimate for April, the company's first month of operations, is 100 units. Sales are expected to increase to 150 units in May, 200 units in June, and then stay at 250 units each month for the rest of the year. National is planning to sell these units for $300 each and to extend credit to its customers up to 60 days. No cash discounts are given. Expected collections of Accounts Receivable are 20% in the month of sale, 40% in the month following sale, and 38% in the second month following sale (2% of Accounts Receivable are expected to be uncollectible).

Required:
1. Prepare a sales budget for the first 6 months of National's operations complete with a computation of expected cash receipts from sales for each month.
2. Does National's credit policy seem wise to you? What would you suggest?

P24-2A Production and Direct Labor Budgets. Greyline Manufacturing Company produces two products, X and Y. Both products require direct labor hours in Departments A and B. Wages are $6 per hour in Department A and $4 per hour in Department B. Greyline expects to sell 800 units of Product X in September and 600 units in October. Expected sales of Product Y amount to 500 units in September and 700 units in October. The company begins each month with finished goods inventory amounting to 50% of the month's expected sales (in units).

The direct labor hour requirements (per unit) for the production of these two products are shown in the table below:

	Product X	Product Y
Direct labor hours required in:		
Department A	1 hour	4 hours
Department B	3 hours	2 hours

Three-fourths of the wages earned by direct laborers are paid in the month earned and one-fourth is paid in the following month. Wages payable to Department A workers totaled $5,400 and wages payable to Department B workers totaled $3,500 at the end of August.

Required:
1. Prepare a direct labor budget for each department for the month of September.
2. Why are production budgets important? Discuss them with reference to Greyline's operations.

P24-3A Production, Raw Materials Purchases, and Direct Labor Budgets. The Snowsports Company will begin operations next January to produce plastic hockey sticks. Sales quantities and direct materials and direct labor cost estimates are as follows:

Units to be Sold		Direct Materials and Direct Labor Costs per Unit	
January	20,000	Direct material	
February	15,000	(4 lbs. @ $1.50 per lb.)	$6.00
March	20,000	Direct labor ($\frac{1}{2}$ hr. @ $3.00 per hr.) . . .	1.50
April	10,000	Total	$7.50

The following information is also available:

(a) Monthly production is to be scheduled so that the inventory of finished hockey sticks (in units) is 50% of the next month's expected sales (in units).

(b) Direct materials inventory (in pounds) at the end of each month should be 25% of the next month's usage requirement. Direct materials are to be paid for in the month following their purchase with no cash discounts. Assume no direct materials are in inventory on January 1.

(c) Wages are paid in the month the labor cost is incurred.

Required: 1. Prepare a production budget showing the required production in January, February, and March.

2. Prepare a raw materials purchases budget for the direct materials needed in the months of January and February.

3. Prepare a direct labor budget for January and February.

4. Is it reasonable for this company to set desired ending finished goods inventory levels as a constant percentage of the next month's expected sales and desired raw materials inventory as a constant percentage of the next month's usage requirement? Discuss.

P24-4A Cash Budget. Palomina Company produces dog food that it sells in 10-pound bags for $6.50 per bag. The following information is available:

(a) Sales estimates for the first 4 months of the year are: January — 50,000 bags, February — 60,000 bags, March — 55,000 bags, and April — 50,000 bags. The ending inventory of dog food each month is 20% of the next month's sales estimate (in bags). All sales are cash sales.

(b) The dog food is made from a mixture of direct materials costing $.08 per pound. Each month's ending inventory of direct materials (in pounds) is 50% of the next month's usage requirement. Payment for direct materials is made in the month of purchase, with no cash discounts taken.

(c) Each bag of dog food requires 0.25 hours of direct labor costing $4 per hour. Three-fourths of each month's direct labor cost is paid in the month incurred and one-fourth is paid in the following month.

(d) Variable factory overhead costs are expected to be $1.40 per bag and fixed factory overhead is $60,000 per month (including $25,000 of depreciation). Factory overhead costs are paid in the month *after* they are incurred.

(e) Variable selling expenses of $1.00 per bag sold and fixed selling expenses of $10,000 per month are paid in the *same* month incurred.

(f) General and administrative expenses totaling $45,000 per month (including $20,000 depreciation) are all fixed. They are paid in the month *after* they are incurred.

(g) Current liabilities on January 1 (all to be paid in January) total $139,200.

(h) The company's cash balance on January 1 is $45,000.

Required: Prepare a cash budget for each of the first 2 months of the year. (Hint: Other budgets may also have to be prepared in order to obtain information for Palomina's cash budget.)

P24-5A   Projected Income Statement. Refer to P24-4A. January's beginning finished goods inventory (10,000 bags) has a cost of $46,400. The cost of goods manufactured in January equals the total manufacturing costs incurred in that month (there are no goods in process inventories). An *average* cost flow assumption is used to compute inventory costs. Assume that Palomina is not a corporation.

Required:　Prepare a projected income statement for the month of January for the Palomina Company.

P24-6A   Flexible Factory Overhead Budget. The production budget of the Mammoth Manufacturing Company has been set at 200,000 units per month during the second quarter of the year (assume a production of 50,000 units per week for 4 weeks per month). All manufacturing cost budgets have been developed from this production budget. For example, the factory overhead budget shown below for April applies to May and June as well. Footnotes stating when factory overhead costs are paid are included below this budget. Utility costs incurred in March were $9,500.

MAMMOTH MANUFACTURING COMPANY
Factory Overhead Budget
April

Budgeted production	200,000 units
Variable overhead costs:	
Utilities	$ 10,000[a]
Supplies	6,000[b]
Maintenance	7,600[b]
Materials handling	12,500[b]
Other variable costs	16,000[b]
Total variable overhead	$ 52,100
Fixed overhead costs:	
Supervisory salaries	$ 18,000[b]
Depreciation of plant and equipment	30,000
Insurance and property taxes on plant and equipment	14,000[c]
Other fixed costs	25,000[b]
Total fixed overhead	$ 87,000
Total factory overhead	$139,100

[a] Paid in *following* month.
[b] Paid in *same* month.
[c] Insurance was prepaid; taxes are paid in December.

The factory may have to close down during the last week in April because of some difficulty the company is having with the renegotiation of a labor contract. If this happens, production in April will fall to 150,000 units. This lost production will have to be made up in May for the company to avoid losing sales.

The company is concerned about the effects that closing the factory down the last week in April will have on its cash budget.

Required:　On one schedule prepare monthly factory overhead budgets (adjusting them where necessary for the effect of the 1-week closing of the factory) for April, May, and June. Include the estimated monthly cash payments for factory overhead costs.

PROBLEMS

Part B

P24-1B Sales Budget. The American Products Company estimates sales for the first 6 months of the year as follows:

Sales	
January	$ 885,000
February	910,000
March	960,000
April	1,400,000
May	1,650,000
June	1,120,000

All sales are on account. No cash discounts are given. A study of Accounts Receivable collections indicates the following:

	Percent of Accounts Receivable Collected
In the month of sale	25%
In the first month after sale	30%
In the second month after sale	30%
In the third month after sale	10%
Uncollectible	5%

Required:
1. Prepare a sales budget for each month of the *second* quarter of the year complete with a computation of expected cash receipts from sales for each month.
2. How might American Products try to get its customers to pay their accounts more quickly? Discuss.

P24-2B Production, Raw Materials Purchases, and Direct Labor Budgets. The Brand Company will begin operations next January to produce Product Z. Sales quantities and direct materials and direct labor cost estimates are as follows:

Units to be Sold		Direct Materials and Direct Labor Costs per Unit	
January	40,000	Direct materials	
February	30,000	(3 lbs. @ $2.50 per lb.)	$ 7.50
March	40,000	Direct labor	
April	20,000	(2 hrs. @ $4.00 per hr.)	8.00
		Total	$15.50

The following information is also available:

(a) Monthly production is scheduled so that the ending inventory of finished goods (in units) is 30% of the next month's expected sales (in units).
(b) Direct materials in inventory (in pounds) at the end of each month should be 50% of the next month's usage requirement. Direct materials are to be paid for in the month of purchase with a 2% cash discount taken. Assume that no direct materials are in inventory on January 1.
(c) Wages are paid 75% in the month that direct labor cost is incurred and 25% in the following month.

Required:
1. Prepare a production budget for January, February, and March.
2. Prepare a raw materials purchases budget for the direct materials needed in the months of January and February.
3. Prepare a direct labor budget for January and February.

P24-3B   Production and Raw Materials Purchases Budgets. Blueline Manufacturing Company produces two products, X and Y. Both products require use of two direct materials, Material A and Material B. Material A costs $5 per pound and Material B costs $1 per pound. Blueline expects to sell 1,600 units of product X in May, 1,200 units in June, and 1,000 units in July. Sales of product Y are expected to be 500 units in May, 700 units in June, and 900 units in July.

The company begins each month with finished goods inventory equal to 25% of the month's expected sales (in units). Direct materials in inventory (pounds) are to be 50% of each month's usage requirement at the beginning of the month.

The direct materials requirements (per unit) for the production of these two products are shown in the table below:

	Pounds of Direct Materials Required	
	per Unit of Product X	per Unit of Product Y
Material A	2 pounds	4 pounds
Material B	1 pound	3 pounds

Accounts payable from purchases of direct materials are paid in the month of purchase. No cash discounts are taken.

Required: 1. Prepare a production budget for product X and product Y for the months of May and June.
   2. Prepare a raw materials purchases budget for direct materials A and B for the month of May.
   3. Why are production budgets important? Discuss with reference to Blueline's operations.

P24-4B   Cash Budget. Pretty Kitten Company produces cat food, which it sells in 10-pound bags for $6.25 per bag. The following information is available:

(a) Sales estimates for the first 4 months of the year are:

January	30,000 bags
February	40,000 bags
March	35,000 bags
April	30,000 bags

The ending inventory of cat food each month is 30% of the next month's sales estimate (in bags). All sales are cash sales.

(b) The cat food is made from a mixture of direct materials costing $.06 per pound. Each month's ending inventory of direct materials (in pounds) is 40% of the next month's usage requirement. Payment for direct materials is made in the month of purchase, with no cash discounts taken.

(c) Each bag of cat food requires 0.2 hours of direct labor costing $4 per hour. Direct labor costs are paid in the month incurred.

(d) Variable factory overhead costs are expected to be $1.25 per bag and fixed factory overhead is $50,000 per month (including $20,000 of depreciation). Factory overhead costs are paid in the month *after* they are incurred.

(e) Variable selling expenses of $1.00 per bag sold and fixed selling expenses of $15,000 per month are paid in the *same* month incurred.

(f) General and administrative expenses totaling $35,000 per month (including $20,000 depreciation) are all fixed. They are paid in the *same* month incurred.

(g) Current liabilities on January 1 (all to be paid in January) total $72,500.

(h) The company's cash balance on January 1 is $75,000.

Required: Prepare a cash budget for each of the first 2 months of the year. (Hint: Other budgets may also have to be prepared in order to obtain information for Pretty Kitten's cash budget.)

P24-5B Projected Income Statement. Refer to P24-4B. January's beginning finished goods inventory (9,000 bags) has a cost of $38,950. January's total manufacturing costs are the cost of goods manufactured for that month (there are *no* goods in process inventories). An *average* cost flow assumption is used to compute inventory costs. Assume Pretty Kitten is not a corporation.

Required: Prepare a projected income statement for the month of January for the Pretty Kitten Company.

P24-6B Flexible Factory Overhead Budget. The production budget of the Mathis Manufacturing Company has been set at 50,000 units per month during the entire coming year. All manufacturing cost budgets have been developed from this production budget. The factory overhead budget for 1 month is shown below:

Factory Overhead Budget

Budgeted production	50,000 units
Variable overhead costs:	
Utilities	$ 3,100
Supplies	2,500
Other	4,500
Total variable overhead	$10,100
Fixed overhead costs:	
Depreciation	$20,000
Supervisory salaries	10,000
Other	16,000
Total fixed overhead	$46,000
Total factory overhead cost	$56,100

All factory overhead costs are assumed to be paid in the month incurred (except depreciation). Management is concerned about the effects that a change in the production budget might have on cash payments by the company.

Required: Prepare a factory overhead budget for a month when production volume is 65,000 units. Estimate the *increase* in cash payments for that month for factory overhead costs over the payments expected at a production volume of 50,000 units.

DISCUSSION CASES

C24-1 The Uses of Budgeting. Hacker Industries produces a large variety of products in several locations. These products are mostly consumer items that the company sells to retail stores throughout the West and Midwest. Demand for many of the company's products is seasonal. The company does not prepare a master budget.

Recently, late raw materials deliveries have caused production delays at several of Hacker's plants. Direct and indirect labor costs have increased greatly over the last few years as have raw materials costs. One sales manager was heard to say, "I'm not even sure which products are most profitable anymore. When I think I have it figured out, production tells me they refuse to make any more because they're running low on Material X or some such thing. That's usually just after we've completed a big, expensive sales campaign for the product, too."

Last month the company had a big scare when it ran short of cash. Fortunately, the company has a line of credit at the bank; however, emergency borrowing is very expensive. The company president's reaction was, "Well, I guess I should have slowed down construction on the new Somerville plant, but I didn't realize you people couldn't keep things going without my attention."

Required: List and discuss the benefits Hacker Industries might receive from budgeting.

C24-2 Performance Evaluation. The combined manufacturing cost budget (for direct materials, direct labor, and factory overhead) for May is shown below along with the actual costs incurred during that month. The budget information was taken from the second quarter budget prepared at the beginning of the year.

Manufacturing Cost Report — May

	Actual	Original May Budget	Excess of Actual Cost Over Budget
Production (units)	21,000	20,000	
Direct materials	$108,000	$100,000	$ 8,000
Direct labor	157,200	150,000	7,200
Factory overhead:			
Variable overhead costs			
Utilities	7,400	7,000	400
Supplies	4,750	4,600	150
Maintenance	1,620	2,500	(880)
Other	5,900	5,600	300
Fixed overhead costs			
Depreciation	16,000	16,000	—0—
Supervisory salaries	6,000	6,000	—0—
Other	11,200	13,000	(1,800)
Total manufacturing costs	$318,070	$304,700	$13,370

Required: Discuss the value of the manufacturing cost report shown above. Suggest an alternative presentation that would be more useful for evaluating the performance of manufacturing and prepare that presentation. Discuss why performance evaluation would be improved by the alternative presentation you prepared.

25

Standard Costs and Variance Analysis

After reading this chapter, you should understand:

- The meaning of standard costs
- How standard costs are set
- The use of a standard cost system to help identify operating problems
- The computation and meaning of direct materials quantity and price variances
- The computation and meaning of direct labor efficiency and price variances
- The computation and meaning of fixed overhead volume and overhead budget variances

In Chapter 22 we discussed cost accounting systems primarily from the point of view of *product costing*. We described two types of cost accounting systems, job order and process cost systems. These systems are widely used for applying direct materials, direct labor, and factory overhead costs to the products produced by manufacturing companies. These same cost accounting systems, however, can also supply information to aid management in *planning* and *controlling* its operations.

In this chapter we emphasize the use of cost accounting systems in controlling company operations. Our discussion focuses on the development of *standard costs* and their use in evaluating the performance of manufacturing activities of companies.

OVERVIEW OF STANDARD COSTS

Definition of Standard Costs

Standard costs are the costs that *should* be incurred in performing an activity or producing a product under a given set of planned operating conditions. Standard costs are predetermined costs established on the basis of a careful study by managerial accountants, by engineers, and by others involved in the activity for which the standards are being set. The conditions that are planned depend upon the factors that are expected to influence costs. For example, the standard direct labor costs to be incurred in a sheet metal cutting operation depend upon having (1) direct materials of the proper size and quality entering the process as needed, (2) cutting machinery in proper adjustment for the particular operation being performed, (3) machine operators with the proper training and experience earning the normal wage rate, and so on. When the conditions specified for an operation are believed to exist, the standard costs are the costs expected to be incurred; that is, they are the *budgeted* costs.

Uses of Standard Costs and Variances

Standard costs are useful in planning and controlling the activities of a company. They are useful in planning because they aid in the development of budgets. Raw materials budgets, direct labor budgets, and factory overhead budgets can be developed from the production budget using standard costs as a means of describing the costs expected to be incurred in planned manufacturing operations. Standard costs are often developed for selling costs related to finished goods warehouse operations, shipping, and delivery, and for some general and administrative expenses incurred in routine clerical functions. Thus they are also helpful in preparing the selling expense budget and the general and administrative expense budget. Standard costs can be thought of as the "building blocks" in budget construction.

Standard costs are also a valuable source of data for decision making. If they reflect current operating conditions, standard costs provide a more reliable basis for estimating costs than do recorded actual costs, which may have been influenced by abnormal conditions or past inefficiencies. It is normally less time-consuming and costly to develop cost estimates from standard costs than to perform an analysis of past actual costs each time a decision is required.

The most valuable use of standard costs, however, is in controlling company operations. They provide the standard against which actual costs are compared to evaluate an activity. If the planned conditions under which an activity is to be performed exist, the standard cost is the amount of cost that should be incurred. If the actual cost incurred differs from the standard, one or more of the planned conditions must not have existed. **A variance is the difference between a standard cost and an actual cost.**

When the actual cost is greater than the standard cost, then the variance is *unfavorable*. When the actual cost is less than the standard cost, the variance is *favorable*. Reporting a variance provides a signal that an operating problem (such as a machine being out of adjustment) is occurring that may require management attention. If actual costs do not differ from standard costs, it is assumed that no operating problems are occurring and no special attention is needed. In other words, *feedback* of variance information helps to implement the *management by exception* principle (as discussed in Chapter 24).

Recording Standard Costs in the Accounts

When a manufacturing company uses a standard cost system, it normally assigns standard costs to each of its inventory accounts. This simplifies cost recording by eliminating the following tasks:

1. Keeping detailed cost records in the subsidiary raw materials inventory ledger and making LIFO, FIFO, or average cost computations to assign *actual* costs to units taken from that inventory. Subsidiary raw materials inventory records can be kept in physical quantities only.

2. Calculating *actual* costs per unit in process costing.
3. Posting actual costs to job order cost sheets in job order costing.

Assigning standard costs to inventory accounts also keeps identical units in inventory from having different costs assigned to them just because problems, such as inefficient production by a new employee, machine breakdown, or use of faulty materials, result in higher costs being incurred in the production of some units than others. Thus costs resulting from inefficiency in manufacturing operations are not recorded in inventory in a standard cost system. They are measured as variances and treated separately from inventories. In this chapter, as the calculations of variances for direct materials, direct labor, and factory overhead are discussed, journal entries to record standard costs in the inventory accounts are shown.

Setting Manufacturing Cost Standards

In order to understand variance computations and to know what they mean, it is necessary to understand how standard costs are set. Standard costs are established for the units of product *output* of manufacturing processes. The standard cost of a unit of product output is set by determining two standards for each *input* (direct materials, direct labor, and factory overhead) to the manufacturing process, a quantity standard and a price standard. **A quantity standard is the amount of an input to a manufacturing process that should be used to produce a unit of product in that process when the process is performed under planned conditions.** For example, an operation might require 5 pounds of a particular direct material per unit of product output and .8 hours of direct labor per unit. These amounts, 5 pounds per unit and .8 hours per unit, are the quantity standards for direct materials and direct labor. **A price standard is the cost that should be incurred to acquire a unit of input for the process.** Price standards, for example, are the cost per pound for direct materials and the cost per hour for direct labor.

Manufacturing companies spend a lot of time and effort designing their products and their manufacturing operations for efficient production. By considering the prices of alternative types, sizes, and qualities of direct materials and the expected direct labor and factory overhead costs that would result from using various kinds of direct labor and machine operations, they attempt to determine the least costly way to manufacture each product. This planning process results in a set of planned conditions for the production of the company's products. Quantity and price standards for direct materials, direct labor, and factory overhead are determined from these planned conditions.

Exhibit 25-1 shows the standard manufacturing cost for one unit of a hypothetical product produced by the Cordex Company. The planned conditions for the production of this product (called a Cordan) provide the basis for all of the illustrations and exhibits in this chapter.

Notice in Exhibit 25-1 how the standard costs per unit of product output are computed by multiplying the quantity standard for each input by its price standard. For example, the $6.00 standard direct materials cost of one Cordan is determined by multiplying the quantity standard (5 pounds per unit of product) times the price standard ($1.20 per pound). Notice also that the standard factory overhead rates

EXHIBIT 25-1
Standard
Manufacturing
Cost — Cordans

CORDEX COMPANY Standard Manufacturing Cost — Cordans		
Inputs	*Standard Quantity and Price*	*Standard Cost per Output Unit*
Direct materials	5 pounds @ $ 1.20	$ 6.00
Direct labor	.8 DLH @ $ 5.00	4.00
Factory overhead		
Variable	.8 DLH @ $ 2.00	1.60
Fixed	.8 DLH @ $10.00	8.00
Total standard cost per unit		$19.60

(price standards for factory overhead) have been set separately for fixed and variable overhead ($2 per hour variable and $10 per hour fixed) and that direct labor hours (DLH) are being used as the basis for applying factory overhead. The quantity standards for factory overhead were established by determining the number of direct labor hours required per unit of product under planned operating conditions (.8 direct labor hours per unit).

STANDARD COSTS AND VARIANCES FOR DIRECT MATERIALS

Direct Materials Quantity and Price Standards

QUANTITY STANDARDS.   A direct materials quantity standard shows the amount of a particular direct material that should be used to produce a unit of product output. Direct materials quantity standards are set to include the actual amount of materials contained in each "good" unit of product output, plus allowances for materials normally lost through cutting, trimming, and other operations, and an allowance for normal amounts of spoiled production. In this way they show the average (normal) quantity of material that should be used per good unit of product output when manufacturing operations are performed under the planned conditions.

PRICE STANDARDS.   Direct materials price standards are set for each required material to be used in producing a company's products. They show the cost per material unit of acquiring direct materials for production. Direct materials price standards are set to include the invoice price (less any discounts expected) to be paid to normal suppliers when materials are purchased in expected quantities, plus any transportation-in costs.

Exhibit 25-2 shows the computations of the direct materials quantity and price standards for the direct materials used by the Cordex Company to produce Cordans, the product whose standard cost is shown in Exhibit 25-1.

Notice the conditions that have influenced the determination of the direct materials quantity standard in Exhibit 25-2. The size and shape of the 25-pound blocks (in relation to the size and shape of the desired product) affect the cutting, trimming, and shaping operations and determine the resulting material content of the product and the allowance for waste. The quality of the direct materials as well as the proper adjustment of the equipment and necessary skill of the laborers are

EXHIBIT 25-2
Direct Materials
Quantity and Price
Standards

CORDEX COMPANY
Direct Materials Quantity and Price Standards for Cordans

Quantity standard (pounds per good unit)[a]:

Material content per completed unit	4.75 pounds
Allowance for waste in cutting, trimming, and shaping operations	.25 pounds
Standard material quantity per unit	5.00 pounds

Price standard (dollars per pound)[b]:

Invoice price	$1.00
Less purchases discount taken	(.02)
Transportation-in charges	.22
Standard price per pound	$1.20

[a] The manufacturing process involves cutting 25-pound blocks of material into 5-pound blocks, followed by trimming and shaping operations in which .25 pounds of material are lost. Material lost through cutting, trimming, and shaping is hauled away at no charge by a local scrap dealer.
[b] Materials are purchased in 25-pound blocks in quantities of 1,000. At that quantity the normal supplier charges $1.00 per pound. If purchased in smaller quantities, the price would be $1.05 per pound. The normal supplier offers terms of 2/10, n/30, and the company intends to take the 2% discount for all material purchases. Materials are to be shipped by rail from the supplier to St. Louis, where they are picked up by a local trucking company and brought to the plant, unloaded, inspected, and stacked in the storeroom at a total cost of $5,500 for the 1,000-block (25,000 pounds) purchase.

considered in determining that no allowance for normal spoilage is necessary for this product. Careful study of these conditions enabled the engineering and production department personnel to determine the standard quantity of direct materials to be used per unit of product output.

The price standards are influenced by the type, size, and quality of the required direct materials, but they are also influenced by several other conditions. Planned purchase quantities affect the invoice price. The company's policy of taking all cash discounts also affects the purchase cost. Finally, shipping by normal carriers as well as unloading and inspecting in the usual manner determine the transportation-in cost per pound of material. Together these conditions determine the standard price per pound to make the required direct materials available for production.

Direct Materials Quantity and Price Variances

DIRECT MATERIALS QUANTITY VARIANCE. When operating conditions that actually occur during production differ from those planned, the total actual quantity of direct materials used to produce a given amount of good product output may differ from the standard direct materials usage. **The standard direct materials usage is the amount of direct materials that *should be used* to produce a given number of good units of product output.** It is computed by multiplying the number of good units of product output times the direct materials quantity standard. For example, 1,000 Cordans should require 5,000 pounds (1,000 units × 5 pounds per unit from Exhibit 25-2) of direct materials.

The direct materials quantity variance is the difference between the actual

and standard direct materials cost that results from actual direct materials usage being more or less than standard direct materials usage. It is computed as the difference between the actual usage of direct materials times the standard price and the standard direct materials usage times the standard price. This computation is illustrated below, assuming 2,000 Cordans are produced during a period and 9,950 pounds of direct materials are actually used in that production:

Direct materials quantity variance:			
Actual usage at standard price	9,950 lbs. @ $1.20	=	$11,940
− Standard usage at standard price	10,000ª lbs. @ $1.20	=	12,000
Direct materials quantity variance	(50) lbs. @ $1.20	=	($ 60) (favorable)

ª 2,000 units × 5 pounds per unit = 10,000 pounds.

The key to computing the direct materials quantity variance is a correct computation of the standard direct materials usage. Remember that the standard direct materials usage is computed by multiplying the *actual* number of good units of product output times the direct materials quantity standard (2,000 units × 5 pounds per unit = 10,000 pounds in the illustration). Notice in the computation that both actual and standard usages are multiplied by the $1.20 price standard for the direct materials. Notice also that the $60 direct materials quantity variance is *favorable* because actual usage is less than the standard allowed for production of 2,000 Cordans. When the actual quantity of direct materials used exceeds standard usage allowed for a given output, the direct materials quantity variance is unfavorable.

DIRECT MATERIALS PRICE VARIANCE.   When direct materials are purchased under conditions other than those planned, the cost per direct material unit may differ from the price standard. If this occurs, it causes a direct materials price variance. **A direct materials price variance is the difference between the actual cost incurred to acquire direct materials and the cost that should have been incurred (at the standard price) to acquire the direct materials.** This variance is computed by multiplying the actual number of direct material units *purchased* times the difference between the actual and standard prices per direct material unit. Direct materials price variances are normally computed at the time materials are purchased. The computation is made as shown below, assuming 25,000 pounds of direct materials for production of Cordans have been acquired by Cordex at an actual cost of $33,750 ($1.35 per pound):

Direct materials price variance:			
Actual purchase cost	25,000 lbs. @ $1.35	=	$33,750
− Standard purchase cost	25,000 lbs. @ $1.20	=	30,000
Direct materials price variance	25,000 lbs. @ $ .15	=	$ 3,750 (unfavorable)

In the computation of the direct materials price variance, the standard purchase cost is found by multiplying the total actual quantity purchased times the direct materials price standard ($1.20 from Exhibit 25-2). As a result, the direct materials price variance can be computed as the difference between the actual and standard purchase cost ($33,750 − $30,000) or by multiplying the actual number of units purchased times the difference between the actual and standard price per unit [25,000 pounds × ($1.35 − $1.20)]. The direct materials price variance is *unfavorable* because the actual purchase price per unit is higher than the standard price. When the actual purchase price per unit is less than the standard price, the direct materials price variance is *favorable*.

Recording Direct Materials Variances

In order to assign standard costs to inventories, variances must be separated from actual costs and recorded separately in variance accounts. Direct materials price variances are removed at the time direct materials are *purchased*. The journal entry made by the Cordex Company to record the purchase of 25,000 pounds of direct materials on account for the production of Cordans is shown below (this journal entry relates to the direct materials price variance computation shown earlier):

Raw Materials Inventory	30,000	
Direct Materials Price Variance	3,750	
Accounts Payable		33,750

To record the purchase of direct materials.

Note in this journal entry that the actual purchase cost of the 25,000 pounds of direct materials (25,000 lbs @ $1.35 = $33,750) is credited to Accounts Payable. The standard cost of these direct materials (25,000 lbs. @ $1.20 = $30,000), however, is added (debited) to Raw Materials Inventory. Thus the Raw Materials Inventory account is being kept at standard cost. Note that the unfavorable direct materials price variance (25,000 lbs @ $.15 = $3,750) is debited to a separate account entitled Direct Materials Price Variance. This balances the journal entry.

As journal entries are described throughout this chapter, you should note that all unfavorable variances are recorded during an accounting period as debits to variance accounts. All favorable variances result in credits to variance accounts. We will discuss the treatment of balances in the variance accounts at the end of an accounting period after our discussion of direct labor and factory overhead variances.

Direct materials quantity variances are recorded as direct materials are *used*. The journal entry made by Cordex to record the use of 9,950 pounds of direct materials to produce 2,000 Cordans is shown below (this journal entry relates to the direct materials quantity variance computation shown earlier):

Goods in Process Inventory	12,000	
Direct Materials Quantity Variance		60
Raw Materials Inventory		11,940

To record the use of direct materials.

Note in this entry that the Raw Materials Inventory is reduced by the standard cost of the *actual* direct materials used (9,950 lbs. @ $1.20 = $11,940). The standard cost of the *standard direct materials usage* (10,000 lbs. @ $1.20 = $12,000), however, is added (debited) to the Goods in Process Inventory account. Thus the Goods in Process Inventory account is also kept at standard cost. Note that the favorable direct materials quantity variance is recorded as a credit to the Direct Materials Quantity Variance account to balance this journal entry. We discuss the use of the direct materials price and quantity variances later in this chapter after direct labor and factory overhead variances have been discussed.

STANDARD COSTS AND VARIANCES FOR DIRECT LABOR

Direct Labor Quantity and Price Standards

QUANTITY STANDARDS. A direct labor quantity standard gives the amount of direct labor time that should be used to produce a good unit of product output from manufacturing operations. Direct labor quantity standards are set by carefully studying the time required to perform the direct labor operations needed to produce a product and allowing for normal amounts of labor time used for personnel rest breaks, machine adjustment and idle time, and production of normal amounts of spoiled units. Direct labor quantity standards show the average direct labor time expected per unit of product output when manufacturing operations are performed under planned conditions.

PRICE STANDARDS. Direct labor price standards normally show the current wage rates per hour for the various types of labor employed in a company's manufacturing operations, that is, for machinists, welders, painters, assembly workers, and so on. Direct labor price standards may also be set to include an allowance for payroll taxes and fringe benefits. Although these additional payroll costs are normally treated as factory overhead costs by companies *not* using standard cost systems, it is common practice for such items to be included in direct labor price standards. The price standard set for each manufacturing operation required to make a product assumes that the operation would be performed by a properly trained operator earning the usual wage rate for that operation.

Exhibit 25-3 shows the computations of the quantity and price standards for the direct labor used in producing Cordans, the product whose standard cost is shown in Exhibit 25-1. For simplicity we assume that the same labor rate is earned by all workers in each direct labor operation.

In Exhibit 25-3 the quantity standard for direct labor was set by adding the standard hours per unit of product for the various required labor operations. Cutting, trimming, and shaping operations in department A (.4 hours) prepare the direct materials so that they are ready for the baking and polishing operations in department B (.4 hours). After the baking and polishing operations are completed, the units are finished. At that time each unit should have had a total of .8 direct labor hours devoted to it. The direct labor price standard of $5 per hour includes the basic wage rate of $4 in both departments plus allowances for payroll taxes and fringe benefits that total $1.

Direct Labor Efficiency and Price Variances

DIRECT LABOR EFFICIENCY VARIANCE. When actual operating conditions during production differ from the planned conditions, the total actual direct labor hours may differ from the standard direct labor usage. **The standard direct labor usage is the number of direct labor hours that** *should be used* **to produce a given number of good units of product output.** The standard direct labor usage, com-

EXHIBIT 25-3
Direct Labor
Quantity and Price
Standards

CORDEX COMPANY
Direct Labor Quantity and Price Standards for Cordans

Quantity standard (direct labor hours per unit)[a]:

Cutting operations	.12 hours	
Trimming and shaping operations	.28	
Total in department A		.40 hours
Baking and polishing operations in department B		.40
Standard direct labor quantity per unit		.80 hours

Price standard (dollars per direct labor hour)[b]:

Basic wage rate	$4.00
Payroll taxes (Social Security and unemployment compensation)	.60
Fringe benefits (vacation pay, insurance, etc.)	.40
Standard price (rate) per direct labor hour	$5.00

[a] Cutting, trimming, and shaping are hand labor operations that take place in department A. Baking and polishing are machine operations in department B.
[b] Payroll taxes are assumed in this exhibit to total 15% of the basic wage rate. Fringe benefits are assumed to be 10% of the basic wage rate. These rates are used for simplicity.

monly referred to as the *standard direct labor hours allowed*, is computed by multiplying the number of good units of product output times the direct labor quantity standard. For example, 1,000 Cordans should require 800 (1,000 units × .8 direct labor hours per unit from Exhibit 25-3) direct labor hours to produce.

The direct labor efficiency variance is the difference between the actual and standard direct labor cost that results from actual direct labor usage being more or less than standard direct labor usage. It is computed as the difference between the standard cost of the actual direct labor hours worked and the standard cost of the standard direct labor usage. The computation is illustrated below, assuming 2,000 Cordans are produced during a period and 1,615 actual direct labor hours are worked:

Direct labor efficiency variance:

Actual hours at standard price	1,615 hours @ $5.00	=	$8,075
− Standard hours at standard price	1,600 hours[a] @ $5.00	=	8,000
Direct labor efficiency variance	15 hours @ $5.00	=	$ 75 (unfavorable)

[a] 2,000 units × .8 hours per unit = 1,600 hours.

The key to computing the direct labor efficiency variance is a correct computation of the standard direct labor usage. Remember that the standard direct labor usage is computed by multiplying the *actual* number of good units of product output times the direct labor quantity standard (2,000 units × .8 hours per unit = 1,600 standard direct labor hours allowed in the illustration). Notice in the efficiency variance computation that both the actual direct labor hours and the standard direct labor hours allowed are multiplied by the $5.00 price standard. Thus the direct labor efficiency variance can be computed by multiplying the direct labor price standard by the difference between actual and standard direct labor usage. Notice also that the $75 direct labor efficiency variance is *unfavorable* because actual usage exceeds standard usage. When actual direct labor hours are less than standard direct labor hours allowed for a given output, the direct labor efficiency variance is *favorable*.

DIRECT LABOR PRICE VARIANCE. **The direct labor price variance is the difference between the actual direct labor cost incurred for a given number of actual labor hours worked and the cost that should have been incurred for those actual hours at the standard direct labor price (rate) per hour.** It is also known as the direct labor *rate* variance. The direct labor price (rate) variance measures the extent to which actual labor costs incurred differ from standard direct labor costs because of differences between actual and standard labor prices. The direct labor price variance is computed by multiplying the actual direct labor hours worked times the difference between the actual direct labor cost per hour and the direct labor price standard. This computation is illustrated below, assuming 1,615 direct labor hours were worked (to produce 2,000 Cordans) at a total cost of $7,913.50 ($4.90 per hour):

Direct labor price variance:			
Actual direct labor cost	1,615 hours @ $4.90	=	$7,913.50
− Actual hours at standard price	1,615 hours @ $5.00	=	8,075.00
Direct labor price variance	1,615 hours @ ($.10)	=	($ 161.50) (favorable)

Note in this computation of the direct labor price variance that the direct labor cost that should have been incurred for the actual hours worked is computed by multiplying the actual hours times the direct labor price standard ($5.00 from Exhibit 25-3). As a result, the direct labor price variance can be computed as the difference between the actual direct labor cost and the standard cost of the actual direct labor hours ($7,913.50 − $8,075) or by multiplying the actual number of hours worked times the difference between the actual and standard price (rate) per hour [1,615 hours × ($4.90 − $5.00)]. The direct labor price variance is *favorable* because the actual direct labor rate per hour is less than the direct labor price standard. When the actual rate per hour exceeds the standard rate, the direct labor price variance is *unfavorable*.

Recording Direct Labor Variances

Direct labor efficiency and price variances are normally recorded at the same time as production takes place. The journal entry to record the use of direct labor in a standard cost system adds (debits) the standard cost of direct labor to the Goods in Process Inventory account. The journal entry made by the Cordex Company to record the use of 1,615 direct labor hours for the production of 2,000 Cordans is shown below (this journal entry relates the computations of both the direct labor efficiency and direct labor price variances shown earlier):

Goods in Process Inventory 8,000.00
Direct Labor Efficiency Variance 75.00
   Direct Labor Price Variance 161.50
   Wages Payable 7,913.50
To record the direct labor cost incurred.

Note in this entry that the actual direct labor cost incurred (1,615 hours @ $4.90 = $7,913.50) is credited to the liability account, Wages Payable. The standard cost for 2,000 Cordans (1,600 standard direct labor hours allowed @ $5 per hour = $8,000), however, is added (debited) to the Goods in Process Inventory account to keep that account at standard cost. Also note that the unfavorable direct labor efficiency variance ($75) is debited and the favorable direct labor price variance ($161.50) is credited to separate variance accounts to balance the journal entry.

STANDARD COSTS AND VARIANCES FOR FACTORY OVERHEAD

Factory overhead includes all manufacturing costs other than direct materials and direct labor costs. It includes such items as depreciation, insurance, and property taxes on factory plant and equipment, utilities, maintenance, supervision, and factory supplies. Because of the large number and variety of these cost items, they are typically combined and applied to units of product produced as a single cost element, *factory overhead* (or simply *overhead*). Recall from our discussion of factory overhead application in Chapter 22 that factory overhead is applied *indirectly* to products by setting predetermined overhead rates. These rates are commonly determined per direct labor hour (or per machine hour) prior to production. Factory overhead is then applied (debited) to Goods in Process Inventory in an amount equal to the predetermined rate multiplied by the number of direct labor hours (or machine hours) used in that production.

Factory Overhead Quantity and Price Standards

QUANTITY STANDARDS.   The quantity standard for factory overhead is the number of direct labor hours or machine hours (whichever is to be used for overhead application) that *should be used* to produce a unit of product output when manufacturing operations take place under planned conditions. If direct labor hours are used as the basis for overhead application, the quantity standard for overhead is the same as the quantity standard for direct labor. If machine hours are used for overhead application, a separate quantity standard showing the expected machine hours required under planned operating conditions to produce a unit of product output would have to be determined.

PRICE STANDARDS.   The price standards for factory overhead are the standard predetermined overhead rates. Separate rates are often established for variable and fixed factory overhead. These rates are computed by determining the amounts of variable and fixed factory overhead budgeted at a given volume of manufacturing activity (measured in standard direct labor hours or machine hours) and dividing those budgeted amounts by that volume. Although either standard direct labor hours or machine hours are used for budgeting and applying factory overhead, standard direct labor hours are much more widely used. We assume the use of standard direct labor hours for budgeting and applying factory overhead in the remaining discussion and illustrations of this chapter.

Exhibit 25-4 shows the computation of standard factory overhead rates at three alternative volumes (expressed in standard direct labor hours) using overhead costs from the flexible overhead budget of the Cordex Company shown in that exhibit.

Notice in Exhibit 25-4 that the fixed factory overhead budget is $20,000 at each of the three volumes shown. This is because fixed overhead costs are not expected to be affected by changes in the volume of manufacturing activity. As a result, however, the *fixed* factory overhead *rate* per standard direct labor hour depends upon the volume of standard direct labor hours at which it is computed. Note in

EXHIBIT 25-4   Flexible Overhead Budget and Rate Computation

CORDEX COMPANY
Flexible Factory Overhead Budget For Cordan Production

	2,000	2,500	3,000
Volume (units per month)	2,000	2,500	3,000
Volume (standard direct labor hours)	1,600	2,000^a	2,400
Factory overhead costs:			
Variable:			
Indirect labor	$ 800	$ 1,000	$ 1,200
Indirect materials	400	500	600
Power	960	1,200	1,440
Other variable overhead	1,040	1,300	1,560
Total variable overhead	$ 3,200	$ 4,000	$ 4,800
Fixed:			
Depreciation on plant and equipment	$16,000	$16,000	$16,000
Property taxes and insurance	2,200	2,200	2,200
Other fixed overhead	1,800	1,800	1,800
Total fixed overhead	$20,000	$20,000	$20,000
Total factory overhead	$23,200	$24,000	$24,800

Standard Overhead Rate Computations at Each Volume

	1,600 Standard Direct Labor Hours	2,000 Standard Direct Labor Hours	2,400 Standard Direct Labor Hours
Variable	$\frac{\$3,200}{1,600 \text{ DLH}}$ = $2.00/DLH	$\frac{\$4,000}{2,000 \text{ DLH}}$ = $2.00/DLH	$\frac{\$4,800}{2,400 \text{ DLH}}$ = $2.00/DLH
Fixed	$\frac{\$20,000}{1,600 \text{ DLH}}$ = $12.50/DLH	$\frac{\$20,000}{2,000 \text{ DLH}}$ = $10.00/DLH	$\frac{\$20,000}{2,400 \text{ DLH}}$ = $8.33/DLH
Total	$\frac{\$23,200}{1,600 \text{ DLH}}$ = $14.50/DLH	$\frac{\$24,000}{2,000 \text{ DLH}}$ = $12.00/DLH	$\frac{\$24,800}{2,400 \text{ DLH}}$ = $10.33/DLH

^{a} Recall that the quantity standard for direct labor is .8 hours per Cordan. Thus the standard direct labor hours allowed for a unit volume of 2,500 units is 2,000 hours (2,500 units × .8 hours per unit).

Exhibit 25-4 that the fixed factory overhead rate is computed to be a different amount at each of the three volumes and that this changes the total factory overhead rate as well. Thus if monthly production volumes are expected to fluctuate and the fixed overhead rate is computed each month at that month's production volume, the fixed overhead (and total overhead) rates would also fluctuate.

To allow fixed factory overhead rates to change because of fluctuating production volume is usually not considered desirable. In order to avoid this problem, the volume of production used in the factory overhead rate computation is usually kept constant for several years at a time.

Variable factory overhead rates are *not* influenced by the volume chosen for the rate computation. The reason for this is that the total budgeted variable factory overhead cost varies directly in proportion to volume. Thus the constant rate at which variable overhead costs are budgeted per standard direct labor hour is the standard variable overhead rate regardless of the volume at which it is computed. Observe in Exhibit 25-4 that the standard variable overhead rate for the company producing Cordans is computed to be $2 per standard direct labor hour at each of the three volumes.

Standard overhead rates are usually computed using a volume that reflects the normal activity or practical capacity of the manufacturing operations. **Normal activity is an average of expected annual production volumes, usually computed for 3 to 5 years into the future.** It is closely related to the average sales volume expected over that future period. **Practical capacity is the volume of activity at which manufacturing facilities are capable of operating per year under *practical* conditions, that is, allowing for usual levels of efficiency.** It is closely related to the physical size of the production facilities, which typically does not change much from year to year. Computing factory overhead rates using the overhead budget at either normal activity or practical capacity provides stability to the fixed factory overhead rate (and therefore the total overhead rate), which would not exist if the expected monthly or annual production volume is used. We assume throughout our discussion of factory overhead variances that normal activity for the Cordex Company is 2,500 Cordans (2,000 standard direct labor hours) per month and that the company has used that volume to set its standard predetermined overhead rates. Those rates are as follows:

Variable overhead rate = $ 2 per standard direct labor hour
Fixed overhead rate = $10 per standard direct labor hour
Total overhead rate = $12 per standard direct labor hour

Applying Factory Overhead Costs in a Standard Cost System

Overhead application is slightly different when a standard cost system is used by a company instead of an actual cost system (as discussed in Chapter 22). When a company does not have a standard cost system, but does apply factory overhead using a predetermined overhead rate per direct labor hour, the amount applied is computed as the *actual direct labor hours worked* times the predetermined overhead rate. When a standard cost system is used, however, the amount of factory overhead applied is computed as the *standard direct labor hours allowed* times the standard predetermined overhead rate. For example, suppose that a company with a predetermined overhead rate of $3 per direct labor hour actually works 105 hours to produce 50 units that should have taken only 100 hours. If the company is *not* using a standard cost system, it would apply $315 (105 actual hours × $3 per hour) of factory overhead to those units. With a standard cost system, however, only $300 (100 standard direct labor hours allowed × $3 per hour) would be applied to those units.

Factory Overhead Variances

Factory overhead variances arise when the amount of factory overhead cost incurred during a period differs from the amount of factory overhead cost applied.

TOTAL OVERHEAD VARIANCE. **The total overhead variance is the difference between total factory overhead cost *incurred* and total factory overhead cost *applied* in a standard cost system.** The computation of the total overhead variance experienced by the Cordex Company during a month when 2,000 Cordans were produced and a total of $24,400 of actual overhead cost was incurred is shown below:

Total overhead variance:

Total overhead cost incurred	$24,400
− Total overhead cost applied (1,600 standard direct labor hours allowed @ $12)	19,200
Total overhead variance	$ 5,200 (unfavorable)

Note in this computation that the *standard direct labor hours allowed* to produce 2,000 Cordans (2,000 units × .8 hours per unit = 1,600 hours) and the total predetermined overhead rate ($12 per hour) were used to compute the total overhead cost applied. When total overhead cost incurred is greater than total overhead cost applied, as in the above computation, the total overhead variance is unfavorable. When the amount incurred is less than the amount applied, the total overhead variance is favorable.

The total overhead variance is usually divided into at least two separate overhead variances to improve management's understanding of the reasons why the total overhead variance occurred. We discuss two overhead variances, the fixed overhead volume variance and the overhead budget variance, which together make up the total overhead variance.

FIXED OVERHEAD VOLUME VARIANCE. **The fixed overhead volume variance is the difference between the amount of fixed overhead budgeted and the amount of fixed overhead applied.** It is computed by subtracting the amount of fixed overhead cost applied (standard direct labor hours allowed times the standard fixed overhead rate per hour) from the total fixed overhead budgeted. It is unfavorable when the fixed overhead applied is less than the fixed overhead budgeted and favorable when the fixed overhead applied is greater than the fixed overhead budgeted.

The fixed overhead volume variance arises *solely* because of the difference between the way fixed overhead is budgeted and the way it is applied. Total fixed overhead is budgeted at the amount expected to be incurred regardless of the volume of manufacturing activity. Fixed overhead, however, is applied based on the predetermined fixed overhead rate times the standard direct labor hours allowed for the number of units of product produced.

The fixed overhead for the Cordex Company is budgeted at a total amount of $20,000 per month (see Exhibit 25-4), or $240,000 per year. Recall that the company uses a normal activity of 2,000 standard direct labor hours per month (24,000 per year) to compute its standard fixed overhead rate of $10 per standard direct labor hour. Fixed overhead is then applied at this rate. During the month when Cordex produces 2,000 units of product, 1,600 (2,000 × .8) standard direct labor hours would be allowed. At this volume $16,000 (1,600 standard DLH × $10 per DLH) of fixed overhead would be *applied* to that output. The amount *budgeted*, however, is $20,000. The fixed overhead volume variance is computed below:

Fixed overhead volume variance:

Fixed overhead budgeted	$20,000
− Fixed overhead applied (1,600 standard DLH @ $10)	16,000
Fixed overhead volume variance	$ 4,000 (unfavorable)

Exhibit 25-5 shows both the amount of fixed overhead budgeted by Cordex and the amount that would be applied at various levels of standard direct labor hours. The $4,000 unfavorable fixed overhead volume variance computed above is also shown.

Notice in Exhibit 25-5 that for all volumes *below* normal activity of 2,000 standard direct labor hours, the amount of fixed overhead budgeted is more than the

EXHIBIT 25-5
Cordex Company
Fixed Overhead
Budgeted and Applied

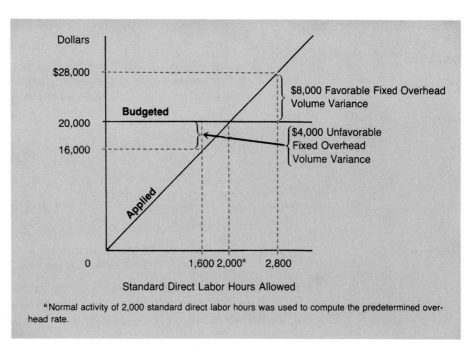

Standard Direct Labor Hours Allowed

[a] Normal activity of 2,000 standard direct labor hours was used to compute the predetermined overhead rate.

amount applied. This results in an unfavorable fixed overhead volume variance. For all volumes *above* normal activity, the amount of fixed overhead budgeted is less than the amount applied and results in a favorable fixed overhead volume variance. For example, if Cordex had produced 3,500 Cordans, 2,800 (3,500 units × .8 hours per unit) standard direct labor hours would have been allowed. Fixed overhead applied would be $28,000 (2,800 standard direct labor hours allowed × $10 per hour). The amount budgeted, however, would still be $20,000. In this case the fixed overhead volume variance would be $8,000 favorable ($20,000 budgeted − $28,000 applied). This variance is also shown in Exhibit 25-5.

The only time that a company would *not* have a fixed overhead volume variance (that is, its volume variance would be zero) is when the number of standard direct labor hours used to apply fixed overhead to actual product output (the standard direct labor hours allowed) is exactly equal to the number used to compute the fixed overhead rate. Note in Exhibit 25-5 that when the standard direct labor hours allowed are 2,000, which is the normal activity level used to compute the predetermined overhead rates, the amount of fixed overhead applied equals the amount budgeted ($20,000) and the fixed overhead volume variance is zero.

It is important to recognize that *there can never be a "variable" overhead volume variance*. The reason for this is that variable overhead is applied in the same way it is budgeted, at a constant rate per standard direct labor hour. For a month when Cordex produces 2,000 Cordans (for which 1,600 standard direct labor hours are allowed) its variable overhead budget is $3,200 (see Exhibit 25-4). This is the same amount that would be applied in that month. The amount of variable overhead budgeted for a given production volume (in units) equals the amount of variable overhead applied to the units produced. For the Cordex Company the variable overhead rate is $2 per standard direct labor hour. The amount of variable overhead budgeted and applied is 1,600 standard direct labor hours allowed × $2 per hour = $3,200.

Since the variable overhead budgeted at standard direct labor hours allowed equals the amount of variable overhead applied, the fixed overhead volume variance can also be computed as the difference between the *total* overhead budgeted and applied (at standard direct labor hours allowed). This is shown in the table below.

	Overhead Budgeted at 1,600 Standard Direct Labor Hours Allowed	Overhead Applied at 1,600 Standard Direct Labor Hours Allowed
Variable overhead	$ 3,200 (1,600 hours @ $2)	$ 3,200 (1,600 hours @ $2)
Fixed overhead	20,000	16,000 (1,600 hours @ $10)
Total overhead	$23,200	$19,200 (1,600 hours @ $12)

$4,000 unfavorable fixed
overhead volume variance

The fixed overhead volume variance is of little use for management control purposes. It shows only that the volume of units produced in a period was more or less than the volume used to set the predetermined standard overhead rate. When it is subtracted from the total overhead variance, however, a remainder is left that provides useful control information. This is the overhead budget variance. We now consider the computation of the overhead budget variance.

OVERHEAD BUDGET VARIANCE. **The overhead budget variance is the difference between total overhead incurred and total overhead budgeted at standard direct labor hours allowed.** The total overhead budgeted at standard direct labor hours allowed is the amount of factory overhead cost that *should* be incurred for the number of units produced. When the actual total factory overhead cost incurred exceeds this budgeted amount, the overhead budget variance is therefore unfavorable. Incurring less cost than budgeted gives a favorable budget variance.

The computation of the overhead budget variance for the month when 2,000 Cordans were produced is shown below. Recall from our computation of the total overhead variance that total overhead cost incurred is assumed to be $24,400.

Overhead budget variance:		
Total overhead incurred		$24,400
− Total overhead budgeted at standard		
direct labor hours allowed (1,600 hours):		
Variable (1,600 hours @ $2.00)	$ 3,200	
Fixed	20,000	23,200
Overhead budget variance		$ 1,200 (unfavorable)

The overhead budget variance arises when expenditures for the individual overhead items differ from those budgeted at the standard direct labor hours allowed. To provide useful control information, the overhead budget variance would normally be reported *item by item* so that management can judge which items need attention. Such a breakdown of the overhead budget variance is shown below in Exhibit 25-6. The actual amounts incurred have been assumed for purposes of illustration, whereas the budgeted amounts have been taken from Exhibit 25-4.

EXHIBIT 25-6   Overhead Budget Variance Report

CORDEX COMPANY
Overhead Budget Variance Report

	Actual Overhead Costs Incurred	Budgeted Overhead at 1,600 Standard Direct Labor Hours Allowed	Overhead Budget Variance
Indirect labor	$ 1,500	$ 800	$ 700 (unfavorable)
Indirect materials	740	400	340 (unfavorable)
Power	1,040	960	80 (unfavorable)
Other variable overhead	1,025	1,040	(15) (favorable)
Depreciation on plant and equipment	16,000	16,000	0
Property taxes and insurance	2,250	2,200	50 (unfavorable)
Other fixed overhead	1,845	1,800	45 (unfavorable)
Total	$24,400	$23,200	$1,200 (unfavorable)

In Exhibit 25-6 five of the seven overhead items in the overhead budget variance report show unfavorable variances. Indirect labor and indirect materials, in particular, show very large variances relative to their budgeted amounts. Together they make up approximately 87% [($700 + $340) ÷ $1,200] of the total (net) overhead budget variance. By directing the attention of Cordex's management to these two items, the overhead budget variance report enables the management by exception principle to be used.

To complete our discussion of overhead variance computations, in Exhibit 25-7 we show how the fixed factory overhead variance and the overhead budget variance together make up the total overhead variance. In Exhibit 25-7 both the total

EXHIBIT 25-7
Cordex Company
Graph of Factory
Overhead Variances

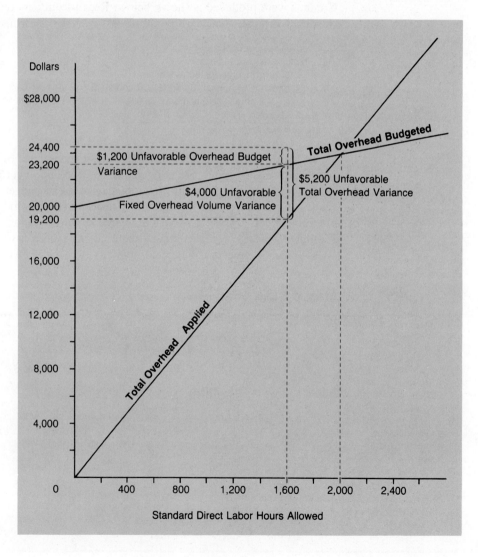

overhead budgeted and the total overhead applied are shown at various levels of standard direct labor hours allowed. The fixed overhead volume variance, the overhead budget variance, and the total overhead variance are shown for the month when Cordex produced 2,000 Cordans (when 1,600 standard direct labor hours were allowed).

Note in Exhibit 25-7 how the $1,200 unfavorable budget variance and $4,000 unfavorable fixed overhead volume variance are added to make up the $5,200 unfavorable total overhead variance. Note also that the $4,000 unfavorable fixed overhead volume variance appears as the difference between the total overhead *budgeted* and the total overhead *applied* at 1,600 standard direct labor hours allowed.

We now describe the journal entries required to record the factory overhead actually incurred, the factory overhead applied, and the two factory overhead variances.

Recording Factory Overhead Variances Factory overhead costs actually *incurred* are recorded as debits to the Factory Overhead account. Factory overhead costs *applied* (at standard) are recorded as credits to the Factory Overhead account (and debits to the Goods in Process Inventory account). Thus the balance in the Factory Overhead account at the end of a period equals the total overhead variance for the period. This balance is usually removed from the account at the end of each month by a journal entry to record the fixed overhead volume variance and overhead budget variance (which together make up the total overhead variance) in separate variance accounts.

Assuming for simplicity that all factory overhead costs except depreciation were paid in cash, the journal entries made by Cordex to record the actual factory overhead cost incurred, the standard factory overhead cost applied, and the two overhead variances are shown below (see Exhibits 25-6 and 25-7 for the amounts used in these journal entries):

Factory Overhead	24,400	
Accumulated Depreciation: Plant and Equipment		16,000
Cash		8,400
To record the actual factory overhead cost incurred.		
Goods in Process Inventory	19,200	
Factory Overhead		19,200
To apply factory overhead.		
Fixed Overhead Volume Variance	4,000	
Overhead Budget Variance	1,200	
Factory Overhead		5,200
To record factory overhead variances.		

Note in the first entry that the actual factory overhead cost incurred ($24,400) is debited to Factory Overhead. In the second entry the standard amount of factory overhead applied to Goods in Process Inventory (1,600 standard direct labor hours $\times$ \$12 total overhead rate = \$19,200) is removed from (credited to) the Factory Overhead account. Thus standard factory overhead costs are recorded in the Goods in Process Inventory account (just like the standard costs for direct materials and direct labor). Note that after the second entry, however, Factory Overhead has a \$5,200 debit balance (\$24,400 debit − \$19,200 credit), which is equal to the total overhead variance. Finally, note in the last entry that the \$5,200 debit balance in Factory Overhead is removed and divided among the two overhead variances that make up the total overhead variance.

By using the journal entries illustrated for recording direct materials, direct labor, and factory overhead in this chapter, the standard manufacturing cost of producing 2,000 Cordans has been recorded in the Goods in Process Inventory account of the Cordex Company. Although we do not illustrate these journal entries, Cordex would transfer the standard cost of completed Cordans (\$19.60 per unit from Exhibit 25-1) from the Goods in Process Inventory to the Finished Goods Inventory when the units are completed. As the Cordans are sold this standard cost would be removed from the Finished Goods Inventory and added to Cost of Goods Sold. In addition to the three inventory accounts, Cost of Goods Sold is thus also recorded at standard cost.

At the end of an accounting period for which financial statements are prepared, the variance accounts for direct materials, direct labor, and factory overhead will have balances. If the company's standards reflect current planned conditions, these balances will be small. The variance account balances are normally closed at the end of the period to the Cost of Goods Sold account. If the total (net) amount of these variances is not small, a more complicated procedure is required. This procedure is beyond the scope of this book.

USING MANUFACTURING COST VARIANCES TO CONTROL OPERATIONS

When the manufacturing operations of a company are running smoothly as they have been planned, the standard costs are the costs that are expected to be incurred. When problems occur in these operations, however, variances arise. If a machine is out of adjustment, it can cause more direct materials usage and result in an unfavorable direct materials quantity variance. The purchase of a less expensive grade of material than needed for the production of a product would cause a favorable direct materials price variance, but it could also cause more direct materials usage and result in an unfavorable direct materials quantity variance. Similarly, assigning a new unskilled employee with a low wage rate to a job requiring a higher paid worker with more skill would cause a favorable direct labor price variance, but it could also lead to unfavorable direct materials quantity and direct labor efficiency variances. Standard cost variances result from problems that change the actual manufacturing conditions from the planned conditions. Variances can be thought of as the "symptoms" of those problems.

Managers attempt to use cost variance information to determine what problems are affecting the efficient performance of their company's manufacturing activities in somewhat the same way a doctor attempts to diagnose a medical ailment. The doctor knows that the symptoms observed in a patient may be the result of a temporary physical condition which will go away without medical help. The doctor also knows that if the symptoms are not the result of a temporary condition, the specific medical problem must be identified before effective treatment can be prescribed. Finally, the doctor knows that an illness may be identified that cannot be cured.

Similarly, variances from standard costs can result from temporary operating problems that will run their course and come to an end without management attention. For example, a small batch of low-quality direct materials that go into a manufacturing process may cause more waste or extra processing time, but these problems disappear when the faulty material is used up. Variances can also be caused by changes in operating conditions that are not controllable, such as labor rate changes resulting from a new union contract or changes in direct materials prices. Variances, however, may result from operating problems that, if identified, could be corrected so that future operations would be more efficient.

In order to make variance computations more helpful to management in identifying the specific problems that are causing the variances, managerial accountants follow three general rules:

1. They try to measure variances as quickly as they can after the variances occur.
2. They try to measure variances in as much detail as is helpful in pinpointing specific problems.
3. They try to report variances to managers who are in a position to identify and correct the problems that are likely to have caused the variances.

Measuring Variances Quickly

Variances should be measured as quickly as possible after they occur so that problems can be recognized early and corrected before they cause too much damage. Although the variance computations illustrated in this chapter for the company producing Cordans were based on a period of a month, many companies compute variances weekly or even daily to help identify problems more quickly. Two practices followed by many companies in computing direct materials variances provide an excellent example of how managerial accountants attempt to follow this general rule. These are discussed below.

Direct materials price variances can be computed either as materials are purchased or as they are used. Most companies compute direct materials price variances at the time of purchase (the way we have illustrated the computation) because these variances are caused by problems arising at the time of purchase. To wait until materials are used (perhaps months after purchase) would delay recognition of those problems.

Direct materials quantity variances can also be computed quickly after they occur. Many companies allow the storekeeper to issue only the standard amount of direct materials required for a given amount of product when the materials requisition is presented. If this amount of material is insufficient to complete production, an additional materials requisition must be presented before more direct materials are issued. As soon as this happens, there is a source document indicating that an unfavorable direct materials quantity variance is occurring and the supervisors of production operations can be alerted.

Measuring Variances in Detail

The reason for measuring variances in detail is that these detailed variance computations provide better clues to help management identify specific problems. Some examples of the kinds of detailed computations that are helpful have already been discussed throughout this chapter. Rather than computing a single total manufacturing cost variance, for example, we discussed computations of separate variances for each input to the manufacturing process (direct materials, direct labor, and factory overhead). In addition, quantity and price variance computations were described for direct materials and direct labor and the overhead budget variance was reported on an item by item basis.

Recall our illustration of the direct labor efficiency variance. The production of Cordans required direct labor hours to be worked in cutting, trimming, shaping, baking, and polishing operations (see Exhibit 25-3). Based on the direct labor quantity standard (.8 DLH per unit) computed in Exhibit 25-3, we determined that the total standard direct labor usage to produce 2,000 Cordans was 1,600 direct labor hours (2,000 × .8). This standard usage was subtracted from the actual 1,615 direct labor hours worked and the excess usage (15 hours) was multiplied by the $5 direct labor price standard to compute the overall $75 unfavorable direct labor efficiency variance. It would be very helpful in identifying the problem(s) causing that variance, however, if the excess labor hours worked in each individual operation or each production department had been measured. Then the direct labor efficiency variance could be computed for the individual operations or departments.

For example, recall that cutting, trimming, and shaping operations are performed in production department A and baking and polishing operations are performed in production department B. Suppose that, of the total 1,615 actual direct labor hours, 835 actual direct labor hours were worked in department A and 780 actual direct labor hours were worked in department B. Exhibit 25-3 shows that the direct labor quantity standard is .4 hours in department A and .4 hours in department B. Thus the standard direct labor usage for 2,000 Cordans is 800 hours in each department. The direct labor efficiency variance can be computed for each department as shown below:

Direct labor efficiency variances:

Department A: (835	−	800)	×	$5.00	=	$175 unfavorable
Department B: (780	−	800)	×	$5.00	=	($100) favorable
Total unfavorable variance					=	$ 75

Note in this computation that the direct labor efficiency variance for department A ($175) is unfavorable because actual direct labor hours exceeded standard direct labor usage. In department B the direct labor efficiency variance is favorable, however. The value of this more detailed direct labor efficiency variance computation is that it helps focus management attention on individual operations or departments. In this way operations that are inefficient can be found. Operations that are especially efficient can also be recognized. Investigations of the causes of both unfavorable and favorable variances can often help improve the efficiency of future operations.

Reporting
Variances

To be useful, manufacturing cost variance information must be communicated to managers who can correct problems in the manufacturing operations by the actions they take or the decisions they make. By measuring variances in enough detail to separate variances incurred in different departments or during different work shifts in the same department, the managerial accountant can direct reports to various managers showing the variances occurring as a result of the operations for which they are responsible. These reports can provide information to the managers that can lead to the identification and correction of operating problems.

Reporting favorable variances to managers is just as important as reporting unfavorable variances. Favorable variances normally indicate that performance of manufacturing activities was better than planned and may indicate opportunities for continued good performance. Employees who have done a particularly good job can be rewarded, and new production methods that they may have developed can be shown to other employees. We should caution, however, that *favorable* variances can sometimes result from potentially serious problems. For example, the $100 favorable direct labor efficiency variance computed for department B could be an indication of hasty and sloppy workmanship by employees that could lead to customer dissatisfaction and lost sales. Thus both unfavorable and favorable variances may be indications of potential trouble.

Of course not all manufacturing cost variances deserve management attention. Some variances result from minor problems that are not longlasting and not serious enough for management to incur the cost of investigating the problems. Other variances may quickly be recognized as resulting from permanent and uncontrollable changes in operating conditions. When this fact is uncovered it suggests the need for revision of the quantity or price standards. For example, a direct labor price variance may be caused by increased wage rates resulting from a new union contract. This change in conditions should be noted and the direct labor price standard should be revised.

By considering the absolute or relative size of variances in relation to the kinds of problems from which they may result, managers direct their attention to the operations that seem most likely to benefit from attention. That is, the managerial accountant's detailed variance analysis can enable managers to use the principle of *management by exception*. Variance computations are especially helpful when they are computed quickly after they occur and reported to the managers who can take corrective action.

A SUMMARY OF
VARIANCE
COMPUTATIONS

Exhibit 25-8 shows, in equation format, the computations of the variances we have discussed. Note particularly the similarity between the direct materials quantity variance computation and the direct labor efficiency variance computation.

EXHIBIT 25-8   Summary of Variance Computations

Direct materials quantity variance	= Direct materials price standard	× (Actual direct materials usage	− Standard direct materials usage)
Direct materials price variance	= Actual direct materials units purchased	× (Actual price per unit of direct materials	− Standard price per unit of direct materials)
Direct labor efficiency variance	= Direct labor price standard	× (Actual direct labor hours	− Standard direct labor hours allowed)
Direct labor price variance	= Actual direct labor hours	× (Actual direct labor cost per hour	− Standard direct labor cost per hour)
Total overhead variance	= Actual total overhead cost incurred	− (Standard direct labor hours allowed	× Standard total overhead rate)
Fixed overhead volume variance	= Total fixed overhead budgeted	− (Standard direct labor hours allowed	× Standard fixed overhead rate per direct labor hour)
Overhead budget variance	= Actual total overhead cost incurred	− [Fixed overhead cost budgeted + (Standard direct labor hours allowed	× Standard variable overhead rate per direct labor hour)]

REVIEW PROBLEM

The records of the Poolside Manufacturing Company reveal the following data:

Input	Standard Quantity and Price	Standard Cost per Output Unit
Direct materials	8 pounds @ $ .20 per pound	$1.60
Direct labor	2 hours @ $2.20 per hour	4.40
Variable overhead	2 hours @ $ .80 per hour	1.60
Fixed overhead	2 hours @ $ .40 per hour	.80
Total standard manufacturing cost per output unit		$8.40

The determination of the factory overhead rates (per direct labor hour) was based on a flexible budget at a normal activity of 20,000 direct labor hours that showed:

	Total	Standard Rate
Variable factory overhead	$16,000	$ .80 ($16,000 ÷ 20,000)
Fixed factory overhead	8,000	.40 ($8,000 ÷ 20,000)
Total factory overhead	$24,000	$1.20

Actual data:

Production: 9,500 units completed, no beginning or ending goods in process inventories.

Direct materials: 100,000 pounds purchased on account at a total cost of $18,000. 79,000 pounds used.

Direct labor: 19,200 hours worked at a total cost of $44,160.

Total factory overhead cost incurred: $23,910 (assume all was paid in cash except for $2,500 depreciation on equipment).

Required: 1. Compute the following variances and indicate whether each is *favorable* or *unfavorable*:
    (a) Direct materials price variance
    (b) Direct materials quantity variance
    (c) Direct labor price variance
    (d) Direct labor efficiency variance
    (e) Total overhead variance
    (f) Fixed overhead volume variance
    (g) Overhead budget variance

2. Prepare journal entries for the Poolside Manufacturing Company to record the above information.

SOLUTION TO REVIEW PROBLEM

1. Variance Computations:

(a) Direct materials price variance:

Actual purchase cost	100,000 pounds @ $.18	= $18,000
− Standard purchase cost	100,000 pounds @ $.20	= 20,000
Direct materials price variance	100,000 pounds @ ($.02)	= ($ 2,000) (favorable)

(b) Direct materials quantity variance:

Actual usage at standard price	79,000 pounds @ $.20	= $15,800
− Standard usage at standard price	76,000 pounds[a] @ $.20	= 15,200
Direct materials quantity variance	3,000 pounds @ $.20	= $ 600 (unfavorable)

[a] Standard direct materials usage = 9,500 units × 8 pounds per unit = 76,000 pounds

(c) Direct labor price variance:

Actual direct labor cost	19,200 hours @ $2.30	= $44,160
− Actual hours at standard price	19,200 hours @ $2.20	= 42,240
Direct labor price variance	19,200 hours @ $ .10	= $ 1,920 (unfavorable)

(d) Direct labor efficiency variance:

Actual hours at standard price	19,200 hours @ $2.20	= $42,240
− Standard hours at standard price	19,000 hours[a] @ $2.20	= $41,800
Direct labor efficiency variance	200 hours @ $2.20	= $ 440 (unfavorable)

[a] Standard direct labor hours allowed = 9,500 units × 2 hours per unit = 19,000 hours

(e) Total overhead variance:

Total overhead incurred	$23,910
− Total overhead applied (19,000 hours @ $1.20)	22,800
Total overhead variance	$ 1,110 (unfavorable)

(f) Fixed overhead volume variance:

Fixed overhead budgeted	$ 8,000
− Fixed overhead applied (19,000 hours @ $.40)	7,600
Fixed overhead volume variance	$ 400 (unfavorable)

(g) Overhead budget variance:

Total overhead incurred		$23,910
− Total overhead budgeted		
Variable (19,000 hours @ $.80)	$15,200	
Fixed	8,000	23,200
Overhead budget variance		$ 710 (unfavorable)

2. Journal Entries:

Direct Materials Purchases

Raw Materials Inventory	20,000	
Direct Materials Price Variance		2,000
Accounts Payable		18,000

To record the purchase of direct materials.

Direct Materials Usage

Goods in Process Inventory	15,200	
Direct Materials Quantity Variance	600	
Raw Materials Inventory		15,800

To record the use of direct materials.

Direct Labor Usage

Goods in Process Inventory	41,800	
Direct Labor Price Variance	1,920	
Direct Labor Efficiency Variance	440	
Wages Payable		44,160

To record direct labor cost incurred.

Factory Overhead Incurred

Factory Overhead	23,910	
Accumulated Depreciation: Equipment		2,500
Cash		21,410

To record actual factory overhead incurred.

Factory Overhead Applied

Goods in Process Inventory	22,800	
Factory Overhead		22,800

To apply factory overhead (19,000 standard direct labor hours allowed @ $1.20 per hour).

Factory Overhead Variances

Fixed Overhead Volume Variance	400	
Overhead Budget Variance	710	
Factory Overhead		1,110

To record factory overhead variances.

GLOSSARY

Direct Labor Efficiency Variance. The direct labor price standard multiplied by the difference between actual and standard direct labor usage.

Direct Labor Price Variance. The actual direct labor hours worked multiplied by the difference between actual direct labor cost per hour and the direct labor price standard.

Direct Materials Price Variance. The actual number of direct materials units purchased multiplied by the difference between the actual and standard prices per unit.

Direct Materials Quantity Variance. The direct materials price standard multiplied by the difference between the actual and standard direct materials usage.

Fixed Overhead Volume Variance. The difference between the total fixed overhead budgeted and the total fixed overhead applied (standard direct labor hours allowed times the standard fixed overhead rate).

Normal Activity. An average expected volume of activity (usually computed over 3 to 5 years into the future) often used in computing standard overhead rates.

Overhead Budget Variance. The difference between total factory overhead incurred and total factory overhead budgeted at standard direct labor hours allowed [(standard direct labor hours allowed times standard variable overhead rate) plus fixed overhead budgeted].

Practical Capacity. The volume of activity at which manufacturing facilities are capable of operating, allowing for usual levels of efficiency.

Price Standard. The cost that should be incurred to acquire one unit of an input (direct material, direct labor, or factory overhead) for a manufacturing process.

Quantity Standard. The amount of an input (direct material, direct labor, or factory overhead) to a manufacturing process that should be used to produce one unit of output from that process.

Standard Costs. The costs that should be incurred in performing an activity or producing a product under planned operating conditions.

Standard Direct Labor Usage. The number of direct labor hours that should be used to produce a given number of good units of product output. It is computed by multiplying the actual number of units produced by the direct labor quantity standard and is commonly called *standard direct labor hours allowed*.

Standard Direct Materials Usage. The amount of direct materials that should be used to produce a given number of units of product output. It is computed by multiplying the actual number of units produced times the direct materials quantity standard.

Total Overhead Variance. The difference between total factory overhead incurred and total factory overhead applied (standard direct labor hours allowed times standard total overhead rate).

Variance. The difference between a standard cost and an actual cost.

QUESTIONS

Q25-1 Define standard costs.

Q25-2 What is a variance?

Q25-3 Distinguish between a direct materials price variance and a direct materials quantity variance.

Q25-4 Why are direct materials price variances usually computed at the time of purchase?

Q25-5 How is the setting of direct materials price standards related to the setting of direct materials quantity standards?

Q25-6 Define standard direct materials usage.

Q25-7 Define standard direct labor usage.

Q25-8 Why is it advisable to compute direct labor efficiency variances separately from direct labor price variances?

Q25-9 Why are standard costs useful in estimating costs for decision making?

Q25-10 Discuss how the reporting of variances is used in controlling manufacturing operations.

Q25-11 What is a fixed overhead volume variance?

Q25-12 Why would the predetermined fixed overhead rate fluctuate if the expected annual volume of activity were used to compute it?

Q25-13 Define practical capacity. How would using the factory overhead budget at practical capacity to compute the standard overhead rates help to stabilize the fixed factory overhead rate?

Q25-14 Why is a standard variable overhead rate not affected by the choice of volume used in computing that rate?

Q25-15 What is an overhead budget variance?

Q25-16 Should all variances be investigated by management to identify the problems causing them? Briefly discuss.

Q25-17 Why would it be useful for the managerial accountant to compute *separately* the standard cost variances we have discussed for individual manufacturing departments or processes?

Q25-18 When should standards be revised?

Q25-19 Can a favorable cost variance result from a serious problem? Give an example.

EXERCISES

E25-1 Direct Materials Variances. The Melton Company has set the standard direct materials cost for one of its products at $12 per unit (4 pounds per unit @ $3 per pound). During March Melton purchased 4,200 pounds of this direct material on account at a total cost of $12,340 and used 3,800 pounds to produce 920 units of product.

Required: 1. Compute Melton's direct materials price and quantity variances for the month of March.
2. Prepare journal entries for the Melton Company to record the purchase and use of this direct material and to record the variances computed in Requirement 1.

E25-2 Direct Materials Variances. The Morgan Company plans to purchase material X as follows:

The company should buy material X in 5-gallon drums (1,000 at a time) at an invoice price of $20.00 per drum and take a 2% cash discount by paying for the material within 10 days. Freight and receiving costs for a shipment of 1,000 drums should total $900.

During March a rush order for one of Morgan's products caused an emergency cash purchase of 1,000 gallons of material X from an alternate supplier. The alternate supplier delivered the material the next day, charging Morgan $4,500 with no cash discount. Freight and receiving costs totaled $180.

Required: 1. Compute the direct materials price standard (per gallon) for material X.
2. Compute the direct materials price variance related to the emergency purchase.

E25-3 Direct Materials Variances. Playtime Products makes large dollhouses. The standard cost of the carpet used for their construction is $8.40 per dollhouse (6 square feet @ $1.40 per square foot). During September, Playtime paid $25,840 to purchase carpet, half of which was used to produce dollhouses during that month. Direct materials variances related to the purchase and use of this carpet during September were:

Direct materials price variance   = $2,040 unfavorable
Direct materials quantity variance   = $112 favorable

Required: Compute the following related amounts.
1. The number of square feet of carpet material purchased in September.
2. The number of dollhouses produced in September.

E25-4 Direct Labor Variances. The Morristown Manufacturing Company incurred $60,500 of direct labor cost in its machine shop during the month of March. This cost was the result of 11,800 direct labor hours worked to produce 4,000 units of product. The direct labor quantity standard is 3 direct labor hours per unit and the direct labor price standard is $5.00 per direct labor hour.

Required: 1. Compute the standard direct labor usage.
2. Compute the direct labor efficiency variance.
3. Compute the direct labor price variance.
4. Prepare the journal entry required to record the standard direct labor cost and the two labor variances for Morristown.

E25-5   Direct Labor Variances Resulting from a Problem. Foster Furniture uses a standard cost system. One model of sofa has a standard direct labor cost of $33 (6 hours per sofa @ $5.50 per hour). During the first week of September, 16 of these sofas were manufactured. Because of illness, one of the regular laborers was replaced during that week by a new untrained employee. A total of 107 direct labor hours were worked at an average labor cost of $5.10 per hour on the sofas.

The direct labor price variance and the direct labor efficiency variance for the production of the sofas resulted from substituting the untrained employee for the regular skilled worker.

Required: 1. Compute the direct labor price variance and the direct labor efficiency variance.
2. How much extra direct labor cost was incurred in the production of the sofas because of the substitution of the untrained employee?

E25-6   Direct Labor Variances. The Brassall Company produced 4,100 gallons of brass polish in January. The direct labor quantity standard for this polish is .2 hours per gallon and the direct labor price standard is $6.00 per hour. During January the following direct labor variances were recorded:

Direct labor price variance   = $109.20 unfavorable
Direct labor efficiency variance   = $120.00 unfavorable

Required: Compute the following related amounts:
1. The actual direct labor hours worked during January.
2. The average actual wage rate paid per direct labor hour in January.

E25-7   Overhead Variances. The Sanford Corporation produces a single product and uses a standard cost system. Fixed and variable overhead costs are applied to this product on a standard machine hour basis. Sanford uses its flexible overhead budget at normal activity of 100,000 standard machine hours to set its standard overhead rates. Summary data from Sanford's flexible budget are shown below:

Standard Machine Hours per Year	Total Overhead Costs Budgeted per Year
80,000	$124,000
90,000	132,000
100,000	140,000
110,000	148,000

The standard machine hour requirement for Sanford's product is 2 machine hours per unit. Last year 45,000 units were produced and actual overhead costs were $132,800.

Required: 1. Compute the fixed and variable overhead rates per standard machine hour. (Hint: Total overhead cost is a *mixed* cost that can be separated into fixed and variable components.)
2. Compute the amount of fixed overhead cost *budgeted* at 80,000, 90,000, 100,000, and 110,000 standard machine hours, respectively.
3. Compute the amount of fixed overhead cost *applied* at 80,000, 90,000, 100,000, and 110,000 standard machine hours, respectively.
4. Compute last year's fixed overhead volume variance.
5. Draw two lines, one representing the amount of fixed overhead *budgeted* and the other representing the amount of fixed overhead *applied,* on a graph using the vertical axis to measure dollars and the horizontal axis to measure standard machine hours. Show the fixed overhead volume variance computed in Requirement 4 on this graph.
6. Compute last year's overhead budget variance.

E25-8   Factory Overhead Variances. The Brimstone Company produces several products. The company's factory overhead rates were determined in 1983 from the flexible overhead budget at its normal activity of 90,000 units (180,000 standard direct labor hours allowed) per year as shown below:

	Factory Overhead Budget at 90,000 Units (180,000 standard direct labor hours allowed)	Standard Factory Overhead Rates per Hour
Variable	$180,000	$1
Fixed	540,000	$3
Total	$720,000	$4

During 1983, 80,000 units were produced and actual factory overhead cost totaled $693,500 (all of which was paid in cash except depreciation of $300,000 on plant and equipment).

Required: 1. Compute the total overhead variance.
2. Compute the fixed overhead volume variance.
3. Compute the overhead budget variance.
4. Prepare journal entries to record (a) factory overhead incurred; (b) factory overhead applied; and (c) the two factory overhead variances.

E25-9   Standard Cost per Unit. The Roberts Company produces product X. Product X is in high demand and Mr. Roberts, the owner, believes that three or four times as many units could be sold as his four employees are capable of making. All four employees work 40 hours per week for 50 weeks a year producing product X. Direct materials and direct labor quantity and price standards are shown below:

Direct materials quantity standard: 1.2 pounds per unit
Direct labor quantity standard: 4 hours per unit
Direct materials price standard: $10 per pound
Direct labor price standard: $6 per hour

Factory overhead is budgeted and applied on the basis of standard direct labor hours. Practical capacity is 8,000 standard direct labor hours. The factory overhead budget at practical capacity shows $40,000 of variable overhead and $16,000 of fixed overhead.

Required: 1. Compute the standard variable and fixed overhead rates per direct labor hour based on the budget at practical capacity.
2. Compute the standard direct materials, direct labor, variable overhead, and fixed overhead costs per unit of product X.

E25-10   Revision of Standards. Refer to E25-9. At the beginning of this year the Roberts Company leased a new machine for $4,000 per year that would allow production of a unit of product X out of 1 pound of direct materials in 3 direct labor hours. Mr. Roberts was so happy that he raised the labor rate he paid his employees to $6.50 per hour. Assume that total variable overhead budgeted at practical capacity is not affected.

Required: 1. Revise the quantity and price standards for direct materials, direct labor, and factory overhead so that they reflect the expected changes brought about because of the new machine.
2. Compute the revised total standard cost per unit of product X.

E25-11   Overhead Rates and Overhead Variances.   The total annual factory overhead budget of the Reynolds Company is given by the following cost equation:

$$\text{Total overhead cost budgeted} \ = \ \$60,000 \ + \ \$2.00\, x$$

$$where: \qquad\qquad\qquad x \ = \ \text{direct labor hours}$$

The Reynolds Company has a practical capacity of 20,000 direct labor hours, but it expects to operate at a normal activity level of 15,000 direct labor hours. The direct labor quantity standard is 5 hours per unit of product. Last year the company produced 2,400 units and incurred $86,000 of overhead costs.

Required: 1. Using the factory overhead budget at *practical* capacity, (a) compute the variable and fixed overhead rates per direct labor hour; (b) compute the overhead budget variance; and (c) compute the fixed overhead volume variance.
2. Using the factory overhead budget at *normal* activity, repeat all of the computations requested in Requirement 1.
3. Discuss the similarities and differences between the computations made in Requirements 1 and 2.

PROBLEMS

Part A

P25-1A   All Standard Cost Variances.   The Pierless Paint Company produces an exterior house paint known as Pierpont 163. Two direct materials are combined in the manufacture of this paint, pier and pont. Pierpont 163 is sold in 1-gallon cans, the standard costs of which are shown below:

Standard cost per gallon: Pierpont 163

Material pier:	.8 gallons @ $4.00 per gallon	$3.20
Material pont:	.5 pounds @ $.60 per pound	.30
Direct labor	.01 hours @ $5.00 per hour	.05
Variable overhead	.01 direct labor hours @ $8.00 per hour[a]	.08
Fixed overhead	.01 direct labor hours @ $22.00 per hour[a]	.22
	Total standard cost per gallon	$3.85

[a] Overhead rates were computed at normal activity of 2,000 standard direct labor hours per month.

Inventory records last month show:

	Opening Inventory	Purchases	Ending Inventory
Material pier	80,000 gallons	120,000 gallons @ $3.80 per gallon	30,000 gallons
Material pont	40,000 pounds	150,000 pounds @ $.62 per pound	91,000 pounds

Additional production information from last month:
Gallons of Pierpont 163 produced: 210,000 gallons
Actual direct labor cost (2,160 hours @ $4.85): $10,476
Actual overhead costs: $63,575

Required: Compute the following variances.
1. Direct materials price and quantity variances for (a) material pier and (b) material pont.
2. Direct labor price and efficiency variances.
3. Overhead budget variance.
4. Fixed overhead volume variance.

P25-2A   Direct Materials Price and Quantity Standards and Direct Labor Quantity Standards.   The Oldtown Clock Company makes walnut veneer clocks that look like antiques. A new clock to be manufactured requires a veneer strip 6 inches wide and 18 inches long. Oldtown's supplier of walnut veneer will sell veneer in 6-inch wide strips that are 8 feet long for $10.00 per strip. The supplier is also willing to sell Oldtown 6-inch wide strips in 6-foot lengths at a price of $8.20 per strip.

The veneer strips must be carefully cut by hand into 18-inch lengths in Oldtown's cutting department. Each 6-inch cut across the strip should take 3 minutes. Direct labor rates in the cutting department are $8.00 per hour. No other manufacturing costs are affected by the company's choice of buying 6- or 8-foot strips. The odd-sized pieces of veneer that are left after cutting have no value.

Required: 1. Assuming the veneer strips are purchased in 6-foot lengths, compute the expected direct materials cost of the veneer and the expected direct labor cost in the cutting department that would be incurred per clock.

2. Assuming the veneer strips are purchased in 8-foot lengths, compute the expected direct materials cost of the veneer and the expected direct labor cost in the cutting department that would be incurred per clock.

3. Considering your answers to Requirements 1 and 2, should Oldtown purchase the veneer strips in 6- or 8-foot lengths?

4. Assuming the veneer strips are purchased in 6-foot lengths, determine (for the veneer strips and veneer cutting operations): (a) the direct materials quantity standard (in feet per clock); (b) the direct materials price standard per foot; and (c) the direct labor quantity standard (in hours per clock).

P25-3A   All Standard Cost Variances.   The Glover Company produces product A for which the following standards have been set:

Direct materials (5 pounds @ $.30 per pound)	$ 1.50
Direct labor (2 hours @ $6.00 per hour)	12.00
Total factory overhead (2 direct labor hours	
@ $3.50 per hour)	7.00
Standard manufacturing cost per unit of A	$20.50

The fixed factory overhead rate was determined from the fixed factory overhead budget of $76,000 at normal activity of 40,000 standard direct labor hours (20,000 units of product A) per month.

Actual data recorded during April:
  Units of product A produced: 13,000
  Direct materials purchases: 100,000 pounds @ $.25 per pound
  Direct materials usage: 65,500 pounds
  Direct labor cost: 26,050 hours @ $6.10 per hour
  Total factory overhead cost: $125,000

Required: Compute the following:
        1. Fixed factory overhead rate per standard direct labor hour.
        2. Variable factory overhead rate per standard direct labor hour.
        3. Direct materials price and quantity variances.
        4. Direct labor price and efficiency variances.
        5. Overhead budget variance.
        6. Fixed overhead volume variance.
        7. Using dollars on the vertical axis and standard direct labor hours on the horizontal axis, graph the amount of total factory overhead budgeted and total factory overhead applied as standard direct labor hours vary. Clearly show the fixed factory overhead volume variance and the overhead budget variance for April on this graph.

P25-4A Direct Labor Variances. The Ranger Company produces Ringos. The president of the company has recently been puzzled by apparent problems causing direct labor price variances that she cannot identify. You are asked to help the president understand the source of the direct labor price variances. The president informs you that 3.5 direct labor hours should be worked to produce each Ringo and that the standard direct labor cost totals $17.50 per Ringo. During April 600 Ringos were produced, 2,100 direct labor hours were worked, and direct labor cost incurred was $10,626.

Required:
1. Given the information supplied above, compute the direct labor efficiency and price variances.
2. Suppose you discover upon further investigation that 420 of the 2,100 direct labor hours were worked in Ranger's Department A and the rest in Department B. Furthermore, you discover that production of each Ringo should require:

Department A:	1 hour	@	$4.50 per hour	=	$ 4.50
Department B:	2½ hours	@	$5.20 per hour	=	13.00
	Total direct labor cost per Ringo				$17.50

and that during April $1,890 of the direct labor cost was incurred in Department A and $8,736 in Department B. Given this additional information, compute the direct labor efficiency and price variances for Department A and Department B, separately.
3. Comment on the results obtained in Requirements 1 and 2.

P25-5A Departmental Labor Efficiency Variances. The Cozyhome Company makes doghouses. These houses are built in two departments. Department A cuts ¾-inch plywood into two shapes (1 and 2) and paints the pieces with quick-drying paint. Doghouses are assembled in Department B using three pieces of shape 1 and two pieces of shape 2. Direct labor quantity standards for the operations of these two departments are shown below:

Department A:
Cutting (shape 1)	.05 hours per piece
Cutting (shape 2)	.10 hours per piece
Painting (shape 1)	.15 hours per piece
Painting (shape 2)	.07 hours per piece

Department B:
Assembly	1 hour per doghouse

On August 18, actual production was as follows:

Department A:
Pieces of shape 1:	80 cut and 80 painted
Pieces of shape 2:	80 cut and 40 painted

Department B:
Doghouses:	22 assembled

Three laborers worked 8 hours each in direct labor operations in Department A and three laborers worked 8 hours each in Department B. All workers earn $5.00 per hour.

At the beginning of the day six pieces of shape 1 and four pieces of shape 2 were ready for assembly.

Required:
1. Compute the standard direct labor cost of one doghouse.
2. Compute the standard direct labor hours allowed in Departments A and B for the work done in the Cozyhome shop on August 18.
3. Compute the direct labor efficiency variances occurring in each of the departments.
4. Write a brief report on the direct labor performance of the two departments including a suggestion of how management might avoid the problem that occurred on August 18 in the company's future operations.

P25-6A All Variances and Journal Entries. The Hammond Manufacturing Company produces Yagis. Standard costs per Yagi are as follows:

	Standard Cost per Yagi
Direct materials:	
Aluminum tubing (144 feet @ $.40)	$57.60
Hardware (1 package @ $5.00)	5.00
Direct labor: (2.5 hours @ $3.80)	9.50
Factory overhead:	
Variable (2.5 hours @ $2.00)	5.00
Fixed (2.5 hours @ $4.00)	10.00
Standard manufacturing cost per Yagi	$87.10

Factory overhead is budgeted and applied on the basis of standard direct labor hours. The overhead rates were set at the practical capacity of 4,000 standard direct labor hours per year.

Actual production and cost data from last year:
Yagis produced: 1,560
Aluminum tubing purchases (on account): 250,000 feet @ $.40 = $100,000
Aluminum tubing used: 226,080 feet
Hardware purchased (for cash): 1,570 packages @ $4.85 = $7,614.50
Packages of hardware used: 1,570 packages
Direct labor cost: 3,990 hours @ $3.85 = $15,361.50
Total factory overhead cost: $25,000 (assume all was paid in cash except for depreciation of $4,500 on equipment)

Required: 1. Calculate the direct materials quantity and price variances for each direct material.
2. Calculate the direct labor efficiency and price variances.
3. Calculate the overhead budget variance.
4. Calculate the fixed overhead volume variance.
5. Prepare all journal entries for the Hammond Manufacturing Company related to the above information.

PROBLEMS

Part B

P25-1B All Standard Cost Variances. The Randall Company produces product A for which the following standards have been set:

Direct materials (6 pounds @ $1.50 per pound)	$ 9.00
Direct labor (3 hours @ $6.00 per hour)	18.00
Total factory overhead (3 direct labor hours @ $4.20 per hour)	12.60
Standard manufacturing cost per unit of A	$39.60

The fixed factory overhead rate was determined from the fixed factory overhead budget of $60,000 at normal activity of 30,000 standard direct labor hours (10,000 units of product A) per month.

Actual data recorded during April:
Units of product A produced: 13,000
Direct materials purchases: 100,000 pounds @ $1.35 per pound
Direct materials usage: 77,200 pounds
Direct labor cost: 39,050 hours @ $6.10 per hour
Total factory overhead cost: $145,600

Required: Compute the following:
1. Fixed factory overhead rate per standard direct labor hour.

2. Variable factory overhead rate per standard direct labor hour.
3. Direct materials price and quantity variances.
4. Direct labor price and efficiency variances.
5. Overhead budget variance.
6. Fixed overhead volume variance.
7. Using dollars on the vertical axis and standard direct labor hours on the horizontal axis, graph the amount of fixed factory overhead budgeted and fixed factory overhead applied as standard direct labor hours vary. Clearly show the fixed overhead volume variance for April on this graph.

P25-2B All Standard Cost Variances. The Coterite Paint Company produces an interior wall paint known as R16-76. Two direct materials are combined in the manufacture of this paint, material 16 and material 76. R16-76 is sold in 1-gallon cans, the standard costs of which are shown below:

Standard cost per gallon: R16-76

Material 16:	.8 gallons @ $5.00 per gallon	$4.00
Material 76:	.4 pounds @ $.60 per pound	.24
Direct labor	.02 hours @ $4.00 per hour	.08
Variable overhead	.02 direct labor hours @ $6.00 per hour[a]	.12
Fixed overhead	.02 direct labor hours @ $15.00 per hour[a]	.30
Total standard cost per gallon		$4.74

[a] Overhead rates were computed at normal activity of 4,000 standard direct labor hours per month.

Inventory records last month show:

	Opening Inventory	Purchases	Ending Inventory
Material 16	80,000 gallons	140,000 gallons @ $4.80 per gallon	45,000 gallons
Material 76	40,000 pounds	140,000 pounds @ $.62 per pound	100,000 pounds

Additional production information from last month:
Gallons of R16-76 produced: 210,000 gallons
Actual direct labor cost (4,320 hours @ $3.85): $16,632
Actual overhead costs: $86,715

Required: Compute the following variances:
1. Direct materials price and quantity variances for (a) material 16 and (b) material 76.
2. Direct labor price and efficiency variances.
3. Overhead budget variance.
4. Fixed overhead volume variance.

P25-3B Departmental Labor Efficiency Variances. Woodcrafters Company makes birdhouses. These houses are built in two departments. Department A cuts ¾-inch plywood into two shapes (1 and 2) and paints the pieces with quick-drying paint. Birdhouses are assembled in Department B using three pieces of shape 1 and two pieces of shape 2. Direct labor quantity standards for the operations of these two departments are shown below:

Department A:
Cutting (shape 1)   .01 hours per piece
Cutting (shape 2)   .02 hours per piece
Painting (shape 1)   .03 hours per piece
Painting (shape 2)   .015 hours per piece
Department B:
Assembly   .2   hours per birdhouse

On August 19 actual production was as follows:

Department A:
Pieces of shape 1: 800 cut and 800 painted
Pieces of shape 2: 800 cut and 400 painted
Department B:
Birdhouses: 220 assembled

Seven laborers worked 8 hours each in direct labor operations in Department A and seven laborers worked 8 hours each in Department B (although there seemed to be a lot of standing around in Department B). All workers earn $5.00 per hour.

At the beginning of the day 60 pieces of shape 1 and 40 pieces of shape 2 were ready for assembly.

Required: 1. Compute the standard direct labor cost of one birdhouse.
2. Compute the standard direct labor hours allowed in Departments A and B for the work done in the Woodcrafters shop on August 19.
3. Compute the direct labor efficiency variances occurring in each of the departments.
4. Write a brief report on the direct labor performance of the two departments, including a suggestion of how management might avoid the problem that occurred on August 19 in the company's future operations.

P25-4B   Direct Materials Variances.   The Clipperton Company produces product DX. The president of the company has recently been puzzled by apparent problems causing direct materials price variances that he cannot identify. You are asked to help the president understand the source of the direct materials price variances. The president informs you that 7 pounds of material should be used to produce each unit of DX and that the standard direct materials cost totals $35 per unit. During April 600 units were produced and 4,200 pounds of direct materials were purchased and used. The direct materials cost incurred was $21,101.

Required: 1. Given the information supplied above, compute the direct materials quantity and price variances.
2. Suppose you discover upon further investigation that 1,100 of the 4,200 pounds purchased and used were direct material A and the rest were direct material B. In addition, you discover that production of each unit should require:

Material A: 2 pounds @ $4.50 per pound = $ 9.00
Material B: 5 pounds @ $5.20 per pound =   26.00
     Total direct materials cost per unit $35.00

and that during April $4,950 of the direct materials cost was for material A and $16,151 was for material B. Given this additional information, compute the direct materials quantity and price variances for material A and material B, separately.
3. Comment on the results obtained in Requirements 1 and 2.

P25-5B   **Direct Materials Price and Quantity Standards and Direct Labor Quantity Standards.** The Newtown Furniture Company makes walnut veneer tables that look like antiques. A new table to be manufactured requires a veneer strip 2 feet wide and 3 feet long. Newtown's supplier of walnut veneer is willing to sell veneer in 2-foot wide strips in 6-foot lengths for $84.00 per strip. The supplier is also willing to sell Newtown the 2-foot wide strips in 3-foot lengths at a price of $42.50 per strip.

If the 6-foot veneer strips are purchased, they must be carefully cut into 3-foot lengths in Newtown's cutting department. Each cut across a strip should take 6 minutes. Direct labor rates in the cutting department are $8.00 per hour. No other manufacturing costs are affected by the company's choice of buying 6- or 3-foot strips.

Required: 1. Assuming that the veneer strips are purchased in 6-foot lengths, compute the expected direct materials cost of the veneer and the expected direct labor cost in the cutting department that would be incurred per table.
     2. Assuming that the veneer strips are purchased in 3-foot lengths, what is the expected direct materials cost of the veneer per table?
     3. Considering your answers to Requirements 1 and 2, should Newtown purchase the veneer strips in 6- or 3-foot lengths?
     4. Assuming that the veneer strips are purchased in 6-foot lengths, determine (for the veneer strips and veneer cutting operations): (a) the direct materials quantity standard (in feet per table); (b) the direct materials price standard per foot; and (c) the direct labor quantity standard (in hours per table).

P25-6B   **All Variances and Journal Entries.** West Manufacturing Company produces Quads. Standard costs per Quad are as follows:

	Standard Cost per Quad
Direct materials:	
Fiberglass poles (130 feet @ $.50)	$ 65.00
Hardware (1 package @ $15.00)	15.00
Direct labor: (2 hours @ $4.50)	9.00
Factory overhead:	
Variable (2 hours @ $2.00)	4.00
Fixed (2 hours @ $5.00)	10.00
Standard manufacturing cost per Quad	$103.00

Factory overhead is budgeted and applied on the basis of standard direct labor hours. The overhead rates were set at practical capacity of 5,000 standard direct labor hours per year.

Actual production and cost data for last year:
   Quads produced: 1,960
   Fiberglass pole purchases (on account): 280,000 feet @ $.53 = $148,400
   Fiberglass pole used: 260,000 feet
   Hardware purchased (on account): 2,500 packages @ $15.60 = $39,000
   Packages of hardware used: 1,975 packages
   Direct labor cost: 3,975 hours @ $4.35 = $17,291.25
   Total factory overhead cost: $31,000 (assume that all was paid in cash except for depreciation of $7,500 on equipment)

Required: 1. Compute the direct materials quantity and price variances for each direct material.
     2. Compute the direct labor efficiency and price variances.
     3. Compute the overhead budget variance.
     4. Compute the fixed overhead volume variance.
     5. Prepare all journal entries for the West Manufacturing Company related to the above information.

DISCUSSION CASES

C25-1 Departmental Performance Evaluation. ". . . and Roy, you know as well as any-one that while our sales volume is down we've got to cut costs. Your department's unit costs are up by 2% this June. We just can't have any more of this or I'll have to find someone who can keep the men working."

Roy Lilley, a production department manager for the JJS Company, left the meeting room very upset. He had just been severely criticized by the production supervisor because of inefficiency in his department. The basis of that criticism was the report shown below:

Department 40-00 (Roy Lilley)
Cost Report — May and June

	May	June
Production (units)	20,000	16,000
Direct labor hours	4,000	3,100
Costs:		
Direct materials	$10,000	$ 8,400
Direct labor	30,000	22,000
Factory overhead	40,000	34,875
Total	$80,000	$65,275
Cost per unit	$ 4.00	$ 4.08

Roy felt that something was wrong. It seemed to him that his department had worked harder than any of the others to keep costs down. This same episode occurred last summer, too, and Roy had almost quit his job because of it.

The cost accounting system used by the JJS Company applied all costs incurred each month to the units produced. Actual total overhead costs, for example, are computed at the end of the month and assigned to the month's production at an actual rate per direct labor hour. In May, total overhead costs had been $100,000 while 10,000 actual direct labor hours were worked in the factory. In June, overhead costs were $90,000 while direct labor hours had dropped to 8,000.

Required: How useful is the cost report in judging the performance of Roy Lilley's department during June? How could a standard cost system be used to prepare a performance report for Department 40-00 that would be more useful to Roy Lilley and to the production supervisor? Discuss.

C25-2 Purposes and Features of a Standard Cost System.
Missouri Briar Company is a manufacturer of corn cob pipes. The company has grown rapidly over the last 10 years. Originally a small supplier of cheaply made pipes for novelty and souvenir shops, the company now supplies large quantities of high-quality pipes to pipe shops throughout the country. Several grades of pipes are sold. The best Grade A pipes smoke more sweetly than the finest imported briar pipes. Demand continues to grow. Profit seems to have leveled off over the last 2 years, however. Pipe production does not seem to be as efficient as it used to be.

Producing a pipe requires several distinctly different operations that require special labor skills. Production starts with "rough cobbing," in which seasoned cobs are cut and drilled. Next comes a critical "sorting" operation, in which the cut and drilled cobs are sorted by quality and shape and sent to different departments set up to produce different grades of pipes.

In these departments, "plugging," "stemming," "sealing," and "finishing" operations are per-formed. More skill is required, and a great deal more time is taken in the production of Grade A pipes than Grade B or C pipes. "Final grading" is the last operation performed. It is an inspection process aimed at maintaining quality. Pipes from Grade A departments that do not pass inspection are downgraded and sold as Grade B or C pipes. Pipes from Grade B departments that do not pass inspection are downgraded and sold as Grade C pipes. Grade C pipes that do not pass inspection are sold as novelties.

During the last 2 years Alex Hrechko, the president of Missouri Briar Company, has noticed that the average direct materials and direct labor cost per pipe have increased considerably, although he is not sure why. Alex is worried that things are out of control.

Some data from the last 3 years are presented in the table below:

| | 1980 | | | 1981 | | | 1982 | | |
| | Pipes Produced | Average Direct Costs | | Pipes Produced | Average Direct Costs | | Pipes Produced | Average Direct Costs | |
		Materials	Labor		Materials	Labor		Materials	Labor
Grade A	20,000	$.90	$1.20	20,000	$.95	$1.30	21,250	$1.00	$1.45
Grade B	30,000	.86	1.10	31,000	.89	1.23	33,750	.94	1.40
Grade C	40,000	.85	1.00	46,000	.88	1.14	53,750	.93	1.35
Novelty	10,000	.84	.95	13,000	.87	1.10	16,250	.91	1.30
Total	100,000			110,000			125,000		

Required: In what ways is the data given deficient for evaluating the performance of the company's manufacturing operations? How could a standard cost system improve the president's ability to control the manufacturing operations of his company? Discuss.

26 Short-Term Decision Making

After reading this chapter, you should understand:

- The nature of the decision-making process
- How to determine what costs and revenues are relevant to a decision
- The nature and analysis of the decision to discontinue producing a product
- The nature and analysis of the decision to make or buy a part or component
- The nature and analysis of the decision to sell a product or to process it further
- The nature and analysis of decisions involving product mix

In the process of operating a company, management is constantly faced with many decisions. For example, management must decide what products to produce, when new products should be added to its existing line, and when old products should be discontinued. It must decide how its products are to be produced, what materials to use, and what manufacturing processes to employ. Decisions must also be made regarding selling prices, the need for advertising, expansion of facilities, and so on. The variety of decisions faced by management is much greater than suggested by these few examples. There is a common element in all decisions, however, which is that they all involve a choice among alternative courses of action.

In this chapter we describe the decision-making process and discuss several forms of analysis that managerial accountants use to help management make decisions. A few common types of decisions are described, and the use of accounting information in making those decisions is illustrated.

THE DECISION-MAKING PROCESS

If an objective can be accomplished in only one way, no decision is necessary. If a problem can be solved in only one way, no decision is necessary. The need for making a decision exists only when a choice is required.

Steps in Decision Making

To describe decision making only as choosing between alternative courses of action would be too simple. Business decision making normally involves the following steps:

1. Recognizing the need for a decision (defining the problem to be solved)
2. Searching for alternative solutions
3. Evaluating the available alternatives
4. Making the decision (choosing the alternative)
5. Carrying out the decision
6. Evaluating the decision and the way it was carried out

Although managerial accounting information may be useful in any or all of these steps, it is particularly helpful to management in evaluating alternatives (step 3). In evaluating decision alternatives the key question is, "What difference does it make?" The managerial accountant prepares an analysis of costs and revenues affected by the choice of alternatives so that the profit impact of the decision is understood. This information can then be weighed by management against any other considerations that are relevant to the decision.

COST AND REVENUE ANALYSIS FOR DECISION MAKING

The profit impact of a decision is often one of the most critical aspects in the evaluation of the decision. To completely understand the profit impact of a decision, a careful analysis of both costs and revenues is necessary. We discuss the analysis of costs first.

For a cost analysis to be helpful in making a decision, it must clearly show all costs affected by the choice of decision alternatives. Costs that are affected by the choice of decision alternatives are called relevant costs. **Relevant costs are future costs that differ in amount depending upon the decision alternative chosen.**

It is important to recognize that a relevant cost is "relevant" only with regard to a specific decision. That is, a cost that is relevant to one decision may not be relevant to another decision. For example, the direct materials cost incurred in producing one of a company's products might be relevant in a decision whether or not to continue producing the product, whereas it might be irrelevant in a decision whether or not to replace an old piece of manufacturing equipment.

An important task for the managerial accountant preparing a cost analysis for a specific decision is to identify the costs that are relevant to the decision. All relevant costs should be included in a cost analysis because incomplete cost information could cause an incorrect decision to be made. Costs that are *not* relevant to a decision, however, should be omitted from the analysis because they would not be helpful in making the decision, and if treated improperly, they also may cause an incorrect decision to be made.

Determining Which Costs Are Relevant

Two steps must be followed in identifying the relevant costs for a particular decision. They are to:

1. Determine the activities that would be necessary to carry out each of the decision's alternatives.
2. Estimate the costs that would be incurred if the activities were undertaken.

DETERMINING ACTIVITIES.   The objective of the first step is to identify all potentially relevant costs and to eliminate from further consideration the costs that are obviously not relevant. The key to identifying potentially relevant costs is to have a good understanding of what activities would be necessary to carry out each of the decision alternatives. The reason is that these activities are the *cause* of all relevant costs. Thus only costs that are incurred as a *result* of performing these activities can be relevant. Therefore two large groups of costs can immediately be eliminated from consideration.

First, no cost incurred prior to making the decision can possibly be relevant. Since the decision must be made before the alternative chosen can be carried out, all costs incurred as a result of the activities necessary to carry out the possible choices must be *future* costs. Thus only future costs can be relevant. Past costs (sometimes called *sunk* costs) can therefore be eliminated from consideration. For example, the cost of a machine purchased last year would not be relevant to a decision as to how that machine should be used in production this year.

Second, future costs incurred as a result of activities that are *not necessary* to carry out the alternatives of the decision under study are not relevant. These costs relate to activities associated with other operations and would be incurred regardless of the alternative chosen in the decision under study. For example, the salaries to be paid this week, next week, or next month to the waiters and waitresses at a local pizza parlor, although future costs, are not relevant to a decision today to replace an old pizza oven with a new oven (unless the size of the new oven affects the number of employees needed).

Recall that the key question in evaluating decision alternatives is "What difference does it make?" Past costs, as well as future costs associated with activities that are not related to the decision's alternatives, remain the same no matter which alternative is chosen. For these costs, "It makes no difference." Hence they are irrelevant and should not be considered in the analysis.

ESTIMATING COSTS.   The costs that remain for further consideration in the analysis are costs required by the decision's alternatives. Even some of these costs may not be relevant, however. A specific cost is relevant only if the total amount to be incurred is affected by the choice of alternatives. This fact cannot always be determined until the amounts of the potentially relevant costs are estimated, however. Thus the cost estimation step serves two purposes, to provide estimates of relevant costs and to further eliminate irrelevant costs.

Consider a decision in which two alternative manufacturing processes to produce a product are being considered. Two potentially relevant costs, direct materials and direct labor, are being examined. Suppose that with Process 1 the product can be produced with 2 pounds of material A in 1 hour of direct labor time. Process 2 requires the use of 4 pounds of material B and 1.2 hours of direct labor time. Direct labor time costs $5 per hour with either process. Material A costs $6 per pound, whereas material B costs $3 per pound. Are either of the costs relevant?

The direct materials cost is not relevant because it costs $12 for the material to produce a unit of product regardless of which process is used (4 pounds @ $3 or 2 pounds @ $6). The direct labor cost, on the other hand, is relevant because with Process 1 one unit will cost $5 (1 hour @ $5), whereas with Process 2 it will cost $6 (1.2 hours @ $5). Note that in estimating these costs we discover the irrelevance of direct materials cost.

Exhibit 26-1 shows the two-step process by which irrelevant costs are separated from relevant costs. Notice in the first step that past costs and costs that are not necessary to carry out decision alternatives are removed. From the costs that remain, costs that would not differ between alternatives are eliminated during the second step. Then the only costs that remain are future costs required to carry out decision alternatives that would be incurred in different amounts depending upon which alternative is chosen. These costs are the relevant costs properly included in the decision evaluation.

EXHIBIT 26-1
Two-Step Process of Identifying Relevant Costs

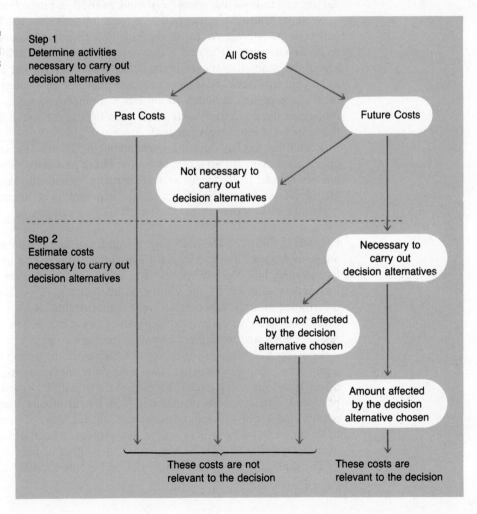

Cost Concepts for Short-Term Decisions

Three additional cost concepts are important in discussions of short-term decision making because they suggest the reason why certain costs might be relevant in a given decision situation. Understanding these concepts can be very helpful to the managerial accountant in searching for potentially relevant costs.

INCREMENTAL COSTS. In some short-term decisions, one of the alternatives may require performing activities that would not have to be performed if that alternative were not chosen. In many other decisions, one of the alternatives may require performing activities at a higher volume than if that alternative were not chosen. When either of these situations occurs, the additional activity usually causes additional costs to be incurred. Cost increases of this type are called incremental costs. **Incremental costs are cost increases resulting from the performance of an additional activity.** They are *always* relevant when the additional activity is not necessary for all of the alternatives to a decision. For example, in a decision whether or not to accept a customer's special order for a number of units of a company's product, the incremental costs of manufacturing, packaging, and shipping the units would be relevant because they would have to be incurred only if the order were accepted.

AVOIDABLE COSTS. In many other short-term decisions, one of the alternatives involves either discontinuing an activity or decreasing its volume. When the volume of an activity is decreased or discontinued altogether, certain costs necessary to support that activity may no longer have to be incurred or may be incurred at a reduced amount. **Avoidable costs are the costs that must be incurred to perform an activity at a given level, but which can be avoided if that activity is discontinued or its volume reduced.** For example, if a company currently buys direct material X to produce a subassembly that it uses in the manufacture of its final product, the cost of direct material X would be avoidable if the company chose to buy the subassembly instead of producing it.

OPPORTUNITY COSTS. Performing the activities necessary for one of the alternatives in a decision sometimes disrupts a company's other profitable activities or reduces its opportunity to engage in future profitable activities. The profit impact of such a disturbance to the company's other activities must be included in the evaluation of the decision alternative under study in order to obtain a complete evaluation. This is commonly accomplished by including *opportunity costs* among the costs to be incurred under that alternative.

An opportunity cost is the profit foregone by following a particular course of action. For example, suppose that a machine is fully utilized in the production of product A. A decision to use that machine for a short time to produce product B would cause decreased production and sales of product A. The profit foregone because of the lost product A sales is an opportunity cost that would be incurred by the decision to use the machine to produce product B. This cost must be considered in evaluating the decision.

Relevant Revenues

If the decision under study has an impact on revenues, the revenues affected are also relevant. The same steps in determining relevant costs are used to determine relevant revenues. **Relevant revenues are future revenues that differ in amount depending upon the decision alternative chosen.** If revenues are not affected by the decision under study, they are no more relevant than costs that are not affected. A decision to raise a production foreman's salary would not directly affect the revenue earned by a company. Thus company revenue would be irrelevant and would not have to be considered in making the decision.

An Illustration of the Process of Determining Relevant Costs and Revenues

In this section we illustrate how the two-step process just described can be used to determine relevant costs and revenues for a simple decision. The illustration is based on a decision under study by the Randolph Company, a family-owned corporation operating in Ohio. The company produces grills and utensils for outdoor barbecuing. Jennifer Randolph, the sales manager, has just returned from a trip to Wyoming where she was offered $10,000 for 200 grills by the director of Ranch Camps of America. As this offer is below the company's normal $60 per grill selling price, she asked her father, the company's president, for an analysis of costs and revenues before deciding whether or not to accept the offer. She gave him the loosely assembled data shown below in Exhibit 26-2, which she found in the company's records.

Mr. Randolph recognized that the data in Exhibit 26-2 could be misleading because the figures were based on records of the company's past operations, whereas the decision involved future operations. Consequently, before looking at the data he thought through the decision in the following way:

Step 1.   There are only two alternatives to the decision. The company can refuse the offer or accept it. If the offer is refused, no cost incurring activities are required and no revenue is received. If the offer is accepted, however, the company must manufacture the 200 grills and ship them to Laramie, Wyoming in order to receive the sales revenue offered. No other activities are required.

EXHIBIT 26-2
Cost Data for the
Ranch Camp Sale

Manufacturing costs per unit:		
Direct materials		$ 20
Direct labor		6
Factory overhead:		
Variable		4
Fixed		5
Total manufacturing cost		$ 35 per unit
Selling costs:		
Commissions to sales personnel	$ 15 per unit	
Advertising	$300 per month	
Trip to Wyoming	$550	

EXHIBIT 26-3
Cost Data for the
Ranch Camp Sale
(Revised)

Manufacturing costs per unit:
Direct materials . . . . $ 20
    Direct labor 6
Factory overhead:
    Variable 4
    Fixed 5
Total manufacturing cost . . . . $ 35 per unit

Selling costs:
~~Commissions to sales personnel~~   ~~$ 15 per unit~~   *omit; activity not required*
~~Advertising~~ . . . .   ~~$300 per month~~ *omit; activity not required*
~~Trip to Wyoming~~ . . . .   ~~$550~~   *omit; past cost*
Shipping costs   *?*

After looking at the data, he penciled in some comments on the projected cost sheet as a result of his thinking in step 1. The data then appeared as shown in Exhibit 26-3.

By thinking through the activities necessary to carry out the alternatives of this decision, Mr. Randolph recognized that three of the costs listed were not relevant. As shown in Exhibit 26-3, he eliminated the cost of his daughter's trip to Wyoming because it was a past cost. He also eliminated advertising and commissions to sales personnel because these costs were related to activities that were not necessary to carry out the alternatives of the decision. The offer had already been made, and therefore no advertising or further selling effort would be necessary. Finally, he recognized that costs related to shipping would have to be incurred if the offer were accepted.

Step 2. Next, after looking at the costs that he felt might be relevant, he tried to estimate these costs. After obtaining a bid of $1,300 to ship the grills to Laramie from a local trucking company, he gathered additional information about manufacturing costs. He found that:

1. The direct materials prices had gone up to $21 per grill.
2. The past direct labor and factory overhead costs per unit were still good estimates of those costs for the coming year. The total fixed factory overhead would not increase because of the additional 200 units produced if the offer were accepted, however.

With this information, Mr. Randolph eliminated the fixed factory overhead from consideration because, although it was a future cost incurred to support necessary manufacturing activity, the amount of the fixed factory overhead would not be affected by the choice of alternatives. Having finally identified and estimated all of the relevant costs, he included the relevant revenue and then presented the analysis shown in Exhibit 26-4 to his daughter.

EXHIBIT 26-4   Relevant Costs and Revenues for the Ranch Camp Sale

	Decision Alternatives	
	Accept Offer (200 units)	Reject Offer
Relevant revenues	$10,000	$0
Relevant costs:		
Manufacturing costs:		
Direct materials ($21 per unit)	$4,200	$0
Direct labor ($6 per unit)	1,200	0
Variable factory overhead ($4 per unit)	800	0
Total manufacturing costs	$6,200	$0
Shipping costs	1,300	0
Total relevant costs	$ 7,500	$0
Increase in company profit	$ 2,500	$0

The analysis in Exhibit 26-4 clearly shows all the costs and revenues affected by the choice of decision alternatives. It shows that accepting the offer would result in an increase in company revenues of $10,000 but an increase in company costs of only $7,500. Thus company profit would be expected to increase (before income taxes) by $2,500. Rejecting the offer produces no revenue or cost increases and, consequently, no profit change. Thus accepting the offer is clearly preferable to rejecting it (by $2,500).

Now that we have described and illustrated the steps involved in separating relevant costs and revenues from irrelevant costs and revenues, we discuss several common short-term decisions and illustrate the use of managerial accounting information in evaluating the alternatives. These common short-term decisions include decisions to: (1) drop an unprofitable product; (2) make or buy a part or component used in production; (3) sell or process a product further; (4) increase advertising expenditures for a product; and (5) adjust the production mix to make the best use of scarce resources. The kinds of decisions discussed can sometimes be extremely complex and under certain conditions can be more properly evaluated as long-term decisions (using methods to be discussed in Chapter 27). We have made the illustrations relatively simple in order to emphasize the treatment of relevant costs and revenues in their evaluation.

DROPPING AN UNPROFITABLE PRODUCT

Over the life of many companies that sell more than one product, the specific products sold will change. New products that the company hopes will be profitable are added and old products that are no longer profitable are dropped. In this section we discuss and illustrate the decision to drop an unprofitable product.

The Nature of the Decision

The profitable lives of most products do not ordinarily come to an abrupt halt. More often there is a gradual decline in profitability. Sales volume falls as consumer demand shifts to other products, resulting in pressure to reduce selling prices. Even the most favorable price–volume combination ultimately fails to produce sufficient revenue to cover the costs incurred to produce and sell the product. At this point the product is no longer profitable and should be dropped.

As a company begins to sense the decline in profitability of one of its products, it normally takes all available steps to slow that decline through price adjustments, increased advertising, the search for new markets, and/or product modification. We do not consider the decisions related to these efforts because they can be very complex. It is important to recognize, however, that a company does not ordinarily allow one of its products to die if its profitable life can be extended. What we are concerned with is the presentation of accounting information to highlight the profitability of individual products so that the product can be dropped when it becomes unprofitable. Proper presentation and analysis, particularly of the cost information, can help a company avoid either carrying the product too long or dropping it too soon. The decision under study has only two alternatives, to drop the product or to continue producing and selling it.

The key to making this decision is to determine the costs that would not have to be incurred (i.e., the *avoidable* costs) if production and sale of the product were discontinued. The costs that can be avoided by discontinuing the activities needed to support production and sales of a given product are certainly relevant to a decision to drop the product. In fact, they are the *only* costs that are relevant. The reason is that these costs are the only future costs that would be incurred in different amounts depending upon which alternative is chosen.

Once the avoidable costs are determined, the decision to drop the product is straightforward. The product should be dropped only if the total avoidable costs exceed the loss in revenue that would be experienced. Under this condition, the total company profit would be higher if the product is dropped than if the company continues to produce and sell it.

An Illustration of the Decision to Drop a Product

The Western Corporation, an old American manufacturer of quality timepieces, has produced many products over the years. Originally a manufacturer of mantel-piece clocks and gold pocket watches, Western's products currently include a mixture of traditional and modern timepieces. Modern devices, digital alarm clocks and wrist chronographs, currently dominate its sales. The product that made the company famous, a pocket watch with a stainless steel case, is still sold, however. Beloved by outdoorsmen for over 80 years for its rugged dependability, this standard pocket watch has sustained its profitability from the time of its introduction.

Currently, however, management has begun to wonder whether the standard pocket watch is really a profitable product or not. Preliminary estimates of next year's operations have been assembled to shed light on this question. They are shown in Exhibit 26-5. This exhibit seems to suggest that the standard pocket watch would be produced and sold at a $215,000 loss.

The profit computation shown in Exhibit 26-5 highlights the distinction between fixed and variable costs and lists the fixed costs so that they can be examined

**EXHIBIT 26-5
Expected Profit
Computation**

THE WESTERN CORPORATION
Expected Profit of Standard Pocket Watches
and Modern Timepieces

	Standard Pocket Watches	All Modern Timepieces	Total
Sales units	50,000	600,000	650,000
Sales revenue	$925,000	$30,000,000	$30,925,000
Less variable costs	750,000	18,600,000	19,350,000
Contribution margin	$175,000	$11,400,000	$11,575,000
Less fixed costs:			
Advertising	$ 60,000	$ 2,500,000	$ 2,560,000
Depreciation: Buildings	120,000	1,200,000	1,320,000
Depreciation: Equipment	45,000	1,100,000	1,145,000
Insurance	20,000	320,000	340,000
Property taxes	12,000	1,600,000	1,612,000
Salaries	78,000	1,320,000	1,398,000
General and administrative	55,000	960,000	1,015,000
Total fixed costs	$390,000	$ 9,000,000	$ 9,390,000
Profit (loss)	($215,000)	$ 2,400,000	$ 2,185,000

individually. The question to consider is, "Which costs can be avoided if the standard pocket watch is dropped?" Consider the following additional information.

1. Variable costs have been carefully separated from fixed costs and applied to products either directly or indirectly through accurate departmental overhead rates. The rate at which variable costs have been assigned to the standard pocket watches is expected to be very close to the rate at which these costs are incurred because of the production and sale of the watches. These costs are consequently judged to be avoidable.

2. The advertising expenses of $60,000 consist of $44,000 specifically related to the pocket watches and $16,000 allocated from general advertising for all company products. Therefore only the $44,000 specifically related to the pocket watches is judged to be avoidable.

3. The $120,000 of depreciation on the factory buildings is a sunk cost because it is based on the *past* purchase cost of the buildings. It is not relevant to this decision. If Western continues to produce pocket watches, however, it will incur a cost related to building usage that can be avoided by discontinuing production of the pocket watches. All of Western's products are produced in the same buildings. If pocket watch production is discontinued, the space currently used for this production can be used to spread out production facilities for other products, thus making their production more efficient. It is estimated that this improved efficiency would increase the profit earned on modern timepieces by

$21,500. With the continued production of pocket watches, this profit increase would be lost. Thus an opportunity cost of $21,500 related to space usage is incurred if the production of pocket watches continues, but it can be avoided by discontinuing production.

4. The $45,000 depreciation on factory equipment is also a sunk cost based on the past purchase cost of factory assets. It is not relevant to this decision. Because of its age, this equipment cannot be sold (it has no residual value). Since it is not expected to be useful in the production of modern timepieces, this equipment would be given to a local scrap dealer (at zero residual value) if the production of pocket watches is discontinued.

5. Discussion with the company's insurance agent suggests that the company's insurance expense for insurance coverage on equipment and inventories would decrease by only $1,500 if production of the pocket watches is discontinued.

6. About $1,000 of property taxes can be avoided if pocket watch production ceases because of the reduction in inventories of pocket watches.

7. Salaries related to pocket watch production, which total $78,000, are for two foremen and a production superintendent. Both of the foremen would be laid off if pocket watch production is discontinued. Their salaries, a total of $40,000, are avoidable. The production superintendent would not be laid off, but would instead become the new manager of the production planning and scheduling department. His salary ($38,000) is not avoidable. When he takes over the new job, however, the company will not have to hire a new manager for production planning from outside the company. The personnel department estimates that to hire such a person would cost the company $46,000. This $46,000 is therefore avoidable if pocket watch production is discontinued. Thus, the total avoidable salaries are $86,000 ($40,000 + $46,000).

8. The $55,000 general and administrative expenses are not expected to be affected by the decision to drop or not to drop the product. They are not avoidable.

As a result of this analysis, we can show the profit effects of a decision to discontinue production and sale of pocket watches by comparing the revenue that would be lost with the costs that would be avoided. This comparison is made in Exhibit 26-6.

Exhibit 26-6 shows the relevant revenue that is earned by continuing production of the pocket watches, but lost if the product is dropped. It also shows the relevant costs that are incurred if production is continued, but avoided if the product is dropped. Revenues that would not be lost and costs that cannot be avoided are not relevant to this decision. Note that the revenue earned by producing the pocket watches ($925,000) *exceeds* the total of the relevant costs ($904,000) that would be incurred by $21,000. Another way of stating this is that the revenue lost by dropping the pocket watch *exceeds* the total of the costs that can be avoided by

EXHIBIT 26-6
Analysis for the
Decision to Drop
a Product

THE WESTERN CORPORATION
Relevant Costs and Revenues for the Decision to
Drop Pocket Watch Production

	Drop	Continue Producing
Sales (units)	0	50,000
Sales revenue	$0	$925,000
Avoidable costs:		
Variable costs	$0	$750,000
Advertising	0	44,000
Opportunity cost for space usage	0	21,500
Insurance	0	1,500
Property taxes	0	1,000
Salaries ($40,000 + $46,000)	0	86,000
Total avoidable costs	$0	$904,000
Profit	$0	$ 21,000

$21,000. Thus profit would decrease by $21,000 if pocket watch production is discontinued. The decision, therefore, would be to continue production.

The relevant costs and revenues shown in Exhibit 26-6 could also be arranged to compare the decision alternatives by computing the contribution margin of $175,000 ($925,000 sales − $750,000 variable costs) that would be lost if the product is discontinued, and deducting from it the fixed costs that can be avoided ($154,000). Since the contribution margin lost exceeds the avoidable fixed costs by $21,000 ($175,000 − $154,000), pocket watch production should be continued. Note that the contribution margin of this product is $3.50 per unit ($175,000 ÷ 50,000 units). Consequently, the contribution margin lost by dropping the product would exceed the avoidable fixed costs ($154,000) as long as sales exceed 44,000 units ($154,000 ÷ $3.50 per unit).

Since sales of pocket watches are expected to be 50,000 units during the coming year, production should be continued. If expected sales were less than 44,000 units, however, the product should be dropped.

THE MAKE OR BUY DECISION

Many products require a long series of manufacturing processes to convert basic direct materials into completed products. These products are seldom produced entirely by a single company. For example, consider the many companies involved in the manufacture of automobiles. There are companies involved in the manufacture of steel, glass, paint, rubber, plastic, and so on. Other companies use these materials to produce parts and components such as lights, fuel pumps, radios, air conditioners, and tires. By the time an automobile is actually completed, many companies have been involved.

The Nature of the Make or Buy Decision

Any company that buys parts or components from other companies periodically questions whether or not it would be less costly to produce one or more of the parts or components itself than to purchase them from outside suppliers. That is, the company has to face a decision whether to make a particular part or component or to buy it.

Many factors affect the make or buy decision. If a company has to buy the required equipment and develop the know-how to produce a particular component, it may be much more costly to make the component than to buy it from the present supplier. A short-term cost advantage can sometimes be obtained by a company, however, when the company has the equipment required for component production and it is not being used fully for other production. The company might be able to produce the component with little or no incremental costs in such a case.

This advantage may not be long-lasting, however, and valuable business relationships with suppliers may be damaged by the decision to make a component. A decision to make a previously purchased component in order to obtain a short-term cost advantage may be unwise if it is likely to be reversed in the near future.

Another reason to make components that are currently being purchased arises from considerations of quality and supplier reliability, which can affect overall costs as well. Poor quality components can cause increases in production costs for a company and can cause customer dissatisfaction with the company's product, leading to loss of sales (resulting in opportunity costs). If the supply of components is unreliable, production delays may result that can also cause increases in production costs or lost sales. When negotiations with suppliers fail to correct these problems, a company may be led to consider producing its own components. The following illustration includes treatment of several of these factors.

An Illustration of the Make or Buy Decision

The Goering Company currently purchases component 311 from an outside supplier for $5.40 per unit for use in the manufacture of one of its products. Due to the discontinuation of another product, the company finds itself with unused machinery capable of producing up to 2,000 units of this component. This equipment cannot be sold. Goering believes it has the necessary production skill to produce the component and, in fact, that it can produce a better-quality component than is available from its current supplier. The company estimates that excess production costs incurred (resulting from the lower quality of the purchased component) in producing its product amount to $.60 for each unit of the purchased component used. This cost could be avoided by making the component of better quality. Estimates of all incremental costs of making the component have been obtained and are shown in the relevant cost comparison for the make or buy decision in Exhibit 26-7.

Note in Exhibit 26-7 that Goering's cost study has revealed no incremental fixed costs associated with making or buying the component. All relevant costs in this particular situation are variable. Thus the relevant cost comparison showing total costs at the expected monthly component requirement of 1,000 units could just as

EXHIBIT 26-7
Analysis for the
Make or Buy
Decision

	Make Component 311	Buy Component 311
THE GOERING COMPANY		
Relevant Costs for the Make or Buy Decision		
Expected monthly requirement (units)	1,000	1,000
Relevant costs:		
Direct materials	$2,200	
Direct labor	1,050	
Variable overhead	550	
Component purchase cost		$5,400
Excess manufacturing costs incurred in production of Goering's product as a result of lower-quality purchased components		600
Total relevant costs	$3,800	$6,000
Relevant costs per unit	$ 3.80	$ 6.00

well have been made by examining the per unit costs. The comparison shows that making 1,000 components per month rather than buying them would save Goering $2,200 ($6,000 − $3,800) per month. A comparison of the per unit variable costs suggests that the company would save $2.20 ($6.00 − $3.80) for each component made. In this case, the company would prefer to make the component regardless of the number of components needed up to the maximum that could be produced with the available equipment. Such a conclusion could not have been drawn, however, if there had been relevant fixed costs incurred as a result of following either or both of the alternatives. Consider the Goering Company's situation if it did not already possess the equipment necessary to produce the component.

Suppose we assume that the Goering Company does not have the equipment necessary to make component 311 but can lease the equipment for a fixed cost of $2,640 per month. All other costs would remain the same. In this case, the cost of making the component would be $6,440 ($3,800 + $2,640) per month and the cost of purchasing it would be $6,000 per month at the expected monthly requirement of 1,000 components. The per unit relevant cost of $6.44 ($6,440 ÷ 1,000) for making the component is meaningful only at the level of 1,000 components, however. If it is compared to the $6.00 per unit cost of buying the component when the quantity of components needed is not 1,000 units, the comparison would be misleading. The reason is that (as you may recall from our discussion of fixed costs in Chapter 23) fixed costs per unit change when the volume changes.

If Goering's need for this component is likely to change, a more general form of analysis may be helpful. The costs of purchasing the component vary at a rate of $6.00 per unit purchased. The total costs of making the component now

EXHIBIT 26-8
Expected Costs of
Making and
Buying Components

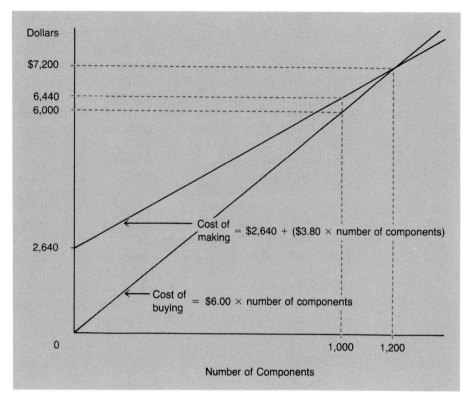

Dollars

$7,200

6,440
6,000

2,640

Cost of making = $2,640 + ($3.80 × number of components)

Cost of buying = $6.00 × number of components

0   1,000   1,200

Number of Components

consist of a fixed cost of $2,640 per month and a variable cost of $3.80 per unit made. Exhibit 26-8 shows a graph of the expected costs for the Goering Company of both purchasing and making the component as the volume of components needed per month varies.

Note from the graph in Exhibit 26-8 that the expected total costs of making the component are higher than those of buying it at a volume of 1,000 units. In fact, the graph shows that total costs to make the component are higher than the total costs to buy it for all volumes below 1,200 units. Notice that for volumes above 1,200 units, however, the total costs of making the component are less than the total costs of buying it. This form of analysis is useful because it not only aids in making the correct current decision (to continue purchasing the component because purchase costs at the expected volume of 1,000 units are less than the expected costs of making the unit), but it also suggests under what (volume) conditions the decision would be reversed. With information from this analysis, the company can make plans for producing the component if production of its main product should require more than 1,200 components per month.

THE DECISION TO SELL OR PROCESS FURTHER

The decision to sell a product or to use it in the manufacture of another product is faced by many companies. For example, a meat packer might sell animal fat or make soap out of it, a textile mill can sell yarn or weave cloth out of it, and kerosene produced in refining oil can be sold or processed further to increase gasoline output.

The Nature of the Decision

Consider a company that can sell all of the units of product A it can produce. Suppose product A can be converted into product B by further processing. In order for the company to produce any units of product B, it must give up sales of product A. The problem is to determine whether or not the company should forego selling some of its units of product A in order to convert them into units of product B. The company faces a *sell or process further decision*.

In this situation, none of the costs incurred to produce product A to the point where it is ready for further processing is relevant to the decision. The reason is that these costs must be incurred whether product A is sold or whether it is processed further and sold as product B. The only costs that can be considered relevant are the incremental costs of selling units of product A (which would be incurred if the units are sold but not if they are processed further) and the incremental costs of further processing and selling units of product B (which would be incurred if further processing occurs but not if it does not occur).

Both the revenue from the sale of product A (if not processed further) and the revenue from the sale of product B (if processed further) are relevant as long as they are different.

An Illustration of the Sell or Process Further Decision

Pringle Paper Products is considering converting some of its fine writing paper into fancy stationery. The company currently is able to sell all of the fine writing paper it can produce, but it believes that its profit might be improved by giving up some of its fine writing paper sales to produce higher priced stationery. Although the plant would not have to be expanded for this new processing, new printing equipment would have to be leased for a fixed cost of $14,000 per year. In addition, packaging equipment currently in full-time use in other production would be reassigned to this new processing, thus reducing production capability slightly for another product. The lost sales for this other product would result in variable opportunity costs of $.025 per box of stationery packaged. Variable costs of converting fine writing paper into fancy stationery include direct labor and variable overhead costs totaling $.40 per box of stationery. Increased delivery costs and the cost of fancy display cartons are expected to cause variable selling costs to be higher for the fancy stationery than for writing paper. The company believes that customer demand will be 40,000 boxes of stationery per year for an indefinite number of years. Estimates of relevant costs and revenues for this decision are shown in Exhibit 26-9.

Exhibit 26-9 shows that the difference between the relevant revenue and relevant cost is $56,000 ($104,000 − $48,000) higher under the "process further" alternative than it is under the "sell" alternative. This means that processing fine writing paper further to produce 40,000 boxes of fancy stationery would result in a profit increase of $56,000. This occurs because the increase in revenue of $90,000 ($140,000 − $50,000) is $56,000 more than the $34,000 ($36,000 − $2,000)

EXHIBIT 26-9
Analysis for the Sell
or Process Further
Decision

	Sell (as fine writing paper)	Process Further (into fancy stationery)
PRINGLE PAPER PRODUCTS Relevant Costs and Revenues for the Sell or Process Further Decision Estimated for 40,000 Boxes of Stationery		
Revenue	$50,000[a]	$140,000
Relevant costs:		
Variable selling costs	$2,000[a]	$ 5,000
Variable labor and overhead costs ($.40 × 40,000)	–	16,000
Variable opportunity costs of using fully utilized packaging equipment ($.025 × 40,000)	–	1,000
Fixed leasing costs	–	14,000
Total incremental costs	2,000	36,000
Difference (relevant revenue minus relevant costs)	$48,000	$104,000

[a] Estimates of costs and revenues are based on the amount of fine writing paper required for 40,000 boxes of stationery.

increase in costs. Thus the decision should be to further process enough fine writing paper to satisfy the demand for fancy stationery.

Notice that the manufacturing costs required to produce the fine writing paper are not shown. The reason is that these costs must be incurred in the same amount regardless of which alternative is chosen and therefore they are not relevant to the decision. Notice also that the revenue increase is $2.25 per box of stationery [($140,000 − $50,000) ÷ 40,000 boxes] and that the increase in relevant *variable* costs is $.50 per box [($5,000 + $16,000 + $1,000 − $2,000) ÷ 40,000 boxes]. Thus each box of fancy stationery sold increases the company's total contribution margin by $1.75 ($2.25 − $.50). Because the incremental fixed cost incurred in further processing is $14,000, the company's profit would increase for any sales volume of stationery in excess of 8,000 boxes ($14,000 ÷ $1.75 per box). That is, 8,000 boxes is the break-even point for stationery sales.

DECISIONS INVOLVING PRODUCT MIX

Multiproduct companies face a common problem. They have to determine how many units of each product to produce and sell. We could propose a rule of thumb for all companies to follow such as, "A company should determine how many units of each of its products can be sold and then produce that many," but such a rule would not be helpful to most companies. If it were helpful, there would be no problem for which a decision would have to be made. There are two reasons that this rule is ineffective for most companies:

1. The rule ignores the fact that many companies can influence the sales volume of their products by the sales activities they perform, such as advertising, the use of promotional campaigns, and the number of sales personnel used.
2. Many companies operate with limited productive capacity and, as a result, cannot produce as much of every product as can be sold.

The problem of deciding how many units of each product a company should produce and sell can be extremely complex. We illustrate only two very simplified situations, but they should be helpful in providing an understanding of the importance of managerial accounting information in product mix decisions.

Deciding How to Spend Advertising Dollars

A SIMPLIFIED DECISION SITUATION.   The first situation we consider involves deciding which products should be advertised. We make the following simplifying assumptions:

1. The company currently spends an initial budgeted amount on advertising for each of several products.
2. A fixed amount of money has been added to the coming year's advertising budget. The question is "On which *one* of the several products should the additional advertising money be spent?"
3. Studies by the sales department can provide reliable estimates of the additional sales volume (in units) that would result from spending the additional advertising money on each of the products.
4. The company has sufficient plant and equipment to produce the additional units of any of the products that would result from the additional advertising.

In this situation, the company's profit would be increased if the contribution margin resulting from increased sales exceeds the increase in advertising cost. The problem is to choose which product should receive the advertising so that the largest possible profit increase is obtained. Since the additional advertising is a fixed amount, the largest profit increase comes from the alternative that produces the largest increase in contribution margin. This is the key to the decision. Managerial accounting information shows the contribution margin per unit for each of the products. Using estimates from the sales department of the additional sales volume that the advertising would produce, the computation required to evaluate the alternatives simply involves multiplying the unit sales increases expected by the contribution margin per unit for each of the products.

AN ILLUSTRATION.   The Merimac Company, which produces three products, has increased its advertising budget by $20,000. The company plans to spend the entire amount of this increase on advertising for one of the three products. Exhibit 26-10 shows the contribution margin per unit information supplied by Merimac's managerial accountant, the sales volume increases estimated by the sales manager, and the computations needed to evaluate the alternatives.

As can be seen in Exhibit 26-10, profit can be increased by spending the additional $20,000 to advertise either product B or product C. Spending the addi-

**EXHIBIT 26-10
Analysis for the
Product Mix Decision**

	Products		
	A	B	C
Selling price per unit	$5	$6	$7
Variable costs per unit	3	5	4
Contribution margin per unit	$2	$1	$3
Sales volume increase resulting from			
additional advertising (units)	× 8,000	× 38,000	× 12,000
Additional contribution margin	$16,000	$38,000	$36,000

**THE MERIMAC COMPANY
Analysis of Product Mix Decision**

tional $20,000 to advertise product A would *decrease* total company profit by $4,000 ($20,000 incremental cost − $16,000 additional contribution margin). The largest profit increase can be obtained by advertising product B. The profit increase would be $18,000 ($38,000 additional contribution margin minus $20,000 additional advertising). Although the contribution margin *per unit* for product B is the lowest of the three products, the increase in its sales volume is highest. It is high enough, in fact, to cause an increase of the total contribution margin for product B that is more than the increase of the total contribution margins for either of the other two products. Thus the additional advertising expenditure should be used for product B.

**Deciding How
Many Units
to Produce**

A SIMPLIFIED DECISION SITUATION.   The second simplified situation we consider involves deciding how many units of each of several products to produce. We make the following simplifying assumptions:

1. Production is limited by a single scarce resource.
2. The combined customer demand for the company's products exceeds its limited production capability.
3. Customer demand for the individual products cannot be influenced during the period over which the decision is implemented.

In this situation, the company would earn the highest profit by choosing the product mix that produces the highest total contribution margin. No fixed costs are involved in this decision. Since production is limited by a single scarce resource, available machine time for example, the problem involves making the most profitable use of this resource. Consequently, the decision maker must know the usage requirements of this resource for each of the products. With the contribution margin per unit information supplied by the managerial accountant, the products making the most profitable use of the scarce resource can be determined. The product that makes the most profitable use of a resource produces the highest contribution margin *per unit of the resource*. The correct decision would be to produce the product making the most profitable use of the scarce resource until its demand is satisfied, then produce the product making the next most profitable use of the resource, and so on, until the scarce resource is fully utilized.

AN ILLUSTRATION.   Three products produced by the Plymouth Company utilize a particular direct material that is in short supply due to a strike at the supplier's plant. Plymouth has only 10,000 pounds of this direct material in its inventory and will receive no more for 3 weeks. During this period it expects to be able to sell 10,000 units of product A, 5,000 units of product B, and 15,000 units of product C. The company must decide how many units of each product to produce and sell during the next 3 weeks. Exhibit 26-11 shows the contribution margins per unit for each product, the direct materials usage requirements of each product, and a computation of the contribution margin earned per pound of direct material.

Notice in Exhibit 26-11 that, although product C provides the *highest* contribution margin per *unit*, it also requires the most direct material to produce a unit. As a result, it produces the *lowest* contribution margin per *pound* of the scarce direct material of any of the products. Since product C requires 2 pounds of direct material to produce a unit and earns $6 of contribution margin per unit, it earns $3 ($6 per unit ÷ 2 pounds per unit) per pound of direct material used. Product B makes the most profitable use of the direct material, followed by product A and then product C. Thus the company should produce as many units of product B as it can until product B's demand is satisfied, then produce product A, and finally product C if any material is still available.

In this illustration, the Plymouth Company should use 2,500 pounds of direct material to produce 5,000 units of product B and use the remaining direct material to produce 7,500 units of product A. Demand for product A would not be completely satisfied and no units of product C would be produced at all, but the total contribution margin earned would be higher than at any other product mix. For example, if the 10,000 pounds of direct material were used to produce 5,000 units of product C, the total contribution margin earned would be $30,000 (10,000 pounds × $3 per pound). If it were used to produce 10,000 units of product A, the total contribution margin would be $40,000 (10,000 pounds × $4 per pound). If 2,500 pounds were used to produce product B and the remaining 7,500 pounds used to produce product A, however, the total contribution margin earned would be

EXHIBIT 26-11
Computation of Contribution Margin per Unit of a Scarce Resource

THE PLYMOUTH COMPANY Computation of Contribution Margin per Pound of Direct Material			
	Product A	*Product B*	*Product C*
Contribution margin per unit	$4	$ 5	$6
Direct materials usage per unit (pounds)	÷ 1	÷ 0.5	÷ 2
Contribution margin per pound of direct material . .	$4	$10	$3

$55,000 [(2,500 pounds × $10 per pound) + (7,500 pounds × $4 per pound)]. No other possible mix can produce a larger contribution margin during the 3 weeks that this material is in short supply.

REVIEW PROBLEM

Northcentral Industries manufactures a wide variety of home appliances including a line of large electric fans. Northcentral has always manufactured its own metal fan blades for these units. Recently, however, a large supplier of many other components used in the company's products has offered to sell fan blades to Northcentral at $500 per thousand. Shipping and receiving costs for these fan blades are estimated to be $58 per thousand.

The manufacturing costs applied to fan blades are shown below:

	Manufacturing Costs per Thousand
Direct materials	$180
Direct labor (32 hours @ $5)	160
Variable overhead[a]	128
Fixed overhead[a]	320
Total manufacturing costs applied	$788

[a] Factory overhead rates were predetermined at a normal activity of 100,000 direct labor hours per year.

Additional Information:
(a) Direct labor, direct materials, and variable overhead costs are judged to be completely avoidable if fan blades are bought instead of made.
(b) Annual fixed overhead costs are judged to be avoidable to the following extent:

Maintenance	$600
Property taxes and insurance	200
Other	100
Total avoidable fixed overhead	$900

(c) If the production of fan blades is discontinued, the supervisor of these manufacturing operations would be able to devote more of his time to other production activities. It is estimated that this would save the company $2,700 per year in manufacturing costs on these other activities.
(d) Northcentral estimates that 30,000 fan blades will be needed per year over the next few years.

Required:
1. Determine whether Northcentral should continue making fan blades or should buy them.
2. Compute the number of fan blades needed per year above which continued production is justified.

SOLUTION TO REVIEW PROBLEM

1.

Annual Costs of Making and Buying 30,000 Fan Blades

	Make	Buy
Direct materials (30 × $180[a])	$ 5,400	–
Direct labor (30 × $160)	4,800	–
Variable overhead (30 × $128)	3,840	–
Fixed overhead	900	–
Opportunity cost of savings obtainable by supervision of other manufacturing activities	2,700	–
Purchase cost (30 × $500)	–	$15,000
Shipping and receiving (30 × $58)	–	1,740
Total costs	$17,640	$16,740

[a] All variable costs are per thousand units.

Since the total costs of purchasing 30,000 fan blades are less than the total (avoidable) costs of making them, the company should *buy* the fan blades.

2. Note that the costs of buying fan blades are entirely variable. They amount to $558 per thousand ($500 + $58). The avoidable costs of making fan blades include both fixed and variable costs, however. Variable costs of making fan blades amount to $468 per thousand ($180 + $160 + $128). Fixed costs of making fan blades (including the opportunity cost) total $3,600.

Thus, by incurring avoidable fixed costs of $3,600 per year, Northcentral is able to save $90 ($558 − $468) per thousand fan blades manufactured instead of purchased. The cost of making the blades will be less than the cost of buying them when the total savings in variable costs exceed the avoidable fixed costs. This occurs at a volume of fan blades that is *greater* than:

$$\frac{\$3,600 \text{ avoidable fixed costs}}{\$90 \text{ variable cost savings per thousand}} = 40,000 \text{ fan blades}$$

Thus continued production of fan blades is justified when more than 40,000 fan blades are needed.

GLOSSARY

Avoidable Cost. A cost that must be incurred in order to perform an activity at a given level but which can be avoided if that activity is discontinued or its volume is reduced.

Decision Making. The process of recognizing problems involving alternatives, searching for alternative solutions, and selecting one solution to be followed on the basis of an evaluation of the alternatives.

Incremental Cost. A cost increase resulting from the performance of an additional activity.

Opportunity Cost. The profit foregone by following a particular course of action.

Relevant Cost. A future cost that differs in amount depending upon the decision alternative chosen.

Relevant Revenue. A future revenue that differs in amount depending upon the decision alternative chosen.

Sunk Cost. A past cost that is irrelevant to a decision because it was incurred prior to the time the decision is being made and, consequently, cannot be affected by whichever decision alternative is chosen.

QUESTIONS

Q26-1 What is a relevant cost?

Q26-2 Why are past costs irrelevant?

Q26-3 Since past costs are irrelevant in decision making, how can keeping past cost records be helpful in the decision-making process?

Q26-4 Why should irrelevant costs be omitted from a decision analysis?

Q26-5 In how much detail do the alternatives in a decision have to be planned before the decision is made?

Q26-6 Distinguish between incremental costs and avoidable costs.

Q26-7 Under what circumstances are avoidable manufacturing costs relevant in the make or buy decision?

Q26-8 Under what circumstances are incremental manufacturing costs relevant in the make or buy decision?

Q26-9 List two incremental costs in a decision to make a previously purchased component that might *not* be avoidable if the decision were reversed a year later. Discuss.

Q26-10 Explain how fixed costs can be incremental costs. Give an example of a situation involving incremental fixed costs and discuss.

Q26-11 Discuss why it might be valuable to distinguish between relevant fixed costs and relevant variable costs for a short-term decision.

Q26-12 Are variable costs ever *not* relevant? Discuss.

Q26-13 Production of product Z has just been discontinued. The company has 40,000 units in inventory that cost $60 per unit to manufacture. At the current selling price of $90 it may take as long as 10 years for the units to be sold. A foreign buyer has just offered the company $2,000,000 for all the units. Is the $60 per unit manufacturing cost relevant in deciding whether or not to accept the offer? List the costs and revenues that you think would be relevant.

Q26-14 What is an opportunity cost? Give an example and discuss.

Q26-15 M. Green, who is paid $4 per hour, is the only person who can operate machine A, which is critical in the production of product X. Product X has a contribution margin of $3 per unit and requires $\frac{1}{4}$ hour of processing on machine A. Sales of product X are limited only by scarce machine A time used in its production. How much does it cost the company if Green becomes sick and leaves work an hour early one day?

Q26-16 A company has 800 pounds of material X in its inventory. The material cost $.50 per pound 6 months ago when it was purchased. Material X can now be purchased for $.55 per pound. If the company sold the inventory on hand, however, it would receive only $.48 per pound. Under what circumstances would the cost of using 100 pounds of the material for a special order be: (a) $48? (b) $50? (c) $55?

EXERCISES

E26-1 Relevant Costs and Revenues. The Arnco Company ended its busy season with 10,000 units of a particular product in inventory that cost $180,000 to manufacture. The company has two choices. It can store the units for 6 months and sell them for $10 each during the following year. Storage would cost $6,000 and Arnco knows at least 40% of the units would spoil during storage. The spoiled units would have no value.

The only other alternative is to have a clearance sale now and sell the units for $6.50 each. Arnco believes that all of the units can be sold if the company spends $10,000 to advertise the sale.

Required: Prepare an analysis showing the relevant costs and revenues of each alternative and decide which alternative should be chosen.

E26-2 Relevant Costs and Revenues. On a chilly Saturday morning Roy Parker bought 20 dozen doughnuts for $36, took 10 gallons of hot coffee, and went to a farm auction. He sold all of the coffee and all but 4 dozen of the doughnuts before heading for home late in the afternoon. Knowing that he could not eat 4 dozen doughnuts himself and that they would be worthless by the next day, he began to consider how he might sell the remaining doughnuts. Only one possibility occurred to him. If he drove across town and left the doughnuts in the lunch room at the plant where he worked, he was sure that workers on the late shift would be happy to buy the doughnuts. He figured the 23-mile round trip to the plant would cost him about $.10 per mile. It would take him about a half hour to make the trip and he decided that it would be worthwhile if he could earn $2.50 (total) on the doughnuts.

Required: Prepare an analysis to determine how much Roy would have to charge per doughnut to reach his profit goal.

E26-3 Incremental Costs. Brookfield Enterprises produces small electrical appliances. The standard manufacturing costs per unit to produce a small toaster are shown below.

Direct materials cost	$ 5.50
Direct labor cost	3.75
Variable overhead cost	4.25
Fixed overhead cost	6.00
Total standard manufacturing cost per unit	$19.50

Variable selling costs to obtain and fill orders normally average $1.50 per unit when the toasters are sold to local customers. Recently, however, Brookfield paid $40,000 to advertise its various products in an international trade magazine.

The company has just received an order from a large mail order merchandising company in Brazil for 500 toasters. The merchandising company is willing to pay all shipping charges except the initial packaging, which would cost $.75 per toaster. The price offered was $9,000 for the toasters.

Required: Compute the total incremental cost that Brookfield would expect to incur if it accepted and filled this order. Should the 500 toasters be sold to the Brazilian company?

E26-4 **Opportunity Costs.** Craftco produces several products that are sold by hobby shops across the country. Production of one product, a small model rocket, uses all available machine hours on machine 12A. The rocket, which provides a contribution margin of $1.65 per unit, requires 0.1 machine hours per unit to produce.

Craftco would like to use machine 12A in the production of other products. This production would take about 200 hours.

Required: Compute the opportunity cost of using 200 machine hours on machine 12A for other production.

E26-5 **Opportunity Costs.** The Maxwell Company owns a lathe that is not currently being used. The lathe, which was purchased 9 years ago for $20,000, has a current book value of $2,000. Maxwell can get $3,800 for the lathe if it is sold now.

Maxwell has just received an order for 40,000 table legs that the company cannot accept unless it keeps the lathe for use in producing the order. If the lathe is kept for this purpose, it will have no residual value after the order is completed.

The direct materials, direct labor, and variable overhead costs that would be incurred to produce the order total $27,500. The customer has offered $30,000 for the table legs.

Required: Prepare a schedule to help the Maxwell Company determine whether the order for the table legs should be accepted.

E26-6 **Dropping a Product.** The Porter Wagon Company produces sleds, scooters, and wagons. Scooters are not as popular as they used to be and the company is considering dropping this product. Porter currently sells 3,000 scooters per year for $15 each. Variable manufacturing and selling costs total $8 per scooter. Fixed costs, which can be avoided if scooters are not produced, total $30,000.

Required: Prepare an analysis to answer each of the following *independent* questions.
1. Given the information presented above, by how much would the company's profit increase if production of scooters is discontinued?
2. If Porter can increase the sales volume of scooters to 4,000 units per year by spending an additional $10,000 per year on advertising, should scooter production be continued?
3. If Porter can increase the sales volume of scooters to 5,000 units per year by reducing its selling price to $13 per unit, should scooter production be continued?

E26-7 **Make or Buy.** The Moorehead Company currently buys component X12 for $1.50 per unit. Moorehead's president has asked for cost estimates for making this product and has received the following report:

Costs of Making Component X12 per Unit

Direct materials	$ .55
Direct labor	.30
Variable overhead	.35
Fixed overhead	.80
Total manufacturing cost per unit	$2.00

If Moorehead makes the component, production would take place in its machine shop. No additional plant and equipment would be necessary; however, the company would have to hire someone to inspect the components before they could be used in producing the company's other products. The inspector's salary would be $12,000 per year.

Required:
1. Compute the incremental costs of making and of buying the component in quantities of 25,000 units per year. Should the company make the component or buy it?
2. Compute the incremental costs of making and of buying the component in quantities of 50,000 units per year. Should the company make the component or buy it?
3. How many units of the component would have to be produced so that the total costs of making them would be equal to the total costs of buying them?

E26-8   Make or Buy.   C. Rice and Company currently makes 20,000 units of component Z13 at a cost of $150,000 per year. Included in this cost are (cancellable) lease payments of $20,000 per year for a drill press used exclusively in the production of this component and $30,000 of other fixed overhead costs that are unavoidable. The remaining costs are variable manufacturing costs.

Required: Prepare an analysis to answer each of the following *independent* questions.
1. If the company could buy 20,000 units of the component for $125,000 per year, should it continue making the component or should it buy it?
2. If the company could buy 20,000 units of the component for $110,000 per year, should it continue making the component or should it buy it?
3. If the company needs 20,000 units of the component per year, below what purchase price per unit would the company prefer to buy the component rather than make it?
4. If the company needs 30,000 units of the component per year, below what purchase price per unit would the company prefer to buy the component rather than make it?

E26-9   Sell or Process Further.   The AR Company sells 1,000 units of product X for $10 per unit. The cost to manufacture product X is $4.50 per unit. Further variable processing costs of $3 per unit for product X would convert this product into product Y, which could be sold for $15 per unit. Variable selling costs are $1 per unit for product X, but for product Y they would be $2 per unit.

Required: Prepare an analysis to answer each of the following questions.
1. Should product X be processed further into product Y?
2. If the selling price per unit of product Y dropped to $13.50 per unit, should product X be processed further into product Y?

E26-10   Sell or Process Further.   The Lattimore Company produces 100,000 pounds per year of Compound W, which has many industrial uses. Compound W costs $.60 per pound to make and $.04 per pound to sell. Its selling price is $1.00 per pound. Lattimore is considering converting 20,000 pounds per year of Compound W into a cleaning solvent through further processing. This cleaning solvent would be sold in quart bottles to grocery and hardware stores for $1.20 per quart. Each quart of cleaning solvent would require $\frac{1}{4}$ pound of Compound W and additional variable processing costs of $.31. Variable selling costs would be $.05 per quart of solvent and the company plans to spend $20,000 per year to advertise the solvent.

Required: Prepare an analysis showing whether the Lattimore Company should process 20,000 pounds of Compound W per year into cleaning solvent.

E26-11   Choosing Which Product to Advertise.   The Marlin Company, which makes and sells two products, has $5,000 to spend on advertising. The company has estimated that using the $5,000 to advertise product A would increase sales of that product by 2,000 units. Marlin is uncertain how many additional units of product B could be sold by spending the $5,000 on it, however. Product A has a contribution margin of $6 per unit and product B has a contribution margin of $2 per unit.

Required: Prepare an analysis to answer each of the following three *independent* questions.
1. If spending the $5,000 on product B would increase its sales by 4,000 units, which product should be advertised?
2. If spending the $5,000 on product B would increase its sales by 8,000 units, which product should be advertised?
3. By how many units would sales of product B have to increase to justify spending the $5,000 on product B instead of product A?

E26-12 Product Mix Decision. Lee Manufacturing can sell a maximum of 4,000 units of product A and 10,000 units of product B. Product A has a contribution margin of $6 per unit and requires 1 machine hour to produce. Product B has a contribution margin of $10 per unit and requires 2 machine hours to produce. Lee currently has 6,400 machine hours available each month.

Required: Prepare an analysis to answer each of the following questions.
1. How many units of products A and B should Lee produce each month to earn the maximum monthly total contribution margin?
2. What is the maximum amount Lee should pay per month to lease one additional machine, which can be used 320 hours per month?

PROBLEMS

Part A

P26-1A Make or Buy Decision. Morris Metal Products currently manufactures component A61, which it uses in the assembly of metal farm structures. Cost estimates to make the component are as follows:

Direct materials	$ 6.00 per unit
Direct labor	5.00 per unit
Variable overhead	3.00 per unit
Fixed overhead	$13,000 per year

Required:
1. Prepare an analysis to answer each of the following *independent* questions.
   (a) Assume that all variable costs are avoidable and that the company needs 2,000 components annually. How much of the fixed overhead must be avoidable in order for the company to prefer to buy the components from an outside supplier at $20 per unit instead of continuing to make them?
   (b) Assume that all variable costs are avoidable, that the company needs 2,000 components annually, and that only $5,000 of fixed costs are avoidable. Below what component purchase price per unit would the company prefer to buy the components from an outside supplier instead of continuing to make them?
   (c) Assume that all variable costs are avoidable, that $1,000 of fixed overhead is avoidable, and that the purchase price of the component is $19 per unit. Below what number of components needed would the company prefer to buy the components from an outside supplier instead of continuing to make them?
2. Suppose fixed overhead costs include:

Rent	$ 5,000
Depreciation: Equipment	3,600
Property taxes	300
Foreman's salary	3,000
Routine maintenance	600
Utilities	500
Total	$13,000

List the fixed costs that you think could be avoided (at least partially) if component A61 is purchased and discuss your reasons for including each cost in the list.

P26-2A   **Deciding Which Product to Advertise.** American Products Company has just completed a study that suggests that sales of its two products could be increased by spending more on advertising. The following table shows how many additional units of each of two products could be sold if advertising for each is increased:

Amount Spent on Product A	Additional Sales of Product A	Amount Spent on Product B	Additional Sales of Product B
$1,000	500 units	$1,000	500 units
2,000	900	2,000	1,000
3,000	1,200	3,000	1,500
4,000	1,400	4,000	2,000

Product A has a contribution margin of $6.00 per unit and product B has a contribution margin of $3.00 per unit. The company has a total of $4,000 to spend on additional advertising.

Required: 1. Compute the increase in the company's profit if the $4,000 is spent on advertising product A alone.

2. Compute the increase in the company's profit if the $4,000 is spent on advertising product B alone.

3. Compute the increase in the company's profit if only $3,000 is spent on advertising product A alone.

4. Compare your answers to Requirements 1 and 3 and explain the answers obtained.

5. Write a recommendation for the company telling them how much additional advertising to spend on each product (up to $4,000 total) in order to increase profit by the greatest amount.

P26-3A   **Dropping a Product.** The Bluejay Company, which sells products X and Y, is considering dropping one of the two products because of sagging sales. Expected profit for the coming year for each of the two products is shown below:

	Product X	Product Y	Total
Sales units	15,000	30,000	45,000
Sales revenue	$120,000	$180,000	$300,000
Less variable costs	45,000	120,000	165,000
Contribution margin	$ 75,000	$ 60,000	$135,000
Less fixed costs:			
Advertising	$ 10,000	$ 20,000	$ 30,000
Depreciation of buildings and equipment	20,000	10,000	30,000
Salaries	40,000	55,000	95,000
General and administrative	3,500	6,500	10,000
Total fixed costs	$ 73,500	$ 91,500	$165,000
Profit (loss)	$ 1,500	($ 31,500)	($ 30,000)

The following amounts of fixed cost can be avoided if product X or Y is dropped.

	Product X	Product Y
Advertising	$10,000	$20,000
Depreciation of buildings and equipment	0	0
Salaries	25,000	45,000
General and administrative	500	1,000
Total avoidable fixed costs	$35,500	$66,000

Required: 1. Prepare a schedule to show the expected profit computation if product X is dropped.

2. Prepare a schedule to show the expected profit computation if product Y is dropped.

3. Prepare a schedule to show the expected profit computation if product Y is dropped and one-third of the customers who would have bought product Y buy product X instead. (Sales of product X increase by 10,000 units.)

4. Think of an item you have bought that, if discontinued, might cause you to buy a different item made by the same company. How are the products related?

P26-4A   Sell or Process Further. The Yardgirl Company makes and sells lawn mowers that are in such high demand that the company has operated both of its departments at their maximum capacity for several years. The company expects to be able to sell all of the mowers it can produce for many years at $160 per mower. The major reason for the popularity of the Yardgirl mower is its quiet and reliable engine. Engines are manufactured in Department A. Engine mounting, assembly, and testing of the mowers take place in Department B. Cost as well as other information relating to the company's operations is shown below:

	Department A	Department B
Expected production (maximum capacity)	20,000 engines	20,000 mowers
Variable manufacturing cost per unit:		
Direct materials	$14	$21 (excluding engines)
Direct labor	11	13
Variable factory overhead	5	16
Total variable manufacturing cost per unit	$30 (per engine)	$50 (per mower)
Fixed factory overhead	$500,000	$200,000

Selling, general and administrative costs:
Variable $20 per mower sold
Fixed $300,000

Yardgirl has recently been offered $70 per engine for 5,000 engines for the coming year and must decide whether or not to accept this offer.

Required: 1. Prepare schedules that show the expected profit for each alternative. State what the company's decision should be.

2. What minimum price per engine would make the offer acceptable?

P26-5A   Incremental Costs. Gordon Dairy is considering leasing five large delivery trucks to replace six smaller trucks currently used for commercial deliveries in the area. Lease payments on these trucks would be $26,000 per year per truck. Gordon now pays $15,000 per year to lease each of the small trucks.

Each of the small trucks currently makes two delivery runs each day, 312 days each year. The average length of these delivery runs is 100 miles, taking 5 hours to complete. The large trucks would have to make only one delivery run each day, 312 days each year. These runs would average 200 miles and would take 8 hours to complete. Drivers earn $5.00 per hour.

Small trucks cost $10 to load and their operating costs average $.20 per mile. The large trucks would cost $20 to load and their operating costs would average $.25 per mile.

Required: 1. Compute the expected costs of making deliveries using the small trucks and the large trucks. What size truck should the dairy use?

2. Suppose the drivers' wages are raised to $6.25 per hour. How is the decision affected?

P26-6A Product Mix Decision. Boothe Electronics manufactures three small electronic games that are in high demand. Unfortunately, one component, a small integrated circuit costing $.50, used in making all three games is in short supply. Boothe's supplier of this component is willing to promise only 10,000 units per month. Manufacturing costs for the three games are shown below:

	Game A	Game B	Game C
Direct materials:			
Integrated circuits	$ .50	$ 2.50	$ 1.50
Other	2.00	3.00	4.00
Direct labor	3.00	4.50	4.20
Variable overhead	1.00	1.50	1.30
Fixed overhead	2.00	3.00	2.60
Total manufacturing costs per unit	$8.50	$14.50	$13.60

Game A sells for $10. Games B and C both sell for $16.00. Variable selling costs are $.50 per game sold for each of the three games. Fixed selling and general and administrative costs total $2,000 per month. Boothe estimates the demand per month for the three games to be: Game A: 7,000 units, game B: 3,000 units, and game C: 2,000 units.

Required: 1. Compute the contribution margin of each of the three games per unit of the scarce resource (the integrated circuit).
2. Determine the combination of production quantities for the three products that gives the highest total monthly contribution margin. Compute this total contribution margin.
3. Prepare an analysis to answer each of the following two *independent* questions.
   (a) What is the highest monthly contribution margin that can be earned if at least 500 games of each type are manufactured per month?
   (b) How much should Boothe be willing to pay for advertising per month to increase demand for game A by 3,000 units per month?

PROBLEMS

Part B

P26-1B Make or Buy Decision. Meyer Tool Company currently manufactures component B61, which it uses in the assembly of its main product. Cost estimates to make the component are as follows:

Direct materials	$ 4.00 per unit
Direct labor	5.00 per unit
Variable overhead	4.50 per unit
Fixed overhead	$25,000 per year

Required: 1. Prepare an analysis to answer each of the following *independent* questions.
   (a) Assume that all variable costs are avoidable and that the company needs 3,000 components annually. How much of the fixed overhead must be avoidable in order for the company to prefer to buy the components from an outside supplier at $15 per unit instead of continuing to make them?
   (b) Assume that all variable costs are avoidable, that the company needs 3,000 components annually, and that only $1,500 of fixed costs are avoidable. Below what component purchase price per unit would the company prefer to buy the components from an outside supplier instead of continuing to make them?
   (c) Assume that all variable costs are avoidable, that $2,500 of fixed overhead is avoidable, and that the purchase price of the component is $18.50 per unit. Below what number of components needed would the company prefer to buy the components from an outside supplier instead of continuing to make them?

2. Suppose fixed overhead costs include:

Rent	$10,000
Depreciation: Equipment	9,600
Property taxes	1,300
Foreman's salary	3,000
Routine maintenance	500
Utilities	600
Total	$25,000

Why might some of the $25,000 of fixed costs that Meyer has assigned to production of component B61 be unavoidable if the company decides to buy rather than make the component?

P26-2B **Deciding Which Product to Advertise.** The Import Products Company has just completed a study suggesting that sales of its two products could be increased by spending more on advertising. The following table shows how many additional units of each of the two products could be sold if advertising for each is increased:

Amount Spent on Product A	Additional Sales of Product A	Amount Spent on Product B	Additional Sales of Product B
$1,000	400 units	$1,000	400 units
2,000	800	2,000	800
3,000	1,100	3,000	1,200
4,000	1,200	4,000	1,600

Product A has a contribution margin of $7.00 per unit and product B has a contribution margin of $6.00 per unit. The company has a total of $4,000 to spend on additional advertising.

Required:
1. Compute the increase in the company's profit if the $4,000 is spent on advertising product A alone.
2. Compute the increase in the company's profit if the $4,000 is spent on advertising product B alone.
3. Compute the increase in the company's profit if only $3,000 is spent on advertising product A alone.
4. Compare your answers to Requirements 1 and 3 and explain the answers obtained.
5. Write a recommendation for the company telling them how much additional advertising to spend on each product (up to $4,000 total) in order to increase profit by the greatest amount.

P26-3B **Dropping a Product.** The Redbird Company sells products X and Y. Redbird is considering dropping one of these products because of slumping sales. The company is currently selling 15,000 units of product X and earning $5 contribution margin per unit of X. It is selling 30,000 units of product Y and earning $2 contribution margin per unit of this product.

Redbird currently incurs $140,000 of fixed cost, $50,000 of which can be avoided if product X is dropped. If product Y is dropped, $68,000 of fixed cost can be avoided.

Required:
1. Compute Redbird's current profit.
2. Compute Redbird's expected profit if product X is dropped.
3. Compute Redbird's expected profit if product Y is dropped.
4. Compute Redbird's expected profit if product Y is dropped and 20% of the expected sales volume of product X is lost as a result.
5. Think of an item that you buy sometimes, which if it were discontinued might cause you not to buy another product made by the same company. How are these products related? Discuss.

P26-4B Sell or Process Further. Earlybird Industries makes and sells clock radios that are in such high demand that the company has operated both of its departments at their maximum capacity for several years. The company expects to be able to sell all of the clock radios it can produce for many years at $40 per unit. The major reason for the popularity of the Earlybird clock radio is its accurate and reliable clock. The clock units are manufactured in department A. They are mounted in the radio unit (purchased from an outside supplier) in department B. Cost and other information on the company's operations are shown below:

	Department A	Department B
Expected production (maximum capacity)	20,000 clocks	20,000 clock radios
Variable manufacturing cost per unit:		
Direct materials	$4	$12 (excluding clocks)
Direct labor	3	3
Variable factory overhead	1	1
Total variable manufacturing cost per unit	$8 (per clock)	$16 (per clock radio)
Fixed factory overhead	$80,000	$50,000

Selling, general and administrative costs:
    Variable $2 per clock radio sold
    Fixed $30,000

Earlybird has recently been offered $15 per clock for 5,000 clocks for the coming year and must decide whether or not to accept this offer.

Required: 1. Prepare schedules that show the expected profit for each alternative. State what the company's decision should be.

            2. What minimum price per clock would make the offer acceptable?

P26-5B Incremental Costs. Golden Bakery is considering leasing two large delivery trucks to replace three smaller trucks currently used for commercial deliveries in the area. Lease payments on these large trucks would be $8,500 per year per truck. Golden now pays $5,000 per year to lease each of the small trucks.

Each of the small trucks currently makes two delivery runs each day, 312 days each year. The average length of these delivery runs is 90 miles, taking 5 hours to complete. The large trucks would have to make only one delivery run each day, 312 days each year. These runs would average 170 miles and would take 8 hours to complete. Drivers earn $4.00 per hour.

Small trucks cost $6 to load and their operating costs average $.15 per mile. The large trucks would cost $20 to load and their operating costs would average $.30 per mile.

Required: 1. Compute the expected costs of making deliveries using the small trucks and the large trucks. What size truck should the bakery use?

            2. Mike Van Hove, the owner of the bakery, favors leasing the large trucks. He estimates that the increased price of gasoline would raise operating costs by $.10 per mile for the large trucks and by $.04 per mile for the small trucks, however. Determine whether or not this increase in gasoline prices should affect the decision for the bakery.

P26-6B Product Mix Decision. Electronics Unlimited manufactures three small electronic games that are in high demand. Unfortunately, one component—a small momentary switch costing $.25, used to make all three games—is in short supply. Due to a strike at the supplier's factory, the company has to operate this month with the 25,000 switches it already has in inventory. Manufacturing costs for the three games are shown on the following page:

	Game A	Game B	Game C
Direct materials:			
Switches	$ .50	$ 2.00	$ 1.50
Other	2.00	3.00	2.50
Direct labor	4.00	5.00	6.00
Variable overhead	2.00	2.50	3.00
Fixed overhead	1.00	1.25	1.50
Total manufacturing cost per unit	$9.50	$13.75	$14.50

Game A sells for $12, game B for $17.50, and game C for $20. Variable selling costs are $1.00 per game sold for each of the three games. Fixed selling and general and administrative costs total $2,000 per month. The company estimates demand this month for the three games to be: Game A: 6,000 units, game B: 3,000 units, and game C: 2,000 units.

Required:
1. Compute the contribution margin of each of the three games per unit of the scarce resource (the momentary switch).
2. Determine the combination of production quantities for the three products that gives the highest total contribution margin this month. Compute this total contribution margin.
3. Prepare an analysis for this company to answer each of the following two *independent* questions.
   (a) What is the highest monthly contribution margin that can be earned if at least 1,000 games of each type are manufactured this month?
   (b) The company can increase the demand for game A by 10,000 units this month by spending $20,000 on advertising. Would it be a good idea to make this expenditure? Discuss.

DISCUSSION CASES

C26-1 Make or Buy Decision. Burrell Manufacturing produces quality tools for woodworking. Burrell has been forced to increase prices by about 40% over the last few years, mostly because of increased costs of purchased components and other direct materials used in the manufacture of its products. Although Burrell will always have a market for its products among craftsmen who appreciate quality, the company is losing much of its business to companies manufacturing low-quality tools. Some of Burrell's departments are operating at about half of their practical capacity.

Jacob Burrell, the company's founder and president, would not allow his name to be associated with poor quality tools. He feels that some price reductions are necessary, however, to keep sales from falling. He is more concerned about providing jobs for his employees than earning a large profit. If sales fall much further he will not be able to do either, however. Not a single employee has been laid off, nor has anyone received less than a full paycheck even though many skilled machinists have pushed brooms and done odd jobs these last few months.

Recently, one of Jake's foremen suggested that the company attempt to manufacture some of the components currently being purchased. The president and his foreman talked at great length, finally choosing a ¾-inch chuck that is used on hand drills, drill presses, and lathes for a careful study. Everyone was quite excited when it was determined that the kind of equipment needed to manufacture the chuck was owned by the company and currently not in use. Production would be no problem for the skilled machinists employed by Burrell.

It took about a week for Jake's accountant to find all the information necessary to prepare the report shown on the following page:

Dec. 15

Dear Jake,

I'm sorry to report that after careful study of the costs of manufacturing ¾-inch chucks, I've concluded that we can't afford to make them. We currently use about 1,000 chucks of this size per month and are now buying them for $6.50 each. The costs to manufacture 1,000 units per month would be:

Direct materials	$1,850
Direct labor	1,900
Variable overhead	1,175
Fixed overhead	3,800
Total	$8,725

I'm sorry to bring you this bad news just before the holidays, Jake. We buy hundreds of other components. Perhaps one of them would be cheaper to make than to buy. I'll be glad to make the cost estimates.

Otto Schmidt

Otto Schmidt

Required: Prepare a brief analysis of this situation and recommend to Mr. Burrell whether his company should make or buy this component and whether it would be worthwhile to also consider making rather than buying other components.

C26-2 Relevant Costs. Sunnydays Nursery School has been in operation for about five years. The school has never had any trouble filling its limits of 36 children for either the morning or afternoon sessions, and 18 children who stay all day and are served a hot lunch. Currently, monthly tuition is $60 for half-day children and $120 for all-day children. The school has a long waiting list of children whose parents want to enroll them for half days.

All-day children have never been accepted at the school unless their parents qualify for aid under the state's day-care program. Under this program the state pays half of the monthly tuition up to a maximum of $100. New regulations that take effect January 1 would require accreditation before state funds can be paid under this program. This would require that at least one teacher be certified by the state for teaching at the preschool level. Currently, none of the school's three teachers can qualify for certification.

The director of the school feels that the loss of state funds would pose a serious threat to the school. She believes that a certified teacher could be hired, although it would cost the school $900 per month.

Tuition could be raised to $75 for half-day children and $150 for all-day children per month. The director is uncertain how this would affect enrollment, however. Alternatively, the school could give up the all-day children who currently receive aid. Several other day-care centers in town (some charging as little as $100 per month) have room to take all of the all-day children.

Monthly operating costs for the school are shown on the following page:

Sunnydays Nursery School
Monthly Operating Costs

Rent	$ 300
Utilities	160
Salaries	2,400
Insurance	100
Toys and supplies[a]	360
Lunches[b]	378
Total monthly cost	$3,698

[a] Variable at rates of $5 per half-day child per month and $10 per all-day child per month.

[b] Variable at a rate of $21 per all-day child per month.

Required: Assume that the director has reviewed all possible choices and has reduced the decision to two possible alternatives: (1) to close the all-day program, not to raise tuition, and not to hire the new teacher; and (2) to keep the all-day program open, to raise tuition, and to hire the new teacher. Discuss how the volume of activity could be measured for the nursery school and why volume is important in the analysis of these two alternatives. List the costs and revenues that you think will be relevant in the analysis of these two alternatives and give a reason for including each on the list.

27

Long-Term Investment Decisions

After reading this chapter, you should understand:

- The nature of investment decisions
- How to associate cash flows with investment proposals
- The payback period computation and its limitations as a basis for investment decisions
- The average rate of return computation and its limitations as a basis for investment decisions
- The net present value computation and its use in a sound, general approach to investment decision making

Recall from the discussion of present values and future values in Chapter 16 that money has a time value. That is, because cash can be invested to earn a return, a dollar today is worth more than a dollar a year from today. The time value of money is a real and important fact of business life and should be considered whenever it is likely to have an impact on business decision making.

Chapter 26 discussed short-term decisions that were made by comparing the costs and revenues that differed between the alternatives of the decisions. In short-term decision making we did not consider the time value of money because the relevant costs and revenues were assumed to involve cash payments and receipts occurring at about the same time. Thus it was not necessary to adjust for timing differences between the cash flows. In contrast, the decisions discussed in this chapter *do* require that we consider the time value of money. In this chapter an understanding of present value computations is assumed. A review of our discussion in Chapter 16 of present value computations and the use of the present value tables shown in Appendix B will be helpful.

**INVESTMENT
DECISIONS AND
THEIR
EVALUATION**

Long-term decisions are decisions that affect cash receipts and payments several years into the future. In this chapter we are concerned with a particular type of long-term decision, the investment decision. **Investment decisions are long-term decisions in which a company (the investor) makes a cash payment (investment) at the time of the decision in order to obtain future net cash inflows totaling more than the investment.** When a cash inflow exceeds a cash outflow, the difference is called a *net* cash inflow. The excess of the net cash inflows over the investment made to obtain them provides a "return" on the investment. It is the prospect of earning this return that makes companies want to invest.

Long-term investment decisions involve cash outflows (payments) early in the period affected by the decision and net cash inflows at future dates (often many years later). Thus it is important that the analysis used to make long-term investment decisions consider the time value of money. Dollars received in the future simply are not worth as much as dollars paid today. As a result any measurement of the expected return on an investment should adjust for the difference in timing between cash inflows and outflows.

Most companies have a large number and wide variety of investment opportunities each year. They can expand factory or office size, replace old equipment, purchase additional new equipment, introduce new products, increase inventories, buy securities of other companies or government units, start an employee training program, or engage in a special advertising campaign. These opportunities normally come to the attention of a company's top management in the form of *proposals* to invest cash. Whenever a company considers investing cash in such proposals to earn a return in future years, the decision is an investment decision.

The return from some investments comes from future cash inflows only. An example of this would be where a company purchases stocks or bonds of another company with no intent to become involved in the other company's activities. The dividends or interest received plus the eventual selling price of the securities (all cash inflows) provide a return when they exceed the amount invested in the securities.

In other cases both future cash inflows and outflows are affected by the investment. For example, a company may invest in additional plant and equipment to be able to produce and sell a larger quantity of a product. If cash inflows from increased sales are more than cash outflows for increased production and selling costs, the increase in net cash inflows provides a return on the investment when it exceeds the amount invested in the additional plant and equipment.

Finally, some investments do not involve increasing cash inflows, but instead involve reducing cash outflows. The effect on a company from a reduction in future cash outflows, however, is the same as from an increase in future cash inflows. The future benefit received by the decrease in cash outflows can also provide a return on the investment. For example, suppose that a local newspaper believes that investing $3,000 today in an employee training program might be expected to save $1,000 in payments for labor costs each year for 5 years. This investment has the same expected return for the newspaper as would investing $3,000 to increase receipts from sales of advertising space in the paper by $1,000 each year for 5 years. In both cases *net* cash inflows of $1,000 per year for 5 years are provided by the investment.

The return on an investment comes from the receipt of future cash inflows or *net* cash inflows (or the reduction of future cash outflows) in an amount totaling more than the investment. For example, if a $100 investment provides a net cash inflow of $121 two years later, a return is earned on the investment. The receipt of $121 can be thought of as the sum of (1) a return *of* the investment ($100), plus (2) a return *on* the investment ($21). Several methods are used to evaluate whether or not to make an investment. Before discussing the basics of good investment decision making, we briefly describe two procedures that have been used over the years (and are still being used) by some companies to make investment decisions.

The Payback Period

The payback period is the length of time required for a return *of* the investment. That is, it is the length of time needed for the future net cash inflows to "pay back" the investment. For example, suppose that an investment of $1,000 would provide net cash inflows of $200 in the first year, $500 in the second, $900 in the third, and $500 in the fourth year following the investment. The payback period can be computed from the following tabulation:

	Amount Unpaid at Beginning of Year	Net Cash Inflow Expected	Amount Left Unpaid at Year End
Year 1	$1,000	$200	$800
Year 2	800	500	300
Year 3	300	900	—

This tabulation shows that $700 of the investment would be paid back by the end of the second year. Since only $300 of the investment would remain unpaid at the end of the second year, and $900 of net cash inflows are expected in the third year, the $300 would be paid back one-third ($300/$900) of the way through year 3. Thus the payback period is $2\frac{1}{3}$ years.

The payback period computation is easier when net cash inflows are expected to be the same each year. For example, an investment of $600 that results in $200 of net cash inflows each year for 5 years would have a payback period of 3 years ($600 investment divided by $200 paid back per year). The computation of the payback period can be shown in equation form below:

$$\text{Payback period} = \frac{\text{Investment}}{\text{Net cash inflow per year}} = \frac{\$600}{\$200} = 3 \text{ years}$$

The payback period computation is sometimes used to determine whether or not an investment proposal should be accepted. This is done by setting a maximum payback period for acceptable investment proposals. An investment proposal with a longer payback period would not be acceptable. In addition, the payback period is sometimes used to judge whether one investment proposal is better than another. The investment proposal with the shorter payback period is judged to be better.

Unfortunately, the payback period is not a good measure for either purpose. To demonstrate that this statement is true, assume that a company is considering three investment proposals, A, B, and C. The amount of investment in each is $600. The cash inflows differ, however. Proposal A would provide net cash inflows of $300 per year for 2 years, while proposal B would provide $200 per year for 5 years. Proposal C would provide $100 each year for 9 years and $1,000,000 in the tenth year. The payback periods of these three investment proposals are shown on the following page:

	Payback Period
Proposal A	2 years ($600 ÷ $300)
Proposal B	3 years ($600 ÷ $200)
Proposal C	6 years ($600 ÷ $100)

If 5 years is the largest acceptable payback period, proposals A and B would be judged acceptable, but proposal C would not (since its payback period exceeds 5 years). In addition, if investment proposals with shorter payback periods are judged to be better, proposal A would be preferred to proposal B. Both of these judgments (the rejection of proposal C and the preference for A over B) are incorrect, however. Although proposal A provides a return *of* its $600 investment faster than proposal B, it provides no return *on* the investment (the $600 total cash inflows exactly equal the $600 investment). Proposal B provides a return of its $600 investment plus a $400 return on the investment and is therefore clearly better than proposal A. Although investment proposal C provides a return of its $600 investment more slowly than proposals A and B, the large size of the return on the investment (over $1 million) makes it unquestionably the best of the three investments.

Although the above example is somewhat extreme, it illustrates the problem of using the payback period to make investment decisions. The problem is that the payback period focuses on the return *of* the investment and completely ignores the return *on* the investment. The payback period computation, by itself, cannot provide a sound basis for investment decisions.

The Average Rate of Return on Investment

Another measure that is sometimes used in making investment decisions is the average rate of return on investment. **The average rate of return on investment is the average return *on* investment per year, per dollar invested.** It is usually expressed as a percent per year. The average rate of return on investment is computed by dividing the total net cash inflows from an investment (the return on investment) by the number of years over which the cash inflows are received times the dollars invested. This computation is shown in equation form below. Total net cash inflows equal total cash inflows minus total cash outflows (including the investment itself).

$$\text{Average rate of return on investment} = \frac{\text{Total cash inflows} - \text{Total cash outflows}}{\text{Years} \times \text{Investment}}$$

For example, suppose that investment proposal D requires an investment of $100 and promises net cash inflows of $20 per year for 4 years and $200 in the fifth year. The average rate of return on investment for proposal D is

$$\text{Average rate of return on investment} = \frac{(\$20 + \$20 + \$20 + \$20 + \$200) - \$100}{5 \times \$100}$$

$$= 36\% \text{ per year}$$

In contrast to the payback period computation, the average rate of return does consider the return *on* investment. The average rate of return on investment, however, also does not provide a good basis for making investment decisions. The reason is that it does not consider the time value of money. For example, consider investment proposal E, which has the same initial investment and cash inflows as proposal D, but the timing of the cash inflows is different. That is, proposal E requires a $100 investment and promises a cash inflow of $200 the first year followed by $20 per year for 4 additional years. Proposal E, like proposal D, also has a 36% per year average rate of return on investment. By averaging the cash flows, the average rate of return on investment computation loses track of the timing differences between the cash flows. Although proposals D and E both have a 36% per year average rate of return, proposal E is better than proposal D because the large inflow ($200) occurs earlier in the life of investment E than it does in proposal D (year 1 rather than year 5); therefore it is worth more to the company because of the time value of money. In order for measurements to provide a correct basis for investment decisions, they must consider the time value of money.

Time-Adjusted Rate of Return on Investment

Fortunately, there is a measure of the rate of return expected to be earned on an investment proposal that correctly considers the time value of money. This measure is called the time-adjusted rate of return (or the *internal* rate of return) of the proposal. **The time-adjusted rate of return of an investment proposal is the compound interest rate that would allow the investment to grow just large enough to provide exactly the proposal's expected cash receipts at the times they are expected.**

Consider two investment proposals, F and G, both of which require an investment of $263.07. Proposal F would provide a cash receipt of $250 after 1 year and $50 after 2 years. Proposal G would provide a cash receipt of $50 after 1 year and $250 after 2 years. These proposals have the same total cash receipts ($300) over the 2 years. Only the timing of the receipts differs. Because of the timing difference, however, proposals F and G have different time-adjusted rates of return. Proposal F has a rate of 12% and proposal G has a rate of 7.45%.

Exhibit 27-1 shows that if the investment of $263.07 grows at 12%, it would be just sufficient to provide the cash receipts of proposal F and that if it grows at 7.45% it would be just sufficient to provide the cash receipts of proposal G. Exhibit 27-1 does not show how these rates are computed; it shows only that these are the correct time-adjusted rates of return for the two proposals.

Exhibit 27-1 shows that the investment of $263.07 in proposal F earns interest of $31.57 ($263.07 × 12%) and thus grows to $294.64 at the end of year 1. The receipt of $250 at the end of year 1 reduces the investment to $44.64 ($294.64 − $250). The $44.64 left invested for the second year earns interest of $5.36, growing to $50. The receipt of $50 at the end of the second year reduces the investment to zero.

Similarly, Exhibit 27-1 shows that the investment of $263.07 in proposal G would earn interest of $19.60 ($263.07 × 7.45%) during year 1, thereby growing to $282.67 by the end of that year. The receipt of $50 at the end of year 1 reduces the amount remaining invested for year 2 to $232.67. This amount earns interest during year 2 of $17.33 ($232.67 × 7.45%). The total amount accumulated at the

EXHIBIT 27-1 Growth and Repayment of Investment in Proposals F and G

Investment Proposal F					
	(1) Investment at Beginning of Year	*(2)* Interest Earned *(at 12%)*	*(3) = (1) + (2)* Total Accumulated at End of Year	*(4)* End-of-Year Cash Receipt	*(5) = (3) − (4)* Remaining Investment at End of Year
Year 1	$263.07	$31.57	$294.64	$250.00	$44.64
Year 2	44.64	5.36	50.00	50.00	0.00
Investment Proposal G					
	(1) Investment at Beginning of Year	*(2)* Interest Earned *(at 7.45%)*	*(3) = (1) + (2)* Total Accumulated at End of Year	*(4)* End-of-Year Cash Receipt	*(5) = (3) − (4)* Remaining Investment at End of Year
Year 1	$263.07	$19.60	$282.67	$ 50.00	$232.67
Year 2	232.67	17.33	250.00	250.00	0.00

end of year 2 is $250. The receipt of $250 at that time reduces the investment to zero.

For each proposal, the time-adjusted rate of return allows the investment to grow just large enough to provide the receipts expected. Since the total receipts over 2 years are $300 for each proposal, the *average* rate of return on investment would be $36.93 ($300 − $263.07) divided by $526.14 (2 × $263.07), or 7.02% for each proposal in spite of the difference in timing of the receipts. The time-adjusted rate of return correctly recognizes the time value of money, however, and shows a higher rate of return (12%) for proposal F than for proposal G (7.45%). Thus the time adjusted rate of return provides a correct basis for investment decision making.

Making Investment Decisions — The General Approach

The general approach to making investment decisions involves the following two steps:

1. Identify acceptable investment proposals by applying a correct method of analysis (one that considers the time value of money) to the estimated cash flows of each proposal.
2. Select from the acceptable proposals the investments that the company should make.

In the next two sections of this chapter we discuss methods that can be used in these two steps. We begin by describing a correct method for identifying acceptable investment proposals.

IDENTIFYING ACCEPTABLE INVESTMENT PROPOSALS

As a general rule, the higher the expected time-adjusted rate of return of an investment proposal, the better the proposal would be for the company. The first thing a company must do to identify *acceptable* proposals is to determine how high the time-adjusted rate of return of a proposal must be to make the investment a desirable one.

The Minimum Acceptable Rate of Return

The time-adjusted rate of return used as a *cutoff* to distinguish between acceptable and unacceptable investment proposals should be the company's cost of capital. **A company's cost of capital is the weighted-average cost (rate of return) it must pay to all sources of investment capital — to short-term creditors, to holders of long-term notes and company bonds, and to stockholders.**

In this text we are not concerned with computing a company's cost of capital. We stress that a proper cutoff rate must be set and used consistently in evaluating investment proposals, however, to identify proposals that would benefit the company and those that would not. Throughout the remainder of this chapter and in the homework materials we refer to this cutoff rate as the company's **minimum acceptable rate of return.**

Using the Minimum Acceptable Rate of Return

The minimum acceptable rate of return can be used in several ways to identify acceptable investment proposals. We briefly consider one method known as the time-adjusted rate of return method, although we concentrate on a second method known as the net present value method, which is easier to use.

THE TIME-ADJUSTED RATE OF RETURN METHOD.   An investment proposal is acceptable to a company when its expected time-adjusted rate of return is greater than the company's minimum acceptable rate of return. This idea suggests one approach to evaluating an investment proposal, computing the proposal's expected time-adjusting rate of return and comparing it with the minimum acceptable rate of return. If the expected time-adjusted rate of return exceeds the minimum acceptable rate of return, the proposed investment is acceptable. If not, the proposal is not acceptable.

This approach is often used to identify acceptable investment proposals. It is not always easy to apply, however. The reason is that determining the expected time-adjusted rate of return of an investment proposal can sometimes be very difficult. Therefore many companies use an equivalent, but easier, approach, which we discuss and illustrate in this section.

THE NET PRESENT VALUE METHOD.   The alternative approach is the net present value method. This method involves a three-step process: (1) finding the present value of the expected future cash inflows from the investment proposal, (2) finding the present value of the cash outflows expected (the required initial investment as well as any future cash outflows), and (3) comparing these two present values.[1] **The net present value of an investment proposal is the present value of its cash inflows minus the present value of its cash outflows.** If the minimum acceptable rate of return is used as the discount rate, the net present value of an investment proposal will always be *positive* whenever the time-adjusted rate of return of the proposal is greater than the minimum acceptable rate of return. Thus an investment proposal can be identified as acceptable or not by discounting its expected cash flows at the minimum acceptable rate of return and looking at its net present value. An investment proposal is acceptable when it has a *positive* net present value, and it is not acceptable when it has a *negative* net present value.

Consider the following simple example. The Dextron Company has an investment proposal that it is evaluating. If Dextron invests $100 today, it would receive a single cash inflow of $133.10 three years from today. Exhibit 27-2 shows the computations of the net present value of this investment proposal, first assuming 8% to be the minimum acceptable rate of return, and then using 12% as the minimum acceptable rate of return.

Note in Exhibit 27-2 that the net present value of the cash flows from accepting the investment proposal are found by subtracting the present value of the cash outflows from the present value of the cash inflows. The present values of these cash flows are computed at the time of the decision (which we assume is when the investment is made) and the minimum acceptable rate of return is used as the discount rate for the present value computations. In these computations the future amount at the end of 3 years is multiplied by the present value of $1 factor (for 3 years) taken from Table 2 in Appendix B. Note also that the initial investment required is *not* discounted because its amount is already stated at its present value at the time of the decision.

The present value (at 12%) of the single cash inflow of $133.10 to be received after 3 years is $94.74 ($133.10 × .711780). This means that if $94.74 is invested at 12%, it will increase to $133.10 in 3 years. Since the larger investment required by this proposal ($100) increases only to $133.10 in 3 years, it must be increasing (earning interest) at a lower rate than 12%. Thus if 12% is the minimum acceptable rate of return, the proposal under study is not acceptable. This is shown in Exhibit 27-2 by the *negative* net present value of $5.26.

When the 8% rate is used, however, the present value of the $133.10 cash inflow is $105.66 ($133.10 × .793832). This means that if $105.66 is invested at 8%, it will increase to $133.10 after 3 years. Since the smaller investment required by this proposal ($100) increases to $133.10 in 3 years, this investment must be increasing at a higher rate than 8%. Thus if the minimum acceptable rate of return is 8%, this

---

[1] Sometimes future cash outflows are subtracted from future cash inflows occurring at the same time. If the result is a net cash *inflow*, its present value is found as part of step (1). If the result is a net cash *outflow*, its present value is found as part of step (2). This procedure simplifies the net present value computation and does not affect the computed amount. It may be necessary at this point to review our discussion in Chapter 16 of present value computations and the use of the present value tables shown in Appendix B.

EXHIBIT 27-2
Net Present Value
Computations

THE DEXTRON COMPANY
Net Present Value Computations

Minimum acceptable rate of return = 12%

	Future Amount		Present Value of $1 Factor[a]		Present Value
Cash inflow at the end of 3 years	$133.10	×	.711780	=	$ 94.74
Cash outflow now (investment)					(100.00)
Net present value					$ (5.26)

Minimum acceptable rate of return = 8%

	Future Amount		Present Value of $1 Factor[a]		Present Value
Cash inflow at the end of 3 years	$133.10	×	.793832	=	$105.66
Cash outflow now (investment)					(100.00)
Net present value					$ 5.66

[a] From Table 2 in Appendix B.

proposal is acceptable. This is shown by the *positive* net present value of $5.66 computed in Exhibit 27-2.

To show that the net present value computations are properly evaluating the acceptability of this investment proposal, observe that the future value of $100 invested at *10%* after 3 years is $133.10 (either by referring to the computations shown in the present value and future value discussion in Chapter 16 or by using Table 1 in Appendix B to compute the future value of $100 invested for 3 years at 10%). This proposal earns a 10% time-adjusted rate of return. Thus if the minimum acceptable rate of return is 12%, the proposal is not acceptable. This is correctly shown by the negative net present value of $5.26 computed in Exhibit 27-2. On the other hand, if the minimum acceptable rate of return were 8%, the proposal that earns 10% would clearly be acceptable. Again the positive net present value of $5.66 computed in Exhibit 27-2 (discounting at 8%) correctly evaluates the proposal.

The time-adjusted rate of return of an investment proposal is the rate that, when used to discount the cash flows resulting from the proposal, gives a net present value of *zero*. It can be found by "trial and error." The procedure involves repeatedly computing the net present value of the cash flows of a proposal at different discount rates until the discount rate that results in a net present value of zero is found. That rate is the time-adjusted rate of return for the investment proposal. Computation of the time-adjusted rate of return can be very time-consuming. Because the acceptability of investment proposals can be judged without actually computing the time-adjusted rate of return as we have just shown, we use the simpler net present value method for the rest of this chapter.

Associating Cash Flows with Decision Alternatives

Perhaps the hardest part of long-term investment decision making is to properly associate cash flows with the decision alternatives. In this section we discuss several factors the managerial accountant should consider in this part of the decision analysis. They include the measurement of relevant cash flows and the treatment of depreciation.

RELEVANT CASH FLOWS. In the chapter on short-term decision making, we stressed the importance of determining the activities required for each of a decision's alternatives so that the relevant costs and revenues could be identified. This kind of careful study is also very important in long-term investment decision making. It is just as important to recognize relevant cash flows as it is to recognize relevant costs and revenues. **Relevant cash flows are future cash flows that differ, either in *amount* or in *timing*, depending upon which decision alternative is chosen.** The reason cash flows (either cash inflows or cash outflows) that differ in amount or in timing are relevant is that their effect on the net present value of each alternative is different.

Cash inflows and outflows that have occurred *prior* to the decision are irrelevant because they cannot be affected by the decision. Cash flows that result from activities *not* required for a decision's alternatives also cannot be relevant (even if they are future cash flows) because they cannot be affected by the alternative chosen. Finally, future cash flows are not relevant if they occur at the same times and their amounts are the same for each alternative. To be relevant to a particular investment decision, cash flows must occur in the future as a result of activities required for the decision's alternatives and must differ in amount or in timing.[2]

Most revenues and expenses of a company result in cash receipts and payments (inflows and outflows) of the same amounts at approximately the same points in time. For example, cash is usually collected from credit sales very soon after the sale. Similarly, wages are normally paid to employees soon after they are earned. As a result, cash receipts from accounts receivable and cash payments for wages in a year are likely to be about the same as the sales revenues and wages expense for the year. When large differences occur, however, they should be considered. Sometimes expenses are prepaid for several years, for example. The amount of the cash payment and the year in which it is paid are important in this analysis, but the annual expense is not.

THE TREATMENT OF DEPRECIATION. Depreciation is a major expense for which the related cash flows occur in different years and in different amounts than does the depreciation expense. For example, if a machine is to be purchased for $1,000 and used until it is sold at the end of 10 years for $100, the total depreciation over the

---

[2] One set of cash flows is being ignored in this chapter, the cash outflows associated with the payment of income taxes. When the decision alternative chosen affects the amount or timing of income tax payments, the income tax payments become relevant cash outflows that must be considered for a proper evaluation of the decision's alternatives. We ignore these cash flows because treating them would only complicate the introductory discussion of this chapter.

10 years is $900. If the straight-line depreciation method is used, the resulting depreciation expense would be $90 in each of the 10 years. No $90 cash outflow occurs in any of those years, however.

Only two cash flows are associated with the purchase and resale of this machine. The first is the cash outflow of $1,000 required to purchase the machine. The second is the $100 cash inflow to be received at the end of year 10. An investment analysis should focus on the amounts and timing of these cash flows and *not* on the $90 yearly depreciation expense in order to properly compute a net present value. It is important to understand that we are not ignoring this major element of cost, but we are simply treating it in a different way.

MEASURING CASH FLOW CHANGES FROM THE "DO NOTHING" ALTERNATIVE. Investment decisions are decisions involving whether or not to do something; to buy a machine or not to buy it, to expand the size of the factory or not to expand it, to introduce a new product or not to introduce it, and so on. We refer to alternatives such as *not* buying the machine, *not* expanding the size of the factory, or *not* introducing the new product as the *"do nothing"* alternative. Choosing the do nothing alternative does not change a company's cash flows. On the other hand, choosing to accept an investment proposal, whether it is to buy a new machine, expand the size of the factory, or introduce a new product, causes changes in the cash flows. In considering an investment proposal it is useful to think of the do nothing alternative as having zero cash flows and the investment alternative as having cash flows equal to the *changes* it causes.

For example, consider the following decision situation. The owner of Mac's Diner is trying to decide whether or not to buy a dishwasher. With its current operations, the diner's cash inflow is expected to be $180,000 per year, whereas an outflow of $130,000 per year is expected. The diner's kitchen would have to be rearranged slightly to make room for the dishwasher, which would have a total cost of $2,000 including installation. The machine is expected to last 4 years, save $1,000 of the diner's $20,000 wage expense per year, and have no residual value.

If the dishwasher is not purchased, the diner's net cash inflows and outflows would not change. If the dishwasher is purchased at the end of year 0 (i.e., the beginning of year 1), however, cash outflows are increased by $2,000 at that time and decreased by $1,000 at the end of each of the next 4 years.[3]

Six cash flow diagrams are presented in Exhibits 27-3 through 27-5. Each exhibit shows cash flows (in thousands of dollars) related to the two decision alternatives, to invest in the dishwasher or not to (to do nothing). In each diagram a horizontal line is drawn to represent time. The numbered points on this "time line" are the *ends* of years 0 through 4. These diagrams show cash inflows as arrows pointing *upward*

---

[3] Although the cash receipts and payments of a company may flow continuously through a year, the assumption that they flow at the end of the year simplifies present value computations. While slightly inaccurate, this assumption is common practice in analyzing investment decisions. We use this assumption throughout this chapter and in all homework materials. We also assume that investments are made at the time of the decision, which we consider to be the end of year 0 (i.e., the beginning of year 1).

EXHIBIT 27-3
Cash Flow Diagrams
(Total Cash Flows)

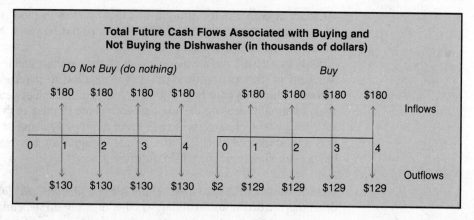

Total Future Cash Flows Associated with Buying and
Not Buying the Dishwasher (in thousands of dollars)

from the time line at the time at which they are assumed to occur. Cash outflows are shown as arrows pointing *downward* from the time line.

Notice in Exhibit 27-3 that no cash flows occurring prior to the decision have been drawn on the diagram. Thus one step has already been taken in determining relevant cash flows. *Past* cash flows have been eliminated from consideration. In Exhibit 27-3 irrelevant future cash flows have not been excluded, however.

Exhibit 27-4 shows the relevant cash flows that remain after eliminating future cash flows that would not differ.

Exhibit 27-4 shows the remaining relevant cash flows after cash receipts and payments that are not affected by the decision alternative chosen have been removed. Notice that the $180,000 of cash inflows that would not be affected by the purchase have been removed. In addition, $110,000 of cash outflows associated with expenses other than wages have been removed. The only relevant cash flows remaining are the wage payments of $20,000, which would be reduced to $19,000 by the purchase of the dishwasher and the $2,000 initial investment required for the purchase. Exhibit 27-4 still does not show the relevant cash flows in the most useful form for analysis, however.

In Exhibit 27-5 the do nothing alternative is shown with no cash flows and the alternative of investing in the dishwasher is shown with cash flows equal to the *changes* in cash flows resulting from the purchase.

EXHIBIT 27-4
Cash Flow Diagrams
(Relevant Cash Flows)

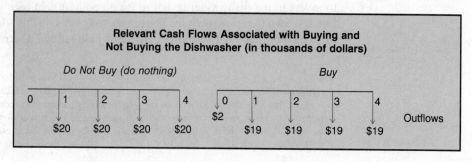

Relevant Cash Flows Associated with Buying and
Not Buying the Dishwasher (in thousands of dollars)

EXHIBIT 27-5
Cash Flow Diagrams
(Changes in Cash
Flows)

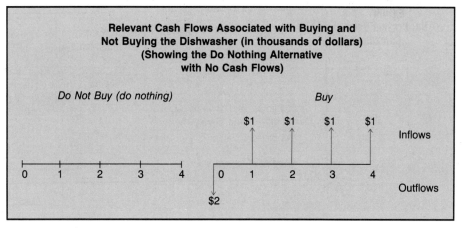

Relevant Cash Flows Associated with Buying and
Not Buying the Dishwasher (in thousands of dollars)
(Showing the Do Nothing Alternative
with No Cash Flows)

In Exhibit 27-5 the cash flow changes associated with buying the dishwasher are shown in contrast to no cash flow changes if the dishwasher is not purchased. Note that although no *actual* cash inflows are caused by purchasing the dishwasher, cash inflows of $1,000 each year are shown for the investment alternative. This is because a decrease in cash outflows is equivalent to an increase in cash inflows. Saving $1,000 in wages provides the same benefit to the diner as receiving an additional $1,000 inflow. Similarly, if purchasing the dishwasher had somehow caused a decrease in cash inflows, this would be equivalent to an increase in cash outflows.

The conversion of the cash flow diagrams in Exhibit 27-4 to those in Exhibit 27-5 is made by subtracting the cash flows at the end of each year for the do nothing alternative in Exhibit 27-4 from the cash flows at the end of each year under both alternatives in that exhibit. This results in zero cash flows if the investment is not made and in cash flows equal to the differences (changes caused by investing) between the two alternatives for the investment alternative.

There are several good reasons why it is helpful to show the changes in cash flows for the investment alternative and zero cash flows for the do nothing alternative. The first reason is that it simplifies net present value computations. Notice in Exhibit 27-5 how much less cluttered the set of cash flow diagrams is than those in the previous two exhibits. There are fewer cash flows for which present values must be computed.

A second reason is that all of the effects on cash flows of an investment proposal (like the purchase of the dishwasher in our illustration) are clearly shown on the cash flow diagram for that proposal. This makes it easier for the decision maker to understand the analysis prepared by the managerial accountant. It also makes it easier for the managerial accountant to check the analysis to make sure all relevant cash flows are included.

The most important reason for showing cash flow changes from those of the do nothing alternative for the investment proposal is that it simplifies identification of acceptable investment proposals. For the investment proposal to be acceptable, it

EXHIBIT 27-6
Net Present Value
Computation

Net Present Value Computation for Investment in the Dishwasher

	Future Amount		Present Value of an Annuity of $1 Factor at 20%[a]		Present Value
Cash inflows (end of years 1–4)	$1,000	×	2.588735	=	$2,588.74
Cash outflow (end of year 0)					(2,000.00)
Net present value					$ 588.74

[a] From Table 4 in Appendix B.

must cause *changes in cash flows* with a *positive* net present value. In addition, measuring cash flow changes from those of the do nothing alternative simplifies comparison of acceptable investment proposals (in cases to be discussed later) where not all of the proposals can be selected for investment.

Computation of the net present value of the proposal to buy the dishwasher (assuming a minimum acceptable rate of return of 20%) is shown in Exhibit 27-6.

Notice in Exhibit 27-6 that the cash outflow of $2,000 for the investment does not need to be discounted, for it is already stated at its end of year 0 value. The four $1,000 cash inflows have to be discounted at 20% to find their value as of the end of year 0. Note that the series of four $1,000 cash inflows is an *annuity* that is discounted using the present value of an annuity of $1 factor from Table 4 of Appendix B. This annuity has a present value of $2,588.74 ($1,000 × 2.588735). Since the net present value ($588.74) is positive, this investment proposal is acceptable.

SELECTING PROPOSALS FOR INVESTMENT

Investment decision making would be much easier if a company could invest in all proposals that it identified as being acceptable. This is not always possible, however. We now consider two situations in which a company must select between two or more investment proposals that have been identified as acceptable.

Mutually Exclusive Investment Proposals

Investment proposals often arise because of alternative ways to perform an activity, do a job, or provide a service. Sometimes there are several alternative ways to perform the same activity, do the same job, or provide the same service, each involving an investment. In this situation the investment alternatives are called mutually exclusive investment proposals. **Mutually exclusive investment proposals are proposals that accomplish the same thing, so that when one proposal is selected, the others are excluded.** For example, a company might be considering air conditioning its offices. Although several makes and models of air conditioners may be available, each with a different set of cash flows, one is sufficient to do the job.

THE ANALYSIS. The evaluation of a set of mutually exclusive investment proposals requires a two-step analysis. In the first step, each investment proposal is compared to the do nothing alternative using the net present value computation to determine its acceptability. If more than one proposal is acceptable (by having a positive net present value), a second step is then necessary. In the second step, one of the acceptable alternatives must be selected. Often the selection is made by choosing the proposal with the highest positive net present value. When the selection is made in this way, the analysis of the first step provides the necessary information for the choice.

AN ILLUSTRATION. Tony's Laundromat operates with 30 washing machines and 20 dryers. Tony is considering adding a do-it-yourself dry-cleaning machine. Two models are currently available.

The first model is a large capacity unit of light-weight construction. Tony believes that the unit would last 4 years if it undergoes a major overhaul costing $3,000 at the end of the second year. This unit costs $13,000 and would have no residual value. Additional cash receipts from this machine are expected to amount to $6,000 the first year, $7,000 the second, $8,000 the third, and $9,000 the fourth year. Additional cash payments for operating expenses related to this machine are expected to equal 25% of additional receipts. Thus cash outflows are expected to be $1,500 in the first year, $4,750 ($3,000 overhaul + $1,750 operating expenses) in the second, $2,000 in the third, and $2,250 in the fourth year.

The second machine is a small capacity unit of heavy-duty construction, also costing $13,000. This unit is expected to last 4 years without an overhaul and to have a residual value of $1,000 at the end of the fourth year. Additional cash receipts from this machine are expected to be $6,000 each year and operating expenses would result in cash payments of $1,000 each year. Tony's minimum acceptable rate of return is 16%.

Exhibit 27-7 shows the cash flow diagrams and net present value computations for each of the two dry-cleaning machines. Each additional cash inflow and outflow caused by the purchase of the machines is shown on the cash flow diagrams. To save computations, however, the cash outflows are subtracted from the cash inflows for each year so that only the *net cash inflows* are discounted in the net present value computation. As long as cash flows occur at the same times, they may be added or subtracted without affecting the net present value computation.

Note in Exhibit 27-7 how the net present value computation for the small machine is simplified by recognizing that the $6,000 additional receipts minus the $1,000 additional payments for the first 3 years can be discounted as a $5,000 *annuity* of three payments. In that computation the present value factor used is the present value of an annuity of $1 for 3 years at 16% taken from Table 4 in Appendix B. All of the other present value factors are taken from Table 2 in Appendix B. Note again that the initial investments are not discounted. The cash outflow for the initial investment required by each alternative, if chosen, would occur at the time of the decision (the end of year 0). This is the point in time at which we are computing

**EXHIBIT 27-7
Net Present Value
Computations**

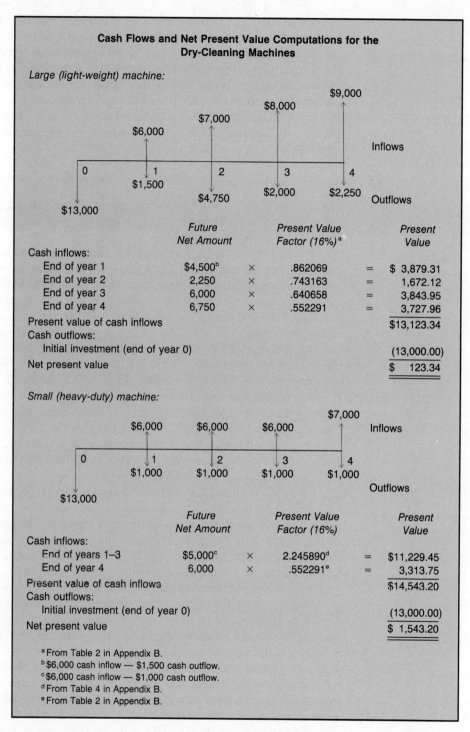

**Cash Flows and Net Present Value Computations for the
Dry-Cleaning Machines**

Large (light-weight) machine:

	Future Net Amount		Present Value Factor (16%)[a]		Present Value
Cash inflows:					
End of year 1	$4,500[b]	×	.862069	=	$ 3,879.31
End of year 2	2,250	×	.743163	=	1,672.12
End of year 3	6,000	×	.640658	=	3,843.95
End of year 4	6,750	×	.552291	=	3,727.96
Present value of cash inflows					$13,123.34
Cash outflows:					
Initial investment (end of year 0)					(13,000.00)
Net present value					$ 123.34

Small (heavy-duty) machine:

	Future Net Amount		Present Value Factor (16%)		Present Value
Cash inflows:					
End of years 1–3	$5,000[c]	×	2.245890[d]	=	$11,229.45
End of year 4	6,000	×	.552291[e]	=	3,313.75
Present value of cash inflows					$14,543.20
Cash outflows:					
Initial investment (end of year 0)					(13,000.00)
Net present value					$ 1,543.20

[a] From Table 2 in Appendix B.
[b] $6,000 cash inflow — $1,500 cash outflow.
[c] $6,000 cash inflow — $1,000 cash outflow.
[d] From Table 4 in Appendix B.
[e] From Table 2 in Appendix B.

the present values. Thus the initial investments are already stated at their present values.

The net present value computations shown in Exhibit 27-7 demonstrate that both investment proposals are acceptable (both net present values are positive). The small, heavy-duty machine would be selected because of its higher net present value, however.[4]

WHEN ONE OF THE INVESTMENT PROPOSALS MUST BE ACCEPTED. Occasionally, several mutually exclusive investment alternatives are considered with the requirement that one *must* be selected. That is, the alternative of not investing at all is not an available choice. This might occur, for example, when facilities must be obtained to satisfy a law. In such situations, the better investment alternative is the one with the highest (most positive) net present value *even if that net present value is negative*.

When not investing is an acceptable alternative, a present value of zero can always be obtained by selecting that alternative. An investment proposal would have to have a positive net present value in order to be preferred to not investing. When one of the investment proposals *must* be accepted (when not investing is unacceptable), however, the preferred investment proposal does not have to have a positive net present value. The proposal with the least negative (most positive) net present value would be chosen.

Suppose, for example, that a recently established safety ordinance requires that additional lights be added to a factory parking lot. The additional lights require a cash outflow, although they will provide no cash inflows. Normally, such an investment would not be made because it would result in a negative present value. Because of the new law, however, not investing in additional lights is not an acceptable alternative. If several proposals for additional lighting would satisfy the safety ordinance, the proposal with the least negative net present value would be chosen.

Capital Rationing   The previous analyses identified acceptable investment proposals. If a company has enough cash available, all acceptable investments would be made (including the investments selected from each set of mutually exclusive proposals). A company sometimes finds itself with a larger number of acceptable investment proposals than it can finance, however. When this occurs, the company must make its investment decisions in a situation known as capital rationing. **Capital rationing occurs when a company cannot obtain sufficient cash to make all of the investments that it would like to make.** A difficult decision problem arises when this occurs. The

---

[4] Choosing the better alternative may become more complicated when the mutually exclusive investment proposals require a different amount of investment or when the number of years over which they affect the company's cash flows differ. Procedures to handle such situations are not discussed in this book.

company must choose which of the acceptable proposals to invest in, which to delay until sufficient funds become available, and which to forget altogether, if necessary.

Many approaches to handling this problem have been suggested. A detailed study of these approaches is beyond the scope of this book, although we do discuss the general idea of two of the approaches.

THE MAXIMUM NET PRESENT VALUE APPROACH.   One approach involves looking at all possible combinations of the acceptable investment proposals that do not require a larger total investment of cash than is available. The combination of investment proposals that provides the highest total net present value would be chosen. For example, suppose that a company has $20,000 cash available for investment during the current budget period and has three proposals that are acceptable because of their positive net present values. These are shown below:

Proposal	Initial Investment Required	Net Present Value
A	$20,000	$12,000
B	10,000	9,000
C	10,000	4,000

Investment in proposal A would consume the entire $20,000 cash available for investment, while both proposals B and C could be undertaken with the $20,000 cash available. Proposals B and C would be selected by the maximum net present value approach as the combination providing the highest total net present value (i.e., $13,000 instead of $12,000).

THE HIGHEST TIME-ADJUSTED RATE OF RETURN APPROACH.   A second approach is to select the proposals with the highest time-adjusted rates of return until the total amount available for investment is used up. This approach is easy to use when the time-adjusted rates of return have been computed, but it can also be used without computing these rates. It would require repeating the net present value computations for the acceptable investment proposals, using higher and higher discount rates and eliminating proposals whose net present values become negative. After enough proposals have been eliminated through this process so that sufficient funds are available for investment in the remaining proposals, the remaining proposals are then selected. The logic of this process is that the least profitable investment proposals (those with the lowest time-adjusted rates of return on investment) will be eliminated first, leaving the most profitable proposals (those with the highest time-adjusted rates of return on investment) as the proposals to be selected for investment.

The Blair Company currently owns a machine that was purchased 5 years ago at a cost of $200,000. It is expected to have a remaining useful life of 5 years and a residual value at the end of that time of $8,000.

Blair can purchase a new machine for $140,000. It would have a 5-year life and a residual value of $38,000. If the new machine is purchased, the old machine would be sold for $40,000 immediately.

No revenues would be affected by the purchase of the new machine, although annual cash payments for three operating costs would be reduced as shown in the table below:

	Annual Cash Payments	
	Old Machine	New Machine
Direct labor	$30,000	$12,000
Power	6,500	4,500
Maintenance	6,000	1,000
Total	$42,500	$17,500

Required:

1. Draw a cash flow diagram of the cash flow changes that would result from purchasing the new machine.
2. Compute the payback period for the additional investment required to purchase the new machine.
3. Compute the average rate of return on the additional investment required to purchase the new machine.
4. Compute the net present value of the additional investment in the new machine (assuming a minimum acceptable rate of return of 14%) and state whether buying the new machine is an acceptable investment proposal.
5. Assume that the Blair Company has only $400,000 cash available for investment during the coming year. The following other investment proposals have been identified as acceptable:

	Required Investment	Net Present Value
Proposal A	$200,000	$21,050
Proposal B	100,000	6,300
Proposal C	100,000	4,100

If the Blair Company selects investment proposals using the maximum net present value approach would the new machine be purchased?

SOLUTION TO REVIEW PROBLEM

1.

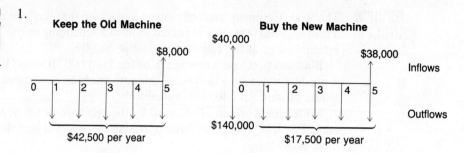

Keep the Old Machine

Buy the New Machine

Cash Flow Changes Resulting from Purchasing the New Machine

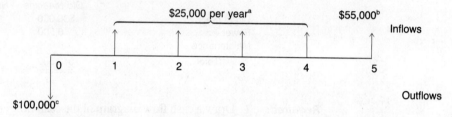

a $42,500 old cash outflows — $17,500 new cash outflows = $25,000 net cash inflows (savings).
b $25,000 net cash inflows + ($38,000 new residual value − $8,000 old residual value).
c $140,000 purchase cost of new machine − $40,000 sales value of old machine.

2. Payback period $= \dfrac{\text{Investment}}{\text{Net cash inflow per year}}$

$= \dfrac{\$100,000 \text{ additional investment}}{\$25,000 \text{ cash savings per year}}$

$= \underline{\underline{4 \text{ years}}}$

3. Average rate of return on investment $= \dfrac{\text{Total cash inflows} - \text{Total cash outflows}}{\text{Years} \times \text{Investment}}$

$= \dfrac{[(4 \text{ years} \times \$25,000 \text{ inflow per year}) + \$55,000 \text{ inflow}] - \$100,000 \text{ outflow for investment}}{5 \text{ years} \times \$100,000 \text{ investment}}$

$= \dfrac{\$55,000}{\$500,000}$

$= \underline{\underline{11\% \text{ per year}}}$

4. Net present value:

	Future Net Amount		Present Value Factor (14%)		Present Value
Cash inflows:					
End of years 1–4	$25,000	×	2.913712[a]	=	$ 72,842.80
End of year 5	55,000	×	.519369[b]	=	28,565.30
Present value of cash inflows					$101,408.10
Cash outflows: Additional investment (end of year 0)					(100,000.00)
Net present value					$ 1,408.10 (Acceptable)

[a] From Table 4 of Appendix B.
[b] From Table 2 of Appendix B.

5. No, the new machine would not be purchased. If only $400,000 cash is available to invest, Blair should select proposals A, B, and C in order to maximize its net present value. Although the proposal to purchase the new machine has a positive net present value and is therefore an acceptable proposal, the Blair Company cannot purchase the new machine without giving up the opportunity to invest in proposals A, B, or C. Since proposals A, B, and C each provide a higher net present value than purchasing the machine, the machine cannot be purchased without lowering the total net present value that the company can obtain with only $400,000 available for investment.

GLOSSARY

Average Rate of Return. The difference between total cash inflows and total cash outflows of an investment, divided by the number of years over which cash inflows are obtained times the amount invested.

Capital Rationing. The situation in which a company is not able to make all acceptable investments because it does not have sufficient cash.

Cash Inflow. A cash receipt.

Cash Flow. A cash inflow or a cash outflow.

Cash Outflow. A cash payment.

"Do Nothing" Alternative. The decision alternative of *not* accepting an investment proposal.

Investment Decisions. Long-term decisions in which an investment is made in order to receive net cash inflows in the future totaling more than the investment.

Minimum Acceptable Rate of Return. The rate of return used as a cutoff to identify acceptable and unacceptable investment proposals. Investment proposals with time-adjusted rates of return in excess of this rate are acceptable.

Mutually Exclusive Investment Proposals. A set of alternative investment proposals, only one of which may be selected.

Net Cash Inflows. Cash inflows in excess of cash outflows. If cash outflows exceed cash inflows, the difference is referred to as a *net cash outflow*.

Net Present Value.   The total present value of an investment's cash inflows minus the total present value of its cash outflows.

Payback Period.   The length of time required for the net cash inflows from an investment proposal to equal the amount invested (i.e., for a return *of* the investment).

Relevant Cash Flows.   Future cash flows of investment decision alternatives that differ, either in amount or timing, depending upon which alternative is chosen.

Time-Adjusted Rate of Return.   The compound interest rate that would enable an investment to grow just large enough to provide exactly the cash receipts expected from the investment.

QUESTIONS

Q27-1   What is an investment?

Q27-2   Why is it necessary to base the analysis of long-term investment decisions on relevant cash flows instead of on relevant costs (or expenses) and revenues?

Q27-3   There is no cash flow associated with depreciation. Discuss.

Q27-4   Why are cash flows that occur before the time of an investment decision (the end of year 0) irrelevant to that decision?

Q27-5   Would a company rather receive $500 one year from now or 2 years from now? Explain.

Q27-6   Would a company rather pay $500 one year from now or 2 years from now? Explain.

Q27-7   A company *must* buy one of two machines. Both of them will need an overhaul costing $500. Is the cost of the overhaul a relevant cash flow in deciding which machine to buy? Discuss.

Q27-8   Define *net* cash inflows and *net* cash outflows.

Q27-9   Cash outflows can be subtracted from cash inflows that occur in the same year before present value computations are made. This would not change the net present value. Discuss.

Q27-10   Why would a $1,000 investment that decreased future cash payments by $250 each year for 6 years be as desirable to a company as another $1,000 investment that increased cash receipts by $250 each year for 6 years?

Q27-11   Distinguish between return *of* investment and return *on* investment.

Q27-12   Why is the payback period an incorrect measure for determining whether an investment proposal is acceptable or for judging whether one proposal is better than another?

Q27-13   The average rate of return on investment is better than the payback period in judging whether or not an investment proposal is acceptable. Discuss.

Q27-14   Define time-adjusted rate of return.

Q27-15   Why is the time-adjusted rate of return better than the average rate of return in determining whether or not an investment proposal is acceptable?

Q27-16 Define the net present value of an investment proposal.

Q27-17 If the cash flows from an investment proposal are discounted at a rate exactly equal to the proposal's time-adjusted rate of return, what would the net present value be? Explain.

Q27-18 The cash flows from an investment proposal are discounted at a rate higher than the proposal's time-adjusted rate of return. Is the net present value positive or negative? Explain.

Q27-19 Why is the minimum acceptable rate of return used as a discount rate to compute the net present value of a company's investment proposals?

Q27-20 Give an example of mutually exclusive investment alternatives. Explain why the alternatives are mutually exclusive.

Q27-21 Should an investment with a negative net present value ever be made? How could this be justified?

Q27-22 Define capital rationing.

EXERCISES

E27-1 **Payback Period.** A company is considering the following investment proposals:

(a) $10,000 invested in a savings account that pays $200 interest (in cash) quarterly.
(b) $10,000 invested in a delivery van, which would reduce delivery expenses so that cash payments are decreased by $1,025 per year for 10 years.
(c) $10,000 invested in land, for which real estate taxes of $100 would be paid each year. The investor expects to be able to sell the land after 10 years for $25,000.

Required: Compute the payback period for the proposals described in (a), (b), and (c).

E27-2 **Payback Period.** The McKenzie Company is considering buying a machine that would increase the company's cash inflows by $2,200 per year for 5 years. Operation of the machine would increase the company's cash payments by $100 in each of the first 2 years, $200 in the third and fourth years, and $300 in the fifth year. The machine costs $5,000 and would have a residual value of $500 at the end of the fifth year.

Required: Compute the payback period for this machine.

E27-3 **Average Rate of Return on Investment.** Refer to E27-2.

Required: Compute the average rate of return on investment for the machine being considered by the McKenzie Company.

E27-4 **Average Rate of Return on Investment.** Tom Hammond is considering investing $4,000 in a large tract of farm land a group of his friends is planning to buy. His share of the expected selling price of the land after 5 years would be $6,800.

Required: Compute the average rate of return on Tom's investment.

E27-5 **Time-Adjusted Rate of Return.** Below are two *related* questions.

(a) If $100 is invested today to earn 12% compounded annually, to what amount would the investment grow in 10 years?
(b) If an investment of $100 grows to $350 in 10 years, is its time-adjusted rate of return greater than or less than 12%?

Required: Prepare an analysis to answer the two questions.

E27-6   Time-Adjusted Rate of Return.   A tract of land is to be purchased that can be sold in 5 years for $100,000. Assume that no other future cash flows would result from ownership of this land.

Required: Prepare an analysis to answer the following two *related* questions concerning the purchase of this land:
1. How much would have to be invested in (paid for) the land for the investment to earn a time-adjusted rate of return of 12%?
2. If $60,000 is paid for the land, is the expected time-adjusted rate of return greater than or less than 12%?

E27-7   Present Value.   Below are descriptions of four sets of cash flows.

(a) A single $100 cash inflow at the end of year 5.
(b) A series of $100 cash inflows at the end of years 1, 2, 3, 4, and 5.
(c) A cash inflow of $300 at the end of year 3 and a cash inflow of $500 at the end of year 5.
(d) A series of cash outflows of $50 at the end of years 1 through 10.

Required: Determine the present value (at the end of year 0) of each of the sets of cash flows using a discount rate of 16%.

E27-8   Present Value.   Below are two *independent* questions.

(a) The Delta Company sells a new type of pecan shelling machine that it claims will save a constant amount of labor costs at a particular company each year for 10 years. Delta suggests that this savings would have a present value (at 20%) of $8,384.94 to the company. What is the amount of the annual labor cost savings being claimed?
(b) The Sigma Company sells a small mechanical apparatus with a complicated solid-state control unit that attaches to an automobile's carburetor. Sigma claims the apparatus will save the average car owner $100 per year in gasoline bills that should be worth over $800 (present value) to the owner using a discount rate of 10%. If the apparatus can save $100 per year, how many years would it have to be used for the present value of the savings to exceed $800?

Required: Prepare an analysis to answer each of the questions.

E27-9   Net Present Value.   Refer to the information in E27-4.

Required: Compute the net present value of the land investment, assuming a minimum acceptable rate of return of 14%.

E27-10   Net Present Value.   Refer to the information in E27-2.

Required: Compute the net present value of the machine investment being considered by the McKenzie Company, assuming a minimum acceptable rate of return of 20%.

E27-11   Net Present Value.   The Carmichael Radio Company, a distributor of radio towers and antennas, is considering buying the entire inventory of the West Tower Company, a manufacturer of extremely large, heavy-duty towers, which is going out of business. These towers would cost $250,000 delivered to Carmichael's warehouse. Carmichael's minimum acceptable rate of return is 20%.

Required: Compute the net present value of Carmichael's investment for *each* of the following assumed patterns of cash inflow that could result from the sale of these towers.
1. Cash inflows of $100,000 each year for 4 years.
2. Cash inflows of $50,000 each year for 8 years.
3. Cash inflows of $200,000 during the first year, $100,000 during the second year, and $50,000 in each of the third and fourth years.

E27-12   Mutually Exclusive Investment Proposals.   The Merimac Company can accept either investment proposal A or investment proposal B (but not both), or it can reject both investment proposals. Proposal A requires an investment of $1,000 and promises increased (net) cash inflows of $350 for 5 years. Proposal B requires an investment of $1,000 and promises increased (net) cash inflows of $375 for 4 years and $250 in the fifth year. The company's minimum acceptable rate of return is 25%.

Required: 1. Prepare an analysis to determine which (if either) of the proposals should be selected for investment.
2. How would the answer to Requirement 1 be altered if one of the two investments must be selected?

E27-13   Capital Rationing.   The Mosely Company has identified the investment proposals shown below as acceptable. Only $50,000 can be made available for investment, however.

Investment Proposal	Required Investment	Net Present Value	Time-Adjusted Rate of Return
A	$10,000	$ 4,000	15%
B	20,000	12,000	14%
C	10,000	5,000	18%
D	30,000	16,000	13%
E	10,000	7,000	21%
F	20,000	13,000	15%

Required: Determine the combination of proposals to be selected using:
1. The maximum net present value approach.
2. The highest time-adjusted rate of return approach.

PROMBLEMS

Part A

P27-1A   Net Present Value.   The Bowler Company is considering purchasing a packaging machine for $20,000 that has a residual value of $100 after 8 years. It would be depreciated using the straight-line method. The machine would reduce labor costs in the shipping department by $6,500 per year. Experience with such machines suggests that $2,000 of finished goods would be ruined per year by the packaging machine. Ownership of the machine would also increase property taxes and insurance (paid annually) by $250 per year. Bowler's minimum acceptable rate of return on investment is 16%.

Required: 1. Prepare an analysis to determine whether the purchase of this machine is an acceptable investment for Bowler.
2. Below what purchase price would the packaging machine be an acceptable investment for Bowler?

P27-2A   Selecting Acceptable Investment Proposals.   A company is considering the following three investment proposals:

Proposal A — An investment of $10,000 promising cash receipts of $3,635 per year for 5 years.

Proposal B — An investment of $10,000 promising a single cash receipt of $24,000 after 5 years.

Proposal C — An investment of $10,000 promising a cash receipt of $2,000 each year for 4 years and $6,000 in the fifth year.

Required: 1. Prepare an analysis to determine the acceptability of each of the investment proposals assuming a minimum acceptable rate of return of 16%.
2. If only one of the three investment proposals can be selected for investment, which one should it be? Write a brief justification for your selection.

P27-3A   **Machine Replacement — Net Present Value.** The Oldtown Manufacturing Company is considering replacing an old machine that cost the company $50,000 five years ago. This machine could be used for 10 more years, at which time it would have a residual value of $5,000. If it were sold now, net receipts from its disposal would be $15,000. Six operators are required to run the old machine, each earning $10,000 per year.

The new machine, which costs $110,000, has an estimated life of 10 years and a residual value of $5,000 at the end of that time. The new machine is subject to straight-line depreciation. The new machine requires only three operators earning $10,000 each per year. Actual direct materials cost would be slightly less with the new machine because materials waste (currently $1,000 per year) could be cut in half.

Maintenance, which currently runs approximately $2,000 per year for the old machine, would be decreased by 25% with the new machine. At present, power costs $30,000 per year. The new machine would require 40% more power. It is estimated that the revenues associated with the product produced by the old machine, $200,000 per year, would not be changed by purchasing the new machine. Oldtown's minimum acceptable rate of return is 14%.

Required: 1. Draw the cash flow diagram representing the cash flow changes that would result from the replacement of the old machine.
2. Compute the net present value of the proposal to replace the old machine. Is this proposal acceptable?
3. What maximum amount should the Oldtown Manufacturing Company be willing to pay for the new machine?

P27-4A   **Machine Replacement, Additional Alternatives.** Several years ago the Abco Company signed a contract to supply 10,000 units of a special product each year to one of its customers at a price of $10.00 per unit. This contract, which runs for 5 more years, must be fulfilled!

Abco is currently producing the product with an old machine that can be kept running for 5 more years if $15,000 of maintenance cost per year is incurred. Other operating costs to produce this product with the old machine (excluding maintenance) total $90,000 per year. The old machine has no residual value now and will have none after the contract is fulfilled.

The West Company has recently offered to sell Abco 10,000 units of this product per year over the next 5 years for $9.50 per unit. Abco had almost decided to accept this offer from West as the best possible way to satisfy its contract when a new machine capable of producing the 10,000 units each year for $85,000 total cash operating costs per year became available. This new machine would cost $75,000 and would have a residual value of $25,000 in 5 years. Abco's minimum acceptable rate of return on investment is 12%.

Required: 1. Is purchasing 10,000 units of the product per year from the West Company preferable to producing them on the old machine? Discuss.
2. Determine the acceptability of the proposal to invest in the new machine by computing the net present value of this investment alternative.
3. If the West Company withdraws its offer to supply the units, would the answer to Requirement 2 change? Discuss, supporting your discussion with computations if necessary.

P27-5A   **Mutually Exclusive Investment Proposals.** The Porter Paper Company has just been ordered by the court to install antipollution controls on the exhaust system of one of its production processes. The company's minimum acceptable rate of return is 20%. Two devices are available on the market.

Device A costs $20,000 and is expected to last 10 years, after which it would have a zero residual value. It costs $500 per year to operate and maintain.

Device B costs $12,000 and would last only 5 years after which it would have a residual value of $1,000. If device B is purchased, Porter would have to replace it in 5 years. The second unit would have an expected cost at that time of $16,000. The second unit would also be expected to have a residual value of $1,000 at the end of its 5-year life. Device B costs $600 per year to operate and maintain.

Required: 1. Determine which pollution control device Porter should purchase by computing the net present value of the investment for each of the devices.
2. How much *per year* would the court have to fine Porter for ignoring the order to ensure that it would be less expensive (in terms of present value of costs) for the company to comply with the court order by purchasing one of the devices.

P27-6A   Introducing a New Product—Net Present Value.   Fowler Industries is considering introducing a new product. Fowler believes it can sell a volume of 20,000 units of this product per year for 20 years at a price of $12.00 per unit. Fowler estimates that the cost of producing the product would be $2.00 per unit. Additional production costs of $25,000 per year would be required during the first 2 years, however, while the production department becomes familiar with the techniques required to produce the new product. Cash payments for advertising this product are expected to be $30,000 per year. Variable selling costs are expected to be about $1.00 per unit sold.

Fowler Industries has already spent $500,000 on research and development of this product. If the new product is introduced, an additional $500,000 would have to be invested immediately to obtain the additional plant and equipment necessary for production. This additional plant and equipment would have a residual value of $100,000 after 20 years. Fowler's minimum acceptable rate of return is 20%.

Required: Compute the net present value of the proposal to introduce this new product and state whether this proposal should be acceptable to Fowler Industries.

PROBLEMS

Part B

P27-1B   Net Present Value.   The Keeler Company is considering purchasing an overhead conveyer system for $150,000 that has a residual value of $5,000 after 6 years. This conveyer system would be depreciated on a straight-line basis. The conveyer system would reduce labor costs in the shipping department by $55,000 per year. Experience with such systems suggests that $5,000 would be spent each year on maintenance to keep it operating properly. Ownership of the new conveyer system would also increase property taxes and insurance (paid annually) by $1,000 per year. Keeler's minimum acceptable rate of return on investment is 12%.

Required: 1. Prepare an analysis to determine whether the purchase of this overhead conveyer system is an acceptable investment for Keeler.
2. Below what purchase price would the overhead conveyer system be an acceptable investment for Keeler?

P27-2B   Selecting Acceptable Investment Proposals.   A company is considering the following three investment proposals:

Proposal A — An investment of $10,000 promising cash receipts of $2,600 per year for 10 years.

Proposal B — An investment of $10,000 promising a single cash receipt of $60,000 after 10 years.

Proposal C — An investment of $10,000 promising a cash receipt of $2,000 each year for 9 years and $13,000 in the tenth year.

Required: 1. Prepare an analysis to determine the acceptability of each of the investment proposals assuming a minimum acceptable rate of return of 20%.
2. If only one of the three investment proposals can be selected for investment, which one should it be? Write a brief justification for your selection.

P27-3B   Machine Replacement — Net Present Value.   The Greenville Manufacturing Company is considering replacing an old machine that cost the company $70,000 five years ago. This machine could be used for 10 more years, at which time it would have a residual value of $6,000. If it were sold now, net receipts from its disposal would be $25,000. The old machine requires five operators to run it, each earning $12,000 per year.

The new machine, which costs $135,000, has an estimated life of 10 years and a residual value of $6,000 at the end of that time. The new machine requires only four operators, each earning $10,000 per year. Actual direct materials cost would be slightly less with the new machine because materials waste (currently $2,000 per year) could be cut in half.

Maintenance on the old machine, which currently runs approximately $1,000 per year, would be decreased by 60% with the new machine. At present, power costs $20,000 per year. The new machine would require 10% more power. It is estimated that the revenues associated with the product produced by the old machine, $150,000 per year, would not be changed by purchasing the new machine. Greenville's minimum acceptable rate of return is 20%.

Required: 1. Draw the cash flow diagram representing the cash flow changes that would result from the replacement of the old machine.
2. Compute the net present value of the proposal to replace the old machine. Is this proposal acceptable?
3. What maximum amount should the Greenville Manufacturing Company be willing to pay for the new machine?

P27-4B   Machine Replacement, Additional Alternatives.   Several years ago the Dane Company signed a contract to supply 5,000 units of a special product each year to one of its customers at a price of $20.00 per unit. This contract, which runs for 5 more years, must be fulfilled!

Dane is currently producing the product with an old machine that can be kept running for 5 more years if $25,000 of maintenance cost per year is incurred. Other operating costs to produce this product with the old machine (excluding maintenance) total $80,000 per year. The old machine has no residual value now and will have none after the contract is fulfilled.

The East Company has recently offered to sell Dane 5,000 units of this product per year over the next 5 years for $18.50 per unit. Dane had almost decided to accept this offer from East as the best possible way to satisfy its contract when a new machine capable of producing the 5,000 units each year for $80,000 total cash operating costs per year became available. This new machine would cost $60,000 and would have a residual value of $15,000 in 5 years. Dane's minimum acceptable rate of return on investment is 16%.

Required: 1. Is purchasing 5,000 units of the product per year from the East Company preferable to producing them on the old machine? Discuss.
2. Determine the acceptability of the proposal to invest in the new machine by computing the net present value of this investment alternative.
3. If the East Company withdraws its offer to supply the units, would the answer to Requirement 2 change? Discuss, supporting your discussion with computations if necessary.

P27-5B   Mutually Exclusive Investment Proposals.   The Smart Rubber Company has just been ordered by the court to install antipollution controls on the exhaust system of one of its production processes. The company's minimum acceptable rate of return is 16%. Two devices are available on the market.

Device A costs $40,000 and is expected to last 20 years, after which it would have a zero residual value. It costs $500 per year to operate and maintain.

Device B, which costs $30,000, is also expected to last 20 years after which it would have a residual value of $1,000. Device B costs $2,150 per year to operate and maintain.

Required: 1. Determine which pollution control device Smart should purchase by computing the net present value of the investment for each of the devices.
2. How much per year could Smart afford to pay in fines to the court to avoid buying one of these devices?

P27-6B **Introducing a New Product — Net Present Value.** Wayne Industries is considering introducing a new product. Wayne believes it can sell 30,000 units of this product per year for 20 years at a price of $9.00 per unit. Wayne estimates that the cost of producing the product would be $3.00 per unit. Additional production costs of $50,000 would be required during the first year, however, while the production department becomes familiar with the techniques required to produce the new product. Cash payments for advertising this product are expected to be $45,000 per year. Variable selling costs are expected to be about $2.00 per unit sold.

Wayne Industries has already spent $300,000 on research and development of this product. If the new product is introduced, an additional $250,000 would have to be invested immediately to obtain the additional plant and equipment necessary for production. This additional plant and equipment would have a residual value of $100,000 after 20 years. Wayne's minimum acceptable rate of return is 20%.

Required: Compute the net present value of the proposal to introduce this new product and state whether this proposal should be acceptable to Wayne Industries.

DISCUSSION CASES

C27-1 **Mutually Exclusive Investment Proposals.** Midus Muffin Shops, a chain of fast-food shops serving breakfast 24 hours a day, is considering opening a shop in Danville. The shop could be opened in one of two ways, either by building the shop between a west-side shopping center and Danville's small college campus, or by buying a vacant building on the edge of the downtown business district. The investment required in either case is $100,000. An extensive analysis of the potential of these two locations, however, suggests that the expected cash inflows and outflows from their operations would be very different.

The downtown location offers a much greater volume of customers than the west-side location for at least 5 years. Furthermore, this volume would be concentrated between 6 A.M. and 11:30 P.M., allowing considerable savings in wages during the early morning hours. The volume of the west-side location would be smaller and more uniform throughout the day and night.

The costs of upkeep at the new west-side building should be considerably less than for the older building downtown, however. Furthermore, an interstate highway currently under construction 100 miles to the north is eventually expected to come through Danville within three blocks of the west-side location after 5 or more years, increasing the potential volume of customers to that shop by a considerable amount.

Required: Assume that you are a consultant to Midus and have been assigned to make a recommendation to the company about what to do in Danville. Write a letter, one or two pages long, to the president of Midus describing the approach that should be used in making this decision, listing the important factors that you expect to influence the decision and requesting specific information from the company that you will need to evaluate the decision's alternatives.

C27-2 **Estimating Cash Flow Changes Resulting from an Investment.** Mary T. lives with her mother and is an administrative secretary for a large architectural company in a small midwestern city. She earns $15,000 per year. She dreams of being an architect, however. New architects in her company start at $21,000 per year. Mary has been accepted at several universities. Because she is bright and ambitious, she believes she can graduate in 3 years (including summer school) unless she works part-time, in which case it would take 4 years. She has been looking at college catalogues for several months, calculating the total costs for tuition, fees, room and board, books and supplies, and so on. She has tabulated these costs and ruled out all but one school because of the high out-of-state tuition. She has estimated the costs per year of attending the state university. They are shown on the following page:

Tuition and fees	$1,800
Room and board	2,500
Books and supplies	400
Automobile	500
Clothes	200
Miscellaneous	200
Annual Cost	$5,600

Although it seems like a lot of money, Mary believes her total cost over 3 years ($16,800) would be paid back before she finishes her first year working as an architect. Before she resigns from her job, she comes to you for your opinion.

Required: Write a letter, one or two pages long, to Mary describing how she should evaluate this decision. Make some tentative calculations using any of the above information she has supplied to you that you feel is relevant and assuming any additional information that is necessary in order to demonstrate how she should consider the monetary aspects of her decision. Disregard income taxes.

APPENDIX A

Royal Crown Companies, Inc. Annual Report 1980 – Financial Section

The following discussion explains certain significant factors which affected the Company's operations during 1980, 1979 and 1978 and discusses the Company's liquidity and capital commitments. The Company's consolidated financial statements and notes thereto and selected financial data (page 30) should be read in conjunction with this discussion as they are essential to evaluate the Company's results of operations and financial condition.

RESULTS OF OPERATIONS
1980 Compared to 1979

Net sales for 1980 were up 4% over 1979. Increases by the soft drink and citrus divisions more than offset lower revenues from fast food. While the entire decline in fast food can be attributed to the sale of 17 Arby's restaurants in early 1980, sales of company-owned restaurants in Ohio and Michigan (comprising over one-half of total units) suffered due to high unemployment in that area, offset by increased royalties and license fees. Eliminating the sales of the 17 restaurants, 1980 sales for the total Company were up 6% over 1979. Soft drink sales advanced on stronger prices and increases in unit shipments. The growth in citrus revenues was principally due to pricing. Billings by the home furnishings division were up slightly, although volume shipments of mirror tiles and bedroom furniture were down.

Cost of sales as a percentage of sales was 1% higher than 1979. Higher sugar and container costs in soft drink operations and higher restaurant fixed costs at Arby's and in home furnishings accounted for one-half of the increase. An inventory write-down of mirror tiles represented the other half. Higher fruit costs in the citrus division were offset by a freeze insurance settlement. Marketing, administrative and other expenses increased 9%, principally due to increased advertising and promotional expenses in soft drink, Arby's and the citrus division. Much of soft drink's increase was related to the introduction of RC 100. Delivery and administrative costs also were up, principally due to inflation.

Interest expense increased 29% over 1979 on both higher average borrowings and interest rates. Capital expenditures, lower than planned profits, especially in the last half of the year, and higher receivables and inventories, especially citrus products, were the primary causes of increased borrowings.

The reduction in the effective tax rate to 42% in 1980 from 44% in 1979 was principally due to higher investment tax credits and a redetermination of the Company's tax liability.

Current assets at December 31, 1980 exceeded current liabilities by 1.57 times versus 1.67 times at December 31, 1979. Long-term borrowings, including capitalized lease obligations, totaled $62.9 million at December 31, 1980 and equaled 61% of shareholders' equity.

1979 Compared to 1978

Net sales increased 8% over 1978 with significant revenue gains achieved by Arby's and the home furnishings division. Eliminating the sales by businesses sold in 1978 and the sales of 35 Arby's restaurants purchased in 1979, comparable net sales were up 11%, as all divisions showed sizable increases. Comparable soft drink sales in 1979 were up 9% over 1978, due entirely to price increases as volume was slightly lower in 1979. Comparable fast food revenues increased 20% primarily from opening new restaurants. The increase of citrus revenues was the result of higher prices as unit volume was lower. Comparable home furnishings sales were up 17% from volume and price; all four companies set revenue records.

Cost of sales as a percentage of sales was 1% lower in 1979. Pricing and production efficiencies from high volume in home furnishings offset higher fruit costs in the citrus division. Marketing, administrative and other expenses were comparable in both years; lower operating expenses at Arby's and in the home furnishings division, together with lower promotional expenses by the citrus division, were offset by higher advertising expenditures and by receivable write-offs in the fourth quarter in the soft drink division.

Interest expense was up 40% over the prior year on higher interest rates and increased borrowings for the purchase of 35 Arby's restaurants and the construction of 19 new units during the year. At December 31, 1979, there were 138 company-owned restaurants, up 54 over the 84 units at year-end 1978.

The effective tax rate in 1979 was 44%; the reduction from the federal statute rate of 46% was due to investment tax credits. The effective tax rate of 20% in 1978 was caused by large investment tax credits on considerably lower taxable earnings.

Current assets at December 31, 1979 exceeded current liabilities by 1.67 times versus 1.98 times at December 31, 1978. Long-term borrowings, including capitalized lease obligations, totaled $61.9 million at December 31, 1979 and equaled 61% of shareholders' equity.

1978 Compared to 1977

The disposition of certain operations and the recognition of other unusual expenses resulted in a pretax charge of $14.9 million to 1978 income. (See Note 12 to consolidated financial statements).

Net sales were up 12% over 1977. Soft drink sales advanced 5%, while the revenues of the three other divisions—fast food (up 29%), citrus (up 28%), and home furnishings (up 9%) —were at record levels. Soft drink unit shipments were slightly below prior year; higher prices accounted for the increase in soft drink revenues. Fast food revenues grew proportionately with the openings of new company-owned Arby's restaurants. Citrus sales were strong in both volume and price. Sales by the home furnishings operations were up in units and generally in prices compared to 1977.

Cost of sales as a percentage of sales was up 4% over 1977, due largely to reduced soft drink and fast food sales in early 1978 causing higher unit fixed costs, increased costs of soft drink and citrus containers, higher meat costs at Arby's and significant increases in lumber and glass costs in home furnishings. Marketing, administrative and other expenses as a percentage of sales were comparable in both years. Significant increases in the 1978 soft drink advertising and promotional expenses to meet strong promotional discounting by competitors were offset by lower operating expenses in other operations.

Interest expense rose 80% over the prior year as a result of both increased borrowings and higher interest rates. Expansion of Arby's restaurants was the major reason for greater borrowings in 1978 over 1977. At December 31, 1978, there were 84 company-owned restaurants open, up 19 from December 31, 1977.

The effective tax rate of 20% in 1978 was down significantly from the 45% in 1977 and was caused by the influence of large investment tax credits upon lower taxable earnings.

LIQUIDITY AND CAPITAL COMMITMENTS

The Company's liquidity during 1980 was reduced due to three related factors—lower than planned income, higher than projected receivables and inventories, and capital expenditures. Adding to these was the payment in 1980 of 1979 income taxes of approximately $11 million, as tax payments in 1979 were based on 1978's low earnings.

Due to the above, the Company's average short-term borrowings during 1980 increased $16 million, which, due to higher interest rates, also decreased profits. While the Company has unused lines of credit and additional borrowing flexibility, the current level of debt is unsatisfactory and is being reduced.

A significant factor causing the lower income was the weak economy which impacted the profits of all divisions, especially fast food and home furnishings. The earnings during the second half of the year were particularly reduced. The slower sales resulted in higher than projected inventory balances in the home furnishings division. Moreover, during much of 1980, heavy price discounting was being practiced by the majority of companies in the citrus industry. The Company's citrus division limited its discounting, which restricted its sales volume and thus maintained the relatively high level of inventories of citrus products which it intentionally established during 1979 at favorable costs.

The weak economy also resulted in an increase in trade receivables, as customers slowed their payments, especially in the soft drink and citrus divisions.

Since the majority of 1980 capital projects were committed by mid-year, curtailment of these expenditures during the last half of 1980 was of limited benefit.

To strengthen the Company's position and reduce borrowings, the following decisions have been made and the following actions are being taken:

a. Operations and products whose profitability does not generate an adequate and rapid return of cash are being placed on a limited timing schedule for improvement. If any are unsatisfactory, the Company will take appropriate action.

b. Efforts will be made to collect receivables more rapidly.

c. Inventory will be reduced. The January 1981 freeze in Florida is expected to limit the citrus crop; it is expected that demand for citrus products will reduce the division's high level of inventory.

d. Capital expenditures have been limited to essential projects, in-progress projects, and new projects having a high rate of cash payout.

Consolidated Balance Sheets
Royal Crown Companies, Inc. and Subsidiaries

In thousands of dollars	December 31	
	1980	1979
ASSETS		
Current assets:		
Cash	$ **4,325**	6,585
Receivables less allowance for doubtful accounts: 1980—$2,008; 1979—$1,940	**42,758**	39,937
Inventories:		
Products finished and in process	**28,274**	26,112
Materials and supplies	**25,106**	25,346
Other current assets	**6,664**	4,982
Total current assets	**107,127**	102,962
Long-term notes receivable less unamortized imputed interest and allowance for doubtful collection: 1980—$4,342; 1979—$5,426	**7,326**	5,136
Property, plant and equipment:		
Land	**13,176**	12,544
Buildings	**48,820**	47,899
Production equipment	**65,067**	61,147
Delivery equipment	**31,007**	24,747
	158,070	146,337
Less accumulated depreciation	**60,495**	51,769
	97,575	94,568
Capitalized leased assets:		
Buildings	**7,974**	8,965
Production equipment	**967**	859
Delivery equipment	**3,841**	4,092
	12,782	13,916
Less accumulated amortization	**5,961**	5,746
	6,821	8,170
Investment in direct financing leases	**3,051**	
Goodwill	**15,160**	16,005
Other assets	**1,075**	1,302
	$238,135	228,143

See notes to consolidated financial statements.

Consolidated Balance Sheets
Royal Crown Companies, Inc. and Subsidiaries

In thousands of dollars	December 31	
	1980	1979
LIABILITIES AND SHAREHOLDERS' EQUITY		
Current liabilities:		
Current portion of long-term debt and capitalized lease obligations	**$ 3,991**	1,339
Notes payable	**20,510**	10,773
Dividends payable	**2,132**	2,132
Accounts payable	**21,751**	21,009
Accrued expenses	**19,393**	15,304
Accrued income taxes	**491**	11,196
Total current liabilities	**68,268**	61,753
Long-term debt	**55,817**	53,723
Capitalized lease obligations	**7,054**	8,210
Deferred income taxes	**2,440**	1,363
Other deferred credits	**1,448**	1,627
Shareholders' equity:		
Preferred stock at no par:		
authorized 3,000,000 shares; none issued		
Common stock at $1 par:		
authorized 12,000,000 shares;		
issued and outstanding 8,199,825 shares	**8,200**	8,200
Capital in excess of par	**8,629**	8,629
Retained earnings	**86,279**	84,638
Total shareholders' equity	**103,108**	101,467
	$238,135	228,143

See notes to consolidated financial statements.

Consolidated Statements of Income and Retained Earnings
Royal Crown Companies, Inc. and Subsidiaries

In thousands of dollars	Year Ended December 31		
	1980	1979	1978
Net sales	**$438,076**	421,375	390,683
Cost of sales	**265,993**	252,340	237,086
Gross profit	**172,083**	169,035	153,597
Marketing, administrative and other expenses	**144,591**	132,401	131,790
Operating profit	**27,492**	36,634	21,807
Interest expense	**(10,047)**	(7,777)	(5,545)
Other income, net	**99**	572	408
Income before unusual write-offs and losses and before income taxes	**17,544**	29,429	16,670
Provision for unusual write-offs and losses			14,950
Income before income taxes	**17,544**	29,429	1,720
Provision for income taxes	**7,375**	12,950	339
Net income:			
1980—$1.24 per share	**10,169**		
1979—$2.01 per share		16,479	
1978—$ .17 per share			1,381
Dividends declared:			
1980—$1.04 per share	**8,528**		
1979—$1.04 per share		8,524	
1978—$1.02 per share			8,352
Retained earnings:			
During the year	**1,641**	7,955	(6,971)
At beginning of the year	**84,638**	76,683	83,654
At end of the year	**$ 86,279**	84,638	76,683

See notes to consolidated financial statements.

Consolidated Statements of Changes in Financial Position
Royal Crown Companies, Inc. and Subsidiaries

In thousands of dollars	Year Ended December 31		
	1980	1979	1978
SOURCE OF WORKING CAPITAL			
From operations:			
Net income	**$ 10,169**	16,479	1,381
Depreciation and amortization	**14,143**	13,060	12,769
Deferred income taxes	**1,077**	639	(2,042)
Provision for unusual write-offs and losses not requiring the outlay of working capital			6,167
Total from operations	**25,389**	30,178	18,275
Increase (decrease) in long-term debt	**2,094**	(526)	16,702
Disposals of property, plant and equipment	**9,627**	449	6,540
Decrease in other assets	**227**	2,106	502
Common stock issued		74	238
	37,337	32,281	42,257
APPLICATION OF WORKING CAPITAL			
Dividends declared	**8,528**	8,524	8,352
Additions to property, plant and equipment	**23,778**	18,005	28,825
Leased assets capitalized	**805**	45	1,856
Increase in long-term notes receivable	**2,190**	933	9,207
Increase in goodwill		5,481	1,115
Decrease (increase) in lease obligations	**1,156**	1,032	(693)
Decrease in other deferred credits	**179**	599	669
Invested in direct financing leases	**3,051**		
Noncurrent tangible assets less noncurrent liabilities of 35 Arby's restaurants purchased		2,482	
	39,687	37,101	49,331
Decrease in working capital	**$ (2,350)**	(4,820)	(7,074)
INCREASE (DECREASE) IN WORKING CAPITAL BY COMPONENT			
Cash	**$ (2,260)**	764	1,774
Receivables	**2,821**	3,879	8,856
Inventories	**1,922**	7,978	(4,749)
Refundable income taxes		(4,154)	4,154
Other current assets	**1,682**	1,636	1,032
Current portion of long-term debt and capitalized lease obligations	**(2,652)**	157	149
Notes payable	**(9,737)**	(3,918)	(6,304)
Accounts and dividends payable	**(742)**	1,854	(7,249)
Accrued expenses	**(4,089)**	(1,820)	(4,906)
Accrued income taxes	**10,705**	(11,196)	169
Net decrease in working capital	**(2,350)**	(4,820)	(7,074)
Working capital at beginning of year	**41,209**	46,029	53,103
Working capital at end of year	**$ 38,859**	41,209	46,029

See notes to consolidated financial statements.

Notes To Consolidated Financial Statements
Royal Crown Companies, Inc. and Subsidiaries

1. Summary of Significant Accounting Policies

All subsidiaries are wholly-owned and are consolidated in the financial statements.

In certain subsidiaries, checks are issued against a centrally-managed bank account to enhance the availability of cash, creating negative cash balances which are reported as zero with the offsetting credit classified as accounts payable. Amounts reclassified were $5,519,000 and $5,543,000 in 1980 and 1979, respectively.

Unamortized imputed discounts to the extent deemed collectible are amortized as income over the term of the related note receivable using the interest method.

Inventories are stated at the lower of cost (computed on the average or first-in, first-out methods) or net realizable value.

Property, plant and equipment are stated at cost, except for some returnable soft drink containers stated at deposit value (less than cost). Depreciation is calculated on a straight-line basis over the estimated useful lives of the assets, generally within the following ranges: buildings: 20-40 years; production equipment: 4-15 years; and delivery equipment: 3-10 years. At the time properties are retired, the assets and the related accumulated depreciation are removed from the accounts; gain or loss is included in income. Maintenance and repairs are charged to income as incurred.

Capitalized leased assets are stated at the lesser of net present values of future minimum payments or fair market values at lease inception dates. Capitalized leased assets are amortized on a straight-line basis over the terms of the leases and interest expense is calculated on outstanding obligations.

Goodwill of $2,289,000 pertaining to companies purchased prior to 1970 has continuing value and is not being amortized; the remaining $12,871,000 is being amortized generally over 40 years.

Franchise fees are recognized as income when the franchise restaurant is opened.

Deferred income taxes are provided to recognize timing differences between financial and tax reporting. Investment tax credits are credited to the current income tax provision as realized.

Advertising costs are charged to income during the year in relation to sales and are fully expensed by the end of the year.

Current pension costs plus past service costs amortized over 30 years are accrued and funded.

No income charges or credits are recorded for stock option transactions.

Net income per share, computed by dividing net income by the average number of shares outstanding during each year after recognizing dilutive options, represents primary and fully diluted earnings.

2. Supplementary Detail

Additional detail of certain financial statement captions is as follows:

In thousands of dollars

	At December 31	
	1980	1979
Receivables:		
Customers	**$33,091**	31,823
Other	**11,675**	10,054
Allowance for doubtful accounts	**(2,008)**	(1,940)
Total	**$42,758**	39,937
Other current assets:		
Deferred income taxes	**$ 2,668**	2,144
Other	**3,996**	2,838
Total	**$ 6,664**	4,982
Goodwill:		
Cost	**$16,293**	16,787
Accumulated amortization	**(1,133)**	(782)
Total	**$15,160**	16,005
Notes payable:		
Banks	**$20,500**	7,000
Other notes	**10**	3,773
Total	**$20,510**	10,773
Accrued expenses:		
Advertising	**$ 6,464**	3,403
Wages, commissions and retirement	**3,144**	3,041
Taxes, other than income taxes	**1,669**	1,527
Interest	**734**	746
Other	**7,382**	6,587
Total	**$19,393**	15,304

	For year ended December 31		
	1980	1979	1978
Other income, net:			
Interest	**$ 1,032**	529	213
Net gain (loss) on assets sold	**(304)**	138	205
Write-off of goodwill	**(494)**		
Other expense, net	**(135)**	(95)	(10)
Total	**$ 99**	572	408
Provision for doubtful accounts included in administrative expenses	**$ 1,210**	3,754	2,128

3. Income taxes

The provision (credit) for income taxes was as follows:

In thousands of dollars	1980	1979	1978
Current:			
Federal	$ 5,825	10,385	1,780
State and foreign	1,029	1,458	678
	6,854	11,843	2,458
Deferred:			
Depreciation	40	389	(330)
Unusual write-offs and losses	158	566	(1,972)
Other, net	323	152	183
	521	1,107	(2,119)
	$ 7,375	12,950	339

Reconciliations of the difference between the federal statutory tax rate and the effective book tax rate follow:

	1980	1979	1978
Federal statutory tax rate	46.0%	46.0	48.0
Investment tax credits	(6.5)	(5.3)	(57.3)
State and foreign taxes, net of federal tax benefits	3.2	2.9	22.2
Amortization of goodwill	2.2	.5	5.8
Redetermination of the tax liability	(2.9)		
Other items, net		(.1)	1.0
Effective book tax rate	42.0%	44.0	19.7

4. Borrowings

The Company has senior notes of $24,836,000 and $24,897,000, payable to private lenders with interest at 8⅝% and 8.8%, respectively. The notes are separately payable in ten equal annual installments commencing June 15, 1983 and June 1, 1984, respectively. An additional note was issued in 1980 to a commercial bank for $5,000,000 with interest approximating the prime rate payable February 4, 1982. The notes require the Company to maintain minimum working capital of $30,000,000 and current assets at least 1½ times current liabilities. The Company must also limit its consolidated borrowings to 1⅓ times total shareholders' equity plus deferred credits less intangible assets and restrict its dividends to $6,000,000 plus 75% of net income after December 31, 1976. Retained earnings available for dividends at December 31, 1980 were $9,000,000.

Other long-term notes with interest rates from 7% to 10% are payable $150,000 in 1982, $120,000 in 1983, $121,000 in 1984, $122,000 in 1985 and $571,000 later. Property, plant and equipment with a net book value of $1,843,000 are pledged as collateral for these notes.

The Company has formal lines of credit with commercial banks totaling $19,000,000 of which $9,000,000 was used at December 31, 1980, requiring compensating balances of $1,500,000. During 1980, the average month-end balance of short-term borrowings from formal and informal banking arrangements was $28,875,000, with an average interest rate of 14.5%. The maximum month-end balance for short-term debt was $39,000,000. The average interest rate at December 31, 1980 was 20.4%.

5. Pension Plans

The Company's pension plans cover substantially all employees who are not members of bargaining units. Pension expense including costs for bargaining units was $1,654,000, $1,427,000 and $1,316,000 in 1980, 1979 and 1978, respectively. The actuarially computed values of vested and non-vested accumulated benefits at the most recent valuation date of January 1980 were $9,023,000 and $2,186,000, respectively, using an assumed average rate of investment return of 7.6% compounded annually. The plans' net assets available for benefits at the valuation date totaled $12,053,000.

6. Stock Option Plans

The Company's 1973 qualified stock option plan, which expired December 31, 1977, authorized the granting of options to purchase common stock at not less than market value at date of grant, exercisable one year after grant and expiring after five years. In each year 1974 through 1977, options for 50,000 shares were granted. In 1978 and 1979, options for 13,000 and 5,000 shares were exercised at a weighted average price of $15.83 and $9.94 per share, respectively. Options for 55,500 shares were held by 18 officers and key employees at December 31, 1980 at a weighted average price of $17.41 per share having a total value of $966,000. Their expiration dates range from April 14, 1981 to May 1, 1982.

The Company's 1975 non-qualified stock option plan authorizes the granting of options to purchase 300,000 shares of its common stock at not less than market value at date of grant. The plan will terminate when all shares have been granted or on a date determined by the Board of Directors. Options are exercisable one year after grant not to exceed in cumulative annual installments one-third of the number of shares covered by each grant and expire after ten years. In 1978, options for 2,000 shares were exercised at $15.63 per share. Options for 179,000 shares were held by 22 officers and key employees at December 31, 1980 at a weighted average price of $15.23 per share having a total value of $2,727,000. Their expiration dates range from July 29, 1985 to November 6, 1989.

No other shares are reserved for officers and employees or for options, warrants, conversions or other rights.

Further information relating to options follows:

	Number of Option Shares	
	Qualified Plan	Non-Qualified Plan
Outstanding at January 1, 1979	106,800	129,500
Granted		55,000
Exercised	(5,000)	
Canceled	(21,000)	(5,000)
Outstanding at December 31, 1979	80,800	179,500
Canceled	(25,300)	(500)
Outstanding at December 31, 1980	55,500	179,000
Became exercisable during:		
1979		23,800
1980		40,000

7. Changes in Common Stock and Capital in Excess of Par

	Common Stock Issued		Capital in Excess of Par
In thousands	Shares	Amount	
Balance January 1, 1978	8,180	$8,180	$8,337
Sale of stock to employees exercising options	15	15	223
Balance December 31, 1978	8,195	8,195	8,560
Sale of stock to employees exercising options	5	5	45
Tax benefits of early disposition of optioned shares			24
Balance December 31, 1979 and 1980	8,200	$8,200	$8,629

8. Leases

The Company as lessee leases real estate, vehicles, production and data processing equipment for periods that vary between three and twenty years. Some leases provide for contingent rentals based upon sales volume, mileage or production. In 1980, 1979 and 1978, rental expenses included $3,561,000, $3,342,000 and $2,362,000 for operating leases; $922,000, $1,108,000 and $1,026,000 for contingent rentals; and $430,000, $253,000 and $133,000 for sublease rentals, respectively.

The Company as lessor leases land, buildings, restaurants and restaurant equipment for periods that vary between one and twenty years. During 1980 the Company purchased 29 restaurants for $5,378,000 to accommodate two Arby's franchisees in their expansion. These locations are subject to direct financing or operating leases. The net book value of property under operating leases is $4,267,000 at December 31, 1980.

The following table shows the Company's future minimum rentals as lessee and lessor:

	Lessee		Lessor	
In thousands of dollars	Capitalized Leases	Operating Leases	Direct Financing Leases	Operating Leases
1981	$ 1,875	3,031	483	417
1982	1,616	2,839	490	513
1983	1,243	2,683	490	486
1984	1,019	2,507	490	456
1985	927	1,901	490	423
Later years	8,604	11,636	5,963	4,336
Total minimum payments	15,284	24,597	8,406	6,631
Less: Amount representing interest	7,237		5,246	
Net present value	8,047		3,160	
Less: Current portion	993		109	
Long-term portion	$ 7,054		3,051	

9. Acquisition and Disposition

The Company purchased during March 1979, effective January 1, 1979, the stock of three closely-held companies whose business was the operation of 35 franchised Arby's restaurants. Of the $8,089,000 purchase price, the Company paid $2,265,000 cash and issued one-year and two-year notes at prime rates not exceeding 11% for the remainder. Net assets and operating results of the three companies are not material to the consolidated financial statements and have been included therein since January 1, 1979. A minority shareholder of the three companies is an executive officer of the Company. In February 1980, Arby's sold property and leasehold interests in 17 Arby's restaurants to an Arby's franchisee for $1,690,000 cash and $3,914,000 notes receivable. The notes are collateralized by the assets sold. The net assets and operating results of these restaurants are not material to the consolidated financial statements.

10. Financial Reporting by Business Segments

The Company's operations involve four businesses. Soft drink operations produce and market principally RC Cola, Diet Rite and Nehi brands to retail stores through franchised and company-owned bottlers. The fast food business involves licensed and company-owned Arby's roast beef restaurants. Citrus operations process and market natural fruit juice products under the Adams and Texsun brands and private labels. Home furnishings involve the production and marketing of Frederick Cooper lamps, Couroc serving trays, Athens bedroom and occasional furniture and Hoyne mirror tiles. Foreign operations and export sales are not material.

The following financial data of the four business segments for 1980, 1979 and 1978 are shown in thousands of dollars.

	Soft Drink	Fast Food	Citrus	Home Furnishings	Corporate	Consolidated
At December 31, 1980 or for year then ended						
Net sales	$220,731	69,880	78,706	68,759		438,076
Operating profit	$ 13,942	6,666	9,704	1,827	(4,647)	27,492
Interest expense						(10,047)
Other income, net						99
Income before income taxes						17,544
Depreciation and amortization expense	$ 6,967	4,442	1,260	1,098	376	14,143
Additions to property, plant and equipment	$ 8,509	9,797	2,164	3,268	40	23,778
Identifiable assets	$ 63,241	71,482	45,651	39,540	18,221	238,135
At December 31, 1979 or for year then ended						
Net sales	$204,399	75,497	73,454	68,025		421,375
Operating profit	$ 14,859	11,058	9,274	5,306	(3,863)	36,634
Interest expense						(7,777)
Other income, net						572
Income before income taxes						29,429
Depreciation and amortization expense	$ 6,722	3,734	1,220	1,082	302	13,060
Additions to property, plant and equipment	$ 5,519	8,910	1,917	1,569	90	18,005
Identifiable assets	$ 60,663	67,582	46,882	39,278	13,738	228,143
At December 31, 1978 or for year then ended						
Net sales	$213,210	47,128	68,419	61,926		390,683
Operating profit	$ 11,119	5,518	8,845	397	(4,072)	21,807
Interest expense						(5,545)
Other income, net						408
Provision for unusual write-offs and losses	$(11,995)	(700)		(2,255)		(14,950)
Income before income taxes						1,720
Depreciation and amortization expense	$ 8,492	1,983	1,110	962	222	12,769
Additions to property, plant and equipment	$ 9,964	15,681	1,530	1,638	12	28,825
Identifiable assets	$ 65,084	46,510	38,962	36,496	12,956	200,008

11. Legal Proceedings

The Company and one of its subsidiaries are defendants in a private action antitrust and patent infringement suit filed in April 1979, in which the plaintiff seeks treble its alleged damages which it claims exceed $4,000,000 as well as attorneys' fees and injunctive relief. The material allegations of the complaint have been denied by the Company and its subsidiary, and the subsidiary has filed a counterclaim seeking a declaratory judgment that the subject patent is void and damages in excess of $1,000,000 for breach of contract, unfair competition and libel. Substantial defenses are available to this action, and in the opinion of the Company the suit will have no material adverse effect upon its consolidated financial position.

12. Provision for Unusual Write-offs and Losses in 1978

In 1978 the disposition of four unprofitable soft drink bottling operations, the sale of a profitable home furnishings subsidiary and the recognition of other unusual expense items resulted in a $14,950,000 pretax charge to 1978 income. The net sales of these operations [Soft drink-$25,061,000; Home furnishings-$3,597,000] and their operating profit (loss) [Soft drink-$(4,831,000); Home furnishings-$190,000] were included in the Company's 1978 consolidated statement of income. The net assets at the date of disposition were $11,696,000 and $2,244,000 for Soft drink and Home furnishings, respectively. The principal proceeds received by the Company from the sales of these operations were long-term notes receivable, collateralized by the assets sold.

13. Quarterly Financial Data (Unaudited)

The following is a summary of selected quarterly financial data for the years ended December 31, 1980, 1979 and 1978 in thousands of dollars except per share data.

	For Quarter Ended			
	Mar 31	Jun 30	Sep 30	Dec 31
1980:				
Net sales	$106,938	107,891	114,698	108,549
Gross profit	40,959	45,633	45,332	40,159
Income before income taxes	6,201	6,500	4,436	407
Net income	$ 3,411	3,575	2,439	744
Earnings per average share outstanding	$ .42	.43	.30	.09
1979:				
Net sales	$ 99,068	104,301	115,109	102,897
Gross profit	38,237	43,265	47,096	40,437
Income before income taxes	5,844	8,195	10,087	5,303
Net income	$ 3,331	4,390	5,548	3,210
Earnings per average share outstanding	$ .41	.53	.68	.39
1978:				
Net sales	$ 89,629	101,114	104,585	95,355
Gross profit	35,575	42,320	41,909	33,793
Income before unusual write-offs and losses and before income taxes	4,081	6,595	4,446	1,548
Provision for unusual write-offs and losses				(14,950)
Income (loss) before income taxes	4,081	6,595	4,446	(13,402)
Net income (loss)	$ 2,185	3,687	2,445	(6,936)
Earnings (loss) per average share outstanding	$ .27	.45	.30	(.85)

Fourth quarter results include pretax charges of approximately $1,800,000 in 1980 and $1,500,000 in 1978 to adjust inventory valued at cost to net realizable value. The 1980 fourth quarter also includes a $500,000 pretax capital loss on the sale of an office facility and a $500,000 write-down of goodwill. Income taxes have also been reduced $500,000 in this quarter as a result of redetermination of the tax liability.

For additional information, refer to Management's Discussion and Analysis.

14. Effects of Changing Prices (Unaudited)

The following supplemental information relating to the effects of general inflation (constant dollar) and changes in specific prices (current cost) has been prepared in accordance with Financial Accounting Standards Board Statement No. 33 "Financial Reporting and Changing Prices." This disclosure is experimental in nature and an understanding of the basic concepts and definitions is required to use the information.

The constant dollar accounting method attempts to reflect general inflation by adjusting for the changing purchasing power of the dollar. Historical costs are converted into constant dollars of equal purchasing power by using the average 1980 U.S. Consumer Price Index for all Urban Consumers (CPI-U). Accordingly, depreciation and amortization expense and cost of sales have been adjusted by the constant dollar amounts of inventories, property, plant and equipment.

The current cost accounting method attempts to restate the Company's financial results for changes in specific costs of the Company's assets rather than for changes in general costs. Inventory, property, plant and equipment are valued at their estimated current cost and depreciation, amortization and cost of sales have been adjusted based on current costs.

Under both methods, depreciation and amortization expense have been recalculated using the same assumptions and accounting policies as those utilized for the historical cost financial statements.

Inflation also affects the Company's monetary assets and liabilities such as cash, receivables and payables which will decrease in value over time. The Company's net monetary liabilities position during 1980 resulted in a purchasing power gain of $8.6 million which substantially offset the adverse effects of the inflation adjustments. Although this gain is excluded from income since it will be realized in the future when liabilities are paid, it is an integral part of the changing prices calculation and should be considered in assessing the impact of inflation on income.

Statement of Income from Continuing Operations Adjusted for Changing Prices

In thousands of average 1980 dollars		For Year Ended December 31, 1980
Income from continuing operations, as reported in the income statement		$ 10,169
Adjustments to restate costs for the effects of general inflation:		
Cost of sales	$(6,379)	
Depreciation and amortization	(6,481)	(12,860)
Loss from continuing operations adjusted for general inflation		(2,691)
Adjustments to reflect the difference between general inflation and changes in specific prices (current costs):		
Cost of sales	547	
Depreciation and amortization	(949)	(402)
Loss from continuing operations adjusted for changes in specific prices		$ (3,093)
Gain from decline in purchasing power of net amounts owed		$ 8,554
Increase in specific prices (current cost) of inventories and property, plant and equipment held during the year		$ 24,212
Effect of increase in general price level		23,363
Excess of increase in specific prices over increase in the general price level		$ 849

At December 31, 1980, current cost of inventory was $55.1 million and current cost of property, plant and equipment net of depreciation was $152.9 million, reflecting the higher value of these assets today compared to their historical cost amounts. The increase in current cost of these assets due to specific price changes was $849,000 higher in 1980 than the increase attributable to general inflation. The inflationary impact on the cost of replacing older plant and equipment was partially offset by raw material price increases that were lower than the CPI-U and the non-capital intensive nature of significant portions of the Company's manufacturing processes.

A critical omission of accounting adjustments for changing prices is the recognition of related tax benefits. While FASB Statement No. 33 requires that income be reduced by the pretax effects of inflation, it does not permit the effective tax rate to be applied on the lower income as income taxes are based on historical earnings under current federal tax laws. This dramatically demonstrates the need for revision of the tax laws to allow businesses to provide for the replacement of capital assets through depreciation charges that reflect inflationary conditions.

As required by FASB Statement No. 33, below is a comparison of selected data adjusted for the effects of changing prices for the past five years. The adjusted data should not be considered precise measurements of the assets and expenses included, but instead as reasonable approximations of the price changes that have occurred. Items left blank for prior periods are not required by FASB Statement No. 33 and are not available.

TO THE SHAREHOLDERS
ROYAL CROWN COMPANIES, INC.

We have examined the consolidated balance sheets of Royal Crown Companies, Inc. and Subsidiaries as at December 31, 1980 and 1979, and the related consolidated statements of income and retained earnings and changes in financial position for the years ended December 31, 1980, 1979 and 1978. Our examinations were made in accordance with generally accepted auditing standards and, accordingly, included such tests of the accounting records and such other auditing procedures as we considered necessary in the circumstances.

In our opinion, the aforementioned consolidated financial statements present fairly the financial position of Royal Crown Companies, Inc. and Subsidiaries at December 31, 1980 and 1979, and the results of their operations and the changes in their financial position for the years ended December 31, 1980, 1979 and 1978, in conformity with generally accepted accounting principles applied on a consistent basis.

Coopers & Lybrand

COOPERS & LYBRAND
Atlanta, Georgia
February 19, 1981

Five-Year Comparison of Selected Supplementary Financial Data Adjusted For The Effects of Changing Prices

In thousands of average 1980 dollars

	For Year Ended December 31				
	1980	1979	1978	1977	1976
Net sales:					
As reported	**$438,076**	421,375	390,683	349,619	287,430
In constant dollars	**438,076**	478,359	493,452	475,404	416,057
Historical cost information adjusted for general inflation:					
Income (loss) from continuing operations	**(2,691)**	7,420			
Earnings (loss) per share of common stock	**(.33)**	.90			
Net assets at year-end	**151,151**	153,816			
Current cost information:					
Income (loss) from continuing operations	**(3,093)**	7,524			
Earnings (loss) per share of common stock	**(.38)**	.92			
Increase in specific prices over (under) increase in the general price level	**849**	(54)			
Net assets at year-end	**156,696**	158,914			
Gain from decline in purchasing power of net amounts owed	**8,554**	8,730			
Cash dividends declared per common share	**1.04**	1.18	1.29	1.22	1.10
Market price per common share at year-end	**14.75**	16.18	19.10	25.50	25.51
Average consumer price index	**246.8**	217.4	195.4	181.5	170.5

Selected Financial Data
Royal Crown Companies, Inc. and Subsidiaries

In thousands of dollars except per share data	For Year Ended December 31				
	1980	1979	1978	1977	1976
Net sales:					
Soft drink	$ **220,731**	204,399	213,210	202,697	174,793
Fast food	**69,880**	75,497	47,128	36,625	6,465
Citrus	**78,706**	73,454	68,419	53,493	46,304
Home furnishings	**68,759**	68,025	61,926	56,804	59,868
Total net sales	**438,076**	421,375	390,683	349,619	287,430
Cost of sales	**265,993**	252,340	237,086	197,378	155,948
Gross profit	**172,083**	169,035	153,597	152,241	131,482
Marketing, administrative and other expenses	**144,591**	132,401	131,790	117,109	97,683
Operating profit:					
Soft drink	**13,942**	14,859	11,119	20,961	22,734
Fast food	**6,666**	11,058	5,518	4,985	984
Citrus	**9,704**	9,274	8,845	8,613	6,412
Home furnishings	**1,827**	5,306	397	4,512	7,440
Corporate expenses	**(4,647)**	(3,863)	(4,072)	(3,939)	(3,771)
Total operating profit	**27,492**	36,634	21,807	35,132	33,799
Interest expense	**(10,047)**	(7,777)	(5,545)	(3,084)	(1,246)
Other income, net	**99**	572	408	1,526	773
Income before unusual write-offs and losses and before income taxes	**17,544**	29,429	16,670	33,574	33,326
Provisions for unusual write-offs and losses			14,950		
Income before income taxes	**17,544**	29,429	1,720	33,574	33,326
Provision for income taxes	**7,375**	12,950	339	14,965	15,896
Net income	$ **10,169**	16,479	1,381	18,609	17,430
Average shares outstanding	**8,199,825**	8,195,867	8,186,509	8,176,325	8,158,550
Per average share:					
Net income	$ **1.24**	2.01	.17	2.27	2.14
Cash dividends declared	$ **1.04**	1.04	1.02	.90	.76
Total assets	$ **238,135**	228,143	200,008	173,039	137,623
Long-term debt plus capitalized lease obligations	$ **62,871**	61,933	56,837	39,442	17,964
Shareholders' equity	$ **103,108**	101,467	93,438	100,171	88,756

Officers

William T. Young
Chairman of the Board and
Chairman of the Executive Committee

Donald A. McMahon
President and Chief Executive Officer

Vice Presidents
Fred M. Adamany
Arnold Belasco
George W. Gray
W. Nolan Murrah, Jr.
Richard J. St. John
Ronald L. White

W. Nolan Murrah, Jr.
Secretary

Ronald L. White
Treasurer

George W. Gray
Controller

Directors

Cason J. Callaway, Jr.,[2]
President and Chief Executive Officer
Callaway Chemical Company
Manufacturer of specialty chemicals

B. H. Hardaway, III
Chairman of the Board
The Hardaway Company
General contractors

David A. Jones,[2]
Chairman of the Board and Chief Executive Officer
Humana Inc.
Investor-owned hospital company

Donald A. McMahon,[1]
President and Chief Executive Officer

David C. Scott,[1,2*]
Chairman of the Board and Chief Executive Officer
Allis-Chalmers Corporation
Manufacturer of capital goods

Fred R. Sullivan,[1]
Chairman of the Board and President
Kidde, Inc.
Multi-market manufacturing and service company

William T. Young,[1*]
Chairman of the Board

[1] Executive Committee
[2] Audit Committee
*Chairman

Principal Subsidiaries and Presidents

Fred M. Adamany, President
Royal Crown Cola Co.
Rolling Meadows, Illinois

Ben R. Adams, President
Adams Packing Association
Auburndale, Florida
Texsun Corporation
Weslaco, Texas

Joseph A. George, Jr., President
National Art Company
Greenwood, Mississippi

Leo Gershanov, President
Frederick Cooper Lamps Co., Inc.
Chicago, Illinois

John S. Roberts, President
Hoyne Industries, Inc.
Rolling Meadows, Illinois

Richard P. McDermott, President
Couroc of Monterey, Inc.
Monterey, California

Jefferson T. McMahon, President
Arby's, Inc.
Atlanta, Georgia

Basil Turbyfill, President
Athens Furniture, Inc.
Athens, Tennessee

Corporate Information
Royal Crown Companies, Inc. and Subsidiaries

Annual Meeting
The Annual Meeting of Shareholders of Royal Crown
Companies, Inc. will be held at 1:00 p.m. on Tuesday,
April 21, 1981, at 100 West 10th Street, Wilmington, Delaware.

Registrar and Transfer Agent
The First National Bank of Boston
100 Federal Street, Boston, MA 02110

Registrar
Columbus Bank and Trust Company
1148 Broadway, Columbus, GA 31901

Transfer Agent
First National Bank of Columbus
101 Thirteenth Street, Columbus, GA 31902

Accountants
Coopers & Lybrand
1200 Equitable Building, Atlanta, GA 30303

Form 10-K Available
The Form 10-K report for Royal Crown Companies, Inc.,
filed annually with the Securities and Exchange Commission,
is available upon request. It may be obtained by writing to:
Investor Relations, Royal Crown Companies, Inc.,
41 Perimeter Center East, N.E., Atlanta, Georgia 30346.

The following are trademarks owned by Royal Crown
Companies, Inc. and its subsidiaries: RC, RC 100, Diet Rite,
Nehi, Arby's, Adams, Texsun, Vintage, Frederick Cooper,
Couroc, Athens, Hoyne.

Dividend Reinvestment
The Automatic Dividend Reinvestment Plan enables shareholders to reinvest their dividends in Royal Crown
Companies, Inc. common stock automatically, conveniently
and at low cost. In addition, participating shareholders may
make periodic cash investments for the purchase of additional Royal Crown Companies stock. Participation is voluntary; shareholders may join or withdraw at any time. For full
details write to: The First National Bank of Boston, Automatic Dividend Reinvestment and Cash Stock Purchase Plan,
P.O. Box 1681, Boston, Massachusetts 02105.

Market Price of Stock and Cash Dividends

Quarter Ended	Market Price Range* ($) High	Low	Close	Cash Dividends Declared (¢)
1980				
March 31	14⅞	10⅝	12	26
June 30	14	11	13⅛	26
September 30	19½	12¾	16¼	26
December 31	16	11⅞	14¾	26
1979				
March 31	16⅜	13	13¼	26
June 30	15¾	13⅛	14⅜	26
September 30	14⅞	13⅛	13⅞	26
December 31	15⅝	11⅞	14¼	26

*New York Stock Exchange

Royal Crown Companies, Inc. common stock is traded on the
New York and Pacific Coast Stock Exchanges. There were
11,607 shareholders of record owning the Company's common shares at December 31, 1980. See Note 4 for dividend
availability.

APPENDIX B

Present Value and
Future Value Tables

TABLE 1: FUTURE VALUE OF $1

N	2.0%	3.0%	4.0%	5.0%	6.0%	8.0%
1	1.020000	1.030000	1.040000	1.050000	1.060000	1.080000
2	1.040400	1.060900	1.081600	1.102500	1.123600	1.166400
3	1.061208	1.092727	1.124864	1.157625	1.191016	1.259712
4	1.082432	1.125509	1.169859	1.215506	1.262477	1.360489
5	1.104081	1.159274	1.216653	1.276282	1.338226	1.469328
6	1.126162	1.194052	1.265319	1.340096	1.418519	1.586874
7	1.148686	1.229874	1.315932	1.407100	1.503630	1.713824
8	1.171659	1.266770	1.368569	1.477455	1.593848	1.850930
9	1.195093	1.304773	1.423312	1.551328	1.689479	1.999005
10	1.218994	1.343916	1.480244	1.628895	1.790848	2.158925
11	1.243374	1.384234	1.539454	1.710339	1.898299	2.331639
12	1.268242	1.425761	1.601032	1.795856	2.012196	2.518170
13	1.293607	1.468534	1.665074	1.885649	2.132928	2.719624
14	1.319479	1.512590	1.731676	1.979932	2.260904	2.937194
15	1.345868	1.557967	1.800944	2.078928	2.396558	3.172169
16	1.372786	1.604706	1.872981	2.182875	2.540352	3.425943
17	1.400241	1.652848	1.947900	2.292018	2.692773	3.700018
18	1.428246	1.702433	2.025817	2.406619	2.854339	3.996019
19	1.456811	1.753506	2.106849	2.526950	3.025600	4.315701
20	1.485947	1.806111	2.191123	2.653298	3.207135	4.660957
21	1.515666	1.860295	2.278768	2.785963	3.399564	5.033834
22	1.545980	1.916103	2.369919	2.925261	3.603537	5.436540
23	1.576899	1.973587	2.464716	3.071524	3.819750	5.871464
24	1.608437	2.032794	2.563304	3.225100	4.048935	6.341181
25	1.640606	2.093778	2.665836	3.386355	4.291871	6.848475
26	1.673418	2.156591	2.772470	3.555673	4.549383	7.396353
27	1.706886	2.221289	2.883369	3.733456	4.822346	7.988061

N	10.0%	12.0%	14.0%	16.0%	20.0%	25.0%
1	1.100000	1.120000	1.140000	1.160000	1.200000	1.250000
2	1.210000	1.254400	1.299600	1.345600	1.440000	1.562500
3	1.331000	1.404928	1.481544	1.560896	1.728000	1.953125
4	1.464100	1.573519	1.688960	1.810639	2.073600	2.441406
5	1.610510	1.762342	1.925415	2.100342	2.488320	3.051758
6	1.771561	1.973823	2.194973	2.436396	2.985984	3.814697
7	1.948717	2.210681	2.502269	2.826220	3.583181	4.768372
8	2.143589	2.475963	2.852586	3.278415	4.299817	5.960464
9	2.357948	2.773079	3.251949	3.802961	5.159780	7.450581
10	2.593742	3.105848	3.707221	4.411435	6.191736	9.313226
11	2.853117	3.478550	4.226232	5.117265	7.430084	11.641532
12	3.138428	3.895976	4.817905	5.936027	8.916100	14.551915
13	3.452271	4.363493	5.492411	6.885791	10.699321	18.189894
14	3.797498	4.887112	6.261349	7.987518	12.839185	22.737368
15	4.177248	5.473566	7.137938	9.265521	15.407022	28.421709
16	4.594973	6.130394	8.137249	10.748004	18.488426	35.527137
17	5.054470	6.866041	9.276464	12.467685	22.186111	44.408921
18	5.559917	7.689966	10.575169	14.462514	26.623333	55.511151
19	6.115909	8.612762	12.055693	16.776517	31.948000	69.388939
20	6.727500	9.646293	13.743490	19.460759	38.337600	86.736174
21	7.400250	10.803848	15.667578	22.574481	46.005120	108.420217
22	8.140275	12.100310	17.861039	26.186398	55.206144	135.525272
23	8.954302	13.552347	20.361585	30.376222	66.247373	169.406589
24	9.849733	15.178629	23.212207	35.236417	79.496847	211.758237
25	10.834706	17.000064	26.461916	40.874244	95.396217	264.697796
26	11.918177	19.040072	30.166584	47.414123	114.475460	330.872245
27	13.109994	21.324881	34.389906	55.000382	137.370552	413.590306

TABLE 2: PRESENT VALUE OF $1

N	2.0%	3.0%	4.0%	5.0%	6.0%	8.0%
1	0.980392	0.970874	0.961538	0.952381	0.943396	0.925926
2	0.961169	0.942596	0.924556	0.907029	0.889996	0.857339
3	0.942322	0.915142	0.888996	0.863838	0.839619	0.793832
4	0.923845	0.888487	0.854804	0.822702	0.792094	0.735030
5	0.905731	0.862609	0.821927	0.783526	0.747258	0.680583
6	0.887971	0.837484	0.790315	0.746215	0.704961	0.630170
7	0.870560	0.813092	0.759918	0.710681	0.665057	0.583490
8	0.853490	0.789409	0.730690	0.676839	0.627412	0.540269
9	0.836755	0.766417	0.702587	0.644609	0.591898	0.500249
10	0.820348	0.744094	0.675564	0.613913	0.558395	0.463193
11	0.804263	0.722421	0.649581	0.584679	0.526788	0.428883
12	0.788493	0.701380	0.624597	0.556837	0.496969	0.397114
13	0.773033	0.680951	0.600574	0.530321	0.468839	0.367698
14	0.757875	0.661118	0.577475	0.505068	0.442301	0.340461
15	0.743015	0.641862	0.555265	0.481017	0.417265	0.315242
16	0.728446	0.623167	0.533908	0.458112	0.393646	0.291890
17	0.714163	0.605016	0.513373	0.436297	0.371364	0.270269
18	0.700159	0.587395	0.493628	0.415521	0.350344	0.250249
19	0.686431	0.570286	0.474642	0.395734	0.330513	0.231712
20	0.672971	0.553676	0.456387	0.376689	0.311805	0.214548
21	0.659776	0.537549	0.438834	0.358942	0.294155	0.198656
22	0.646839	0.521893	0.421955	0.341850	0.277505	0.183941
23	0.634156	0.506692	0.405726	0.325571	0.261797	0.170315
24	0.621721	0.491934	0.390121	0.310068	0.246979	0.157699
25	0.609531	0.477606	0.375117	0.295303	0.232999	0.146018
26	0.597579	0.463695	0.360689	0.281241	0.219810	0.135202
27	0.585862	0.450189	0.346817	0.267848	0.207368	0.125187

N	10.0%	12.0%	14.0%	16.0%	20.0%	25.0%
1	0.909091	0.892857	0.877193	0.862069	0.833333	0.800000
2	0.826446	0.797194	0.769468	0.743163	0.694444	0.640000
3	0.751315	0.711780	0.674972	0.640658	0.578704	0.512000
4	0.683013	0.635518	0.592080	0.552291	0.482253	0.409600
5	0.620921	0.567427	0.519369	0.476113	0.401878	0.327680
6	0.564474	0.506631	0.455587	0.410442	0.334898	0.262144
7	0.513158	0.452349	0.399637	0.353830	0.279082	0.209715
8	0.466507	0.403883	0.350559	0.305025	0.232568	0.167772
9	0.424098	0.360610	0.307508	0.262953	0.193807	0.134218
10	0.385543	0.321973	0.269744	0.226684	0.161506	0.107374
11	0.350494	0.287476	0.236617	0.195417	0.134588	0.085899
12	0.318631	0.256675	0.207559	0.168463	0.112157	0.068719
13	0.289664	0.229174	0.182069	0.145227	0.093464	0.054976
14	0.263331	0.204620	0.159710	0.125195	0.077887	0.043980
15	0.239392	0.182696	0.140096	0.107927	0.064905	0.035184
16	0.217629	0.163122	0.122892	0.093041	0.054088	0.028147
17	0.197845	0.145644	0.107800	0.080207	0.045073	0.022518
18	0.179859	0.130040	0.094561	0.069144	0.037561	0.018014
19	0.163508	0.116107	0.082948	0.059607	0.031301	0.014412
20	0.148644	0.103667	0.072762	0.051385	0.026084	0.011529
21	0.135131	0.092560	0.063826	0.044298	0.021737	0.009223
22	0.122846	0.082643	0.055988	0.038188	0.018114	0.007379
23	0.111678	0.073788	0.049112	0.032920	0.015095	0.005903
24	0.101526	0.065882	0.043081	0.028380	0.012579	0.004722
25	0.092296	0.058823	0.037790	0.024465	0.010483	0.003778
26	0.083905	0.052521	0.033149	0.021091	0.008735	0.003022
27	0.076278	0.046894	0.029078	0.018182	0.007280	0.002418

TABLE 3: FUTURE VALUE OF ORDINARY ANNUITY OF $1

N	2.0%	3.0%	4.0%	5.0%	6.0%	8.0%
1	1.000000	1.000000	1.000000	1.000000	1.000000	1.000000
2	2.020000	2.030000	2.040000	2.050000	2.060000	2.080000
3	3.060400	3.090900	3.121600	3.152500	3.183600	3.246400
4	4.121608	4.183627	4.246464	4.310125	4.374616	4.506112
5	5.204040	5.309136	5.416323	5.525631	5.637093	5.866601
6	6.308121	6.468410	6.632975	6.801913	6.975319	7.335929
7	7.434283	7.662462	7.898294	8.142008	8.393838	8.922803
8	8.582969	8.892336	9.214226	9.549109	9.897468	10.636628
9	9.754628	10.159106	10.582795	11.026564	11.491316	12.487558
10	10.949721	11.463879	12.006107	12.577893	13.180795	14.486562
11	12.168715	12.807796	13.486351	14.206787	14.971643	16.645487
12	13.412090	14.192030	15.025805	15.917127	16.869941	18.977126
13	14.680332	15.617790	16.626838	17.712983	18.882138	21.495297
14	15.973938	17.086324	18.291911	19.598632	21.015066	24.214920
15	17.293417	18.598914	20.023588	21.578564	23.275970	27.152114
16	18.639285	20.156881	21.824531	23.657492	25.672528	30.324283
17	20.012071	21.761588	23.697512	25.840366	28.212880	33.750226
18	21.412312	23.414435	25.645413	28.132385	30.905653	37.450244
19	22.840559	25.116868	27.671229	30.539004	33.759992	41.446263
20	24.297370	26.870374	29.778079	33.065954	36.785591	45.761964
21	25.783317	28.676486	31.969202	35.719252	39.992727	50.422921
22	27.298984	30.536780	34.247970	38.505214	43.392200	55.456755
23	28.844963	32.452884	36.617889	41.430475	46.995828	60.893296
24	30.421862	34.426470	39.082604	44.501999	50.815577	66.764759
25	32.030300	36.459264	41.645908	47.727099	54.864512	73.105940
26	33.670906	38.553042	44.311745	51.113454	59.156383	79.954415
27	35.344324	40.709634	47.084214	54.669126	63.705766	87.350768

N	10.0%	12.0%	14.0%	16.0%	20.0%	25.0%
1	1.000000	1.000000	1.000000	1.000000	1.000000	1.000000
2	2.100000	2.120000	2.140000	2.160000	2.200000	2.250000
3	3.310000	3.374400	3.439600	3.505600	3.640000	3.812500
4	4.641000	4.779328	4.921144	5.066496	5.368000	5.765625
5	6.105100	6.352847	6.610104	6.877135	7.441600	8.207031
6	7.715610	8.115189	8.535519	8.977477	9.929920	11.258789
7	9.487171	10.089012	10.730491	11.413873	12.915904	15.073486
8	11.435888	12.299693	13.232760	14.240093	16.499085	19.841858
9	13.579477	14.775656	16.085347	17.518508	20.798902	25.802322
10	15.937425	17.548735	19.337295	21.321469	25.958682	33.252903
11	18.531167	20.654583	23.044516	25.732904	32.150419	42.566129
12	21.384284	24.133133	27.270749	30.850169	39.580502	54.207661
13	24.522712	28.029109	32.088654	36.786196	48.496603	68.759576
14	27.974983	32.392602	37.581065	43.671987	59.195923	86.949470
15	31.772482	37.279715	43.842414	51.659505	72.035108	109.686838
16	35.949730	42.753280	50.980352	60.925026	87.442129	138.108547
17	40.544703	48.883674	59.117601	71.673030	105.930555	173.635684
18	45.599173	55.749715	68.394066	84.140715	128.116666	218.044605
19	51.159090	63.439681	78.969235	98.603230	154.740000	273.555756
20	57.274999	72.052442	91.024928	115.379747	186.688000	342.944695
21	64.002499	81.698736	104.768418	134.840506	225.025600	429.680869
22	71.402749	92.502584	120.435996	157.414987	271.030719	538.101086
23	79.543024	104.602894	138.297035	183.601385	326.236863	673.626358
24	88.497327	118.155241	158.658620	213.977607	392.484236	843.032947
25	98.347059	133.333870	181.870827	249.214024	471.981083	1054.791184
26	109.181765	150.333934	208.332743	290.088267	567.377300	1319.488980
27	121.099942	169.374007	238.499327	337.502390	681.852760	1650.361225

TABLE 4: PRESENT VALUE OF ORDINARY ANNUITY OF $1

N	2.0%	3.0%	4.0%	5.0%	6.0%	8.0%
1	0.980392	0.970874	0.961538	0.952381	0.943396	0.925926
2	1.941561	1.913470	1.886095	1.859410	1.833393	1.783265
3	2.883883	2.828611	2.775091	2.723248	2.673012	2.577097
4	3.807729	3.717098	3.629895	3.545951	3.465106	3.312127
5	4.713460	4.579707	4.451822	4.329477	4.212364	3.992710
6	5.601431	5.417191	5.242137	5.075692	4.917324	4.622880
7	6.471991	6.230283	6.002055	5.786373	5.582381	5.206370
8	7.325481	7.019692	6.732745	6.463213	6.209794	5.746639
9	8.162237	7.786109	7.435332	7.107822	6.801692	6.246888
10	8.982585	8.530203	8.110896	7.721735	7.360087	6.710081
11	9.786848	9.252624	8.760477	8.306414	7.886875	7.138964
12	10.575341	9.954004	9.385074	8.863252	8.383844	7.536078
13	11.348374	10.634955	9.985648	9.393573	8.852683	7.903776
14	12.106249	11.296073	10.563123	9.898641	9.294984	8.244237
15	12.849264	11.937935	11.118387	10.379658	9.712249	8.559479
16	13.577709	12.561102	11.652296	10.837770	10.105895	8.851369
17	14.291872	13.166118	12.165669	11.274066	10.477260	9.121638
18	14.992031	13.753513	12.659297	11.689587	10.827603	9.371887
19	15.678462	14.323799	13.133939	12.085321	11.158116	9.603599
20	16.351433	14.877475	13.590326	12.462210	11.469921	9.818147
21	17.011209	15.415024	14.029160	12.821153	11.764077	10.016803
22	17.658048	15.936917	14.451115	13.163003	12.041582	10.200744
23	18.292204	16.443608	14.856842	13.488574	12.303379	10.371059
24	18.913926	16.935542	15.246963	13.798642	12.550358	10.528758
25	19.523456	17.413148	15.622080	14.093945	12.783356	10.674776
26	20.121036	17.876842	15.982769	14.375185	13.003166	10.809978
27	20.706898	18.327031	16.329586	14.643034	13.210534	10.935165

N	10.0%	12.0%	14.0%	16.0%	20.0%	25.0%
1	0.909091	0.892857	0.877193	0.862069	0.833333	0.800000
2	1.735537	1.690051	1.646661	1.605232	1.527778	1.440000
3	2.486852	2.401831	2.321632	2.245890	2.106481	1.952000
4	3.169865	3.037349	2.913712	2.798181	2.588735	2.361600
5	3.790787	3.604776	3.433081	3.274294	2.990612	2.689280
6	4.355261	4.111407	3.888668	3.684736	3.325510	2.951424
7	4.868419	4.563757	4.288305	4.038565	3.604592	3.161139
8	5.334926	4.967640	4.638864	4.343591	3.837160	3.328911
9	5.759024	5.328250	4.946372	4.606544	4.030967	3.463129
10	6.144567	5.650223	5.216116	4.833227	4.192472	3.570503
11	6.495061	5.937699	5.452733	5.028644	4.327060	3.656403
12	6.813692	6.194374	5.660292	5.197107	4.439217	3.725122
13	7.103356	6.423548	5.842362	5.342334	4.532681	3.780098
14	7.366687	6.628168	6.002072	5.467529	4.610567	3.824078
15	7.606080	6.810864	6.142168	5.575456	4.675473	3.859263
16	7.823709	6.973986	6.265060	5.668497	4.729561	3.887410
17	8.021553	7.119630	6.372859	5.748704	4.774634	3.909928
18	8.201412	7.249670	6.467420	5.817848	4.812195	3.927942
19	8.364920	7.365777	6.550369	5.877455	4.843496	3.942354
20	8.513564	7.469444	6.623131	5.928841	4.869580	3.953883
21	8.648694	7.562003	6.686957	5.973139	4.891316	3.963107
22	8.771540	7.644646	6.742944	6.011326	4.909430	3.970485
23	8.883218	7.718434	6.792056	6.044247	4.924525	3.976388
24	8.984744	7.784316	6.835137	6.072627	4.937104	3.981111
25	9.077040	7.843139	6.872927	6.097092	4.947587	3.984888
26	9.160945	7.895660	6.906077	6.118183	4.956323	3.987911
27	9.237223	7.942554	6.935155	6.136364	4.963602	3.990329

Index

Boldface numbers refer to pages with definitions.